CONTEMPORARIES OF ERASMUS
A BIOGRAPHICAL REGISTER OF THE
RENAISSANCE AND REFORMATION

VOLUME 3

N–Z

Contemporaries of
ERASMUS

A BIOGRAPHICAL REGISTER OF THE

RENAISSANCE AND REFORMATION

VOLUME 3

N – Z

Peter G. Bietenholz
University of Saskatchewan

Editor

Thomas B. Deutscher
University of Saskatchewan

Associate Editor

University of Toronto Press

Toronto / Buffalo / London

The research and publication costs of the
Collected Works of Erasmus are supported by the
Social Sciences and Humanities Research Council of Canada.
The publication costs are also assisted by
University of Toronto Press.

ISBN 0-8020-2575-7

Printed on acid free paper

Canadian Cataloguing in Publication Data
Main entry under title:
Contemporaries of Erasmus
Supplement to: Erasmus, Desiderius, d. 1536. Works.
Collected works of Erasmus.
Includes indexes.
Contents: v. 1. A–E. – v. 2. F–M. – v. 3. N–Z.
ISBN 0-8020-2507-2 (v. 1). – ISBN 0-8020-2571-4 (v. 2). –
ISBN 0-8020-2575-7 (v. 3)
1. Erasmus, Desiderius, d. 1536 – Dictionaries,
indexes, etc. 2. Renaissance – Biography.
3. Reformation – Biography. I. Bietenholz, Peter G.,
1933–   II. Deutscher, Thomas Brian, 1949–
III. Erasmus, Desiderius, d. 1536. Works. Collected
works of Erasmus.
PA8500 1974 suppl.   199.492   c85-098027-5

Collected Works of Erasmus

The aim of the Collected Works of Erasmus
is to make available an accurate, readable English text
of Erasmus' correspondence and his
other principal writings. The edition is planned
and directed by an Editorial Board, an Executive Committee,
and an Advisory Committee.

Contents

Editorial Notes
xi

Biographies
1

Works Frequently Cited
489

Short-Title Forms for Erasmus' Works
494

Contributors
497

Illustration Credits
499

Illustration Index
501

Editorial Notes

In assembling *Contemporaries of Erasmus*, the following principles have been applied, with an appropriate degree of flexibility in view of the diversity of available material and fields of scholarly specialization among contributors.

- No biography is offered unless the person in question could be plausibly identified. On the other hand, even persons known merely by their first names are included in the register, provided the references to them warranted investigation. It is hoped that our short notes will encourage further research and eventually lead to further identification of those so mentioned.
- Both first and second names are given in the appropriate vernacular, provided predominant forms could be established; Latin forms often seemed preferable for unidentified or obscure persons. Humanist names in Latin or Greek were preferred wherever they seemed less uncertain than their vernacular counterparts or were deemed to be more widely known.
- Persons known by place of birth rather than by family name are indexed under their first names, unless contemporaries already tended to use the place name as a surname.
- In accordance with English-language custom, popes, emperors, queens, and kings are indexed under their first names, given in English; other members of royal houses, both legitimate and illegitimate, are similarly indexed.
- All members of noble houses are listed together under the family name, with first names in the appropriate language. In some cases, however, the names of a house and a territory are identical or, as with many German princes, the territorial name, often in Anglicized form, is in general use, as with Albert of BRANDENBURG, archbishop of Mainz.
- Women are listed under their maiden names, when known, rather than under names adopted in marriage. Cross-references are provided to married names.
- Cross-references are provided to name forms and identifications proposed by Allen but now abandoned. Cross-references are also given for variant name forms, Latin or vernacular, wherever expedient.
- An asterisk has been used with the name of an individual to indicate that a biography on that individual is included in *Contemporaries of Erasmus*; the asterisk precedes the name under which the biography is indexed.
- For names of places, modern vernacular forms are used, with the exception of those

for which there is a form commonly accepted in current English usage (for example The Hague, Brussels, Louvain, Cologne, Milan). Current political frontiers are respected in the choice of place names rather than historical geography; this practice was adopted as being the most acceptable to an international readership, despite the occasional anachronisms that result.

- References to the correspondence and works of Erasmus are incorporated in each article without an obligation to completeness. *Contemporaries of Erasmus* is not intended as a substitute for the indexes that complement the CWE.
- Contributors were given latitude in the preparation of the bibliographies that accompany their articles so that they could be arranged thematically, alphabetically, or chronologically, as was thought most appropriate for the particular biography.
- Abbreviated references are used for works frequently cited throughout *Contemporaries of Erasmus*. A list of these works, offering fuller data, will be found at the end of each volume. On occasion, however, the full reference to a work cited in abbreviated form in the text of an article will be found in the bibliography following that entry.

The biographies are signed with the names of their authors or co-authors. Initials identify the members of the team in the research office generously provided by the University of Saskatchewan:

| PGB | Peter G. Bietenholz | IG | Ilse Guenther |
| TBD | Thomas B. Deutscher | CFG | Catherine F. Gunderson |

The biographies contributed by members of this team frequently reflect their fields of competence, but just as often they had to be compiled with local research facilities because of limits on time and available funds.

BIOGRAPHIES

Volume 3

N–Z

BIOGRAPHIES

Volume 3

N–Z

Ottmar NACHTGALL of Strasbourg,
1487–5 September 1537
Ottmar Nachtgall (Nachtigall, Luscinius) was
born in Strasbourg and received his early
education from Jakob *Wimpfeling. Johann
Geiler became interested in him and served as
his counsellor and adviser. Nachtgall went to
Paris in 1508, studied philosophy and literature, and became profoundly interested in
classical literature. Since he was training for a
career in the church, he proceeded to Louvain
for theology and canon law, thence to Padua,
and finally to Vienna, where he studied
musical composition under Wolfgang Grefin-
ger. He travelled to the East, traversing Hungary and Transylvania to Greece. By 1511 he
was in Augsburg and in 1514 returned to
Strasbourg. A friend of Jakob *Sturm, Nikolaus
*Gerbel, and Thomas *Vogler, all members of
the humanist circle, he attached himself to his
old tutor, Wimpfeling, and to Sebastian *Brant.
He was given a benefice as vicar and organist at
St Thomas' and won special attention from
Erasmus, who met him on his visit to Strasbourg in 1514 (Epp 302, 305).

Nachtgall introduced the study of Greek in
the city, preparing Greek grammars and Greek
texts for the use of adults interested in learning
the language. He was recommended for a
benefice in one of the city's chapters in 1519,
but the appointment ran into heavy opposition
in Rome. He went there to settle the matter and
discovered he would have to stoop to corrupt
practices to obtain the post. Refusing to do
this, he lost the prebend and then, in 1520, lost
his place as organist; the chapter stated that it
had decided to terminate the position, but it
was reinstated thereafter. Nachtgall returned
to his humanist studies, at this point encouraged by *Zasius of Freiburg and by Erasmus,
who respected him for his knowledge of
Greek. Nachtgall worked on an edition of
Aulus Gellius and revised his own Greek
grammar while the controversies regarding
*Luther swirled around him, engaging many of
his friends.

Nachtgall remained a Catholic, although he
was embittered by the failure of the church to
encourage and support scholars like Wimpfeling, Erasmus, and himself. Increasingly alienated from the Strasbourg intellectuals for
religious reasons, he left the city in 1523 to
settle in Augsburg, welcomed by the bishop,
Christoph von *Stadion, Anton *Fugger (Ep
2192), and Konrad *Peutinger. He attempted to
support himself by writing and was commissioned by Johann Schrot, abbot of St Ulrich's,
to prepare an explanation of the Psalms based
on the version of the Septuagint (Augsburg: S.
Ruff for S. Grimm 1524). In 1525, through the
patronage of the Fuggers, he was named
preacher and canon of St Maurice's, Augsburg, in succession to Johann *Speiser. Departing somewhat from his earlier Erasmian stance,
he soon emerged as a principal spokesman of
the Catholic faction. On 6 and 8 September
1528 he denounced Luther and the Anabaptists from the pulpit. He was then forbidden by
the city council to continue preaching, and by
the end of the month retired to Freiburg (Ep
2264), where he attempted, without success, to
obtain a university chair. He was given a post
as preacher in the cathedral and assigned the
ground-floor apartment of a house built by the
imperial counsellor, Jakob *Villinger, as his
residence.

This housing assignment brought him into
conflict with Erasmus, who had arrived from
Basel shortly after Nachtgall. Erasmus was
given the floor just above Nachtgall. By 1530
trouble had erupted (Epp 2308, 2310). Erasmus
asserted that he should have the whole house
and should by no means be confined to only
one floor. His letters to his friends were full of
complaints about Nachtgall, and Erasmus was
willing to listen to any calumny against his
neighbour. Matthias *Kretz reported, for example, that Nachtgall had joined the Anabaptists and had only recently returned to the
Catholic church (Epp 2430, 2445). Nachtgall
tried to smooth things over and wrote to
Erasmus on 4 April 1531 (Ep 2477) that he was
departing on a pilgrimage to the region of
Marseille and would turn over his keys of the
house to him. He offered to undertake any
commissions Erasmus might have in Besançon, Lyon, or other towns along the way, and
Erasmus entrusted him with Ep 2466, adding a
commendatory postscript, and probably other
letters, including one to *Sadoleto (Allen Ep
2474 introduction). But he never forgave
Nachtgall, suspecting him of intrigues at the
court of *Ferdinand (Ep 2565). He continued to
entertain any sort of gossip against Nachtgall

(Ep 2728), although an uneasy friendship appears to have been restored on the surface (Epp 2676, 2818). In 1531 Nachtgall declined a position at Munich offered to him by Duke William of *Bavaria. Public preaching may never have been his true calling, and he withdrew increasingly into his studies. He retired to the Carthusian monastery near Freiburg to which he left all his belongings.

BIBLIOGRAPHY: Allen and CWE Ep 302 / ADB XIX 655–7 / Schmidt *Histoire littéraire* II 174–208, full bibliography in II 412–18 / Josef Rest 'Neues über Ottmar Nachtgall' *Zeitschrift für Geschichte des Oberrheins* 77 (1923) 45–59 / BRE Ep 54 and passim / AK II Ep 586 and passim / G. von Pölnitz *Anton Fugger* (Tübingen 1958–) I 55–6 and passim / *Matrikel Freiburg* I 278 / For Nachtgall's importance as a composer: *Die Musik in Geschichte und Gegenwart* ed F. Blume et al (Kassel-Basel 1949–73) VIII 1327 / Friedrich Roth *Augsburgs Reformationsgeschichte* 2nd ed (Munich 1901–11) I 129–31, 306–9, and passim
MIRIAM U. CHRISMAN

Maerten van NAERDEN d January 1567
Maerten van Naerden (Martinus de Narden, de Nardis, or Nardenus), the son of Jacob van Naerden, matriculated in the Cologne faculty of arts on 4 November 1505 and was a MA by 1508, when he matriculated at Orléans; at Orléans he obtained his licence in canon and civil law in January 1513. For a period he was a lawyer at The Hague, but in 1526 the central government appointed him to the council of Friesland, together with Everardus *Nicolai. Erasmus sent both of them his greetings in a letter to *Haio Herman, who was by then their colleague (Ep 2261); unluckily Erasmus must have taken Haio's 'Nardenus' for 'Hardenus,' thus long preventing identification. From 1527 Maerten van Naerden acted as the council's first councillor and vice-president. From 1 July 1537 to 13 August 1538 he was an extraordinary councillor of Holland, and on 2 July 1538 he was appointed to the presidency of the council of Utrecht. Hector van *Hoxwier succeeded him in the last function when Naerden went to Groningen, where he was lieutenant to the governor and president of the court of justice (Hoofdmannenkamer) from 29 August 1541. He was allowed to retire from that office on 4 August 1557 and spent the rest of his life as an ordinary member of the council of Holland at The Hague, to which he was appointed on 22 October 1557. He died and was buried at The Hague. He had been married to Auck van Donia and afterwards to Petronella Osbrechtsdochter, who survived him by more than eighteen years.

BIBLIOGRAPHY: A.J. Van der Aa et al *Biographisch woordenboek der Nederlanden* (Haarlem 1852–78, repr 1965) XIII 21 / J. van Kuyk in NNBW III 901–2 / *Matrikel Köln* II 586 / *Matricule d'Orléans* I-2 283–4 / J.S. Theissen *Centraal gezag en Friesche vrijheid* (Groningen 1907) 123, 148, 152, 154, 228, 462
C.G. VAN LEIJENHORST

Giovanni NANNI *See Johannes* ANNIUS

NARCISUS (Ep 1281 of 20 May 1522)
Narcisus, an unidentified physician attached to the court of *Charles V, is mentioned in a letter from Juan Luis *Vives to Erasmus. He is also listed as a member of the emperor's train during his visit to England in 1522.

BIBLIOGRAPHY: Allen Ep 1281 / LP III-2 p 969
PGB

Galeottus NARNIENSIS *See Galeotto* MARZIO

Engelbert II of NASSAU 17 May 1451–31 May 1504
Engelbert (Engelbrecht) II of Nassau was the son of John IV, count of Nassau-Dillenburg-Dietz, and Maria, countess of Loon and Heinsberg, Westphalia. As lord of Breda he had large estates in the Netherlands. On 19 December 1468 he married Cimburga of Baden and in 1473 he received the order of the Golden Fleece. Loyal to the dukes of Burgundy, he followed Charles the Rash of *Burgundy on his campaigns and was councillor to Mary, his daughter, and her husband, *Maximilian I. As a military commander he distinguished himself especially at Guinegatte on 7 August 1479, where his action helped to turn a seemingly lost battle into a victory for Maximilian. He rose to become governor of Brabant, Limburg, and Luxembourg. In 1487 he was taken prisoner by the French but managed to work in support of the peace agreement between Maximilian and King *Charles VIII of France

that was signed in Frankfurt in 1489. On 22
July 1489 he was released from captivity on
payment of a ransom. Under Philip the
Handsome of *Burgundy he continued to be
greatly respected and was lieutenant-general
of the Netherlands from 1501 during Philip's
absence in Spain. During the last years of
his life he tried in vain to prevent hostilities
between Karel van *Egmond, whom he had
brought up, and Duke Philip. He died in
Brussels and was buried in the church of
Breda. His nephew Henry III of *Nassau
erected a marble monument to him that bore
his likeness, the work of the Italian sculptor
Thomas of Bologna.

Engelbert II attended the presentation of
Erasmus' *Panegyricus* (ASD IV-1 27) to Philip the
Handsome.

BIBLIOGRAPHY: NNBW I 819–20 / ADB VI 128 /
Hermann Wiesflecker *Kaiser Maximilian I.*
(Vienna-Munich 1971–   ) I 147–8 and
passim   IG

Henry III of NASSAU 12 January 1483–
11/14 September 1538
Henry III, count of Nassau-Dillenburg, a son of
Count John V and Elizabeth, the daughter of
Landgrave Henry of Hesse, was born in
Siegen, east of Cologne, and brought up in
part by his uncle, Engelbert II of *Nassau. In
1499 he went to the Netherlands, entered
the service of Philip the Handsome of *Burgundy, and accompanied him on his journey to Spain, France, Savoy, and Germany
from 1501 to 1503. In 1504 he inherited the
territories of his uncle in the Low Countries,
and in 1506 he received the order of the
Golden Fleece; from 1507 to 1513 and again
from 1516 he was commander in the wars
against France and Gelderland, earning the
esteem of *Maximilian I and the future
*Charles V, although *Margaret of Austria
found him too hawkish. After the death of his
first wife, Françoise, the daughter of Jacques
de Savoye, count of Romont, he married
Claude de Chalon, the heiress of Orange, in
1515. Henry was one of the tutors of Prince
Charles and governor of Holland and Zeeland
from 1515 until 1522, when he accompanied
the Emperor to Spain. After the death of his
second wife he married Mencia de *Mendoza,
the daughter and heiress of Rodrigo, marquis

of Zenete. Since the marriage remained childless, her extensive possessions did not fall to
the Nassau family. Henry III remained in
Spain until 1529. As grand chamberlain he
followed the emperor to the coronation in
Bologna, attended the diet of Augsburg in
1530, and returned to Spain in 1534, meeting *Francis I of France in the Dauphiné (Ep
2977) on the way. The following year he
resumed his negotiations with the French king
in Paris. He died in 1538 in Breda and his
son, René de *Chalon, inherited his possessions as well as the rich territories of his
mother, Claude.

In 1518 Erasmus privately expressed disappointment at Henry III's pardoning of some
members of the Black Band (Epp 829, 832). But
he sent respectful greetings to him in 1520 and
1521 through Nicolaas *Everaerts and Alexander *Schweiss (Epp 1092, 1192; cf Ep 982),
suggesting that he had at some time received
favours from Count Henry. However, the
student Erasmus had met in Orléans (Ep 147)
was not Count Henry but his cousin in a
bastard line, Hendrik van *Nassau-Breda.

BIBLIOGRAPHY: Allen and CWE Ep 829 / NNBW
I 1073–5 / ADB XI 551–2 / F. Walser and R.
Wohlfeil *Die spanischen Zentralbehörden und der
Staatsrat Karl V.* (Göttingen 1959) passim /
Michel Baelde *De collaterale raden onder Karel V
en Filips II* (Brussels 1965) 287–8 and passim
                                                    IG

Jan and Hendrik van NASSAU-BREDA
d 3 March 1505 and 25 September 1517
Jan and Hendrik van Nassau-Breda (Johannes
and Henricus de Nassouwen de Breda) were
the sons of Jan, castellan of Heusden (d 1505) –
a natural son of John IV of Nassau – and of
Adriana van Haestrecht (d 1512). On 30
August 1496 the brothers matriculated together in Louvain; in 1500 both were studying in
Orléans with their tutor, Jacob de *Voecht.
Erasmus, who stayed in Voecht's house, had a
high opinion of their character and application
(Epp 147, 157, 159). After Jan, who had been a
canon of Breda since 1494, died in Orléans,
Hendrik returned to Breda, where he was a
town councillor from 1513 to 1517, wine
inspector in 1514, and master of the butchers'
guild from 1515 to 1517. He married Catharina
van Merwen and had three sons. He signed his

will on 16 September 1517 and died nine days later.

The brothers are incorrectly identified in Allen and CWE Ep 147.

BIBLIOGRAPHY: *Matricule d'Orléans* II-1 208–9 IG

NASSAU *See also René de* CHALON

NATALIS (Epp 95 and 101, May 1499)
Erasmus' reference to 'Natalis, the Minorite theologian,' who journeyed between Paris and Tournehem, may concern Noël de Longastis, documented at Paris 20 December 1485–1486. He was the only Franciscan graduate in theology in Paris who bore the name Natalis during the period in question. Longastis received his licence in theology on 20 December 1485, ranking thirteenth of twenty-one graduates, and received his doctorate on 13 February 1486. He would thus have begun his theological studies around 1474 and would have been born between 1450 and 1455.

BIBLIOGRAPHY: Paris, Bibliothèque Nationale MS Lat 5657-A f27 verso

JAMES K. FARGE

Philibert NATUREL d 22 July 1529
Philibert Naturel (Naturelli, proper name: Preudhomme, Proudhomme) was born around 1450 as a member of the Burgundian family de Plaine. He received a doctorate in civil and canon law and embarked upon an ecclesiastical career in the course of which he became provost of the cathedral chapter of Utrecht on 11 February 1500. He was a member of the privy council of the Netherlands from 1484 and was appointed grand chancellor of the order of the Golden Fleece on 30 November 1504. Naturel spent most of his life in the diplomatic service of the house of Hapsburg. In 1492 he went to Rome as envoy of Philip the Handsome, duke of *Burgundy, and two years later, after Philip's father, *Maximilian I, became emperor, Naturel served as his ambassador to the papal court. In the following years he undertook a number of missions, mostly in Italy, and gained some prominence among Maximilian's diplomats. From 1502 he was primarily entrusted with missions to France; in particular he participated in the negotiations leading to the treaties of Blois and Haguenau in

1504 and 1505. Subsequently he returned to the service of Philip the Handsome, where he advocated Franco-Burgundian peace and friendship with sufficient zeal to be accused by critics in Germany of treasonable sympathy with France. After some years of reduced activity he served the future *Charles V as resident ambassador to the court of France from 1517 until his weakened health forced him to retire in 1523 or 1524. He died at Mechelen and was buried at the abbey of Villers, between Brussels and Namur, of which he had been commendatory abbot.

Erasmus met Naturel at Louvain. When staying with Jean *Desmarez in early 1503 he referred to Naturel as his neighbour and encouraged Willem *Hermans to seek the patronage of the provost of Utrecht (Ep 178).

BIBLIOGRAPHY: Allen Ep 178 / *Négociations diplomatiques entre la France et l'Autriche durant les trente premières années du* XVIe *siècle* ed E. Le Glay (Paris 1845) I xxii and passim / Alexandre Henne *Histoire du règne de Charles-Quint en Belgique* (Brussels-Leipzig 1858–60) II 226–7 and passim / C.J.F. Slootmans *Jan metten lippen* (Rotterdam-Antwerp 1945) 258–71 and passim / *Deutsche Reichstagsakten* Jüngere Reihe (Gotha-Göttingen 1893–) I and II passim / *Monasticon Belge* ed U. Berlière et al (Maredsous-Liège 1890–) IV-2 389–90 / F.A.F.T. de Reiffenberg *Histoire de la Toison d'Or* (Brussels 1830) 354–61

INGE FRIEDHUBER

Johannes NAUCLERUS c 1425–1510
Johannes Nauclerus (Verge or Vergenhans) was born near Tübingen of a noble family in the service of the counts of Württemberg. In about 1450 he was appointed tutor to Count Eberhard, later known as 'the Bearded,' who was at that time five years old. When Eberhard began his rule in 1459 he secured for Nauclerus the provostship of the Stuttgart chapter (1459–70). From 1461 to 1464 Nauclerus was parish priest in Weil der Stadt. He was a doctor of canon law and chaplain of the cathedral of Basel in the spring of 1464 when he matriculated at Basel, where he lectured until 1465. A year later he travelled to Rome, where he was employed in the papal chancery. In 1477, at the time when the University of Tübingen was founded, Nauclerus was parish priest in Brackenheim,

near Urach, and canon at Sindelfingen. As a
close friend of his former pupil Count Eberhard, he was appointed professor of canon law
and was also the first rector of the new
university; from 1482 to 1509 he was chancellor. He accompanied Count Eberhard on his
pilgrimage to Rome in 1484 and died in
Tübingen.

Nauclerus' major publication was a universal chronicle, *Memorabilium omnis aetatis ...
commentarii*, compiled from Italian humanist
as well as more traditional sources at the request of *Maximilian I. It was printed in
Tübingen by Thomas *Anshelm in 1516, with a
commendatory letter by Erasmus (Ep 397),
who praised the printer and tried to excuse
the lack of elegance in the author's style. In
his *Tractatus de symonia* (Tübingen: J. Otmar
1500) Nauclerus criticized the practice of
simony.

BIBLIOGRAPHY: Allen and CWE Ep 397 / ADB
XXIII 296–8 / *Matrikel Basel* I 45 / *Matrikel
Tübingen* I 2, II xxvi / Eduard Fueter *Histoire de
l'historiographie moderne* trans E. Jeanmaire
(Paris 1914) 226–7 / Hermann Haering in
Lebensbilder aus Schwaben und Franken ed H.
Miller, R. Uhland, et al (Stuttgart 1940–72) V
1–25, with a portrait of Nauclerus   IG

Fridericus NAUSEA of Waischenfeld,
d 6 February 1552

Nausea is a twisted Latin translation of the
name Friedrich Grau or Grawe of Waischen-
feld, in the diocese of Bamberg. Nausea
attended the school of Zwickau and the
University of Leipzig, where he matriculated in
the spring of 1514 and was the tutor of barons
Paul von Schwarzenberg and Karl Schenk von
Limburg. In 1518 he accompanied Schwarzenberg to Italy, visiting Pavia, Padua, Venice,
and Bologna. When Schwarzenberg returned
to Germany, Nausea obtained a doctorate of
laws in Padua (1523) and continued to study
theology in Siena. A year later he entered the
service of Lorenzo *Campeggi, accompanying
him to Germany, Hungary, and back to
Bologna in 1525. Nausea helped to bring about
the pact of Regensburg (1524) between Archduke *Ferdinand, Duke William IV of *Bavaria,
and Cardinal Matthäus *Lang, who pledged
themselves to enforcing the edict of Worms
against *Luther. In recognition of his services

Fridericus Nausea

he was made papal notary in 1524. He was
appointed cathedral preacher in Frankfurt am
Main, but the reformed party prevented him
from exercising his functions; he therefore
accepted the same position in Mainz. There he
caught the attention of Johannes *Fabri, bishop
of Vienna, and after visiting Rome (1533–4)
and obtaining a theological doctorate in Siena
(1534), he joined King Ferdinand as a court
preacher and was appointed a councillor in
1539. A year earlier he had been appointed
coadjutor to Bishop Fabri, whom he succeeded
as bishop of Vienna from 1541 to 1552. He died
in Trent while attending the council.

As a leading exponent of the irenic movement at the court of Vienna chosen to discuss
Christian unity with *Melanchthon and *Bucer, Nausea was greatly inspired by Erasmus'
works and held him in lasting respect. In
Venice he lent the printer Gregorio de'
*Gregori his copies of some of Erasmus' works
for reprinting (1522–6). As early as 1524 he
addressed Erasmus in a public appeal for
support of his conciliatory efforts: *Ad magnum
Erasmum ... oratio* (Vienna: J. Singriener 1524);
this touched off a correspondence which in

Andrea Navagero, by Raphael

spite of interruptions (Epp 1834, 2847) lasted until Erasmus' death, although unfortunately all of Nausea's letters are missing and probably some of Erasmus' too. Early in 1526 Nausea called on Erasmus on his way from Bologna to Frankfurt (Epp 1632, 2906; AK III Ep 1095), and apparently received from him as a parting present a ring (Ep 1834). Erasmus' letters are warm and direct, although they fail to voice truly personal feelings. Nausea on his part sent Erasmus copies of his works (Epp 1577, 1632, 2847) and let his admiration for Erasmus be known at court (Ep 2906). After Erasmus' death he vented his grief and likewise his enthusiasm for Erasmus' work in his *In magnum Erasmum Roterodamum nuper vita defunctum monodia* (Cologne: J. Gymnich 1536), attributing to him a divine mission and Christ-like features. Dedicated to Ferdinand, the pamphlet is an early indication of the growing influence of the Erasmian group at the court of Vienna. It is reprinted in LB among the preliminary pieces.

When Nausea succeeded Georg *Keck as provost of Waldkirch, in the Breisgau, he had an opportunity of renewing his relations with old friends of Erasmus such as Ludwig *Baer

and *Beatus Rhenanus. The result of these contacts was the printing of Nausea's work about the council of Trent, *Dialogus super Tridentini concilii progressu et successu* (Basel: J. Oporinus 1552), which concealed the author's name behind a pseudonym but in Protestant Basel netted the printer a spell in the city jail. Nausea's publications also include poetry such as *Disticha ... in ... Lactantii ... opera* (Pavia: J. de Burgofranco 1519), text books such as *In artem poeticen* and *Syntagma de conficiendis epistolis* (Venice: G. de' Gregori 1522), many sermons, a *Christlich Bettbüchlein* in memory of Anne of Hungary (Vienna and Leipzig 1538), a *Catechismus catholicus* (Cologne: heirs of J. Quentel 1553), and a collection of letters addressed to him together with a list of his publications: *Epistolarum miscellanearum ... libri x* (Basel: J. Oporinus 1550).

BIBLIOGRAPHY: Allen Ep 1577 / ADB XXIII 321–5 / AK V Ep 2405, VIII Ep 3494, and passim / BRE Epp 406, 410 / *Matrikel Leipzig* I 532 / Hedwig Gollob *Bischof Friedrich Nausea (1495–1552)* (Nieuwkoop 1967) / Bruce Mansfield *Phoenix of His Age* (Toronto 1979) 8–11 / Andreas Flitner *Erasmus im Urteil seiner Nachwelt* (Tübingen 1952) 22–5 / Martin Steinmann *Johannes Oporinus* (Basel 1966) 85–7

IG & PGB

Andrea NAVAGERO of Venice, 1483–July 1527

Andrea Navagero, a member of a patrician family of Venice, was educated first at the Latin classes of *Sabellico in Venice itself and from about 1501 in the University of Padua under various tutors who certainly included the Hellenist *Musurus. During the early years of the century Andrea was associated with Girolamo *Aleandro and Paolo *Canal in a literary circle with interests in both neo-Latin and Italian poetry (Venice, Biblioteca Marciana, MS it. Cl. IX, 203/6757). However, by 1508 his romanticism had turned bellicose, and he joined the Venetian general Bartolomeo d'*Alviano both in his attempt to found an academy in the newly conquered town of Pordenone and on the battlefield of Agnadello. Crushed by the defeat and by commercial disasters in his family, he considered becoming a priest but was persuaded to remain in Venice by the offer of two hundred ducats per year as state historiographer and librarian of the Marciana. He received this post only in 1516, not in 1506 as stated by Allen. Throughout the second decade of the century Andrea dedicated himself to scholarly pursuits, making a great contribution to the Aldine texts of Quintilian and Virgil (1514), Lucretius (1515), and Terence (1517), although his own works remained scattered in anthologies until assembled by J.-A. Volpi (Padua 1718), and his history did not progress beyond a draft. This was perhaps because of his sudden, and to him unexpected, return to public life with his election as ambassador to *Charles v on 10 October 1523. It was while resident at the Spanish court that he was reported to have attacked Erasmus' style (Ep 1791), but by 7 April 1526, nearly a year before this letter was written, he had already been appointed Venetian ambassador to France, although he had not yet taken up the post. He died of plague soon after his arrival at Blois in July 1527.

Navagero had a great influence on Spanish Renaissance poetry. In the summer of 1526 he met in Granada the Spanish poet Juan Boscán Almogávar (d 1542), who was dissatisfied with his own work. Navagero introduced Boscán to the Italian hendecasyllable, canzone, terza rima, and octava rima, and suggested that he experiment in these new forms. Boscán and a younger friend (and better poet), Garcilaso de la Vega (1501?–36), did so, revolutionizing Spanish poetry and inaugurating the 'Siglo de Oro' in poetry. In the first edition of the works of the two poets, published posthumously, Boscán narrates in the prologue of Book Two (which contains his first Spanish poetry in the Italian manner) his meeting with Navagero (*Las obras de Boscan y algunas de Garcilasso de la Vega repartidas en quatro libros*, Barcelona: Garles Amoros 20 March 1543, f D iiij recto–verso).

It seems that Erasmus never referred to Navagero, who was almost certainly in Pordenone at the time of his visit to Venice in 1508. But since Navagero was regarded even by Aldo *Manuzio (dedication to *Rhetorica ad Herennium*, 1514) as an almost fanatical Latinist, and since he had a long association with Aleandro, his reported hostility to Erasmus was probably genuine.

BIBLIOGRAPHY: Allen Ep 1791 / E.A. Cicogna

Elio Antonio de Nebrija

Delle iscrizioni veneziane (Venice 1524–53) VI 173–348 / P. Papinio 'Nuove notizie intorno ad Andrea Navagero' *Archivio veneto* 3 (1872) 255–7
M.J.C. LOWRY

Elio Antonio de NEBRIJA
1441/1444–2 July 1522
Antonio de Nebrija (Aelius Antonius Nebrissensis, Nebricenis) was the son of Juan Martínez de Cala e Hinojosa and Catalina de Xarama y Ojo, small landowners of Lebrija, or Nebrija, where he was born. He adopted the name Aelius or Elio as a symbolic claim to classical ancestry. At the age of fourteen, after his first studies in Lebrija, he entered the University of Salamanca, where he followed the courses of Pascual de Aranda and Pedro de Osma and received his bachelor's degree. Between about 1460 and 1470 he studied in Italy at the University of Bologna and other institutions, where he was exposed to the ideas of Italian humanists. He then retuned to Spain at the invitation of Alonso de Fonseca, the archbishop of Seville, in whose service he remained until the latter's death in 1473. On 4 July 1475 he signed a contract as a lecturer with

the University of Salamanca, and shortly afterwards he was entrusted with the chair of grammar and poetry. At Salamanca he married and had his first children, thus closing the doors to an ecclesiastical career, which he seems to have considered at one time. At Salamanca, and again later in Seville, Nebrija fought to improve the teaching of Latin and Greek and began his important studies of Spanish grammar. Fully committed to his research, in 1486 or 1488 he accepted the patronage of Juan de Zúñiga, then master of the military order of Alcántara and later archbishop of Seville, which allowed him the freedom to alternate his studies with occasional teaching at the University of Seville. At this time Nebrija became an acknowledged authority in philological and biblical studies.

By 1505 the deaths of Archbishop Zúñiga and of *Isabella of Castile, who had also been one of his patrons, led Nebrija to accept the offer of a chair at the University of Salamanca, which he had refused in 1503–4. Between 1504 and 1506 the inquisitor-general, Diego de Deza, grew suspicious of Nebrija's philological approach to the study of the Scriptures and confiscated his papers. The humanist addressed an *Apologia* (Alcalá? 1516?) to Cardinal *Jiménez de Cisneros, who as early as 1502 had invited him to join the group of scholars which he was assembling at Alcalá for the preparation of the Complutensian Polyglot Bible. As a result, all Nebrija's papers were returned to him. The *Apologia* was remarkably similar to Erasmus' dedication (Ep 182) to his edition of the *Adnotationes* on the New Testament of Lorenzo *Valla (Paris 1505), which Nebrija was probably unable to read before composing his own work. On 21 March 1509 Nebrija was appointed royal chronicler. He left Salamanca for the University of Alcalá in 1513, to participate in the completion of the Polyglot Bible. Even then he maintained an attitude of detachment from the project, disagreeing with the cardinal's insistence that the Latin Vulgate was to be corrected using Latin manuscripts but not revised through a comparison with the Greek and Hebrew texts. Nebrija died at Alcalá and was buried in the College of San Ildefonso. He was praised by Erasmus in a letter of 1520 to Juan Luis *Vives (Ep 1111) and in the course of his controversy with Diego *López Zúñiga (ASD IX-2 70, 114, 178).

Nebrija, the greatest Spanish humanist of his generation, is best remembered for his studies of Latin and Spanish grammar and of the Scriptures: *Institutiones grammaticae* (Seville 1481), *Introductiones latinae* (Salamanca 1481), *Lexicon hoc est dictionarium ex sermone latino in hispaniensem* (Salamanca 1492), *Gramática ... sobre la lengua castellana* (Salamanca 1492), three *Quinquagenae* of critical notes on the Scriptures (1514–16), and *De litteris graecis et hebraicis cum quibusdam annotationibus in scripturam sacram* (1563). Other works included *Muestra de las antigüedades de España* (1499), *Juris civilis lexicon* (1506), *Artis rhetoricae compendiosa coaptatio ex Aristotile, Cicerone et Quintiliano* (Alcalá 1515?), *Rerum a Fernando et Elisabe Hispaniarum regibus gestarum decades duae* (Granada 1545), and editions of Pomponius Mela (Salamanca 1498) and Persius Flaccus (Lyon 1512).

BIBLIOGRAPHY: Allen Ep 487 / P. Lemus y Rubio 'El Maestro Elio Antonio de Lebrixa' *Revue hispanique* 22 (1910) 459–508 and 29 (1913) 13–120 / Bataillon *Erasmo y España* 22–38 and passim / Antonio Odriozola 'La caracola del bibliófilo nebrisense. Extracto seco de bibliografía de Nebrija en los siglos xv y xvi' *Revista de bibliografía nacional* 7 (1946) 3–114 / F. Rico *Nebrija frente a los bárbaros: El canon de gramáticos nefastos en las polémicas del humanismo* (Salamanca 1979) / Felix G. Olmedo *Nebrija (1444–1522)* (Madrid 1942)

ARSENIO PACHECO

Francesco NEGRO of Venice, b 17 April 1452
Francesco Negro was born in Venice of Giorgio Cernoëvich (Latin *Niger*), a refugee of noble family from Senj in Croatia, then under Hungarian rule, and his wife, Elena, originally of Treviso. He sometimes called himself Pescennius Franciscus Niger after Pescennius Niger Justus (an opponent of Septimius Severus and briefly emperor in Byzantium), from whom he claimed descent. Negro studied at Venice and Padua, where, supporting himself by teaching, he took degrees in both civil and canon law in 1476. Ordained in 1477 or 1478, he became parish priest of the collegiate church of San Giovanni Decollato, in Venice, in 1481. By 1483 he was hoping to be named bishop of Krk (Veglia) in Croatia but, perhaps the victim of intrigue by a rival, was suspected by the Venetian government of plotting the restoration of his cousin

Giovanni Frangipane, the deposed tyrant of Veglia. Negro was imprisoned, tortured, and found guilty but released some months later after writing a defence, 'De humanae conditionis miseria.' In spite of dedicating his 'Peri Archon,' a praise of the Venetian state, to Doge Agostino Barbarigo in 1498 (Vatican Library, MS Vat. Lat. 4033) and sending a second copy to Leonardo Loredano, doge from 1501 to 1521 (Venice, Biblioteca Nazionale Marciana, Lat. VI 6), Negro was never able to re-establish himself in Venice.

From 1484 to 1494 Negro taught publicly and privately at Rome, Padua, and Arad, then in Hungary, now in Romania. A manuscript of the *Mathesis* of Julius Firmicus Maternus which he found in Hungary was printed by Aldo *Manuzio (Venice 1499). Called to Ferrara in October 1494 by Duke Ercole I to instruct his son, Cardinal Ippolito d'*Este, Negro remained in the service of the cardinal, if not always in his court, until 1505, travelling with him to Hungary and Rome, where in 1497 or 1498 Negro was named protonotary apostolic. Probably in 1503 or 1504 Negro was called to Vac, Hungary, to found a public gymnasium and was named canon by Bishop Nicola Báthori. Having left the service of the cardinal, he wandered through southern Italy – Rome, Bari, Santa Severina in Calabria, Cosenza, Paola, Naples, Ischia – living precariously by private and public teaching and by serving the ecclesiastical hierarchy. The last certain record of Negro is his letter to Cardinal Ippolito of 16 August 1515 from Rome, but a new dedication of the 'Peri Archon' (Vatican Library, MS Vat. Lat. 4033), apparently in his hand, may show him alive in 1523.

WRITINGS AND BIBLIOGRAPHY: In 'Cosmodystychia,' 1513–4, a religious work dedicated to Pope *Leo X (Vatican Library, MS Cod. Vat. Lat. 3971), Negro listed thirty-eight works completed or in progress, primarily on grammar, rhetoric, and pseudo-science. In addition to *Opusculum scribendi epistolas* (Venice: H. Lichtenstein 1488), which Erasmus criticized harshly (Ep 117; see also *De conscribendis epistolis*, ASD I-2 267, and the pirated edition of an early draft of this treatise, *Libellus de conscribendis epistolis*, Cambridge: J. Siberch 1521, B3 recto), Negro's chief published works are *Brevis grammatica*, ed J.L. Santritter (Venice, T. Francus 1480); an epithalamion for

Archduke Sigmund of Austria (n p, pr, d, but perhaps Padua: M. Cerdonis 1485: British Library); *Regulae elegantiarum* in *Augustini Dati Praecepta eloquentiae* (Paris 1498); a funeral oration for Duke Ercole I (n p, pr, d, but perhaps Ferrara: L. de Valentia 1505: British Library); *Historia Theodosiae Martyris* (of three parts – life, martyrdom, miracles – the last was published by G. Henschenius, *Acta Sanctorum Aprilis*, Antwerp 1675, I 63–5). Orations, poems, and letters survive in manuscript; cf P.O. Kristeller *Iter Italicum* (London-Leiden 1965–   ). Some have been published, with autobiographical passages of 'Peri Archon' and 'Cosmodystychia,' in two important studies of Negro: P. Verra 'Cinque orazioni dette dall'umanista Francesco Negri nello studio di Padova' *Archivio veneto-tridentino* 1 (1922) 194–236 and G. Mercati *Ultimi contributi alla storia degli umanisti* (Vatican City 1939) II 24–109, 1*–68*. Earlier studies are G. degli Agostini *Notizie ... scrittori viniziani* (Venice 1752–4) II 473–87; G. Tiraboschi *Storia della letteratura italiana* new ed (Florence 1809) VI 924–5, 1048; Allen and CWE Ep 117

JUDITH RICE HENDERSON

Vulturius NEOCOMUS *See Gerard* GELDENHOUWER

Jacobus NEPOS of Tettnang, d by 1527

Nepos (Näf, Nef) was born at Tettnang, between Friedrichshafen and Ravensburg. He is first heard of as Erasmus' famulus at Antwerp in the autumn of 1516 and accompanied him from there on (Ep 534). In May 1517 he was sent to Basel with manuscripts for Johann *Froben to print, such as More's *Utopia* and *Epigrammata*, which he had apparently copied (Epp 584, 732). The importance of this mission reflects Erasmus' trust in him (Ep 597). In July he returned to Louvain, apparently picking up letters for Erasmus at Strasbourg, Mainz, and Cologne (Epp 595, 600, 612, 614, 615). Thereafter he was repeatedly sent to Antwerp (Epp 702, 708, 736). He continued to copy letters sent or received by Erasmus into the Deventer book and sometimes corrected the work of his colleagues (Hand C; Ep 772 introduction; Allen's introductions to Epp 629, 750). In May 1518 he accompanied Erasmus to Basel but was soon sent back to Louvain on an errand (Ep 852). When Erasmus returned to Louvain Nepos stayed on as a corrector in Froben's press, at first engaged in the monumental task of the second edition of the New Testament (Epp 886, 904) and readily accepted by the *Amerbach sons as one of the editorial team (AK II Ep 771, perhaps implying that he was unusually short).

In the autumn of 1519 Nepos' name was entered into the university register with an unusual reference to his proficiency in Greek and Latin. He was restless at this time and dreamt of opening his own press but was deterred by the amount of capital he would have to borrow. Instead he married the handsome daughter of a printer, Michael Furter, and after two short visits to Bern in the winter of 1519–20 announced a course of lectures on Homer at the university; he also taught Greek privately to a group of boys. Following the example of *Glareanus, who had departed for Paris, he kept a boarding house for his pupils, relying on Glareanus and *Zwingli to send him boys. Among his pupils were the nephews of Cardinal Matthäus *Schiner. References to him in the letters of his fellow humanists, which had been frequent for a time, taper off from 1522 on, but in archival documents at Basel he is still mentioned late in 1524 and is mentioned as being deceased in 1527.

Nepos may be credited with exercising some influence on editorial decisions and once rejected a manuscript by *Myconius. On the other hand he wished to publish a dialogue by Zwingli, which is now lost. Apparently he worked on Erasmus' *Farrago* (BRE Ep 136) and the *Antibarbari*. In 1520 he also co-operated with the Basel printer Andreas *Cratander, whose Homer edition may well have been inspired by him. He evidently knew a good deal about Cratander's editions of the satirical dialogues *Julius exclusus* and *Henno rusticus*, both of which he may in his mind have attributed to Erasmus. His obvious sympathy with the reformers is confirmed by the fact that he was the addressee of the dedicatory preface (24 June 1521) of an *Anzeigung* against the bull condemning Luther, whose author was Urbanus *Rhegius, hiding behind a pseudonym.

BIBLIOGRAPHY: Allen and CWE Ep 595 / *Opuscula* 238, 245 / *Matrikel Basel* I 341 / Z VII Epp 94, 133, 137, 138, 148, VIII Epp 301, 333,

and passim / AK II Ep 739 and passim / BRE Epp 125, 129, 152, 157, and passim / O. Clemen 'Jacobus Nepos' *Zentralblatt für Bibliothekswesen* 21 (1904) 179–82 / Bierlaire *Familia* 51–4 and passim / E. Egli 'Ein biographisches Trümmerfeld' *Zwingliana* 1 (1897–1904) 454–6 / O. Farner 'Zwinglis Entwicklung zum Reformator nach seinem Briefwechsel bis Ende 1522' *Zwingliana* 3 (1913–20) 161–80, esp 169 / R. Wackernagel *Geschichte der Stadt Basel* (Basel 1907–54) III 185, 217, 94* / E. Hilgert 'Johann Froben and the Basel University scholars, 1513–1523' *The Library Quarterly* 41 (1971) 141–69, esp 164–5   PGB

Konrad NESEN of Nastätten, 1495–25 June 1560
Konrad Nesen (Nesenus, Nysenus), the brother of Wilhelm *Nesen, is practically unknown prior to the date of his matriculation at the University of Wittenberg on 14 June 1525. In particular, he cannot be traced to either Paris or Louvain; it seems clear that his brother was largely responsible for the composition and publication of the *Dialogus bilinguium ac trilinguium*, which bore Konrad's name (CWE 7 appendix). In Wittenberg he studied law and, like his late brother, was a friend of *Melanchthon, who in 1529 recommended him unsuccessfully to Philip of *Hesse (*Melanchthons Briefwechsel* I Ep 814). In 1530 he became *praeceptor* at the court of King *Ferdinand, but it is not clear what functions were reflected by that title. In 1532 he returned to Wittenberg and there obtained a licence in law. From 1533 to his death he was syndic of the city of Zittau in Lusatia and took a leading part in introducing the Reformation there. From 1541 he was also one of the city's burgomasters.

In 1529 Christoph von *Carlowitz associated Konrad with an old friend of Wilhelm, Ludovicus *Carinus, who bore Erasmus a grudge (Ep 2085).

BIBLIOGRAPHY: Allen Ep 2085 / ADB XXIII 437–8 / *Matrikel Wittenberg* I 126 / de Vocht CTL I 399 and passim / *Melanchthons Briefwechsel* I Ep 1092 / *Melanchthons Werke in Auswahl* ed R. Stupperich et al (Gütersloh 1951–75) VII-2 312   MICHAEL ERBE & PGB

Wilhelm NESEN of Nastätten, 1493–6 July 1524
Wilhelm Nesen (Nesenus, Nessenus) was born

at Nastätten, between Koblenz and Mainz, the son of a peasant. In 1511 he went to study at Basel, where he took his MA in 1515. During his studies he became the friend of Huldrych *Zwingli and Henricus *Glareanus. He also worked as a corrector for the presses of Michael Furter and Johann *Froben (1515–16) and took care of Erasmus' edition of Seneca's *Lucubrationes* (Epp 328, 329). Erasmus dearly liked Nesen when they met in the course of the former's visit to Basel. In 1516 Erasmus dedicated to him the second edition of *De copia* (Ep 462). Nesen in turn became deeply devoted to the older scholar (Epp 469, 473, 534). In 1517 Nesen, who also kept a private school in Basel, planned to visit Italy with Bruno *Amerbach (Epp 595, 816), but by January 1518 he was in Paris (Epp 630, 768) with his young friend Ludovicus *Carinus, supervising two sons of the Frankfurt patrician Nikolaus *Stalburg. He studied Greek under Cyprianus *Taleus and met Nicolas *Bérault and Guillaume *Budé (Epp 925, 931). In March 1519 Nesen paid a brief visit to Erasmus at Louvain (Epp 924, 925, 994). In July he left Paris for good and moved to Louvain with the Stalburg sons and Carinus (Epp 994, 1002). He found lodgings in the College of the Lily, where Erasmus himself lived. The time of his move from Paris to Louvain coincides with the publication of the *Dialogus bilinguium ac trilinguium* (Paris: J. Bade for C. Resch 1519), a fierce attack upon the Louvain theologians, which may in large measure be the work of Wilhelm, although it was published under the name of his brother, Konrad *Nesen (CWE 7 appendix). In Louvain Nesen attempted to lecture privately on Pomponius Mela within the framework of the new Collegium Trilingue but was refused the university's permission to do so. A prank apparently played on the rector of the university by Nesen's students did not help matters (CWE Ep 1046 introduction), nor did Nesen's appeal to the council of Brabant on 7 January 1520, although Erasmus supported him loyally (CWE Ep 1057 introduction).

In the spring of 1520 Nesen was among those friends who defended Erasmus against Edward *Lee, and he even seems to have been the editor of the *Epistolae aliquot eruditorum* published to this effect [Antwerp: M. Hillen 1520]. He may also have undertaken a mission to Germany in order to launch a campaign by

Erasmus' admirers against Lee (CWE Epp 1083, 1088 introductions). Seeing no future for himself in Louvain, he left before 31 August 1520 (Ep 1126) and on 14 September was appointed director of the Frankfurt Schola patriciorum financed by Stalburg and others. With the anonymous *Epistola de Magistris Nostris Lovaniensibus* and the *S. Nicolai vita* [Sélestat: L. Schürer 1520] Nesen continued to attack the conservative theologians of Louvain, a vendetta watched by Erasmus with mixed feelings (Ep 1165). Nesen also became an adherent of *Luther, whom he met twice when the reformer passed through Frankfurt on his way to and from the diet of Worms in 1521. He was therefore attacked by Johannes *Cochlaeus, then dean of St Mary's at Frankfurt, and probably obliged to give up his position in Frankfurt, in which he was replaced by Carinus at the beginning of 1523. In February Luther dedicated to him his pamphlet *Adversus armatum virum Cokleum* (Wittenberg: [J. Rhau] 1523) and in April Nesen began to study civil law at Wittenberg and gave lectures on classical authors and ancient geography. In the spring of 1524 he accompanied *Melanchthon and Joachim *Camerarius on a journey to southern Germany and stayed for a while at Frankfurt. After his return to Wittenberg he was drowned on 6 July in a boating accident on the Elbe.

After Nesen's departure from Louvain there is no evidence of continued direct relations between him and Erasmus. In the winter of 1521–2 Erasmus had evidently lost confidence in him (Epp 1244, 1257), and Nesen's move to Wittenberg seems to have sealed the alienation. Erasmus was informed of Nesen's death by Melanchthon. Although he reacted to the news with warmth and praise for Nesen's great loyalty to him, he added that for himself their friendship had been decidedly unfortunate (Ep 1523). Melanchthon soon realized that Erasmus' memories of Nesen were increasingly bitter, and in 1528 he attempted to exculpate his dead friend (Ep 1981), apparently without success. In sharp contrast to his earlier praise for Nesen's editing of *De copia* (Ep 630), Erasmus now reproached him with negligence in seeing Seneca's *Lucubrationes* through the press (Epp 1479, 1804, 2056, 2091, 2227). Another and possibly more significant reason for Erasmus' unhappy memories were Nesen's anonymous lampoons, in the preparation of which Erasmus had had a share, although he may subsequently have regretted their publication. While Erasmus could not be expected to refer openly to these matters, he did criticize Nesen's machinations in conjunction with his adherence to Luther and even suspected him of having incited Luther to write pamphlets against *Henry VIII and Cochlaeus (Ep 1729; LB X 1250C, 1268C).

BIBLIOGRAPHY: Allen Ep 329 / Reedijk poem 103 / ADB XXIII 438–41 / *Matrikel Basel* I 307 / AK II Ep 494 and passim / BRE Ep 28 and passim / BA *Oekolampads* I 175–6, 191, and passim / *Melanchthons Briefwechsel* I Ep 325 and passim / Z VII Ep 215 and passim / de Vocht CTL I 391–401, 466–9, and passim / Martin Spahn *Johannes Cochlaeus* (Berlin 1898, repr 1964) 60–1 and passim / Schottenloher II 92

MICHAEL ERBE & PGB

Hermann von NEUENAHR

c 1492–30 October 1530

Count Hermann von Neuenahr (Neuenar, Nuenar, Newenaer, Nova Aquila) was a son of Count Wilhelm and Walburgis von Manderscheid. He received a prebend at the Cologne cathedral chapter as early as 1495 and was a canon when he matriculated at the University of Cologne on 14 November 1504. He studied under Johannes *Caesarius, and when a Cologne embassy departed for Rome in 1508, Neuenahr and Caesarius went along with it, registering in 1509 at the University of Bologna. After his return he was elected provost of Aachen and in January 1524 provost and archdeacon of the Cologne chapter, offices that were combined with the chancellorship of the University of Cologne. Neuenahr was a close collaborator of Archbishop Hermann von *Wied, with whom he was related through the marriage of his brother, Wilhelm von Neuenahr. In the spring of 1519 he undertook a mission to Rome (BRE Ep 103) and later in the year he was in Frankfurt for the election of *Charles V. In 1530 he accompanied his archbishop to the diet of Augsburg, where he fell ill. On 9 August he was close to death (Ep 2360). Erasmus attributed his untimely death to his disregard for his health (Ep 2508).

From Ep 442 it may be surmised that Erasmus had met Neuenahr in Caesarius' company when travelling through Cologne in 1515. Subsequently he took the initiative in writing to the count, who answered enthusiastically (Ep 442). From then on their correspondence continued until Neuenahr's death. Of the ten preserved letters exchanged by them, seven were written by Erasmus. In September 1518 Erasmus again spent some delightful days in Neuenahr's company, resting at the count's castle of Bedburg, west of Cologne (Ep 867). They clearly found each other congenial and took care to have their mutual affection shared by a steadily widening circle of common friends such as *Vives (Ep 1082), *Capito (Ep 1165), *Sobius (Ep 1775), Ferry de *Carondelet (Ep 2002), *Riquinus (Ep 2246), and Gerhard von *Enschringen who in turn provided links between Neuenahr and both Johann Sturm and the printer Johann *Schott at Strasbourg (Epp 1078, 1082). As a result, Neuenahr contributed to the great *Herbarium* of Otto *Brunfels. A vital aspect of Neuenahr's friendship with Erasmus was their joint support for the cause of humanism in general and for *Reuchlin in particular (Epp 610, 680). Erasmus made no secret of his reservations about Neuenahr's publication of Giorgio *Benigno's *Defensio Reuchlini* and his share in the *Epistolae trium illustrium virorum* (Epp 680, 703, 808, 830, 1106); on the other hand he never tired of repeating the story of Neuenahr's amusing revenge against Jacob of *Hoogstraten, a leading anti-Reuchlinist (Ep 877, etc). In the end he succeeded in arranging a truce of sorts between Neuenahr and Hoogstraten (Epp 1078, 2045; ASD IX-1 135–8). In turn, he approached Neuenahr in an effort to stop the circulation in Cologne of the *Julius exclusus* (Epp 636, 1053), and he must have appreciated Neuenahr's attack upon his own critic, Edward *Lee (Ep 1078). Later he tried to enlist Neuenahr's aid in his quarrel with *Eppendorf (Ep 1991).

In the course of his visits with Neuenahr, Erasmus probably also met Hermann's brother, Wilhelm von Neuenahr, who in 1519 married Anna von Wied, a niece of the archbishop of Cologne, Hermann von Wied. In March 1520, it was Wilhelm not Gumpert von Neuenahr, as stated in Allen, who sent greetings to Erasmus (CWE Ep 1078).

BIBLIOGRAPHY: Allen Ep 442 / ADB XXIII 485–6

/ Knod 371 / *Matrikel Köln* II 570 / Ludwig Geiger in *Zeitschrift für vergleichende Literatur-Geschichte und Renaissance-Literatur* n s 2 (1888–9) 456–82 / Ludwig Geiger *Johann Reuchlin* (Leipzig 1871, repr 1964) 366–7 and passim / Hutten *Operum supplementum* I 427–9 and passim / Hermann Keussen *Die alte Universität Köln* (Cologne 1934) passim / *Herbarium* ed Otto Brunfels (Strasbourg 1530–6) II-2 116–28   EUGEN HOFFMANN & PGB

Gumpert and Wilhelm von NEUENAHR *See Hermann von* NEUENAHR

Jan de NEVE of Hondschoote, d 25 April 1522
Jan de Neve (Jean de Nève, Nepotis, Nevius, Naevius) of Hondschoote, now in the French Département du Nord, matriculated at the University of Louvain on 27 February 1492 and ranked third among those promoted to MA on 12 April 1494. While studying theology he taught arts courses in the College of the Lily. From 1509 he was involved in a complicated dispute over the regency of the Lily which led to litigation with Leo *Outers and eventually, on 26 August 1517, to a settlement that left Neve in sole possession of the regency. He had resided in the Lily throughout this period and seems to have exercised the functions of regent, as he now continued to do until his death, although from 1521 paralysis made it necessary for him to appoint a co-regent in the person of Jan *Heems.

His teaching (Ep 1932) and the regency of the Lily absorbed most of Neve's energies. He did not pursue theology beyond a bachelor's degree and never moved up to the theological faculty. Nor did he publish, although he played an active role in university councils and committees, in which he was well served by his conciliatory nature (Ep 696). Being a priest, he was nominated to benefices within the gift of the university in 1515, 1517, and 1521. He was also elected for a term each as rector (28 February 1515) and dean of arts (30 September 1516).

Under Neve's regency the Lily attained a significance for the new learning that may have been unparalleled at Louvain prior to the foundation of the Collegium Trilingue. Among his colleagues were men of the stature of Johannes *Custos, Maarten van *Dorp, and above all, Erasmus himself, who may have been introduced to Neve by Dorp on a visit to Louvain in 1514 and who dedicated to him his edition of *Catonis praecepta* (Ep 298). When Erasmus returned to Louvain in the summer of 1517 the Lily offered a most congenial ambiance for his studies and his leisure. He moved to the college as soon as the dispute over the regency was resolved (Ep 643) and lived there until his departure from Louvain in 1521, referring to Neve as his host with warmth and genuine gratitude (Epp 651, 695). The two men were united by a firm, sincere friendship, and there are traces of missing correspondence when Erasmus was away from Louvain (Epp 849, 1222). He also left some money with Neve for safekeeping (Ep 2352). In the autumn of 1519 Neve and Nicolas *Coppin succeeded in settling the disagreements between Erasmus and the conservative theologians, although the truce turned out to be short-lived (CWE Ep 1022 introduction, Ep 1225). After Neve's sudden death from a stroke (Ep 1921), Erasmus recalled him with great warmth and – the true mark of friendship – felt no need to gloss over a certain vindictiveness, the only weak spot he had found in Neve's character (Ep 1347). Earlier, in the *Familiarium colloquiorum formulae* he had used Neve's name to typify great storytellers (ASD I-3 140).

BIBLIOGRAPHY: Allen and CWE Ep 298 / *Matricule de Louvain* III-1 79 / de Vocht *Literae ad Craneveldium* Ep 26 and passim / de Vocht MHL 179–87, 354, 366–7, and passim / de Vocht CTL I 200 and passim / H. de Jongh *L'Ancienne Faculté de théologie de Louvain* (Louvain 1911) 120 and passim   PGB

NICASIUS (Ep 85 of 14 December [1498?])
The addressee of this letter, Nicasius, chaplain of Cambrai, was in a position to give Erasmus' greetings to Michel *Pavie. Nicasius has not been identified.

Pope NICHOLAS V 15 November 1397–24/25 March 1455
Tommaso Parentucelli was born in Sarzana, in Liguria, the son of a physician. He studied in Bologna and Florence, where he tutored young noblemen, then entered the service of Cardinal Niccolò Albergati in Bologna, mov-

Pope Nicholas v

ing with him to Rome in 1426. In 1444 Parentucelli became bishop of Bologna in succession to Albergati, and two years later cardinal. On 6 March 1447 he was elected pope in succession to Eugenius IV, and in July 1447 he was officially recognized by the Emperor *Frederick III. With the assistance of highly respected cardinals such as Nicolaus *Cusanus, and relying on his own diplomatic skill, he was able to end the schism with the council of Basel and win over most of the remaining conciliarists. In consequence he proclaimed a jubilee for the year of 1450. Numerous pilgrims came to Rome, contributing so lavishly to the wealth of the city that plans could be made to rebuild the residence of the popes, although additional funds had to be raised.

On 16 March 1452 Frederick III came to Rome to be crowned by the pope, who also hoped to achieve reunification with the church of Byzantium. In May 1453, however, Constantinople was stormed by the Turks. Nicholas' attempts to arouse enthusiasm for a crusade against the conquerors were in vain, and from 1454 he was ill. His last diplomatic successes were the peace of Lodi in 1454 and the

foundation on 25 February 1455 of a league that secured peace in Italy for a quarter of a century.

Nicholas V was a great patron of the arts; among others, the painter Fra Angelico da Fiesole and the architect Leon Battista Alberti were supported at his court. He was the first pope to take an interest in humanistic studies and gathered an important collection of classical texts in manuscript, a nucleus of what was later to become the Vatican library. He also assisted famous humanistic scholars, especially Lorenzo *Valla, who lived at his court (Ep 34).

BIBLIOGRAPHY: Allen and CWE Ep 34 / R. Morghen in EI XXIV 766–7 / J. Gill in *New Catholic Encyclopedia* (New York 1967–74) X 443–5 / LThK VII 979–80 / Pastor II 3–314 / F.X. Seppelt et al *Geschichte der Päpste* 2nd ed (Munich 154–) IV 307–26   IG

NICHOLAS of Luxembourg documented at Louvain in 1520
Nicholas of Luxembourg (Nicolaus Lutzenburgus), one of the masters of the school of St Maartensdal, the Louvain monastery of the

canons regular of St Augustine, is known only from the references in Epp 1070, 1071, which show him in familiar contact with Erasmus.

BIBLIOGRAPHY: W. Lourdaux *Moderne Devotie en christelijk humanisme: de geschiedenis van Sint-Maarten te Leuven van 1433 tot het einde der XVIe eeuw* (Louvain 1967) 69–77   PGB

Felipe NICOLA documented 1522–30
From 1522 to 1524 Felipe Nicola was a minor figure in the imperial chancery in Spain. Erasmus sent him a friendly letter on 29 April 1526, with greetings for Sancho *Carranza de Miranda and his friends at court (Ep 1701). In 1530 Nicola was in Cremona and wrote to Johannes *Dantiscus at Augsburg expressing his desire to return to the chancery, seeking news of the diet, and voicing his opposition to the religious innovations of the German reformers. A letter which Nicola sent to Hieronymus Perbonus in 1529 was published by the latter in his *Oviliarum opus* (Milan: V. Meda 1533).

BIBLIOGRAPHY: Allen Ep 1701 / Bataillon *Erasmo y España* 223 and passim / de Vocht *Dantiscus* 59   TBD

**NICOLAAS of 's Hertogenbosch,
NICOLAUS Buscoducensis
or Sylvaducensis**
See Nicolaas van BROECKHOVEN

NICOLAAS of Middelburg (LB X 1681D)
In his *Responsio adversus febricitantis libellum* of 1529, directed against Luis de *Carvajal, Erasmus recalled a conversation he had had at Antwerp in the house of Nicolaas of Middelburg, a physician. He believed that the occurrence lay about twenty-six years in the past. Nicolaas of Middelburg has not been identified.   MARCEL A. NAUWELAERTS

Everardus NICOLAI 1497/8–10 May 1561
Everardus (Everaert) Nicolai was the second son of Nicolaas *Everaerts. In 1526 he was appointed to the council of Friesland at Leeuwarden, and Erasmus sent him greetings in a letter to his colleague *Haio Herman of Friesland (Ep 2261, 31 January 1530). In 1533 he moved to Mechelen to join the grand council but returned to Leeuwarden as president of the council of Friesland in 1541. Finally in 1557

he became president of the grand council in Mechelen.

Nicolai was married to Genoveva, a daughter of Aert van der *Goes, who bore him five children.

BIBLIOGRAPHY: Allen Ep 2261 / C.M.G. ten Raa in NBW VII 656–62 / NNBW III 914–15 / de Vocht CTL II 431 / Michel Baelde *De collaterale raden onder Karel v en Filips II* (Brussels 1965) 260–1 and passim   JAMES D. TRACY

Johannes NICOLAI bishop of Apt, d March/ April 1533
In 1528 Erasmus sent greetings to the governor of Avignon (Ep 2049). The papal vice-legate and governor of the city of Avignon from 1519 was Johannes Nicolai (Jean de Nicolaï), who since 13 June 1515 had been bishop of Apt (Département de Vaucluse). According to Eubel, Nicolai was a doctor of canon and civil law and provost of nearby Saint-Paul-Trois-Châteaux, and had administered Apt from 1515 as coadjutor of an ailing relative. A patron of learning and of the University of Avignon and a Christian humanist who instituted public lectures on the Epistles of St Paul, he was highly regarded by Andrea *Alciati, whose memories of Avignon were otherwise not pleasant. He was also a friend of Jacopo *Sadoleto and especially of Jean Montaigne of Avignon, who informed Bonifacius *Amerbach on 6 May 1533 of Nicolai's recent death. Alciati had earlier mentioned Nicolai's friendship with Amerbach and his admiration for Erasmus.

The name Nicolai is frequent in southern France. The governor of Avignon should not be confused with Jean de Nicolaï of Bourg-Saint-Andéol, lay councillor of the Parlement of Toulouse in 1492 and first president of the Chambres des comptes of Paris from 1508 to 1521, or with Jean Nicolaï of Arles (d before 18 May 1581), the author of several juridical works (cf Masson).

BIBLIOGRAPHY: Allen Ep 2049 / AK III Epp 1067, 1354, IV Ep 1749 / *Le lettere di Andrea Alciato giureconsulto* ed Gian Luigi Barni (Florence 1953) Epp 51, 95 / *Gallia christiana* I 369–70 / Eubel III 125 / Jacopo Sadoleto *Opera* (Verona 1787–8, repr 1964) I 133–7 / C. de Vic, J. Vaissète, et al *Histoire générale de Languedoc* (Toulouse 1872–1904, repr 1973) XI-2 183, 186,

223, XII 292 / J.-H. Albanès *Gallia christiana novissima* (Montbéliard 1899–) I 275–6 / For Jean de Nicolaï of Bourg-Saint-Andéol: Fleury Vindry *Les Parlementaires français au XVIe siècle* (Paris 1909–12) II 178 / Paul Masson et al *Les Bouches-du-Rhone, Encyclopédie départementale* (Marseille-Paris 1913–37) IV-2 355   PGB

Nicolaus NICOLAI *See Nicolaus* GRUDIUS

Petrus Hieronymus NICOLAI d probably before 1532
The son of Nicholaas *Everaerts who dined with Erasmus at Antwerp in the spring of 1520 (Ep 1092) was probably the eldest, Petrus Hieronymus Nicolai (Everardi or Everaerts), whose life is not well known. He was promoted doctor of both laws at Louvain on 22 May 1520 and entered the Premonstratensian order at Middelburg; he was priest at Middelburg from 1518 to 1520 and held the cure of Flushing from about 1524.
    BIBLIOGRAPHY: Allen and CWE Ep 1092 / de Vocht CTL II 431 / NNBW VI 497–8
                                    JAMES D. TRACY

NICOLAUS *See* NICHOLAS, NICOLAAS

Bernardus NIGER documented 1529–c 1537
Bernardus Niger was a student at Dole in the Franche-Comté when he addressed Ep 2135 to Erasmus (27 March 1529). He was a friend of *Viglius Zuichemus and Karel *Sucket and was probably himself a Netherlander. In 1530 he wrote to Bonifacius *Amerbach (AK III Ep 1419) that he was on the point of joining Viglius at Bourges, where *Alciati was teaching. It is conceivable that he was a relation of Philippus Nigri or Le Noir (d 4 January 1563), bishop of Antwerp, who was also connected with Viglius.
    BIBLIOGRAPHY: Allen Ep 2135 / C.P. Hoynck van Papendrecht *Analecta Belgica* (The Hague 1743) I 73, 129 / For Nigri: BNB XV 734–7
                                              PGB

FRANCISCUS NIGER *See Francesco* NEGRO

Adolf van der NOOT of Brussels, 3 June 1486–31 March 1543
The Van der Noot family ranked traditionally on the borderline between aristocracy and patriciate, and its members frequently served as diplomats and court or civic officials. Adolf van der Noot (Notius) was the son of Pieter, master of the forests of Brabant, and Angelica van der Heyden. On 30 August 1500 he matriculated in Louvain as an arts student. In 1510 he went to Bologna, where he received a doctorate in civil and canon law. Just two years later he became a member of the council of Brabant in his native Brussels, and in January 1532 he succeeded Jeroen van der *Noot as chancellor of Brabant. In this capacity he played a role in the repression of the Ghent riots between 1537 and 1540. In 1540 he resigned the chancellorship and was appointed lieutenant of the feudal court of Brabant.
    Adolf was lord of Oignies and a knight of the Golden Fleece. He was married to Philippotte, a daughter of Jan van Watermael, councillor of Brabant, and subsequently to Margriet van Pede (d 17 May 1557). Adolf and his second wife were buried in St Gudula's, Brussels; their daughters married high officials.
    The chancellor of Brabant was mentioned to Erasmus by Conradus *Goclenius, who was involved in a long litigation over his claims to a prebend of the Antwerp chapter. Mentioning Adolf's high regard for Erasmus, Goclenius asked his friend to write to the chancellor in his support. Erasmus complied, but the fact that the name of the addressee is missing from his letter suggests that he did not know the chancellor personally (Epp 3124, 3130).
    BIBLIOGRAPHY: Allen Ep 3124 / *Matricule de Louvain* III-1 206 / de Vocht CTL II 127, III 99–102, IV 19 / de Vocht *Busleyden* 22 / de Vocht *Literae ad Craneveldium* 294 / Knod 377 / J. de Azevedo-Coutiño-y-Bernal *Généalogie de la famille van der Noot* (n p 1771) 71 / Arthur Gaillard *Le Conseil de Brabant* (Brussels 1898–1902) III 338, 350 / V. de Ryckman de Betz and F. de Jonghe d'Ardoye *Armorial et biographies des chanceliers et conseillers de Brabant* (Hombeek 1956) I 108–9 / *Relation des troubles de Gand sous Charles-Quint par un anonyme* ed M. Gachard (Brussels 1946) 256, 350
                          HILDE DE RIDDER-SYMOENS

Jeroen van der NOOT of Brussels, 1463–18 February 1541
Jeroen was the third son of Wauter van der Noot, councillor of Brabant and ducal cham-

berlain, and Digne van Grimbergen-van As-
sche. He matriculated at the University of
Louvain on 30 August 1478, and in 1485–6
studied law at Orléans, becoming a licentiate in
civil and canon law. In 1495 he succeeded his
father as a member of the council of Brabant in
Brussels, and later he was chancellor of
Brabant. Having lost his eyesight, he resigned
the chancellorship in 1531 and retired with an
annuity of five hundred Rhenish guilders. His
wife, Maria, was a sister of Jan and Hendrik
van *Nassau-Breda; she died on 2 January
1521, aged forty, giving birth to her nineteenth
child. Jeroen made wills on 16 February 1523
and 5 April 1532. He was buried with his wife
in the Carmelite church of Brussels. A painting
of Jeroen and his family in the Visitation chapel
of that church was destroyed in 1695 when the
French bombarded Brussels, but several copies
exist.

In 1520 Erasmus wrote to Joost van der
*Noot, a relative of Jeroen, asking him to use
his influence with the chancellor in favour of
Wilhelm *Nesen, who was refused permission
to lecture at the University of Louvain (Ep
1057). Two years later he addressed himself
directly to Jeroen, asking him to impose silence
on Nicolaas *Baechem Egmondanus and other
critics at Louvain (Ep 1300). He wrote in the
same vein to the president of the great council
of Mechelen, Joost *Lauwereyns (Ep 1299).

BIBLIOGRAPHY: Allen Ep 1300 / BNB XXVI 374 /
Matricule de Louvain II-1 381 / *Matricule d'Or-
léans* II-1 122–3 / de Vocht CTL I 462–3 and
passim / de Vocht *Literae ad Craneveldium* Ep
66 / Arthur Gaillard *Le Conseil de Brabant*
(Brussels 1898–1902) III 338 / V. de Ryckman
de Betz and F. de Jonghe d'Ardoye *Armorial
et biographies des chanceliers et conseillers de
Brabant* (Hombeek 1956) I 104–7 / J. de
Azevedo-Coutiño-y-Bernal *Généalogie de la
famille van der Noot* (n p 1771) 7–8 / E. Lejour
*Inventaire des archives de la famille Van der
Noot* (Brussels 1954) 8 / C. van den Bergen-
Pantens 'Quelques oeuvres relatives a la
famille Van der Noot au xve siècle' *Brabantica*
9 (1968) 218–20, with a reproduction of the
family painting
                          HILDE DE RIDDER-SYMOENS

Joost van der NOOT of Brussels, died c 1525
Joost van der Noot (Notius) belonged to the
patrician branch of his family. His father, Jan,
was repeatedly alderman and burgomaster of
Brussels between 1500 and 1537; his mother,
Francisca Schoof, was the daughter of a
patrician of Louvain. Joost matriculated on 11
May 1510 in Louvain and on 26 January 1516 in
Bologna, where he studied law. In 1520
Erasmus addressed him as a councillor of
Brabant (Ep 1057), an office that he seems to
have retained until his untimely death in his
thirties, around 1525. He is not mentioned,
however, in the standard literature on the
council of Brabant. He was married to Barbara
Madoets.

When the University of Louvain refused to
let Wilhelm *Nesen lecture, Erasmus wrote in
his support to Joost van der Noot, enclosing as
a gift a copy of his recently published *Farrago*
(Ep 1057, of 7 January 1520).

BIBLIOGRAPHY: Allen and CWE Ep 1057 / de
Vocht CTL I 462 / Knod 377 / *Matricule de Louvain*
III-1 392 / J. de Azevedo-Coutiño-y-Bernal
Généalogie de la famille van der Noot (n p 1771) 29
/ P. Leynen and H. van Parijs 'Quelques
lignages de docteurs en droit de Bologne (xvie
siècle)' *Les Lignages de Bruxelles* 8 (1969) 132
                          HILDE DE RIDDER-SYMOENS

Brixius NORDANUS See PUISTUTH

NORFOLK See Thomas HOWARD, *duke of
Norfolk*

Christian NORTHOFF of Lübeck, documented 1496–1532
Christian (Carsten), a son of Johann and a
brother of Heinrich *Northoff (Noorthoven,
Noerthoest, Noorthovius, Nordhave) is first
documented as one of Erasmus' younger
friends in Paris through a sequence of didactic
and sometimes amusing letters Erasmus addressed to him (Epp 54–6), apparently expecting a reward (Ep 55). By August 1497, when
Erasmus addressed to him the stylish and witty
Ep 61 composed in the name of his brother,
Christian had left Paris. In the course of that
year Erasmus continued to write to him,
linking him with the famous humanist Rudolf
von *Langen at Münster (Epp 70, 72). During
his stay at Paris Christian seems, like his
brother, to have been tutored by Augustinus
Vincentius *Caminadus. A 'Christianus,' an

'Augustinus,' and an 'Erasmus' are the speakers in Erasmus' *Familiarum colloquiorum formulae* (ASD I-3 27–70; Ep 130). It is possible that this earliest version of the *Colloquia* was composed specifically for the benefit of the Northoff brothers and other north-German students of Caminadus.

Meanwhile Christian had returned to Lübeck, where he spent his life as a highly respected merchant (Epp 61, 70). On 31 August 1497 Christian and three brothers and sisters endowed a vicary in St Mary's church, and in 1498 he bought a house in the Schüsselbuden. In 1500 he was at Rome with his brother Heinrich and on 9 April registered as a 'citizen and merchant of Lübeck' in the German institution, Santa Maria dell'Anima. In 1515 he was one of the governors of the monastery of St Anne in Lübeck, and in 1522 he belonged to the executive of St Anthony's fraternity. In 1518 he had an oxen slaughtered for the benefit of the poor. The name of his wife was Anneke Klinckrade, and they had several children. The year of his death is given as 1532 or 1535.

BIBLIOGRAPHY: Allen Ep 54 / Wilhelm Jannasch *Reformationsgeschichte Lübecks ... 1515–1530* (Lübeck 1958) 99, 363 / *Die Bau- und Kunstdenkmäler der Freien und Hansestadt Lübeck* (Lübeck 1906–) II 163, 212 / *Liber confraternitatis S. Mariae de Anima* ed C. Jaenig (Rome 1875) 113 / Lübeck, Archiv der Hansestadt Lübeck, MS Personenkartei 225 passim

PGB

Heinrich NORTHOFF of Lübeck, documented 1489–1500

A Heinrich Northoff is mentioned in the Lübeck sources only in 1489 as half-brother of the better-known Hans Northoff. Perhaps the same Heinrich matriculated at the University of Rostock on 21 May 1492 with his friend Bernhard *Schinkel. Both received a BA the following year, and in the summer of 1496 they continued their studies at the University of Louvain, where Heinrich was registered on 6 July as a student of canon law. In the academic year beginning 20 September 1496 the two friends were in Paris, where Heinrich and his brother Christian *Northoff were living with and being tutored by Erasmus and Augustinus Vincentius *Caminadus. As Erasmus was then a good friend of Caminadus, the Lübeck

students came to know him quite well. He may have composed his *Familiarium colloquiorum formulae* for their benefit (ASD I-3 27–70; Ep 130), and in August 1497 he wrote in Heinrich's name the entertaining Ep 61 to Christian, who had left Paris. This letter indicates that Erasmus was then living under the same roof as Heinrich and Caminadus.

Early in 1497 Heinrich received a MA in Paris. By February 1498 he seems to have joined Christian (Epp 70, 72). There is no need to assume that he subsequently returned to Paris, since Ep 82 may date from November 1497. Erasmus later used Heinrich's name as a recommendation when introducing himself to Adolf *Greverade (Ep 141). On 1 April 1500 Heinrich was in Rome, where he lived at the German institution, Santa Maria dell'Anima, signing the register as a cleric from Lübeck and a notary of the Sacred Palace. No more is known about him thereafter.

BIBLIOGRAPHY: Allen Ep 54 / *Matrikel Rostock* I 262, 268 / *Matricule de Louvain* III-1 141 / *Liber confraternitatis S. Mariae de Anima* ed C. Jaenig (Rome 1875) 113 / Lübeck, Archiv der Hansestadt Lübeck, MS Personenkartei 225 / Paris, Archives de l'Université (Sorbonne), MS Registre 91

PGB

NOTIUS *See van der* NOOT

Gerardus NOVIOMAGUS *See Gerard* GELDENHOUWER

Luis NÚÑEZ CABEZA DE VACA of Jaén c 1465–12 December 1550

Luis Núñez Cabeza de Vaca of Jaén was a tutor to the future *Charles v from approximately 1504 to 1512, for a time sharing tutorial duties with Adrian of Utrecht, the future Pope *Adrian VI. In December 1507 and June 1512 *Margaret of Austria recommended him to the Emperor *Maximilian for preferment. In 1515 and 1521 he was a member of Charles' council, and in May 1522 he accompanied him to England. By 14 October 1523 he was bishop of the Canaries. He was transferred to Salamanca on 22 June 1530 and to Palencia in 1536.

On 19 October 1517 Erasmus named Cabeza de Vaca as one who had recommended the baptized Jewish physician and scholar Matthaeus *Adrianus (Ep 686). In the summer of 1527 the bishop served as vice-president of the assembly called by the inquisitor-general, Alonso *Manrique, to judge the orthodoxy of the works of Erasmus (Ep 1847).

Shortly after his elevation to the see of Salamanca, Cabeza de Vaca asked Alonso *Fernández, archdeacon of Alcor, to write a life of the saintly Friar Hernando de Talavera, the first archbishop of Granada, the archdeacon's former protector and tutor. The edition of Félix G. Olmedo (Madrid 1931) includes a dedication to Cabeza de Vaca.

BIBLIOGRAPHY: Allen Epp 686, 1847 / Bataillon *Erasmo y España* 337   LUIS A. PÉREZ

Konrad NYDER of Eppingen, documented 1523–46
Konrad Nyder was born in Eppingen, thirty kilometres south-east of Heidelberg, and matriculated at the University of Heidelberg on 23 November 1523. Later he moved to Koblenz, married the daughter of a burgher, and in 1532 was himself admitted to the citizenship of Koblenz. On this occasion the official register refers to him as a doctor of medicine. As it turned out, however, he did not yet possess a doctorate; as a result he was dismissed from his position as town physician, which he had held for four years, and hurried off to Italy, where he acquired the missing degree (Ep 2968). In fact he signed himself 'doctor of arts and medicine' in Ep 2984. On his way home from Italy, in the autumn of 1534, he visited Simon *Grynaeus at Basel, giving him a letter from Johannes *Sinapius, and at Freiburg called on Erasmus with letters of reference from Giovanni *Manardo and Anselmus *Ephorinus. Erasmus agreed to recommend him to Johann von *Metzenhausen, archbishop of Trier (Epp 2968, 2984). It seems that Nyder was restored to his position in Koblenz and also named physician to the archbishop. At the same time Erasmus had recommended Nyder to his friend Christoph *Eschenfelder (Epp 2984, 3003). In 1546 Nyder sold a house in Koblenz.

BIBLIOGRAPHY: Allen Ep 2984 / *Matrikel Heidelberg* I 535 / L. Keil 'Humanisten in den Trierer Landen im Anfang des 16. Jahrhunderts' *Trierische Chronik* 16 (1920) 188–9 / The reference in BA *Oekolampads* II 256 may not be to Nyder.   HANSGEORG MOLITOR

Jan OBRECHT (Ep 201 of [4 November 1506])
Little is known about Jan Obrecht, to whom Erasmus sent Ep 201 from Florence. Since the letter was to be relayed to Obrecht by Jacob *Mauritszoon of Gouda (Ep 202), it is likely that Obrecht lived at or near that town. Erasmus' intention to meet him in the summer of 1507 was not realized because Erasmus was at Bologna at that time. He may have been a kinsman of Willem *Obrecht and Jacob Obrecht, Erasmus' music teacher (cf Allen I 56–7).

BIBLIOGRAPHY: Allen and CWE Ep 201
C.G. VAN LEIJENHORST

Willem OBRECHT of Delft, documented 1506–7
Willem Obrecht of Delft (Delfinus), probably a relative of Jan *Obrecht, to whom Erasmus sent Ep 201, was a licentiate in canon and civil law. At Bologna, where Erasmus met him, he was tutoring Matthias, Marcus, and Petrus *Laurinus, who were the sons of Hieronymus *Laurinus, chamberlain and treasurer to Duke Philip the Handsome of *Burgundy.

BIBLIOGRAPHY: Allen Ep 201 / E. Friedlaender and C. Malagola *Acta Nationis Germanicae Universitatis Bononiensis* (Berlin 1887) 268
C.G. VAN LEIJENHORST

Vincentius OBSOPOEUS *See Vincentius OPSOPOEUS*

Pompeius OCCO 1483–22 November 1537
Pompeius (Poppe, Popius) Occo was born in Ostfriesland (near Emden?); his father's name was Haynck. Around 1494 he joined his uncle, the physician Adolph Occo, at Augsburg. On Adolph's death in 1503 he inherited his rich library (Ep 485) and thus became the owner of an autograph manuscript of Rodolphus *Agricola's *De inventione dialectica*, which was edited after much delay by *Alaard of Amsterdam, and of the Treviso Seneca that Erasmus later used for his own edition (Epp 903, 2056, 2091, 2108). In January 1504 Occo matriculated at Cologne in the faculty of arts, but he returned to Augsburg the next year. Chosen to be factor of the Fugger family in Holland, he settled in Amsterdam in 1511. Soon he also became factor and banker to the Danish king *Christian II, and was involved in collecting the dowry attached to Christian's marriage with *Isabella

Pompeius Occo, by Dirck Jacobszoon

56), written by Alaard with woodcuts by Jacob Corneliszoon. He was guildmaster of the Heilig Kruisgilde and churchwarden, until 1519, of the Heilige Stede and from 1521 to 1526 of the Nieuwe Kerk of Amsterdam. Pope *Leo x granted him the title 'Comes S. Palatii et Aulae Lateranensis' in 1515. He married Gerbrich Claesdochter (1491–1558/9), by whom he had six children, including Sybrand (1514–88), his successor, and Anna, the wife of Haio Herman. A portrait by Dirck Jacobszoon is now in the Amsterdam Rijksmuseum; an altar-piece by Jacob Corneliszoon in the Koninklijk Museum voor Schone Kunsten at Antwerp depicts him with his wife. Alaard of Amsterdam composed a long *Comploratio* and an epitaph on his death.

BIBLIOGRAPHY: Allen Ep 485 / J.F.M. Sterck *Onder Amsterdamsche humanisten* (Hilversum-Amsterdam 1934), and in NNBW VI 1075–6 / O. Nübel *Pompejus Occo* (Tübingen 1972) / On his portraits see E.J. Dubiez in *Ons Amsterdam* 10 (1958) 194–202 and B. Haak in *Bulletin van het Rijksmuseum* 6 (1958) 27–37

C.G. VAN LEIJENHORST

of Austria. In August 1521 Occo received the king in his house, aptly called the 'Paradise,' in the Kalverstraat (Ep 485), the foundations of which were uncovered by archaeologists in 1980. Occo's ties with Christian resulted in his imprisonment between August and November 1522, as the relations between Christian and the Hapsburgs had steadily worsened. However, Occo remained loyal to Christian, even in the period between his expulsion from Denmark and his final defeat (1523–32). During the years that followed he took great pains to retain some of his influence in Scandinavia.

Occo occupied a special place in the cultural life of Amsterdam, maintaining relations with well-known humanists such as Cornelis *Croock, Alaard of Amsterdam, and Nicolaas *Kan, who was his kinsman. Erasmus knew him only indirectly, through Alaard and *Haio Herman, but sent him greetings in Ep 1978. Occo had several books printed, including a prayer-book entitled *In melius singula* (Occo's device; Paris: Joannes du Pré 20 December 1519) and the *Passio Domini nostri Jesu Christi* (Amsterdam: Doen Pietersz 2 April 1523; NK

Bernardino OCHINO of Siena, c 1487–1564/5
In March 1521 Erasmus had heard of a Carmelite preaching at the French court that the coming of Antichrist was bound to be near, seeing that his four precursors were already present: *Lefèvre d'Etaples, *Reuchlin, Erasmus himself, and finally an Italian Franciscan ('Minoritam nescio quem': Epp 1192, 1212). Allen suggested that the reference may be to Bernardino Ochino, who later became famous as general of the Capuchins, the most celebrated preacher of his generation in Italy, and finally a leading Italian reformer in exile. There is no evidence, however, that Ochino's reputation had spread abroad as early as 1521; in fact nothing seems to be known about his life in that period.

BIBLIOGRAPHY: Allen Ep 1192 / EI XXV 161–2 / RGG IV 1555–6 / LThK VII 1090   PGB

Jan OCKEGHEM d 6 February 1497
Jan (van) Ockeghem (Okeghem, Ockenheim) was probably born in Dendermonde, in Flanders, between 1420 and 1425. He is first documented as a chorister of the cathedral of Antwerp from 1443 to 1444. From 1448 he was a

member of the chapel of Duke Charles I of
Bourbon. By 30 September 1453 he had joined
the chapel of the royal court of France and
thereafter remained in the service of King
*Charles VII and his successors as a singer,
composer, chaplain, and master of the royal
chapel. He was also appointed treasurer of the
abbey of St Martin of Tours and freed from the
usual residence requirement of that office.
Apart from a visit to his birthplace and another
to Spain, Ockeghem spent the rest of his life at
the royal court and in Tours, where he died.

As a composer, Ockeghem had considerable
influence on the development of polyphonic
music; his main works are twelve masses of
striking originality, among them the *Missa
Prolationum*, and the *Requiem*, the earliest
extant polyphonic mass for the dead; he also
composed ten motets and about twenty
chansons.

Erasmus did not really like polyphonic music
(LB IX 899A–C), preferring the use of plainchant
in church services. Nevertheless he wrote an
epitaph for Ockeghem (Reedijk poem 32); it
was first published in Josse *Bade's edition of
the *Adagia* and *Epigrammata* (1506–7) and was
later set to music by Johannes Lupi. One may
speculate that Erasmus could have known the
composer after his arrival at Paris in the
summer of 1495.

BIBLIOGRAPHY: J.C. Margolin *Recherches Eras-
miennes* (Geneva 1969) 92, 96 / J. Robijns in NBW
VI 736–54 / L.L. Perkins in *The New Grove
Dictionary of Music and Musicians* ed S. Sadie
(London 1980) XIII 489–96 / D. Plamenac in *Die
Musik in Geschichte und Gegenwart* ed F. Blume
(Halle-Basel 1949–   ) IX 1825–38 / *The New
Oxford History of Music* ed J.A. Westrup et al
(London 1957–74) III 254–60   IG

ODILIA (Reedijk poems 29–31)
Erasmus wrote three epitaphs for one Odilia
and her son, which Reedijk has tentatively
dated from 1494–5. It is possible that the
unidentified Odilia was buried at Brussels.

Giovanni Angelo ODONI of Penne,
born c 1510, died after April 1551
Giovanni Angelo Odoni (Odone, Oddone,
Odonus) was born at Penne, near Pescara, to a
wealthy family. His father was a physician,
and he had four older sisters and a younger

brother, Cesare. At Penne Giovanni Angelo and his brother studied the humanities under a master named Uranio, who used
the *Adagia, De copia*, and other works of Erasmus as texts. It is not certain whether this
Uranio can be identified with the Giovan
Battista Uranio who composed a poem in praise
of the *De liberorum educatione* of Count Iacopo
da Porcia (Strasbourg: J. Schott 1510).

The contact between Odoni and Erasmus
was deepened and enriched at Bologna, where
the two brothers went around 1528 to pursue
university studies, Giovanni Angelo in medicine and Cesare in law. The channels for the
diffusion of Erasmian ideas at Bologna were
not only books – which Giovanni Angelo read
avidly – but also the preachers who in those
years spoke from the prestigious pulpit of San
Petronio. Between 1533 and 1534 Giovanni
Angelo became a member of a small group of
persons who hoped to effect in Italy a type of
religious reform inspired by the ideas of
Erasmus on the one hand and by those of
Martin *Bucer on the other. Fileno *Lunardi, a
law student, was also a member of the group,
and Ortensio *Lando perhaps participated in
several of its meetings. The group was also in
contact with a number of persons in Ferrara,
for example, the physician Johannes *Sinapius.
The most powerful figure in the group was a
nobleman of influential family, a doctor in
canon and civil law, in his sixties, experienced
in political affairs, who as a religious propagandist hid under the pseudonym 'Eusebio
Renato' but can probably be identified with
Battista *Fieschi.

The Bolognese group dedicated itself to the
composition and diffusion of evangelical
works and entered into correspondence not
only with Bucer and Strasbourg but also with
Wittenberg, through Hans von der Planitz,
ambassador of the elector of Saxony to *Charles
V during the meeting he had at Bologna with
*Clement VII in 1533. From the reformers across
the Alps the Italians sought assistance for their
editorial endeavours (a work of the Bolognese
group was not accepted by Venetian printers),
political support for the convocation of a
universal council for the reform of the church,
and, above all, doctrinal guidance.

In 1534 Odoni and Lunardi, armed with
letters of introduction from Sinapius to Simon

*Grynaeus and to Erasmus, travelled via Basel to Strasbourg to study theology under Bucer and Wolfgang *Capito. Odoni stayed at Strasbourg for three years. In addition to following the lectures of Bucer, with whom he boarded, and Capito, he participated in the life of the reforming community and made trips to Zürich, to Lyon, where he visited Ortensio Lando and met Etienne *Dolet, and in the spring of 1535 to Freiburg, where he visited Erasmus (Ep 3020). At the same time he translated two works of Erasmus into Italian: the colloquy *Uxor μεμψίγαμος sive coniugium* and the *Liturgia Virginis Matris*. These he sent to his sisters at Penne.

In 1535, shortly before his visit to Erasmus, Odoni sent him Ep 3002. The core of this long composition was a program for religious reform, presented in such a way as to attract the greatest number of followers in Italy. In this letter Erasmus' criticisms against the paganized curia and the worldly hierarchy were combined with the tradition of Italian anticlericalism, from Dante to *Machiavelli. Because of its program and its propaganda value, Odoni had the letter and Erasmus' reply published, but neither the publication nor Erasmus' letter has survived.

Returning to Italy in 1537 Odoni found work with a monastic community and then, in the same year, with Agostino Gonzaga, bishop of Reggio Calabria, as a theological consultant. He probably accompanied the bishop to his diocese, with the intention of using his protection to spread the reform. On 20 April 1544, after a long period when little is known about his work, he acquired a doctorate in medicine at the University of Bologna. In 1551 he was denounced to the Inquisition of Bologna by Pietro Manelfi as a 'great Lutheran.' Manelfi's testimony indicated that Odoni had been active for some years at Vicenza where he expounded on the Scriptures in heretical gatherings, and then at Padua, where he was in contact with Anabaptists. An inquisitorial process at Venice revealed that in the same years he was in contact with the heterodox physician Girolamo Donzellino. The outcome of these denunciations is not known.

Giovanni Angelo Odoni was an exemplary representative of a generation of Italians who through contact with Erasmus came to embrace the Reformation. His genius, his teaching, and his human qualities, which his letters bear witness to, did not bear fruit because they were totally bound up with a lost cause. His personal conflict was identifiable with the failure of the Reformation in Italy.

BIBLIOGRAPHY: Allen Ep 3002 / H.L. and J. Baudrier *Bibliographie lyonnaise* (Lyon 1895–1921) VIII 32–3 / L. Perini 'Gli eretici italiani del '500 e Machiavelli' *Studi storici* 10 (1969) 883–901 / S. Seidel Menchi 'Sulla fortuna di Erasmo in Italia' *Revue suisse d'histoire* 24 (1974) 537–634 / S. Seidel Menchi 'Passione civile e aneliti erasmiani di Riforma nel patriziato genovese del primo cinquecento' *Rinascimento* 18 (1978) 119–21 / J.V. Pollet *Martin Bucer* (Paris 1958–62) II 45, 478

SILVANA SEIDEL MENCHI

Johannes OECOLAMPADIUS of Weinsberg, 1482–22/3 November 1531
Johannes Oecolampadius, the reformer of Basel, was born in the Swabian town of Weinsberg. His father, Johannes Husschin (or Hussgen), was a well-to-do citizen; his mother came from Basel. At the age of seventeen he enrolled in the University of Heidelberg, where he became acquainted with the humanist reform movement led by Jakob *Wimpfeling. After a brief stay at Bologna he returned to Heidelberg and continued the study of theology. From 1506 to 1508 he tutored the Palatinate princes at Mainz, then finished his studies, took holy orders, and in 1510 began to preach regularly at Weinsberg, where a benefice had been created for him. While on a leave of absence he studied Greek and Hebrew at Tübingen and under Johann *Reuchlin in Stuttgart (1513–15). During this period he also met *Melanchthon and established a lifelong friendship with Wolfgang Faber *Capito. When in the summer of 1515 Capito moved to Basel as a professor of theology and cathedral preacher, Oecolampadius followed him and took up work as a corrector in Johann *Froben's printing firm. In the winter of 1515–16 he assisted Erasmus in editing the Greek New Testament (see below). After another period of residence at Weinsberg he accepted the post of penitentiary of the cathedral of Basel in 1518. Shortly afterwards, however, he was appointed cathedral preach-

er in Augsburg. Before he went there the University of Basel conferred a theological doctorate upon him (Ep 904).

In Augsburg Oecolampadius suddenly found himself in the midst of the heated debates about *Luther's writings. He was favourably impressed by them because they confirmed his own views about the necessity of ecclesiastical reform. At the same time the tension between his own apprehensions and Luther's much harsher criticism of the Roman church created great insecurity in his mind. In order to clarify his beliefs he left his post and entered the Brigittine monastery of Altomünster, near Augsburg, as a monk (Epp 1095, 1102). There he wrote two tracts on the mass and on confession which showed that he had actually broken with the Catholic tradition. They were published in 1521 and caused a great deal of unrest among the monastic community. In January 1522 Oecolampadius fled from Altomünster (Ep 1258). He became chaplain of Franz von *Sickingen at the Ebernburg, near Frankfurt, but in November of the same year he returned to Basel. This time it was the printer Andreas *Cratander who employed him as a corrector and allowed him to resume his work on the translations of patristic texts which he had begun before going to Augsburg. In December 1522 he began to correspond with *Zwingli, and in the spring of 1523 he gave his first courses at the university. He started out with a commentary on Isaiah, and, because he lectured partly in German, he became a very great popular success. In spite of the opposition of some conservative members of the university the city council appointed him professor of theology, along with Conradus *Pellicanus. Two years later he also became preacher at St Martin's.

In this double position as teacher and preacher Oecolampadius became the leader of the Reformation movement in Basel. Although his influence was strong he never attained a position comparable to that of Zwingli in Zürich. His opponents were to be found in the university, in the cathedral chapter, and among the wealthy merchants. Among his most ardent followers were a number of very active parish priests, reform-minded monks, and many guild members, such as tradesmen and artisans.

Johannes Oecolampadius

Oecolampadius also served the cause of the Reformation outside Basel. At the disputation of Baden (1526) he headed the evangelical party, and at the disputation of Bern (1528) he helped Zwingli lead it towards victory. He also attended the Marburg colloquy with Zwingli. He had criticized Luther's doctrine of the Eucharist in two writings: *De genuina verborum Dei: 'hoc est corpus meum' etc. expositione* (Basel: n pr 1525) and *Antisyngramma*, published in his *Apologetica* (Zürich: C. Froschauer 1526). He also wrote against the anabaptists and published a number of sermons and commentaries on the prophets. In his last year he was instrumental in bringing about reformation at Ulm, Memmingen, and Biberach.

After many delays and setbacks caused by the hesitant policy of the city council, the breakthrough in the religious renewal in Basel came in February 1529, and at the critical moment Oecolampadius was not at the centre of events. The crucial decisions of the city council were the result not so much of evangelical preaching as of a popular uprising led by the guilds. Once the die had been cast, however, Oecolampadius became very active

Wibrandis Rosenblatt, wife of Oecolampadius

much as to say a true theologian' (Ep 373). To Oecolampadius fell the honour of writing the epilogue to the edition; here he praised Erasmus as the greatest scholar of his age. Oecolampadius also made important contributions to Erasmus' edition of the works of Jerome (1516).

Although correspondence was kept up after Oecolampadius had moved to Augsburg, it became increasingly evident that the two men had gone their different ways in religious thought. When both were back in Basel again, they differed sharply in their judgments on Luther. This became particularly visible in the course of the debates about Erasmus' *De libero arbitrio,* which Oecolampadius attacked in public (Ep 1526). In turn, his own tract *De genuina ... expositione* was criticized by Erasmus (Ep 1636) and therefore banned from the Basel bookstores. After 1525 Erasmus ceased to pass judgment on Oecolampadius publicly. His reservations, however, still appeared occasionally in his private letters (Epp 1644, 1674, 1679, 1697, 1717, 1835, 1977, 1979; the last two references concern Oecolampadius' marriage to Wibrandis *Rosenblatt). At one time he began to write, but subsequently suppressed, a treatise against Oecolampadius' eucharistic position, with part of which he tended to agree (Epp 1616, 1717, 1893). When in the spring of 1529 rumours were spread that Erasmus had attempted to deride Oecolampadius in the latest edition of the *Colloquia,* he tried to settle the matter in a very friendly letter (Ep 2147). A last meeting took place in Froben's garden shortly before Erasmus' departure for Freiburg. The two men parted in peace (Epp 2158, 2196). In 1530 and 1531 Oecolampadius once more contributed to one of Erasmus' editorial enterprises. He agreed that his own translations of certain writings of St John Chrysostom should be included in the great edition published by the Froben press, and he even revised some of them.

An authoritative portrait of Oecolampadius by Hans Asper (n d) is in the Öffentliche Kunstsammlung Basel (reproduced in CWE 4 304). Another portrait by Hans Asper, dated 1550, painted after the one just mentioned and now in a private collection in Zürich, is reproduced in E. Staehelin *Das Buch der Basler Reformation* (Basel 1929), facing p 112; see also p

again; he prepared the new church ordinance (issued on 1 April 1529), promoted church discipline, and became head preacher (*antistes*) at the cathedral. His idea of a lay presbytery, however, was only partly accepted. Although unsuccessful in this respect, Oecolampadius became an inspirer and a forerunner of Calvin. He died in Basel shortly after Zwingli's death in the battle of Kappel.

After an initial period of close friendship, the relationship between Oecolampadius and Erasmus was characterized by mounting tension, although there was never an open breach. When the two scholars worked together in 1515 and 1516 they did not hide their admiration for each other. Erasmus left to Oecolampadius the task of correcting the Hebrew quotations in the annotations to the Greek New Testament. In addition to this Oecolampadius checked the dogmatic correctness of Erasmus' annotations and, together with Nikolaus *Gerbel, read the proofs. For this work Erasmus thanked him in the preface to the annotations and called him 'a man eminent for his knowledge of the three tongues no less than for his piety which is as

263. A third portrait by an unknown artist (probably late seenteenth century and also based on Asper's works) is in the Old Aula of the University of Basel; it is described by P.L. Ganz 'Die Basler Professorengalerie in der Alten Aula des Museums an der Augustiner-gasse' *Basler Zeitschrift für Geschichte und Altertumskunde* 78 (1978) 31–162, cf 131. A copy of a medallion attributed to Hans *Holbein the Younger, 1530, is now in a private collection in Switzerland (reproduced in BA *Oekolampads* I, frontispiece, and *Das Buch der Basler Refor-mation*, frontispiece; see also p 262).

BIBLIOGRAPHY: Allen and CWE Ep 224 / RGG IV 1567–8 / *Briefe und Akten zum Leben Oekolampads* ed E. Staehelin 2 vols (Leipzig 1927–34, repr 1971) / *Oekolampad-Bibliographie* ed E. Staehelin 2nd ed (Nieuwkoop 1963) / E. Staehelin *Das theologische Lebenswerk Oekolampads* (Leipzig 1939, repr 1971) / E. Staehelin 'Erasmus und Oekolampad in ihrem Ringen um die Kirche Jesu Christ' *Gedenkschrift zum 400. Todestage des Erasmus von Rotterdam* (Basel 1936) / E. Staehe-lin 'Oecolampadiana' *Basler Zeitschrift für Ge-schichte und Altertumskunde* 65 (1965) 165–94
HANS R. GUGGISBERG

Floris OEM van Wijngaarden of The Hague, d 1531
Floris, a son of Jan Oem (Oom) van Wijngaar-den and Catherina van Egmont van Ysselstein, matriculated at the University of Louvain on 30 August 1482, with his brother, Ysbrand Oem. He was a Louvain MA in 1485 and stayed on to teach. On 29 November 1491 he was admitted to the university council, and on 11 June 1493 he received a doctorate in civil and canon law. On 28 February 1494 he was elected rector. He returned to Holland and from 14 March 1496 to 8 August 1510 he held an appointment as councillor-in-ordinary in the council of Holland. From 1500 to 1510 he was deputed to reorganize the finances of the bankrupt city of Leiden. In doing so, he made enemies and was removed from the council. He then became the pen-sionary of Dordrecht from 1513 and served the town's interests so devotedly as to incur the displeasure of the central government. As a result he was banned from Dordrecht from 6 December 1518 to September 1520. A fervent defender of orthodoxy, he was a

personal friend of Frans van der *Hulst, and also of Pope *Adrian VI, who informed him about the news of his election six days after he had heard it himself (Burmannus; cf Ep 1668). In 1522 and 1527 he took an active part in the repression of Lutheranism, and on 12 September 1523 he anonymously attacked Erasmus in a Dutch pamphlet (Ep 1469). The critic's identity was revealed three years later by his son Jan *Oem, who also credited Floris with a share in creating the Collegium Trilingue (Ep 1668). Floris was married to Arnoldina van Duvenvoorde; their children, in addition to Jan, included a son who had been a pupil of Jan *Beren (Ep 1668), pre-sumably the Herman Oem of Dordrecht who matriculated at Louvain on 29 August 1523, and probably the Cornelis whose daughter was to marry a son of Frans van *Cranevelt.

BIBLIOGRAPHY: Allen Ep 1668 / P.L. Müller in ADB XXIV 345–6 / J. van Kuyk in NNBW III 926–8 / de Vocht CTL I 7, II 259–60, and passim / N. van der Blom *Erasmus en Rotterdam* (Rotterdam-The Hague 1969) 79 ff / *Matricule de Louvain* II-1 462, III-1 30, 107, 703 / R. Fruin *Verspreide geschriften* VI (The Hague 1902) 138–75 / *Memorialen van het Hof (den Raad) van Holland, Zeeland en West-Friesland* ed A.S. de Blécourt et al (Haarlem-The Hague 1929) xlv / C. Burmannus *Hadrianus* VI (Utrecht 1727) 398 / Oem's short autobiography was edited by R. Fruin in *Handelingen en Mededeelingen van de Maatschap-pij der Nederlandsche Letterkunde te Leiden* (1866) 143–53 / There is also a manuscript diary by him of meetings of the states of Holland, 1513–19, in the Gemeente-archief, Dordrecht
C.G. VAN LEIJENHORST

Jan OEM van Wijngaarden d 4 May 1567
Jan, a son of Floris *Oem van Wijngaarden, matriculated at the University of Louvain on 28 February 1523; he became a licentiate of canon and civil law in 1526. In February of that year he wrote to Erasmus (Ep 1668), indicating that he was living in the house of Jan *Vullinck, notary to the university, and that Pope *Adrian VI had provided him with a prebend of St Lambert's, Liège. He also said he knew Conradus *Goclenius, Adrianus Cornelii *Bar-landus, and Joost *Vroye, probably from having attended their lessons. Ep 1668 was answered by Erasmus with the short and

reserved Ep 1699. On 11 July 1527 Oem took up residence at Liège. In 1539 he was involved in the prosecution of heretics. Not until 1544 was he ordained at Herckenrode by the suffragan bishop of Liège, Gedeon van der Gracht. He was acting as an assessor to the official of Liège in 1545, and succeeded as the official and scholaster of St Lambert's on 30 June 1559. In 1532 Barlandus dedicated his *Libri tres de rebus gestis ducum Brabantiae* (Louvain: R. Rescius for B. Gravius 1 May 1532; NK 237) jointly to Jan Oem and another canon of St Lambert's, Arnold van den Vogelsanck.

BIBLIOGRAPHY: de Vocht CTL I 7, II 345–6 / *Matricule de Louvain* III-1 693 / E. Daxhelet *Adrien Barlandus* (Louvain 1938) 118–24, 326–8

C.G. VAN LEIJENHORST

Johannes OESIANDER *See Johann Albrecht*
WIDMANSTETTER

Anna OFFENBURG of Basel,
d before 1 October 1539
Anna was a natural daughter of Henmann Offenburg and thus a half-sister of Egli *Offenburg. She married Henricus *Glareanus on 1 November 1522, a development that aroused the interest of his humanist friends including Erasmus (Ep 2217; AK II Epp 896, 902). Later she moved to Freiburg with her husband. Her health was failing by the spring of 1537 when she went to the spa of Baden; two years later she died, childless.

BIBLIOGRAPHY: Allen Ep 1316 / NDB VI 425 / O.F. Fritzsche *Glarean* (Frauenfeld 1890) 76–7 and passim   PGB

Johann Egli OFFENBURG of Basel,
d after 1560
Egli (or Egloff) was the son of Henmann Offenburg, burgomaster and commander of the Basel troops at Marignano. He matriculated at the University of Basel in 1514 and studied under Henricus *Glareanus, who later married his natural half-sister, Anna *Offenburg (Ep 1316). In 1525 he became a member of the great council. Firmly opposed to the Reformation, he accompanied Heinrich *Meltinger on his flight from Basel in February 1529 and subsequently renounced his citizenship. In September Erasmus recommended him warmly to Cardinal Jean of *Lorraine as the carrier of Ep 2217, but the cardinal evidently could not find employment for him, for in the same year he is mentioned as the steward of the bishop of Basel at Pfeffingen, in the Birs valley. He was also in possession of the Schauenburg, an estate and castle near Basel which his family had held for generations, and he became lord of Büren (Solothurn). After his second wife, Verena Baer, died in 1537, he married Barbara von Sigolzheim.

BIBLIOGRAPHY: Allen Ep 2217 / *Matrikel Basel* I 322 / DHBS V 185 / W. Merz *Oberrheinische Stammtafeln* (Aarau 1912) 43 / *Basler Chroniken* I 82, 85, V 311 / R. Wackernagel *Geschichte der Stadt Basel* (Basel 1907–54) III 161, 288, 511, 513   PGB

Gabriël OFHUYS d 22 June 1535
Born around 1475, Gabriël Ofhuys entered the deanery of St James on the Koudenberg in Brussels and became a canon regular of St Augustine, perhaps influenced by the better-known historian and preacher Gaspar Ofhuys (d 1523). On 26 July 1501 Gabriël took his vows in the Carthusian monastery of Scheut at Anderlecht, near Brussels. In 1505 he made a second profession in Louvain but subsequently returned to Brussels, where he died. Allen identifies him with the person to whom Jacques *Lefèvre d'Etaples dedicated his *Contemplationes Remundi* (Paris: G. de Gourmont 1505).

Gabriël was probably related to Karel *Ofhuys, who in 1516 asked Erasmus to give greetings to Gabriël (CWE Ep 480A; Allen Ep 692). Gabriël worshipped Erasmus and some time in 1521 asked him for some verses, probably an epigram to be affixed to a painting by him. Erasmus complied and sent his poem, which is lost, together with a letter on 14 October 1521 (Ep 1239). Gabriël also had an unidentified brother, who in 1529 was captain of the archers with King *Ferdinand (Ep 2130).

BIBLIOGRAPHY: Allen Ep 692 / J. de Grauwe *Prosopographia Cartusiana Belgica (1314–1796)* (Ghent-Salzburg 1976) 109 / Reedijk 400

GILBERT TOURNOY

Karel OFHUYS of Brussels, documented 1486–1516
Born around 1470, Karel Ofhuys belonged to a well-known Brussels family. He registered at

the University of Louvain on 27 February 1486. Other than that he is known only from an admiring letter he wrote Erasmus from Paris in the autumn of 1516 (CWE Ep 480A; Allen Ep 692). He urged Erasmus to publish a commentary on the Pauline Epistles and also demonstrated his acquaintance with other works by Erasmus, including the *Enchiridion*, which he must have read at the time of its publication in 1503.

BIBLIOGRAPHY: Allen Ep 692 / *Matricule de Louvain* III-1 9   GILBERT TOURNOY

Nicolaus OLAHUS of Sibiu, 10 January 1493–14 January 1568
Miklos Oláh, better known under the Latin form of his name, Olahus (Olaus, Holachus), was born at Sibiu (Szeben, Hermannstadt), in Transylvania. His family originated in Wallachia and had risen to the lesser nobility. Olahus was distantly related to King *Matthias Corvinus. From 1509 to 1510 he attended the cathedral school of Oradea (Várad) under the patronage of the humanist bishop Sigismundus Thurzo. As he never went abroad for a university education he must have acquired his polished style and wide-ranging knowledge of the classics through extensive reading. In 1510 he was a page at the court of King *Vladislav II in Buda and remained there for the next six years, until the powerful chancellor, Bishop György Szathmári, appointed him his secretary in 1516. That same year he took holy orders. The good will of his powerful patron brought him a number of benefices: he was made canon of Pécs (Fünfkirchen, Quinquecclesiae) in 1518 and of Esztergom (Gran) in 1522.

While at the court in Buda, Olahus became a member of the Erasmian circle in the Hungarian capital which had developed around Jacobus *Piso and included, among others, István *Brodarics, László *Szalkay, the *Thurzo brothers, Queen *Mary, and her chaplain, Johann *Henckel. In March 1526 Olahus was appointed secretary to both King *Louis II and the queen. Later that year he accompanied the king on the military campaign which ended in the disaster at Mohács on 29 August. Olahus, however, was dispatched by the king on 26 August to ride back to Buda with Louis' last greetings to the queen and instructions to flee

Nicolaus Olahus

to Bratislava (Pressburg, Pozsony) if the battle against the Turks was lost. Remaining loyal to the queen, Olahus followed her and supported the claims of her brother *Ferdinand to the Hungarian crown against *John Zápolyai, the candidate of the majority of the Hungarian nobles. Olahus remained a major promoter of the Hapsburg cause throughout his long career.

Olahus was appointed canon of Székesfehérvár by Ferdinand in 1527. He accompanied Queen Mary to Znojmo (Znaim) in Moravia, where they were joined by Henckel, who after some hesitation had also opted for the Hapsburgs. Accompanied by Olahus and Henckel, Mary travelled to Linz, Passau, Innsbruck, and Augsburg, where the imperial diet was meeting. It was from here that on 1 July 1530 Olahus wrote his first letter to Erasmus, in which he expressed the hope that Erasmus would come to the diet and help resolve the religious problem (Ep 2339). Olahus was eager to see the end of the Protestant-Catholic controversy, in order that the diet could turn its attention to the Turkish problem and take steps to liberate Hungary. On 1 October 1530 he personally addressed the diet, trying to stir the deputies to action. He was to be disappointed, however, because the religious situation prevented any attention being given to the Hungarian problem. In his frequent letters to Erasmus, he painted an increasingly depressing picture of the conditions in his homeland (Epp 2396, 2399, 2409). Following the conclusion of the diet, he accompanied the queen back to Austria. On 10 February 1531, Mary left Krems for Brussels following her appointment as regent of the Netherlands. Olahus remained at her side (Ep 2463). Further away from his homeland, he was even more homesick than formerly in Austria, although the friendship of *Ursinus Velius and many leading humanists in the Netherlands (among them *Goclenius, *Cranevelt, *Schepper, Petrus Nannius, and *Dantiscus) and also his correspondence with Erasmus mitigated his loneliness. Olahus, who longed each day for the chance to return to Hungary, could not understand why Erasmus, who had the opportunity, did not return to his native Netherlands (Ep 2607). Much of the subsequent correspondence between the two men revolved around the problem of Erasmus' return to Brabant. As the major promoter of this project Olahus was delighted when after some hesitation Erasmus appeared to have made up his mind and, in the summer of 1533, his departure for the Netherlands seemed imminent (Epp 2613, 2646, 2693, 2741, 2759, 2762, 2785, 2792, 2828), but wet and unpleasant weather prevented him from setting out (Ep 2860). At the beginning of November Erasmus was still writing to Olahus that he was coming (Ep 2877), but he never did. In January 1534 Erasmus complained to Olahus about the attack of Nikolaus *Ferber of Herborn, and Olahus persuaded Mary to order that the offending book be suppressed (Epp 2898, 2915). In April Erasmus privately warned Olahus of the vicious character of Pieter van *Montfoort whom he had earlier recommended. He also indicated that news had reached him that Olahus was planning to return to Hungary. Although Erasmus wished him well, he showed disappointment at the prospect of losing this ardent supporter and admirer at the court in Brussels (Ep 2922). In reply, Olahus once again urged Erasmus to return to the Netherlands (Ep 2948). The preserved correspondence between the two comes to an end at this point. When Olahus learnt two years later of Erasmus' death, he composed an elegy and epitaphs for Erasmus in elegant Latin (reprinted among the preliminary pieces in LB I).

Because of the unsettled conditions in Hungary, Olahus remained in Brussels, but his imagination was filled with the vision of his distant, devastated homeland. This led him in 1536 to undertake the composition of a historical geography which he called *Hungaria* (Bratislava 1735). The next year he wrote *Athila* (Frankfurt 1581), which was an account of the early history of Hungary. In both works he contrasted the glories of the past with the misery of the present.

The death of King John Zápolyai in 1540 raised the hope that internal conditions in Hungary might become more settled. With the consent of Queen Mary, Olahus had gone to Vienna in 1539, and in the service of Ferdinand he returned to his native land in 1542. He was made a member of the royal council and elevated to the bishopric of Zagreb (1543). His rise in power continued, and in 1548 he became bishop of Eger, a position he held until his appointment as archbishop of Esztergom in May 1553. While primate of Hungary, he was also appointed chancellor of the realm and used his great influence to advance the Catholic cause, thus becoming a major figure in the history of the Counter-Reformation. He was instrumental in bringing the Jesuits to Hungary in 1561. A year later he founded the Jesuit college of Trnava (Nagyszombat), the city in which he was buried. A central figure in Hungarian humanism, Olahus links the Erasmian circle of the court of Buda prior to Mohács with the Catholic revival under the Hapsburgs.

BIBLIOGRAPHY: Allen Ep 2339 / *Magyar életrajzi lexikon* (Budapest 1967–9) II 316 / *Magyar irodalmi lexikon* (Budapest 1963–5) II 395 / Jozsef Szemes *Oláh Miklos* (Esztergom 1936) / Pál Schleicher *Oláh Miklos és Erasmus* (Budapest 1941) / Ferencz Kollányi 'Oláh Miklos és Rotterdami Erasmus' *Uj Magyar Sion* (1885) 585–604, 736–58 / Pongrác Sörös 'Ötven év Oláh Miklos életéböl' *Katholikus Szemle* (1903) 327–43, 416–432 / Corneliu Albu 'La correspondance de Nicolaus Olahus avec Erasme' *Revue Roumaine d'Histoire* 7 (1968)

515–523 / de Vocht *Literae ad Craneveldium* Ep 275 and passim / de Vocht CTL III 36–44 and passim / de Vocht *Danticus* 110–12 and passim / The following modern editions of Olahus' works exist: *Hungaria, Athila* ed K. Eperjessy and L. Juhász (Budapest 1938); *Carmina* ed J. Fógel and L. Juhász (Leipzig 1934); L. Juhász 'De carminibus Nicolai Olahi in mortem Erasmi scriptis' in *Gedenkschrift zum 400. Todestage des Erasmus von Rotterdam* (Basel 1936) 316–25. Olahus' correspondence was edited by Arnold Ipolyi (Budapest 1875)

L. DOMONKOS

Pedro Juan OLIVAR of Valencia,
d after 8 January 1553
Pedro Juan Olivar (Oliver, Olivarus, Olivarius) is said by Nicolás Antonio to have studied Greek in Alcalá with Dominicus Cretensis and subsequently in Paris with Jacobus Rhodius, a nephew of Marcus *Musurus. Among his teachers in Paris was also *Lefèvre d'Etaples. As he was later associated with the court of *Charles v he may have accompanied the future emperor to the Netherlands in 1520. On 1 August 1521 he matriculated at the University of Louvain and began to study theology under the guidance of Jacobus *Latomus. He also made the acquaintance of Erasmus before the latter left the Netherlands towards the end of 1521 (Ep 1791). Latomus recommended him to the generosity of Erard de la *Marck, bishop of Liège, but it seems that Olivar moved on to England. Perhaps with the assistance of his compatriot Juan Luis *Vives he lived in London and perhaps in Oxford, met *Linacre, and may have been introduced to Archbishop *Warham. Altogether he is said to have spent three years in England before returning to Brussels, from where he wrote to Frans van *Cranevelt on 13 January 1524, having borrowed from him *Valeriano's Greek grammar and Erasmus' *Adagia* together with his New Testament. It seems that he had taken service with a diplomat, conceivably Girolamo *Aleandro.

On 13 March 1527 Olivar wrote to Erasmus from Valladolid (Ep 1791), where the court was in residence and where he enjoyed a measure of intimacy with the chancellor, *Gattinara, and his secretary, Alfonso de *Valdés. Olivar's letter shows the confident enthusiasm which Erasmus' supporters at the imperial court at that time possessed. The letter was accompanied by the articles of the churchmen assembled at Valladolid to examine Erasmus' works and by Olivar's Latin translation of a letter by Valdés concerning these articles. In 1528 and 1529 Olivar was in Valencia (Ep 2163), corresponding with Diego *Gracián and Valdés. But for the energetic opposition of a zealous anti-Erasmian, Professor Juan de Celaya, the city council would have offered Olivar a chair of Greek and Latin at the University of Valencia. During this period he translated into Latin a treatise by Chrysostom which Erasmus had recently edited in Greek (Ep 1661). Meanwhile the Spanish Erasmians were increasingly subject to persecution. By 1531, however, Olivar was requested by Jerónimo Suárez, bishop of Mondoñedo, to examine the dialogue *Lactancio* by his old friend Alfonso de Valdés. He did not find any heresies but indicated passages that seemed dangerous or too explicit.

In the spring of 1535 Olivar moved to France. In Poitiers he published some notes on Cicero's *Somnium Scipionis*, which are dedicated to Juan Martín Población, physician to *Eleanor of Austria, queen of France. Perhaps through Población he made friends at the French court and met Guillaume *Budé in 1537. In this period he also met Stephen *Gardiner. On 6 June 1542 he was at Oxford and from there he dedicated to Gardiner his *De prophetia*. Finally, after 1544 he spent three years in the service of *George of Austria, bishop of Liège, with whom he travelled in England, Germany, and Spain. He is last documented on 8 January 1553 at Cologne, when he dedicated his treatise on the presence of Christ's body and blood in the Eucharist to the archbishop of that city.

Olivar's works include *Scholia in Ciceronis fragmentum de Somnio Scipionis* (Poitiers: J. and E. Marnef 1535); *Summa capita in Ciceronis philosophiam moralem una cum aliis quibusdam libellis* (Poitiers 1535); *Pomponii Melae de situ orbis libri tres ...* (Paris: C. Wechel 1536); *Annotationes in Ciceronis opus de finibus bonorum et malorum libri v* (Paris: S. de Colines 1537); *Aristotelis praedicamentorum liber* (Paris 1538); *Aristotelis de interpretatione liber* (Paris 1538); *Porphyrii Isagoge. Accesserunt in eundem libellum castigationes iuxta necessariae ac eruditae* (Paris:

C. Wechel 1538); *De prophetia et spiritu prophetico liber lectu dignissimus* (Basel: J. Oporinus 1543); *Dilucida et clara confirmatio praesentiae corporis et sanguinis Christi in sacramento altaris...* (Cologne: M. Soter 1553); *Annotationes in secundum Plinii librum* (Paris: C. Wechel 1536).

BIBLIOGRAPHY: Allen Ep 1791 / Bataillon *Erasmo y España* 231–2, 316–17, 482, 511, and passim / de Vocht *Literae ad Craneveldium* Ep 86 / de Vocht CTL II 198–9 / Fermin Caballero *Alonso y Juan de Valdés* (Cuenca 1875) / Emile Legrand 'Bibliographie hispano-grecque 1477–1560' I nos 76, 78, 79 in *Bibliographie hispanique 1915* (New York 1915) / A. Palau *Manual del Librero hispano-americano* (Barcelona 1948–77)
MILAGROS RIVERA & PGB

Johannes OLPEIUS *See Hans HOLBEIN*

Severinus OLPEIUS (documented 1527)
Severinus Olpeius is the name of an unidentified student who had lived in the house of Jan *Antonin at Cracow for the greater part of the winter of 1526–7. In April he went to Basel carrying Ep 1810. When he returned to Poland he was given letters by Erasmus and Bonifacius *Amerbach, none of which are known to have arrived (Epp 1915, 1916; AK III 1210, 1220). In February 1528 Jan (II) *Łaski wrote that Severinus had not been to see him (Ep 1954).

Jacobus OMPHALIUS of Andernach,
11 February 1500–25 October 1567 '
Jacobus Omphalius was born at Andernach, on the Rhine below Koblenz. He attended the schools of his native town and matriculated in Cologne as a student in the faculty of arts on 24 September 1515. Little is known about the higher education he acquired during the 1520s. In about 1524 he accompanied his fellow townsman Johannes *Guinterius from Utrecht to Louvain, where he made the acquaintance of Johannes Sleidanus, Johann Sturm, Bartholomaeus *Latomus, Andreas Vesalius, Nicolaus *Clenardus, and other notable scholars and academics. At Louvain he studied Latin and Greek and later accompanied some well-to-do students on their journey to France. In Paris he was registered as MA in 1529–30 and taught Latin authors in the Collège de Lisieux, associating with Erasmus' friend Philippus

*Montanus and the printer Gerard *Morrhy (Ep 2311), who was concerned lest Omphalius attract the wrath of the Paris theologians by having his students read Erasmus' *Colloquia* (Ep 2633). In 1532 he was proctor of the Anglo-German nation of the University of Paris.

Three years later Omphalius went to Toulouse, where he earned a doctorate of both laws on 1 December 1535. His influential friends there, such as Jean de *Boyssoné and Nicolas *Bérault, whom he urged to write to Erasmus (Epp 3082, 3083), helped him secure a professorship at Toulouse in early 1536, but within the same year he had returned to Germany by way of Paris. On 8 October 1537 the Archbishop of Cologne, Hermann von *Wied, appointed him assessor at the imperial court in Speyer in succession to Hartmann *Moer. During his activity at Speyer he corresponded with Bonifacius *Amerbach, renewing a friendship formed seven years earlier (AK V Ep 2171) and became involved in a suit brought to the imperial court by the Basel printers Hieronymus *Froben and Nicolaus *Episcopius (AK V Epp 2239, 2240). His letters to Amerbach also reveal Omphalius' acquaintance with *Viglius Zuichemus and others. In 1540 Omphalius left Speyer for Cologne, where he was promoted to the post of a councillor to Archbishop Hermann von Wied. He now entered the most productive period of his life, in terms of both his political and his literary careers. He took an active part in Hermann von Wied's unsuccessful attempt to introduce the Reformation in the archbishopric of Cologne, especially after his appointment as Wied's chancellor in December 1545. Following the archbishop's resignation on 25 February 1547, Omphalius at first remained in the service of his successor, Adolf von *Schaumburg, while privately trying to secure financial compensation for his former master.

In about 1551 Omphalius became a councillor to William V, duke of *Cleves, but continued to live at Cologne, where he frequently served as legal adviser to the city and was at one time professor of law (before 1565). During this last period of his life he carried out several diplomatic missions in the service of the duke. On 15 May 1559 he acquired the status of hereditary nobility. Despite Omphalius' enthusiasm for the attempted reform of Cologne, Höveler (14–15) suggests that he did not publicly adhere to Protestantism until about 1563.

Omphalius was married to Elisabeth von Bellinghausen, who was from an influential Cologne family, and accordingly he was very prosperous. However, in about 1562 he incurred considerable losses as a private creditor and thereafter found himself continually in financial difficulties. He died in Cologne and was buried at Wiesdorf on the Rhine, in close proximity to his estate 'zum Büchel.'

It is not clear whether Erasmus knew Omphalius personally. In 1530 Morrhy reported that Omphalius meant to write to Erasmus (Ep 2311) and by about the same time Omphalius seems to have been in touch with Amerbach. There is, in fact, evidence for a friendly correspondence between Omphalius and Erasmus (Ep 2779: Erasmus' reference to another Omphalius residing at Paris remains a puzzle). Upon Erasmus' request, Omphalius assisted in the suppression of Julius Caesar *Scaliger's first *Oratio* (Ep 2635), and in his only preserved letter to Erasmus (Ep 3094) Omphalius expressed his approval of Erasmus' defence against Pietro *Corsi, *Responsio ad Petri Cursii defensionem.*

Omphalius' numerous writings and the ancient and contemporary works he edited are listed by Höveler (23–8) and in AK VII 198. A work which may be specifically mentioned here is *De elocutionis imitatione ac apparatu liber unus* (Basel: H. Froben 1537), which was dedicated to Cardinal Jean *Du Bellay from Paris on 1 March 1537. Seven years later a quarrel developed when Omphalius and the cardinal happened to meet each other at Cologne. Two later editions of this book (Cologne: A. Mylius 1591, 1602) contain Omphalius' *Epistolae scriptae ad familiares*, edited by his son Bernardus (see Höveler 24).

The well-known French humanist and jurist François Bauduin (1520–73) dedicated to Omphalius his *Notae ad libros I & II Digestorum seu Pandectarum* (Basel: J. Oporinus 1557).

BIBLIOGRAPHY: Allen Ep 2311 / AK V Ep 2171, VII Ep 3140, and passim / de Vocht CTL III 363 / *Matrikel Köln* II 752 / Johann Joseph Höveler 'Jacobus Omphalius Andernacus, ein berühmter Humanist und Staatsmann des 16.

Jahrhunderts' *Jahresbericht des Progymnasiums zu Andernach für das Schuljahr 1899–1900* (Andernach 1900) 3–28 (with bibliography) / Gotthold Bohne 'Die juristische Fakultät der alten Kölner Universität in den beiden ersten Jahrhunderten ihres Bestehens' *Festschrift zur Erinnerung an die Gründung der alten Universität Köln im Jahre 1388* (Cologne 1938) 109–236, esp 211 / Michael Erbe *François Bauduin (1520–73)* (Gütersloh 1978) 17, 215 / *Jülich-Bergische Kirchenpolitik am Ausgange des Mittelalters und in der Reformationszeit* ed Otto R. Redlich (Bonn 1907–14) I 324 / J.A.R. von Stintzing *Geschichte der deutschen Rechtswissenschaft* (Munich-Leipzig 1880–1910) I 101, 483–5 / Johann Gropper *Briefwechsel* ed R. Braunisch (Münster 1977–   ) I passim / *Correspondance de Nicolas Clénard* ed A. Roersch (Brussels 1940–1) Ep 10 and notes   KASPAR VON GREYERZ

Quirinus OP DEM VELDE *See Theoderich* MICHWAEL

Giambattista OPIZZONI of Pavia, documented 1509–25

Giambattista Opizzoni (Opizo) was born at Pavia to a noble family originally from Tortona. In 1509 he occupied a chair of medicine at the University of Pavia, where he had probably studied. He later moved to Venice, where he participated in the movement for the restoration of scientific knowledge through observation and through the application of philological methods to classical authors such as Euclid, Pliny the Elder, and Dioscorides. On 1 July 1515 Opizzoni embarked at Venice on a pilgrimage to the Holy Land. The pilgrimage, known to Erasmus through the account of Peter *Falck (Ep 512), provided Opizzoni with the opportunity to make scientific observations. On his return to Venice he collaborated with Gianfrancesco *Torresani and Georgius *Agricola in the publication of the Aldine Greek edition of Galen, completed in five volumes in 1525. Although the edition of Galen was his greatest claim to fame, Opizzoni also developed an extensive collection of Greek, Chaldaic, and Arabic manuscripts and was known among scholars for his erudition. Georgius Agricola praised him in his *Bermannus* (Basel: J. Froben 1530).

In August 1525, when Torresani refused to

look at a corrected copy of the latest edition of the *Adagia* (Basel: H. Froben 1523) sent to him by Erasmus, it was Opizzoni who held the work for safe keeping (Epp 1594, 1595). In October Erasmus informed Torresani that, time permitting, he intended to write to Opizzoni (Ep 1628), but no letter has been found.

BIBLIOGRAPHY: Allen Ep 1594 / *Memorie e documenti per la storia dell' Università di Pavia e degli uomini illustri che v'insegnarono* (Pavia 1878) I 122 / C. Castellani *La stampa a Venezia dalla sua origine ad Aldo Manuzio seniore* (Venice 1889) 42 / M. de Diesbach 'Les pèlerins fribourgeois à Jérusalem 1436–1640' *Archives de la Société d'histoire du canton de Fribourg* 2–2 (1891) 267 / A. Ferriguto *Almorò Barbaro: L'alta cultura del settentrione in Italia nel quattrocento* (Venice 1919) 278, 366 / R. Röhricht *Deutsche Pilgerreisen nach dem Heiligen Lande* (Innsbruck 1900, repr 1967) 208 / Julius Salernus 'Pro Ticinensibus contra Cremonenses oratio' MS of the Biblioteca Universitaria di Pavia, sec. XVIII, fondo 'Ticinesi' no 40, f 82

MARCO BERNUZZI

Vincentius OPSOPOEUS died c August 1539
Vincentius Opsopoeus (Obsopaeus, Obsopius, Heydnecker, Heidecker) was the son of a cook in Bavaria. After a teaching engagement at the choir school of Salzburg, he matriculated in Leipzig on 23 April 1524. Showing an interest in the teachings of the Wittenberg reformers, he translated *Luther's commentary on the Epistle to the Galatians into German, *Die Epistel S.Pauli an die Galater* (Wittenberg: n p 1525) and edited a collection of his letters, *Martini Lutheri epistolarum farrago* (Haguenau: J. Setzer 1525) and his commentary on Jonah in Latin translation (Haguenau: J. Setzer 1526). Late in 1524 he went to Nürnberg, where he probably resumed teaching, and where he belonged to the circle around Willibald *Pirckheimer; he also remained in contact with the reformers. In 1526 Luther wrote a letter of recommendation for Opsopoeus (w *Briefwechsel* IV Ep 1003). From c 1528 he was rector of the newly founded Latin school in Ansbach, where he died.

In 1524 Opsopoeus began to edit a series of Greek authors, partially in Latin translation. Thus he produced, mostly with the Haguenau press of Johann Setzer, first editions of Polybius (1530), Heliodorus (1531), and Diodorus Siculus (1539) and translated Lucian's *Hermotimus* (1527) and subsequently several more of his works. His translations of books I, II (1527) and later IX of Homer's *Iliad* were less successful; Helius *Eobanus Hessus did not think highly of them. Opsopoeus also published a selection of the Psalms in a Latin verse translation, *Psalmi omnium selectissimi ... Latino carmine redditi* (Haguenau: J. Setzer 1532) and a book on the art of toasting, *De arte bibendi libri tres* (Nürnberg: J. Petreius 1536).

Opsopoeus owned a rich library, which is now at Erlangen. In a letter to Pirckheimer of 28 May 1528 (Ep 1997) Erasmus severely criticized Opsopoeus' Greek edition of the letters of St Basil and St Gregory of Nazianzus (Haguenau: J. Setzer 1528). He wished to translate these letters into Latin, but Opsopoeus' edition turned out to be so poor that he was inclined to abandon his plan unless Pirckheimer could provide him with the manuscript used by Opsopoeus. It would seem that the manuscript, perhaps from Opsopoeus' own library, actually reached him after some delay (Epp 2028, 2214).

BIBLIOGRAPHY: Allen Ep 1997 / ADB XXIV 408 / Luther w *Briefwechsel* III Ep 707, IV Ep 1003, and passim / *Melanchthons Briefwechsel* I Epp 329, 330, and passim / *Matrikel Leipzig* I 589 / August Jegel 'Der Humanist Vinzenz Heidecker gen. Opsopoeus' *Archiv für Kulturgeschichte* 30 (1940) 27–84 / Josef Benzing *Lutherbibliographie* (Baden-Baden 1966) nos 65, 427–9, 1887, 2283 / C. Krause *Helius Eobanus Hessus* (Gotha 1879, repr 1963) II 19–20   IG

Antoine Honorat, sieur d'ORAISON documented 1503–44
Antoine Honorat (Honoré, Oresonus, Oroysonius, Aurisonius) was a grandson of Antoine Honoré d'Aqua, whose ancestors had held high offices in the service of the house of Anjou. In 1503 the will of his maternal great-aunt, Marguerite d'Oraison, dame de Ribiers, induced him to substitute the title of Oraison (between Apt and Digne, Département des Alpes de Haute Provence) for that of Aqua. He was also viscount of Cadenet and baron of Boulbon, in the same region. In 1512 he married Catherine de Clermont-Lodève,

the sister of Cardinal François de Clermont, papal legate at Avignon. Jean Baptiste de *Laigue, bishop of Senez, was Oraison's younger brother.

In 1522 Oraison was acting on a royal commission in Provence. In 1528 Andrea *Alciati referred to him as an old friend who had requested him to write a juridical treatise on duelling; this *Liber de singulari certamine* was dedicated to *Francis I on 1 March 1529 but apparently not published until 1541 (Paris: J. Kerver). Erasmus repeatedly sent Oraison greetings through Joachim *Martens and Franciscus *Cassander, who apparently had a learned discussion with Oraison on Augustine in 1530 (Epp 2049, 2296, 2442).

BIBLIOGRAPHY: Allen Ep 2049 / *Bulletin des Amis du château de Pau* 59 (1973) 22–4, 26 / *Gallia christiana* I 76, 369, 410 / AK III Ep 1261 / *Catalogue des actes de François I* (Paris 1887–1908) I 307 and passim

MICHEL REULOS & PGB

Jean-Baptiste d'ORAISON *See Jean-Baptiste de LAIGUE*

Nicaise de l'ORME *See Nicaise DELORME*

ORTENBURG *See Gabriel de SALAMANCA, count of Ortenburg*

Andreas OSIANDER d 17 October 1552
On the basis of Osiander's own remarks, 1496 may be accepted as the year of his birth. On 9 July 1515 he matriculated at the University of Ingolstadt. He studied Hebrew with Johann Böschenstein but also acquired a good command of Greek, so that later on he earned *Luther's unreserved praise for his knowledge of the biblical languages (Luther W XLVIII 651). His models were *Reuchlin and Erasmus. In 1520 he became a priest, celebrating his first mass in Gunzenhausen, a small town in the diocese of Eichstätt, conceivably his birthplace. In the same year he began to teach Hebrew in the Augustinian monastery of Nürnberg and for the first time was in touch with supporters of the Reformation. In 1522 he was appointed parish priest of St Lawrence's, a cure which he was to hold for twenty-seven years.

After the imperial government (Reichsregi-

Andreas Osiander

ment) had left Nürnberg in 1524 Osiander headed a group of preachers who began to refashion church services according to the ideas of the reformers (Ep 1394). When the Nürnberg city council convened a religious colloquy in March 1525 Osiander represented the evangelical side and led it to victory as the council rallied to its cause. He also played a leading part in the implementation of the new religious order. Despite some opposition from members of the council as well as the citizenship at large, he reorganized public worship and other areas of civic life related to the church, while at the same time warding off the more radical innovations sought by the Anabaptists and Sacramentarians. Osiander was by nature intractable, but his position in the city was initially so strong that the council included him among Nürnberg's delegates to the diet of Augsburg (1530) and the religious conferences of Marburg (1529) and Haguenau and Worms (1540–1) as well as the political meeting at Schmalkalden (1539), not to mention others. On these occasions he proved unyielding in his opposition to Catholics and Zwinglians alike and often clashed with *Melanchthon, who took a more conciliatory stance. After 1541 the council no longer appointed him to foreign missions. In 1548, when the council was prepared to accept the terms of *Charles v's interim, he judged that the Gospel was being betrayed and left Nürnberg.

Albert (I) of *Brandenburg-Ansbach, duke of Prussia, had formed a favourable opinion of Osiander during repeated visits to Nürnberg, and it was to him that the latter now turned. In January 1549 he was appointed preacher of the Altstädter church at Kaliningrad (Königsberg) and given a chair at the university. His last years there were, however, overshadowed by the bitter debates caused by his controversial doctrine of divine justice. Osiander's writings consist for the most part of expositions of Scripture, sermons, and essays on the theological controversies of the day, composed at the request of the Nürnberg council and subsequently Duke Albert. Some of these are of considerable interest but have tended to be neglected by modern scholars because of their excessively polemical style. Since 1975, however, a comprehensive critical edition of his works (ed Gerhard Müller et al, Gütersloh) has been in progress. His portrait in the vestry of St Lawrence's, Nürnberg, appears to be authentic (Seebass Osiander 278–95).

In 1527 Erasmus mentioned Osiander in the context of the Eucharistic controversies which were then dividing the Protestant camp (Ep 1901). Osiander, for his part, recognized the importance of Erasmus' philological approach to the study of Scripture while dismissing his theology as frigid and conducive to scepticism (Seebass Osiander 72).

Osiander had an interest in astronomy and played a minor role in the publication of Nicolaus Copernicus' De revolutionibus orbium coelestium (Nürnberg: J. Petreius 1543), writing a preface for it which shows limited awareness of the work's significance.

BIBLIOGRAPHY: Allen Ep 1344 / RGG IV 1730–1 / ADB XXIV 473–83 / Gottfried Seebass Das reformatorische Werk des Andreas Osiander (Nürnberg 1967) / Wilhelm Möller Andreas Osiander (Elberfeld 1870) / Emanuel Hirsch Die Theologie des Andreas Osiander und ihre geschichtlichen Voraussetzungen (Göttingen 1919) / Martin Stupperich Osiander in Preussen 1549– 1552 (Berlin-New York 1973) / Gottfried Seebass Bibliographia Osiandrica (Nieuwkoop 1971) / Gerhard Müller 'Edition der Werke des Andreas Osiander' Theologische Literaturzeitung 97 (1972) 567–71 / David C. Steinmetz Reformers in the Wings (Philadelphia 1971) 91–9 / Gerald Strauss Nuremberg in the Sixteenth Century (New York 1966) 252–3 and passim

RAINER VINKE

Diego OSORIO of Burgos, documented 1519–27
Don Diego Osorio, a nobleman from Burgos, held the royal office of corregidor of Córdoba when he acted as a patron to Juan *Maldonado. When the plague struck Córdoba in the winter of 1519–20 Maldonado was a guest at Osorio's castle of Vallejera. Maldonado's Latin comedy Hispaniola, written in 1519 and published six years later, is dedicated to Osorio.

Osorio is mentioned repeatedly in the correspondence of Erasmus. In November 1527 Maldonado described him as an enthusiastic admirer and defender of Erasmus and forwarded his greetings, adding that the corregidor was too modest to write to Erasmus directly (Ep 1908). Six months earlier Juan Luis *Vives had already sent Erasmus a copy of a letter from Maldonado to Osorio describing the meeting at Burgos between Pedro de *Vitoria and Alonso Ruiz de *Virués (Ep 1836). Erasmus in turn sent greetings to Osorio in a letter to Maldonado (Ep 1971). The reference in Ep 2163, however, concerns Iacobus a *Catena rather than Osorio, as Allen tentatively suggested. For the Jacobus Burgensis greeted in Ep 2050 see Petrus *Decimarius.

BIBLIOGRAPHY: Allen Ep 1908 / Bataillon Erasmo y España 216, 222, 274

MILAGROS RIVERA

Katrijn van OSSEGHEM See Johann POPPENRUYTER

Konstanty OSTROGSKI c 1460–10 August 1530
Konstanty Ostrogski (Constantine, duke of Ostrog in Volhynia) was grand hetman of Lithuania from 1497, castellan of Vilno from 1511, and voivode of Troki, near Vilna, from 1522. Because the grand duchy of Lithuania

was united with Poland under one crown, Ostrogski led the Lithuanians in a number of joint military actions. They defeated the Tartars at Wiśniowiec (28 April 1512), the Muscovites at Orsza (8 September 1514), and again the Tartars on the Olszanica river beyond Kaniow (27 January 1527). This latter victory was brought to Erasmus' attention in Ep 1803. Ostrogski earned rich rewards from King *Sigismund I and great esteem from the Polish statesmen. He was an Orthodox Christian and the patron of Orthodoxy in Lithuania.

BIBLIOGRAPHY: Allen Ep 1803 / PSB XXIV 486–9 /The Cambridge History of Poland ed W.F. Reddaway et al (Cambridge 1941–50) I 268 and passim / J. Wolff Kniaziowie litewsko-ruscy od końca czternastego wieku (Warsaw 1895) 347–51 / W. Pociecha Królowa Bona. Czasy i ludzie Odrodzenia (Poznań 1949–58) I–IV / Z. Wojcie-chowski Zygmunt Stary (Warsaw 1946)

HALINA KOWALSKA

Leo OUTERS of Bergues-Saint-Winoc, d 17 December 1530

A native of Bergues-Saint-Winoc, diocese of Thérouanne, Outers matriculated on 30 August 1481 at the University of Louvain, where he graduated MA and licentiate of law and taught in the College of the Lily. In August 1499 and August 1502 he was elected rector of the university for a term. From 1494 he was the regent of the Lily, sharing his position with a co-regent. When Jan de *Neve succeeded to the regency litigation about the respective claims of Outers and Neve ensued. Since both were personal friends of Erasmus, his move to the Lily was somewhat delayed until the contestants reached an agreement on 26 August 1517, in which Outers gave up his claims in return for compensation (CWE Ep 643). From September Erasmus occupied the room that had formerly been Outers' and later that year sent cordial greetings to him (Ep 735).

Soon after his second rectorate Outers moved to Liège, where he had been installed as canon of St Lambert's on 31 December 1500. In 1519 he was elected provost of St Paul's, Liège, and subsequently presented to that church a very fine stained-glass window depicting the coronation of the Virgin with the donor kneeling in a corner. He also received some other benefices and from 1517 was chancellor of Erard de la *Marck, archbishop of Liège.

BIBLIOGRAPHY: Allen Ep 735 / Matricule de Louvain II-1 439 / de Vocht MHL 125–6, 180–7 and passim / de Vocht CTL I 92–3 and passim / Inventaire des archives de l'Université de Louvain, 1426–1797 ed Henry de Vocht (Louvain 1927) 122 / O.-J. Thimister Histoire de l'église collégiale de Saint-Paul (Liège 1890) 257 / J. de Theux de Montjardin Le Chapitre de Saint-Lambert à Liège (Brussels 1871) II 348–9 / J. Helbig De Glasschil-derkunst in België (Antwerp 1943) I 148 and passim / M.A. Nauwelaerts 'Erasme à Louvain: Ephémérides d'un séjour de 1517 à 1521' Scrinium Erasmianum I 3–24 esp 8 / Yvette Vanden Bemden Les vitraux de la première moitié du XVIe siècle conservés en Belgique, Corpus vitrearum Belgique IV (Ghent-Ledeberg 1981)

FRANZ BIERLAIRE

Richard PACE d 28 June 1536

Richard Pace (Paceus) was probably born in Hampshire, in or near Winchester, around 1483. While a youth he served as a page in the household of Thomas Langton, bishop of Winchester, who was greatly impressed by the boy's musical ability. Langton offered to support Pace while he studied in Italy, and in his will he left Pace an annuity of ten pounds a year for seven years.

Pace went first to Padua. In 1501, at the time of Langton's death, he was described as being a student at Bologna. In 1508, when Pace was studying with Niccolò *Leoniceno at Ferrara, he and Erasmus first met. One of Erasmus' letters to Charles *Blount, Lord Mountjoy, praises Pace as 'a young man ... well versed in knowledge of Greek and Latin letters ... and ... modest withal'; Erasmus understood that Pace was collecting classical allegories such as Erasmus had intended to include in an expanded edition of his Adagia, but he now decided to leave this to the English scholar (Ep 211; see also Adagia I vi 81). However no such work by Pace was ever published. Erasmus, who was on his way to Rome, left a number of his papers with Pace, including the Antibarbari, De ratione studii, and De copia. When Pace left Ferrara he entrusted these papers to William *Thale. In 1511 Erasmus was attempting to find out what had happened to his manuscripts, especially that of De copia, which he feared might be published in an unauthorized edition. In fact Thale appears to have sold some of Erasmus' effects and to have given away the rest. Erasmus eventually recovered books I and II of the *Antibarbari*, but the bulk of his papers never reached him again (Allen I 121n; Epp 30, 66, 211, 244, 260, 283, 350; preface to *Antibarbari*: CWE 23 16–17 = Ep 1110).

In 1509 Pace entered the service of Cardinal Christopher Bainbridge, Langton's nephew, who had been appointed *Henry VIII's representative in Rome. Pace assisted Bainbridge faithfully until the cardinal's death in 1514 and thereafter spent some time investigating the charge that Bainbridge had been poisoned on the orders of Silvestro *Gigli. Erasmus was disappointed that Pace had forsaken learning for a diplomatic career, and in 1513 he wrote *Ammonio that Pace was pleasing 'the Midases rather than the Muses.' But he added that no one was 'more affectionate, more upright, than he' (Ep 283; there is a similar comment in *Ciceronianus* ASD I-2 677).

Pace was able to transfer to Cardinal *Wolsey's service in 1515, and for the next decade he was employed extensively in diplomatic missions on the continent. It was at Constance, while negotiating with the Swiss and the Emperor *Maximilian I, that Pace wrote his most famous work, *De fructu qui ex doctrina percipitur* (Basel: J. Froben 1517); Pace tells us that it was composed in a public bath ('hypocausto'). The work, which is scrappy, sometimes pompous, sometimes vulgar, distressed Erasmus for several reasons. 'You immortalised me as disgracefully poor,' he wrote Pace in March 1518, 'though anyone might almost take me for a regular Midas' (Ep 787). Erasmus regretted that Pace had included overly personal anecdotes and had stirred up theological controversies best left dormant, and he criticized the book as lacking unity and coherence (Epp 776, 783, 796). *Bombace, he said, should have known better than to recommend its publication (Ep 800).

Pace spent the years between 1517 and 1519 in England, acting as secretary to Henry VIII and travelling with him from one royal palace to another. He was granted a coat of arms in 1518. In October of that year he delivered an oration (later printed by *Pynson as *Oratio in pace*: STC 19081a) before the ambassadors from France, Spain, Venice, and the papacy gathered to sign the treaty of London pledging universal peace and concerted resistance to the Turks.

In April 1519 Pace wrote Erasmus praising his paraphrase on Corinthians and expressing the hope that Erasmus would return to England (Ep 937). The prospect was attractive to Erasmus for various reasons (Ep 964 introduction), but in the end Erasmus did not receive a sufficiently precise offer of support, and he remained in the Netherlands. It was there that he met Pace in May 1519: Pace was sent to represent England at Frankfurt, where the German princes were negotiating over the succession to the Emperor Maximilian, who had died. His instructions were to press for the election of Henry VIII, but if that proved impossible to support *Charles of Spain rather than *Francis I. Pace brought letters to Erasmus and Erasmus wrote letters of introduction for Pace to friends who would be at Frankfurt (Epp 968–70). The two scholars probably travelled together for a time, either from Antwerp to Brussels or from Brussels to Mechelen (Epp 968, 971 introductions).

In the autumn of 1519 Pace succeeded John *Colet as dean of St Paul's (and later acquired the deaneries of Exeter and Salisbury). In the spring of 1520 he was appointed lecturer in Greek at Cambridge, but it appears that he never actually took up the post. In 1520 Pace was on the continent again for the famous meeting at the Field of Cloth of Gold, but he missed seeing Erasmus, who met a number of his English friends at Calais in July. Here Erasmus shook hands with Edward *Lee as a sign of reconciliation for which Pace had been working (Epp 1074, 1097, 1118; CWE Ep 999 introduction).

Pace returned to England, but in 1521 he set out again on several European embassies which were to occupy him for four years. Initially he was to advocate the election of Wolsey as pope following the death of *Leo X, but *Adrian VI was named before Pace reached Rome. While at leisure in Rome Pace translated some short treatises of Plutarch; they were printed at Venice in 1523 (B. dei Vitali). After spending some months in Venice and Switzerland Pace was again sent to Rome in 1524, when Adrian died. At this time Pace invited

Erasmus to join him (Ep 1423). Following the
election of *Clement VII Pace was ordered to
Lombardy, then back to Venice. On the way he
saw his friends *Pole and *Lupset at Padua.

While in Venice in 1525 Pace was taken
seriously ill. The Signory sent physicians to
him, and without their aid Pace believed that
he would have died. Pace begged Wolsey to
secure Henry VIII's permission for him to
return to England. He reached London in
November. Several of Erasmus' letters comment on Pace's illness, which affected his mind
(Epp 1595, 1624, 2031, 2033). In 1526 coadjutors
were appointed for his deaneries. In 1528 he
appeared to be better, and Erasmus wrote in
the hope of resuming their old correspondence
(Ep 1955). But Pace's condition was beyond
cure. At the time of Wolsey's fall Erasmus
heard that Pace had been imprisoned; the
confinement was in fact due to his sickness (Ep
2253). Erasmus' last letter to Pace, dated 22
March 1530, laments his friend's past calamities
(Ep 2287). Pace lived on, in obscurity, until
1536. He was buried at St Dunstan's, Stepney.

No authentic likeness of Pace is known to
survive.

BIBLIOGRAPHY: Allen and CWE Ep 211 / DNB XV
22–4 / Diplomatic dispatches in LP / Jervis Wegg
Richard Pace (London 1932) / Introduction to *De
fructu qui ex doctrina percipitur* ed Frank Manley
and Richard S. Sylvester (New York 1967) / J.
Le Neve *Fasti Ecclesiae Anglicanae 1300–1541* ed
J.M. Horn et al (London 1962–) III 5, IX 5
STANFORD E. LEHMBERG

PACIMONTANUS *See Anselmus* EPHORINUS,
Balthasar HUBMAIER

Otto von PACK d 8 February 1537
Otto von Pack (Pack de Delitzsch) was the son
of a noble family of the Saxon province of
Meissen. He matriculated at the University of
Leipzig in 1499, turned to legal studies, and
eventually obtained a doctorate in civil and
canon law, also from Leipzig (1521). Meanwhile he had entered the service of Duke
George of *Saxony. He was present at the
Leipzig disputation in 1519 and represented
the duke at four diets between 1522 and 1526.
During that time he began to embezzle sums of
money with the help of forged documents, and
when detection seemed inevitable in January

1528 he went to the young landgrave, Philip of
*Hesse, and showed him a copy of a document
purporting to have been signed at Wrocław on
behalf of King *Ferdinand, some ecclesiastical
princes including Cardinals Albert of *Brandenburg and Matthäus *Lang, and Duke
George of Saxony. According to Pack these
princes had allied themselves to eliminate the
Lutherans in their territories and conquer
Hesse and Electoral Saxony. Philip of Hesse,
deeply alarmed, tried to gain King *John
Zápolyai as an ally and started preparations for
war. Martin *Luther succeeded in restraining
Philip, while Duke George exposed Pack's
document as a fraud. Pack fled from Hesse but
was captured in Holland in 1536 and executed
in 1537.

Erasmus had no direct connection with Pack;
however, when Pack was in the service of
George of Saxony, Erasmus somehow got hold
of a letter from *Eppendorf to Pack and
concluded that the two were intimate (Epp
1934, 2086). Perhaps wrongly, he suspected
Pack of having put into Eppendorf's hands a
compromising letter of his own addressed to
Duke George (Epp 1923, 1951). After Pack had
been unmasked as an impostor, Erasmus tried
to use the letter to Pack, which was still in his
possession, as a threat against Eppendorf, but
the latter refused to be intimidated (Epp 2086,
2099).

BIBLIOGRAPHY: Allen Ep 1934 / ADB XXV 60–2 /
Matrikel Leipzig I 430, II 38, 46, and passim /
Luther w *Briefwechsel* IV Ep 1246 and passim /
Bruno Gebhardt et al *Handbuch der Deutschen
Geschichte* 9th ed (Stuttgart 1976) II 78 / R.
Kötzschke and H. Kretschmer *Sächsische Ge-
schichte* (Frankfurt am Main 1965) 185   IG

Jan van PAESSCHEN of Brussels, documented 1504–32
Jan van Paesschen (Paschasius, de Pascha,
Pasqua) was born in Brussels, the son of
Arnold and Marie Picquot. He was brought up
by his maternal uncle, Jean Picquot, canon of
Mechelen, and it was at Mechelen that he
joined the Carmelite order and began his study
of theology. On 6 February 1504 he was
promoted doctor of theology at Louvain, but
his name is not found in the matriculation
register of that university.

From 1505 Jan van Paesschen was prior of

Frederick II, elector Palatine

the monastery of his order at Mechelen, where in the following year Nicolaas *Baechem was received as a novice. Together they attacked Erasmus, opposed the Collegium Trilingue of Louvain, and resisted the study of Greek. In 1523 Jan van Paesschen was a member of the committee of theologians collaborating with the inquisitor, Frans van der *Hulst; he also wrote an account of the execution of Hendrik *Vos and Jan van den *Esschen. He is last heard of in 1532, when he resigned the priorate at Mechelen to Maarten Cuypers.

Erasmus may have referred to Jan van Paesschen in 1524 (Ep 1437). Three years later Conradus *Goclenius let Erasmus know that after the recent death of Baechem Jan van Paesschen had taken his place and had begun to denounce Erasmus and the Collegium Trilingue (Ep 1788). In a letter to Frans van *Cranevelt of 6 December 1526, Pieter de *Corte confirmed this turn of events and offered a summary of Jan's sermons. The news troubled Erasmus, and in March 1527 he appealed to Archbishop Jean de *Carondelet for support (Ep 1806). When Jan van Paesschen continued his invective he complained

in October 1528 to Erard de la *Marck and again to Carondelet (Epp 2054, 2055). No more is heard about the Carmelite in Erasmus' subsequent letters (unless he is to be identified with a Paschasius mentioned in Ep 2876).

None of Jan van Paesschen's writings were published during his lifetime. He was primarily a preacher, and some of his sermons were preserved in manuscript. These are mentioned by Paquot together with a manuscript chronicle of the Carmelite monastery of Mechelen, 'Liber memorabilium, quae contingerunt in conventu Mechliniensi ab anno 1508 ad annum 1530' all now missing. A devotional work in Flemish was published posthumously in Louvain (J. Welle 1563, 1568, and 1576), where it was also printed in French translation: *La peregrination spirituelle vers la terre saincte* (J. Bogard 1566); it was instrumental in establishing the practice of the stations of the Cross.

BIBLIOGRAPHY: Allen Ep 1437 / J.N. Paquot *Mémoires pour servir à l'histoire littéraire* (Louvain 1763–70) V 20–6 / F. Donnet in BNB XVI 458–60 / de Vocht CTL II 339–43 / de Vocht *Literae ad Craneveldium* Ep 213 / H. Thurston *Stations of the Cross* (London 1906) 82–92 / Irenaeus Rosier *Biographisch en bibliographisch overzicht van de vroomheid in de Nederlandse Carmel* (Tielt 1950) 70

MARCEL A. NAUWELAERTS

Clemens and Christophorus PALAEOLOGUS documented 1517–18 and 1520
Monks of the Greek monastery of St Catherine's on Mount Sinai repeatedly travelled in Europe to raise funds for their house. One who did so from 1517 to 1518 gave his name as Clemens Palaeologus (Ep 594). Another, or possibly the same man, was called Christophorus Palaeologus by Erasmus, who gave him Ep 1132 for Cardinal *Wolsey (Ep 1132). One may perhaps wonder whether the name of the famous Byzantine dynasty was chosen because it sounded familiar to European ears.

BIBLIOGRAPHY: Allen and CWE Ep 594 / AK II Epp 583, 635–6   PGB

Frederick II, elector PALATINE 9 December 1482–26 February 1556
Frederick, the fourth son of the Elector Philip and Margaret, the daughter of Louis IX of

Bavaria-Landshut, was born in Winzingen castle, near Neustadt an der Weinstrasse. He and his brothers received a good education which was supervised by Johann *Reuchlin from 1497 to 1499. From 1501 he attended the Burgundo-Hapsburg court in the Netherlands, becoming a good friend of Philip the Handsome, duke of *Burgundy, after whose death he continued his attachment to the Hapsburg dynasty. In 1508 he followed the Emperor *Maximilian I on his campaign against Venice; he afterwards returned to Brussels but was sent away in disgrace after an abortive romance with Princess *Eleanor of Austria. He played an important role in the election of *Charles v in 1519 and from 1521 to 1525 served the Hapsburg cause at the Reichsregiment of Nürnberg. He was also one of the Hapsburg commanders in the wars against the Turks (1529 and 1532). In 1535 the emperor finally granted him his reward; he forced his fourteen-year-old niece Dorothea, the daughter of *Christian II of Denmark, to marry Frederick. Thereafter Frederick took up his wife's claim to the Scandinavian kingdoms, a cause that precipitated his financial ruin. In 1540 he presided over the religious colloquy at the diet of Regensburg.

Frederick had been count of the Upper Palatinate since the death of his father in 1508. In 1544, after the death of his brother Louis v, elector *Palatine, he succeeded to the electoral state. Realizing that the greater part of the population was evangelical, he introduced a Protestant church ordinance in 1546 and joined the army of the Schmalkaldic League with a small force; however he withdrew when the emperor called him to account. After the emperor's victory at Mühlberg he observed a policy of neutrality. He died in 1556, after several years of poor health.

Frederick II is mentioned in Ep 2993 (1534) as one of the signatories of the treaty of Donauwörth.

BIBLIOGRAPHY: Allen Ep 2993 / NDB V 528–30 / ADB VII 603–6 / A. Hasenclever *Die kurpfälzische Politik in den Zeiten des schmalkaldischen Krieges* (Heidelberg 1905)   IG

George, count PALATINE 10 February 1486–27 September 1529
George, a younger brother of Louis v, elector

Dorothea, countess Palatine

*Palatine, received a good education with his brothers. From 1499 he began to accumulate ecclesiastical preferments, becoming a canon of Mainz, Cologne, Trier, and Speyer, and also provost of the chapters of Mainz and of St Donatian's, Bruges. On 12 February 1513 he was elected bishop of Speyer and by papal dispensation permitted to keep all his other benefices. In 1511 he matriculated at the University of Heidelberg and in 1515 took holy orders. When Johann *Reuchlin's *Augenspiegel* was condemned in Cologne and Mainz, Pope *Leo x turned the affair over to George in November 1513; he appointed Thomas *Truchsess to examine the work, and in due course it was pronounced free of heresy (Epp 290, 300).

Bishop George tried to eradicate abuses within his diocese; he forbad the clergy to have *Luther's books in their possession, and in 1524 he dismissed his Lutheran suffragan, Anton *Engelbrecht. During the peasant revolt in 1525 he fled to Heidelberg; when the peasants threatened to attack Speyer he contacted their leaders personally and made many concessions in the compact of Udenheim

Henry, count Palatine

(5 May 1525), but his attempt to avoid bloodshed failed. In 1529 Bishop George attended the diet of Speyer and died soon afterwards.

Bishop George is also mentioned in a letter by Maternus *Hatten (Ep 1289).

BIBLIOGRAPHY: Allen Ep 290 / ADB VIII 698–9 / Ludwig Geiger *Johann Reuchlin* (Leipzig 1871, repr 1964) 298–304 / *Matrikel Heidelberg* I 479 / Eubel III 303   IG

Henry, count PALATINE 1487–3 January 1552

Henry, a younger brother of Louis V, elector *Palatine, received a good education with his brothers; from 1497 to 1499 Johann *Reuchlin supervised their instruction. In 1510 Henry matriculated at the University of Heidelberg. He was successively appointed canon of Cologne, provost of Aachen, and coadjutor to his brother George, count *Palatine, bishop of Speyer. From 16 March 1524 Henry was bishop of Worms and from 15 July 1524 bishop of Utrecht. As the diocese was repeatedly being ravaged by the troops of Gelderland, he resigned in 1529, allowing the temporalities to

go to *Charles V, and left Holland, retiring to his see of Worms. He was also coadjutor and from 27 August 1540 bishop of Freising. He died in Worms.

Count Henry is mentioned by some of Erasmus' correspondents as appointing Jakob *Sturm as his secretary in 1518 (Ep 612), as attending the diet of Speyer in 1526 (Ep 1739), and as having acquired the famous library of the Heidelberg humanist Johann von *Dalberg in 1526 (Ep 1774).

BIBLIOGRAPHY: Allen and CWE Ep 612 / ADB XI 625–6 / *Matrikel Heidelberg* I 475, II 541 / Eubel III 198, 316, 336   IG

Louis V, elector PALATINE 2 July 1478– 16 March 1544

Louis ('the Peaceful') was the eldest son of the elector Philip and Margaret, the daughter of Duke Louis IX of Bavaria-Landshut. He was born in Heidelberg. With his brothers, George, Henry, and Frederick, counts *Palatine, he received a good education which was supervised by Johann *Reuchlin from 1497 to 1499. When his father died in 1508, Louis succeeded to the government of the Palatinate. In a move designed to prevent renewed quarrelling between the two branches of the Wittelsbach family (for another move cf Ep 1454) he married Sibylla, the daughter of Albert IV of Bavaria. Throughout his rule he endeavoured to find peaceful settlements to existing conflicts. He also improved Palatine relations with the Emperor *Maximilian I, which had been suffering from the aftermath of the war of the Bavarian succession (1503–4). Since he took no part in major wars, he had more resources available for cultural purposes; the palace of Heidelberg was enlarged and a number of important buildings were erected in the city.

Louis also pursued a conservative policy in religious matters, opposing the reformers, whom he considered as fanatics. In 1523 he joined Landgrave Philip of *Hesse and the archbishop of Trier, Richard von *Greiffenklau, in their campaign against his vassal Franz von *Sickingen and the rebel knights; Erasmus noted especially the clashes between the elector and Ulrich von *Hutten (Epp 1356 and 1934). In the peasant revolt of 1525 he showed himself less uncompromising than other princes; after the peasants' defeat, he refrained from

Louis v, elector Palatine

Otto Henry, elector Palatine

severe punitive action. He also showed a measure of religious toleration: Anabaptism found a foothold in his county, and, true to his character, Louis was, it seems, personally opposed to the death penalty and for a time reluctant to carry it out (Ep 1928). From about 1529 he changed his attitude, however, perhaps to please the Hapsburg government. In 1532 the religious compact of Nürnberg between *Charles v and the Protestant princes of Germany was brought about in large measure by the conciliatory endeavours of Louis, who refused to join any confessional alliance. He died in Heidelberg after three years of illness.

BIBLIOGRAPHY: Allen Ep 1356 / ADB XIX 575–7 / Richard Benz *Heidelberg* (Constance 1961) 83, 119, and passim / *The Mennonite Encyclopedia* (Scottdale 1955–9) III 402   IG

Otto Henry, elector PALATINE 10 April 1502–12 February 1559
Otto Henry (Ottheinrich) was the elder son of Ruprecht, count Palatine and Elizabeth, the daughter of Duke George of Bavaria-Landshut. His parents both died in 1504 during the war of the Bavarian Succession; in

the ensuing peace treaty Otto Henry and his younger brother, Philip, count *Palatine, received part of the territories of their maternal grandfather with the title of dukes of Neuburg. In 1520 Otto Henry attended the coronation of *Charles v in Aachen and in 1521 the diet of Worms. On 15 April 1521 he departed for Jerusalem – a pilgrimage of which he kept a diary – and after his return began to rule his tiny duchy of Neuburg in July 1522. In the same year his rights to the succession to the Palatinate were recognized, provided that Louis v and Frederick II, electors *Palatine, died without children. In 1529 Otto Henry married Susanna, the widow of Margrave Casimir of Brandenburg-Ansbach; she did not bear him any children and died in 1543.

Otto Henry was at first opposed to the Lutherans and still asserted this stand at the diet of Augsburg in 1530, but gradually he was attracted by the Protestant faith and in 1542 introduced the Reformation in Neuburg. By this time his financial situation was becoming increasingly difficult, and in 1544 he turned over control of his government to the estates of Neuburg, who assumed responsibility for his

Philip, count Palatine

---

debts. He received an annuity and withdrew to Heidelberg, where he lived as a private citizen. In 1552, after Maurice of Saxony and his allies, including Otto Henry's stepson, Albert of *Brandenburg-Ansbach, had defeated the forces of the Hapsburgs, he returned to Neuburg. In 1556, after the death of Frederick II, he became elector, introduced the Reformation in the Palatinate, and reorganized the University of Heidelberg. He died three years later at Heidelberg. Otto Henry is best known for his cultural interests; he owned important collections of books, paintings, and other works of art.

Ep 2947 (1534) mentions Otto Henry's part in the peace negotiations that led to the reinstatement of Duke Ulrich of *Württemberg.

BIBLIOGRAPHY: Allen Ep 2947 / ADB XXIV 713–19 / Richard Benz *Heidelberg* (Constance 1961) 94–114   IG

Philip, count PALATINE 12 November 1503–4 July 1548
Philip was the younger son of Ruprecht, count Palatine, and Elizabeth of Bavaria-Landshut and a younger brother of Otto Henry, elector

*Palatine. He was born in Heidelberg. Both his parents died in 1504, and the brothers were brought up in Neuburg, on the Danube, the capital of the tiny duchy they had inherited. At first intended for the church, Philip was instructed by capable tutors. He matriculated in Freiburg on 6 June 1516 and studied under *Zasius until 1518. The portrait of him painted by Hans Baldung, which is now in the Bayerische Staatsgemäldesammlung of Munich, dates from this time. From 1519 to 1521 he studied in Padua, where he contracted the pox, which was to plague him for the rest of his life, flaring up periodically. Since his hopes for a successful career in the church did not materialize, Philip returned to Neuburg and his brother, Otto Henry. Throughout their lives the brothers remained closely attached to each other, and Otto Henry later wrote a biography of his younger brother.

In 1523 Philip entered the service of Archduke *Ferdinand but soon moved to the court of Frederick II, elector *Palatine, who had been his guardian until 2 June 1522, although he returned frequently to Neuburg. He attended the diet of Speyer in 1529 and in the same year, on 11 October, distinguished himself during the defence of Vienna against the Turks. He was knighted by the Emperor *Charles V, whose coronation at Bologna he attended in 1530. On 1 May 1532 he received the order of the Golden Fleece and soon thereafter King Ferdinand appointed him governor of Württemberg, replacing the deposed Duke Ulrich of *Württemberg. This position was welcome for financial reasons since the income from their tiny duchy was insufficient for the two brothers. In Württemberg Philip collected an army against the Turks but soon had to fight against the troops of Philip of *Hesse and Duke Ulrich, who was trying to recapture Württemberg. In 1534 Philip, wounded during the battle at Neckarsulm and plagued by his illness, was unable to withstand Ulrich's successful campaign and had to return to Neuburg. In 1536 he recruited a cavalry force and joined Charles V for his campaign into France, but no commensurate financial reward was forthcoming. Philip also attempted to overcome his financial difficulties by marriage. His suit for the hand of Christine, the widowed daughter of *Christian II of Denmark, was not successful, however. For several years he hoped to marry Princess *Mary, the daughter of King *Henry VIII. From 1539 on he went repeatedly to England and a marriage contract was drawn up, but Louis V, elector *Palatine, refused to ratify it because the contract described Mary as a bastard. Philip spent much time in England until King Henry's death on 28 January 1547; then he returned to Neuburg, severely ill, and died there the following year.

Early in 1534 Franciscus *Ricius was sent to Württemberg on a diplomatic mission to count Philip, the governor (Ep 2917).

BIBLIOGRAPHY: ADB XXVI 18–27 / Richard Benz *Heidelberg* (Constance 1961) 103–6 / *Matrikel Freiburg* I-1 227 / 'Herzog Philippsen Leben und Sterben kurz verzeichnet durch seinen Bruder Ottoheinrich' in M.P. von Freyberg *Sammlung historischer Schriften und Urkunden* (Stuttgart-Tübingen 1827–36) IV 241–76   IG

Aonio PALEARIO of Veroli, 1503–3 July 1570 Antonio della Pagliara (Paglia) is best known under the Italianized form of his humanist name, Aonius Palearius. He was born in Veroli, Lazio, the son of Matteo della Pagliara of Salerno and Clara Iannarilli of a prominent family of Veroli. He had three sisters, all of whom died in childhood. From 1520 to 1529 Aonio studied humanities and classical languages at the University of Rome. Next he spent a year at Perugia in the service of Ennio *Filonardi, his patron, who was then papal governor of that city. In 1530 he went to Siena, where he made friends among the young patricians and found employment as a teacher and tutor. From 1531 to 1532 and again from 1534 to 1536 he interrupted his stay at Siena to continue his studies at the University of Padua. There he met Pietro *Bembo and composed his poem *De animorum immortalitate*, known today from a number of reprints, the first of which was arranged by Jacopo *Sadoleto (Lyon: S. Gryphius 1536). Paleario also involved himself deeply with the religious debate at Padua and became acquainted with the work of *Luther and also of Erasmus, who kept in touch with Padua through correspondence with *Viglius Zuichemus and others. On 5 December 1534 Paleario wrote to Erasmus (CWE Ep 2980A) outlining his own thoughts on church reform, no doubt within the context of

hopes raised everywhere by the recent election of Pope *Paul III, who had made the summoning of an ecumenical council his first priority. It is not known whether Erasmus answered, or even received, this letter, which presents the earliest known documentation of Paleario's religious thought and one of the most important. Its theme was later taken up in Paleario's letter about the council addressed to Luther, *Melanchthon, Calvin, and *Bucer (20 December 1544) and in his most significant theological work, *Actio in pontifices Romanos* (n p, 'editio Voegeliana' c 1600), which is the text of an address he had hoped to present to the council.

After his return to Siena, Paleario resumed his private teaching, tutoring in particular some young members of the influential Bellanti family. In 1537 he married Marietta Guidotti of Colle di Valdelsa, a Florentine town fifteen kilometres north-west of Siena, where he acquired a property and settled down. His eldest daughter was born in 1538 and was followed in due course by two more daughters and two sons. In Colle Paleario soon found himself at the centre of a conventicle attended by sympathizers of the Reformation. In 1542 he was accused of heresy before Francesco Baldini Piccolomini, archbishop of Siena. Sadoleto intervened in his favour and eventually he was acquitted for lack of evidence. In an oration *Pro se ipso*, composed between 1543 and 1544 and published in the collection of his writings, he reacted to the charge that he was 'siding with the Germans' by defending these latter and praising Erasmus along with *Oecolampadius, Melanchthon, Luther, *Bugenhagen, and Bucer for the great profit to be gained from their writings (Basel n d, 368–9, 372–3). Not surprisingly, his orthodoxy remained suspect, and as a result he failed to obtain the chair of Latin at the University of Siena. In 1546 the city council of Lucca appointed him to teach the *bonae literae* in their college. He moved to Lucca but continued to spend his vacations at Colle, where he had left his family. In 1556 he left Lucca for a chair of classical literature at Milan. There he had to submit to another trial for heresy (1559–60) but once again was acquitted. In 1567 his works were reprinted in Basel without the deletions demanded by the Italian authorities, and a third trial was initiated. In the meantime many of his protectors, such as Sadoleto, had died, and he was faced with the general intransigence of post-Tridentine Italy. The inquisitor of Milan turned the case over to the Roman Inquisition and, after repeated adjournments, Paleario went to Rome in 1568 and was imprisoned. He conducted his defence with dignity and acumen, refused to recant in public, and on 3 July 1570 suffered the ultimate penalty.

BIBLIOGRAPHY: Aonio Paleario *Epistolarum libri IV* ... (Lyon: S. Gryphius 1552, repr Basel: J. Oporinus, n d) / Aonio Paleario *Opera* ed F.A. Hallbauer (Jena 1728) / The *Actio in pontifices Romanos* was re-edited by G. Paladino in his *Opuscoli e lettere di riformatori italiani del cinquecento* (Bari 1927) II / The letter to Erasmus was discovered and edited by Silvana Seidel Menchi 'Alcuni atteggiamenti della cultura italiana di fronte a Erasmo' in *Eresia e riforma nell'Italia del cinquecento: Miscellanea I* (Florence-Chicago 1974) 67–133, esp 116–33 / Giuseppe Morpurgo *Un umanista martire, Aonio Paleario, e la riforma teorica italiana* (Città di Castello 1912) / Salvatore Caponetto *Aonio Paleario (1503–1570) e la riforma protestante in Toscana* (Turin 1979) / Valerio Marchetti *Gruppi eretici senesi del cinquecento* (Florence 1975) 25–49 / Dirk Sacré 'Parerga Paleariana' *Humanistica Lovaniensia* 32 (1983) 197–217 / Dirk Sacré 'Aonii Palearii carmina iuvenilia II' *Humanistica Lovaniensia* 34 (1985)

SILVANA SEIDEL MENCHI

Camillo PALEOTTI of Bologna, c 1482–1517
Camillo Paleotti was born at Bologna around 1482 to the renowned jurist Vincenzo Paleotti and his second wife, Dorotea Foscherari. Camillo, one of eleven children to survive his father, studied letters under Filippo (II) *Beroaldo, his brother-in-law, and Antonio Codro *Urceo. In 1504 he became lecturer in poetry and rhetoric at the University of Bologna, where he taught at the side of Beroaldo. In 1506, when Pope *Julius II drove the Bentivoglio family from Bologna, he was appointed chancellor and secretary of the governing council of the city. He and his brothers became disillusioned with the government of Julius and in May 1511 welcomed the seizure of the city by Annibale (II) *Bentivoglio. Camillo served the Bolognese senate as chancellor,

while his brother Alessandro, a professor of canon law, became the city's official representative to the schismatic council of Pisa. After Julius II recaptured Bologna in June 1512, Camillo and Alessandro were imprisoned in the Castel Sant'Angelo at Rome. Camillo was freed several months later, while Alessandro languished in his cell until after the election of *Leo x in early 1513. Leo x not only restored the Paleotti family to its former privileges but also elevated Annibale, Camillo's eldest brother, to the senate of Bologna.

Meanwhile Camillo found a place in the humanist circles of Rome. He became personal secretary to Cardinal Bernardo Bibbiena and an intimate friend of the humanist Pietro *Bembo. He accompanied the cardinal on diplomatic missions to Florence in 1515 and to Emilia in 1516. By the fall of 1516, however, he was weakened by a disease, probably tuberculosis, and returned to Rome. He died in February or March 1517.

Paleotti may have met Erasmus when the latter stayed at Bologna between 1506 and 1507, but there was no correspondence between them. On 6 December 1517 Paolo *Bombace informed Erasmus that 'our Paleotti' and the hellenist Marcus *Musurus had died (Ep 729), and Erasmus mourned their deaths, along with those of the humanists Fausto *Andrelini and Andrea *Ammonio, in Ep 855.

Paleotti left only fragmentary works, now in the Archivio Isolani of Bologna. One of his poems, the *Sylva cui titulus amor*, appeared in an edition of Aelius Donatus' grammar published at Vienna in 1513.

BIBLIOGRAPHY: CWE Ep 729 / Paolo Prodi *Il cardinale Gabriele Paleotti (1522–1597)* (Rome 1959–67) I 36–7
TBD

Lucas PALIURUS *See Lukas* KLETT

Blosius PALLADIUS of Sabina, d 12 August 1550
Blosius Palladius was the Latin name taken by Biagio Pallai of Sabina, near Rome. Little is known of his early life. He went to Rome at the beginning of the sixteenth century and remained there most of his life. He was a scriptor in the curia and was made one of the *riformatori* of the Studio of Rome by *Leo x. He served as private papal secretary for *Clement VII, *Paul

III, and Julius III and was eventually made
bishop of Foligno (in 1540; he resigned in
1547). A respected orator and elegant poet,
Palladius was connected with the salon of the
courtesan Imperia and was an important
member of the Roman Academy, which he led
for a time. He edited two important poetic
collections originating from the academy: *Sub-
urbanum Augustini Chisi* (Rome: J. Mazzocchi
1512) and the *Coryciana* (Rome: L. de Henricis
and L. Perusinus 1524) in honour of Johannes
*Corycius. An oration for the knights of
Rhodes (*Anecdota litteraria*, Rome 1773, II 163
ff) and another celebrating the erection of a
statue of Leo x (*Oratio ... complectens fere
historiam Romanam*, Rome 1735) attest to his
rhetorical skill. He died in Rome a wealthy man
and left his money to charity.

Unlike most humanists connected with the
Roman Academy, Palladius was favourable to
Erasmus (Ep 3047, 20 August 1535). As papal
secretary for Paul III he authored two briefs
dealing with Erasmus (Epp 3021, 3034).

BIBLIOGRAPHY: Allen Ep 3021 / Cosenza III
2555 / EI XXVI 121 / Maria Corrao *Un letterato del
secolo XVIe della corte di Leone x Blosio Palladio*
(Palermo 1910) / *Atti del Convegno su Angelo
Colocci* (Jesi 1972)   JOHN F. D'AMICO

John PALSGRAVE of London,
died c 12 September 1554

Palsgrave was educated at Cambridge, possibly at Corpus Christi College, and was
admitted a BA in 1504. Before 1513 he had gone
to study in Paris and there gained a MA. At the
end of 1516, with a recommendation to
Erasmus from Thomas *More, he went to
Louvain intending to study law (Ep 499). By
mid-1517 he had apparently returned to
England (Ep 607), but was back and in touch
with Erasmus later that year (Epp 623, 688). He
was incorporated at Oxford and became a
bachelor of theology there in 1532. He had
been ordained acolyte by 1513 and became a
canon and prebendary of St Paul's, London, in
1514. Other preferment followed, but it was as
a scholar and teacher that Palsgrave was best
known. By early 1513 he was schoolmaster to
*Mary Tudor, the sister of *Henry VIII, and on
her marriage to *Louis XII in 1514 he accompanied her to France. By 1525, after he had
written his treatise on French grammar, he

became tutor to Henry, duke of Richmond, an
illegitimate son of Henry VIII. In his efforts to
give the boy a humanistic education he sought
the support of More, who seems to have
befriended him. The sons of several noblemen
about the court also became his pupils, and he
may for a time have conducted a select school at
Blackfriars. In spite of his reputation as an
enlightened teacher, financial reward did not
result, and in 1533 he was collated by
Archbishop *Cranmer to the rectory of St
Dunstan in the East. In 1545 he was instituted
to the rectory of Wadenhoe (Northamptonshire), where he died.

Palsgrave's connection with Erasmus was
slight, possibly limited to his visit to the
continent in 1517 when he acted as the bearer
of letters from More.

Palsgrave's *Lesclarcissement de la langue fran-
coyse*, with dedication to Henry VIII, published
in 1530 (STC 19166), was the best French
grammar to appear in the sixteenth century. As
an experiment in teaching Latin he prepared an
English translation of Gulielmus Fullonius'
Acolastus for use in schools. He may also have
been the author of 'Le Myrouer de Verite,' a
translation of 'A Glasse of the Truth' purported
to have been written by Henry VIII.

BIBLIOGRAPHY: Allen and CWE Ep 499 / DNB XV
170–2 / Emden BRUO 1501–40 429–30 / McConica 120–1 and passim / John Le Neve et al *Fasti
ecclesiae Anglicanae* 2nd ed (London 1962–5) V
57   ELIZABETH CRITTALL

Johannes PALUDANUS or de PALUDE *See
Jean DESMAREZ*

Petrus PALUDANUS

In Ep 1193 Erasmus protested that he had
never known anyone by the name of Petrus
Paludanus. A letter attributed to him and
addressed to Paludanus had been published in
the first unauthorized edition of the *Formula* in
1519 or 1520 (CWE 25; Allen XI 366–7). In Epp
3099, 3100 Erasmus repeated that he knew
nothing of Paludanus; however, the text of the
letter printed in the *Formula* is largely identical
with his Ep 71, addressed to Robert *Fisher. If
Paludanus existed, the similarity between the
two letters might have been a reason for
Erasmus to disown him. On the other hand,
the text is not particularly elaborate, so it is

unclear why a letter-writer of Erasmus' calibre would have needed to repeat it in a second letter. In Ep 3100 he recalled that the *Formula* had been composed for a stupid English pupil of his in Paris. This description may fit Robert Fisher, the recipient of Ep 71, but since it was not published until 1521 it is not easy to explain how the Basel(?) editors of the *Formula* could have copied from it at least a year earlier. Nor is there a convincing hypothesis for Paludanus' identity, assuming that he actually existed. A Petrus, who was the son of 'magister Henricus de Palude,' registered in 1494 in the University of Louvain (*Matricule de Louvain* III-1 111) and a Flemish Carmelite named Petrus Paludanus entered a note in a manuscript written for the Brethren of the Common Life in Gouda now in the British Library (MS Harley 4906: 'De vita activa et comtemplativa' attributed to Jerome).   PGB

Niccolò Mario PANIZZATO of Ferrara, d 18 August 1529

Niccolò Mario Panizzato (Paniceatus, Paniciatus) was the son of a notary of Ferrara and studied in the faculty of arts of the University of Ferrara under Battista Guarino. In the 1480s Guarino recommended him as tutor to Isabella, the daughter of Duke Ercole I d'Este, describing him as learned in Latin and Greek and pointing out that he had already taught for two years at the university and had written many poems and orations, some of which he had delivered in public. However, Isabella's illness prevented Panizzato from beginning his lessons, and he continued to teach at the university. On 25 October 1490 he delivered the commencement lecture before the rectors of the university. On 4 August 1504 he wrote to Isabella, who had married Francesco Gonzaga, marquis of Mantua, seeking her assistance in his quest for promotion to the chair of rhetoric vacated by the death of Guarino. The choice, however, probably fell upon Guarino's son, Alessandro, and in 1510 the journal of the university reports strife between the students of Panizzato and those of the younger Guarino (Archivio storico di Ferrara, Secolo XVI, Busta 55, *Zornale del 1510*, 50). Panizzato later held the chair of Latin rhetoric and poetry, by himself in the academic year 1521–2 and with Alessandro Guarino and Celio *Calcagnini in

1523–4. One of his students was Ludovico *Ariosto, who mentioned him in the *Orlando furioso* (XLVI 14). Panizzato died at Ferrara and was buried in the church of San Vitale.

In 1525 Erasmus and Panizzato exchanged greetings through Calcagnini (Epp 1576, 1587).

Panizzato wrote a number of poems, including nine Latin epigrams celebrating the marriage of Alfonso I d'*Este and Lucrezia Borgia in 1502, printed under the title *Borgias* (see also Civica Biblioteca di Ferrara, MS 256). Ferrante Borsetti published two of his compositions, dedicated to Daniele Fino, a learned citizen of Ferrara, in *Historia almi Ferrariae gymnasii* (Ferrara 1735) II 93–5. Panizzato also delivered a number of funeral orations, while other works are found in the Civica Biblioteca di Ferrara (MSS 70, 436–7). Described as 'modest and shy' by Battista Guarino, Panizzato was criticized by the Portuguese humanist Henrique *Caiado, who characterized him as 'more austere in speech than in morals.'

BIBLIOGRAPHY: Allen Ep 1576 / G. Antonelli *Indice dei manoscritti della civica biblioteca di Ferrara* (Ferrara 1884) 48, 148, 207, 210 / G. Baruffaldi (Giacomo Guarini) *Supplementum et animadversiones ad Ferrariensis gymnasii historiam* (Bologna 1740–1) I 359, II 28 / G. Baruffaldi the Younger *Vita di Ludovico Ariosto* (Ferrara 1807) 88–9 / G. Bertoni *La biblioteca estense e la coltura ferrarese ai tempi del duca Ercole I* (Turin 1903) 167 / L.N. Cittadella *I Guarini, famiglia nobile ferrarese oriunda di Verona* (Bologna 1870) 59 / A. Franceschini *Nuovi documenti relativi ai docenti dello studio di Ferrara nel secolo XVI* (Ferrara 1970) 11, 13–16, 19–21, 23, 266 / G.G. Giraldi 'De poetis suorum temporum' in *Opera omnia* (Louvain 1696) 554–5 / A. Luzio *I precettori di Isabella d'Este* (Ancona 1887) 21 / G. Pardi *Lo studio di Ferrara nei secoli XV–XVI* (Ferrara 1903) 179 / L. Ughi *Dizionario storico degli uomini ferraresi* (Ferrara 1804, repr 1969) 114–15 / B. Zambotti *Diario ferrarese dall'anno 1476 sino al 1504* ed G. Pardi (Bologna 1934–7) in *Rerum Italicarum scriptores* XXIV, pt 7, 210, 267–8   PAOLO PISSAVINO

Giovanni Domenico PANIZZONE documented 1531–48

Giovanni Domenico Panizzone (Panizonus, Panyzonus) was a secretary to Francesco II *Sforza, duke of Milan. After having been

issued credentials dated 8 May 1531 he went to
Zürich to negotiate with the Swiss cantons
about common action against the ruthless
Giangiacomo de' Medici, lord of Musso on
Lake Como. Until September 1548 he returned
regularly to Switzerland as the Milanese
ambassador, representing the last Sforza duke
and, after his death in 1535, the governor of
*Charles v. Many of the letters and papers he
wrote in the course of his missions have
survived, including a letter to *Zwingli, whom
he met several times in the summer of 1531. In
November and December 1533, in March 1534,
and again in November 1535, he met at Lucerne
with Léonard de *Gruyères, the envoy of
Charles v, through whom he exchanged
greetings with Erasmus (Ep 3075).

BIBLIOGRAPHY: Z XI Epp 1272, 1281, 1284 / P.
Ghinzoni 'Ulrico Zwingli e Francesco II Sforza'
Bollettino storico della Svizzera italiana 15 (1893)
137–52 / *Amtliche Sammlung der älteren eidgenössischen Abschiede* ed K. Krütli et al (Lucerne
1839–86) IV-1b 977, IV-1c 230, 295, 588, IV-1d
passim   PGB

PANNONIUS *See Matthaeus FORTUNATUS,
JANUS Pannonius*

Antoine PAPILLON d 1525
Information about the life of Antoine Papillon
(Papilion, Papilio) is scarce. He was a member
of the Grand Conseil at Paris, which was
primarily concerned with legal and ecclesiastical affairs. As a protégé of *Margaret of
Angoulême he seems on occasion to have
followed the court of her brother, King
*Francis I. About 1524 Margaret secured his
appointment as first master of requests to the
dauphin, Prince *Francis. Papillon's library
included a copy of Paolo *Emilio's *De rebus
gestis Francorum*, which he had bought on 1
June 1517, the first edition of Thomas *More's
Utopia (1516), and several Basel editions
including Erasmus' Suetonius (1518). He sympathized with the ideas of the reformers and on
7 October 1524 wrote from Lyon to Huldrych
*Zwingli after having met Antoine *Du Blet on
his return from Zürich. A friend of Michel
d'*Arande, François *Lambert, and Henricus
Cornelius *Agrippa, he translated *Luther's *De
votis monasticis* (1521) into French for Margaret,
but this translation now appears to be lost.

In August 1525 Erasmus reported Papillon's
recent death in terms that suggest personal
acquaintance or at least previous correspondence between them (Epp 1599, 1600). In the
following year he spoke of grave suspicions
that Papillon might have been poisoned by his
enemies (Ep 1722).

BIBLIOGRAPHY: Allen Ep 1599 / Z VIII Epp 346,
380 / Herminjard I Epp 98, 125, 132 / N. Weiss in
*Bulletin de la Société de l'histoire du protestantisme
français* 71 (1922) 61–2 / *Catalogue des actes de
François I* (Paris 1887–1908) VII 418   PGB

Antoine PAPIN of Ath, d 19 or 29 August 1541
Little is known about Antoine Papin (Papinius)
of Ath, in Hainaut, who entered the Benedictine abbey of Gembloux, near Namur, which
joined the Bursfeld congregation in 1505.
Papin was installed as abbot of Gembloux on 10
February 1518. Soon afterwards he sent five of
his monks to St Truiden in support of the
reform there undertaken by the abbot, Willem
*Bollart. Some years later, however, Papin
seems to have been guided by self-interest
when he interfered in the affairs of the abbey of
Villers-la-Ville (Tilly), in Brabant. On 22
January 1531 he received *Charles v at Gembloux, and two years later he strained the
resources of his abbey so as to lend the emperor
eighteen hundred florins. He restored or
constructed several buildings and increased
the library, which still held a fine collection of
manuscripts assembled during Gembloux's
heyday in the twelfth century. Erasmus, who
had been given a list of the Gembloux
manuscripts, asked in 1519 for a codex of St
Cyprian to be loaned to him, and Papin sent it
promptly (Epp 975, 984).

BIBLIOGRAPHY: Allen Ep 975 / *Gallia christiana*
III 525–7 / *Monasticon Belge* ed U. Berlière et al
(Maredsous-Liège 1890–) I 24, 162, IV-2 390 /
LThK IV 643   PGB

Theophrastus PARACELSUS of Einsiedeln,
c 1493–24 September 1541
Theophrastus Philippus Aureolus Bombastus
of Hohenheim called himself Paracelsus from
1529. Born at Einsiedeln in Switzerland, he
was the son of Wilhelm of Hohenheim, a
medical practitioner, and of a bondswoman of
the Benedictine abbey of Einsiedeln. After an
early education with his father he studied with

Theophrastus Paracelsus

His extensive writings were mostly published after his death, eventually exerting an enormous influence on later medical and chemical thought in most parts of Europe. His iconoclastic yet highly original and often extremely progressive views have made him a key and highly controversial figure in the development of modern science.

Erasmus had met Paracelsus only once, perhaps in Froben's house, when he obtained written medical advice concerning his liver and kidney ailments. Some time later (about March 1527) Erasmus wrote a letter requesting further *consilia*. Paracelsus replied to this by sending drugs and recommending specific remedies (Epp 1808, 1809; Allen has the order of letters reversed). Erasmus' letter indicates a clear confidence in Paracelsus as medical adviser, even though in general he was a champion of the humanistic Galenic tradition of medical practice that was completely rejected by Paracelsus. It is probable that the physician referred to about 16 September 1528 in a letter to Joachim *Martens (Ep 2049) is Paracelsus.

BIBLIOGRAPHY: Allen Ep 1808 / W. Pagel in *Dictionary of Scientific Biography* ed C.C. Gillispie (New York 1970–80) x 304–13: good brief summary with bibliography / W. Pagel *Paracelsus* (Basel 1958) / R.H. Blaser 'Neue Erkenntnisse zur Basler Zeit des Paracelsus' in *Nova Acta Paracelsica* 6 (1953): Supplementum / W.A. Murray 'Erasmus and Paracelsus' BHR 20 (1958) 560–4 / AK III Ep 1244 and passim

CHARLES B. SCHMITT

various ecclesiastics including Johannes *Trithemius. Paracelsus probably also studied at several Italian universities, including Ferrara, though no direct documentation is known to survive. After practising medicine in various places, including Venice, Scandinavia, and probably also the Middle East, he settled in Strasbourg in 1525. In the winter of 1526–7 he was called to Basel as a consultant to Johann *Froben and there met Erasmus, who was on intimate terms with Froben. In March 1527 he was appointed town physician and authorized to lecture on medical topics at the University of Basel (having the support of Erasmus, among others), even though his appointment was not approved by the academic authorities. As a professor Paracelsus broke many academic conventions: for example, he lectured in his Swiss-German dialect rather than Latin, he rejected the traditional Galenic teachings, and he publicly burnt Avicenna's *Canon*. After Froben's death in October 1527 he lost support and was dismissed the next year. His later life was marked by further disputes and travels – in France, Germany, Switzerland, and Austria.

Thomas PARCIUS (Ep 773, of 21 February 1518)
Thomas Parcius (perhaps Parker, Perkins, Percy, Darcy) has not been identified. In addressing Ep 773 to him, Erasmus gives him the title of secretary of the city of Calais; however, the historians and chroniclers of Calais only mention a Lord Thomas Darcy who owned estates in the territory of Calais. The heading of Erasmus' letter may err in respect of both the name and the addressee's office. 'Secretary of the city of Calais' may be an incomplete reference for 'the king's secretary at Calais.' At the time of the English occupation this official was one of the leading functionaries, together with the deputies, the comptrol-

lers, the mayor of the city, and the mayor of the staple. In 1518 the king's secretary was John Benolt (Benoult, Brettowlte).

BIBLIOGRAPHY: Allen and CWE Ep 773 / F. Lennel *Histoire de Calais* (Calais 1910) II 211 / LP II 3805 and passim / Calais, Bibliothèque municipale, MS 183: 'Chronique de Calais' by Turpin I 8–9   ANDRÉ GODIN

Lazarus a PARENTIBUS of Genoa, documented 1527
In May 1527 Erasmus gave Crato *Stalburg an introductory letter addressed to Lazarus a Parentibus, a citizen and resident of Genoa (Ep 1818). As Erasmus mentioned specifically that Stalburg's journey was a business trip, it is quite likely that Lazarus was also a merchant; perhaps he was the unnamed merchant of Genoa who in September 1525 had taken a letter from Juan Luis *Vives at Bruges to Erasmus at Basel (Ep 1613). He has not otherwise been identified.

BIBLIOGRAPHY: Allen Ep 1818 / de Vocht CTL II 25–6   IG

Michel PARMENTIER of Lyon, c 1481–c 1561
A native of Lyon, Michel Parmentier was a bookseller and publisher there at the Ecu de Bâle, a major centre for the sale and distribution of Basel publications in France that was established initially by Johann *Schabler, alias Wattenschnee, and carried on in the 1520s by Schabler's nephew Jean Vaugris and after Vaugris' death in 1527 by Parmentier alone. Though Parmentier married and spent his life in Lyon, he acquired citizenship in Basel in 1526 and had agents working for him in Bordeaux, Toulouse, and Avignon. He also served as an intermediary for correspondence between scholars; Erasmus used his services for letters to Jacopo *Sadoleto in 1534 (Epp 2930, 2972). The few editions Parmentier published on his own were mostly legal and medical works, along with the *Epigrammata* of the poet Jean Voulté. His bookselling activities were much more extensive, and his inventory showed considerable breadth, including works by Erasmus, *Luther, and *Cochlaeus. His personal contacts were increasingly with Protestants. His partner, Jean Vaugris, had been one of Lyon's earliest converts to the new

religion, and at least three of Parmentier's four daughters married Protestants. Parmentier was about eighty years old in 1561, when he testified about the past and present condition of two Lyon hospitals, but he may not have lived to see the reformed regime in Lyon from 1562 to 1563, when his son-in-law, the merchant-publisher Jean-François de Gabiano, served as an elder of the church. He was surely dead by January 1565, when another daughter remarried an important Protestant notary.

BIBLIOGRAPHY: Allen Ep 2930 / J. and H. Baudrier *Bibliographie lyonnaise* (Lyon 1895–1921) x 387–405 / J. Plattard 'A l'écu de Bâle' *Revue du seizième siècle* 13 (1926) 282–5 / Peter G. Bietenholz *Basle and France in the Sixteenth Century* (Geneva-Toronto 1971) ch 1 / P. Roode and L. Desgraves 'Relations entre les imprimeurs et les libraires de Bordeaux et de Lyon aux XVIe et XVIIe siècles' in *Nouvelles études lyonnaises* (Geneva 1969) 65–79 / Lyon, Archives départementales du Rhône, MS 3E8029, 247 verso–248 recto / Archives municipales de Lyon, MS GG128, piece 82
                              NATALIE ZEMON DAVIS

Juan de la PARRA died c May 1521
Very little is known about Juan de la Parra, who was for some time a member of Don Juan de Zúñiga's 'Academy' at Zalamea. According to Pietro Martire d'Anghiera he was appointed personal physician to *Ferdinand when the prince was still in his cradle. In a letter from Valladolid he described the illness and death in 1506 of Philip the Handsome, duke of *Burgundy. He accompanied Ferdinand to the Netherlands in 1518 and, while still in the prince's service, died at Worms during the diet of 1521, a victim of a plague epidemic that also took the lives of Guillaume (I) de *Croy, lord of Chièvres, and Luigi *Marliano. Clearly on intimate terms with his young charge, Juan de la Parra acted as Ferdinand's tutor as well as his physician and read with him Erasmus' *Institutio principis christiani*. Erasmus wrote to Juan de la Parra in February 1519, recommending Juan Luis *Vives as a teacher for Ferdinand (Ep 917). Shortly before his death Juan de la Parra had been named bishop of Almeria, but he never took possession of his see.

BIBLIOGRAPHY: Allen and CWE Ep 917 / *Series*

episcoporum ecclesiae catholicae ed P.B. Gams (Regensburg 1873) 5 / Eubel III 105 / Pietro Martire d'Anghiera *Opera* (Graz 1966) 641 (Ep 722) / Juan Luis Vives *Opera omnia* (Valencia 1782–90, repr 1964) II 320 / *Deutsche Reichstagsakten* Jüngere Reihe (Gotha-Göttingen 1893–) II 911   PGB

Jacobus de PARTIBUS *See Jacques* DESPARTS

PARVUS *See Guillaume and Jean* PETIT

Johannes PASCHASIUS or PASQUA *See Jan van* PAESSCHEN

Lambertus PASCUALIS (LB IX 965C)
Lambertus Pascualis is identified as a Carthusian at Koblenz by Johann *Dietenberger, who states that Pascualis drew his attention to Erasmus' statements concerning divorce. As a result he is mentioned in passing in Erasmus' reply to Dietenberger (LB IX 965C). A dedicatory epistle by Pascualis is found in an edition of *Denis the Carthusian's *In epistolas canonicas commentarii* and other works (n p 1530; copies in the British Library and the Bibliothèque Nationale, Paris).   PGB

Antonio PASINI of Todi, d 1469
Antonio Pasini from Todi was commonly referred to as 'Tudertinus.' He translated some of the lives of Plutarch which were printed a number of times, beginning around 1470.
Erasmus mentioned Pasini in the *Ciceronianus* as a translator found unacceptable by the Ciceronians (ASD I-2 662).
BIBLIOGRAPHY: Cosenza IV 3483 / Girolamo Tiraboschi *Storia della letteratura italiana* (Rome 1782–97) VI-2 153   TBD

Silvio PASSERINI of Cortona, c 1469–20 April 1529
A native of Cortona, Silvio Passerini was the son of Rosado Passerini, a prior of the commune, and of Margherita di Niccolò del Braca, and a grandson of the city's noted lawyer and reformer of its statutes, Mariotto Passerini. His great uncle, Niccolò Passerini, had been treasurer to Eugenius IV. Silvio was one of the most assiduous and successful benefice hunters at the court of *Leo X and also enjoyed the favour of *Clement VII. He was a protonotary before his appointment as datary in 1514 and was created cardinal on 1 July 1517, taking the title of San Lorenzo in Lucina and holding *in commendam* the dioceses of Sarno (1518–19 and 1525–29), Barcelona (1525–29), and Assisi (1526–29). From 1521 he was also bishop of his native city.

Contemporaries regarded Passerini as hard and avaricious. In 1516, when through the good offices of Andrea *Ammonio and Silvestro *Gigli, bishop of Worcester, Erasmus turned to Leo X for dispensations allowing him to set aside his religious habit and to hold more than one benefice (Epp 517, 518, 519), Passerini, as apostolic datary, was the appropriate official to approach. Gigli complained that Passerini was 'so hard-hearted' (Ep 552) and indicated the need to throw him 'a sop of some sort' to 'stop him from barking too much' (Ep 479). Financial extortion marked Passerini's years as legate for the city of Perugia, duchy of Spoleto, and province of Umbria (1520–7). The Perugians were obliged to pay him so much that 'within a short time he [had] accumulated a great sum' sufficient to build himself 'a palace outside Cortona' (Bonazzi II 82) known as Il Palazzone, for which he commissioned the architect Giovanni Battista Caporali and the painter Luca Signorelli. In Florence, which he governed in 1519 in the absence of Cardinal Giulio de' Medici (Clement VII), and from 1524 after Giulio had become pope, his hardness and insensitivity towards Florentine political traditions, coupled with the heavy cost of papal campaigns in Lombardy, alienated the Medici from the people. On 26 April 1527 there was an abortive rebellion. In May the Sack of Rome forced him to negotiate an end to Medici power in Florence, and on 17 May he left for Parma with his two wards, Ippolito and Alessandro de' *Medici. Together with the other cardinals who were at liberty during the pope's captivity in Castel Sant'Angelo, Passerini was invited by Cardinal *Wolsey to assemble at Avignon to assume the government of the church. However he remained at Parma, whence on 15 December he and the other free cardinals sent a letter of congratulation to Clement on his escape to Orvieto. Passerini died at Città di Castello on his way to Rome, and his body was taken to Rome for burial in San Lorenzo in Lucina.

BIBLIOGRAPHY: Allen Ep 479 / T. Alfani
'Memorie perugine' and 'Ricordi del Bontempi'
in *Archivio storico italiano* 16 ii (1851) 331, 333 / L.
Bonazzi *Storia di Perugia* (Perugia 1875–9) II 82 /
EI XXVI 463 / A. Ciaconius *Vita et res gestae
Pontificum Romanorum et S.R.E. Cardinalium*
(Rome 1677) III 400 / G. Garimberto *La prima
parte delle vite overo fatti memorabili d'alcuni papi e
di tutti i cardinali passati* (Venice 1567) 475–6 /
J.R. Hale *Florence and the Medici: The Pattern of
Control* (London-New York 1977) 314–7 and
passim / Rosemary Devonshire Jones *Francesco
Vettori: Florentine Citizen and Medici Servant*
(London 1972) 145–6 and passim / F. Nerli
*Commentari de' fatti civili occorsi dentro la città di
Firenze dall'anno 1215 al 1537* (Augusta 1727) 142
/ L. Passerini *Storia e genealogia delle famiglie
Passerini e De' Rilli* (Florence 1874) table IV / P.
Pellini *Della historia di Perugia* (Perugia 1970) III
345–6, 355 and passim / Cecil Roth *The Last
Florentine Republic* (New York 1925, repr 1968)
13–16 and passim / G. Vasari *Vite de' più
eccellenti pittori, scrittori e architetti* (Milan 1809)
VI 366–7   ROSEMARY DEVONSHIRE JONES

Pope Paul III, by Pietro Buonaccorsi

D. de PATERNINA documented 1524–5
On 2 February 1525 D. de Paternina, a
secretary of Cardinal Lorenzo *Campeggi,
signed Ep 1542 to Erasmus. He also helped
Campeggi prepare a *Constitutio ad removendos
abusus et ordinatio ad cleri vitam reformandam*
(Regensburg: P. Kohl 1524 and several reprints; Ep 1480).

Pope PAUL III 29 February 1468–
10 November 1549
Born at Canino, Alessandro, the son of
Pierluigi Farnese and Giovanella Gaetani,
came from a noble family whose patrimony
south of Lake Bolsena had made them important in the history of the papal states from the
twelfth century. A true child of the Renaissance, he was educated in its most illustrious
centres. After instruction in Rome under
*Pomponius Laetus, he went to Florence in
July 1486 to continue his Greek and Latin
studies under Demetrius *Chalcondyles and
Angelo *Poliziano. Here he became the friend
of Giovanni de' Medici, the future *Leo x.
    When Farnese returned to Rome the erudi-
tion noted by Erasmus (Ep 3000), the charm
which had commended him to Lorenzo (1) de

*Medici, and the diplomatic skill which main-
tained him in favour with five popes assured
him a promising ecclesiastical career. In July
1491 he became apostolic secretary and notary
in the court of Innocent VIII. *Alexander VI
made him treasurer-general on 6 September
1492, and in promoting him to the cardinalate
in 1493 was probably as sensitive to the
strategic position of the Farnese lands as to the
beauty of Giulia Farnese, whose liaison with
the pope caused her brother to be dubbed the
'petticoat' cardinal. Nomination to the legation
of the papal states on 14 November 1494
enabled Farnese to monitor his own fiefs at the
same time. In 1499 he received his first
bishopric, Corneto and Montefiascone, which
he held until 1519. In October 1502 Alexander
VI gave him the much-prized legation of the
Marches. Alessandro remained on excellent
terms with Alexander VI's rival and successor,
*Julius II, who confirmed him in the Marches
on 5 June 1504 and legitimized his sons,
Pierluigi and Paolo, though not his daughter,
Costanza. The legitimization of a third son,
Ranuccio, awaited the favour of Leo x.
    Farnese's administration of his next bishop-

ric, however, marks a moral turning point in his career. He received Parma, the best-loved of his dioceses, on 28 March 1509, and appointed as vicar-general Bartolommeo Guidiccioni, a most conscientious man. He himself, after representing Julius II at the opening of the Lateran council on 3 May 1512, in an uncommon display of ecclesiastical energy visited his diocese in 1516 to give effect to the council's decrees. In 1519 a diocesan synod set up by him introduced new constitutions for the reform of the clergy. In June 1519 he was ordained priest. Even if he typified a Renaissance prince in his nepotism, patronage, love of spectacle, and addiction to astrology, Farnese was henceforth among those cardinals who sponsored the new spirit of Catholic reform. His wealth owed much to the rich benefices bestowed on him by Leo x, the friend of his youth, and enabled him to build the Farnese palace, which he greatly enlarged after becoming pope. He received a series of cardinal bishoprics beginning during Leo's pontificate with Frascati (15 June 1519) and continuing under *Clement VII with Palestrina, Sabina, Porto, and finally Ostia in 1524. Despite the strained relations arising from Giulio de' Medici's election to the papacy instead of his own, Farnese won Clement VII's confidence and became dean of the Sacred College in 1524. During the Sack of Rome he shared in the pope's captivity in Castel Sant'Angelo, emerging to become legate in Rome, while the exiled Clement VII occupied the Farnese palace in Viterbo. He accompanied Clement to meetings with *Charles v in Bologna in 1530 and 1532.

Unanimously elected pope on 13 October 1534 (Ep 2988), Farnese took the name Paul III. In his customary letter of congratulation Erasmus associated the name with its Greek connotations of 'quiet' and 'tranquillity' and with the Latin 'modesty.' Expressing his wishes for the peace of the church and for a council, and commenting on the pope's exceptional learning and experience in ecclesiastical matters, Erasmus passed lightly over the pope's moral lapses (Ep 2988). But the appointment of two of his grandchildren, Alessandro *Farnese, a son of Pierluigi, and Guido Ascanio *Sforza, a son of Costanza, to the cardinalate in the first nomination of his pontificate on 18 December 1534 aroused the ire of his contem-

poraries (Ep 2998). If Erasmus did not, apparently, comment on this or on Paul III's appointment of Alessandro Farnese as vice-chancellor of the church on 13 August 1535, Christoph von *Stadion may have had Alessandro in mind when he wrote in November of the pope's desire to enrich his kinsmen (Ep 3073). Erasmus did not live to see Ascanio made treasurer of the papal camera on 22 October 1537 or Pierluigi become gonfalonier of the church in January 1537, duke of the newly formed duchy of Castro in October, and – against the wishes of both the emperor and the Sacred College – duke of Parma and Piacenza in 1545. Pierluigi's son Ottavio became the Emperor Charles v's son-in-law by marrying his natural daughter, *Margaret in 1538 and acquired the duchy of Camerino in 1540.

In his determination to call a general council (Ep 3048) Paul III forwarded Catholic reform and came closer to fulfilling Erasmus' hopes. Early in his pontificate the secular powers were invited to attend a council (Ep 2998), and from his first bull of 2 June 1536 convoking one to meet at Mantua to the eventual opening of the council at Trent on 13 December 1545 he laboured incessantly for it against opposition from cardinals, German Protestants, and secular rulers and prepared positively for it by various reform commissions. Failing to get a bull of reform from the work of the first two commissions, instituted in November 1534 to inquire into morals and into the administration of the papal states, Paul III realized the need to create cardinals committed to reform. The men of devoted Christian lives and conspicuous learning like the imprisoned John *Fisher (Ep 3048), Reginald *Pole, Gasparo *Contarini, Gianpietro Carafa (*Paul IV) and Girolamo *Aleandro whom the pope now raised to the purple effaced the scandal of his first nomination and eventually ended the predominance of cardinals created by the Medici. By the bull Sublimis Deus of 23 August 1535 Paul appointed a commission, distinguished by Pole, Contarini, and Carafa among others, to examine the condition of the church and to suggest reform. Their report, published in January 1538, contributed substantially to the work of the council of Trent. Paul III's recognition of the Society of Jesus in 1540 and of the Ursulines in 1544, his encouragement of the Barnabites and Theatines, and his initiative in the foundation of the Somaschi further emphasize his commitment to change. For the defence of the faith a reformed Inquisition was created in Rome in 1542. The pope's wish to bring *Henry VIII back to Rome was not fulfilled (Ep 2983).

Especially erudite himself (Ep 3000) – a priority after his accession was the restoration of the Roman university ruined during the Sack of 1527 – Paul III cherished men of learning (Ep 2971) and may have sought to defend Erasmus from the attacks of Pietro *Corsi (Ep 3007), even though the latter dedicated his *Defensio pro Italia ad Erasmum Rotterodamum* (Rome 1535) to the pope. Believing that the possession of a classical style was necessary to refute the Protestant charge of linguistic barbarism and scholastic subtlety, Paul exhorted Erasmus to put his eloquence and erudition at the service of the church (Ep 3021), hinting that such support would not go unrecognized. In March 1535 it was rumoured that the new pope intended to make Erasmus a cardinal (Ep 3007) and provide him with adequate revenue. In August 1535 Paul's hint was substantiated in the offer of the provostship of Deventer (Ep 3033), and by the late summer and autumn of 1535 Erasmus was writing to Bartholomaeus *Latomus, Piotr *Tomicki and Conradus *Goclenius (Epp 3048, 3049, 3052) as if the offer of a cardinal's hat were already assured in Rome. The pope was well-disposed towards him and six cardinals favoured him (Ep 3052). Of these, three were evidently Pietro *Bembo (Ep 3026), Nikolaus von *Schönberg (Ep 3047), and Antonio *Pucci (Ep 3011). What Erasmus hoped for at the time when Ludwig *Baer set off for Rome with his congratulatory letter of 23 January 1535 (Ep 2988) is uncertain. In October 1535 he wrote to Léonard de *Gruyères that Paul wished to make him rich, but even if he were offered ten provostships he would not accept one of them (Ep 3063). Why should he, on the threshold of death, accept responsibilities which he had up till now refused? To Tomicki Erasmus indicated that poverty, age, and infirmity prevented him from accepting a cardinalate (Ep 3049). Erasmus died before the pope's third nomination on 22 December 1536.

In politics Erasmus advised the pope to remain neutral (Ep 2988), but he did not live to see Paul's desire to foster peace among Christian princes (Ep 2983) triumph in the truce of Nice signed between *Francis I and Charles V on 18 June 1538. Before Erasmus' death Paul III's 'genius for impartiality' had been severely tested by Charles V's anti-French policy in the spring of 1536. After the imperial victory at Tunis in June 1535, to which Paul's own galleys had contributed, Charles V had occupied the duchy of Milan on the death of Francesco II *Sforza (Ep 3073). The French had retaliated by invading the lands of Charles' protégé, Charles II of *Savoy, and during his victorious sojourn in Rome the emperor had made an angry speech against Francis I in the pope's presence (Ep 3121). To avert war Paul III had hastily dispatched Agostino *Trivulzio on a peace mission to France. Not, however, until the peace of Crépy of 1544 was a more lasting political settlement achieved. On 13 December 1545 the inaugural mass of the long-awaited council of Trent was celebrated. Nevertheless the last years of the aged pope were politically and domestically clouded by the assassination of his beloved son Pierluigi on 10 September 1547 and the revolt of his pampered grandson Ottavio.

The bright eyes of this choleric old man, whose fiery temper, according to the Venetian ambassador, was normally remarkably well controlled, gleam out of Titian's portrait in the Museo di Capodimonte, Naples. Paul III's patronage, magnificent in its commissions to Michelangelo for St Peter's basilica, the Sistine chapel, Capella Paolina, and the Farnese palace, was nevertheless limited by the empty treasury (Ep 3011), which induced him to increase taxes and gave rise to revolts in the papal states. Paul's Mannerist-style tomb in St Peter's, Rome, the work of Michelangelo's student Giacomo della Porta, with its effigy of the pope, his right hand raised in blessing, and its allegorical figures of Wisdom and Justice, aptly commemorates the pope who epitomized two epochs.

BIBLIOGRAPHY: O. Panvinio *Pontificum Romanorum vitae* (Cologne 1626) /A. Ciaconius *Vitae et res gestae Pontificum Romanorum et S.R.E. Cardinalium* (Rome 1677) / C. Capasso *Paolo III (1534–1549)* (Messina 1923–4) / L. Marchal in DTC XII 9–20 / L. Dorez *La Cour du Pape Paul III* (Paris 1932) / A.F. Verde *Lo*

Pope Paul IV

---

studio fiorentino (Florence-Pistoia 1973–   ) III-1
30–32 / Pastor XI and XII / Hubert Jedin *A
History of the Council of Trent* trans E. Graf
(London 1957–   ) I 76 and passim, II 9, 11,
and passim / Karl Schätti *Erasmus von Rotterdam und die Römische Kurie* (Basel 1954)

ROSEMARY DEVONSHIRE JONES

Pope PAUL IV 28 June 1476–18 August 1559
Gianpietro Carafa was born at Capriglio in the
kingdom of Naples, the son of Antonio Carafa
and Vittoria Camponesca, and a nephew of
Cardinal Oliviero Carafa, protector of the
Dominican order. At the age of sixteen
Gianpietro entered the Dominican convent in
Naples, where he studied theology and received the tonsure in 1494. He entered his
uncle's household in Rome by 1496; by 1500 he
was an official of the apostolic camera, in 1503
an apostolic protonotary, and on 30 July 1505
bishop of Chieti, where he was resident in 1507
and 1512. He was active in the sixth and
seventh sessions of the fifth Lateran council in
1513 and in November 1513 was sent as papal
nuncio to England.

Erasmus met Gianpietro in London in 1514

and described him to William *Gonnell as a man
of consummate learning (Ep 287), praising him
further in a letter to *Leo X on 21 May 1515 not
only for the encouragement he had given to
Erasmus himself but for his knowledge of
Greek, Latin, Hebrew, and theology (Ep 335).
Other sources confirm his intellectual brilliance, particularly his astonishing memory,
which enabled him to quote with ease from
Scripture and the works of Thomas Aquinas.
Erasmus wrote to him on 23 December 1515 (Ep
377) and apologized for the misunderstanding
that he had been thought to ask for money
whereas he only wanted good will; he mentioned that his edition of the New Testament
was finished. Erasmus met him again in
Brussels and had a friendly supper with him in
the spring of 1516 (Ep 412). On hearing that
Carafa's position at the court was not without
problems, Erasmus showed sincere concern
(Epp 628, 640). When the nuncio had gone to
Spain with the future *Charles V he sent
greetings and inquired about his well-being
(Epp 695, 752, 794 of 1517–18).

From the future Emperor Charles, Gianpietro received the archbishopric of Brindisi in
1518. *Adrian VI, who had met him in Spain,
recalled Gianpietro to Rome, where he participated in the Oratory of Divine Love and in 1524
joined St Gaetano Thiene in founding the
Theatine congregation of priests. After an
interview with *Clement VII on 3 May he
renounced his benefices and on 14 September
made his profession in the new congregation,
which was established in Rome in a house
which he had bought and fitted with cells.
Erasmus, writing on 30 August 1524, had
heard that Gianpietro was in Rome but apparently had no more details (Ep 1478). After
the Sack of Rome Gianpietro escaped, arriving
in Venice in June 1527; he remained there until
he was created a cardinal on 22 December 1536
by Pope *Paul III. He then resumed his
bishopric of Chieti. Gianpietro was a member
of the reform commission of 1536 and contributed to the reform proposals of the *Consilium de
emendanda ecclesia*. In 1537 he served on the
commission for the reform of the penitentiary
and in January 1538 was one of a commission of
nine cardinals entrusted with making preparations for a council. In 1542 he played a leading
role in the establishment of the Roman Inquisi-

tion. He was appointed archbishop of Naples on 29 February 1549.

On 23 May 1555 Carafa was elected Pope Paul IV. Autocratic, intolerant, and irascible, he extended the scope and severity of the Inquisition to the point of arresting Cardinal Giovanni Morone on suspicion of heresy and attempting to recall Cardinal Reginald *Pole from England to face similar charges. He also promulgated stern legislation against criminals and moral offenders. He failed to recall the council of Trent, suspended since 1552, and from 1556 to 1557 engaged in a futile war with Philip II of Spain in an effort to free Italy from foreign domination. In January 1559 he promulgated the Index of prohibited books, which included a condemnation of all the works of Erasmus. The Pauline Index aroused such opposition that it was modified, then withdrawn. The Tridentine Index of 1564 was more moderate in its treatment of Erasmus and other authors. During Paul's pontificate his nephews, Cardinal Carlo Carafa and Giovanni Carafa, duke of Paliano, behaved scandalously, the latter murdering his pregnant wife because he suspected her of adultery. Paul IV disgraced them in 1559, and they were executed under Pius IV in 1561. The Roman populace celebrated the death of Paul IV by freeing the prisoners of the Inquisition and burning down its headquarters.

BIBLIOGRAPHY: Allen and CWE Ep 287 / The most useful biographical article to date is by Hubert Jedin in *Enciclopedia Cattolica* (Vatican City 1949) IX 736–42 / See also Eubel III 24, 255, 311, and passim; Pastor XII–XIV; G. Schwaiger in LThK VIII 200–2; the description by Bernardo Navagero in E. Alberi *Relazioni degli ambasciatori veneti al Senato* 2nd ser III (Florence 1848) 378–81 / On his earlier career see P. Paschini *S. Gaetano Thiene, Gian Pietro Carafa e le origini dei chierici teatini* (Rome 1926)

D.S. CHAMBERS

PAUL of Middelburg 1445–14 December 1533 Paul (Paulus de Middelburgo) was born at Middelburg, on the island of Walcheren. He received his first schooling at Bruges and continued his studies at Louvain, tackling philosophy, theology, and medicine. After he had been ordained priest in his native town he became professor of astronomy in the Universi-

Paul of Middelburg

ty of Padua in 1479. Two years later he entered the service of Federigo da Montefeltro, duke of Urbino, as his personal physician and astrologer. After the duke's death in 1482 Paul lived for some time in the Netherlands. He advocated a reform of the calendar and engaged in a dispute over its theological implications, especially with Petrus de Rivo, a Louvain doctor of law. For example, Paul argued that Good Friday was actually a Monday. Between about 1487 and 1494 both sides to this dispute produced a number of pamphlets. Paul finally returned to the question with his *Paulina, de recta Paschae celebratione* (Fossombrone: O. Petrutius 8 July 1513); this may well be the work Erasmus had particularly in mind when writing Ep 326.

Meanwhile Paul had been appointed to the see of Fossombrone, near Urbino, on 30 July 1494 and was thus in a position to participate in the fifth Lateran council, which was also concerned with the reform of the calendar. The results of the council debates, however, fell far short of Paul's expectations; all he finally did was incite Nicolaus Copernicus to take up the matter. Paul died in Rome and was buried in

Santa Maria dell'Anima. Apart from his treatises on calendar reform he wrote mathematical works of no great originality and astrological prognostics. Of the latter we possess those for the years 1479–84, 1486, and 1524; the forecast for 1484 also covers the twenty years following.

Erasmus later defended Paul, his compatriot, against Agostino *Steuco, who denied, however, that he had shown a lack of regard for Paul (Epp 2465, 2513). In his defence of the fourth and fifth editions of the New Testament he noted that Paul too had occasionally found fault with the Vulgate (LB VI preliminary texts).

A fine painting, now at Windsor Castle, and variously attributed to Justus of Ghent, Melozzo da Forlì, and Pedro Borruguete, shows Duke Federigo and his son listening to the lecture of a humanist, perhaps Paul of Middelburg.

BIBLIOGRAPHY: Allen and CWE Ep 326 / NNBW III 860–1 / D.J. Struik 'Paulus van Middelburg (1445–1533)' *Mededeelingen van het Nederlandsch Historisch Instituut te Rome* 5 (1925) 79–118 / Lynn Thorndike *A History of Magic and Experimental Science* (New York 1923–58) IV and V passim   C.G. VAN LEIJENHORST

Anton PAUMGARTNER of Augsburg, c 1518–10 June 1581
Anton, the third son of Johann (II) *Paumgartner and Regina Fugger, received a good education at home and was tutored for some time by Franciscus *Rupilius; subsequently he was sent to France and Italy to learn languages, business, and manners. In 1533 he represented his father's firm in Venice (Ep 2879); thereafter he shared his time between Venice and Augsburg. He married Regina Honold in February 1540. Like his brothers, on 10 March 1541 he signed an agreement on the future sharing of his father's inheritance. But, used to a life of luxury, he kept squandering a great deal of money and offended his wife with his frequent infidelities, so that she left him in July 1543. His evident mismanagement of his affairs caused Johann, his father, to exclude him from the inheritance (18 June 1543), buying him off with an annuity of 1800 florins. Thereafter he seems to have been more careful with his money; he managed not to get involved in the financial ruin which beset his brothers be-

tween 1563 and 1565 and even to hold on to the family estate of Baumgarten which he obtained by giving up his annuity. He lived comfortably in Augsburg and on his estates until his death. Michael Lindener dedicated to him *Rastbüchlein* (n p 1558), a collection of frequently salacious burlesques.

Erasmus refers in Ep 2879 to Anton Paumgartner's good education and his knowledge of foreign languages.

BIBLIOGRAPHY: Wilhelm Krag *Die Paumgartner von Nürnberg und Augsburg* (Munich-Leipzig 1919) 103–5 and passim / Karl Otto Müller *Quellen zur Handelsgeschichte der Paumgartner von Augsburg (1480–1570)* (Wiesbaden 1955) 14*–15*, 40, 42–8, and passim   IG

David PAUMGARTNER of Augsburg, 1521–18 April 1567
David, the youngest son of Johann (II) *Paumgartner and Regina Fugger, was still living at home in 1533 (Ep 2879) when Franciscus *Rupilius was supervising his studies. In 1537 he was studying at Padua under his tutor Johann Muschler, but a year later his father, objecting to his tutor's methods of instruction, made him return to Augsburg. After his father's death in 1549, David and his brother Johann Georg *Paumgartner split the inheritance, David receiving the Bavarian estates of Hohenschwangau, Baumgarten, and Konzenberg and Kaltern in the Tirol. The two brothers shared the town house at Augsburg and jointly administered their interests in mining. David succeeded his father as a councillor of Augsburg. On 15 March 1546 he married Ursula, of the noble family of Freiburg von Eissenberg.

In his initial period of prosperity, David acquired additional property such as several farms in Waltenhofen, near Kempten (1557), and the market of Thannhausen, between Ulm and Augsburg (1560). From 1553 the brothers lost interest in the mining business. David relinquished his citizenship of Augsburg and lived partly in Hohenschwangau and partly at the court of King *Ferdinand I, where he enjoyed an influential position. He lent considerable sums of money not only to the Hapsburg family but also to a number of noblemen, and as a result he got into financial difficulties. In 1561 he borrowed money from Margrave George

Frederick of Brandenburg-Ansbach, pledging
Hohenschwangau and Kaltern as security;
unable to repay, he lost them, and also
Thannhausen, near Krumbach, in 1565. The
financial ruin of the Herbrot firm of Augsburg
(1562) also added to his troubles, and in the
end he retained only Konzenberg, where his
wife lived. Depressed by the desperate financial situation, he joined Wilhelm von Grumbach, a Franconian knight, who was involved
in a private war against Würzburg. After
Grumbach had been declared an outlaw in
April 1563, David tried to intercede for him at
the court in Vienna in 1565 and 1566. When
this failed he joined Grumbach at Gotha and
they were captured in the storming of the castle
of Grimmenstein. He died on the scaffold in
Gotha.

Erasmus referred to David's natural gifts in
Ep 2879. In 1535 he dedicated to him his
Precationes aliquot novae (Epp 2994, 2995). By
mistake he had misread David's name as Daniel
(also in Ep 2879), and this name was printed on
a few copies of the *Precationes* (such as one sent
to Julius *Pflug; cf Ep 3016), while most other
copies show David's name correctly.

BIBLIOGRAPHY: NDB I 663 / Wilhelm Krag *Die
Paumgartner von Nürnberg und Augsburg*
(Munich-Leipzig 1919) 102–6 and passim / Karl
Otto Müller *Quellen zur Handelsgeschichte der
Paumgartner von Augsburg (1480–1570)* (Wies-
baden 1955) 14*–21*, 69, 112, and
passim   IG

Johann (I) PAUMGARTNER of Augsburg,
1455–19 October 1527
Johann Paumgartner, the youngest son of
Anton Paumgartner (d 1475) of Nürnberg and
Klara Arzt, went to Augsburg in 1485 to join
his brother Franz (d 1503), who had settled
there as a merchant. In the same year he
married Felicitas Rehlinger, of an Augsburg
patrician family. Franz and especially Johann
became very prosperous from selling the silver
mined near Schwaz in the Tirol. Their firm was
repeatedly able to lend money to the Emperor
*Maximilian I, receiving repayments with high
interest in the form of silver from those mines.
Johann's assistance was especially appreciated
when Maximilian's finances were depleted
after the war with the Swiss confederation. On
2 October 1499 Johann was ennobled and on 18

*Johann (I) Paumgartner, by Hans Burgkmair
the Elder*

August 1502 he was named councillor, assigned the estate of Ehrenberg, near Füssen,
and entrusted with the financial administration of the Tirol. The family firm, in which his
son, Johann (II) *Paumgartner, was active from
1512 on, also dealt in spices, cloth, and grain
provisions for the emperor's troops, but the
main wealth came from the trade in silver and
copper. For the most part these metals were
sold in Venice, where the firm had its own
premises. From 1513 Paumgartner also had his
own melting plant in Kundl in the Tirol.

Johann (I) had six daughters, all of whom he
married to rich and influential businessmen.
His son married Regina, a sister of Anton
*Fugger, and on 7 November 1520 took over
the business from his father. Johann (I) died in
Augsburg. A woodcut portrait by Hans Burgkmair the Elder is reproduced in Müller.

Johann Paumgartner is mentioned in Epp
2602 and 2879 as an influential personality and
councillor to Maximilian and *Matthias
Corvinus.

BIBLIOGRAPHY: NDB I 663 / Wilhelm Krag *Die
Paumgartner von Nürnberg und Augsburg*
(Munich-Leipzig 1919) 32–44 and passim / Karl

Otto Müller *Quellen zur Handelsgeschichte der Paumgartner von Augsburg (1480–1570)* (Wiesbaden 1955) 3*–9* and passim   IG

Johann (II) PAUMGARTNER of Augsburg, 1488–20 September 1549

Johann Paumgartner (Pangartner, Panngarten, Baumgarten), the son of Johann (I) *Paumgartner and Felicitas Rehlinger, was sent to Venice, France (Ep 2879), the Netherlands, and England to gain business experience. After his return he joined his father's firm and on 28 July 1512 married Regina, a sister of Anton *Fugger. From 12 November 1515 on he was authorized to close deals on behalf of the firm and, when his father retired on 7 November 1520, he took over the business. Like his father, he gave financial support to the Hapsburgs, particularly before the election of *Charles V and during the wars against the Turks (cf Ep 2879). In return he received much of the silver mined in the Tirol, which he sold for the most part in Venice. Profits were high; moreover his loans to the Hapsburgs helped Paumgartner to gain an influential position at court. In 1541 he was appointed imperial councillor and became 'Freiherr von Paumgarten zu Paumgarten,' etc in 1543.

The Paumgartner firm owned important shares in silver and copper mines in the Tirol (Falkenstein, Klausen, Sterzing, etc) and also, from 1549 on, in some cinnabar and mercury mines in Krain. Excessive mining exhausted the deposits, however, and the mining industry in the Tirol declined after 1530. As security and payment for his loans Johann received not only metals but also property such as the estate of Kaltern (Caldaro), near Bolzano (South Tirol). From 1524 on Johann invested a great deal of his wealth in property; in Bavaria and Burgau he bought the estates of Schwabmünchen (1526), Konzenberg (1530), and Obenhausen (1533) and the castle and village of Baumgarten (1533); in 1535 he acquired Hohenschwangau, near Füssen, and Erbach, southwest of Ulm, while Kenzingen, in the Breisgau, was bought in 1543. The castle of Hohenschwangau became the main seat of the family and was rebuilt between 1538 and 1547 by an architect and artists from Italy.

Johann Paumgartner took great care in providing a good education for his children, especially the sons, Johann (III), Johann Georg, Anton, and David *Paumgartner. In the administration of his property he received legal advice from his friend Udalricus *Zasius, whom he consulted in 1535 in connection with a 'Familienstatut' regulating the inheritance. Zasius dedicated to Paumgartner his *In usus feudorum epitome* (Basel 1535; cf AK IV Epp 1869, 1896); when Zasius died in 1535, Paumgartner sent his son, Johann Ulrich *Zasius, to Italy with his own sons to study in Padua (Ep 3129) and assisted him in other matters. By an agreement signed on 10 March 1541, Johann distributed his possessions among his sons. However he was subsequently shocked by the extravagant habits of his third son, Anton, and deprived him of most of his share. Johann (III), the eldest son, died before his father.

Paumgartner was a member of the executive of the Augsburg merchant guild from 1520 to 1536, but, unlike the majority of his fellow citizens who favoured the Reformation, he was an ardent Catholic. After the Catholic clergy and the bishop had been forced to leave Augsburg in 1537, Paumgartner either attended the imperial court or lived on his estates. From 1539 he was actively engaged in endeavours to reintroduce Catholicism in Augsburg; he also tried to reconcile the city with Charles V although it had joined the Schmalkaldic League. However his efforts failed despite the support of the burgomaster, Wolfgang Rehlinger, a Lutheran. From 1543 on he also attempted to persuade Philip of *Hesse to side with the emperor. In Augsburg opposition against Paumgartner hardened in 1546, when his money helped to finance Charles V's preparations for the Schmalkaldic war. When he refused to return to the city, the Augsburg council ordered the occupation of his estates of Konzenberg and Baumgarten. After Charles V had gained control of southern Germany Johann and his son David took an active part in the peace negotiations with Ulm and other cities; however, they refused to intercede on behalf of Augsburg, and the city had to surrender on harsh conditions. On 23 July 1547 Paumgartner entered Augsburg in the entourage of Charles V and helped to establish a patrician city government on 3 August 1548. A year later he died in Augsburg.

Aware of Anton Fugger's friendship with

Erasmus, Paumgartner too sought to establish a connection with him. In February 1532 Zasius wrote to Erasmus, indicating that Paumgartner would like to become his friend and would be happy if Erasmus dedicated a book to him (Ep 2602). Erasmus at once wrote a polite letter (Ep 2603) and a month later wrote again to acknowledge Paumgartner's gift of pure gold (Ep 2621). A lively correspondence ensued, with Paumgartner's secretary, Christoph *Gering, occasionally writing on behalf of his master, while Johann Georg, then a student in Padua, also wrote to Erasmus. The latter praised Paumgartner in a dedicatory epistle addressed to Johann Georg (Ep 2695); to Paumgartner himself he dedicated *Aliquot homiliae divi Joannis Chrysostomi* (Basel: H. Froben 1533; Ep 2774), for which Paumgartner sent him a gold goblet (Ep 2809). Some of Erasmus' letters to Paumgartner were sent through Johann *Koler, whom he asked for more detailed information about the Paumgartner family (Ep 2868) because he planned to write something in their praise. Franciscus *Rupilius, too, was a source of information (Ep 2867). Erasmus' panegyric was contained in Ep 2879 (cf also Ep 2961), addressed to Juan de *Vergara but obviously destined for wider circulation. Soon thereafter Paumgartner wrote to Erasmus, delighted to be counted among his friends and touching on the state of international affairs, while ordering Gering to send the scholar a gift of wine (Ep 2900). After some delay because he had been travelling (Epp 2906, 2936, 2937), Paumgartner probably learnt from Koler of the panegyric and promised Erasmus another present (Epp 2939, 2947). Koler (Epp 2983, 2993, 3050) and Rupilius (Ep 3007) helped to keep the connection alive in spite of the delays caused by Paumgartner's frequent business trips.

The death of his friend Zasius was deeply regretted by Paumgartner (Ep 3129), whose patronage was by no means limited to Erasmus. He reacted with equal sincerity to the news of Erasmus' death; he offered Bonifacius *Amerbach his friendship in the wake of the deaths of the two scholars and asked him to send him a copy of all Erasmus' works as well as a copy of his will (AK IV Ep 2066). Amerbach responded by dedicating to him the *Catalogi duo* of Erasmus' works (Basel: H. Froben 1537; Ep

3141). Paumgartner reacted by ordering a set of Erasmus' works for each of his three sons (AK V Ep 2115). However, he seems to have disappointed his Basel friends, who were hoping for a substantial subsidy towards the cost of printing the *Opera omnia* (AK V Ep 2156).

BIBLIOGRAPHY: Allen Ep 2603 / NDB I 663–4 / AK IV Epp 1869, 1896, 2066, 2084, and passim / Wilhelm Krag *Die Paumgartner von Nürnberg und Augsburg* (Munich-Leipzig 1919) 38–106 / Karl Otto Müller *Quellen zur Handelsgeschichte der Paumgartner von Augsburg (1480–1570)* (Wiesbaden 1955) 9*–14* and passim   IG

Johann (III) PAUMGARTNER of Augsburg, 16 August 1513–24 October 1541
Johann, the eldest and most talented son of Johann (II) *Paumgartner and Regina Fugger, received a good education, like his brothers, and was tutored for some time by Franciscus *Rupilius. He seems to have visited Italy (Ep 2879); afterwards in 1530–1 he was studying law in Bourges, and in 1530 his father sent a copy of Gregorius *Haloander's edition of the *Corpus iuris civilis* to Andrea *Alciati and a valuable ring to *Viglius Zuichemus who were Johann's professors. From 1533 on he attended the court of Queen *Mary of Hungary in the Low Countries (Ep 2879), returning to Germany before 21 March 1536 to become active in his father's business. On 3 January 1537 he married Anna, the sister of Bishop Christoph von *Stadion. On 10 March 1541 he and his brothers signed an agreement of inheritance, but he died before his father.

Erasmus was in contact with Johann during the latter's sojourn in the Netherlands (Ep 2879). In 1535 he sent him a copy of his *Precationes*, a work dedicated to Johann's brother David *Paumgartner. The book reached Louvain, but unfortunately *Goclenius misunderstood Erasmus' instructions and gave it to one of his friends. By the time the mistake was discovered, Paumgartner had already returned to Germany (Ep 3111).

BIBLIOGRAPHY: de Vocht CTL II 384 / Wilhelm Krag *Die Paumgartner von Nürnberg und Augsburg* (Munich-Leipzig 1919) 101–2 / Karl Otto Müller *Quellen zur Handelsgeschichte der Paumgartner von Augsburg (1480–1570)* (Wiesbaden 1955) 14*, 39, 44, and passim   IG

Johann Georg PAUMGARTNER of Augsburg, c 1515–29 June 1570
Johann Georg, the second son of Johann (II) *Paumgartner and Regina Fugger, received a good education with his brothers. When in 1531 *Viglius Zuichemus passed through Augsburg on his way to Italy, Johann Georg accompanied him to Padua to study there under his supervision. On the way south they visited Erasmus and *Zasius at Freiburg (Ep 2868) and also Bonifacius *Amerbach and other humanists at Basel. Johann Georg was still in Padua in December 1535 (Ep 3078). Eager to establish contact with scholars, he wrote to Erasmus, and they exchanged several letters thereafter (Epp 2683, 2809). Erasmus addressed to him a dedicatory letter in *Herwagen's edition of Demosthenes (August 1533, Ep 2695), while *Cochlaeus dedicated to him his *Vita Theodorici regis quondam Ostrogothorum* (Ingolstadt: A. Weissenhorn 1544) and Henricus *Glareanus his *Liber de asse* (Basel: M. Isengrin 1550), after he had met Johann Georg when the latter visited Freiburg in the winter of 1549–50.

After his return to Augsburg Johann Georg was active in the family firm. On 10 March 1541 an agreement of inheritance was signed by him and his brothers. His eldest brother, Johann (III) *Paumgartner, died and Anton *Paumgartner was excluded from the inheritance; as a result Johann Georg received, according to his father's will of 1543, Erbach, near Ulm, Kürnberg and Kenzingen in the Breisgau, and property in Schwabmünchen, near Augsburg, and elsewhere. The family house in the Annagasse in Augsburg and mining property were to be shared between him and his brother David *Paumgartner.

Johann Georg enjoyed an influential position at the court of King *Ferdinand I but resided mainly in Augsburg or on his estates and neglected the family business. When David encountered financial difficulties in 1563 and pledged some family property as security for his debts, Johann Georg protested, but to no avail. He refused to pay David's debts in Augsburg and remained on his estates outside the city. However, while attending the wedding of Sidonia Fugger in Augsburg he was arrested on 5 March 1565 and detained, at first in his own house in the Annagasse and from 21 August 1565 in the debtors' prison, from which he was not released until 3 May 1570. He did not recover from the illness he had contracted in prison and died shortly after his release.

Johann Georg married late in life, on 9 April 1554. His wife, Anna von Kainach-Leonrod, bore him two daughters and two sons and spared no effort to effect his release from prison.

BIBLIOGRAPHY: Wilhelm Krag *Die Paumgartner von Nürnberg und Augsburg* (Munich-Leipzig 1919) 106–118 and passim / AK VII Ep 3337 / Karl Otto Müller *Quellen zur Handelsgeschichte der Paumgartner von Augsburg (1480–1570)* (Wiesbaden 1955) 14*–21*, 52–5, 224, 249–50, and passim IG

Michel PAVIE d 17 May 1517
Michel Pavie (Pavia, Pavius, Pavye) was born in the diocese of Amiens. He took his BA in Paris in March 1479 and his MA in 1480. He taught arts for a time, perhaps from 1480 to 1484, at the Collège de Sainte-Barbe, but entered the Collège de Navarre to begin theological studies in 1484; he studied there under the famous Jean Raulin. In 1491 he was made vice-principal of arts students at Navarre and was rector of the university from 15 December 1492 to March 1493. He received his doctorate on 11 December 1496, his disputations having been presided over by Jean de Rely, bishop of Angers and confessor of King *Charles VIII. He was in Cambrai in 1498 when Erasmus greeted him as 'my old teacher' (Ep 85), and he became dean of the church of Cambrai on 2 October 1506. Vincentius *Theoderici addressed a letter to him in 1514 in his edition of Petrus de Palude, referring to Pavie as the confessor of the future *Charles V, an office that he may already have held for some years. As confessor he was also a member of Charles' privy council, and in 1516 he preached the sermon at a solemn commemorative service held at Brussels for *Ferdinand II of Aragon, recently deceased. Pavie died in Brussels and was buried at Nizelle.

BIBLIOGRAPHY: Allen Ep 85 / *Auctarium chartularii Universitatis Parisiensis* ed Charles Samaran et al (Paris 1894–1964) IV 713 / Jean de Launoy *Regii Navarrae gymnasii Parisiensis historia* (Paris 1667) II 963 / J. Houdoy *Histoire artistique de la cathédrale de Cambrai* (Lille 1880,

Geneva 1972) 127 / Karl Brandi *Kaiser Karl v.*
new ed (Darmstadt 1959–67) I 49 and passim /
O. Lehnhoff *Die Beichtväter Karls v.: ihre
politische Tätigkeit und ihr Verhältnis zum Kaiser*
(Göttingen 1932) / F. Walser and R. Wohlfeil
*Die spanischen Zentralbehörden und der Staatsrat
Karls v.* (Göttingen 1959) 124

JAMES K. FARGE

Ambrosius PELARGUS of Nidda, 1493–
5 July 1561
Ambrosius Pelargus (Storch) was born in 1493
in Nidda (Hesse) of unknown parentage.
Apart from his entry into the Dominican order
in Frankfurt, his friendship there with Johann
*Dietenberger, and his matriculation in the
University of Heidelberg on 5 March 1519, little
is known of his early life and education. His
later career can be conveniently described in
three stages.

From 1525 to 1529 Pelargus served as
preacher and lecturer at the Dominican house
in Basel. While there he joined Augustinus
*Marius in a dispute with *Oecolampadius
over the mass. His first work, the *Apologia
sacrificii eucharistiae,* appeared first in Latin
(Basel: J. Faber Emmeus July 1527) and was
then quickly translated into German for the
benefit of the magistrates (August 1527). His
argument that only the infallible authority of
the church can settle a dispute in which both
sides appeal to Scripture seems to have won
some support among the magistrates. However, Oecolampadius' appeals to *Zwingli and
his response to Pelargus of 1528 called forth
from Pelargus another work, the *Hyperaspis-
mus sive propugnatio apologiae* (Basel: J. Faber
Emmeus January 1529), in which he again took
up the question of the authority of Scripture
and tradition. With the help of Zürich and
Bern, Oecolampadius successfully appealed to
the magistrates to confiscate the book. Though
the book was soon released again, Pelargus,
fearing for his safety, fled to Freiburg at the
end of January 1529, thus preceding the
exodus of Catholics during the Reformation
tumults in early February.

At Freiburg, Pelargus entered the university
on 3 March 1529 and became *baccalaureus
biblicus* and *sententiarius* that same year. Between 1530 and 1532 he wrote several small
works, among them one against the Anabap-

tists (21 December 1530), one against those
who thought baptism to be unnecessary (1531),
one against Oecolampadius' opinion that
children should be baptized at the age of three
or four (1530), one arguing that the Anabaptists should be punished with death (27
February 1531), one against the iconoclasts (9
September 1531), and a dialogue between a
Catholic and a Protestant on the mass (1532).
These works then appeared in his *Opuscula*
(Cologne: J. Gymnich August 1534). It was at
Freiburg too that Pelargus' exchange with
Erasmus began (see below). On 28 February
1533 Pelargus received his doctorate in theolo-
gy from the University of Freiburg, and in July
1533 he moved with the Dominicans to Trier.

As a preacher and professor in Trier,
Pelargus published his correspondence with
Erasmus, *Bellaria epistolarum Erasmi Rot. et
Ambrosii Pelargi vicissim missarum* (Cologne: H.
Fuchs March 1539). He also translated from
Greek into Latin the Divine Liturgy of St John
Chrysostom, *Divina ac sacra liturgia S. Ioannis
Chrysostomi* (Worms: S. Wagner 1541), and in
the winter of 1540–1 took part in the colloquy
at Worms, and also perhaps the one at
Regensburg in 1546. On 16 May 1546 he was
appointed proctor for the archbishop of Trier,
Ludwig von Hagen, at the council of Trent. At
the council he played an important role in the
discussions on justification, sacraments, and
residency requirements for bishops, and on 7
February 1552 he preached to the gathered
council. At the beginning of 1561 Pelargus
handed his teaching duties at Trier over to the
Jesuits, and a few months later he died. He was
buried in the Dominican church at Trier.

It was primarily at Freiburg that Pelargus'
exchanges with Erasmus took place. Soon after
Pelargus arrived there at the beginning of 1529,
he was recommended to Erasmus in a letter
from Antonio *Hoyos (Ep 2104). In June of that
year Pelargus opened correspondence with
Erasmus in a friendly and light-hearted letter
which reveals him to be one of Erasmus'
admirers (Ep 2169). Erasmus' polite response,
in which he remarked on criticisms of his work
and invited Pelargus' comments (Ep 2170), was
the beginning of an amicable exchange in
which Pelargus offered minor criticisms of
Erasmus' exegetical work (Epp 2181, 2184,
2186). Erasmus' replies (Epp 2182, 2185)

indicate that he placed a high value on the insights of Pelargus, who knew Greek (cf Ep 2471) and had pursued classical studies.

Thus again in 1532 Erasmus evidently requested Pelargus' criticisms and suggestions before publishing the second edition of his *Declarationes ad censuras Lutetiae* (Basel: H. Froben September 1532). Pelargus complied by writing *Iudicium Pelargi de Declarationibus Erasmi* (first published in the *Bellaria* of 1539), in which he pointed out some offensive passages and chided Erasmus for misleading the young and making light of the religious calling. There followed a friendly exchange in July 1532 in which jokes are traded (for example, Epp 2672, 2673) and serious matters are discussed (exegetical points: Ep 2671; celibacy, monastic poverty, etc: Epp 2674–6). This good-natured exchange was marred only by Pelargus' complaint that Erasmus now seemed less friendly towards him (Ep 2670).

Pelargus' complaint foreshadowed what was to become a serious strain on the friendship a few months later. In September 1532 Pelargus wrote to Erasmus informing him that Erasmus' letter to Thomas *More of 5 September 1529 (Ep 2211) had come to his attention. In this letter Erasmus had spoken of two monks who had initiated the tumult in Basel. Pelargus was convinced that Erasmus was referring to Marius and himself, and he bitterly accused Erasmus of betraying their friendship (Ep 2721). In his reply (Ep 2722) Erasmus denied having attacked Pelargus and pointed out that in the letter to More no names were mentioned. He further noted that Pelargus should have complained earlier so that the letter could have been altered or omitted in the *Epistolae floridae* of 1531 in which it was published. Though Pelargus was not immediately mollified by this explanation (cf Epp 2723, 2724), the dispute does seem to have been resolved in about October 1529 with the help of Ludwig *Baer (Ep 2725). But Erasmus reported on 5 October 1532 that Pelargus, angered by the letter to More, had aroused Ottmar *Nachtgall to slander him (Ep 2728). Further, Erasmus reported on 12 June 1533 that Pelargus neither visited nor wrote (Ep 2818) – an indication that relations between the two were still cool.

A series of nine letters from the end of June 1533 demonstrates that friendly relations had by then been restored (Epp 2832–40). These letters all concern Pelargus' impending departure from Freiburg; they are full of jokes about a gift Erasmus had sent, and the series is concluded with warm farewells.

After Pelargus' departure for Trier in July 1533, there is only one extant letter from him to Erasmus; on 1 September 1534 he described Trier and its university and requested from Erasmus a letter of commendation to the archbishop, Johann von *Metzenhausen (Ep 2966). Erasmus complied with Pelargus' request within the month (Ep 2968), but, as a letter of 6 October 1534 to *Melanchthon shows, he still regarded Pelargus' loyalty as questionable and suspected Pelargus of attacking him 'sine nomine' in his *Opuscula* (Ep 2970). Whether Pelargus for his part still harboured any ill will for Erasmus is doubtful. When he published their correspondence in the *Bellaria* (1539), he stated in the preface that although this publication might be seen as injurious to Erasmus' memory, he had no such intention, but felt that everything written by Erasmus was worth publishing. Yet here too there was a note of ambiguity, for Pelargus was clearly worried about suspicion over the authenticity of these letters.

BIBLIOGRAPHY: Allen Ep 2169 / LThK VIII 251–2 / J. Quetif and J. Echard *Scriptores Ordinis Praedicatorum* (Paris 1721) II 158–9 / N. Paulus *Die deutschen Dominikaner im Kampf gegen Luther* (Freiburg 1903) 190–212 / H. Jedin *History of the Council of Trent* trans E. Graf (London 1957–) I 38 and passim, II 20, 114, and passim / A. Keil 'Ambrosius Pelargus. Ein Verkünder der Wahrheit in schwerer Zeit' *Archiv für mittelrheinishe Kirchengeschichte* 8 (1956) 181–223 / W. Mann 'Eine humanistische Schrift über die hl. Messe aus dem vortridentinischen Deutschland' *Archiv für mittelrheinische Kirchengeschichte* 13 (1961) 197–233 / *Matrikel Heidelberg* I 517 / *Matrikel Freiburg* I 273 / *Aktensammlung zur Geschichte der Basler Reformation* ed E. Dürr et al (Basel 1921–50) II 685ff and passim   DENIS R. JANZ

Joyce PELGRIM documented 1504–14
The bookseller Joyce Pelgrim, very likely the 'Jodocus bibliopola' of Ep 232, was probably a native of the Netherlands. In 1504 an edition of

the *Ortus vocabulorum* was printed for him in Paris by Jean Barbier. Soon afterwards he became a partner of Henry Jacobi, a stationer at London and Oxford. Both Pelgrim and Jacobi did business in St Paul's churchyard, London, Pelgrim at the sign of St Anne, Jacobi at the sign of the Trinity, which was subsequently taken over by Philippe, presumably a son of the Paris publisher Jean de *Coblencz. Franz *Birckmann also had connections with the Trinity. From 1506 to 1508 Pelgrim and Jacobi commissioned books to be printed for them by Wolfgang Hopyl in Paris, Dirk *Martens in Louvain, and other continental firms. Between 1511 and 1513 Pelgrim's trips between London and Cambridge found an echo in Erasmus' letters (Epp 232, 278). In 1510 he sued a competitor before the court of the University of Oxford, and in 1514 he went to Oxford in connection with Jacobi's estate.

BIBLIOGRAPHY: DNB XV 687–8 / E.G. Duff *A Century of the English Book Trade* (London 1905) 117–18 / E.G. Duff *The Printers, Stationers and Bookbinders of Westminster and London* (London 1906, repr 1977) 194–5 and passim / STC 23940a   PGB

Conradus Pellicanus, by Hans Asper

Conradus PELLICANUS of Rouffach,
8 January 1478–6 April 1556
Conradus Pellicanus (Konrad Kürschner) was born in the Alsatian town of Rouffach. In 1491 he went as a student to Heidelberg. Two years later he entered the Franciscan monastery at Rouffach, and in 1495 he was sent to Tübingen to continue his studies. The most prominent among his teachers was Paulus *Scriptoris, who awakened his interest in philology and his critical attitude towards scholasticism. In 1499 Pellicanus began to study Hebrew and soon established personal contacts with Johann *Reuchlin. He took holy orders in 1501 and in the same year finished his Hebrew grammar, *De modo legendi et intelligendi Hebraeum*, which was the first work of its kind compiled by a Christian scholar. It was printed at Strasbourg by Johann *Schott in 1504 (as an appendix to an edition of Gregor *Reisch's *Margarita philosophica*). Pellicanus became a lecturer in theology in the Franciscan monastery of Basel in 1502. Johann *Amerbach secured his services as a collaborator in his press, and the reform-minded bishop Christoph von *Utenheim also befriended him. After prolonged sojourns at Rouffach and Pforzheim and several journeys as a secretary of the Franciscan provincial, Kaspar Schatzgeyer, Pellicanus was elected warden of the Basel monastery in 1519. He continued to pursue his humanist interests and allowed the convent to become a centre of Reformation propaganda. In 1523 the city council appointed *Oecolampadius and him to professorships in theology at the university. Three years later, however, he accepted *Zwingli's invitation to move to Zürich, where the Reformation had already been established. Here he taught Greek and Hebrew until his death and was one of the most prominent contributors to the Zürich translation of the Bible.

Pellicanus' thought had been strongly influenced by the Alsatian humanist tradition as represented by *Wimpfeling. Like Zwingli he was also indebted to the intellectual impulses of Erasmus, an indebtedness he never hesitated to acknowledge. His personal relations with the Dutch humanist were, however, not without problems. Pellicanus had known

Erasmus since 1515. He had helped him with his edition of the works of Jerome and later with other patristic editions. Since 1521 Pellicanus had belonged to the circle of close friends who surrounded Erasmus in Basel. In the fall of 1525, however, a crisis broke out when Pellicanus was reported to have spread the news that Erasmus' views on the Eucharist were identical with those of Oecolampadius. Erasmus reacted very harshly with an indignant letter in which he accused Pellicanus of disloyalty and treachery (Ep 1637). Pellicanus claimed that his own views corresponded with the New Testament and with the teachings of the church Fathers. Criticizing the vehemence of Erasmus' attack and the vagueness of his dogmatic statements he nevertheless expressed his wish that the friendly relations might continue (Epp 1638, 1639). Erasmus, however, remained adamant (Epp 1640, 1644). He particularly resented Zwingli's support of Pellicanus and later accused the Hebrew scholar of being responsible for the publication of the correspondence relating to the controversy (Zürcher 260). A conversation between the two estranged friends failed to clear the matter up (Ep 1674), and in August 1526 Erasmus attacked Pellicanus in another angry letter (Ep 1737). After that the two scholars ceased to communicate with each other for almost ten years. Eventually reconciliation was brought about shortly before Erasmus' death, the initiative having come from Pellicanus (Ep 3072; AK V Ep 2456). During and after the controversy Pellicanus never ceased to consider himself a disciple of Erasmus. His irenic turn of mind made it impossible for him to accept the breach as final.

Apart from his Hebrew grammar, Pellicanus' major scholarly achievement was his commentary on the entire Bible: Commentaria Bibliorum (Zürich: C. Froschauer 1532–9) in seven volumes. Of considerable documentary interest is his autobiography, the Chronicon, edited by B. Riggenbach (Basel 1877).

On 7 August 1526 Pellicanus married Anna Fries of Zürich; apart from their son, Samuel *Pellicanus, they had a daughter, Elisabeth, 24 August 1528–7 July 1537 (Ep 3072). Anna Fries died in 1536, and on 20 January 1537 Pellicanus married Elisabeth Kalb, his former servant.

There are three portraits of Pellicanus: 1/ Hans Asper, n d, Zürich, Kunsthaus, reproduced in Zürcher Bildnisse aus fünf Jahrhunderten, with text by M. Fischer, H. Hoffmann et al (Zürich 1953) 16 (in DHBS this painting is incorrectly attributed to Hans *Holbein the Younger); 2/ another portrait, school of Hans Asper, now in a private collection in Zürich, reproduced in Das Buch der Basler Reformation ed E. Staehelin (Basel 1929), facing p 64; 3/woodcut after Tobias Stimmer, in Nicolaus Reusner Icones sive imagines virorum literis illustrium ... 2nd ed (Strasbourg: B. Jobin 1590) 202.

BIBLIOGRAPHY: Allen Ep 1637 / DHBS V 240–1 / RGG V 208 / AK I Ep 189 and passim / B. Walde Christliche Hebraisten Deutschlands am Ausgang des Mittelalters (Münster 1916) / H. Meylan 'Erasme et Pellican' in Colloquium Erasmianum (Mons 1968) 244–54 / K. Maeder Die Via Media in der Schweizerischen Reformation (Zürich 1970) / Christoph Zürcher Konrad Pellikans Wirken in Zürich 1526–1556 (Zürich 1975) / Y. Charlier Erasme et l'amitié d'après sa correspondance (Paris 1977) 192, 290, and passim / Paul R. Nyhus 'Caspar Schatzgeyer and Conrad Pellican: The triumph of dissension in the early sixteenth century' ARG 61 (1970) 179–204 / BA Oekolampads I 584–5 and passim   HANS R. GUGGISBERG

Elisabetha PELLICANUS See Conradus
PELLICANUS

Samuel PELLICANUS of Zürich, 1 June 1527–17 September 1564
Samuel Pellicanus (Pellikan) and his sister, Elisabeth, are mentioned with joy and pride in Ep 3072 by their father, Conradus *Pellicanus. Samuel was educated at Basel from about 1542 and matriculated at the university on 2 February 1543. Sickness prevented him from undertaking a journey to Italy, but in 1545 he visited Friesland. In 1547 he married Elisabeth Clauser of Zürich, who in due course bore him eleven children. He was a schoolteacher at Zürich and Winterthur, and from 1557 to 1564 he was in charge of a hostel for pupils located at the 'Fraumünster' in Zürich. He died of the plague.

BIBLIOGRAPHY: AK VI Ep 2604 and passim / Matrikel Basel II 32   PGB

Guillaume PELLICIER of Mauguio,
d December 1567

Guillaume, the son of Milan Pellicier and
Maritone Guérin, was apparently born in
Mauguio, near Montpellier, in 1498 or 1499. He
became a licentiate in canon law and, being a
priest, became the protégé of his uncle, also
named Guillaume Pellicier, bishop of Maguelonne. In 1526 or 1527 the uncle resigned this
see in favour of his nephew, a transfer carried
through with the help of *Margaret of Angoulême and her almoner, Michel d'*Arande. By
1528 Pellicier was a councillor to King *Francis
I; at this time he sent greetings to Erasmus (Ep
2049), who was also in touch with a circle of
admirers at the University of Montpellier
formed around Petrus *Decimarius. With royal
support and after a trip to Rome in 1535
Pellicier succeeded the following year in
moving the chapter and see of Maguelonne to
Montpellier, where he continued to reside
when he was not at court. In 1539 he was
appointed French ambassador to Venice,
where he presented his credentials on 30 June.
While in Venice he secured, again with the
help of his patroness, Margaret of Angoulême,
the position of a master of requests and also the
abbacy of Echarlis in the diocese of Sens. In the
summer of 1542 he had to leave Venice in
disgrace, perhaps as a result of his spying
activities.

Returning to his diocese, Pellicier resumed
his episcopal duties, which he seems to have
exercised conscientiously, as might be expected of a friend of Margaret and Guillaume
*Briçonnet, bishop of Meaux. He did, how-
ever, provide favours for various members of
his family and lived with a Greek woman
named Cassandra, who bore him five children.
In 1547 he was among the French delegation
attending the council of Trent assembled at
Bologna, but he soon returned, perhaps for
reasons of health. Subsequently his enemies
pressed charges of heresy and treason against
him, and in November 1551 he was jailed. His
trial continued until 1557 in a climate of
complex intrigue. To some degree his trial
seems to have reflected the tensions between
powerful court factions; at any rate, Pellicier's
eventual exoneration appears to have coincided with the ascendancy of Charles, cardinal of
Lorraine. The last decade of Pellicier's life was
spent back in his diocese.

Pellicier distinguished himself by his scholarly interests. At Venice he formed a collection
of 225 Greek manuscripts and books. His
merits as a classical scholar – he was studying
the elder Pliny in particular – were later
recognized by Joseph Scaliger. He contributed
to the progress of botany, and Etienne *Dolet
praised him for his knowledge of medicine. In
fact many medical works were present in his
library. At Montpellier in 1534 he caused the
statutes of the medical school to be revised.
When three students of medicine, Guillaume
*Carvel, Etienne du Temple, and Etienne *Des
Gouttes, were tried for heresy (1528–9),
Pellicier endeavoured to restrict his involvement as far as possible, and Erasmus may well
have assumed that the 'bishop' was sympathetic to the defendants (Ep 2050). Pellicier also
befriended François *Rabelais, who studied
and taught at Montpellier from 1530 to 1531
and from 1537 to c 1539. The two men
corresponded during Pellicier's embassy to
Venice in 1540 and 1541.

BIBLIOGRAPHY: Allen Ep 2049 / *Correspondan-
ce politique de Guillaume Pellicier, ambassadeur de
France à Venice, 1540–1542* ed A. Tausserat-
Radel (Paris 1899) / Louise Guiraud *Le Procès de
Guillaume Pellicier* (Paris 1907) / Louise Guiraud
La Réforme à Montpellier (Montpellier 1918) I
93–9 and passim / *Catalogue des actes de François I*
(Paris 1887–1908) VI 154 and passim / Roland
Antonioli *Rabelais et la médecine* (Geneva 1976)
43, 52–4, 204–5, 214–20   PGB

Jaime PÉREZ de Valencia c 1408–90

Jaime Pérez (Jacobus de Valentia) was born at
Ayora, in the Spanish province of Valencia. He
entered the Augustinian order and taught
philosophy and theology in his convent and at
the University of Valencia. He served his order
as a prior, as provincial in 1455, and as
vicar-general in 1461. In 1468 he became titular
bishop of Christopolis in Thrace and from 1476
he served as suffragan in the diocese of Porto,
under Cardinal Rodrigo de Borja, later Pope
*Alexander VI. He wrote commentaries on the
Psalms and Canticles, first published at Valencia between 1484 and 1486, and later by Josse
*Bade at Paris in 1506 and 1507 and a number of

times thereafter. He also wrote a *Tractatus contra Judaeos* (Valencia 1484). In 1517 Symphorien *Champier, attempting to settle a disagreement between Erasmus and Jacques *Lefèvre d'Etaples over the interpretation of Psalm 8:6, cited Pérez and other authors (Ep 680A).

BIBLIOGRAPHY: Allen and CWE Ep 680A / *Enciclopedia universal ilustrada europeo-americana* (Barcelona-Madrid 1907(?)–) XLIII 711 / *Nomenclator literarius theologiae catholicae* ed H. Hurter (New York 1906) II 1032–3

LUIS A. PÉREZ

Niccolò PEROTTI of Fano, 1429–14 December 1480
Niccolò Perotti was born in Fano, in the Marches, in 1429. He studied with Vittorino da Feltre and Guarino *Guarini of Verona. Going to Rome with William Grey, he studied there under Lorenzo *Valla and joined the service of Cardinal *Bessarion. From 1449 he was a prominent member of *Nicholas v's team of translators of Greek texts, producing among other works the first Latin version of Polybius I–V (1452–4). In 1455 he became a papal secretary. In 1456 he took orders, becoming archbishop of Siponto in 1458 and serving as papal governor in Viterbo (1464–9), Spoleto (1471–2), and Perugia (1474–7). He died near Sassoferrato.

Perotti remained active as a scholar throughout his career and engaged in bitter polemics with Poggio *Bracciolini, Giovanni Andrea Bussi, and Domizio *Calderini. His most popular work, the *Rudimenta grammaticae*, was a brief introduction to Latin grammar and syntax (Rome: C. Sweynheym and A. Pannartz 1473). Erasmus recommended it to William *Blount, Lord Mountjoy, (Ep 117) and ranked it along with the similar work of Giovanni *Sulpizio as a competent textbook (*De ratione studii* ASD I-2 114–15, 148; CWE 24 667). Perotti's most original work was the *Cornucopiae* (Venice: P. Paganini 1489), a commentary on Book I of Martial that ran to more than one thousand columns and included detailed discussions of the etymology, formation, and derivatives of almost every word in the text. Erasmus, like many of his contemporaries, regarded the *Cornucopiae* as a useful reference work, though he regretted that some editions of it contained interpolations (Epp 1175, 1725, 2446). He took one adage from the *Cornucopiae* (II i 44), adding a detailed commentary.

BIBLIOGRAPHY: Allen Ep 117 / Remigio Sabbadini in EI XXVI 789 / Giovanni Mercati *Per la cronologia della vita e degli scritti di Niccolò Perotti* (Rome 1925) / Revilo P. Oliver *Niccolò Perotti's Version of the Enchiridion of Epictetus* (Urbana 1954)   ANTHONY GRAFTON

Aemilius PEROTTUS *See Emile* PERROT

Antoine PERRENIN documented 1525–38
Contrary to Allen's suggestion, the Antonius greeted by Erasmus in Ep 2050 is not the imperial secretary Antoine Perrenin; see the biography of Petrus *Decimarius.

Nicolas PERRENOT de Granvelle
d 27 August 1550
Nicolas Perrenot de Granvelle was born between 1484 and 1486, the son of Pierre, an affluent citizen of Ornans in the Franche-Comté. He received an excellent education. While studying at the University of Dole he became acquainted with Mercurino *Gattinara, who was then president of the Parlement of Dole. When Gattinara became grand chancellor to the future Emperor *Charles V in 1518, he invited Perrenot to attend the court. In the meantime Perrenot had obtained his doctorate and a position as advocate of the district of Ornans. He married Nicole, the sister of François *Bonvalot, in 1513. Because of his connections with Gattinara he quickly advanced in his career: on 12 December 1518 he became councillor of the Parlement of Dole and on 18 September 1519 councillor and master of requests at the Netherlands court. From 17 June 1521 he held the same offices in the administration of the regent, *Margaret of Austria, who soon came to place great trust in him. His efforts in preparing the meeting with *Henry VIII at Calais (July 1520, Ep 1106) led Gattinara to recommend Perrenot to the emperor. On 15 September 1524, he was appointed to the council of state, a position which he held until his death.

In 1526 Charles V appointed Perrenot to his delegation for the peace negotiations with King *Francis I of France in Madrid. In this capacity he undertook a mission to Paris but

was detained in Vincennes until March 1528.
While he was in France his father and a friend,
Léonard de *Gruyères, succeeded in obtaining for him the title and estate of Granvelle
(8 July 1527). When Gattinara died in 1530
Granvelle succeeded him as imperial chancellor, but he was never given the title of
grand chancellor, only those of first councillor and keeper of the seals. While Don Francisco de los Cobos supervised Spanish affairs,
Granvelle reported in Charles' council on
German and Netherlandish matters. Cobos
remained for the most part in Castile, whereas
Granvelle accompanied the emperor to the
Netherlands, to the diets in Germany, on his
journeys to Italy, and also on military campaigns, such as the expedition to Tunis (1535).
Since Granvelle and his master were in
remarkable agreement on political and religious questions, the chancellor played a
key role in all policy decisions, directing and
co-ordinating the initiatives of the imperial
government. Charles v showed his appreciation for the councillor's abilities in a letter
written after Granvelle's death to his son
Philip: 'Mon fils, ... nous avons perdu un
bon lit de repos.'

Some of the most important moments in
Granvelle's career included his presence at the
diet of Augsburg in 1530 and his preparation in
1537 and subsequent staging of the conference
of Nice (1538) between Charles v and Francis i.
In 1540 he went to Germany in an effort to work
out an understanding between Catholics and
Protestants in meetings held at Worms. This
same goal he pursued at the diet of Regensburg
in 1541 and at subsequent diets from 1543 to
1546, earning a fair measure of trust on the part
of the Protestants. It was Granvelle who
succeeded in drawing Maurice of Saxony to the
side of the emperor, and with his son Antoine
he laid the groundwork for the peace of Crépy
(1544). In 1545 he was instrumental in bringing
about the council of Trent; from 1546 to 1548 he
participated with Charles v in the Schmalkaldic
war and in the retributive diet of Augsburg. In
1550 poor health forced Granvelle to leave the
court and retire to Besançon in the Franche-
Comté, but the diet insisted that he be recalled.
Soon after his arrival in Augsburg he died. Jean
Vandenesse left a detailed report of his death,
his lying in state, and his last journey to

Nicolas Perrenot de Granvelle, by Titian

Besançon. Granvelle was buried in the family
chapel, which he had built and designated as
his final resting place.

It is known that Granvelle was unsympathetic to Erasmus even though he was clearly
influenced by his ideas. There is no record of
direct relations between them, but in March
1533 Jean (ii) de *Carondelet wrote from
Brussels to Granvelle in an effort to facilitate
Erasmus' return to the Netherlands (Epp 2784,
2785).

Of Granvelle's writings we possess letters
and reports now in the archives and libraries of
Besançon, Brussels, Madrid, Simancas, and
Vienna. They indicate the wide range of his
correspondence with the emperor, his family,
and various diplomats and friends. Only a
small portion of his extant papers are published, among others by Karl Lanz in *Corres-
pondenz Kaiser Karls v.* (Leipzig 1844–6).

BIBLIOGRAPHY: Allen Ep 2784 / ADB IX 580–2 /
BNB VIII 185–97 / Jean Vandenesse 'Journal des
voyages de Charles-Quint de 1514 à 1531' in
Collection des voyages des souverains des Pays-Bas
ed L.P. Gachard and C. Piot (Brussels 1874–82)
II / A. Castan 'Granvelle et le petit empereur de

Besançon 1518–1538' *Revue historique* 1 (1876)
78–139 / Elie Perrin *Nicolas Perrenot de Granvelle, Ministre de Charles-Quint* (Besançon 1901)
/ Maurice van Durme 'A propos du quatrième
centenaire de la mort de Nicolas Perrenot de
Granvelle' BHR 13 (1951) 270–94 / Maurice van
Durme 'Nikolaas Perrenot van Granvelle en
het protestantisme in Duitsland 1530–1550' in
Miscellanea L. van der Essen (Brussels 1947) II
649–55 / Kurt Herting 'Granvella und die
Reunionsbestrebungen von 1540/41' in *Jahrbuch der Philosophischen Fakultät der Universität
Göttingen* (1924) 12–14 / Karl Brandi *Kaiser Karl
v.* new ed (Darmstadt 1959–67) II 45–6 and
passim / Michel Baelde *De collaterale raden onder
Karel v en Filips II* (Brussels 1965) 295 passim
ROSEMARIE AULINGER

Emile PERROT of Paris, documented 1524–51
Emile Perrot (Milo, Aemilius Perottus) was
born in Paris at the beginning of the sixteenth
century. He matriculated at the Collège du
Cardinal Lemoine, where he was taught by
Guillaume *Farel. By 1524 he had become a
teacher of grammar in the college and sent
letters and greetings to Farel, who had fled to
Basel. At the same time Jean *Lange included
Perrot among the most fervent of Erasmus'
French admirers (Ep 1407). Perrot maintained
relations with *Lefèvre d'Etaples, *Baïf, Guillaume Scève, Jean Canaye, and others.

While sympathetic to the evangelical current, Perrot concentrated on the pursuit of his
career. Abandoning Paris he moved to Toulouse to study law. In 1529 he went to Turin
and later to Padua to pursue his studies, still
corresponding with Farel and watching keenly
for any signs of evangelical progress in his
surroundings. In 1531 he accompanied Jacques
d'Albret, bishop of Nevers, to Rome. The next
year he received his doctorate in civil law from
the University of Padua. He was subsequently
named to the Parlement of Paris, where he was
received on 10 July 1551.

Perrot published a commentary on a section
of the Digest entitled *Ad Galli formulam et ei
annexam Scaevolae interpretationem glossae*
(Lyon: S. Gryphius 1533). He also published
some dedicatory verses in Jean Imbert's *Insti-
tutionum forensium Galliae ... libri quattuor*
(Lyon: S. Gryphius n d).

BIBLIOGRAPHY: Allen Ep 1407 / Herminjard I

Epp 83, 98, 105; II Epp 252, 267, 285 / *Guillaume
Farel, 1489–1565, Biographie nouvelle*
(Neuchâtel-Paris 1930, repr 1978) 289–90 /
Ferdinand Buisson *Sébastien Castellion* (Paris
1892) I 38 / Edouard Maugis *Histoire du
Parlement de Paris de l'avènement des rois Valois à
la mort d'Henri IV* (Paris 1913–16) I 220
HENRY HELLER

PETER of Brussels (Allen Ep 2737, of 13
November 1532)
In Epp 2737, 2739 Henricus Cornelius *Agrippa of Nettesheim mentioned a letter-carrier
for Cardinal Lorenzo *Campeggi who took
charge of one of his letters to Erasmus. The
editors of Allen suggested that the messenger
was one Peter of Brussels; this has not been
substantiated.

PETER Rareş *voivode* of Moldavia, d 1546
Petru Rareş (Petryllus) was the illegitimate
son of Stephen the Great (1457–1504), ruler of
Moldavia. Following the death of his father in
1504, he grew up at the Polish court as an exile.
In 1527 he was raised to the Moldavian throne
by a group of local nobles (*bojars*), as Peter IV,
called the 'Thin-Bearded.' He was caught in
the major clash of forces represented by
*Suleiman the Magnificent, *Sigismund I of
Poland, *John Zápolyai, king of eastern Hungary, and *Ferdinand of Hapsburg, ruler of
Bohemia and western Hungary. Surrounded
by more powerful neighbours, Peter Rareş
tried to survive in whatever way he could. In
1529 he was able to secure several fortified
places in Transylvania and conquered the city
of Bistrita (Bistritz, Beszterce), which had been
settled by Saxons. Not content with these new
acquisitions, he began a war with Poland over
the possession of the region of Pokutia, in
southern Galicia. In 1531 the conflict with King
Sigismund ended in a disastrous defeat for the
Moldavians at the battle of Obertyn (Epp 2600,
2606), described in a poem by Andrzej
*Krzycki. In an effort to outmanoeuver King
John Zápolyai, Peter Rareş made a pact with
Ferdinand of Hapsburg in 1535 and swore
allegiance to him. While negotiations with
Vienna were in progress Peter also had secret
dealings with the Turks and with John
Zápolyai. He was a master of the art of
double-dealing. Incensed at the news that

Moldavia was making overtures to Ferdinand, Suleiman invaded the region in 1538 and forced Peter to flee. He spent almost two years as a prisoner of John Zápolyai in Transylvania while Suleiman placed his own candidate on the Moldavian throne. Following the death of Zápolyai in 1540, Rareş escaped from his prison, made complete submission to Suleiman, and in February 1541 was restored to his position as *voivode* by Turkish troops. For the next five years he ruled under Ottoman protection but again entered into secret negotiations to betray Suleiman to the forces of Ferdinand.

BIBLIOGRAPHY: Ion Ursu *Die auswärtige Politik des Peter Rareş* (Vienna 1908) / Nicholas Iorga *A History of Roumania, Land, People Civilization* (London 1925) 96–7 and passim / R.W. Seton-Watson *A History of the Roumanians* (Cambridge 1934) 55–9 (with a portrait from a contemporary fresco) and passim / *A History of the Romanian People* ed A. Otetea (New York 1972–5) 212 and passim / A. Krzycki *Carmina* ed K. Morawski (Cracow 1888) 112–6

L. DOMONKOS

Guillaume PETIT of Montvilliers,
d 8 December 1536
Guillaume Petit (Parvy, Parvus) was born around 1470 at Montvilliers, at the mouth of the Seine. He had at least one brother, Jean. The kinship with the Paris bookseller Jean *Petit (whose father and grandfather were Paris butchers) claimed for him by Guillaume *Budé (Ep 522) is not otherwise established. Petit entered the Dominican order at the convent of Rouen and was sent to Paris to study. He received his licence in theology on 14 February 1502, ranking eighth of seventeen, and his doctorate on 26 December. He was the prior of the Evreux convent from 1506 to 1508 but was frequently in Paris during this time. In 1507 the Dominican general chapter named him inquisitor-general of France, and in 1508 he became prior of the convent at Blois, where the royal court was often in residence. In that year he published a letter to the king's confessor, Antoine Du Four, whom Petit succeeded in 1509. When *Francis I acceded to the throne in 1515, he also took Petit as his confessor, and named him royal librarian as well. With royal authority and funds at his disposition, Petit acquired many manuscripts. He employed a *familia* of copyists and oversaw the publication of many of these manuscripts (especially those concerning French history) by such scholars as *Lefèvre d'Etaples, Josse *Bade, Josse *Clichtove, and Robert Fortuné. The number of dedicatory epistles to Petit (at least twenty-one) indicates that he was a generous patron of the above and of Jacques *Merlin, Johannes *Annius, Agostino *Giustiniani, Jean Chéradame, and others. Petit's catalogue of the royal manuscripts at Blois, made in 1518, is still extant. Along with Guillaume Budé and Guillaume *Cop, Petit was one of the 'three Williams' who urged Francis I to invite Erasmus to Paris for the sake of the trilingual college which the humanists were promoting (Epp 522, 523, 537). After hints from Budé in Ep 568 and perhaps another letter from Budé which he suppressed, Erasmus, however, began to have doubts about Petit's support, and his doubts were confirmed by Budé (Epp 725, 744, 778).

Petit gave the eulogies for King *Louis XII, Queen Anne of Brittany, Massimiliano Visconti, and the queen mother, Louise of *Savoy, and he preached the homily on the eve of Francis I's major victory at Marignano in 1515. In 1518 Francis I called Petit 'the most capable man in the kingdom' when he named him bishop of Troyes. He moved him to the see of Senlis in 1527. Here Petit undertook major restoration of the cathedral, which had been damaged by fire in 1504, and had his own effigy carved in the rood screen.

As a friend of humanists, Petit opposed the attempts of the faculty of theology and the Parlement of Paris to censure Lefèvre d'Etaples and Erasmus, but he personally denounced as heterodox the court sermons of the Meaux reformer Michel d'*Arande in 1523 and warned the clergy of Troyes against the spread of Lutheran heresy. Petit was frequently an intermediary between the faculty of theology and the king. The faculty wrote to Petit on 28 August 1523 delegating him to convince the king that Louis de *Berquin should be prosecuted as a heretic, but Petit wrote back in reply to convey the king's displeasure at the faculty's pursuit of Erasmus. Petit's role in the politics of religious conciliation practised by Francis I until 1534 was not unimportant. He faithfully carried out the court's wishes to press the faculty for a favourable decision about the divorce of *Henry VIII. He was appointed to direct a royal commission to reform the faculty and the whole university on 29 April 1533. He was irate about the faculty's alleged condemnation of *Margaret of Navarre's *Miroir de l'âme pécheresse* in 1533. But the faculty was happy to have Petit's support in opposing the proposed colloquy with Philippus *Melanchthon in 1535. Of the four university faculties, only the theologians supported Petit's bid to become *conservateur des privilèges apostoliques* of the university. Petit died in 1536 and was buried in the sanctuary of his cathedral of Senlis. A large portrait was still extant at Montélimar in the nineteenth century. Petit has been thought to be the ecclesiastic represented at Francis I's left hand in a miniature depicting Antoine Macault's presentation of his translation of Diodorus Siculus (Chantilly, Musée Condé MS Fr 1672), but some authors believe that person to be Antoine *Duprat.

Petit's works include an edition of Paul the Deacon's *De origine et gestis regum Langobardorum* and Liutprand, bishop of Cremona's *Rerum gestarum per Europam libri sex* (Paris: Josse Bade for self and Jean Petit 1514). He also edited Claude de Seyssel's *Explicatio primi capitis evangelii Lucae* (Paris: Josse Bade 1514, 1515). He wrote *Viat de salut tres necessaire et utile à tous chrestiens, pour parvenir à la gloire eternelle* (Troyes? 1526?; Paris: Olivier Mallard for Galliot du Pré 1538; Lyon: Olivier Arnoullet 1539; Paris: Jean Réal 1540); *Oratio habita in concilio prouincie Senonensis Parrhisi celebrato die XIII Feb. a.d. MDXXVIII* (Paris: Josse Bade 1528); *Hortus fidei, apostolorum et Niceni concilii articulos continens* (Paris: Galliot Du Pré 1537); *La Formation de l'homme et son excellence, et ce qu'il doibt accomplir pour avoir Paradis* (Paris: Olivier Mallard for Galliot Du Pré 1538, Jean II Petit and Arnoul L'Angelier 1540, Gilles Corrozet 1540); and *Très Dévotes Oraisons à l'honneur de la très sacrée et glorieuse vièrge Marie* (Paris: Simon de Colines n d, Olivier Mallard for Galliot Du Pré 1538).

BIBLIOGRAPHY: Allen and CWE Ep 522 / Farge no 386 / J. Quétif and J. Echard *Scriptores ordinis praedicatorum* (Paris 1719–21) II-1 100–2 / P. Renouard *Imprimeurs et libraires parisiens du XVIe siècle* (Paris 1964–   ) II 57 and passim / Rice *Prefatory Epistles* Ep 68 and passim / J. Tremblot 'Les armoiries de l'humaniste Parvy' BHR 1 (1941) 7–29   JAMES K. FARGE

Jean PETIT of Paris, documented 1495–1530
Jean (I) Petit (Parvus) came from a wealthy Parisian family of butchers. By 1495 he opened a bookstore in the rue Saint-Jacques near the monastery of the Mathurins or Trinitarians, under the sign of the Golden Lion; subsequently he moved to the sign of the Golden Fleur-de-lys. Guillaume *Budé once claimed that he was a kinsman of the royal confessor Guillaume *Petit (Ep 522). One of the four important *libraires-jurés* to the University of Paris, he possessed considerable wealth and became the foremost bookseller and publisher of Paris in the first quarter of the sixteenth century, publishing more than a thousand volumes between 1501 and 1520. Most Paris printers were working to his orders at one time or another; in doing so, they often used typographical material which belonged to Petit. With his assistance Josse *Bade was able to establish his own press in 1503. Bade was subsequently his partner in publishing many first editions. Petit maintained branch stores in Lyon and Rouen, and his business connections reached from one end of Europe to the other. By December 1530 his own activity came to an end, although his business was continued, at the same address, by his son and partner, Jean (II) Petit.

Acting at the prompting of Johann *Froben and his associates, in April 1518 Erasmus warned Petit, who was rumoured to be planning a reprint of the great Basel edition of Jerome (Epp 796, 802, 815). That reprint of Jerome never came to pass during Petit's lifetime, but he did publish Bade's edition of the *Adagia* in conjunction with the printer (1506, 1507, and 1515), the *Moria* in conjunction with Gilles de *Gourmont (1511), and together with Pierre *Gromors the adage *Dulce bellum inexpertis* (1523) and *Breviores aliquot epistolae* (1525).

BIBLIOGRAPHY: Allen Ep 263 / Renouard *Répertoire* 339–41 / A. Claudin *Histoire de l'imprimerie en France* (Paris 1901) II 532–9 / Philippe Renouard *Bibliographie des impressions et des oeuvres de Josse Bade Ascensius* (Paris 1908) I 22–3 / Philippe Renouard 'Quelques documents sur les Petit, libraires parisiens, et leur famille' *Bulletin de la Société de l'histoire de Paris et de l'Ile-de-France* 23 (1896) 133–53

GENEVIÈVE GUILLEMINOT

Johannes PETRI of Langendorf,
d 19 or 29 April 1511

The earliest reliable records of the Franconian Johannes Petri (or Hammelberg) date from 1488, when he acquired the citizenship of Basel on 5 November and membership in the 'Safran' guild on 16 November. He worked as a printer, sometimes on his own but more frequently in partnership with Johann *Amerbach or with Johann *Froben, who was a close relative. With Froben he published several voluminous editions of the glossed Vulgate (1498, 1506–8, 1509; cf LB IX 136B), and others in association with Amerbach as well. In the partnership arrangements between these three Franconians Petri's responsibilities were primarily commercial. He visited the fairs, bought and sold books, and negotiated crucial orders from Anton Koberger. In 1500 he married Barbara Mellinger of Basel. In moving to Basel he established a precendent followed by his nephew Adam Petri, who later founded with his son Henricus one of Basel's most important and enduring publishing houses.

BIBLIOGRAPHY: AK I Ep 27 and passim / NDB V 638–9 / Grimm *Buchführer* 1374–6 / I. Stockmeyer and B. Reber *Beiträge zur Basler Buchdruckergeschichte* (Basel 1840) 134–5 / P. Heitz and C.C. Bernoulli *Basler Büchermarken bis zum Anfang des 17. Jahrhunderts* (Strasbourg 1895) xv–xvi, 2–5 / Benzing *Buchdrucker* 30 / O. von Hase *Die Koberger*, 3rd ed (Amsterdam-Wiesbaden 1967) 80, 111, and passim   PGB

Johannes PETRI *See also* JAN *of Delft, Jean-Pierre de* VARADE

Alfonso PETRUCCI of Siena, February 1492–4 July 1517

Alfonso was a son of Pandolfo Petrucci, ruling lord of Siena; his tutor was Severo Varini, a Cistercian monk. He held the Sienese bishopric of Sovana from 1510 to 1513, was created a cardinal on 10 March 1511, and obtained the bishopric of Massa Marittima the same year. His only surviving letters are about horses, dogs, and hunting, and there is no evidence that he had any intellectual interests; he may have been mentally unbalanced. After the banishment of his brother Borghese from the government of Siena and *Leo x's support in March 1516 for the pro-Medicean Rafaello Petrucci in his place, he negotiated against the pope with Francesco Maria *della Rovere, duke of Urbino. He tried to bring about Spanish intervention at Siena and was the main instigator of the plot against the pope's life which his own master of the household, Antonio Nini, revealed under torture. Alfonso was tricked into returning to Rome with a safe conduct, and on arrival with Cardinal Bandinello *Sauli on 18 May he was at once imprisoned in Castel Sant'Angelo. Deprived of his dignities on 22 June he was secretly executed, probably by strangulation. Erasmus mentioned his degradation in Ep 607 of 17 July 1517.

BIBLIOGRAPHY: Allen and CWE Ep 607 / Eubel III 12, 237, 305 / Pastor VI 344 and passim / Sanudo *Diarii* VII 260 and passim / Alessandro Ferrajoli *La congiura dei cardinali contro Leone x* (Rome 1919) / Fabrizio Winspeare *La congiura dei cardinali* (Florence 1957)   D.S. CHAMBERS

PETRUS Ep 17, of 1489?

Cornelis *Gerard's friend Petrus, to whom Erasmus sent greetings in Ep 17, was tentatively identified by Allen as the 'Petrus in Poel' (Marienpoel, near Leiden) mentioned in a letter from Willem *Hermans to Gerard.

BIBLIOGRAPHY: Allen Ep 17 / Hermans' letter was printed by P.C. Molhuysen in *Nederlandsch archief voor kerkgeschiedenis* n s 4 (1907) 61–2   C.G. VAN LEIJENHORST

PETRUS documented at Tournehem, 1498–1500

Petrus (Pierre), a good friend of Jacob *Batt and a married man (Epp 123, 138), was no doubt, like Batt, in the service of Anthony of *Burgundy and his family in the castle of Tournehem. Otherwise he has not been identified. Erasmus met him at Tournehem and sent greetings to him in his letters to Batt (Epp 80, 129).   ANDRÉ GODIN

PETRUS (Epp 2098, 2118) *See Peter* BITTERLIN

PETRUS (Epp 2793, 2799) *See* FELSENMEYER

Konrad Peutinger, by Christoph Amberger

PETRUS *See also* PETER, *Petrus* CYPRIUS

PETRYLLUS *voivode* of Moldavia *See* PETER RAREȘ

Johann PEUERLE or PEURLE *See Johannes* AGRICOLA

Konrad PEUTINGER of Augsburg,
15 October 1465–28 October 1547
Although Konrad's father, Johann Peutinger
(Peutunger, Beitinger), a wealthy merchant,
died in the year of his son's birth, his guardian,
Ulrich Höchstetter, provided an excellent
education for the orphan. After attending
school in Augsburg and studying in Basel
(1479–80) Peutinger travelled to Italy in 1482.
There he attended the lectures of the renowned law professor Jason Mainus and of the
humanists Matthaeus Collatius and Ermolao (I)
*Barbaro in Padua, and of the elder Filippo
*Beroaldo in Bologna (1485). He also associated
with Giovanni *Pico della Mirandola and
Angelo *Poliziano in Florence, and finally with
*Pomponius Laetus in Rome. He was intro-
duced to Pope Innocent VIII and to Cardinal

Rodrigo de Borja, the future Pope *Alexander
VI. Around 1488 Peutinger returned to Germa-
ny, where he visited the court of the Emperor
*Frederick III in Aachen. After his return to
Augsburg he entered the civil service and on 9
September 1497 received a permanent appoint-
ment as town clerk, an office which involved a
great number of tasks.

From his student years Peutinger had taken
a keen interest in the study of the classics and
of history. He always managed to combine
humanistic scholarship with the legal and
political duties of his civic office, duties which
he likewise found to be congenial. He deserves
much credit for the new *Stadtgerichtsordnung* of
1507 which provided a firm basis for Augsburg's judicial system. He also concerned
himself with poor relief and for this purpose
translated into German *Oecolampadius' treatise on the distribution of alms. As an
accomplished diplomat he often represented
Augsburg at imperial diets and similar gatherings. His working relationship with the Emper-
or *Maximilian I, who named him a councillor,
was close and enduring (Epp 611, 863). In 1491
Peutinger went to Rome and probably used
this opportunity to acquire a legal doctorate in
Italy. In 1496 he participated in the diet of
Lindau; in 1499 he was a representative of the
Swabian League in Tübingen, Reutlingen, and
Esslingen; in 1505 he went to Cologne and the
following year to the imperial court in Graz and
Vienna, also visiting Hungary. In 1513 he
followed Maximilian to the Netherlands and
pleaded on behalf of the Swabian League for
the outlawed Götz von Berlichingen. In 1517
he was in Munich and negotiated an agreement about the boundaries between the
Bavarian territories and the city of Augsburg.
The death of Maximilian I did not end his
connections with the imperial court. In 1520 he
was at Bruges in the entourage of *Charles V
and on this occasion met Erasmus and Thomas
*More (Epp 1129, 1247); in 1521 he participated
in the diet of Worms. In general, his connections with the imperial court provided a
number of valuable privileges for Augsburg:
the judgments of her law courts were not to be
appealed elsewhere; imperial civil servants
residing in Augsburg and Augsburg citizens
who surrendered their citizenship were not to
be exempt from her fiscal measures (1506); all

former privileges were confirmed and new coinage rights were secured despite the protests of the bishop, Christoph von *Stadion.

At Worms Peutinger renewed his acquaintance with Martin *Luther, who had met him previously on a visit to Augsburg in 1518. Peutinger was not at first unsympathetic to the views of Luther. When Erasmus met the Dominican Johannes *Faber of Augsburg in Cologne and developed with him proposals for the settlement of the Lutheran conflict, it is significant that he thought of Peutinger as a man well suited to support their plan at the imperial court. In a long letter from Cologne dated 9 November 1520 (Ep 1156) he invited Peutinger to do so. It became increasingly clear that Peutinger was not prepared to go beyond the reforming tendencies advocated by Erasmus. At the diet of Augsburg in 1530 he did not express his personal opinion when it was his duty to deliver Augsburg's protest against the rejection of the Lutheran confession. After Augsburg had turned Protestant, Peutinger could no longer represent the city in religio-political matters; in 1534 he resigned from his office amid expressions of public gratitude. In 1538 he was elevated to the rank of patrician and in 1547, shortly before his death, the Emperor Charles v raised him to the hereditary nobility.

After his retirement from public service Peutinger was able to devote himself entirely to the study of the arts and sciences, an activity in which he was joined and supported by his wife, Margarethe *Welser (Ep 1247). Maximilian I called on Peutinger to assist in works which would glorify himself and the Hapsburg dynasty; thus Peutinger advised him on the arrangement of his funeral monument in Innsbruck. On other occasions too he conveyed Maximilian's own ideas to the artist, as in the case of Jörg Breu's renovation of the old city hall of Augsburg. During his studies in Italy Peutinger learnt to appreciate the importance of epigraphy; and his own city of Augsburg offered a greater abundance of archaeological evidence than any other city in Germany. With the support of Maximilian I Peutinger published a volume of Augsburg inscriptions: Romanae vetustatis fragmenta in Augusta Vindelicorum et eius diocesi ([Augsburg]: E. Ratdolt 1505). To be able to continue

his humanistic studies by consulting Greek sources in the original Peutinger began to learn Greek at the age of forty.

In 1715 Peutinger's library, manuscripts, and other texts were bequeathed by the last surviving member of the Peutinger family to the Augsburg Jesuits (see a catalogue published by C.G. von Murr in Journal zur Kunstgeschichte und zur allgemeinen Litteratur, part 13, Nürnberg 1784, 311–18). When the Jesuit order was disbanded, some of these treasures were brought to Munich while others remained in the city library of Augsburg; valuable manuscripts can also be found in Vienna and Stuttgart. One of the most significant pieces from Peutinger's estate is the so-called Tabula Peutingeriana, a road-map of the late Roman empire.

The entries made in the Ratsbücher of the Augsburg council by Peutinger in his capacity of city clerk also deserve mention, since he complemented them with historical notes. In 1496 he discovered the chronicle of Ursberg which was edited by Johann Mader in 1515. Peutinger was also instrumental in the publication of Conradus Celtis' edition of Guntherus' Lingurinus (Augsburg: E. Oeglen 1507). In 1515 he published his editions of Jordanes and Paulus Diaconus (Augsburg: J. Miller). He did not complete his work on several volumes: a collection of letters (suggested by Maximilian I); and his editions of Macrobius' De somnio Scipionis, of Antonius Musa (begun in 1513), and of Apuleius Celsus' De herbarum medicaminibus. A work of considerable importance is Peutinger's Sermones conviviales de mirandis Germaniae antiquitatibus (Strasbourg: M. Schürer 1506), in which he disputed *Wimpfeling's findings about the borders of ancient Germany.

Predated by Peutinger's friendship with *Pirckheimer (Ep 318), *Beatus Rhenanus (BRE Ep 33), *Hutten (Ep 611), and Oecolampadius, Erasmus' relations with Peutinger were based on mutual respect and affection (Ep 1247), although they did not lead to a sustained correspondence. At the Frankfurt spring fair of 1529 Peutinger purchased copies of Erasmus' Vidua christiana and Responsio adversus febricitantis libellum and proceeded to study them at great length (Ep 2153). While Erasmus lived at Basel, Peutinger's son Claudius Pius had

Johann Pfefferkorn

studied there in 1524, and at the time of
Erasmus' death associates of the Froben press
were in touch with Peutinger and his son about
a manuscript (Ep 3134; AK IV Ep 2020).

BIBLIOGRAPHY: Allen Ep 318 / ADB XXV 561–8 /
Schottenloher II 133–5, VII 189 / Heinrich Lutz
Conrad Peutinger in Abhandlungen zur Geschichte der Stadt Augsburg: Schriftenreihe
des Staatsarchives Augsburg 9 (Augsburg n d),
with a valuable bibliography / *Matrikel Basel* I
161 / BA *Oekolampads* I 83–4, 132–4, 336, and
passim   ROSEMARIE AULINGER

Johann PFEFFERKORN c 1469–after 1521
Johann Pfefferkorn (Pepricornus, etc) was
born as a Jew in Moravia and was by profession
a butcher. He was baptized in Cologne around
1504 and found employment as steward of the
hospital. After his conversion he became a
fanatical opponent of Jewish ritual and learning, convinced that all Jews could be converted
to Christianity if their books were confiscated
and they were compelled to attend mass. These
ideas he stated in his *Judenspiegel* (Nürnberg
and Cologne 1507, Latin ed 1508), *Judenbeichte*
(Nürnberg and Cologne 1508, also a Latin ed),

Osternbuch (Cologne 1509), and *Judenfeind*
(Cologne 1509) – pamphlets that reflect Pfefferkorn's close connections with the Cologne
Dominicans and Ortwinus *Gratius. In order to
obtain official approval for the confiscation of
books, he travelled in 1509 to the court of
*Maximilian I. On the way he visited the
emperor's sister Kunigunde, the widow of
Duke Albert IV of Bavaria, and secured a letter
of recommendation to her brother, on the basis
of which he easily obtained from the emperor a
document ordering the confiscation of all
Jewish books opposed to Christianity (19
August 1509). On his return trip he visited
Johann *Reuchlin in Stuttgart but failed to win
his support. Pfefferkorn succeeded in having
Jewish books confiscated in Frankfurt, Mainz,
Bingen, and other towns. However, Uriel von
Gemmingen, archbishop of Mainz, was asked
by the emperor to obtain an independent
judgment from scholars at the universities of
Mainz, Erfurt, Heidelberg, and Cologne as
well as from the inquisitor, Jacob of *Hoogstraten, and from Reuchlin. It was Reuchlin's
authoritative report (6 October 1510) that
thwarted Pfefferkorn's plan. It stated that only
two specific books could be considered as
slanderous attacks upon Christianity, and that
these had been forbidden by the rabbis
themselves; the rest were harmless or could be
considered as a source of learning. Meanwhile
the confiscated books had been returned to the
Jews in June and July 1510.

Pfefferkorn attacked Reuchlin in April 1511
in his *Handspiegel* (Mainz). Reuchlin replied in
his *Augenspiegel* (Tübingen 1511), pointing out
thirty-four false statements in the *Handspiegel*.
Reuchlin's defence was severely criticized in
Cologne, especially by Hoogstraten and Arnold of *Tongeren. Pfefferkorn's next pamphlet, the *Brandspiegel* (Cologne 1512), was
even more violent. The emperor imposed
silence on both parties and forbad the distribution of Reuchlin's *Augenspiegel* (7 October
1512). This started the protracted proceedings
against Reuchlin in which Pfefferkorn was not
directly involved. He expressed his hatred
against the Jews once more in his *Sturmglocke*
(Cologne 1514). When he found himself a
prominent target of the first part of the *Epistolae
obscurorum virorum* in 1515, he wrote the
Beschirmung (n p), which Gratius translated

into Latin. His *Streitbüchlein* (n p 1517), in which he tried to defend his personal honour, contained attacks on Reuchlin and Erasmus. After Pope *Leo x's final decision against Reuchlin (23 June 1520), Pfefferkorn wrote his last and especially spiteful pamphlet, *Mitleidige Klage* (Cologne, 21 March 1521). This is the last known date of Pfefferkorn's life.

In Erasmus' correspondence, Pfefferkorn's name was mentioned for the first time in 1516 by Gerard *Geldenhouwer, who drew Erasmus' attention to the *Beschirmung* (Ep 487). Personally attacked by Pfefferkorn in his *Streitbüchlein*, Erasmus expressed deep contempt for this spiteful, uneducated man (Epp 694, 697, 700, 701, 703, 713, 856), who, unable to write Latin, was assisted by learned men such as Ortwinus Gratius and became a tool of the sinister Dominicans. After 1517 Erasmus lost interest in Pfefferkorn, although he continued to refer to his pamphlets in a general fashion (Epp 1006, 1238) and to use his name in abusive terms (Epp 1085, 1305).

BIBLIOGRAPHY: Allen and CWE Ep 487 / Ludwig Geiger in ADB XXV 621–4 / Ludwig Geiger *Johann Reuchlin* (Leipzig 1871, repr 1964) 209–20 and passim / *Encyclopaedia Judaica* (Jerusalem 1972–) XIII 355–7 / S.W. Baron *A Social and Religious History of the Jews* 2nd ed (New York 1952–76) XIII 184–91 / Hutten *Operum supplementum* 53–4 and passim   IG

Julius PFLUG of Eytra, 1499–3 September 1564

Julius Pflug was born at Eytra, near Leipzig, a son of Caesar Pflug, councillor to Duke George of *Saxony. Julius studied from 1510 at Leipzig, where Petrus *Mosellanus was among his teachers, and from 1517 in Bologna. During a brief visit to Saxony he was named archdeacon of Lower Lusatia on 17 September 1519. He returned to Bologna and in January 1521 went to Padua. He returned to Saxony in the summer of 1521 and resumed his study of law at Leipzig, receiving his licence in 1524. He was named assessor at the superior court of Leipzig (Oberhofgericht) and continued to receive ecclesiastical preferment, including the provostship of Zeitz (1523) and canonries at Merseburg (1528), Mainz (1530), and Naumburg (1532). Meanwhile, in October 1525 he again left for Italy, this time in the company of

Julius Pflug, by Friedrich Hagenauer

Gregorius *Haloander. At Rome he attended the lectures of Lazzaro *Bonamico until the Sack of 1527 led to his departure for Venice and eventually Saxony (1528).

Of an irenical mind but true to the Catholic faith, Pflug endeavoured to reconcile the Lutherans with the Roman church and became adviser to both Duke George and the Emperor *Charles V. He participated in the Leipzig colloquy (1534), the diet at Regensburg (1541), and the colloquy of Worms (1557). From the death of Duke George to that of Cardinal Albert of *Brandenburg he lived at Mainz. On 20 January 1541 he was elected bishop of Naumburg but could not take possession of his see until after the Schmalkaldic war (28–9 November 1546). In the following winter he helped draft the text of the Augsburg Interim. He attempted to restore Catholic discipline throughout his diocese, but from 1555 had to resign himself to the fact that his efforts were doomed to failure. He died as the last Catholic bishop of Naumburg.

From November 1551 to March 1552 Pflug attended the council of Trent, where he kept a diary which remains a valuable source of historical information. Apart from his funeral oration for his teacher Petrus Mosellanus, Pflug published a treatise *Von christlicher Busse* (Cologne: G. Calenius at the press of J. Quentel 1562) and some circumstantial writings, also in German (cf Schottenloher III 319). Of great importance is his voluminous correspondence, a good deal of which is now accessible in an excellent critical edition by J.V. Pollet.

Pflug's correspondence with Erasmus apparently began in 1530 with an approach, now lost, by Pflug, who offered his friendship and referred to Erasmus' quarrel with *Eppendorf. Well aware of Pflug's influence with Duke George, Eppendorf's prince, Erasmus answered warmly (Ep 2395), and in fact Pflug did his best to bring about a truce (Epp 2400, 2406, 2450–3, 2492). From his first letter (Ep 2395) Erasmus recognized in Pflug a kindred spirit and, encouraged by Pflug to show the way towards religious reconciliation (Ep 2492), was glad to develop his views on this topic (Ep 2522). Pflug also mediated in the controversy between Agostino *Steuco and Erasmus (Epp 2513, 2522). Although Steuco was an old friend, Pflug deplored his disdain of German humanist learning (Ep 2806). Erasmus had the last word in this affair by publishing Pflug's letter with his *De concordia* (1535), which is dedicated to Pflug (Ep 2852), in testimony to their shared concern for irenicism. The last record of their contacts is Erasmus' Ep 3016, in which he thanked Pflug for his appreciation of the *Precationes* and announced the completion of the *Ecclesiastes*.

BIBLIOGRAPHY: Allen Ep 2395 / ADB XXV 688–91 / DTC XII-1 1366–9 / LThK VIII 429–30 / Schottenloher II 138, III 319–20 / Pflug *Correspondance* I 276–87 and passim / J.V. Pollet 'Origine et structure du *De sarcienda ecclesiae concordia* (1533) d' Erasme' *Scrinium Erasmianum* II 183–95 / Knod 406 / Joseph Lecler *Histoire de la tolérance au siècle de la réforme* (Paris 1955) I 238 and passim (English trans London 1960)   MICHAEL ERBE & PGB

Thomas PHAEDRA or PHEDRUS *See Tommaso* INGHIRAMI

Gulielmus PHARELLUS *See Guillaume* FAREL

Johannes PHAUNUS *See John* FAWNE

Franciscus PHILIPPI (Ep 1138 of 1 September 1520)
In a letter to William *Burbank, a member of Cardinal *Wolsey's entourage, Erasmus returned the compliments of Franciscus Philippi, 'a most promising young man.' Allen identified him tentatively with Francisco Felipe or Felipez, initially perhaps a page and later a trusted adviser to Queen *Catherine of Aragon. After her death *Henry VIII gave him a pension which was last paid in May 1540 (LP XVI 380). No other identification has been suggested; if Felipe is meant here, Erasmus may have thought him younger than he actually was.

BIBLIOGRAPHY: Allen and CWE Ep 1138 / LP II 3446 and passim / Garrett Mattingly *Catherine of Aragon* (Boston 1941) 253–4 and passim   PGB

Johannes PHILIPPI of Kreuznach, documented 1483–1519
A native of Kreuznach, south of Bingen in the Rhineland, Philippi (Jean Philippe, Philippus Alemannus) is first documented as a student in Paris, where he was registered with the German nation in 1483. He remained in Paris and began working as an associate of the printer Georg Wolf in 1494. He printed for different Paris publishers and on his own account; his last known book is dated 1519. On 15 June 1500 he completed the first edition of the *Adagia*, which was sold at his own address under the sign of the Trinity in the rue Saint-Marcel and in Enguilbert de Marnef's shop under the sign of the Pelican in the rue Saint-Jacques. The text had been corrected by Augustinus Vincentius *Caminadus, a friend of Erasmus who repeatedly lodged with him in Paris. Caminadus himself published an edition of Virgil with Philippi's press in 1505. Erasmus complained about the printer's errors in Philippi's *Adagia* (Ep 181); later he mentioned this edition as proof of the independence of his *Adagia* from those of Polidoro *Virgilio (Ep 1175). Philippi reprinted the *Adagia* in 1505; he also published Cicero's *De officiis*, which was edited by Erasmus in about 1501.

BIBLIOGRAPHY: Allen Ep 1175 / Renouard *Répertoire* 344–5 / A. Claudin *Histoire de l'imprimerie en France* (Paris 1901) II 235–40 / M.

Mann Phillips *The 'Adages' of Erasmus* (Cambridge 1964) 41–3   GENEVIÈVE GUILLEMINOT

PHILIPPUS (Ep 116 of [November 1499])
Philippus (Philip) is described by Erasmus as a lawyer and friend of Johannes *Sixtinus; Erasmus met him at a dinner in Oxford in the company of Richard *Charnock and John *Colet. He has not been identified.   PGB

Jacobus PHILOMUSUS *See Jakob* LOCHER

PHIMOSTOMUS *See Johann* DIETENBERGER

Petrus PHOENIX
documented at Dole 1514–50
During his visit to Besançon in the spring of 1524 Erasmus was greeted by a doctor of laws whom he had known formerly at Mechelen when the imperial court was there. At the end of the year, when writing to Eustachius *Andreas, he sent greetings to this old friend and his brother (Epp 1533, 1610). In February 1528 he wrote to one Felix, a doctor of laws, in Burgundy and probably at Dole, about some details of the visit of 1524 (Ep 1956). Allen suggested that these references might all concern the same person and that he could be Petrus Phoenix, although there is no evidence for his presence at Mechelen.

Petrus Phoenix (Pierre Fénix), probably of Lure, between Belfort and Vesoul, was a student at Dole when appointed master of the municipal school on 27 November 1514. Subsequently he obtained academic degrees and became rector of the University of Dole for 1524, professor of law, and finally a member of the Parlement of Dole. He died between 1550 and 1553.

BIBLIOGRAPHY: Allen Ep 1956 / Julien Feuvrier *Un Collège franc-comtois au XVIe siècle* ed E. Monot (Lons-le-Saunier 1907) 118, 129, 261, 263 / P.-A. Pidoux *Un Humaniste comtois, Gilbert Cousin* (Lons-le-Saunier 1910) 21 / Auguste Castan *Catalogue des incunables de la Bibliothèque publique de Besançon* (Besançon 1893) 277, 500   PGB

Johannes Matthaeus PHRISSEMIUS
of Frickenhausen, d 1532
Johannes Matthaeus Phrissemius (Frissen, Frischemius, Ott, Orter), of Frickenhausen am Main, near Würzburg, matriculated at the universities of Leipzig in 1508 and Cologne on 3 October 1510. On 21 May 1512 he graduated BA and in 1516 he was a MA. It seems that he intended to study theology but was considered unsuitable by the theological faculty on account of his humanistic propensities. While teaching at the faculty of arts (1517–23) he eventually took up canon law, receiving his baccalaureate on 11 December 1522, his licence on 20 October 1524, and his doctorate on 22 August 1525. Meanwhile he remained a member of the faculty of arts, whose dean he was in 1522 and 1526. In these years his Catholic orthodoxy was questioned more than once. Among his students was Heinrich Bullinger, who studied at Cologne from 1519 to 1522 and subsequently succeeded *Zwingli as leader of the church of Zürich. Phrissemius was chancellor of the city of Cologne from 1525 to 1528, representing the city in many legal actions. In 1532 the Elector Hermann von *Wied named him chancellor of the archbishopric, but he died before he could take up his duties.

In 1528 (Ep 1978) Erasmus judged Phrissemius to be a promising but somewhat immature young scholar on the basis of his edition of Rodolphus *Agricola's *De inventione dialectica* (Cologne: H. Fuchs 1527, reprinted in Paris 1529, and repeatedly thereafter). In a letter of 27 March 1529 Phrissemius encouraged *Alaard of Amsterdam to undertake an edition of Agricola's works. This letter was printed in Alaard's edition of Agricola's *Lucubrationes* (Cologne: J. Gymnich [1539]).

BIBLIOGRAPHY: Allen Ep 1978 / *Matrikel Leipzig* I 486 / *Matrikel Köln* II 664 / Leonhard Ennen *Geschichte der Stadt Köln* (Cologne 1863–80) IV 102–3, 177–8 / Karl and Wilhelm Krafft *Briefe und Dokumente aus der Zeit der Reformation im 16. Jahrhundert* (Elberfeld 1876) 187 / Joseph Hartzheim *Bibliotheca Coloniensis* (Cologne 1747) 187   HANSGEORG MOLITOR

Paulus Constantinus PHRYGIO of Sélestat,
c 1485–1 August 1543
Phrygio (Paul Seidensticker or Costenzer) was educated at Sélestat, in Alsace, before matriculating in 1495 at the University of Basel and in 1499 at Freiburg, where he obtained a MA in 1500. About 1503 he was teaching at a school at Colmar, and in 1508 at Sélestat. In 1510 he was

lecturing in theology at Basel, where he obtained a theological doctorate on 6 September 1513. Subsequently he was parish priest at Eichstätt, north-west of Ingolstadt, and from 1519 at Sélestat. His commitment to the Reformation is shown in 1521 by an anonymous pamphlet, *Oratio Constantini Eubuli* [Sélestat: L. Schürer]. For religious reasons he was forced to leave Sélestat in 1525 together with Johannes *Sapidus and went to Strasbourg. After Basel was reformed in 1529 he was called back to that city as pastor of St Peter's and as professor, positions that had already been declined by *Bucer. At first his lectures were ancillary to those of *Oecolampadius, but from 1532 he held the newly established Old Testament chair although he was not especially noted as a Hebrew scholar. In 1533 he became rector of the university for two consecutive terms and also godfather to Basilius, the son of his colleague Bonifacius *Amerbach. From 1535 to the end of his life he was professor of New Testament at Tübingen, replacing Simon *Grynaeus, whom the University of Basel could not spare any longer.

Phrygio was encouraged by Grynaeus to undertake an extensive chronicle of world history (Basel: J. Herwagen 1534), although *Beatus Rhenanus considered him scarcely qualified for this enterprise. He also composed commentaries on Micah (Strasbourg: K. Müller 1538) and Leviticus (Basel: H. Petri 1543). Erasmus included him in his poem in praise of Sélestat and its humanists (1514–15; Reedijk poem 98) and there is another reference to him in Ep 1285.

BIBLIOGRAPHY: Allen Ep 1285 / ADB XXVI 92–3 / *Matrikel Basel* I 237 / BRE Ep 289 and passim / BA *Oekolampads* II 292, 640, and passim / AK I Ep 484, IV Epp 1802–6, V Ep 2181, and passim / R. Thommen *Geschichte der Universität Basel, 1532–1632* (Basel 1889) 99–102 / P. Kalkoff in *Zeitschrift für die Geschichte des Oberrheins* 51 (1897) 618, 52 (1898) 275–6 / Marie-Joseph Bopp *Die evangelischen Geistlichen und Theologen in Elsass und Lothringen von der Reformation bis zur Gegenwart* (Neustadt a.d. Aisch 1959) 416

PGB

PHRYSIUS *See Rienck van* BURMANIA, *Haio* CAMMINGHA, GERARD *of Friesland,* HAIO HERMAN *of Friesland,* JAN *of Friesland, Zacharias* DEIOTARUS

Angelo PIATTI documented at Milan, 1519–29

In September 1520 Georg *Schirn, a Cistercian monk at the monastery of Sant'Ambrogio Maggiore, Milan, wrote to Erasmus (Ep 1142), directing him to address his reply to the abbot. Angelo Piatti (Angelus Plattus), who is not known otherwise, was abbot of Sant'Ambrogio for the years 1519–20, 1522–4, and 1529. It seems that the abbot was elected, or re-elected, annually.

BIBLIOGRAPHY: Allen Ep 1142 / Bartholomaeus Aresius *Insignis basilicae et imperialis coenobii S. Ambrosii maioris Mediolani abbatum chronologica series* (Milan 1674) 66, 68   PGB

Enea Silvio PICCOLOMINI *See Pope* PIUS II

Galeotto II PICO della Mirandola 31 May 1508–20 November 1550

Galeotto was the son of Ludovico Pico della Mirandola and Francesca, the daughter of the Milanese condottiere Gian Giacomo Trivulzio. In 1502 Ludovico Pico had captured the family territories of Mirandola and Concordia from his elder brother, Gianfrancesco *Pico. Ludovico died in battle in 1509, and in 1514, after years of strife within the family, Gianfrancesco received the territory of Mirandola while young Galeotto was left with Concordia. The settlement did not, however, end the strife between the two factions of the family. On 16 October 1533 Galeotto and forty armed men broke into the castle of Mirandola and murdered Gianfrancesco and his son Alberto. *Charles V pronounced the imperial ban against him, but Galeotto managed to keep his state through bribery. Galeotto had long sympathized with the French, and in 1536 he placed himself directly under the protection of *Francis I, waging wars for him and receiving honours and an annuity in return. A kinsman of the Gonzaga dukes of Mantua and the Rangoni of Modena, Galeotto was also in close contact with Duke Ercole II d'Este. His two daughters married into the French house of Rochefoucauld. Galeotto died at Paris.

Galeotto and his crimes were mentioned by Franciscus *Ricius in a letter to Erasmus (Ep 2917). Two of Galeotto's letters survive, one to Francis I and the other to Cardinal Ippolito d'*Este.

BIBLIOGRAPHY: Allen Ep 2917 / Corrado
Argegni *Condottieri, capitani, tribuni* series 19 of
Enciclopedia biografica bibliografica 'Italiana' (Milan 1936–7) II 428 / F. Ceretti *Il conte Galeotto
Pico* (Modena 1882) / Charles B. Schmitt
*Gianfrancesco Pico della Mirandola (1469–1533)
and His Critique of Aristotle* (The Hague 1967)
16–30   ANNA GIULIA CAVAGNA

Gianfrancesco PICO della Mirandola 1469–16 October 1533

Gianfrancesco Pico (Picus Mirandulanus) was
born the son of Galeotto I Pico and Bianca
Maria d'Este, the illegitimate daughter of
Niccolò III d'Este. His uncle was Giovanni
*Pico, whose works he prepared for post-
humous publication (first ed Bologna: B.
Hector 1496). Gianfrancesco succeeded his
father as ruler of the independent principate
of Mirandola in 1499, though the title was
disputed and much of his later life was marked
by the problems caused by this. Quite early
in his life (about 1492) he fell under the influence of Girolamo *Savonarola; he wrote a
biography of the friar and other works defending his cause.

Pico wrote many works of philosophy,
theology, and poetry, in addition to leaving
behind a sizeable correspondence. His most
important and longest work is *Examen vanitatis
doctrinae gentium* (first ed Mirandola: G. Mazzocchi 1520), an extended attack upon pagan
philosophy and science and defence of Christianity. In the *Ciceronianus* Erasmus had a
speaker criticize Pico as being 'too much a
philosopher and theologian' and also referred
to his epistolary exchange with Pietro *Bembo
entitled *De imitatione* (1512–13; first ed Basel: J.
Froben 1518); see ASD I-2 604, 664; Ep 2088; cf
Ep 2632. Pico was murdered by his nephew
Galeotto II *Pico, a fact referred to by Erasmus
and his correspondents (Epp 2906, 2917).
Though Erasmus and Pico were in Italy at the
same time there is no evidence that they ever
met.

BIBLIOGRAPHY: Allen Ep 2088 / Charles B.
Schmitt *Gianfrancesco Pico della Mirandola (1469–
1533) and His Critique of Aristotle* (The Hague
1967) / *Desiderio Erasmo da Rotterdam, Il
Ciceroniano o dello stile migliore* ed A. Gambaro
(Brescia 1965) xxxv–xlix
                            CHARLES B. SCHMITT

Giovanni Pico della Mirandola

Giovanni PICO della Mirandola

24 February 1463–17 November 1494
Giovanni Pico della Mirandola was born at the
family castle at Mirandola. His father, Gianfrancesco I, count of Mirandola, died about the
time of his birth. Giovanni was raised by his
mother, Giulia Boiardo, the aunt of the poet
Matteo Maria Boiardo. His two sisters, Caterina and Lucrezia, married into petty princely
families of the Romagna – Caterina's husband
was Leonello Pio da Carpi, the father of
Alberto *Pio Carpi, Erasmus' opponent; Lucrezia married Pino Ordelaffi da Forlì. His two
brothers, Galeotto Pico della Mirandola and
Anton Maria, were typical non-intellectual
aristocrats of their time, feuding vociferously
over the family estates. Giovanni Pico's mother
planned an ecclesiastical career for the younger and less aggressive son and took him to
Bologna in 1477 to study canon law. Giulia
died 13 August 1478, and Giovanni, now
under the protection of his brother Anton
Maria, withdrew from Bologna and the study
of canon law.

In May 1479 Pico was at the University of
Ferrara, where he became a close friend of

Battista Guarini and probably studied classics and the humanities under him. He also wrote a considerable number of Italian and Latin poems. It was also at this time that he began to study philosophy. The year was notable for the beginning of a friendship with the Dominican preacher Girolamo *Savonarola, and for a famous visit to Florence where he met and began lasting friendships with Marsilio *Ficino, Angelo *Poliziano, Girolamo Benivieni, and notably Lorenzo (II) de' *Medici.

In the fall of 1480 Pico moved to Padua and was certified as a student on 16 December 1480, attending the university for the academic years 1480–1 and 1481–2. His studies concentrated on Aristotle and Averroes under Nicoletto Vernia at the Studio and Elia del Medigo, the Jewish Averroist, either privately or at extra-university lectures. Agostino Nifo knew him and remarked on Pico's interest in Siger of Brabant. Pico also became a friend of Ermolao (I) *Barbaro, the Venetian humanist, at this time. Elia del Medigo translated excerpts of Hebrew and Arabic works for Pico, helping him in his desire to study Averroism as deepened by Hebrew philosophy. Pico also became a friend of Girolamo Ramusio, another translator of Arabic texts.

The years 1482–3 saw him visiting Pavia, a rival centre for scholasticism in Northern Italy. He also arrived at a settlement of his family estate with his brothers. He continued to write poetry and sent his Latin sonnets to Poliziano. Apparently upset by Poliziano's faint praise, he destroyed the greater part of them. In 1484 he moved to Florence and began a very active life, participating in the discussions of Ficino's Platonic Academy, yet still retaining his deep interest in Averroes, whereas Ficino had attacked Averroes in his Theologia Platonica. Pico studied Greek, possibly with Poliziano. Elia del Medigo had come to Florence and continued translating Aristotle and Averroes for Pico. At this time Pico conceived the idea of reconciling Plato and Aristotle, considering Aristotle the last true Platonist. His commitment to a new synthesis built around scholastic philosophy reinforced by Arabic and Hebrew studies led him in June 1485 to compose his famous letter to Ermolao Barbaro attacking humanism and praising philosophy, De genere dicendi philosophorum. This letter had been

prompted by one from Barbaro and was answered by Barbaro and much later by *Melanchthon.

In July 1485 Pico went to Paris, probably seeking the source of scholastic philosophy there. We do not know what his studies and contacts were, but it seems probable that he decided while there to make a public exposition of his ideas of philosophical and theological unification. After returning to Florence in March 1486, he set out for Rome in May. However, on 10 May he apparently 'kidnapped,' with or without her connivance, Margherita, the wife of Giuliano Mariotto de' Medici, and was captured and imprisoned. Whatever the circumstances, Lorenzo secured his release and Pico retired to Perugia with Elia del Medigo, where he engaged in preparatory studies for his appearance in Rome. While there he seems to have written De ente et uno, intended as part of his ultimate reconciliation of Plato and Aristotle. Flavius Mithridates (Guglielmo de Moncada) translated writings of the Cabbala for Pico. Pico himself began to study Hebrew, Aramaic, and Arabic. In the fall of 1486 Pico wrote his Commento to Girolamo Benivieni's Canzona d'amore a work in the genre of poetic theology, not dissimilar to Ficino's commentary on Plato's Symposium. Pico also projected a major work of poetic theology but, as in the case of his reconciliation of Plato and Aristotle, did not live to complete it. He was also planning at this time a commentary on Plato's Symposium, but it remained unwritten.

By 12 November 1486 Pico had written his nine hundred theses, which he offered to debate with any challengers in the manner of the medieval quodlibetals. This was published by Eucharius Silber as Conclusiones sive theses DCCCC (Rome, 7 December 1486). The debate scheduled for Epiphany 1487 was suspended by order of Pope Innocent VIII. On 20 February 1487 a papal commission to examine Pico's theses was created and on 2 March it began to examine the Conclusiones. Thirteen of the nine hundred theses were found objectionable (seven condemned, six called dubious) on 5 March. The condemnation was based on Averroistic statements and deviations from church tradition inspired by the Cabbala. It is notable that the theses and not the person of

Pico were condemned. Whatever the character of the condemnation, and whether valid or justifiable or not, Pico's reply, the *Apologia* published 31 May 1487, defended his position. But on 31 July he declared his submission to the church. However, Innocent VIII, who had been shown a post-dated copy of the *Apologia*, condemned all the theses on 5 August 1487 and published a bull of condemnation on 15 December. On 6 January 1488 Pico was on the road travelling to Paris, where he apparently expected to find theological supporters. Innocent issued orders for his arrest, and he was picked up near Lyon and placed in the dungeon of Vincennes. Through the influence of Lorenzo de' Medici *Charles VIII of France ordered his release. In March he was released, left France, and settled in Florence under the protection of Lorenzo, who made a number of vain attempts to secure Pico's absolution from Innocent VIII. After the death of Lorenzo and Innocent in 1492 the new pope, *Alexander VI, responded favourably to Pico's appeal on 18 June 1493.

After 1488 Pico spent the rest of his life in Florence, with few visits elsewhere. In 1488 another Jewish friend and translator, Jochanan ben Isaac Alemanno, came to Florence. Pico made further studies of Hebrew and Hebraic religious thought and used the Cabbala as an instrument for reconciling philosophy and theology. He began writing his commentaries on the Psalms (published only fragmentarily) and in 1489 wrote and published his commentary on Genesis 1:1–27, the *Heptaplus* (Florence: Bartolomeo di Libri 1489). Presumably during these years he was working on his monumental project of reconciling Plato and Aristotle to which *De ente et uno* belonged. In 1492 he dedicated this work to Poliziano. In 1493 he wrote his *Disputationes adversus astrologiam divinatricem*. This work – along with the inaugural oration with which he prefaced his *Conclusiones*, known subsequently as *Oratio de dignitate hominis* – was posthumously published for the first time by his nephew, Gianfrancesco *Pico della Mirandola, in the editions of his works of 1496, the *Commentationes* and the *Disputationes* (Bologna: Benedictus Hector).

In 1489 Pico's influence contributed to the issuing of an invitation to Savonarola to visit Florence. During this time of deepening spirituality Pico became very close to the friar, although it is unlikely that he modified his earlier philosophical views in any notable way. He died dressed in a Dominican habit and was entombed in San Marco in Florence.

Erasmus was well aware of Pico's fame and stature as a scholar, as remarks in several letters (Epp 126, 324, 1347) and in the *Ciceronianus* (ASD I-2 663–4) indicate. He also had a sense of kinship with Pico, who like himself had found the theology of the schools too narrow and had been accused of heresy (LB VI [27], IX 60C, 102E). It is difficult to trace any direct influence of Pico's writings on Erasmus, although one scholar claims that Erasmus' *Enchiridion* was based on Pico. Certainly Pico was highly admired in English Erasmian circles, as Thomas *More's translations of several of his minor works and of the biography by Gianfrancesco attest. Despite his short life and the incompleteness of his work, Pico attained great fame in his own age for his brilliance, erudition, and devotion to truth. Modern scholars have shared much of this admiration for a career that combined a defence of intellectual freedom with a search for a unity of truth contained in all the great intellectual and religious traditions of man.

As yet there is no complete edition of Pico's works. After the compilation of the *Commentationes* by Gianfrancesco Pico in 1496, the *Opera omnia* were published at Venice by Bernardino de' Vitali in 1498, at Strasbourg by Johann Prüss in 1504, and frequently thereafter. A critical edition for the Edizione nazionale dei classici del pensiero italiano was begun by Eugenio Garin: three volumes have appeared including the *De hominis dignitate* and the *Disputationes adversus astrologiam divinatricem* (Florence 1942–52), with a fourth volume projected. A critical edition of the *Conclusiones DCCCC* was prepared by Bohdan Kieszkowski (Geneva 1973, Travaux d'humanisme et renaissance CXXXI). For corrections and alternative readings see José V. De Pina Martins' *Jean Pic de la Mirandole: Un portrait inconnu de l'humaniste: Une edition très rare de ses Conclusiones* (Paris 1976) 45–82. Incomplete and confused collections of Pico's letters are found in the various *Opera omnia* and in the *Auree epistole*, first published by Michel Le Noir at Paris in 1499.

More recently, Léon Dorez published 'Lettres inédites de Joannes Pico' in *Giornale storico della letteratura italiana* 25 (1895) and Eugenio Garin published a number of letters with Italian translations in *Prosatori latini del quattrocento* (Milan-Naples 1952) 796–833.

BIBLIOGRAPHY: Allen Ep 126 / F. Bonnard in DTC XII 1605–7 / P.O. Kristeller in *Encyclopedia of Philosophy* ed P. Edwards (New York 1967) VI 307–11 / D. Berti 'Intorno a Giovanni Pico della Mirandola' *Rivista Contemporanea* 16 (1859) 7–56 / F. Calori Cesis *Giovanni Pico della Mirandola* (Mirandola 1897) / L. Dorez and L. Thuasne *Pic de la Mirandole en France (1485–88)* (Paris 1897) / U. Cassuto *Gli Ebrei a Firenze nell'età del Rinascimento* (Florence 1918) / I. Pusino 'Der Einfluss Picos auf Erasmus' *Zeitschrift für Kirchengeschichte* 46 (1928) 370–82 / J. Festugière 'Studia Mirandulana' *Archives d'histoire doctrinale et littéraire du Moyen Age* 7 (1932) 143–250 / L. Thorndike *A History of Magic and Experimental Science* (New York 1923–58) IV 485–511, 529–43 / P. Kibre *The Library of Pico della Mirandola* (New York 1936) / G. Semprini *La filosofia di Pico della Mirandola* (Milan 1936) / E. Garin *Giovanni Pico della Mirandola. Vita e dottrina* (Florence 1937) / E. Garin *La cultura filosofica del Rinascimento italiano* (Florence 1961) 71, 113, and passim / E. Garin *Giovanni Pico della Mirandola* (Parma-Mirandola 1963) / A. Dulles *Princeps Concordiae: Pico della Mirandola and the Scholastic Tradition* (Cambridge, Mass, 1941) / E. Cassirer 'Giovanni Pico della Mirandola' *Journal of the History of Ideas* 3 (1942) 123–44, 319–44; repr in *Renaissance Essays* ed P.O. Kristeller and P. Wiener (New York 1968) 11–60 / B. Nardi 'La mistica averroistica e Pico della Mirandola' *Umanesimo e Machiavellismo* ed E. Castelli (Padua 1949) 55–74; also in B. Nardi *Saggi sull'Aristotelismo Padovano dal secolo XIV–XVI* (Florence 1958) 127–46 / Q. Breen 'Giovanni Pico della Mirandola on the Conflict of Philosophy and Rhetoric' *Journal of the History of Ideas* 13 (1952) 384–426; repr in Q. Breen *Christianity and Humanism* (Grand Rapids 1968) ch 1 / D.P. Walker 'Orpheus the Theologian and Renaissance Platonists' *Journal of the Warburg and Courtauld Institutes* 16 (1953) 100–20; repr in his *The Ancient Theology* (London 1972) ch 1 / D.P. Walker *Spiritual and Demonic Magic From Ficino to Campanella* (London 1958) / P.M. Cordier *Jean Pic de la Mirandole* (Paris 1957) / E. Wind *Pagan Mysteries in the Renaissance* (New Haven 1958) / E. Monnerjahn *Giovanni Pico della Mirandola* (Wiesbaden 1960) / F.A. Yates *Giordano Bruno and the Hermetic Tradition* (London 1964) 50, 84–116, and passim / F.A. Yates 'Giovanni Pico della Mirandola and Magic' *L'opera e il pensiero di Giovanni Pico della Mirandola nella storia dell'umanesimo* (Florence 1965) I 159–96 / P.O. Kristeller 'Giovanni Pico della Mirandola and His Sources' *L'opera e il pensiero di Giovanni Pico della Mirandola* I 35–142 (includes important appendices, list of manuscripts, and bibliography) / G. Di Napoli *Giovanni Pico della Mirandola e la problematica dottrinale del suo tempo* (Rome 1965) (includes extensive bibliography) / C. Trinkaus *'In Our Image and Likeness': Humanity and Divinity in Italian Humanist Thought* (London-Chicago 1970) ch 10 and 753–60 / H. De Lubac *Pic de la Mirandole: Etudes et discussions* (Paris 1974)   CHARLES TRINKAUS

PIETER and PIETER Gerard *See* ERASMUS' *family*

PIETER, PIERRE *See also* PETRUS

Albert PIGGE of Kampen,
c 1490–26 December 1542
Albert Pigge (Pighius) of Kampen, an uncle of the humanist Stephanus Winandus Pighius, matriculated at Louvain on 28 February 1507. Two years later he took his MA degree, standing first on the list. He then studied theology under the future Pope *Adrian VI among others, and by 9 May 1515 had received the degree of bachelor of theology and had taken orders. The story that he studied at Cologne and received a doctorate in theology is not substantiated by university records. From 1518 to 1522 he was at Paris, where he published *Adversus prognosticatorum vulgus ... astrologiae defensio* (H. Estienne 18 March 1519), two short works on calendar reform, the second of which bore a dedication to *Leo X dated 1520, and a reply to the *Nova astronomia* of Marcus of Benevento (S. de Colines 3 May 1522). F. Husner reports that Erasmus possessed a volume of astrological *Prognostica* written by Pigge. In 1522 Adrian VI called him to Rome and made him his chamberlain (*cubicularius*), an office he retained under

*Clement vii through the influence of Girolamo
*Aleandro. In 1525, acting in consultation with
the datary, Gian Matteo *Giberti, he wrote to
the theologians of Louvain to have them cease
their attacks on Erasmus (Ep 1589). Having
survived the Sack of Rome in 1527 (Ep 1850), he
was almost killed when a bridge collapsed at
Bologna in 1530. In March 1531 he was sent to
present King *Ferdinand i with a consecrated
hat and sword.

Pigge was rewarded with many benefices,
but when *Paul iii appointed him provost and
archdeacon of St John's at Utrecht on 1 August
1535 he had to return to the Netherlands. In
the last years of his life he played a notable role
in defending the Roman Catholic church
against the Reformation. In 1538 he published
his *Hierarchiae ecclesiasticae assertio* (Cologne:
Melchior of Neuss). In letters of 1 October 1540
Paul iii requested him to take part in the
theological colloquy which began on 14 January 1541 at Worms and was continued at
Regensburg. He obeyed without much enthusiasm and arrived at Worms on 25 November
1540. However, he proved to be so uncompromising that he incurred the displeasure of both
parties. He especially disagreed with the
tactics of Johann Maier of *Eck, and to clarify
their disagreement he wrote the *Controversia-
rum ... explicatio*, first printed in two parts at
Ingolstadt and Venice, then at Cologne (Melchior of Neuss 1542). After visits to Venice and
Cologne he returned to Utrecht, where he
died. He was buried in St John's and Jacobus
*Latomus composed an epitaph for him.

Other polemical works by Pigge included the
De libero hominis arbitrio (Cologne: Melchior of
Neuss, August 1542), the *Ratio componendorum
dissidiorum et sarciendae in religione concordiae*
(Cologne: Melchior of Neuss, March 1542),
and an *Apologia* against Martin *Bucer (Mainz:
n pr March 1543). His arguments, especially on
the role of tradition in determining doctrine,
influenced discussions at the council of Trent.
Several manuscripts in the Biblioteca Vaticana
contain writings by Pigge (Vat. Lat. 3917, 3922,
4575–6, 6176, 7804; Ottob. lat. 774, 1735), parts
of which have been edited by Hubert Jedin.

BIBLIOGRAPHY: Allen Ep 1589 / J. Verzijl in
NNBW x 733 / ADB xxvi 125–6 / RGG v 383 /
LThK viii 502 / *Matricule de Louvain* iii-1 329 /
de Vocht *Literae ad Craneveldium* Ep 97 and

passim / H. Jedin *Studien über die Schriftsteller-
tätigkeit Albert Pigges* (Münster 1931) / M.E.
Kronenberg in *Het Boek* 28 (1944–6) 107–58, 226
/ C.N. Fehrmann in *Kamper Almanak* (1955–6)
169–213 / G. Melles *Albertus Pighius en zijn strijd
met Calvijn over het liberum arbitrium* (Kampen
1973) / F. Husner 'Die Bibliothek des Erasmus'
in *Gedenkschrift zum 400. Todestage des Erasmus
von Rotterdam* (Basel 1936) 228–59, esp 238
                                    C.G. VAN LEIJENHORST

Vincenzo PIMPINELLA of Rome,
d 13 October 1534
Little definite is known of the life of Pimpinella
(Pimpinellus) other than that he was a Roman.
He was a member of the Roman Academy, the
Coryciana, during the pontificate of *Leo x. He
taught at the University of Rome, where he
lectured on the Greek New Testament as well
as Latin classical authors. He was a poet and
orator of some prominence in Rome. In the
conclave which elected *Adrian vi he was
selected to give an oration to the assembled
cardinals. By 1525 he had entered the curia,
and on 3 July 1525 was appointed archbishop
of Rossano, in Calabria. He resigned his
diocese and served as governor of the Marches
in 1527 and 1528. Pope *Clement vii appointed
him nuncio to the court of the King *Ferdinand
to deal with the Turkish threat in Hungary
(1529–32). He was present at the diet of
Augsburg, where he delivered an oration on 20
June 1530. However, he was overshadowed by
Cardinal Lorenzo *Campeggi.

In 1529 (Ep 2225) Pimpinella renewed a
dispensation, probably for eating meat, granted earlier to Erasmus by Cardinal Campeggi
(Ep 1542). Pimpinella seems to have had
respect for Erasmus' talents.

BIBLIOGRAPHY: Allen Ep 2225 / Gerhard
Müller 'Vincenzo Pimpinella am Hofe Ferdinands I., 1529–1532' *Quellen und Forschungen
aus italienischen Archiven und Bibliotheken* 40
(1960) 65–88 / Anthony Hobson 'The Printer of
the Greek Editions "in Gymnasio Mediceo ad
Caballinum Montem"' *Studi di biblioteconomia e
storia del libro in onore di Francesco Barberi* (Rome
1976) 331–5   JOHN F. D'AMICO

Jean de PINS d 1 November 1537
Born about 1470 of an aristocratic family of
Languedoc, Jean de Pins (Pinus) was the third

son of Gaillard, seigneur de Pins and de Muret, and of Clermande de Saman. Orphaned in early youth, he was educated by his eldest brother, Barthélemy, seigneur de Pins, de Roquette, and de Justaret, at Toulouse, Poitiers, and Paris and in Italy. At Bologna he studied under Filippo (I) *Beroaldo and Antonio Codro *Urceo, perhaps learning Greek. In 1497, the year of his return to France, he was ordained priest. Ceding his rights in the family estates to Barthélemy, Jean de Pins returned to Italy. At Bologna he published a letter and verses (addressed to Ferry de *Carondelet) in the works of Codro Urceo, edited by Filippo (II) *Beroaldo (J.A. de Benedictis 1502), and lives of Beroaldo the Elder and St Catherine of Siena (B. Hector 1505), dedicated respectively to Etienne *Poncher, bishop of Paris, and Louis d'Amboise, bishop of Albi. In 1507 he followed the latter as secretary to Savona for the interview between *Louis XII and *Ferdinand II of Aragon. By 1508, when he returned to France, Jean de Pins had been named protonotary apostolic. He was appointed councillor to the Parlement of Toulouse. Having come to the attention of Chancellor Antoine *Duprat, Jean de Pins followed the French court to Milan in 1515 and was named to the senate of the newly occupied city. The same year he went to Rome with Guillaume Gouffier, seigneur de Bonnivet, to arrange the Bologna conference between King *Francis I and Pope *Leo X. Between 1516 and 1520, while serving the king as ambassador to Venice, Jean de Pins studied Greek under Marcus *Musurus, collected manuscripts and books for the royal library at Fontainebleau, and published a life of St Roch and a Latin translation of the romance of Paris and Vienne, *Allobrogica narratio*, dedicated respectively to the chancellor and to his sons Antoine and Guillaume (Venice: A. de Bindonis 1516). A translation of Dio Cassius which he announced in a letter to Duprat was apparently never completed. Two Aldine editions, the orations of Gregory of Nazianzus edited by Marcus *Musurus (1516) and the Horace edited by Francesco *Torresani (1519), were dedicated to Jean de Pins. In 1520 he was sent to Rome as ecclesiastical delegate in order to assist the ailing French ambassador, Alberto *Pio, prince of Carpi. He was named bishop of Pamiers by a papal bull of 6 January 1521, but because the see was contested, he was given

that of Rieux in 1523. Until his death on 1 November 1537, Jean de Pins was the patron and protector of the humanist circle at nearby Toulouse. In accordance with his will of 27 April 1537, which named his nephews as his heirs, Jean de Pins was buried in the Carmelite monastery at Toulouse on 6 November.

Erasmus, who met Jean de Pins at Bologna, was favourably impressed by his scholarship (Ep 928; *Ciceronianus* ASD I-2 673–4). The letter which Erasmus wrote in 1532 (Ep 2628) requesting Jean de Pins's manuscript of Josephus for Hieronymus *Froben was intercepted and cast suspicion of heresy on the bishop, but he discomfited his accusers when he was called to read the letter before the Parlement (Ep 2665). E.V. Telle has interpreted this incident as part of the French reaction to the *Ciceronianus* (*Colloquia Erasmiana Turonensia* I 410–11). The friendship of Erasmus and Jean de Pins continued until Erasmus' death (Ep 2757, 2969, 2976, 3018, 3083).

Some of Jean de Pins' letters are preserved in manuscript in the Bibliothèque Nationale, Paris, and in a seventeenth-century collection by François Graverol, Bibliothèque Municipale de Nîmes, MS 75. Charron (p ix) mentions a manuscript of orations. His *De vita aulica libellus* (Toulouse: Jacques Colomiès n d), with a dedication dated 1540, is now very rare.

BIBLIOGRAPHY: Allen Ep 928 / *Gallia christiana* XIII 169B–C, 192E–194A, instrumenta 138B–D / R.C. Christie *Etienne Dolet* rev ed (London 1899) 59–73 and passim / Preserved Smith *Erasmus: A Study of his Life, Ideals, and Place in History* (New York 1923) 411–15, 447–52 / Jean de Pins 'Un ambassadeur français à Venise et à Rome (1515–1525), Jean de Pins, évêque de Rieux' *Revue d'histoire diplomatique* (July–December 1947) 215–46 (January–December 1948) 88–113 / Gentil Cormery *Jean de Pins, évêque de Rieux (1470–1537)* (Albi-Castres 1933) / Jean de Pins 'Jean de Pins et Longueil' BHR 12 (1950) 183–9 / Etienne-Léonard Charron *Mémoires pour servir à l'éloge historique de Jean de Pins* (Avignon 1748) / P. Tamizey de Larroque 'Sur Jean de Pins, évêque de Rieux' *Revue de Gascogne* 13 (1872) 47–8

JUDITH RICE HENDERSON

Alberto PIO prince of Carpi, 23 July 1475–7 January 1531
Alberto Pio, born at Carpi, was a son of

Leonello, prince of Carpi, and Caterina, a sister of Giovanni *Pico della Mirandola. Leonello having died in 1477, Pico saw to the education of Alberto and his brother, Leonello, choosing the humanist Aldo *Manuzio as their tutor. Alberto later supported Manuzio's Greek press at Venice and employed one of his associates, Marcus *Musurus, as his tutor and librarian in the early 1500s. In 1495 Manuzio dedicated his edition of Aristotle's *Organon* to Alberto. Meanwhile, before 1500, Alberto's control over Carpi was bitterly contested by his uncle Marco Pio and cousin Giberto, who on a number of occasions forced him into exile. Alberto found refuge at Ferrara, where he studied under Pietro *Pomponazzi (Ep 1587) and formed friendships with Pietro *Bembo, Celio *Calcagnini, Jacopo *Sadoleto, and Ludovico *Ariosto, who addressed at least two of his poems to him (*Opere minori* ed C. Segre, Milan 1954, 'Lirica latina' IX, XIV). In 1500 Giberto Pio sold his portion of Carpi to Ercole I d'Este, duke of Ferrara, and there began an uneasy period in which Alberto shared his state with his more powerful neighbour. He sought support from Francesco Gonzaga, marquis of Mantua, and at one point was betrothed to Margherita, his natural daughter. In 1505 Francesco sent Alberto on the first of a series of diplomatic missions to France, and in 1509 the prince of Carpi helped to negotiate the League of Cambrai against Venice by reconciling *Louis XII of France with the Emperor *Maximilian I. Maximilian, as overlord of Carpi, favoured Alberto by annulling the sale of part of its territory to the Este. In 1510 Louis XII sent Alberto to the court of *Julius II to prevent a reconciliation between the pope and Venice. However his mission failed, and Julius organized a Holy League against the French. In the ensuing confrontation Alberto changed sides and for a time lost Carpi to the French and Alfonso I d'*Este. On 29 May 1512 Maximilian renewed Alberto's investiture for all of Carpi, and after the defeat of the French he was once again able to secure his state.

In 1513 Cardinal Giovanni de' Medici was elected Pope *Leo X. Alberto became imperial ambassador at Rome and enjoyed the favour of the new pope, whom he probably met in the 1490s at Ferrara. In this peaceful period in his life Alberto participated in the activity of the Roman Academy and developed contacts with Baldesar *Castiglione, Raphael, and Bramante. In 1518 he strengthened his ties with the Medici pope by marrying a relative of his, Cecilia Orsini. Meanwhile he did not forget Carpi but devoted much of his income to the architectural embellishment of the city. After the death of Maximilian in 1519 the new emperor, *Charles V, did not renew Alberto's appointment as imperial ambassador. Once again the prince of Carpi turned to France for support, eventually becoming ambassador of *Francis I at Rome. He supported Francis even after the battle of Pavia in February 1525, and as a result was finally deprived of Carpi by the imperial general Prospero Colonna. He gave his support to the anti-imperialist League of Cognac and during the Sack of Rome of 1527 remained close to *Clement VII, seeking refuge with him in the Castel Sant'Angelo. He fled to France, where he was honoured by the king. He died in Paris three days after taking the Franciscan habit (Ep 2441).

During the last six years of his life Alberto engaged in a famous controversy with Erasmus, the focal point of which was the crucial question of Erasmus' relationship with Martin *Luther and the Protestant Reformation. In May 1525 Erasmus reported to his friend Celio Calcagnini that he had heard that Alberto Pio was attacking him at Rome, saying that he was neither a philosopher nor a theologian and that he possessed no sound doctrine (Ep 1576). Although Calcagnini replied expressing surprise that Alberto would act in this manner (Ep 1587), Erasmus decided to confront him by writing a letter reproaching him for his attacks and denying the charge that he had inspired and defended Luther (Ep 1634). Alberto drafted a lengthy *Responsio* to Erasmus pressing his claims that there were many points in common between Luther and Erasmus and that Erasmus' attacks on theologians and monks had aided the German reformer. The work, which was signed on 15 May 1526, circulated widely in manuscript, and a copy reached Erasmus by September, along with another polemic which Erasmus attributed to Girolamo *Aleandro (Ep 1744). Erasmus later defended himself in a letter to Clement VII (Ep 1897) but delayed replying to Alberto himself, at least ostensibly because he could not locate him after the Sack of Rome (Ep 2066). By December 1528 he heard that Alberto was in Paris

planning to print his *Responsio* and implored
him to wait until he received his reply (Ep
2080). His letter arrived too late, since Alberto's work was issued by the press of Josse
*Bade on 7 January 1529. In March (Ep 2118)
Erasmus published his own *Responsio* (Basel:
H. Froben; LB IX 1095–122), in which he
vehemently denied encouraging Luther
through his works or through his silence. By
June 1530 Erasmus heard that Alberto was
preparing another reply, collecting all passages in which Luther and Erasmus agreed (Ep
2328, 2329). The *Tres et viginti libri in locos
lucubrationum variarum D. Erasmi Rotterodami*
was published by Bade on 9 March 1531, two
months after Alberto's death. It was designed
to prove Alberto's charges against Erasmus
once and for all, and to urge Erasmus to admit
and correct his errors. Erasmus' reply was both
swift and violent. The *Apologia adversus
rhapsodias Alberti Pii* was printed in June 1531
(Basel: H. Froben) and accused Alberto of
including numerous lies and false citations in
his work (LB IX 1123–96). As a final insult
Erasmus made Pio the subject of the colloquy
Exequiae seraphicae (ASD I-3 686–99) first printed
in September 1531. Agostino *Steuco later
reproached Erasmus for so violently attacking
a dead man (Ep 2513). Erasmus' controversy
with the prince of Carpi did not end, as he
might have hoped, with the *Apologia*. The
Spanish scholar Juan Ginés de *Sepúlveda,
who had served Alberto at Rome in the
mid-1520s, defended his former patron in the
Antapologia (Rome: A. Bladus 1532 and Paris:
A. Augereau 1532). However the tone of the
Antapologia was courteous, and Erasmus wisely decided to avoid further strife by not
replying (Ep 2701).

BIBLIOGRAPHY: Allen Ep 1634 / G. Tiraboschi
Biblioteca Modenese (Modena 1781–6) IV 156–
201 / G. Tiraboschi *Storia della letteratura italiana*
(Modena 1787–94) VII-1 291–301 / P. Guaitoli
'Memorie sulla vita di Alberto Pio' in *Memorie
storiche e documenti sulla città e sull'antico
principato di Carpi* I (Carpi 1877) / A. Morselli
'Notizie e documenti sulla vita di Alberto Pio:
Lettere inedite' in *Memorie storiche e documenti
sulla città e sull'antico principato di Carpi* IX-1
(Carpi 1931) 51–131 / C.H. Clough 'The Pio di
Savoia Archives' in *Studi offerti a Roberto Ridolfi*
ed B. Biagiarelli and D. Rhodes (Florence 1973)
197–219 / C. Vasoli *Alberto III Pio da Carpi* (Carpi

1978) / On the relations between Erasmus and
Pio see R. Marcel 'Les dettes d'Erasme envers
l'Italie' in *Actes du Congrès Erasme, Rotterdam,
27–29 octobre 1969* (Amsterdam-London 1971)
171 / M.P. Gilmore 'Erasmus and Alberto Pio,
Prince of Carpi' in *Action and Conviction in Early
Modern Europe: Essays in Memory of E.H.
Harbison* ed T.K. Rabb and J.E. Seigel (Prince-
ton 1969) 299–318 / M.P. Gilmore '*De modis
disputandi*: The apologetic works of Erasmus' in
*Florilegium historiale: Essays presented to Wallace
K. Ferguson* ed J.G. Rowe and W.H. Stockdale
(Toronto 1971) 62–88; French trans in *Colloquia
Erasmiana Turonensia* II 713–36 / E. Garin
'Erasmo e l'umanesimo italiano' BHR 33 (1971)
7–17   MARCO BERNUZZI & TBD

Giambattista PIO of Bologna, c 1460–1540
Giambattista Pio was born in Bologna and
studied under the humanist Filippo (I) *Beroaldo. He taught at Bologna, Ferrara, Milan,
Bergamo, Rome, and Lucca. In 1534 he was
appointed to the University of Rome by Pope
*Paul III, and it was in Rome that he died.

Pio was an editor of classical texts, especially
Lucretius and Ovid, as well as a translator from
the Greek. His most famous work was the
Annotationes linguae latinae graecaeque (Bologna:
J.A. de Benedictis 1505). He also published
editions of Fulgentius (Milan: U. Scinzenzeler
1498), Plautus (Milan: U. Scinzenzeler 1500),
and Valerius Flaccus (Bologna: H. de Benedictis 1519).

Erasmus mentioned Pio several times as an
important Italian scholar. He and his correspondents were generally critical of Pio's
abilities (Allen I 15; Epp 256, 1479, 1482) and
occasionally cited his grammatical errors (Ep
729; *Opuscula* 189–90). Erasmus also found
fault with Pio's style (ASD I-2 667, I-4 36).

BIBLIOGRAPHY: Allen Ep 256 / Cosenza IV
2826–9 / Carlo Dionisotti *Gli umanisti e il volgare
fra quattro e cinquecento* (Florence 1968) 78–110
                            JOHN F. D'AMICO

Jan PIPE documented 1505–31
Jan Pipe obtained the seventh prebend of the
chapter of St Donatian's, Bruges, in 1505 but
resigned in 1507 and went to study at Louvain,
matriculating on 8 June. In 1510 he was
appointed to the fourth prebend, which he
held until 2 August 1531. He was a close friend
of Jan van *Fevijn, who wrote fondly of him in

1526 when asking Frans van *Cranevelt to help
Pipe in some litigation. Pipe is perhaps
identical with one Nicolaus Fistula, a friend of
Fevijn, to whom Erasmus sent greetings in Ep
1012 (1520). Barring discovery of a Nicolaus,
perhaps a relative of Jan, one may assume that
it was Jan whom Erasmus had met in Fevijn's
company and whose name he remembered
incorrectly.

BIBLIOGRAPHY: CWE Ep 1012 / de Vocht
Epistolae ad Craneveldium Ep 174 / *Matricule de
Louvain* III-1 334   IG & PGB

Charitas PIRCKHEIMER of Nürnberg,
21 March 1467–19 August 1532
Charitas, the sister of Klara and Willibald
*Pirckheimer, was born in Eichstätt and called
Barbara at baptism. In 1479 she entered the
convent of St Clare at Nürnberg, of which she
was elected abbess in 1503. Like many female
members of the Pirckheimer family, Charitas
possessed a degree of literary education which
was quite unusual at her time, as was noted by
Erasmus in his colloquy *Abbatis et eruditae* (ASD
I-3 407). Willibald encouraged her studies and
in 1513 dedicated to her his first translation
from Plutarch and in 1520 his edition of
Fulgentius. He also brought about contacts
between her and Albrecht *Dürer as well as
Conradus Celtis, who celebrated her in an ode
and in 1502 dedicated to her his edition of
Hrosvita of Gandersheim. She also maintained
friendly relations with Christoph Scheurl and
Sixtus Tucher, provost of St Lorenz's at
Nürnberg, a distinguished legal scholar.

From the early beginnings of the Reformation Charitas was firmly opposed to *Luther
(see her Ep 60, *Quellensammlung* III). It was due
to her energetic interventions that her convent
escaped closure when the reformed party won
the upper hand in Nürnberg. She was,
however, powerless when from 1525 the Poor
Clares were no longer permitted to hold mass
and to receive novices. Under the title of
Denkwürdigkeiten she composed a chronicle of
her struggle for the preservation of the convent
during the years 1524–8, a struggle in which
she was able to count on the support of her
brother and at certain times also of *Melanchthon (Eckert and Imhoff 314ff). In Ep 409
Willibald conveyed to Erasmus the greetings of
Charitas and Klara, adding that both were
eagerly studying Erasmus' books. There does

Klara Pirckheimer

not seem to be any evidence for a direct
exchange of letters between Charitas and
Erasmus (as was claimed by Eckert and Imhoff
37). Charitas' grave was identified in 1959 in
the churchyard of the convent of St Clare.

BIBLIOGRAPHY: Allen and CWE Ep 409 /
Ludwig Geiger in ADB XXVI 817–19 / *Caritas
Pirckheimer Quellensammlung* ed Josef Pfanner
et al (Landshut 1961–7), four parts containing
her prayer book, the *Denkwürdigkeiten*, her
correspondence, etc / Wilhelm Loose *Aus dem
Leben der Charitas Pirckheimer, nach Briefen*
(Dresden 1870) / Johannes Kist *Charitas Pirck-
heimer* (Bamberg 1948) / Josef Pfanner in
Fränkische Lebensbilder II (Würzburg 1968) 193ff
/Willehad Paul Eckert and Christoph von
Imhoff *Willibald Pirckheimer* (Cologne
1971)   BARBARA KÖNNEKER

Klara PIRCKHEIMER of Nürnberg,
1480–5 February 1533
Klara, the sister of Charitas and Willibald
*Pirckheimer, was probably born at Munich. In
1494 she entered the convent of St Clare at
Nürnberg. She was appointed abbess in 1532
in succession to her sister Charitas but died a
few months later. She in turn was succeeded

Katharina Pirckheimer, daughter of Willibald Pirckheimer

by Willibald's daughter Katharina, the last abbess of St Clare. Klara was no exception to the remarkable level of education and culture for which the female members of the Pirckheimer family were famous (see the colloquy *Abbatis et eruditae* ASD I-3 407). Willibald dedicated to her his edition of Nilus' *Sententiae morales* (Nürnberg: F. Peypus 1516); in the same year he conveyed Klara's greetings to Erasmus (Ep 409).

BIBLIOGRAPHY: Allen and CWE Ep 409 / See also J. Pfanner's biography of Charitas Pirckheimer and his edition of her letters

BARBARA KÖNNEKER

Willibald PIRCKHEIMER of Nürnberg, 5 December 1470–22 December 1530
Willibald Pirckheimer was the last male descendant of a patrician family settled in Nürnberg since the fourteenth century. For some time the Pirckheimer firm had been one of the leading commercial houses of Europe, but towards the end of the fifteenth century it was bankrupt. Willibald's father, Johann, had married Barbara Löffelholz, another patrician, and instead of joining the family business had become a lawyer in the episcopal court of Eichstätt. Thus

Willibald was born in Eichstätt, the fourth of twelve children. His two brothers died young and eight of his sisters entered various convents as adolescents.

In 1475 Pirckheimer's father moved to Munich as a councillor to Duke Albert IV of Bavaria. There the boy was privately educated and permitted to accompany his father on missions to the Tirol, Switzerland, and Italy. At the age of sixteen he was sent back to the court of Eichstätt to be instructed in courtly refinements and military matters. In 1488 or 1489 he went to Italy and for a few years studied law in Padua and Pavia. There he acquired a comprehensive humanistic education in the fields of literature, philosophy, history, and science. The thoroughness of his learning would later assure him a leading position among the German scholars of his day. He did not graduate, however, because his father was planning that he should have a civic career at Nürnberg, where men with doctorates were ineligible to sit on the city council.

In 1495 Pirckheimer returned from Italy, married Crescentia Rieter, from a Nürnberg patrician family, and was elected as one of the forty-two members of the city's governing council. In 1499 he served as captain of the Nürnberg contingent in the war between *Maximilian I and the Swiss, a campaign he described in his *De bello helvetico*, which was completed in 1526 but not published until 1610. In the army camp he formed a personal relationship with Maximilian, who appointed him imperial councillor – a title he is first given in a letter of 20 August 1514 (*Pirckheimer Briefwechsel* Ep 328). In 1526 *Charles V confirmed him in this dignity.

Pirckheimer served on the Nürnberg council from 1495 to 1502 and from 1505 to 1523, attending to legal and educational matters as well as exercising administrative duties. Primarily on his initiative teaching positions in classical literature were instituted at the schools of St Lorenz and St Sebald in 1509. For some time he commanded as *Viertelsmeister* a contingent of the Nürnberg militia, and for several years he served as one of five councillors who annually elected the new city council. His main responsibility, however, was to represent Nürnberg at diets, in the numerous quarrels with the Franconian nobility, and in the continuous litigation with the margraves of

*Brandenburg-Ansbach, who were attempting to extend their powers at the expense of the free imperial city.

Pirckheimer's missions took him to many cities in Southern Germany and along the Rhine, to Austria, and finally, in 1519, to Switzerland. While he proved himself to be a skilful diplomat and won the friendship of many statesmen and scholars, his policies and his personal conduct were repeatedly questioned by his fellow-citizens and led to conflicts with his colleagues; these were caused partly by his short temper and his critical attitude towards Nürnberg's system of government but also by his life-style and his pursuit of interests incompatible with the fashions of the Nürnberg patriciate. The city was dominated by commercial interests, and humanism was given a cool reception unless it proved to be of commercial value. A school of poetry founded in 1496 was forced to close in 1509 for lack of students. Pirckheimer, however, was unencumbered by business concerns, and as a man of considerable wealth pursued his personal tastes and scholarly interests whenever his civic duties left him time to do so. He spent his money on the promotion of arts and letters as well as on the enlargement of the sizeable library he had inherited from his father. It was also considered strange among his peers that he failed to remarry after his wife had died in 1504 following the birth of their sixth child, and that he made his house a refuge for poets (Pirckheimer *Opera* 327) as well as opening his door to many local and itinerant artists and scholars.

Pirckheimer's great reputation among the German humanists was at first based not on his scholarly and literary work but on the universality of his interests as a collector, promoter, and patron. He published his own writings relatively late in life and carried more weight as an editor and translator than as an author in his own right. Among his literary efforts are the *Apologia seu podagrae laus* (Nürnberg 1522), an ironical eulogy of gout, from which he suffered in old age, fashioned in the manner of Erasmus' *Moria*. He also composed an obituary of Albrecht *Dürer (1528), his lifelong friend and sometime collaborator. Of the works he edited, the most important was an edition of St Fulgentius (Haguenau 1520), deriving from the library of Johannes *Trithemius. Most of his

Willibald Pirckheimer, by Albrecht Dürer

work, however, consisted of translations, which reflect the wide scope of his scholarly interests. He translated from Greek into Latin as well as from both classical languages into German. Among his translations are several works of Plutarch and dialogues of Lucian (Eckert-Imhoff 371), Aristophanes' *Plutus* (unpublished), a number of pseudo-Platonic dialogues (Nürnberg 1523), the *Sententiae morales* by Nilus (Nürnberg 1516), the orations of Gregory of Nazianzus (Nürnberg 1521, Basel 1531), the *Characteres* of Theophrast with the first edition of the Greek text (Nürnberg 1527), Xenophon's *Hellenica* (Nürnberg 1532), and Ptolemy's *Geography* (Strasbourg and Nürnberg 1525), which greatly impressed Erasmus (Epp 2493, 2760). One might also mention the unpublished translation of Horapollo's *Hieroglyphica*, from which Pirckheimer drew significant inspiration for the *Ehrenpforte* (1517) and the *Triumphzug* (1526), collective works undertaken for Maximilian I for which Pirckheimer provided the outline and Dürer some of the illustrations.

When he first sought contact with Erasmus, Pirckheimer had published a single Latin translation: Plutarch's *De his qui tarde a numine corripiuntur libellus* (Nürnberg 1513). Late in 1513 he wrote *Beatus Rhenanus of his relief that recent rumours about the death of 'our' Erasmus were false (*Pirckheimer Briefwechsel* Ep 291). A year later he asked Beatus formally to introduce him to Erasmus and, if possible, arrange for an encounter with the great scholar (Ep 318). The latter wish was not realized, for Erasmus never visited Nürnberg despite repeated invitations (Epp 555, 1095, 1480). However, a friendship developed and deepened over the years as a frequent exchange of letters allowed the two men to share their scholarly interests and their very similar outlook on contemporary issues. Their correspondence survives only in part; in particular many of Pirckheimer's letters were burnt after his death by Thomas *Venatorius (Ep 2537).

Erasmus' first letters (Epp 322, 362) reflect his satisfaction that a man of Pirckheimer's rank and position would seek his friendship. Pirckheimer for his part played the role of the student, sending Erasmus his Plutarch translation for comment (Epp 326A, 375). The first letter did not reach Erasmus, but the Plutarch may be identified with the short work which Erasmus acknowledges having received in Bruges from Thomas *More (Ep 362). The quarrel surrounding *Reuchlin led to a more personal exchange of opinions. In October 1517 Pirckheimer sent Erasmus a defence of Reuchlin which he had recently published in Nürnberg together with his translation of Lucian's *Piscator* (Ep 685). Erasmus was sympathetic but had misgivings about the prominence given to himself in a list of 'true theologians' inserted in Pirckheimer's defence of Reuchlin (Eckert-Imhoff 258); he thought that Pirckheimer had over-reacted in giving such a high profile to the controversy (Ep 694). Both men then justified their opinions at great length (Epp 747, 856).

A similar exchange took place with respect to Erasmus' quarrel with Edward *Lee (Epp 1085, 1095, 1139), but in this case it was Pirckheimer who counselled moderation in view of the unequal standing of Erasmus and his opponent. Similar differences of opinion continued to occur from time to time but never troubled their relationship since they involved tactical questions rather than principles and were always accompanied by assurances of mutual

friendship and trust (Epp 1344, 1480, 1880, 1893).

Like many humanists Pirckheimer initially favoured *Luther, accepting his attacks on church corruption as a continuation of the Reuchlin affair (cf his letter to Johann Tschertte of November 1530, Eckert-Imhoff 362ff). At one time he found himself unexpectedly in the front lines of the battle when Johann Maier of *Eck suspected him of being the author of the dialogue *Eckius dedolatus* and added his name to the papal bull condemning Luther in 1520 (Ep 1182). The matter was never clarified, but today it is considered unlikely that Pirckheimer was responsible for the satire, and he himself denied it consistently. However, it took a great deal of effort and the intercession of Girolamo *Aleandro (Ep 1244) to acquit Pirckheimer in August 1521 of the condemnation contained in the papal bull. Erasmus too tried to be of assistance, recommending that Pirckheimer approach *Leo x directly, but the letter did not reach Nürnberg until after the pope's death (Ep 1244).

In the following years Pirckheimer's letters to Erasmus combined bitter complaints about the repressive measures taken by Rome against the reformers with the beginnings of a more critical attitude towards Luther. Since Nürnberg was the political centre of the empire, Pirckheimer had a good understanding of the developments. In 1523 he was viewed with great suspicion by the nuncio, *Chierigati, despite Erasmus' effort to recommend him to the papal diplomat (Epp 1336, 1344). As late as 1524, when there was no hope of a reconciliation, Pirckheimer tried to remain objective and fair to both sides and assured Erasmus of Luther's sympathy for him, even as Erasmus was mailing out copies of *De libero arbitrio* (Ep 1480). Earlier on he had tried in vain to dissuade Erasmus from publishing his *Spongia* against *Hutten (cf his letter of 10 August 1523 to Hieronymus *Emser, Eckert-Imhoff 355ff). In the end Pirckheimer had fully revised his stand and changed from a supporter to an opponent of the Reformation. In doing so, he acted out of concern for the *bonae literae*, a concern which he shared with Erasmus, but also out of disappointment with the Reformation's failure to bring about moral renewal. His change of heart also reflected personal concerns. In 1525 the Nürnberg council, of which he was no longer a member, planned to close all convents in the city; the Pirckheimer family stood to suffer greatly since seven of Willibald's sisters and three of his daughters lived in nunneries, including his sister Charitas *Pirckheimer, who was abbess of the convent of St Clare. To Pirckheimer this meant coercion under the pretext of evangelical freedom; he appealed to *Melanchthon, through whose intervention the decision to close the convents was averted, but the situation remained critical, and in 1529 Pirckheimer composed a defence of the nuns of Nürnberg, asking the council to protect their rights.

Pirkheimer's realignment with the old church further strengthened his friendship with Erasmus (Ep 1512), who hung two portraits of Pirckheimer, Dürer's engraving and a medal, on opposite walls of his study (Ep 1543). He enlisted Pirckheimer's help in securing Dürer's portrait engraving of himself, dated 1526 (Epp 1536, 1558, 1729). Earlier, in 1523, he had appealed for his friend's help in providing a printer's privilege for Johann *Froben from the court of *Ferdinand (Epp 1341, 1344). In turn, in 1525 Erasmus dedicated to Pirckheimer his edition of Chrysostom's *De sacerdotio*, exhorting his friend to continue his fight against the enemies of the *bonae literae* (Epp 1558, 1560).

In the final years of his life Pirckheimer found himself obliged to defend the church as well as humanism. In 1526 he published a treatise against *Oecolampadius, *De vera Christi carne et vero eius sanguine*, followed in 1527 by a rejoinder to Oecolampadius' defence (BA *Oekolampads* nos 318, 402, 458, 465). In these treatises Pirckheimer defended the Catholic doctrine of the Eucharist against the symbolic interpretation of Oecolampadius in a fashion which was too close to Luther's position for Erasmus' taste (Ep 1717). Generally speaking, Erasmus was unhappy with this dispute since, as he confided to Pirckheimer, he would have inclined towards Oecolampadius' interpretation had it not been opposed by the church, whose authority he respected despite doubts (Epp 1717, 1729, 1893, 2147).

Increasingly the correspondence tended to be dominated by Erasmus' reports of unrest and tumult arising everywhere on account of the Reformation (Epp 1603, 2158) and his complaints about attacks and slander (Epp 1408, 1417, 1717). At great length Erasmus described his quarrel with *Eppendorf in Epp 1991 and 1992 and lamented his deteriorating health (Epp 1408, 1440, 1452, 1543, 1558, 1603). Shortly after Pirckheimer's death Erasmus edited in conjunction with Hans Straub, a son-in-law of the late scholar, Pirckheimer's translation of the orations of Gregory of Nazianzus with a dedicatory epistle addressed to Duke George of *Saxony (Ep 2493). Only a few of these translations had been published previously, in 1521 and 1528.

Pirckheimer died in Nürnberg, the last of his name; he was buried in St John's churchyard. His only grandchildren were the offspring of his daughter Felicitas, who had married Hans Imhoff. In 1606 another Hans Imhoff, Willibald's great-grandson, published at Nürnberg a *Tugendbüchlein* which contained some of Pirckheimer's German translations and a short biography based in part on his own notes. Erasmus' Ep 2493, which is really an obituary for Pirckheimer, praises especially his human qualities and his civic and political virtues. As he was to do again in Ep 2760, he lauded among his friend's writings the translations of Gregory of Nazianzus and Ptolemy. The tone of this obituary accords well with Erasmus' judgment of Pirckheimer in the *Ciceronianus*, where his commitment to public service was seen as the only obstacle to his undivided devotion to scholarship (ASD I-2 687).

BIBLIOGRAPHY: Allen Ep 318 / Ludwig Geiger in ADB XXVI 810–17 / Willibald Pirckheimer *Opera politica, historica, philologica et epistolica* ed M. Goldast (Frankfurt 1610, repr 1969) / Willibald Pirckheimer *Briefwechsel* ed E. and S. Reicke (Munich 1940–   ) / Niklas Holzberg *Willibald Pirckheimer: Griechischer Humanismus in Deutschland* (Munich 1981) / Karl Hagen *Deutschlands literarische und religiöse Verhältnisse im Reformationszeitalter mit besonderer Rücksicht auf Willibald Pirkheimer* (Frankfurt 1868, repr 1966) / Paul Drews *Willibald Pirckheimers Stellung zur Reformation* (Leipzig 1887) / Emil Reicke *Willibald Pirckheimer* (Jena 1930) / Hans Rupprich 'Willibald Pirckheimer: A study of his personality as a scholar' in *Pre-Reformation Germany* ed G. Strauss (New York 1972) 380–435 / *Willibald Pirckheimer, 1470–1970:*

Dokumente, Studien, Perspektiven (Nürnberg 1970) contains W.P. Eckert 'Erasmus von Rotterdam und Willibald Pirckheimer' (11ff) and K.B. Glock 'Willibald Pirckheimer-Bibliographie' (111ff) / W.P. Fuchs 'Willibald Pirckheimer' *Jahrbuch für Fränkische Landesforschung* 31 (1971) 1ff / W.P. Eckert and Christoph von Imhoff *Willibald Pirckheimer, Dürers Freund, im Spiegel seines Lebens, seiner Werke und seiner Umwelt* (Cologne 1971), contains selections of his writings in German translation / Gerald Strauss *Nuremberg in the Sixteenth Century* (New York 1966) 247–8 and passim / L.W. Spitz *The Religious Renaissance of the German Humanists* (Cambridge, Mass, 1963) 155–96 and passim   BARBARA KÖNNEKER

Jacobus PISO of Medgyes, d March 1527
Born at Medgyes, in Transylvania, Piso travelled to Italy, where he studied at Bologna under Filippo (I) *Beroaldo. He continued his education in Rome and received a legal doctorate in 1501. Upon his return to Hungary he entered the service of King *Vladislav II. He probably took holy orders in 1505 or 1506 and a year later was sent to Italy as royal ambassador. At Rome he met Erasmus (Epp 216, 850, 1206), who turned his attention to literature and was to have a profound effect on his intellectual development. Piso's reputation was such that in 1510 *Julius II sent him to Poland as his ambassador in order to gain the support of the Polish monarch for a war against the Turks. His mission did not produce the desired results, and Piso returned to Rome. In 1514 *Leo x again sent him to Poland, with instructions to bring about a peace between King *Sigismund I and Basil IV, prince of Muscovy. Instead of making peace the Poles won a resounding victory at Orsza (8 September) which was celebrated by Piso in his *Epistola ... de conflictu Polonorum et Litvanorum cum Moscovitis*, addressed to Johannes *Corycius. It was published in *Jani Damiani Senensis ad Leonem X ... elegeia* (Basel J. Froben 1515), a volume which also included four important letters by Erasmus. After leaving Poland Piso made a brief visit to Rome and then returned to Hungary in early 1515. He was appointed tutor to Alexius *Thurzo. The same year he became royal secretary and attended the gathering of rulers at Vienna. In 1516 Piso was entrusted with the education of *Louis II, the ten-year-old king of Hungary (Ep 850). He became provost of Pécs (Fünfkirchen, Quinqueecclesiae) and emerged as one of the most trusted and respected men at the royal court. His last important diplomatic mission was to the Polish court in 1523 (Ep 1662). Following the disastrous battle of Mohács on 29 August 1526, where Louis II died on the battlefield, Piso accompanied the widowed Queen *Mary to the relative safety of Bratislava (Pressburg, Pozsony), in north-western Hungary. The death of the king who had been his pupil, the loss of his house and possessions in Buda, and the increasing threat of the Turkish danger threw him into a deep depression and affected his health. He died at Bratislava in March 1527 (Ep 1917).

Jacobus Piso was one of the main channels through which Erasmian influences entered Hungary. He met Erasmus in Rome in 1509; they became friends and, while both were in Italy, exchanged many letters, of which only Ep 216 has survived. Too busy to keep up a regular correspondence, Piso sent Erasmus a handsome gift in 1526 accompanied by two letters, one of them actually four years old; Erasmus replied warmly (Epp 1297, 1662, 1754). There is also a trace of further correspondence (Ep 1910). Piso's house in Buda became a centre of humanistic influence, and it was there that a number of Hungarian scholars as well as members of the royal court met to discuss the writings of Erasmus. Prominent members of this circle were László *Szalkay, István *Brodarics, Nicolaus *Olahus, Queen Mary, and her confessor, Johann *Henckel. *Ursinus Velius also joined this illustrious group whenever he visited Buda. It was Piso who introduced Erasmus to the Thurzo family. Known for the elegance of his Latinity (*Ciceronianus* ASD I-2 689) and the beauty of his poetry, Piso was crowned poet laureate by the Emperor *Maximilian I. A volume of his poems was published by his friend Georg *Werner in 1554 at Vienna. There are modern editions of his poems in *Analecta nova ad historiam renascentium in Hungaria litterarum spectantia* ed J. Ábel and I. Hegedüs (Budapest 1903) 408–22 and in *Fünf Gedichte von Jacob Piso* ed Hermann Hinz (Sibiu-Hermannstadt 1914).

BIBLIOGRAPHY: Allen Ep 216 / *Magyar életrajzi lexikon* (Budapest 1967–9) II 419 / *Magyar*

irodalmi lexikon (Budapest 1963–5) II 507 / Jenö
Ábel *Magyarországi humanisták és a Dunai tudos
társaság* (Budapest 1880) / Lajos Némethy
'Adalekok Piso Jakab életiratához' in *Történel-
mi Tár* (1885) 764–7 / Imre Trencsényi-
Waldapfel *Erasmus magyar barátai* (Budapest
1941) / AK II Ep 856a / *Acta Tomiciana* (Poznań-
Wrocław 1852–   ) I–VII passim

L. DOMONKOS

Bonaventura PISTOFILO of Ferrara,
d July 1535
A member of a family originating in Pontremoli,
Tuscany, Bonaventura Pistofilo (Ventura Zam-
bati, Pistophilus) studied at the University of
Ferrara, first medicine under Niccolò *Leoniceno, then law, in which he obtained a degree.
His respect for Leoniceno was manifest in a
funeral monument which he erected in his
honour in the church of San Domenico,
bearing an epitaph by Celio *Calcagnini.
Pistofilo married Margherita, the daughter of
the celebrated poet Tito Vespasiano Strozzi,
and was on intimate terms with his brother-in-
law, Ercole Strozzi. Tito Vespasiano dedicated
to Pistofilo the fourth Latin sermon of his
Sermonum liber, praising his knowledge and
refined manners (*Strozii poetae pater et filius*,
Venice: Aldo Manuzio 1513, 142–6). In 1505
Pistofilo became chancellor to the elder Strozzi,
a judge of the Savi, the highest magistracy of
Ferrara. In 1510, after the death of his
father-in-law, he became secretary to duke
Alfonso I d'*Este, and in 1516 and 1518 he was
sent on diplomatic missions to *Francis I of
France. His official correspondence ended on 9
June 1535; he died in July of the same year and
was buried in an elegant tomb in the church of
San Paolo, destroyed in an earthquake in 1570.
He left behind a large collection of coins
(Calcagnini *Epistolicarum quaestionum et episto-
larum familiarium libri*, in *Opera aliquot*, Basel,
H. Froben 1544, 207) and a vast library, willed
to Bartolo Ferrini.
   In addition to being active in affairs of state,
Pistofilo was a poet and historian who took
great interest in intellectual matters. In 1525
Floriano *Montini described him as an admirer
of Erasmus who had read his *De libero arbitrio*
against *Luther (Ep 1552). He was a patron of
Celio Calcagnini, who frequently mentioned
him in his correspondence (*Epistolicarum quae-

stionum libri 114–15 and passim), and who
dedicated to him his *De libero animi motu ex
sententia veterum philosophorum* (1525; Ep 1587)
and his *Quod caelum stet, terra moveatur vel de
perenni motu terrae* (c 1520). Ludovico *Ariosto
praised him in the *Orlando furioso* (XLVI 18) as a
learned, faithful, and diligent secretary. Pietro
*Bembo, writing to Pistofilo on the death of
Duke Alfonso I, praised him as a man of
ingenuity (*Opere*, Venice 1729, III 224). The
Ferrarese writers Giovambattista Giraldi Cin-
thio (*Commentario delle cose di Ferrara et de'
principi d'Este*, Venice 1556, 150) and Giglio
Gregorio Giraldi (*De poetis suorum temporum* in
Opera omnia, Louvain 1696, II 565) praised him
for his faithfulness, prudence, and elegant
style of letter-writing.
   Pistofilo's most important work was a biography of Duke Alfonso I, published by Antonio
Cappelli in *Atti e memorie delle Regie Deputazioni
di storia patria per le provincie modenese e parmense
3 (1865) 489–555. Two of his sonnets were
published by Girolamo Baruffaldi in *Rime scelte
di poeti ferraresi antichi e moderni* (Ferrara 1713):
'Ne al mercante alcun perir di nave' and 'Se un
già col cantar dolce la sua sposa.' His 'La presa
dell' armata de' Venetiani,' 'La presa di Bastia,'
and various poems remain in manuscript in the
Biblioteca Comunale of Ferrara (G. Antonelli
Indice dei manoscritti ..., Ferrara 1884, nos 68,
70, 437). Baruffaldi (*Dissertatio de poetis ferra-
riensibus*, Ferrara 1698, 33) mentions 'La passione di Cristo in terza rima' by Pistofilo.
   BIBLIOGRAPHY: Allen Ep 1552 / A. Maresti
*Raccolta delle armi antiche e moderne de' nobili
ferraresi* (Ferrara 1695) / G. Tiraboschi *Storia
della letteratura italiana* (Milan 1822–6) VII 62
and passim / F. Borsetti *Historia almi Ferrariae
gymnasii* (Ferrara 1735) II 388 / L. Ughi
Dizionario storico degli uomini ferraresi (Ferrara
1804) 114–15 / G. Catalano *Vita di Ludovico
Ariosto ricostruita su nuovi documenti* (Geneva
1930) 150, 476–7 / G. Mercati *Codici latini
Pico-Grimaldi-Pio e di altra biblioteca ignota del
secolo XVI esistenti nell'Ottoboniana ...* (Vatican
City 1938) 202 / W.L. Gundersheimer *Ferrara,
The Style of the Renaissance Despotism* (Princeton
1970)   PAOLO PISSAVINO

Matthias PISTOR of Leiningen, documented
1501–26
Matthias Pistor of Leiningen, south-west of

Simon Pistoris

Worms, matriculated at the University of Heidelberg on 11 January 1501. The only other source of information about him is Ep 1739A, a letter he addressed to Erasmus, probably in 1526 and from Speyer; he styles himself MA, is expecting the arrival of his patron, Henry, count *Palatine, bishop of Utrecht, and mentions connections with Johannes *Fabri and Johann *Schlupf. He also states that he had written to Erasmus twice before, evidently without receiving a reply.

BIBLIOGRAPHY: Allen Ep 1739A / *Matrikel Heidelberg* I 440   KONRAD WIEDEMANN

Simon PISTORIS of Leipzig, 28 October 1489–3 December 1562
Simon Pistoris (Pistorius, Becker) was the son of another Simon (d 1523), who was a physician at Leipzig and a member of the city council. He studied at Leipzig, where he took his BA in 1505. He proceeded to study law both at Leipzig and at Wittenberg (1507–8), graduated at Leipzig in 1509 as a bachelor of law, and went on to study at Pavia (1510–11). After his return to Germany he took his licence in law (1512) and his doctorate (1514), both at Leipzig,

where in 1515 he was appointed professor of civil law. In 1519 he became *professor ordinarius* and began to serve as assessor at the superior court (Oberhofgericht) of ducal Saxony. At the Leipzig disputation of 1519 he welcomed the participants with an oration and made the acquaintance of *Luther, who at first esteemed him but later on detested him when it became clear that he would not break with the church of Rome. In 1523 he became the chancellor of Duke George of *Saxony and kept this office until the duke's death in 1539. Despite the triumph of the Reformation in ducal Saxony, he resumed the chancellorship in 1541, after having refused a chair at the University of Ingolstadt offered to him on the initiative of *Viglius Zuichemus. He served Duke (from 1547 Elector) Maurice until he retired in 1549. Thereafter he lived, and eventually died, on his estate of Seusslitz, near Meissen.

When writing to Duke George in July 1520, Erasmus mentioned Pistoris among some distinguished scholars of the University of Leipzig (Ep 1125). Pistoris and Erasmus corresponded personally, but their letters are often complementary to the important correspondence between Erasmus and Duke George, and on occasion Erasmus dispatched letters to both at the same time (Epp 1561, 1940, 1943). Pistoris' first preserved letter to Erasmus (Ep 1521) is an exculpation of his friend Hieronymus *Emser, whom Erasmus suspected of having written the harsh Ep 1448 in the duke's name. Pistoris' contention that Duke George had spoken for himself is borne out by the accompanying letter from the duke (Ep 1520). Greetings and messages were also conveyed in letters exchanged between Erasmus and Pistoris' friends and colleagues such as Emser (Ep 1773), *Cochlaeus (Ep 1974), and Julius *Pflug (Ep 2522). In April 1526 Pistoris reiterated the duke's pleasure, already expressed by George himself, at the publication of the *Hyperaspistes* (Epp 1691, 1693). Another subject of discussion was the dismissal of *Ceratinus, whom Erasmus had recommended to Leipzig as professor of Greek (Epp 1693, 1744). Above all, it was in the embarrassing quarrel with *Eppendorf that Pistoris rendered Erasmus valuable assistance (Epp 1934, 1940, 1943, 1951, 2333, 2344, 2406, 2450). Pistoris also consulted Erasmus about some of

the problems arising at the time of the diet
of Augsburg in 1530. From such letters as have
survived it would appear that Erasmus was
reluctant to answer (Epp 2333, 2344). In his
last preserved letter to Pistoris (Ep 2450)
Erasmus praised Pflug and recommended
Andreas von *Könneritz.

Pistoris' energies were absorbed by the
duties of his office. He did not publish any
major works, although some of his memoranda
were later published by his son Modestinus
Pistoris, together with his own *Consilia* (Leipzig 1587–8).

BIBLIOGRAPHY: Allen 1125 / ABD XXVI 186–9 /
Matrikel Leipzig II 660 and passim / *Matrikel
Wittenberg* I 23, III 810 / Schottenloher II 144 /
Pflug *Correspondance* I Ep 60 and passim
MICHAEL ERBE & PGB

Christophorus PISTORIUS documented 1527–31

Christophorus Pistorius (Beck) wrote to Erasmus in September 1527 from Ansbach (Ep
1881), where he served as a tutor to the
five-year-old Albert (II) of *Brandenburg-
Ansbach. He wrote after having read and liked
the second part of Erasmus' *Hyperaspistes*.
Pistorius' letter coincided with the return to
Franconia of Margrave George of
*Brandenburg-Ansbach, who was going to
lead Ansbach-Bayreuth firmly into the Protestant camp. Pistorius consequently became
provost of Wülzburg, formerly a Benedictine
abbey near Eichstätt, which in 1523 had come
under the influence of Margrave George and
been transformed into a chapter of canons. For
some time Catholic and reformed canons
coexisted there. On 26 February 1531 Pistorius,
'formerly preceptor of margrave Albert,' resigned the provostship to another man, who in
turn resigned to him the parish of Hof,
forty-five kilometres north of Bayreuth.

Pistorius is perhaps identical with a Franconian who studied at the University of
Heidelberg and was registered on 9 May 1514
as Christoph Beck, of Eisenheim near Gerolzhofen, in the diocese of Würzburg. He
obtained a MA in 1516 and a doctorate in civil
and canon law in 1521.

BIBLIOGRAPHY: Johann Baptist Götz *Die
Glaubensspaltung im Gebiete der Markgrafschaft
Ansbach-Kulmbach in den Jahren 1520–1535* (Frei-

Pope Pius II

burg 1907) 196–7 / *Matrikel Heidelberg* I 495, II
437, 522, 536–7
PGB

Pope PIUS II

18 October 1405–14/15 August 1464
Enea Silvio Piccolomini (Aeneas Sylvius) was
born at Corsignano (later re-named Pienza in
his honour), near Siena, to Silvio Piccolomini
and Vittoria Forteguerri. Although his family
was noble, it was impoverished in Aeneas' time
and his early life was relatively simple. He
studied humanities at the University of Siena
(1423). In 1431 he entered the service of
Cardinal Domenico Capranica, whom he accompanied to Basel as his secretary. In 1432 he
passed to the service of Nicodemo della Scala,
bishop of Freising, then to that of Bartolomeo
Visconti, bishop of Novara, and in 1435 to that
of Cardinal Niccolò Albergati. In 1435 he went
to Scotland on a diplomatic mission on behalf of
the council of Basel. From 1436 to 1438 he was
again in Basel and attended the sessions of the
council there. In 1439 he became secretary to
the anti-pope Felix v. His reputation as a poet
resulted in his coronation as poet laureate by
the Emperor *Frederick III on 7 July 1442. He

was appointed to the imperial chancellery in 1443. While in the emperor's service Piccolomini helped reconcile the emperor to Pope Eugenius IV (1445). He entered the papal service and was made bishop of Trieste (1447), then Siena (1450). He was active in promoting papal plans for a crusade and was created cardinal of St Sabina on 18 December 1456. On 19 August 1458 he was elected pope. His pontificate was marked by much activity in favour of a crusade, culminating in his journey to Ancona in a vain attempt to launch an expedition. He died in Ancona.

Piccolomini was a respected Latin author of romance, poetry, and history. His writings on German topics, the *Germania* (1457), *Historia Friderici III* (before 1458), and *Historia bohemica* (1458), as well as his *Commentarii concilii basiliensis* (1440; repudiated when he became pope), made him a popular writer in the German humanistic circles frequented by Erasmus. He also wrote a number of works on education including *De liberorum educatione* (1450) and the *Artis rhetoricae praecepta* (1456). His autobiographical memoirs (*Commentaria*), composed while he was pope, were first printed at Rome in 1584 and offer rich insight into his learning and policies. In addition numerous collections of his letters were published, beginning in the 1470s.

Erasmus had a generally positive attitude towards Piccolomini. He praised him for his eloquence (Ep 23) and as a letter-writer (Ep 1206) and urged Christian *Northoff to divide his workday as Aeneas Sylvius did (Ep 56; ASD I-3 69). Erasmus also cited him in his replies to Noël *Béda (LB IX 488c) and in other works (ASD I-3 272; LB V 957F) and several times referred to his promotion of a crusade (Ep 2285; LB V 359F).

BIBLIOGRAPHY: Allen Ep 23 / Giuseppe Bernetti *Saggi e studi sugli scritti di Enea Silvio Piccolomini, Papa Pio II (1405–1464)* (Florence 1971) / J. Mitchell *The Laurels and the Tiara: Pope Pius II 1458–1464* (Garden City, NY 1962) / G. Paparelli *Enea Silvio Piccolomini: l'umanesimo sul soglio di Pietro* (Ravenna 1978) / Pastor III / Berthe Widmer *Enea Silvio Piccolomini in der sittlichen und politischen Entscheidung* (Basel 1963)   JOHN F. D'AMICO

Albertus PIUS *See Alberto* PIO

Gérard de PLAINE c 1480–31 August 1524
Gérard de Plaine (Pleine, de Plana), subsequently known as seigneur de la Roche, was a son of Thomas de *Plaine, chancellor of Burgundy. He matriculated at the University of Louvain on 30 January 1496. By 1504 he was a master of requests at the court of Philip the Handsome, duke of *Burgundy. On 8 November 1511 he was named president of the privy council of the regent, *Margaret of Austria, serving in this capacity until January 1515. After the future *Charles V had come of age, Gérard was replaced by Jean *Le Sauvage, but he retained his position as master of requests, with an increased salary. In 1519 he went to Germany to promote the election of Charles V as emperor, and in 1520 he undertook a diplomatic mission to England. In the following year he participated in the meeting of Charles V and *Henry VIII at Calais, where Erasmus too was present (Ep 1106). In 1522 he accompanied the emperor to Spain as a member of his council of state and an expert in the affairs of the Low Countries. He also continued to serve as a diplomat and was sent on an important mission to Pope *Clement VII in the summer of 1524; however, he died shortly after his arrival in Rome.

Being a second son, Gérard founded a new line, styling himself after his estates of La Roche (Dijonais) and Courcelles (Hainaut). In 1502 he married Barbe de Neufchâtel, and, after her death, Anne de Ray in 1514. Erasmus recalled having met him in the entourage of his father some time after his first wedding (Ep 1432). In March 1522 Erasmus wrote to Gérard in Spain, after he had been informed of the councillor's interest in his writings; he took advantage of the occasion to complain about the attacks of Nicolaas *Baechem Egmondanus and Diego *López Zúñiga (Ep 1432).

BIBLIOGRAPHY: Allen Ep 1432 / *Matricule de Louvain* III-1 133, III-2 400 / Karl Brandi *Kaiser Karl V.* new ed (Darmstadt 1959–67) I 45 and passim / Ursula Schwarzkopf *Die Rechnungsführung des Humbert de Plaine über die Jahre 1448–1452* (Göttingen 1970) / de Vocht *Literae ad Craneveldium* Ep 114 and passim / de Vocht MHL 239 / F. Walser and R. Wohlfeil *Die spanischen Zentralbehörden und der Staatsrat Karls V.* (Göttingen 1959) / Andreas Walther *Die*

*burgundischen Zentralbehörden unter Maximilian
1. und Karl v.* (Leipzig 1909) / *Deutsche
Reichstagsakten* Jüngere Reihe (Gotha-
Göttingen 1893–   ) I–III passim / LP II 3018 and
passim   HEIDE STRATENWERTH

Thomas de PLAINE c 1444–20 March 1507
Thomas de Plaine, seigneur de Maigny
(Magny-sur-le-Thil), etc, a son of Humbert de
Plaine and Isabelle de Thoisy, was descended
from a family of merchants, officials, and
lawyers of the Franche-Comté that had risen to
prominence in the service of the dukes of
Burgundy. Thomas matriculated at the University of Louvain on 31 January 1459. He was
named master of requests and embarked on a
career in the legal administration, becoming a
member of the great council of Mechelen under
Duke Charles the Rash of *Burgundy and
president of the council of Flanders. Duke
Philip the Handsome of *Burgundy appointed
him chancellor of Burgundy in 1497, an office
that he held to his death. During Philip's
journey to Spain from 1501 to 1503 his
chancellor was a member of the council of
regency; he was also one of the executors of
Philip's will. He was survived by his wife,
Jeanne le Gros, and several children, among
them Gérard de *Plaine, seigneur de la Roche.
   In the summer of 1498 Erasmus reported how
the chancellor had responded with an address
of thanks on behalf of his master to the
presentation of the pope's golden rose (Ep 76).
Erasmus had personal contact with Thomas de
Plaine (Ep 1432), perhaps in connection with
the presentation of his *Panegyricus* in the
course of an official ceremony at the castle of
Brussels at Epiphany 1504. On this occasion
too the chancellor made a speech of thanks on
behalf of Duke Philip (ASD IV-1 27, 93).

BIBLIOGRAPHY: Allen Epp 76, 179 / *Matricule
de Louvain* II-1 59 / de Vocht *Busleyden* 293–4
(editing a letter to the chancellor from Busleyden) / Andreas Walther *Die burgundischen
Zentralbehörden unter Maximilian 1. und Karl v.*
(Leipzig 1909) passim
                                    HEIDE STRATENWERTH

Petrus PLATEANUS d 27 January 1551
Petrus Plateanus, the son of poor parents, was
born, according to his own statement, near

's Hertogenbosch (Ep 2216) and received his
education in the school of the Brethren of the
Common Life in Liège. He studied at first at
the Collegium Trilingue in Louvain (a Petrus
Joannis de Buscoducis matriculated at Louvain
on 31 August 1524; *Matricule de Louvain* III-1
729). In 1525 he went to Wittenberg, where he
matriculated on 1 April. On the recommendation of *Melanchthon, he was appointed rector
of the town school at Jáchymov (Joachimsthal).
He married Magdalene Lochmann of Zwickau
in 1528 and formed a close friendship with
Georgius *Agricola, the town physician in
Jáchymov, whose interest in metallurgy he
shared. Agricola also aroused his interest in
medicine, and when he left for Chemnitz (Karl-
Marx-Stadt), Plateanus decided in 1531 to go to
the University of Marburg, where he graduated MA in 1533. He may have studied medicine
while teaching ethics and rhetoric. In 1535 his
friend Agricola recommended him for the
headship of the Latin school of Zwickau, and
he was appointed on 5 May. Enrolment at the
school had been declining for some years, but
with the support of the town council, which
also lent him money to buy a house (1536–7),
Plateanus efficiently reorganized the school so
that it became one of the best in the area, highly
praised by *Luther (w *Briefwechsel* IX Ep 3698).
Plateanus' curriculum provided for eight classes with compulsory examinations twice a year
and reinvigorated the study of Greek. Enrolment rose to eight hundred students in 1544,
and as larger facilities were needed the old
Cistercian monastery was renovated and handed over to Plateanus on 10 October 1542. The
Schmalkaldic war had drastic consequences for
Zwickau, and Plateanus was among the many
citizens who left. On 21 August 1547 he was
appointed pastor and superintendent of
Aschersleben, in Saxony, and remained there
with his family of four sons and a daughter
until his death. His eldest son, Theodorus,
later became a well-known physician.
   Plateanus' 'Schulordnung' for Zwickau is
preserved in manuscript. He also wrote a
Latin grammar for his school, *Introductionis
grammaticae libri duo* (Leipzig 1543), and in his
Marburg years an epistolary report about the
Anabaptists of Münster which was published
as an appendix to Johannes *Cochlaeus' *XXI*

Bartolomeo Platina, by Melozzo da Forli

Gymnasium zu Zwickau *Jahresbericht* (1878)
1–33 / Georgius Agricola *Ausgewählte Werke* ed
H. Prescher (Berlin 1955–) II 61–5, 312

IG

Bartolomeo PLATINA of Piadena, 1421–
21 September 1481
Bartolomeo Sacchi was born at Piadena, near
Cremona, and was named 'Platina' after his
birthplace. After youthful experience as a
mercenary soldier, he entered the service of
Lodovico Gonzaga of Mantua and became
tutor to the Gonzaga children. He studied at
Mantua under Ognibene Bonisoli and then,
with a recommendation from Lodovico Gonzaga, went to Florence, where he studied
under Johannes *Argyropoulos. His stay in
Florence (1458–61) brought him the lasting
friendship of Jacopo and Donato *Acciaiuoli,
as well as Pierfilippo Pandolfini. In 1462
Platina went to Rome, probably as secretary to
the recently appointed Cardinal Francesco
Gonzaga, and soon began to take part in the
life of the Roman Academy around Julius
*Pomponius Laetus.
  Platina's rash and extreme protests against
the abolition of the College of Abbreviators, in
which he had purchased membership, led to
his imprisonment in Castel Sant'Angelo on the
orders of Pope Paul II (1464) and to a temporary
halt in his career at the curia. From 1468 to 1469,
when Paul believed that members of Pomponius' circle had entered into a conspiracy
against him, Platina was again imprisoned and
tortured as one of the prime suspects.
  After Paul's death, Platina returned to the
curia, where through the patronage of *Sixtus
IV he acquired several benefices in addition to
the librarianship of the Vatican library. He was
librarian from 1475 until his death and was
responsible for systematically building the
library's holdings. He died a respected member
of the papal court, as attested to by the
distinguished mourners who attended his
funeral. His tomb survives in Santa Maria
Maggiore in Rome.
  Erasmus respected Platina as a stylist and a
historian, who in his *Liber de vita Christi et
omnium pontificum* (Venice: J. de Colonia and J.
Manthen 1479) treated St Jerome with harsh
and unwarranted criticism (*Opuscula* 138). He

articuli Anabaptistarum ... confutati (Leipzig
1534).
  In 1529 Plateanus was instrumental in the
publication of Agricola's dialogue *Bermannus*;
he wrote a preface for it, dedicated to Heinrich
von Könneritz. Eager to have his friend's book
printed by Hieronymus *Froben, he sent it to
Erasmus for approval (Ep 2216). Erasmus
concurred and wrote a second preface (Ep
2274), addressed to Andreas and Christian von
*Könneritz, who were studying in Freiburg.
He also seems to have answered Plateanus'
letter, which expressed sincere admiration for
Erasmus on the part of the headmaster and
other leading citizens of Jáchymov. Other
letters followed (Ep 2782), but none are
preserved. In March 1533 Plateanus visited
Erasmus in Freiburg; Erasmus managed a polite
expression of pleasure despite his unusually
poor health (Ep 2782).
  BIBLIOGRAPHY: Allen Ep 2216 / ADB XXVI
241–3 / de Vocht CTL II 576 / Luther W
Briefwechsel IX Ep 3698 / *Matrikel Wittenberg* I 124
/ E.E. Fabian 'M. Petrus Plateanus, Rector der
Zwickauer Schule von 1535 bis 1546' in

also knew and enjoyed his book on cooking, *De honesta voluptate et valetudine libri x* (Venice: L. de Aquila and S. Umber 1475; ASD I-1 125), as well as his dialogues and his panegyric on Cardinal *Bessarion (ASD I-2 666). Platina's major works also include editions of Josephus' *Bellum iudaicum* (Rome: A. Pannartz 1475) and Varro's *De lingua latina* (Rome: G. Lauer c 1471) as well as a history of Mantua (Vienna 1675) and a short life of Vittorino da Feltre (ed G. Biasuz, Padua 1948).

BIBLIOGRAPHY: F. Arisi *Cremona literata* (Parma 1702–41) I 310–23 / G. Gaida's preface to Platina's *Liber de vita Christi* in *Rerum Italicarum scriptores* (Città di Castello 1913–32) I-1 / Vladimiro Zabughin *Guilio Pomponio Leto: Saggio critico* (Rome-Grottaferrata 1909–12) I 74–86 and passim / A. Luzio and R. Renier 'Platina e i Gonzaga' *Giornale storico della letteratura italiana* 3 (1889) 430–40 / A.J. Dunston 'Pope Paul II and the humanists' *Journal of Religious History* 7 (1972–3) 287–306 / Egmont Lee *Sixtus IV and Men of Letters* (Rome 1978) 11–12, 110–19, and passim

EGMONT LEE

Angelus PLATTUS *See Angelo* PIATTI

Ludwig PLATZ of Melsungen, documented from 1497, d 1547
Ludwig Platz was born at Melsungen, twenty-three kilometres south-east of Kassel, and matriculated at the University of Erfurt toward the end of the winter term of 1497. He graduated BA in the autumn of 1499 and MA in the spring of 1504. During a major outbreak of the plague in 1505 he and Helius *Eobanus were among the many professors and students who moved first to Melsungen and, when the epidemic reached there too, to Frankenberg, where lectures were continued. Soon after returning to Erfurt Platz was co-opted to the council of the faculty of arts and, beginning with the summer term of 1508, was elected to various offices, being dean for the summer term of 1515 and the winter term of 1519. In the same year he was promoted licentiate in theology, and for the summer term of 1520 he was rector. Even though he did not specifically belong to the circle of Eobanus and *Mutianus Rufus, Platz supported the new learning, and during

his term as rector he continued the humanistic reforming efforts already under way. In reply to a complimentary message Erasmus praised the rector in Ep 1127 for his determined and constructive approach to reform, which avoided disruption: 'Theology, frigid and quarrelsome, had sunk to such a pitch of futility that it was essential to recall it to the fountain-head. Even so, I would rather see correction here than destruction, or at least toleration until some better approach to theology is forthcoming.' Over the following decades the university was to pursue educational policies which were in full agreement with the principles expressed by Erasmus in his letter. Eobanus too praised Platz in his *De non contemnendis studiis* (Erfurt 1523).

In 1519 the city council had appointed Platz a fellow of the Collegium Maius, the principal college in the faculty of arts. In years to follow the city failed to fill the fellowships which fell vacant; in the end the only two fellows left in the Collegium Maius were Dr Jacobus *Theoderici and Platz. As a result his administrative burden was steadily growing; from 1527 he was regularly either dean or treasurer of the faculty. In 1533 he visited his former pupil Euricius *Cordus at Marburg; cf Cordus' *Botanologicon* (Cologne: J. Gymnich 1534). Without abandoning the traditional church he was for some time sympathetic to the teachings of Martin *Luther. Not until 1536, when he was close to seventy according to Eobanus (*Epistolae familiares* Ep 142), did he take a wife, thus forfeiting his fellowship in the Collegium Maius and his participation in university affairs. He was also the curate of Walschleben, ten kilometres north of Erfurt, but installed his brother Nikolaus Platz there as a vicar. No writings by Ludwig are mentioned in the sources.

BIBLIOGRAPHY: Allen and CWE Ep 1127 / *Matrikel Erfurt* II 202, 341 / G. Bauch *Die Universität Erfurt im Zeitalter des Frühhumanismus* (Wrocław 1904) 144–5 / E. Kleineidam *Universitas Studii Erffordensis* (Leipzig 1964–80) passim / Helius Eobanus Hessus *Epistolae familiares* (Marburg 1543 etc)

ERICH KLEINEIDAM

PLEINE *See Gérard and Thomas de* PLAINE

PLETHON See Georgius GEMISTOS PLETHON

Jacques PLUMION of Saint-Omer,
documented 1491–1519
The archives of the Saint-Omer chapter preserve some traces of the life of this friend of
Erasmus and Jacob *Batt, who was a canon of
Saint-Omer (Ep 161). A document of 11 July
1491, bearing the seal of Guillaume Cappel,
rector of the University of Paris, attests to the
application Plumion (Plumio) had shown as a
student of law. This certificate fails to reveal,
however, whether Plumion had returned from
Paris as a doctor, a licentiate, or a bachelor of
canon law.

A second document, a copy of the will
written on 6 October 1519 by Jacques Plumion,
'priest, dean and canon of the chapter of
Saint-Sauveur at Saint-Omer,' reveals the
spiritual quality of his mind. Customary
commonplaces apart, the very personal accents
of a fervent and deeply rooted piety find
expression in a peaceful contemplation of
death. Paying only scant attention to bequests
and donations, Plumion's will is for the most
part an exercise in religious devotion and thus
admirably confirms the reports given to Erasmus by the physician *Ghisbert about the
dignified way in which the disciples of Jean
*Vitrier were facing their last hour. Erasmus,
who at the end of his own life was to write De
praeparatione ad mortem, was bound to be
impressed by such examples of Christian
composure.
BIBLIOGRAPHY: Saint-Omer, Bibliothèque
municipale, MS 932: 'Catalogue des archives
capitulaires' by A. Giry, II G 467, 483
ANDRÉ GODIN

Juan Martín POBLACIÓN
documented 1506–35
Juan Martín Población (Poblatio), of the diocese of Palencia, is documented for the first
time on 20 November 1506, when he signed
the matriculation register of the University
of Montpellier. In June 1520 Juan Luis *Vives
mentioned him among some Spanish and
Portuguese scholars he had met on a recent
visit to Paris. Vives stressed his expertise
'in the whole of mathematics' (Ep 1108), a
comment which is borne out by his book on
the astrolabe, De usu astrolabii compendium

(Paris: H. Estienne n d). In 1521 Vives praised
Población's medical skills in the notes of his
edition of Augustine's De civitate Dei. In May
1522 Población accompanied *Charles v when
the emperor visited England on his way back
to Spain. In 1529 Vives mentioned him among
the humanist protégés of Alonso *Manrique,
archbishop of Seville, when dedicating his De
pacificatione to the archbishop.

In 1530 Población appears to have returned
to Paris in the entourage of *Eleanor, the new
queen of France and sister of Charles v. As her
physician he was attached to the French court
and became a French subject. Although he has
traditionally been associated with *Francis I's
royal college as a predecessor of the mathematician Oronce Finé, it does not appear that he
held an official appointment. In 1532 he
published a Spanish translation of Cebes,
based on the Greek text (Paris: S. de Colines).
In 1535 Pedro Juan *Olivar dedicated to him his
edition of Cicero's Somnium Scipionis, styling
him 'Johannes Martinus Siliceus Poblacio' and
chief physician to the queen.
BIBLIOGRAPHY: Allen and CWE Ep 1108 / Abel
Lefranc Histoire du Collège de France (Paris 1893)
131, 232 / Emile Legrand 'Bibliographie
hispano-grecque 1477–1560' I no 63 in Bibliographie hispanique 1915 (New York 1915) /
Bataillon Erasmo y España 101, 189, 511 /
Matricule de Montpellier 10
MILAGROS RIVERA

POGGIO, POGIUS See Poggio BRACCIOLINI

Edmund de la POLE earl of Suffolk,
1471/2–4 May 1513
A son of John de la Pole, second duke of
Suffolk, and Elizabeth, a sister of Edward IV,
Edmund succeeded to his father's dukedom,
which he then surrendered to the crown,
agreeing to be known as earl of Suffolk (26
February 1493). In 1498 he was indicted for
murder in the King's Bench and in the summer
of 1499 he fled overseas. On 20 August a royal
proclamation forbad anyone to leave the
kingdom without a licence, delaying Erasmus'
departure for Paris (Ep 108). Pole was soon
pardoned, returned to England, and was
received back into favour; but in 1501 he again
fled to the continent. He was outlawed; all his
titles were forfeited and his friends impris-

oned. In 1504 he was seized by Karel van
*Egmond, duke of Gelderland, while on his
way to Friesland. In 1506 he was delivered to
*Henry VII by Philip the Handsome, duke of
*Burgundy, and confined to the Tower of
London. Upon the accession of *Henry VIII he
was exempted from the general pardon of 1509
and was executed in 1513, when his brother
Richard was serving in the French army, then
at war with England.

BIBLIOGRAPHY: Allen Ep 108 / DNB XVI 21–3 /
G.E. C[okayne] *The Complete Peerage of England*
ed V. Gibbs et al (London 1910–59) XII-1 451–3 /
LP I 1911(2), 2072 and passim / J.D. Mackie *The
Earlier Tudors 1485–1558* (Oxford 1952) 167–70
and passim / J.J. Scarisbrick *Henry VIII* (London
1968) 32–3   R.J. SCHOECK

Reginald POLE 1500–17 November 1558
Reginald was the son of Sir Richard Pole and
Margaret Plantagenet, countess of Salisbury.
After an early education at home, he was sent
for five years to the charterhouse at Sheen and
from there to Oxford, matriculating at Magdalen College where his studies were directed by
Thomas *Linacre and William *Latimer. In 1515
Pole received his BA. His mother had always
intended him for the church, and after gradua-
tion he was presented with a number of
benefices. Nevertheless, in February of 1521 he
requested that his cousin, *Henry VIII, send
him to Italy for further study at the University
of Padua. The king agreed and provided him
with one hundred pounds per annum. At
Padua he studied under Niccolò *Leonico
Tomeo (Ep 2526) and formed close friendships
with *Longueil, *Bembo, and *Lupset. After
the death of Longueil, Pole wrote his biography and prefixed it to his friend's collected
writings (Florence 1524). In August 1525,
Lupset wrote to Erasmus describing Pole's
virtues and talents, an introduction which
occasioned Erasmus' first letter to him the
following October in which the young Polish
scholar Jan (II) *Łaski was commended to him
(Epp 1595, 1627).

Returning to England in the winter of 1526–7
(Epp 1761, 1817), Pole continued his studies at
Sheen and in August 1527 was elected dean of
Exeter, although still a layman. The events
surrounding the king's divorce proceedings
greatly saddened his cousin. Consequently, in

Reginald Pole

1529 he sought permission to study in Paris in
order to avoid any taint of complicity in the
issue. However, Henry ordered Pole to consult
the Paris faculty of theology on the question.
Pole reluctantly did as requested and elicited a
reply favourable to the king. In July 1530 Pole
returned to the monastery at Sheen.

Although the king offered Pole the archbishopric of York or the see of Winchester after the
death of Cardinal *Wolsey, Pole refused and
began to anger Henry by his obvious hostility
to the divorce. Prudently, Pole undertook
another visit to the continent in 1532, again
supported by a royal pension. After residing
briefly at Avignon, he returned to Padua,
where he established a large household of
scholars and students. He resumed his reading
of the classics but increasingly devoted himself
to the study of philosophy and theology as
well. It was at this time that he met Gasparo
*Contarini, Lodovico Priuli, Gian Pietro Carafa
(the future Pope *Paul IV), and his own future
secretary and biographer, Lodovico Beccadelli.

The king's divorce and marriage to *Anne
Boleyn and his disinheriting of Princess *Mary
caused Pole much anguish, although he still

hoped that some peaceful accommodation might be possible between the king and Rome. However, in 1533, Thomas *Cromwell, distrusting Pole, wrote to him for his honest thoughts on the king's proceedings. The response was not forthcoming until May 1536 when *Pro ecclesiasticae unitatis defensione* appeared, a treatise which vigorously rejected the divorce and the reconstitution of the English church. Henry was furious and demanded Pole's immediate return.

Instead, Pole accepted an invitation from Pope *Paul III to visit Rome, arriving in November 1536. With his friend Contarini, he was appointed to the commission which prepared the *Consilium de emendanda ecclesia*, and on 22 December he was raised to the Sacred College of Cardinals. He was appointed papal legate to England the following February. The arrest and execution of his mother and brother in England convinced him that only a Catholic alliance could restore his country to full communion with the church. He embarked upon missions to *Charles V and *Francis I to discuss such a league but met with no success. In 1540 he was recalled to Rome and made governor of the patrimony of St Peter. The pope appointed Pole as one of the three legates to open the council of Trent, a duty which occasioned his *De concilio*. By November 1546 he was back in Rome, and during the conclave of 1549 he narrowly missed election to the papacy.

The death of Edward VI and the accession of Mary filled Pole with renewed hope for England. The pope reconfirmed his legatine powers, but the situation in England was still too uncertain to permit his return. In the meantime, Pole was charged with the mediation of peace between the Emperor and *Henry II of France. Finally, on 12 November 1554 Parliament reversed the act of attainder against him, and eight days later he arrived in England as papal legate. On 30 November he formally absolved his nation from schism and the following January Parliament passed an act restoring the supremacy of the papacy. In March 1556 Pole was consecrated archbishop of Canterbury, two days after his ordination as a priest. In the following year severe difficulties developed between Pole and Pope Paul IV, his old associate. In part the problem was

political, caused by the pope's war with Spain. However, Paul also doubted Pole's orthodoxy. During the summer of 1558, in the midst of these tribulations, Pole fell ill, dying on 17 November, the same day as his queen.

Pole's devotion to his church could not be doubted, given the sacrifices he endured for his belief in a united Christendom. However, Paul IV's violent assaults on his former friend were not unjustified. Pole, together with Contarini, Priuli, and Giovanni Morone, was closely associated during the 1530s with the movement of Italian evangelism identified with Juan de *Valdés and the *spirituali*. Desirous of eradicating abuses in the church, dedicated to the efficacy of Scripture and the supremacy of faith, and convinced of the value of humanistic erudition, these men owed much to the spirit and writings of Erasmus. Indeed, the somewhat distant and formal, while still sincere, friendship between Erasmus and Pole is clearly animated by a shared concern for the integrity of a humane faith compatible with good letters. When praising Pole's virtues to Erasmus in August 1525, Lupset noted how he had always defended Erasmus against his detractors (Ep 1595), an act of friendship which Erasmus effectively acknowledged in a letter of the following March in which he reported to Pole the viciousness of *Luther's answer to his *De libero arbitrio* and announced the *Hyperaspistes* (Ep 1675). The correspondence between Pole and Erasmus continued intermittently (Ep 2526), and there is some evidence for letters now missing (Epp 1675, 2593). On leaving Padua in the autumn of 1526, Pole and Lupset visited Johann von *Botzheim in Constance (Ep 1761) and might have passed through Basel on their way to England, but there is only inconclusive evidence for a visit with Erasmus, who mentioned Pole in a letter to Germain de *Brie at just this time (Ep 1817). Further contacts between Pole and Erasmus were occasioned by Simon *Grynaeus' visit to England in 1531 and the lending of a manuscript of Chrysostom from Pole's library (Ep 2526). In December 1535 Erasmus was apparently in possession of an account of the death of John *Fisher and Thomas *More, which Pole had translated from English into Italian (Ep 3076).

In the *Ciceronianus* (ASD I-2 678–9, March

1528) Erasmus observed that Pole was capable of writing in a Ciceronian style but had not yet published anything under his own name. In fact, Pole's style is usually not elegant and not designed to establish a literary reputation. Of his major works there appeared in his lifetime the early, anonymous (and Ciceronian) life of Longueil (Florence: heirs of F. Giunta 1524), his *Pro ecclesiasticae unitatis defensione libri quatuor* (Rome: A. Bladus c 1537), and the *Discorso di pace* (Rome: A. Bladus 1555). The *Consilium delectorum cardinalium de emendanda ecclesia* was published in 1538 (Rome: A. Bladus). *De concilio* saw print only after his death (Rome: P. Manuzio and Venice: G. Ziletti 1562), as did *De summo pontifice* (Louvain: J. Fowler 1569). Pole's correspondence, containing also the *Vita del Cardinale Reginaldo Polo* by his secretary, Lodovico Beccadelli, was edited in five volumes by A.M. Quirini (Brescia 1744–57, repr 1967). *On Justification* was found among Pole's papers and published posthumously (Louvain: J. Fowler 1569). Several of his formal orations also saw print.

A portrait of Pole by Sebastiano del Piombo survives in the Hermitage, Leningrad, and an anonymous portrait once attributed to Titian is at Lambeth Place, London.

BIBLIOGRAPHY: Allen Ep 1627 / DNB XVI 35–46 / Emden BRUO 1501–40 453–5 / Lodovico Beccadelli *The Life of Cardinal Reginald Pole* trans B. Pye (London 1766) / Dermot Fenlon *Heresy and Obedience in Tridentine Italy: Cardinal Pole and the Counter-Reformation* (Cambridge 1972) / Wilhelm Schenk *Reginald Pole, Cardinal of England* (London 1950) / F.G. Lee *Reginald Pole, Cardinal Archbishop of Canterbury* (New York 1888)   KENNETH R. BARTLETT

Lancellotto de' POLITI of Siena,
1484–8 November 1553
Lancellotto de' Politi (Ambrosius Catharinus Politus, Ambrogio Catarino), a member of a respected family in Siena, studied philosophy and law in his home town and obtained a doctorate of civil and canon law. When he taught philosophy and law in Siena, Giovanni Maria del Monte, later Pope Julius III, was one of his students. At the age of twenty-two Politi began to make the rounds of famous universities in Italy and excelled in numerous disputations. In 1514 he taught civil law in Rome and in

1515 was sent to Florence by Pope *Leo x. There he became acquainted with the writings of Girolamo *Savonarola. Deeply impressed, he took up theology, entered the Dominican order (probably in 1517), and, in honour of St Catherine of Siena, adopted the name Ambrosius Catharinus Politus.

His first publication, a defence of the Catholic faith against Martin *Luther, *Apologia pro veritate catholicae fidei* (Florence: G. Giunta December 1520, new ed by J. Schweizer and A. Franzen, Münster 1956), dedicated to the Emperor *Charles v, was well received by the curia and by the papal nuncio, Girolamo *Aleandro. Luther saw a copy in March 1521 and replied with *Ad librum eximii Magistri Nostri M. Ambrosii Catharini ... responsio* (Wittenberg 1 April 1521; Luther w VII 701ff). In the same month Politi published a second book against Luther, *Excusatio disputationis contra Martinum Lutherum* (Florence: F. Giunta 1521), which was likewise welcomed by Aleandro and also by Johannes *Cochlaeus. Luther did not reply and Politi now began to attack other targets including Cardinal *Cajetanus and especially Bernardino *Ochino, who, like Politi, was from Siena. His *Annotationes in excerpta quaedam ... cardinalis Cajetani* (Paris: S. de Colines 1535) contained a strong attack on Erasmus (cf Ep 3127), whom he considered a prominent source of Protestant heresies. His *Speculum haereticorum contra Bernardinum Ochinum* (Rome 1537) was accompanied by *De casu hominis et peccato originali liber unus*, which contained another attack on Erasmus.

Politi had been prior of the Dominicans at Siena by 1520. He was in Rome from 1529 to 1532 and from 1538 to 1539 but lived in France during the intervening years, where he can be traced at Paris, Lyon, and Toulouse. After a second stay in France Politi returned to Italy for good in 1544 and found that the new emphasis on justification by faith had had considerable success among the common people. Therefore he chose the vernacular when presenting such rebuttals as *Compendio d'errori et inganni Luterani contenuti in un libretto ... intitolato 'Trattato utilissimo del benefitio di Christo crucifisso,' Resolutione sommaria contra le conclusioni Luterane ...*, and *Reprobatione de la dottrina di frate Bernardino Occhino ...* printed in one volume in 1544 (Rome: G. Cartolari). Politi attended the

Angelo Poliziano, by Niccolò Fiorentino

council of Trent from 1545 to 1547 and delivered an oration on 4 February 1546. On the recommendation of the council he was nominated bishop of Minori, in the kingdom of Naples, by Pope Julius III (24 August 1546). The problem of justification and certitude of grace was focal to a new controversy with his fellow-Dominican Dominicus Soto, which started with an attack by Politi in 1547 and continued with various rejoinders until 1551. Politi's *Expurgatio ... adversus apologiam fratris Dominici Soto* (Venice 1547) made Erasmus responsible for the wide dissemination of heresy. His *De consideratione et iudicio praesentium temporum ...* (Venice: G. Giolito 1547) offered yet another refutation of Lutheran views. It was re-edited by Cochlaeus (Mainz: F. Behem 1548). Politi, who also dealt with the problems of predestination, original sin, and the Immaculate Conception, eventually wrote a commentary to the letters of St Paul, *Commentaria ... in omnes divi Pauli ... epistolas* (Venice: V. Valgrisi 1551). On 3 June 1552 he was nominated archbishop of Conza, in the kingdom of Naples. His last censure of Erasmus, ... *Opusculum de coelibatu adversus*

impium Erasmum, was printed in Siena (L. Bonetti 1581), long after his death.

Erasmus was well aware of Politi's attacks on his writings (Epp 1908, 3127) but refrained from replying. He mentioned him in the *Spongia* (ASD IX-1 166–7) as one of Luther's many opponents and stated in Ep 1275 that his arguments against Luther on behalf of the pope's powers were not too well founded.

BIBLIOGRAPHY: Allen Ep 1275 / M.-M. Gorce in DTC XII-2 2418–34 / DHGE XI 1502 / LThK I 426–7 / F. Lauchert *Die italienischen literarischen Gegner Luthers* (Freiburg 1912) 30–135 / Eugénie Droz *Chemins de l'hérésie* (Geneva 1970–   ) III 208–327 / Benedetto di Mantova *Il Beneficio di Cristo* ed S. Caponetto (Florence 1972) 346–422, 529   IG

Angelo POLIZIANO of Montepulciano, 14 July 1454–28/9 September 1494

Angelo Ambrogini, born in Montepulciano, in Tuscany, the son of Benedetto and Antonia Salimbeni, is generally known under the name of Poliziano, coined on the Latin name of his native city (Mons Politianus). After the murder of his father in 1464 Angelo was sent to Florence, where he followed the courses given at the Studio by Cristoforo *Landino, Johannes *Argyropoulos, Demetrius *Chalcondyles, Andronicus Callistus, and Marsilio *Ficino. Recognition of his poetic talent came when he was only sixteen, as the result of his translation of the second book of the *Iliad*, dedicated to Lorenzo (il Magnifico) de' *Medici (1470). Close relations between the head of the Medici family and Poliziano are documented from 1472; in 1475 the humanist was chosen as tutor to Lorenzo's son Piero and later also to Giovanni, the future Pope *Leo X. Poliziano remained in Lorenzo's household until May 1479. During this period he composed Latin and Greek lyrics; continued, until 1474 and the end of fifth book, his translation of the *Iliad*; and began the unfinished *Stanze per la giostra di Giuliano de' Medici*, inspired by the joust won by Lorenzo's brother on 29 January 1475. Furthermore he wrote the *Sylva in scabiem* (1475); compiled the *Raccolta aragonese* and wrote its prefatory epistle (1476–7); wrote the *Detti piacevoli* (1477–9) and the *De Pactiana coniuratione commentarium* (1478, published in Florence during the same year); and translated

Epictetus' *Enchiridion* (1479, published in Bologna in 1487), Plutarch's *Amatoriae narrationes* (1479), and Alexander of Aphrodisias' *Problemata* (1479).

After a disagreement with Lorenzo's wife, Clarice Orsini, and a series of misunderstandings with his patron, Poliziano left Florence and travelled to Venice, Padua, Verona, and Mantua. Within a two-day period in Mantua (possibly 12–14 June 1480), he wrote the drama *Orfeo* at the request of Cardinal Francesco Gonzaga.

Later in the summer of 1480 there was a reconciliation with Lorenzo, and Poliziano returned to Florence to resume his responsibilities as tutor to Piero de' Medici, though no longer to Giovanni. At the same time he was appointed to the chair of Greek and Latin eloquence at the Studio. The programs of Poliziano's earlier university courses included almost exclusively classical poets and rhetoricians: Quintilian and Statius (1480–1), Ovid (1481–2), Virgil and Theocritus (1482–3), Virgil and Hesiod (1483–4), Horace and Persius (1484–5), Homer and Juvenal (1485–6), and then Homer every academic year until 1490. Poliziano gathered some of the introductory lectures prepared for his courses (*Manto, Rusticus, Ambra, Nutricia*) under the comprehensive title of *Sylvae*. Other introductory discourses composed during this period concerned Quintilian and Statius, Persius, and Homer. In addition to the works motivated by his academic obligations, Poliziano probably composed during these years the *Canzoni a ballo* and the *Rispetti*, wrote the prefatory epistle for the first edition of Leon Battista Alberti's *De re aedificatoria* (29 December 1485) and the prologue for the performance of Plautus' *Menaechmi* (presented by the clerics of San Lorenzo on 12 May 1488), and published the *Miscellaneorum centuria* (1489), considered to be his masterpiece as a philologist.

After 1490 Poliziano, possibly under the influence of his friend Giovanni *Pico della Mirandola, focused his attention at the Studio on works of a philosophical nature. Consequently during the last three years of his university career he lectured on works by Aristotle, Porphyry, and Gilbertus Porrettanus and wrote the prolusions *Panepistemon* (1490, published in 1492), *Dialectica* (1491), and *Lamia*

(published in 1492). Poliziano's activity outside the Studio during the final years of his life include his translations of Heriodanus' *Histories* (published in 1493), Plato's *Charmides* (not completed), Hippocrates' *Aphorisms*, and Galen's *Commentaries* (now lost) and his contributions to an edition and commentary of the Pandects (left incomplete). His well-known controversies with Paolo *Cortesi, Georgius *Merula, Michael *Marullus, and Bartolomeo *Scala also developed during the period from 1490 to 1494. Poliziano died during the night of 28–9 September 1494 and was buried in the church of San Marco in Florence.

Erasmus' attitude towards Poliziano is epitomized in Ep 471 to Johann *Reuchlin, where – to use the words of Eugenio Garin (*Ritratti di umanisti* 185) – Poliziano, Pico, Rodolphus *Agricola, and Ermolao *Barbaro are presented as men of such magnitude that in the eyes of the Dutch scholar 'an encounter with them seemed sufficient to give sense to [the] life' of an individual. Other Erasmian classifications of the outstanding contributors to the progress of humanistic learning in fifteenth-century Italy included Poliziano (Epp 126, 531, 1347, 1479; ASD IX-1 196; *Opuscula* 176, 185). It is evident, therefore, that the homage paid by Erasmus to the Tuscan humanist in the letter to Reuchlin is not a passing comment but a firm judgment. Aside from showing considerable familiarity with details of Poliziano's life (Epp 145, 188, 337) the works of Erasmus provide evidence of an interest in the personality of the Italian sustained by the Dutch humanist from his early years to the end of his life (Epp 61, 126, 1206, 2466) and encomiastically summarized in the *Adagia* (II ix 1) and in the *De conscribendis epistolis* (ASD I-2 226). Characteristically Erasmus' appreciation is not uncritical: he declares that Poliziano himself could make mistakes (Ep 1482), and, without contradicting his basic attitude, he compares the uncommon merits of older and younger humanists, such as Rodolphus Agricola and Guillaume *Budé, to the achievements of the master from Montepulciano (*Adagia* I iv 39; Epp 531 and 1479).

Given the quality of the work and its European popularity, it is not surprising to see that Poliziano's *Miscellaneorum centuria* is mentioned and even quoted by Erasmus on several occasions (Epp 126, 373, 1635; *Adagia* I iv 8, II ii

65, III vii 3). In Ep 1175 the Dutch humanist explicitly declared that he cited Poliziano in the *Adagia* because in his works he found references to authors still unknown to him. Actually the *Adagia* contain many other references to the Italian humanist; furthermore Poliziano is quoted in the *De pueris instituendis* and quite extensively in the *De conscribendis epistolis* (both in ASD I-2); the latter shows how attentively Erasmus read the letters of the Italian humanist and studied his epistolary style. In the *Ciceronianus* Erasmus declared that the Italian humanist proved to be 'a rare miracle of nature' in all the literary genres he attempted, regardless of his rejection of the Ciceronian style (ASD I-2 664). Further on in the dialogue the Dutch humanist attentively analysed the historical and cultural significance of Poliziano's controversies with Paolo Cortesi and Bartolomeo Scala (ASD I-2 705–7). Erasmus concluded with an unconditional acceptance of the principles stated by Poliziano, who had anticipated the Erasmian positions by objecting to the adoption of Cicero as the sole model of style and by defending an eclectic approach to imitation as the best means to cultivate an independent but elegant style.

The first edition of Poliziano's collected vernacular works was published in Bologna, without the authorization of the author, 'per Platone delli Benedetti' on 9 August 1494; Aldo *Manuzio published the first edition of the Latin and Greek works (*Opera omnia Angeli Politiani*) in July 1498, followed by Sebastianus *Gryphius (Lyon 1536–9) and Nicolaus *Episcopius (Basel 1553). In 1839 Angelo Mai published the long-lost translation of books II to V of the *Iliad*, after retrieving a manuscript in the Biblioteca Apostolica Vaticana: see *Spicilegium Romanum* ed A. Mai (Rome 1825–38) II 1–100. Modern editions of Poliziano's unpublished works include: *Prose volgari edite e inedite e poesie latine e greche edite e inedite* ed I. Del Lungo (Florence 1867); G. di Pierro 'Zibaldoni autografi di Angelo Poliziano nella R. Biblioteca di Monaco' *Giornale storico della letteratura italiana* 55 (1910) 1–32; G. Presenti 'Diario odeporico-bibliografico inedito di Angelo Poliziano' *Memorie del R. Instituto Lombardo*, 3rd ser, 14 (1916) 229–42; and F. Garin 'La *Expositio Theocriti* di Angelo Poliziano nello Studio fiorentino' *Rivista di filologia classica* 42 (1914)

272–82. Alessandro Perosa discovered in Parma and subsequently published Poliziano's *Sylva in scabiem* (Rome 1954). For Poliziano's letters see A. Campana 'Per il carteggio del Poliziano' *La Rinascita* 6 (1943) 437–72.

The dispersion of Poliziano's library began very shortly after his death. This problem is authoritatively discussed by Ida Maier in *Les Manuscrits d'Ange Politien* (Geneva 1965). The portraits of Poliziano that are undoubtedly authentic are in the fresco 'The approval of the rules of the Franciscan order' by Domenico Ghirlandaio in the Sassetti chapel of the church of Santa Trinità in Florence (painted c 1483) and in the fresco 'Zacharias in the temple' painted by Ghirlandaio in 1490 in the Tornabuoni chapel of the church of Santa Maria Novella in Florence. Niccolò Fiorentino portrayed Poliziano in three medals about 1494.

BIBLIOGRAPHY: CWE Ep 61 / The basic modern biographical study of Poliziano is still Isidoro del Lungo *Florentia: Uomini e cose del quattrocento* (Florence 1897), completed and corrected by Angelo Picotti 'Tra il poeta e il Lauro (Pagine della vita di Agnolo Poliziano)' *Giornale storico della letteratura italiana* 65 (1915) 263–303 and 66 (1916) 52–104, repr in *Ricerche umanistiche* (Florence 1955) / More recent biographical studies consulted during the course of the compilation of the present entry are: the article by E. Bigi in DBI II 691–702, s v *Ambrogini, Angelo*; Bruno Maier 'Agnolo Poliziano' in *Orientamenti culturali: Letteratura italiana; I maggiori I* (Milan 1956) 245–305; Ida Maier *Ange Politien: La formation d'un poète humaniste* (Geneva 1966) / For critical reference see the studies included in the commemorative volume *Il Poliziano e il suo tempo: Atti del IV convegno internazionale di studi sul rinascimento* (Florence 1957) and the masterly profile by Eugenio Garin 'Poliziano e il suo ambiente' in *Ritratti di umanisti* (Florence 1967), English trans in his *Portraits from the Quattrocento* (New York 1973) 160–89   DANILO AGUZZI-BARBAGLI

Edmund POLLARD *See Edmundus* POLUS *arduus*

Edmundus POLUS arduus
(Ep 449 of 13 August [1516])
The young man whose name had been recorded in this way was recommended to

Erasmus by Henry *Bullock in Cambridge.
Conceivably his name was Pollard, and a
dominus Pollard, whose first name is not
known, is in fact documented in the University
of Cambridge between 1521 and 1525.

BIBLIOGRAPHY: Allen and CWE Ep 449

Johannes POMERANUS *See Johann*
BUGENHAGEN

Pietro POMPONAZZI of Mantua,
1462–18 May 1525
Pietro (Petrus, Perettus) Pomponazzi was born
in Mantua and hence sometimes called Petrus
Mantuanus. He studied philosophy and medicine at the University of Padua under Francesco de Neritone (di Nardò), a Thomist whose
philosophical principles he adopted when
young. In 1487 Pomponazzi was awarded a
doctorate in medicine and the following year
was appointed a *lector extraordinarius*, lecturing mainly on Aristotle's *Physics*. He was
nominated *professor ordinarius* in 1495, and in
1499 he was elected to the chair of philosophy
on the death of Nicoletto Vernias, the Aristotelian; Pomponazzi had originally argued against
Vernias in defence of Thomism, but his secular
Aristotelianism was increasingly influencing
the younger man.

The war of the League of Cambrai closed the
Studio at Padua in 1509, and Pomponazzi
migrated to Ferrara, where after 1510 he
lectured on Aristotle's *De anima*. In 1511 he was
appointed to the chair of philosophy at
Bologna for a four-year term, although he was
unable to take up the appointment until the
next year because of the war. Pomponazzi was
reconfirmed in this chair in 1515 with the
highest stipend then paid to a professor of
philosophy.

The following year saw the publication of
Pomponazzi's most famous work, *De immortalitate animae* (Bologna: Giustiniano da Ruberia),
which argued that there could be no rational
proof of the soul's immortality: such beliefs
rested only on the authority of Scripture, the
teachings of the church, and faith. The book
caused enormous controversy. The patriarch
and doge of Venice were moved to condemn
the text and the author as heretical and sent it
to *Bembo in Rome. Bembo, however, found no
fault in it, nor did Pope *Leo x. Encouraged by

Pietro Pomponazzi

his friends, Pomponazzi wrote an *Apologia*
(Bologna: Giustiniano da Ruberia) of his
opinions in 1517, responding to his detractors,
and in 1519 he directed his *Defensorium*
(Bologna: Giustiniano da Ruberia) against
Agostino Nifo, a Thomist who had attacked *De
immortalitate animae*. The University of Bologna
stood by Pomponazzi resolutely, reappointing
him to his chair in 1518 for a further eight years
at double his previous salary. Pomponazzi
died in Bologna.

Although there is no evidence of a direct
connection between Erasmus and Pomponazzi, Erasmus was at least aware of the debate in
Italy on the views of Aristotle on the immortality of the soul (Ep 916). Pomponazzi was clearly
the 'Petretus Mantuanus' who taught Celio
*Calcagnini and Alberto *Pio in their youth (Ep
1587).

A collected edition of Pomponazzi's writings
appeared in the last year of his life: *Tractatus
acutissimi, utillimi et mere peripatetici* (Venice: O.
Scoto 1525) containing *De intensione et remis-
sione formarum ac de parvitate et magnitudine, De
reactione, De modo agendi primarum qualitatum,
De immortalitate animae, Apologiae libri tres,*

Contradictoris tractatus doctissimus, Defensorium autoris, and *De nutritione et augmentatione.* An edition of his *Opera* (Basel: H. Petri 1567) included *De naturalium effectuum admirandorum causis seu de incantationibus* and *De fato, libero arbitrio, praedestinatione, providentia Dei libri v.* There also appeared in 1563 *Dubitationes in quartum Meteorologicorum Aristotelis librum* (Venice: Francesco dei Franceschi). Left in manuscript in the library of the Fraternità de' Laici in Arezzo are commentaries on certain books of Aristotle's *Physics,* on *Metaphysics* xII and the *Parva naturalia.*

A portrait of Pomponazzi survives in the Pinacoteca Ambrosiana at Milan.

BIBLIOGRAPHY: Cosenza IV 2902–6 / *The Renaissance Philosophy of Man* ed E. Cassirer et al (Chicago 1948) 257–381 / A.H. Douglas and R.P. Hardie *The Philosophy and Psychology of Pietro Pomponazzi* (Cambridge 1910, repr 1962) / Bruno Nardi *Studi su Pietro Pomponazzi* (Florence 1965) / F. Fiorentino *Pietro Pomponazzi: studi storici su la scuola bolognese e padovana del secolo xvI* (Florence 1868) / A. Poppi *Saggi sul pensiero inedito di Pietro Pomponazzi* (Padua 1970)   KENNETH R. BARTLETT

Julius POMPONIUS LAETUS of Diano, 1428–98
The illegitimate son of Giovanni, count of Sanseverino, and an unknown mother, Pomponius Laetus early left his native Diano (Tegiano), near Salerno, and later refused any association with the Sanseverino family. After an educational voyage through Sicily he moved to Rome, where he studied under Lorenzo *Valla and Pietro Oddi da Montopoli, and subsequently remained in the city, eventually acquiring Roman citizenship.

He soon became the centre of an intellectual circle later known as the Roman Academy. Originally a spontaneous and often light-hearted group of intellectuals, most of whom had ties to the papal court, the Academy devoted itself to literary discussions, archaeological excursions, and eventually the production of Roman plays and a more formal corporate life. Beginning about 1465, Pomponius taught rhetoric at the Studio of Rome but was dissatisfied with his salary and determined to leave the city in 1467, going first to Venice, with the intention of embarking on a long voyage to the east.

Pomponius' association with the Academy and the discovery of an apparent conspiracy of several of its members against Pope Paul II in 1468 prompted the pope to demand Pomponius' arrest in Venice and his extradition to Rome. He was imprisoned in Castel Sant'Angelo and tortured but released within months. In 1470 he returned to teaching rhetoric at the Studio of Rome.

Pomponius spent the rest of his life in Rome, acquiring considerable fame and some modest wealth through his teaching. Only two brief absences are recorded, occasioned by voyages to Germany (1479–80) and to the Black Sea area (1482–3).

Pomponius' central role in the increasingly formalized activities of the Academy reflects the wide respect he enjoyed among scholars active in Rome towards the end of the century. His death was widely lamented, and his funeral was attended by a large congregation of scholars and dignitaries at the papal court.

Erasmus regarded Pomponius as a Latin stylist and orator with little concern beyond elegant expression and no knowledge of Greek (ASD I-2 666; *Opuscula* 184). In reality his intellectual interests ranged considerably farther. He is responsible for editions of several Latin authors and commentaries upon them, including Nonius Marcellus' *Doctrina de proprietate latini sermonis* (Rome: G. Lauer n d), Festus' *De verborum significatione* (Rome: G. Lauer n d), Festus' *De gestis Alexandri* (Rome: G. Lauer c 1470), and others. Pomponius also studied the agricultural methods of antiquity, conducting experiments in his own vineyard. The most important work of his later years concerned the historical sources and the antiquities of Rome, including numismatics and topography. As a historian and antiquarian he became the most important continuator of Flavio *Biondo's work. Contrary to a commonly accepted view (Ep 347), Pomponius was not ignorant of Greek, although his serious work concerned only Latin authors.

BIBLIOGRAPHY: Vladimiro Zabughin *Giulio Pomponio Leto: Saggio critico* (Rome-Grottaferrata 1909–12) is clearly the most comprehensive and authoritative study of

Pomponius, superseding earlier treatments and preferable to many later ones / A.J. Dunston 'Pope Paul II and the Humanists' *Journal of Religious History* 7 (1972–3) 287–306 / Egmont Lee *Sixtus IV and Men of Letters* (Rome 1978) 47 and passim   EGMONT LEE

Constantino PONCE DE LA FUENTE *See Christophorus FONTANUS*

Etienne PONCHER of Tours,
1446–24 February 1525
Etienne Poncher (Poncherius) belonged to a family that had risen to prominence in the administration of royal finance – just like the *Briçonnet, Semblançay and *Budé families, who were all interrelated with the Ponchers. After studies in both civil and canon law, he took holy orders and embarked on the intertwined careers of prelate and diplomat. He was a canon of Saint-Gatien, Tours, in 1482, of Saint-Martin, Tours, in 1491, and of Notre Dame, Paris, in 1492, and chancellor of the bishop of Paris in 1496. On 3 February 1503 he became bishop of Paris and in the same year resigned his benefices at Tours. In 1508 he became commendatory abbot of Saint-Benoît-sur-Loire. On the other hand, he was appointed to the Parlement of Paris as clerical councillor in 1485 and became *président aux enquêtes* in 1493.

*Louis XII, who thought very highly of Poncher, named him to his privy council, and Georges (I) d'*Amboise used him as his right-hand man. Accompanying Amboise to Milan, he was appointed chancellor of the duchy of Milan in July 1502. He briefly returned to France in April 1503 to take possession of his diocese, but in July he returned to Milan. After Amboise had called him back to the French court in the spring of 1504, he came to have some influence on the affairs of the country; in particular he advocated the marriage of *Claude de France with the future *Francis I. He also accompanied Louis XII to Savona for his meeting with *Ferdinand II of Aragon in 1507 and participated, albeit without conviction, in the negotiations leading to the League of Cambrai in 1508. After the death of Georges d'Amboise, in May 1510, the cardinal's functions were shared between four

Etienne Poncher

courtiers. As one of them, Poncher undertook a series of missions in Italy, visiting Mantua, Milan, Parma, Modena, Piacenza, and again Milan, where he took in hand the preparation of the council of Pisa. By the end of 1511 he relinquished the office of chancellor of Milan and returned to France, where he succeeded in part to the functions of the chancellor, Jean de Ganay, when the latter died in June 1512. Until the death of Louis XII he was keeper of the seals and in this capacity appointed Girolamo *Aleandro in 1514 as his secretary, but he was never nominated chancellor. In fact that coveted position eluded him definitively with the ascent of Francis I, who gave it to Antoine *Duprat.

Under Francis I Poncher was from 1515 a member of the council of regency and participated in all negotiations with the Hapsburgs and England, attending the Noyon meetings of May and August 1516 and conducting missions to Brussels (January–February 1517, Ep 522), Cambrai (March 1517, Ep 569), London (September 1517 and August–October 1518), and Montpellier (May 1519, Ep 924). In March 1519 he was named archbishop of Sens (Ep 924) and primate of the realm, while his nephew François *Poncher succeeded him as bishop of Paris. From 1518 Nicolas *Bérault was his secretary. Poncher died on the day of the battle of Pavia.

Like such men as *Standonck, Raulin, *Lefèvre d'Etaples, and *Clichtove, Poncher was keenly aware of the need to bring about reforms of both the monasteries and the parish clergy. Cautiously favourable to the ideals of humanism, he took alarm at the quarrel over the three Magdalens in 1517 and induced John *Fisher to take a stand in this matter (Epp 936, 1016). He was much praised as a patron of letters (Epp 522, 569, 925), and Erasmus compared him in this regard to Jérôme and Gilles de *Busleyden (Ratio verae theologiae LB V 78A). He took a leading part in the negotiations over Erasmus' invitation to Paris (Epp 522, 531) and seems to have conceived a genuine enthusiasm for installing him as head of the royal college Francis I intended to set up (Epp 569, 1003). By 10 February 1517 Erasmus had an interview with him at Brussels on this subject (Epp 522, 1434), and in 1518 and 1519 he encouraged Guillaume Budé to renew the royal invitation (Epp 810, 896, 994). In the course of the Brussels interview Poncher also mentioned that Lefèvre d'Etaples had taken exception to Erasmus' criticisms (Apologia ad Fabrum LB IX 20B, 31E–F).

BIBLIOGRAPHY: Allen Ep 529 / M.-C. Garand 'La carrière religeuse et politique d'Etienne Poncher, évêque de Paris (1503–1519)' in: Congrès scientifique du VIIIe centenaire de Notre-Dame de Paris, 1964: Recueil des travaux (Paris 1967) 291–343
MARIE-MADELEINE DE LA GARANDERIE

François PONCHER of Tours,
d 1 September 1532
François Poncher, born in Tours by 1480, was the favourite (Ep 522) of his powerful uncle, Etienne *Poncher, whom he joined in Milan by 1503. He became canon of Notre Dame, Paris, before receiving the last minor orders in May 1505; he was not ordained priest until 16 April 1511. Meanwhile in 1510 he had entered the Parlement of Paris as one of the ecclesiastical councillors. He succeeded his uncle as abbot of Saint-Maur-des-Fossés and in 1519 as bishop

of Paris. After his uncle's death he attempted to secure his abbey of Saint-Benoît-sur-Loire and other benefices by improper means. An investigation against him was begun in 1526 and in 1529 evidence was presented to show that he had conspired against *Francis I when the king was a prisoner in Spain. In 1531 he was imprisoned in Vincennes, where he died the following year.

Girolamo *Aleandro dedicated to him an edition of Sallust (Paris 1511), Nicolas *Bérault an edition of Appian (Paris 1521), and Guillaume *Du Maine a Greek dictionary (Paris 1523).

BIBLIOGRAPHY: Allen Ep 522 / Gallia christiana VII 159–60 / Louis Delaruelle Répertoire ... de la correspondance de Guillaume Budé (Toulouse-Paris 1907) 16 / M.-C. Garand in Congrès scientifique du VIIIe centenaire de Notre-Dame de Paris, 1964: Recueil des travaux (Paris 1967) 331 / Le Journal d'un bourgeois de Paris ed V.-L. Bourrilly (Paris 1910) 370 and passim
MICHEL REULOS & PGB

Antoine de PONS 2 February 1510–1586
Antoine de Pons, count of Marennes and baron of Oléron, was the son of François de Pons and Marguerite de Coëtivy. As a child he was placed in the court of *Francis I. In 1528 he was with the forces of Lautrec fighting for control of Naples, but he was captured by the Spaniards at Aversa. Returning to France, he served as a gentleman of the chamber of the king. By January 1534 he was in Ferrara, where he married Anne de Parthenay, a lady-in-waiting to Renée of France, the wife of Ercole II d'*Este. Anne de Parthenay was the daughter of Madame de Soubise, who was the principal French confidante of Renée and was much resented by Ercole. After Soubise was forced to leave Ferrara in March 1536, Pons became the main adviser to the isolated Renée and was suspected of being little more than a French agent. He travelled to France in 1539, ostensibly to see to his affairs, but returned to Ferrara in 1540. For fear of offending France, Ercole tolerated Pons at his court until 1544, when he began proceedings against him and his wife under the pretext that they were plotting against his life. They fled Ferrara in disgrace, returning to France. Anne de Parthenay died soon afterwards, and in 1556 Pons, who at

Ferrara had been sympathetic towards Protestant beliefs, married an ardent Catholic, Marie de Montchenu. He became a persecutor of Huguenots, leading his own troops against them during the wars of religion. With 250 fiefs under his control, Pons served as councillor of state, governor of Saintonge and cavalier of the Holy Spirit.

On 3 April 1536 Antoine de Pons sent Erasmus greetings through the German professor of medicine Johannes *Sinapius, who described him as first among the courtiers of Ercole (Ep 3113).

BIBLIOGRAPHY: Allen Ep 3113 / Eugène and Emile Haag *La France protestante* (Paris 1846–59, repr 1966) VIII 287 / Bartolomeo Fontana *Renata di Francia, Duchessa di Ferrara* (Rome 1893–9) I 178–81, II 100, and passim / *Nouvelle biographie générale* (Paris 1853–66) XL 759 / E. Rodocanachi *Renée de France, Duchesse de Ferrare* (Paris 1896) 73–4 and passim   TBD

Giovanni Pontano, by Adriano Fiorentino

Giovanni PONTANO of Cerreto,
7 May 1429–September 1503

Giovanni (Giovianus) Pontano was born at Cerreto, near Spoleto in Umbria. Having lost his father at an early age, he went to study at Perugia, where his uncle Tommaso was chancellor of the commune. In 1447 he attached himself to the court of Alfonso I (the Magnanimous) of Naples, then waging war against Florence. In Naples his most important mentor was Antonio Beccadelli (Panormita), who made him a member of his literary circle, later called the Academy, where he received the name Gioviano. He also studied astrology under Lorenzo Bonincontri and Greek under George of *Trebizond and Gregorius *Tiphernas. In 1461 he married Adriana Sassone (d 1490), who bore him several children. In 1471 he became a citizen of Naples and succeeded Beccadelli in the leadership of the Academy, giving guidance and inspiration to young scholars such as Alessandro d'*Alessandro, Pietro Summonte, and Jacopo *Sannazaro. In addition to his literary activity, he was also one of the leading statesmen of Naples, serving the Aragonese kings as tutor, secretary, councillor, and diplomat. However, when *Charles VIII of France conquered the kingdom in 1495 Pontano greeted the new regime with an enthusiastic oration, deprecating his former patrons. Within the year the French abandoned Naples, the Aragonese dynasty returned, and Pontano was removed from public office. He devoted his last years to completing his literary works.

Pontano, the most important humanist of fifteenth-century Naples, composed many works of poetry, social commentary, and philosophy. His poems, which celebrated human love and the wonders of nature, were gathered in the collections *Amorum libri* (begun in 1455), *De amore coniugali, Hendecasyllabi seu Baiae* (c 1490–1500), *Eridanus* (begun 1483), and *Lepidina* (c 1496). Other poems included the *De hortis Hesperidum* (c 1500), a georgic on Naples and the cultivation of citrus fruits, the *Tumuli* (1502) or funeral epigrams, the *De laudibus divinis* or religious hymns, the *Urania* (completed in 1500) on astrology, and the *Meteora* (c 1490) on meteorology. Of his prose works the most innovative were his dialogues *Charon* (c 1469), *Antonius* (1470s), and *Asinus* (c 1487–8), which combined satire with moral teaching. His treatises on political and social virtues included *De principe* (1468) written for the future *Alfonso II of Aragon, king of Naples,

De obedientia (1472), on the proper behaviour of subjects, and five works on the use of money, written between 1490 and 1493: De liberalitate, De beneficentia, De magnificentia, De splendore, and De conviventia. In his last years (c 1498–1501) Pontano also completed his De bello neapolitano, a history of the war of Ferdinand I of Naples against Angevin claimants to his throne, and composed the philosophical treatises De fortuna and De prudentia and the dialogue Aegidius, dealing with the question of fate and the role of human reason and virtue in confronting it. Finally his tract De sermone and dialogue Actius dealt with the theories of poetic and historical writing respectively. Pontano's Opera underwent numerous publications in the sixteenth century, the most complete being the Basel edition of 1556, by Henricus Petri.

Pontano is mentioned frequently in the correspondence and works of Erasmus as a master of Ciceronian style and a standard against which Erasmus was judged. In 1527, for example, Pedro Juan *Olivar of Valencia informed Erasmus that Baldesar *Castiglione and other Italian envoys at the Spanish court maintained that the style of Erasmus was nothing compared with that of Pontano (Ep 1791). Erasmus himself was familiar with Pontano's De principe, Meteora liber, Urania, and a number of the dialogues. Although he at times expressed respect for Pontano's erudition and eloquence (Ep 1885) and the even flow and pleasing sound of his style (Ep 1479; ASD I-2 699), Erasmus was critical of the Neapolitan poet, characterizing him as one who was close to the apes of Cicero (Ep 531), and as an idol of those who valued the name 'Ciceronian' more than the name 'Christian' (Ep 1885). He also pointed to the anticlericalism and obscenities found in Pontano's dialogues, complaining that these were not attacked by critics of his own Moria (Ep 337), De pueris instituendis, and New Testament (LB IX 92E, 110F). In the Ciceronianus Erasmus praised Pontano profusely, perhaps with tongue in cheek, but suggested that he handled secular themes in such a way that one could scarcely tell whether he was a Christian or not. He noted a lack of popular appeal in Pontano's writings and denied that he was truly a Ciceronian, for he used many words not found in Cicero (ASD I-2 699–700).

BIBLIOGRAPHY: Allen Ep 337 / EI XXVII 850–3 / Giovanni Pontano I trattati delle virtù sociali ed Francesco Tateo (Rome 1965) / Vincenzo Prestipino Motivi del pensiero umanistico e Giovanni Pontano (Milan 1963) 117–220 / Mario Santoro Fortuna, ragione e prudenza nella civiltà letteraria del Cinquecento (Naples 1966) 23–65 and passim / Francesco Tateo Umanesimo etico di Giovanni Pontano (Lecce 1972) / Francesco Tateo L'umanesimo meridionale (Bari 1972) 5–62, 72–5, and passim / Felix Gilbert Machiavelli and Guicciardini (Princeton 1965) 90, 203–5, and passim / Myron P. Gilmore Humanists and Jurists (Cambridge 1963) 43–9 and passim

TBD

Gerhaus POPPENRUYTER of Nürnberg, d after 1515

Gerhaus, the sister of Erasmus' friend Johann *Poppenruyter, lived in her native Nürnberg, where she became the second wife of Wolfgang Ochsenfelder (d before 1 November 1496). In 1515 Erasmus recommended her to Willibald *Pirckheimer and Pirckheimer in return assured him that he had helped her (Epp 359, 362). Among the five children Gerhaus bore her husband was the merchant Sebald Ochsenfelder. After Johann Poppenruyter's death at Mechelen, Ochsenfelder was co-heir with his uncle, the priest Sebald Poppenruyter, who also lived in Nürnberg. On 28 January 1534 Sebald Poppenruyter ceded his share in the inheritance to his nephew.

BIBLIOGRAPHY: Otto Schottenloher in ARG 45 (1954) 115–16

PGB

Johann POPPENRUYTER of Nürnberg, c 1457–d before 24 January 1534

Johann Poppenruyter (Poppenreuter, Popparuterius) was born in Nürnberg, the son of Ulrich, a smith (d before 1488), and Elsbeth (last documented in 1501). He learnt the trade of a gunsmith and by 1498 had established a foundry of guns well known for their quality; King *Louis XII of France ordered fifty-two guns from him. By 1503 he had become senior gunsmith to Philip the Handsome, duke of *Burgundy, married Katrijn van Osseghem (Oxenen), and settled in Mechelen, where he bought a house in Old Brussels Street; additional houses were acquired in 1508, 1511, 1512, 1522, 1530, 1531, and 1532. He also owned property in Antwerp, Bergen op Zoom,

Heffen, and Liezele. In 1512 King *Henry VIII of England ordered from him twelve large guns which were named for the twelve apostles. On 16 February 1514 he became a citizen of Mechelen, and in 1515 he was appointed gunsmith to the future *Charles v with an annual salary. Albrecht *Dürer visited him in Mechelen on 7 June 1521 and made a sketch of one of his guns.

Poppenruyter's first wife, Katrijn, had died childless in 1512. His second wife, Heylwich, the daughter of Hendrik Michiel van Nieuvenhuyse, also bore him no children. She survived him, carrying on the business with the help of her second husband, Remi de Halut. Poppenruyter had, however, seven illegitimate children born between 1511 and 1521, who are mentioned in his will dated from Mechelen, 6 December 1533.

Johann Poppenruyter was no doubt the 'Johannes' to whom Erasmus in 1503 dedicated his *Enchiridion*, written, he says, at the request of Johannes' wife, who would have liked to see her husband become more devout and faithful (Epp 164, 698, 1556). Erasmus maintained a genuine friendship with the Mechelen gunsmith and his family. He visited them at Mechelen in 1515, probably on his return journey from London to Basel, and in a letter from Mechelen recommended Johann's sister, Gerhaus *Poppenruyter, to *Pirckheimer (Epp 359, 362). In his *Apologia contra Latomi dialogum* (LB IX 85 D–E) in 1519 he mentioned Poppenruyter by name as a representative of his trade. According to an earlier suggestion the *Enchiridion* and perhaps also three epigrams about an irreverent courtier may have been addressed by Erasmus to Jan de Trazegnies (Reedijk poems 58–60; Allen Ep 164; de Vocht CTL II 381).

BIBLIOGRAPHY: Allen Ep 1556 / CWE Ep 164 / de Vocht *Busleyden* 124 / NBW VII 739–43 / Otto Schottenloher 'Erasmus, Johann Poppenruyter und die Entstehung des *Enchiridion militis christiani*' ARG 45 (1954) 109–16   IG

Hervé de PORSMOGUER See Hervé de PORTZMOGUER

Leonardo de PORTIS of Vicenza,
c 1464–15 September 1545
Leonardo de Portis (da Porto, Porzio) was a jurist of Vicenza who composed *De sestertio*,

pecuniis, ponderibus et mesuris antiquis libri duo. The work was edited by Giambattista *Egnazio and published at Venice, probably in 1520. It was reprinted almost immediately by Johann *Froben at Basel, in 1524 by Francesco Giulio *Calvo at Rome, and in 1530 by Hieronymus *Froben at Basel. Since the same matters were dealt with by Guillaume *Budé in *De asse* (Paris 1515), the question of precedence and charges of plagiarism arose. Although Egnazio insisted that Portis' book had been written around 1511, Erasmus stated that the works were so similar that one could well have been based on the other (Epp 648, 1840). In *Adagia* v ii 16 he suggested that Janus *Lascaris had been called upon to judge the matter.

BIBLIOGRAPHY: Allen and CWE Ep 648 / Louis Delaruelle *Répertoire ... de la correspondance de Guillaume Budé* (Toulouse-Paris 1907, repr n d) Epp 19, 24, 163 / Roberto Weiss *The Renaissance Discovery of Classical Antiquity* (Oxford 1969) 176–7   TBD

Hervé de PORTZMOGUER d 10 August 1512
Hervé de Portzmoguer (Herveus, Porsmoguer) has become a legendary figure of Breton history, but despite the wealth of literature on his account, very little information is available about him. His very name has been twisted to the point of calling him 'Primauguet,' which was the official French version prior to the studies of Auguste Jal. There is good reason to believe that he was a member of the family of Portzmoguer (*portus-maceria*: port-wall or rampart) mentioned among the noble houses of Brittany from 1446 and disappearing only in the nineteenth century. Two different branches of this family lived in the neighbouring parishes of Plouarzel and Ploumoguer, in the diocese of Léon. Both villages still exist, and the name of Porsmoguer is still used for a small bay to the north of Pointe Saint-Mathieu, the most westerly point of Brittany.

Hervé is documented as the commander of the vessel *Marie-la-Cordelière*, a carrack that had been built at Morlaix for Queen Anne of Brittany, who presented it to *Louis XII of France on the occasion of their wedding (January 1499). Originally the ship's name was just *Marie*, but in witness of her devotion to St Francis Queen Anne added *La Cordelière* (in Latin *Chordigera*). The queen was particularly fond of the big ship; according to the chronicler

Alain Bouchard it had cost her 'un gros argent,' and when she went to Brest she marvelled at the *Cordelière* and visited her twice.

It is not known whether Hervé was a sea captain or rather an army officer in command of the *Cordelière*. The naval engagement of 10 August 1512 in which the ship was involved has been described with passionate enthusiasm both by French and English chroniclers. According to their accounts an English squadron was observed in the vicinity of Saint-Mathieu and Portzmoguer attacked without awaiting further orders. As a result of his courageous and perhaps rash initiative the *Cordelière* engaged two English vessels at the same time, the *Sovereign*, under the command of Charles *Brandon, the future duke of Suffolk, which lost a mast and had to withdraw, and the *Regent*, commanded by Thomas Knyvet. The *Regent* and the *Cordelière* came into contact and amid the hand-to-hand fighting both caught fire and sank, with the loss of more than eleven hundred men including Portzmoguer. According to a tradition which is definitely not historical, Portzmoguer was giving a ball aboard the *Cordelière* when the English squadron appeared and he rushed out to sea to meet them, so that the fair ladies came to share the glorious end of their cavaliers.

Germain de *Brie commemorated the event in a poem, *Chordigerae navis conflagratio* (Paris: J. Bade 1513), which led to his appointment as secretary to Queen Anne but also brought about a quarrel with Thomas *More and a casual reference to Portzmoguer in one of More's letters to Erasmus (Ep 1087). Another commemorative epic is Humbert de Montmoret's *Herveis* (Paris: H. Le Fevre n d; copy in Paris, Bibliothèque Nationale).

BIBLIOGRAPHY: Allen Ep 1087 / August Jal *Dictionnaire critique de biographie et d'histoire* (Paris 1872, repr 1970) II 992–4 / Prosper-Jean Levot *Biographie bretonne* (Vannes-Paris 1852–7) II 648–50 / More Y III-2 434 passim / François Rabelais *Le Quart Livre* ch 21

GEORGES KOUSKOFF

Leonardo PORZIO *See Leonardo de* PORTIS

William POTKYN documented 1492–1538
The first record of William Potkyn (Potkinus) as a notary public dates from a visitation of

Merton Priory on 16 November 1492, and although he continued to serve both archbishops *Warham and *Cranmer in the capacity of notary public until 1538, only fragmentary references to his activities have survived. He is mentioned in 1511 as the notary in the proceedings against William Carter and in 1520 as the person purchasing the advowson of certain benefices, while in 1524 his name appears in the subsidy of the archbishopric of Canterbury. Occasional letters to and from the archbishops of Canterbury also refer to Potkyn as one in charge of various official deeds. In 1522 we also find Potkyn, then proctor of the Court of Arches, presenting the Doctors' Commons with a gilt salt-cellar in memory of his brother Peter. In 1537 Potkyn was licensed to practise as a notary and a tabellion, while on 20 October 1538 he received a dispensation to hold a benefice. He must have either resigned as notary public shortly afterwards or died, for by 1538 that office had been filled by Anthony Hues.

Potkyn seems to have kept the account of Erasmus' Aldington annuity, for Erasmus complained both to Thomas *Bedyll and to Warham of Potkyn's allegation that his receipts were incorrect (Epp 782, 892, 893; CWE Ep 823 introduction). In 1524 he is mentioned again as having just transferred ten pounds to Erasmus (Ep 1488).

BIBLIOGRAPHY: Allen and CWE Ep 782 / A. Heales *The Records of Merton Priory* (London 1898) 309 / LP I 438 (p 256), III 1030, IV 639, 1263, 3176, VI 311 737(7), 783, 881, 1315, 1341, XII-2 703 (iii), addenda 574 / *The Acts and Monuments of John Foxe* ed G. Townsend (London 1847) V 649 / *Faculty Office Registers, 1534–49* ed D.S. Chambers (Oxford 1966) 92, 152/ G.D. Squibb *Doctors' Commons* (Oxford 1977) 81, 130 / *Miscellaneous Writings and Letters of Thomas Cranmer* ed J.E. Cox (Cambridge 1846) 249, 254, 264, 265, 348 / I.J. Churchill *Canterbury Administration* (London 1933) I 25, 181, 191 / C. Jenkins 'Cardinal Morton's Register' *Tudor Studies* ed R.W. Seton-Watson (London 1924) 27–8   MORDECHAI FEINGOLD

Lieven van POTTELSBERGHE d 29 July 1531
Lieven van Pottelsberghe (Pottelsberge, Pottelbergius) was the son of another Lieven and Livine Snibbels. A knight and lord of Vinder-

houte, Merendree, Wissenkerke, etc, he spent
most of his life in Ghent, where he also died.
His wife, Livine van Steelant, bore him three
sons and a daughter. One of his sons was
recommended in 1512 for the award of a
benefice; this recommendation came from
*Maximilian I and indicates the emperor's
appreciation of Lieven's services. He was
secretary of the city of Ghent and from 1507 to
1508 receiver-general for subsidies and the
county of Flanders. In 1514 he was a member of
the council of Flanders and later was appointed privy councillor and master of requests. He
was a patron of the arts, and his portrait by
Gerard Hoorenbout is in the Museum voor
Schone Kunsten, Ghent.

In Ep 751 Erasmus referred to his personal
acquaintance with Pottelsberghe at the time of
his appointment to a canonry at Courtrai
(1516); Pottelsberghe seems to have been of
service to Erasmus, who resigned the prebend
in exchange for an annuity.

BIBLIOGRAPHY: Allen Ep 751 / BNB XVIII 82–4 /
Herbert Kreiten in *Archiv für österreichische
Geschichte* 96 (1907–8) 242, 276 / A. van der
Veegaete in *Hand Maatschappij van Geschiedenis
der Oudheid … Gent* 3 (1948) 93–103 / *Monasticon
Fratrum Vitae Communis* I : *Belgien und Nord-
frankreich* ed W. Leesch et al (Brussels 1977)
addenda / P. van Peteghem 'Centralisatie in
Vlaanderen onder Keizer Karel (1515–1555)'
(doctoral thesis, Rijksuniversiteit Gent,
1980) MARCEL A. NAUWELAERTS & PGB

**Jozine and Lodewijk van PRAAT or PRAET, a
PRATO** *See Louis of* FLANDERS

Jacobus PRAEPOSITUS *See Jacob* PROOST

Nicolaus PRAEPOSITUS Edanus (Ep 1054 of
19 December 1519)
The name of Nicolaus Praepositus Edanus, to
whom Erasmus' letter is addressed, has not
been found elsewhere. P.S. Allen tentatively
suggested identifying him with Jacob *Proost;
see also CWE Ep 1054.

Wolfgang PRANTNER *See Wolfgang*
BRANTNER

PRATENSIS *See Etienne* DESPREZ, FELICE *da
Prato*

Lieven van Pottelsberghe, by Gerard Hourenbout

Kilian PRAUS documented 1522–5
Little is known about Kilian Praus (Chilianus,
or Clemens, Πρᾶος, Braxatoris [=brewer, in
German *Brauer*]). For several years he was a
monk of the Benedictine abbey of St Georgen-
berg, near Schwaz in the Tirol, but he cannot
be traced in the surviving records of this abbey,
which has suffered considerable damage over
the years. Praus was apparently already
known to Erasmus when he set out from his
monastery at the beginning of May 1522 in
order to obtain a degree in theology. He carried
a letter of recommendation to Erasmus from his
abbot, Leonhard *Müller, explaining that the
house was too poor to provide proper support
for Praus (Ep 1279). He travelled in the
company of his kinsman Simon *Schaidenreisser, and after visiting Johann von *Botzheim at
Constance (Ep 1285) both matriculated at the
University of Basel.

In the first place it was *Beatus Rhenanus
who seems to have taken a warm interest in
Kilian, helping him to obtain his BA and make
further plans for study (BRE Ep 419). Presumably with his recommendation, in 1523 Praus
moved from Basel to Sélestat (BRE Epp 418–19),

where he may have been working for a printer. Having met *Hutten and Heinrich *Eppendorf at Basel, he soon had to defend himself against Erasmus' suspicions that he was siding with these former friends turned opponents (Ep 1449). There is no reason, however, to doubt his sincere admiration for Erasmus, and P.S. Allen suggested that he might be identical with an unnamed supporter willing to take Erasmus' side against Otto *Brunfels (Ep 1614).

At the height of the peasant war and religious unrest Praus left Sélestat for Strasbourg, where he had settled by August 1525. Failing to find work with the printers, he had accepted Eppendorf's hospitality and devoted himself to the study of Greek (BRE Ep 239). No more is known about him thereafter.

Kilian is not a common name; it may be noted that Schaidenreisser is found next to a Kilian not only in the matriculation register of Basel but also in that of Wittenberg. In the winter term of 1515 the registrant immediately ahead of Schaidenreisser is one Kilian Schultz of Jessen, on the river Elster east of Dessau in Saxony. The name Brauer-Braxatoris occurs frequently in that region at the time; the name Prauss is found too. Moreover, Schaidenreisser came from that same region. If Praus were Schultz, the student at Wittenberg, his first acquaintance with Erasmus could conceivably be dated from a joint visit of Schaidenreisser and Praus to Erasmus in about 1515–16, since Praus might be the 'theologus' mentioned in Ep 482.

BIBLIOGRAPHY: *Matrikel Basel* I 351 / *Matrikel Wittenberg* I 59   PGB

Ludwig PRAYTTER documented in 1531
'Praytter' is Johann *Löble's spelling (Ep 2497) of the name of the steward of the 'Heilig Kreuz' estate, near Colmar in Upper Alsace, that formerly belonged to Jakob *Villinger. It seems that Praytter also managed the other Villinger properties in the region of the Upper Rhine, including the house 'zum Walfisch' at Freiburg (Ep 2505). A Ludwig Breithar of Strasbourg was registered at the University of Basel in 1460–1 (*Matrikel Basel* I 15)   PGB

Georgius PRECELLIUS (Ep 398 of 5 April 1516)
Georgius Precellius of Ulm wrote to Erasmus

from that city, where he was perhaps a parish priest. He is probably identical with one Georg Precellius who in 1505 was a priest of modest rank (*Frühmesser*) in Albeck and in 1531 priest of Radelstetten; both towns are located in the territory of Ulm. A Georg Pratzel or Bratzel of Eisensheim, near Gerolzhofen, in the diocese of Würzburg, matriculated at the University of Heidelberg in 1496 and was a MA in 1499.

BIBLIOGRAPHY: Allen Ep 398 / Albrecht Weyermann *Neue historisch-biographisch-artistische Nachrichten von Gelehrten und Künstlern ... aus Ulm* (Ulm 1829) 394 / *Matrikel Heidelberg* I 420, II 425 / We wish to acknowledge the assistance of Dr Hans Eugen Specker, Stadtarchivdirektor, Ulm.   PGB

Friedrich PRECHTER of Strasbourg, documented 1485–before 1546
Friedrich Prechter (Brechter) was a member of one of the two major business and banking families in Strasbourg. His father, Johann, moved from Haguenau to Strasbourg in 1473. Friedrich himself purchased his citizenship in 1485. The Prechters, who were involved in large-scale financial investment and in Europe-wide commerce, were second only to the Ingolts in the production of paper in Strasbourg and in the Alsatian paper trade. Friedrich Prechter furnished paper to Anton Koberger from 1494 to 1527, as well as to the press of Johann *Amerbach in Basel. He also was a major business partner of the *Fugger banking house (Ep 2808). In 1536 Johann (II) *Paumgartner instructed Bonifacius *Amerbach to send him by way of Prechter a copy of each of Erasmus' works and of his will. Prechter's son, also Friedrich, was a member of the Strasbourg city council. He died in 1528, predeceasing his father, whose death is first mentioned in a lawsuit in 1546.

BIBLIOGRAPHY: AK I Ep 140, IV Ep 2066 / François Joseph Fuchs 'Les Prechter de Strasbourg, une famille de négociants banquiers du XVIe siècle' *Revue d'Alsace* 95 (1956) 146–94 / Grimm *Buchführer* 1435 / Oscar von Hase *Die Koberger* 3rd ed (Amsterdam-Wiesbaden 1967) 67–70 and Ep 42 / A. Schulte *Die Fugger in Rom, 1495–1523* (Leipzig 1904) II 221 and passim / Götz von Pölnitz *Anton Fugger* (Tübingen 1958–) I 68, 396–7, and passim
MIRIAM U. CHRISMAN

PRETIOANNES, PRESTER JOHN See LEBNA
DENGAL, *emperor of Ethiopia*

Leonardus PRICCARDUS d 18 April 1541
The origins of Priccardus (Pricard, Prickert,
Prycker) are not clear. Hashagen and de Vocht
suggest that he may have been a relative of
'Reyn. Prijcardus Aquensis' (ie 'of Aachen'),
who matriculated at the University of Cologne
in 1495.

On 24–7 July 1485 and in 1486 Priccardus –
then an apprentice barber – participated in the
staging of religious plays in Metz. Impressed
by the youth's performance, Canon Jean
Chandelly took charge of Priccardus, sending
him to the local Latin school and later to the
University of Paris, where he earned a BA in
1492 and a MA in 1493. When he returned to
Metz Priccardus became a teacher at the school
of Saint-Sauveur. On 17 September 1506 he
received a canonry at St Mary's in Aachen after
papal nomination. It is not known when he
obtained a benefice in the diocese of Liège and
when he secured a canonry at St Adalbert's in
Aachen. A benefice that he held at the parish
church of Körrenzig, near Erkelenz, between
Aachen and Mönchengladbach, within the
collation of St Adalbert's chapter, is mentioned
on 28 June 1533 Priccardus continued to live in
Aachen, where he died.

Late in 1525 we find Priccardus visiting the
court of Duke John III of *Cleves, in the
company of the vice-provost of St Mary's,
Werner *Huyn van Amstenrade. The two
canons sought the duke's support for the
chapter in its litigation with the city council of
Aachen. Priccardus may not have been very
prosperous; having borrowed money from his
friend Jérôme de *Busleyden he was unable to
pay back the entire sum after Busleyden's
death.

Priccardus was an important, perhaps the
central, figure among the group of Aachen
Erasmians formed by his fellow canons Johann
von *Vlatten, Werner Huyn, Johann *Schoenraid, Johann *Sudermann, and Aegidius *Ha-
sebart. He was, moreover, acquainted with
other Rhenish humanists such as Konrad von
*Heresbach, and Busleyden dedicated a qua-
train to him.

Erasmus met Priccardus in Aachen in September 1518 (Ep 867) and stayed at his house

during a second visit to Aachen late in 1520. He
praised his host warmly in Ep 1169. Priccardus'
only extant letter to Erasmus (Ep 972) is an
eloquent testimony to a friendship based on
humanistic values and informed Erasmus that
word about Edward *Lee's critique of the New
Testament had reached Aachen. In response
Erasmus defended himself against his detractors (Ep 993). In a subsequent letter to
Priccardus (Ep 1170) Erasmus went to great
lengths to try to explain away his ambiguous
comments on the Aachen canons made in Ep
867 and extended greetings to all of Priccardus'
colleagues, especially to Vlatten. It seems that
the correspondence between the two humanist
friends continued after 1520, although no more
letters have survived. A mark of Erasmus'
esteem for Priccardus may be found in the
colloquy *Convivium poeticum* of 1523, where he
is probably portrayed as 'Leonardus' (ASD I-3
344). In the dedication to Vlatten of his edition
of Cicero's *Tusculanae quaestiones* of the same
year he praised Priccardus' knowledge of the
classics and his experience in many fields (Ep
1390). The last we hear of their friendship is
that in 1529 Erasmus sent the Aachen canon a
copy of his edition of Lactantius' *De opificio* (Ep
2130).

Latin verses inscribed on a church bell
installed in Aachen in 1535 and fragments of a
manuscript on the origin of the famous Aachen
relics, both the work of Priccardus, are
mentioned in a seventeenth-century chronicle
of Aachen.

BIBLIOGRAPHY: Allen Ep 972 / *Matrikel Köln* II
369 / de Vocht *Busleyden* 255–6 / *Auctarium
chartularii universitatis Parisiensis* ed Charles
Samaran et al (Paris 1894–1964) VI 703, 723, 725
/ Anton Gail 'Johann von Vlatten und der
Einfluss des Erasmus auf die Kirchenpolitik
der Vereinigten Herzogtümer' *Düsseldorfer
Jahrbuch* 45 (1951) 12, 30–1 / Justus Hashagen
'Hauptrichtungen des rheinischen Humanis-
mus' *Annalen des Historischen Vereins für den
Niederrhein* 106 (1922) 25 / *Nomina admodum
reverendorum perillustrium atque generosorum
dominorum canonicorum regalis ecclesiae B.M.V.
Aquisgranensis* ed Antonius Heusch (Berlin
1892) 13, 16 / *Des Peter à Beeck … Aquisgranum
oder Geschichte der Stadt Aachen* ed and trans
Peter S. Käntzeler (Aachen 1874) 81–2, 259 /
'Freundesbriefe Conrads von Heresbach an

Johann von Vlatten (1524–36)' ed Otto R. Redlich *Zeitschrift des Bergischen Geschichtsvereins* 41 (1905) 170 / Eduard Teichmann 'Ein Aachener als Darsteller der Titelrolle in zwei Metzer Mysterien' *Zeitschrift des Aachener Geschichtsvereins* 20 (1898) 295–8

KASPAR VON GREYERZ

René de PRIE 1451–9 September 1519
The son of Antoine de Prie, baron of Buzançais, and Madeleine d'Amboise, a cousin of Cardinal Georges (I) d'*Amboise, René owed his advancement to the latter. Appointed bishop of Bayeux on 3 August 1498, he was a signatory of the treaty of Etaples and a witness at *Louis XII's marriage in 1499. Created a cardinal on 18 December 1506, René became known generally as the cardinal of Bayeux. He was present with Louis XII at the Savona meeting in 1507 and went to Rome in October 1509, but he took fright after *Julius II's imprisonment of Cardinal François de Clermont in June 1510 and barricaded himself in his palace. Instead of joining Julius II at Bologna in October he accompanied Cardinal Guillaume (I) *Briçonnet to Milan, taking part in the schismatic council which met at Pisa. He was deprived of his benefices by the pope on 24 October 1511, as Andrea *Ammonio reported to Erasmus in a letter of 28 November (Ep 247). According to the Florentine Francesco Pandolfini in a letter of 5 March 1512, a majority of the rebel cardinals wanted René to be antipope, but Louis XII favoured Cardinal Bernardino López de *Carvajal. After his reinstatement by *Leo X René was restored to the bishopric of Limoges on 18 August 1514 (having first been nominated in 1510) and presided at the marriage of Louis XII and *Mary Tudor. He died on 9 September 1519 and was buried at Notre-Dame-de-Lyre (Evreux), of which, among other monastic houses, he was titular abbot.

BIBLIOGRAPHY: Allen and CWE Ep 247 (incorrectly giving his name as René de Brie) / Eubel II 101, III 11, 127, 222 / Pastor VI 264, 285, and passim / Sanudo *Diarii* VI 517 and passim / Renaudet *Préréforme* 544, 551–6 / Augustin Renaudet *Le Concile gallican de Pise-Milan* (Paris 1922) 2, 638, and passim

D.S. CHAMBERS

Silvester PRIERIAS c 1456–1523
Silvestro Mazzolini is known more commonly as Prierias (Prieras), so called after his birthplace, Priero in Piedmont. Of unknown parentage, Prierias entered the Dominican order at Genoa at the age of fifteen (c 1471) and was ordained a priest in about 1479. From 1491 to 1508 he served as a prior in the Dominican houses of Milan, Verona, and Genoa and as professor of logic at Bologna (1499) and of metaphysics at Padua (1501). In 1508 he was elected vicar-general of his order in the province of Lombardy, and he held this post until 1510, when he became prior of the house at Bologna. He also served as inquisitor at Brescia from 1508 to 1511, when he took up the same post in Milan. In 1513 he became prior at Cremona. In the summer of 1514 Prierias was appointed professor of Thomistic theology at Rome, an office which he held for the rest of his life. *Leo X also named him master of the sacred palace on 15 December 1515 on the recommendation of the Dominican master-general, *Cajetanus. As the pope's theologian and Rome's censor of books, Prierias was called on to give an opinion in the *Reuchlin affair in 1516. His stand against Reuchlin earned him much hatred among German humanists.

Again in his role as censor, Prierias concerned himself with *Luther's theses on indulgences of 1517. In June 1518 he was appointed theological examiner for the case, whereupon he immediately became Luther's first Italian literary opponent, publishing *In praesumptuosas Martini Lutheri conclusiones de potestate papae dialogus* [Rome: E. Silber June 1518]. Luther's scornful reply of 1518, *Ad dialogum Silvestri Prieratis de potestate papae responsio* (Luther W I 644–86, IX 782–7), called forth three more polemical works from Prierias before his death in Rome early in 1523: *Replica F. Silvestri Prieratis Sacri Palatii ap. magister ad F. Martinum Luther*, written in October 1518, published by Luther (Leipzig: M. Landsberg January 1519, repr in Luther W II 48–56); *Epithoma responsionis ad M. Luther* (Perugia: n pr 1519, repr in Luther W VI 325–48); and *Errata et argumenta M. Lutheri recitata, detecta, repulsa et copiosissime trita* (Rome: n pr 1520).

Prierias earned the contempt of Erasmus by his first polemical work against Luther. In

October 1518 Erasmus described this work as ill-judged (Ep 872) and in 1520 he reported that Prierias' work was disliked by all (Ep 1167). Prierias spoke as immoderately as Luther on the subjects of indulgences (Ep 1033) and the papal primacy (Ep 1275). According to Erasmus, so inept was Prierias' defence of the papal primacy that the pope himself silenced him (Epp 1581, 1909; there is good reason to doubt this claim). But Prierias' bad Latin and weak argumentation were not the only reasons for Erasmus' disapproval. He also felt that Prierias' clumsy attempts to refute Luther were only serving to widen the rift (*Apologia adversus rhapsodias Alberti Pii* LB IX 1119D). His stupid and overly hasty reply to Luther had stirred up a hornets' nest (*Apologia adversus Petrum Sutorem* LB IX 789E) and added fuel to the fire (*Apologia adversus rhapsodias Alberti Pii* LB IX 1141E). Prierias did not reciprocate Erasmus' contempt and disdain. Wishing perhaps to enlist Erasmus' support against Luther, Prierias wrote a friendly letter to Erasmus inviting him to Rome (referred to in Ep 1342). Erasmus wrote to Prierias c 19 January 1523 assuring him that he would never defect to the Lutheran side (Ep 1412). It is unlikely that Prierias received this letter before his death early in 1523.

Prierias' most popular work was the *Summa summarum quae Silvestrina dicitur* (Bologna: n pr 1514), a manual for confessors. Other non-polemical works include the *Rosa aurea* (Bologna: n pr 1503), which was made up of expositions on the Gospels for the whole year, and his *Malleum in falsas assumptiones Scoti contra divum Thomam in primo Sententiarum* (Bologna: n pr 1514).

BIBLIOGRAPHY: Allen and CWE Ep 872 / LThK VIII 735 / J. Quetif and J. Echard *Scriptores ordinis praedicatorum* (Paris 1721) II 55–8 / F. Lauchert *Die italienischen literarischen Gegner Luthers* (Freiburg 1912) 7–30 / Pastor VII 363–7 and passim / H. Oberman 'Wittenbergs Zweifrontenkrieg gegen Prierias und Eck' *Zeitschrift für Kirchengeschichte* 80 (1969) 331–58 / Joseph N. Scionti 'Sylvester Prierias and his opposition to Martin Luther' (doctoral thesis, Brown University 1967) / Carter Lindberg 'Prierias and his significance for Luther's development' *The Sixteenth Century Journal* 3 no 2 (1972) 45–64 /

Thomas N. Tentler *Sin and Confession on the Eve of the Reformation* (Princeton 1977) 32, 34–7, and passim

DENIS R. JANZ

Jacob PROOST of Ieper, 1486–30 June 1562
Jacob Proost (Probst, Praepositus) of Ieper (Ypres), in West Flanders, had apparently become a member of the Saxon congregation of the Austin friars and, at a date unknown, had been taught by Martin *Luther (Ep 980). With other members of the Saxon congregation he entered the Antwerp house of his order founded in 1513 and in 1518 became prior; however he returned to Wittenberg at some point after May 1519 (Ep 980). He continued the study of theology and received his licence in 1521. On his return to Antwerp he began to preach the teachings of Luther but was compelled to recant in public on 9 February 1522. He left his convent and again went to Wittenberg, where he married a young woman from Luther's household. In May 1524 he was called to Bremen as a minister, and from 1534 to 1559 he was the superintendent. He died in Bremen. He was a friend of *Lefèvre d'Etaples and also corresponded for some years with *Melanchthon.

Erasmus evidently knew Proost. In May 1519 he described him to Luther as a 'genuine Christian,' a great admirer of the Saxon friar, and almost the only priest of his acquaintance 'who preaches Christ' (Ep 980). Early in 1522 when he heard that the Inquisition had moved Proost from Antwerp to Brussels, he was eager to learn of his fate (Epp 1254, 1256, 1258). In 1529 his opponent Frans *Titelmans reminded him discreetly of his earlier sympathy for the 'heretic' (Ep 2245).

BIBLIOGRAPHY: Allen Ep 980 / BNB XVIII 282–6 / A. de Decker *Les Augustins d'Anvers* (Ghent 1884) / H. de Jongh *L'Ancienne Faculté de théologie de Louvain* (Louvain 1911) 194 / de Vocht CTL I 426–7 and passim / Floris Prims *Geschiedenis van Antwerpen* (Brussels-Antwerp 1927–49) XVIII 188–9, 288 / P. Fredericq *Corpus documentorum inquisitionis haereticae pravitatis neerlandicae* (Ghent 1889–1902) IV passim / Schottenloher II 154

MARCEL A. NAUWELAERTS

Antonio PUCCI of Florence, 1484/5–
12 October 1544

A gifted son of the pro-Medici Florentines
Alessandro Pucci and Sibilla di Tommaso
Sassetti and a nephew of Cardinal Lorenzo
*Pucci, Antonio obtained doctorates in both
philosophy and theology at the University of
Pisa. At fourteen he became a canon of
Florence's cathedral. His distinguished public
exposition of Scripture and his uncle's patronage brought him to the papal court, where he
became a protonotary and a canon of St Peter's.
On 5 May 1514 he preached the sermon at the
opening of the ninth session of the fifth
Lateran council and in spite of being a clerk of
the apostolic camera he stressed the need for
reform. In November 1518 he succeeded his
uncle as bishop of Pistoia, in October 1529 as
major penitentiary, and in September 1531 as
cardinal, being referred to in Erasmus' correspondence by his title of Santi Quattro
Coronati. He was translated to Santa Maria in
Trastevere in 1541 and raised to cardinal
bishop of Albano in 1542 and of Sabina in 1543.

Successive popes sent Pucci on missions to
Switzerland, France, and Spain. In August
1517 he replaced Ennio *Filonardi, nuncio of
*Leo x in Switzerland, taking with him from
Rome his uncle's secretary, Paolo *Bombace
(Ep 729). Erasmus asked Pucci for assistance in
obtaining a commendatory brief from the pope
for his revised edition of the New Testament,
published at *Froben's press in Basel in 1519
(Ep 860; see also Epp 864, 865; LB IX 751D–E).
Pucci himself visited Erasmus at the press (Ep
855) – a mark of honour occasioned by
Erasmus' illness (Ep 852) – and bought a copy
of Jerome (BRE Epp 88, 116). Although in
dedicating his edition of Cyprian to Lorenzo
Pucci Erasmus expressed gratitude to Antonio
(Ep 1000), he wrote severely of Antonio to
Nicolaas *Everaerts in an outburst of criticism
of those entrusted with dealing with Martin
*Luther (Ep 1188). Since Pucci was in Zürich in
1518, he would be the papal legate whom
Jacobus *Nepos assumed to be the target of the
dialogue *Henno rusticus* (z VII Ep 148), but the
person in question could have been Leo's
commissioner for indulgences, Giovanni Angelo Arcimboldi. Presumably with reference to
Pucci's recruiting campaign for Swiss merce-

naries in 1521, *Zwingli wrote that no one felt
safe when this Roman harlot ('Glycera') was
around (z VII Ep 176 1521). In April Pucci led six
thousand Swiss troops to Italy for Leo's
anti-French offensive. *Clement VII twice sent
Pucci to France (March 1525, autumn of 1528),
the second occasion being preceded by a short
nunciature in Spain (summer of 1528). After
being a hostage for Clement VII after the Sack of
Rome in 1527, he accompanied him to Bologna
in 1530 for *Charles v's coronation.

During the pontificate of *Paul III the Pucci
connection with the Medici was especially
evident. Erasmus heard a rumour associating
Antonio with the sudden death in August 1535
of Ippolito de' *Medici (Ep 3059) for which his
bitter rival, Alessandro de' *Medici, duke of
Florence, was held responsible. The rumour is
understandable: Pucci was in Florence during
that summer (Ep 3047), and the pope's choice
of him as his legate at Alessandro's wedding
ten months later indicates his acceptability to
the duke. His successor, Duke Cosimo, resort-
ed to Pucci as cardinal penitentiary for
concessions from the pope. Pucci stubbornly
resisted the reform of that office, not fully
accomplished until after his death. As desired,
he was buried near the Medici pope Clement
VII in Santa Maria sopra Minerva, Rome.

Wolfgang *Capito dedicated to Pucci a
translation of a homily of Chrysostom (Basel:
A. Cratander October 1519) and Urbanus
*Rhegius eulogized Antonio and his uncle
Lorenzo in his *De dignitate sacerdotum* (Augs-
burg: J. Miller 1519). Antonio himself wrote
fourteen eucharistic homilies (Bologna: A.
Giacarelli 1551). He also wrote Latin couplets
to commemorate the visit of Paul III to the Villa
Igno in the diocese of Pistoia.

BIBLIOGRAPHY: Allen Ep 860 / A. Ciaconius
*Vita et res gestae Pontificum Romanorum et S.R.E.
Cardinalium* (Rome 1677) III 522–3 / P. Litta
Famiglie celebri italiane (Milan 1819–85) x table vi
/ A.F. Verde *Lo studio fiorentino* (Florence-
Pistoia 1973–   ) III-1 / C.-J. Hefele *Histoire des
conciles* (Paris 1907–21) VIII-1 429–30 / Letters
regarding Pucci's Swiss mission are in *Archivio
storico italiano* 3rd ser, 20, 21 (1874–5) / A.
Pieper *Zur Entstehungsgeschichte der ständigen
Nuntiaturen* (Freiburg 1894) / A. D'Addario
Aspetti della controriforma a Firenze (Rome 1972)

84, 86, 468 / A. Rosati *Memorie per servire alla storia de' vescovi di Pistoia* (Pistoia 1766) / Pastor x 10 and passim, xi 7, 195, and passim / B. Varchi *Storia fiorentina* ed L. Arbib (Florence 1838–41) iii 336 / F. Vettori 'Sommario' in *Scritti storici e politici* ed E. Niccolini (Bari 1972) 190

ROSEMARY DEVONSHIRE JONES

Lorenzo PUCCI of Florence,
1458–16 September 1531
Pucci was a son of the Florentines Antonio Pucci and Maddalena di Giramonte Gini; his stepmother was Piera, a daughter of Gianozzo Manetti, and his brother Puccio was a jurist who married Girolama Farnese, a sister of Alessandro (later *Paul iii). From 1474 Lorenzo studied law at the University of Pisa and lectured on the Institutes in 1478–9. By April 1484 he was in Rome and wrote to Lorenzo (i) de' *Medici asking for his support in an attempt to buy an office as auditor of the papal camera; in 1488 he is recorded as an apostolic protonotary and *cubicularius* and in 1497 as an abbreviator in the papal chancery. Correspondence in 1493 reveals him in the midst of the Borgia court, convinced that Giulia Farnese's daughter resembled Pope *Alexander vi. His career in the papal camera continued under *Julius ii; he was one of its clerks in 1509 when Erasmus visited Rome, and he held the office of datary from March 1511 until September 1513. In July 1512 Julius ii sent him to Florence to try to detach the republic from its French alliance.

Under *Leo x Lorenzo rose rapidly; he was appointed bishop of Melfi on 12 August 1513 and was the first cardinal to be appointed by the new pope, on 29 September of the same year. He was thereafter commonly known by his title of Santi Quattro Coronati. Much favoured, he lived in the papal palace at the Vatican, along with cardinals Bernardo Dovizi da Bibbiena and Giulio de' Medici, the future *Clement vii. He was appointed in 1513 to a subcommittee which was to consider reform of the central offices of the curia and is thought to have obstructed any proposals for change. In November 1517 he was appointed to the commission considering the organization of a crusade, and on 28 September 1520 he became cardinal penitentiary, an office which he held until October 1529 and which made him

responsible for the controversial sale of indulgences (according to Paolo Giovio he declared that nothing sold by the pope could be illegitimate). He was nevertheless entrusted with drafting reform proposals for the penitentiary in November 1524. During the Sack of Rome in May 1527 he managed to take refuge in Castel Sant'Angelo in spite of having been thrown from his horse. Lorenzo accompanied Clement vii to Orvieto; there, in December 1527 and March 1528, and subsequently in Rome, he dealt in his capacity of penitentiary with successive embassies from *Henry viii over the matter of the king's divorce, taking a rigorous attitude. Erasmus noted his death in Ep 2628.

Overlooking Lorenzo's dubious reputation, Erasmus cultivated him as a patron, thanks to the good offices of his nephew Antonio *Pucci and of Paolo *Bombace, who was a member of his household and prevailed upon his master to secure papal approval for the second edition of Erasmus' New Testament (Epp 865, 905). In return Erasmus dedicated to him his edition of Cyprian (Ep 1000), and in June 1521 he was informed by Bombace that Lorenzo had delivered a letter from himself to Leo x (Ep 1213). Thereafter Erasmus sent his greetings to Lorenzo through Bombace (Epp 1236, 1411) and expressed pleasure at the continued favour shown him by Pucci (Epp 1213, 1631); but he complained to *Botzheim in 1523 that Lorenzo had not given him any money for the dedication of Cyprian (Allen i 43).

There is a portrait of Lorenzo by Sebastiano del Piombo in the Haus, Hof- und Staatsarchiv in Vienna.

BIBLIOGRAPHY: There appears to be no biographical article available, much less a monograph. For the earlier part of Lorenzo's career see A.F. Verde *Lo studio fiorentino* (Florence-Pistoia 1973–) ii 438–43, iii-1 572–3; J. Burchardus *Liber notarum* ed E. Celani (Città di Castello 1906–59) passim; LP iv passim; G.B. Picotti 'Per le relazioni fra Alessandro vi e Piero de' Medici' *Archivio storico italiano* 73 (1915) 37–100 / For the later part and in general see Creighton, Eubel, Pastor, Sanudo, Paris de Grassis and other sources noted under Leo x; also W. von Hofmann *Forschungen zur Geschichte der kurialen*

Behörden (Rome 1914) 97–8, 102; E. Göller *Die päpstliche Pönitentarie* (Rome 1911) II 111; H. Jedin *A History of the Council of Trent* trans E. Graf (New York 1957–   ) I 131

D.S. CHAMBERS

Philipp PUCHAIMER documented 1528–36
The origins of Philipp Puchaimer (Buchammer) remain obscure so far, and so does the end of his life. He may perhaps be identical with one 'Philippus Buchhaimer ex Wardea' (one of several towns named Wörth) who matriculated at Vienna on 16 August 1510. He is not reliably documented until 16 October 1528, when Johannes *Cochlaeus wrote to Fridericus *Nausea from Aschaffenburg asking him to send Puchaimer a Pliny. On the following day Puchaimer himself wrote to Nausea, repeating the request amid expressions of support for the cause of humanistic letters. Not long thereafter he wrote again to acknowledge receipt of the book and to offer Nausea his friendship and the use of his own library.

On 21 August 1529 Johann *Sichard dedicated to Puchaimer his edition of Caelius Aurelianus' *Tardarum passionum libri v* and other medical texts (Basel: H. Petri 1529), thanking Puchaimer for his assistance. Sichard referred to him as the physician of Albert of *Brandenburg, archbishop of Mainz. It seems likely that he already held this position the preceding year when he wrote to Nausea from Aschaffenburg, where Albert resided. *Beatus Rhenanus met him in 1530 at Augsburg, probably during the diet. On 2 March 1531 he received from Puchaimer Etienne de L'Aigue's commentary on Pliny the Elder (Paris 1530). His answer (dated 3 March; BRE Ep 274) contains a description of the splendours of Anton *Fugger's house at Augsburg, where he had been introduced by Puchaimer. It was published as an appendix to Beatus Rhenanus' *Res Germanicae* (Basel: H. Froben 1531). Erasmus referred to this description when writing to Fugger a year later (Ep 2476). On 20 September 1535 Johann *Huttich wrote to Beatus Rhenanus (BRE Ep 292) asking him to use his influence with Puchaimer in favour of Jakob *Ziegler, who wished to retire to Mainz. On 6 November 1536, when Georgius *Sabinus married *Melanchthon's daughter at Wittenberg, Puchaimer was present as a member of a delegation

conveying the good wishes of Cardinal Albert.

BIBLIOGRAPHY: Allen Ep 2476 / *Matrikel Wien* II-1 369 / *Epistolae ad Nauseam* 56–8 / Georg Theodor Strobel *Neue Beyträge zur Litteratur besonders des sechzehnten Jahrhunderts* (Nürnberg-Altdorf 1790–4) III-1 66

KONRAD WIEDEMANN

Giovanni Antonio PUGLIONI *See Giovanni Antonio* BUGLIO

PUISTUTH (Ep 2957, of 12 August 1534)
The name Puistuth, applied by *Viglius Zuichemus to one of the Anabaptist leaders of Münster, appears to be an epithet or nickname. It does not appear in the sources of Münster Anabaptism and the person in question has not been identified. There is no basis for the identification with Brictius thon Norde (Brixius Nordanus) proposed in Allen Ep 2957:85–7n.

ROBERT STUPPERICH

Richard PYNSON died c January 1530
A Norman by birth, Pynson was a student at the University of Paris in 1464. After learning printing at Rouen he settled in London around 1490, taking over the business of William de Machlinia, an early law printer. In 1508 he was appointed printer to the king, succeeding Guillaume Faques (Fawkes). In his earlier years he printed a wide variety of proclamations, year-books, and literary works – including works by Chaucer, Lydgate, and *Skelton – as well as editions and translations of the classics. His typographical art was the finest produced in England; he was the first in England to use Roman type (1509) and the first to print an English book on arithmetic (Cuthbert *Tunstall *De arte supputandi* 1522, STC 24319). He published *Henry VIII's *Assertio septem sacramentorum adversus Martinum Lutherum* in 1521 (STC 13078) and the king's letters to *Luther in 1528 (STC 13084–7). Among other anti-Lutheran tracts he published in 1523 *De libero arbitrio adversus Melanchthonem* (STC 24728) by the Franciscan Alphonsus de Villa Sancta. Specializing in law books, he published about four hundred titles in his forty-year career.

In 1513 Pynson printed the first edition of one of Erasmus' translations from Plutarch, *De tuenda bona valetudine precepta* (STC 20060; Epp 268, 273). McConica argues for a number of

Pynson's books from 1516 as being part of an 'Erasmian reform movement,' to which his publication of *Savonarola's *Sermo in vigilia nativitatis domini* (STC 21800) may be seen as a forerunner; he also published works by William *Lily (1513 and 1522, STC 15601.3 and 15606.7) and John *Colet (1511 and 1513, STC 5544–5). An otherwise unknown publication of Pynson's press is mentioned by Andrea *Ammonio in 1513 (Ep 280), and in 1520 he printed Thomas *More's *Epistolae ad Germanum Brixium* (Ep 1096).

BIBLIOGRAPHY: Allen Ep 1096 / DNB XVI 530–1 / LP I 364 and passim / H.R. Plomer *A Short History of English Printing, 1476–1900* 2nd ed (London 1915) / H.B. Lathrop 'The first English printers and their patrons' *The Library* 4th ser 3 (1922) 69–96 / H.S. Bennett *English Books and Readers 1475 to 1557* (Cambridge 1952) 182–5 / Stanley Morison *First Principles of Typography* 2nd ed (London 1962) / McConica 54–5, 65, and passim   R.J. SCHOECK

Antonius PYRATA of Sibiu, d 21 August 1534
Antonius Pyrata (Pirata, properly Goldenmünzer, Guldenmünster, also called Bruder Feindtselig) was a Dominican from Sibiu (Hermannstadt), in Transylvania, and appeared in Constance around 1498, preaching to the Dominican friars and nuns. His special gift for the pulpit was praised both by Johannes *Fabri and by Erasmus (Ep 1342), who had evidently met him during his visit to Constance in the autumn of 1522 (Ep 1331). His exhortations were at first directed against vice, including superstition and curial corruption, but with the beginning of the Reformation he was soon the leading public opponent of the new faith at Constance. From 1520 to 1523 he was vicar-general of the German province of the Non-Observant Dominicans, and in 1522 Bishop Hugo von *Hohenlandenberg sent him to Zürich in an effort to prevent the apostasy of the Dominican nuns there. From 1524 he preached in the cathedral of Constance while the position of preacher remained formally open after the dismissal of Johann *Wanner. In 1527 he was invited to become preacher at Innsbruck; Jakob *Stürtzel was instructed to offer him incentives and a benefice was in fact assigned to him in July 1528, but in the end he continued in the position he had recently

assumed at Radolfzell and died in the monastery of Katharinental in the Swiss canton of Thurgau.

BIBLIOGRAPHY: Allen Ep 1342 / Jörg Vögeli *Schriften zur Reformation in Konstanz* ed A. Vögeli (Tübingen-Basel 1972–3) II-2 865 and passim / Rublack *Reformation in Konstanz* 248–50 and passim / Nikolaus Paulus *Die deutschen Dominikaner im Kampf gegen Luther* (Freiburg 1903) 313–23 / Diethelm Heuschen *Reformation, Schmalkaldischer Bund und Österreich in ihrer Bedeutung für die Finanzen der Stadt Konstanz, 1499–1648* (Tübingen-Basel 1969) 63–5   PGB

Guilelmus de QUERCU, QUERQUO See *Guillaume* DUCHESNE

Francisco de QUIÑONES d 27 October 1540
Francisco de Quiñones (Quignon, Francisco de los Angeles), the son of Fernando de Quiñones, count of Luna in León, was born around 1475–80. He was a relative of the Emperor *Charles V and became his personal friend when the latter came to Spain. As a boy Francisco served as a page to Cardinal *Jiménez before studying at the universities of Alcalá and Salamanca. Before 1507 he entered the order of Franciscan Observants at the monastery of Santa María de los Angeles, in the province of La Coruña, founded by Juan de la Puebla. He was elected vicar-general of the Spanish province of his order in 1521, commissary-general of the Franciscan Observants outside Italy in 1522, and minister-general of the entire order in 1523, retaining this last office to the end of 1527. During his tenure as minister-general new branches of the Franciscan movement with a commitment to special austerity were coming into existence, the Reformed, the Recollects, and the Capuchins; their strict interpretation of the Franciscan rule and missionary zeal conformed to Quiñones' own ideals. For some time he had planned to go to New Spain as a missionary and was instrumental in the dispatch of the missionaries called the 'twelve apostles' to Mexico in 1524.

In his Roman residence the Franciscan general surrounded himself with scholars and humanists such as Juan Ginés de *Sepúlveda and Diego *López Zúñiga. From 1526 he also served as a diplomatic mediator between Pope *Clement VII and Charles V and came to form a close relationship with Charles' ambassador at the curia, the Erasmian Miguel Mai. After the Sack of Rome Quiñones played an important role in negotiating the liberation of Clement VII. On 7 December 1527 he was nominated to the cardinalate of Santa Croce di Gerusalemme, but the publication was deferred for some time. From 1530 to 1533 he was also bishop of Coria in Spain, while in 1531 Clement named him governor of Veroli, where he was eventually to die, and in 1532 governor of Campagna. He was also charged with a revision of the Roman breviary and together with his associates in this enterprise instituted some sweeping reforms in their edition, first published in 1535 (Rome: A. Bladus). Quiñones' breviary ran to more than a hundred editions, but it was sharply criticized in various places, including the Sorbonne and the council of Trent. In 1556 the pope prohibited the continued use of it, and in 1568 it was definitively suppressed.

When Luis de *Carvajal's Apologia diluens nugas Erasmi was reprinted in Paris at the instigation of Juan de *Zafra, a preface to Quiñones was added (LB X 1684), which prompted some critical remarks on the part of Erasmus although he apparently did not think the cardinal was directly associated with Carvajal's attack (Epp 2126, 2205). In 1532 Erasmus learnt from Sepúlveda that, at the death of López Zúñiga, critical notes concerning the fourth edition of Erasmus' New Testament (1527) had remained in the hands of Quiñones. In accordance with the wishes of the late author, the notes were subsequently copied and sent to Erasmus, who at one point considered writing directly to Quiñones but in the end decided otherwise (Epp 2637, 2701, 2729). One Christophorus Oroscius dedicated to Quiñones from Salamanca his Annotationes in interpretes Aetii, etc (Basel: R. Winter 1540).

BIBLIOGRAPHY: Allen Ep 2126 / Diccionario de historia eclesiástica de España ed Quintín Aldea Vaquero et al (Madrid 1972–5) III 2037–8 / P. Battifol Histoire du brèviaire romain 3rd ed (Paris 1911) 274–98 / J.W. Legg The Second Recension of the Quignon Breviary (London 1908–12) / J. Messeguer Fernández 'El P. Francisco de los Angeles de Quiñones, OFM, al servicio del Emperador y del Papa' Hispania 73 (1958) 1–41 / J. Messeguer Fernández 'Bibliographie hispano-grécque 1477–1560' I no 82 in Bibliographie hispanique 1915 (New York 1915) / Pastor X 33–5 and passim / Bataillon Erasmo y España 326, 368, 405–7, and passim / Eubel III 20, 160 / Otto Lehnhoff Die Beichtväter Karls V. (Alfeld 1932) 34 / Hugolin Lippens in Archivum Franciscanum historicum 44 (1951) 65; 45 (1952) 6   MILAGROS RIVERA & PGB

Guilhelmus QUINONUS
(Ep 2380 of 6 September 1530)
Erasmus wrote to Guilhelmus Quinonus in reply to a letter now missing. Quinonus knew Philippus *Montanus and may have lived in Paris. Erasmus also referred to the attacks of Gerard *Geldenhouwer, whose name he either did not give or suppressed in the published version of his letter. It seems likely that Quinonus too had mentioned Geldenhouwer.

Quinonus has not been identified, nor has his title of 'mandator' been explained. The editors of Allen Ep 2444 suggested that he was a member of the order of St John but failed to substantiate their hypothesis. A 'Wilhelmus filius Heynrici Quinon,' cleric of the diocese of Liège, matriculated at the University of Louvain on 20 August 1486 as an arts student in the College of the Pig (Matricule de Louvain III-1 16).   PGB

Jean QUINTIN See QUINTINUS (Ep 2444)

QUINTINUS (Ep 2444 of 9 March 1531)
There is no evidence either to corroborate or to cast doubt on the tentative identification in Allen of Quintinus, who was presumably staying at Paris, with Jean Quintin (Quintinus Haeduus or Aeduus) of Autun (c 1509–61). Quintin was educated in Poitiers and by 1536 had become professor of canon law in Paris. Although he held a rich benefice of the order of the knights of St John, he sympathized with the Protestants in his younger years. At the estates general of Orléans (1560–1) he was the speaker for the clergy. He published several works on canon law. The editors of Allen IX noted certain similarities between this letter and another, addressed six months earlier to Guilhelmus *Quinonus; both letters were published by Erasmus in the Epistolae floridae of September 1531.

BIBLIOGRAPHY: Allen 2444 / *Histoire ecclésiastique des églises reformés au royaume de France* ed G. Baum and E. Cunitz (Paris 1883–9) I 428–9 and passim

MICHEL REULOS & PGB

QUIRINUS Hagius of The Hague, documented 1524(?)–35

Quirinus Hagius is probably identical with the Quirinus Ghysberti of The Hague who matriculated at the University of Louvain on 18 April 1524 (as, four weeks later, did Nikolaas *Kan of Amsterdam, who later preceded Quirinus in Erasmus' service). Quirinus reached Freiburg in 1532 (Ep 2644) and was engaged by Erasmus. Towards the end of August Erasmus sent him to England (Epp 2704, 2707). Returning by way of the Low Countries, he was back in Freiburg towards the end of November (Epp 2728, 2817), his mission accomplished to his master's satisfaction (Epp 2741, 2759, 2777, 2794, 2804, 2817). In April 1533 he was dispatched again to the same destinations. Having entire confidence in his honesty (Ep 2799), Erasmus hoped that this time he might have better success in obtaining payment of his English annuity, and in fact he did so (Epp 2810, 2815). Quirinus delivered letters and messages to Charles *Blount, Baron Mountjoy, and Thomas *More, and in the second half of June reached Brussels (Epp 2828, 2830, 2831). In July he travelled the Low Countries as far as Holland, gathering letters to take back to Erasmus (Epp 2841–4, 2848, 2851, 2876, 2922). Not until November did Erasmus mention his return to Freiburg (Ep 2876). On 4 November 1533 Quirinus matriculated at the University of Freiburg as a cleric of the diocese of Utrecht and began to attend the lectures of Udalricus *Zasius (Ep 2906). Early in 1534 we learn that master and famulus had parted company; Erasmus was convinced that Quirinus had embezzled some money entrusted to him in England and used part of it to buy a new outfit (Epp 2906, 2918). He sent a warning to his Antwerp banker, Erasmus *Schets, in case Quirinus turned up there (Ep 2896). In fact it is not known what became of Quirinus after that date. It is clear, however, that he must be the 'monster' or 'viper' of whom Erasmus kept complaining, the trusted famulus who had betrayed him, leaving his feelings deeply hurt (Epp 2944, 2946, 2947, 2976). The 'heretics'

must have planted the man in his household so as to learn secrets that could be used against Erasmus (Ep 2940). Bonifacius *Amerbach's attempt to calm Erasmus (Ep 2943) had no effect. As late as September 1535 Erasmus complained that 'Hagius' was incapable of keeping any secret and that he had corrupted Quirinus *Talesius and perhaps even turned Karel *Uutenhove against Erasmus (Ep 3052).

BIBLIOGRAPHY: *Matricule de Louvain* III-1 725, III-2 224 / *Matrikel Freiburg* I-1 287 / Bierlaire *Familia* 93–5 / de Vocht CTL II 182, 469, 498–9 / de Vocht MHL 48–51

FRANZ BIERLAIRE & PGB

Jean QUONUS documented c 1514–18

Very little is known about Jean Quonus. He was the prior of the charterhouse of Longuenesse, near Saint-Omer, and had taught himself Hebrew by the time Erasmus paid him a visit in June of 1516 (Ep 471). Such was his admiration for Johann *Reuchlin and his works that when Erasmus produced a letter he had received from Reuchlin Quonus begged him to leave it behind. The prior's passionate admiration for Reuchlin, his desire to perfect his knowledge of Hebrew with the help of Reuchlin's books, and also his lively interest in the Cabbala, 'that field of sublime studies,' speak from nearly every line of an ardent letter Quonus wrote to *Lefèvre d'Etaples (on 24 July 1514?) upon hearing a rumour that Reuchlin, 'that superman,' was expected in Paris. Reuchlin did not fail to publish this enthusiastic letter in his 1519 collection of letters received from admirers and friends directly following the letters from Erasmus. Quonus' name also figures in the opening lines of the book between those of *Beatus Rhenanus and Richard *Cox amid the 'accomplished scholars of Germany and vigorous defenders of Reuchlin.' In 1517 and as late as the beginning of 1518 Erasmus was still attempting to retrieve a letter from Reuchlin which was in Quonus' hands (Epp 673, 762).

Like *Vitrier, *Edmond, and some of the Benedictines and Cistercians in the abbeys of St Bertin and Clairmarais-lez-Saint-Omer, Quonus represents the attempt to combine the ideals of piety and humanistic study that existed within the monastic communities in the smaller cities of northern Europe.

BIBLIOGRAPHY: Allen Ep 471 / *Illustrium*

François Rabelais

---

virorum epistolae ... ad Ioannem Reuchlin (Haguenau 1519) / RE Ep 201, pp 80, 223 / Saint-Omer, Bibliothèque municipale MS 378: 'Epistolae familiares, sermones latini et capitulares Clarimarescentium' ANDRÉ GODIN

Anton RABE *See Antonius* CORVINUS

François RABELAIS d 9 April 1553
Rabelais was probably born in 1483 at La Devinière, a farm owned by his lawyer father near Chinon, in Touraine. His father, Antoine Rabelais, was well known in the region, having the various titles of 'sénéchal de Lerné,' 'assesseur du lieutenant du bailli de Touraine,' and 'seigneur de Chavigny.' There is scant evidence upon which an account of his early years may be based. He perhaps received his schooling at a combination of local institutions such as the abbey of Seuilly and the Franciscan monastery at La Baumette, or possibly even at a school in Angers. He may also have spent some years reading law in one of the nearby university towns (Angers or Poitiers).

Having no doubt been a Franciscan novice in earlier years, Rabelais became a friar at Fontenay-le-Comte, in the Vendée, where he stayed until 1526. By April 1521 he had become a priest. In the monastery a fellow monk, Pierre *Lamy, encouraged him in 1520 to initiate a correspondence with the eminent scholar Guillaume *Budé. During the early 1520s Rabelais and Lamy assiduously applied themselves to the study of Greek, and Rabelais advanced sufficiently to translate into Latin some of Herodotus and Lucian. When their superiors objected to their studies and confiscated their books, Lamy ran away. For his part Rabelais sought and received permission to transfer to the Benedictine monastery of St Pierre at nearby Maillezais, where the abbot, Bishop Geoffroy d'Estissac, was sympathetic to humanistic studies. He took Rabelais into his service as secretary and became a loyal patron to him during the coming years.

Some time in the course of the years 1526–30 Rabelais left Maillezais, perhaps with the purpose of studying medicine in Paris, where he may have exchanged his monk's habit for the attire of a secular priest. Possibly his children François and Junie were born during this period. In 1540 Rabelais appealed successfully to Rome to have the stigma of their illegitimacy removed. Presumably he had studied medicine several years before signing the matriculation list at the University of Montpellier on 17 September 1530, since as early as 1 December he became a bachelor of medicine. In 1530 he lectured at Montpellier on such topics as Hippocrates' *Aphorismi* and Galen's *Ars parva*. From June 1532 he was in Lyon, where Sebastianus *Gryphius published his editions of Giovanni *Manardo's *Epistolae medicinales* (1532, dedicated to André Tiraqueau); *Hippocratis ac Galeni libri aliquot* (15 July 1532, dedicated to Geoffroy d'Estissac); and the *Testamentum* attributed to Lucius Cuspidius (4 September 1533, dedicated to Amaury Bouchard). On 1 November 1532 he had been appointed physician to the hospital (Hôtel-Dieu) at Lyon. In the same year, a popular story with themes from folklore was printed in Lyon and achieved immediate success: *Les Grandes et Inestimables Chronicques du grant et enorme geant Gargantua ...* This anonymous work of modest quality provided Rabelais with a scheme on which he was to elaborate his own *Gargantua* and *Pantagruel*. In 1532 Claude

Nourry of Lyon published *Pantagruel*, using an anagram of the author's name on the title page: 'maistre Alcofrybas Nasier.' Rabelais followed up the success of *Pantagruel* by publishing in the autumn of 1532 a parodic *Pantagruéline Prognostication* for 1533 (Lyon: F. Juste). He no doubt also promptly undertook the composition of his *Gargantua*. While *Pantagruel* had been published first, the sequence was reversed in the complete editions to follow the chronological order of the story.

On 15 January 1534 Rabelais accompanied Jean *Du Bellay, bishop of Paris, on his mission to Rome as the bishop's private physician. While exploring the ruins of ancient Rome, he conceived the idea of writing a description of the city. But after his return to the Hôtel-Dieu of Lyon (1 August 1534), he was content to re-edit Bartolomeo Marliani's *Topographia urbis Romae* (Lyon: S. Gryphius 1534) with a dedication to Du Bellay. Perhaps late in 1534 *Gargantua* (Lyon: F. Juste) was published, followed by Rabelais' *Almanach pour l'an 1535* and the *Pantagruéline Prognostication* modified for 1535 (followed by similar ones in 1537 and 1542).

After the placards affair (17–18 October 1534) official opposition to all presumed Protestants and evangelicals stiffened considerably. It seems that, owing to his irregular status outside his order, Rabelais thought it prudent to leave the Hôtel-Dieu in February 1535 and remain out of sight for a while, until Jean Du Bellay, now a cardinal, invited him to join him for another mission to Rome. They set out on 15 July and arrived there on 31 July, having gone by way of Ferrara, where Rabelais quite possibly may have met with Clément Marot, then in exile after the placards affair. Three letters to his earlier patron, Geoffroy d'Estissac (30 December 1535, 28 January, and 15 February 1536), tell us about events in Rome and Rabelais' interests and preoccupations, among them horticulture. He also sought and received from *Paul III absolution for his apostasy from the order. He was allowed to return to a Benedictine monastery and later in the year entered Cardinal Du Bellay's monastery of Saint-Maur-les-Fossés, which was to be secularized. By 17 August 1536 Rabelais' name was on a list of canons at Saint-Maur.

Following the outbreak of hostilities with

*Charles v in the summer of 1536 Rabelais probably accompanied Jean Du Bellay to the northern provinces, where he was to check the defence preparations. In 1537 Rabelais seems to have moved about considerably in France. A poem which Etienne *Dolet wrote to celebrate his pardon (19 February 1537) for having killed a man in self-defence describes a banquet of humanists in Paris, which Rabelais attended along with Dolet, Budé, Marot, and others. Not long afterwards Rabelais returned to Montpellier, where he became a licentiate on 3 April and a doctor of medicine on 22 May and lectured on Hippocrates' *Prognostica* (18 October 1537–14 April 1538). After accompanying his cardinal to the meeting of Aigues-Mortes between *Francis I and Charles v he set out for Lyon, where he resided until 1540. His son Théodole, who died in infancy, may have been born around this time.

By early 1540 Rabelais was in the employ of Guillaume Du Bellay, seigneur de Langey, acting lieutenant-general of the French forces stationed in Piedmont. As his personal physician he accompanied him on his travels back and forth between Turin and France. When passing through Lyon, possibly in April 1542, Rabelais arranged with his publisher, François Juste, to bring out a revised and expurgated edition of *Gargantua* and *Pantagruel* (Lyon 1542). The text attenuated some of the obvious attacks on the Paris theologians, replacing 'les Sorbonicoles,' for example, by 'les magistres,' and prudently suppressing incriminating wording such as a whole list of suspect oaths in chapter XVII of *Gargantua*. In the same year, however, Etienne Dolet produced an unauthorized reprint of the unexpurgated work (Lyon 1542), and on 2 March 1543 the Paris faculty of theology condemned both the expurgated and the unexpurgated editions. Meanwhile Rabelais had once again set out for Turin with Langey, arriving there on 12 May 1542, but owing to the latter's poor health they were obliged to head back to France, and on 9 January 1543 Langey died near Roanne. It fell to Rabelais to accompany his body on the journey to Le Mans for burial in the cathedral (5 March). On 30 May 1543 Rabelais' friend and patron Bishop Geoffroy d'Estissac also died. In the meantime a sequel to *Gargantua* and *Pantagruel*, Rabelais' *Tiers Livre* (Paris: C,

Wechel early 1546), was nearing completion, and on 19 September 1545 Francis I issued a royal privilege for its publication. Rabelais dedicated it to the king's sister, *Margaret of Angoulême, queen of Navarre. Despite this double royal patronage, the Paris faculty of theology listed it among censured books (31 December 1546). In the course of 1546 Rabelais travelled to Metz, perhaps in order to be abroad if the French authorities chose to prosecute him. On 3 August of that year Dolet was burned in Paris as a heretic. Following the death of Francis I on 31 March 1547, Rabelais joined Cardinal Du Bellay in Rome and remained in Italy until 1549. In 1548 there were two printings of an incomplete *Quart Livre* (Lyon: P. de Tours), including only the prologue and eleven chapters.

After the birth of Louis, the second son of King *Henry II, on 3 February 1549, Cardinal Du Bellay sponsored a festival in Rome to celebrate this event, which was described by Rabelais in his *Sciomachie* (Lyon: Jean de Tournes for S. Gryphius 1549). In the autumn of 1549 Cardinal Du Bellay and Rabelais returned to France. Rabelais spent the summer of 1550 at Saint-Maur, where the cardinal was convalescing after another trip to Rome. At this time he was presented to Cardinal Odet de Châtillon, who secured a royal privilege for the reprinting of all the revised books of the story of *Gargantua* and *Pantagruel* and any continuations (6 August 1550). This encouraged Rabelais to complete the *Quart Livre* (Paris: M. Fezandat 1552), which he dedicated to Odet de Châtillon in a prefatory letter dated 28 January 1552. At the request of the faculty of theology, the Parlement in Paris condemned it and forbad its sale; however, the ban was lifted in May. As the end of his life approached, Rabelais resigned his two cures on 9 January 1553. If the traditional date assigned to his death is correct, he died on 9 April.

In 1562 there appeared under Rabelais' name and the title *L'Isle Sonante* (n p) sixteen chapters of the *Cinquiesme Livre*. The entire text was published in 1564 by another anonymous printer. Many critics feel that it should not be entirely ascribed to Rabelais. The large number of editions of the story of *Gargantua* and *Pantagruel* leaves no doubt as to his continued popularity, but not until the present century

has Rabelais' thought been accurately assessed in the complex ideological and religious context of his own times.

In February 1533 Bonifacius *Amerbach thanked Erasmus' secretary, Gilbert *Cousin, for a copy of Rabelais' edition of the (supposititious) *Lucii Cuspidii Testamentum* (AK IV Ep 1717). M.A. Screech has found this book with Cousin's dedication, in the Öffentliche Bibliothek of the University of Basel. The only direct connection known to exist between Rabelais and Erasmus is Rabelais' letter of 30 November 1532 (Ep 2743) which Erasmus never published. Without expecting Erasmus even to know his name, Rabelais acknowledged his intellectual and moral debt to him in terms of exalted gratitude. Despite the excessive but conventional flattery, there is no doubt but that the underlying sentiment is authentic. Although there were significant differences in their backgrounds and temperaments, the two men shared a number of kindred views and interests. Both had experienced the monastic life but had elected to live in secular society where they had widespread contacts among humanists and publishers. Both men were obliged to seek patrons, although Erasmus managed to retain a greater degree of personal independence. Both were thoroughly acquainted with university life and both had performed an intellectual pilgrimage to Italy. While remaining in the Roman church both were followers of the 'philosophia Christi' and close to the evangelism current among some circles of their friends. Both men desired ecclesiastical reform and satirized abuses in the religious institutions and practices of their day. Both condemned war, albeit with qualifications, and sought moral and civic improvement through humanist education.

Yet Rabelais drew his inspiration from a host of sources other than those of Erasmus, extending his exuberant quest for knowledge into such areas as law, natural science, medicine, sports, folklore, and popular culture. While thoroughly versed in Greek and Latin he elected to write in the vernacular. Febvre, Lebègue, Plattard, and Screech have documented the frequent use he made of Erasmus' writings and editions of classical texts as a source of information and, indeed, inspiration. In many cases he borrowed maxims or *exempla* from the *Adagia* or *Apophtheg-mata*. An important instance of this type of borrowing, since it bears upon the interpretation of *Gargantua*, is Rabelais' allusion to the *Sileni Alcibiadis* in the prologue to *Gargantua*, which is based on *Adagia* III iii 1. Other works by Erasmus also figure as sources of inspiration to Rabelais: the *Colloquia*, the *Moria*, the *Enchiridion*, the *Querela pacis*, and Erasmus' pedagogical treatises.

Further investigation, however, reveals that the fundamental design and thought of Rabelais' books differ considerably from what he could have found in Erasmus' writings. In *L'Evangélisme de Rabelais* (1959) Screech provides abundant evidence for the complexity of Rabelais' religious thought on the basis of a comparison with the positions of *Luther, Calvin, and their Catholic opponents as well as Erasmus. Recent critics have also begun to explore the inspiration Rabelais drew from such fields as folklore, language and signs, French legends, and popular culture, where Erasmus could not serve him as a guide.

BIBLIOGRAPHY: Allen Ep 2743 / *Matricule de Montpellier* 60 / Jean Larmat *Rabelais* (Paris 1973) / Donald M. Frame *François Rabelais, A Study* (New York 1977) / M.A. Screech *Rabelais* (Ithaca, NY 1979) / Jean Plattard *La Vie de François Rabelais* (Paris-Brussels 1928) / Lucien Febvre *Le Problème de l'incroyance au XVIe siècle: La religion de Rabelais* rev ed (Paris 1947) / V.-L. Saulnier *Le Dessein de Rabelais* (Paris 1957) / Raymond Lebègue 'Rabelais, the last of the French Erasmians' *Journal of the Warburg and Courtauld Institutes* 12 (1949) 91–100 / M.A. Screech 'Rabelais, Erasmus, Gilbertus Cognatus and Boniface Amerbach ... ' *Etudes Rabelaisiennes* 14 (1977) 43–6 / The best recent critical editions of Rabelais' work with notes, variant readings, and bibliographies have appeared in the series *Textes littéraires français* (Geneva, Droz): *Pantagruel* ed Saulnier (1965); *Gargantua* ed Calder and Screech (1970); *Tiers Livre* ed Screech (1964); *Quart Livre* ed Marichal (1947); *Pantagruéline Prognostication* ed Screech (1974) / A large scale critical edition of the *Oeuvres*, undertaken by Abel Lefranc and other scholars in 1913 is still not complete: *Oeuvres* (Paris: Champion, Geneva: Droz 1913–   ) / *Rabelais: Oeuvres complètes* ed Jacques Boulenger and Lucien Scheler (Paris 1955), with a comprehen-sive bibliography of Rabelais editions (II 997–1018)

HARRY R. SECOR

Tommaso RADINI TEDESCHI of Piacenza, 15 March 1488–May 1527
Tommaso Radini (Rhadinus, Rodaginus, Todisco, Thomas Placentinus) belonged to a noble family of German origin that had settled at Piacenza. There he entered the Dominican order while he was still quite young. He studied philosophy and theology and taught at the University of Rome. In 1521, in the absence of Silvester *Prierias, the master of the sacred palace, he was for a while in charge of the papal household. Radini died during the Sack of Rome in May 1527.

Radini's first publications were *Calipsychia sive de pulchritudine animae* (Milan: G. da Ponte 1511), dedicated to *Maximilian I, and *Sideralis abscysus* (Pavia: J. de Burgofranco 1511). More important was his *Oratio ad principes et populos Germaniae* (Rome: J. Mazzocchi August 1520), an attack upon Martin *Luther, in particular his opposition to scholastic philosophy. Radini was at that time unknown, and both Luther and Philippus *Melanchthon thought that the book was written by Hieronymus *Emser under a pseudonym. Melanchthon replied in his *Didymi Faventini adversus Thomam Placentinum oratio pro Martino Luthero theologo* [Wittenberg 1521] with an important presentation of the Protestant viewpoint. Radini's answer was his *Oratio in Philippum Melanchthonem* (Rome: J. Mazzocchi 1522), highly praised by Johannes *Cochlaeus in his *Commentaria de actis et scriptis Martini Lutheri* (Mainz: F. Behem 1549). Radini is mentioned in Epp 1167, 1185 and in the *Spongia* (ASD IX-1 166).

BIBLIOGRAPHY: Allen Ep 1167 / Luther w *Briefwechsel* II Ep 345 / *Melanchthons Briefwechsel* I Epp 109, 126, 135 / F. Lauchert *Die italienischen literarischen Gegner Luthers* (Freiburg 1912) 177–99   IG

RAPHAEL Volaterranus *See Raffaele* MAFFEI

Thomas RAPP of Durlach, documented 1487–1521
Thomas Rapp (Rappius) of Durlach, east of Karlsruhe, matriculated at the University of Heidelberg on 31 October 1487 and was a BA in

1489 and a licentiate in theology on 27 February 1492. He spent most of his life at Strasbourg, where he was a member of the literary society and participated in the banquet given for Erasmus in August 1514 (Ep 302). Erasmus praised his 'charming open-hearted character' (Ep 305). In 1515 *Beatus Rhenanus called him 'professor of liberal arts' when dedicating to him his edition of Seneca's *Ludus de morte Claudii Caesaris*, published by Johann *Froben in Basel together with Erasmus' *Moria* (BRE Ep 44 and p 602). In 1520 Rapp called himself vicar of Strasbourg cathedral when writing to Beatus Rhenanus about a manuscript of Tertullian he had found for him in the monastery of Hirsau (BRE Epp 179, 207). Because of his connections with Hirsau and his friendship with the Hirsau monk Nicolaus *Basellius, he is probably the Thomas mentioned in Ep 391.

BIBLIOGRAPHY: Allen and CWE Ep 302 / *Matrikel Heidelberg* I 388, II 420 / BRE Ep 44 and passim   PGB

Ulrich (IX) von RAPPOLTSTEIN documented from 1506, d 25 July 1531

Ulrich (IX) von Rappoltstein came from a family of Alsatian knights with estates in the region of Sélestat, Colmar, and Guebwiller and with a long tradition as patrons of the arts. As early as 1331, Ulrich (VII) commissioned two Strasbourg poets to complete Wolfram von Eschenbach's *Parsival*. The family began to collect books equally early, establishing the basis of an important library. Ulrich (IX), who inherited the Rappoltstein estate and title from his uncle, continued the family tradition. He patronized the printer Amandus Farckall, who established the first printing shop in Colmar. The inventory of Ulrich's books in his own hand shows a broad interest in the religious and social issues of his time. He matriculated at the University of Freiburg on 18 April 1506 with his brother Georg, boarded with the famous *Zasius, and associated with Basilius *Amerbach. He and his wife, Anna Alexandria von Fürstenberg, secretly favoured the reformers and attempted to protect Paul *Volz from the Hapsburg government of Ensisheim (Ep 1607).

BIBLIOGRAPHY: Allen Ep 1607 / *Matrikel Freiburg* I 169 / AK I Ep 357, VI Ep 2769a / BRE Ep 241 / Lina Baillet 'La bibliothèque des Sei-

gneurs de Ribeaupierre, humanistes alsaciens' in *Les Lettres en Alsace* (Strasbourg 1962)
MIRIAM U. CHRISMAN & PGB

Leonhard REBHAN of Ingolstadt, documented 1506–30

Rebhan (Rebhahn, Rephanus) matriculated at the University of Basel in 1506 but did not receive his BA until 1522. By that time he was canon of St Peter's and the chapter's preacher. A year later he was prepared to meet Wolfgang Wissenburg, an exponent of reform, in a public debate. In 1526–7 he was rector of the university, an office that was frequently held by men who were not faculty members. Also in 1526 he was a member of Basel's delegation to the disputation of Baden, and in the summer of 1527 he submitted to the city council a substantial exposé on the question of the mass; he also signed another, submitted by Augustinus *Marius and other theologians opposed to the reformers. At the request of Ludwig *Baer, Erasmus wrote to him on 6 June 1529, encouraging him to come to Freiburg (Ep 2171). On 2 August 1530 he participated with other exiled members of his chapter in a meeting at Neuenburg, Breisgau and was elected negotiator for the group.

BIBLIOGRAPHY: Allen Ep 2171 / *Matrikel Basel* I 281 / *Aktensammlung zur Geschichte der Basler Reformation* ed E. Dürr et al (Basel 1921–50) II 611–34, 677, III 243, IV 553–4, 583–92, and passim / E. Staehelin *Buch der Basler Reformation* (Basel 1929) plate opposite 128 and passim / R. Wackernagel *Geschichte der Stadt Basel* (Basel 1907–54) III 357, 359, 484, 509 / BA *Oekolampads* I 490 and passim   PGB

Clemens RECHBERGER of Basel, d 1545

Very little is known about Clemens Rechberger, who was no doubt a relative of Bonifacius *Amerbach's brother-in-law, Jakob *Rechberger, and matriculated at the University of Basel in the autumn of 1525. The reason for his being a witness to Erasmus' first will on 13 June 1527 (Allen VI 506) is probably that by this time he was the trusted famulus of Bonifacius Amerbach. On 3 June 1533 he wrote to Amerbach from Solothurn inviting him to attend his first mass at Zurzach. He died shortly before July 1545, leaving one child.

BIBLIOGRAPHY: AK III Ep 1183, IV Ep 1752 /
Matrikel Basel I 359   PGB

Jakob RECHBERGER d August 1542

Jakob Rechberger (Rechburger) was descended from a family from Zurzach, in the Aargau,
where his father, Lupold, was the official of
Klingnau. Jakob was a brother of Iteljohann
Rechburger, doctor of law, who had entered
the service of Wilhelm van *Honstein, bishop
of Strasbourg, and eventually became his
chancellor. Jakob became a spice merchant and
settled at Basel, receiving his citizenship in
1506. Despite the pleas of Iteljohann (AK I Ep
296), he was not considered an appropriate
match for Margarete *Amerbach, so in 1506 she
ran away from home to marry him. Within a few
years, however, Johann *Amerbach, Margarete's father, was reconciled to his son-in-law,
and excellent relations prevailed between
various members of the two families. Rechberger served from 1515 to 1534 in the executive of
the 'Safran' guild, and in February 1526 he was
a trustee of the parish of St Martin's and in this
capacity engaged in negotiations with Johannes *Oecolampadius. Like Bonifacius *Amerbach, Rechberger at first refused to receive
communion under the new rite. Although he
eventually accepted Basel's accession to the
reformed camp, no breach developed between
him and his Catholic relatives in the Aargau. In
1536 he was suffering badly from gout (Ep
3095), and he was also sick at the time his wife
died in 1541 (AK V Ep 2453).

BIBLIOGRAPHY: Allen Ep 3095 / AK I Ep 297
and passim / BA *Oekolampads* I 471 / *Wappenbuch
der Stadt Basel* ed W.R. Staehelin (Basel
[1917–30]) / *Aktensammlung zur Geschichte der
Basler Reformation* ed E. Dürr et al (Basel
1921–50) II 254, IV 485   PGB

Johann RECHLINGER *See Johann* REHLINGER

Ida van RECHTERGEM *See Erasmus* SCHETS

Wigand von REDWITZ 1476–20 May 1556

Wigand von Redwitz (Redwig, Rabitz), who
had made a pilgrimage to Jerusalem, was a
canon from 1490. On 18 June 1522 he was
elected prince-bishop of Bamberg, receiving
papal confirmation on 7 January 1523. At first

Wigand von Redwitz

he offered only weak resistance to Lutheranism, but after the first manifestations of social
unrest, he decreed on 11 June 1524 that the
terms of the edict of Worms of 1521 must be
observed in the bishopric. The peasant revolt
touched off an uprising among the citizens of
Bamberg in April 1525. The bishop tried to
intervene but soon had to withdraw to
Altenburg while monasteries and castles in the
principality suffered heavily. With the help of
the army of the Swabian League, the city of
Bamberg was eventually subdued and the
bishop was able to return. Now he was
resolutely opposed to the Reformation, although he did try to eradicate some abuses
within the church. In 1528 the machinations of
Otto von *Pack caused Redwitz to clash with
the Landgrave Philip of *Hesse. Much more
dangerous, however, were the raids of Margrave Albert Alcibiades of Ansbach-Kulmbach,
who ransacked the bishoprics of Bamberg and
Würzburg in 1552 and demanded that half the
territory of Bamberg be ceded to him. The city
of Bamberg was occupied by Albert Alcibiades'
army and the bishop had to flee to Forchheim.

On 29 August 1552, however, the margrave was declared an outlaw and subsequently he was forced to give up his conquests.

In 1554, when he was over seventy, Redwitz resigned his see, and his coadjutor, Georg Fuchs von Rügheim, succeeded him on 6 February 1555. The bishop of Bamberg is mentioned in Ep 2993 as one of the princes adhering to the treaty of Donauwörth.

BIBLIOGRAPHY: Allen Ep 2993 / DHGE VI 466 / ADB XLII 442–5 / Eubel III 128 / *Deutsche Reichstagsakten* Jüngere Reihe (Gotha-Göttingen 1893–) III 222 and passim   IG

Raffaele REGIO of Bergamo, d 17 July 1520
Raffaele Regio (Regius) was born in Bergamo around 1440, if Erasmus' guess that he must have been seventy in 1508 is anywhere near correct (Ep 1347). Of his early education we know little except that he studied in Venice at the School of St Mark under Benedetto Brugnolo; see Alessandro Falconi's *Oratio in laudibus Benedicti Brugnoli* (Venice: B. de' Vitali 1502). In 1482 Regio was appointed lecturer in classical literature in the University of Padua but was superseded in 1486 by a rival named Giovanni Calfurnio, who he claimed had bribed the rector and the students. The quarrel led indirectly to a series of part-academic, part-personal polemics on scholarly matters, including a discussion of selected passages of Persius, Quintilian, and Pliny (Venice: G. Anima Mia 1490), a commentary on Ovid's *Metamorphoses* (Venice: B. Zanni for O. Scoto 1492), and a number of editions of various philosophical and rhetorical works of Cicero. The most important in this category included a decisive refutation of the commonly accepted view that the *Rhetorica ad Herennium* was the work of Cicero himself (Venice: O. Scoto 1492). Though he is not mentioned in official documents during the 1490s, Regio seems to have been able to continue work at Padua until the death of Calfurnio eased his position in 1503. He took a special interest in the affairs of eastern European students, to one of whom, Jan Lubranski of Posnań, he later dedicated his translation of Plutarch's *Regum et imperatorum apophthegmata* (Venice: G. dei Rusconi 1508).

Regio was also well known to various members of the circle of Aldo *Manuzio, and Erasmus was plainly impressed by him as a person in 1508, describing the aged Regio hurrying to hear *Musurus' lecture at seven o'clock in the morning and in bitter weather that kept the younger men of Padua in their beds (Ep 1347). However, there was no lasting scholarly or personal contact between them. Erasmus clearly knew Regio's translations from Plutarch and compared them with Filelfo's version (Epp 2422, 2431); but he normally refers to Regio only to point out a commonplace, whether of vigour in old age (Ep 1347) or of the fallibility of the most learned men (Epp 1479, 2422, 2431, 2466).

Forced to leave Padua by the war of the League of Cambrai, Regio took refuge in Venice and on 23 January 1512 was appointed public lecturer in Latin, a post which he had been voted to but had not taken up four years earlier. In this capacity he pronounced a lost funeral oration over the dead Aldo Manuzio and was described to Erasmus by John *Watson (Ep 450). But the embers of old conflicts heated even his final years, since a pupil of Calfurnio, Marino *Becichemo, began in 1512 to lecture in competition with him and tempted away many of his students. Regio died in 1520, leaving his books to the monastery of San Giorgio.

BIBLIOGRAPHY: Allen and CWE Ep 450 (Allen mistakenly referred to Regio in his notes to Epp 2611, 2617, which in fact concern Raffaele *Maffei) / A. Medin 'Raffaele Regio a Venezia: epigrammi per la sua morte' *Archivio veneto-tridentino* 1 (1922) 237–44

M.J.C. LOWRY

Johannes REGIOMONTANUS of Königsberg, 6 June 1436–c 8 July 1476
Johann Müller or Molitor called himself Regiomontanus after the small town of Königsberg, thirty kilometres north-west of Bamberg, where he was born. He matriculated at the University of Vienna on 14 April 1450, graduated BA in 1452, and in 1457 joined the faculty as a colleague of his great teacher, Georg von Peuerbach, to whom he owed his thorough training in mathematics and astronomy. He became acquainted with Cardinal *Bessarion, who visited Vienna in 1460, and in 1461 he followed the cardinal to Italy. Eager to master the Greek language, he stayed with Bessarion at first in Rome and from 1463 in

Venice, where he also had an opportunity to lecture and to search for ancient manuscripts. In his Italian years he completed the *Epitome* of Ptolemy's *Almagestum*, based on a new translation of the Greek text which had been begun by Peuerbach (but was not published until 1496). In this text Regiomontanus offered critical observations which later proved useful to Copernicus. From 1467, if not earlier, Regiomontanus lived in Hungary in the service of King *Matthias Corvinus. In 1471 he moved to Nürnberg and installed a press in his own house in an effort to provide accurate editions of mathematical and astronomical texts, a field till then neglected by the printers. He also wrote works of his own and designed astronomical instruments. In 1475 he went to Rome, perhaps in response to an invitation by Pope *Sixtus IV, who wished to consult him on the reform of the calendar. Regiomontanus died in Rome the following summer.

Regiomontanus had also been preparing a new edition of Ptolemy's *Geographia*. This was never published, but his notes on the errors of an earlier translation by Jacopo Angeli were appended to Willibald *Pirckheimer's Latin translation of the *Geographia* (Strasbourg: J. Grüninger 1525). This work is mentioned by Anselmus *Ephorinus (Ep 2606) and, with generous praise, by Erasmus himself (Ep 2760).

BIBLIOGRAPHY: Allen Ep 2606 / ADB XXII 564–81 / Edward Rosen in *Dictionary of Scientific Biography* ed C.C. Gillispie (New York 1970–80) XI 348–52 / Ernst Zinner *Leben und Wirken des Johannes Müller genannt Regiomontanus* rev ed (Osnabrück 1968) / *Short-Title Catalogue of Books Printed in German-Speaking Countries ... from 1455 to 1600 now in the British Museum* (London 1962) 719   RAINER VINKE & PGB

Urbanus REGIUS *See Urbanus* RHEGIUS

Johann REHLINGER von Horgau of Augsburg, d 1552
Johann (Hans) Rehlinger (Rechlinger, von Rehlingen) belonged to an old patrician family in Augsburg that was related by marriage to the Höchstetter family. Nothing appears to be known as yet about his education, but in some sources he is given the title of doctor. Johann Rehlinger married Anna Dietenhaimer (1486–1536). Their daughter Anna (1505–48) married

Anton *Fugger on 4 March 1527. A rich businessman, Rehlinger invested between 1529 and 1536 in mercury and cinnabar mines in Idrija (Slovenia) with Johann (II) *Paumgartner. He was a member of the Augsburg city council but in 1531 lost his seat temporarily because of his opposition to the Lutheran party (Ep 2480). He and others who had been removed from the council for the same reason were soon re-installed, however (Ep 2631). In 1536 he retired from his civic offices in Augsburg and was assigned a pension.

Rehlinger was brought to Erasmus' attention when *Viglius Zuichemus tutored his grandsons, Heinrich and Quirin Rehlinger, at Bourges and subsequently at Padua. In 1532 Erasmus exchanged greetings with the young Rehlingers (Ep 2594).

BIBLIOGRAPHY: Allen Ep 2594 / de Vocht CTL III 462 / NDB V 715 (s v Anton Fugger) / Götz von Pölnitz *Anton Fugger* (Tübingen 1958–) I 87, 480, 501, and passim / W. Krag *Die Paumgartner von Nürnberg und Augsburg* (Munich-Leipzig 1919) 62   IG

Peter REICH von Reichenstein d 14 April 1540
Peter Reich (Rich von Rychenstein) was descended from a noble family from the Birs valley, south of Basel, whose members served the bishops of Basel continuously from the thirteenth century to the French revolution. A canonry at the Basel cathedral chapter was pledged to Peter in 1499, and he was already a canon when he registered at the University of Basel in 1508. In 1516 he studied at Ingolstadt and in 1518 at Bologna. In 1527 he was arch-priest and in 1529, in the wake of Basel's reformation, he left for Freiburg with the rest of the chapter whose *custos* he now became. In 1540 he was also provost of Saint-Ursanne in the Jura. At Basel he enjoyed a discreet income from his paternal inheritance and owned a large, pleasant house which for a time in 1531 he put at the disposal of Anselmus *Ephorinus and his friends (Ep 2539). When Erasmus left Freiburg in 1535 Reich purchased his house 'zum Kind Jesu' (Epp 3056, 3059; AK IV Ep 1989), and five years later he died at Freiburg. Johann *Sichard dedicated his edition of the historian Justin to him (Basel: A. Cratander 1526).

BIBLIOGRAPHY: Allen Ep 2539 / DHBS V 427 (for the family) / W. Merz *Oberrheinische Stammtafeln* (Aarau 1912) 46 / *Wappenbuch der Stadt Basel* ed W.R. Staehelin (Basel [1917–30]) / *Atkensammlung zur Geschichte der Basler Reformation* ed E. Dürr et al (Basel 1921–50) I 471–5, IV 166–7, 503, V 366–7, VI 304–5, and passim / *Matrikel Basel* I 291 / R. Wackernagel *Geschichte der Stadt Basel* (Basel 1907–54) III 431 and passim / Knod 437   PGB

Simon REICHWEIN *See Simon* RIQUINUS

Dietrich REIFFENSTEIN *See Johann*
REIFFENSTEIN

Johann REIFFENSTEIN d 1528
Johann Reiffenstein (Reyffenstein, Ryffenstain) was the youngest son of Wilhelm Curio Reiffenstein zu Bommersheim, a steward in the service of Count Botho von Stolberg (in the Harz mountains, east of Göttingen). In 1500 Botho married the heiress Anna von Königstein-Eppstein (Königstein in the Taunus, north of Wiesbaden), and the possessions of the two houses were thereafter largely under joint administration, while several members of the Reiffenstein family continued to be attached to the counts. About 1520–2 Johann was studying at Louvain with Conradus *Goclenius and had the opportunity of meeting Erasmus (Epp 1982, 2732). From 1523 he was one of the students boarding with *Melanchthon in Wittenberg. His close connection with the reformer is reflected by the fact that he was permitted to edit a *Farrago aliquot epigrammatum Philippi Melanchthonis et aliorum quorundam eruditorum* (Haguenau: J. Setzer 1528). In reply to a letter Erasmus had sent him early in 1528 by Frans van der *Dilft, Melanchthon wrote Erasmus two letters (Epp 1981, 1982), both dated from Jena on 23 March; on the same day he also wrote letters to Goclenius and to Johann's brother, Wilhelm Reiffenstein (*Melanchtons Briefwechsel* I Epp 664–7). These were given to Dilft and Johann Reiffenstein respectively for delivery. Whether Reiffenstein departed with Dilft or immediately after him is not clear. Nor is there any confirmation that Reiffenstein actually reached Basel. In the early summer of that same year Reiffenstein died, apparently from heart failure, in the

course of a hunt in the Taunus; perhaps he had never returned to Wittenberg. The accidental death was described in a lengthy poem by Jacobus Micyllus in his *Sylvarum libri v* (Frankfurt: P. Braubach 1564) 33–41.

In October 1532 Melanchthon gave to Johann Reiffenstein's nephew, Dietrich (Theodoricus), another letter for delivery to Erasmus at Freiburg (Ep 2732). Contrary to the hypothesis stated in Allen's edition, this Dietrich was probably a son not of Melanchthon's well-known friend Wilhelm Reiffenstein (c 1482–1538), but of another son of Wilhelm Curio Reiffenstein (cf *Melanchthons Briefwechsel* I Ep 695, II Ep 1287). This Dietrich has not been identified; he may be identical with the Theodericus Reyffenstein of Königstein who matriculated at Wittenberg on 30 June 1525 (*Matrikel Wittenberg* I 126).

BIBLIOGRAPHY: Allen Ep 1982 / ADB XXVII 691–3, cf XXXVI 328 / *Melanchthons Briefwechsel* I Ep 380 and passim / Philippus Melanchthon *Werke in Auswahl* ed R. Stupperich et al (Gütersloh 1951–75) VII-1 Ep 101 and passim / Eduard Jacobs 'Die Humanistenfamilie Reiffenstein' *Vierteljahrsschrift für Kultur und Litteratur der Renaissance* 2 (1887) 71–96 / Eduard Jacobs 'Kleine Beiträge zur Wappen- und Siegelkunde' *Zeitschrift des Harzvereins* 20 (1887) 256–87, esp 262–7 / For contemporary namesakes of this Johann Reiffenstein see *Matrikel Tübingen* I 219, *Matrikel Wittenberg* I 133

MICHAEL ERBE

Jost von REINACH of Basel, documented 1486–1536
The noble and very numerous von Reinach family took their name from Reinach in the Aargau, where their castle was located. Jost von Reinach (Rinach, a Rina) belonged to the second generation of a branch domiciled at Basel. In 1486 he matriculated at the University of Freiburg. He became a canon of Basel in 1510 and in 1516 was already the owner of the impressive house in the Münsterplatz called after his family. Later he was also canon of Chur and provost of Lindau. He is best known for the scandal he caused in October 1524 when he was arrested and briefly imprisoned by the city council in violation of his canonical privileges. His offence was that he had kidnapped one Katharina Lautenschlager, the

daughter of a poor taylor, and kept her hidden from her parents. It seems that his earlier girl friends were deemed less virtuous so that a similar scandal had previously been avoided.

In February 1529 Jost was at Constance presenting the plight of the Basel chapter which was in exile in the wake of the city's reformation. In the course of a similar mission a few months later he met Johannes *Fabri, still a non-resident member of the chapter, with whom he had corresponded in 1522 (BRE Ep 221). With a letter of introduction dated 1 July 1530 and addressed to Christoph von *Stadion, bishop of Augsburg, and other bishops (*Aktensammlung* IV 500–1), he was sent to the diet then opening in Augsburg. He also carried letters from Erasmus to Lorenzo *Campeggi and Duke George of *Saxony (Epp 2341, 2342, 2344). By the end of September he was still in Augsburg. He was negotiating for the chapter again in July 1533.

BIBLIOGRAPHY: J. Kindler von Knobloch *Oberbadisches Geschlechterbuch* (Heidelberg 1898–1919) III 432 / *Aktensammlung zur Geschichte der Basler Reformation* ed E. Dürr et al (Basel 1921–50) I 147–52, 168, 471, 475, III 269, IV 133, 136, 467, 475, 594, 603, VI 289–90, and passim / *Basler Chroniken* VII 328 / R. Wackernagel *Geschichte der Stadt Basel* (Basel 1907–54) III 389, 77* / BRE Ep 221 / *Matrikel Freiburg* I 83
PGB

Johann REINHARD *See Johann* GRÜNINGER

Gregor REISCH of Balingen, c 1467–9 May 1525
Gregor Reisch (Rusch) of Balingen, Württemberg, registered at the University of Freiburg on 25 October 1487 and was a MA in 1489. On 9 May 1494 he matriculated at Ingolstadt, probably as tutor to a count of Zollern. He was already working on his *magnum opus*, the *Margarita philosophica*, most parts of which were completed by 1496. Once published (Freiburg: J. Schott 1503), it was often reprinted and soon became an indispensable encyclopaedia. It is still studied as a major document of the popular science of that time. Meanwhile Reisch had entered the Carthusian monastery outside Freiburg. After a short spell from 1501 as prior of the Buxheim house near Memmingen, he returned to Freiburg as prior in 1502 and

before 1510 became superior of the Rhenish province of his order. From 1502 to 1510 he gave private instruction to the young Johann Maier of *Eck. In 1510 he published at Basel an important edition of the statutes of his order. From 1510 he was an adviser to *Maximilian I in cultural and scientific matters (Ep 3139), hearing the emperor's last confession at Wels in 1519. In 1523 he suffered a stroke; he died in the city of Freiburg while the charterhouse was in the hands of rebellious peasants.

Before Erasmus' appearance at Basel in 1514, Reisch had been a principal consultant to Johann *Froben and his partners with regard to their great edition of St Jerome. Erasmus politely respected Reisch's role in this enterprise (Epp 308, 309) but realized that only under his own direction could the edition attain a high standard of textual criticism. After the publication of the first edition of his New Testament in 1516 Erasmus emphasized that his efforts had won Reisch's praise (Epp 413, 456).

BIBLIOGRAPHY: Allen and CWE Ep 308 / G. Münzel *Der Kartäuserprior Gregor Reisch und die Margarita philosophica* (Freiburg 1937) / Robert von Srbik *Maximilian I. und Gregor Reisch* ed A. Lhotsky (Vienna 1961) / *Matrikel Freiburg* I 87 / AK I Ep 488 and passim   PGB

Simon von REISCHACH documented 1485(?)–1515
Simon von Reischach (Ryschach, Reuschach) was probably descended from the noble Swabian family of that name. If so, the future chancellor of Friesland was probably the 'Simon de Rischach' who matriculated at the University of Tübingen on 5 January 1485. He was later a doctor of laws and entered the service of Duke George of *Saxony, who in 1511 sent him on an embassy to England in the course of which he may have met Erasmus (Epp 1122, 1125). Probably in 1512 he was appointed chancellor of Friesland by the duke and kept this charge until Friesland was sold to the future *Charles V in 1515. In 1512 he was sent to the court of *Louis XII of France in an effort to prevent a French alliance with Karel van *Egmond and Edzard I Cirksena, dukes of Gelderland and Eastern Friesland. Nothing is known about him after his departure from Friesland.

BIBLIOGRAPHY: Allen and CWE Ep 1122 /
NNBW II 1190–1 / *Matrikel Tübingen* I 55
                                    MICHAEL ERBE

Aegidius REM of Augsburg, d 15 September
1536
Aegidius, the younger brother of Lukas *Rem,
was born in Augsburg around 1485. Being
destined for an ecclesiastical career, he was
sent to Paris for study and there received his BA
and MA (1504–6). Subsequently he went to
Pavia, where he was promoted doctor of civil
and canon law in 1513. After his return from
Italy he entered the service of Cardinal
Matthäus *Lang. Until 1519 he divided his time
between Lang's household and assignments
that took him to the court of Rome. He was a
canon of Passau from 15 June 1514 and was also
appointed a councillor in Lang's ecclesiastical
principality of Salzburg. In 1525 he was in the
castle above Salzburg when the peasant rebels
besieged it, and that same year he recalled
these events in his *Bellum rusticum Saltzburgen-
se*. In 1526 he was appointed bishop of
Chiemsee, in Bavaria, and henceforward lived
in the residence of the bishops of Chiemsee at
Salzburg, where he died. Aegidius Rem
maintained contacts with many humanists
including Konrad *Peutinger, Caspar *Ursinus
Velius, and Riccardo *Bartolini, but he probably did not know Erasmus personally. He was
a friend and patron of Johann *Koler (Ep 2993),
to whom he dedicated a Latin edition of
Agathias' *De bello Gothorum* (Augsburg: S.
Grimm and M. Wirsung 1519).

BIBLIOGRAPHY: Allen Ep 2993 / Ernst von
Frisch 'Der "Salzburger Bauernkrieg" des
Egidius Rem in seiner ursprünglichen Fassung
von 1525' *Mitteilungen der Gesellschaft für
Salzburger Landeskunde* 82–3 (1942–3) 81–91 /
F.A. Veith *Bibliotheca Augustana de vita et scriptis
eruditorum* (Augsburg 1735) 149ff / Paul von
Stetten *Geschichte der adeligen Geschlechter der
freien Reichsstadt Augsburg* (Augsburg 1762)
158ff / Conradin Bonorand *Joachim Vadian und
der Humanismus im Bereich des Erzbistums
Salzburg* (St Gallen 1980) 178–9 / *Deutsche
Reichstagsakten* Jüngere Reihe (Gotha-
Göttingen 1893–   ) II and III passim
                                    INGE FRIEDHUBER

Lukas REM of Augsburg, 14 December 1481–
22 September 1541
Lukas Rem belonged to one of several branches
of the highly respected Augsburg merchant
family of that name. He was a son of Hans Rem
and Magdalena, the aunt of Bartholomäus and
Margarethe *Welser. After an apprenticeship
in Venice Rem joined the Welser firm and was
initially employed in its offices at Milan and
Lyon. Two longer assignments took him to
Portugal, where he achieved his greatest
success: in difficult negotiations with the
Portuguese he established a permanent office
at Lisbon for the Welsers and their business
partners in southern Germany and in sugar
plantations in the Canaries; he also gave them
an important share in the trade with India.
From 1510 he headed the Welser offices in
Lyon and Antwerp. His successful handling of
their affairs did not, however, prevent the
emergence of disagreements between the
Welsers and their factor which led in 1517 to a
parting of the ways. Rem returned to Augsburg and with his brothers Hans and Andreas
founded his own company, which he directed
profitably until his death.
   In 1518 Rem married Anna Ehem of Augsburg, who bore him seven children, three of
whom died at an early age. From 1527 he
favoured Protestantism and although he exercised great discretion in his public position, his
children were christened by evangelical preachers. After years of failing health he suffered
a stroke in 1535 from which he never fully
recovered. He died at Augsburg. From 1494 to
1540 Rem kept a diary. Written without literary
pretensions, his notes offer an interesting
record of his family life and financial situation,
his many travels, and his restless business
activity. As a document of economic history
this diary has considerable importance.
   A number of contacts between Rem and
Erasmus are recorded during 1535, when the
Augsburg merchant forwarded Damião de
*Gois' letters to Erasmus, and presumably also
the latter's answers (Epp 2987, 3019, 3043,
3076, 3078). In a letter to Gois Erasmus reacted
with concern to the news of Rem's stroke (Ep
3043). Erasmus and Rem apparently did not
exchange letters, but messages and news were
passed on by Johann *Koler (Epp 2993, 3050).

Rem is portrayed as St Luke on an altar-piece that he commissioned from Quinten *Metsys, and which is now in the Alte Pinakothek, Munich.

BIBLIOGRAPHY: Allen Ep 2987 / Wilhelm Vogt in ADB XXVIII 187–90 / Hubert von Welser in *Lebensbilder aus dem Bayerischen Schwaben* ed G. von Pölnitz et al (Munich 1952–) VI 166–85 / 'Tagebuch des Lucas Rem aus den Jahren 1494–1541' ed B. Greiff *Jahresberichte des historischen Vereins von Schwaben und Neuburg* 26 (1860) i–xxii, 1–100 / Götz von Pölnitz *Anton Fugger* (Tübingen 1958–) I 100 and passim

INGE FRIEDHUBER

Wolfgang REM of Ulm, d after March 1532
Wolfgang Rem (Roem) of the Kötz or Khaetz branch of that family matriculated in 1505 at the University of Bologna. Two years later he was a doctor of civil and canon law when he applied unsuccessfully for the position of assessor at the imperial law court (Reichskammergericht), then located at Regensburg. In 1508, however, he was an advocate at the Reichskammergericht, and the following year he was a procurator. In a source of 1508 he is given the title of councillor to the Emperor *Maximilian I, and it was at the recommendation of Austria that he was appointed assessor at the Reichskammergericht in 1511. In 1518 he was a councillor of the city of Ulm, but from some time prior to 1530, when contacts between him and Erasmus are first documented, he appears to have resided permanently in Augsburg. Two years earlier he was already representing Augsburg as *Bundesrichter* or *tribunus* (Ep 2269) in the tribunal of the Swabian League, and in 1531 he applied to the city to raise his salary in this position.

Rem was married to Ursula Rötengatter, and their son, Wolfgang Andreas *Rem, became a correspondent of Erasmus. The father's own contacts with Erasmus were in part effected through Johann *Koler, a good friend of the family (Epp 2269, 2545), who conveyed the greetings of both father and son in his letter to Erasmus of 17 March 1532 (Ep 2627). There is also a letter from Udalricus *Zasius to Rem dated 1526.

BIBLIOGRAPHY: Allen Ep 2269 / Knod 442 / Winterberg 31 / *Deutsche Reichstagsakten* Jüngere Reihe (Gotha-Göttingen 1893–) VII-1 413

PGB

Wolfgang Andreas REM of Ulm, 28 February 1511–31 August 1588
Wolfgang Andreas, the son of Wolfgang *Rem, was born at Worms, where his father was probably attending to some business connected with the imperial law court. His father later settled at Augsburg, where Ottmar *Nachtgall instructed the boy in Greek and Latin. He also attended a number of universities, matriculating on 27 August 1523 at Ingolstadt and, after a stay at Padua, on 20 December 1526 at Tübingen, where he studied under Georg *Simler. In Dole he attended the lectures of Petrus *Phoenix and obtained a licentiate in law on 23 January 1529. It was no doubt the presence of the famous Andrea *Alciati which finally attracted Rem to Bourges, where he was promoted doctor of civil and canon law on 23 June 1530. Later in his life, in 1546, while a delegate to the council of Trent, he also matriculated at Bologna.

At an early age Rem had begun to receive ecclesiastical preferment. In 1526 he was provost of St Maurice's, Augsburg, and in 1531 he received a canonry in the Augsburg cathedral chapter, rising to be cellarer, dean, and from 1580 provost of that chapter. Residing at Augsburg, he served consecutive bishops as a legal expert and was often sent to represent them on missions abroad. His only known writing is an oration in memory of Bishop Christoph von *Stadion (d 1543), Erasmus' friend and admirer. While attending the diet of Regensburg in 1531 he was named councillor to King *Ferdinand, and in 1545 at the diet of Worms he was appointed councillor to the Emperor *Charles V. From 1545 to 1547 he represented his bishop, Cardinal Otto Truchsess von Waldburg, at the council of Trent.

In Augsburg young Rem's interest in Erasmus must have been awakened by his teacher, Nachtgall, and his father's circle of friends. In Bourges he struck up a friendship with Karel *Sucket, who after Rem's departure reported that he had received a letter from the latter, echoing the hopes that those in high places set on Erasmus' ability to mediate between Catholics and Protestants (Ep 2373). In January 1531

Erasmus sent a friendly reply to a letter from Rem, who, like Anton *Fugger and others, had encouraged him to settle at Augsburg or at least attend the diet (Ep 2419). There are some references to and greetings from Rem in other letters exchanged between Erasmus and correspondents in Augsburg (Epp 2475, 2627), including a promise on Erasmus' part to write to Rem in the near future (Ep 2565).

BIBLIOGRAPHY: Allen Ep 2419 / ADB XXVIII 190 / Knod 442–3 / Matrikel Tübingen I 257 / Pflug Correspondance III 234–5 / Schottenloher II 168 / H. Jedin A History of the Council of Trent trans E. Graf (London-St Louis 1957–   ) II 20 and passim   PGB

REMACLUS ARDUENNA of Florennes, c 1480–1524

Remaclus was born about 1480 at Florennes, a country town in the Belgian Ardennes (hence: Arduenna, Remacle d'Ardenne). He studied at Louvain and while still very young entered the service of Jean de Hornes, bishop of Liège. Between 1499 and 1506 a Remacle of Liège is repeatedly documented in Paris, apparently as an agent of the printer Thielman (I) Kerver. In 1507 Remaclus Arduenna went to study at Cologne, where in the same year he published a small volume of verse entitled Epigrammaton libri tres. After his return to Brabant in 1509 he successively served the Spaniard Luis *Nuñez Cabeza de Vaca, who was tutor to the future *Charles V, the Milanese physician Luigi *Marliano, and finally the Brabant councillor Alois Bont, in whose train he set out for Scotland in 1510, following him at least as far as London. There he supported himself by teaching while he wrote his drama Palamedes, which was published with an introductory letter dated 1 January 1512 and addressed to Pietro *Griffi, assistant collector of the papal revenues in England. Still in 1512 he went to Paris, where his Palamedes was printed again by Gilles de *Gourmont. In the French capital Remaclus met the Scottish humanist James Foullis, whom he addressed in the prefatory letter to his Eclogue (printed at Paris by Gourmont about 1512). In Paris Remaclus also made the acquaintance of the Italian humanist Fausto *Andrelini, whose Livia he imitated in his Amorum libri tres, published by Josse *Bade in 1513. This collection of mostly erotic verse

devoted to a girl named Jordana is dedicated to Joris van *Halewijn. At his return to Brabant Remaclus was appointed an archducal secretary and succeeded in securing the favour of *Margaret of Austria. He was a fervent adversary of *Luther and was mentioned as such in the Acta academiae Lovaniensis (Opuscula 324). He actually wrote a work against Luther's errors, as recorded by Erasmus in his Spongia (ASD IX-1 168), and assisted the papal legate Girolamo *Aleandro, who came to the Netherlands in 1520 in order to repress Luther's rebellion. In 1520 the emperor granted him the title of court historiographer. Remaclus died in 1524 at Mechelen, where he was buried in the church of Saints Peter and Paul.

Remaclus probably met Erasmus in London, but there is no evidence of their acquaintance before 1 June 1516, the date of Erasmus' first and only known letter to Remaclus (Ep 411). This letter, however, gives an indication of familiarity. In March 1518 Erasmus mentioned in a letter to Pierre *Barbier that Remaclus was suffering from a skin disease and 'non admodum osculabilis' (Ep 803). Some years after Remaclus' death Johannes *Cochlaeus recalled that the name 'Cochlaeus' was bestowed on him by Remaclus during his stay in Cologne (Ep 2120).

BIBLIOGRAPHY: Allen Ep 411 / E. Juste 'Notice sur les épigrammes latines de Remacle d'Ardenne (1507)' Annales de la Société archéologique de Namur 4 (1855–6) 169–97 / E. Juste 'Deuxième notice sur Remacle d'Ardenne de Florennes, poète de la Renaissance' Annales de la Société archéologique de Namur 7 (1861–2) 166–75 / de Vocht Busleyden 218–22 / J. IJsewijn and D.F.S. Thomson 'The Latin poems of Jacobus Follisius or James Foullis of Edinburgh' Humanistica Lovaniensia 24 (1975) 102–52 / J. IJsewijn and D.F.S. Thomson 'The Eclogue of Remaclus Arduenna' Humanistica Louvaniensia 24 (1975) 153–60 / Renouard Répertoire 366 / G. Tournoy-Thoen 'Les premiers épithalames humanistes en France' in Mélanges à la mémoire de Franco Simone (Geneva 1980) I 199–224.

GODELIEVE TOURNOY-THOEN

Jacobus REMIGII documented 1515–20

Jacobus Remigii was prior to the Dominicans of Brussels when he received his theological licence from the University of Louvain on 10

September 1515 and his doctorate on 1 September 1517. On 30 September 1517 he joined the Collegium strictum of the faculty as a 'regens' professor. In 1520 he was elected definitor of the province of his order.

Erasmus claimed that when the *Epistolae obscurorum virorum* were for sale in Louvain Remigii bought numerous copies as presents for his friends because he thought the book was written in praise of his order (Epp 808, 2045).

BIBLIOGRAPHY: Allen and CWE Ep 808 / de Vocht MHL 190–1 / H. de Jongh *L'Ancienne Faculté de théologie de Louvain* (Louvain 1911) 170–1, 40*–2*   IG

Hermann von RENNENBERG d 28 January 1585

Count Hermann was a brother of Kaspar von *Rennenberg; together they studied in 1533 at the University of Freiburg and were for a while members of Erasmus' household (Ep 2810). Unlike his brother, Hermann eventually proceeded to Italy and registered at the University of Bologna in 1536. He was a canon of St Lambert's, Liège, and provost of Zutphen, in Gelderland, resigning in 1559. Among his other benefices were the archdeaconry of Kempen, in the ecclesiastical principality of Liège, and the provosty of the Holy Cross, Liège. In 1566 he became provost of St Saviour, Utrecht and subsequently of the Campine, in the diocese of Liège.

BIBLIOGRAPHY: Allen Ep 2810 / Knod 443 / *Matrikel Freiburg* I-1 285 / AK IV Ep 1831 / *Cornelii Valerii ab Auwater epistolae et carmina* ed H. de Vocht (Louvain 1957) 110–14

FRANZ BIERLAIRE & PGB

Kaspar von RENNENBERG
1511–22 February 1544

Kaspar von Rennenberg (Rennenburg, Rennenberch, Rhenenberg) was a son of Count Wilhelm II von Rennenberg, bailiff of Born in the duchy of Jülich (now in the Dutch province of Limburg), and his second wife. On 3 February 1528 he received a canonry of St Lambert's, Liège. In 1529–30 he studied at the University of Bourges, where he became a friend of *Viglius Zuichemus, with whom he later corresponded (Epp 2810, 2854). On 2 June 1530 he matriculated at the University of

Orléans. In May 1533 Kaspar and his brother, Hermann von *Rennenberg, were living with Erasmus in Freiburg (Ep 2810), but by June ill health forced Erasmus to terminate this arrangement (Ep 2818). It would seem that subsequently they occupied part of the house 'zum Walfisch,' Erasmus' first residence at Freiburg (Ep 2919). In April 1534 they left Freiburg and Erasmus lost touch with them for a while (Ep 2924). They had at one time intended to follow Viglius to Italy, but he advised them against this project and they proceeded to Cologne. Subsequently Erasmus was again in correspondence with them (Ep 3031A). Kaspar rose to be *custos* of the chapter of St Lambert and undertook several diplomatic missions for the prince-bishop of Liège.

BIBLIOGRAPHY: Allen Ep 2810 / *Matricule d'Orléans* II-2 184–5 / *Matrikel Freiburg* I-1 285 / AK IV Ep 1831   FRANZ BIERLAIRE

Leonardus REPHANUS See Leonhard REBHAN

Konrad RESCH of Kirchheim,
d after 5 August 1552

Konrad Resch (Rösch) of Kirchheim, on the Neckar near Bottwar, was the son of a sister of Johann *Schabler and is first recorded in Lyon and Paris in 1508 and 1509 in connection with his uncle's book trade. In Lyon he married Katharina Klein (or Schwab), whose parents belonged to the colony of German printers and merchants. From 1515 Resch managed Schabler's business at Paris and in the same year he went from Basel to the Frankfurt book fair (Ep 330), where his presence is also documented for 1518 (AK II Ep 617), 1520, 1522, 1525, 1536, and 1543 (AK V Ep 2582). In 1518 he became a French subject, and in 1523 he held an official appointment as bookseller to the University of Paris. By this time he was fully in charge of the bookstore under the 'Ecu de Bâle' in the rue Saint-Jacques, which he sold on 1 August 1526 to Chrétien *Wechel. In moving the headquarters of his book trade to Basel, he was probably responding to the growing gulf between Catholic and Protestant governments which was bound to affect his business. He did not own a press at Paris or Basel but commissioned several printers to produce specific titles at his expense, including a Greek lexicon (1521) which he may have wished to improve, enlisting the help of Guillaume *Budé and probably of Erasmus too (Ep 1328). His Paris publications were embellished with plates imported from Basel that he probably owned himself. His business necessitated many trips to Lyon and to Basel, where he acquired citizenship and membership in the 'Safran' guild in 1522, four years before he was to settle there.

With his move to Basel in 1526 Resch was formally declared Schabler's heir (revoked in 1534) and appears as the recognized head of the bookstore 'zum roten Ring' on the Fischmarkt. While the nature of his partnership with Schabler remains unclear there is no indication that he owned capital in the *Froben press, whose products he distributed. He continued to travel to Paris and in 1532 paid a long visit to old Guillaume *Cop (AK IV Ep 1646), but he also maintained business connections with Lyon and Montpellier and at one time even with Wittenberg, combining his book trade, as was usual, with the remitting of money. The dissemination of anti-Catholic literature played a considerable role in his French business, and in 1538 the Basel council wrote to the Paris authorities in an effort to allay the suspicions aroused by his activities. In 1529 Sebastian *Franck appears to have been a guest in his house as does Jean Calvin from 1535 to 1536. He also helped Michael *Servetus to find a printer for his explosive De Trinitatis erroribus, published in 1531. His widow lived long enough to lodge Petrus Ramus when he came to Basel in 1568. In his later years Resch became a friend of Andreas *Cratander, who had earlier distrusted him (AK III Ep 1396), and the trustee for his widow. Thomas Platter too appreciated the sound advice of the kindly old man, whose financial expertise was borne out by his great affluence. Resch provided a touch of humour when he suggested that Bruno *Amerbach and his wife, who was Resch's aunt, should sleep in separate beds to permit Bruno finally to produce a much delayed edition of *Capito's Hebrew grammar (AK II Ep 643).

Erasmus was indebted to Resch for the conveyance of mail between Basel, Paris, and other destinations (Epp 1319, 1620, 1733); more significantly, however, he was frequently affected by Resch's business connections with the Froben press. Thus it was probably with Erasmus' and Froben's consent that Resch published attacks upon Erasmus by Edward *Lee (Ep 1037), Jacobus *Latomus (Ep 934; AK II Ep 715), and Diego *López Zúñiga (1522), the latter two accompanied by Erasmus' rejoinders. On the other hand, he certainly did not have Erasmus' approval when he agreed to distribute Noël *Béda's Annotationes (1526) directed against the Erasmian New Testament. Resch had Erasmus' paraphrases to the gospels of Matthew and John reprinted at Paris in 1523 but took no chances with Luke, which he had examined by the theological faculty (Allen VI 66–7). In general it appears that Resch endeavoured to balance his co-operation with controversial authors and opposing religious camps in the name of good business. In 1529 Erasmus was anxious to see Budé's recent Commentarii linguae graecae, but the book was not at once available in Basel because Resch took good care not to import it from Paris so that he could arrange for a local reprint by Johann *Bebel (Epp 2223, 2224). These irritations, however, were minor, and Erasmus remained indebted to Resch for the publication in Paris of a number of his works, including several of the New Testament paraphrases and also the controversial De interdicto esu carnium.

BIBLIOGRAPHY: Allen and CWE Ep 330 / AK II Ep 529, 643, III Ep 1423, IV Ep 1754, and esp VI Ep 2851, and passim / E. Droz Chemins de l'hérésie (Geneva 1970–6) I 95–9, 122–6 / P.G. Bietenholz Basle and France in the Sixteenth Century (Geneva-Toronto 1971) 29–30, 33–40, 347–50 / Grimm Buchführer 1391–3 / Herminjard I Ep 20 and passim / Renouard Répertoire 368 / Philippe Renouard Documents sur les imprimeurs, libraires ... à Paris de 1450 à 1600 (Paris 1901, repr 1969) 6, 235 / T. Platter Lebensbeschreibung (Basel 1944) 123   PGB

Rutgerus RESCIUS of Maaseik, d 2 October 1545
Rutgerus Rescius (Ressen, Dryopolitanus) was born at Maaseik, in Limburg, around 1497. He went to Paris, where he studied Greek under Girolamo *Aleandro and graduated BA between September 1513 and March 1514. When Aleandro gave up teaching in December 1513 Rescius began himself to teach Greek privately; among his pupils was Ludolf *Cock (Ep 2687).

In 1514 he taught at Alkmaar and on 4 October 1515 matriculated at the University of Louvain with a view to studying law. At the same time he entered the service of Dirk *Martens, the printer, living in his house until 1518 and assisting him with books involving Greek printing. As of 1 September 1518 he was appointed to the prestigious chair of Greek at the newly founded Collegium Trilingue. His salary was modest, in keeping with his status as a young scholar and his lack of teaching experience. He worked hard, however, and succeeded both in bettering his position and in gaining increased recognition as a Greek scholar. In 1527 he was offered a chair in Paris as one of *Francis I's royal lecturers, but he decided to stay in Louvain.

In about 1525 Rescius married Anna Moons (d 1 January 1585) of Louvain and moved with her to a house that she or her family owned. This entailed neglect of some of the supervisory duties in the Trilingue, where up till then he had had his room and board. This resulted in difficulties with the governors of the college, and the problems gradually multiplied as Rescius' family grew and his financial situation worsened. In 1529, when Dirk Martens retired definitively from the printing trade and left Louvain, Rescius founded his own press with the collaboration and financial participation of Johann Sturm of Schleiden. Sturm, who was later to gain distinction as the rector of the Strasbourg Gymnasium, was then one of Rescius' students and a boarder in his house. While Rescius' press produced some creditable editions of Greek Fathers of the church and classics including Homer and Xenophon, it demanded a good deal of attention and thus led to further charges that he was neglecting his duties at the Trilingue. In January 1536 Rescius launched his reprint of *Viglius Zuichemus' first edition of Theophilus Antecessor's Greek paraphrase of the *Institutiones iuris civilis*. To boost sales of the book he announced a series of lectures on that author beginning on 5 March. This step inevitably involved the Trilingue in a damaging conflict with the faculty of law. After the death of Conradus *Goclenius (25 January 1539) Rescius acted for a few days as temporary head of the Trilingue. It was suspected, however, that in one instance he had abused his powers for

personal profit, and the appointment of a permanent successor to Goclenius was hastened. The incident led to litigation between the college and its professor of Greek, which ended only with the latter's death.

The earliest known contacts between Rescius and Erasmus relate to Rescius' work as a corrector in Martens' print shop (Ep 546), and with Erasmus' move to Louvain in July 1517 their contacts intensified (Epp 617, 748, 904). When Rescius' appointment to the Greek chair of the Trilingue was under consideration, Erasmus paid him the compliment that despite his youth he was 'more learned than he gives himself out to be,' but he would have preferred a professor of established reputation (Ep 691). When a provocative prank on the part of Wilhelm *Nesen and his students led on 1 December 1519 to the unwarranted arrest of Rescius, Erasmus took immediate steps to free him (Ep 1046; de Vocht CTL I 470–8); in the ensuing litigation he provided at least moral support (Ep 1240). Although there is no evidence of frequent and enduring epistolary contacts between them, Erasmus had evidently been persuaded that the Trilingue was being well served by its professor of Greek. When the college thought of getting rid of Rescius as a result of his marriage, Erasmus defended him warmly (Epp 1768, 1806A) and in October 1527 advised him to work on improving relations with his colleagues rather than accept the royal lectureship in Paris (Ep 1882). In retrospect, however, writing to Goclenius in May 1532, he judged that the Trilingue had been blind to the consequences when it permitted Rescius to live with his family (Ep 2466). In the matter of Rescius' lectures on Theophilus he recognized that the professor's action might be harmful to the college; the letter he wrote Rescius about this time is unfortunately lost (Ep 3130). Throughout these years it was the letters of Goclenius that permitted Erasmus to keep informed about Rescius' doings (Epp 1994A, 2063, 2352, 3111), and on occasion he asked Goclenius to greet Rescius on his behalf (Ep 3052).

BIBLIOGRAPHY: Allen Ep 546 / BNB XIX 155–60 / *Matricule de Louvain* III-1 521 / *Correspondance de Nicolas Clénard* ed A. Roersch (Brussels 1940–1) I Ep 22 and passim / Alphonse Roersch *L'Humanisme belge à l'époque de la Renaissance*

(Brussels-Louvain 1910–33) I 37–55 / de Vocht
CTL I–IV passim (with detailed examinations of
all relevant letters in Erasmus' correspondence)   MICHAEL ERBE & PGB

André de RESENDE of Evora, d 1573
Resende was born of a noble family in Evora
around 1500. Among the Portuguese Resende
was second only to his friend Damião de *Gois
in his admiration for Erasmus. He was a noted
humanist poet, greatly devoted to the use of
mythology, and in his later years he engaged in
archeological studies related to Portugal's
past.

Resende began his higher education at the
University of Lisbon when he was thirteen
years old. In 1518 he went to Spain to continue
his studies at Alcalá and Salamanca, and in
1527 he attended the University of Paris,
where he befriended Nicolaus *Clenardus. He
entered the Dominican order and became a
priest. In his *Carmen* (see below), he says that
he was seized by an ardent desire 'to see and
hear' the great humanist, and in 1529 he
undertook 'the arduous trip' to Louvain,
evidently believing that Erasmus had returned
there. Resende became a close friend of
*Goclenius, a professor at the Collegium
Trilingue who was a confidant of Erasmus.
Resende was disgusted by the conservative
theologians' attacks on Erasmus and abandoned Louvain (Ep 2570). In 1531 he was in
Brussels for the festivities celebrating the birth
of prince Manuel and described the celebrations in a poem, *Genethliacon principis Lusitani*
(Bologna: G.B. Phaelli 1533), of which Erasmus
heard (Ep 2914). He never returned to Louvain
but rather attached himself to the Portuguese
ambassador, Pedro de *Mascarenhas (Ep
2570).

Resende expressed his dedication to Erasmian humanism in several poems and speeches. In the *Angeli Andreae Resendi Lusitani in
Erasmimastigas iambi* (LB I (17)–(18)) he voiced
strong criticism of the impious and luxurious
life of the clergy. Without mincing words
Resende stated that he preferred a thousand
times what the enemies of Erasmus called his
'nonsense' to the subtleties of the Scotists. In
his *Carmen ... adversus stolidos politioris literaturae oblatratores* (Basel: H. Froben September
1531), one of his longest poems, which he
dedicated to Goclenius, Resende's praise of

Erasmus knows no limits: he is the Cicero of the
age and the new Apollo; Germany is most
fortunate because Erasmus has taught the
people to love Greece and Rome and to turn
away from Mars. In contrast to his adversaries
in Spain, the royal princes in Portugal adored
him. Erasmus, who was greatly pleased with
the poem, sent it to Hieronymus *Froben, who
published it without the author's knowledge
(Ep 2500). Resende, however, had not thought
of having the poem in print: he belonged to the
Dominican order, which would not look kindly
on his defence of Erasmian humanism against
his conservative detractors. When Erasmus
was informed of his reaction he wrote to
Goclenius that he had assumed at the time that
Resende was a 'free man' (Ep 2644).

Resende returned to Portugal in 1533. The
following year *John III asked him to deliver a
speech on the occasion of the opening of the
new academic year at the University of Lisbon.
Although Resende was faced by an audience
unsympathetic to his ideas, his address was a
strong endorsement of Erasmian humanism.
He told the professors to teach ancient
languages and to read the church Fathers with
their students because it would lead them to a
better understanding of their religion. He
rejected the claim of some of the professors that
they were Christians rather than Ciceronians.
Good style, he contended, was not detrimental
to theology.

After Resende's return to Portugal, Erasmus
inquired about him in several letters (Epp 2914,
3043, 3076). Erasmus' death was a great shock
to Resende, who expressed his sorrow in
several poems. The night before Erasmus died,
Resende reported in a poem (*L'itinéraire érasmien* 90) he sent to Damião de Gois, that the
Muses had told him in a dream of the coming
sad event. He regretted the fact that Erasmus
could not give the final polish to his work, thus
echoing the advice Gois had once given to
Erasmus (Ep 3043). Resende was not wrong in
predicting that Erasmus' enemies would vent
their antagonism against him without restraint
after his demise. Looking into the future,
Resende ended his poem on a note of hope,
however. He felt certain that later generations
would restore Erasmus' reputation.

Resende remained in close contact with the
king and his brother *Henry, who both valued
his advice. In 1533 Prince Henry sent him to

Salamanca to invite Nicolaus Clenardus to
become his teacher in the ancient languages,
and the Flemish humanist accepted the offer.
Resende divided his time between Evora,
Lisbon, and Coimbra and was active writing
and delivering speeches. He spent his old age
quietly in Evora because his enthusiasm for
Erasmian humanism was no longer appreciated in his native land.

BIBLIOGRAPHY: Allen Ep 2500 / de Vocht CTL
II 395–403 and passim / Elisabeth Feist Hirsch
Damião de Gois (The Hague 1967) 64–6 and
passim / Anselmo Braankamp Freire *Noticias da
vida de André de Resende* (Lisbon 1926) / José
Manuel Guerreiro 'André de Resende e o
humanismo em Portugal' *A Cidade de Evora.
Boletim da Commissão Municipal do Turismo* 37–8
(1955–6) 5–53 / A. de Resende *L'Itinéraire
érasmien d'André de Resende (1500–73)* Textes
choisis, ed and trans Odette Sauvage (Paris
1971). This valuable edition is enhanced by
notes and a bibliography; unfortunately the
dates given are not always correct / A. de
Resende *Oracão de sapiência* (*Oratio pro rostris*),
facsimile, transcription and translation into
Portuguese by Miguel Pinto de Meneses with
introduction and notes by Moreira de Sá
(Lisbon, 1956). The notes contain extensive
bibliographies / A. de Resende *Libri quatuor de
antiquitatibus Lusitaniae ... a Jacobo Menoetio
Vasconcello recogniti ...* (Evora 1593)

ELISABETH FEIST HIRSCH

Johann REUCHLIN of Pforzheim, 1454/5–
30 June 1522
Reuchlin (Capnio) was born on 28 December,
1454 or 22 February 1455 in Pforzheim, Baden,
where his father, Georg, was employed as a
steward of the Dominican monastery. Reuchlin
probably attended the Latin school in his home
town. On 19 May 1470 he matriculated at the
University of Freiburg but soon afterwards
became a chorister in Pforzheim. As a tutor of a
son of Margrave Charles I of Baden he had an
opportunity to study in Paris in 1473; from 1474
he attended the University of Basel, receiving
his BA in September 1474 and his MA in 1477.
That same year he returned to Paris to study
Greek under Georgius *Hermonymus. Thereafter he studied law in the universities of
Orléans (matriculated January 1479) and Poitiers, receiving a bachelor's degree in Roman
law from the former and a licence from the latter

Johann Reuchlin

(14 June 1481). In the winter of 1484–5 he was
promoted doctor of laws at the University of
Tübingen, where he matriculated on 9 December 1481 and was teaching Greek. Meanwhile,
in the spring of 1482 he accompanied Count
Eberhard the Bearded of Württemberg on a
journey to Florence and Rome. Thereafter he
remained in Eberhard's service until the
count's death (24 February 1496), residing in
Stuttgart from 1483 but frequently travelling on
diplomatic errands, notably to Italy in 1490 and
to the imperial court in Linz in 1492. On this
latter occasion he obtained the honorific title of
count palatine and was raised to the rank of
hereditary nobility. When he performed legal
work for private clients such as the Dominican
order (1482–1511) he seems to have done so
without charge. As a result of two marriages to
daughters of the upper bourgeoisie he became
moderately well-to-do (Ep 457). Through his
first wife, who was his senior by about five
years, he came into possession of an estate at
Ditzingen, near Stuttgart. Between 1502 and
1505 he married again.

From 1496 to 1498 Reuchlin lived in political
exile in Heidelberg, there joining the circle
of Johann von *Dalberg. In 1498 he spent

some time in Rome as an envoy of Philip, elector Palatine, and subsequently returned to Stuttgart. In 1500 the Swabian League created a three-member tribunal which Reuchlin joined in 1502 as appointee of the princes. When the tribunal was moved from Tübingen to Augsburg in 1512–13, he retired to private life, taking up residence in Stuttgart. Amid the disturbances caused in 1519 by the war against Duke Ulrich of *Württemberg, he sought refuge in Ingolstadt, where he matriculated on 21 October 1519. From March 1520 he held an appointment as professor of Greek and Hebrew, but after a year he returned to Stuttgart. In the winter term of 1521–2 he taught Greek and Hebrew in Tübingen. By then he was ailing, and after the waters of Bad Liebenzell had brought no relief, he died in Stuttgart.

While Reuchlin promoted the study of Greek and introduced neo-Latin comedy in Germany, it was his pioneering work in the study of Hebrew language and of the Cabbala that earned him his historical significance. He used his extensive travels to establish contact with other humanists and learned Jews and to acquire manuscripts and printed works for his library, which was one of the largest private book collections of his time. In old age he surrounded himself, both in Stuttgart and during his teaching spells at Ingolstadt and Tübingen, with a circle of talented disciples.

Reuchlin produced a Latin dictionary, *Vocabularius breviloquus*, commissioned by the Basel printer Johann *Amerbach. Anonymously published in 1478, it was frequently reprinted. He also translated a number of short texts from Greek and Hebrew and composed two Latin comedies, *Scaenica progymnasmata* (1498) and *Sergius vel caput capitis* (1504); a manual on preaching, *Liber congestorum de arte praedicandi* (1504); and a diplomatic address (1498). His principal scholarly works are a Hebrew grammar and dictionary, *De rudimentis hebraicis* (1506, reprinted 1974), complemented by *De accentibus et orthographia linguae hebraicae* (1518); and the cabbalistic dialogues *De verbo mirifico* (1494) and *De arte cabalistica* (1517), both reprinted in 1964. He also wrote in German three books on the Jewish question: *Tütsch Missive, warumb die Juden so lang im Ellend sind* (1504); *Augenspiegel* (1511, repr 1961); and *Ain* *clare Verstentnus* (1512); a fourth book on the same issue was written in Latin: *Defensio contra calumniatores suos Colonienses* (1513).

When Johann *Pfefferkorn began his campaign for the suppression of all Hebrew books, the Emperor *Maximilian I sought the advice of several experts. Of these Reuchlin was the only one to oppose Pfefferkorn in his assessment (6 October 1510, printed with the *Augenspiegel*, ed A. Leinz-von Dessauer 1965). This stand involved him in a bitter literary confrontation with Pfefferkorn, the Dominicans, and the theologians of Cologne and in 1513 led to inquisitorial proceedings induced by Jacob of *Hoogstraten. On 29 March 1514 Reuchlin was acquitted by the court of the bishop of Speyer, George, count *Palatine, but Hoogstraten appealed the case to Rome. Matters went well for Reuchlin until the proceedings were halted by Pope *Leo x in August 1516. In the meantime the controversy spread well beyond Germany as both parties attacked each other in print and sought support for their positions. Reuchlin demonstrated his reputation in the scholarly world with the publication of a selection of letters addressed to him: *Clarorum virorum epistolae latinae, graecae et hebraicae* (March 1514; enlarged May 1519) with prefaces by the Tübingen humanists Johann Hiltebrant and Philippus *Melanchthon. This was followed by the publication of an anonymous satirical parody, *Epistolae obscurorum virorum ad … Ortvinum Gratium* (1515–17) of which Johannes *Crotus Rubianus and Ulrich von *Hutten were the principal authors. It was probably also Hutten who composed the *Triumphus Reuchlini* which appeared between 1518 and 1519 under a pseudonym (Ep 923). In October 1517 Willibald *Pirckheimer published his *Epistola apologetica*, and Giorgio *Benigno's *Defensio* of Reuchlin (Ep 680) was edited a month earlier by Hermann von *Neuenahr in Cologne, the citadel of his opponents. While the flood of polemical pamphlets kept swelling, Franz von *Sickingen even threatened to use force to make the Dominicans adopt a conciliatory stand (1519–20). The controversy surrounding Reuchlin was now being linked with the early conflicts around *Luther. A pamphlet of 1521, originating in Strasbourg, showed Luther, Hutten, and Reuchlin as 'patroni libertatis'

(*Festgabe* 1955, 175; it also offers the only contemporary portrait of Reuchlin). Reuchlin, however, kept his distance when Luther deferentially courted his favour in a letter of 14 December 1518 (w *Briefwechsel* I Ep 120). When Melanchthon, his grand-nephew, disregarded a request to leave Wittenberg, Reuchlin withdrew an earlier promise to bequeath his library to him and left it instead to the collegiate church of Pforzheim for public use (remnants of this library are now in the Landesbibliothek of Karlsruhe). For some time Reuchlin had belonged to a pious fraternity associated with the order of St Dominic; in 1516 he joined another, of Augustinian orientation. A widower since about 1519, he became a member of the Stuttgart Salve Regina fraternity in the summer of 1521; apparently he was a priest at this time (*Festgabe* 1955, 102). On 23 June 1520, however, a Roman tribunal found him guilty. Reuchlin appealed and, apart from considerable financial losses, remained unscathed.

In April 1514 Reuchlin initiated a correspondence with Erasmus, who was then residing in England (Ep 290). By this time Reuchlin was sixty years old, had completed the major part of his scholarly work, and was known everywhere on account of the controversy over Hebrew literature. That Ep 290 was indeed the first letter exchanged between the two humanists is indicated by Allen Epp 300:1, 37 and 324:1, although Allen and more recently Krebs (142) and Gundersheimer (44) thought otherwise. Erasmus answered Ep 290 from London with a letter, now lost, which was given to Cornelis *Batt and then handed over to Franz *Birckmann (Ep 573); he also wrote again from Basel (Ep 300). The absence of any Erasmian letters in the *Clarorum virorum epistolae* of March 1514 strongly suggests that Reuchlin had not received any by then. The collection of May 1519, on the other hand, contained five letters by Erasmus (who incidentally did not appreciate their inclusion; cf Ep 1041). Moreover, Ep 290 contains a synopsis of the whole Reuchlin controversy which would appear to be out of place if there had been prior exchanges.

Since Reuchlin assumed that his opponents had spread word of the proceedings of the Inquisition against him as far as England, he wished to restore his reputation by sending

Erasmus news of the favourable decision handed down at Speyer (Ep 290). Thanks to Erasmus, Reuchlin gained friends in England, notably John *Fisher and John *Colet (Epp 300, 324, 432, 457, 471, 562, 592, 593, 653, 713, 784). Erasmus himself was initially sceptical but inclined towards Reuchlin's cause after reading the polemical exchanges. Although critical of his long-winded style and immoderate tone (Epp 300), he did praise him highly in a letter to *Wimpfeling (Ep 305) of September 1514, which was published in December.

Ep 300 also gave Erasmus an opportunity to explain his plans for the *Novum instrumentum* and inquire after a Greek manuscript of the New Testament which Reuchlin had borrowed from the Dominican monastery of Basel. Reuchlin did not answer this query (cf Ep 324). On 1 March 1515 Erasmus raised the problem of their respective shares in Johann Amerbach's edition of Jerome (Ep 324). This ambitious and difficult scholarly project had been tackled without any knowledge of Erasmus' research (Ep 396 introduction; AK I Ep 335), and as early as 1509 Reuchlin had agreed to take part (AK I Epp 420, 425). Initially Reuchlin was asked to correct the Hebrew and some difficult Greek passages, for which purpose he visited Basel in July and August 1510 (AK I Epp 434, 438, 441), but in addition he studied manuscripts in various places (AK I Epp 442, 451, 469). At the end of 1510 Johannes *Cono, a former student of Reuchlin, was invited with the latter's consent to join the project as a Greek scholar (AK I Ep 443). In April 1511 Reuchlin began to submit his contribution, and by August 1512 he considered his task to be completed (AK I Ep 451, 460, 469). There was, however, some disagreement as to his stipend, and the printer, Adam Petri, reserved public recognition primarily for Cono's work (AK I Ep 469). This was the delicate situation providing the background for Ep 324. After Cono's death Erasmus assumed responsibility for the scholarly side of the Jerome edition and lost no time in seeking to regain Reuchlin's co-operation. Shortly afterwards, in April 1515, the two men met at the Frankfurt fair (Epp 326B, 967) and enjoyed one another's company. Probably on this occasion Reuchlin made Erasmus a present of three Nile-reed pens (Ep 457), one of which Erasmus later presented to Wilhelm *Nesen with a suitable epigram (Reedijk poem 103). Reuchlin's contribution to the edition of Jerome was prominently and publicly acknowledged in Erasmus' letter to *Leo x (Ep 335). If Erasmus failed to mention Reuchlin in his dedicatory epistle addressed to William *Warham (Ep 396), another preface by the editors, Bruno and Basilius *Amerbach (AK II Ep 551), acknowledged the significance of Reuchlin's contribution, as did *Beatus Rhenanus, who was also involved in the edition (Allen I 63).

After the Frankfurt meeting of April 1515, which remained their only personal encounter, Reuchlin sent the Greek manuscript of the New Testament which Erasmus needed (LB IX 246B, 311D, 354C, 1049D; CWE Ep 384 introduction). Immediately after the publication of the *Novum instrumentum* Johann *Froben returned the manuscript to Reuchlin together with a copy of the edition but without a covering letter from Erasmus (Epp 418, 471). Reuchlin thanked Erasmus anyway and also reported on the progress of the legal proceedings in Rome. Erasmus had intervened on behalf of Reuchlin shortly after their meeting in Frankfurt. In letters addressed to cardinals Raffaele *Riario and Domenico *Grimani in Rome (Epp 333, 334) he emphatically took Reuchlin's side. These letters were soon printed, but as the controversy became more involved and widespread Erasmus' discomfort grew. From the beginning (Ep 300; cf Ep 967; ASD IX-1 202) he had expressed his disapproval of the bitter tone of the polemic (Epp 622, 636, 808, 824, 856; CWE Ep 694 introduction) and the direct and personal attacks which differed substantially from his own more subtle and generalized irony. On balance he rejected the *Epistolae obscurorum virorum* (Epp 622, 636, 808), although he was not insensitive to their wit (ASD IX-1 140, Ep 2045; cf Ep 1135). He tried to prevent the publication of the *Triumphus Reuchlini* (Epp 636, 951; ASD IX-1 202). For Pfefferkorn he felt a deep-seated hatred (CWE Ep 694 introduction, Ep 856). He also detested his supporters (Epp 808, 824, 856); only his relations with Hoogstraten were complex and not entirely negative. He had no doubt that Reuchlin was being treated unjustly and that all good men were on his side, but he believed that Reuchlin should have reacted with meekness and patience because the controversy

arising from his spirited defence was so damaging to Christianity. He once said that for the sake of peace he would be prepared to sacrifice the entire Old Testament (Ep 701; cf Ep 703). The task of silencing Pfefferkorn belonged to the ecclesiastical and secular authorities (Epp 694, 701, 703). Erasmus was not very optimistic about the outcome of Reuchlin's trial (Epp 622, 653). Thus he had reason not to wish to be known as a supporter of Reuchlin, a role that he claimed had been assigned to him by Pirckheimer and the *Illustrium virorum epistolae* (Epp 694, 856, 1041, 1217). Moreover, he was a member of the theological faculty of Louvain, which despite his private complaints (Ep 713) was not prepared to depart from the stand against Reuchlin it had officially taken in 1515. He was indeed a 'homo pro se' (*Epistolae obscurorum virorum* II Ep 59).

When Reuchlin's case became connected with Luther's Erasmus himself was increasingly exposed to attacks and had even more reason to consider his position carefully and define his stand. He drew a clear distinction between his concern for *bonae literae* on the one hand and the affairs of Reuchlin and Luther on the other (Ep 967, 1033), but he also defended Reuchlin against Hoogstraten (Ep 1006), for Reuchlin's commitment to the *bonae literae* was much stronger than Luther's. When Erasmus' effort to dissociate himself from Luther became increasingly more determined, he accused Luther of harming Reuchlin as well as himself and the cause of *bonae literae* in general (Epp 1141, 1188, 1202). Erasmus emphasized that Reuchlin was not on Luther's side (Epp 1143, 1155, 1167; *Opuscula* 324); nevertheless he dissociated himself further from Reuchlin (Ep 1167). In particular he had never cared for the Cabbala and the Talmud (Epp 967, 1006, 1033), and Reuchlin's polemics continued to annoy and concern him (Epp 967, 1033, 1173). Respect for the scholar did not prevent a critical remark on occasion (LB VI 984E, 985F, ASD IX-2 136; Ep 1167), although an unfavourable comparison of Reuchlin's Hebrew scholarship with that of *Capito (Ep 413, printed in October 1519) was most likely prompted by momentary enthusiasm for the latter. The comment was removed when the letter was reprinted in August 1521, but this did not keep Hutten from dwelling on the point as late as 1523 (ASD IX-1 126, 142).

Between 1514 and 1517 Reuchlin and Erasmus continued to exchange letters. Immediately after his return from England in August 1516 Erasmus conveyed to Reuchlin Fisher's admiration for him and suggested that he send his young grand-nephew, Melanchthon, to England (Ep 457). A month later he thanked Reuchlin for a letter (Ep 418) that had been long in reaching him and described the admiration felt for Reuchlin by the Carthusian prior Jean *Quonus at Saint-Omer (Ep 471). It was not until March 1517 that Reuchlin replied, apparently from the Frankfurt book fair, sending copies of De arte cabalistica for Erasmus himself and for Fisher (Ep 562). Fisher's was held up by Thomas *More, who apparently wanted a chance to look it through (Ep 592), while Colet was disappointed that he had not received a copy even though he was critical of the book's subject (Ep 593). A year after receiving his copy Fisher had apparently still not reacted (Ep 824). It seems that Erasmus followed up by sending Fisher a Latin translation of Pfefferkorn's Streydtpuechlyn (1517); at the same time he reported that it had been the future Pope *Adrian VI who had caused the University of Louvain to censure Reuchlin (Ep 713; ten years later he blamed Jacobus *Latomus for this action, Ep 1804).

For a period of three years between November 1517 and November 1520 Erasmus did not, it seems, write again to Reuchlin. It is unlikely that letters were lost; rather this was a period in which the advent of Lutheranism was inducing Erasmus to review his relationship with Reuchlin. Hutten informed Erasmus of the considerate treatment Reuchlin had received during the occupation of Stuttgart in 1519 (Epp 986, 999). Erasmus' own report to Fisher in August 1520 about Reuchlin's conduct during the political chaos of 1519 and the reasons for his move to Ingolstadt was derived from hearsay and partly false (Ep 1129). Hutten later presented it as a deliberate slight to Reuchlin (Spongia ASD IX-1 142–5). When Erasmus was at Cologne in November 1520 a rumour of Reuchlin's death, when shown to be false, prompted his last known letter to Reuchlin; it reaffirmed their joint stand in defence of bonae literae (Ep 1155). Reuchlin died less than two years later, on 30 June 1522, and Erasmus immediately composed the Apotheosis Capnionis (ASD I-3 267–73) for the

new edition of his Colloquia (published in July or August). He sent a copy of it to John Fisher (Ep 1311) and another to Rome for Jakob *Ziegler, including for the latter a copy of Reuchlin's translation of Athanasius (Ep 1330). Making a saint of Reuchlin in this uncanonical fashion earned him censure from the theological faculty of Paris four years later; he wrote a careful reply (Declarationes ad censuras Lutetiae LB IX 936–7). An even more vehement attack on his attitude to Reuchlin had earlier been launched from quite a different direction. In his Expostulatio of 1523 Hutten charged him with double-faced ambiguity; this led Erasmus to reply at some length in the Spongia (ASD IX-1 134–45, 202). Commemorating his dead friends of various nationalities in the same year, Erasmus thought Reuchlin the only German worthy of mention (Ep 1347). In later years he continued to see Reuchlin as his own precursor and the champion of bonae literae who first attracted the hatred of the uncultured monks (LB IX 789D; Epp 1601, 1634, 1744). In the Ciceronianus he classed Reuchlin with *Wimpfeling as representatives of an early and imperfect period of the Latin renascence (ASD I-2 684–5), a judgment corresponding to Reuchlin's self-evaluation (Ep 562).

BIBLIOGRAPHY: Allen Ep 290 / ADB XXVIII 785–99 / RGG V 1074–5 / LThK VIII 1260–1 / Schottenloher II 169–72, V 228–9, VI 476, VII 195 / Josef Benzing Bibliographie der Schriften Johannes Reuchlins im 15. und 16. Jahrhundert (Bad Bocklet 1955) / Johann Reuchlins Briefwechsel ed Ludwig Geiger (Stuttgart 1875, repr 1962) / Matricule d'Orléans II-1 99–101 / Ludwig Geiger Johann Reuchlin, sein Leben und seine Werke (Leipzig 1871, repr 1964) / Guido Kisch Zasius und Reuchlin (Constance 1961) / Martin Sicherl Zwei Reuchlin-Funde aus der Pariser Nationalbibliothek (Wiesbaden 1963) / Lewis W. Spitz The Religious Renaissance of the German Humanists (Cambridge, Mass, 1963) 61–80 / F. Secret Les Kabbalistes Chrétiens de la Renaissance (Paris 1964) 44–72 / Max Brod Johannes Reuchlin und sein Kampf (Stuttgart 1965), cf Hermann Goldbrunner 'Reuchliniana' Archiv für Kulturgeschichte 48 (1966) 403–410 / Dorothea Glodny-Wiercinski 'Johann Reuchlin – "Novus Poeta"?' Germanisch-Romanische Monatsschrift n s 21 (1970) 145–152 / James H. Overfield 'A new look at the Reuchlin affair' Studies in Medieval

and Renaissance History 8 (1971) 165–207 /
Johann Reuchlin *La Kabbale* ... intro, trans,
notes by François Secret (Paris 1973) / Charles
Zika 'Reuchlin's "De verbo mirifico" and the
magic debate of the late fifteenth century'
Journal of the Warburg and Courtauld Institutes 39
(1976) 104–138 / Hermann Greive 'Die hebrä-
ische Grammatik Johannes Reuchlins' *Zeitschrift
für die alttestamentliche Wissenschaft* 90 (1978)
395–409 / Heiko A. Oberman *Wurzeln des
Antisemitismus. Christenangst und Judenplage im
Zeitalter von Humanismus und Reformation*
(Berlin 1981) / Giulio Vallese *L'apoteosi di
Reuchlin* (Naples 1949, 3rd ed 1964) / Manfred
Krebs 'Reuchlins Beziehungen zu Erasmus von
Rotterdam' in *Johannes Reuchlin 1455–1522,
Festgabe seiner Vaterstadt Pforzheim zur 500.
Wiederkehr seines Geburtstages* ed Manfred
Krebs (Pforzheim 1955) 139–155 / Werner L.
Gundersheimer 'Erasmus, Humanism, and the
Christian Cabala' *Journal of the Warburg and
Courtauld Institutes* 26 (1963) 38–52 / Johannes
Beumer 'Erasmus von Rotterdam und sein
Verhältnis zu dem Deutschen Humanismus mit
besonderer Rücksicht auf die konfessionellen
Gegensätze' in *Scrinium Erasmianum* I 164–201 /
Carl S. Meyer 'Erasmus and Reuchlin' *Moreana*
24 (1969) 65–80 / Paul Oskar Kristeller 'A
little-known letter of Erasmus, and the date of
his encounter with Reuchlin' in *Florilegium
historiale* (Toronto 1971) 52–61 / Douglas H.
Parker 'Erasmus in the Letters of Obscure Men'
Renaissance and Reformation 11 (1975) 97–107 /
Yvonne Charlier *Erasme et l'amitié d'après sa
correspondance* (Paris 1977) 169–173 / P.G.
Bietenholz 'Erasmus and the German public,
1518–1520 ...' *The Sixteenth Century Journal* 8
Supplement (1977) 61–78 / P.G. Bietenholz
'Erasmus und die letzten Lebensjahre Reuch-
lins' *Historische Zeitschrift* 240 (1985) 45–66 /
Charles Zika 'Reuchlin and Erasmus: Human-
ism and occult philosophy' *Journal of Religious
History* 9 (1977) 223–46 / Siegfried Frey 'Das
Gericht des Schwäbischen Bundes und seine
Richter 1488–1534' in *Mittel und Wege früher
Verfassungspolitik* ed Josef Engel (Stuttgart
1979) 224–81   HEINZ SCHEIBLE

Felix REX of Ghent, d October 1549
Felix Rex (Conincx, de Coninck) of Ghent
received the nickname of Polyphemus, perhaps because he liked to display his knowl-

edge of several languages (Ep 2071). Reminded
of the giant Polyphemus in Homer, Erasmus
also called him Cyclops, pointing out that he
was no wiser and no less bibulous (Ep 2121); he
also created a lively caricature of the man in his
colloquy *Cyclops sive evangeliophorus* (ASD I-3
603–9; Ep 2147).

Rex had apparently been employed by the
*Froben press before entering the service of
Erasmus as a famulus. He carried letters for
Erasmus on a trip to the Low Countries, which
he undertook in the autumn of 1528. On his
return he talked, apparently without sadness,
of the death of his wife and child, but his
reports should always be taken with a grain of
salt (Epp 2068, 2071, 2072). In December 1528
Rex was sent to Alsace (Ep 2081) and in
February 1529 to the Franche-Comté. In Besançon he came to blows with Ludovicus *Carinus, who attempted to have him arrested in
Dole as well as Basel (Epp 2101, 2112). Erasmus
forestalled further trouble by sending Rex in
March on another mission, this time to deliver
copies of the *Vidua christiana* to *Mary, queen
of Hungary, and King *Ferdinand (Epp 2110,
2121, 2173, 2230, 2313). From Speyer, where he
met the court of Ferdinand, he sent Erasmus an
enthusiastic letter on 23 March signed 'Faustus
celebris' (Ep 2130) and then went on to Mary's
court at Znojmo (Znaim) in Moravia (Epp 2211,
2334). King Ferdinand had appointed him an
archer (Epp 2130, 2211), and he talked about
enlisting against the Turks (Ep 2230); however,
he preferred to stay in Bohemia for a while,
tippling in his usual fashion, or so Erasmus
assumed, and writing to his master, who
refused to answer (Ep 2288). Eventually he
started on his way home, and in June 1530 he
was at Augsburg, where the diet was being
held. He was careful to secure recommendations from Erasmus' friends in high places (Epp
2334–6, 2339) but apparently failed to appease
his master (Ep 2342) and was sent back to
Augsburg (Epp 2386, 2391, 2392, 2402, 2406,
2415, 2490). After another short stay with
Erasmus at Freiburg early in January 1531 (AK
IV Ep 1488), he returned to Augsburg, allegedly on his way to the service of Ferdinand (Epp
2430, 2437, 2438, 2445). In April he was again at
Augsburg, gathering letters for Erasmus (Epp
2475, 2480), but once again he did not return
direct to him (Epp 2490, 2582). Instead he went

to the court of the Elector John of *Saxony, having obtained recommendations from *Luther, *Melanchthon, and *Jonas. When he finally went back to Freiburg in February 1532 he was given highly creditable references (Epp 2609, 2610, 2728) but was taken in by Erasmus with mixed feelings, as usual (Ep 2661). In July 1532 he delivered Erasmus' letters to the diet of Regensburg (Epp 2679, 2685, 2687). This was the last mission he undertook for Erasmus, who let him go for good after his return (Epp 2692, 2737). Eventually he made up his mind to go to Poland; on his way there he visited Cologne, Frankfurt, and the court of Hesse. Erasmus predicted a sad end for him (Ep 2728), but in that he was mistaken. After a spell of service with Bishop Johannes *Dantiscus, Rex settled at Kaliningrad (Königsberg), where Albert of *Brandenburg, duke of Prussia, appointed him his librarian on 5 December 1534. He married a religious refugee from Holland, and two letters of 1543 show him influenced by Sebastian *Franck and committed to the cause of religious toleration. In January 1545 he also attempted to re-establish contact with his old acquaintances at Basel and asked Bonifacius *Amerbach for a souvenir of Erasmus (AK VI Ep 2681). Perhaps the most colourful of Erasmus' famuli, freeloading, entertaining, versatile, and evidently capable, Rex finally died at Kaliningrad of the plague.

BIBLIOGRAPHY: Allen Ep 2130 / A. Roersch L'Humanisme belge à l'époque de la Renaissance (Brussels-Louvain 1910–33) I 83–99 / M.A. Nauwelaerts in Commémoration nationale d'Erasme (Brussels 1970) 156 / Bierlaire Familia 78–81 / de Vocht CTL I 278, IV 99, and passim / de Vocht Dantiscus 396 and passim / Alfred Hegler Beiträge zur Mystik in der Reformationszeit (Berlin 1906) 31–44   FRANZ BIERLAIRE

Richard REYNGHEER See Jean (I) LE SAUVAGE

Richard REYNOLDS d 4 May 1535
Richard Reynolds (Reginaldus) received his education at Cambridge, graduating BA in 1505–6 and proceeding MA in 1508–9. In 1509 he became a university preacher, while his election to a fellowship at Corpus Christi College followed in 1510. He should not be confused with his namesake, a member of Christ's College, Cambridge, who was admit-

ted MA in 1514. Reynolds graduated bachelor of divinity in 1513 and by 1515 had joined the Brigittine monastery of Syon, where he became confessor-general. Apart from John *Fisher, Reynolds was probably the most celebrated English theologian of the age. Reginald *Pole, who had known Reynolds from the time of his own student days at Sheen, highly praised the latter's learning and piety, claiming that he was the only English monk to have mastered the principal languages of Latin, Greek, and Hebrew. The breadth of Reynolds' learning is suggested by the ninety-four volumes he bestowed upon his monastery. Another friend of Reynolds was Thomas *More, who at one point availed himself of Reynolds' services as an intermediary to arrange a conference with the 'Holy Maid of Kent,' Elizabeth Barton. In spite of repeated attempts at persuasion, Reynolds obstinately refused to acknowledge the supremacy of the king and was finally executed at Tyburn on 4 May 1535. Erasmus mentioned Reynolds' execution in August and September 1535 (Epp 3048, 3056). A print depicting Reynolds' execution is to be found in C. Hazart Kerckelycke Historie ... (Antwerp 1669) III facing 266, while another is included in Hamilton's biography of Reynolds.

BIBLIOGRAPHY: Allen Epp 3048, 3056 / R. Pole Defense of the Unity of the Church trans J.G. Dyer (Westminster, Maryland, 1965) 253 / J. and J.A. Venn Alumni Cantabrigienses (Cambridge 1922–54, repr 1974) I-3 445 / LP VIII 565–6, 609, 616, 659, 661, 663, 666, 726, 786, 904, 1096, 1125 / A. Hamilton The Angel of Syon (Edinburgh-London 1905) / W. Roper The Life of Sir Thomas More ed E.V. Hitchcock (London 1935) 60, 80 / D. Knowles The Religious Orders in England (Cambridge 1948–59) III 214–18 / Rogers Ep 214   MORDECHAI FEINGOLD

Thomas RHADINUS See Tommaso RADINI TEDESCHI

Urbanus RHEGIUS of Langenargen, May 1489–23 May 1541
Rhegius (Urban Rieger) was born in Langenargen, near Constance, most likely as the son of Konrad Rieger, a priest. After obtaining his MA in 1516 he adopted the name of Regius and from 1525, with only one exception, he used the spelling Rhegius. From about 1504 he

attended the Latin school in Lindau. On 19 June 1508 he matriculated at the University of Freiburg, where he boarded with the jurist Udalricus *Zasius and studied under Johann Maier of *Eck and Matthias Zell. He was a friend of Wolfgang *Capito, and on 22 May 1510 he obtained his BA.

In 1512 Rhegius followed Eck to the University of Ingolstadt, where he matriculated on 11 May and graduated MA in the spring of 1516. During the following two years of obligatory teaching in the faculty of arts, he was fond of expounding the works of such authors as *Lefèvre d'Etaples and St Jerome. In August 1517 the Emperor *Maximilian crowned him poet laureate in recognition of the verse published during his studies. In the spring of 1516 he approached Erasmus, whom he did not then know personally, and conveyed to him the offer from Duke Ernest of *Bavaria of a post at the University of Ingolstadt (Ep 386). Erasmus declined politely and recommended Henricus *Glareanus instead (Epp 392, 394).

Rhegius, who had been a priest since February 1519, already possessed some Greek and Hebrew when he matriculated at Tübingen on 20 August 1519 to take up theology. In the summer of 1520 he succeeded *Oecolampadius as cathedral preacher in Augsburg. A condition of his appointment was that he obtain a doctorate in divinity. To do so, he matriculated at Basel in the summer of 1520; on 21 November he was back in Augsburg and presented his doctoral diploma to the cathedral chapter. He also kept in touch with Erasmus (Ep 1103), whose Latin version of the Epistle to Titus and accompanying paraphrase he translated into German (Augsburg: S. Grimm 1522).

On 30 May 1521 Rhegius preached a sermon against indulgences which led to a conflict with the canons; as a result the chapter appointed a successor without dismissing Rhegius formally. In November 1521 he left Augsburg and returned to Langenargen. From September 1522 to the end of the following year he served as preacher at Hall, in the Tirol, but his advocacy of *Luther's teaching caused the bishop of Bressanone to remove him. It may be an indication of his popularity at Hall that no successor could be installed until 1528.

In August 1524 the council of the city of Augsburg hired Rhegius as preacher at St Anna's and the Franciscan church. He soon emerged as a leading spokesman of the reform party, marrying Anna Weissbrucker on 16 June 1525 and offering communion in both forms during a Christmas service that year. Meanwhile his search for an appropriate theology continued. At times he was critical of Luther and leaned towards *Zwingli's positions. After the publication of De libero arbitrio in 1524 he also turned away from Erasmus, to whom he had written in enthusiastic terms as recently as January 1522 (Ep 1253). When Anabaptism gained popularity in Augsburg during 1527–8, Rhegius co-operated with the city council in attacking the sect. He attended the disputation of Bern in January 1528 (Ep 2430) and took a leading part in the religious debates during the diet of Augsburg in 1530. Together with *Melanchthon and *Brenz he advocated a conciliatory approach towards the representatives of the Roman church. But no formula for consensus was found, and when the city of Augsburg was not even prepared to sign the Confessio Augustana, Rhegius accepted an invitation by dukes Ernest and Francis of *Brunswick-Lüneburg to go to their capital as a preacher. On his way there he visited Luther in Koburg, probably at the beginning of September 1530. The meeting was decisive for Rhegius, who from this time on remained a convinced, if conciliatory, Lutheran.

In Celle important theological and organizational tasks awaited Rhegius. From the summer of 1531 he was superintendent of the whole duchy of Brunswick-Wolfenbüttel, and in this capacity he introduced the reformation in the city of Lüneburg and between 1535 and 1537 in Hannover. Cities like Bremen and Brunswick repeatedly asked for his counsel, and he played a decisive role in reorganizing churches and schools in the entire north-west of Germany. He supported *Bucer's proposal for the Wittenberg concord, and in February 1537 at a meeting in Schmalkalden he remained Luther's loyal supporter despite the difficult question of resisting the emperor. He signed the articles of Schmalkalden without accepting Melanchthon's qualifying addendum regarding the papacy. Although he had no more hope of any accord with the Catholic side, in 1540 he acceded to the duke's request that he participate in the religious discussion of Haguenau.

From there he returned a sick man and died at Celle the following year, survived by his wife and sixteen children.

In his early writings Rhegius was concerned with systematic theology, but later he turned to more practical issues. In his last years he composed a number of catechisms and many sermons; he also counselled princes and cities with appropriate memoranda. A woodcut portrait of Rhegius in the Westfälisches Landesmuseum of Münster is very likely authentic. His brother, who delivered Ep 386, has not been identified.

BIBLIOGRAPHY: Allen Ep 386 / ADB XXVIII 374–8 / *Realencyklopädie für protestantische Theologie und Kirche* ed J.J. Herzog et al 3rd ed (Leipzig 1896–1908) XVI 734–41 / *Matrikel Freiburg* I-1 183 / *Matrikel Tübingen* I 226 / *Matrikel Basel* I 344 / Maximilian Liebmann *Urbanus Rhegius und die Anfänge der Reformation* (Münster 1979) / Gerhard Uhlhorn *Urbanus Rhegius* (Elberfeld 1870) / Otto Seitz *Die Theologie des Urbanus Rhegius, speziell sein Verhältnis zu Luther und Zwingli* (Gotha 1898) / Robert Stupperich 'Urbanus Rhegius und die vier Brennpunkte der Reformation in Westfalen' *Westfalen* 45 (1967) 22–34 / Heinz Holeczek *Erasmus Deutsch* (Stuttgart-Bad Canstatt 1983–) I 116–17, 297   RAINER VINKE

Johann von RHEIDT *See Johann von* RIEDT

Beatus RHENANUS *See* BEATUS *Rhenanus*

Caelius RHODIGINUS *See Lodovico* RICCHIERI

Godofredus RHODUS Stegrius documented 1520–36
No identification has been proposed as yet for the poet Godofredus Rhodus Stegrius. The last part of his name perhaps indicates that he came from Estaires, between Hazebrouck and Lille. In 1520, evidently as a young man, he wrote a Latin poem which contained profuse praise of Erasmus. It is not known to exist today, but it earned its author a delightful letter from Erasmus, who was clearly impressed (Ep 1178). After Erasmus' death Rhodus composed an elegy in praise of his achievements and his ascent to heaven, which was first printed in *Catalogi duo operum Erasmi* (Antwerp, c 1 May

Raffaele Riario, by Melozzo da Forlì

1537) and may now be read near the end of the introductory matter in LB I.

BIBLIOGRAPHY: Allen Ep 1178   PGB

Raffaele RIARIO 3 May 1461–9 July 1521
Raffaele was the son of Antonio Sansoni and Violante Riario, whose mother, Bianca della Rovere, was sister to Pope *Sixtus IV. Little is known about his education; he was an apostolic protonotary and already living in the Vatican with his great-uncle before he became a cardinal on 10 December 1477. His first title-church was San Giorgio al Velabro, and he continued to be known as the cardinal of San Giorgio although he was promoted to successive cardinal bishoprics from Albano in 1503 to Ostia in 1511. In January 1483 he became apostolic chamberlain and in 1484 protector of the Augustinian friars. He was ordained priest in April 1504.

Raffaele was in Florence in April 1478 and was arrested for presumed complicity with the Pazzi and his uncle Girolamo Riario in the conspiracy against the Medici. However he returned safely to Rome on 20 June and from 17 September 1479 became archbishop of Pisa (until 1499). In October 1483 the title-church of San Lorenzo in Damaso was bestowed on him, and he started building there the massive palace later known as the 'Cancelleria' (allegedly spending on it his winnings at dice); he moved into the palace in 1497 but two years later fled from Rome for fear of *Alexander VI, taking refuge with the Orsini of Monterotondo. He returned to Rome in 1503 when the election of his uncle *Julius II restored his fortunes.

Raffaele accompanied Julius II to Perugia and Bologna in 1506, and it is possible Erasmus first met him at Bologna in the winter of 1506–7; certainly Raffaele made him particularly welcome in Rome in 1509, as Erasmus recalled repeatedly (Epp 296, 334). Writing to Raffaele himself about work in progress and his longing to return to Rome, he also asked the cardinal's intercession for *Reuchlin (Ep 333). That Erasmus was particularly dear to Raffaele is mentioned in the *Compendium vitae* (Allen I 51; CWE 4 409). Erasmus also recalled that Raffaele had introduced him to Tommaso *Inghirami, whom he saw performing in an adaptation of a tragedy by Seneca in front of Raffaele's palace (Ep 1347); this palace by 1510 was filled with statues, pictures, and columns of marble. Raffaele was well known as a collector of antique and pseudo-antique sculpture.

Raffaele had accompanied Julius II to Bologna in 1510 (though he did not join him at the siege of Mirandola); despite his high standing and widespread expectations he received few votes in the conclave which elected *Leo X, but he remained eminent in the court of Rome and in 1515 warmly invited Erasmus to go back there in a letter (Ep 340) which Erasmus did not receive until much later. Disaster befell Raffaele again through his passive complicity in an anti-Medicean plot; probably out of sympathy for his relative Duke Francesco Maria *della Rovere, dispossessed as duke of Urbino by papal policy, Riario supported cardinals *Petrucci and *Sauli in their conspiracy to have the pope murdered and was allegedly the candidate intended to succeed Leo. Raffaele was imprisoned on 4 June 1517 in Castel Sant'Angelo and after confession was condemned to the deprivation of his dignities including his palace; subsequently he was fined 150,000 ducats and released with the pope's forgiveness, but in spite of this and a moving scene of reconciliation with Leo at Christmas 1518, when both wept, it seems that Raffaele never properly recovered his influence. Although Erasmus was aware of his involvement (Ep 607), he apparently considered Raffaele's influence with Leo X to be high again in 1518 when he asked him to seek papal approval for his edition of the New Testament (Ep 860). In October 1520, after spending the summer at Caprarola, Raffaele left Rome for Naples, where he stayed at the Palazzo Colonna on Monte Oliveto; he evidently suffered a stroke in the spring of 1521 and became partly paralysed, dying on 9 July; his will is dated 3 July 1521 and Cardinal Giulio de' Medici (later *Clement VII) was his executor. In spite of his own wishes his body was brought back to Rome and buried in the church of Santi Apostoli, where it was found intact during the course of rebuilding in 1708.

An early portrait of Raffaele is in Melozzo da Forlì's painting of Sixtus IV appointing *Platina as librarian (Vatican, Pinacoteca); he has also been identified in Raphael's 'Miracle of Bolsena' (Vatican, Stanze). His head appears on a medal of 1478 bearing the inscription 'Virtus' and on another after 1483 inscribed 'Liberalitas' (Hill, nos 791, 333). Certainly his munificence as a literary patron is evident from numerous dedications, although none from Erasmus.

BIBLIOGRAPHY: Allen and CWE Ep 333 / A. Schiavo 'Profilo e testamento di Rafaelle Riario' *Studio Romani* 8 (1960) 414–29, though without explanation Schiavo dates Raffaele's birth a year earlier than is usually accepted / Pastor V 123 and passim / Eubel II 18 and passim / F. Albertini *Opusculum de mirabilibus ... urbis Romae* ed A. Schmarsow (Heilbronn 1866) / A. Ferrajoli 'La congiura dei cardinali contro Leone X' *Miscellanea della R. Società romana di storia patria* (Rome 1919) 101–03 / A. Schiavo *Il palazzo della cancelleria* (Rome 1914) / P.O. Kristeller *Iter Italicum* (London-Leiden 1965–) I 25, 32, II 55, 126, and passim / L. Thorndike *A History of Magic and Experimental Science* (New York 1923–58) IV 408 / E. Wind *Pagan Mysteries in the Renaissance* rev ed (London 1967) 177–8 / G.F. Hill *A Corpus of Italian Medals of the Renaissance before Cellini* (London 1930) nos 333, 791   D.S. CHAMBERS

Lodovico RICCHIERI of Rovigo, 1469–1525
Lodovico Ricchieri (Caelius Rhodiginus) was
born at Rovigo; he studied philosophy at
Ferrara under Niccolò *Leoniceno and probably also law at Padua. At Ferrara he met Celio
*Calcagnini. He was professor of Greek and
Latin at Rovigo from 1491 until the death of his
protector, Girolamo Silvestri, in 1499, and
again in 1503. On 26 May 1504 he was deprived
of his job and his voice in the council of Rovigo
because of his high-handedness in dealing
with the city. For the next twenty years he was
a wanderer, teaching at Bologna, Vicenza,
Padua, and other cities. In 1508 he held the
chair of eloquence at Ferrara, then ruled by
Alfonso I d'*Este, who financed a trip by
Ricchieri to France. In 1515 *Francis I appointed him to the chair of Greek at Milan, a post
formerly held by Demetrius *Chalcondyles, but
he held this only at the pleasure of the French.
He returned to Rovigo in 1523 and died there
between February and July 1525, according to
Celio Calcagnini because his hopes were
dashed by the defeat of Francis I at Pavia (Ep
1587).

In 1516 Ricchieri published the *Antiquarum
lectionum libri* (Venice: A. Manuzio), a collection of notes on the classics and on general
topics in sixteen books, each with a separate
dedication including one to Jean *Grolier, then
treasurer of Milan. The work was reprinted at
Basel by Johann *Froben in 1517. Erasmus
complained that Ricchieri had borrowed from
the *Adagia* without acknowledgment and that
he had clumsily tried to correct *Adagia* I vii 56
and II iii 42. Ricchieri may also have been the
'someone from Italy' accused of ignorance and
stupidity in *Adagia* II ix 1. *Beatus Rhenanus
was also of the opinion that Ricchieri was an
author of little merit (Epp 556, 575). Ricchieri
himself was informed of Erasmus' comments
by Francesco Giulio *Calvo and Francesco
*Sacchetti and wrote to him on 22 April 1522
protesting his good intentions and promising
to dedicate a book of a new edition of the work
to him (Ep 949). He died before he could fulfil
his promise, and the next edition of the
Antiquarum lectionum libri, edited by his nephew Camillo and by G.M. Goretti, appeared at
Basel (H. Froben and N. Episcopius) only in
1542. As the years passed Erasmus grew less
hostile towards Ricchieri and indeed valued

his work (Epp 1576, 2446). In the *Ciceronianus*
he echoed Calcagnini's comment (Ep 1587) that
Ricchieri was a good and Christian man (ASD
I-2 671).

Ricchieri was also the author of commentar-
ies on Virgil (1566), Ovid (1513), and Horatius
Flaccus (Basel 1545), for which he used works
of Erasmus, Aldo *Manuzio, and Angelo
*Poliziano. He was erroneously credited with
the *De orthographia* of the pseudo-Apuleius.
His pupils included Paolo Giovio, Giulio
Bordoni, and Julius Caesar *Scaliger.

BIBLIOGRAPHY: Allen Ep 469 / EI XXIX 242–3 /
C. Cessi *La 'cacciata' di Celio Rodigino da Rovigo*
(Rovigo 1897) / Cosenza IV 3034–5 / G. Oliva
Celio Rodigino (Rovigo 1869) / G. Toffanin *Il
cinquecento* in *Storia letteraria d'Italia* 7th ed
(Milan 1973) 14
                       ANNA GIULIA CAVAGNA & TBD

Bartolomeo RICCI of Lugo, 1490–1569
Bartolomeo, born at Lugo, in the Romagna,
was the son of Cornelio Ricci, a member of a
declining noble family. He studied under
Urbano Rassetti and, at Bologna, under Romolo *Amaseo. At Padua he met Andrea
*Navagero, who recommended him to Marcus
*Musurus. At Venice he was tutor in the
household of Senator Giovanni Cornaro, the
brother of Caterina the former queen of
Cyprus, and in 1513 he corresponded with
Pietro *Bembo. In 1534 he returned to Lugo as a
teacher. During a serious illness in 1538 he
wrote to Paolo *Manuzio entrusting him with
his writings for publication and giving his
library to Agostino Albiosi. In 1540 Celio
*Calcagnini secured an appointment for him at
the court of Ferrara as the tutor of the sons of
Ercole II d'*Este, to whom he wrote a letter
explaining the teaching methods he hoped to
employ, based on the personality of each
pupil. At Ferrara he got involved in a dispute
with the scholar Gaspare Sardi. He died there,
praised by Gabriello Falloppio, Carlo Sigonio,
and Giovan Battista Giraldi.

An exponent of Ciceronianism, Ricci left
many works: comedies, orations, letters and
the *Apparatus latinae locutionis* (Venice: J.
Mantonius and Sabbio brothers 1533). He also
wrote the treatise *De imitatione* (Venice: sons of
Aldo Manuzio 1545), praised by Roger Ascham
in *The Scholemaster* (London: J. Daye 1570), in

which he took up a theme already developed by Angelo *Poliziano and Pietro Bembo, arguing that imitation was not a mechanical exercise but a vital link between the individual and the past.

Erasmus heard of Ricci's book on locution through *Viglius Zuichemus (Ep 2791). After he expressed interest in the work (Ep 2810) Viglius informed him that Johann *Bebel had taken a copy to Basel (Ep 2854).

BIBLIOGRAPHY: Allen Ep 2791 / Cosenza IV 3043 / *Dizionario enciclopedico della letteratura italiana* (Rome-Bari 1966–70) IV 542 / E. Garin *L'educazione in Europa (1400–1600)* (Bari 1957) 115–17 / *L'epistolario Manuziano* ed E. Pastorello (Florence 1957) 326 / L. Ughi *Dizionario storico degli uomini illustri ferraresi* (Ferrara 1804) II 128   ANNA GIULIA CAVAGNA

RICCI *See also Franciscus, Hieronymus, and Paulus* RICIUS

Peter RICH *See Peter* REICH

Pierre RICHARD of Moulins, documented c 1506–27 November 1554
Pierre Richard was born in Moulins, in central France. He studied arts at the Collège de Sainte-Barbe in Paris under the illustrious Jacques Almain, taking his MA around 1506. He taught arts at the same college and was proctor of the nation of France in 1512. He was a *socius* of the Collège de Sorbonne and obtained his licence in the faculty of theology on 16 February 1520, ranking fifteenth in the class of nineteen. His doctorate in theology was completed on 19 December 1520. Richard was active on the faculty of theology regularly from 1521 to 1550, and he also helped direct the affairs of the Collège de Sorbonne. From 1517 to 1529 he was the curé of Moulins but resided in Paris. On 16 August 1532, Richard became a canon of the cathedral chapter of Paris. He was also the curé of Saint-Jacques de la Boucherie in Paris from 1536 to 1552. From 1539 he was a *provisor* of the Hôtel-Dieu of Paris. On 1 July 1542 the Parlement of Paris appointed Richard to a panel of five theologians constituted to receive accusations of heresy.

Allen has confused Pierre Richard of Moulins with Pierre Richard of Coutances, a professor at the Collège d'Harcourt, whose

doctorate in theology was completed on 22 November 1496 and who was the author of several works of piety. Féret, who did distinguish the two, nevertheless made several errors of attribution.

The correspondent of Ludwig *Baer about whom Erasmus was concerned (Ep 1610) was certainly Pierre Richard of Moulins, whom Baer would have known both at Sainte-Barbe and at the Sorbonne and continued to greet in letters to Paris until 1539 (Basel MSS). It was Pierre Richard of Moulins who sat on the faculty of theology committee which reported favourably on Pierre *Cousturier's *De tralatione Bibliae* (Paris 1525), which was so critical of Erasmus. In March 1525 Richard was also delegated to examine Cousturier's *Apologeticum in novos Anticomaritas praeclaris beatissimae virginis Mariae laudibus detrahentes*, and Richard's 'Epistola ad Stephanum Gentilem, priorem Sancti Martini de Campis, in qua multa contra homines sui temporis theologorum contemptores edisserit' was published in this work of Cousturier (Paris: Jean Petit 1526). Earlier he had edited with Robert Duval, the *Epitome* of Valerius Maximus (Paris: Jean Barbier for Bertrand Macé 1509).

BIBLIOGRAPHY: Allen Ep 1610 / Farge no 416 / P. Féret *La Faculté de théologie de Paris et ses docteurs les plus célèbres. Époque moderne* (Paris 1900–10) II 64 / Herminjard VIII 60 / J. Meurgey *Histoire de la paroisse de Saint-Jacques de la Boucherie* (Paris 1926) / Basel, Öffentliche Bibliothek of the University, MS G I 26 ff 4, 8
                    JAMES K. FARGE

Pierre RICHARDOT of Morey,
d 25 December 1541
Pierre was the eldest son of Berthod Richardot, a petty noble, and his wife, Marguerite Lulier. He was born about 1503 in Morey, near Vesoul (Département de la Haute-Saône), as was his more famous brother, François, who was at first a friend of Calvin, and subsequently a canon of Besançon and the bishop of Arras (cf AK VI Ep 2970). Pierre, who held a doctorate in law, was at first a member of the household of Léonard de *Gruyères. After the death of Désiré *Morel in July 1533 he succeeded him as the official of Archdeacon Ferry de *Carondelet. On 4 July 1534 he was appointed to a Besançon canonry, remaining in this position

until his early death. On 7 January 1540 he was instructed by the chapter to go to Flanders to press charges against Simon Gauthiot d'Ancier and on 14 June he reported on the success of his mission and the death of his companion, Léonard de Gruyères.

Erasmus wrote to Richardot in November 1533 in reply to an admiring letter (Ep 2880; cf Ep 3075). Their correspondence, although apparently not frequent, continued on a tone of warmth and humour, and Richardot also played his part in the elaborate arrangements made for keeping Erasmus supplied with his favourite wine (Epp 3102, 3115). Erasmus' warm feelings for Pierre may have had to do with the fact that he was a close friend of his famulus Gilbert *Cousin (Ep 3080), who was likewise acquainted with François Richardot. When Erasmus attempted to persuade Cousin to return to him he counted on Pierre to support his request (Ep 3122).

BIBLIOGRAPHY: Allen Ep 2880 / Gilbert Cousin *Opera* (Basel 1562) I 300–2, 328, 352, printing two letters from Cousin to Pierre, appealing for support against his enemies and expressing grief at the death of Erasmus / A. Castan 'La Rivalité des familles de Rye et de Granvelle au sujet de l'archevêché de Besançon' *Mémoires de la Société d'émulation du Doubs* VI-6 (1891) 13–130, esp 58–95 / Gauthier 132   PGB

RICHARDUS (Ep 1610 of c September 1525) Richardus, chaplain to Nikolaus von *Diesbach, coadjutor to the bishop of Basel, is not otherwise known. In 1524 he, Thiebault *Biétry, and Georges *Ferriot accompanied Erasmus on his trip from Porrentruy to Besançon.

Martin RICHTER of Redwitz, documented 1512–49
Martin Richter of Redwitz, in Franconia (eighty kilometres north of Nürnberg), matriculated at the University of Leipzig for the summer term of 1512. He was unable to pay more than a fraction of his registration fee, and when he met Jakob *Ziegler in Leipzig he soon gave up formal study and instead became Ziegler's inseparable companion and secretary. He accompanied Ziegler throughout his restless life including sojourns in Hungary and Italy; he met his friends, copied Ziegler's

writings in his beautiful hand (Ep 1330), and also wrote many of his letters. Ziegler liked to call Richter his brother by choice or adoption, and his correspondents, including *Luther and Erasmus (Ep 1330), echoed the phrase.

In the spring of 1529, when his master had moved to Venice, Richter was sent back to Germany. He visited *Pirckheimer in Nürnberg and Luther in Wittenberg; he submitted to the latter a manuscript copy of Ziegler's polemic against *Clement VII. After an interview with Philip of *Hesse, Richter went to Strasbourg (December 1530), where he arranged with Martin *Bucer for Ziegler's subsequent move to that city. In Basel he found a publisher for Ziegler's commentary on Pliny the Elder (H. Petri 1531) and met *Oecolampadius, and in Zürich he met *Zwingli; both men assisted in providing the means for Ziegler's transfer to Strasbourg. Richter then returned to his master in Italy but subsequently moved with him to Strasbourg and indeed seems to have accompanied him on all his further travels until Ziegler's death occurred at Passau in 1549. The remainder of Richter's life has not been traced.

BIBLIOGRAPHY: Allen Ep 1330 / Karl Schottenloher *Jacob Ziegler* (Münster 1910) xvi, 35, 40–1, 100–5, 118, 267, 290, 346–7, 379, 397, and an appendix with illustrations in Richter's hand found in one of Ziegler's manuscripts at Erlangen / Pflug *Correspondance* I Ep 74 and passim / BA Oekolampads II 577, 641 / *Matrikel Leipzig* I 517   PGB

Bartholomaeus RICIUS *See Bartolomeo* RICCI

Franciscus RICIUS d 1578
Franciscus was the younger son of Paulus *Ricius. By 1526 he had followed Paulus and his brother, Hieronymus *Ricius, into the service of *Ferdinand I. In 1532 he succeeded his brother as provost of Trent; it can be assumed that he was in holy orders. Ferdinand used him on a number of diplomatic missions. In February 1534 he sent him from Innsbruck to Philip, count *Palatine, governor of Württemberg, and in the following month Ricius wrote to Erasmus from Tübingen (Ep 2917), recalling a recent visit to Freiburg and a letter from Erasmus delivered to him at Innsbruck. On 20 November 1536 he was sent to Constantinople as Ferdinand's ambassador, returning the

following year; he also went twice to Spain for negotiations with the government of *Charles v. In 1560 he is said to have retired from the court to the monastery of Mühlstadt, but subsequently he agreed to break his retirement and undertook the visitation and reformation of some monasteries. He resigned the provostship of Trent in 1575 and died three years later at Mantua in the course of a journey in Italy.

BIBLIOGRAPHY: Allen 2917 / Constant von Wurzbach *Biographisches Lexikon des Kaiserthums Österreich* (Vienna 1856–91) XXXVI 284 / *Matrikel Tübingen* I 276   PGB

Hieronymus RICIUS d 22 February 1570
Hieronymus was the elder son of Paulus *Ricius. He matriculated at Vienna on 13 October 1513, indicating Pavia as his home town. On 13 November 1515 he registered at the University of Freiburg to study both arts and medicine but left again the following February to complete his study of medicine elsewhere. At his request Udalricus *Zasius wrote to his father to testify to his good conduct at Freiburg. In 1516 he introduced himself to *Reuchlin in a letter dated from Augsburg, where Paulus lived at the time, sending the famous Hebrew scholar a copy of his father's edition of the *Porta lucis* (RE Ep 221). Two years later Hieronymus published in Augsburg (S. Grimm and M. Wirsung) a Latin translation of *Ficino's treatise *Consiglio contro la pestilenza* dedicating it to Bernhard Adelmann and signing himself as a native of Pavia. Like Paulus, Hieronymus entered the service of *Ferdinand I and became physician to his wife, Queen Anne. In 1530 he was among her attendants during the diet of Augsburg.

On 29 January 1527 King Ferdinand presented Ricius as a candidate for the provostship of Trent, and he was duly elected. In Trent at about this time he restored Hilarius *Bertholf and Michael Scopegius to health (*Vadianische Briefsammlung* IV appendix Ep 11). On 24 February he pronounced an oration at Prague on the occasion of Ferdinand's coronation as king of Bohemia. In 1531 the estate of Sprinzenstein was transferred to him and the following year he resigned the provostship of Trent to his brother, Franciscus *Ricius. In 1537 he received the estate of Neuhaus, on the

Danube, and the following year he married Helene Jöchl von Jöchelsthurm. On 21 February 1555 he was authorized to call himself 'von und zu Sprinzenstein,' dropping the old family name of Ricius.

In 1529 Ricius introduced himself to Erasmus in a letter of laboured humility, making no reference to either Paulus or Franciscus (Ep 2131). Erasmus sent him some polite lines in reply (Ep 2150).

BIBLIOGRAPHY: Allen Ep 2131 / Constant von Wurzbach *Biographisches Lexikon des Kaiserthums Österreich* (Vienna 1856–91) XXXVI 285–6 / *Genealogisches Handbuch des Adels* (Glücksburg-Limburg 1951–) XXIII 403 / *Matrikel Freiburg* I 224 / *Matrikel Wien* II-1 401 / *Die Chroniken der deutschen Städte vom 14. bis ins 16. Jahrhundert* (Leipzig etc 1862–) XXIII 295 / Udalricus Zasius *Epistolae* ed J.A. Riegger (Ulm 1774) II 464–5   PGB

Paulus RICIUS d 1541
Paulus Israelita, called Ricius (Ritius, Ritzius, Rizzi, Ricci), was of Jewish descent but was baptized prior to meeting Erasmus at Pavia, probably in September 1506 (Ep 549). His second name was apparently adopted from an early patron, Stefano Ricci, who also became his godfather. Paulus, who at one time was a student of Pietro *Pomponazzi, lectured at Pavia on philosophical and medical problems. In 1507 he published there through the press of Jacobus de Burgofranco a collection of writings, the *Compendium* or *Sal foederis*, adducing passages from the Talmud and the Cabbala in defence of the Christian religion (subsequent ed, Augsburg: S. Grimm and M. Wirsung 1514). Burgofranco published in 1510 Ricius' *De sexcentum et tredecim Mosaicae sanctionis edictis*, another cabbalistic work that had been preceded by *Aphoristicae in cabalistarum eruditionem ... isagogae* and other texts (Pavia: B. de Garaldis 1509). His translations of some works by Averroes were published in Milan in 1511. During his Italian years Ricius also established connections with the court of France and with Cardinal Matthäus *Schiner, and for some time he served as physician to the bishop of Bressanone (Brixen), in the South Tirol.

By 1514 Ricius settled in Augsburg, where several presses, above all that of Grimm and

Wirsung, began to publish his writings, old and new, in steady succession. These included *In apostolicum simbolum juxta Peripateticorum dogma dialogus* (1514); his Latin edition of the famous *Porta lucis* by Joseph Gikatilla (1516; Ep 798), which *Pellicanus had consulted in Augsburg two years earlier, perhaps in manuscript; a commentary on the first Psalm, 'Beatus vir' (1519); and *Talmudica ... commentariola* (1519). The latter was the first Latin translation of part of the Mishna, undertaken according to Ricius in compliance with the request of the Emperor *Maximilian I for a Latin Talmud. In the same year his *De anima coeli compendium* prompted an attack by Johann Maier of *Eck and defences and rejoinders on both sides.

In 1516, if not earlier, Ricius was named personal physician to the Emperor Maximilian I, after whose death in 1519 he eventually came to serve *Ferdinand I in the same capacity. He was a staunch supporter of *Reuchlin; in a letter to *Hutten he mentioned Reuchlin and Erasmus with singular praise (Augsburg, 10 November 1518; Hutten *Opera* I Ep 94) and subsequently he defended Reuchlin in an *Apologetica ... oratio* against Jacob of *Hoogstraten (Nürnberg: F. Peypus 1523). Reuchlin in turn recommended Ricius in May 1518 to Frederick the Wise, elector of *Saxony, who was trying to attract a Hebrew scholar to the University of Wittenberg. Reuchlin said that his own rank was too low to approach Ricius and suggested that the elector contact Cardinal Matthäus *Lang, whom Ricius was then serving as his personal physician (RE Ep 256).

Ricius did not go to Wittenberg, but in 1521 he is said to have taught Hebrew at the University of Pavia. He continued, however, to serve Ferdinand, who in 1530 was trying to obtain for him a coadjutorship to the see of Trent. In 1530 he attended his master at the diet of Augsburg, and by letters patent of 15 November 1530 he was raised to noble rank as baron of Sprinzenstein, an estate in the Mühlviertel of Upper Austria. He is also said to have married the noble Bianca von Zimmern, who bore him two sons, Hieronymus and Franciscus *Ricius. If Bianca was indeed the mother of his sons – the dates are not easy to reconcile – Paulus' marriage must have taken place by 1500 at the latest. For one born a Jew,

his professional career and social rank were exceptional and remarkable.

Paulus continued his literary activity with an appeal for the war against the Turks, launched during the diet of Speyer in 1529: *Ad principes ... oratio* (Augsburg 1530: subsequent reprints relate the speech to another diet of Speyer in 1544). His *Statera prudentium* (Regensburg 1532) advanced proposals for a reconciliation between Catholics and Protestants. It aroused the ire of Girolamo *Aleandro, who was soon in a position to send Ricius' retraction to Rome. Finally, in *De coelesti agricultura* (Augsburg: H. Steiner 1541), published together with some of his earlier writings, Ricius presented a synthesis of his studies attempting a rapprochement between Aristotelian philosophy and the Cabbala. It included an apology against the late Jacob of Hoogstraten, who had argued that the Cabbala was heretical and blasphemous. Related to Ricius' medical activity is an ophthalmological prescription printed in Oswald Gäbelkhover's *Arzneybuch* (ed of 1618).

The cordial relations between Erasmus and Ricius were resumed when they met at Antwerp in the spring of 1517 (Epp 548, 549) and in Cologne in November 1520 (Ep 1160). In 1518 a letter from *Budé apparently refers to efforts undertaken at the instigation of *Francis I to attract Ricius to Paris (Ep 810). In the wake of Reuchlin's condemnation in Rome in June 1520, Ricius no doubt played his part in persuading Erasmus to voice support for the aged scholar, and even induced him to soften his disapproval of cabbalistic studies (Epp 798, 1160). In 1525 Erasmus obtained good results from a prescription for his stone ailment that Ricius had supplied (Epp 1558, 1603) and repeatedly sent his greetings to him when addressing letters to *Pirckheimer in Nürnberg (Epp 1560, 1611).

BIBLIOGRAPHY: Allen Ep 548 / *Enciclopedia Judaica* (Jerusalem 1971–2) XIV 163–4 / *The Jewish Encyclopedia* (New York 1901–16) X 404–5 / François Secret *Les Kabbalistes chrétiens de la Renaissance* (Paris 1964) 87–97 and passim / Karl Schadelbauer in *Festschrift zum 80. Geburtstag Max Neuburgers* Wiener Beiträge zur Geschichte der Medizin 2 (Vienna 1948) 423 / Gerhard Eis 'Verschollene Schriften von Paulus Ricius?' *Medizinische Monatsschrift* 9 (1955) 180–2 /

Hutten *Opera* IV 137 / *Die Chroniken der deutschen Städte vom 14. bis ins 16. Jahrhundert* (Leipzig etc 1862–) XXIII 269 / Winterberg 31 / RE Epp 221, 256   PGB

Jakob RIDDER of Kalkar, d 6–7 May 1529
Jakob Ridder (de Ridder, Rydder) was born around 1462 in Kalkar, east of Cleves, where his father, Gerhard, occupied several civic offices. Jakob entered the Dominican monastery in his home town, where he continued his studies and was ordained priest in 1483. He moved on to another Dominican house of the Dutch province and in pursuit of further studies was sent to Cologne in September 1488, to Oxford the following year, and to Paris in September 1490. After a term as prior of the Leeuwarden house he went in 1496 to Rostock, where he acquired his licence in theology. Thereafter he served as lector and prior in Utrecht (until 1501) and as prior of Asperen (from 1504 as 'perpetuus vicarius'), while in 1503 he was delegated to reform the Dominican houses of Zierikzee, Groningen, and Winsum. After being named titular bishop of Hebron (10 July 1506), he was appointed coadjutor to the bishop of Utrecht, Friedrich von *Baden, on 12 March 1507 and accorded an annual stipend of two hundred Rhenish guilders. His activity as the suffragan of Utrecht can be documented by a number of altars he consecrated and other liturgical functions he attended throughout the diocese.

Between 20 and 28 February 1518 Ridder bestowed the requisite holy orders on Philip of *Burgundy, the new bishop of Utrecht, as well as taking part in the episcopal consecration. From the time of Philip's accession he was able to share the burden of his duties with a second coadjutor, whom Philip may have appointed at the urging of his flock. Gerard *Geldenhouwer contended once that Ridder had bought his office with the profits of public lechery. His health failing, Ridder resigned his coadjutorship at the beginning of 1529 and retired to his old monastery of Kalkar, where he soon died. In Ep 811 Erasmus reacted politely to Geldenhouwer's assurance that Ridder thought highly of him.

BIBLIOGRAPHY: Allen Ep 811 / NNBW II 1207 / J.F.A.N. Weijling *Bijdrage tot de geschiedenis van*

de wijbisschoppen van Utrecht tot 1580 (Utrecht 1951) 280–90 and passim / *Matrikel Rostock* I 286   PGB

Jakob RIECHER *See Jakob* RIEHER

Johann von RIEDT of Cologne, d October 1535
Johann von Riedt (Ryth, Rijeth, Reidt, Rheidt, Reyda) was the son of the Cologne patrician Johann von Riedt and his second wife, Katharina Vratz (or Pilgram). This family should be distinguished from several others known in part under identical name forms; in particular Johann von Riedt must not be confused with Johann von Rheidt, who like him was burgomaster of Cologne but was executed in 1513.

Johann von Riedt matriculated at the University of Cologne in November 1484 and was a member of the Cologne city council from 1514, serving as burgomaster in 1522–3, 1525–6, 1528–9, 1531–2, and 1534–5. He signed the protocols of the diets of Speyer and Augsburg in 1529 and 1530 as the delegate of Cologne. He is known to have advocated the reform of the university but was equally opposed to the Lutheran reformers and to the conservative scholastic theologians. He married a widow, Katharina Kannengiesser, the daughter of the burgomaster Gottfried Rinck. They had a son, Johann, who became a Jesuit and founded the 'Gymnasium zu den drei Kronen' in Cologne, another son named Gottfried, and a daughter, Ursula.

It is not known when and where Riedt had met Erasmus; however Johann's younger brother, Heinrich, was studying at Orléans at the time of Erasmus' visit there in 1500. The Cologne burgomaster renewed earlier contacts in 1528 when Christoph von *Carlowitz, who had just been to Cologne, visited Erasmus in Basel and stayed for a while in his house. On 1 October Erasmus answered a missing letter from Riedt, mentioning Carlowitz and Joachim van *Ringelberg, another young man who recently passed through Cologne on his way to Basel, where he published his *Institutiones astronomicae*, dedicated to Riedt. Erasmus also recommended Jacobus *Ceratinus, who had apparently used him as a reference, for a

position at the University of Cologne (Ep
2058). In April 1530 Peter *Medmann suggested that Erasmus should immortalize Riedt in
his writings (Ep 2304). Riedt was also a friend
of Jacobus *Sobius.

BIBLIOGRAPHY: Allen Ep 2058 / Matrikel Köln
II 161 / Anton Fahne Geschichte der Kölnischen,
Jülichschen und Bergischen Geschlechter in Stamm-
tafeln (Cologne-Bonn 1848–53) I 355 and
passim / Leonard Ennen Geschichte der Stadt
Köln (Cologne-Neuss 1863–80) III passim /
Briefe an Desiderius Erasmus von Rotterdam ed
Joseph Förstemann and Otto Günther (Leipzig
1904) 409 and passim / Joseph Hartzheim
Bibliotheca Coloniensis (Cologne 1747) 195–6 /
Wolfgang Herborn 'Zur Rekonstruktion und
Edition der Kölner Bürgermeisterliste bis zum
Ende des Ancien Régime' Rheinische Vierteljah-
resblätter 36 (1972) 89–183 / Briefe und Documente
aus der Zeit der Reformation ed Karl and Wilhelm
Krafft (Elberfeld [1875]) 664–5 / Conrad Var-
rentrapp Hermann von Wied und sein Reforma-
tionsversuch in Köln (Leipzig 1878) passim /
Matricule d'Orléans II-1 198 (s v Hinricus
Ryt)   EUGEN HOFFMANN

Jakob RIEHER of Basel, documented from
1504, died c 1536
Jakob Rieher (Riecher, Rechner, Reicher) belonged to a Basel family of innkeepers, money
changers, and holders of public office. He
matriculated at the University of Basel in the
spring of 1504 and received a BA the following
year. At some point he entered the service of
Cardinal Matthäus *Schiner, who once referred to him as 'doctor Jacobus.' In 1514
Schiner recommended him for a canonry of St
Peter's, Basel, and the city council followed the
recommendation. Also thanks to Schiner he
was made papal chamberlain and canon of
Cremona, and in 1523 provost of Thann, in
Upper Alsace. He held no canonry there,
however, and apparently never took up
residence in Thann. In February 1525 the Basel
council asked him to resign the canonry of St
Peter's, pointing out that he had enough
benefices elsewhere and apparently had no
intention of residing at the chapter. He replied
that owing to his long and unrewarding
service with Schiner he had not so far been able
to live at Basel and asked for one more year of

grace to wind up his affairs. By the time Basel
became reformed he was listed as a resident
canon and in April 1529 swore an oath of
loyalty to the new religious order.

In the winter of 1527 the provost of Thann
was asked to inspect a bundle of Erasmus'
letters that had mistakenly been left behind at
Thann, and Erasmus subsequently took advantage of his presence at Basel to approach
him on this matter (Ep 1922). By 1536 Theobald
Molitor had assumed the provostship of
Thann.

BIBLIOGRAPHY: Allen Ep 1922 / Matrikel Basel I
273 / Historisch-biographisches Lexikon der
Schweiz (Neuchâtel 1921–34) V 627 / Korrespondenzen und Akten zur Geschichte des Kardinals
Matth. Schiner ed Albert Büchi (Basel 1920–5) I
325, II 469–70 / Aktensammlung zur Geschichte
der Basler Reformation ed E. Dürr et al (Basel
1921–50) I 204–5, III 438 / AK II Ep 672 / Karl
Scholly Die Geschichte und Verfassung des
Chorherrenstiftes Thann (Strasbourg 1907) 179 /
Another Jakob Rieher of Basel, a Dominican
and a bachelor of theology, matriculated at
Vienna in 1456; see Matrikel Wien II-1 46
                                                      PGB

RIFFALDUS, RIFFAULT See Jean and Jérôme
RUFFAULT

RIMACLUS See REMACLUS ARDUENNA

Jodocus a RINA See Jost von REINACH

Johann RINCK of Cologne, d 1566
Johann Rinck (Rynck), the son of another
Johann, who was burgomaster of Cologne (d
1516), and of Gertrud von Bacharach, matriculated on 11 October 1508 at the university of his
native city, where he graduated bachelor and
licentiate in law in 1513 and 1514 respectively.
From 1514 he continued his studies in Bologna
and there received a doctorate of civil and
canon law on 10 July 1517. In the same year he
was syndic of the German nation. On his
return to the University of Cologne he obtained another doctorate in civil and canon law
in 1518, with Petrus Clappis acting as his
promoter. In the same year he became a
member of the faculty of law, retaining his
membership until his death, although after 20

September 1560 his health prevented him from attending faculty meetings. He had been elected rector of the university for the academic year 1558–9 but had to resign prematurely on 17 March 1559, again for reasons of failing health. From 1518 he was also a member of the Cologne city council, where he supported the liberal reforms promoted for a time by Archbishop Hermann von *Wied and his advisers. His loyalty to the church of Rome was not in doubt, however, and in a faculty meeting of 7 November 1545 he demanded measures against 'heretical books.'

Rinck continued a family tradition of support for the new learning which had begun with his father. The elder Johann Rinck was a patron and correspondent of Sebastian *Brant and Jakob *Wimpfeling, perhaps even a distant relative of the latter, who mentioned him in his *Diatriba* (Haguenau 1514). The preserved correspondence between the younger Rinck and Erasmus does not reveal the beginnings of their connection. It may be noted, however, that Rinck was a friend and correspondent of Johannes *Cochlaeus (Ep 3004), who admired Erasmus, and that his gift of a silver-gilt cup to Erasmus early in 1530 arrived simultaneously with another cup given by Duke John III of *Cleves (Ep 2277); this may have been more than a coincidence. Rinck's cup was announced to Erasmus in a letter now missing, which asked Erasmus to state his views on the war against the Turks. Erasmus promptly did so in *De bello turcico*, which is addressed to Rinck (Ep 2285; LB V 345–68). The correspondence continued in a warm, congenial spirit, with one of Rinck's (Ep 3004) and three more of Erasmus' letters surviving (Epp 2355, 2534, 2618), the last of which is the dedicatory preface to Erasmus' *Precatio pro pace ecclesiae* (1535; LB V 1215–18).

BIBLIOGRAPHY: Allen Ep 2285 / Matrikel Köln II 630 / Knod 452–3 / Anton Fahne *Geschichte der Kölnischen, Jülichschen und Bergischen Geschlechter* (Cologne-Bonn 1848–53) I 361 / Hermann Keussen *Regesten und Auszüge zur Geschichte der Universität Köln* (Cologne 1918) 488 / Leonard Ennen *Geschichte der Stadt Köln* (Cologne-Neuss 186,–80) IV 372 / Schmidt *Histoire littéraire* I 233 / Joseph Knepper *Jakob Wimpfeling* (Freiburg 1902) 278, 287 / Cologne, Historisches Archiv der Stadt Köln, MS Test

3/265 (Rinck's will dated 5 March 1544) and MSS Universitätsakten   FRANK GOLCZEWSKI

Joachim van RINGELBERG of Antwerp, c 1499–after 1531

Joachim Sterck (Fortius) van Ringelberg, a native of Antwerp, was brought up in the Burgundian court from the age of twelve. On 5 January 1519 he matriculated in the University of Louvain. In the College of the Lily he learnt Latin and studied rhetoric; he must also have attended the Collegium Trilingue, where he studied Greek and in due course the sciences. In 1527 he went abroad, visiting Cologne, Mainz, and Heidelberg on his way to Basel. In October 1528 Erasmus mentioned two recent meetings with Ringelberg which had given him great pleasure (Ep 2058), but in December he associated him with the public agitation of the reformed party (Ep 2079). Erasmus also composed some Latin verses (Reedijk poems 118, 119) for publication with Ringelberg's *Institutiones astronomicae* (Basel: V. Curio 31 October 1528 and, together with additional works, Paris: C. Wechel 1530). From April to June 1529 Ringelberg is documented in his native Antwerp. Thereafter he first returned to Louvain and then went to France. After a stay in Paris, from September to December 1529, he taught in Orléans and Bourges. On 1 January 1531 he was in Lyon. After that no more is heard of him.

A first, as yet incomplete, edition of his *Opera* was published at Lyon (S. Gryphius) in 1531 (repr 1967); a complete edition followed at Basel (B. Westheimer) in 1541 under the title *Lucubrationes*. This comprises twenty-seven treatises, including five letters. Ringelberg's writings, many of which were also published separately, deal with the Latin language, philosophy, science including astronomy, and also mathematics. The most popular among them was *De ratione studii*, which was reprinted several times and as late as 1622 in Leiden and 1786 in Harderwijk; an English translation by G.B. Earp appeared in London in 1830.

BIBLIOGRAPHY: Allen Ep 2058 / H. Bosmans in BNB XIX 346–59 / de Vocht CTL II 192–5 / L. Indestege in NBW VI 877–91 (with bibliography)   MARCEL A. NAUWELAERTS

Simon RIQUINUS of Montabaur, documented 1519–1547/8

Simon Riquinus (Rychwyn, Reichwein) was born in the town of Montabaur, north-east of Koblenz, as he proudly recalled in one of his contributions to Sebastian Münster's *Cosmographia* (1554; 494). He was probably born around 1502, as this would give him an appropriate age for university entrance when he matriculated at Cologne in November 1519, giving his name as 'Simon Rychwyn, alias Dythemius.' The assumed name 'Dythemius' presumably reflected the fact that Simon had a twin brother, Johann, who later joined him as a teacher in the school of Diest. For six years Simon continued his studies at Cologne, completing the syllabus of the faculty of arts (MA in 1522) and probably also tackling medicine. At the same time he tutored counts Anton and Salentin von *Isenburg, thus honouring the wishes of his father, who encouraged him to seek employment at the electoral court of Trier. Simon's own preference, however, was for humanistic studies and teaching (Ep 2298).

From 1525 Riquinus was headmaster of a newly founded school at Diest, in Brabant. To secure his acceptance of this position, the mayor and the town clerk of Diest had personally visited him in Cologne. His salary of a hundred florins and fringe benefits was sufficient to retain him in Diest until 1528. Next he apparently went to Paris (Ep 2077) and to Louvain, where he presumably completed his medical studies since from there on he practised as a physician. Having married an heiress from Trier, Margarete Klebisch, he was able to live in style. His house at Louvain was open to visitors; among them was the Saxon Janus *Cornarius, whose conduct left Riquinus with a negative impression (Ep 2246). The beginnings of his friendship with Erasmus may well have gone back to Erasmus' visit to Cologne in the autumn of 1520; since both were friends of Hermann von *Neuenahr, it may have been Neuenahr who brought them together. Another link was perhaps Joachim *Martens of Ghent, who may have associated with Riquinus and Louis de *Berquin in Paris; Riquinus may even have visited Basel personally in the autumn of 1528 (Ep 2077; AK III Ep 1395). In February 1530 Erasmus mentioned Riquinus

and Martens as young medical scholars of great promise in his preface to Georgius *Agricola's *Bermannus* (Ep 2274).

During his years at Diest Riquinus must have formed some connections with the court of Jülich-Cleves because the territory of Diest depended politically on the dukes, who appointed a stadholder there. By September 1529 he had left Louvain to become personal physician to Duke John III of *Cleves, an appointment that brought him into close contact with *Heresbach, *Vlatten, and other members of the duke's court. His letter to Erasmus of 1 January 1530 (Ep 2246) appears to be written from the court. Along with it Riquinus sent a copy of his *Iudicium* concerning the 'English sweat' (Cologne: J. Soter October 1529). Such a fever had then infested the region of the Nether Rhine, and Erasmus may have inquired about it, perhaps because he was looking for cogent reasons to decline pressing invitations from Cologne and Jülich-Cleves. By 1533 Riquinus lived in Trier, where he is last documented in 1547/8. He practised medicine and was on friendly terms with Ambrosius *Pelargus, who praised him highly when writing to Erasmus on 1 September 1534 (Ep 2966). In 1540 Riquinus was personal physician to the elector of Trier, Johann von *Metzenhausen; he accompanied his master to the conference of Haguenau and attended him during the attack of fever which led to the elector's sudden death. Riquinus retained his position as court physician under Metzenhausen's second successor, Johann von Isenburg, who may well have been among the young men Riquinus had tutored at Cologne. Riquinus was survived by his second wife, Barbara Walter, who in 1557 married Dietrich Flade, the mayor of Trier, who was later executed as a warlock.

When Sebastian Münster was preparing his admirable *Cosmographia universalis* (Basel: H. Petri 1544) he approached Archbishop Johann von Isenburg with the request to find him a collaborator suitably qualified to deal with the region of Trier. Isenburg referred him to Riquinus, whose contributions to Münster's work provide impressive evidence for the extent and thoroughness of his learning. He supplied illustrations of the cities of Trier and Cologne, the latter of which was published by

Münster with a generous acknowledgment of Riquinus' assistance (*Cosmographia* 1554; 501). Moreover, a map of the Eifel was drawn by Riquinus himself, who accompanied it with a careful description, citing Salvian and other authors of late antiquity.

BIBLIOGRAPHY: Allen Ep 2246 / de Vocht CTL II 387–9 / L. Keil in *Trierische Chronik* 17 (1921) 82–9 / Anton J. Gail 'Johann von Vlatten und der Einfluss des Erasmus von Rotterdam auf die Kirchenpolitik der Vereinigten Herzogtümer' *Düsseldorfer Jahrbuch* 45 (1951) 2–109, esp 32–7 / Sebastian Münster *Cosmographia universalis* (Basel: H. Petri 1554) 81–4, 481–2, 494–6, 501–5 / Georgius Agricola *Ausgewählte Werke* ed Hans Prescher (Berlin 1955–   ) II 314 / Emil Zens 'Dr. Dietrich Flade, ein Opfer des Hexenwahns' *Kurtrierisches Jahrbuch* 2 (1962) 41–69, esp 44 / E. Wickersheimer 'Deux régimes de santé: Laurent Fries et Simon Reichwein à Robert de Montréal' *T'Hémecht: Zeitschrift für Luxemburger Geschichte* 10 (1957) 59–71

ANTON J. GAIL

Michael RISCH of Pirna, documented 1497–1525

Michael Risch (Rysch) was descended from a family of Pirna, on the Elbe above Dresden, whose name is represented from time to time in the matriculation registers of German universities. Michael matriculated at Leipzig in the summer term of 1497 and graduated BA in the winter term of 1498–9. In the summer of 1502 he was among the first class of students to register at the newly opened University of Wittenberg, and in the spring of 1506 he was among the first students of the new University of Frankfurt an der Oder, having graduated MA in the meantime. Subsequently he translated Erasmus' *Paraphrasis in Johannem* into German and published it [Leipzig: W. Stöckel 1524] with a preface dated from Pirna, 10 November 1524. He was a friend of Hieronymus *Emser, who informed Erasmus in February 1525 that he had arranged for the printing (Ep 1551). Emser was later to publish his own German New Testament in an effort to meet the Protestant reformers on their own ground; no doubt he wished the German paraphrase to serve the same purpose. Two years earlier Stöckel had published the four gospels in a German version

based on Erasmus' Latin translation. No more is known about Risch.

BIBLIOGRAPHY: Allen Ep 1551 / *Matrikel Leipzig* I 420, II 366 / *Matrikel Wittenberg* I 5 / *Matrikel Frankfurt* I 2 / Heinz Holeczek *Erasmus Deutsch* (Stuttgart-Bad Cannstatt 1983–   ) I 110, 118, 288, 297   MICHAEL ERBE & PGB

Georg RITHAIMER of Mariazell, d 1543

Georg Rithaimer (Rithamer, Riedheim, Ritheimer, Rytheymerius) of Mariazell, in Styria, matriculated at the University of Vienna in the spring of 1505 and subsequently taught there in the field of the liberal arts. He lectured on Aristotle and other Greek authors (*De anima* in 1515, *Insolubilia* in 1516), and in 1529 he was appointed professor of Greek. In 1520 and 1521 he corresponded with *Vadianus, evidently an old friend, who spoke highly of his scholarly knowledge.

Rithaimer is mentioned in a letter from Andreas von *Trautmannsdorf (Ep 2398).

BIBLIOGRAPHY: Allen Ep 2398 / *Matrikel Wien* II-1 331 / Joseph von Aschbach *Geschichte der Wiener Universität* (Vienna 1865–88) II 346–7 / *Vadianische Briefsammlung* II Ep 177 and passim   IG

Eustachius van der RIVIEREN of Zichem, d 16 April 1538

Eustachius van der Rivieren (de Rivis, a Fine, de Zichinis, Zichemus) of Zichem, in Brabant, matriculated in the University of Louvain on 31 August 1499 as a student of the College of the Lily. In 1500 he graduated with high standing and joined the Dominicans, who urged him to continue his studies. He matriculated again on 2 October 1508 and eventually obtained a doctorate in divinity on 1 September 1517. He was admitted to the academic senate and elected dean of the faculty on 28 February 1525 and 1530, and on 31 August 1532. On 3 May 1517 he was prior of the house of the Dominicans in Louvain, an office he seems to have held intermittently until his death. As mentioned in the *Spongia* (ASD IX-1 168–9), he attacked *Luther in *Errorum Martini Lutheri brevis confutatio* (Antwerp: M. Hillen May 1521) and *Sacramentorum brevis elucidatio* (Antwerp: S. Cocus and G. Nicolaus July 1523), both dedicated to Erard de la *Marck.

Eustachius may perhaps have been the Dominican prior of Louvain who attacked Erasmus in 1520 (Epp 1144, 1147, 1164–6). When Pieter de *Corte, who then happened to be the rector of the university, was promoted master of divinity on 12 July 1530, Rivieren took advantage of his position as dean of the theological faculty to launch into a bitter attack against the *bonae literae* (Ep 2353). Some months earlier, in the autumn of 1529, a Louvain theologian had accused Erasmus in the presence of Quirinus *Talesius of holding heretical views. Perhaps this critic was again Rivieren; Erasmus protested in a letter carried by Ottmar *Nachtgall (Ep 2264), and he may have received a reassuring reply (Ep 2277). Rivieren certainly had not changed his mind. On 26 December 1530 he dated the preface to his *Apologia pro pietate in Erasmi Roterodami Enchiridion canonem quintum* (Antwerp: G. Vorsterman 1531), another denunciation of heretical views incongruously prefaced with praise of Erasmus' erudition. Like Rivieren's earlier attacks on Luther, it was inscribed to Erard de la Marck, who took pains to assure Erasmus of his displeasure with the dedication (Ep 2629). While Erasmus decided that Rivieren's arguments were too childish to warrant any reply (Epp 2500, 2522, 2956), he persuaded Hieronymus *Froben to print a *Carmen ... adversus stolidos politioris literaturae oblatratores* (Basel September 1531) by André de *Resende in which Rivieren was ridiculed (Ep 2500).

BIBLIOGRAPHY: Allen Ep 2353 / *Matricule de Louvain* III-1 190, 361 / de Vocht CTL II 271, III 131–7, and passim / Joseph Coppens *Eustachius van Zichem en zijn strijdschrift tegen Erasmus* (Amsterdam 1974) / H. de Jongh *L'Ancienne Faculté de théologie de Louvain* (Louvain 1911) 167–70 and passim / Rivieren's attacks on Luther were re-edited by Frederik Pijper in *Bibliotheca reformatoria Neerlandica* (The Hague 1903–) III / There is also a critical edition of the attack on Erasmus by Joseph Coppens (Brussels 1975)   IG & PGB

Adrianus a RIVULO documented 1524–8
In his native Flemish tongue Adrianus a Rivulo (Rivo) was probably called van der Beeken. It is uncertain, however, that he was identical with one Adrianus Beca of Dendermonde who

matriculated in Louvain on 31 August 1518 as a fee-paying student of the College of the Lily, where Erasmus had his rooms. According to Daxhelet, Rivulo was a native of Antwerp. He was a private student of Adrianus Cornelii *Barlandus who in August 1524 dedicated to him his *Germaniae inferioris urbium ... catalogus*, published with the second edition of his *Dialogi* (Louvain: P. Martens 1524). From this dedicatory letter (Daxhelet 298–9) it is learnt that Rivulo had by then gone to Basel and was staying with Erasmus. In July 1525 he returned to Louvain, carrying Ep 1584 for Barlandus. Erasmus was reminded of Rivulo through his renewed contacts with Frans van der *Dilft, as the two young Flemings had been members of his household together in the winter of 1524–5, and in March 1528 he wrote a letter to Rivulo, trying to keep in touch (Ep 1979). No more is known about Rivulo.

BIBLIOGRAPHY: Allen Ep 1584 / Etienne Daxhelet *Adrien Barlandus* (Louvain 1938, repr 1967) 18 and passim / Bierlaire *Familia* 64 / *Matricule de Louvain* III-1 594
                                                     FRANZ BIERLAIRE & PGB

Jan ROBBYNS of Mechelen, d 28 December 1532
Jan Robbyns (Robijns, Robynus), a son of Jacob, a town councillor of Mechelen, received his MA from the University of Louvain on 18 May 1484. He entered the service of Nicolas *Ruistre, the future bishop of Arras, and began to gather ecclesiastical preferment. He was curate of St Catherine's, Mechelen; from 27 December 1501 dean of the chapter of St Rombout, Mechelen; canon of Cambrai and St Gommarus', Lier; and scholaster of the church of St Gillis, Bruges, a benefice which he exchanged in 1528 for the parish of St Pieter at Attenhoven. He also held chaplaincies of Notre Dame and the chapel of the Holy Spirit at Mechelen, exchanging the latter on 15 November 1521 for the chaplaincy of Notre Dame, Heffen.

When Nicolas Ruistre founded the College of Arras at Louvain in 1508, Robbyns and the future Pope *Adrian VI drew up the statutes of the new foundation. Adrian appointed Robbyns executor of his will; other close friends of the dean of Mechelen were Jérôme de *Busleyden and Frans van *Cranevelt (Epp 1317, 1850). When the Collegium Trilingue was being founded in Louvain Robbyns acted as adviser to Busleyden's executors. He lived on the Wollenmarkt at Mechelen in a house he had purchased on 28 March 1510. He had a brother, Walter, and several sisters, and died in 1532 at Mechelen. In his will, signed that same year, he left part of his possessions to the Louvain College of Pope Adrian VI, founded in 1524, and to the Trilingue.

Erasmus and Robbyns were friends. Erasmus fully appreciated Robbyns' continuing support of the Trilingue (Ep 1001), and his three known letters to Robbyns (Epp 805, 1046, 1435) are all concerned with the appointment of professors to the college and the difficulties they experienced at times. Robbyns' answer to the last letter, his only letter to Erasmus known to us, expressed the wish that Erasmus might promptly return to Louvain (Ep 1457, of 28 June 1524). A letter from Robbyns to Philippus Maioris, dean of Cambrai, is published by Henry de Vocht in Literae ad Craneveldium (Ep 98).

BIBLIOGRAPHY: Allen Ep 178 / de Vocht Literae ad Craneveldium xlv, 46–8, and passim / de Vocht MHL 390–2 / de Vocht Busleyden 98–100 and passim / de Vocht CTL I 8–12 and passim / H. de Vocht Inventaire des Archives de l'Université de Louvain (Louvain 1927) nos 2401, 2732 / Mechelen, Archief en Stadsbibliotheek MS 'Crayons généalogiques des familles de Grau, Robijns et van den Driessche, dit du Trieu' / Mechelen, Archief van het Aartsbisdom MS 'Notae' by E. Steenackers

MARCEL A. NAUWELAERTS

ROBERTET (Ep 1375, of 7 July [1523])
Of bourgeois origin, the Robertet family produced a number of high court officials and secretaries of state in the sixteenth century. It has not been determined which Robertet wrote and signed Ep 1375 inviting Erasmus to Paris – a letter to which *Francis I added an autograph postscript and his own signature. Perhaps he was Claude Robertet, notary and secretary to the king from 1519, a son of Florimond, the treasurer of France. Claude and his brother François were good friends and correspondents of Guillaume *Budé. Conceivably the writer of Ep 1375 was Florimond himself, who despite his great age did not die until 29 November 1527.

BIBLIOGRAPHY: Allen Ep 1375 / Louis Delaruelle Répertoire ... de la correspondance de Guillaume Budé (Toulouse-Paris 1907, repr n d) 147, 220, and passim / Rogers Epp 137, 156 / Le Journal d'un bourgeois de Paris ed V.-L. Bourrilly (Paris 1910) 275 and passim / G. Robertet Les Robertet au XVIe siècle (Paris 1888)   PGB

ROBERTO da Lecce, ROBERTUS Liciensis
See Roberto CARACCIOLO

Adolphus ROBOREUS or ROBORIUS See Adolf EICHHOLZ

Jan ROBYNS Carmelite monk, documented at Louvain, 1519
In Ep 946 of about 22 April 1519, a letter probably addressed to Jan *Briart of Ath, Erasmus referred to an unidentified licentiate in theology who, in sermons at Louvain and subsequently at Mechelen, spread lies about him (cf Allen Ep 948:162–5). Henry de Vocht tentatively identified Erasmus' critic with a Carmelite by the name of Jan Robyns who received his licence in Louvain on 21 February 1519; during the ceremony Briart made a speech before conferring the degree upon Robyns. The licentiate may have been identical with one Jan Robyns of Schoonhoven who was a student in the faculty of arts by 1510, but as de Vocht points out, the name is very common. P.S. Allen had suggested that the licentiate might be Ruard *Tapper, although he did not receive his licence until 3 June 1519.

BIBLIOGRAPHY: de Vocht MHL 197–9 / de Vocht CTL I 313, 349 / H. de Jongh L'Ancienne Faculté de théologie de Louvain (Louvain 1911) 44*   MARCEL A. NAUWELAERTS

Jan ROBYNS See also JAN ROBBYNS

François de ROCHEFORT See François DU MOULIN

Guy de ROCHEFORT d 15 January 1508
Guy de Rochefort (Guido a Rupeforti) was descended from a noble family of the Franche Comté. Like his elder brother Guillaume (d

1492), he was at first in the service of Charles the Rash, duke of *Burgundy, but subsequently came to serve *Louis XI of France. He was named secretary and on 15 March 1482 first president of the Parlement of Dijon. In the wake of his brother, who was appointed chancellor of France in 1483, Guy moved to Paris and on 9 July 1497 was himself appointed chancellor in succession to Robert Briçonnet, archbishop of Reims. He is credited with the creation in 1497–8 of the Grand Conseil, an off-shoot of the king's council especially concerned with legal and ecclesiastical matters. In the days of *Louis XII scholars such as Guillaume *Budé saw in him their principal supporter in a court otherwise unsympathetic to their efforts. In particular he favoured the humanist circle around Robert *Gaguin, including Charles and Jean *Fernand and also the Italians Girolamo *Balbi and Fausto *Andrelini, both of whom dedicated some of their work to Rochefort. Aware that Budé warmly praised the French chancellor in De asse, Erasmus wrote in 1516 that his own patron, the Burgundian chancellor Jean *Le Sauvage, was following Rochefort's example (Ep 480).

BIBLIOGRAPHY: Allen Ep 480 / Renaudet Préréforme 118 and passim / M.-M. de la Garanderie La Correspondance d'Erasme et de Guillaume Budé (Paris 1967) 317 / M.-M. de la Garanderie Christianisme et lettres profanes (Lille-Paris 1976) II 29 / G. Budé Opera omnia (Basel 1557, repr 1966) II 312–13 / David O. McNeil Guillaume Budé and Humanism in the Reign of Francis I (Geneva 1975) 13, 31–2, and passim   MICHEL REULOS & PGB

ROCHUS (Ep 1837) See Rochus HYEMS

Godschalk ROESMONT See Godschalk ROSEMONDT

Servatius ROGERUS of Rotterdam, d 3 January 1540
Servatius was a young fellow-monk of Erasmus at Steyn. Like Erasmus, he was a native of Rotterdam (Ep 3). Albert Hyma's arguments (The Youth of Erasmus, Ann Arbor 1930, 56, 172) that the two were cousins are unconvincing. While he was at Steyn, Erasmus may have dedicated a number of poems to Servatius

(Reedijk poems 5–8) and wrote him at least nine letters (Epp 4–9, 11, 13, 15), expressing his love in passionate terms. Allen's arrangement of the nine surviving letters – which may not be correct – creates the impression that Servatius at first reciprocated Erasmus' affection but later tired of the friendship and was remiss in replying. In the end, Erasmus sought simply to win his friend to the study of the humanities, chiding him for his lack of industriousness. Although Erasmus never published these letters himself, this need not imply that the attachment they reveal would have been compromising, because they are conventional and rhetorical throughout. On the other hand, it is unlikely that they are merely epistolary exercises, for however rhetorical and conventional significantia may be, there still has to be a significatum; although expressed in a gush of rhetoric, Erasmus' feelings may still have been basically true and sincere.

After Erasmus entered the service of Bishop Hendrik van *Bergen in 1492 or 1493, Servatius paid him a visit, perhaps in 1494 (Ep 39). Nevertheless, between his departure from Steyn and the writing of Ep 185, probably late in 1505, Erasmus seems to have maintained little contact with his old friend. Servatius and Willem *Hermans viewed Erasmus' initial successes from a distance (Epp 92, 142). A new situation arose when Servatius was chosen to be the eighth prior of Steyn on Claes *Warnerszoon's death in 1504. Erasmus then found it necessary to keep him informed of his movements (Epp 185, 189, 200, 203). In 1514 Servatius wrote to Erasmus urging him to return to his order in Holland. Erasmus replied with Ep 296, explaining why he was not suited to the monastery and justifying his scholarly way of life. In 1517 Erasmus obtained a final dispensation allowing him to set aside his habit and possess benefices (Ep 517). Although he did not publish Ep 296, copies were circulated and it was eventually printed. In 1533 Erasmus complained that it had been misquoted and held against him (Ep 2892), for example by Agostino *Steuco in Ep 2513. Before 1533, when a certain Robert Janszoon is named as the prior of Steyn, Servatius left that monastery to become rector of Marienpool, an Augustinian convent near Leiden, where he died.

BIBLIOGRAPHY: Allen and CWE Ep 4 / Allen 1
Appendix 3 / Dalmatius van Heel OFM *De
reguliere kanunniken van het klooster Emmaus*
(Gouda 1949) 23 / R.L. DeMolen 'Erasmus as
adolescent ...' BHR 38 (1976) 7–25
                              C.G. VAN LEIJENHORST

Eberhard ROGGE documented 1536
Eberhard Rogge (Roggius, Rhogius) was a
nephew of his namesake, the burgomaster of
Chełmno (Kulm in Western Prussia). The elder
Eberhard Rogge was a good friend of *Melanchthon, and when in May 1536 the nephew,
then a young man, was on his way to Basel,
Melanchthon gave him a letter for Erasmus (Ep
3120). It stated that the purpose of Rogge's
journey was to see and salute Erasmus and that
he was known to Simon *Grynaeus and
Sigismundus *Gelenius. Also carrying a letter
from Tiedemann *Giese (Ep 3112), Rogge called
on Erasmus a few weeks before his death. On 6
June Erasmus managed to answer Melanchthon's letter and also compose a short note
addressed to Giese for Rogge to take back with
him (Epp 3126, 3127). By 23 November Jakob
von Warten or Barthen at Gdansk had heard
from Rogge about his visit to Erasmus and the
latter's subsequent death – news that Warten
passed on to Johannes *Dantiscus.
BIBLIOGRAPHY: Allen Ep 3112 / de Vocht
Dantiscus 282   MICHAEL ERBE

Wilhelm von ROGGENDORF 1481–August
1541
Wilhelm, Freiherr zu Roggendorf und Mollen-
burg, was the second son of the Austrian
nobleman Kaspar von Roggendorf, Burggraf of
Steyr. At the age of thirteen he became page to
Philip the Handsome of *Burgundy; in 1503 he
was his councillor and chamberlain to his wife,
*Joanna. After Philip's death he continued to
serve in the administration of the Hapsburg
Netherlands. In 1506 he was a member of
*Maximilian 1's embassy to England, and
subsequently he undertook other diplomatic
missions. In March 1519 he was appointed
governor of Friesland. He held this most
difficult position until 1521 and then held a
military command in the Netherlands before
returning to Austria to plan and organize, with
Count Nikolaus von Salm, the defence of
Vienna against the besieging Turks in 1529. In

1530 King *Ferdinand appointed him chief
chamberlain. He continued to serve with
distinction as a commander in the war against
the Turks and was gravely wounded in
Hungary. He died of the after-effects of his
wound.
   Wilhelm von Roggendorf, who was once
host to Albrecht *Dürer in Antwerp in 1520 and
asked him to draw his coat of arms, is
mentioned in Ep 2409.
BIBLIOGRAPHY: Allen Ep 2409 / NNBW III
1086–8 / *Die Korrespondenz Ferdinands I.* ed
Wilhelm Bauer and Robert Lacroix (Vienna
1912–   ) II 389–90, 612, 614 / J.A. Goris and G.
Marlier *Albrecht Dürer, Diary of his Journey to the
Netherlands 1520–1521* (Greenwich, Conn,
1971) 66 / E.H. Kneschke *Neues allgemeines
Deutsches Adels-Lexicon* (Leipzig 1859–70) VII
553   IG

Hendrik ROL of Grave, died c 9 September
1534
Hendrik Rol (Roll, Rulle, Hendrik van Hilver-
sum, etc) was born in Grave, North Brabant,
and entered the Carmelite monastery of Haarlem. However he soon left to become chaplain
to the family of Gijsbrecht van Baek, bailiff
(*Drost*) of IJsselstein, who sympathized with
the reformers and whose wife later joined the
Anabaptists. Rol is reported to have visited
Augsburg at the time of the diet of 1530 and the
Strasbourg reformers a year later. In 1531 he
went to Wassenberg, in Jülich, where he
joined the circle around such future Anabaptist leaders as Johann *Klopreis. Although he
was not formally baptized until 5 January 1534,
he opposed infant baptism from the time of his
arrival in Münster, where in 1533 he was the
evangelical preacher of St Giles (St Ilgen). On
21 February 1534 he left Münster to win
support for the Anabaptist community there.
He first went to Wesel, where he had some
success, but in Maastricht, where he arrived on
2 August 1534, he was arrested one month later
and was executed about 9 September.
   Rol is mentioned in Ep 2957. Rol's two
pamphlets, *Die slotel van dat secret des nachtmaels
onses Heeren Jezus Christus* (1532) and *Eyne ware
Bedijnckijnge*, exhibit original and by the
standards of radical reformers moderate views
on the question of the Eucharist. They were
edited by Samuel Cramer in *Bibliotheca reforma-*

toria Neerlandica (The Hague 1903–   ) v 1–123.

BIBLIOGRAPHY: Allen Ep 2957 / *The Mennonite Encyclopedia* (Scottdale, Pa, 1955–9) II 704–5 / ADB XXIX 75–6 / NNBW X 827–8 / G.H. Williams *The Radical Reformation* (Philadelphia 1962) 347–9 and passim / Wilhelm Kohl 'Heinrich Roll, Beiträge zu seiner Biographie' in *Studia Westfalica ... Festschrift für Alois Schröer* (Münster 1973) 185–94 / A.F. Mellink *De Wederdopers in de Noordelijke Nederlanden 1531–1544* (Groningen 1953) passim   IG

Lukas ROLLENBUTZ of Zürich, documented 1505–30

Lukas Rollenbutz was descended from a good Zürich family and became a canon of St Augustine at the monastery of St Leonhard's, Basel, which had earlier connections with his family. He is first documented as the last prior of St Leonhard's on 10 February 1505. Under his guidance the canons surrendered their house and its possessions to the city council of Basel on 1 February 1525 in a bid to forestall confiscation by the Windesheim congregation. The cowl which they ceased to wear (Ep 1547) was exchanged for the habit of secular priests. The suspicions of the Windesheim congregation were fully justified, for Rollenbutz clearly favoured the reformers. In 1520 he was eager to meet Martin *Luther in the event that both attended a chapter of their orders (Luther w *Briefwechsel* II Ep 266). In the same year he was connected with *Beatus Rhenanus and in 1527 also with Huldrych *Zwingli, to whom in 1530 he was going to send Erasmus' *Epistola contra pseudevangelicos* and, on another occasion, a polemical tract by François *Lambert.

BIBLIOGRAPHY: Allen Ep 1547 / DHBS V 537 / BRE Ep 172 / Z IX Ep 670, X Ep 958 / *Urkundenbuch der Stadt Basel* ed R. Wackernagel et al (Basel 1890–1910) IX 382, X 23–30 / Beat Matthias von Scarpatetti *Die Kirche und das Augustiner-Chorherrenstift St. Leonhard in Basel* (Basel-Stuttgart 1974) 331–44 / E. Egli 'Aus Zwinglis Bibliothek' *Zwingliana* 2 (1905–14) 247–9, esp 248 / Rudolf Wackernagel *Geschichte der Stadt Basel* (Basel 1907–54) III 320, 364–5, 55*
                                                        PGB

ROMBOLDUS (Allen I 49, CWE 4 406)

Romboldus (in Dutch Rombout) is the name given by Erasmus to one of the Brethren of the Common Life at 's Hertogenbosch (c 1484–7) in the *Compendium vitae* several decades after the described events. Two sources deal with the nearly three years (from about 1484) Erasmus had been 'wasting' in the house of the Brethren at 's Hertogenbosch, the *Compendium vitae* and Ep 447 of 1516, where without mention of a name Romboldus is unmistakenly described as the brother who always seemed to take a special delight in young Erasmus' gifts (Ep 447:132–7). Romboldus was probably a 'repetitor' or tutor in the house of the Brethren, or possibly a teacher at the local chapter school, for the Brethren of 's Hertogenbosch had no school of their own. Erasmus could not learn much from Romboldus and also resisted his pressing solicitation to join the Brethren. Afterwards he may have regretted this decision, for had he joined the Brethren rather than a monastic order he would not have been compelled to take irrevocable vows. It seems then that the well-intentioned Romboldus was a bright spot in an otherwise rather gloomy period, and there is no real reason to suppose that he is the unpleasant and hard-handed *kriomuxos* of the adage *Sicula aula* (see H. Kämmel in *Neue Jahrbücher für Philologie und Pädagogik* 44, 1874, 316–17), as N. van der Blom did (*Hermeneus* 40, 1968–9, 222), or to connect the unflattering words said about the Brethren in *De pronuntiatione* (ASD I-4 29) particularly with 's Hertogenbosch and Romboldus (Hyma 130–1, M. Cytowska in ASD I-4 29:508–17n; the town mentioned there is Deventer).

BIBLIOGRAPHY: M.A. Nauwelaerts 'Erasmus en de latijnse school van 's-Hertogenbosch' in *Miscellanea Mgr P.J.M. van Gils* (Maastricht 1949) II 449–58 / M.A. Nauwelaerts *Latijnse school en onderwijs te 's-Hertogenbosch tot 1629* (Tilburg 1974) 191–203 / A. Hyma *The Youth of Erasmus* 2nd ed (New York 1968) 128–42
                                        C.G. VAN LEIJENHORST

Jacques ROMEROIE of Bruges, documented 1524–5

Jacques Romeroie matriculated at the University of Louvain on 31 August 1524; together with some other students from Bruges he was one of the paying students at the College of the Lily. He is probably identical with the Jacobus Rommerus (Ep 1899) who from 1524 to 1525 was the amanuensis of Maarten van *Dorp (d 31

William Roper, by Hans Holbein

May 1525) and under Dorp's supervision collated Erasmus' manuscript of St Augustine's *De Trinitate* with another belonging to the abbey of Gembloux. The subsequent life of Romeroie has not been traced.

BIBLIOGRAPHY: *Matricule de Louvain* III-1 730 / de Vocht *Literae ad Craneveldium* Ep 107 introduction / de Vocht MHL 249   PGB

Jacobus ROMMERUS *See Jacques* ROMEROIE

Margaret ROPER *See Margaret* MORE

Thomas ROPER of London, died c 26 February 1598
Thomas was the eldest son of William *Roper and Margaret *More. In a letter dated Christmas 1523 Erasmus sent felicitations on Thomas' recent birth (Ep 1404). After studies at Louvain, where he matriculated on 20 July 1548, Thomas was admitted to Lincoln's Inn, London, in 1557. There he completed legal studies and subsequently succeeded his father as prothonotary (chief clerk) of the Court of King's Bench in 1577. He was buried in the

Roper family vault at St Dunstan's, Canterbury.

BIBLIOGRAPHY: Allen Ep 1404 / *Matricule de Louvain* IV-1 369 / William Roper *Life of Thomas More* ed E.V. Hitchcock (London 1935) xxx–xxxi and passim / P. Hogrefe 'Sir Thomas More's connection with the Roper family' *Publications of the Modern Language Association of America* 47 (1932) 523–33 / R.J. Schoeck 'Anthony Bonvisi, the Heywoods and the Ropers' *Notes and Queries* 197 (26 April 1952) 178–9 / E.E. Reynolds *Margaret Roper* (London 1960) passim   R.J. SCHOECK

William ROPER c 1496–4 January 1578
William was the son of John Roper, a gentleman established in Kent and a close legal associate of both Sir John (1) *More and Sir Thomas *More. In 1518 William was admitted to Lincoln's Inn, called to the Bar in 1525, and called to the Bench of Lincoln's Inn in 1535. Before he died on 7 April 1524 John Roper secured for his son the lucrative office that he had himself held, that of prothonotary (or chief clerk) of the Court of King's Bench, and William retained this office until 1577 (when he passed it on to his son Thomas). In 1529 he was elected a member of Parliament; under Queen *Mary he served again as a member of Parliament (1554, 1555, and 1558) and also as sheriff of Kent.

By the time of his admission to Lincoln's Inn Roper had entered the household of Thomas More, whose daughter Margaret *More he married on 2 July 1521 (Ep 1233). In Ep 1404 (1523) Erasmus congratulated Margaret on the birth of their first son, Thomas *Roper, and there were other children: another son, Anthony, and three daughters, Elizabeth, Margaret, and Mary. One of the few More family members who did not go into exile under Elizabeth, William died in England; he was not buried at Chelsea with his wife but in the Roper vault at St Dunstan's, Canterbury, where the head of Thomas More is said to rest. There is a miniature watercolour of him on paper by Hans *Holbein, now in the Metropolitan Museum of Art, New York.

A lawyer and not a humanist, William Roper is the author of the splendid life of More that exists in more than thirteen sixteenth-century manuscripts and was first printed in 1626. It is historically important both as an early English biography and as the foundation of all subsequent biographies of More. Erasmus is cited once only, as a witness of More's 'cleere unspotted consciens.'

BIBLIOGRAPHY: Allen Ep 1404 / DNB XVII 215–16 / E.E. Reynolds in *New Catholic Encyclopedia* (New York 1966–79) XII 665–6, with a reproduction of Holbein's watercolour / E.E. Reynolds *Margaret Roper* (London 1960) / R.J. Schoeck 'William Rastell and the prothonotaries' *Notes and Queries* 197 (13 September 1952) 398–9 / R.J. Schoeck 'Anthony Bonvisi, the Heywoods and the Ropers' *Notes and Queries* 197 (26 April 1952) 178–9 / P. Hogrefe 'Sir Thomas More's connections with the Roper family' *Publications of the Modern Language Association of America* 47 (1932) 523–33

R.J. SCHOECK

ROSARIUS *See Sébastien* ROSIER

Godschalk ROSEMONDT of Eindhoven, d 5 December 1526

Born around 1483 of a respected family of Eindhoven, now in the Dutch province of North Brabant, Godschalk Rosemondt (Roesmont, Rosemundus) matriculated on 6 November 1499 at the University of Louvain. He was promoted MA on 26 July 1502 and while commencing the study of theology he taught arts subjects at his college, the Falcon, from 1504. In April 1515 he was a licentiate in theology and the following year he received his doctorate. Having taken holy orders, he was appointed to several benefices within the gift of the faculty of arts, and in October 1515 he became a member of the theological faculty and succeeded to one of the lesser professorships. In 1520 he finally obtained one of the principal chairs that had been made vacant by the death of Jan *Briart and the corresponding primary prebend in the chapter of St Peter's. He had been dean of the theological faculty for the winter terms of 1518–19 and 1520–1 and for the winter term of 1520 he served as the rector of the university. As a personal friend of Pope *Adrian VI he was one of the executors of his will in 1524 and was also appointed the first president of Pope's College endowed by

Adrian VI. He retained this position until his death, which followed several months of very grave illness (Epp 1732, 1766, 1768).

As a highly respected theologian Rosemondt was occasionally involved in the trials of heretics. He also published several devotional works in the vernacular, which proved highly successful (for details see Coppens and Inderstege). The most widely read among them, in the view of Inderstege, is also the most significant and even lends itself to a comparison with Erasmus' *Moria* and *Colloquia*, at least in terms of style and intent. This is the *Boecxken van der biechten* (Antwerp: H. Eckert 6 March 1517, reprinted many times). It was followed by an analogous work in Latin, which is, however, no mere translation: *Confessionale* (Antwerp: A. van Hoogstraten 14 May 1518). Reprinted three times to 1525, it is shown in Tentler's analysis to be a work of learning and pastoral wisdom.

Rosemondt clearly viewed the multiple feuds between Erasmus and Louvain's conservative monks and theologians with an open mind and even a measure of sympathy for Erasmus. When Rosemondt was rector, Erasmus felt encouraged to lodge a formal complaint with him against Nicolaas *Baechem Egmondanus and others while at the same time attempting to clarify his position with regard to *Luther (Ep 1153). Rosemondt reacted by summoning the two protagonists into his presence; neither Erasmus nor Baechem expected to be reconciled and, in fact, the rector endeavoured in vain to find common ground between their positions. Erasmus reported the meeting at length to Thomas *More (Ep 1162) and suggested that it confirmed Rosemondt in his favourable opinion of Erasmus (see also Epp 1173, 1217, 1581). Erasmus again appealed to him for help against Laurens *Laurensen, whom the rector did indeed help to silence (Epp 1164, 1581), and other critics (Ep 1172). Over the years he retained his high regard for Rosemondt's sense of justice (Epp 1173, 1582), and after the theologian's death he echoed *Goclenius' praise of him (Epp 1768, 1821).

BIBLIOGRAPHY: Allen Ep 1153 / *Matricule de Louvain* III-1 194, 637 / L. Inderstege in NBW VI 820–31 / NNBW V 612–13 / de Vocht *Literae ad Craneveldium* Ep 213 and passim / de Vocht CTL I

356 and passim / H. de Jongh L'Ancienne Faculté de théologie de Louvain (Louvain 1911) 165–7 and passim / On Rosemondt's Confessionale and its editions see C. Coppens in Ex officina: Bulletin van de Vrienden van de Leuvense Universiteitsbibliotheek 2 (1985) 13–36, 94–108 and Thomas N. Tentler Sin and Confession on the Eve of the Reformation (Princeton 1977) 37–8 and passim

PGB

Wibrandis ROSENBLATT of Säckingen, 1504–1 November 1564

Wibrandis was the daughter of Hans Rosenblatt, bailiff of Säckingen, in the Breisgau, and a colonel in the wars of *Maximilian I. Her mother, Magdalena Strub, was from Basel, where Wibrandis grew up during the years her father spent in Maximilian's service and where in 1524 she married Ludwig Keller, MA. Keller died on 25 July 1526, leaving her with a one year old daughter. Her second marriage to Johannes *Oecolampadius, probably on 15 March 1528, led to cynical remarks by Erasmus (Epp 1977, 1979, 2054) and especially Bonifacius *Amerbach, who contrasted her ('elegans, succulenta') with the 'living corpse' of her theologian husband, who was twenty-two years older than his bride (AK III Ep 1253). Oecolampadius himself emphasized that she was poor, pious, and had 'born the cross' for several years (BA Oekolampads II 162, 183). He praised her domestic virtues; she also bore him three children.

After his death Wibrandis married Wolfgang Faber *Capito on 11 April 1532 (Ep 2613) and as a result moved to Strasbourg. This marriage was urgently recommended by Martin *Bucer, wheras Capito, it seems, had set his heart on another. Wibrandis had five children by him before he died in November 1541. In the spring of 1542 she married Bucer, her last husband, who accepted responsibility for the four children still in her charge and in turn had reason to praise her care of his own children from a previous marriage; they also had two more. In 1549 she followed Bucer to his exile in England but returned to Strasbourg in 1550 to fetch more members of the family and possessions; she was back in England in time to see him die in March 1551. She returned briefly to Strasbourg and from 1553 to her death lived once more with her family at Basel, where she died of the plague and was buried in Oecolampadius' tomb in the cathedral. Some of her letters are printed in BA Oekolampads. They show a moral strength in keeping with the physical energy she had displayed throughout her life, and a readiness to speak her mind freely.

BIBLIOGRAPHY: BA Oekolampads II 143–4, 722–4, 784–7, 818–33, 841–4, 851–4, and passim / Z IX Ep 699 and passim / R.H. Bainton Women of the Reformation in Germany and Italy (Boston 1974) 79–96

PGB

Sébastien ROSIER at Nozeroy, Franche-Comté

Sébastien Rosier (Rosarius), a friend of Gilbert *Cousin, was perhaps one of the youths whose visit to Freiburg is mentioned in Ep 3123 of about May 1536. His presence at Freiburg, however, has not been documented.

BIBLIOGRAPHY: Allen Epp 2381, 3123 / Gilbert Cousin Opera (Basel 1562) I 218, 304, 317–19; cf 335.

PGB

Johannes ROSINUS d 18 November 1545

Johannes Rosinus was born in Silesia. A poet laureate, he contributed verses to several books printed at Vienna between 1528 and 1539, sometimes in conjunction with Georg von *Logau. He also wrote a history of the Turkish siege of Vienna in 1529 (Augsburg 1538). He was a friend of Johannes Alexander *Brassicanus and Caspar *Ursinus Velius, while Johannes *Fabri was his patron and may have been instrumental in winning him the favour of *Ferdinand I, who named him royal chaplain, court tutor, and provost of Zwettl, in Lower Austria. In 1544 he was appointed provost of St Stephen's, Vienna, and chancellor of the university.

In 1526 the theological faculty accused Rosinus of heterodox opinions after a sermon he had preached at St Stephen's, but he defended himself resolutely and prevailed. As a member of Fabri's retinue he went to Cologne and Aachen in 1531 for the election and coronation of Ferdinand as king of the Romans. On this occasion he also went to Freiburg to visit Erasmus, who recalled this visit with great warmth in Ep 2455, written in reply to a letter and a poem sent by Rosinus.

BIBLIOGRAPHY: Allen Ep 2455 / Michael Denis

Wiens Buchdruckergeschichte bis MDLX (Vienna 1782–93) I 364–5, nos 283, 285, 382, 407

PGB

Cornelius ROSNER (Ep 2984 of 20 December 1534)
Cornelius Rosner was apparently a colleague of Johannes *Dryander and a rival of Konrad *Nyder, both physicians connected with Koblenz and the electoral court of Trier. He has not been identified. A Hieronymus Rosener of Koblenz matriculated at the University of Erfurt for the summer term of 1509 (*Matrikel Erfurt* II 261).

PGB

Andreas RÖSSLIN prior of the Dominicans at Freiburg, d 1536
Erasmus' account of Erasmius *Froben's spell as servant-pupil in the house of a prior (Ep 2236) requires further elucidation. Allen assumed that the prior lived in Freiburg and tentatively suggested Andreas Rösslin, a Dominican who lectured on divinity in the university.

Sebastian von ROTENHAN 1478–June 1532
Sebastian von Rotenhan (Rotenhaen, Rubrigallus) was born in Rentweinsdorf, in Lower Franconia, the eldest son of Matthäus von Rotenhan, a knight. He matriculated at the University of Erfurt in 1493, studying mainly mathematics, history, geography, and law. Three years later he went to Ingolstadt and in 1498 to Bologna, where he studied under Filippo (I) *Beroaldo; he obtained a doctorate of laws in Siena on 31 October 1503. From 1507 to 1512 he was assessor at the imperial law court (Reichskammergericht) in Speyer; then he travelled extensively through Germany, Spain, France, England, Greece, and Turkey. He was in Palestine in 1514 and became a knight of the Holy Sepulchre. After his return he worked again at the Reichskammergericht in Speyer (1516–19), was a councillor of Albert of *Brandenburg, archbishop of Mainz (1519–21), and then joined the household of Konrad von *Thüngen, bishop of Würzburg.
    Rotenhan's major contribution to scholarship was the first edition of the *Chronicon* of Regino of Prüm (Mainz: J. Schöffer 1521); it was dedicated to the Emperor *Charles v. Rotenhan was a friend of Ulrich von *Hutten, but more

conservative in his views. In 1524 he defended the fortress on the Marienberg, near Würzburg, against the rebellious peasants, but he also mediated between bishop and peasants. He attended the diet of Augsburg in 1530 as imperial councillor. Rotenhan never married and died in Rentweinsdorf near the end of June 1532.
    Rotenhan's main interests lay in the field of geography. He designed the first map of Franconia, printed with an imperial 'privilege' in Ingolstadt on 4 January 1533 and edited by Petrus *Apianus, to whom he had handed over the map shortly before his sudden death. A copy of the map is in the Bibliothèque Nationale at Paris. Rotenhan published a pamphlet containing geographical names and their explanations and a translation of his knightly mottoes in ten languages, *Prisci aliquot Germaniae ac vicinorum populi* [Augsburg: H. von Erfurt 1520?].
    Rotenhan must have written to Erasmus prior to August 1520 offering him his support againt the attacks of Edward *Lee. In Ep 1134 Erasmus thanked him for his kind offer.

BIBLIOGRAPHY: Allen Ep 1134 / ADB XXIX 299–301 / Knod 462–3 / BRE Ep 258 / *Matrikel Erfurt* II 175 / *Deutsche Reichstagsakten* Jüngere Reihe (Gotha-Göttingen 1893–   ) I–III passim / On Rotenhan as geographer see Walter M. Brod in *Mainfränkisches Jahrbuch für Geschichte und Kunst* 11 (1959) 121–42, 12 (1960) 69–78

IG

Bernhard ROTHMANN of Stadtlohn, c 1495–24 June 1535
Bernhard (Bernt) Rothmann (Rottman) was born in Stadtlohn, west of Münster, the son of a blacksmith. He was a schoolmaster in Warendorf, east of Münster, then went to Mainz in 1524 to obtain a MA, and by 1529 had received a chaplaincy at the chapter of St Maurice's near Münster (Ep 2957). After further journeys which allowed him to visit *Melanchthon in Wittenberg and apparently also *Capito in Strasbourg, he returned to Münster in 1531 and was appointed to the parish of St Lambert. His sermons soon became popular as he emerged as one of the chief clerical spokesmen of the reform party. On 23 January 1532 he published his confession of faith in thirty articles, largely moderate and

Lutheran. Under the influence of the Anabaptist preachers who arrived from Wassenberg in Jülich, Rothmann's views became steadily more radical, and so did his pastoral practice. By February 1534 the city was controlled by the Anabaptists under the leadership of Jan *Mathijszoon and *Jan of Leiden. Rothmann, their intellectual leader (Ep 2957), had numerous pamphlets printed on a press installed in his own house: for example, *Eyne Restitution ... gesunder christlicher Leer* (Münster 1534); *Van der Verborgenheit der Schrifft des Rykes Christi* (Münster February 1535); and *Van der Wrake unde Straffe des Babilonischen Grüwels* (December 1534), an explicit appeal to take up arms in defence of the Anabaptist theocracy, of which Erasmus was sent a copy (Ep 3060). Rothmann apparently died in the storming of Münster on 24 June 1535, although his body was not found afterwards (Epp 3031, 3031A, 3041).

BIBLIOGRAPHY: Allen Ep 2957 / RGG V 1200 / ADB XXIX 364–70 / *The Mennonite Encyclopedia* (Scottdale, Pa, 1955–9) IV 367–70 / George H. Williams *The Radical Reformation* (Philadelphia 1962) 363–81 and passim / *Die Schriften Bernhard Rothmanns* ed R. Stupperich (Münster 1970)   IG

ROTTPERGERIN (Ep 1374 of 6 July 1523)
Wolfgang Faber *Capito asked Erasmus to greet the printer Andreas *Cratander and one 'Rottpergerin.' This woman, who evidently lived at Basel, has not been identified. She may have come from the region of the castle of Rotberg, south of Basel. One Ursula von Rotberg was a nun of the 'Steinenkloster' at Basel in 1524; whether she belonged to the noble von Rotberg family is not clear.   PGB

R[O]US (Ep 3132, of 15 July 1536)
Attempts to identify 'quendam Dominum de R[o]us Atrebatum, Caesaris Yconomum' should probably await a new critical edition of this letter as there appear to be several candidates.

Gérard ROUSSEL of Vaquerie, d 1555
Gérard Roussel (Rufus, Ruffus) was born about 1480 in Vaquerie, near Amiens. He studied arts in Paris at the Collège du Cardinal Lemoine under Jean Pelletier and became an associate of *Lefèvre d'Etaples as early as

1501. Lefèvre's version of the *Dialectica* of George of *Trebizond was corrected by Roussel for the press of Henri Estienne in 1508. Three years later Roussel wrote a preface to the logical works of Boethius published at the same press (Rice *Prefatory Epistles* Ep 82). In 1521 he published his first work, a commentary on Boethius' *Arithmetic* (Paris: S. de Colines) with a dedicatory preface addressed to Lorenzo *Bartolini (Rice *Prefatory Epistles* Ep 132). The next year he brought out a new translation of Aristotle's *Magna moralia* (Paris: S. de Colines) with a commendatory preface by Josse *Clichtove (Rice *Prefatory Epistles* Epp 135, 136).

By the spring of 1521 Roussel had gone to Meaux to work beside Lefèvre. At the time he already had a living at Busancy, in the diocese of Reims. At Meaux he was first assigned the cure of St Saintin and later was made a canon and treasurer of the cathedral chapter. Writing to Erasmus from Meaux at the beginning of 1524 (Ep 1407) Jean *Lange noted that Roussel counted as one of Erasmus' champions in France. However true that may be, Roussel's own letters indicate that he was far more struck by the evangelical ideas of *Oecolampadius and *Zwingli. Although fearful of both persecution by conservatives and social upheaval, he attempted to promote these ideas by preaching and by establishing a conventicle at the cathedral where the laity could study the Pauline Epistles.

In October 1525 Roussel fled Meaux with Lefèvre and together they took refuge at Strasbourg. He remained there until recalled to France in the spring of the next year by *Margaret of Angoulême, soon to be queen of Navarre. On his return he became Margaret's confessor and almoner. His preaching at the Louvre in 1531 and in the following two years attracted considerable attention. Erasmus, for example, noted the scandal they aroused among conservatives (Ep 2810). On the other hand, German Protestants and English agents interpreted them as signs that an irenic religious policy was being pursued by the French court. Indeed, *Francis I induced even the pope to approve Roussel's teaching (October 1533). Roussel was rewarded by the provision of the abbeys of Userche and Clairac and in 1536 with the bishopric of Oleron (Ep 2961). In later years he accompanied Margaret

of Navarre to the south following her with-
drawal from the French court. He was stabbed
to death by a Catholic fanatic while delivering a
sermon from the pulpit.

In addition to his editions of Boethius and
Aristotle, Roussel apparently wrote a commentary on Romans (1524) and began a translation
of the Bible (1525–6), both of which have been
lost. As noted by Erasmus in 1527 (Ep 1795), he
may also have collaborated with Lefèvre on a
translation into Latin of Chrysostom's commentary on Acts. Two late works, the 'Fami-
liere exposition du symbole de la foy et oraison
dominicale, en forme de colloque' and the
'Somme de visite de diocese,' are preserved in
Paris, Bibliothèque Nationale MS Fr 419.

BIBLIOGRAPHY: Allen Ep 1407 / Rice *Prefatory
Epistles* Ep 82 and passim / Henry Heller
'Nicholas of Cusa and early French evangeli-
cism' ARG 63 (1972) 6–21, esp 13–16 / Henry
Heller 'Marguerite of Navarre and the reform-
ers of Meaux' BHR 33 (1971) 271–310, esp 282–5
/ Henry Heller 'An unknown letter from
Clement VII to Gérard Roussel' BHR 38 (1976)
489–94 / Charles Schmidt *Gérard Roussel,
prédicateur de la reine Marguerite de Navarre*
(Strasbourg 1845 repr 1970) / *Melanchthons
Briefwechsel* II Ep 1336 / Paris, Archives de
l'Université de Paris (Sorbonne) MS Registre 89
ff 12 verso, 104 verso   HENRY HELLER

Crotus RUBEANUS or RUBIANUS *See Johannes CROTUS Rubianus*

Johann RUDOLFINGER documented in
Strasbourg 1505–34

Johann Rudolfinger (von Rudolphingen, Ru-
dalfingius), a vicar of the Strasbourg cathedral,
was a member of the literary society and took
part in the dinner arranged for Erasmus during
his visit to the city in August 1514 (Ep 302).
Erasmus described him as 'that master of
harmony not only in his music but also in his
character' (Ep 305). In 1525 he obtained the
citizenship of Strasbourg. Rudolfinger published nothing of his own but was an intimate
of the humanist group. Thomas Wolf, canon of
three Strasbourg chapters, presented him with
a manuscript of his dialogues (1505). Ottmar
*Nachtgall dedicated his little treatise *Musicae
institutiones* (Strasbourg: J. Knobloch 1515) to
Rudolfinger and Symphorianus Pollio. Music

Johann Rudolfinger, by Hans Baldung Grien

was indeed Rudolfinger's special interest.
Before September 1517 he had given encouragement to the composer Sixtus Dietrich, and
in 1534 Dietrich dedicated to him his *Epicedion*
for Thomas Sporer, a fellow musician. This was
printed at Strasbourg at the expense of
Rudolfinger, in whose name Johannes *Sapidus composed a preface, while a woodcut by
Hans Baldung Grien presents Rudolfinger as a
septuagenarian. Erasmus was again entertained by him when passing through Strasbourg in September 1518 (Ep 867) and the two
often exchanged greetings (Epp 342, 369, 383,
633, 883).

BIBLIOGRAPHY: Allen and CWE Ep 302 / BRE Ep
1 and passim / AK II Ep 591, IV Ep 1862 / Schmidt
Histoire littéraire II 70, 181

MIRIAM U. CHRISMAN & PGB

Johannes RUELLIUS, Jean RUEL *See Jean DU
RUEL*

Jean RUFFAULT of Lille, 1471–30 November
1546

Jean Ruffault (Riffault, Ruffaldus) was the son
of another Jean, a citizen of Lille, and Jeanne de

la Porte, also known as d'Espierre. The elder Jean was receiver for the ducal government and later lieutenant of the bailiff of Lille. His son started his career as a simple clerk in the audit office of his native city and rose through the ranks, becoming second greffier in 1493, first greffier in 1497, auditor in 1502, and *maître extraordinaire* in August 1504, and in December 1506 he came to fill the top position of *maître ordinaire*, which he retained until 1532. Meanwhile he had also been appointed ducal councillor and on 26 March 1515 was named *trésorier général des finances*. When the collateral councils were set up in 1531 Ruffault was confirmed as treasurer-general within the framework of the new council of finance. In 1542 he was in addition appointed greffier of Brabant. As a financial expert, he was frequently called upon to join diplomatic negotiations such as the ones leading to the 'Ladies' Peace' of Cambrai in 1529; he also had to deal with the revolt of Ghent in 1539–40.

Ruffault, a knight, owned the estates of Frelin, Neuville, Mauvaux, and Lamsaert as well as other properties for the most part in the regions of Lille and Brussels. Greatly favoured by Philip the Handsome, duke of *Burgundy, and subsequently by *Charles v, he was able to accumulate a considerable fortune. His biographers credit him with a keen intelligence and a talent for organization. He was a generous patron of the parish church of St Etienne, Lille, and with his wife, Marie Carlin (d 1534), was buried in a family chapel they had built in the churchyard. Among their ten children were Jérôme *Ruffault; Jean, who squandered the family fortune; Marie, who married chancellor Engelbert van Daele; and Françoise, who became the wife of Matthias *Laurinus.

Erasmus' connections with Ruffault all seem to have hinged around the payment of his annuity as councillor to Charles v. It appears that he wrote personally to the treasurer-general (Epp 1287, 1545), while such friends as the Laurinus family (Epp 1342, 1848) and Gilles de *Busleyden (Ep 1461) did their best to ensure a sympathetic hearing. Ruffault actually did what he could to help Erasmus and obtained the release of payments in 1523 and perhaps 1525 (Epp 1342, 1380, 1585, 1643). Matthias Laurinus, no doubt through Ruffault, intervened again in 1527 when it was decided

that in order to receive regular payments Erasmus must return to the Low Countries; however, on this occasion they had no success (Ep 1871).

BIBLIOGRAPHY: Allen Ep 1287 / BNB XXXVII 703–5 (with additional bibliography) / J. Gaillard *Bruges et le Franc* (Bruges 1857–　) I 364, VI 242 / A. Wauters *Histoire des environs de Bruxelles* (Brussels 1855, repr 1969) I 42, II 229, 234 / A. Henne *Histoire du règne de Charles-Quint en Belgique* (Brussels-Leipzig 1858–60) III 247, IV 381 / de Vocht CTL IV 185 / de Vocht *Literae ad Craneveldium* Ep 140 / J. Verkooren *Inventaire des chartes et cartulaires du Luxembourg: Comté puis Duché* (Brussels 1921) V 509 / D. Walther *Die burgundischen Zentralbehörden unter Maximilian I. und Karl V.* (Leipzig 1909) 80 / *Analecta Belgica* ed C.P. Hoynck van Papendrecht III-2: *Vita Viglii ab Aytta Zuichemi* (The Hague 1743) 432 / J. Bartier *Légistes et gens de finances au XVe siècle: Les conseillers des Ducs de Bourgogne sous Philippe le Bon et Charles le Téméraire* (Brussels 1955) 65

HILDE DE RIDDER-SYMOENS

Jérôme RUFFAULT of Lille, d 16 November 1562

A son of Jean *Ruffault, Jérôme was born at Lille around 1500. Together with two of his brothers, Jean and Hugues, he studied at the University of Louvain, matriculating on 28 February 1517. From 1520 to 1522 Ruffault and the Englishman Nicholas Wotton were the favourite pupils of Juan Luis *Vives, who had high praise for Ruffault's diligence and conduct. The latter was still in Louvain in October 1524 when he wrote to Vives, who had meanwhile gone to England, about the publication of the Spaniard's *Introductio ad sapientiam* (de Vocht *Literae ad Craneveldium* Ep 122). It is possible that Ruffault was then attending lectures in theology, for by this time he had been received into the Benedictine order in the abbey of St Vaast at Arras. As early as 10 April 1523 he had been named coadjutor to the abbot, Martin Asset, an appointment which he owed to his well-connected father and the intercession of *Charles v. In 1526 he was elected abbot of St Adriaan's, Geraardsbergen (Grammont), in succession to Jan de Broedere. After Asset's death in 1537 Ruffault also became abbot of St Vaast's, but continued to reside at Geraardsbergen. At this time he gave up his claims to an annuity of four hundred Rhenish guilders settled upon the abbey of Middelburg. Eventually he left the administration of St Adriaan's in the hands of his prior, Jan Zittard, and from 1559 to his death he resided in Arras. In Geraardsbergen he earned reproach for his prodigality and lack of firmness, but at St Vaast's he was laid to rest under an epitaph that seems to reflect a positive view of his achievements.

As a student in Louvain Ruffault cearly moved in humanist circles. He helped with the edition of Vives' *Introductio ad sapientiam* (Louvain: D. Martens 1524), complaining to *Cranevelt about the manuscript (de Vocht *Literae* Epp 122, 144). From Mechelen, where he attended the weddings of his sisters, he had earlier sent Cranevelt a copy of Vives' *Veritas fucata* (Louvain: D. Martens 1523), which contained echoes of the master's conversations with his pupils Wotton and Ruffault (de Vocht *Literae* Epp 41, 52). Vives also brought Ruffault to the attention of Erasmus, mentioning that Jérôme had written to his father in support of Erasmus' claims to his annuity from Charles (Epp 1303, 1306). In 1529, when Levinus *Ammonius encouraged Erasmus to move to Ghent, he mentioned the proximity of Geraardsbergen and the friendship of Abbot Ruffault as incentives (Ep 2197). Erasmus did not return to the Netherlands, but Vives enjoyed the hospitality of his former student at Geraardsbergen.

BIBLIOGRAPHY: Allen Ep 1303 / NBW x 548–51 / *Matricule de Louvain* III-1 548; cf 561, 723 / de Vocht *Literae ad Craneveldium* Ep 41 and passim / de Vocht CTL II 190–1, IV 112, 185, 524 / H. Fremaux 'Histoire généalogique de la famille Ruffault originaire de la Flandre wallonne, 1313 à 1621' *Souvenirs de la Flandre wallonne* 2nd ser 5 (1885) 70 / A. de Cardevacque and A. Terninck *L'Abbaye de Saint-Vaast* (Arras 1865) 253–5 / E. Soens *De Abdij van Sint-Adriaan te Geraardsbergen: Haar pachthoeven en molens* (Aalst 1914) 21–2 / G. van Bockstaele 'Abbaye de Saint-Adrien à Grammont' in *Monasticon Belge* ed U. Berlière et al (Maredsous-Liège 1890–) VII-2 103–5 / R. Fruin *Het archief der O.L.V. abdij te Middelburg* (The Hague 1901) 469–70 / C. Noreña *Juan Luis Vives* (The Hague 1970) 68 / *Dirk Martens 1473–1973: Catalogus*

van de tentoonstelling te Aalst, Stedelijk Museum (Aalst 1973) 202, 204–5

HILDE DE RIDDER-SYMOENS

Gerardus RUFFUS or RUFUS *See Gérard ROUSSEL*

Johannes RUFFUS Fabri
documented 1527–31
Johannes Ruffus Fabri was the warden of the Franciscan monastery at Rouffach, in Upper Alsace, from 1527 to 1531. A former member of the Franciscan house at Basel, he wrote in December 1527 to his old friends there, mentioning a bundle of Erasmus' letters which had gone astray (Ep 1922). No more is known about Ruffus.

BIBLIOGRAPHY: *Alemannia Franciscana Antiqua* VII (Ulm 1961) 129   PGB

Nicolas RUISTRE of Luxembourg,
c 1442–15 November 1509
Nicolas Ruistre (le Ruistre, de Ruter, Ruterius) entered the court of Philip the Good, duke of *Burgundy, as a boy and seems to have received his education there. He became a secretary but soon rose to the position of a master of requests and councillor under Charles the Rash, duke of *Burgundy. Ruistre continued to occupy very influential positions under Mary and Philip the Handsome, duke of *Burgundy; he was appointed a secretary of the council of finance on 26 December 1487, one of the four treasurers on 14 March 1497, and one of the four masters of requests in attendance to the duke. The services of Ruistre, who meanwhile had taken holy orders, were rewarded by ample preferment; he became a canon of St Donatian's in Bruges (1484), archdeacon of Brabant (4 December 1484), provost of St Bavo's, Haarlem (1485), and also a canon of St Gudula's, Brussels, of Lier, and of Dendermonde. On 10 June 1487 he became provost of St Peter's, Louvain, and thus chancellor of the university. On the advice of his friend Jan *Robbyns he founded a new college for students in Louvain, the college of Arras (15 September 1508).

In 1501 Ruistre was nominated bishop of Arras and was consecrated on 7 August 1502. His importance at court increased; he was one of the envoys sent to negotiate with King

*Louis xII of France in Lyon and Blois (1501), and one of the six councillors to whom the management of the provinces was entrusted on 26 December 1505 when Philip the Handsome left for Spain. It was thanks to Ruistre that Erasmus was entrusted with composing his *Panegyricus* (ASD IV-1 23–93) to welcome the prince on his earlier return from Spain in January 1504. The preface is therefore addressed to Ruistre (Ep 179). In the preceding year Erasmus presented to Ruistre his Latin translation of three declamations by Libanius (Louvain: D. Martens July 1519) together with a dedicatory preface (Ep 177) and an epigram (Reedijk poem 75).

BIBLIOGRAPHY: Allen Ep 177 / de Vocht *Busleyden* 305–7 and passim / de Vocht CTL I 8–9 and passim   IG

RUIZ *See Pedro Ruiz de la* MOTA, *Alonso and Jerónimo Ruiz de* VIRUÉS

Johannes RULLUS of Cracow, d June 1532 Rullus (Rol) came from an immigrant Alsatian family which had settled in Cracow. After studies at the universities of Cracow and Vienna (1517) he lived in Cracow and mingled with the booksellers and printers. He belonged to the circle of young humanists centred around Leonard *Cox. In 1527 he moved to Wrocław, where he was appointed rector of the parish school of St Mary Magdalene. He was sympathetic to the Reformation and in November 1527 visited Joachim *Camerarius in Nürnberg. In Wrocław he made close contacts with that city's humanists but continued to maintain ties with his friends in Cracow, especially Andrzej *Trzecieski and Jan (II) *Łaski, who attempted without success to secure a lectureship for Rullus at the Lubranski academy in Poznań. Rullus collected an impressive library, including fourteen books by Erasmus. Trzecieski recommended Rullus to Erasmus (Ep 1895).

Rullus died in Wrocław in June 1532. Verses of his were appended to M. Pyrser's edition of Erasmus' *De constructione* (Cracow: H. Wietor 1523) and to Leonard Cox's *Libellus de erudienda iuventute* (Cracow: H. Wietor 1526).

BIBLIOGRAPHY: Allen Ep 1895 / *Matrikel Wien* II-1 443 / H. Barycz *Z dziejów polskich wędrówek naukowych za granicę* (Wrocław 1969) / H.

Barycz *Z epoki renesansu, reformacji i baroku* (Warsaw 1971) / G. Bauch in *Programm der Evangelischen Realschule* II *in Breslau* (Wrocław 1901) 15–25 / G. Bauch *Geschichte des Breslauer Schulwesens in der Zeit der Reformation* (Wrocław 1911) 71–2, 123 / *Erasmiana Cracoviensia in diem natalem Erasmi Roterodamensis quingentesimum edita* Zeszyty Naukowe Uniwersytetu Jagiellońskiego 250 (Cracow 1971) 26, 35–6 / *Lasciana nebst den ältesten evangelischen Synodalprotokollen Polens 1551–61* ed H. Dalton (Berlin 1898) Ep 21   HALINA KOWALSKA

Franciscus RUPILIUS documented 1514–41 Franciscus Rupilius (Rothut) is first documented on 28 April 1514 when he wrote to Joachim *Vadianus from Bruck an der Mur in Styria, perhaps after meeting him at Vienna. By 1530 he was studying in Bourges under Andrea *Alciati, where he was a friend of *Viglius Zuichemus. He was apparently also Viglius' contemporary at Padua in 1532 (Epp 2682, 2716) and was later in a position to recommend him successfully to Matthias *Held. Rupilius had obtained a doctorate in law (Ep 3011) before he joined the household of Johann (II) *Paumgartner in 1527 to supervise the education of Paumgartner's sons. He lectured in Rome in 1530 and was there again from 1534 to 1535, when with Paumgartner's support he obtained canonries at Bressanone (Brixen) and Regensburg (Epp 3007, 3011). In 1536 he was in Padua with two Paumgartner sons and Johann Ulrich *Zasius. By September 1537 he had returned to Germany and was apparently staying with Paumgartner, who instructed him to write to Basel concerning the planned edition of Erasmus' *Opera omnia* (AK V Ep 2156). On 10 March 1541 he was a witness to the agreement distributing Paumgartner's inheritance among his sons. In 1556 a Sigmund Rothut the Old held an investment in the Paumgartner firm.

The correspondence between Rupilius and Erasmus began before July 1532 (Ep 2682). Erasmus intended to write a eulogy on the Paumgartner family and had asked for more specific information; this was supplied by Rupilius in 1533 (Epp 2867, 2868). While in Rome from 1534 to 1535 Rupilius met Ambrosius von *Gumppenberg, and both offered their services in support of Ludwig *Baer (Ep 3007) and perhaps also Franz (II) *Baer (Ep 2929). Rupilius wrote to Erasmus repeatedly, but only Ep 3007 survives. It shows his great respect for Erasmus and his eagerness to be of service to him and mentions Pietro *Corsi's Defensio pro Italia ad Erasmum. In 1535 Johann *Koler learned from Rupilius that Pope *Paul III had granted Erasmus the provostship of Deventer (Ep 3050).

BIBLIOGRAPHY: Allen Ep 2867 / AK IV Ep 1924a /Wilhelm Krag Die Paumgartner von Nürnberg und Augsburg (Munich-Leipzig 1919) 101 / Epistolae ad Nauseam 156–8, 161–4, 178 / U. Zasius Epistolae ed J.A. Riegger (Ulm 1774) II 434 / Vadianische Briefsammlung I Ep 35 / Analecta Belgica ed C.P. Hoynck van Papendrecht II-1: Viglii ab Aytta Zuichemi epistolae selectae (The Hague 1743) Epp 12, 70, 84 / Karl Otto Müller Quellen zur Handelsgeschichte der Paumgartner von Augsburg (1480–1570) (Wiesbaden 1955) 59   IG & PGB

Johann RUSER of Ebersmunster,
d 28 October 1518

Johann Ruser was born in Ebersmunster (Ebersheimmünster), near Sélestat. He worked in the printing shop of Matthias *Schürer in Strasbourg. *Beatus Rhenanus dedicated his edition of the younger Pliny's letters to Ruser (Strasbourg: M. Schürer 1514), and he was one of the members of the Strasbourg literary society identified by Jakob *Wimpfeling in his letter of compliments to Erasmus in 1514 (Ep 302; cf Ep 305). Ruser later became a priest of the order of St John and taught at Sélestat. In 1517 he corresponded with Erasmus with regard to providing Schürer with work, so he clearly maintained an interest in the press (Ep 606). In August 1517 Erasmus wrote Ruser to say that he had finished his edition of Quintus Curtius and would like Schürer to print it (Ep 633). In a long dedicatory letter addressed to Paul *Volz, which served as the preface to the 1518 Froben edition of the Enchiridion, Erasmus sent greetings to the Sélestat literary society, including *Sapidus, Wimpfeling, and Ruser. In that same year Ruser died in the house of the order of St John at Sélestat.

BIBLIOGRAPHY: Allen and CWE Ep 302 / BRE Epp 36, 66, and passim

MIRIAM U. CHRISMAN

Johann Jakob RUSSINGER See Konrad SCHMID

Nicolaus RUTERIUS See Nicolas RUISTRE

Thomas RUTHALL of Cirencester,
d 4 February 1523

Thomas Ruthall was born in Cirencester, in Gloucestershire; his date of birth is unknown. Virtually nothing is known of his parentage except that his mother's name was possibly Avenyng. He was educated at Oxford, becoming a bachelor of canon and civil law by 1488, a licentiate in 1490, and a doctor of canon law in 1499; he was ordained in 1488. In 1500 he was incorporated at Cambridge. Before then, however, he entered the king's service and was employed first as a royal ambassador and then as *Henry VII's secretary. Ecclesiastical preferments followed, among them the deanery of Salisbury (not Lincoln as has sometimes been said), a canonry at Wells, and the archdeaconry of Gloucester. He was chancellor of Cambridge University from 1503 to 1504. In 1509 he was appointed bishop of Durham, thus joining the circle of courtier bishops endowed with great powers of patronage. Ruthall continued as secretary to *Henry VIII until 1516 and then was keeper of the privy seal until his death. He accompanied the king to France in 1513 but returned to assist with preparations for the threatened Scots invasion. He was present at the Field of Cloth of Gold in 1520 and was at Calais with *Wolsey in 1521. He died at Durham Place, London.

As a dispenser of patronage, Ruthall was a disappointment to Erasmus (Epp 282, 332). He seems, indeed, to have avoided involvement (Ep 239). Erasmus tried to gain his support by messages sent through Andrea *Ammonio (Epp 219, 236, 240) and by dedicating to him his translation of Lucian's Timon in 1506 (Ep 192) and his edition of Seneca's Lucubrationes in 1515 (Ep 325). Ruthall had earlier bestowed upon Erasmus some assurance of goodwill (Ep 243) and gifts of money, in not very large amounts, at various times (Epp 280, 281, 295). The Seneca, however, apparently remained unacknowledged. More than twenty years later Erasmus recalled that the carelessness of Franz *Birckmann, who never delivered the presentation copy to Ruthall, combined with his own impetuous reminders had cost him the bishop's friendship (Ep 2091). No subsequent contacts are recorded except for Erasmus' gesture in sending Ruthall his *Paraphrasis in Galatas* at the height of his controversy with Edward *Lee (Ep 974).

BIBLIOGRAPHY: Allen Ep 192 / DNB XVII 492–3 / Emden BRUO III 1612–13 / John LeNeve *Fasti Ecclesiae Anglicanae, 1300–1541* 2nd ed (London 1962–) III 5 / *The Itinerary of John Leland* ed Lucy Toulmin Smith (London 1906–10) I 129   ELIZABETH CRITTALL

Walter RUYS of Grave, d 29/30 May 1534
Walter Ruys (Gualterus Ruysius Gravius) a native of Grave, near Nijmegen, joined the Dominicans at Nijmegen and was sent to complete his education at Louvain. From there he sent Erasmus a letter, now lost, urging him to gather his paraphrases together into a single volume (Ep 1472) and probably referring to Maarten *Lips (Ep 1473). On 26 July 1524 Erasmus sent him a friendly reply (Ep 1472) and about six months later again showed his interest in Walter's studies (Ep 1547).

In 1525, however, an *Apologia* against his *Exomologesis* and *De esu carnium* appeared under the pseudonym of Godefridus Ruysius Taxander (Antwerp: S. Cocus and G. Nicolaus 21 March 1525; NK 1840). Erasmus soon knew that it had originated from the Dominican camp (Ep 1571), but it took him several months to reach the conclusion that four persons were responsible for the attack: Vincentius *Theodorici, *Cornelis of Duiveland, Govaert *Strijroy, and – surprisingly – Walter Ruys, who had added some flowery figures of speech (Ep 1655; cf Epp 1608, 1621). The four critics parted company (Epp 1621, 1686), one of them vanishing to Gelderland (Ep 2045). Ruys was, in fact, chosen prior of the Dominicans at Nijmegen, perhaps by 1527. In 1531 he may have been succeeded by one Henricus Vaeck. He edited a collection of baptismal and other rites, containing 251 (according to the title 113) *praefationes* which were apparently drawn from a post-Gregorian *sacramentarium* (Cologne: J. Soter 1530).

BIBLIOGRAPHY: Allen Ep 1472 / G.A. Meyer in NNBW II 1246 / G.A. Meyer *Dominikaner klooster en statie te Nijmegen* (Nijmegen 1898) 60–3, 237 / S.P. Wolfs in *Numaga* 15 (1968) 94–121 / de Vocht *Literae ad Craneveldium* Epp 148, 149
                                      C.G. VAN LEIJENHORST

Louis RUZÉ c 1468–January 1526
Louis Ruzé (Ruzeus) seigneur de la Harpinière et de Melun, was descended from a bourgeois family traditionally connected with the Parlement of Paris and allied by marriage to the *Briçonnet, the Semblançay, and the *Poncher families. Ruzé successively held the offices of *conseiller* of the city of Paris (1500), *conseiller* to the Parlement (1511), and from 1516 *lieutenant civil* of the provostship of Paris. The duties of this latter office included judiciary powers in civil law cases but also the enforcement of regulations concerning the book trade and the issuing of printing permits and royal 'privileges' as a safeguard against unauthorized reprints. These functions were exercized by Ruzé with special consideration for the interests of the humanists, many of whom were his friends or protégés. Paris editions of St Cyprian (B. Rembolt 1512), Quintilian (J. Bade 1519), *Poliziano (J. Bade 1519), and Plutarch (J. Bade 1521) are dedicated to Ruzé. Christophe de *Longueil enjoyed his patronage, and Ruzé became so attached to him that in 1519 he was very reluctant to let Longueil return to Italy. Another favourite protégé was Jacques *Toussain, who belonged to Ruzé's household from 1518 to 1524. The chroniclers of the day recorded a personal calamity that befell Ruzé on 10 June 1521 when his wife, Marie Quattrelivres, eloped in the company of two burglars.

Erasmus first came to know Ruzé indirectly through his correspondence with *Bérault (Ep 925), *Brie (Ep 569), and especially *Budé. To Budé Ruzé was an intimate friend, as was François *Deloynes, whom he mentions frequently in the same breath as Ruzé. One of Ruzé's brothers was Budé's brother-in-law, and Ruzé himself became the godfather of Budé's son Louis.

An eager reader of Erasmus' writings (Ep 493), Ruzé was particularly upset in 1517 and 1518 by Erasmus' unsparing *Apologia ad Fabrum* (Epp 744, 810), and thereafter he seems to have had mixed feelings with regard to Erasmus. From Liège, where a diplomatic mission had taken him in March 1519, he wrote to Erasmus, encouraging him to move to Paris. Flattering though it was, this letter may well have annoyed Erasmus by its touch of chauvinism and its insistence on placing Budé's reputation on an even footing with Erasmus' own (Ep 926). The tone of aloofness in Erasmus' answer (Ep 928) may well reveal a measure of latent conflict. Soon after this exchange Ruzé and Erasmus may have met in Mechelen. It was Ruzé (Ep 935) who first made Erasmus aware of Longueil's famous letter to Jacques *Lucas (Ep 914) with its unflattering comparison between Erasmus and Budé. It can be assumed that Ruzé's own view did not differ greatly from that expressed by Longueil. However that may be, Erasmus continued to send greetings to Ruzé (Epp 1024, 1066, 1185), and in 1524 Jean *Lange counted Ruzé among Erasmus' friends at Paris (Ep 1407).

BIBLIOGRAPHY: Allen Epp 493, 926 / Louis Delaruelle Répertoire ... de la correspondance de Guillaume Budé (Paris-Toulouse 1907) passim / M.-M. de la Garanderie La Correspondance d'Erasme et de Guillaume Budé (Paris 1967) passim / M.-M. de la Garanderie 'Les relations d'Erasme avec Paris au temps de son séjour aux Pays-Bas méridionaux' in Scrinium Erasmianum I 29–53 / Le Journal d'un bourgeois de Paris ed V.L. Bourrilly (Paris 1910) 83–5

MARIE-MADELEINE DE LA GARANDERIE

Peter RYCH *See Peter* REICH

Simon RYCHWYN *See Simon* RIQUINUS

Jacob RYDDER *See Jakob* RIDDER

Johann RYNCK *See Johann* RINCK

Matthias von SAARBURG d 3 December 1539
Matthias von Saarburg (Sarburgensis, a Saraecastro), who was of noble birth, had obtained a MA before 27 May 1499 when he was appointed to teach at Trier, where a small university had been founded in 1473. He was dean of arts on 1 February 1502. In 1503 he matriculated in Bologna and may have obtained his doctorate in both laws there. After his return to Trier he was in possession of the parish of Niederprüm by 1506. In 1518 he was

in Koblenz as a canon of St Castor's and official for the archbishop of Trier, Richard von *Greiffenklau. In 1525 he was vice-chancellor and rector of the university and dean of St Simeon's, Trier, a chapter to which he left a large part of his library. Matthias von Saarburg proved very helpful to scholars such as Johann *Sichard and Ulricus *Fabricius who were trying to locate old manuscripts.

Erasmus was Saarburg's guest at Koblenz when he was returning from Basel to Louvain in September 1518 (Ep 867). Ep 880, a short letter of thanks, is probably addressed to him. He told Erasmus about the circumstances that had apparently impelled Jacob of *Hoogstraten to leave Cologne (cf Ep 877). In November 1521 Erasmus was again on his way to Basel and was once more hospitably received by Saarburg (Ep 1342). In 1528 Saarburg was approached by Justin *Gobler as part of a concerted effort to locate a manuscript of Tertullian's De spectaculis (Ep 1946).

BIBLIOGRAPHY: Allen and CWE Ep 867 / Knod 470 / Paul Lehmann Johannes Sichardus (Munich 1911) 191–203   IG

Marcantonio SABELLICO of Vicovaro, 1436–1506
Marcantonio Cocci was born of poor parents in Vicovaro in central Italy, and received his early schooling in his home town. He continued his studies in Rome under Julius *Pomponius Laetus, Gaspar Veronese, and Porcelio Pandone. While in Rome he took part in the life of Pomponius' Roman Academy and there adopted his humanistic *nom de guerre*.

In 1473 Sabellico was called to Udine to teach rhetoric but also continued his studies in dialectics, mathematics, and Greek. His interest in historical writing led him to compile *De vetustate Aquileiae patriae* in six books [Venice: Antonio de Avinione 1482]. But his hope of achieving permanent employment at Udine on the strength of his work was shattered when he was dismissed from his position in 1483. He then spent fifteen months at Verona, where he completed twenty-two of the thirty-three books of his history of Venice. In 1485 he presented this work (published in Venice: A. Torresani 1487) to the doge and senate of Venice, and soon afterwards he was appointed to the second public lectureship in the humanities at the school of San Marco, with Giorgio *Valla occupying the first lectureship. On Valla's death in 1500 Sabellico took over the first lectureship. He also served as librarian to the collection of books which Cardinal *Bessarion had given Venice but which was as yet without a permanent home.

Sabellico repaid the republic's largesse by writing and publishing further works in praise of Venice as well as a description of the city in three books and a dialogue on the Venetian magistrates (Venice: A. de Strata 1489). In addition he continued his literary studies and produced commentaries on Pliny the Elder, Valerius Maximus, Livy, Horace, and other authors. Several of his orations and his philosophical, moral, and historical minor works attest to both his productiveness and his rise to considerable prominence in Venice. Towards the end of his life he published his historical *magnum opus*, a universal history from the Creation, under the title *Enneades seu rhapsodiae historiarum* (Venice: B. dei Vitali 1498). His *Opera omnia* were published at Basel (J. Herwagen) in 1560.

Erasmus quoted a proverb from Sabellico in *Adagia* III x 98 and expressed respect for him as a rhetorician and historian in the *Ciceronianus* (ASD I-2 668). Later judgment of his work has not been as positive. Sabellico's historical work has been severely criticized for its uncritical acceptance of defective sources, his overt and transparent glorification of Venice, and his general preference for narrative effect over factual accuracy. Sabellico died in Venice.

BIBLIOGRAPHY: Apostolo Zeni in his preface to the 1718 ed of Sabellico's *Historiae rerum Venetarum* in *Degl'istorici delle cose veneziane* (Venice 1718–22) I / G. Tiraboschi *Storia della letteratura italiana* (Milan 1782–97) VI-1 56–7 / E. Fueter *Geschichte der neueren Historiographie* (Munich-Berlin 1925) 30–5 / Gaetano Cozzi 'Cultura politica e religione nella "pubblica storiografia" veneziana del'500' *Bollettino dell'Istituto di storia della società e dello stato* 5–6 (1963–4) 219–22 / Felix Gilbert 'Biondo, Sabellico, and the beginnings of Venetian official historiography' in *Florilegium Historiale: Essays Presented to Wallace K. Ferguson* ed J.G. Rowe and W.H. Stockdale (Toronto 1971) 275–93 / Martin Lowry *The World of Aldus Manutius* (Oxford 1979) 24, 28–9, and passim / A. Pertusi 'Gli inizi della storiografia umanistica nel quattrocento' in *La storiografia veneziana fino al secolo XVI* ed A. Pertusi (Florence-Venice 1970) 269–313   EGMONT LEE

Georgius SABINUS of Brandenburg, 23 April 1508–2 December 1560
Georg, the son of Balthasar Schuler, is best known under the name he used as a poet, Georgius Sabinus. From 1523–4 he was educated at Wittenberg under *Melanchthon but did not matriculate at the university until the winter term of 1532–3. In 1530 he accompanied Melanchthon to the diet of Augsburg and in the same year published his *Elegiae* (Wittenberg: J. Klug), which were later to be increased to a total of six books and to include the best of his work as a noted neo-Latin poet. According to Ellinger, however, the elegance of his style is rarely matched by an ability to express deep feelings. In 1533 he left for Italy, where Pietro *Bembo came to take an interest in him and his work, while Girolamo *Aleandro issued a diploma creating him a poet laureate. In August 1534, as he was preparing to return to Germany from Venice, he persuaded Giambattista *Egnazio to give him a letter of introduction to Erasmus (Ep 2964). By the beginning of October he was in Freiburg and obtained from Erasmus some flattering lines to take back to Melanchthon (Ep 2970). On 6 November 1536 Sabinus married Melanchthon's daughter Anna, a girl of about fourteen years of age. The marriage was not to be a happy one, and after Anna's death (26 February 1547) Sabinus married again in 1550. Meanwhile, in 1538 the Elector Joachim II of Brandenburg appointed him to a chair of rhetoric at the University of Frankfurt an der Oder. In 1544 Albert I of *Brandenburg-Ansbach, duke of Prussia, invited him to Kaliningrad (Königsberg), where he became the rector of a ducal college which was quickly promoted to the status of a university, with Sabinus retaining the rectorate. He later fell out with the duke and at the beginning of 1555 returned to Frankfurt an der Oder, where he was again appointed professor and councillor to Joachim II. He undertook diplomatic missions for the elector of Brandenburg which took him back to Italy and also to Poland. He died at Frankfurt.

Sabinus was a friend of Joachim *Camerarius and of his fellow poets *Eobanus Hessus and Johannes *Dantiscus. He corresponded occasionally with Bembo, in whose entourage at Padua he had also met Damião de *Gois. Among his works there are contributions to classical and historical scholarship such as a commentary on Ovid's *Metamorphoses* under the title *Fabularum Ovidii interpretatio* (Wittenberg: G. Rhau 1555) and *Narratio deliberationis Maximiliani imperatoris de bello turcico* (Leipzig: V. Bapst 1551), but his reputation rests on his collected *Poemata* (Strasbourg: K. Müller 1544; enlarged new editions 1558 and 1563).

BIBLIOGRAPHY: Allen Ep 2964 / Georg Ellinger in ADB XXX 107–11 / Georg Ellinger *Geschichte der neulateinischen Literatur Deutschlands im sechzehnten Jahrhundert* Berlin-Leipzig 1929–33) II 65–75 and passim / *Matrikel Wittenberg* I 148 / *Melanchthons Briefwechsel* I Ep 1023, II Epp 1328, 1347, and passim / *Der Briefwechsel des Justus Jonas* ed G. Kawerau (Halle 1884–5, repr 1964) I Ep 233 and passim / Elisabeth Feist Hirsch *Damião de Gois* (The Hague 1967) 108–9 / de Vocht *Dantiscus* 369–70 and passim / Fritz Gause *Die Geschichte der Stadt Königsberg* (Cologne-Graz 1965–   ) I 294–7, 304   PGB

Jean SABUNYER (Ep 3094, of 10 February 1536)
Writing from Toulouse, Jacobus *Omphalius mentioned that Jean Sabunyer (Sabonier), a man of great authority and influence at the court of *Francis I, had written to Erasmus; Omphalius suggested that Erasmus should reply. Nothing is known about such an exchange of letters, nor has it been possible to identify Sabunyer. It may be noted, however, that in dedicating his *De elocutionis imitatione* (Basel 1537) to Cardinal Jean *Du Bellay, Omphalius mentioned Sabunyer again; he had apparently helped to bring about contacts between the author and the cardinal.
MICHEL REULOS & PGB

Francesco SACCHETTI (Ep 949 of 22 April 1519)
Lodovico *Ricchieri mentioned in his letter to Erasmus that a passage in the 1517–18 edition of the *Adagia* had been brought to his attention by 'Franciscus Saccetus Ticinensis, vir bene doctus et senatorius.' Surviving records do not permit a firm identification of this Francesco Sacchetti of Pavia. He was conceivably Francesco, the son of Francesco di Riccardo Sacchetti. The elder Francesco was a doctor of medicine and professor of logic and law at Pavia from 1449 to 1469 and seems to have died in or before 1473. A minor in 1473, the younger Francesco was also a doctor of arts and of medicine and is given the title of royal and ducal senator. He was taken prisoner by French troops after the battle of Pavia in 1525 and is said to have died in captivity at Naples. His widow, Giovanna Elisabetta dal Pozzo, was alive in 1539.

BIBLIOGRAPHY: Allen Ep 949 / *Memorie e documenti ... dell' Università di Pavia* (Pavia 1878) I 39–40, 158 / Pavia, Archivio civico MS 'Schedario Marozzi,' family Sacchetti col 451 (an often unreliable source of information)
ANNA GIULIA CAVAGNA

Bartolomeo SACCHI *See Bartolomeo* PLATINA

Jacopo SADOLETO of Ferrara, 12 July 1477–18 October 1547
The Sadoletti belonged to the middle ranks of the new bourgeoisie of Ferrara and Modena. Jacopo's father, Giovanni (c 1440–1511), was appointed to the University of Ferrara as professor of law in 1488, shortly after his marriage to Francesca Machiavelli. Jacopo probably spent his childhood in Modena and Pisa, attending Este schools, before going to the University of Ferrara, where he studied under Niccolò *Leoniceno.

Some time between 1498 and 1499 Sadoleto left his family to continue his studies in Rome in the household of the austere and cultivated Oliviero Carafa, then dean of the Sacred College, where Sadoleto remained for twelve years. The surviving literary yield of this period is limited to *De Cajo Curtio*, a poem; *De Laocoontis statua*, celebrating the discovery of the statue on the Esquiline; and *De bello suscipiendo contra Turcos* (c 1510), a complaint of peace inferentially against *Julius II and the *Este dukes. His classical formation developed during these years as much through his association with the humanists and artists of the Roman Academy as from his studies in Carafa's household. In 1511 he took minor orders.

Jacopo Sadoleto

Perhaps the most decisive turning point after his decision to forswear a career under the Este dukes came with the election of *Leo x and the new pope's selection of Sadoleto and Pietro *Bembo to the apostolic secretariat on 11 March 1513. This appointment set the course of Jacopo's career in the church and embellished his reputation as a Latinist. It also established the tension between the active and the contemplative life from which he never escaped, obligating both the scholar and later the reformer in him to Rome and the curia for the rest of his life. To the twelve benefices, canonries, and pensions he received in 1513, Leo x added the diocese of Carpentras, in the papal state of Venaissin in southern France, in 1517. But Sadoleto had by then come to see his real vocation as the life of leisured scholarship, while he was being drawn ever more deeply into the frenzied demands of Leonine diplomacy and the prosecution of *Luther.

Following the death of Leo x in 1521, Sadoleto went to Carpentras briefly in 1523 before being recalled by *Clement vii at the end of the year to resume his position as domestic secretary, becoming involved in all the humilia-

tions of the pope by *Charles v and the Lutherans. In mid-April of 1527, two weeks before the Sack of Rome, Sadoleto hastily left for his diocese, hoping to retire there permanently on the ground that he had earned remission from curial service, so as to achieve 'a free and self-determined manner of living.' The bishop had rejected common cause with the priestly estate, convinced that he could serve the church in its travails more constructively through his literary vocation. Although he contested every future summons to Rome during the last twenty years of his life, he also became a zealous and caring prelate at Carpentras – an authentic reformer and an aggressive defender of his people in their troubled relations with the temporal government of the Comtat Venaissin. He was also a prodigal nepotist.

Between 1527 and 1536 the erstwhile poet produced three works of exegesis and three long treatises, dividing his efforts between the cause of good letters and the defence of Christian orthodoxy. While he knew that he could not please both Bembo and Reginald *Pole with the same treatise, Sadoleto looked upon Erasmus as one of the few to whom he did not have to justify his double interest. The first long work to emerge in this period and the most frequently published of all Sadoleto's books was *De pueris instituendis* (1530), a thoroughly secular defence of liberal studies which promises that the fusion of the liberal arts in philosophy brings forth not only Augustine's *sapientia* but similitude to the 'divine original.' He further elaborated the case for philosophy with his *Hortensius*, completing *De laudibus philosophiae* which he had begun in 1521: intellect rather than grace is the culmination of human dignity. But before finishing the book Sadoleto began his long commentary on Romans, in which he undertook to argue from an inherent justice which the believer activates by his *bona voluntas* in the beginnings of salvation, ostensibly without the foregoing operation of grace. Erasmus' admonitions were not sufficiently heeded: the commentary, published at Lyon (S. Gryphius) in 1535, was disapproved by the Paris faculty of theology and placed under a ban in the Vatican, pending correction and revision.

But these difficulties were ignored by *Paul

III, when he asked the bishop through Gasparo *Contarini to return to Rome to assist in preparations for the council, an invitation which became a summons also to participate in a special commission on the reformation of the church. The briefs went out a week after Erasmus' death.

Sadoleto arrived around 1 November 1536 and delivered a scolding and even bitter oration at the opening of the first session of the Commission of Nine: *Aleandro, Badia, Contarini, Carafa (the future *Paul IV), Cortese, Fregoso, *Giberti, Pole, and Sadoleto. The oration centred on the responsibility of the curia for the corrupt condition of the church in the recent past and the loss of its authority in Germany, England, and Eastern Europe. Three weeks later Sadoleto was one of three reform prelates included among the nine new cardinals nominated 22 December 1536, 'recalled anew,' he said, 'from a harbour into the storm.'

On 9 March 1537 the *Consilium de emendanda ecclesia* was presented to the pope and the Sacred College, together with a dissenting version of it by Cardinal Sadoleto, who insisted that at least parts of his memorial be read after Contarini delivered the majority report. Although the substance of Sadoleto's proposals is unknown, from Aleandro's account of Jacopo's defeat it seems reasonable to infer that they were too extreme, departing too wildly from the 'search for precedents' which characterized the reform measures of the majority. We do know that he was not assigned to any of the smaller commissions on reform which replaced the Nine.

While strongly supporting the early convocation of the council, Sadoleto turned to his own efforts at conciliation from 1537 to 1539. Unwilling to yield on matters of doctrine or on the authority of the church, he was deeply committed to its reformation and the recovery of Christian unity. Like Erasmus, he believed in the prospects of *rapprochement* through discussions between humanist moderates and intellectuals of both sides – not *Luther himself (who once described Sadoleto as 'able and cultivated ... but crafty and artful in the Italian manner'), *Oecolampadius, or Calvin, but men like *Melanchthon, Johann Sturm, and *Bucer.

Sadoleto sent a brief and respectful letter to Melanchthon in June 1537, written, he said, as an invitation to friendship. Melanchthon finally decided not to answer it, but news of Sadoleto's overture spread rapidly, drawing the fire and fury of *Cochlaeus, *Eck, *Nausea, and Johannes *Fabri – the hard core of the Catholic party in Germany. Sadoleto sent another letter to the eccentric and heterodox dean of Passau, Rudbert von *Mosham, in October, which Eck found even more outrageous than the letter to Melanchthon. A year later he wrote somewhat more cautiously to Johann Sturm at Strasbourg, a communication which was placed on the Index in 1559. In July 1538 he wrote his general treatise on the schism in Germany, in which he combined polemical refutation of Lutheran theology with abundant concessions on the subject of corruption in Rome. While acknowledging the legitimacy of grievances in Germany, he wrote with assurances that they could be resolved in the council. And in March 1539 he wrote the *Epistola ad senatum populumque Genevensem*, an appeal for the unity of the faith, addressed to members of the Calvinist community and not to its leadership – a loosely constructed exhortation which the thirty-year-old Calvin assaulted with passion and great intellectual force.

In 1542, at the age of sixty-five, Sadoleto was recalled to Rome to work for the council, now to be held at Trent. He drafted the bull of convocation in May, setting out in August as papal legate to *Francis I, who had declared war on the emperor in July. His mission was a failure, serving only to reveal again the indifference of the princes to the pope's effort to secure peace before the council opened in November. After attending a colloquy with the emperor at Busseto in June 1543, Sadoleto returned for the last time to Carpentras, now suffering from the depredations of French and Swiss troops and racked by religious violence which ended in the slaughter of the Waldensians in over twenty towns and villages, climaxing a campaign of repression which Sadoleto had vainly tried to prevent.

Dispirited and in debt, he was called back to Rome in 1545 for the last time. The council finally opened at the end of the year, and Sadoleto was assigned to the special commission on conciliar affairs. From his votes there it seems clear that no other member was less partisan, less attached to national interest, or more independent of the pope's dynastic ambitions than the bishop of Carpentras. To the anti-curial Venetian ambassador he was 'the very model of sound learning, high principles and innocence in this court,' willing once again to support an unpopular minority or to stand alone.

Sadoleto died on 18 October 1547 at the age of seventy and was buried in San Pietro in Vincoli, his third titular church in Rome. His remains were transferred to the cathedral at Carpentras, which he had helped to build, in 1646.

No member of the curia under either of the Medici popes was a more consistent advocate or defender of Erasmus than Sadoleto, through whom Erasmus received the first expression of favour from Leo x in 1515 (Ep 338). Erasmus, however, was soon to create divisions in Rome, both among the humanists of the Roman Academy and in curial circles. Sadoleto's defence of Erasmus between 1518 and 1521 reflects certain anomalies of his own career in the curia in that he drafted briefs and bulls in the name of *Leo x for the prosecution of Luther while defending Erasmus against critics and enemies who were charged with the execution of the pope's anti-Lutheran policy.

In August 1518 Sadoleto wrote the brief which cited Luther to the Auditor of the Camera and another which instructed the legate *Cajetanus to take Luther into custody. First Alberto *Pio and then Aleandro attacked Erasmus for his toleration of Lutherans, and indeed for what to Aleandro was a clandestine role in Luther's apostasy. Sadoleto was among those suspected of secretly informing Erasmus of the nuncio's accusations in his reports from Germany; he provoked Aleandro's wrath again by the papal brief which he sent to Erasmus acknowledging his loyalty and good will towards the Holy See (Epp 1180, 2443).

But Sadoleto also drafted the brief of 18 January 1521 which enjoined Charles v to execute the ban against heretics in Germany and to help 'rid the Lord's vineyard of reptiles.' Erasmus looked upon these measures as fatefully mistaken, while still declining in 1522 to write against Luther despite the pope's request through Sadoleto that he do so (Epp 1180, 1313). He openly deplored Leo x's turn to

severity, convinced that its only effects would be to inflame the radicals and alienate the moderates (Ep 1555).

Sadoleto defended Erasmus against *López Zúñiga's attacks on the New Testament in 1520, later recalling – rather grandiosely – that the Spaniard had not dared to write anything against Erasmus while Sadoleto was in Rome (Epp 1213, 1302, 2385). But during the later years of Clement VII's pontificate, while still presenting himself as a steady partisan of Erasmus, Sadoleto repeatedly tried to dissuade him from polemical engagement with Catholic rigorists (Epp 2272, 2385). In reply to the bishop's counsels of moderation and to the suggestion that he was needlessly contentious, Erasmus cited both the indifference of his critics to the need for reform and the facts of corruption, and the errors of the Roman curia in dealing with Luther. He pointed out that if Luther had been ignored at the outset, the present firestorm would not have come about, or would certainly not have been so widespread (Ep 2315). If only the matter had been entrusted to people like Sadoleto, it would now be less exacerbated everywhere (Ep 2443). It was not Erasmus who had generated so much anger and alienation in Germany, as Aleandro charged, but Aleandro and his kind, always too quick to suspect his loyalty and orthodoxy and too slow in their gratitude for his defence of the faith (Ep 2443).

Erasmus also assumed the role of *admonitor* and *corrector* of Sadoleto. In May and June 1532 Sadoleto described the difficulty he was having with his new work on Romans, while thanking Erasmus for Hieronymus *Froben's Greek Basil, dedicated to Sadoleto (Epp 2611, 2648). In sending the first volume of his commentary to Freiburg a year later Jacopo explained that he wanted Erasmus' criticism all the more because of the 'new path' he had taken into the reading of St Paul (Ep 2816). Erasmus read it during the summer and asked Bonifacius *Amerbach for his views of it, fearful that he had displeased Sadoleto by the straightforwardness of his admonitions (Epp 2927, 2928). Although Erasmus' criticism has not survived, it would appear that Sadoleto made little use of it in the first volume of his commentary and none in the second and third (Ep 2973). Erasmus wrote to Damião de *Gois in

December 1535 to say that he had anticipated the problems which Sadoleto was encountering from the Paris theologians and that he had done everything in his power to warn him (Ep 3076). Although Sadoleto protested his continuing affection for Erasmus in a letter of 8 December 1534 (Ep 2982), there is no surviving correspondence between them from that date to Erasmus' death in July 1536 and no further exchange of manuscripts.

Renaudet observed that 'Sadoleto probably remained the most loyal friend Erasmus had' (*Erasme et l'Italie* 239). The one visible stain on this loyalty is a comment Sadoleto made in 1530 about Erasmus to Fregoso: after praising Erasmus for his eloquence and erudition, he added, 'I know a little, but less than you imagine, about his integrity, honour, and ingenuousness.'

Sadoleto's published works can be consulted in the following major editions: *Jacopi Sadoleti S.R.E. Cardinalis epistolae* ed V.A. Costanzi (Rome 1759–67); *Lettere del Card. Iacopo Sadoleto e di Paolo suo nipote* ed A. Ronchini (Modena 1872); *Jacobi Sadoleti ... opera quae extant omnia* (Verona 1737–8, repr 1964). For manuscripts in Rome see Douglas 229–30, and in Carpentras and Avignon see Reinhard vii-viii.

BIBLIOGRAPHY: Allen Ep 1511 / Richard M. Douglas *Jacopo Sadoleto 1477–1547* (Cambridge, Mass, 1959) / Wolfgang Reinhard *Die Reform in der Diözese Carpentras unter den Bischöfen Jacopo Sadoleto, Paolo Sadoleto, Jacopo Sacrati und Francesco Sadoleto 1517–1596* (Münster 1966)   RICHARD M. DOUGLAS

Paolo SADOLETO of Modena, 1508–72
Paolo Sadoleto's father, Jacopo, was a cousin of Cardinal Jacopo *Sadoleto and like so many of the Sadoletti family worked as a lawyer and minor official in the court of the Este regime. Paolo was born in Modena, and after a period of study under Lilio Giraldi in Ferrara he went to Rome in 1527 to enter the household of his elder kinsman, then serving as domestic secretary to *Clement VII. An early adept at Greek and Latin, Paolo quickly won the favour of his 'uncle' and became in turn his protégé, confidant, spokesman, coadjutor, and successor in the diocese of Carpentras, north-east of Avignon in the papal state of Venaissin.

Indeed the career of the younger Sadoleto became something of a mirror of the elder's, although for all his early promise as a classical scholar and poet, his pursuit of letters was less determined than the cardinal's. Paolo left no legacy of published treatises or verse and is accessible to us only through his letters and Jacopo's.

Jacopo managed to provide Paolo with two benefices before he was twenty, to which another five were added later. The zealous reformer spent four years in efforts to wear down the opposition of Clement VII to the designation of Paolo as coadjutor 'cum iure successionis' to the diocese, the bull of appointment not being signed by the pope until 1535.

Not long after joining Jacopo in Rome, Paolo accompanied him in an abrupt departure for Provence in April 1527 as part of the exodus which fled the city before the arrival of Charles de Bourbon and the *Landsknechte*. The two reached Carpentras three days before the Sack of Rome. The strong association between 'uncle' and 'nephew' as they addressed each other, continued for two decades, until Jacopo's death in 1547.

Paolo's exertions as coadjutor began before the diploma of confirmation was signed. The dutiful young scholar also became the bishop's itinerant procurator, defending Jacopo's honour, literary reputation, and orthodoxy on missions to Sebastianus *Gryphius in Lyon in 1528, to the court of *Francis I in 1532 on matters related to the Comtat Venaissin, and to Rome in 1535 to cultivate support from the new pope, *Paul III, for Jacopo's controversial commentary on Romans. The interlocutor in the bishop's dialogue *De pueris instituendis* became the industrious deputy of a proud, trusting, and often dependent patron.

The only difference between them apparently developed out of their antithetical responses to the Waldensian (Vaudois) heretics in the papal state of Venaissin. Jacopo was pacific and conciliatory, constantly influenced by his dread of violence and his interest in people whom he wanted to protect against the repressive policy of papal authorities and the militant bishop of Cavaillon, and from French military officers fearful that a 'Swiss canton' was emerging east of the Rhone. Paolo, on the other hand, supported a strategy of force, approved by Francis I and the vice legate in Avignon, Alessandro *Campeggi, which led to an armed 'crusade' that destroyed twenty towns and villages in the spring of 1545.

Jacopo died in Rome two years later. By this time Paolo was a consequential figure in his own right. He was appointed rector of the Comtat Venaissin in 1541, was twice a candidate for the secretariat of the council of Trent, and succeeded his cousin as bishop of Carpentras. In 1552 he was called to Rome to become diplomatic secretary to Julius III; he disclosed a certain zeal for the life of the court and the company of notables but he left abruptly after two years to return to his see and the chronic crises of heretical agitation in the county. He served as rector again from 1560 to 1561 before joining Cardinal Ippolito II d'Este on a mission to Paris, following him to Rome the next year, where he remained until 1564.

Paolo died in 1572. He seems to have been more a prelate-activist than a scholar-prelate in the manner of his mentor. Paolo too valued the 'freedom and peace of mind' which he found in Provence, but it was a sense of pastoral duty rather than a hunger for study which drew him from Rome to Provence and away from what he admitted to be a competing desire for 'public reputation and recognition.'

The principal interest in Erasmus' one letter to Paolo (Ep 2864) lies in the sentence which describes Jacopo as 'the first among my closest friends' (1533).

BIBLIOGRAPHY: Allen Ep 2864 / *Jacobi Sadoleti epistolarum appendix: Accedunt Hieronymi Nigri et Pauli Sadoleti vitae ...* (Rome 1767) / Richard M. Douglas *Jacopo Sadoleto 1477–1547* (Cambridge, Mass, 1959) 52, 66–7, and passim / Wolfgang Reinhard *Die Reform in der Diözese Carpentras unter den Bischöfen Jacopo Sadoleto, Paolo Sadoleto, Jacopo Sacrati und Francesco Sadoleto 1517–1596* (Münster 1966) 30–9, 104 ff
RICHARD M. DOUGLAS

SAEVERUS *See* SEVERUS

Benet SAFONT of Barcelona, d 1535
Benet Safont was the son of a physician famous in Catalonia. He joined the Order of the Holy Trinity for the Redemption of Captives, which had been founded by 1200 to secure the freedom of Christians who had fallen into the hands of the Muslims. In 1520 he was elected general of this order. In 1527 Pedro Juan *Olivar described him to Erasmus as a man of authority and a firm supporter of Erasmus' cause (Ep 1791).

BIBLIOGRAPHY: Allen Ep 1791
MILAGROS RIVERA

Guilhelmus SAGARUS, SAGHER *See Willem Janszoon* ZAGERE

Niccolò SAGUNDINO of Venice, d after September 1533
The grandson of a better known Greek humanist and translator who bore the same name and came to Venice from the Greek island of Negroponte, or Euboea, during the fifteenth century, Niccolò grew up under the immediate influence of his father, Alvise, an important state secretary who was widely employed by the republic on missions in the eastern Mediterranean. Of the date of his birth and of his early education nothing is known; but since he apparently studied under Marcus *Musurus after the latter's appointment as Greek lecturer in Venice (1512), it is likely that his earlier instruction also took place there. No trace of the minor post in public service which Allen says he held by 1504 can be found and there is nothing to suggest that he played any significant part in the circle of Aldo *Manuzio or met Erasmus during 1508. But it would have been natural for him to follow his father's career, and he evidently moved in literary circles, for when he visited Marino Sanudo's library on 5 December 1511 he came with Musurus and Alberto *Pio and was by this time called 'secretary' by the diarist.

In 1515 Sagundino accompanied the Venetian ambassador, Sebastiano *Giustiniani, to England and, though he suffered from both homesickness and the 'English sweat,' he found time to enjoy the companionship of Erasmus and Thomas *More. Both are mentioned in terms of friendship and respect in a letter of 22 April 1517 which Sagundino sent to congratulate Musurus on his recent appointment as archbishop of Monemvasia (Ep 574). On 30 May (Ep 584) Erasmus asked More to have Sagundino send him a copy of this letter, along with a letter from Sebastiano Giustiniani

(Ep 559) which he had lost. Sagundino sent two copies on 22 June, adding a new letter of praise and affection to Erasmus (Ep 590). On 22 August he again sent greetings to Erasmus through Francesco *Chierigati (Ep 639). But though Sagundino had some reputation as a musician, his literary interests do not seem to have competed with his professional ambitions and contact with Erasmus was not maintained. Returning to Venice in 1519, Sagundino followed the path of promotion within the civil service, attaining the important rank of secretary to the Council of Ten in 1532.

BIBLIOGRAPHY: Allen Ep 574 / Sanudo *Diarii* XIII 293 and passim   M.J.C. LOWRY

Antonio SALAMANCA *See Antonio* HOYOS *de Salamanca*

Gabriel de SALAMANCA count of Ortenburg, d 12 December 1539
Gabriel, the son of Gonzales de Salamanca, appeared in Germany in the entourage of Archduke *Ferdinand and soon became a powerful nobleman in his court. By February 1521 he was chancellor of the Tirol and in 1523 treasurer-general, at first for the Tirol and later for all of Austria; on 15 March 1524 he was raised to the rank of count of Ortenburg in Carinthia. For some time opponents had been accusing him of massive fraud, and in 1526 he was forced to give up his Austrian offices; however, he received a lifelong pension as compensation (on 3 May 1526). Gabriel continued to enjoy the favour and trust of Ferdinand and, to some extent, also of the Emperor *Charles V and proved indispensable in their financial dealings with Anton *Fugger and his associates. Between 1526 and 1538 he was able to raise a considerable part of the huge sums that were needed for Ferdinand's coronation as king of Hungary, for court expenses, and for the war against the Turks. In March 1527 he was sent to England in an effort to gain King *Henry VIII's support against the Turks. Gabriel was appointed governor (*Landvogt*) of Upper Alsace on 23 July 1527 and on 19 July 1528 *Hauptmann* of the county of Gorizia (Görz) which was leased to him. Ferdinand also assigned to him the castle and town of Bruck an der Leitha in Lower Austria. In 1537 he was named imperial councillor and again given the task of recruiting troops against the Turks.

In 1523 Gabriel married Elisabeth von Eberstein; his second wife, whom he married in 1533, was Elisabeth of Baden. His death occurred in Alsace and he was survived by four sons. When Gabriel's nephew, Antonio *Hoyos de Salamanca, came to Freiburg in 1529, Erasmus recalled his previous – and lost – correspondence with Gabriel, who had rendered him some service (Epp 2096, 2098; cf perhaps Ep 2008).

BIBLIOGRAPHY: Allen Ep 2096 / ADB XXIV 437–8 / AK VI Ep 2819 / de Vocht *Literae ad Craneveldium* Epp 227, 229 / Götz von Pölnitz *Anton Fugger* (Tübingen 1958–) I 65, 74, II 23–4, 43, 93–9, and passim / Wilhelm Bauer *Die Anfänge Ferdinands* (Vienna 1907) 167   IG

Johannes SALIUS, SALIANUS, SALINGER *See Johann* SALZMANN

Jean SALMON Macrin of Loudun, 1490–1557
Jean Salmon was called Maigret or Macrinus, Macrin – no doubt in view of his constitution. He was born at Loudun, in Poitou, and educated in Paris, studying under Jacques *Lefèvre d'Etaples and Girolamo *Aleandro. He was a friend of Germain de *Brie and Guillaume *Budé. At first he enjoyed the protection of Cardinal Antoine *Bohier and after Bohier's death was close to the *Robertet family. By 1530 he had become the protégé of Guillaume and Jean *Du Bellay, who secured for him an appointment as *valet-de-chambre* to King *Francis I. Modelling himself after Catullus and Horace, he was a fertile Latin poet, untiring in the praise of his patrons and their causes. In his *Carminum libri quatuor* (Paris: S. de Colines 1530), addressed to Guillaume Du Bellay, reference is made to Erasmus and Thomas *More. His *Naeniae* (Paris: M. de Vascosan 1550) are occasioned by the loss of his wife, Gillonne de Boursault.

Erasmus returned greetings from Salmon in his answer to a letter from Nicolas *Bourbon (Ep 2789).

BIBLIOGRAPHY: Allen Ep 2789 / A. Cioranescu *Bibliographie de la littérature française du seizième siècle* (Paris 1959) 637–8 / V.-L. Bourrilly *Guillaume du Bellay* (Paris 1905) 116–18 and passim / Rogers Ep 86

MICHEL REULOS

Giovanni Salviati, by Giuseppe Pazzi

Giovanni SALVIATI of Florence, 24 March 1490–28 October 1553

A son of the Florentines Jacopo Salviati and Lucrezia de' Medici, Giovanni was a nephew of Pope *Leo x and an uncle of Duke Cosimo i of Florence. He studied the humanities at the Studio of Florence. Before Leo x's great creation of cardinals in July 1517 in which hè was made a cardinal deacon (Sts Cosmas and Damian), he had already been an apostolic protonotary, and in 1518 was appointed bishop of Fermo. During his uncle's pontificate he received the administration of the diocese of Ferrara (1520) and in *Clement vii's that of Volterra (1530). *Paul iii promoted him successively to the cardinal bishoprics of Albano (1543), Sabina (1544), and Porto (1546).

Salviati played a notable part in politics but was not successful in any of his major ambitions. He was legate in Lombardy in 1524 and 1525 prior to the disastrous French defeat at Pavia. He set out for Spain in July 1525, not accompanied, as his father had recommended, by Niccolò *Machiavelli, and failed to ensure the implementation of the peace terms negotiated by Clement vii with the imperial viceroy,

Charles de Lannoy, after *Francis i's defeat. But his report from Alcalá on 22 September of *Margaret of Angoulême's visit to her beloved brother in captivity illuminates a tender episode in Margaret's life. Immediately after his return from Spain Salviati became legate to France (September 1526–August 1529; cf Ep 2066). He was involved in the Anglo-French discussions at Amiens (June 1527) on the liberation of Clement vii from Castel Sant'Angelo, but not, as he would have liked, in the peace concluded between France and the Empire in August 1529 at Cambrai while he himself was there. By October, when Erasmus was hoping that the papal legate's presence would restrain Noël *Béda (Ep 2225), Salviati had probably already left France for Rome. He was present at the imperial coronation at Bologna in 1530, was in Rome during Clement vii's second meeting with the emperor in 1532, and then accompanied the pope to Marseille to meet Francis i in 1533. After Clement's death in 1534 Salviati sided with Cardinal Ippolito de' *Medici against his half-brother, Alessandro de' *Medici, whose rule in Florence was becoming increasingly unpopular. After Alessandro's assassination in 1537 Salviati joined a group of Florentine exiles in an armed march on the city and its new duke, Cosimo i de' Medici. However the intervention of Spanish troops forced the exiles to disband and Salviati accepted Duke Cosimo. Imperial opposition blocked his chances of election as pope after the death of *Paul iii in 1549. He died in Ravenna, but his body was interred in the cathedral of Ferrara.

A cultured man, Salviati was the first in Rome to receive the printed edition of Machiavelli's *Arte della guerra*; he numbered among his household the Spanish Hellenist and anti-Protestant polemicist Francisco Torres.

BIBLIOGRAPHY: Allen Ep 2066 / Giuseppe Canestrini and Abel Desjardins *Négotiations diplomatiques de la France avec la Toscane* (Paris 1859–86) ii 782–842 / L. Cardella *Memorie storiche dei cardinali* (Rome 1792–7) iv 58–61 / A. Ciaconius *Vita et res gestae Pontificum Romanorum et S.R.E. Cardinalium* (Rome 1677) iii 382–407 / Rosemary Devonshire Jones *Francesco Vettori: Florentine Citizen and Medici Servant* (London 1972) 230 and passim / G. Molini *Documenti di storia italiana* (Florence 1836–7) i and II / Pastor VII 203, VIII 69, IX 51, X 4, XI 7, XIII 3, and passim / R. Ridolfi *The Life of Niccolò Machiavelli* trans Cecil Grayson (Chicago-London 1963) 179, 212, and passim / R. Ridolfi *The Life of Francesco Guicciardini* trans Cecil Grayson (London 1967) 184 and passim / A.F. Verde *Lo studio fiorentino* (Pistoia 1977) III-1 498   ROSEMARY DEVONSHIRE JONES

William SALYNG prior of Merton, c 1470–14 March 1520
William Salyng (Seiling) was an Augustinian canon of the priory of Merton, in Surrey, when he became a scholar of St Mary's College, Oxford, in January 1485. In 1502 he was a bachelor of theology, and in 1504 he was a doctor. He was elected prior of Merton on 16 March 1502 and retained this position until his death. In 1509 Bishop Richard *Foxe admonished him for being absent from his priory under the pretext of study at Oxford. By 1517 he was a friend of Johannes *Sixtinus and Andrea *Ammonio (Ep 624).

Salyng should not be confused with the classical scholar William Selling, a Benedictine who was prior of Christ Church Cathedral priory, Canterbury, from 1478 until his death in 1494.

BIBLIOGRAPHY: Allen Ep 624 / Emden BRUO III 1635   R.J. SCHOECK

Jakob von SALZA 14 August 1481–25 August 1539
Jakob von Salza was born on his father's estate of Schreibersdorf, near Lubán (Lauban) in Silesia. He matriculated at the University of Leipzig in the winter term of 1498–9 and in 1502 moved to Bologna, where he was syndic (1505) and procurator (1507) of the German nation. On 3 July 1508 he received a doctorate of laws in Ferrara. After his return from Italy King *Vladislav II of Hungary and Bohemia in 1510 appointed him chief administrator or *Landeshauptmann* of the principality of Glogau in Silesia (in the region of today's Polish city of Głogów). In 1511 while participating in a tournament at Wrocław he had the misfortune of gravely wounding another participant; this is said to have led to his entering the church. He received canonries of the chapter of Głogów and the Holy Cross chapter at Wrocław and also in 1513 at the cathedral

chapter of Wrocław, where he was elected *scholaster* in 1516. In 1519 he accompanied the chancellor of Bohemia, Ladislaus von Sternberg, to Frankfurt am Main, the scene of the imperial election of *Charles v. On 1 September 1520 his fellow canons elected him bishop of Wrocław in succession to Jan (II) *Thurzo, and on 24 July 1521 he received papal confirmation. He continued to show great ability as an administrator, and in 1536 King *Ferdinand I appointed him *Oberlandeshauptmann* for the entire region of Silesia. In his secular as well as his ecclesiastical office he strove, with little success, to stall the progress of the Protestant Reformation. He died at Nysa (Neisse).

There is a passing reference to the bishop of Wrocław in Jakob *Ziegler's Ep 1260 to Erasmus.

BIBLIOGRAPHY: Allen Ep 1260 / NDB X 312–13 / ADB XIII 538–40 / *Matrikel Leipzig* I 427 / Knod 476 / Pflug *Correspondance* I Ep 16 and passim / Johann Heyne *Dokumentierte Geschichte des Bisthums und Hochstifts Breslau* (Wrocław 1860–8, repr 1969) III 730–41 / Gerhard Zimmermann *Das Breslauer Domkapitel im Zeitalter der Reformation und Gegenreformation* (Weimar 1938) 471–3 / Schottenloher II 257 (no 19670), III 160, VII 204   MICHAEL ERBE

Johann SALZMANN of Steyr, d 1530
Johann Salzmann (Salczman, Saltzman, Salinger, Salius, Salianus) from Steyr, in Upper Austria, matriculated at the University of Vienna in April 1497, unable to pay his fees. Information about his subsequent life is incomplete. After obtaining a medical doctorate – where is not known – he visited Annaberg in the Erz mountains in 1507. On 19 June of that year he dedicated a poem about Annaberg to the city fathers and mentioned in its preface that the preceding year *Maximilian I had crowned him with the poet's laurel in reward for his earlier poem about Carinthia, which is not known to exist. The poem on Annaberg was printed in Michael Barth's *Annaberga* (Basel: J. Oporinus 1557). In 1510, at the time of a plague epidemic in Hungary, Salzmann was town physician of Sibiu (Hermannstadt), in Transylvania, as he stated in dedicating to the town magistrates (on 12 August) *De praeservatione a pestilentia et ipsius cura opusculum* (Vienna: H. Wietor 16 November 1510), a work that

follows traditional lines. A German version of his plague treatise, *Eine nutzliche Ordnung und Regiment wider die Pestilentz* (Vienna: J. Singriener 1521), has a preface signed by Salzmann in Graz on 15 September of that year. This preface is a eulogy of Archduke *Ferdinand, whose personal physician Salzmann had meanwhile become, perhaps in succession to Juan de la *Parra, who had died in the spring of 1521. Salzmann retained this position to his own death; he was also a member of the medical faculty of Vienna from 1513 to his death and was elected rector of the university for the winter term 1522–3 and again for the following summer term.

In the second half of July 1520 Salzmann apparently travelled from Freiburg to the Netherlands, taking along Epp 1120–1 for Erasmus, whom he probably met at Bruges at the court of *Charles v. Erasmus later recalled that their conversation turned to *Reuchlin, whom Salzmann evidently supported (ASD IX-1 144–5).

BIBLIOGRAPHY: Allen and CWE Epp 1120, 1129 /*Matrikel Wien* II-1 254, III-1 28, 31 / Harry Kühnel *Mittelalterliche Heilkunde in Wien* (Graz-Cologne 1965) 103 / Joseph von Aschbach et al *Geschichte der Wiener Universität* (Vienna 1865–98) II 97–8, III 9, 379 / R.F. Kaindl *Geschichte und Kulturleben Deutschösterreichs von der ältesten Zeit bis 1526* (Vienna 1929) 387   PGB

Johannes SAMBORKIUS *See Jan* ZAMBOCKI

Richard SAMPSON c 1484–25 September 1554
A friend of both Erasmus and Thomas *More, Richard Sampson studied canon law at Trinity Hall, Cambridge, and received his bachelor's degree in civil law in 1506. After studies at Paris, Perugia, and Siena he received his doctorate in civil law at Cambridge in 1513 and in canon law in 1520; he occupied a chair of canon law at that university from 1512 to 1518. He also served Cardinal *Wolsey as chaplain and in September 1514 was appointed Wolsey's vicar-general in the diocese of Tournai, which had been conquered from the French. Wolsey's possession of the diocese was contested by the French bishop Louis *Guillard, and, according to a letter of Erasmus (Ep 360), Sampson was excommunicated by the rival ecclesiastical authorities in 1515. In 1517

Sampson received the archdeaconry of Cornwall, the first of many benefices which he accumulated. In 1518 Tournai was restored to the French and Sampson returned to England. From 1523 to 1540 he was dean of the Chapel Royal; he also served *Henry VIII as ambassador to the court of *Charles v in Spain from 1522 to 1525 and in 1529 undertook another mission to the emperor and Pope *Clement VII on the matter of the royal divorce. He became bishop of Chichester in 1536, exchanging this for Coventry and Lichfield in 1543. The author of an *Oratio* in defence of the royal supremacy (London: T. Berthelet c 1535; STC 21681), Sampson also published commentaries on the Psalms (London: T. Berthelet 1539 and J. Herford 1548; STC 21679–80) and on Paul's Epistles to the Romans and 1 Corinthians (London: J. Herford 1546; STC 21678) and may be the author (known only by surname) of several musical compositions, perhaps in connection with his office in the Chapel Royal.

Sampson's friendship with Erasmus began during the latter's stay at Cambridge from 1511 to 1514 and was renewed at Tournai probably in 1515 (Ep 806). According to More's letter to Erasmus of February 1516 (Ep 388), Sampson played a role in efforts to obtain a prebend for Erasmus at Tournai. The plan did not succeed, but in a letter to Johannes de *Molendino of January 1518 (Ep 755), Erasmus referred to Sampson as his benefactor; this prompted Sampson to write Ep 780, asking Erasmus to regard him instead as a friend. Erasmus replied with Ep 806, again expressing his gratitude. In September 1520 Erasmus described the English ecclesiastic as 'the incomparable Doctor Sampson, whose nature is as open and as friendly as anything one could wish to see' (Ep 1138).

BIBLIOGRAPHY: Allen and CWE Ep 388 / DNB XVII 719–21 / Emden BRUC 505–6 / *The New Grove Dictionary of Music and Musicians* ed Stanley Sadie (London 1980) XVI 459

R.J. SCHOECK

Felino SANDEIS 1444–6 September 1503
One of the most eminent canon lawyers of the later fifteenth century, Felino Sandeis (Sandei, Sandeo) taught at both Padua and Pisa before being summoned to join the rota in Rome by *Sixtus IV in 1484. His *consulta* were widely circulated by contemporary printers, and he was cited amongst other legal authorities by

Bonifacius *Amerbach in a letter on *Henry VIII's divorce (Ep 2267). Rewarded by the papacy with the bishoprics of Adria and Penna (1495), then Lucca (1501), he bequeathed his library to Lucca, where he died. The 467 volumes which can still be identified in the Biblioteca Capitolare provide an important example of a working library, which contained not only manuscripts but a large variety of early printed texts.

BIBLIOGRAPHY: Allen Ep 2267 / G. Ghilarducci *Il vescovo Felino Sandeis e la Biblioteca Capitolare di Lucca* (Lucca 1972) / Ludwig Hain *Repertorium bibliographicum* (Stuttgart 1826–38, repr 1948) IV 269–78   M.J.C. LOWRY

Michael SANDER died c September 1529
Michael Sander (Sanderius, Zanderus, Sanderi de Soweyden) was born in the diocese of Worms and studied at Bologna from around 1492 to 1501, obtaining a doctorate in civil and canon law. By January 1512 he was secretary to Cardinal Matthäus *Schiner, frequently signing his letters. He accompanied Schiner on his ceaseless travels and apparently went to Rome in the summer of 1512. On 3 February 1514 Schiner obtained for him a canonry at Novara and in May 1515 he was appointed commendatory abbot of San Christoforo, near Bergamo. He was also a canon of St Thomas', Strasbourg, and dean of the chapter of Wrocław. Before 1520 he became an apostolic protonotary.

Between 1518 and 1521 Sander's frequent visits to Zürich are documented through the correspondence of *Zwingli and *Beatus Rhenanus, which dealt with his book purchases in Basel and also with Zwingli's appointment to Zürich (z VII Epp 46, 50, 188; BRE Ep 98). He was at Ghent in July and August 1521 and evidently met Erasmus in the Netherlands before the humanist moved to Basel (Ep 1242). Between 1520 and 1522 Schiner also sent him repeatedly to London for negotiations with Cardinal *Wolsey, and after Schiner's death in September in 1522 he appears to have been to some extent in the English service (LP III 3103). On 7 September 1523 he was appointed to a canonry at Constance with the support of the papal nuncio Ennio *Filonardi, who was then in Constance. Sander did not expect to take up residence and therefore declined the occupancy of the house of his predecessor. His fellow-canon Johann von *Botzheim, who soon

came to see in him a source of his troubles with the Roman curia (Ep 1530), noted the vehemence of his interventions in the conflict between the reform party of Constance and the bishop, Johannes *Fabri (Ep 1401). Still keeping in touch with Erasmus (Ep 1424) Sander went to Rome at the beginning of 1524, where Cardinal Lorenzo *Campeggi had named him master of ceremonies.

BIBLIOGRAPHY: Allen Ep 1242 / LP III 985, 1375, 1860 / *Korrespondenzen und Akten zur Geschichte des Kardinals Matth. Schiner* ed A. Büchi (Basel 1920–5) I 128 and passim / Manfred Krebs *Die Protokolle des Konstanzer Domkapitels* (Karlsruhe 1952–9) VI 311, 326, and passim   PGB

Cornelia SANDRIEN of Antwerp, c 1496–1526
Cornelia Sandrien (Sanders, Sandria) was the daughter of Claus Sandrien called Daneels and Martine van Ghoorle. In 1514 she married Pieter *Gillis, town secretary of Antwerp; they had nine children: Nicolaas, Martine, Jan, Joachim, Jeroom, Anna, Margriet, Lucia, and Petronella.

On the occasion of their marriage Erasmus composed an epithalamium (Reedijk 384–5) which, however, could not be completed and printed in time for the wedding (Ep 312). These verses later came to be part of a colloquy, *Epithalamium Petri Aegidii*, on which Erasmus was still working after his arrival at Basel late in 1521. It was published in Johann *Froben's *Colloquia* edition of August–September 1525 (ASD I-3 410–16). Erasmus and Cornelia exchanged greetings (Epp 434, 715, 818, 849). After Cornelia's death, Erasmus encouraged Pieter to look for a new wife (Ep 1740 of 29 August 1526). By January 1530 he composed two epitaphs for Cornelia (Ep 2260; Reedijk poems 126–7).

BIBLIOGRAPHY: Allen Ep 715 / Floris Prims *Antwerpiensia 1936. Tiende Reeke* (Antwerp 1937) 172–3 / Franz Bierlaire *Erasme et ses Colloques: le livre d'une vie* (Geneva 1977) 77   MARCEL A. NAUWELAERTS

Jacopo SANNAZARO of Naples, 28 July 1457 or 1458–6 August 1530
Jacopo Sannazaro (Sannazzaro, Nazarius) was born to a prominent Neapolitan family and spent much of his early life on the country

estate of his mother, Masella Santomango of Salerno. In the early 1480s he settled permanently in Naples, where he became a poet at the court of King Ferdinand I (1458–94) and a member of the Neapolitan Academy, then led by Giovanni *Pontano. Pontano gave Sannazaro the name Actius Syncerus, the meaning of which is uncertain. Actius may have meant 'of the sea shore' and Syncerus 'sincere.' In 1501 King Frederick I of Naples (1496–1501), the last of his line, lost his throne in an agreement between *Louis XII of France and *Ferdinand II of Aragon and in compensation received the duchy of Anjou and a pension. Sannazaro followed his king into voluntary exile. When Frederick died in 1504, Sannazaro returned to his estate at Naples and assumed leadership of the academy upon the death of Pontano. Sannazaro died on 6 August 1530 and not, as commonly stated, on 24 April.

Sannazaro was famous throughout Italy as the author of the *Arcadia*, an Italian pastoral romance consisting of a series of eclogues joined by prose. Although Sannazaro finished most of the work by 1489, it was not published until 1502, in an unauthorized edition at Venice. In 1504 Pietro Summonte, a friend of Sannazaro, published an improved text at Naples, and throughout the sixteenth century new editions appeared approximately every second year. Sannazaro's Latin poems, which Ellinger judged to be outstanding, included the *De partu Virginis*, a heroic treatment of the Nativity, borrowing metaphors from the pagan classics; the *Eclogae piscatoriae*, bucolic poems dealing with fishermen; and the *Elegiae* and *Epigrammata*, collections of miscellaneous poetry. His Latin *Opera* were published by the Aldine press at Venice in 1535.

Of Sannazaro's works, Erasmus possessed the *De partu Virginis* and the *Eclogae piscatoriae* in the Roman edition of 1526 (F.M. Calvo), which included briefs from *Leo X and *Clement VII and a letter by Cardinal Egidio *Antonini of Viterbo (Ep 1840). In the *Ciceronianus* Erasmus mentioned these two works, criticizing the former for its mixture of pagan motifs with a sacred theme. He argued that religious language should suffice for a sacred work, and that religious poetry could not move its readers to piety if it were a patchwork of Homeric and Virgilian phrases, let alone of

words gathered only from Cicero (ASD I-2 700–1).

BIBLIOGRAPHY: Allen Ep 1840 / EI XXX 737–40 / Jacopo Sannazaro *Arcadia* and *Piscatorial Eclogues* trans and intro Ralph Nash (Detroit 1966) / Georg Ellinger *Geschichte der neulateinischen Literatur Deutschlands im sechzehnten Jahrhundert* (Berlin 1929–33) I 59–62 and passim / Cosenza IV 3175–82 / Francesco Tateo *L'umanesimo meridionale* (Bari 1972) 143–210 / William J. Kennedy *Jacopo Sannazaro and the Uses of Pastoral* (London-Hanover, NH 1983)   TBD

Pietro SANTERAMO of Messina, documented 1484–1504

Pietro Santeramo (Sancteramus, Sancteranus) of Messina taught in the faculty of arts of the Studio of Palermo around 1480. He was a colleague of the Sicilian humanist Lucio Marineo, whom he accompanied to Spain in 1484 and with whom he taught at the University of Salamanca. In his *Opus de rebus Hispaniae memorabilibus* (Alcalá: M. de Eguía 1533, f 113) Marineo praised one of Santeramo's works, 'De Granatensi bello,' for its rich and elegant style. In a letter to Cataldo Parisio, Marineo further praised Santeramo as one of the most illustrious Sicilians of his age.

After his time in Spain, Santeramo travelled to Paris and to the Netherlands, where in 1496 he met Erasmus at Bergen in the household of Hendrik van *Bergen, bishop of Cambrai. In 1498 Erasmus included a letter from Santeramo to Fausto *Andrelini in *De conscribendis epistolis* as an exemplary letter of friendship (ASD I-2 510). According to Allen (Ep 71 introduction), Santeramo had probably given the letter to Erasmus for delivery to Andrelini in Paris. In 1515, in one of his dedicatory epistles for the second volume of his edition of Jerome, Erasmus recalled Santeramo as 'a very amusing and well-read person,' and repeated an anecdote about a trick which the Sicilian had played on Andrelini in Paris (Ep 326). Santeramo had long since returned to Sicily, writing to Marineo from Messina on 10 July 1497. He wrote two other letters to his former colleague, the last from Naples on 6 August 1504.

BIBLIOGRAPHY: Cosenza IV 3188 / N. Antonio *Bibliotheca hispana* (Rome 1672) 372 / L. Marineo *Epistolarum familiarum libri decem et septem* (Valladolid: A.G. de Brocar 1514) book V 18 and passim / A. Mongitore *Bibliotheca sicula sive de scriptoribus siculis* (Palermo 1724) II 158

PAOLO PISSAVINO

Johannes SAPIDUS of Sélestat, 1490–8 June 1561

Johannes Sapidus (Witz) was born in Sélestat, in Upper Alsace. He was not, as is sometimes asserted, the nephew of Jakob *Wimpfeling. He attended the Sélestat grammar school, at that time under the direction of Hieronymus *Gebwiler. In the company of *Beatus Rhenanus he continued his education at the University of Paris, where they both pursued their humanist interests. On his return to Sélestat, Sapidus was appointed rector of the grammar school in 1512 on a permanent basis, Gebwiler having resigned in 1509 to take on the reform of the chapter school in Strasbourg.

Under Sapidus the Sélestat school flourished, drawing students not only from Alsace but from Switzerland and Lorraine. By 1517 there were nine hundred students. Sapidus struck out even more boldly against the old grammar texts than had his predecessors. He emphasized Latin writing based on the classical texts themselves and introduced Greek to the curriculum. His enthusiastic acceptance of the Reformation, however, drew him into conflict with Wimpfeling, who threatened to turn him over to the Inquisition. He was also embroiled with the city council. In 1526 he left Sélestat for Strasbourg to continue his career as an educator.

On his arrival Sapidus was asked by the reformers to direct the new Latin school which had been organized in the old Dominican convent. When the Strasbourg Gymnasium was established in 1538, Sapidus' school was absorbed in the new institution, under the direction of the Luxembourg humanist Johann Sturm, who was Sapidus' son-in-law. Although every attempt was made to give Sapidus the status and prestige he felt were his due, his teaching and his relationship with the students had already deteriorated because he was increasingly irritable and waspish with them. The parents complained to the magistrates and Johann Sturm, and he was finally made professor of poetry. Some of his energies then flowed into writing. He wrote a biblical play, *Anabion sive Lazarus redivivus* (Strasbourg:

K. Müller 1539), to celebrate the opening of the new school building in 1539, and dedicatory poems for the works of his friends, as well as *Epitaphia* (Strasbourg: W. Rihel 1542) and other verses (Ep 3069).

Sapidus' friendship with Erasmus began with the latter's journey to Basel in 1514. Sapidus met the older scholar in Sélestat and escorted him to his destination, a service which Erasmus rewarded with a quatrain (Ep 305). A warm interchange of letters and poems followed. Sapidus composed a poem in honour of the humanist in 1516, *Ad sodales Erasmo Roterodamo consuetudine iunctissimos*, which Erasmus published in the *Epistolae elegantes* with an encouraging letter addressed to Sapidus as 'teacher of the liberal arts,' emphasizing the importance of his calling which should not be undermined by minor problems like a cut in salary (CWE Ep 391A; Allen Ep 364). Sapidus wrote another poem on Erasmus' national origins that same year, which Erasmus also published (LB III 1556 A–B; cf Ep 421). Sapidus was also eager to share Erasmus with his own friends. He introduced *Oecolampadius to Erasmus, a fruitful encounter since the former stayed on in Basel to help Erasmus prepare the *Novum instrumentum* (Ep 354). In 1516 Sapidus sent along yet another friend, Beat *Arnold (Ep 399).

There was a particularly close relationship between Erasmus, Paul *Volz, and Sapidus (Epp 368, 372). In 1518 in the last paragraph of the dedicatory letter to Volz (Ep 858), which became the preface to the 1518 Froben edition of the *Enchiridion*, Erasmus admonished Volz to tell Sapidus that he should remain a scholar, true to himself. In a sense Erasmus was using the younger scholar as an example for all his readers. The three remained close and shared common interests despite their differences in religion. In 1520 Erasmus dedicated to Sapidus the first edition of the *Antibarbari* (Ep 1110). In November 1535 Volz informed Erasmus that Sapidus was the author of an epigram attacking Etienne *Dolet, who had previously criticized Erasmus (Ep 3069). In another poem in honour of a silver cup Erasmus had presented to Volz, Erasmus found a false quantity which called for correction (Ep 3114). This poem, together with a long elegy and an ode to Andrzej *Krzycki which Sapidus had composed under the impact of Erasmus' death, is reprinted amid the preliminary pieces in LB I.

On Sapidus' death in 1561, Johann Marbach, president of the Strasbourg church, preached the funeral eulogy, which was later published. Achilles Pirmin Gasser, one of his former students in Sélestat, wrote an epitaph for him.

BIBLIOGRAPHY: Allen and CWE Ep 323 / Gustav Knod in ADB XXX 369–71 / Johannes Ficker and Otto Winckelmann *Handschriftproben des sechzehnten Jahrhunderts* ... (Strasbourg 1905) II 78 / M.U. Chrisman *Bibliography of Strasbourg Imprints, 1480–1599* (New Haven 1982) 146 and passim / Marie-Joseph Bopp *Die evangelischen Geistlichen und Theologen in Elsass und Lothringen von der Reformation bis zur Gegenwart* (Neustadt a.d. Aisch 1959) 464 / Schmidt *Histoire littéraire* I 96 and passim / BRE Ep 105 and passim / AK I Ep 405 and passim
MIRIAM U. CHRISMAN

Samuel SARFATI died c 1519
In Ep 240 Erasmus refers to a Jewish physician who cured Pope *Julius II of a serious illness in August 1511; a similar reference occurs in the *Julius exclusus* (*Opuscula* 76). In the *Acta contra Lutherum* (*Opuscula* 323–4) a Jewish physician is made responsible for the pope's death.

Among the physicians of Julius II two Jews from Provence are mentioned. Samuel Sarfati (Sarfadi, Sarfatti), called Gallo, arrived in Rome in 1498 and died around 1519. Jacob ben Emmanuel, known as Bonetus (Bonet) de Lattes (Lates), was physician to *Alexander VI, Julius II, and *Leo X until 1515; he is the author of several medical works.

BIBLIOGRAPHY: Allen and CWE Ep 240 / *Opuscula* 76 / *The Julius exclusus of Erasmus* trans P. Pascal, annot J.K. Sowards (Bloomington 1968) 53, 117 / For Sarfati: *Encyclopaedia Judaica* (Jerusalem 1971–2) XIV 878–9 / For Bonetus: *The Jewish Encyclopedia* (New York [1901–16]) III 305; Rice *Prefatory Epistles* Ep 8   PGB

SASBOUDUS (Epp 16, 296)
In a letter evidently dating from his years in the monastery of Steyn (Ep 16 of 1488?) Erasmus addressed a friend named Sasboudus (Sasbout), who has not been identified. It is possible, however, that he is identical with the Sasboudus mentioned a quarter of a century

later in a letter to Servatius *Rogerus, the prior of Steyn (Ep 296 of 1514). In both letters Sasboudus appears to be associated with an unidentified Henricus. The Sasboudus mentioned in Ep 296 was married. It is thus possible that he was a childhood friend and the only layman among Erasmus' early correspondents. They may have been educated together (Ep 16:45–6) at Deventer or 's Hertogenbosch. Although Sasboudus may well have come from the region of Delft, as Allen suggested, there is no reason for relating him to Joost *Sasbout of Delft.

BIBLIOGRAPHY: Allen and CWE Ep 16
C.G. VAN LEIJENHORST

Joost SASBOUT of Delft, 4 March 1487–14 November 1546
Joost Sasbout (Iodocus Sasboldus Delphius), lord of Spalant, was a native of Delft and a kinsman of the well-known Cornelis Muys (Musius) of Delft. He matriculated at Louvain on 8 October 1506. After having obtained his MA he left Louvain to study canon and civil law, receiving his doctorate in or before 1513. In 1515 he was appointed ordinary councillor in the council of Holland. In 1526 he was sent as an imperial commissioner to Friesland; he made such a favourable impression that the governor, Georg Schenck, wished to have him as the new president of the council of Friesland, but instead Gregor Bertholff of Aachen was appointed to that office in 1527. On 7 November 1543 Sasbout took the oath as chancellor of Gelderland, the duchy having given up its struggle for independence. He died at Arnhem comforted by the fact that he had written his own epitaph; otherwise, his qualities as a poet may be seen in verses he wrote in tribute to Maarten van *Dorp, edited by de Vocht in MHL 399–400, 402. His wife was Catherine van der Meer; their son Arnold (d 1583) likewise became chancellor of Gelderland.

Sasbout and Erasmus knew each other, it seems, rather superficially (Ep 2645); Erasmus regularly sent him greetings (Epp 1092, 1188, 2644), and after 1532 they exchanged some letters (Epp 2645, 2844; cf Epp 2851, 2923). In Ep 3037 of 10 August 1535 Erasmus was told that his famulus *Quirinus Hagius had misrepresented his theological views in the presence of, among others, Sasbout; to reduce the effect of this embarrassing event Erasmus wrote a letter to Sasbout which is referred to in Epp 3052 and 3061 but is now lost.

BIBLIOGRAPHY: Allen Ep 1092 / J. van Kuyk in NNBW II 1265–6 / Matricule de Louvain III-1 323 / de Vocht Literae ad Craneveldium Ep 113 / de Vocht MHL 399 / de Vocht CTL II 199–200 / J.S. Theissen Centraal gezag en Friesche vrijheid (Groningen 1907) 148–9

                                        C.G. VAN LEIJENHORST

Gabriel SAUCIUS (Ep 2008 of 16 July 1528)
In a letter to Caspar *Ursinus Velius, Erasmus sent greetings to Gabriel Saucius, who has not been identified. P.S. Allen wondered whether Gabriel de *Salamanca might be intended.

Stanislaus SAUER of Lwówek, d 21 January 1535
Stanislaus Sauer, (Sawr, Saurus) was born around 1469 at Lwówek (Löwenberg), in Silesia, the son of a patrician who was a member of the town council. He studied at Cracow (1486–90), graduating BA, and subsequently at Bologna under Filippo (I) *Beroaldo (Mutianus Ep 472) and in 1502 obtained a canonry at the chapter of St Thomas, Racibórz (Ratibor); at the same time he was appointed a notary in the chancery of the bishop of Wrocław. In the spring of 1504 he matriculated at the University of Vienna as a canon of Wrocław, in 1506–7 he completed his studies in Italy, obtaining a doctorate in canon law at Padua, and subsequently he returned to his canonry at Wrocław, henceforward devoting his life to scholarship. He was a friend of Conradus *Mutianus Rufus and also corresponded with Caspar *Ursinus Velius and with Joachim *Vadianus; in 1516 he lent the latter a manuscript from the library of his chapter containing Lorenzo *Valla's De libero arbitrio (Vadianische Briefsammlung supplement I Ep 11). He was an ardent student of Jerome and made a collection of his sayings; in 1509 he also erected a monument to him in the church of the Holy Cross, Wrocław. He took a special interest in history and collected pieces relevant to the history of Silesia, Poland, and Hungary into a manuscript volume, now in Munich, from which Allen derived Ep 850. In recent years his chronicle of the bishopric of Wrocław

under Jakob von *Salza has been published and also a report on the beginnings of the reform movement at Wrocław, addressed to a delegation of the cathedral chapter that had gone to Rome for negotiations (Schottenloher VII 204).

In 1522 Jakob *Ziegler advised Erasmus to contact Sauer concerning another manuscript of the Wrocław chapter containing Pontius' life of Jerome. Ziegler's contacts with Sauer must have dated from an earlier period as he was not certain whether the latter was still alive.

BIBLIOGRAPHY: Allen Ep 1260 / Matrikel Wien II-1 321 / Der Briefwechsel des Conradus Mutianus ed K. Gillert (Halle 1890) II Epp 402, 472 / Schottenloher VII 204 / Karl Schottenloher Jakob Ziegler (Münster 1900) 55 / Johann Heyne Dokumentierte Geschichte des Bistums und Hochstifts Breslau (Wrocław 1860–8) III 303, 533, 632 / Gustav Bauch in Zeitschrift des Vereins für Geschichte und Altherthum Schlesiens 38 (1904) 323–6, 40 (1906) 189, 41 (1907) 139 / Gerhard Zimmermann Das Breslauer Domkapitel im Zeitalter der Reformation und Gegenreformation (Weimar 1938) 471–3   MICHAEL ERBE

Georg SAUERMANN of Wrocław,
d 31 October 1527
Georg Sauermann (Sauromannus, Sauramanus, Saurman) was the son of Konrad, a merchant and patrician of Wrocław (Breslau) who was ennobled by *Charles V in 1530. The family, later to be known as Saurma, has played a fairly prominent role in the history of Silesia. Georg matriculated in the spring term of 1508 at the universities of both Wittenberg and Leipzig. In 1509 he entered the University of Bologna, being described in the register as a canon of Löbau, in Lusatia. In 1513–14 he was rector of Bologna and on 3 June of the latter year was promoted doctor of civil and canon law. In Bologna he met Ulrich von *Hutten and Julius *Pflug (Pflug Correspondance I Ep 3), while Romolo *Amaseo congratulated him on his rectorate with a Panegyricus (Bologna: B. Hector 1513). Shortly before his departure for Rome, he composed an oration on the death of the Emperor *Maximilian, Ad Carolum Hispaniorum regem et Ferdinandum archiducem Austriae post obitum avi oratio (Bologna: H. de Benedictis 28 February 1519). It was re-

Bandinello Sauli, by Sebastiano del Piombo

printed by Johann *Froben in a collection of *Panegyrici* (Basel December 1520), including also Erasmus' *Panegyricus*.

Meanwhile Sauermann continued to receive preferment. According to Amaseo's *Panegyricus* he was provost of Głogów (Glogau) and a canon of Wrocław. From about 1512 he was also provost of St John's cathedral chapter, and in 1520 he was dean of the Holy Cross, also in Wrocław. In the early spring of 1520 he went to Rome, where he was well received by *Leo x. With the pope's recommendations he set out for Spain and in May met the newly elected Emperor Charles v at Corunna. He entered Charles' service and accompanied him back to the Netherlands. On the occasion of the emperor's departure from Spain he composed a *Hispaniae consolatio* (n p n d, with a dedication to Pedro Ruiz de la *Mota, dated from Louvain, August 1520). Charles v appointed him procurator at the papal curia, and in the autumn of 1520 he returned to Rome, where he spent his remaining years living with a Roman woman, who bore him a son, Julius Clemens. Both father and son are recalled by Georg von *Logau in his *Hendecasyllabi* (Vienna: H. Wietor

1529). On *Adrian vi's election to the papacy he composed an oration addressed to the new pope (Rome: J. Mazzocchi 1 May 1522) and subsequently edited another, delivered by Girolamo *Balbi. Although a critic of the faults of the traditional church, he published a severe attack upon the Lutheran reformers, *De religione ac communi concordia* (Rome: L. de Henricis 1524), and in the same vein he edited Andrzej *Krzycki's *De afflictione ecclesiae* (Rome 1527), with a dedication to Stanislaus *Thurzo dated from Rome, 1 April 1527. During the Sack of Rome in the following month he was badly manhandled and died a few months later of his injuries. In 1550 a monument was erected to him in the German national church of Santa Maria dell'Anima.

In 1522 and 1523 Erasmus sent greetings to Sauermann at Rome in letters to Pierre *Barbier and Marcus *Laurinus (Epp 1294, 1342). In the latter he mentioned the dean of Wrocław among some friends of long standing, perhaps an indication that they had already met in Italy in 1509 prior to their simultaneous presence at Louvain in 1520. In June 1527 he mentioned that Sauermann had been preparing a work, apparently in connection with the Ciceronian discussions in Rome (Ep 1840), while a year later he regretted not having remembered Sauermann in the *Ciceronianus* (Ep 2008).

BIBLIOGRAPHY: Allen Ep 1342 / *Matrikel Wittenberg* I 26 / *Matrikel Leipzig* I 489 / Knod 478 / Pflug *Correspondance* I 76, 97–8, 491 / W. Pirckheimer *Opera* (Frankfurt 1610, repr 1969) 311 / ADB XXX 417 / H. Heckel in *Schlesische Lebensbilder* IV (Wrocław 1931) 6–12 / A. Weltzel *Geschichte des Geschlechtes der Saurma und Sauerma* (Racibórz 1869) / Gustav Bauch 'Ritter Georg Sauermann, der erste adelige Vorfahr der Grafen Saurma-Jeltsch' *Zeitschrift des Vereins für Geschichte und Alterthums Schlesiens* 19 (1885) 146–81; also 38 (1904) 334–6 / A.J. Schmidlin *Geschichte der deutschen Nationalkirche in Rom, S. Maria dell'Anima* (Freiburg-Vienna 1906) 349 / Gerhard Zimmermann *Das Breslauer Domkapitel im Zeitalter der Reformation und Gegenreformation* (Weimar 1938) 483–7
MICHAEL ERBE

Bandinello SAULI of Genoa, d 29 March 1518
Sauli was a Genoese protégé of *Julius ii. On 5 October 1506 he was appointed bishop of

Malta and on 6 May 1507 an apostolic secretary; in 1509 he obtained the bishopric of Gerace and Opido. He was with the papal court at Ravenna when he was created a cardinal on 10 March 1511. *Leo x also favoured him, and on 5 August 1513 he was appointed bishop of Albenga. In April 1515 he rented the palace of Francesco Maria *della Rovere, duke of Urbino, in Rome. His attachment to the duke may in fact help explain why he became involved in the conspiracy of cardinals against Leo x, which came to light in 1517, though Francesco Guicciardini and Paolo Giovio suggested it was because Leo had not given him the bishopric of Marseille. Sauli and Cardinal Alfonso *Petrucci were arrested on 19 May, and Cardinal Raffaele *Riario on 29 May. On 22 June all three were sentenced to be deprived of benefice, degraded from the rank of cardinal, and handed over to the secular arm. However, only Petrucci was executed. Riario was pardoned and restored on 24 July and Sauli on 31 July, the latter with a fine of twenty-five thousand ducats. Erasmus, writing to Cuthbert *Tunstall on 17 July, commented upon the degradation of two cardinals (Ep 607). Sauli spent the last months of his life in retirement in Rome. There is a portrait of him by Sebastiano del Piombo in the Kress Collection, Washington.

BIBLIOGRAPHY: Allen Ep 607 / Eubel III 12, 209, 243 / A. Ferrajoli La congiura dei cardinali contro Leone x (Rome 1919) 51–3 / Pastor VI 344, VII 171–95 and passim / Sanudo Diarii XXIV 288 and passim   D.S. CHAMBERS

Georgius SAURAMANUS, SAUROMAN-NUS See Georg SAUERMANN

Stanislaus SAURUS See Stanislaus SAUER

Girolamo SAVONAROLA of Ferrara, 21 September 1452–23 May 1498

Girolamo Savonarola, the son of Niccolò di Michele dalla Savonarola and Elena Bonacorsi, was born at Ferrara. He was educated in the humanities, possibly under Battista Guarino, and was tutored by his grandfather Michele, who instilled in him a profound religious fervour and a love for St Thomas Aquinas and the Scriptures. At the age of twenty he was already concerned about the corrupt state of the church and the world, composing the poems De ruina mundi (1472) and De ruina ecclesiae (1475). On 25 April 1475 he entered the Dominican convent of San Domenico at Bologna, where he was ordained priest. After studying theology at Bologna and Ferrara he was sent to the convent of San Marco in Florence in 1482 as reader in theology. In 1487 he returned to Bologna as master of studies at the Dominican Studium generale, and in 1488 he preached in Ferrara and in Lombardy. In the 1480s his sermons were already attracting considerable attention because of their prophetic and apocalyptical tone, focusing on the evils of the church and the inevitability of divine retribution. Among his listeners was Giovanni *Pico della Mirandola, who may have been behind the request of Lorenzo (I) de' *Medici in 1490 that Savonarola return to Florence. In July 1491 Savonarola was elected prior of San Marco, which he hoped to make the centre for the reform of the entire church. On 22 May 1493 the basis for his work seemed established when San Marco was separated from the Lombard congregation of the order and placed in a new Tuscan congregation, of which Savonarola became vicar-general.

However, the events of 1494 presented Savonarola with even greater opportunities. In September the descent of *Charles VIII of France into Italy seemed to fulfil Savonarola's prophecies of divine retribution. In November the surrender of Florence to the French and the expulsion of Piero de' Medici caused the confused populace to turn to Savonarola for leadership. On 21 November the Signoria asked him to intervene personally with Charles, who was then occupying the city. Through his interview with the king Savonarola was at least partly responsible for saving the city from destruction and securing the peaceful departure of the French on 28 November. For the next three and a half years Savonarola and his followers held sway over the Florentine republic. Savonarola intensified his campaign for moral reform, organizing religious processions and the burning of vanities. But if he attracted a large body of disciples, he also earned the enmity of many citizens. His opponents, objecting to his plans for reform and to his endorsement of pro-French policies, conspired with Pope *Alexander VI in bringing

Girolamo Savonarola, by Fra Bartolomeo

about his downfall. On 13 May 1497, after earlier attempts to silence the friar, whose sermons were focusing more and more on the depravity of the papal court, Alexander excommunicated Savonarola. The divisions between the opponents and adherents of Savonarola increased, and his cause was undermined by the departure of Charles VIII from Italy in 1495 and the failure of the French to return in force to the peninsula. Savonarola's fall came suddenly in the spring of 1498. On 8 April, the day after an ordeal by fire to test the divine inspiration of Savonarola's teachings had failed to take place, a mob invaded San Marco and Savonarola was made a prisoner of the now hostile Signoria. Interrogated under torture he was forced to deny that his prophecies were from God. In May he and two fellow Dominicans were tried by ecclesiastical commissioners from Rome, condemned as heretics and schismatics, and hanged and burnt in the Piazza della Signoria.

Erasmus' attitude towards Savonarola was unsympathetic, shaped by his dislike of the Dominican order rather than his hatred of ecclesiastical corruption. In his important letter of 19 October 1519 to Albert of *Brandenburg

(Ep 1033) he placed the blame for religious turmoil in Germany squarely on the mendicant orders, giving Savonarola as an example of the audacity of the Dominicans if left unbridled. He returned to this theme in Ep 1173 and defended his remarks in a letter to the Dominican Vincentius *Theoderici of March 1521 (Ep 1196). He also mentioned Savonarola briefly in his *Ecclesiastes* (LB V 985F).

Savonarola composed many religious pamphlets published at Florence by the presses of Bartolomeo dei Libri, Antonio Miscomini, and Piero Pacini. These included *Della umiltà* (1492), *Dell'amore di Gesù Christo* (1492), *Della vita viduale* (1495?), *De simplicitate vitae christianae* (1496), *Triumphus crucis* (1497), and *Tractatus de vitae spiritualis perfectione* (1497). He also wrote an *Apologia* for the congregation of San Marco (1497?), *Trattato contro gli astrologi* (1495), *De veritate prophetica* (1497), *Trattato circa el reggimento e governo della città di Firenze* (1498), and *Compendium totius philosophiae* (Venice: A. Pincio 1534). In addition many of his sermons and letters were published.

BIBLIOGRAPHY: Allen Ep 1033 / *Bibliotheca savonaroliana* (Florence 1898) / M. Ferrara *Bibliografia savonaroliana* (Florence 1958) / Roberto Ridolfi *Vita di Girolamo Savonarola* (Rome 1952, English trans by Cecil Grayson London 1959) / Girolamo Savonarola *Le lettere* ed R. Ridolfi (Florence 1933) / Girolamo Savonarola *Poesie* ed Mario Martelli (Rome 1968) / J. Schnitzer *Savonarola* Italian trans by E. Rutili (Milan 1931) / P. Villari *La storia di Girolamo Savonarola e dei suoi tempi* new ed (Florence 1930) / Donald Weinstein *Savonarola and Florence: Prophecy and Patriotism in the Renaissance* (Princeton 1970)
                                   MARCO BERNUZZI & TBD

Charles II, duke of SAVOY 10 October 1486–17 August 1553
Charles II (also III), the son of duke Philip II and his second wife, Claudia de Brosse, succeeded Philibert II of *Savoy, his half-brother, on 10 September 1504. In 1521 he married Beatrice of Portugal, the sister-in-law of the Emperor *Charles V, thus initiating a policy of reliance upon the power of the Hapsburgs. While his efforts to retain control of Geneva failed and his domestic policies showed little imagination, the Hapsburg alliance (Ep 2177) gained him the county of Asti (in

1530). However, the prize he coveted, Monferrato, eluded him in 1536 when Charles v assigned it to his rival, Frederico *Gonzaga of Mantua. In 1536 his lands were invaded by France and all but the strategically unimportant parts of Piedmont and the region of Nice were occupied by either the French or the Bernese. Unable to play any role in the continuing conflicts between the emperor and France, Charles retired to Vercelli on the eastern border of his dominions after the death of his wife in 1538, and there he spent his last years, living quietly and modestly. He was survived by one son, Emmanuel Philibert, who recovered Savoy and the greater part of Piedmont in the treaty of Cateau-Cambrésis of 1559.

On 7 September 1523 *Luther addressed a letter to Charles II, hoping that he might be won over to the Reformation (Luther w *Briefwechsel* III Ep 657), but his hopes proved unfounded and he received no reply. Erasmus, who soon learnt about this letter from Philibert de *Lucinge (Ep 1413), later wrote to Duke Charles complaining about the attacks of Jean *Gachi and attempting to clarify his own position (Ep 1886). Although his letter apparently did not receive a direct answer, he was soon satisfied that the matter had been settled (Epp 1892, 2033, 2045, 2126).

BIBLIOGRAPHY: Allen Ep 1413 / DBI XX 294–304 /EI IX 51, XXX 932, 942   PGB

Louise of SAVOY 11 September 1476–22 September 1531

Louise of Savoy was the daughter of a cadet of the house of Savoy, who was later to become duke of Savoy as Philip II, and of Margaret of Bourbon, whose brother was to become duke of Bourbon. Louise's brother was Duke Philibert II of *Savoy. At twelve she was married to Charles of Valois, count of Angoulême, who died in 1496, leaving her with two children: *Margaret, born in 1492, and *Francis, born in 1494. King *Charles VIII died childless in 1498, and because his successor, *Louis XII (1498–1515), had no sons, Francis was heir presumptive. During these years Louise's life was shaped by the hope that 'her Caesar' would one day become king, as he did on 1 January 1515.

Francis I was twenty at his accession and his mother not yet forty. Until her death it was she,

Louise of Savoy

according to Lemonnier, who was the real head of the government. Even if such a claim may seem too sweeping, it is a fact that, before crossing the Alps to fight in Italy in 1515 and again in 1525, Francis appointed his mother regent. He trusted her judgment, and with some justification, for during his long imprisonment (1525–6) she managed to hold the country together and preserve the monarchy in his name. And it was she who negotiated with *Margaret of Austria the Peace of Cambrai (the 'Ladies' Peace') in 1529, bringing to a close the first period of war between Francis I and *Charles V. There would seem to have been a division of labour which permitted Francis to devote himself to warring, hunting, and pursuing mistresses, while Louise attended effectively to the business of administration and diplomacy.

On the other hand, Louise's claim to have provided good government encounters the objection that she confused it with the pursuit of personal objectives. If it can be said that the rebellion of the duke of Bourbon in 1523 was provoked by the pressing of her personal claims to estates claimed by the duke, then she bears a heavy responsibility for creating

conditions in which Charles v and *Henry vIII
could plan the dismemberment of France. The
financier Jacques de Semblançay may or may
not have been guilty of diverting funds, but the
financial gain she obtained by his disgrace in
1527 shows that she was not a disinterested
party. Her conduct in these two cases indicates
tenacity rather than wisdom.

Erasmus made several incidental references
to Louise in his correspondence, but the only
thing that interested him was her religious
policy. Would she foster or frustrate reform?
He described her as 'religiosissima et pruden-
tissima' (Ep 1854), but this was in a quite formal
letter to her daughter. In the case of *Berquin,
who was accused of heresy, he seems to have
credited her in 1526 with cautious support
(Epp 1717, 2188), but these remarks are
outweighed by what he says about her role in
encouraging persecution in the latter half of
the decade (Ep 2038).

Louise's *Journal*, though it unfortunately
does not mention any event after 1522, tells us
a good deal about her religious outlook. It is
written in anything but an evangelical spirit,
though it does reveal attitudes that the church
would not have approved. Belief in astrology is
implied in her obsession about dates. The
muttering of prayers and paternosters was of
no use in war, she noted, except for those who
do not know how to conduct it. The *Journal*,
however, exhibits conventional piety as well as
disillusioned pragmatism. Its author could
hardly have had much understanding of what
Erasmus or *Lefèvre d'Etaples or her own
daughter were striving for.

Royal controversy with the Paris faculty of
theology and its allies in the Parlement of Paris
may have created the illusion of an alliance
between the crown and the reformers, but
what really mattered to Louise is revealed most
clearly in her response to the Remonstrances of
10 April 1525, drawn up by the Parlement after
the disaster of Pavia. Parlement called for a
restoration of the Pragmatic Sanction, under
which abbeys and cathedral chapters elected
their abbots and bishops, and abolition of the
Concordat of 1516, which had given the king
the power to select the candidates for most of
these offices. Louise conceded nothing in
substance; on the contrary, she exercised her
powers as regent to appoint, under the terms
of the Concordat, her chief minister, Chancellor *Duprat, to two of the greatest benefices:
the archbishopric of Sens and the abbey of
Saint-Benoît-sur-Loire, and she caused these
appointments to stick, against the opposition
of the cathedral chapter and abbey. What was
at stake in these constitutional battles was not
reform of abuses or of doctrine, but royal
patronage.

On another of the Parlement's remonstrances, Louise offered no resistance. This was the
one that called for the suppression of heresy
and asserted that royal protection of suspected
heretics was to blame for allowing it to spread.
To remedy the situation she was asked to
request the pope to authorize a special tribunal
of 'judges delegate' to pursue the heretics,
wherever they might be found, even in high
places. She agreed, and it was this tribunal that
prosecuted Berquin and other reformers. It
was in this atmosphere that the Paris theologians attacked the works of Erasmus and of
Lefèvre d'Etaples. This was the end of
peaceful reform from within the church which
Lefèvre had attempted at Meaux with the
support of Louise's daughter, Margaret. Erasmus was justified in his negative conclusion.

BIBLIOGRAPHY: Allen Ep 1692 / Henry Lemonnier in *Histoire de France* ed Ernest Lavisse v-1
(Paris 1911) 195–7 / Henry Hauser 'Etude
critique sur le *Journal* de Louise de Savoie'
Revue historique 86 (1904) 280–303 / Louise de
Savoie *Journal* in Samuel Guicheron *Histoire
généalogique de la royal maison de Savoie* new ed
(Turin 1780) 457–64 / Roger Doucet *Etude sur le
gouvernement de François Ier dans ses rapports
avec le Parlement de Paris* (Paris 1921–6) esp II /
J.H. Shennan *The Parlement of Paris* (London
1968) / Christopher W. Stocker 'The politics of
the Parlement of Paris in 1525' *French Historical
Studies* 8 (1973) 191–212 / Gilbert Jacqueton *La
Politique extérieure de Louise de Savoie* (Paris
1892); this appears to be the only serious book
devoted to Louise, and it is limited to foreign
policy / Two popular works may be mentioned;
their opposite assessments tend to balance
each other: Millicent (Garrett) Fawcett *Five
Famous French Women* (London 1905–7) and
Dorothy Moulton (Piper) Mayer *The Great
Regent: Louise of Savoy, 1476–1531* (London
1966) / See also Paule Henry-Bordeaux *Louise de
Savoie, 'roi de France'* (Paris 1954)

GORDON GRIFFITHS

Philibert II, duke of SAVOY 10 April 1480–
10 September 1504
Philibert, the son of Philip II, duke of Savoy,
and of his first wife, Margaret of Bourbon, was
educated at the court of France before he
succeeded his father as ruler on 7 November
1497. The actual power, however, lay mostly in
the hands of his illegitimate half-brother, René
de Villars, who was led to support the French
by the promise of territorial gains in Lombardy.
Thus Philibert was at the side of *Louis XII
when he held his solemn entry into Milan in
1499. Later, when the French alliance was
judged to be unrewarding and even dangerous
for Savoy, Philibert's marriage to *Margaret of
Austria was arranged and celebrated at Brussels on 26 September 1501, and in 1502 Villars
was compelled to flee to France. Erasmus
mentioned Philibert's reception (1503) of his
brother-in-law, Philip the Handsome of *Burgundy, in his *Panegyricus* of 1504, (ASD IV-1 15,
31, 46).
    BIBLIOGRAPHY: ASD IV-1 15 / EI XV 286 / Jacques
Freymond *La Politique de François Ier à l'égard de
Savoie* (Lausanne 1959) 26–30   PGB

*Frederick III, elector of Saxony, by Lucas
Cranach the Elder*

SAXO CAROLUS or SASSENKERL *See
Gotskalk* ERIKSEN

Albert, duke of SAXONY 31 July 1443–
12 September 1500
The younger son of the Elector Frederick II,
Albert (Albrecht) ruled the Saxon lands jointly
with his brother, Ernest, from 1464 to 1485
when they were divided under the terms of the
treaty of Leipzig. Albert thus became the
founder of the Albertine line of the house of
Wettin. His lands included the cities of
Leipzig, Dresden, and Meissen, while the
electoral dignity fell to the Ernestine branch.
Well-educated and energetic Albert was married to a daughter of George , king of Bohemia,
in 1459. When his father-in-law died in 1471 he
attempted to succeed to the crown of Bohemia,
but failed. Thereafter he served the house of
Hapsburg in the Burgundian Wars, and in 1479
he went to Jerusalem as a pilgrim. In 1488 he
came to the rescue of *Maximilian I, who was in
danger of losing the inheritance of his Burgundian wife. Albert was appointed governor of
the Netherlands, and in 1493 his services were
rewarded with the regency and revenues of
Friesland, but he was never able to establish

full control over that territory. In his own
country he built a castle at Meissen and rebuilt
the cathedral of Freiberg. His active role in the
development of the rich silver mine at Schnee-
berg is described in Georgius *Agricola's *Bermannus*. In 1520 Erasmus paid tribute to
Albert's military prowess – he is called 'der
Beherzte' in German – and stated that he knew
him in his boyhood, if only by name (Epp 1122,
1125).
    BIBLIOGRAPHY: Allen Ep 1122 / ADB I 314–18 /
NDB I 174–5 / R. Kötzschke and H. Kretzschmar
Sächsische Geschichte (Frankfurt a. M. 1965)
140–2 and passim / G. Agricola *Ausgewählte
Werke* ed Hans Prescher (Berlin 1955–) II
123–4, 140–2, and passim   PGB

Frederick III, elector of SAXONY 17 January
1463–5 May 1525
Frederick III, called the Wise, was a son of
Elector Ernest of Saxony and Elizabeth, a
daughter of duke Albert III of Bavaria-Munich.
John, elector of *Saxony, was his younger
brother and Duke George of *Saxony was his
cousin. Frederick was born in Torgau and
received a humanistically oriented education
in the monastery school at Grimma and at the

court of Dieter II of Isenburg, archbishop of Mainz. Deeply religious by nature, he eagerly absorbed the devotional ideas of the late Middle Ages. Thus he was to accumulate a large collection of relics in the castle church of Wittenberg, and in 1493 he went on a pilgrimage to the Holy Land. He was interested in theology, jurisprudence, and history, commissioning *Spalatinus in 1510 to write a chronicle of Saxony. More unusual perhaps was the manual skill that he demonstrated, particularly on the lathe.

Frederick took over the government in 1486. In the preceding year the territories of the Wettiner dynasty had been partitioned, with the exception of the territory of Wittenberg, whose ruler always had to be the Saxon elector. Thus Frederick came to rule what was to be known as the Ernestine territories (in Saxony and Thuringia) in addition to the electorial lands. Until Frederick's death the Ernestine duchy was ruled jointly by him and his brother, John, who co-operated harmoniously at all times. On the other hand, Frederick's relations with Duke George, his Albertine cousin, remained tense, and this was partly responsible for the ineffectiveness of Frederick's intervention during a period of unrest in Erfurt (1509–16). In the end, the earlier impasse between the sovereign rights of the archbishop of Mainz and the protectorate exercised by Saxony persisted in Erfurt because Frederick was unwilling to use force. He was by nature cautious and defensive, and these qualities were reflected in his policies. He preferred diplomacy to force, and he excelled in its use. At home his rule was patriarchal, but with the help of outstanding advisers he modernized the administration. For a while Frederick maintained close ties to *Maximilian I and even lived at his court. He undertook diplomatic missions for the emperor and in 1498 was appointed his deputy (Statthalter), while on the other hand he was increasingly committed to a federalist approach to constitutional reform in the empire. When Maximilian wished to ensure the succession of his grandson as the next emperor, Frederick persistently refused to commit his vote. During the election campaign following Maximilian's death he showed greater restraint than his fellow electors in acceptng money and pledges

from the Hapsburg and French candidates. In June 1519 he voted – not without misgivings – for *Charles v, after refusing to be a candidate for the imperial crown himself (Epp 1001, 1030). When it came to spelling out the electors' terms for Charles' election, Frederick played a leading role.

Frederick was a patron of the arts. He kept an orchestra at his court and corresponded with humanists, artists such as *Dürer, and historians like *Aventinus and *Trithemius; he also supported *Reuchlin. In 1502 he founded the University of Wittenberg; in 1518 and 1519 he reformed it, responding generously to the demands of *Luther and the humanists, whose position had been strengthened by the appointment of *Melanchthon to a newly established chair of Greek. Yet he insisted on the continuation of lectures in canon law. In 1517 he prevented the preaching of Albert of *Brandenburg's indulgence in his territory so as to protect the Wittenberg indulgences. The rumour that he encouraged Luther's attack on indulgences is unfounded. But when Luther was summoned to Rome, he followed Spalatinus' advice and in 1518 at the diet of Augsburg persuaded the cardinal-legate *Cajetanus to content himself with interrogating Luther in Augsburg; in addition he ensured that Luther had legal counsel. The interregnum following the death of Maximilian in January 1519 gave him an opportunity to protect Luther by the subtle use of dilatory tactics while maintaining his own neutrality. Thereafter he prevailed upon Charles v to summon Luther to the diet of Worms in 1521 and also obtained for him a letter of safe conduct. He actually saw Luther for the first time when the latter appeared before the plenary session of the diet. He never spoke to him personally, but as advised by his councillors provided for Luther's safety after the hearing at Worms. He even won from Charles v the concession that he was never officially informed of the edict of Worms.

Frederick kept a low profile during the unrest in Wittenberg in 1521 and 1522 but eventually tolerated Luther's return. In 1524 he secretly supported the introduction of reform in the territory of Magdeburg but prevented the reformers from gaining a decisive victory in his own lands. Ignoring the advice of Spalatinus, he protected the rights of ecclesiastical institutions, partly because he feared the consequences of unilateral secularization for both his own person and his territory. Although he was impressed with Luther's teaching he took communion in both forms only on his deathbed. When the peasant riots spread to Thuringia and his brother and cousin were preparing for an armed confrontation with the peasants, he was lying ill in his castle of Lochau; he too had promised help, but in the end he maintained that one could not know what role God had planned for the common man.

Frederick was not married but had two sons, Sebastian and Fritz von Jessen, from his long liaison with Anna Weller; he also had a daughter by an unknown mother. From 1518, if not earlier, he was ailing. Plagued with kidney stones and gout, he was seriously ill from the beginning of 1525 and died on 5 May at Lochau. He was buried in the castle church of Wittenberg.

The elector bought Erasmus' works for the library of Wittenberg (Ep 501), and Erasmus dedicated his edition of Suetonius to Frederick and Duke George in 1517 (Ep 586). In 1519–20 the relations between Erasmus and the elector of Saxony were both intensive and historically significant. In the spring of 1519, through Justus *Jonas, Frederick sent Erasmus a medal bearing his portrait, together with a letter, which is now lost (Epp 963, 978). Erasmus responded with a warm declaration of sympathy for Luther (Ep 939). His reaction, whether calculated or spontaneous, certainly pleased the elector (Ep 963). Erasmus' public praise of Frederick's role in the imperial election (Epp 1001, 1030) prepared the way for a personal meeting with the elector at Cologne on 5 November 1520 (Ep 1155 introduction; ASD IX-1 182). The conversation soon turned to Luther, and Erasmus once more encouraged Frederick to support Luther, and to resist all pressures to send him to Rome for trial. Erasmus afterwards agreed to set his views down in writing, and despite his embarrassment over the unauthorized publication of this document, the famous *Axiomata pro causa Lutheri* (*Opuscula* 329–37), Erasmus later recalled the Cologne interview with pleasure (Ep 1512). He and the elector maintained respect for each other even after Erasmus had attacked Luther in *De libero*

arbitrio. Erasmus recalled Frederick's generosity towards Melanchthon (Ep 1624) and praised his integrity in a letter to his successor (Ep 1670).

There are in existence paintings, engravings, pencil drawings, and medals of Frederick, including some by Lucas Cranach the Elder and Albrecht Dürer.

BIBLIOGRAPHY: Allen Ep 586 / F.H. Schubert in NDB V 568–72 / G. Spalatinus *Friedrichs des Weisen Leben und Zeitgeschicht* ed C.G. Neudecker and L. Preller (Jena 1851) / Paul Kirn *Friedrich der Weise und die Kirche* (Leipzig-Berlin 1926) / Paul Kalkoff *Ablass und Reliquienverehrung an der Schlosskirche zu Wittenberg unter Friedrich dem Weisen* (Gotha 1907) / Paul Kalkoff *Luther und Friedrich der Weise* (Leipzig 1919) / H. Bornkamm 'Kurfürst Friedrich der Weise (1463–1525)' ARG 64 (1973) 79–84 / *Deutsche Reichstagsakten* Jüngere Reihe (Gotha-Göttingen 1893–) I–IV passim / *Des kursächsischen Rates Hans von der Planitz Berichte aus dem Reichsregiment in Nürnberg 1521–23* ed E. Wülcker (Leipzig 1899) passim / Walter Friedensberg *Geschichte der Universität Wittenberg* (Halle 1917) passim / Irmgard Höss *Georg Spalatin (1484–1545)* (Weimar 1956) / Irmgard Höss 'Der Brief des Erasmus von Rotterdam an Kurfürst Friedrich den Weisen vom 30. Mai 1519' ARG 46 (1955) 209–13 / Hermann Wiesflecker *Kaiser Maximilian I.* (Vienna 1971–) I and IV passim / Heinz Holeczek 'Die Haltung des Erasmus zu Luther nach dem Scheitern seiner Vermittlungspolitik 1520/21' ARG 64 (1973) 85–112 / Ingetraut Ludolphy 'Die religiöse Einstellung Friedrichs des Weisen ... vor der Reformation als Voraussetzung seiner Lutherpolitik' *Jahrbuch für die Geschichte des Protestantismus in Österreich* 96 (1980) 74–89

IRMGARD HÖSS

George, duke of SAXONY 27 August 1471– 17 April 1539
George – called 'der Bärtige' (the Bearded) – was the eldest son of duke Albert of *Saxony, founder of the Albertine line of the Saxon dynasty, and Zdeňka (Sidonia), daughter of King George Poděbrady of Bohemia. The electors Frederick the Wise and John of *Saxony were his cousins; Landgrave Philip of *Hesse was his son-in-law. George spent his childhood partly at the imperial court in

George, duke of Saxony, by Lucas Cranach the Elder

Vienna. His mother intended him to be a priest, so he received an excellent education, covering theology as well as secular subjects. Later on he was to show a solid grasp of the intricate theological disputes of his time. In 1484 he became a canon of Mainz but resigned this prebend to his youngest brother when his father went off to fight in Friesland in the service of *Maximilian I and needed George to govern his duchy. During his twelve years as governor George developed into one of the most experienced and capable princes of Germany. After the death of his father, who from 1498 had been in charge of all Friesland, George initially gave Friesland to his brother Henry. Later he took it back and himself tried to break the widespread resistance to Saxon rule, but the task exceeded his financial resources and in 1515 he sold Friesland to the future *Charles v for a hundred thousand florins. Although instalments of this sum were paid irregularly at best, he remained loyal to the Hapsburg dynasty.

George's predominant concern was always with interior policy. He was personally in control of the civil service, paid attention to minute details, and drafted a great number of letters and decrees. His subjects knew that they could approach him with their grievances, and he gained great respect for his sense of justice. Despite many disagreements with his Ernestine cousins regarding religious matters and the joint management of mines, he always succeeded in maintaining the peace by way of bilateral talks. He greatly improved the economic position of his country, thereby giving proof of his acumen for business and finance. The mining town of St Annaberg was founded in 1494 and enjoyed his special attention, but older centres benefited as well, with Leipzig and Dresden doubling their population during his period of government. Dresden was developed into a prestigious capital. The duke personally endowed the hospital of St Jacob's, which accommodated one hundred disabled persons. In Leipzig he commissioned new buildings for the university on a generous scale. Churches such as the cathedral of Meissen were restored and enlarged.

George understood very well that the church was in need of reform, and when *Luther launched his Ninety-five Theses he was sympathetic. In 1519 he compelled a reluctant university to hold the Leipzig disputation and offered his castle as a meeting place, ignoring the opposition of the bishop of Merseburg. He attended the debates and when Luther was obliged to acknowledge the condemned teachings of Jan Hus, Duke George turned against him once and for all. At the diet of Worms in 1521 he added his own grievances to the *Gravamina* of the German nation against the Holy See but insisted on co-operation with Rome in the matter of reforms and called for an ecumenical council. He declared himself in favour of enforcing the edict of Worms against Luther and henceforward endeavoured to keep his duchy clear of Lutheran influences. He personally took issue with Luther's teachings, for instance in an open letter addressed to King *Henry VIII (Ep 1495). In other letters he tried in vain to keep Prince George of Anhalt and Landgrave Philip of Hesse from abandoning the Catholic church. He even composed theological treatises, for instance one on the Eucharist (Ep 1951). But he did not hesitate to interfere with the ecclesiastical institutions of his state, enforcing monastic reform.

Civil disobedience George would not tolerate, and he believed that the peasant revolt of 1525 was the result of Luther's teaching. He joined forces with Landgrave Philip and other Lutheran princes to subdue the peasants and must share the responsibility for the executions carried out in the wake of the revolt. He wished to continue his alliance with the evangelical princes but found that his anti-Lutheran stance was unacceptable to them. In 1526 he therefore joined with the Catholic princes in the defensive league of Dessau. He discovered the intrigues of his councillor Otto von *Pack just in time to avoid a military confrontation with Philip of Hesse. In the end he was unable to prevent the spread of Lutheranism in his duchy, although he prohibited the distribution of Luther's New Testament and in its place circulated the German version by Hieronymus *Emser, for which he himself had written a preface. After all his sons by his marriage with Barbara, the sister of King *Sigismund I of Poland, had died he was unable to prevent the succession of his brother Henry, who had become a Lutheran. Thus all his efforts to maintain Catholicism were doomed. He died in Dresden and was buried in the cathedral of Meissen.

Duke George had a positive attitude towards humanism. Even though the authors of the *Epistolae obscurorum virorum* saw Leipzig as a citadel of scholasticism, second only to Cologne, George in fact made sure of a continuing humanist presence. The Englishman Richard *Croke was followed by Petrus *Mosellanus as a teacher of Greek, and Duke George would have liked to attract Erasmus himself to his university (Epp 527, 553, 809). Capable teachers were appointed to the Latin schools of the duchy, and the duke himself employed humanists such as Emser, *Cochlaeus, who became his chancellor in 1533, and Christoph von *Carlowitz.

Duke George was the only secular prince to correspond with Erasmus on a regular basis. From his first approach to Erasmus after the publication of the New Testament (Ep 514) and Erasmus' dedication of his Suetonius to George and Frederick of Saxony (Ep 586) until 1531 no fewer than twenty-one letters by Erasmus and ten by Duke George are extant. Erasmus praised Duke George as a patron of the new learning, especially at the University of Leipzig, which seemed to him in fruitful competi-

tion with the younger University of Wittenberg (Epp 948, 1125). After the diet of Worms in 1521 when the divergence between the religious policies of George and Frederick became fully visible, Erasmus' connections with George intensified while his contacts with Frederick, which had been so crucial for a while, weakened because his advice was no longer needed in Wittenberg. Duke George did not mince his words when he urged Erasmus to take up his pen against Luther (Ep 1340). He thus played his part in prompting him to write *De libero arbitrio* (Allen I 35), of which he was sent a copy as soon as it was off the press (Ep 1495). George congratulated the author but also said that he wished the book had come sooner (Epp 1503, 1520). After the publication of the first part of the *Hyperaspistes* he again urged Erasmus to continue the controversy (Epp 1691, 1693, 1776), and in December 1527 Erasmus sent him the second part of the work (Epp 1927, 1929). In 1531 Erasmus addressed the duke in a dedicatory preface to *Pirckheimer's translation of the orations of Gregory of Nazianzus (Ep 2493).

Duke George showed his appreciation of Erasmus with occasional gifts (Epp 1126, 1326, 1691), while Erasmus felt sufficiently confident to recommend to the duke his protégés Jacobus *Ceratinus (Epp 1564, 1565), Frans van der *Dilft (Ep 1942), and Christoph von Carlowitz (Epp 2085, 2122). Initially he also praised the virtues of Heinrich *Eppendorf (Ep 1283), but subsequently his complicated quarrel with Eppendorf frequently became an unpleasant topic in their correspondence.

Among the portraits of Duke George there is a woodcut by E. Sachse showing him in his youth, an oil portrait by Lucas Cranach the Elder at Munich and another on Cranach's altarpiece in the chapel of St George, Meissen cathedral (1534). The same chapel preserves his effigy on his funeral slab. His likeness is also preserved on a gold medal of 1537.

BIBLIOGRAPHY: Allen Ep 514 / E. Werl in NDB VI 224–7 / H. von Welck *Georg der Bärtige, Herzog von Sachsen* (Brunswick 1899) / *Akten und Briefe zur Kirchenpolitik Herzog Georgs von Sachsen* ed Felician Gess (Leipzig 1905–17) to be continued by E. Werl / Waldemar Goerlitz *Staat und Stände unter den Herzögen Albrecht und*

John, elector of Saxony, by Lucas Cranach the Elder

Georg (Leipzig-Berlin 1928) / Gisela Reichel 'Herzog Georg der Bärtige und Erasmus von Rotterdam' (doctoral thesis, University of Leipzig 1942) / Otto Vossler 'Herzog Georg der Bärtige und seine Ablehnung Luthers' *Historische Zeitschrift* 184 (1957) 272–91 / Elisabeth Werl 'Herzogin Sidonia von Sachsen und ihr ältester Sohn Herzog Georg *Herbergen der Christenheit* 3 (1959) 8–19 / Karlheinz Blaschke *Sachsen im Zeitalter der Reformation* (Gütersloh 1970) passim / Helga-Maria Kühn *Die Einziehung des geistlichen Gutes im albertinischen Sachsen 1539–1553* (Cologne-Graz 1966) 8–17
                                    IRMGARD HÖSS

John, elector of SAXONY 30 June 1468–16 August 1532
John, later called 'the Steadfast' (Johann der Beständige), the younger brother of Frederick the Wise, elector of *Saxony, was born at Meissen. In the course of his carefully planned education he spent some time at the court of the Emperor *Frederick III. His personal ambitions lay in the field of military excellence, and his patronage of art and scholarship did not exceed the limits of princely convention. In

accordance with his father's will he and Frederick the Wise succeeded jointly to the rule of the Ernestine territories in Saxony and Thuringia in 1486; only the district of Wittenberg, the electorate proper, fell exclusively to his elder brother in conformity with imperial law. The personal closeness of the two brothers ensured harmonious collaboration between themselves and at first with the imperial policies of *Maximilian I, whom John served above all in a military capacity. From 1500, however, both brothers gradually moved towards opposition to Maximilian's schemes. When John married Margaret of Anhalt as his second wife in 1513, the terms of co-rulership were revised and John was installed in Thuringia, choosing Weimar as his residence. At an early date he came to support *Luther, who dedicated *Von weltlicher Obrigkeit* to him in 1523, and openly adopted the principles of the Reformation; he even supported reformers of a more radical bent such as Jakob Strauss at Eisenach and Wolfgang Stein, his court preacher at Weimar. Initially he also had an open mind towards Thomas Müntzer; it was only after his inflammatory sermon of 13 July 1524 that he came to oppose Müntzer, and from March 1525 he discussed concerted measures against the rebelling peasants with Landgrave Philip of *Hesse. When mediation failed and the death of Frederick the Wise (5 May 1525) left him elector and sole ruler of the Ernestine states, he eventually participated in the military actions jointly conducted by Hesse and Albertine Saxony and also in the punishment of the rebels. He concluded further alliances with Philip of Hesse and subsequently with Albert of *Brandenburg-Ansbach, duke of Prussia, and at the diet of Speyer (1526) he openly advocated the cause of the reform party. The favourable outcome of the diet encouraged him to undertake the comprehensive reorganization of his territorial church by means of visitations. Misled by the machinations of Otto von *Pack (1528), he was only with difficulty dissuaded from attacking the ecclesiastical principalities of Franconia, but subsequently he forswore all schemes of military aggression in the interests of peace throughout the Empire. Attending the diets of Speyer (1529) and Augsburg (1530) accompanied by *Melanchthon (Epp 2128,

2130, 2310), he personally strove for reconciliation with the Catholic camp, partly under the weight of dynastic considerations (Epp 2141, 2338). After the disappointing results of Augsburg, however, he joined the defensive Schmalkaldic League and lodged a protest against the election of *Ferdinand as Roman king. When an alliance with Bavaria against the Hapsburgs was proposed at Saalfeld (October 1531), John gave his consent but left further negotiations in the hands of his son, John Frederick of *Saxony; in his own mind the concern for peace prevailed. He died at Schweinitz and was buried in the castle church of nearby Wittenberg without having been invested formally with the electoral territories.

In his only known letter to John (Ep 1670, 2 March 1526), Erasmus pleaded with him to restrain Luther's attacks against himself; the letter remained unanswered. At the height of the Pack crisis in 1528 Melanchthon assured Erasmus of his efforts to commit the elector to a policy of moderation (Ep 1981). Another indirect connection between Erasmus and the elector resulted in the winter of 1531–2 from the stay of Felix *Rex at John's court after a visit to Wittenberg (Epp 2609, 2610, 2728).

A portrait of John (c 1510) by Lucas Cranach the Elder from the 'Fürstenaltar' of Dessau is now at Halle in the Landesgalerie Moritzburg. Another one (c 1532–5) from Cranach's workshop forms the centrepiece of the triptych now in the Kunsthalle of Hamburg.

BIBLIOGRAPHY: Allen Ep 1670 / Thomas Klein in NDB X 522–4 (with bibliography) / Carl Hinrichs *Luther und Müntzer* (Berlin 1952) / Johannes Kühn *Die Geschichte des Spyerer Reichstages von 1529* (Leipzig 1929) / Ekkehart Fabian *Die Entstehung des Schmalkaldischen Bundes und seiner Verfassung 1524/29–1531/35* 2nd ed (Tübingen 1962) / *Geschichte Thüringens* ed H. Patze and W. Schlesinger III: Irmgard Höss and Thomas Klein *Das Zeitalter des Humanismus und der Reformation* (Cologne-Graz 1967) / George H. Williams *The Radical Reformation* (Philadelphia 1962) 53–7 and passim
IRMGARD HÖSS

John Frederick, elector of SAXONY 30 June 1503–3 March 1554
John Frederick, the son of John of *Saxony and

John Frederick, elector of Saxony, by Lucas Cranach the Elder

Sophie of Mecklenburg, was named after his father and his uncle, Frederick the Wise of *Saxony, to whom he was as dear as a son. John Frederick came to be known as 'the Magnanimous' ('der Grossmütige'). Among his tutors was *Spalatinus, who may have stimulated his enduring interest in history; but on balance the young man was more attracted to the knightly virtues and grew up to be a passionate participant in tournaments. He continued to live at his father's court, and even after his marriage to Sibyl of Jülich-Cleves in 1526 and the birth of their first children, he was not permitted to set up a residence of his own. From childhood he was keenly interested in religion and as early as 1520 he defended *Luther before his uncle, the elector. He continued to support Luther unwaveringly in his stand against such radical reformers as Thomas Müntzer.

From the time his father succeeded to the electorate (1525) John Frederick was entrusted with important tasks such as negotiating an alliance and common diplomatic stand with Hesse (at Friedewald, November 1525). In the *Pack affair of 1528 he advocated militancy. During his father's absence at the diet of

Sibyl of Jülich-Cleves, wife of John Frederick, elector of Saxony

Speyer (1529) John Frederick acted as a regent, and the following year he accompanied him to the diet of Augsburg.

When he became elector in 1532 John Frederick subjected his clergy to a new visitation in 1533 and abolished the monasteries, deriving from this measure the means to improve the funding of the University of Wittenberg (1536). Having learnt his lesson in the Pack affair, John Frederick generally advocated peace and compromise; he played the role of a mediator in the conflict over the return of Duke Ulrich of *Württemberg. In 1535 he went to Vienna and was invested but failed to resolve other differences with King *Ferdinand. Consequently he approved the constitution of the Schmalkaldic League and caused the league to reject the papal proposals for a general council (1536). He refused, however, to accept as *casus foederis* any war caused by the bigamous marriage of Philip of *Hesse and sent his theologians to attend the religious colloquies of 1540 and 1541. In the following years, however, he could not resist the lure of territorial gains at the expense of the cathedral chapter of Naumburg-Zeitz and had the

reformer Nikolaus von *Amsdorf installed as the bishop. After continued opposition to the interests of the Hapsburgs, he attempted another reconciliation in 1544, failing to realize that *Charles v had already resolved to crush the Schmalkaldic League. Not until the Regensburg diet of June 1546 did he recognize the emperor's true intentions. Belatedly he began to arm and, taking the field in person, was captured by the emperor's troops at Mühlberg on 24 April 1547. Sentenced to death and then reprieved, he remained in captivity until the successful rebellion against Charles v engineered by his cousin Maurice of Saxony (of the Albertine line) restored his freedom on 27 August 1552. As he had been deprived by the emperor of his electoral title and territory, he entered into negotiations with his Albertine cousins but had only obtained some minor concessions when he died at Weimar.

In theological matters John Frederick considered Luther as the ultimate authority and sponsored efforts towards the collection of his writings and sermons as a basis for a future edition of his complete works. There were no direct ties between the elector and Erasmus, and in Erasmus' correspondence John Frederick is mentioned only in passing (Epp 2947, 3031A). However, a list of the elector's library drawn up in 1519 includes Erasmus' *Institutio principis christiani*, and the first work dedicated to John Frederick (in 1520) by Spalatinus, his former teacher, was a German translation from Plutarch based on Erasmus' Latin rendering of *De discrimine adulatoris et amici*. Among the surviving portraits of John Frederick there are three by Lucas Cranach the Elder and one by Titian.

BIBLIOGRAPHY: Thomas Klein in NDB x 524–5 (with bibliography) / Georg Mentz *Johann Friedrich der Grossmütige, 1503–54* (Jena 1903–8) / Irmgard Höss *Georg Spalatin* (Weimar 1956) / Hans Volz 'Luthers Schmalkaldische Artikel' *Zeitschrift für Kirchengeschichte* 68 (1957) 259–86 / *Die Schmalkaldischen Bundesabschiede* ed E. Fabian (Tübingen 1958–   ) I and II passim / *Geschichte Thüringens* ed H. Patze and W. Schlesinger III: Irmgard Höss and Thomas Klein *Das Zeitalter des Humanismus und der Reformation* (Cologne-Graz 1967) / Carl Hinrichs *Luther und Müntzer* (Berlin 1952)

IRMGARD HÖSS

Elizabeth SAY *See William* BLOUNT, *fourth Baron Mountjoy and William* SAY

William SAY of Essenden, d 4 December 1529
Sir William was the eldest son of Sir John Say (d
1478), speaker of the House of Commons. He
owned estates at Essenden and elsewhere in
Hertfordshire, as well as Hawford, in Essex.
His first wife was Genevese, a daughter of
John Hill. After her death he married Elizabeth, a daughter of Sir John Fray and widow of
Sir Thomas Waldgrave. With Elizabeth he had
two daughters, another Elizabeth who became
the wife of Erasmus' pupil William *Blount,
fourth Baron Mountjoy, and died before 21
July 1506, and Mary, who married Henry
*Bourchier, second earl of Essex. Say and his
two wives were buried at Broxbourne Church,
Hertfordshire.
    Erasmus visited Say in Blount's company in
the summer of 1499 (CWE Ep 103 introduction)
and afterwards wished to show that he
remembered Say's kindness to him (Epp 115,
120).
    BIBLIOGRAPHY: Allen and CWE Epp 105, 115 /
DNB XVII 877 / G.E. C[okayne] *The Complete
Peerage of England* ed V. Gibbs et al (London
1910–59) IX 340   PGB

Riccardo SBRUGLIO of Cividale di Friuli,
c 1480–after 1525
Riccardo Sbruglio (Sbrulius, Sbrolius) of Cividale, near Udine, was in Venice on 13 December 1506 and in Constance early in 1507. Here a
poem on the Sforzas that he had composed
attracted the attention of the Emperor *Maximilian I, who recommended him to the Elector
Frederick of *Saxony. As a result Sbruglio was
sent to teach in Wittenberg, where he was
registered in the spring term of 1507 and won
the enduring friendship and admiration of
Christoph Scheurl, who was then rector.
When *Spalatinus arrived in Wittenberg, he
too thought highly of Sbruglio. In 1512 Scheurl
compared him to Ovid and Baptista *Mantuanus but was unable to secure him a teaching
position at Nürnberg (Scheurl Epp 58, 59). In
the spring of 1513 Sbruglio matriculated in
Frankfurt an der Oder and in 1516 at Cologne.
In 1515 he visited *Mutianus Rufus at Gotha; in
1517 he was at Freiburg, and when *Zasius'
Lucubrationes (Basel: J. Froben) were published

a year later he contributed some verses. In the
same year he taught in Ingolstadt, where he
had connections with Urbanus *Rhegius. On
the recommendation of Spalatinus, Sbruglio
was appointed poet and historiographer by the
Emperor Maximilian. In November 1518 he was
in Augsburg. Wherever he went he produced
verses in honour of local princes and dignitaries. Reaction to them was mixed: Mutianus,
*Eobanus Hessus, Hermannus *Buschius, and
*Hutten were critical of Sbruglio and his talent
but Erasmus, Zasius, Bonifacius *Amerbach,
*Pirckheimer, and *Vadianus showed appreci-
ation. No one seemed willing to retain his
services for any length of time.
    Sbruglio wrote to Erasmus in November
1518, but his letter is not preserved (Ep 1001).
However, while he was in Louvain from 1519
to 1520 he composed a poem reproving
Erasmus' critics at the theological faculty (Ep
1159). At Louvain he may have met Erasmus or
just missed him; at any rate they met at Cologne
in November 1520, and Erasmus wrote a letter
to him (Ep 1159). Subsequently Erasmus
honoured him again by making him one of the
speakers in his colloquy *Convivium poeticum*
(ASD I-3 344–59), first published in August
1523. In the summer of 1524 Sbruglio was at
Salzburg, and in the spring of 1525 he was in
Hungary with Fridericus *Nausea among the
retinue of the papal nuncio *Campeggi. No
more is heard of him after that date.
    Sbruglio's numerous poems for various
occasions include an *Epithalamium* for Gabriel
de *Salamanca (Vienna: J. Singriener 1523) and
*In divi Caroli Maximi Caesaris ... ex Hispania ...
reditum elegia,* and *In divi Maximiliani Caesaris
obitum naenia* (both Augsburg: S. Grimm and
M. Wirsung 1519).
    BIBLIOGRAPHY: Allen Ep 1159 / AK II Epp 579,
738 / *Matrikel Wittenberg* I 21 / G. Ellinger
*Geschichte der neulateinischen Literatur Deutsch-
lands im sechzehnten Jahrhundert* (Berlin-Leipzig
1929–33) I 350–2 / *Christoph Scheurl's Briefbuch*
ed F. von Soden and J.K.F. Knaake (Potsdam
1867–72, repr 1962) I Epp 58, 59   IG

Bartolomeo SCALA of Colle di Val d'Elsa,
17 May 1430–14 July 1497
Bartolomeo Scala was born at Colle di Val
d'Elsa, near Siena, to a miller named Giovanni
di Francesco. He studied the humanities and

Bartolomeo Scala

who accused him, among other things, of being a Ciceronian. Their conflict was noted by Erasmus in Ep 337 as well as in the *Ciceronianus* (ASD I-2 667–8, 706) and in *De conscribendis epistolis* (ASD I-2 537).

Scala managed to combine scholarship with his public duties and produced a number of works, the most important being the *Historia Florentinorum*. Begun in the mid-1480s and still incomplete at Scala's death, it was edited for publication by L. Oligero (Rome 1677). Other works included *De legibus et iudiciis dialogus* published by L. Borghi in *Bibliofilia* 42 (1940) 256–82; a collection of fables entitled *Apologi centum* edited by C. Müllner (Vienna 1896); a political treatise entitled *Apologia contra vituperatores civitatis Florentinae* (Florence 1496); and unpublished treatises on philosophical sects and on marriage. His oration to Innocent VIII was published in 1484 (Rome: B. Guldinbeck).

BIBLIOGRAPHY: CWE Ep 337 / Alison Brown *Bartolomeo Scala, 1430–1497, Chancellor of Florence: The Humanist as Bureaucrat* (Princeton 1979) / N. Rubinstein 'Bartolomeo Scala's *Historia Florentinorum*' *Studi di bibliografia e di storia in onore di T. de Marinis* (Verona 1964) 49–59 / Donald J. Wilcox *The Development of Florentine Humanist Historiography in the Fifteenth Century* (Cambridge, Mass, 1969) 177–202 and passim   TBD

law at the Studio of Florence, possibly under Carlo Marsuppini, and law at Milan under Francesco *Filelfo. In 1457 he became secretary to Pierfrancesco de' Medici, nephew of the *de facto* ruler of Florence, Cosimo. With Medici support he became chancellor of the Guelph party on 24 October 1459 and chancellor of Florence on 24 April 1465. The latter post Scala held until his death, surviving even the fall of the Medici in 1494. Scala introduced reforms into the chancellery, centralizing it to make it a more effective instrument of Medici rule. He received Florentine citizenship in 1471 and served in the highest elective offices of the commune including gonfalonier of justice in May 1486 and life member of the Council of Seventy in July of the same year. In 1484 he was sent to congratulate Innocent VIII on his elevation to the papacy and was honoured by the pope with a knighthood. In 1468 he married Maddalena Benci, by whom he had a son and five daughters, including Alessandra, who married the poet Michael *Marullus Tarcaniota.

A careful Latin stylist, Scala engaged in a heated controversy with Angelo *Poliziano,

Julius Caesar SCALIGER of Padua, d 21 October 1558

Julius Caesar Scaliger claimed to be the son of Benedetto and Berenice della Scala, of the ancient ruling family of Verona; he gave his birth date as 23/4 April 1484, and the place as Riva, on Lake Garda. His young manhood, by his account, included long stints as a soldier and a period of study in Bologna.

In fact Scaliger lied; he was the son of Benedetto Bordon, a manuscript illuminator of Padua, where he was probably born. He took a doctorate in arts at Padua in 1519 and worked on an Italian translation of Plutarch during the early 1520s. It was when he came to Agen, in southern France, in 1524 as personal physician to the bishop, Antonio della Rovere, that he established as his permanent fantasy the claim to be a della Scala, although he had used the name before. He also established himself as a physician in Agen. Prospering, he became a naturalized French citizen in 1528 and married Andiette de la Roque Lobejac, and in 1532–3 he served as a consul in the town. His wife brought him considerable property and bore him fifteen children; one of their sons, Joseph Justus, became even more famous than his father as a scholar. For the rest of his life Scaliger remained a solid citizen, respected widely as a philosopher and doctor and eagerly sought out by young medical students.

Scaliger's literary career began with an attack on Erasmus. In 1529 he read the *Ciceronianus*. Becoming enraged at Erasmus' denigration of Cicero, he wrote an oration in reply in which he not only refuted Erasmus' arguments but blackened his character, claiming that he was a drunkard and had worked for Aldo *Manuzio as a proof-corrector. He sent a copy of the oration to the students of the Collège de Navarre at Paris with a covering letter (*Epistolae aliquot nunc primum vulgatae*, Toulouse 1620, 12–13). Not only did the students fail to return this oration to Scaliger's messenger or encourage Scaliger himself to publish it, they communicated its contents, so Scaliger claimed, to Erasmus himself, forcing him to remonstrate harshly with them (*Epistolae* 7–11, 20–1, 25). Though Scaliger's manuscript was eventually returned, the work did not appear until 1531: *Oratio pro M. Tullio Cicerone contra Erasmum* (Paris: G. Gourmont and P. Vidoue September 1531). As soon as a copy reached Basel, Bonifacius *Amerbach sent it to Erasmus (Ep 2564); Erasmus in turn immediately decided that the work was really by Girolamo *Aleandro and that 'Julius Caesar Scaliger' was a mere pseudonym. He described the work itself as slanderous and raving (Ep 2565), and apparently never took the trouble to read it carefully (Ep 2810). And he continued to say and imply that Aleandro had written the work (Epp 2575, 2577, 2579, 2581, 2613). Indeed, he even attempted to have it suppressed (Epp 2577, 2635).

On 1 April 1532 Aleandro wrote at length to deny that he had written Scaliger's oration (Epp 2638, 2639); on 30 November *Rabelais wrote to assure Erasmus that Scaliger was a real person and a clever doctor, though irreligious (Ep 2743). Erasmus, however, considered that at best Scaliger had been a mere agent suborned by Aleandro (Ep 3127), and in

JULIUS CÆSAR SCALIGER.

Julius Caesar Scaliger

a letter of 18 March 1535 he explicitly denied that Scaliger had written the oration (Ep 3005). This letter fell into Scaliger's hands. The denial that he had written the first oration inflamed Scaliger further. He wrote a second oration and sent it to the printer, along with Erasmus' letter (see *Epistolae* 32–8). And he wrote a third oration (*Epistolae* 35).

At this point, however, friends intervened. Scaliger suppressed his third oration, which apparently does not survive. He also came across the preface to Cicero's *Tusculanae quaestiones* that Erasmus wrote for Johann *Froben's 1523 edition of the work (Ep 1390), and in which Erasmus said that he was finding Cicero more and more to his taste as he grew older. Scaliger evidently found not the original edition but the 1536 reprint, and misread the preface as evidence that Erasmus had seen the error of his ways. Accordingly he wrote to Erasmus' correspondent Jacobus *Omphalius that he was willing and even eager to be reconciled with Erasmus (*Epistolae* 55–9). Erasmus never responded, and Scaliger allowed his second oration to be printed at the end of the year. But his change of heart was apparently genuine. In his collection of epitaphs, the *Heroes* (Lyon: S. Gryphius 1539), he included one for Erasmus between those for Virgil and Cicero. This began: 'Tune etiam moreris? ah quid me linquis Erasme / Ante meus quam sit conciliatus amor?'

In his later years Scaliger won much greater fame for far more serious works, above all, his brilliant systematic treatments of Latin gammar (Lyon: S. Gryphius 1540), poetics (Lyon: A. Vincent 1561), and natural philosophy (Paris: F. Morel 1557).

BIBLIOGRAPHY: Allen Ep 2564 / J.C. Scaliger *Epistolae aliquot nunc primum vulgatae* (Toulouse 1620) / R.C. Christie in *Encyclopaedia Brittanica* 11th ed (Cambridge 1910–11) XXIV 283–4 / J.E. Sandys *A History of Classical Scholarship* Cambridge 1903–8) II 177–8 / C.B. Schmitt in *Catalogus Translationum et Commentariorum* II (Washington, DC, 1971) 271 / Paul Lawrence Rose in *Dictionary of Scientific Biography* ed C.C. Gillispie (New York 1970–80) XII 134–6 / Vernon Hall Jr 'The Life of Julius Caesar Scaliger (1484–1558)' *Transactions of the American Philosophical Society* n s 40 (1950) 85–170; cf the review by Paul O. Kristeller in *American Historical Review* 57 (1952) 394–6 / C.R.J. Clements 'Literary theory and criticism in Scaliger's *Poemata*' *Studies in Philology* 51 (1954) 561–84 / J.F.C. Richards 'The *Elysium* of Julius Caesar Bordonius (Scaliger)' *Studies in the Renaissance* 9 (1962) 195–217 / Myriam Billanovich 'Benedetto Bordon e Giulio Cesare Scaligero' *Italia medioevale e umanistica* 11 (1968) 187–256 / Jean-Claude Chevalier *Histoire de la Syntaxe* (Geneva 1968) / Rose Mary Ferraro *Giudizi critici e criteri estetici nei Poetices libri septem (1561) di Giulio Cesare Scaligero* (Chapel Hill 1971)

ANTHONY GRAFTON

Jan SCARLEY of 's Hertogenbosch, d 23 September 1540

In Ep 1717 Erasmus referred, without mentioning a name, to the rector of the University of Louvain, who attempted to impose silence on his critics in the theological faculty in compliance with instructions received from Pope *Clement VII, presumably those conveyed by Ep 1589 of 12 July 1525. Erasmus' vague reference may concern Jan Scarley (Scarlei, Scarleye), MA and bachelor of theology, who

was rector from 24 February to 31 July 1525, when he was succeeded by the theologian Willem of *Vianen. Scarley taught liberal arts at the College of the Castle and was perhaps more likely than his theologian successor to take the action described by Erasmus.

BIBLIOGRAPHY: Allen Ep 1717 / NNBW V 667 / *Matricule de Louvain* III-1 514, 741–51, and passim / de Vocht *Literae ad Craneveldium* 385 / de Vocht CTL III 260–1, 384   PGB

Agostino SCARPINELLI of Naples, documented 1520–35

Although a Neapolitan, Scarpinelli is first encountered in the suite of the Milanese Luigi *Marliano, bishop of Tuy, physician and councillor to Ludovico *Sforza and subsequently to the Emperor *Charles V. Scarpinelli was attendant on Marliano at the imperial court and accompanied his patron to the diet of Worms (Epp 1195, 1198), where the bishop died of the plague in 1521.

After the death of Marliano Scarpinelli returned to Italy where he apparently entered the service of Francesco II *Sforza, duke of Milan, a transfer of allegiance probably aided by his close association with Marliano. At Pavia in 1522 Scarpinelli was appointed resident ambassador at the English court, despite the fact that he knew no English and was already quite advanced in age, a circumstance which perhaps would hinder his journey and for which Sforza apologized to King *Henry VIII and Cardinal *Wolsey.

The tenure of Scarpinelli's embassy in England was to last for ten years and be marked by neglect and poverty. Indeed, the duke's failure to send Scarpinelli sufficient money on which to live and his negligence in supplying formal letters of credence resulted in the Neapolitan not being recognized in England as a duly accredited ambassador.

Throughout the 1520s and early 1530s, Scarpinelli continued to support his master's claim to his duchy and sent him well-considered and documented dispatches. Nevertheless, the duke made no reply for long periods of time and left Scarpinelli in dire distress, to the point that he wrote to the Milanese ambassador in Rome on 23 August 1526 that he had consumed his own patrimony in the duke's service and was now destitute, a dramatic confession reinforced by a letter of 29 April 1527 in which Scarpinelli claimed to be dying of hunger in a prison and unable to escape without some payment. These desperate entreaties were repeated with regularity until 1531, although in September 1530 Scarpinelli was confirmed in his post and promised seventeen hundred ducats, and was even subsequently commended by the duke for the loyalty of his service.

Scarpinelli requested his recall on 6 June 1531, asking for just enough money to pay his creditors in England and depart the country with honour. His request was granted on 25 January 1532, and he left England soon after, arriving in Rome on 27 September of that year.

Despite the misfortunes of his mission to England, Scarpinelli was considered a man of great ability. He was deeply interested in classical studies, especially Cicero, and was perhaps the 'Meister Augustin' who received two woodcuts from Albrecht *Dürer at Antwerp in August 1520.

Scarpinelli may have met Erasmus at the imperial court as early as 1516 or 1517. On 13 December 1520 Erasmus wrote to him from Louvain, telling him of his difficult trip home after his visit to Germany (Ep 1169). He sent another friendly note in 1524 (Ep 1478). Scarpinelli wrote to Erasmus from Ferrara early in 1535, and the former ambassador was still active until at least 18 March 1535, probably still in the service of the Francesco Sforza (d 1535), given Erasmus' mention of him in a letter to Pietro *Merbelli, secretary to that same duke (Ep 3005).

BIBLIOGRAPHY: Allen Ep 1169 / *Calendar of State Papers, Venetian* IV 68–70 and passim / *Calendar of State Papers, Milan* I passim / LP III-2 nos 2680–1, 2683, 3279

KENNETH R. BARTLETT

Girardus SCASTUS (Reedijk poem 50)
Perhaps in the spring of 1501 Erasmus composed a series of epigrams, one on six new bells for a church that had been struck by lightning and seven others meant to be engraved upon these bells. A prelate by the name of Girardus Scastus is mentioned in the first epigram. For suggestions towards an identification of this prelate see Reedijk poems 50–7. Recently Nicolaas van der Blom proposed an emenda-

tion to Erasmus' text that would eliminate 'Scastus'; he also proposed to identify the church with the cathedral of Chartres and Girardus with Erard de la *Marck; see *Hermeneus* 53 (1981) 29–41.

C.G. VAN LEIJENHORST

Cornelius Duplicius SCEPPERUS *See Cornelis de* SCHEPPER

Daniele SCEVOLA of Ferrara, documented 1509
Daniele Scevola was a physician at Ferrara who met Erasmus when he stopped in Ferrara for a short time after leaving Padua in December 1508. On 22 December 1509 he wrote to Erasmus at Siena, seeking news of his activity and sending greetings from Niccolò *Leoniceno (Ep 216A). Erasmus left Italy in the summer of 1509 and probably did not receive the letter.

BIBLIOGRAPHY: CWE Ep 216A / P.O. Kristeller 'Two unpublished letters to Erasmus' *Renaissance News* 14 (1961) 6–14 TBD

Johann SCHABLER of Bottwar, died c 1540
Johann Schabler (Scabeller, frequently called Wattenschnee), a native of Bottwar, near Marburg, matriculated in the University of Basel in the autumn of 1473. From 1483 he was in Lyon, where after an initial venture into local publishing he established an outlet for the products of the *Froben and *Amerbach press and other publishers, collaborating closely with such international booksellers as Wolfgang *Lachner in Basel and the Koberger firm of Nürnberg. The Lyon store operated from 1521 to 1523 under the direction of Michel *Parmentier, Schabler's manager, who seems to have taken it over after that time (AK II Epp 763, 769, 955). Schabler's wife, Claudia Vaugris, was a native of the Lyon region and a close relative of Benoît *Vaugris.

On 28 December 1494 Schabler acquired membership in Basel's 'Safran' guild and on 24 January 1495 citizenship, paying cash on both occasions, but he continued his itinerant life, and the transfer of his business to the Rhine was gradual at best. Around 1504 he started another store at Paris in the rue Saint-Jacques, using as his ensign 'l'écu de Bâle,' which subsequently also appeared in front of the

Lyon store. In 1522 Schabler bought from Lachner's estate the book store 'zum roten Ring' on the Fischmarkt at Basel (Ep 1508), which after his death continued to thrive in the hands of Konrad *Resch, his nephew, who appears to have taken over the Paris store at the time Schabler moved to the Fischmarkt. In addition to taking over Lachner's store Schabler also provided a significant share of the capital requirements of the Froben press after the death of Lachner. His resulting influence in the press was not welcome to *Beatus Rhenanus (CWE Ep 1014; cf Ep 1704; BRE Epp 125, 128, 129). Schabler had a large stake in the sale of the great Froben edition of Jerome, produced under the direction of Erasmus (AK II Epp 752, 755); his name is also given occasionally in the imprints of books he commissioned to be printed, for example, by Johann *Bebel.

Very little is known about Schabler's daughter, Anna. She was born in 1498 and, being then a widow (AK II Ep 636), married Bruno *Amerbach in the autumn of 1518, when Johann Froben reprinted Erasmus' *Encomium matrimonii* in their honour (Ep 604). The character, beauty, and wealth of Anna and above all the happiness of the young couple visibly impressed those who knew them (AK II Epp 636, 643), but in May 1519 Anna died of the plague (AK II Ep 657), deeply mourned by her humanist friends (AK II Epp 668, 684). Bruno had just opened negotiations with his father-in-law about her dowry (AK II Epp 657, 673, 676) when he too was carried off (Ep 1084).

BIBLIOGRAPHY: Allen Ep 1508 / ADB XLI 244–5 / AK I Ep 134 and passim / K. Stehlin *Regesten zur Geschichte des Basler Buchdrucks* (Leipzig 1887–90) nos 312, 2054, and passim / R. Wackernagel *Geschichte der Stadt Basel* (Basel 1907–54) III 202–3, 34*–35* / Grimm *Buchführer* 1389–90 / P.G. Bietenholz *Basle and France in the Sixteenth Century* (Geneva-Toronto 1971) 27–31 and passim / P. Heitz and C.C. Bernoulli *Basler Büchermarken bis zum Anfang des 17. Jahrhunderts* (Strasbourg 1895) xxvii–xxviii, 72–3 / BA *Oekolampads* I 210–11, 475 — PGB

Johann Matthäus SCHAD of Mittelbiberach, documented 1515–46

Little is known as yet about Johann Matthäus Schad of Mittelbiberach, near the city of Biberach in Swabia. He was a son of the knight and imperial councillor Dr Johann Schad and a younger relative of Dr Joachim Schad, who matriculated at Heidelberg in 1486 (*Matrikel Heidelberg* I 382) and from about 1512 to his death in August 1519 acted in Constance for the absentee provost of the cathedral chapter, Cardinal Matthäus *Lang. Johann Matthäus was conceivably named after the cardinal, who was a close relative – perhaps Johann's nephew – and patron of the Schad family. On 3 February 1515 Johann Matthäus registered at the University of Tübingen. In June or July 1518 he was admitted to a canonry at Constance in his absence. He continued his studies in the University of Louvain, where he matriculated on 23 June 1522 as provost of Constance. In fact Lang must have resigned the provostship to him shortly before that date. On 16 June 1523 Schad sent the chapter a letter from Louvain, explaining that he wished to continue his studies for the time being and would not be able to take up residence in Constance; as a result Jörg Fergenhans was appointed as his administrator. On 19 November 1525 he wrote to Erasmus from Padua, where he seems to have associated with Leonard *Casembroot and Christoph *Truchsess von Waldburg (Epp 1648–50), whereas he knew Cornelis de *Schepper and Johannes *Dantiscus from his student days at Louvain. Schad seems to have retained the provostship when the Constance chapter was forced to leave the city in the Reformation, and seems to have lived with his father on the family estates near Biberach. Unless he was succeeded by a younger brother of whom nothing has so far been heard, he would be identical with the Johann Joachim Schad, provost of Constance, who in 1536 was involved in litigation between his family and the Protestant city of Biberach. In 1546 Johannes *Cochlaeus dedicated Filippo Archinto's *Christianum de fide et sacramentis edictum* (Ingolstadt: A. Weissenhorn 1546) to provost Johann Joachim.

BIBLIOGRAPHY: Allen Ep 1648 / *Matrikel Tübingen* I 204 / *Matricule de Louvain* III-1 675 / Manfred Krebs *Die Protokolle des Konstanzer Domkapitels* (Karlsruhe 1952–9) VI 108–11, 289, 292, and passim / Jörg Vögeli *Schriften zur Reformation in Konstanz* ed A. Vögeli

(Tübingen-Basel 1972–3) II-2 1100–1 / *Die Beschlüsse der Oberdeutschen Schmalkaldischen Städtetage* ed Ekkehart Fabian (Tübingen 1959–60) III 333–40 / de Vocht *Dantiscus* 301–2 / Pietro Martire d'Anghiera *Opera* (Graz 1966) 553 Ep 560   PGB

Peter SCHADE *See Petrus* MOSELLANUS

Valentin SCHAFFNER *See Valentinus* CURIO

Simon SCHAIDENREISSER of Bautzen, documented 1515–73
Simon Schaidenreisser (Minervius) was born in Bautzen, east of Dresden, a town belonging to the 'Hexapolitan' League of Lusatian cities. He obtained a BA in Wittenberg in 1516. For the spring term of 1522 he matriculated at Basel with his kinsman and friend Kilian *Praus; on their way to Basel they had enjoyed the hospiality of Johann von *Botzheim at Constance. Botzheim states (Ep 1285) that Schaidenreisser claimed to be acquainted with Erasmus from an earlier occasion. He may therefore be the Simon Hexapolitanus who approached Erasmus and was helped by him, perhaps at Basel in the summer of 1515 or in the Netherlands a year later (Ep 482). Since Hexapolitanus called Erasmus the 'leading light of Germany,' it may be assumed that he was himself German. A letter from Praus (Ep 1449) suggests that in the spring of 1524 Schaidenreisser was still in Basel and was in contact with Erasmus and Heinrich *Eppendorf. Thereafter his whereabouts are unknown until 1532, when he was a teacher of poetry in Munich. Three years later he was in the service of the town council of Munich and from 1538 to 1573 he was a judge (*propraetor*) in Munich. Schaidenreisser produced an edition of Ludwig Senfl's settings of Horace and other classical poets, modelled after Petrus Tritonius (Nürnberg 1534). He also produced the first German translation of the *Odyssey* (Augsburg: A. Weissenhorn 1537) in prose, and of Cicero's *Paradoxa* (Augsburg: A. Weissenhorn 1538).
BIBLIOGRAPHY: Allen v xxi / CWE Ep 482 introduction (there is no evidence for Schaidenreisser's presence in Brussels) / ADB XXX 552–3 / *Matrikel Wittenberg* I 59 / *Matrikel Basel* I 351 / Winfried Zehetmeier 'Simon Minervius

Schaidenreisser: Leben und Schriften' (doctoral thesis, University of Munich 1962)   IG

Kaspar SCHALBE of Eisenach, d after 1526
Kaspar Schalbe (Schwalbe) belonged to a highly respected family of Eisenach in the Thuringian forest, west of Erfurt. He was no doubt a relative – perhaps the son – of Heinrich Schalbe, at whose table Martin *Luther was a regular guest at the age of about fifteen, helping a son with his studies in return. Kaspar Schalbe matriculated in Erfurt in 1504, obtaining a BA in 1506 and a MA in 1510. He was a friend of Conradus *Mutianus Rufus, to whom he presented a work of Erasmus in 1513; in 1515 Mutianus referred to Schalbe as a poet, and Euricius *Cordus dedicated three of his satirical poems to him. By 1524 Schalbe had become a follower of Luther (Ep 1425) and had married. He is again documented in 1526; a reference in 1532 may refer to another Schalbe.
   In company with Justus *Jonas, Schalbe visited Erasmus in 1519 in Louvain and recalled the encounter enthusiastically in Ep 977. Erasmus too was impressed by the callers, especially Jonas (Epp 978, 982), and thanked Schalbe for a letter and the visit in Ep 981. In 1520 Erasmus sent greetings to Schalbe in a letter to Jonas (Ep 1157).
   BIBLIOGRAPHY: Allen Ep 977 / Luther w *Briefwechsel* I Ep 3, III Ep 587 / *Matrikel Erfurt* II 236 (the reference 'sacerdos uxoratus' may be a later addition) / Heinrich Boehmer *Martin Luther: Road to Reformation* trans J.W. Doberstein and T.G. Tappert (New York 1957) 18–19   IG

Adolf von SCHAUMBURG
1511–20 September 1556
Adolf von Schaumburg (Schauenburg, Schauwenberg) was the son of Jobst, count of Holstein and Schaumburg-Pinneberg, and Maria of Nassau-Dillenburg. He probably studied at Louvain and soon began to receive ecclesiastical preferment, becoming a canon of the Cologne cathedral chapter on 23 December 1529 and a domiciliar of Mainz on 9 February 1532 (not followed by a full canonry); in addition he was a member of the chapter of St Gereon's, Cologne, serving as dean from 1529 and as provost from 1533. On 17 December of

that year the cathedral chapter of Cologne elected him coadjutor to the archbishop, Hermann von *Wied, while papal confirmation for this appointment was granted on 27 August 1535. When Hermann von Wied attempted to lead his ecclesiastical principality into the Protestant camp, he was excommunicated by Pope *Paul III on 16 April 1546. On 3 July the pope appointed Schaumburg administrator of Cologne, and the chapter elected him as the next archbishop on 24 January 1547, thus forcing Hermann von Wied to resign. On 3 May 1547 Schaumburg was ordained priest, and during the diet of Augsburg he was consecrated bishop on 18 April 1548. To tackle much-needed reforms, he convened a synod of his archdiocese in 1549. From 1551 to 1552 he attended the second session of the council of Trent. With the inspiration and the practical support of Johann *Gropper he cleansed his church of all Protestant inclinations; as a prince of the Empire he proved himself a faithful ally of the house of Hapsburg. He died at Brühl, was buried in the cathedral of Cologne, and was succeeded in the archsee by his brother, Anton von Schaumburg.

There is no record of direct relations between Schaumburg and Erasmus. Tielmannus *Gravius reported in 1533 that he was fully occupied in the service of the then coadjutor (Ep 2894).

BIBLIOGRAPHY: Allen Ep 2894 / NDB I 83–4 / Hans Foerster Reformbestrebungen Adolfs III. von Schaumburg (1547–56) in der Kölner Kirchenprovinz (Münster 1925) / Leonard Ennen Geschichte der Stadt Köln (Cologne-Neuss 1863–80) IV passim / Gustav Wolf Aus Kurköln im 16. Jahrhundert (Berlin 1905) passim / Reinhold Schwarz Personal- und Amtsdaten der Bischöfe der Kölner Kirchenprovinz von 1500–1800 (Cologne 1914) / Die Protokolle des Mainzer Domkapitels seit 1450 ed Fritz Herrmann (Paderborn 1924–32) III passim / Johannes Gropper Briefwechsel I 1529–1547 ed Reinhard Braunisch (Münster 1977) passim   ROLF DECOT

Georg SCHENCK von Tautenburg

d 2 February 1540

Georg Schenck (Schenk) von Tautenburg (Toutenburg, Tautenberch) was descended from a noble family of Thuringia. His parents were Wilhelm Schenck and Kunigunde von Tettau. Georg came to Utrecht in 1496 with the new bishop, Friedrich von *Baden, who put him in charge of the castle of Vollenhove in 1502. He occupied the same position and other offices under Bishop Philip of *Burgundy. In the wake of his marriage to Anna de Vos van Steenwijk he acquired a number of estates in Drente. In 1521 he succeeded Wilhelm von *Roggendorf as governor of Friesland and thus came to bear the brunt of the war against Karel van *Egmond, duke of Gelderland. Although his success varied, he was able to establish firm control for the Hapsburg government in the region of Overijssel, of which he became governor in 1528. In 1531 he was received into the order of the Golden Fleece. In letters addressed to Erasmus he is remembered for his action in preventing a large group of Anabaptists from setting out for Münster in March 1534 (Epp 2957, 3031A). He died at Vollenhove from the after-effects of an old wound.

BIBLIOGRAPHY: Allen Ep 2957 / NNBW III 1132–6 / ADB XXXI 66 / de Vocht Literae ad Craneveldium Ep 263 and passim   IG

Cornelis de SCHEPPER of Nieuwpoort,

d 22/28 March 1555

Cornelis de Dobbele (Cornelius Duplicius Scepperus) was born around 1502–3 at Nieuwpoort, in Flanders, the son of Jan, a future mayor of Dunkirk, and his second wife, Gislaine de Severin. The family, which may have come from Ghent, belonged to the nobility of Flanders and had adopted the name de Schepper (de Shipper) in honour of Cornelis' grandfather, Jan, who had ended his career as vice-admiral of Flanders. Cornelis was first tutored by an uncle, who was a priest in Esquelbecq, near Dunkirk; he then proceeded to Paris, where Gérard *Roussel was among his teachers. After studies that included mathematics and the sciences, he went to Louvain, where he matriculated in 1522, took up languages at the Collegium Trilingue, and formed an enduring friendship with Conradus *Goclenius. He also completed his Assertionis fidei adversus astrologos ... libri sex (Antwerp: Franz Birckmann 1523; dedicated to Erard de la *Marck). Meanwhile he had entered the service first of chancellor Gotskalk *Eriksen and soon thereafter of his master, King *Christian II of Denmark, who arrived in the Netherlands as a refugee. In October and November 1523 he accompanied King Christian to Wittenberg, where early in 1524 he published with Melchior Lotter two pamphlets in defence of the legitimate claims of his master, *Illustrissimi ... Christierni ... ad emissos contra se Lubecensium articulos ... responsio* and *Illustrissimi ... Christierni ... ad duas epistolas ... responsio*. In serving Christian's cause, first as a secretary and later as his vice-chancellor, Schepper displayed a remarkable measure of ability and loyalty in his publications as well as in negotiations at the imperial court in Spain. He returned from Spain in time to comfort *Isabella, the wife of Christian II and sister of *Charles v, on her deathbed. Afterwards he wrote an epitaph for her tomb and an elegy, which well expresses his deep sense of affection for the royal couple (1526). Christian rewarded his faithful service with a new coat-of-arms, the nominal lordship of Yaemtland in Norway in 1529, and the highest Danish distinction, the order of the elephant, in 1530.

Schepper continued to advocate the cause of King Christian, although in 1526 he had moved on to the service of Charles v. On the recommendation of *Margaret of Austria, who sent him to Spain, he was appointed councillor and secretary, and soon was close to the chancellor, *Gattinara (Ep 1747). He embarked on a remarkable series of diplomatic missions, in the course of which he came to visit every corner of Europe. In the spring of 1528 he was in Scotland to negotiate an alliance against England; in the summer of that same year he was in Poland to rally support for *Ferdinand's claims to Hungary. After his return (Ep 2063) – if not on an earlier occasion – he was married at Bruges to Anna Isabella (Elizabeth) Donche, the widow of Petrus *Laurinus. The match was later mentioned with approval by Erasmus, who was well aware of the bride's considerable wealth (Epp 2792, 2799). In 1531 Schepper participated in the peace negotiations between kings Ferdinand and *John Zápolyai; while travelling through Germany he probed extensively into the confused religious situation of the German territories. His first embassy to Constantinople in 1533 was largely successful; when the second, undertaken in 1534 (Ep 2917), failed to produce satisfactory re-

sults, no blame was laid on the ambassador. In 1537 he took an active part in the resolution of a conflict between Margaret's government and the city of Ghent, and in 1538 he participated in the peace negotiations with France and the papal government at Nice and Villefranche. In 1539 he made preparations for Charles v's journey through France, and in 1540 he negotiated again with John Zápolyai. In 1541 he spent several months at the French court as ambassador of *Mary of Hungary, who had succeeded her aunt Margaret as the regent of the Netherlands. Over the following two years he devoted much attention to the dispute between Charles v and William v of *Cleves. In 1545 he went to England as Charles' special envoy, and in 1546 he undertook two more missions to the kings of England and France, ensuring their neutrality as the emperor was preparing for his war against the Schmalkaldic League.

His diplomatic missions apart, Schepper was appointed to Charles' privy council in 1533, becoming a regular member in 1535. In 1534 he was named to the regency council for the Netherlands and in 1538 to the Netherlandish council of state. These appointments led to considerable involvement with the administration of the Netherlands. From 1546 to 1547 Schepper devoted his energies exclusively to his administrative duties, which included financial responsibilities and the organization of military supplies, naval affairs, and public works. After the death of his first wife on 20 August 1548 he married Margaretha Loonis. He had no children. In 1551 he wrote a preface to J.C. Calvete de Estrella's *De Aphrodisio expugnato*, which was republished in a collection, *Rerum a Carolo v ... in Africa bello gestarum commentarii* (Antwerp 1554). He also left speeches and letters in manuscript.

It is not possible to say whether or when Erasmus met Schepper, but it is clear that he held him in high esteem, while Schepper viewed Erasmus with sincere admiration. He belonged to the group of Erasmus' supporters at the court of Charles v who regularly did their best to protect their hero from the attacks of conservative theologians in Spain, at Louvain, and elsewhere (Epp 1747, 1791, 1847, 2163). Another connection between Erasmus and Schepper existed in the person of Erasmus'

Erasmus Schets

---

former famulus Lieven *Algoet, who had
entered the service of Mary of Hungary (Epp
2567, 2587, 2792, 2798). Their common friends
included Alfonso de *Valdés, Frans van
*Cranevelt, Adolf van der *Noot, and Johan-
nes *Dantiscus, who kept up a correspondence
with Schepper; but above all it was Goclenius
who kept each posted of the other's progress
(Epp 1994A, 2063, 2587); in 1535 he passed on
to Erasmus some details about the death of
Thomas *More that Schepper had apparently
learnt from Eustache *Chapuys (Ep 3061).

BIBLIOGRAPHY: Allen Ep 1747 / *Matricule de
Louvain* III-1 686 / BNB V 709–18 / ADB XXXI 93–7 /
de Vocht *Dantiscus* 14–24, 327, and passim / de
Vocht CTL II 166–71 and passim / de Vocht
Literae ad Craneveldium Ep 249 and passim /
Jules de Saint-Genois 'Recherches sur Cor-
neille de Schepper ... ' *Messager des sciences
historiques et Archives des arts et de la bibliographie
de Belgique* 5th ser 5 (1856) 1–27 / C.P. Serrure
in *Messager des sciences et des arts de la Belgique*
1 (1833) 180–4 / Herminjard I Ep 97 / Michel
Baelde *De collaterale raden onder Karel v en
Filips II* (Brussels 1965) 306–7 and passim /
Schepper's dispatches were edited by J. de
Saint-Genois and G.A. Yssel de Schepper in
Missions diplomatiques de C.D. de Schepper
(Brussels 1856)

ALBRECHT LUTTENBERGER & PGB

Erasmus SCHETS of Maastricht, d 13 May
1550
Erasmus Schets (Schetz, Schetus, Schetanus)
was born in Maastricht, north of Liège. He
moved to Antwerp, where on 27 July 1511 he
married Ida, a daughter of Frans van Rechtergem, a business friend originally from Aachen
who had trading connections with Spain and
the Portuguese Indies. Schets himself spent
some time in Portugal (Ep 1681). Once he had
established himself at Antwerp he gradually
rose to prominence as a merchant and banker,
lending huge sums to the Hapsburg government of the Netherlands. He specialized in
trading metals, importing, for example, copper
from Prussia, and often competed against, but
on occasion also associated with, the house of
Fugger. Anton *Fugger was unable to challenge his leading position as supplier of guns
and munitions to the Netherlandish government. In the spring of 1530 he went to Liège
(Ep 2352), where on 30 December 1529 his
brother Willem had died as archdeacon of the
cathedral chapter, leaving Schets his heir. In
1539 he built in Antwerp the fine house called
'van Aken' (of Aachen) where he entertained
*Charles v in 1545. The same year he bought
the lordship of Grobbendonk, which he left to
his son Gaspar *Schets. Three more sons were
born from his marriage with Ida van Rechtergem, who died in 1548; they were Melchior,
Balthasar, and Koenraad.

The correspondence between Schets and
Erasmus began in 1525 and continued until
Erasmus' death; more than seventy letters have
been preserved. Schets introduced himself to
Erasmus when forwarding letters from Spain;
he also drew Erasmus' attention to his excellent
connections with Spain through Francisco de
*Vaylle, who had married a sister of Ida van
Rechtergem (Ep 1541). The candid admiration
of the Antwerp businessman appealed to
Erasmus, and he asked Schets to take over from
Pieter *Gillis as the transfer agent for his
English annuities (Epp 1583, 2159). Mutual
trust and affection developed, which included
Ida and Schets' son Gaspar (Epp 1993, 1997).

Erasmus asked for Ida's help in the purchase of Dutch linen and at the same time sent a golden ring as a gift for her (Epp 1654, 1671). The letters between Erasmus and Schets went back and forth at short intervals and invariably dealt with financial transactions; but if Schets had become Erasmus' regular banker, the advice he tendered on many occasions ranged far beyond the field of finance. In 1527 Erasmus remarked that Schets' Latin might sometimes be at fault, but never his trustworthiness (Ep 1862). When Tielmannus *Gravius announced the recent death of Erasmus to Schets on 1 August 1536, he clearly knew what a deep personal loss the Antwerp financier had suffered (Ep 3136).

BIBLIOGRAPHY: Allen Ep 1541 / de Vocht CTL III 358 and passim / Götz von Pölnitz *Anton Fugger* (Tübingen 1958–) II 231, 263, 280, III 92, and passim / Floris Prins *Geschiedenis van Antwerpen* (Brussels-Antwerp 1927–49) XVII 194–5 / Liège, Archives de l'Etat, MSS Cathédrale, registre 266 f 161 (communication from Professor Léon-E. Halkin)

MARCEL A. NAUWELAERTS & PGB

Gaspar SCHETS of Antwerp, 20 July 1513– 9 November 1580

Gaspar, the eldest son of Erasmus *Schets, matriculated at the University of Louvain on 26 February 1531. Gifted in the field of liberal arts, he composed Latin poems and in 1540 received the dedication of the last work of *Eobanus Hessus, a Latin version of the *Iliad* (Basel: R. Winter). His first wife, Margaretha van der Bruggen, bore him two daughters, Isabella and Agnes; his third wife (according to an inscription formerly in Our Lady's church at Mechelen) was Katrien van Ursel, whose elevated social rank facilitated entry into the higher nobility for Schets and his sons. Katrien had a large number of children, among them Lanceloot, Melchior, Jan Karel (NBW IV 745–7), and Koenraad.

After the death of his father in 1550 Gaspar succeeded to the lordship of Grobbendonk, to which he added successively Heist-op-den-Berg, Hingene, and in 1559 Rumst. A major supplier of funds to the Hapsburg governments, sometimes on equal footing with the house of Fugger, he was appointed by King Philip II his factor in charge of the Antwerp

exchange, a position which he retained until 1577. In 1564 he was promoted to the office of treasurer-general for the Netherlands.

A sparkling and colloquial letter which Erasmus addressed to young Gaspar in 1534 has survived (Ep 2897). It expresses appreciation of Schets' literary gifts, of which Erasmus had recently received a sample. In the following year Schets travelled in Germany, visiting Eobanus at Erfurt, and Frankfurt am Main at the time of the autumn fair, where he was expected to meet Hieronymus *Froben (Ep 3067). He may also be the Gaspar recommended by Erasmus in the course of that summer to Tielmannus *Gravius, who was afterwards in touch with Schets' father (Ep 3041).

BIBLIOGRAPHY: Allen Ep 2897 / A. Wauters in BNB VIII 314–24 / de Vocht CTL III 358–61 / Götz von Pölnitz *Anton Fugger* (Tübingen 1958–) II 263, III 78, 466, 577, and passim / *Matricule de Louvain* IV-1 49 / Michel Baelde *De collaterale raden onder Karel V en Filips II* (Brussels 1965) 307–8 and passim

MARCEL A. NAUWELAERTS

Willem SCHETS *See Erasmus* SCHETS

Matthäus SCHINER of Mühlebach, c 1465– 1 October 1522

Matthäus Schiner (Schinner) was the son of Peter and the nephew of Nikolaus Schiner (c 1437–1510), bishop of Sion from 1497 to 1499. He was born of peasant stock at Mühlebach, near Ernen (Valais, Switzerland), and received his first education from his uncle Nikolaus, who was then a parish priest at St Niklaus, and at the cathedral school of Sion. It is uncertain whether Schiner also attended schools in Zürich and Bern. Some time between 1485 and 1489 he received further schooling and acquired a good knowledge of Italian at Como, under the guidance of the humanist Theodorus Lucinus.

In the spring of 1489 Schiner took holy orders at Como and in Rome. In 1497, when political upheaval in the bishopric of Sion raised his uncle to the episcopal see, he was appointed a canon of the cathedral chapter and in 1499 became his uncle's successor as bishop of Sion. An adamant opponent of French political influence in the Valais and northern

Matthäus Schiner

the death of Leo x he returned to Rome, where he contracted the plague an died.

Erasmus probably first met Schiner during the summer of 1516 (Ep 447), presumably in the Netherlands. On this occasion he was made aware of Schiner's role in the Jetzer scandal at Berne which is mentioned first in Ep 447 and subsequently on repeated occasions (Epp 1033, 1164) until the colloquy *Exequiae seraphicae* of 1531 (ASD I-3 693). Between 1517 and 1521, while he was at the imperial court in Flanders, Schiner invited Erasmus to dine with him on several occasions (Epp 948, 1155, 1164, 1248). Erasmus had great respect for his host, whom he called 'a man of learning and unfettered judgment' (Ep 948). In the course of these meetings Schiner apparently encouraged Erasmus to continue his paraphrase of the New Testament, and he seems to have commended this enterprise during his travels in Germany and Switzerland. Erasmus rewarded him with dedications to the Epistles of St James and St John (Epp 1171, 1179) and subsequently a letter published with his paraphrase of St Matthew (Epp 1248, 1255; LB IX 801D).

During the final one and a half years of Schiner's life, Erasmus wrote repeatedly to the cardinal, although only one letter intended for actual dispatch (Ep 1249) and presumably the fragment of another (Ep 1295) survive. As Schiner began to take a more vigorous stand against *Luther and the Reformation, Erasmus was quick to praise Schiner's determination while defending himself against the widespread allegations that he was a Lutheran at heart (cf Epp 1248, 1249). He seems to have convinced his influential friend of his religious integrity, for when Erasmus' orthodoxy was challenged at the imperial court Schiner was amongst those who energetically intervened in his favour (Ep 1342; ASD IX-1 178).

When Schiner was back in Rome following the election of Pope *Adrian VI in 1522, he twice wrote to Erasmus offering him generous terms should he consent to come to Rome in order to serve the church's campaign against the Reformation (Ep 1295). Erasmus made much of Schiner's offer (Epp 1299, 1300, 1302, 1305, 1311, 1342) but stayed in Basel, excusing himself on the grounds of illness and the dangers of travel. No doubt the poignant

Italy, he became a close confidant of Pope *Julius II, who made him bishop of Novara, a cardinal in 1511, and a papal legate in 1512. Exiled from his bishopric of Sion through the 'Matze' (a traditional form of popular uprising) in 1510 and again in 1517, Schiner continued to move around as a highly talented diplomat who helped to bring about the involvement of Swiss troops in the Italian wars, which ended with their defeat at Marignano in 1515. As a result Schiner fell into disfavour with *Leo x and had to avoid Italy. From his base at Zürich (1517–21) he served the Hapsburg government on several diplomatic missions.

A skilful linguist and orator, the cardinal was initially a friend of Huldrych *Zwingli but soon came to disapprove of his enthusiasm for the Reformation. Schiner assisted the papal nuncio, Girolamo *Aleandro, on his anti-Lutheran mission to the diet of Worms in 1521. He maintained friendly relations with such notable humanists and supporters of the new learning as Johannes *Fabri, Henricus *Glareanus, Peter *Falck, Heinrich Wölflin (Lupulus), Christoph von *Utenheim, Claudius *Cantiuncula, and Jakob *Wimpfeling. After arguments of Bishop Johannes Fabri, who advised him to decline Schiner's offer (BRE Ep 221), carried more weight.

BIBLIOGRAPHY: Allen Ep 447 / DHBS VI 20–1 / LThK IX 404 / Albert Büchi *Kardinal Schiner als Staatsmann und Kirchenfürst: Ein Beitrag zur allgemeinen und schweizerischen Geschichte von der Wende des XV.–XVI. Jahrhunderts* (Zürich-Fribourg 1923–37) / *Kardinal Matthäus Schiner und seine Zeit* in *Blätter aus der Walliser Geschichte* 16 (1967–8), esp Peter Arnold 'Kurzbiographie von Matthäus Schiner' 5–60 / Carl J. Burckhardt 'Kardinal Matthäus Schiner' in *Raron: Burg und Kirche* ed Alfred A. Schmid (Basel 1972) 139–75 (with illustrations) / Albert Büchi 'Kardinal Schiner und der Humanismus' *Schweizerische Rundschau* 20 (1919–20) 100–20 / *Korrespondenzen und Akten zur Geschichte des Kardinals Matth. Schiner* ed Albert Büchi (Basel 1920–5) / Hans von Greyerz 'Der Jetzerprozess und die Humanisten' *Archiv des Historischen Vereins des Kantons Bern* 31 (1932) 245–99 / Robert Durrer 'Das Madrider Kardinalsporträt von Raffael und die Bildnisse Matthäus Schiners' *Monatshefte für Kunstwissenschaft* 6 (1913) 1–17 (with illustrations)

KASPAR VON GREYERZ

Arnold and Bernhard SCHINKEL of Lübeck, d 1497 and 1501, respectively

During his stay in Paris Erasmus wrote to a man of Lübeck about the progress of his son, who was then living with Erasmus as a paying pupil; money for the youth's upkeep was to be remitted through Erasmus' young friend Heinrich *Northoff, also of Lübeck (Ep 82). Erasmus did not publish this letter until 1519, giving the date of 1497, but no names. On slight evidence P.S. Allen assigned to it the date of December 1498. It is possible, though by no means certain, that this letter dated from November 1497 and that the man of Lübeck and his son were Arnold and Bernhard Schinkel (Scinkel); it seems unthinkable that Erasmus and Bernhard should not have known each other.

Only two students from the diocese of Lübeck registered with the German nation of the University of Paris in the period 1494–9. One was Heinrich Northoff, the other Bernhard Schinkel. Bernhard was a son of Arnold Schinkel (d 30 November 1497) and his wife, Ursula (died c 1481). Arnold is documented as

a rich Lübeck merchant from 1466. Shortly before his death he committed an inheritance that was coming to him to the endowment of an altar in St Mary's, and Bernhard's younger brother, Friedrich, was its first vicar. Arnold was buried there, and rivalling the pious patronage of the *Greverade and Northoff families, the Schinkels had a rich altarpiece created for this chapel, which was destroyed in the second world war. Bernhard is last mentioned in Lübeck documents in 1502 as co-heir together with his brothers and sisters of a house on the market square. It seems that he had died at Paris in late September or early October of 1501: Paris, Archives de l'Université (Sorbonne) Registre 91 f 42 verso.

Since he was a good friend of Heinrich Northoff, Schinkel may have been the youth tutored by Erasmus, although Ep 82 suggests a certain seniority of Northoff with regard to Erasmus' charge which is not in evidence during the joint course of their preceding studies. Schinkel and Northoff matriculated together at the University of Rostock on 21 May 1492 and both received a BA the following year. In the summer of 1496 both registered at the University of Louvain as students of canon law, Schinkel on 10 June and Northoff on 6 July. In the course of the academic year beginning 20 September 1496, probably in the first half, both moved to Paris. Ep 82 mentions that books belonging to Erasmus' pupil were lost in transit from an Antwerp merchant to a Paris merchant; this detail would fit Schinkel's progress from Louvain to Paris (and not conflict with another reference to the lost books in Ep 80). Schinkel seems to have graduated MA at Paris shortly after Northoff, in 1497–8, possibly at quite a young age. If the references to the youth of Lübeck in Epp 80–2 concern Schinkel, *puer* in Allen Ep 80:15 should not be translated as 'servant-pupil.'

BIBLIOGRAPHY: *Matrikel Rostock* I 262, 268 / *Matricule de Louvain* III-1 139 / John McGinley ed 'Five years of accounts (1494–5 through 1498–9) from the fourth book of the receptors of the German nation at the University of Paris' (MA thesis, University of Notre Dame, Indiana 1973) partially editing Paris, Archives de l'Université (Sorbonne) MS Registre 91 / *Lübecker Ratsurteile* ed Wilhelm Ebel (Göttingen 1955–67) I no 446, 696, 739 / *Die Bau- und*

Kunstdenkmäler der Freien und Hansestadt Lübeck
(Lübeck 1906–   ) II 171–2, 212, 220–1, 389 /
P.G. Bietenholz 'Schüler und Freunde des
Erasmus in Lübeck und Montpellier' ARG 75
(1984) 78–92 / Lübeck, Archiv der Hansestadt
Lübeck MSS Personenkartei 270 passim

JAMES K. FARGE & PGB

Georg SCHIRN (Ep 1142 of 10 September
1520)
Georg Schirn (Georgius Schirnus Alemannus),
who styled himself 'theologorum minimus,'
was a monk of the Cistercian house of
Sant'Ambrogio Maggiore, Milan. Together
with his letter to Erasmus (Ep 1142), he sent
one to *Beatus Rhenanus (BRE Ep 178). Schirn
or Tschirn is a name sometimes found in Silesia,
but it has not been possible to identify Georg.

Johannes SCHLECHTA *See Jan* ŠLECHTA

Lorenz SCHLEHENRIED of Würzburg,
d 9 July 1556
On his journey from Basel to Paris in the
autumn of 1528 the Würzburg canon Daniel
*Stiebar was accompanied by an attendant
named Laurentius (Epp 2065, 2069). Laurentius can be identified from the matriculation
register of the University of Basel, where
Lorenz (Laurentius) Schlehenried (Schleen-
riedt, Schleerich) was listed just ahead of
Stiebar and another Würzburg canon, Johann
Truchsess von Wetzhausen. The name 'Laurentius' is not frequent among Basel students,
nor were matriculants from Würzburg; in fact
the combination does not occur a second time
in the whole *Matrikel*. Schlehenried's family
belonged to the Franconian gentry. On 18
August 1529 he matriculated at Heidelberg,
where he received a BA on 18 June 1530 and in
1532 was admitted to study law as a licentiate in
arts. On 20 May 1536 he registered at the
University of Freiburg with his charge, Count
Konrad von Castell, aged seventeen and a
domiciliar of Würzburg. The count later resigned his canonry to become a Protestant and
ended his career as a councillor to the Emperor
Maximilian II. Still in the company of Konrad
von Castell, Schlehenried matriculated early in
1539 at Orléans, where in 1541 he was the
procurator of a German nation that had
dwindled in numbers and was short of funds.

Schlehenried strove to redress the situation
and to this end wrote a letter to the influential
Johann *Gogreve, who had himself been
procurator during his studies at Orléans.
    The counts of Castell continued to patronize
Schlehenried, who in 1543 was in Ingolstadt
preparing himself for the doctorate in law. A
year later, however, he attached himself to the
Fugger family, accompanying Ulrich Fugger to
Bologna, where he was to oversee the young
man's studies. Soon, however, his commitment
to Protestantism became sufficiently obvious to
prevent him from continuing in the employ of
the Fuggers. He remained in Italy for the time
being and must have made contact with the
Protestant circle around Renée of France,
duchess of Ferrara. In the winter of 1551–2 a
former member of that circle, the poetess and
humanist Olimpia Morata, who was then
married in Schweinfurt, wrote to him in search
of news from her family. Prior to his return
from Italy Schlehenried obtained his doctorate
in civil and canon law in 1553 at Bologna. On 11
January 1554 he was appointed to a lectureship
in canon law at the University of Tübingen in
succession to Gebhard Brastberger, who was
promoted to the chair of canon law. Schlehenried's academic career in Tübingen was cut
short, however, by his death of the plague,
which occurred at Lauingen. His wife had died
shortly before him.
    BIBLIOGRAPHY: Detlef Illmer in *Matricule
d'Orléans* II-2 335–8 / *Matrikel Basel* I 361 /
Matrikel Heidelberg I 545, II 447, 481 / *Matrikel
Freiburg* I 302 / *Matrikel Tübingen* I 373 / AK VIII
Ep 5362 n 10   PGB

Dominik SCHLEUPNER of Nysa,
d 3 February 1547
Dominik, the son of Nikolaus Schleupner, a
goldsmith, was born at Nysa (Neisse), in
Silesia, around 1480. In 1498 he matriculated at
Cracow and obtained his BA there two years
later. By 1503 he was at Wrocław as notary and
assistant secretary of the consistory; by 5 July
1504 he was *subcustos* of the cathedral. As a
protégé of the Wrocław bishop Johannes (II)
*Thurzo, he was nominated to a vacant
canonry at the cathedral chapter of Wrocław
on 8 April 1516. Prior to occupying his prebend
he had to have the customary three years of
university studies and matriculated at Witten-

berg (7 April 1519) and Leipzig (15 November 1520). On 30 May 1522 he had returned to Wrocław and was confirmed in the occupancy of his prebend; in addition he held other benefices at Nysa, Racibórz, and Wrocław, where he was *custos* of the Holy Cross chapter (1512) and a canon of St Giles' (1513).

From his student days at Wittenberg Schleupner maintained close contacts with *Luther and *Melanchthon, and after his move to Leipzig he preached in the Lutheran fashion at the church of the Benedictine nuns of St George's. At Luther's suggestion the Nürnberg council invited him to their city, and on 14 April 1522 he preached a probationary sermon at St Sebald's (Nürnberg, Staatsarchiv MS Rst Nürnberg, Ratsverlässe 675 f 12 recto). In the following summer he was still at Wrocław but during the winter of 1522–3 he had moved to Nürnberg and was engaged in Lutheran preaching, as *Pirckheimer reported to Erasmus on 17 February (Ep 1344). On 23 February he was appointed preacher at St Sebald's, occupying an office that had been created from a bequest by Sebald Schreyer (d 1520) and was made permanent a year later when the council assigned him a fixed salary (Nürnberg, Staatsarchiv MSS Rst Nürnberg, A-Laden Akten S I L 74 no 26 f 3 verso; and Ratsbücher 12 ff 221–2; Ratsverlässe 700 f 9). In the spring and summer of 1524 the bishop of Wrocław, Jakob von *Salza, and his cathedral chapter attempted to save Schleupner for the traditional faith by offering him the position of cathedral preacher, but he rejected their overtures and soon thereafter resigned all his Silesian benefices.

In Nürnberg the reorganization of state and church according to Lutheran principles was gaining momentum, and Schleupner played a prominent role in the process. An ordinance for church services (c May 1524), probably drafted by him, is preserved in the Scheurlsches Familienarchiv at Nürnberg-Fischbach (MS C f 92 verso–93 recto, 107). Late in 1524 he opposed the circulation of Thomas Müntzer's *Ausgedrückte Entblössung* in a memorandum which is missing today. By the turn of 1525 he joined Thomas *Venatorius in endorsing *Osiander's *Grosser Ratschlag* addressed to the Nürnberg council, and in March 1525 he participated in the religious colloquy held at

Nürnberg. In the spring of 1526 he intervened in the liturgical controversy, rejecting the exclusive use of German in the liturgy proper; in another opinion of 1527 he opposed the compulsory taking of communion. Between 1528 and 1533 he participated in Nürnberg's negotiations with Brandenburg-Ansbach about church ordinance and visitation, and in 1530 he composed a memorandum to protest against the outcome of the diet of Augsburg (Nürnberg, Staatsarchiv MS Fst Ansbach, Religionsakten 17 f 269 recto–272 recto, 307 recto–310 recto). In 1531 he participated in the drafting of a catechism, and in the controversy concerning the treatment of Anabaptists (1528–33) he opposed the death penalty. As preacher of St Catherine's where the council had transferred him in 1533, he took part in the prosecution of the Anabaptist Peter Riedemann, and in 1542 he signed with others Nürnberg's *Bedenken* against Kaspar Schwenckfeld. When he died five years later he was buried in the churchyard of St Rochus'; an epitaph cast in bronze is preserved. Schleupner had married Dorothea Schmidmaier on 20 February 1525. After her death (22 August 1527) he married Margareta Apel on 11 December 1527, prompting Pirckheimer to set down his twenty-eight propositions *Contra digamiam episcoporum*.

BIBLIOGRAPHY: Allen Ep 1344 / ADB XXXI 472–3 / Gerhard Zimmermann *Das Breslauer Domkapitel im Zeitalter der Reformation und Gegenreformation, 1500–1600* (Weimar 1938) no 221 / Konrad Müller 'Dominikus Schleupner, ein Schlesier auf der Nürnberger Sebalduskanzel' *Jahrbuch für Schlesische Kirche und Kirchengeschichte* n s 33 (1954) 45–58 / Kurt Engelbert 'Die Anfänge der lutherischen Bewegung in Breslau und Schlesien' *Archiv für schlesische Kirchengeschichte* 18 (1960) 121–207, esp 141–2, 19 (1961) 165–232, esp 215–16 / Johannes Kist *Die Matrikel der Geistlichkeit des Bistums Bamberg, 1400–1556* (Würzburg 1965) no 5440 / Matthias Simon *Nürnbergisches Pfarrerbuch* (Nürnberg 1965) no 1211 / *Quellen zur Nürnberger Reformationsgeschichte* (Juni 1524–Juni 1525) ed Gerhard Pfeiffer (Nürnberg 1968) passim / Peter Zahn *Die Inschriften der Friedhöfe St. Johannis, St. Rochus und Wöhrd zu Nürnberg* (Munich 1972) no 605 / Hans Dieter Schmid *Täufertum und Obrigkeit in Nürnberg* (Nürnberg

1972) 255–6 and passim / Andreas Osiander *Gesamtausgabe* ed Gerhard Müller (Gütersloh 1975–) I and II passim / *Acta Capituli Wratislaviensis 1500–1562* ed Alfred Sabisch (Cologne-Vienna 1972–) I-1–II-2 passim / Harold J. Grimm *Lazarus Spengler* (Columbus 1978) passim / G. Seebass 'Dominikus Schleupners Gutachten zum Stand der Reformation in Nürnberg 1526' *Zeitschrift für bayerische Kirchengeschichte* 47 (1978) 27–50 / *Melanchthons Briefwechsel* I Epp 103, 111, and passim

FRANZ MACHILEK

Albert (I) von SCHLICK d 1548
A letter, now lost, from Erasmus to Bernhard von *Cles reached the latter after considerable delay at Prague and was actually given to him by a Baron Albert von Schlick (Ep 2504). The member of this important family of Bohemian nobles in question is probably Albert (I) (Albrecht) von Schlick (Slick), a son of Hieronymus (I), the founder of the Elbogen (now Loket, on the river Ohře or Eger) line of the house, and Klara (?) von Zelking. He was a chamberlain of King *Ferdinand and prefect (*Landvogt*) of Lusatia and fought in the wars in Hungary. His first wife was a Schlick and the second was Elisabeth von Ungnad.

BIBLIOGRAPHY: Allen Ep 2504 / Pflug *Correspondance* II Ep 157 / Georg Agricola *Ausgewählte Werke* ed H. Prescher (Berlin 1955–) II genealogical table of the von Schlick family opposite p 320   PGB

Johann SCHLUPF of Bittelbrunn,
died c March 1527
Johann Schlupf (Schlupp) was very likely born at Bittelbrunn, near Engen, north-west of Lake Constance, and went to school at Engen. On 22 March 1493 he obtained a chaplaincy in the castle of Hewen, near Engen, perhaps to provide him with the means for his further education. In 1501, when he registered in the University of Freiburg, he already had his MA. He obtained a licence in theology and on 30 August 1503 became a member of the faculty of divinity. Even prior to his arrival at Freiburg he had been nominated to the parish of Überlingen, on Lake Constance, and from 1506, it seems, he exercised his priestly office there. In 1515 he persuaded Cardinal Matthäus *Schiner, who was passing through Überlingen, to

grant an indulgence for the benefit of his parish church.

When several cities in the neighbourhood began to opt for the Reformation, Schlupf worked hard to save Überlingen for the old faith. In 1521 he urged the burning of *Luther's books, and in 1523 he used his pulpit to attack the reform-minded ministers of Constance, thus touching off an official feud between the two cities which was to continue for years. In May 1526 he was among the delegates of the bishop of Constance attending the disputation of Baden. Johann von *Botzheim and Michael *Hummelberg, who knew him well but did not share his religious convictions, judged him to be fanatical and ignorant. Hummelberg ridiculed him in a satirical epitaph. Schlupf is mentioned in Ep 1739A.

BIBLIOGRAPHY: Allen VIII Ep 1739A / *Blarer Briefwechsel* I Epp 29, 35, 85 / Christian Roder 'Zur Lebensgeschichte des Pfarrers Dr. Johannes Schlupf ... ' *Freiburger Diözesan-Archiv* 43 (1915) 257–89 / *Matrikel Freiburg* I-1 145 / *Amtliche Sammlung der älteren Eidgenössischen Abschiede* ed J.K. Krütli et al (Lucerne 1839–82) IV-1a 930   PGB

Konrad SCHMID of Küssnacht, 1476/7–11 October 1531
When summing up the last days of Ulrich von *Hutten, Erasmus mentioned a priest outside the city of Zürich with whom Hutten had stayed for a few days (Ep 1437). The reference is too vague for conclusive identification. Allen suggested Konrad Schmid, commander of the order of St John at Küsnacht (canton Zürich). Erasmus might also have intended Hans Klarer, the priest-physician with whom Hutten stayed on the island of Ufenau from early August 1523 to his death (cf z VIII Ep 320), or possibly Johann Jakob Russinger, abbot of Pfäfers (z VII Ep 245).

BIBLIOGRAPHY: Allen Ep 1437 / z VIII Ep 308, XI Ep 1122, and passim / E. Egli 'Komtur Schmid von Küsnacht' *Zwingliana* 2 (1905–12) 65–73 / Heinrich Bullinger *Werke* ed Fritz Büsser et al (Zürich 1972–): *Briefwechsel* I Ep 15 and passim (for Schmid)   PGB

Johann von SCHMISING of Münster, documented 1517–60
Johann von Schmising (Smising, Smysinck)

was descended from a noble family from the region of Münster, in Westphalia, and was a kinsman of Hermannus *Buschius. There is no information about his parentage and his education except that he matriculated at the University of Cologne on 5 September 1517. In 1528 he is documented as a canon of Osnabrück. Thirty years later he was dean of the Osnabrück chapter. The last reference to him dates from 1560. In 1532 he was, according to Ludolf *Cock, canon of Münster (Ep 2687).

BIBLIOGRAPHY: Allen Ep 2687 / Johann Carl Bertram Stüve *Geschichte des Hochstifts Osnabrück* (Jena 1853–73) II 179 / Hermann Hamelmann *Geschichtliche Werke* ed H. Detmer et al (Münster 1902–13) I-3 137, 194 / *Matrikel Köln* II 786   ROBERT STUPPERICH

Georg SCHMOTZER of Constance,
d after 5 January 1550

Georg Schmotzer registered at the University of Tübingen on 26 April 1503 and received his MA in 1506. He had taken orders before matriculating at Freiburg on 27 January 1508 to study law under Udalricus *Zasius. In 1514, after obtaining a doctorate in law, he became professor of Institutions and was also put in charge of the monthly disputations in the faculty of law. He served in these functions until 1525, for two terms as rector of the university. In 1525 he joined the Hapsburg government at Ensisheim as councillor but was permitted to retain his chair at Freiburg for another two years. When he vacated it Zasius attempted in August 1527 to interest Bonifacius *Amerbach in applying for the position. In February 1529 Schmotzer excused himself from undertaking an embassy to Savoy because of illness. On his retirement in 1547 he returned to Freiburg and in 1549 the Austrian government appointed Andreas von *Könneritz and him to carry out a visitation of the university. In the last years of his life he acted as guardian for the children of Jakob *Stürtzel. The name of Schmotzer's wife was Veronika Hesser.

Schmotzer's friendly correspondence with Bonifacius Amerbach continued until the summer of 1549. No doubt it was Amerbach who advised Erasmus to appeal to Schmotzer in 1527 (Ep 1922) when some of his letters were confiscated. Amerbach was ready to support

Erasmus with a letter of his own (AK III Ep 1221).

BIBLIOGRAPHY: Allen Ep 1922 / *Matrikel Freiburg* I-1 181 / Winterberg 63–4 / Schreiber *Universität Freiburg* II 321–2 / AK II Ep 648, III Epp 1180, 1201, VII Ep 3172, and passim / *Deutsche Reichstagsakten* Jüngere Reihe (Gotha-Göttingen 1893–) VII-1 481   PGB

Harmen SCHOENMAKER of 't Zand,
d February 1535

Harmen Schoenmaker (Herman or Peter Schomaker or Schumacher), originating from 't Zand, a village northwest of Appingedam in the province of Groningen, was an Anabaptist leader who purported to be the new Messiah. Not content with rebaptizing, he even seems to have practised circumcision (Ep 2999). On 24 January 1535 the stadtholder of Friesland, Georg *Schenck von Tautenburg, reported to the bishop of Münster, Franz von *Waldeck, that Schoenmaker had been captured, and so did Tielmannus *Gravius to Erasmus on 3 February (Ep 2990). On 26 February, *Viglius Zuichemus stated that he had died in prison (Ep 2999) apparently of natural causes, before he could be sentenced and executed. Schoenmaker was also mentioned in the so-called *Bichtbok* of 1534.

BIBLIOGRAPHY: Allen Ep 2990 / P.G. Bos in *Nederlandsch archief voor kerkgeschiedenis* n s 6 (1909) 18–28 / A.F. Mellink *De wederdopers in de Noordelijke Nederlanden* (Groningen 1954) passim / *Documenta anabaptistica Neerlandica* ed A.F. Mellink (Leiden 1975) I 111–12, 114, 118–19, 122–3, 124–5 / K.-H. Kirchhoff *Die Täufer in Münster* (Münster 1973) 230 / George H. Williams *The Radical Reformation* (Philadelphia 1962) 379

C.G. VAN LEIJENHORST

Johann SCHOENRAID dean of Aachen,
d 1541

Johann Schoenraid (Schoenraed, Schoenroide, Schonrad, Sconenrad) matriculated at Cologne as a student at the faculty of arts on 12 May 1490 and was still studying there in June 1492. He became a canon of St Mary's in Aachen on 3 October 1504. In 1512 he probably registered in Santa Maria dell'Anima, the German institution at Rome. The date of 1524 is mentioned for his appointment as dean of St Mary's chapter, but it is possible that he already occupied this office in 1520, as is suggested by Ep 1170. In 1535 he is given the titles of dean, apostolic protonotary, and a Lateran count. Two years later, Canon Johann Pallart became his coadjutor. Like Leonardus *Priccardus, Schoenraid was a leading member of the party of Erasmians in Aachen (Ep 2130). He died early in 1541 and was succeeded in his canonry by Hermann Pastoris on 20 April 1541.

Schoenraid was one of the canons who played host to Erasmus during his visit to Aachen in September 1518. He may have been the canon who was recommended to Erasmus by Hermann von *Neuenahr and guided him to the house of the precentor, Johann *Sudermann (Ep 867). In May 1519 Schoenraid sent greetings to Erasmus (Ep 972). In March 1529 Erasmus' messenger Felix *Rex entrusted to Johann Schoenraid copies of Erasmus' *Vidua christiana* for Tielmannus *Gravius and Leonardus Priccardus (Ep 2130).

Johann Schoenraid is not to be mistaken (as in Allen Ep 2130:116n) for a younger Johann Schoenraid who was a canon of St Mary's in Aachen from 1522 until 1540, when he resigned and got married.

BIBLIOGRAPHY: Allen and CWE Ep 972 / *Matrikel Köln* II 277 / Eduard Adenaw 'Archäologische Funde in Aachen nach dem Jahr 1898' *Zeitschrift des Aachener Geschichtsvereins* 36 (1914) 123 / *Nomina admodum reverendorum perillustrium atque generosorum dominorum canonicorum regalis ecclesiae B.M.V. Aquisgranensis* ed Antonius Heusch (Berlin 1892) 12, 14–16 / Hermann Friedrich Macco *Aachener Wappen und Genealogien: Ein Beitrag zur Wappenkunde und Genealogie Aachener, Limburgischer und Jülicher Familien* (Aachen 1908) II 131 and table 93 (the Schoenraid coat of arms) / *Des Peter à Beeck ... Aquisgranum oder Geschichte der Stadt Aachen* trans and ed Peter S. Käntzeler (Aachen 1874) 83

KASPAR VON GREYERZ

Johann SCHÖFFER of Mainz, c 1475–c 1531
Johann Schöffer (Scheffer) was the second son of Peter (I) Schöffer and Christine, the daughter of Johann *Fust. He matriculated in the University of Leipzig in the summer semester of 1492 and was a BA in 1494. After his father's death in 1503 he took over the management of the printing press 'zum Humbrecht,' also called 'Schöfferhof,' in the Schustergasse, Mainz.

Assessing correctly the growing demand for humanistic books and taking advantage of his connections with such members of the archiepiscopal court as *Hutten and Heinrich *Stromer, Schöffer was able to publish some three hundred titles between 1503 and 1531. Nikolaus *Carbach and Wolfgang *Angst worked as correctors for him. He also held some civic offices.

Schöffer is mentioned in Ep 1054 as the publisher of *Collectanea antiquitatum in urbe atque agro Moguntino repertarum* by Johann *Huttich, a book that Erasmus wanted to acquire.

BIBLIOGRAPHY: Allen Ep 1054 / Benzing *Buchdrucker* 296 / *Matrikel Leipzig* I 389, II 341
IG

Peter (II) SCHÖFFER of Mainz, c 1480– January 1547
Peter, the third son of Peter (I) Schöffer, learnt the trade of a type cutter and was at first associated with the family press. After his father's death in 1503 he inherited the house 'zum Korb' in Mainz and set up a printing press there, but he had to sell the house on 4 August 1512 because his business failed to prosper. Among the fourteen books known to have been printed by him at Mainz some music scores have been noted for their typographical excellence. In 1518 he began printing in Worms and soon moved his entire business to that city (Ep 1804), publishing sixty books there, among them a number by Reformation and Anabaptist writers. In 1529 he moved to Strasbourg, where he married Anna Pfintzer, a widow, and was admitted to citizenship on 14 December. He continued in the printing business, producing some twenty-seven titles, partly in association with Johann Schwintzer and partly with Matthias Apiarius, who, like Schöffer, specialized in musical scores. Later he moved to Basel and Venice. Seven books have been identified as his products in Venice. He finally returned to Basel, where he cut type until his death. In 1531 Peter's son, Ivo, took over from his uncle, Johann *Schöffer, as the head of the family press in Mainz.

In 1527 Erasmus had seen a pamphlet,

written in German with scandalous illustrations, that Schöffer had sent from Worms (Ep 1804). In 1530 in Strasbourg he printed *Bucer's reply to Erasmus' *Epistola contra pseudevangelicos*, and Erasmus continued to view his activities with understandable suspicion (Ep 2510).

BIBLIOGRAPHY: Allen Ep 1804 / Benzing *Buchdrucker* 297, 416, 478 / M.L. Gölner in *The New Grove Dictionary of Music and Musicians* ed Stanley Sadie (London 1980) XVI 700   IG

Pieter SCHOMAKER *See Harmen* SCHOENMAKER

Nikolaus von SCHÖNBERG of Meissen, 11 August 1472–c 7–9 September 1537
Nikolaus von Schönberg (Schomberg, Schoneberg), born in Meissen, in Saxony, was the eldest son of Dietrich, a nobleman and a judge. He matriculated at Leipzig in 1485 to study law. Passing through Prato in 1496 on his way to Rome, he heard Girolamo *Savonarola preach a sermon and was moved to enter the Dominican monastery of San Marco in Florence on 29 October 1497; he made his profession on 31 October 1498. Within a short time he was elected prior of the Dominican houses, first of Lucca, then of Siena, and finally of San Marco (1506–7). In 1507 he was named assistant to the general of his order and the following year procurator general, a position which he owed to his friend the future Cardinal *Cajetanus, who was then elected general of the Dominicans. Under Pope *Julius II he was a preacher at the Vatican and from 1510 professor of theology at the Studio of Rome.

In January 1517 Pope *Leo x appointed Schönberg to undertake a mission to France, and on 17 March 1518 he was sent to Hungary and Poland in efforts to gain support for the papal crusade. No pledges were made, and Schönberg also failed in his endeavour to mediate in the conflict between Poland and the Teutonic knights; nor could he carry out a planned visit to Muscovy. On his return he was closely associated with Cardinal Giulio de' Medici, later Pope *Clement VII, and was appointed archbishop of Capua on 12 September 1520. He did not reside there for long as he was called back to Rome by Pope *Adrian VI and thereafter lived mainly in the Holy City. As

Nikolaus von Schönberg

a close adviser to Clement VII he advocated friendly relations with the government of *Charles v. On 11 March 1524 he left Rome and as papal nuncio visited the courts at Blois, Burgos, and finally London. By 16 June he had returned, his peace mission a failure, as Erasmus regretfully told his friends (Epp 1466, 1470). A similar mission in the autumn had no better success. He was in Rome during the Sack in 1527 and helped to arrange a truce with the imperial army. Schönberg was now in poor health, but in 1530 he attended the emperor's coronation at Bologna. Pope *Paul III finally named him cardinal on 21 May 1535 (Epp 3047, 3066). He resigned as archbishop of Capua not later than the spring of 1536.

Schönberg's interest in astronomy may have been aroused when his secretary, Johann Albrecht *Widmanstetter, expounded the ideas of Nicolaus Copernicus before Clement VII in 1533. In 1536 Schönberg requested and apparently received a manuscript copy of Copernicus' *De revolutionibus*. Widmanstetter's scriptural translations encouraged Schönberg to undertake paraphrases of parts of the Gospels and Epistles, which remained in

Widmanstetter's library (now in Munich) together with parts of Schönberg's correspondence. According to Ambrosius von *Gumpenberg, Schönberg also held Erasmus in high esteem (Ep 3047).

Schönberg died in Rome and was buried in Santa Maria sopra Minerva, where a commemorative inscription survives. Giorgio Vasari mentons a painting by Giuliano Bugiardini which showed Schönberg with Clement VII, and Fra Bartolomeo portrayed him in a fresco at San Marco, of which Schönberg was then prior.

BIBLIOGRAPHY: Allen Ep 1466 / *Matrikel Leipzig* I 347 / LThK IX 451 / Pflug *Correspondance* I Ep 107 and passim / Pastor XII 549, XIII 365, and passim / A. Walz 'Zur Lebensgeschichte des Kardinals Nikolaus von Schönberg' *Mélanges Mandonnet* (Paris 1930) II 371–82 / See also the important articles by Hans Striedl listed in the biography of Widmanstetter

IG

Christoph SCHÖNFELD *See Simon* SUNFELDUS

Johann SCHONRAD *See Johann* SCHOENRAID

Cornelis van SCHOONHOVE of Ghent, d 10 July 1528
Cornelis van Schoonhove received a licence in arts at Paris in 1493–4, and on 22 September 1495 enrolled in the study of canon law at Louvain. He became an advocate at Bruges and in 1510 or 1511 fiscal advocate at Ghent. He had three sons and a daughter by his first marriage, to Johanna Anneron, and two daughters by his second marriage, to Pierine Pyps. He died at Ghent.

Schoonhove is mentioned in Ep 1214 of 21 June 1521, in which Erasmus thanked Abbot *Hugenoys for a gift he had received through the fiscal advocate. Willem van *Schoonhove, his son, stayed with Leonard *Casembroot at Padua in August 1525 (Ep 1594).

BIBLIOGRAPHY: Allen Ep 1214 / Paul van Peteghem 'Centralisatie in Vlaanderen onder Keizer Karel (1515–1555)' (thesis, Rijksuniversiteit Gent 1980) / *Matricule de Louvain* III-1 130

MARCEL A. NAUWELAERTS

Gisbert van SCHOONHOVE of Bruges, d 28 May 1524
Schoonhove (Sconhove, de Scoonovia, Schoonoven) matriculated at Cologne on 13 October 1489 under the name Gysbertus de Scoenhovia. He was a member of the chapter of St Donatian at Bruges from 1490, receiver in 1497, and precentor in 1514. He died at Bruges.

Erasmus must have met Schoonhove during his visits to Bruges. In 1519 or 1520 he sent greetings to the precentor through Jan van *Fevijn, another member of the cathedral chapter (Ep 1012).

BIBLIOGRAPHY: CWE Ep 1012 / *Matrikel Köln* II 269 / de Vocht CTL II 179

MARCEL A. NAUWELAERTS

Willem van SCHOONHOVE of Ghent, documented 1525–7
Willem was probably born at Ghent, the son of Cornelis van *Schoonhove and Johanna Anneron. He studied medicine at Padua, where in 1525 he was staying with Leonard *Casembroot (Ep 1594). On 17 August 1527 he matriculated at the University of Montpellier.

BIBLIOGRAPHY: *Matricule de Montpellier* 51

MARCEL A. NAUWELAERTS

Pieter de SCHOT of Ghent, documented c 1500–16
Schot (Schotte, Scotus) was master of a Latin school at Ghent, where Adrianus Cornelii *Barlandus was his pupil at the end of the fifteenth century and the beginning of the sixteenth. Barlandus mentioned him in his publications of 1512, praising him and his school. He was still writing to Pieter about November 1516 by way of his brother, Cornelius *Barlandus, who had also been taught by Pieter (Ep 492).

BIBLIOGRAPHY: Allen Ep 492 / A. Roersch in BNB XXII 19–21 / H. de Jongh *L'Ancienne Faculté de théologie de Louvain* (Louvain 1911) 122 / E. Daxhelet *Adrien Barlandus, humaniste belge, 1486–1538* (Louvain 1938) 241

MARCEL A. NAUWELAERTS

Johann SCHOTT of Strasbourg, 19 June 1477– c 1548
Johann Schott (Scottus, Scotus) was born into an old Strasbourg family whose members had

served on the city council since the thirteenth century. His paternal grandfather, Friedrich Schott, was a well-known sculptor, and his maternal grandfather was Johann Mentelin, the first Alsatian printer. His father, Martin, married Mentelin's youngest daughter and eventually inherited the Mentelin shop through his brother-in-law, Adolf Rusch. Johann, then, represented the third generation in the family business. Able, astute, and committed, he carried the business to new levels of productivity.

Johann received a good education. He matriculated at Freiburg in 1490 and then moved on to Heidelberg in 1492, receiving his BA the following year. He was at Basel in 1497 but received no degree. On the death of his father in 1499 he returned to Strasbourg to take over the printing business. He must have served part of his apprenticeship as a printer in the family shop or in Basel since by 1500 he had brought out a book under his own signature. From 1503 to 1504 he was apparently in Freiburg, publishing an edition of Gregor *Reisch's *Margarita philosophica*. In this early period he published humanist works and classical editions including texts in Greek, working closely with Ottmar *Nachtgall.

With the advent of the Reformation, Schott greatly increased his production. This was not a matter of mere profit. He began to print the work of *Luther and *Hutten when it was still dangerous to do so. He personally protected Otto *Brunfels and Michael Herr when they fled the Carthusian convent. Publishing the books of the reformers was to him a matter of profound religious commitment, and this brought him into sharp conflict with Erasmus. It began in 1522 when Schott published pieces by Luther and *Melanchthon which revealed Luther's judgment of Erasmus as being materialistic and lax in his religious views (*Iudicium D. Martini Lutheri de Erasmo ...*; a German version, 1523, also by Schott; Epp 1348, 1374, 1496). This was followed by an explosion over Hutten, who attacked Erasmus in his *Expostulatio* (1523). Hutten died shortly thereafter, but Erasmus insisted on replying to his dead opponent in a bitter and vehement tract, the *Spongia*. Otto Brunfels wrote a response to the *Spongia* which matched it in tone. Schott was

the printer of both Hutten's *Expostulatio* and Brunfels' defence. Erasmus was infuriated and complained to the Strasbourg town council in March 1524 (Ep 1429). In a second letter to the council, written in August (Ep 1477), Erasmus claimed that Brunfels and Schott had reacted with violent threats. Both were cited before the council, but there is no record of any decision. Erasmus' letters over the next few months reflect his obsession with the matter and his deep-seated hatred of Schott, who tried without success to have his side of the story presented to Erasmus (Epp 1459, 1496, 1934). At one point Erasmus was convinced that it all stemmed from Schott's jealousy of Johann *Froben (Ep 1437). Six years later he jumped to the conclusion that another attack from Strasbourg had again been printed by Schott (Epp 2293, 2441).

After the tumultuous years of the early Reformation, Schott became increasingly interested in scientific publication. He created a team of natural scientists and artists to print Otto Brunfels' important work on botany. Since the last book issued by his press is dated 1548, it is assumed he died in that year.

BIBLIOGRAPHY: Allen Ep 1429 / ADB XXXII 402–4 / Benzing *Buchdrucker* 412 / Charles Schmitt *Martin et Jean Schott 1481–1499, 1500– 1545* (Strasbourg 1893) / Miriam U. Chrisman *Bibliography of Strasbourg Imprints, 1480–1599* (New Haven 1982) 415–16 and passim

MIRIAM U. CHRISMAN

SCHRIJVER *See Cornelius and Johannes GRAPHEUS*

Johann SCHUDELIN of Vaihingen, documented 1517–21
Johann Schudelin, from Vaihingen, northwest of Stuttgart, is documented only for his short tenure of office as headmaster of the Latin school at Memmingen from about January (or perhaps only from Christmas) 1517. On 15 April 1521 he received leave to enter into a contract with the nearby abbey of Ottobeuren, as of Michaelmas (29 September). Subsequent efforts to retain him at Memmingen were apparently unsuccessful, and on 14 August 1521 one Paul Höpp was hired to take over Schudelin's position at Michaelmas. Schude-

lin's name is not found in the Memmingen tax register of 1521. Erasmus sent Schudelin a complimentary letter (Ep 1234) at the suggestion of Gabriel *Stendelin.

BIBLIOGRAPHY: Allen Ep 1234 / H. Schallhammer 'Das Schulwesen der Reichsstadt Memmingen von den Anfängen bis 1806' *Memminger Geschichtsblätter 1962* (1963) 12, 77; *Memminger Geschichtsblätter 1964* (1965) 16, 60 / Additional data from the MS 'Ratsprotokoll' of Memmingen were kindly supplied by Uli Braun, *Heimatpfleger* of the city of Memmingen.

PGB

Georg SCHULER See Georgius SABINUS

Peter SCHUMACHER See Harmen SCHOENMAKER

Valentin SCHUMANN of Leipzig, d 1542

Schumann (Valentinus Dammander) was the son of a Leipzig burgher and was himself admitted to citizenship in 1514. From 1513 to his death he published a large number of books from his press, which was located in the Ritterstrasse except for the peak years of his activity, 1522–31, when he occupied larger premises in the Grimmischen Gasse. With an eye to the needs of the local university community he printed both classical and humanist authors. From 1518 to 1521 he also published works by *Luther and such sympathizers of Luther as *Hutten and *Oecolampadius; thereafter he avoided reformed authors. For a period in 1524 and 1525 he may have left Leipzig to operate a press that Hieronymus *Emser had set up in Dresden for the dissemination of his own writings. After Schumann's death the Leipzig press was continued for a short while by his heirs, including one Joachim Schumann, presumably his son.

In 1515 Emser induced Schumann to reprint Erasmus' *Enchiridion*, which was then in short supply in Saxony (Ep 553); Schumann reprinted his own edition in 1519. In 1516 he reprinted from Dirk *Martens' first edition Erasmus' Epp 333–5, 337 and in 1519 Erasmus' Latin version of the New Testament. Above all, however, the *Short-Title Catalogue* identifies him as the anonymous printer of the first edition of Erasmus' *Axiomata pro causa Lutheri* in 1521 (Ep 1155). In 1522 he reprinted German versions of

the gospels of Matthew and John and the Epistle to the Galatians that were based on Erasmus' Latin translation.

BIBLIOGRAPHY: ADB XXXIII 57–9 / Benzing *Buckdrucker* 262, 264 / *Short-Title Catalogue of Books Printed in German-speaking Countries … from 1455 to 1600* (London 1962) 284 / Heinz Holeczek *Erasmus Deutsch* (Stuttgart-Bad Cannstatt 1983–) I 52–5, 122–3, 288, and passim

PGB

Heinrich SCHÜRER of Waldshut, documented 1526–44

In 1526 Bonifacius *Amerbach described to Erasmus the plight of one Heinrich Schürer, and in Epp 1689, 1690 (cf Epp 1709, 1710) Erasmus made a vigorous effort to support the young man's case at the court of King *Ferdinand. Schürer had lost two properties in the aftermath of disturbances at Waldshut, on the Rhine above Basel, in 1524 and 1525 which resulted from a convergence of peasant war and Anabaptist preaching and ended with severe repression and punishment by the Hapsburg government. Schürer took his case to Ensisheim, the seat of the Hapsburg regional administration and law court, evidently without success. He also accepted a loan from Amerbach which he was slow to repay. It is conceivable that he worked at this time for the Froben press, which would help explain Erasmus' zeal for his cause. In 1530 he invited Bonifacius, his brother Basilius *Amerbach, and Gertrud *Lachner, the wife of Johann *Froben, to attend his first mass at Säckingen, Baden, signing himself chaplain at Säckingen. It seems that even then he was still trying to obtain satisfaction from the Hapsburg government and was again asking Erasmus to help him, although now with little success (Epp 2326, 2331, 2344). In 1543 he was parish priest at Bremgarten, Aargau, and in 1544 chaplain at Baden, Aargau.

BIBLIOGRAPHY: AK III Epp 1104, 1484, V Ep 2572, VI Ep 2629 / For the events at Waldshut: Baumann 'Zur Geschichte der Stadt Waldshut 1526–30' *Zeitschrift für Geschichte des Oberrheins* 34 (1882) 313–41 and J. Loserth 'Die Stadt Waldshut und Vorder-Österreichische Regierung in den Jahren 1523–1526' *Archiv für Österreichische Geschichte* 77 (1891) 1–149

PGB

Matthias SCHÜRER of Sélestat, d before
March 1520
Matthias Schürer (Schurerius) was born in
Sélestat by 1470. His mother's sister, Katharina
Dammerer, was married to the Strasbourg
printer Martin (I) Flach. Her second marriage
was to Johann (I) Knobloch, another Strasbourg printer. After attending the Sélestat
grammar school, Matthias went on to the
University of Cracow, earning his BA in 1491,
and his MA in 1494. By 1500 he was in
Strasbourg serving as apprentice to his cousin
Martin (II) Flach, who had taken on the
printing shop after his father's death. Schürer
continued his training under Johann (I) Prüss
between 1504 and 1506 and Knobloch between
1506 and 1508. Then, his seven-year apprenticeship completed, he opened his own press
and book store. In the brief twelve years which
were left to him he made the literature of
classical Rome available in the city. In the
previous twenty years only 16 editions of the
Greek and Latin classics had been printed in
Strasbourg, whereas Schürer printed 101 editions of Greek and Latin authors and an equal
number of works by contemporary humanists.
A member of the literary society, he provided
the materials needed by the humanists and
helped to kindle the interest of educated
laymen in the ancient world.

Schürer's choice of classical authors was
influenced in part by his own tastes. He had an
obvious bias towards poets and historians,
publishing Horace, Virgil, eleven editions of
Ovid, Cornelius Nepos, Suetonius, and Sallust. He was the first Strasbourg printer to
publish Cicero (seventeen editions) and also
printed Pliny the Younger.

In 1509, only a year after he had established
his own press, he began to publish works by
Erasmus, beginning with an unauthorized
edition of the Adagia (Allen I 17). Despite this
boldness he enjoyed a pleasantly supportive
relationship with Erasmus; indeed after the
Strasbourg banquet in 1514 Erasmus described
him as a man to whom he was much attached
(Ep 305). In the preface to Schürer's edition of
De copia (1514) Erasmus commended Schürer
because he was willing to print books for the
use of the scholarly community without
thought of profit (Ep 311; cf Reedijk poem 98).
At the same time Erasmus entrusted him with

the first edition of the Parabolae (Ep 312), and in
the spring of 1515 they enjoyed each other's
company when travelling together from Strasbourg to Frankfurt (Epp 326B, 328, 330).

In answer to repeated requests for fresh
printer's copy (Epp 369, 383, 612) Erasmus
wrote in July 1517 that he regretted he had
nothing to give Schürer for publication at that
time (Ep 606). In August Erasmus decided to
give him his revised text of Quintus Curtius
(Epp 633, 693). The following spring Erasmus
wrote Johann *Froben that if he did not want to
print the Enchiridion, he was to send it to
Schürer (Ep 795). Erasmus gave his work to no
other Strasbourg printer during Schürer's
lifetime, and the latter had a virtual monopoly
on Erasmian publication in the city. Unfortunately Schürer's planned edition of Rodolphus
*Agricola, to which Erasmus attached great
importance, never materialized (Epp 311, 606,
612, 633).

Schürer's career was cut short. In 1518
Erasmus was concerned by his ill health (Epp
801, 883); by early 1520 he was dead. He was a
scholar who had mastered the new technology
to serve his fellow humanists.

BIBLIOGRAPHY: Allen Ep 224 / Benzing
Buchdrucker 413 / Grimm Buchführer 1448–9 /
François Ritter Histoire de l'imprimerie alsacienne
(Strasbourg-Paris 1955) 160–70 / Miriam U.
Chrisman 'Le métier et la main: Mathias
Schürer, humaniste-imprimeur' in Grandes Fi-
gures de l'humanisme alsacien (Strasbourg 1978)
159–72 / Miriam U. Chrisman Bibliography of
Strasbourg Imprints, 1480–1599 (New Haven
1982) 416–17 and passim

MIRIAM U. CHRISMAN

Engelbert Ysbrantz SCHUT of Leiden,
died c 1503
Engelbert Schut (Enghelbertus or Engbardus
Leydensis), who was probably born around
1410, matriculated in 1435 at Cologne in the
faculty of arts, was a BA on 18 May 1436, a
licentiate on 5 April 1438, and a MA probably
soon afterwards. His subsequent whereabouts
are unknown until 29 January 1458, when he
was appointed rector of the Leiden municipal
school. From 1464 he was the headmaster of
another Leiden school of lesser importance,
the so-called bijschool. When he stopped
teaching in 1483, the town government contin-

ued to avail itself of his knowledge of Latin for the composition of official documents.

Schut corresponded with Wessel *Gansfort, with whom he may have gone to school at Zwolle. His most gifted pupil was Jacob Hoeck, twice rector of the University of Cologne and later dean of Naaldwijk. It has long been thought that Schut was the father of the painter Cornelis Engelbrechts, but Bangs casts doubt on the assumption. Schut was the author of the poem *De moribus mense* and of a *De pane dyalogus*, published with Petrus de Rivo's *Libellus quo modo omnia in meliorem partem sunt interpretanda* (Leiden: Jan Seversz 20 March 1509; NK 1708). He also wrote a 'Tractatus metricus de locis rhetoricis' which is perhaps identical with the section 'De locis rhetoricis' in *De arte dictandi* (Gouda: G. Leeu c 1480).

Erasmus praised Schut lavishly in a poem of around 1488–9 (Reedijk poem 11; cf Ep 28) and in a contemporary letter to Cornelis *Gerard (Ep 29). This apparently failed to have the desired effect, and much later in *De conscribendis epistolis* (ASD I-2 231) he showed contempt for Schut's medieval learning. Reedijk suggested that Erasmus perhaps had Schut in mind when writing the *Conflictus Thaliae et Barbariei* (LB I 893–4), where Barbaries is associated with the Zwolle school.

BIBLIOGRAPHY: Allen and CWE Ep 28 / F.S. Knipscheer in NNBW IX 593–4 / M. van Rhijn *Studiën over Wessel Gansfort en zijn tijd* (Utrecht 1933) 127–34 / Reedijk poem 11 and p 383 / J.D. Bangs *Cornelis Engelbrechtsz.'s Leiden. Studies in Cultural History* (Assen 1979) 10

C.G. VAN LEIJENHORST

Johann Jakob SCHUTZ von Traubach of Ensisheim, d 28 November 1524

Johann Jakob Schutz (Schütz) von Traubach was born into a noble family in Ensisheim, Alsace; his father was secretary of the archives there. On 24 March 1511 he matriculated at the University of Freiburg with his brother Johann Wolfgang, and two years later he graduated BA. Later he was probably forced to leave his home town because of his religious beliefs. In July 1523 he established himself in Sélestat, living with a former nun. From the moment of his arrival he was in debt.

Whether from conviction or from self-interest, Schutz was determined to establish Lutheranism in Sélestat, despite the firm efforts of the burgomaster, Melchior *Ergesheimer, to maintain the Catholic faith. Schutz was in league with one of the priests, Paulus *Phrygio, the rector of the school; Lazarus Schürer, the printer; and Sebastian Rosenhammer, a goldsmith. He outlined a plan to them which would create discontent and discredit Ergesheimer, thus clearing the way for the reform.

Schutz proceeded to forge an exchange of letters between Ergesheimer and the Hapsburg governor in Ensisheim. The first letter had Ergesheimer describing the growth of a Lutheran group in Sélestat, naming Schürer, Rosenhammer, Phrygio, and Schutz as the leaders. The next had the governor agreeing that the movement must be stopped and suggesting that Austrian troops be allowed to enter the city to extirpate the heresy, and the third had Ergesheimer agreeing. Having manufactured his evidence, Schutz then showed the letters to Lutheran sympathizers in Sélestat and, more important, to influential persons in Strasbourg, including Wolfgang *Capito. Capito reported to the Strasbourg council that the governor at Ensisheim planned to persecute the Lutherans and besiege Strasbourg.

Schürer and Rosenhammer, frightened by the fact that they might be implicated, revealed the forgery to Ergesheimer. Legal procedures were begun and a careful study of the authenticity of the documents was made. Ergesheimer, who had been in prison during most of the investigation, was declared innocent of all charges, and in November 1524 Schutz was executed by decapitation, then quartered. Erasmus mentioned his fate in connection with his quarrel with *Eppendorf over the authenticity of one of his own letters (Ep 1992; *Admonitio adversus mendacium* LB X 1688C–D).

BIBLIOGRAPHY: Allen Ep 1992 / Paul Adam *Histoire religieuse de Sélestat* (Sélestat 1967–75) I 186–92 / *Matrikel Freiburg* I 196

MIRIAM U. CHRISMAN

Philipp von SCHWALBACH 1503–after 1527

Philipp von Schwalbach was descended from a noble family from the Rhineland whose estates were located to the east of Wiesbaden. His parents were Johann von Schwalbach zu Niederhofheim and Niederulmen and Brigitta Wambold von Umstadt; his wife was Margarethe von Mittelbach. On 17 March 1523 Schwalbach was appointed assessor at the law court of the archbishop of Mainz. From 7 June 1525 he was assistant steward (*Untervizedom*) of the Mainz chapter, while the *Vizedom* (*Wiztum*) was Martin von Heusenstamm. Schwalbach probably still held the same position in April 1527 when Henricus *Caduceator informed Erasmus that he was living in Schwalbach's house as tutor to his five children (Ep 1811).

BIBLIOGRAPHY: Johannes Maximilian Humbracht *Die höchste Zierde Teutsch-Landes und Vortrefflichkeit des Teutschen Adels* (Frankfurt 1767) no 271 / *Die Protokolle des Mainzer Domkapitels* ed Fritz Herrmann (Paderborn 1924–32) III 351 / Valentin Ferdinand von Gudenus *Codex diplomaticus anecdotorum res Moguntinas ... illustrantium* (Göttingen 1743–68) I 945   KONRAD WIEDEMANN

Kaspar SCHWALBE *See Kaspar* SCHALBE

Alexander SCHWEISS of Herborn, d 1533–6
Alexander Schweiss (Schweis) was born at Herborn, in Hesse, apparently of a modest family. The year of his birth is not known, nor is the course of studies he pursued. In 1511 he is documented for the first time as secretary to the council of the Landgraviate of Hesse; according to his own statements he had entered the service of a prince, presumably the landgrave of Hesse, by 1504. By 1516 at the latest he became secretary to Henry III of *Nassau-Dillenburg, part of whose ancient family estates were in the immediate vicinity of Schweiss' birthplace; as a prominent Hapsburg dignitary in the Netherlands, Henry came to enjoy the personal confidence of *Charles v. Schweiss accompanied his master on many journeys and campaigns and won his esteem and trust. For several years he exchanged frequent letters with Henry's brother, William (the Rich) of Nassau, and with Willibald *Pirckheimer.

Schweiss' great familiarity with the affairs of Germany combined with his knowledge of languages led to quick advancement after he had gone to Spain with his influential master in

1522. On 24 July 1523 the emperor raised him to noble status and the following year he joined Charles' chancery as a secretary. In 1529 and 1530 he followed the imperial court to Italy and subsequently to the diet of Augsburg, where as Henry of Nassau's protégé he wielded influence out of proportion with his secretarial rank. In the summer of 1529 he played a prominent role in the litigation between Hesse and Nassau concerning the succession in the county of Katzenelnbogen. Later that year he joined Henry of Nassau in efforts to remove obstacles from the course of an embassy dispatched by the Protestant estates to present their case to the emperor. At the diet he was chosen to translate the Augsburg Confession into French and to read before the assembly the Catholic 'Confutatio' in reply to the confession. It seems that after the diet he committed himself unequivocally to the side of the Catholic forces. In the course of his years in the imperial chancery Schweiss earned many rewards and proofs of Charles' favour; as a result he was well-to-do when he left the court in 1533. It is not clear whether he lived for three more years in retirement, as is sometimes claimed. He was married to Barbara von Siegburg who bore him several daughters.

It seems that Erasmus and Schweiss maintained sporadic contact (Ep 1119). In March of 1521 Erasmus chose Schweiss as the recipient of a carefully worded letter, no doubt written in the hope of reaching Henry of Nassau and other members of the imperial government (Ep 1192). In this letter he endeavoured to explain his own difficult position between the Lutheran reformers and the conservative theologians and also to convince the court of the need to prevent further polarization in the religious dispute. In 1530 Schweiss signed on behalf of the emperor a letter patent acknowledging Erasmus' capacity to make a will (Ep 2318). Petrus *Apianus mentioned Schweiss in the preface of his *Quadrans astronomicus* (Ingolstadt 1532).

BIBLIOGRAPHY: Allen Ep 1192 / F. Otto in ADB XXXIII 365–6 / F. Otto in *Annalen des Vereins für Nassauische Altertumskunde und Geschichtsforschung* 28 (1896) 340 / Otto Meinardus *Der katzenelnbogische Erbfolgestreit* (Wiesbaden 1899–1902) passim (containing Schweiss' correspondence with William of Nassau and his letters of nobility) / T.M. Roest van Limburg in *Kunstkroniek* n s 14 (1905–6) 18–24

ALBRECHT LUTTENBERGER

Philipp SCHWITZER of Montbéliard, died c 8 February 1529

On 13 April 1529 Erasmus wrote from Basel to his friend Ludwig *Baer, who had recently preceded him in moving to Freiburg, offering him a notable account of the last few months in the life of an unnamed Anabaptist (Ep 2149). This man, for whom Erasmus shows little sympathy, was Philipp Schwitzer of Montbéliard (Mömpelgard), in the Franche Comté; conceivably he was of Swiss descent. According to the unpublished record of Schwitzer's trial at Lucerne (8 February 1529), he was a priest who had adopted Anabaptist views three years earlier and had subsequently baptized others, including some eight fellow priests. According to Erasmus he had been imprisoned for some time in Montbéliard before he appeared in Basel at the height of the agitation that ended with the suppression of Catholic worship. The judicial records of Basel confirm Erasmus' report that Schwitzer's public calls for penance in the city streets led to his arrest. He seems to have admitted his Anabaptist views freely, and he refused to swear the required 'Urfehde.' On 27 January he was released under threat of immediate execution if he were ever to be caught again in Basel. He showed considerable courage in moving on to Lucerne, a city noted for its staunch Catholicism. There he repeated his public appeals for penance and again stood firmly by his views in the following trial. He was executed by drowning.

BIBLIOGRAPHY: Willy Brändly 'Täuferprozesse in Luzern im XVI. Jahrhundert' *Zwingliana* 8 (1944–8) 65–78, esp 70–2 / *Aktensammlung zur Geschichte der Basler Reformation* ed E. Dürr et al (Basel 1921–50) III 261–3 / P.G. Bietenholz 'Erasmus and the Anabaptists' *Erasmus in English* 2 (1971) 8   PGB

Christoph SCHYDLOWITZ *See Krzysztof SZYDŁOWIECKI*

Giovann'Angelo SCINZENZELER of Milan, documented 1500–26

Giovann'Angelo was the son of Ulrich Scin-

zenzeler, so called after his home town of Zinzenzell, in Bavaria, who began to print books at Milan in 1477, often under contract with Lombard publishers such as Giovanni Da Legnano. Giovann'Angelo is first documented in 1500 as a bookseller in connection with a dispute between himself and the Greek scholar Demetrius *Chalcondyles, who appealed to Duke Ludovico *Sforza. At about that time Giovann'Angelo also took charge of his father's press; in fact his name is found for the first time in the colophon of Niccolò Tedeschi's *Lectura super quinque libros Decretalium*, 20 June 1500, which he printed for Giovanni Da Legnano. Until 1522 he continued to work for the publishing firm of the Da Legnano family, printing 120 volumes for them, while his total production amounted to 227 books, for the most part legal text books for the use of universities. Giovann'Angelo's press was most active in the years 1500 to 1513; afterwards his production declined both in numbers and in quality. The list of his titles reflects the tastes prevailing at the time, especially among the educated public. It includes Italian and Latin classics, tales of chivalry, legal volumes, and also works of religious orientation such as books of devotion, missals, and writings by Iacopo da Varazze, Isidorus de *Isolanis, Girolamo *Savonarola, Teodoro da Suigo, and Luigi Bigi Pittorio. In 1506 and again in 1512 he printed for the Da Legnano the *Libellus proverbiorum* (Balsamo nos 53, 100), a collection of classical adages gathered by Polidoro *Virgilio and edited by the priest Pollio Gerus Vadius (Ep 1175). The last works positively identifiable as his are an edition of Ludovico *Ariosto's *Orlando furioso* (30 May 1526) and Olimpo Baldassare degli Alessandri's *Linguaccio* (June 1526). No more is heard of him thereafter.

BIBLIOGRAPHY: Allen Ep 1175 / ADB XXXIII 478 / L. Balsamo *Giovann'Angelo Scinzenzeler tipografo a Milano (1500–1526)* (Florence 1959) / *Storia di Milano* (Milan 1953–62) VII 879, X 865 / P. Ascarelli *La tipografia cinquecentina in Italia* (Florence 1953) 81   ANNA GIULIA CAVAGNA

SCOPEGIUS (Epp 2321, 2615 of 1530–2)

A certain Scopegius was believed by Erasmus to be one of the authors of Martin *Bucer's *Epistola apologetica*.

SCOPUS (Ep 103 of the summer of 1499) 'Scopus' is perhaps a nickname for one of Erasmus' friends at Paris, 'suddenly converted from a poet to a soldier.' He may also be mentioned in Ep 95. No identification has been proposed.

SCOTTUS, SCOTUS *See Pieter de* SCHOT, *Johann* SCHOTT

SCRIBONIUS *See Cornelius and Johannes* GRAPHEUS

Paulus SCRIPTORIS of Weil der Stadt, d 1504 Paulus Scriptoris was born in Weil der Stadt, west of Stuttgart. He studied in Paris and became warden of the Franciscan monastery of Tübingen as well as a lecturer in the faculty of arts. In addition to more conventional topics he lectured on Ptolemy, Euclid, and the use of the astrolabe. In 1499 he designed a globe for Johann von *Dalberg. Conradus *Pellicanus, who came to Tübingen in 1495, became his favourite student and always remembered him with gratitude (Ep 1638). *Staupitz and *Eck were also among his students. He was still warden in 1499 but shortly thereafter was suspended from his offices on account of unorthodox statements on matters of doctrine. Pellicanus later perceived a resemblance between his position and that of *Luther. In 1501 he was transferred to Basel. Fearing arrest, he went in 1502 to Vienna and Rome. After his safe return he was in Heilbronn and was to be sent to Toulouse as lecturer of theology, but before he could go there the bishop of Basel, Christoph von *Utenheim, sent him to Schussenried, in Alsace, to reorganize the Benedictine monastery of St Alban. On his way there he died in Kaysersberg.

Scriptoris' only publication is a commentary on John Duns Scotus' commentary on Peter Lombard: *Lectura* ... (Tübingen: J. Otmar 1498).
BIBLIOGRAPHY: Allen Ep 1638 / ADB XXXIII 488–9   IG

Lucas SCUPPEGIUS documented 1521–34 Very little is known about Lucas Scuppegius (perhaps Lukas Schüpgen or Tschiek), who in 1521 was a judge in Jáchymov (Joachimsthal), the famous mining centre in Bohemia. He also was the town's burgomaster in 1523, 1525, and

1527. In 1525 he was arrested by the rebelling miners. He is mentioned in Erasmus' correspondence with two other prominent inhabitants of Jáchymov: in 1529 Petrus *Plateanus mentioned Scuppegius' devotion to Erasmus and urged Erasmus to send him greetings in his reply (Ep 2216); subsequently Erasmus did send his compliments to him when writing to Georgius *Agricola (Epp 2529, 2918).
BIBLIOGRAPHY: Allen Ep 2216 / G. Agricola *Ausgewählte Werke* ed H. Prescher et al (Berlin 1955–) II 324   MICHAEL ERBE

SEBASTIANUS (Ep 2554 of 9 October 1531) It has not been possible to identify Sebastianus, whose premature death, evidently at Freiburg, is mourned in this letter from Anselmus *Ephorinus. Presumably he was the friend and neighbour of Erasmus whose death is mentioned in Ep 2555.

Andreas SEBRIDARIUS *See Andrzej* ZEBRZYDOWSKI

William SEILING *See William* SALYNG

SELIM I Ottoman Sultan, d 20 September 1520 Selim I (Selimus, Zelimus), known as *Yavuz Sultan Selim*, or Selim the Grim, was the son of *Bayezid II and Aisha Khatun, the daughter of Ala'al-Daula, ruler of the Dhu'l Kadr, in Kurdistan. He was born in 1467/8 or 1470/1. Towards the end of Bayezid's reign he was the governor of Trebizond. As Bayezid was ageing, a struggle for the succession developed between Selim and his brother Ahmed. Bayezid himself favoured Ahmed, but with the support of the janissaries Selim forced his father to abdicate on 24 April 1512, an event reported by Erasmus in *De bello turcico* (LB V 352A).

In the first year of his reign, Selim eliminated his brothers and nephews. He then turned to the east, where Shah Ismail, the head of the religious order known as the *Safawiyya*, had made himself the master of Persia, and where the rapid progress of Shi'ism was threatening the very existence of the Ottoman Empire. Selim, who had a personal grievance against Ismail for supporting Ahmed, first rounded up the Shi'ites in his own empire, killing or imprisoning forty thousand. He then declared

Selim 1

war on Ismail and utterly routed his forces at Çaldiran on 23 August 1514, entering Tabrīz on 5 September.

In 1515 the Ottomans conquered eastern Anatolia and Kurdistan, and Selim personally took Kemah in May. Annoyed by the un-cooperative attitude of the aged Ala'al-Daula, his grandfather, during the march against Ismail, Selim sent an army against him. Ala'al-Daula was killed, his sons captured and executed, and his lands incorporated into the Ottoman Empire.

After the Battle of Çaldiran, the beys of Kurdistan declared for Selim, and the towns and citadels still remaining in Persian hands were captured during 1515 and early 1516. Selim's successes and especially his annexation of the Dhu'l Kadr had altered the balance of power in this region and made war between the Ottomans and their Mameluke neighbours inevitable. In the summer of 1516 the Mame-luke sultan, Kānsūh al-Gauri, arrived with a large army at Aleppo, intending to support Ismail and recover Marash. Selim marched against him and, having defeated the Egyp-tians at Mardj Dābik, north of Aleppo, on 24

August 1516, annexed Syria. Kānsūh himself was killed. Selim offered Tuman Bay, the new Mameluke sultan, peace on condition that he accept Ottoman suzerainty, but the Mameluke reaction caused Selim to resume war. His army defeated an Egyptian army at Gaza on 31 September 1516, but the decisive battles, in which both Selim and Tuman Bay participated, took place at Rīdānīyya and Cairo (23–30 January 1517) and gained Egypt for Selim (Ep 729). In Cairo Selim received the submission of the sharif of Mecca, and henceforth Ottoman sultans bore the prestigious title of *Khādim al-Haramaīn al-Sharifain*. Among the hostages sent to Istanbul was al-Mutawakkil, the last Abbasid caliph, who was later interned until after Selim's death. There is no basis for the tradition that al-Mutawakkil had formally renounced the caliphate in Selim's favour: the latter had in any case been called caliph even before the conquest of Egypt.

From the outset Selim had given priority to the situation in the east and throughout his reign maintained peaceful relations with the European states. His vast conquests of Muslim lands altered the religious and political balance of the Ottoman Empire, making it the great Sunni power in opposition to Shi'ite Persia.

Selim had spent 1517 and the early part of 1518 in Egypt and Syria, returning to Istanbul in July 1518. Meanwhile two Shi'ite uprisings had to be suppressed: that of Ibn Hanush in Syria and that of Shah Veli near Tokat. In Istanbul the equipment of a great fleet, intended for the conquest of Rhodes, was begun, but before the preparations were complete Selim died suddenly on 20 September 1520. Harsh and warlike by nature, Selim was also a celebrated poet, his *diwan* being entirely in Persian.

BIBLIOGRAPHY: Allen Ep 729 / M. Süreyya *Sicill-i Osmânî* (Istanbul 1890–7) / J.H. Kramers in *Encyclopaedia of Islam* (Leiden-London 1913–38) IV 214–17 / S. Altundağ in *Islam Ansiklopedisi* (Istanbul 1940–) x 423–34 / S. Tansel *Yavuz Sultan Selim* (Ankara 1969)

FEHMI ISMAIL

Jean de SELVE sieur de Cormières, 1475–10 December 1529
Selve (Selva) was born at La Roche-Canillac, sixteen kilometres south-east of Tulle (Cor-

rèze) in the Bas Limousin, where the family had been established since the fourteenth century. He served in a number of judicial and diplomatic posts under *Louis XII and *Francis I. We hear of him first as a councillor in the Parlement of Toulouse. In 1499 he went to the Parlement of Normandy, of which he became *premier président* in 1507. In 1514 he was charged by Louis XII with the task of restoring relations with England and negotiating Louis' marriage to *Mary Tudor. As reward for his success he was appointed *premier président* of the Parlement of Bordeaux. He was sent back to England to renew the treaty after the accession of Francis I (1 January 1515). After the victory of Marignano (13 September 1515) he was appointed vice-chancellor of the duchy of Milan, and he remained in this post until the loss of Milan in 1520. Then he became *premier président* of the Parlement of Paris (17 December 1520), which he remained until his death in December 1529. In this capacity he presided over the treason trials of Semblançay and Bourbon. The probity of Selve is an argument (Clément-Simon) against those who have asserted that both were victims of the malevolence of the king's mother, Louise of *Savoy.

After the king's capture at Pavia (24 February 1525) Selve found himself at the centre of negotiations for Francis' release. In a speech before the combined chambers of the Parlement (22 March) he pointed out that what was at stake was the public welfare, the preservation of a monarchy and of a realm (Paris, Archives Nationales MS Reg. Parl. x^{1a} 1527, f 229 recto). Subsequently his role was to seek accommodation between the regent, who was attempting to maintain the royal authority in the name of her son, and the Parlement, which sought to reclaim its position as the supreme court of royal justice and wished to reverse royal tendencies toward absolutism.

Evidently Selve gained the regent's confidence, for she sent him and *Tournon to Spain to negotiate the treaty of peace that would liberate Francis. The major stumbling block was *Charles V's claim to Burgundy. As the jurist of the embassy, Selve argued that Burgundy was an inalienable part of France. When it became clear that Charles would not sign a treaty unless it included the surrender of Burgundy, Francis made a secret declaration in the presence of Selve and Tournon, just a few hours before signing the treaty of Madrid (14 January 1526), that the cession would be null and void.

Back on French soil (17 March 1526), Francis kept Selve at his side as one of his privy councillors. He was involved in the negotiation of the League of Cognac (signed 22 May) against Charles V, and when in December 1527 Francis consulted an assembly of notables, it was Selve who, as spokesman for the judiciary, argued that the king was in no way obliged to fulfil the terms of the treaty of Madrid, which had been extorted under duress (Clément-Simon 115–17). Upon the conclusion of the new period of hostilities Selve was again a member of the French delegation for the negotiation of peace. The peace of Cambrai, which confirmed the French possession of Burgundy (signed 5 August 1529), is known as the 'Ladies' Peace' because it was presided over by *Margaret of Austria and Louise of Savoy, but it should also be recognized as the fruit of the labours of devoted servants of the French crown, with Selve prominent among them.

Selve was evidently regarded by humanists as their advocate at court, if we may judge from the number of works dedicated to him, including a volume of *Alciati's *Dispunctiones* (Milan: A. Minuziano 1518), *Campester's *Apologia* against *Luther (Paris: S. de Colines 1523) and *Lefèvre's edition of the Psalter (Paris: S. de Colines 1524). It was at the suggestion of Nicolas *Bérault (Ep 1598) that Erasmus dedicated to Selve his *Apologia* (Basel: August 1525) against Pierre *Cousturier (Ep 1591), proposing that with the king a prisoner it should be Selve's role to sustain the cause of learning. The letters of many learned men, Erasmus added, convinced him that Selve was the only one who possessed not only the talent, knowledge, and power of discernment but also the natural goodness and courteous character to do so. Selve could hardly fulfil Erasmus' expectations while engaged in diplomatic negotiation in Spain, but as soon as he and the king were back in France (17 March 1526), Selve found himself in the middle of *Berquin's case, which Erasmus regarded as a test of the future of humane letters in France. The king had ordered the Parlement to release

Berquin. Parlement replied in a lengthy defence of its actions and asked Selve to explain
them to the king (Paris, Archives Nationales MS
Reg. Parl. x^{1a} 1529 f 199 verso, 9 April 1526).
We do not know what Selve's attitude to the
case may have been at this time, but at least he
was familiar with it when he found himself
among the twelve judges appointed by the
pope at the request of the king to hear
Berquin's appeal. The decision in this final trial
of Berquin was that he was a pertinacious
heretic, and he was sentenced to perpetual
imprisonment. Selve's name is first among
those who passed this sentence. When Berquin appealed, it was Selve, in his capacity of
premier président, who convened the Parlement
and presided over the deliberations which
ended in the death sentence (16 April 1529).
Selve himself died in the following December.

According to Allen, the *Tractatus de beneficio*
(Paris: F. Regnault n d) was Selve's only
publication, but mention should be made of his
memoir on Burgundy, reproduced in most of
the manuscripts recording the negotiations of
Madrid and Toledo in 1525, according to
Michel François (*Tournon* 39 n3). For the
assembly of notables see Théodore Godefroy
Le Cérémonial françois (Paris 1649) II 473–90,
including Selve's address of 20 December 1527.

BIBLIOGRAPHY: Allen Ep 1591 / Michel Fran-
çois *Le Cardinal François de Tournon* (Paris 1951)
34–43 and passim / *Correspondance politique de
Odet de Selve* ed Germain Lefèvre-Pontalis
(Paris 1888) xi–xiii / Germain Lefèvre-Pontalis
'Les de Selve, diplomates limousins du XVIe
siècle' *Bulletin de la Société des lettres, sciences et
arts de la Corrèze* 19 (1897) / G. Clément-Simon
'Un conseiller du roi François Ier, Jean de
Selve' *Revue des questions historiques* 73 (1903)
45–120 / *Le Journal d'un bourgeois de Paris* ed
V.-L. Bourrilly (Paris 1910) for frequent refer-
ences to Selve, and for text of the sentence
against Berquin in 1529, 423–7 / Paris, Archives
Nationales, MS Reg. Parl. x^{1a} 1527–9

GORDON GRIFFITHS

Juan Ginés de SEPÚLVEDA of Pozoblanco,
c 1490–17 November 1573
Juan Ginés de Sepúlveda was born in Pozoblanco, a small village near Córdoba. He was
the son of Ginés Sánchez Mellado and María
Ruiz, artisans of humble origins. Nothing is

known about him until he entered the
University of Alcalá, where he studied under
Sancho de Miranda between 1510 and 15
December 1513. He received his BA on 3
October 1511, and on 13 November 1512 he
became a theology student at the college for
poor students. In December 1513 Sepúlveda
received a scholarship for the College of San
Antonio at Sigüenza, and on 14 February 1515
Cardinal *Jiménez de Cisneros recommended
him for the Spanish college of Bologna, at
which he was accepted on 28 May 1515. He is
referred to then as a cleric, and we must
therefore assume that he received his first
orders while in Sigüenza.

In Bologna Sepúlveda studied under Pietro
*Pomponazzi and received his doctoral degree
in arts and theology shortly before 15 May
1523, when he referred to himself as a doctor
for the first time in his Latin translation of
Aristotle's *De generatione et interitu* (Rome). He
ceased to be a student on 23 June 1523. In
Bologna he enjoyed the friendship and patronage of Alberto *Pio, prince of Carpi, Ercole
Gonzaga, *Adrian VI, and above all Giulio de'
Medici, the future *Clement VII, who encouraged him in his task of translating Aristotle's
works. In 1522 at Bologna Sepúlveda had
dedicated to Giulio his edition of the *Parva
naturalia* of Aristotle (n p n d), in which he
explained to his patron the plan and objectives
of his Aristotelian translations. While still a
student Sepúlveda had also published a letter
addressed to Santiago Arteaga, rector of the
Spanish college, which had been included in
Fortunio García's *Commentarii ad Legem Gallus*
(Bologna 1517), and his *Liber gestorum Aegidii
Albornotii* (Bologna: H. de Benedictis 1521).

After leaving Bologna, Sepúlveda spent two
years commuting between Rome and Carpi,
where in the residence of his friend and patron
Alberto Pio he enjoyed the company and
friendship of Trifón de Bizancio, Pietro Pomponazzi, Juan Montes de Oca, Andrés Barro,
and many other leading scholars of the time.
On 19 August 1523 he published his *Dialogus de
appetenda gloria, qui inscribitur Gonsalus* (Rome:
M. Silber), and on the following day his
translation of Aristotle's *De mundo*, which he
dedicated to Ercole Gonzaga. By 1526 he had
become the official translator of Aristotle's
works for the papal court, and on July of that

same year he published at Rome *De fato et libero arbitrio*, attacking *Luther's propositions. As a complement to his Aristotelian translations, he published a translation of the commentaries of Alexander Aphrodisias (Rome: M. Silber 1527) dedicated to Clement VII. When the imperial troops sacked Rome, Sepúlveda took refuge in Naples, where he suffered the city's siege of May to September 1528, until he was called to Gaeta by Cardinal *Cajetanus.

On returning to Rome, Sepúlveda entered the service of Cardinal Francisco de *Quiñones, whom he accompanied on his mission to prepare for *Charles V's coronation as emperor in Bologna. Between August 1529 and February 1530 Sepúlveda followed the emperor on his journeys and was made a canon of Córdoba cathedral, resigning that position in 1533 to his nephew, Pedro de Sepúlveda. In 1529 Sepúlveda published his *Cohortatio ad Carolum V ut bellum suscipiat in Turcas* (Bologna: G.B. di Phaelli). In 1531 he published at Rome *De ritu nuptiarum et dispensatione* (also London: J. Cawood 1553) on *Henry VIII's divorce and the *Democrates primus, seu de convenientia militaris disciplinae cum christiana religione* (Rome: A. Bladus 1535), as well as translations of Aristotle's *Libri meteororum quatuor ... de animalibus ... de generatione et corruptione* (Paris 1532) and *Ethics* (1534).

In 1536 Sepúlveda's career took a new direction when he left the papal court and became the official chronicler and chaplain of Charles V, with a yearly honorarium of eighty thousand maravedies. In December he returned to Spain, where he resided either at the court or in Córdoba or Pozoblanco. He was occasionally called to serve as an adviser to the Inquisition, and in 1542 he was selected to be one of the tutors of Philip II. Although his translations of Aristotle ended with the publication of *De republica libri VIII* (Paris: M. de Vascosan 1548), he wrote many original works: *De ratione dicendi testimonium ... dialogus qui inscribitur Theophilus* (Valladolid 1538), *De correctione anni mensiumque Romanorum* (Venice: G. Giolito de' Ferrari 1546), and *De regno et officio regis* (Lérida: P. Robles 1570). His chronicles, *De rebus gestis Caroli V* and *Historia Philippi II*, were published in the four-volume edition of his works at Madrid in 1780. However, Sepúlveda is best known for his

polemics defending the Spanish conquest of America and subjugation of the Indians against Bartolomé de las Casas: *Democrates alter seu de justis belli causis*, published by M. Menéndez y Pelayo in 1892 and by A. Losada in 1951 (a Spanish ed: Seville: J. Cromberjer 1541), and *Apologia pro libro de justis belli causis* (Rome 1550). The first collection of his works was printed by Simon de Colines at Paris in 1541, and his *Epistolarum libri septem* were published in 1557 (Salamanca: J.M. de Terranova and J. Archario). He died at Pozoblanco and was buried in its parish church.

Erasmus first heard of Sepúlveda in the years 1526–8, probably as the author of *De fato et libero arbitrio* against Luther. In the *Ciceronianus*, first published in 1528, he mentioned the Spaniard as a scholar of considerable promise (ASD I-2 691). Later Sepúlveda would state that he was not entirely pleased with this reference, because he felt it was patronizing for a man who had already published many works and translations (Bataillon 407 n12). In the following years Erasmus heard rumours that Sepúlveda was assisting his patron Alberto Pio in the composition of a new attack on himself (Epp 2261, 2329, 2375). This attack was the *Tres et viginti libri in locos lucubrationum variarum D. Erasmi Rotterodami*, published in 1531 (Paris: J. Bade) after Pio's death. Erasmus replied with a vicious attack, the *Apologia adversus rhapsodias Alberti Pii* (Basel: H. Froben 1531). Sepúlveda came to the defence of his deceased patron, publishing the *Antapologia pro Alberto Pio* in 1532 (Rome: A. Bladus; Paris: A. Augereau) and sending it to Erasmus with Ep 2637, dated 1 April. The *Antapologia* dealt with Erasmus in a balanced, respectful manner, and the humanist responded with a conciliatory letter on 16 August (Ep 2701).

After these initial contacts, Erasmus and Sepúlveda exchanged several letters that were rather professional in tone, dealing with the transmission to Erasmus of the notes of his deceased opponent Diego *López Zúñiga and above all with exegetic and philological points concerning the Scriptures and the writings of the church Fathers (Epp 2729, 2873, 2905, 2938, 2951, 3096). Of particular interest are three letters (Epp 2873, 2905, 2938) on the Vatican Greek manuscript B of the Bible (Vaticanus 1209), the authenticity of which Sepúlveda

Michael Servetus

defended against the criticisms of Erasmus.

BIBLIOGRAPHY: Allen Ep 2637 / J. Mercier in DTC XIV 1905–7 / Angel Losada *Juan Ginés de Sepúlveda a través de su 'Epistolario' y nuevos documentos* (Madrid 1949) / Aubrey F.G. Bell *Juan Ginés de Sepúlveda* (Oxford 1924) / A. Morel-Fatio *Historiographie de Charles-Quint* (Paris 1913) 42–72 / Bataillon *Erasmo y España* 407–10, 421–5, 632–3, and passim

ARSENIO PACHECO

Michael SERVETUS of Villanueva di Sigena, c 1511–27 October 1553
Servetus (Miguel Servet, alias Revés) was a son of the notary Antón Servet and of Catalina Conesa, both of the old nobility. Between 1525 and 1526 he was in the service of Juan de Quintana, the future confessor of *Charles V. In 1528–9 he studied law at the University of Toulouse, but he returned to the service of Quintana and with him attended the coronation of the emperor at Bologna on 24 February 1530. From Bologna he travelled to Basel, where he stayed for more than six months at the house of *Oecolampadius, then to Strasbourg, where he was acquainted with Martin

*Bucer. In 1531 he published *De Trinitatis erroribus libri septem* (n p) at the press of Johann Setzer in Haguenau, but the work was condemned by the Swiss reformers and led to the initiation of procedures against him by the Inquisition of Saragossa and to an order for his capture by that of Toulouse. Erasmus, in a letter to Bucer of 2 March 1532 (Ep 2615), mentioned this work as the 'libellus de tribus personis.' In the opinion of Bataillon, Servetus attempted to submit his work to Erasmus, but the latter – who had much earlier been accused of sympathies for Arianism – hastened to make it known that there was nothing in common between the heretic Servetus and himself. In 1532 Servetus tried without success to allay criticism of his theological position in the more conciliatory *Dialogorum de Trinitate libri duo* (n p), also printed by Setzer.

Changing his name to Villanovanus (Villeneuve), Servetus then travelled to France, where he worked as a corrector for printing presses at Lyon. He prepared an edition of Ptolemy's *Geography* (Lyon: M. and G. Trechsel 1535) and, having met the physician and humanist Symphorien *Champier, defended him in an apology against Leonhard Fuchs ([Lyon] 1536). He also spent time at Paris, where he studied medicine and published a treatise on the use of syrups, the *Syruporum universa ratio* (Paris: S. de Colines 1537). He also lectured on astrology and published the *Apologetica disceptatio pro astrologia* [Paris 1538], which drew the ire of the Paris faculty of medicine and resulted in a trial to curb his teaching. Servetus then moved to Charlieu, where he practised medicine. In 1540 he returned to Lyon, where he began a second edition of the *Geography* (Vienne: G. Trechsel 1541) and an edition of Sante Pagnini's Latin translation of the Bible (Lyon: G. Trechsel 1542). In 1541 he settled in Vienne, where he served as physician to Archbishop Pierre Palmier.

In 1546 Servetus began an exchange of letters on theological issues with Jean Calvin, whom he had once contacted at Paris. When Calvin broke off his correspondence, Servetus completed his fundamental work, the *Christianismi restitutio*, published in secret by Balthazar Arnoullet at Vienne in 1552 or 1553. In addition to his theological views, the work contained an important section on the circulation of the blood. Denounced as a heretic by a close friend of Calvin, Servetus was imprisoned by the Inquisition at Vienne in 1553. He escaped on 7 April but was apprehended at Geneva on 13 August. With Calvin acting as his principal accuser, Servetus was tried and convicted of spreading heresy, and was burnt at the stake. His execution spurred Sebastianus Castellio to publish *De haereticis, an sint persequendi* ... (ostensibly Magdeburg: G. Rausch 1554, but in fact Basel: J. Oporinus 1554), thus igniting the greatest toleration controversy of the sixteenth century.

BIBLIOGRAPHY: Allen Ep 2615 / José Baron Fernandez *Miguel Servet: su vida y su obra* (Madrid 1970) / Bataillon *Erasmo y España* 427 and passim / Roland H. Bainton *Hunted Heretic: the Life and Death of Michael Servetus 1511–1553* (Boston 1953) / Jerome Triedman *Michael Servetus: A Case Study in Total Heresy* (Geneva 1978) / Bruno Becker *Autour de Michel Servet et de Sébastien Castellion* (Haarlem 1953) / John F. Fulton *Michael Servetus, Humanist and Martyr* (New York 1953) / E.M. Wilbur *A History of Unitarianism* (Cambridge, Mass, 1945) I 49–75, 113–85, and passim

MILAGROS RIVERA & TBD

Girolamo SESTOLA of Ferrara, documented 1516–34
Girolamo Sestola was a secretary of Alfonso I d'*Este, duke of Ferrara. In the summer of 1516 he was sent on a mission to England, and on his trip he met Erasmus (Ep 611). He was still attached to the court of Ferrara in 1534.

BIBLIOGRAPHY: CWE Ep 611 / A. Frizzi *Memorie per la storia di Ferrara* 2nd ed (Ferrara 1847–8) IV 278 / LP II 2117, 2149, and p 1472 / Bartolomeo Fontana *Renata di Francia, Duchessa di Ferrara* (Rome 1889–99) I 152–4, 181, 185

TBD

SEVENBERGEN *See Maximiliaan van* BERGEN

SEVERUS (Epp 1169, 1195, 1198, and 1271)
In letters to Agostino *Scarpinelli and Luigi *Marliano, dating from the time just before and during the diet of Worms in 1521, Erasmus sent greetings to a common friend referred to as Saeverus or Severus (Epp 1169, 1195, 1198). A year later Juan Luis *Vives mentioned a monk

named Severus as being tutor to the grandchildren of Fadrique *Alvarez de Toledo, duke of Alba (Ep 1271). Allen suggested that the monk, no doubt a Spaniard, might be identical with the friend of Scarpinelli and Marliano; all one can say is that the passage does not rule out the monk's presence at the imperial court. Nor does it seem likely that the Severus of Erasmus' acquaintance was Wolfgangus Severus (Schiverius, Schiefer) from the region of Linz, who was an admirer of Erasmus, a correspondent of *Beatus Rhenanus (1521) and Thomas *Blarer (1523), and a political agent for Archduke *Ferdinand. Appointed as tutor to the future Maximilian II, he lost his position at the court in 1539, perhaps in view of his friendship with *Melanchthon and *Camerarius.

BIBLIOGRAPHY: Allen Ep 1169 / BRE Ep 203 / *Blarer Briefwechsel* I Ep 62 / J.H. Zedler *Universal-Lexikon aller Wissenschaften und Künste* (Halle-Leipzig 1732–50) XXXVII 707 / J.G. Schelhorn *Ergötzlichkeiten* (Ulm-Leipzig 1762–4) I 89–94

PGB

Bona SFORZA *See* BONA *Sforza, queen of Poland*

Francesco II SFORZA duke of Milan,
4 February 1495–1 November 1535
Francesco II or Francesco Maria was the second son of Ludovico *Sforza, duke of Milan, and of Beatrice d'Este. After Ludovico was stripped of Milan and imprisoned by *Louis XII of France in 1500, Francesco and his elder brother, Massimiliano, were raised at Innsbruck by their cousin Bianca Maria Sforza, the wife of the Emperor *Maximilian I. In 1512 the French were defeated by the Swiss and Massimiliano became duke of Milan. However, the brothers' return to Milan was short-lived because *Francis I defeated the Swiss at Marignano in September 1515 and once again took the city. On 4 October Massimiliano renounced the duchy to Francis I, and Francesco became the Sforza claimant. In 1516 an effort by Cardinal Matthäus *Schiner and Galeazzo *Visconti to recover the duchy for him through a Swiss-imperial alliance failed. In November 1521, however, imperial and papal forces under Ferrante Francesco d'Avalos, marquis of Pescara, conquered Milan, and Francesco Sforza became duke, entering the city in April 1522.

Sforza was not happy with his lot as an

Francesco II Sforza

Charles at Bologna and adhered to a new league against the French (Ep 2726). On 13 October 1534 his ties with the emperor were strengthened when he married by proxy Christina, the daughter of *Christian II of Denmark and of Charles' sister *Isabella. However Christina was too young to have children, and on the death of Sforza a year later Milan was taken over directly by the imperial government.

Erasmus wrote to Sforza on 16 October 1535 asking him to repress the 'Bellum civile inter Ciceronianos et Erasmicos,' attributed to Gaudenzio *Merula (Ep 3064). On 7 November Petrus *Merbellius wrote to inform Erasmus of the duke's death (Ep 3070).

BIBLIOGRAPHY: Allen Ep 3064 / Gino Franceschini in *Storia di Milano* (Milan 1953–62) VIII 83–333 / Federico Chabod *Lo stato di Milano e l'impero di Carlo v* (Rome 1934; repr *Lo stato e la vita religiosa a Milano nell'epoca di Carlo v* 1971) 3–225 at 20–6 and passim / C.M. Ady *A History of Milan under the Sforza* (London 1907) 222–50 and passim / N. Guastella 'Tre pretesi delitti di Francesco II Sforza' *Archivio storico lombardo* 76 (1949) 115–67   TBD

apparent puppet of the Emperor *Charles v and began to conspire against him. In October 1525 Sforza's chancellor, Girolamo Morone, was arrested by the imperial commander, Pescara, after trying to win him over to a league against Charles. Imperial troops then besieged Sforza in the castle of Milan. Although he supported the League of Cognac against the emperor, on 24 July 1526 he surrendered his stronghold and fled to Venetian territory. After the Sack of Rome in May 1527 Sforza gathered French and Venetian troops and threatened Milan, but by April 1528 he had been abandoned by Venice and by his own commander. Although Charles v considered giving Milan to his brother King *Ferdinand or Federico *Gonzaga, among other candidates, he was persuaded by *Clement VII and Mercurino *Gattinara, the imperial chancellor, to reinstate Sforza, who was by then sickly and without an heir. Sforza met Charles at Bologna in November 1529 and after agreeing to make heavy payments to the imperial treasury was allowed to return to Milan under the watchful eyes of the imperial ambassador, Marino *Caracciolo. In February 1533 Sforza again met

Guido Ascanio SFORZA 25 November 1518–6 October 1564

Guido Ascanio, the first-born son of Bosio II Sforza, count of Santa Fiora, and Costanza, the illegitimate daughter of Cardinal Alessandro Farnese, the future Pope *Paul III, was born at Rome. He studied at Bologna and on 18 December 1534, when he was only sixteen, was created cardinal with his cousin Alessandro *Farnese by the recently elected Paul III. Richly endowed with benefices, he became bishop of Parma on 13 August 1535, legate to Bologna and the Romagna in March 1537, papal chamberlain on 22 October 1537, legate to Hungary in 1540, and patriarch of Alexandria on 6 April 1541. When Cardinal Farnese was on diplomatic missions Sforza, called the cardinal of Santa Fiora, often replaced him in the direction of affairs of state and official correspondence. In the conclaves of 1550–5 he was the leader of the pro-Spanish faction. He was briefly imprisoned by the anti-Spanish Pope *Paul IV in August and September 1555. Later he was a force behind the election of Pius IV and the destruction of the Carafa family.

Ludovico Sforza

Gian Galeazzo Sforza, nephew of Ludovico Sforza

Conradus *Goclenius mentioned the elevation of Sforza and Farnese to the cardinalate in a letter to Erasmus (Ep 2998).

Sforza was noted as a patron of artists and humanists. He developed a large personal library, founded an academy at his palace, and constructed a chapel at Santa Maria Maggiore.

BIBLIOGRAPHY: Allen Ep 2998 / EI XXXI 573 / Eubel III 23, 270, and passim / A. Haidacher in LThK IX 712 / Pastor XI–XV *ad indicem*   TBD

Ludovico SFORZA duke of Milan,
1452–17 May 1508

Ludovico was the fourth son of Francesco I Sforza, duke of Milan, and his wife, Bianca Maria Visconti. He was called 'il Moro' because his second name was Maurus, later changed to Maria. In 1479 Ludovico became duke of Bari, succeeding his brother Sforza Maria. Between 1479 and 1480, through a mixture of force and diplomacy, he assumed the regency over his young nephew Gian Galeazzo Sforza, who had become duke of Milan in 1476. Ludovico maintained a brilliant court, extending patronage to Leonardo da Vinci, the architect

Bramante, the Greek scholar Demetrius *Chalcondyles, and the historian Giorgio *Merula, among others. On 17 January 1491 he married Beatrice d'Este of Ferrara, by whom he had two sons, Massimiliano and Francesco II *Sforza.

In the early 1490s, however, Ludovico's position was threatened by the growing hostility of Ferdinand, king of Naples, and his son Alfonso, duke of Calabria, whose daughter Isabella was married to the unfortunate Gian Galeazzo. Ludovico made an alliance with *Charles VIII of France, encouraging his plans to conquer the kingdom of Naples. However, after Charles crossed the Alps in September 1494 and easily conquered Naples in February 1495, Ludovico grew fearful lest the French revive claims to the duchy of Milan. In March 1495 he joined a number of Italian states, Spain, and the Emperor *Maximilian I in a league against the French, and Charles VIII abandoned Italy almost as quickly as he had entered it. Meanwhile Ludovico became duke of Milan in his own right on the death of Gian Galeazzo in October 1494, and on 26 March 1495 he formally received investiture from the emperor, who obtained in return 400,000 ducats and the hand of Bianca Maria Sforza, the sister of Gian Galeazzo. In 1499, however, Ludovico paid a harsh price for his earlier encouragement of the French. The new king of France, *Louis XII, invaded Ludovico's territory and occupied Milan. The duke fled to the Tirol in September 1499 and with the assistance of Swiss mercenaries managed to reconquer Milan early in 1500. However, his army was captured by the French at Novara on 8 April 1500 when his Swiss refused to do battle with their compatriots in French pay. Ludovico was betrayed to the French and spent the rest of his life as a prisoner in France, dying in the castle of Loches.

Robert *Gaguin mentioned Ludovico in Ep 46 to Erasmus, in which he described the campaign of Charles VIII in Italy. Erasmus alluded to his capture and imprisonment in De conscribendis epistolis (ASD I-2 304).

BIBLIOGRAPHY: C.M. Ady A History of Milan under the Sforza (London 1907) 115–95 / Franco Catalano in Storia di Milano (Milan 1953–62) VII 311–519 and passim   TBD

Richard SHURLEY documented 1509–27 `
The sole reference to Shurley (Shirley) in Erasmus' correspondence also provides the first glimpse into his career. It appears that early in 1509 Shurley was in Italy, where William *Thale gave him certain of Erasmus' manuscripts that had been entrusted to him by Richard *Pace (Ep 244). Soon afterwards Shurley may have travelled to England, for he was presented to the living of Pembridge, Herefordshire, on 29 October 1509. Apparently he did not remain long in England, since in 1511 he was awarded a degree in canon law from the University of Turin. Later he was associated with the English hospice of St Thomas in Rome, where accounts for the period 1520–5 bearing his name have survived. Having served as the warden of the hospice from 1522 to 1523, Shurley was removed by order of Cardinal *Wolsey, who instituted John *Clerk, bishop of Bath and Wells, in his place. From 1525 to 1526, however, Shurley was again warden and, according to Gasquet, he acted as warden when he served as the commissary to Bishop Clerk in 1527.

BIBLIOGRAPHY: Allen Ep 244 / LP I 218 (63), III 2416 / G.B. Parks The English Traveler to Italy

(Rome 1954–   ) I 363, 640 / D.S. Chambers 'English representation at the court of Rome in the earlier Tudor period' (doctoral thesis, University of Oxford 1962) 508–9 / F.A. Gasquet A History of the Venerable English College, Rome (London 1920) 51

MORDECHAI FEINGOLD

John SIBERCH of Siegburg, c 1476–1554
Johann Lair (Laer) of Siegburg, on the river Sieg above Bonn, was known in England as John Siberch (Siburgus). The son of Peter and Lena Lair, he matriculated in the faculty of arts at the University of Cologne on 5 December 1492 and probably took minor orders at some later date. Although nothing is known of Siberch's studies or life for the next two decades, by 1517 he was engaged in the local book trade as an employee of the bookseller Hans Beck. Some time between 1514 and 1520 Siberch married one of the daughters of the Cologne bookseller Gerhard Amersfoort, whose other daughters were married to the publisher Franz *Birckmann and the printers Johannes *Grapheus of Antwerp and Servaes of Sassen of Louvain. Siberch acted as a travelling bookseller during this period prior to his departure for England in 1520 or 1521, where he set up the first press at Cambridge. Siberch was probably encouraged by Richard *Croke, whom he had met at some earlier date in Leipzig. He also received a loan of twenty pounds from the university chest, which was never repaid. Fourteen books were published by Siberch during his stay in England. Some time before 1527 Siberch closed down his press and apparently worked for a time for his brother-in-law Franz Birckmann in Antwerp. Again virtually nothing is known of his movements for the following two decades. He was, however, ordained a priest in 1538 and in 1544 he was at Siegburg, where he received a benefice and remained until his death in 1554.

Siberch's connections with Birckmann and Grapheus were bound to put him in touch with Erasmus. In the spring of 1518 he arrived in Louvain from Cologne, and Erasmus expressed surprise that he had not brought a letter from Johannes *Caesarius (Ep 808). In Cambridge in 1521 he produced the unauthorized first edition of Erasmus' De conscribendis epistolis, probably from a manuscript copy given by Erasmus to Robert *Fisher in 1498 (Ep 71 introduction). As might be expected, Erasmus was enraged (Ep 1284), and within a year he had rewritten the book, which was then published by Johann *Froben. Erasmus' anger, however, does not appear to have been long-lasting, for in December 1525 he sent regards to Siberch, which were duly conveyed by Robert *Aldridge (Epp 1656, 1766).

BIBLIOGRAPHY: Allen and CWE Ep 808 / O. Treptow *John Siberch* abridged and trans by J. Morris and T. Jones (Cambridge 1970) / E.P. Goldschmidt *The First Cambridge Press in its European Setting* (Cambridge 1955) / Grimm *Buchführer* no 520   MORDECHAI FEINGOLD

Rutgerus SICAMBER *See Rutgerus* SYCAMBER

Johann SICHARD of Tauberbischofsheim, d 9 September 1552
Johann Sichard (Sichart, Sichardus) was born in Tauberbischofsheim, south-west of Würzburg, the son of Georg, a tradesman. At first he attended the school of his home town, but later his uncle, Martin Golias, dean of Aschaffenburg, enabled him to attend the Latin school in Erfurt. He matriculated in Ingolstadt on 30 October 1514 and obtained his MA in 1518. From 1519 to 1521 he taught in Munich. The register of the University of Freiburg describes him as a cleric when listing his name on 3 June 1521, but in the same year he married Eva Hesler. While studying law, he worked as a private tutor. Because of his connection with the Lutheran reform movement he failed to be appointed to a chair in Freiburg, but on the recommendation of Udalricus *Zasius he became lecturer in Roman law and perhaps also in rhetoric at Basel in 1523 (AK II Ep 962). In 1524 he succeeded to the legal chair vacated by Claudius *Cantiuncula. Besides teaching he edited and prepared for printing Latin manuscripts he had found in libraries in monasteries and also served as adviser to the Basel printers *Cratander, *Bebel, and Henricus Petri. In 1530 he returned to Freiburg and obtained a doctorate of laws on 28 November 1531. In 1535 the reorganized University of Tübingen appointed him to a legal chair, for which he had been recommended by Simon *Grynaeus, and he served his first term as rector. He distinguished himself as a teacher and was repeated-

ly re-elected rector and also dean of laws. He also served as legal adviser to Duke Ulrich of *Württemberg and in 1544 prepared a legal exposé of the duke's claims for presentation at the diet. He died in Tübingen.

Although Sichard was well acquainted with Bonifacius *Amerbach, there is little evidence of personal contact between him and Erasmus. Erasmus was asked to greet Sichard by Jan *Antonin in 1526 (Ep 1660) and by *Cochlaeus in 1529 (Ep 2120), and in 1527 (Ep 1899) *Goclenius referred to his projected edition of Terence. In his Basel years (1526–30) Sichard edited more than twenty volumes, partly of Latin literature and partly of legal studies, including many rare texts and some first editions. Sichard's own *Praelectiones in libros codicis Justiniani*, edited by J.M. Fickler, Basel 1565, and *Responsa iuris*, edited by J.S. Gödelmann, Frankfurt 1599, were famous for their clarity.

BIBLIOGRAPHY: Allen Ep 1660 / ADB XXXIV 143–6 / *Matrikel Freiburg* I-1 251 / *Matrikel Tübingen* I 281 and passim / R.E. Feine 'Johann Sichard' in *Schwäbische Lebensbilder* (Stuttgart 1940–72) V 60–72 / Paul Lehmann *Johannes Sichardus und die von ihm benutzten Bibliotheken und Handschriften* (Munich 1912) with an extensive bibliography of Sichard's editions / Winterberg 66–8 / Guido Kisch *Johannes Sichardus als Basler Rechtshistoriker* (Basel 1952) / BRE Ep 266 and passim / AK II Ep 962, III Ep 1029, and passim   IG

Eustachius de SICHEM *See Eustachius van der* RIVIEREN

Franz von SICKINGEN 2 March 1481–7 May 1523
Franz von Sickingen (Cinglius, Sichinius, Sychinus) was born in the Ebernburg, near Kreuznach, the only son of Schwicker von Sickingen, chief steward to the elector Palatine, and his wife, Margarethe von Hohenburg. At an early age he came into the possession of a considerable inheritance, the income from which he normally spent on hiring mercenaries. Thus prepared, he embarked on a series of private feuds (Ep 582), often without just reason, attacking among others the principalities of Worms (1514), Lorraine (1516), and Metz and Hesse (1518). On the strength of his

Franz von Sickingen, by Hieronymus Hopfer

military exploits he secured for himself a position comparable to princely rank. Having invoked the imperial ban against him, the Hapsburg administration had no means of enforcing that ban, and when Sickingen entered into negotiations with the court of France, the Hapsburgs preferred to draw him into their own service. In the spring of 1519 he was induced to join the Swabian league for their war against Ulrich of *Württemberg (Epp 923, 986), and later that year the newly elected *Charles v appointed him councillor and field commander. He supported *Reuchlin (Ep 986; Hutten *Operum supplementum* I 438ff) and was persuaded by Ulrich von *Hutten to adopt the cause of the reformers. In January 1520 he extended an offer of protection to *Luther (Hutten *Opera* I Ep 150), and in the following autumn Hutten found asylum in his Ebernburg. Soon thereafter he also gave asylum to Martin *Bucer and Johannes *Oecolampadius, who as Sickingen's chaplain introduced a reformed liturgy in the spring of 1522 (Ep 1523). Both Bucer, in his dialogue *Neukarsthans*, and particularly Hutten contrived to present Sickingen in the role of champion of

the true gospel. Hutten also urged him to adopt his proposals for a general 'Pfaffenkrieg' against the ecclesiastical princes, but Sickingen refused, at least as long as his connection with the Hapsburg government appeared to offer a better opportunity for fulfilling his personal ambitions. Fighting for the Hapsburgs against France in the summer of 1521, however, brought him no closer to his goal, and so he placed himself at the head of the disgruntled imperial knights. In August 1522 the knights met at Landau and formed a league designed to wage war against the ecclesiastical princes. Sickingen himself lost no time in launching his own attack against Richard von *Greiffenklau, archbishop of Trier. For a second time the imperial ban was invoked against him, and the troops of Trier joined with their allies from Hesse and the Palatinate to besiege him in his castle of Landstuhl. There he was wounded and died. His efforts to exploit the widespread feelings of anticlericalism for the benefit of the imperial knights thus met with complete failure. Far from improving the position of the knightly class, Sickingen's last stand served to seal its demise.

Hutten wrote of Sickingen with elaborate and enthusiastic praise when reporting to Erasmus the outcome of the war in Württemberg (Ep 986). In Erasmus' reply his brief reference to Sickingen was friendly, if non-committal (Ep 999). He did, however, meet Sickingen personally in November 1520, when both were in Cologne after the coronation of Charles v; their talk on this occasion was about Luther (Epp 1155 introduction, 1166). In February 1523 (Ep 1342) Erasmus recalled how he had come close to meeting Sickingen for a second time when travelling from Louvain to Basel in 1521; he noted how thoroughly Sickingen's fortunes had changed in the mean time. In the *Spongia* (ASD IX-1 129–31) Erasmus claimed that in the end Sickingen had refused to lend Hutten any further support; the correctness of this statement cannot, however, be substantiated from other sources (cf Strauss 440).

BIBLIOGRAPHY: Allen Ep 582 / Heinrich Ulmann in ADB XXXIV 151–8 / Heinrich Ulmann *Franz von Sickingen: Nach meistens ungedruckten Quellen* (Leipzig 1872) / Karl Hans Rendenbach *Die Fehde Franz von Sickingens gegen Trier* (Berlin

1933) / David Friedrich Strauss *Ulrich von Hutten* new ed (Meersburg-Leipzig 1930) passim   BARBARA KÖNNEKER

SIGISMUND I king of Poland, 1 January 1467–1 April 1548

Sigismund was born in Cracow, the fifth son of Casimir IV Jagiełło, king of Poland and grand duke of Lithuania, and Elisabeth, a daughter of the Emperor Albert II. In 1498 he was commissioned to administer the duchy of Głogów by his brother *Vladislav II, king of Bohemia and Hungary. In 1501 he undertook the administration of Opava, and in 1504 he was appointed Vladislav's governor in Silesia and Lusatia. After the death of his brother Alexander, Sigismund was acclaimed grand duke of Lithuania on 20 October 1506, and that same year he was elected king of Poland on 8 December. His coronation took place on 24 January 1507 in Cracow. Initially he attempted to follow the dynastic policies of his predecessors: resistance to the Hapsburgs, the maintenance of peaceful relations with Turkey, and the advancement of Polish influence in Hungary. In 1512 he married Barbara, a daughter of István Zápolyai, duke of Szepes (Spiš) and *voivode* of Transylvania. However, several factors forced Sigismund to change his political course, such as war between Muscovy and Lithuania (1507–8), war with Moldavia (1509), and Turkish invasions (1510, 1512). Another war with Muscovy resulted in the loss of Smolensk, which was not recovered despite the victory at Orsza on 8 September 1514.

Above all Sigismund was becoming aware of the threat presented by a coalition of the Emperor *Maximilian I, Muscovy, and the order of Teutonic knights. At a summit in Vienna in July 1515 the Hapsburgs and the Jagiellonians drew up a treaty of succession which opened the door to Hapsburg rule in Bohemia and Hungary through the marriage of the children of King Vladislav – the future *Louis II Jagiełło and Anne – with the grandchildren of the emperor – *Mary and *Ferdinand or *Charles. After King Vladislav's death Sigismund took care of Louis and was able to exercise a vote in the imperial election. Through his representatives Sigismund voted for Charles of Hapsburg on 28 May 1519.

Sigismund I, king of Poland

Undoubtedly he was counting on Charles' support in his war with the grand master of the Teutonic order – Albert (I) of *Brandenburg-Ansbach. This war, begun at the end of 1519, ended with the truce of Torun on 5 April 1521, despite many Polish military successes. Sigismund was simultaneously faced with the onslaught of the Tartars and the war between Lithuania and Muscovy, which ended with a five-year truce in December 1522. In response to pressure from the emperor and the pope to join an anti-Turkish crusade, Sigismund held himself in reserve and remained uncommitted, despite the fact that in 1524 he was forced to defend himself once more against the incursions of the Turks.

In 1524 Sigismund decided to improve relations with France, acceding to the desires of the French supporters in Poland, particularly his second wife, *Bona Sforza, and her entourage. As a result of this Sigismund signed a truce with Turkey in 1525 and ended hostilities with the Teutonic order by means of the Cracow treaty of 9 April 1525. He accepted the secularization of the order into a Protestant duchy held by Albert of Brandenburg as a vassal of Poland. This act caused Sigismund to be accused of sympathy for Lutheranism, a charge without foundation. From the outset of the Reformation he attacked its influence in Poland, issuing a series of anti-Lutheran edicts between May 1520 and September 1523. In 1525 and 1526 he suppressed a Lutheran insurrection at Gdansk with an armed force.

The Hungarian defeat and the death of Louis II at Mohács on 29 August 1526 once again directed Sigismund's attention to Hungarian affairs. At first, under pressure from Queen Bona, he thought of pursuing his own rights to the land of his fallen nephew, but he abandoned these personal aspirations after the election of Ferdinand to the Bohemian throne on 24 October 1526 and the election of *John Zápolyai, the brother of Sigismund's first wife, Barbara, to the Hungarian throne by the national party on 10 November of that year. After repulsing a Tartar invasion in 1527 and extending the treaty with Muscovy he was able to give more attention to moderating the explosive Hungarian situation. Here his efforts were rewarded with the signing of a one-year truce between Ferdinand and Zápolyai in 1530.

A second war with Moldavia (1530-1) was decided by a Polish victory at Obertyn on 22 August 1531. This war, complicated by a Turkish invasion of Hungary, led to a flurry of diplomatic activity by Sigismund. The result was the conclusion of a lasting peace with Turkey on 1 May 1533. Peace in the south allowed Lithuania to resume war with Muscovy in order to regain lost lands. However, this third war between Lithuania and Muscovy (1534-7), despite Polish support, did not bring about significant results.

The last decade of Sigismund's reign, though free from war, was a time of armed preparedness for further threats from Muscovy, Moldavia, and Turkey. During these years the initiative passed to his wife, Bona. After the conclusion of peace between Ferdinand and John Zápolyai in 1538, Sigismund agreed to the marriage of his daughter Isabel to John in 1539. After John's death it was expected that Sigismund would act as the protector of Isabel and her newly born son, John Sigismund, in the defence of their rights to Hungary. However Sigismund did nothing to prevent Ferdinand from acquir-

ing the whole of Hungary. The renewed close ties with the Hapsburgs indicated by the marriage of Sigismund's son, *Sigismund II Augustus, with Elizabeth, the daughter of Ferdinand, in 1543 did not involve Poland in a war with Turkey. In 1544 Sigismund transferred the administrative duties in Lithuania to his son, who had been elevated to grand duke of Lithuania and elected king of Poland during his father's lifetime in 1529.

During his entire reign Sigismund based his support upon a narrow elite of magnates and acted in close harmony with his intimate advisers, Krzystof *Szydłowiecki and Piotr *Tomicki. By so doing he ignored the political aspirations of the middle gentry. This neglect brought about a number of tumultuous diets and a growth of unrest in domestic politics. At the end of Sigismund's reign Poland was torn by a sharp conflict between the magnates and the gentry. The gentry increasingly came to accept Reformation programs in order to attack the power of the church. Sigismund was a patron of the arts, maintaining artists at his court and constructing a Renaissance castle on Cracow's Wawel hill and the royal chapel in the Cracow cathedral.

From his first marriage with Barbara, who died in 1515, Sigismund had a daughter, Jadwiga, who married Joachim the elector of Brandenburg. His marriage with Bona produced a son, Sigismund Augustus, and four daughters: Isabel, who married John Zápolyai; Sophia, who married Henry, duke of Brunswick; Anne, who married the Polish king Stephen Batory; and Catherine, who married John Vasa, king of Sweden. Sigismund died in Cracow and was buried in the royal chapel in the Cracow cathedral, where there is a monument made by Italian craftsmen.

Sigismund was frequently mentioned in the correspondence of Erasmus (Epp 1452, 1652, 1662). Jan (II) *Łaski, visiting Basel in 1526, encouraged Erasmus to write to him. The result was Ep 1819, dated 15 May 1527, in which Erasmus praised Sigismund for his pursuit of peace. The king thanked Erasmus in a letter of 19 February 1528, extending an invitation to Poland and sending a gift of one hundred ducats (Ep 1952). This letter was written at the instigation of Erasmus' Polish friends who

251 SILBERBERG

were royal advisers, Szydłowiecki and Andrzej *Krzycki (Ep 1954). The publication of Ep
1819 (Cracow: H. Wietor 1527) without the
author's knowledge earned Erasmus considerable criticism from supporters of the Hapsburgs, since it contained a reference to John
Zápolyai as 'king of Hungary' (Epp 2030,
2032).

Erasmus thanked Sigismund for his gift and
invitation in a letter of 28 August, a letter
characterized by unlimited praise and advice to
continue a peaceful political program (Ep
2034). He mentioned Sigismund's generosity
and his invitation in letters to friends in
western Europe (Epp 2029, 2054, 2299). Sigismund wrote to Erasmus a last time with a
recommendation for Jan, the son of Seweryn
*Boner (Ep 2520). In 1531 Johannes *Dantiscus
sent Erasmus a medallion of Sigismund (Ep
2643).

BIBLIOGRAPHY: Allen Ep 1652 / *Korespondencja
Erazma z Rotterdamu z Polakami* ed M. Cytowska
(Warsaw 1965) / Z. Wojciechowski *Zygmunt
Stary* (Warsaw 1946) / E. Zivier *Neuere Ge-
schichte Polens* (Gotha 1915) / W. Pociecha
Królowa Bona: Czasy i ludzie Odrodzenia (Poznań
1949–58) I–IV / *The Cambridge History of Poland*
ed W.F. Reddaway et al (Cambridge 1941–50)
I 300–347   HALINA KOWALSKA

SIGISMUND II **Augustus** king of Poland,
1 August 1520–7 July 1572
Sigismund Augustus was the son of *Sigismund I and his second wife, *Bona Sforza. He
was given a thorough education according to
Italian standards. Owing to the efforts of his
mother he was proclaimed grand duke of
Lithuania as early as 18 October 1529. On 18
December of that year he was elected king of
Poland during the diet of Piotrków. His
coronation took place in Cracow on 20 February 1530. From 6 October 1544 he carried out
administrative duties in Lithuania, assuming
the kingship of Poland only after the death of
his father in 1548.

In 1531 Anselmus *Ephorinus reminded
Erasmus of a request that he dedicate his
edition of Terence to Jan and Stanisław
*Boner, explaining that among other things
this would win them the favour of Sigismund
Augustus (Ep 2554). In his dedication (Ep 2584)
Erasmus included words of praise for the

Sigismund II Augustus, king of Poland

virtues of the young king and his love of
learning.
BIBLIOGRAPHY: Allen Ep 2554 / *The Cambridge
History of Poland* ed W.F. Reddaway et al
(Cambridge 1941–50) I 348–68 / E. Zivier *Neuere
Geschichte Polens* (Gotha 1915)
HALINA KOWALSKA

Johann SILBERBERG of Klein-Basel, documented 1480; died before 5 November 1526
Silberberg (properly Tunsel, Tonsel, Thunsel,
also Argentimontanus) came from a good
Klein-Basel family and adopted the name of its
house. He was registered at the University of
Basel in 1481, and was a BA in 1484 and a MA in
1487. In 1491 he studied at Bologna, obtaining
a doctorate in canon law in 1492 and another in
medicine. Back at Basel, he was rector of the
university in 1497 and at the same time a
member of the faculty of law, later also
becoming a member of the medical faculty.
Although he was rector again for a term in 1502
and received a licence in civil law at Basel in
1503, he held no university chair and his
principal activity was the practice of medicine
(Ep 1825). In 1504 he was registered in the

University of Heidelberg; in 1506 he was again in Basel and lived until 1515 in the Rheingasse near the *Amerbach home. In the religious controversy he inclined to the old faith and helped defend it at the Baden disputation of 1526. He also treated Bishop Christoph von *Utenheim.

Silberberg was married to Anna Münch von Rosenberg. In Ep 1825 Erasmus reported to Jan *Antonin that he had died of the plague. This event must have occurred before 5 November 1526, when it was mentioned by *Beatus Rhenanus (AK III Ep 1154).

BIBLIOGRAPHY: Allen Ep 1825 / Matrikel Basel I 170, 247, 267 / Matrikel Heidelberg I 451 / Knod 532 / Wappenbuch der Stadt Basel ed W.R. Staehelin (Basel [1917–30]) / AK I Ep 387 and passim / R. Wackernagel Geschichte der Stadt Basel (Basel 1907–54) III 129, 131, 18* / Albrecht Burckhardt Geschichte der medizinischen Fakultät zu Basel (Basel 1917) 18–19   PGB

Fernando de SILVA

The imperial ambassador mentioned by Erasmus in Ep 2879 may be either Fernando de Silva, count of Cifuentes and ambassador in Rome, or Miguel Mai, whom he succeeded in April 1533.

BIBLIOGRAPHY: Allen Ep 2879

SILVIUS (Epp 865, 905, 2798, 2874)

Silvius (Sylvius) – his vernacular name could conceivably have been Dubois – was said to be a young French scholar ('philologus') by Paolo *Bombace, who had met him when Silvius visited Rome in the autumn of 1518 (Ep 865). In 1533 Erasmus recalled Silvius' story with many curious additions and suggested that the name might be fictitious (Epp 2798, 2874). Silvius is not identified.   PGB

SILVIUS See also François and Jacques DUBOIS, Johannes Sylvius EGRANUS

Andreas SILVIUS of Bruges, documented 1533–70

Ep 2779 is preserved only in a seventeenth-century copy made by J.F. Gronovius, who suggested in a marginal note that the addressee was Andreas Silvius (Sylvius) of Bruges. If Gronovius is right, Silvius was in Paris in March 1533 when Erasmus sent him Ep 2779 and a copy of a new preface for the edition of his Jerome to be published by Claude Chevallon (Paris 1533). From Ep 2779 we learn that several preceding letters between Silvius and Erasmus are missing, that Silvius was in close touch with such Paris friends of Erasmus as Germain de *Brie and Jacobus *Omphalius, and that he had sought Erasmus' advice about a position offered to him.

Some twenty years later, in 1554, Andreas Silvius of Bruges matriculated in the University of Louvain and at about this time was the tutor to Petrus *Vulcanius' son, Bonaventura, while in 1556 he seems to have tutored the son of Reinerus Gemma Phrysius. By 1564 Silvius had moved to Italy, where he obtained a position of some authority and showed kindness to Joachim *Camerarius' son. In the same year he translated into Latin a commentary on Aristotle's De generatione by John of Alexandria, the Grammarian, called Philoponus (Venice: G. Scoto 1564). Silvius also contributed a preface (dated 22 November 1570) to Girolamo Mercuriale's Variarum lectionum libri quatuor (Venice: P. and A. Meietti 1570) in which he thanked Cardinal Antoine Perrenot de Granvelle and other members of the same family for the kindness they had shown him.

BIBLIOGRAPHY: Allen Ep 2779 / de Vocht CTL II 183, 563 / Matricule de Louvain IV-1 485 / Correspondance de Bonaventura Vulcanius ed H. de Vries de Heekelingen (The Hague 1923) Ep 237   IG

Desiderius de SIMANDRIS documented 1532–47

Very little appears to be known about Desiderius de Simandris. He was a secretary to King *Ferdinand and in 1532 and 1533 he received payments from the Fugger bank. In 1534 Erasmus met him at Freiburg and asked him to take charge of a letter to Georgius *Loxanus (Ep 2986). His signature on a receipt dated 15 March 1547 indicates that by that time he had transferred to the service of *Charles v.

BIBLIOGRAPHY: Götz von Pölnitz Anton Fugger (Tübingen 1958–) I 587, 604, III 757
                PGB

François SIMARD, SIMARIUS See SYMARD

Georg SIMLER of Wimpfen, d 1535/6
Georg Simler (Symler), born in Wimpfen on the
Neckar, was said to have studied under
Ludwig *Dringenberg at the famous Latin
school in Sélestat. Around 1500 he was
appointed rector of the Latin school in Pforzheim, where *Melanchthon became his pupil
(1507–9). Simler moved to Tübingen, where he
matriculated on 1 July 1510, was promoted MA
on 15 July, and eventually became a highly
respected professor of Roman law. Here
Melanchthon was again his student and junior
colleague from 1512 to 1518. In the course of his
regular co-operation with the printer Thomas
*Anshelm at Pforzheim and Tübingen, Simler
published a short *Rationarium evangelistarum* in
1502 and edited Rhabanus Maurus' *De institutione clericorum* in 1505. He contributed verses
to Rhabanus Maurus' *De laudibus sanctae crucis*
(1503) and to several works of *Reuchlin
published by Anshelm. Simler himself was a
good friend of Reuchlin. His work on Latin and
Greek grammar, *Observationes de arte grammatica* (Tübingen: T. Anshelm 1512), was highly
praised by Jakob *Spiegel but caused a
controversy with Heinrich *Bebel. In 1535
Simler was ill and seems to have died soon
thereafter.

When Erasmus recommended Heinrich
*Schürer to Lukas *Klett in early 1526, the latter
introduced the young man to his friend Simler,
who spoke of his great respect for Erasmus (Ep
1709).

BIBLIOGRAPHY: Allen Ep 1709 / Karl Hartfel-
der in ADB XXXIV 350–2 / Karl Hartfelder *Philipp
Melanchthon als Praeceptor Germaniae* (Berlin
1889, repr 1964) 36–7 and passim / *Matrikel
Tübingen* I 176 / RE Epp 99, 108 / BRE Ep 24
IG

SIMON (Ep 474) *See Jaspar van* HALMALE

SIMON (Ep 2966) *See Simon* RIQUINUS

SIMON Hexapolitanus *See Simon*
SCHAIDENREISSER

Jean SIMON de Champigny of Paris,
d 23 December 1502
Jean Simon, a son of Jean Simon lord of
Champigny, was born at Paris. A protégé of

King *Charles VIII, he was a councillor in the
Parlement of Paris, a canon of Paris, and
archdeacon of Soissons. Elected bishop of
Paris by the cathedral chapter, he was approved in the consistory of 29 October 1492
and, after lengthy litigation, was consecrated
by Tristan de Salazar, archbishop of Sens, on
22 September 1494. Simon encouraged reformed religious orders and in 1495 published
synodal decrees. He died of the plague and
was buried in the cathedral of Paris.

Erasmus mentioned Simon in Ep 74 as an
admirer of Cornelis *Gerard.

BIBLIOGRAPHY: Allen Ep 74 / DBF VIII 328 /
Gallia christiana VII 156–7 / Renaudet *Préréforme*
2, 205–7, and passim   TBD

Jacopo SIMONETTA of Milan, c 1475–
1 November 1539
Jacopo was born in Milan to the Milanese
historian Giovanni Simonetta, the author of a
life of Duke Francesco Sforza to whom he had
been secretary, and Caterina Barbarvaria. He
was educated at Padua and Pavia. A student in
civil and canon law of the distinguished jurists
Alessandro Tartagni, Bartolomeo Cipolla,
Giasone del Maino, and Bartolomeo Sozzini,
he held a post in the College of Jurisprudence
in Milan from 1498 before departing for Rome.
His treatise *De reservationibus beneficiorum* (first
printed at Cologne by Johann III Gymnich in
1583) brought him to the notice of *Julius II,
who appointed him a consistorial advocate
(1505) and auditor of the rota and employed
him to settle the long-standing dispute between Florence and Siena over the city of
Montepulciano (1511). *Clement VII made him
bishop of Pesaro on 17 July 1528 and drew
upon his judicial expertise in *Henry VIII's
divorce case: the decision in Queen *Catherine's favour on 23 March 1534 was greatly due
to Simonetta's able presentation of her case in
the consistory of 27 February. In a letter to
Erasmus, Piotr *Tomicki placed Simonetta
among other men of 'learning' and 'integrity'
whom *Paul III raised to the cardinalate on 21
May 1535 (Ep 3066). Initially cardinal priest of
San Ciriaco, he was translated in November
1537 to Sant'Apollinare. Paul III also favoured
him with the administration of the dioceses of
Perugia (1535), Lodi (1536), and Nepi (1538).

An admirer of Erasmus (*Epistolae ad Nauseam* 168) and highly esteemed by the reforming cardinals Jacopo *Sadoleto and Reginald *Pole, for the last three years of his life Simonetta was closely associated with Catholic reform and with the attempts to call a general council of the church. One of four eminent cardinals entrusted in the consistory of 20 April 1537 with the reform of the curial offices, starting with the datary, he remained a member of this commission in March 1539 when its number was increased to eight to cope with the reform of a further four departments, including the rota. He was a member of the commission appointed in the consistory of 8 April 1536 which drew up the bull summoning a council to convene at Mantua. When the venue of the council was changed to Vicenza he was among nine cardinals appointed on 7 January 1538 to deal with all matters connected with it, and as one of Paul III's legates (appointed 20 March) he left Rome on 2 April for Vicenza. The arrival on 9 August of the bull proroguing the council put an end to his mission. In April 1539 he was reappointed legate only to be frustrated once more by the decision of 21 May to postpone the council indefinitely. He was buried in Santa Trinità dei Monti, built at the request of St Francis of Padua, founder of the Minimites, whose canonization Simonetta had advocated during the pontificate of *Leo x.

BIBLIOGRAPHY: Allen Ep 3066 / A. Ciaconius *Vitae et res gestae Pontificum Romanorum et S.R.E. Cardinalium* (Rome 1677) III 570–1 / P. Argelati *Bibliotheca scriptorum Mediolanensium* (Milan 1745) II-1 1398–1400 / G. Tiraboschi *Storia della letteratura italiana* (Milan 1822–6) 1098–9 / C. Papadopoli *Historia gymnasii Patavini* (Venice 1726) II 44–5 / Jacopo Sadoleto *Opera omnia* (Verona 1737–8) I lib viii, Ep 5, II lib xiv, Epp 7, 8 / Reginald Pole *Epistolarium* (Brescia 1748) III appendix pp 6–7 / J. Nardi *Istorie di Firenze* (Florence 1858) I 56–7, 385 / LP VII 230, 282, and passim / Pastor x 219, XI 77, and passim / Hubert Jedin *A History of the Council of Trent* trans E. Graf (London 1957–   ) I 311 and passim

ROSEMARY DEVONSHIRE JONES

Johannes SINAPIUS of Schweinfurt, c 1505–61

Johannes Sinapius (Senf, Senff) was the son of Kaspar, a city councillor in Schweinfurt, on the Main. He attended the local Latin school and matriculated in Erfurt at Easter 1520; there he was a friend of Joachim *Camerarius. In the summer of 1523 he matriculated in Leipzig and obtained a BA on 13 July. He studied mainly Greek under Petrus *Mosellanus, after whose death he enrolled in Wittenberg on 7 May 1524 to pursue his Greek studies with *Melanchthon. On 28 September 1526 he matriculated in Heidelberg, where the chair of Greek was held by Simon *Grynaeus, whom he had met briefly in Wittenberg. On 6 August 1527 he obtained his MA and thereafter began to teach arts courses. In his first publication, *Defensio eloquentiae* (Haguenau: J. Setzer 1528), he commended *Luther and particularly Erasmus for their part in the renewal of learning and religion. One of Sinapius' students in 1528 was Johann *Fichard, who remained in Heidelberg until 1530, living in the house of Johann *Lotzer, the elector's physician. Sinapius dedicated to Lotzer his *Declamatio* against the opponents of the new learning (Haguenau: J. Setzer 1530).

When Grynaeus left for Basel, Sinapius succeeded him as professor of Greek in May 1529; he was, however, discouraged by the lack of response to his ideas and made plans to study medicine in Italy. Prior to March 1531 he went to Freiburg to see Erasmus (Ep 2461), who advised him to study in Ferrara under Giovanni *Manardo (Epp 2716, 2956, 3113). Sinapius resigned his Heidelberg chair in October 1531 and visited *Bucer in Strasbourg (18 October) and Grynaeus in Basel, where he may have worked briefly as a corrector for the printers Johann *Bebel and Andreas *Cratander on an edition of a Latin translation of Plutarch's *Vitae* (1531; with the Greek text 1533); as a parting present Cratander may have given to Sinapius a copy of his recent edition of Theophrastus' *Characters* in Greek and Latin with Cratander's autograph dedication, now in the British Library.

In 1532 Sinapius arrived in Ferrara, where he obtained a medical doctorate and was admitted to teach medicine. At the same time he entered the service of Duke Ercole II d'*Este and his wife, Renée of France, as a court physician and supervisor of their children's education. Because of his comfortable position, after much hesitation (1535–7) he declined an invitation to the University of Tübingen issued by Ambrosius *Blarer on Grynaeus' recommendation. Above all he hoped to marry Françoise de Boussiron, a lady in the duchess' retinue. Jean Calvin, who had met both of them when visiting Ferrara in 1536, pleaded Sinapius' suit in his letters to Françoise, and the marriage took place in 1538. The publication of *Epithalamia diversorum in nuptias Joannis Sinapii Germani et Franciscae Bucyroniae Gallae* (Basel: M. Isengrin 1539) underlines Sinapius' importance as a purveyor of Italian medical and humanistic texts for the Basel printers. The volume also includes a poem by his former student Johann Fichard. At the request of Jacobus Micyllus, Sinapius contributed a Latin translation of the *Podagra* to an edition of Lucian's works which also listed Erasmus, Melanchthon, and Willibald *Pirckheimer as contributors (printed by Christian Egenolf, Frankfurt 1538).

Around 1545 Sinapius decided to return to Germany. After lengthy negotiations involving Daniel *Stiebar, among others, Sinapius was appointed court physician to Melchior Zobel von Guttenberg, prince-bishop of Würzburg, a position he held from May 1548 until the end of his life. In 1549 he contributed a history of his native city (reprinted in F. Stein *Monumenta Suinfurtensia historica*, Schweinfurt 1875, II 370ff) to Sebastian Münster's *Cosmographia*. Sinapius' later years were filled with sorrow; military conflicts raged around Schweinfurt, and above all the death of his wife (28 June 1553) was a blow from which he never recovered. His health deteriorated further in 1557, and the following year Bishop Melchior Zobel was murdered by a band of soldiers. Sinapius continued to serve under his successor but died three years later.

From his early days at Wittenberg Sinapius had been sympathetic to the reformers, and the progress of religious persecution in Italy was a factor in his decision to return to Germany. He also helped such Italian reformers as Celio Secondo Curione, Olimpia Morata, and Giovanni Angelo *Odoni to establish their links with the north. Perhaps his move to the Catholic court of Würzburg may be understood in terms of an overriding allegiance to the cause of Erasmus. Their correspondence continued

until Erasmus' death (Epp 2956, 3113), although several letters have not been preserved (Epp 2716, 3002).

BIBLIOGRAPHY: Allen Ep 2461 / *Matrikel Erfurt* II 315 / *Matrikel Leipzig* I 588, II 577 / *Matrikel Wittenberg* I 121 / *Matrikel Heidelberg* I 540, II 444–5 / Hugo Holstein 'Johannes Sinapius, ein deutscher Humanist' *Jahres-Bericht über das Königliche Gymnasium in Wilhelmshaven* 19 (1901) 3–19 / Herminjard IV Epp 619, 676, VI Ep 83, VIII Ep 1175, and passim / Victor Scholderer 'A 16th century association copy' *British Museum Quarterly* 20 (1956) 55–6 / AK IV Ep 1654 / BRE Ep 285 / P.G. Bietenholz *Der italienische Humanismus und die Blütezeit des Buchdrucks in Basel* (Basel 1959) 47, 69, 145–6   IG

Johannes SINTHEIMIUS, a SINTHIS *See Jan* SYNTHEN

Albertus SIXTINUS *See Johannes* SIXTINUS

Johannes SIXTINUS of Bolsward, d 1519
Johannes Sixtinus (John Sextun), a native of Bolsward, in Friesland, studied at Oxford and then pursued an ecclesiastical career in England. In 1499, when he was staying at St Mary's College, the prior of which was Richard *Charnock, he met Erasmus and exchanged several complimentary letters with him (Epp 112, 113, 116). For several years they lost sight of one another, although Ep 181 of 1504 shows that Erasmus had not lost interest in Sixtinus. On 11 October 1502 Sixtinus had received a prebend in St Probus' church, Cornwall, from John Arundell, bishop of Exeter, whom he served as registrar from 1502 to 1504. Around 1504, after the bishop's death, Sixtinus travelled to Italy, where he studied law at Bologna (Ep 244) and perhaps at Ferrara. In 1507–8 he was again in England, staying at Magdalen College, but he returned to Italy and obtained a doctorate in civil law from the University of Siena on 27/8 July 1510. Shortly before this he had been appointed archpriest of Haccombe, Devon.

In October and November 1511 Sixtinus was in London, where he renewed his epistolary contacts with Erasmus (Ep 235), ending the latter's fears that he would print or otherwise take advantage of a manuscript copy of *De copia* which William *Thale had given him in Italy

Pope Sixtus iv, by Melozzo da Forlì

(Epp 244, 248, 249). In August 1513, Sixtinus and Augustijn *Agge travelled to Brabant and Friesland, carrying a letter from Erasmus for Jan *Becker at Middelburg (Epp 273, 291); Sixtinus seems to have returned to England by November 1513 (Ep 280). In about 1515 he became rector of Eggescliffe, in Durham, and in 1516 he was in London again, entertaining Erasmus' courier, Pieter *Meghen. On 9 April 1517 he was the witness at the ceremony by which Andrea *Ammonio, acting on behalf of *Leo x, formally absolved Erasmus of censures caused by his failure to wear the habit of the canons regular (Ep 517). In the same year Erasmus contacted Sixtinus again when Ammonio died (Ep 655) and when *Jan of Friesland needed help in migrating to England (Ep 668); on various other occasions they exchanged letters (Epp 775, 828; cf Epp 782, 786, 849, 892). Sixtinus died in London between 24 March 1519, when he made up his will, and 7 May following, when it was proved; among other things his testament indicated his wish to be buried in the Pardon churchyard of St Paul's. Erasmus still remembered him with affection in Ep 1347 of 1523.

In 1517 Erasmus met a brother of Sixtinus at

Antwerp (Epp 655, 668); in his will Sixtinus mentioned only one brother, Albertus (cf S. Knight *The Life of Dr John Colet* 2nd ed, Oxford 1823, 192–3).

BIBLIOGRAPHY: Allen Ep 113; IV xxi / Emden BRUO III 1675 / J. and J.A. Venn *Alumni Cantabrigienses* (Cambridge 1922–54) I-4, 45 makes the implausible inference that Sixtinus studied at Cambridge in 1462–3

C.G. VAN LEIJENHORST

Pope SIXTUS iv 1414–12 August 1484
Francesco della Rovere (da Savona) was born at Celle, near Savona in Liguria, to Leonardo, a cloth merchant, and Luchina Monleone. He entered the Franciscan order at an early age and studied philosophy and theology at Padua and perhaps Bologna, receiving a doctoral degree. A popular professor and a distinguished preacher, he attracted the attention of Cardinal *Bessarion, protector of the Franciscan order, and around 1459 became his confessor. He was called to Rome to be procurator-general for his order, then vicar for Italy. At Christmas 1462 he engaged in a debate before *Pius II on the nature of the precious blood and later wrote a treatise, *De sanguine Christi* [Rome: J.P. de Lignamine 1471]. In 1464 he was elected general of his order and instigated a number of reforms. On 18 September 1467 he became cardinal of San Pietro in Vincoli.

On 9 August 1471 Francesco emerged from the conclave following Paul II's death as Pope Sixtus iv. His election was hailed by many who saw him as a pontiff who could bring peace to Italy and rally Europe against the Turks. Sixtus was in earnest in his efforts against the Turks but was soon distracted by family concerns. His nepotism was manifested early in his pontificate, when he conferred cardinals' hats on his nephews, Pietro Riario and Giuliano della Rovere (the future *Julius II). His desire to aggrandize his family and to consolidate the papal states led to a series of wars in the second half of his pontificate: first with Florence after the failure of the Pazzi conspiracy – in which he was implicated – to overthrow the Medici (1478), then with Naples, and finally with Venice. His death came less than a week after the signing of the unfavourable peace of Bagnolo (7 August 1484) with Venice.

In the *Julius exclusus* Julius was mistakenly

described as the nephew of Sixtus by his sister.
Julius was the son of Sixtus' brother Raffaele.
The dialogue pictured Sixtus as warlike,
ambitious, and avaricious, and brought up an
unfounded rumour that he was Julius' father
(*Opuscula* 71, 81). In *De bello turcico* Erasmus
mentioned that Sixtus fled Rome for France
after the Turks sacked Otranto in 1480 (LB V
351F).

An able administrator and generous patron
of the arts, Sixtus was attentive to the
rebuilding of Rome, started the Capitoline
Museum, and greatly expanded the Vatican
library, the latter under the direction of
Giovanni Antonio Bussi, succeeded by Bartolomeo *Platina. Among the many humanists
receiving positions in the curia and in the papal
states under Sixtus were Domizio *Calderini,
Sigismondo de' Conti, Niccolò *Perotti, and
Giovanni Antonio *Campano. Sixtus' favoured
artist was Melozzo da Forlì, whose portrait in
the library frescoes is the definitive one of this
intelligent but remiss pontiff.

BIBLIOGRAPHY: Pastor IV 197–471 / Egmont
Lee *Sixtus IV and Men of Letters* (Rome 1978)

DE ETTA V. THOMSEN & TBD

John SKELTON c 1460–21 June 1529

John Skelton (Sceltonus, Schelton, Skeltoni-
des, Skeltonus, Skelkonus), possibly a native
of Norfolk, Cumberland, or Yorkshire, studied
at Cambridge, where he took his degree at
Peterhouse around 1478–9. By the early 1480s
he began to write poetry for the nobility and
royalty; he is credited with composing *The Deth
of Kyng Edwarde the Fourth* around 1483. He
migrated to Oxford, where around 1488 he was
made laureate in rhetoric, an honour more
similar to a degree in rhetoric than to the
modern concept of poet laureate. By 1490 he
translated a selection of Cicero's letters and the
Bibliotheca historica of Diodorus Siculus into
English and wrote a Latin comedy, 'Achade-
mios,' now lost. In about 1492 he was made
laureate at Louvain and in 1493 at Cambridge.

Around 1495 Skelton was named tutor to the
future King *Henry VIII, for whom he wrote a
Speculum principis (c 1501), first published by
F.M. Salter in *Speculum* 9 (1934) 25–37. In 1498
he was ordained priest. He continued to write
poetry, composing love lyrics, religious verses,
and an exposé of court life entitled *The Bouge of
Court* (c 1499). Around 1502 he fell into

John Skelton

discredit at court and may have spent some
time in prison. In 1504 he retired to the rectory
of Diss, in East Anglia. Here he developed a
unique form of verse called the 'Skeltonic,'
which consisted of rhyming couplets with lines
varying from three to eleven syllables. Skelton
used his new creation in such poems as *Devout
Trental for Old John Clarke*, an attack on a
deceased enemy; *Philip Sparrow*, a parody of
the Christian burial service; and *Ware the Hawk*,
a tirade against a neighbouring rector who
trained his falcon in church.

In 1512 Skelton returned to the court, where
Henry VIII gave him the lofty title *orator regis*.
The poems of his second period at court
included *The Manner of the World Nowadays*,
condemning contemporary society; *A Ballade of
the Scottysche Kynge* (1513), celebrating the
English victory over the Scots at Flodden; *The
Tunning of Elynour Rumming* (1522), a description of a drunken woman; and *Speke Parrot*
(1521), *Collyn Clout* (1522), and *Why Come Ye
Nat to Court* (1522–3), satirizing the abuses of
the clergy and – under a thin veil – Cardinal
*Wolsey. He also wrote a morality play entitled
Magnyfycence (1516), an allegory of the political
situation at Henry's court. In his last years he

wrote the *Garlande of Laurell*, summing up his poetic achievements. He died at Westminster and was buried in the church of St Margaret. Many stories, for the most part fictitious, were told of his misadventures and practical jokes; these were published in a collection entitled *Merie Tales Made by Master Skelton* (London: T. Colwell 1567). The first edition of his collected works was published under the title *The Pithy, Pleasaunt and Profitable Workes of Maister Skelton* (London: T. Marshe 1568). Although his reputation suffered in succeeding centuries, interest in his work revived with the publication of his poems in 1843 by Alexander Dyce, and today he is recognized as the greatest English poet between Chaucer and Thomas Wyatt (d 1542). The most recent edition of his works is that of Philip Henderson (London 1931, rev eds in 1948, 1959).

Erasmus probably met Skelton during his trip to England in 1499, when he and Thomas *More visited the royal children at Eltham castle. Shortly after he described Skelton as 'the great light and ornament of English letters' (Ep 104), although, as Edwards notes, it was probably not the poet or the rhetorician that Erasmus sought to win, but the tutor to the king's son. At the same time Erasmus wrote a poem in Skelton's praise (Reedijk poem 46), which he never published. This, combined with the fact that in the 1507 edition of the *Prosopopoeia* Erasmus deleted a reference to Skelton (Reedijk poem 45, line 130), suggests that their acquaintance never grew into friendship. As Edwards (p 69) has observed, Erasmus and Skelton had little in common. Skelton saw little good in the new learning and would have been irritated by Erasmus' pacifism and love of Greek. After 1499 Erasmus did not mention the poet in his correspondence, while Skelton for his part criticized Erasmus' *Moria* and his translations of the New Testament in *Speke Parrot* (lines 48–9, 158–9). However, as Heiserman (p 80) notes, Skelton's analysis of flattery in the play *Magnyfycence* parallels Erasmus' discussion of the same topic in the *Institutio principis christiani*. There at least they did agree.

BIBLIOGRAPHY: Allen and CWE Ep 104 / DNB XVIII 327–32 / Emden BRUC 529–30 / STC 22593–620 / L.J. Lloyd 'John Skelton and the New Learning' *Modern Language Review* 24 (1929) 445–6 / L.J. Lloyd *John Skelton* (Oxford 1938) / William Nelson *John Skelton: Laureate* (New York 1939, repr 1964) / H.L.R. Edwards *Skelton* (London 1949) / A.R. Heiserman *Skelton and Satire* (Chicago 1961) / S.E. Fish *John Skelton's Poetry* (New Haven-London 1965)

R.J. SCHOECK & TBD

Marcin SŁAP Dąbrówski d before 19 November 1550

Marcin Słap of Dąbrówka (Dambrowski) was the son of Jan and Jadwiga. The family belonged to the gentry and owned the Dąbrówka estate, in the vicinity of Poznań. In 1525 and 1526 Marcin is found among the clergy of the collegiate church of Our Lady in Poznań; later he was appointed priest of Skórzewo, near Poznań. He became a client of Andrzej *Krzycki, who sent him abroad in the spring of 1528 as a companion to Andrzej *Zebrzydowski. From Erasmus' Ep 2201 to Kryzcki it appears that Słap spent some time with Zebrzydowski in Erasmus' household in Basel. In the autumn they left for Paris (Ep 2078) but then returned to Erasmus and soon afterwards parted company. Zebrzydowski left for Padua, while Słap remained with Erasmus and moved with him to Freiburg, earning his warm praise (Ep 2201). His separation from Zebrzydowski was caused by disagreements, and it seems that Erasmus wrote on his behalf to Krzycki, defending Słap against Zebrzydowski's charges (Ep 2351). In October 1529 Słap returned to Poland, perhaps at the request of Kryzcki, whose entourage in Cracow he joined for a while before departing again for western Europe on 13 March 1530. On 28 March he was at Torgau and delivered to *Melanchthon a letter from Kryzcki, inviting him to Poland. Słap then journeyed to Freiburg and brought Erasmus letters and also a gift from his master (Epp 2375–7). Erasmus sent him to Besançon for a fresh supply of wine (Epp 2348, 2397) and subsequently gave him a letter of recommendation to Conradus *Goclenius as he set out for the University of Louvain, where he arrived on 31 May 1530, as he told Erasmus in an affectionate letter (Epp 2351, 2352).

Subsequently Słap went to Padua, where he matriculated on 20 August 1534 to study law. On 13 May 1536 he wrote Erasmus from Rome

(Ep 3121), but the latter was probably dead by the time the letter reached Basel (AK IV Ep 2041). In all likelihood Słap met Anselmus *Ephorinus in Rome, and it is possible that they returned to Poland together. It is uncertain where Słap had obtained the doctorate of civil and canon law which he possessed by the time he was appointed to the cathedral chapter of Poznań as archdeacon of Pszczew on 28 March 1538. In 1540 he became chancellor to Łukasz of Górka, bishop of Włocławek, and in 1543 dean of Włocławek, but ultimately he settled in Poznań. After the death of Bishop Sebastjan Branicki he was elected administrator of the diocese of Poznań (15 November 1544–9 February 1546). Thereafter he was vicar-general and official of the next bishop of Poznań, Paweł Wolski, and then chancellor of his successor, Benedykt Izdbienski. In 1550 he became archdeacon of Poznań, but in that same year he died in Piotrków.

BIBLIOGRAPHY: Allen Ep 2351 / *Korespondencja Erazma z Rotterdamu z Polakami* ed M. Cytowska (Warsaw 1965) / H. Barycz *Polacy na studiach w Rzymie w epoce Odrodzenia* (Cracow 1938) 96–7 / H. Barycz *Z dziejów poskich wędrówek naukowych za granicę* (Wrocław 1969) 206–7, 216–17 / H. Barycz 'Die ersten wissenschaftlichen Verbindungen Polens mit Basel' *Vierteljahresschrift für die Geschichte der Wissenschaft und Technik* 5 (1960) Sonderheft 2 40–2 / K. Morawski 'Beiträge zur Geschichte des Humanismus in Polen, II: Die Berufung Melanchthons nach Polen' *Sitzungsberichte der Kaiserlichen Akademie der Wissenschaften, Phil.-Hist. Classe* 118 (Vienna 1889) 24 / W. Pociecha 'Rzym wobec starań o sprowadzenie Melanchtona do Polski' *Reformacja w Polsce* 9–10 (1937–8) 418 / J. Nowacki *Dzieje archidiecezji poznańskiej, II: Archidiecezja poznańska w granicach historycznych i jej ustrój* (Poznań 1964) 215, 265 / *Acta Tomiciana* (Poznań-Wrocław 1852–   ) XII Ep 59, XIV Ep 488 / de Vocht CTL II 393–5 / Bierlaire *Familia* 87–8 and passim

HALINA KOWALSKA

Jan ŠLECHTA 24 January 1466–
29 August 1525
Jan Šlechta (Sslechta, Slechta Kostelecius) was a son of Mikuláš (d 1508), a member of the lower gentry who in 1464 settled at Všehrdy (Schehorn, Czehern) in the predominantly German speaking district of Žatec (Saaz), in western Bohemia. Mikuláš owned a number of villages, including Blevice, near Velvary north-west of Prague. Jan was born either at Všehrdy or at Blevice of Johanna of Vřesovice, Mikuláš' second wife.

During his studies at the University in Prague – reduced to the faculty of arts after the stormy Hussite era – Šlechta was introduced to classical literature and humanistic ideas by Řehoř Pražský (Gregorius Pragensis) and received his BA in the fall of 1484. There is some evidence to suggest that he continued his studies at Bologna (A.P. Šlechta 86; Tiuhlář *Listář* 225).

Following his election as king of Hungary (15 July 1490) *Vladislav II decided to move his court and the royal Bohemian chancery from Prague to Buda. Jan Šlechta was appointed to the staff of the chancery as notary to replace personnel who refused to go to Hungary. He was subsequently promoted to protonotary and royal secretary and received many grants of properties and privileges, including a coat of arms with the head of a wolf. Possibly in 1492 he began to use the name Šlechta. In the latter years of his career at Buda he belonged to the inner circle of royal advisers.

On 4 October 1504 in Bohemia he married Magdalena of Strašnice (Strassnitz), the widow of Prokop of Habřina, who had two sons under age, Václav and Mikuláš. Later that year or in 1505 he resigned his post in Hungary and settled with his family at the castle in Kostelec nad Labem, about twenty kilometres northeast of Prague (Ep 1021). He took care of his extensive estates but also made frequent trips to Prague, where he served in the supreme court and attended sessions of the Bohemian diet as one of the wealthiest members of the lower gentry. He maintained personal contacts with humanist friends at the university and continued his correspondence with several leading humanists in Bohemia and abroad.

In 1507 Šlechta entrusted his son Jan to Master Václav Písecký in Prague for humanistic training. It is not known whether Jan was illegitimate or born of a prior and unrecorded marriage, or where and when he continued his studies after Písecký left for Italy in the company of Sigismundus *Gelenius (1509) and died of plague in Venice (1511).

Šlechta died at Kostelec on 29 August 1525 and was buried beside his father in St Martin's church (for his epitaph, see Truhlář *Humanismus* 188 and A.P. Šlechta 109, 116). His widow survived him until 1542. He remained a Roman Catholic, but many of his best friends were members of the Utraquist (Hussite) church, and towards the end of his life he appears to have leaned toward the Utraquist position. In view of his harsh statements on the Czech Brethren (Ep 1021) it is possible that, while at the royal chancery with Augustin Käsenbrod, he influenced King Vladislav, who after 1500 took repressive measures against them.

Šlechta's main interest lay neither in the political nor in the religious sphere. From his student days in Prague to the end of his life he cultivated personal and literary contacts with the humanists of his day. During his sixteen years at Buda (1490–1505; cf Ep 950) he developed lasting friendships with Bohuslav Hasištejnský of Lobkovice (1460–1510), Stanislaus *Thurzo, Johannes Dubravius (1486–1553), Augustin Käsenbrod (Moravus, 1467–1513), Řehoř Hrubý (the father of Sigismundus *Gelenius), Girolamo *Balbi, Conradus Celtis, Caspar *Ursinus Velius, and others. He exchanged letters and books with them and was active in the Sodalitas Danubiana (later Sodalitas litteraria Ungarorum). His brief but important correspondence with Erasmus (1518–19) drew Erasmus' attention to the religious scene in Bohemia. The three letters known today (Epp 950, 1021, 1039) were printed in the two major collections of Erasmus' correspondence (1521, 1529) and were therefore bound to be widely noted. In 1540 they were discussed by the reformers in Strasbourg (Gindely 40, 68). Erasmus' irenic advice to the confessionally divided Bohemians prepared the way for his major initiatives for religious reconciliation in Germany (Epp 1149, 1155 introductions).

Šlechta's extant literary works are few. A few Latin poems and epitaphs indicate a mediocre talent. In realistic self-assessment, he soon ceased to compose verse. His one major work, 'Mikrokosmos,' was a philosophical treatise written as a dialogue in the Platonic tradition; in it Šlechta discussed the basic issues of human existence, in particular the relationship between man and the universe, and between body and soul. Completed in

1500, the manuscript circulated among his humanist friends, who were asked for their comments. Not until 30 April 1522 did he send the final text to Stanislaus Thurzo, together with a dedicatory letter, which is extant (*Dva listáře* 93–7) although the work itself is missing. Of major interest is his correspondence published by Josef Truhlář. It consists of forty-six letters written by Šlechta in Latin and Czech, dealing in part with business and legal matters, while thirteen are addressed to his humanist friends. Twenty-four letters are addressed to him by other humanists, and twenty-five other letters and documents were issued at the royal court.

In spite of his close friendship with many humanists and his elegant style in Latin prose, Šlechta was neither a scholar nor a philosopher. He was, however, a keen observer of and eager participant in human life in all its dimensions.

BIBLIOGRAPHY: Allen and CWE Ep 950 / *Ottuv slovnik naucnv* (Prague 1888–1909) XXIV 666–7 / Anton Gindely *Quellen zur Geschichte der Böhmischen Brüder* ... (Vienna 1859) 40, 68 / *Listář Bohuslava Hasištejnského z Lobkovic* ed Josef Truhlář (Prague 1893) / *Dva listáře humanistické: Racka Doubravského a Václava Píseckého s doplňkem Listáře Jana Šlechty ze Všehrd* ed Josef Truhlář (Prague 1897) / Josef Truhlář 'Život a působení Jana Šlechty ze Všehrd' *Časopis musea král. českého* 53 (1879) 441–58 / Josef Truhlář *Počátky humanismu v Čechách* (Rozpravy České akademie věd, Prague 1892) 48–50 / Josef Truhlář *Humanismus a humanisté v Čechách za krále Vladislava* (Prague 1894) II 66–8 and passim / F.M. Bartoš 'Erasmus und die böhmische Reformation' *Communio Viatorum* 1 (1958) 116–23 and 246–57 / A.P. Šlechta *Jan Šlechta ze Všehrd a jeho rod* Svazek 1 (vol 4 of *Z pravěku do novověku*, Prague 1925) / Jarold Knox Zeman *The Anabaptists and the Czech Brethren in Moravia 1526–1628* (The Hague-Paris 1969) 138–9 and passim / P.S. Allen *The Age of Erasmus* (Oxford 1924) 276–98 / A bio-bibliography of Šlechta will be included in *Rukovět' humanistického básnictví v Čechách a na Móravě* V: *Enchiridion renatae poesis latinae in Bohemia et Moravia* by Antonín Truhlář, Karel Hrdina, Josef Hejnic, and Jan Martínek (scheduled for publication in Prague) J.K. ZEMAN

Pieter de SMET *See Petrus* VULCANIUS

Andrew SMITH documented in London
1522–9
Of Andrew Smith very little seems to be known
beyond the exercise of his duties as a public
notary, such as witnessing of contracts. On 6
April 1526 his name appeared in connection
with an ecclesiastical commission and in July
1529 he was involved in the examination of
witnesses in the matter of *Henry VIII's
divorce.

Erasmus sent him greetings in September
1524 when writing to Zacharius *Deiotarus (Ep
1491).

BIBLIOGRAPHY: Allen Ep 1491 / LP III 2163, IV
2073, 5791 (p 2588), and passim   PGB

Robert and John SMITH documented
1512–18
Of John Smith (Smyth) nothing certain is
known beyond the years of his service with
Erasmus and Thomas *More. In particular, it
has not been possible to identify him with any
one of the bearers of that name listed by Emden
in BRUC and BRUO. His father, Robert, was
apparently a man capable of providing his son
with an education, although he was himself
without Latin, and was connected with William *Gonnell at Cambridge or nearby Landbeach. Allen drew attention to one Robert
Smith who was a bailiff and afterwards an
alderman of Cambridge. He was excommunicated by John *Fawne, vice-chancellor of the
University of Cambridge, about October 1512.
John would seem to have entered Erasmus'
service as a boy, soon after Erasmus' arrival in
Cambridge in August 1511 (Ep 241). He was
know to Roger *Wentford, the headmaster of
St Anthony's, London, whose pupil he may
have been for a while (Epp 241, 276, 277).
Erasmus felt great affection for his servant-
pupil, but John's father did not like him living
in the house of a foreigner, and on 1 November
1513 Erasmus had to return him to his father. In
a letter to Robert he said pointedly that he had
been 'better than a father' to the boy (Ep 276).
Following interventions by Gonnell and Wentford, John joined Erasmus again prior to his
departure for Basel in July 1514. He accompanied his master on this trip and on subsequent
stays in England and elsewhere and enjoyed

his confidence as well as the affection of his
friends (Epp 279, 353, 452, 455, 460, 473, 556,
575, 581, 594). By August 1517 John was
looking for a new master in England (Ep 644)
but for the time being continued to serve
Erasmus (Ep 768), copying his letters into the
Deventer Letter-book (Allen I appendix VIII;
CWE Ep 772 introduction). Early in March John
was sent to England with letters and requests
for papers, money, and horses. His mission
accomplished, albeit not to the master's entire
satisfaction (Epp 822, 823, 829, 888), Smith
returned to Louvain, only to leave for good by
the end of April. His mother wanted him back,
and Thomas More had offered him a position in
his household (CWE Ep 820 introduction).
Erasmus recommended him warmly to his
friends (Epp 829, 832) and six months later sent
him a short letter which shows again his
fondness for the youth (Ep 895).

BIBLIOGRAPHY: Allen and CWE Ep 276 /
Bierlaire *Familia* 49–51   FRANZ BIERLAIRE

Georgius SMOTZERUS *See Georg* SCHMOTZER

Johannes SMYSINCK, SMISING *See Johann
von* SCHMISING

Reyner SNOY of Gouda, d 1 August 1537
Reyner Snoy of Gouda, near Rotterdam, did
not at first exhibit special intellectual gifts and
consequently trained as a blacksmith. After a
short time, however, he resumed his studies
and soon made up for lost time. He matriculated at Louvain on 14 January 1496, entering
the faculty of arts, and subsequently went to
Bologna, where he was awarded a medical
doctorate. After his return to Holland he
became the personal physician to Adolph of
*Burgundy, lord of Veere. In 1513 he went on
an embassy to *James IV of Scotland in the name
of the future *Charles V (cf his *De rebus Batavicis*
100), and much later he undertook a similar
mission to *Christian II of Denmark after the
king had been forced to flee his country in
1523. He is said to have practised medicine in
England for some time, but by 1524 and 1533,
when he can be traced more reliably, he was in
the service of Adolph of Burgundy. In his old
age he returned to his native Gouda and was
made an alderman but soon resigned so as to
devote himself exclusively to religious studies.

He died with the words 'It is getting late, my friends' on his lips and was buried in St John's, Gouda. *Alaard of Amsterdam wrote an epitaph for him, and Cornelis *Gerard considered him as his patron, dedicating to him the two parts of his *Batavia*. The name of Snoy's wife was Aleidis, and they had two daughters, Aleidis and Maria.

Little is known about Snoy's connections with Erasmus. The fact that he edited a collection of Erasmus' early poems with the title of *Silva carminum* may well indicate that they had known each other during the years Erasmus spent at the monastery of Steyn, near Gouda (c 1487–92). In two letters of 1506 addressed to Jacob *Mauritszoon (Epp 190, 202) Erasmus sent greetings to Snoy, praising his erudition. A suggestion that Snoy was the physician addressed in Ep 132 (Walvis 248–9) is unconvincing. In 1516 Snoy addressed Ep 458 to Erasmus, recalling his friendship with Willem *Hermans and announcing his own history of Holland in fifteen books. However, the posthumous edition by his grand-nephew Jacobus Brassica (Cool) comprises only thirteen books. It is possible that the important Gouda manuscripts 1323 (first part) and 1324 are in Snoy's hand.

The following writings by Snoy have appeared in print: a preface to the reader in his relative Franciscus *Theodoricus' *Precatiunculae* (Gouda: Collaciebroeders [1512]; NK 1756); Erasmus' *Silva carminum* edited with an introduction by Snoy (Gouda: Aellaerdus Gauter 1513; NK 871), reproduced photolithographically by C. Ruelens (Brussels 1864); *Psalterium Davidicum paraphrasibus illustratum* (Antwerp: M. Hillen 1535; NK 1907; cf however NK 01109), a popular work, often reprinted and translated; *Antilutherus: Dialogus super doctrina Lutherana* (Gouda: In sponsa solis [c 1540]; NK 1906); *De libertate christiana* (Antwerp: J. Gravius 1550); *De rebus Batavicis libri XIII*, finished 1519, edited by Jacobus Brassica in F. Sweertius *Rerum Belgicarum annales* 1-2 (Frankfurt 1620). A list of his unpublished works (theological, philosophical, medical, and historical) is contained in De Graaf 11–13.

BIBLIOGRAPHY: Allen Ep 190 / A.J. van der Aa et al *Biographisch woordenboek der Nederlanden* (Haarlem 1852–78) XVII-2 814–6 / Reedijk 133–4 / *Matricule de Louvain* III 132 / I. W[alvis]

Beschryving der stad Gouda (Gouda-Leiden [1713]) I 244–9 / B. and M.E. de Graaf *Doctor Reynerus Snoy Goudanus* (Nieuwkoop 1968)

C.G. VAN LEIJENHORST

Jacobus SOBIUS of Cologne, d before 25 January 1528

Jacobus Sobius (Sob, Sobbe), a descendant of a well-known Cologne family, matriculated at the university of his native city on 10 June 1508 and received his BA the following year. Living in the Bursa Corneliana, he enjoyed the instruction of teachers such as Johannes Greselius, Johann Gruther, Peter Ubels, and Gerlach von Düren, who were sympathetic to humanism. Above all, he and Henricus *Glareanus were students of Johannes *Caesarius. In life-long association with Caesarius and Hermann von *Neuenahr, Sobius remained at the very centre of the Cologne humanist movement. From 1512 to 1516 he travelled extensively visiting Conradus *Mutianus at Gotha in 1514 and subsequently teaching at the Latin school of Freiberg, Saxony, which had been established by Johannes Aesticampianus.

Having returned to Cologne, Sobius received the degree of MA in 1516. He was a doctor of laws in 1519 when he accompanied Neuenahr to Frankfurt, the scene of the imperial election. On 30 June 1519 he addressed from Frankfurt to the newly elected *Charles V a patriotic-humanistic manifesto on behalf of the German nobility, subsequently published as *Oratio Germaniae nobilium ad Carolum Caesarem* (Sélestat: L. Schürer 1519). In Cologne he taught at the Bursa Corneliana until its demise in 1523. On 25 July 1523 he was appointed orator (envoy) by the city of Cologne under a contract stipulating a salary of twenty-five florins (Oberländer Gulden) and a suit of clothes annually and also raising the matter of university reform. On 23 October 1523 Sobius took his oath of office. From a letter he wrote to the Cologne council that was accompanied by the complaints of two students, it can be gathered that he received a formal mandate to submit proposals for reforming the university (Keussen 'Regesten' 234–9).

An assessment of Sobius' position in the religious controversy hinges upon the authorship of the dialogue *Henno rusticus* circulated under the pseudonym of Philalethes civis

Utopiensis and probably first printed in an anonymous edition by Andreas *Cratander in Basel (critical edition in Hutten *Opera* IV 485–514). This lampoon of an unnamed papal legate has normally been attributed to Sobius on the strength of an explicit statement to this effect by Henricus Cornelius *Agrippa. However, a letter to *Zwingli (z VII Ep 148) by Jacobus *Nepos dating from the time when the manuscript was printed in Basel would seem to cast some doubt on the traditional attribution. Sobius' publications include a Latin translation of the life of St Anthony of Egypt, published in 1516 with a prefatory letter that expresses his support of *Reuchlin, a Latin edition of Josephus (Cologne: E. Cervicornus 1524), and a Livy (Cologne: P. Quentel 1525).

In December 1526 Sobius wrote to Erasmus about the forwarding of mail and his contacts with Hans *Bogbinder; he also encouraged Erasmus to move to Cologne (Ep 1775).

BIBLIOGRAPHY: Allen Ep 1775 / ADB XXXIV 529–30 / Joseph Hartzheim *Bibliotheca Coloniensis* (Cologne 1747) 153–4 / *Matrikel Köln* II 626 / Hermann Keussen 'Regesten und Auszüge zur Geschichte der Universität Köln 1388–1559' *Mitteilungen aus dem Stadtarchiv von Köln* 36–7 (1918) esp 374–89 / Karl Krafft 'Mittheilungen aus der niederrheinischen Reformationsgeschichte' *Zeitschrift des Bergischen Geschichtsvereins* 6 (1869) 193–340, esp 228–40 / Ludwig Geiger *Johann Reuchlin* (Leipzig 1871, repr 1964) 351, 365   EUGEN HOFFMANN & PGB

Francesco SODERINI of Florence,
10 June 1453–17 May 1524

Francesco (Cardinalis Vulterranus) was the third son of Tommaso Soderini, a prominent Florentine statesman, and Dianora Tornabuoni, a sister to Lucrezia, the wife of Piero de' Medici. Lorenzo (I) de' *Medici ('il Magnifico') was his first cousin and Piero Soderini, gonfalonier of Florence from 1502 to 1512, his brother. He was taught Latin, probably by Giorgio Antonio Vespucci, a friar of San Marco, but there is no evidence he ever learnt Greek. He studied law at the University of Pisa from 1473 to 1478. Marsilio *Ficino wrote to Francesco in encouragement and praised him to Pierfilippo dal Corno of Perugia, one of his teachers. Francesco was himself teaching law at Pisa in 1477–8 and wrote a (lost) treatise on

the Decretals. On 11 March 1478 he obtained the administration of the bishopric of Volterra, by which title he was thereafter commonly known; in 1486 he was ordained priest.

Francesco's career took a new direction in November 1480 when he was among the Florentine ambassadors to *Sixtus IV concerning the raising of the interdict imposed after the Pazzi conspiracy; he was noted for his eloquence on this occasion. In 1484 he went to Rome again to congratulate Innocent VIII on his accession. In 1487 he was appointed an apostolic secretary, and in 1488 he became an auditor of contradicted letters in the papal chancery. He undertook various diplomatic missions for the Florentine republic after the fall of the Medici, accompanying *Charles VIII when he left Florence for Naples in November 1494 and serving as resident ambassador in France during 1496 and 1497; from December 1498 to September 1499 he was ambassador in Milan; from September 1501 to June 1502 and from November 1502 to June 1503 he was again resident ambassador in France; although he would have missed Erasmus in Paris, he may have made other intellectual contacts when there in February and March 1502. In late June 1502 he went on a mission to Cesare Borgia at Urbino and was accompanied by Niccolò *Machiavelli, some of whose political ideas he may have shared. He was a keen supporter of Machiavelli's Florentine militia project (as letters to his brother Piero and to Machiavelli of 4 March 1506 testify) and recommended Don Miguele, Cesare Borgia's brutal henchman, as commander in 1505. On 31 May 1503 he was made a cardinal by *Alexander VI. An important figure owing to his brother's position, he initially enjoyed the favour of *Julius II. He was appointed bishop of Cortona on 6 March 1504 and of Saintes in 1505. In 1506 he accompanied the pope to Perugia and Bologna. Erasmus may have met him then or at Rome in 1509; in 1508 he obtained the titulary church and palace of Santi Apostoli and according to Paolo *Cortese received visitors in his library so that he could continue reading as soon as they left. He accompanied the pope on his military expedition to Bologna in the winter of 1510–11; though Julius II suspected him in 1511 for his pro-French allegiance, he was not involved in the schism of rebel cardinals. In spite of his brother's fall and the return of the Medici to Florence in 1512 Francesco supported *Leo x's election; Leo appointed him legate in Rome when he went to Florence and Bologna in December 1515.

Francesco's anti-Medicean political interest remained active, however, and he was implicated in the conspiracy of Cardinal *Petrucci against Leo which came to light in 1517. On 8 June he was excommunicated but subsequently received a pardon with a fine of 12,500 ducats – an act of papal clemency which did not please the young Lorenzo (II) de' *Medici, then ruling Florence, or his mother, Alfonsina. Francesco had first taken refuge at Palestrina, of which he had become cardinal-bishop on 18 July 1516, and then in the Colonna fief of Fondi, where by papal permission he remained until Leo's death. He actively opposed Cardinal Giulio de' Medici (*Clement VII) in the ensuing conclave and *Adrian VI failed to bring about a reconciliation. On 27 April 1523 Soderini was arrested for conspiring both to encourage *Francis I to invade Italy and to provoke an anti-imperial rising in Sicily. He was imprisoned in Castel Sant'Angelo, where he fell ill, but was released for the conclave of September 1523, and the cardinals made his pardon a condition of Clement VII's election. In December 1523 he was promoted to the cardinal-bishoprics of Porto and Ostia and after months of illness died at Rome on 17 May 1524.

In a letter of 21 February 1524 Erasmus wrote that he had sent Soderini many letters (Ep 1424) and in June 1525 described him to *Béda as a man of learning who nevertheless had not once written to him in encouragement (Ep 1581). He was not celebrated as a liberal patron, but did make some (unfulfilled) testamentary provisions to found a college in Paris for Italian students of canon law and theology. A portrait believed to be of Francesco and attributed to Lorenzo Lotto by Bernard Berenson was sold at Sotheby's in 1929; its present whereabouts are unknown.

BIBLIOGRAPHY: Allen Ep 1424 / Biographical details (but without full references) are provided by L. Passerini 'Sigillo del Cardinale Francesco Soderini' *Periodico di numismatica e sfragistica* 6 (1874) 298–310, which includes a reproduction of Francesco's seal, and F.M.

Apollonj Ghetti 'Nuovi appunti su Francesco Soderini Cardinale Volterrano' *L'Urbe* 39 (1976) no 3–4 1–14, no 5 1–17 / In general see Eubel II 25, 271, and passim, Pastor VI, 129, and passim, Sanudo I 97–8 and passim / Much further material and extensive discussion is in K.J.P. Lowe 'Francesco Soderini (1453–1524), Florentine patrician and cardinal' (doctoral thesis, London 1985); from this the same author has already published 'Cardinal Francesco Soderini's proposal for an Italian college in Paris in 1524' *History of Universities* 4 (1984) 167–78 / On Francesco's university career see A. Verde *Lo studio fiorentino* (Florence-Pistoia 1973–) III-1 316–19 / For his role in diplomacy and Florentine military reform see G. Canestrini and A. Desjardins *Négotiations diplomatiques de la France avec la Toscane* I (Paris 1859); N. Machiavelli *Legazioni e commissarie* ed S. Bertelli (Milan 1964) I and *Lettere* ed S. Bertelli (Milan 1961); N. Rubinstein 'Machiavelli and the world of Florentine politics' in *Studies on Machiavelli* ed M.P. Gilmore (Florence 1972) esp 13–16; R.P. Cooper 'Machiavelli, Francesco Soderini and Don Michelotto' *Nuova Rivista Storica* 66 (1982) 342–57 / On events in 1517 see A. Ferrajoli *La congiura dei cardinali contro Leone x* (Rome 1919) 70–80 / Some unpublished letters and other writings are noted in P. Kristeller *Iter Italicum* (London-Leiden 1965–)   D.S. CHAMBERS

Heinrich Ritze SOLDEN *See Euricius* CORDUS

Jan Benedykt SOLFA of Trzebiel, 1483–31 March 1564
Solfa was the son of Benedykt and signed his name Johannes Benedictus or Benedicti. He came from the small town of Trzebiel, in Lower Lusatia, hence he was called Lusatus. On 23 February 1505 he commenced his studies at the University of Cracow, receiving the degrees of BA in 1507 and MA in 1512. In 1512–13 he lectured at the faculty of arts. He then went to Italy, securing a doctorate in medicine from Bologna on 11 February 1516. He also spent some time in Rome and Venice. In November he returned to Cracow, which became his main domicile and was where he eventually died. Solfa's medical practice brought him fame and wealthy protectors including Johannes *Dantiscus, Nicolaus Copernicus, and Piotr *To-

micki. He was court physician to King *Sigismund I from 1523 and later physician to the cathedral and chapter of Cracow. Giving medical advice took him to Warmia, Gdansk, and Wrocław. Thanks to his powerful patrons he received many ecclesiastical benefices: he was canon and from 1547 provost of Warmia, canon of Głogów, Wrocław (from 1538), Vilno, Warsaw, Sandomierz, and Cracow (from 1547), and *custos* of Łowicz. On 11 July 1535 he was raised to the rank of gentry by Sigismund I. Solfa made a study of syphilis and the English sweat and was also interested in mental illness, hallucinations, and prophecy. He devoted much attention to philosophical and theological problems, in particular the fate of the soul after the death of the body, which was the subject of his only known letter to Erasmus (Ep 2601).

Solfa's most important works are: *De morbo gallico*, known only from a reprint in Aloysius Lusinus Utinensis' *De morbo gallico omnia quae extant apud omnes medicos* (Venice: G. Ziletti 1566); *Regimen de novo et prius Germaniae inaudito morbo quem passim anglicum sudorem ... appellant* (Cracow: H. Wietor 1530), dedicated to Krzystof *Szydłowiecki; *De visionibus et revelationibus naturalibus et divinis* (Cracow: H. Wietor 1545), dedicated to Jan Tarnowski, castellan of Cracow; *De humatione corporum mortuorum et refrigerio animarum a corpore exutarum libellus* (Cracow: Lazarz 1564).

BIBLIOGRAPHY: Allen Ep 2601 / ADB XXXIV 565 / W. Kożuszek *Jan Benedykt Solfa – lekarz polskiego Odrodzenia* (Wrocław 1966) / J. Lachs *Lekarze krakowskiej kapituły katedralnej, Przeglad Lekarski* 44 (1905) 465–6 / W. Pociecha *Królowa Bona: Czasy i ludzie Odrodzenia* (Poznań 1949–58) I–IV / *Acta Tomiciana* (Poznań-Wrocław 1852–) Epp 58, 95, 274, 415, XVI Epp 99, 621, 638, 645, 648, 650, 661, 662, XVII Epp 89, 132, 193, 514 / *Matricularum Regni Poloniae summaria* (Warsaw 1910–14) IV 13546, 17895 / *Korespondencja Erazma z Rotterdamu z Polakami* ed M. Cytowska (Warsaw 1965)

HALINA KOWALSKA

Jacob SOTI of Aardenburg, documented 1520–47
In the spring of 1520 a young man was sent from Courtrai to Louvain to study liberal arts at the College of the Lily. In Ep 1094 Jan de

*Hondt gave his name as Jan (Johannes) Soti and mentioned that he was sent by the canon and precentor Jacob van *Thielt; he also commented that he was a native of Aardenburg (eighteen kilometres north-east of Bruges) and was poor but well prepared for university on account of his intelligence and knowledge of Latin and music.

This Jan Soti is most likely identical with the Jacobus Soti of Courtrai who registered at the University of Louvain on 28 August 1520 as a student of the Lily and the Jacob Soti (Sothy) listed from 1522 among the 'vicarii perpetui' of the Courtrai chapter. In 1524 Jacob Soti was appointed chaplain of St Nicaise and in 1526 choirmaster (*phonescus*) with the active support of Jacob van Thielt. In 1530 and 1532 Soti received special awards for having served as choirmaster without a salary. In 1547 he was appointed chaplain of St Willebrord's, Hulst, in Zeeland, a benefice within the gift of the Courtrai chapter.

BIBLIOGRAPHY: *Matricule de Louvain* III-1 636 / C. Caullet *Musiciens de la Collégiale Notre-Dame à Courtrai* (Courtrai-Bruges 1911) 10, 58, 149, 161, 169–70, 173 PGB

Mariano SOZZINI of Siena
In Ep 2267 to Erasmus, Bonifacius *Amerbach, discussing the divorce case of *Henry VIII of England, mentioned Mariano Sozzini as a jurist who held that a pope could annul a marriage if it was not consummated, even after a long period of cohabitation. Allen identified him as the older Mariano Sozzini (1401–67), but John Tedeschi has more recently argued in favour of his younger namesake (1482–1556), pointing out that the latter was among the jurists at Padua paid by the English for their legal opinion on the divorce. However, as Tedeschi points out, the younger Mariano supported the king's position; the argument mentioned in Ep 2267, on the other hand, favoured the legal position of *Catherine of Aragon, which was based on the premise that her marriage to Henry was valid because the pope had the right to dispense them from the effects of her earlier marriage to Prince *Arthur, which was never consummated. Therefore it is still unclear which Mariano is cited by Amerbach.

BIBLIOGRAPHY: Allen Ep 2267 / *Italian Refor-*

Georgius Spalatinus

---

mation Studies in Honor of Laelius Socinus ed John
Tedeschi (Florence 1965) 282–7, 292–8

TBD

Gianbattista SPAGNUOLI *See Baptista*
MANTUANUS

Georgius SPALATINUS of Spalt, 17 January
1484–16 January 1545
Georgius Spalatinus is the name commonly
used by the son of Georg Burckhardt, a tanner
at Spalt, thirty-five kilometres south-west of
Nürnberg. The name of Spalatinus' mother is
not known. He first attended the chapter
school of St Nicholas' in Spalt, then from 1497
the Latin school at St Sebald's in Nürnberg,
where he was taught by the humanist Heinrich
Grüninger of Munich. In 1498 he matriculated
at the University of Erfurt, where he graduated
BA in 1499 and belonged to the circle of
students around the Thuringian humanist
Nikolaus Marschalk. In his first publication,
Laus musarum ... (Erfurt 1501, Volz no 1), he
referred to himself as Marschalk's 'puer amanuensis.' Accompanying his teacher, he registered on 18 October 1502 at the newly founded

University of Wittenberg and there obtained
his MA on 2 February 1503. He proceeded to
study law, returning to Erfurt in the winter of
1504–5. There he joined the circle of humanists
headed by *Mutianus Rufus. In the autumn of
1505 Mutianus obtained for him the position of
librarian and teacher of novices in the monastery of Georgenthal, near Gotha, where he
made friends with Henricus *Urbanus, the
monastery's steward, and began to apply
humanist principles to his study of the Bible.
   In 1507 Spalatinus obtained the parish of
Hohenkirchen, which he left in the charge of a
vicar. A public notary from 1507, he took holy
orders in 1508. In the same year he was called
to Torgau to tutor John Frederick of *Saxony,
the nephew of the Elector Frederick the Wise of
*Saxony. Similar appointments followed in the
wake of this first one. In 1511 Spalatinus went
to Wittenberg as mentor to two other nephews
of Frederick, dukes Otto and Ernest of
*Brunswick-Lüneburg, who were attending
the university there; from 1514 he was also
mentor to the elector's natural son, Sebastian
von Jessen. In 1510 he was asked to prepare a
chronicle of Saxony, and in 1512 he became
director of a new library to be established at the
castle of Wittenberg. In 1511 he received a
canonry of the chapter of St George in
Altenburg, but because of his illegitimate birth
he needed papal dispensation to possess his
canonry and did not obtain this until 1515.
During this second period of residence in
Wittenberg he came to know *Luther. Initially
it was because of the *Reuchlin controversy
that he asked Johann *Lang to introduce him to
Luther, but soon a frequent exchange of ideas
and a close friendship developed between
them.
   In September 1516 Spalatinus joined the
elector's chancery as private secretary to
Frederick the Wise, whom he later advised in
religious matters. In 1518 Pope *Leo x conferred upon him special powers to grant
absolution, and in 1522 he became court
preacher. He used his steadily growing influence to promote the university reform demanded by Luther and *Melanchthon in 1518. In the
controversy over indulgences he mediated
between Luther and the elector and, weather-
ing several crises, managed to ensure Frederick's continued protection of his friend. To do

so, he often had to restrain Luther while on the other hand urging the elector to stand firm. He strongly objected to the more radical movements which followed in the wake of Luther's reform.

Spalatinus first wrote to Erasmus in December 1516 (Ep 501) after Luther had prompted him to relay his critical comments on Erasmus' *Annotationes* on the New Testament. In fact Spalatinus' letter is based on one he had received from Luther (w *Briefwechsel* I Ep 27), which not only touches upon justification but also spells out Luther's reservations with regard to humanism. This first friendly approach was followed by others (Epp 711, 978, 1001), which bore fruit in 1519. On the eve of the Leipzig debate Erasmus cautiously expressed his sympathy for Luther's stand, although, like Spalatinus himself, he counselled moderation (Epp 939, 979, 980).

In 1520 relations between Spalatinus and Erasmus were at their most intimate as Spalatinus translated several of Erasmus' shorter works into German, among them the *Querela pacis* together with Ep 288, the *Institutio principis christiani*, and *Sileni Alcibiadis* (*Adagia* III iii 1; Volz nos 6, 9, 17–19, 24). Even though several of these were not printed until 1521 or 1522, the accompanying dedications were all dated from 1520. In the autumn of that year Spalatinus accompanied Frederick the Wise to Cologne, where *Charles v held court in the wake of his solemn coronation. Erasmus too attended the court and on 5 November met the elector in a private audience, with only Spalatinus present as a translator. Afterwards the latter accompanied Erasmus back to his room and was present when he put the famous *Axiomata pro causa Lutheri* (*Opuscula* 329–37) on paper. The subsequent printing of this confidential document was arranged without Spalatinus' knowledge (Höss 182–3; ASD IX-1 182; Ep 1512). As Luther prepared to appear before the diet of Worms, Erasmus shared Spalatinus' concern for the reformer's safety (Ep 1192A).

Luther's reformation was running its course, and in view of the accompanying disturbances Erasmus tried once more to influence Luther by writing to Spalatinus in March 1523 (Ep 1348); the message again was to show restraint. Although Spalatinus shared this concern he took the final step that very spring of breaking

with the papal church. In the following year, when Erasmus published *De libero arbitrio* as a public attack on Luther, he explained this decision to Spalatinus (Ep 1497), who at about the same time received a copy of the book by way of Wittenberg (*Melanchthons Briefwechsel* I Ep 343). His reaction is not known, and there are no traces of further correspondence until much later.

Meanwhile Spalatinus accompanied the elector on all his diplomatic journeys, especially to the diets (Augsburg 1518, Worms 1521, and Nürnberg 1522 and 1523–4), but he could not persuade Frederick to take personal charge of the reorganization of church affairs. After Frederick's death Spalatinus became minister of Altenburg, giving his inaugural sermon on 6 August 1525. On 19 November he married Katharina Heidenreich, alias Streubel, the daughter of a burgher of Altenburg, thus provoking a serious quarrel with his fellow canons at St George's. His two daughters by this marriage were Hanna (b 16 January 1532) and Katharina (b 28 August 1533). In 1526 he attended the imperial diet of Speyer in the retinue of the Elector John of *Saxony. From 1527 on he was active preparing and conducting church visitations and thereby assisted the establishment of a territorial church controlled by the sovereign. On 22 December 1528 he was named superintendent of the Altenburg church district. During the religious colloquies of 1530 to 1532 he was a member of the advisory council to the Elector John and to Duke John Frederick. When John Frederick, his former pupil, became elector, Spalatinus was consulted even more frequently; when the University of Wittenberg was reorganized in 1536, he was confirmed as supervisor of the library, and in 1537 he played an active role in the reformation of the Albertine districts of Freiberg and Wolkenstein, a development Duke George of *Saxony was unable to prevent because they belonged to his younger brother, Duke Henry. After the death of Duke George in 1539 Spalatinus also helped reform Albertine Saxony. Although he usually kept busy in defiance of a delicate constitution, he had to endure serious illness in 1522, 1527, 1535, when he made his will on 13 October, and 1537. With advancing years he suffered from gallstones, and by October 1544 his final illness began. He died four months later in Altenburg and was buried in St Bartholomew's. Neither his grave nor the monument is extant.

Spalatinus' literary output consists of forty-nine works, most of them minor and translations rather than original compositions (see Volz). Of his historical works only two were printed during his lifetime (Volz nos 39, 47). His important biography of Frederick the Wise was edited by Christian Neudecker and Ludwig Preller (Jena 1851). A manuscript of his Saxon chronicle (in three volumes, illustrated by a pupil of Lukas Cranach) is in the arts collection of Coburg castle (MSS 3–5); the other historical writings are for the most part in the Staatsarchiv of Weimar. The manuscript of an early religious tract is in the Stadt- und Kreisbibliothek of Gotha. Of later theological treatises the following are noteworthy: an instruction to the congregation in the city of Schweinfurt (1534: Volz no 37) and a treatise about the Eucharist (1543: Volz no 48). His most extensive work is a translation of Petrarch (1532; Volz no 34).

The following portraits exist: an oil painting by Lukas Cranach the Elder of the young Spalatinus, inscribed 'anno etatis 26, anno Domini 1509,' now in the collection gathered by F.J. von Lipperheide, Berlin; a woodcut by Cranach inscribed 'Christo Saluatori Deo Opti. Max. Georgius Spalatinus Peccator. MDXV'; a model for a medal with the circumscription 'Anno domini 1518. Georgivs Spalatinvs' in the Zentralmuseum of Friedenstein castle, Gotha; an oil painting by Lukas Cranach the Younger described as 'effigies G. Spalatini, MDXXXVII' in the Staatliche Kunsthalle of Karlsruhe (sometimes attributed to Lucas Cranach the Elder).

BIBLIOGRAPHY: Allen Ep 591 / ADB XXXV 1–29 / Georg Mentz 'Die Briefe Georg Spalatins an Veit Warbeck' ARG 1 (1904) 197–246 / Willy Flach 'Georg Spalatin als Geschichtschreiber' in Zur Geschichte und Kultur des Elbe-Saale-Raumes, Festschrift für Walter Möllenberg (Burg 1939) / Irmgard Höss Georg Spalatin 1484–1545 (Weimar 1956) / Irmgard Höss 'Georg Spalatin' in Fränkische Lebensbilder (Neustadt-Aisch 1978) VIII 35–50 / Irmgard Höss 'Der Brief des Erasmus von Rotterdam an Kurfürst Friedrich den Weisen vom 30. Mai 1519' ARG 46 (1955) 209–13 / Irmgard Höss 'Georg Spalatins Traktat "De Sacramento Venerabile Eucharistiae et de Confessione" vom Jahre 1525' ARG 49 (1958) 79–86 / Hans Volz 'Bibliographie der im 16. Jahrhundert erschienenen Schriften Georg Spalatins' Zeitschrift für Bibliothekswesen und Bibliographie 5 (1958) 83–119 / Otto Herding 'Die deutsche Gestalt der Institutio principis Christiani des Erasmus: Leo Jud und Spalatin' in Aus Adel und Kirche, Festschrift für Gerd Tellenbach (Freiberg-Vienna 1968) 534–51

IRMGARD HÖSS

Engelbert van SPANGEN d 28 November 1544

Engelbert, the younger brother of Filips van *Spangen, was born in Breda and on 10 December 1499 entered the abbey of St Bertin at Saint-Omer, where his maternal uncle Antoon van *Bergen was abbot. He was appointed Antoon's coadjutor on 2 October 1511 and by 1514 was preparing to take on a major share of administrative duties (Ep 291). On 12 January 1532 he succeeded to the abbacy. In 1538 he granted hospitality to refugee monks from England, and despite the strained financial position in which the abbey found itself, he succeeded in restoring the abbot's apartment. His sister was the mother of Gérard d'Haméricourt, who became his successor as abbot of St Bertin.

BIBLIOGRAPHY: Allen and CWE Ep 291 / H. de Laplane Les Abbés de Saint-Bertin (Saint-Omer 1854–5) II 89–102 PGB

Filips van SPANGEN c 1477–1529

Filips van Spangen (Philippus Hispanus) was the eldest son of another Filips, heer van Spangen in Schieland, north of Rotterdam, and of Anna van *Glimes. In 1509 he succeeded his father in the lordship. Filips was a patron of Jan *Becker of Borsele, who owed to him his prebend at Middelburg and met him again when he visited Middelburg in the spring of 1514. On this occasion they talked of their common admiration for Erasmus, and Spangen read the Enchiridion on the spot (Ep 291).

Spangen sold one of his hereditary lordships and remained unmarried. At his death he left two natural daughters.

BIBLIOGRAPHY: Allen and CWE Ep 291 / F.V. Goethals Dictionnaire généalogique et héraldique des familles nobles du royaume de Belgique (Brussels 1849–52) IV [393–4] PGB

Richard SPARCHEFORD d 16 June 1560
Richard Sparcheford (Sparkford, Sperchefordus) studied at Oxford, where he graduated BA on 1 July 1510, having already taken holy orders, and proceeded MA on 4 July 1513. Shortly thereafter Sparcheford entered the service of Cuthbert *Tunstall as chaplain. He might therefore have become acquainted with Erasmus either in England before the latter's departure to the continent in July 1514 or in Brussels the following year, when Tunstall frequently met Erasmus during his embassy to the future *Charles V. By 1517 Erasmus had already written to Sparcheford, recommending to him his servant-pupil John *Smith and encouraging Sparcheford in his own studies (Ep 644). Sparcheford was also befriended by Christopher *Urswick, to whom, together with Tunstall, he served as executor and to whose rectorship of Hackney he succeeded through the offices of Cardinal *Wolsey on 28 March 1522 (LP III 2136, 2145). In rapid succession Sparcheford became rector of St Botolph's, Bishopsgate, London, on 20 September 1525, resigning by October 1535; vicar of Sawbridgeworth, Hertfordshire, from 3 October 1527 until 1555; canon of York and prebendary of South Newbald from 1524 to 1537; and canon of St Paul's, London, on 31 March 1534, resigning in February 1537. During most of his early career he appears to have remained in Tunstall's service, and the latter presented him with a copy of Linacre's translation of Galen's *De temperamentis* (Cambridge: J. Siberch 1521), now in the Bodleian Library.

From the mid-1530s Sparcheford devoted most of his energies to the bishopric of Hereford. Already the archdeacon of Salop (Shropshire), he had been commended in 1535 to Edward *Fox, bishop-elect of Hereford, as one who had faithfully served his predecessor (LP IX 245). In October 1538 Sparcheford was commissioned to survey the bishopric, while in 1539 he signed the Act of the Six Articles and the following year the act annulling Henry's marriage to Anne of Cleves. He was installed as a canon of Hereford and prebendary of Piona Parva on 1 April 1539.

The continuation of friendly relations with Erasmus is revealed by an exchange of letters in 1527, when Sparcheford sent Erasmus a copy of *Linacre's *De emendata structura latini ser-*

monis (London 1524) and in return received a volume of Chrysostom (Epp 1867, 1896).

BIBLIOGRAPHY: Allen Ep 644 / Emden BRUO 1501–40 530 / LP III 2136, 2145 (28), 2577, IV 1254, 4029 (2, 3), 4175, VII 923 (iv), IX 245, 334, X 75, 316, XIII-2 600, XIV-1 1065 (4), XV 861 / J. Le Neve *Fasti Ecclesiae Anglicanae 1300–1541* 3rd ed (London 1962–7) II 8, 41, V 31, VI 72

MORDECHAI FEINGOLD

Johann SPEISER of Forchheim, documented 1504–31
Johann Speiser (Speyser, Spyser) of Forchheim, in Bavaria, diocese of Bamberg, was already a priest when he matriculated at the University of Basel in 1508. In 1511 he received a doctorate in canon law and for some time was a procurator at the episcopal court. Indeed, barring an error in the colophon date, he was in Basel as early as 1504, when he edited the *Rosetum exercitiorum spiritualium* (Basel: Jacob of Pforzheim 1504).

Soon after receiving his doctorate Speiser must have moved to Augsburg. The position of curate at the church of St Maurice's chapter had traditionally been filled by one of the canons but from 1510 the parishioners, led by the rich and influential Jakob Fugger, protested against the inadequacy of this arrangement. In 1512 they were authorized to appoint a preacher and maintain him at their own expense. The choice fell upon Speiser, who was clearly Fugger's candidate. After further representations in Rome the chapter was obliged to provide a canonry for the preacher. Christoph von *Stadion and Johann *Eck showed some interest in the position, but Speiser prevailed and on 20 September 1518 was confirmed by the chapter. In the course of these developments the Fuggers acquired long-lasting rights of patronage with regard to the appointment of preachers and possibly the entire chapter of St Maurice's (Ep 2430). In 1518 Speiser dedicated to Jakob Fugger his German translation of a Latin report by Jakob Mennel about the elevation to the cardinalate of Albert of *Brandenburg: *Von der eerlichen und in teutschen Landen seltzsamesten gaistlichen Geschicht ...* [Augsburg 1518]. Subsequently he became associated with the pro-Lutheran party of Augsburg and their leading exponent, Johann Frosch. He also entered into a controversy with the Dominican Johannes *Faber about predestination and other matters. In 1523 he published two sermons on Romans and justification (Augsburg: [M. Ramminger]). From 1522 Stadion, now bishop of Augsburg, was pressing for the removal of Frosch and also of Speiser, while the city council protected them. Speiser enjoyed firm support among his parishioners, but with Stadion and Eck requesting his citation to Rome and considering the religious conservatism of Fugger, his patron, he returned in 1524 to preaching in accordance with the tenets of the Roman church. His parishioners rebelled, and Fugger had to replace him as preacher of St Maurice's with Ottmar *Nachtgall. It seems that Speiser remained in Augsburg. In 1531 Matthias *Kretz let Erasmus know that his mental health was poor and that he was frequently delirious (Ep 2430). Erasmus' reply (Ep 2445) made it clear that he did not know, or could not remember, Speiser.

BIBLIOGRAPHY: Allen Ep 2430 / Friedrich Roth Augsburgs Reformationsgeschichte 2nd ed (Munich 1901–11) I 86, 120–6 / Friedrich Zoepfl Geschichte des Bistums Augsburg und seiner Bischöfe (Munich-Augsburg 1955–   ) II 36, 53, 159–61 / Matrikel Basel I 290 / Rudolf Wackernagel Geschichte der Stadt Basel (Basel 1907–54) II-2 730   IG & PGB

Francesco SPERULO of Camerino
Born at Camerino, in the Marches, Francesco Sperulo (Sperula, Spherulus, Speroli) was a poet at the court of Giulio Cesare da Varano, lord of Camerino, before travelling to Rome at the end of the fifteenth century. Here he participated in the Academy of *Pomponius Laetus and later in the literary circle which met in the house of Paolo *Cortese. He enjoyed the favour of *Alexander VI and of his son, Cesare Borgia, attending the latter's court at Cesena with Pier Francesco Giustolo, Serafino Ciminelli d'Aquila, Vincenzo Orfino, and Vincenzo Calmeta. He composed a panegyric and several Latin poems in hexameters in Cesare's honour. Later he was a member of the literary circle in Rome which surrounded Johannes *Corycius, and several of his poems were included in the Coryciana collection edited by Blosius *Palladius (Rome 1524). From 19 January 1524 until 19 January 1526 he was bishop of San Leo, in the

Marches. Two orations, delivered while he was bishop of San Leo, were published: one advocating peace between the Emperor *Charles V and *Francis I of France, the other celebrating a victory of *Sigismund I of Poland over the Tartars. The Biblioteca Apostolica Vaticana contains in manuscript his 'Villa Julia Medica versibus fabricata' (Vat. Lat. MS 5812); Girolamo Tiraboschi notes that he composed a discussion of the life of man entitled 'Antropographia' or 'Antropopaedia.'

In his reply to Pietro *Corsi (Ep 3032) Erasmus mentioned Sperulo and Filippo (II) *Beroaldo among the many friends he made during his travels in Italy.

BIBLIOGRAPHY: Allen Ep 3032 / Eubel III 223 / Lodovico Jacobilli Bibliotheca Umbriae sive de scriptoribus provinciae Umbriae (Foligno 1658) 121 / P. Savini Storia della città di Camerino (Camerino 1895) 283 / G. Tiraboschi Storia della letteratura italiana (Milan 1822–6) VII 1979–80 / P.O. Kristeller Iter Italicum (London-Leiden 1965–   ) II 55, 335, and passim / C. Beuf Cesare Borgia, the Machiavellian Prince (Toronto-New York 1942) 178 / G. Garnett 'A laureate of Caesar Borgia' English Historical Review 17 (1902) 15–19 / M. Mallet The Borgias: The Rise and Fall of a Renaissance Dynasty (London 1969) 217 / F. Ubaldini Vita di Mons. Angelo Colocci ed V. Fanelli (Vatican City 1969) appendix IV, 114   PAOLO PISSAVINO

Jakob SPIEGEL of Sélestat,
c 1483–after 30 June 1547
Jakob Spiegel (Spigel, Spiegellius, Specularis), born in Sélestat, Lower Alsace, was the son of Magdalene, the sister of Jakob *Wimpfeling (Ep 2088), and her first husband, Jakob Spiegel, a baker. He attended the local Latin school. After his father's death in 1493 he was brought up by his uncle in Speyer. From 1497 he studied in Heidelberg, where he obtained a BA in 1500, then continued his law studies in Freiburg under Udalricus *Zasius. On the recommendation of Jakob *Villinger he received a position in the imperial chancery in 1504. In 1511–12 he resumed his studies in Tübingen and subsequently obtained a doctorate of both laws (perhaps in Vienna). In 1513 he was professor of law at the University of Vienna but subsequently returned to the Hapsburg chancery, where he served as

imperial secretary until the death of the Emperor *Maximilian I in 1519. Returning to Sélestat, he became a member of the literary society, but in 1520 he entered the chancery of *Charles v and was present at the diet of Worms in 1521. That same year both Martin *Bucer and Otto *Brunfels asked him to support their appeal to the papal nuncio Girolamo *Aleandro for permission to leave their monastic orders. While Bucer's request was finally granted, Spiegel advised against granting the same permission to Brunfels. A letter of recommendation from Erasmus (Ep 1323) helped Spiegel to obtain employment with Archduke *Ferdinand in 1523. Three years later the fall of the chancellor, Gabriel *Salamanca, led to Spiegel's resignation. He retired to Sélestat, receiving a small pension, while his half-brother, Johannes *Maius, succeeded to his position as secretary. As a private lawyer in Sélestat Spiegel retained some connection with the court of Charles v (Ep 2572); he was named count palatine in 1536 and attended the conference of princes at Haguenau in 1540 and the diets of Speyer in 1542 and Worms in 1545. Spiegel assembled an excellent library. He is last mentioned in a document of 30 June 1547.

Through Spiegel, Wimpfeling was commissioned to gather the Gravamina Germanicae nationis for Maximilian I and to add to them his proposals to remedy the injustices suffered by Germany at the hands of the pope. Spiegel submitted the manuscript to two other imperial secretaries in 1511, but by that time Maximilian I had shifted his policy. Spiegel continued to serve as a literary agent for his uncle. He arranged for the publication of Wimpfeling's attack on the monastic orders and other clerics, Expurgatio contra detractores (Strasbourg: J. (II) Prüss 1513), and included several of his own letters. When the attacks on Wimpfeling became intolerable it was Spiegel, joined by Konrad *Peutinger of Augsburg, who requested Maximilian I to seek papal intervention to call off the monastic orders. Pope *Leo x responded favourably and silenced Wimpfeling's critics. In 1515 Spiegel again arranged the imperial intervention which secured a small chaplaincy in Sélestat for his uncle. Thus Spiegel served as both aid and protector to the humanist. Spiegel demonstrated a similar

familial concern for his young half-brother, Johannes Maius, and in 1517 encouraged Maximilian to bestow the poet's laurel upon Ulrich von *Hutten. At a meeting of the Sélestat literary society during Lent 1520, a list of the 'friends of literature' was drawn up which included Erasmus, Zasius, *Luther, *Melanchthon, and *Capito. At this time, following the death of Maximilian I, Spiegel urged Wimpfeling to publish the Gravamina Germanicae nationis and his Remedia, written in 1511 but withheld at first at Spiegel's advice (Sélestat: L. Schürer 1520). He added to the text an edict of Maximilian I forbidding the cumulation of benefices and simony as crimes of lèse-majesté. This was probably no more than a draft since no edict of this sort is recorded.

Spiegel's aid and support was not limited to members of his family. He presented Hieronymus *Gebwiler's Panegyris Carolina (Strasbourg: J. (II) Prüss 1521) to the Emperor Charles v and in 1525 attempted to arrange an appointment at the University of Freiburg for Ottmar *Nachtgall, who had been forced to leave Strasbourg because of his religious convictions. In 1524 Johann von *Botzheim hoped for Spiegel's assistance when he was investigated for heresy (Ep 1519).

In 1515 Spiegel was eager to meet Erasmus (Ep 323), who had already lauded him in public (Reedijk poem 98), but apparently did not make his acquaintance until later. In 1518 Spiegel addressed to Erasmus his preface for Erazm *Ciołek's speech advocating a crusade. The text of this letter (Ep 863) emphasizes the close ties between Spiegel and Hutten. In 1519 Spiegel republished in Augsburg (S. Grimm & M. Wirsung) Erasmus' hymn on St Anne (Reedijk poem 22), adding some scholia. In the autumn of 1521, when Erasmus was on his way to Basel, he finally met Spiegel at Strasbourg (Ep 1342), and in November 1522 he recommended him with great warmth to Archduke Ferdinand (Ep 1323). This letter did not, however, reach Ferdinand at once (Ep 1344), and Spiegel was not at hand to support Erasmus' request for a privilege for Johann *Froben (Epp 1342, 1353). Two letters from Spiegel in 1531 show him still eager to be helpful to Erasmus on every occasion (Epp 2572, 2590).

Spiegel commented on the Staurostichon, a

poem by Gianfrancesco *Pico della Mirandola (Tübingen: T. Anshelm 1512), and a work by Prudentius (Sélestat: L. Schürer 1520). He also edited the letters of Johannes *Trithemius (Haguenau: P. Braubach 1536). His most important work was his *Lexicon iuris civilis* (Strasbourg: J. Schott 1538), which was frequently reprinted.

BIBLIOGRAPHY: Allen and CWE Ep 323 / ADB xxxv 156–8 / *Matrikel Heidelberg* I 426 / *Matrikel Freiburg* I 202 / *Matrikel Tübingen* I 185 / Schmidt *Histoire littéraire* I 88 and passim / W. Friedensburg 'Beiträge zum Briefwechsel der katholischen Gelehrten Deutschlands im Reformationszeitalter' *Zeitschrift für Kirchengeschichte* 16 (1869) 470–99, esp 494–5 / Jean Lebeau 'Erasme, Sebastian Franck et la tolérance' in *Erasme, l'Alsace et son temps*, Exposition 20 November 1970 (Strasbourg 1970)

MIRIAM U. CHRISMAN

Ambrogio SPIERA of Treviso, d 1487
Ambrogio Spiera, whose given name was Antonio, was the son of Bartolomeo, rector of the public grammar school of Treviso, in Venetian territory. He studied at his father's school and in 1432 was enrolled in the notaries' guild. He then entered the Servite order, studying dialectics and philosophy with Marco Giacomo di Padua and receiving a degree in theology after undergoing a public examination before the superiors of his order in the cathedral of Padua in 1444. After a period of teaching he was called to Rome, where he preached and is said to have delivered a sermon before Pope *Nicholas v. In 1454 he became procurator general of the Servites. He composed the *Quadragesimales de floribus sapientiae* (Venice: Vindelinus de Spira 1472; new editions in 1481, 1485, 1488), a broad and complex collection of dogmatic, philosophical, legal, and conciliar ideas. He died in Rome of the plague.

In Ep 575 to Erasmus *Beatus Rhenanus dismissed Spiera's work as a 'summary compilation.'

BIBLIOGRAPHY: Allen Ep 575 / Conrad Gesner *Bibliotheca* (Zürich 1583) 37 / Arcangelo Giani *Annalium sacri ordinis Fratrum Servorum B. Mariae Virginis* (Lucca 1719–25) I 489–92 / Augusto Serena *La cultura umanistica a Treviso nel secolo decimoquinto* (Venice 1912) 76–9, 253

ANNA GIULIA CAVAGNA

Nicolaas SPIERINCK d winter 1545–6
Nicolaas Spierinck (Sperinck, Speryng), who was of Dutch origin and a kinsman of Arnold *Birckmann, worked in Lille and Antwerp before his arrival in Cambridge, most probably in 1505, where he took up employment as a stationer and bookbinder. By 1514 Spierinck was living in the parish of Great St Mary, where he subsequently served as a church warden in 1517 and 1522. In 1534 Spierinck was appointed an official university stationer and printer together with Garrett *Godfrey and Segar Nicholson. Gray identifies forty-three volumes bound by Spierinck, including Erasmus' *De conscribendis epistolis* (John *Siberch's edition of 1521) and *Antibarbari* in one volume. There is no direct evidence that Erasmus met his countryman, Spierinck, during his years at Cambridge, 1511–14; however in 1525, in a letter to Robert *Aldridge, he greeted Godfrey, Siberch, and a bookseller by the name of Nicholas, who may safely be identified with Spierinck (Epp 1656, 1766).

A 'Nicolaus Dulf alias Spierynck' of the diocese of Utrecht matriculated on 17 November 1495 in Louvain as a law student.

BIBLIOGRAPHY: Allen Ep 1656 / G.J. Gray *The Earlier Cambridge Stationers and Bookbinders and the First Cambridge Printer* (London 1904) 43–53 / *Matricule de Louvain* III-1 131

MORDECHAI FEINGOLD

Luigi SPINOLA of Genoa, documented 1508–35
Luigi (Gian Luigi, Ludovico) Spinola was the son of Stefano *Spinola and Battistina Sauli. He was born, probably at Genoa, between 1498 and 1508, for his name does not appear in his father's will, dated 3 April 1498, but in a codicil added to the will on 28 April 1508. He enjoyed a humanistic education, with the Hellenist Giacomo Furnio, a pupil of Ermolao *Barbaro, among his teachers. According to one source he married Maria Spinola degli Spinola di Lucoli, while another source states that he married Brigida Catteneo in 1527 and later Maria Doria. He had one son, Pier Francesco, the author of a summary of the history of Francesco Guicciardini (Biblioteca Universitaria di Genova, MS E I 15).

Frail health prevented Spinola from undertaking a career in commerce, as was customary in his family, and also from engaging in public life. Nevertheless, he was greatly interested in the events of 1528: the constitutional reform introduced in Genoa by Andrea *Doria and the change in foreign policy accompanying this reform. Between 1528 and 1530, Spinola, an enthusiastic supporter of Doria, wrote a treatise entitled 'De reipublicae institutione,' which celebrated the new constitutional order and predicted an age of splendour for the republic of Genoa. Spinola dedicated the work to Doria and sent copies to Giambattista *Egnazio, the influential Genoese patrician Sinibaldo Fieschi, Giovan Battista Negri, and ultimately Erasmus. However the treatise was never printed.

In the summer of 1529, when the imperial court passed through Genoa on the way to Bologna, Johannes *Dantiscus, ambassador of the king of Poland to *Charles v, stayed in the Spinola household and formed a friendship with Luigi, which was reinforced when the latter visited him at Bologna. The two exchanged a number of letters, the principal themes of which were political and religious conditions in Europe, over which it was hoped Erasmus would have a beneficial influence either through the court of Charles v or through a council of the church.

Spinola's name was mentioned to Erasmus himself in March 1535 by Giovanni Angelo *Odoni, who listed the Genoese patrician among the most enthusiastic supporters of Erasmus in Italy (Ep 3002). On 8 April 1535 Spinola wrote to Erasmus, praising him and telling him how his family, beginning with his father, Stefano, derived moral and cultural inspiration from his work. The affection of the Spinola family for Erasmus is attested to in other documents: the Italian translation of Erasmus' *De praeparatione ad mortem* (Venice 1539) was dedicated to Caterinetta Spinola Lomellini, while the translation of *De pueris instituendis* (Venice: G. Giolito 1545, 1547) was dedicated to Perinetta Grimaldi, who also came from the Spinola family. In his letter Luigi Spinola also asked Erasmus for his comments on 'De reipublicae institutione,' parts of which depended directly on the *Enchiridion* (Ep 3008).

The date of Spinola's death is unknown. His epitaph, probably written by himself, was published by G.G. Musso in 1958, along with letters to Giambattista Egnazio and Sinibaldo Fieschi. His letters to Dantiscus and excerpts from 'De reipublicae institutione' were published by S. Seidel Menchi in 1978. Three manuscripts of Spinola's treatise survive: in the Biblioteca Estense, Modena (Raccolta Campori, MS 487 Gamma Y 2 32), in the Biblioteca Durazzo, Genoa (MS A III 28), and in the Biblioteca Universitaria, Genoa (MS B I 15).

BIBLIOGRAPHY: Allen Ep 3008 / N. Battilana *Genealogie delle famiglie nobili di Genova* (Genoa 1825–6) II 20 / M. Deza *Istoria della famiglia Spinola* (Piacenza 1624) / *Il 'Liber nobilitatis Genuensis'* ed G. Guelfi Camajana (Florence 1965) / G.G. Musso 'La cultura genovese fra il quattro e il cinquecento' *Miscellanea di storia ligure* 1 (1958) 184–7 / G. Pallavicino 'Genealogiae Genuenses' MS in the Archivio storico comunale, Genoa, 105 E 5, f 28 / S. Seidel Menchi 'Passione civile e aneliti erasmiani di riforma nel patriziato genovese del primo cinquecento' *Rinascimento* 18 (1978) 87–134 esp 130ff / de Vocht *Dantiscus* 59–60, 63–4, 406

SILVANA SEIDEL MENCHI

Pasquale SPINOLA of Genoa, died c 1530
Pasquale Spinola, a son of Stefano *Spinola and a brother of Luigi *Spinola, was born at Genoa before 3 April 1498, when his name appeared in his father's will with those of his brothers Ambrogio and Giovanni. He married Maria Gentile. He supervised the commercial interests of his family in England, where he was documented in 1528 and where he died of the plague. According to Luigi, he admired Erasmus and visited him at Freiburg, perhaps during a business trip (Ep 3008).

BIBLIOGRAPHY: Allen Ep 3008 / LP IV-2 2429, 4006, 4499, 4500, 5011

SILVANA SEIDEL MENCHI

Stefano SPINOLA of Genoa
A member of a powerful patrician family of Genoa, the Spinola di San Luca, Stefano was the son of Ambrogio and the father of Luigi and Pasquale *Spinola. In 1480 he married Battistina, a daughter of Bandinello Sauli. Notarial documents suggest that he was an important merchant and entrepreneur: on 14 December 1489 and 17 February 1491 he entered into a contract with Paolo di Costa and Damiano de Francis Luxardo to finance the transport of salt from Ibiza to Genoa, while on 9 September 1498 he became a partner in the construction of a ship. Between 1491 and 1511 he also filled a

number of important public offices, including ambassador to the duke of Milan in 1494 and 1496, reformer of the laws in 1497, and censor in 1511. He had twelve legitimate and illegitimate children, of which five were mentioned in his will of 3 April 1498 and three others in a codicil added to the will on 28 April 1508. His will endowed each of his daughters with a dowry of six thousand lire and set aside a large sum for the care of the poor. In 1516 the eldest son, Ambrogio, obtained in his name the annulment of the marriage of his daughter Maddalenetta to Battista Spinola.

Luigi Spinola mentioned Stefano in a letter to Erasmus of 8 April 1535, describing him as an admirer of Erasmus who had first been drawn to him after reading a copy of the *Enchiridion* brought to him from Spain by one of his sons (Ep 3008). The fact that Luigi referred to his father in the past imperfect tense suggests that he was dead in 1535.

BIBLIOGRAPHY: For Spinola's will see Genoa, Archivio di stato, Notaio Vincenzo Borlasca, Filza unica, doc 107 (also doc 12, 48) / F. Federici 'Alberi genealogici delle famiglie di Genova' Genoa, Biblioteca Franzoniana, Cod Urbani 129 115 verso, 118 recto

SILVANA SEIDEL MENCHI

SPRINZENSTEIN *See* RICIUS

Johannes STABIUS of Steyr, d 1 January 1522
Johannes Stabius (Stab, Stabe, Stöberer) of Steyr, in Upper Austria, attended the famous school of Sélestat. He studied in Ingolstadt and taught mathematics there. In 1497 he became a professor at the University of Vienna, where he taught mathematics, geography, and astronomy. Stabius also won recognition as a poet; for a Sapphic ode addressed to the Emperor *Maximilian I in 1501 he received the poet's laurel from Conradus Celtis, the foremost Austrian humanist poet at the time. He also participated in the gatherings of Vienna's literary societies. Highly esteemed by Maximilian, he was made royal historiographer and accompanied the emperor on his travels. He was also appointed dean of the chapter of St Stephan's.

In 1516 Stabius sent greetings to Erasmus through Willibald *Pirckheimer (Ep 409). A year later he met Ulrich von *Hutten in

Augsburg (Ep 611). Jakob *Spiegel reported that Stabius was present at the diet of Augsburg in 1518 (Ep 863), and Fridericus *Nausea mentioned him in the dedication to King *Ferdinand of his *Monodia* on the death of Erasmus (Ep 3139).

Stabius never produced the major work on the history of Austria and the Hapsburg family which he had undertaken to write. But he and his friend Albrecht *Dürer worked from 1512 on the famous *Ehrenpforte* (*Triumphal Arch*) of Maximilian, for which he composed the general program and the text tracing the emperor's ancestry back to Shem and Noah. In the course of his genealogical researches, which also influenced the program of Maximilian's elaborate tomb, Stabius vigorously criticized the historical fabrications of Johannes *Trithemius. Stabius was an important geographer, working on maps of Austria and, in collaboration with Dürer, publishing a world map in 1515. He edited an Irish astronomical tract based on a medieval Latin version of a work by Messahalah (Ma Sha Allah ibn-Misr) *De scientia motus orbis* (Nürnberg: J. Weissenburger 1504), and published a *Horoscopion omni generaliter congruens climati* (Nürnberg: H. Höltzel 1512). He also discovered an important manuscript of Gregory of Nyssa which was published at Strasbourg (M. Schürer 1512).

BIBLIOGRAPHY: Allen Epp 409, 3139 / ADB XXXV 337 / BRE Ep 24 and passim / S. Laschitzer 'Die Genealogie Kaiser Maximilians I.' *Jahrbuch der kunsthistorischen Sammlungen des allerhöchsten Kaiserhauses* 7 (1888) 1–199, esp 20–9 and passim / *Johann Cuspinians Briefwechsel* ed H. Ankwicz von Kleehoven (Munich 1933) 6–7 / F.M. Mayer, R. Kaindl, and H. Pirchegger *Geschichte und Kulturleben Österreichs* (Wien-Stuttgart 1958–65) II 158 / H. Rupprich in R. Newald et al *Geschichte der deutschen Literatur* (Munich 1957–) IV-1 679–80 / Willi Kurth *The Complete Woodcuts of Albrecht Dürer* (New York 1963) 33–5, 38, and plates   IG

Christoph von STADION March 1478–15 April 1543
Christoph was born to the knight Nikolaus von Stadion and Agatha von Gültingen in the castle of Schelklingen, west of Ulm. In 1490 he began to study at the University of Tübingen, where he graduated BA in 1491 and MA in 1494.

In the latter year he moved to the University of Freiburg to study theology, and from 1497 he was at Bologna, devoting himself to legal studies. In 1503 he was elected procurator of the German nation in Bologna, and in 1506 he received a doctorate in law from the University of Ferrara and returned to Germany. On 29 August 1506 he was named to a canonry of the cathedral chapter of Augsburg, and following the requisite year of residence he was fully invested with his prebend on 3 September 1509. By 1512 or earlier he was appointed official to the bishop, Heinrich von Lichtenau. In 1512 he went to Rome on business for the bishopric. In 1515 he was dean of the chapter, in 1517 he was appointed coadjutor to Bishop Heinrich, and on 12 April he was elected bishop of Augsburg. Within the framework of the church of Rome he advocated reforms, with regard to the Protestant reformers he recommended a moderate course of action, and in the peasant war of 1525 he attempted to mediate. At the diet of Augsburg in 1530 he worked for a rapprochement between the religious parties (Epp 2355, 2384). In his bishopric and especially in the city of Augsburg he was unable to stall the progress of Protestantism, and in 1537 he was compelled to remove his chapter from Augsburg to the town of Dillingen, where he had a castle and often resided. He died in April 1543 while attending the diet of Nürnberg.

Stadion's interest in learning is reflected in a number of books dedicated to him by Johann *Eck, Johannes *Cochlaeus, Ottmar *Nachtgall, Petrus *Apianus, Vincentius *Opsopoeus, and others (Allen Ep 2029 introduction). Relations between Erasmus and the bishop of Augsburg began in 1528 with the inception of a correspondence which continued until Erasmus' death. Twelve letters are extant today, but additional contacts resulted from Erasmus' frequent exchanges of letters with the Augsburg canon Johann *Koler, who was close to Stadion. The bishop's interest in Erasmus and his writings is not surprising in view of his own conciliatory views and efforts at mediation. Erasmus in turn soon counted Stadion among the handful of bishops who were sincere supporters of *bonae literae* and were able to reconcile piety and reason (Epp 2164, 2410, 2879). The first exchange of letters was induced by Augus-

tinus *Marius. Stadion's letter is missing, but Erasmus' reply of August 1528 (Ep 2029) indicates that the bishop had shown himself to be acquainted with some of Erasmus' writings. Erasmus also complained about those who saw in him a precursor of Lutheranism. In his next letter of October Stadion spoke out boldly against intransigent Catholics who rejected the very thought of church reform, no matter how justified, and again stated his debt to Erasmus' writings (Ep 2064).

In his very first letter Stadion had invited Erasmus to Augsburg (Epp 2029, 2145), but because Erasmus was unable to accept the invitation, the bishop travelled to Freiburg early in 1530 specifically to meet Erasmus and to present him with valuable gifts (Epp 2277, 2299, 2308, 2410). While Erasmus' personal presence at the diet of 1530 was ruled out by the state of his health, he corresponded with Stadion intensively and very privately, fully approving the bishop's plan for mediation (Epp 2332, 2359, 2362, 2366, 2452). In April 1531 Stadion admitted to Erasmus the growing strength of the Lutherans in his diocese; he also informed him of conflicting assessments of the Turkish threat (Ep 2480). News on the same (Ep 2787) and other political matters also occurs in some of the later exchanges. In a most revealing letter of April 1533 Stadion supported marriage for priests and the use of vernacular languages in liturgical prayers; he also discussed the dogmatic controversy between Cardinal *Cajetanus and the Paris faculty of theology (Ep 2787). Four months later he sent Erasmus two horses, of which he was to choose and keep one, and a gift of forty crowns (Ep 2856).

The old humanist clearly took great comfort from his exchanges with the congenial bishop of Augsburg. To show his appreciation publicly he dedicated to Stadion what were possibly two of the most important publications of his last years, the Froben edition of St John Chrysostom of 1530 (Ep 2359) and the *Ecclesiastes* of 1535 (Ep 3036). In his continued commitment to irenicism and Catholic reform Stadion remained faithful to the legacy of Erasmus. In February 1537 Johann (II) *Paumgartner tried to secure exclusively for Stadion the text of the lost proposal for church reform which Erasmus had sent to Pope *Adrian VI (AK v Ep 2115), and after the bishop's death Hieronymus *Froben attempted, apparently without success, to obtain additional letters from his correspondence with Erasmus (AK VI Ep 3002).

BIBLIOGRAPHY: Allen Ep 2029 / Friedrich Zoepfl in NDB III 242–3 / ADB IV 224–7 / Knod 542 / Friedrich Zoepfl in *Lebensbilder aus dem Bayerischen Schwaben* (Munich 1959) VII 125–60 / Schottenloher I 515, III 102, 104 / Pflug *Correspondance* I Ep 115 and passim

MICHAEL ERBE

Edward STAFFORD third duke of Buckingham, 3 February 1478–17 May 1521
Edward Stafford was born at Brecknock Castle, the eldest son of Humphrey, second duke of Buckingham, and Katherine Woodville, the sister of Edward IV's queen. The Staffords were descended from Edward III, and this closeness to the throne was fatal to their house. Duke Humphrey was executed for rebelling against Richard III in 1483, but the attainder was reversed in 1485 by *Henry VII, who restored Edward to the dukedom and committed him and his lands to the wardship and custody of his mother, Lady Margaret *Beaufort. As he grew to manhood Buckingham attained honours (becoming a knight of the Bath in 1485, a knight of the Garter in 1495, and a privy councillor in 1509) and some military commands (against Cornish rebels in 1497 and in France in 1513) but never the predominant place in government to which he felt entitled by his high birth. In particular he claimed the office of lord high constable by hereditary right, though he was only granted it for the day of *Henry VIII's coronation. His wife was a Percy, and their children married into the Howard, Neville, and Pole families. Buckingham became the unofficial leader of aristocratic opposition to the king's low-born ministers and was therefore set on a collision course with Cardinal *Wolsey. Much of his time was spent administering his scattered estates; and his attempt in 1520 to raise a force for protection against his recalcitrant Welsh tenantry perhaps aroused genuine fears that he was about to repeat his father's rebellion. He was eventually tried and condemned on extremely tenuous charges of treason and executed on Tower Hill.

Conventionally devout, he shared the young king's love of pageantry and martial sports. He was also a patron of learning and the arts. A story that he was at Cambridge cannot be substantiated but, like his father, he was a benefactor of the Benedictine hostel there, known (after the second duke as) Buckingham College until its refoundation in 1542 as Magdalene. Duke Edward achieved only a posthumous and incidental mention in Erasmus' correspondence when in 1534 his son Henry *Stafford was rumoured to have stabbed the king (Ep 2961).

A portrait of Buckingham, probably contemporary, hangs in the Master's Lodge at Magdalene College, Cambridge.

BIBLIOGRAPHY: Allen Ep 2961 / DNB XVIII 854–5 / G.E. C[ockayne] *The Complete Peerage of England* ed V. Gibbs et al (London 1910–59) II 390–1 / C. Rawcliffe *The Staffords, Earls of Stafford and Dukes of Buckingham 1394–1521* (Cambridge 1978) 33–44, 93–103

C.S. KNIGHTON

Henry STAFFORD first Baron Stafford, 18 September 1501–30 April 1563
Henry, called earl of Stafford until 1521, was the only son of Edward *Stafford, third duke of Buckingham, and Eleanor, a daughter of Henry Percy, fourth earl of Northumberland. He came to court in 1516 at *Wolsey's suggestion (before relations between cardinal and duke deteriorated), and by 1519 he had married Ursula Pole, a daughter of the countess of Salisbury. In that year he became chief steward of the Stafford lands and was present in 1520 at *Henry VIII's meetings with *Francis I and *Charles V. He lost his title when his father was executed for treason but in September 1522 received back some of the family manors in Cheshire, Shropshire, and Staffordshire. In 1528 he was admitted to Gray's Inn and had become a bencher of the Middle Temple by 1551; this legal training equipped him for a modest administrative career. After Wolsey's fall he made an unsuccessful claim for full restoration of honours, and for the rest of Henry VIII's reign he was active in local government (as recorder of Stafford in 1532 and a justice of the peace from 1536). Edward VI's first Parliament restored him in blood and declared him to be Baron Stafford by a new

creation, and he sat as such in the next
Parliament. Under *Mary I he became chamberlain of the exchequer and received further
grants of his father's property. In February
1558 he was allowed the precedence of his
ancestors in the Stafford barony. His final
appointment was as lord-lieutenant of Staffordshire in 1559, and he died at Caius Castle,
Shropshire, four years later. Despite his
father's disgrace he found favour with Henry
VIII and his children; it is therefore surprising
to hear of a rumour which reached Erasmus in
1534 that he had stabbed the king (Ep 2961).
Stafford seems in fact to have kept careful step
with the political and religious upheavals of his
time. He was a Henrician Protestant, approving of monastic dissolutions and destroying, at
Thomas *Cromwell's behest, a statue of 'St
Erasmus' in Stafford. He supported and
condemned Edward Seymour, duke of Somerset, at the appropriate moments and was
rewarded by Mary for loyalty to herself and for
his father's service to her mother. Perhaps he
showed his true allegiance by dissenting from
the 1559 Act of Uniformity.

For Wood's claim that he attended the
universities of Oxford and Cambridge there is
no substantiation, though it would be plausi-
ble to suppose that he spent some time at
Buckingham (now Magdalene) College, Cambridge. He certainly had a smattering of
Renaissance learning, for he translated Edward *Fox's De vera differentia regiae potestatis et
ecclesiae and published his work in 1548 with a
dedication to Somerset as The true dyfferens
betwen the regall power and the ecclesiasticall power
(London: W. Copland; STC 11220). In 1553 he
published a translation of two of Erasmus'
epistles against the Lutherans, but no copy of
this has survived. He is also said to have
assisted the publication of the Mirror for
Magistrates.

BIBLIOGRAPHY: Allen Ep 2961 / DNB XVIII
858–9 / G.E. C[ockayne] The Complete Peerage of
England ed V. Gibbs et al (London 1910–59) II
391n, XII i 183–4 / C. Rawcliffe The Staffords,
Earls of Stafford and Dukes of Buckingham
1394–1521 (Cambridge 1978) 40, 102, 136 /
Anthony à Wood Athenae Oxonienses ed P.
Bliss (London 1813–20) I 266–7

C.S. KNIGHTON

Crato STALBURG of Frankfurt,
1502–10 February 1572
Crato Stalburg (Stalberg, Stalberger), a son of
Nikolaus *Stalburg, was born in Frankfurt am
Main. He was educated jointly with his brother
Nikolaus and may have accompanied him to
Basel when Nikolaus matriculated there in
1515 (Matrikel Basel I 329). Both followed their
teacher, Wilhelm *Nesen, to Paris in 1517 and
in July 1519 to Louvain (CWE Ep 994:n1; BRE Ep
132). Like Erasmus they boarded in the College
of the Lily, and Crato presumably played his
part in the turbulence caused by Nesen and his
students (CWE Ep 1046). Meanwhile, on 22
November 1518 at Basel *Beatus Rhenanus
dedicated to the two brothers the unauthorized first edition of Erasmus' Familiarum
colloquiorum formulae, commending their keen
interest in the classical languages (BRE Ep 80).
In 1522 and 1523 Crato was for some time a
member of Erasmus' household at Basel (Ep
1818; AK II Ep 902), and Erasmus honoured him
by giving his name to one of the speakers in his
colloquy Convivium poeticum (ASD I-3 344–59;
first published in 1523). Stalburg's connection
with Erasmus continued as he entered upon a
career in commerce. When his business took
him to Italy in 1527 he carried Erasmus' letter
for Lazarus a *Parentibus (Ep 1818). By the
spring of 1528 he had apparently returned to
Basel (AK III Ep 1251). By 1530 he was directing
his business from Lyon and forwarded mail
from Andrea *Alciati in Avignon to Hieronymus *Froben at Basel (AK III 1425, 1448).
Probably in August 1538 Froben sent him mail
for transmission to Rome (AK V Ep 2206). In
1536 he visited the Frankfurt patrician Hieronymus von Glauburg in Milan, delivering to
him a letter from his brother, Johann von
Glauburg. In 1540 he bought a house at Genoa
near the porta nuova and pursued his affairs
from there. In the fashion of foreign merchants he took a common-law wife, who
bore him five children.

By 1554 Stalburg returned to Frankfurt and
henceforward lived in a house on the Korn-
markt. The woman from Genoa took her
children to Frankfurt and was sent off with a
financial settlement. While only two of the
children remained with Stalburg at Frankfurt,
the others were subsequently remembered in
his will. Stalburg never married. In 1556 he was

Nikolaus Stalburg

---

elected to the city council, in 1569 he was mayor, and on 24 April 1571 he was appointed to the office of *Schöffe*. Following the death of his brother Daniel, who had conducted his silk trade as a member of a large merchants' company, Crato renewed the partnership agreement with one of Daniel's former associates, Jakob von Botzheim, and directed the business mostly from Frankfurt. Another of his business partners was Michele della Porta in Milan. While he never quite equalled the worth of his father, Crato's tax assessment for 1556 indicated a fortune of twenty thousand florins.

BIBLIOGRAPHY: Allen Ep 1673 / de Vocht CTL II 24–6 and passim / Preserved Smith *A Key to the Colloquies of Erasmus* (London 1927) 24 / *Frankfurtisches Archiv für ältere deutsche Literatur und Geschichte* ed J.G. von Fichard (Frankfurt am Main 1812) II 133 / Achilles Augustus von Lersner *Der Weit-Berühmten Freyen Reichs-, Wahl- und Handelsstadt Franckfurt am Mayn Chronica* (Frankfurt am Main 1706–34) II-1 154 / Alexander Dietz *Frankfurter Handelsgeschichte* (Glashütten 1970–) I 307 and passim / Friedrich Bothe *Die Entwicklung der direkten*

Besteuerung in der Reichsstadt Frankfurt bis zur Revolution 1612–14 (Leipzig 1906) 160 / Frankfurt, Stadtarchiv MS 'Geschichte der Geschlechter von Frankfurt' by Johann Karl von Fichard, vol 286 'Stalburger' f 24; MS Judicialia s 545 (Crato Stalburg's will); MS Bürgermeisterbuch 1560 f 133 recto

KONRAD WIEDEMANN

Nikolaus STALBURG of Frankfurt, 1469–15 November 1524

Nikolaus or Claus Stalburg, called 'the Rich,' was born at Frankfurt am Main. He was the son of another Claus and Margarethe von Ergersheim. His family had joined the Frankfurt patriciate, but as an old family of merchants the Stalburgs continued their active engagement in commerce whereas most of their peers were content to live off their investments. In 1499 Claus married Margarethe vom Rhein, who bore him fourteen children, among them Crato *Stalburg.

Stalburg's business was mostly in silk fabrics and jewelry. Being worth fifty to sixty thousand florins at the time of his death, he was the richest merchant in Frankfurt. Apart from huge sums invested in his business, he owned a great deal of real estate. The respect he commanded among his fellow citizens is reflected in the public offices to which he was elected; from 1497 he was city councillor, from 1516 *Schöffe*, or magistrate, and for the years of 1505, 1514, and 1521 he was mayor. His interests were not confined to his business, as is shown by an inventory of his possessions made after his death. Among other things he owned a large library covering predominantly the fields of theology, classical literature, and history, and including many books in German or German translation. Stalburg's support of humanistic ideals is further documented by the fact that he engaged Wilhelm *Nesen as the tutor of his sons Nikolaus and Crato. Philippus *Melanchthon was his friend. He also commissioned portraits of himself and his wife, which have survived and are now in the Städelsche Museum of Frankfurt. In 1515 he had the painter Jörg Ratgeb redecorate the refectory of the Carmelite monastery. A comparison of his two wills of 1501 and October 1518 indicates his adoption of reformed ideas. His religious stand is further documented by his support of

Hartmann Ibach, who began to preach the gospel in St Catherine's church.

BIBLIOGRAPHY: Allen Ep 1673 / Friedrich Bothe *Frankfurter Patriziervermögen im 16. Jahrhundert* (Berlin 1908) 1–54 (full treatment of Stalburg's life and affairs) / *Melanchthons Briefwechsel* 1 Ep 435

KONRAD WIEDEMANN

Henry STANDISH d 9 July 1535

Henry Standish (Standicius, Standiis, Standisshe, Stenditius, Standysche, Standysh) was ordained priest on 18 September 1489, hence must have been born not later than 1468. He had entered the Franciscan order at an early age and studied at the University of Oxford and possibly at Cambridge, receiving his doctorate in theology at Oxford before January 1502. He was warden of Greyfriars, the London convent of the Franciscans, from around 1508 until 1515. From 1505 until 1518 he was also provincial minister of the order in England, and he apparently attended its general chapter in Rome in 1506. He was also a popular preacher and delivered sermons before the court in 1511 and often from 1515 to 1520. In 1515 he became involved in a controversy over clerical privilege which arose from the affair of Richard Hunne, a prosperous merchant tailor suspected of Lollard sympathies who had been found strangled in the Lollards' tower in the Tower of London late in 1514, while in the custody of the bishop of London, Richard *Fitzjames. Although the bishop declared Hunne a suicide, exhumed his body, and burned it as that of a heretic, a London coroner's jury returned a verdict of murder against the bishop's chancellor, William Horsey. When Richard *Kidderminster, abbot of Winchcombe, attacked the decision of the coroner's jury and denounced an act of Parliament of 1512 which excluded robbers and murderers from benefit of clergy, Standish entered the fray on the side of royal and parliamentary authority, giving a number of public lectures and participating in two widely celebrated debates before *Henry VIII at Blackfriars in 1515. The convocation of Canterbury cited Standish to appear on a charge of heresy, but he enjoyed the protection of king and Parliament; by way of compromise, charges against

Margarethe vom Rhein, wife of Nikolaus Stalburg

both Standish and Horsey were dropped. The Hunne affair and the debate of Kidderminster and Standish were long remembered and became burning issues in the polemical controversies of William *Tyndale, Thomas *More, and Christopher Saint-German from 1529 to 1534.

In 1518 Henry VIII rewarded Standish by naming him bishop of Asaph, which he remained until his death. In 1524 he served the king on a minor diplomatic mission to Hamburg. He also took part in the trials of Thomas Bilney and others for heresy in 1527 and in 1531, and he was one of *Catherine of Aragon's council in the divorce proceedings of 1529, although the queen distrusted him because of his favour with the king. On 13 March 1533 he was one of three bishops to consecrate Thomas *Cranmer as archbishop of Canterbury. He assisted in the coronation of *Anne Boleyn in June 1533 and accepted the royal supremacy on 1 January 1535. His will was dated 3 July 1535, and he was buried at Greyfriars. He bequeathed forty pounds for the support of scholars at Oxford, five marks to the library of the Franciscan convent at Oxford, and all his books to Thomas Cudnor, a Franciscan doctor of theology.

Erasmus seems to have met Standish during one of his trips to England, probably in 1515. He disliked the Franciscan from the first, both for the rigidity of his views and for his unscrupulousness in debate, and he let pass few opportunities to ridicule him. Erasmus' first reference to Standish may occur in his letter of May 1515 to Maarten van *Dorp, in which he speaks of drinking wine with a certain Franciscan 'a Scotist of the first rank,' who criticized Erasmus' plans for the edition of St Jerome, despite his own apparent ignorance of Jerome's works (Ep 337). In October 1516 Thomas More mentioned Standish ironically as 'that prince among the Franciscan divines' (Ep 481), while Erasmus, writing to Pierre *Barbier, referred to Standish's popularity in England with the comment that 'some black theological planet must now be lord of the ascendant' (Ep 608). In letters to Henry *Bullock (Ep 777), Maarten *Lips (Ep 843), and Philippus *Melanchthon (Ep 1113), Erasmus further referred to Standish as a 'beast' who spoke against his editions of the New Testament and of Jerome, and who supported his arch-enemy, Edward *Lee. In 1517 he made Standish the butt of the adage Esernius cum Pacidiano (Adagia II v 98), describing the Franciscan's controversy with an Italian Servite friar over the question of Franciscan poverty. The controversy, which is said to have occurred around Easter 1517, attracted the interest of the entire court and was played out with considerable melodrama by the two protagonists. According to Margaret Mann Phillips, this adage stands alone in launching a satirical attack on a person mentioned by name.

Erasmus' animosity towards Standish abated little with the passage of time. By July 1520 he had heard that Standish had attacked his rendition of John 1:1 as 'In principio erat sermo' in a sermon at St Paul's. The Franciscan, the report continued, was taken to task at court by Thomas More and a theologian, probably John *Stokesley. After first trying to evade their questions, Standish turned to the king and queen, imploring them to do something about the alleged heresies of Erasmus. He was soon confounded by the arguments of More and of the other friend of Erasmus, until the king

finally saved him from further embarrassment by changing the topic of conversation. Standish's behaviour provided an ample target for Erasmus' barbs, and the incident was described or mentioned in letters to Hermannus *Buschius (Ep 1126), Martin *Luther (Ep 1127A), More (Ep 1162), Justus *Jonas (Ep 1211), Noël *Béda (Ep 1581), and Alfonso de *Valdés (Ep 2126), and in the Apologia to Nicolaas *Baechem (LB IX 433C–D). In 1526 Erasmus was quite worried when he heard that Standish had been entrusted with the examination of heretics and the burning of books, and he sent complaints to Cardinal *Wolsey (Ep 1697) and to François *Du Moulin (Ep 1719). That Standish enjoyed the favour of the court and became a bishop was doubtless a source of irritation to Erasmus (Ep 2615). Nevertheless, in one of his last references to Standish, Erasmus conceded that there was less reason for bitterness with him than with other opponents (Ep 2205). Although it was once believed that Standish was the abbot of the colloquy Abbatis et eruditae (ASD I-3, 403–8), Craig R. Thompson has argued convincingly against such an identification.

BIBLIOGRAPHY: Allen and CWE Ep 608 / DNB XVIII 880–1 / Emden BRUC 549–50 / Emden BRUO III 1756–7 / Erasmus Colloquies trans and ed C.R. Thompson (Chicago 1965) 217 / A.F. Pollard Wolsey: Church and State in Sixteenth-Century England (London 1929, repr 1966) 44–51 and passim / H. Maynard Smith Pre-Reformation England (London 1938) 30 and passim / H. Maynard Smith Henry VIII and the Reformation (London 1948) 263, 299 / G.R. Elton Reform and Reformation England, 1509–1558 (Cambridge, Mass, 1977) 53–7 and passim / D. Knowles The Religious Orders in England (Cambridge 1948–59) III 53–5, 94 / R.J. Schoeck ' … The affair of Richard Hunne' in Proceedings of the Third International Congress of Medieval Canon Law, Strasbourg 1968 ed Stephan Kuttner (Rome 1971) 237–54 / R.J. Schoeck 'Common law and canon law in their relation to Thomas More' in St. Thomas More: Action and Contemplation ed R.S. Sylvester (New Haven, Conn, 1972) 1–14 / Louis Bouyer 'Erasmus in relation to the medieval biblical tradition' in The Cambridge History of the Bible ed G.W.H. Lampe (Cambridge 1963–70) II 491–505

R.J. SCHOECK

Jan STANDONCK of Mechelen, d 5 February 1504

Jan Standonck (van Standonck, Standoncus, Standoneus) was the son of Cornelis van Standonck and Elisabeth Ysschot, *petits bourgeois* in the parish of St Catherine in Mechelen. The date of birth 16 August 1443 cited by some authors (following an eighteenth-century engraving) does not correspond with other evidence about Standonck, and the year 1453 is more probable. After primary schooling in the *groote school* of Mechelen, he went to the school of the Brethren of the Common Life in Gouda, from which he emerged devoted to an ideal of education closely linked to reformed piety and cloistered discipline, humility, and self-abnegation. He matriculated in the faculty of arts of Louvain *gratis quia pauper* on 27 November 1469 but went to Paris, probably in 1471, where he earned bed and board by working for the canons regular at Ste Geneviève, and where a legend began about his studies in the Tour Clovis by moonlight. He received his MA in 1474 and was regent at the Collège de Sainte-Barbe until 1476, when he moved to the Collège de Montaigu to begin a remarkable career there which would last to the end of his life. At the same time he began the fourteen-year long course of studies in the faculty of theology and was received as a *socius* of the Collège de Sorbonne on 24 January 1484 (not 1480). He served the nation of Picardy as proctor from 16 December 1477 to 12 January 1478 and as elector and examiner during several other terms. His election as rector of the university (from 16 December to 16 March 1486) was opposed by many of the *martinets* (students not affiliated with any college). He was prior of the Sorbonne in 1488 and lector in ethics in the faculty of arts in 1489. He received his licence in theology on 23 January 1490, ranking eighth of twenty-two, and his doctorate on 21 June 1490. He had been made an imperial notary in 1480 and an apostolic notary in 1483.

Standonck became confessor to Louis Malet de Graville, admiral of France, and was a close collaborator of Jean de Rély, confessor to King *Charles VIII. A meeting with St Francis of Paola in 1491 profoundly influenced Standonck, and from this time he increased his ascetic practices. A provincial council of Sens

Jan Standonck, by Jean-Baptiste Guyard

in 1485 had already inspired several prominent Paris clerics to embrace a reformed monastic life, and Standonck, at a convocation of bishops and theologians convened by the king at Tours in 1493, proposed strict measures to ensure a reformed clergy and to promote a church devoted to the poor. As canon of Beauvais from 11 September 1493 and of Notre-Dame de Paris from 10 May 1496, he preached reform untiringly in Picardy and in the Paris region. He allied with Jean *Emery and Nicolas de *Hacqueville, clerical councillors in the Parlement of Paris, to enforce monastic discipline in monasteries of the Paris region. He personally convinced the Windesheim congregation of canons to send monks from Holland to restore discipline at the abbey of Château-Landon (diocese of Sens), and their hard-fought victory there (led by Jan *Mombaer) inspired them to attempt a reform of St Victor of Paris. The success of the latter project, accomplished in part by Erasmus' friend Cornelis *Gerard, was only ephemeral. Further reforms were attempted at Livry and at Cysoing (diocese of Tournai). Standonck helped all these reforms by sending disciplined clerics from the Collège de Montaigu, which he had been directing since 1483, and which became a training centre for the reform. He gradually expanded the facilities of Montaigu to take in not only paying students but also the poor, to whom he gave bed and board and instruction, but on whom he forced his own ideal of asceticism. It was this college that Erasmus inhabited briefly in 1495–6 and that he later excoriated in the colloquy Ἰχθυοφαγία. While admitting Standonck's good intentions, Erasmus condemned his lack of prudence and judgment and blamed Standonck's regime for the impaired health of many students (ASD I-3 531). Among the students who came out of Montaigu during Standonck's tenure, however, were Jacobus *Latomus and Noël *Béda, Erasmus' most vehement enemies at the universities of Louvain and Paris.

Standonck was exiled from France from 16 June 1499 until May 1500, having opposed King *Louis XII on three issues: the appointment of Cardinal Guillaume (I) *Briçonnet, already bishop of Saint-Malo and abbot of Grandmont, as archbishop of Reims; the king's divorce from Jeanne of France to marry Anne of Brittany; and the king's attempt to restrict the privileges of the University of Paris. During his exile, Standonck went first to Cambrai, where Bishop Hendrik van *Bergen, Erasmus' first patron, welcomed him and presented him to Philip the Handsome, duke of *Burgundy, and to Count Engelbert II of *Nassau-Breda. Bergen entrusted an existing college in Cambrai to Standonck's care. At Valenciennes, Thomas *Warnet, sharing Standonck's exile, founded another college affiliated with Montaigu. At Mechelen in 1500 Standonck brought in some Brethren of the Common Life from Deventer to direct another sister school, while at Louvain the later Pope *Adrian VI transformed still another school under the aegis of Standonck. In May 1500 Standonck not only returned to Paris but was received in audience by the king. In Ep 135 (which Allen dates November 1500), Erasmus said that Standonck 'returned the other day' from Louvain. This probably refers to the return in May, since there is no evidence of another sojourn in the Low Countries in 1500. During his remaining years Standonck continued his work for the reform of monasteries and devoted much

energy to the formation of a quasi-monastic congregation which linked the Collège de Montaigu and its four affiliated colleges under the jurisdiction of the Carthusian prior in Paris and which gave pride of place to asceticism and virtue. He made a last visit to the daughter schools in 1502. He died in Paris on 5 February 1504 and was buried at the entrance to the chapel sanctuary at the college. The inscription reads simply 'Remember the poor man Standonck.'

Besides the reference to Standonck in Ἰχθυοφαγία cited above, Erasmus also criticized Standonck in De pueris instituendis (ASD I-2 56). Rabelais' scathing reference to Montaigu (Gargantua I 37), however, is probably descriptive of the later regime of Pierre Tempete. The poet Jean Molinet spoke for the large number of Standonck's admirers when he wrote, 'Le bon Stondon, plus pur que n'est or fin.' An eighteenth-century engraving of Standonck by Jean-Baptiste Guyard (Paris, Bibliothèque Nationale, Estampes N 2, reproduced in Godet La Congrégation de Montaigu, frontispiece), based on a painting by Jean-Baptiste-Claude Robin, was probably drawn from a window portrait of Standonck formerly in the library of the Collège de Sorbonne.

BIBLIOGRAPHY: Allen Ep 73 / ASD I-2 56 / BNB XXIII 588–99 / Auctarium chartularii universitatis parisiensis ed Charles Samaran et al (Paris 1894–1964) III 373 and passim, IV passim / M. Godet La Congrégation de Montaigu, 1490–1580 (Paris 1912) / P. Debongnie Jean Mombaer de Bruxelles, abbé de Livry, ses écrits et ses réformes (Louvain-Toulouse 1929) / A. Renaudet 'Jean Standonck, un réformateur catholique avant la Réforme' in Humanisme et Renaissance (Geneva 1958) 114–61 / Renaudet Préréforme passim / William Gregory 'Liber de origine congregationis canonicorum regularium reformatorum in regno Franciae' (Paris, Bibliothèque Ste-Geneviève MS 574, Bibliothèque Nationale MS Latin 15049) / Claude Héméré 'Sorbonae origines, disciplina, viri illustres' (Paris, Bibliothèque de l'Arsenal MS 1166 ff 475ff, Bibliothèque Nationale MS Lat 5494 ff 206ff)   JAMES K. FARGE

Johann von STAUPITZ d 28 December 1524
Johann von Staupitz, born between 1460 and 1469, belonged to a noble family of the region

of Meissen, in Saxony. The future Elector
Frederick the Wise of *Saxony was one of his
childhood friends. Staupitz studied at Cologne
(1483) and Leipzig (1485, 1489), where he was
promoted MA. In 1485 he made his profession
at the Munich house of the Austin friars. In
1497 he was sent to Tübingen for further
studies and obtained a doctorate of theology
on 7 July 1500. For the next two years he was
prior of the Augustinian monastery in Munich,
then Frederick the Wise appointed him the first
biblical professor and dean of theology at the
new University of Wittenberg. In 1503 he was
elected vicar-general of the Observants or
Reformed Congregation of his order in Germany. With the support of the general of the
Augustinian order, Egidio *Antonini of Viterbo, he attempted to reunite the Observant and
Conventual factions in Saxony and from 1509
was provincial of both congregations. His
administrative duties did not permit Staupitz
enough time for his teaching at the university;
he therefore suggested that Martin *Luther be
appointed to the chair of biblical studies, and
this was done in 1512.

From 1512 Staupitz travelled extensively on
his order's business, visiting Rome, the Netherlands, and various regions of Germany. In
1517, when the controversy about indulgences
began to heat up, Staupitz at first stood by
Luther, but in 1520, when events had taken a
very serious turn and pressures on him to take
disciplinary action against Luther were mounting, he resigned as vicar-general of the
Observants and accepted the invitation of
Cardinal Matthäus *Lang to go to Salzburg as
preacher and councillor. When Rome demanded that he abjure Luther's heresies (Ep 1166),
he replied that he had never embraced them. In
1521 Lang obtained his transfer from the
Austin friars to the Benedictine order and the
following year his appointment as abbot of St
Peter's in Salzburg. From 1522 he resumed his
friendly correspondence with Luther but was
no longer willing to take his side. Staupitz died
in Salzburg.

Apart from a new constitution for the
Observants (Nürnberg 1504) and his sermons
(unpublished manuscript in Salzburg), Staupitz wrote a number of other works including
the *Libellus de executione aeternae praedestinationis* (Nürnberg: F. Peypus 1517), *Von der Liebe*

Johann von Staupitz

Gottes ([Munich: J. Schobser] 1518), and *Eyn
Buchleyn von der Nachfolgung des willigen Ster-
bens Christi* (Nürnberg: H. Höltzel 1523). From
1559 his entire work appears on successive
Indexes of the Catholic church.

Erasmus apparently had no personal contacts with Staupitz, although he expressed a
high opinion of him in Ep 872.

BIBLIOGRAPHY: Allen Ep 872 / ADB XXXV
529–33 / RGG VI 342–3 / David Steinmetz
*Misericordia Dei: The Theology of Johannes von
Staupitz in Its Late Medieval Setting* (Leiden 1968)
/ David Steinmetz *Reformers in the Wings*
(Philadelphia 1971) 18–29 / *Matrikel Tübingen* I
116 / *Matrikel Leipzig* I 347, II 313 / *Matrikel
Wittenberg* I 1 / Luther W *Briefwechsel* II Ep 366
and passim   IG

Sigismund STEINSCHNIDER documented
at Basel 1522–3
Little is known about 'Sigismund called Steinschnider' (Steinschneider) besides the facts
and circumstances indicated by Erasmus in
Epp 1353 and 1496. Chronicles confirm that the
provocative meal of pork on Palm Sunday 1522,
which caused Erasmus to write his *Epistola de*

esu carnium (Allen Ep 1274:14n), was held in Steinschnider's house and that he was executed by quartering a year later at Ensisheim, the seat of the Hapsburg administration in the Upper Rhine region. His offence is given as blasphemy against the sacraments and the Virgin Mary. Sigismund may be the Steinschnider mentioned in the *Aktensammlung zur Geschichte der Basler Reformation* ed E. Dürr et al (Basel 1921–50) I 34–5. A Christoph Steinschnider matriculated at Basel in 1521: *Matrikel Basel* I 348.

BIBLIOGRAPHY: Allen Ep 1274 / *Basler Chroniken* I 36–7, 383–4, VII 306   PGB

Petrus STELLA of Orléans, 1480–28 October 1537

Pierre Taisant de l'Estoille, born to a prominent Orléans family, became internationally known under his Latin name, Stella. He studied at Orléans and became a member of the faculty of law there in 1512. He married and had a son, Louis, who became a noted teacher of Greek, but after his wife's death he took holy orders in 1525. He made a successful second career in ecclesiastical politics and resigned his professorship in 1531 to move to Paris as a member of the Parlement. He died in Orléans.

Stella was the leading member of the faculty of law at Orléans. Among his students were François Daniel, Nicolas Duchemin, François Connan, and Jean Calvin. His scholarly opinions seem to have been derived chiefly from Guillaume *Budé. Although he wrote a few minor legal commentaries, he is best known for his disputes with Andrea *Alciati and Udalricus *Zasius. Stella objected to Zasius' critique of Budé's interpretation of Digest 12, 6, 19/1 and 12, 6, 44. Following the publication of Zasius' *Lucubrationes* in 1518, Stella opened a polemic (*Repetitio legis* Orléans: J. Hoys 1518; 2nd ed, expanded Paris: C. Wechel 1528) which remained lively until 1532, attracting the interest of Budé, Alciati, Claudius *Cantiuncula, Bonifacius *Amerbach, and *Viglius Zuichemus (Ep 2210). In a pamphlet added to the second edition Stella extended the attack to include Alciati. This led to a reply by Alciati published under the name of his student Aurelio Albuzio (Basel: H. Froben 1529). Duchemin issued an *Antapologia* against Alciati with a foreword by the young Calvin – his first

publication. Both of these disputes helped to raise hostilities between French scholars and those from other countries.

BIBLIOGRAPHY: Allen Ep 2210 / AK III Ep 1021 and passim / L.-G. Michaud et al *Biographie universelle* 2nd ed (Paris 1854–65) XIII 447–8 / Jacques Boussard 'L'Université d'Orléans et l'humanisme au début du XVIe siècle' *Humanisme et Renaissance* 5 (1938) 209–30 / Godehard Fleischer *Ulrich Zasius und Petrus Stella* (Freiburg 1966)   STEVEN ROWAN

Gabriel STENDELIN documented 1521–31

Gabriel Stendelin (Stendelinus) has not been identified. Writing from Aldenburg on 11 February 1531 an anonymous correspondent of *Agrippa of Nettesheim refers to him as a close friend and Agrippa's 'compater.' In 1521 he encouraged Johann *Schudelin, the schoolmaster of Memmingen, to write to Erasmus, who in his reply called Stendelin 'a man whom I like for many reasons' (Ep 1234). Uli Braun, the *Heimatpfleger* of the city of Memmingen, has kindly informed us that Stendelin's name has not been found in the archives of Memmingen.

BIBLIOGRAPHY: Allen Ep 1234 / H. Cornelius Agrippa of Nettesheim *Opera* (Lyon n d, repr 1970) II 956   PGB

Joachim STERCK van Ringelberg *See Joachim van RINGELBERG*

Jan STERCKE of Meerbeke, d 5 April 1535

Jan Stercke (Johannes Fortis Merbecanus) of Meerbeke, near Ninove, west of Brussels, matriculated on 31 August 1495 at Louvain as a paying student of the College of the Falcon. He graduated MA on 10 April 1498 and was appointed professor of physics and logic while studying theology. On 28 February 1510, 1 January 1512, and 30 September 1530 he was elected dean of the faculty of arts for a term. On 24 November 1514 the faculty appointed him president of the College of St Donatian, which was undergoing a prolonged crisis, in succession to Jean *Desmarez. As a priest, Stercke was the beneficiary of the faculty's privilege of nominating one of its members for the first vacant benefice within the gift of the sees of Tournai (1515) and Cambrai (1517).

When Jérôme de *Busleyden envisaged the founding of a college for the study of Latin,

Greek, and Hebrew, it was Stercke who, in close co-operation with Erasmus, composed the rules for the new college in 1516 and 1517. He prepared several drafts, and a final version became part of the will Busleyden dictated to Nicolas *Wary on 22 June 1517. After Busleyden's death Stercke was appointed the first president of the new Collegium Trilingue in the autumn of 1518. While initially retaining the presidency of St Donatian (until c 1520) in addition to his new duties, he set up operations at the Trilingue and secured its legal autonomy within the framework of the university. A very efficient administrator, he encouraged his staff to demand adequate remuneration; when enrolment rose and lecture halls proved to be too small, he purchased an additional house in 1524 which, after some rebuilding, provided a lecture hall for over six hundred, as Erasmus pointed out proudly (Ep 1564). Well aware of the importance of suitable teachers, Stercke secured the appointments of Conradus *Goclenius and Jan van *Campen to the chairs of Latin and Hebrew in 1519 and supported the latter in years to come against his many critics. He clearly would have liked Erasmus to return to Louvain (Ep 1322). On 21 January 1526 Stercke retired from his position as president of the Collegium Trilingue but remained in close contact with the college. After the death of his successor, Nicholas Wary, he acted as one of the executors of Wary's will and helped Wary's successor, Joost van der *Hoeven.

Stercke remained a friend and supporter of Erasmus throughout his life. Only one of his letters to Erasmus had been preserved (Ep 1322), but they exchanged greetings at a later date (Ep 1973). Stercke's death is mentioned in a letter from Goclenius (Ep 3037).

BIBLIOGRAPHY: Allen Ep 1322 / de Vocht CTL I 14–16, II 60–3, and passim / de Vocht Busleyden 90–2, 120 / de Vocht Literae ad Craneveldium 384 and passim / Matricule de Louvain III-1 129 / Correspondance de Nicolas Clénard ed A. Roersch (Brussels 1940–1) Ep 27 and passim   IG

Agostino STEUCO of Gubbio, 1497/8–18 March 1548

Steuco (Augustinus Eugubinus, Steuchus) was the son of Theseo Stuchi and was given the name Guido at baptism. When he joined the Augustinian canons at Gubbio in 1512 or 1513 he took the name Agostino, which he retained for the remainder of his life. He studied at the University of Bologna under Pietro *Pomponazzi and Romolo *Amaseo, among others. Ordained about 1520, he became librarian of the rich collection of the Grimani family at the convent at Sant'Antonio in Venice in 1525, and four years later became prior of the convent of San Marco in Reggio Emilia, at which time he corresponded with Erasmus. In 1536 he entered direct into the service of Pope *Paul III, being made bishop of Kisamos (Crete) and Vatican librarian in 1538. At the request of the pope he travelled to Bologna in 1547 to participate in the council recently transferred from Trent, but fell ill and went to Venice, where he died.

Steuco published a number of works, particularly on the Scriptures, but also including *Pro religione christiana adversus Luteranos* (Bologna: G.B. Phaellus 1530), *De perenni philosophia* (Lyon: S. Gryphius 1540), and *Contra Laurentium Vallam, de falsa donatione Constantini* (Lyon: S. Gryphius 1547). In 1531 Erasmus wrote a long letter to Steuco (Ep 2465) concerning his *Recognitio veteris testamenti* (Venice: A. Manuzio and A. Torresani 1529), to which Steuco replied (Ep 2513) at equal length and in a tone critical of Erasmus. Further references to Steuco and his criticisms, which evidently angered Erasmus, are to be found in various other letters (Ep 2806, 2892, 2906, 2956, 2961, 3019).

J.V. Pollet has shown that Erasmus was the first to render the controversy public by including Ep 2465 in his *Epistolae floridae* of September 1531. Steuco retaliated reluctantly by appending both letters (Epp 2465, 2513) to his *In psalmorum XVIII et CXXXVIII interpretatio* (Lyon: S. Gryphius 1533), a volume dedicated to Julius *Pflug. Meanwhile Pflug himself had written to Erasmus, regretting Steuco's attack (Ep 2806), and Erasmus now proceeded to publish Pflug's letter together with his own commentary on Psalm 83, *De sarcienda ecclesiae concordia* (LB V 469–506), specifically composed for this occasion.

BIBLIOGRAPHY: Allen Ep 2465 / T. Freudenberger *Augustinus Steuchus aus Gubbio* (Münster 1935) / C.B. Schmitt, introduction to reprint of *De perenni philosophia* (New York-

*Alexander Stewart, by Jacques Le Boucq of
Valenciennes*

London 1972) v–xvii (recent bibliography) /
J.V. Pollet 'Origine et structure du *De sarcienda
ecclesiae concordia* (1533) d'Erasme' in *Scrinium
Erasmianum* ii 183–95 / Pflug *Correspondance* i
276–8 and passim   CHARLES B. SCHMITT

Alexander STEWART c 1493–9 September
1513
Alexander Stewart was the illegitimate son of
*James iv, king of Scotland, and Marion Boyd.
Shortly after the death of his uncle, James
Stewart (CWE Ep 48:8n), in December 1504,
young Alexander was chosen to succeed him
as the archbishop of St Andrews, even though
he was still a minor. Subsequently his father
was in frequent correspondence with Pope
*Julius ii, attempting to secure the see for his
son, and he eventually succeeded in gaining
metropolitan status for the archbishops of St
Andrews. The young archbishop remained in
Scotland until the beginning of 1507, at which
time he departed for the continent, probably in
a joint ambassadorial mission with James
Hamilton, earl of Arran, to King *Louis xii of
France. After the completion of the embassy,
Stewart continued his tour of the continent as
part of his general education, his tutor being

Sir Thomas Halkerston. In 1508 he arrived at
Padua, where he was joined by his brother,
James *Stewart, earl of Moray, and the two
were instructed by Erasmus in logic and in
rhetoric. Erasmus admired the character, intellect, and piety of the young archbishop,
qualities he commemorated in his *Adagia* (ii v 1)
and *De conscribendis epistolis* (ASD i-2 261–2).
Alexander Stewart also appears to have been
registered at the University of Padua for the
study of canon law, for in December 1508 he
was granted an indulgence to study civil law
by Julius ii. Owing to fear of war, however,
that very same month Erasmus and his two
students departed from Padua, first for Ferrara, and then for Siena. In Siena Erasmus
provided his charge with a thorough-going
plan of study before he left for Rome. At the
end of the winter he returned to Siena and took
Alexander with him to Rome, where they spent
Holy Week 1509, and subsequently to Naples.
Alexander then returned home to Scotland.
Before his departure he gave Erasmus a golden
ring encasing an antique gem. It showed a bust
which Erasmus thought to be the god Terminus
and whence he derived his motto 'Cedo nulli'
(Ep 1558; plates in CWE 2 150). After his return
to Scotland Stewart was appointed chancellor
of Scotland, served as a noted patron of
learning, and by all indications was heading
for a brilliant political career. In 1513, however,
he joined his father in the disastrous invasion
of England, and on 9 September he was killed
at Flodden. Erasmus grieved over the death of
his young friend and in the years to come he
occasionally recalled the time they had spent
together in Italy (Epp 604, 1824, 2283, 2886) as
well as the expertise the youth had displayed
in imitating his handwriting (Epp 1992, 2874;
LB x 1688c).

  BIBLIOGRAPHY: Allen and CWE Ep 604 / DNB
xviii 1154–5 / LP i-1 212 (note) and passim / J.K.
McConica 'The riddle of "Terminus"' *Erasmus
in English* 2 (1971) 2–7 / *Compota thesaurariorum
Scotorum: Accounts of the Lord High Treasurer of
Scotland* ed T. Dickson and J.B. Paul (Edinburgh 1877–1916) i 378, iii 162, 176, 370, iv
72   MORDECHAI FEINGOLD

James STEWART earl of Moray, c 1499–
1544/5
A natural son of *James iv, king of Scotland,
and Janet Kennedy, James was created earl of

Moray and Lord Abernethy and Strathearn on 12 June 1501. In September 1523 he was one of the guardians of *James v and shortly thereafter he was appointed lieutenant-general of the French forces in Scotland. From 1532 to 1536 he was warden of the East and Middle Marches. From 1539 to 1540 he was sheriff of Aberdeen. Pursuing a military career, he was noted as a staunch supporter of the church of Rome and an opponent of any rapprochement with England. He died between 2 December 1544 and 14 March 1545.

Like his older half-brother, Alexander *Stewart, James was sent to Italy for study, and in the winter of 1508–9 both were tutored by Erasmus in Siena (Epp 2283, 2886). James is not mentioned, though, in Erasmus' references to the trip to Rome and Naples on which he accompanied Alexander the following spring. Later on it was primarily Alexander whom Erasmus recalled with great affection, but he did not forget James, who had been barely ten at the time of their encounter and a child of great promise. Erasmus inquired about him when writing to Hector *Boece in March 1530, wondering whether he was still alive (Ep 2283).

BIBLIOGRAPHY: Allen Ep 604 / DNB XVIII 1182–3 / G.E. C[ockayne] *The Complete Peerage of England* ed V. Gibbs et al (London 1910–59) IX 179–80 / J.K. McConica 'The riddle of "Terminus"' *Erasmus in English* 2 (1971) 2, 6

PGB

Daniel STIEBAR von Buttenheim of Rabeneck, 1503–7 August 1555

Daniel Stiebar (Stieber, Stibarus) von Buttenheim zu Sassenfurth belonged to a large family of Franconian nobles that was divided into several branches. He was born in Rabeneck, between Bamberg and Bayreuth. In 1515 he began his studies at the University of Erfurt, where he met Joachim *Camerarius in 1518. Their common studies were the beginning of a lifelong friendship and correspondence. In 1517 Stiebar became a domiciliar (aspirant canon) at the Würzburg chapter. He took up residence at Würzburg and gradually attracted the attention of the bishop, Konrad von *Thüngen. Early in 1527 he obtained leave to resume his studies in preparation for an administrative career in the ecclesiastical state of Würzburg. Camerarius offered and proba-

bly gave financial assistance during his academic travels in 1527 and 1528 (AK III Ep 1303). For the summer term of 1527 Stiebar registered at the University of Basel with Johann Truchsess von Wetzhausen and Lorenz *Schlehenried. He seems to have shared quarters with Moritz von *Hutten, the future bishop of Eichstätt, and he established relations with *Beatus Rhenanus and Henricus *Glareanus. In particular he must have impressed his law teacher, Bonifacius *Amerbach, who was to correspond with him for many years and in August 1528 asked Erasmus to let Stiebar live in his household. Erasmus had no bed available but offered Stiebar a place at his table (Ep 2036). He too thought highly of the young man, and his first impressions were fully confirmed by the ease and good humour (Epp 2079, 2745) of their subsequent relations, which were also characterized on Stiebar's side by tact and faithful admiration. After a month he left for Paris in the company of Philippus *Montanus (Epp 2065, 2069), probably carrying Epp 2046–8, and reported afterwards on *Budé's unkind reception of Ep 2047 (AK III Epp 1303, 1311). In the spring of 1529 he returned to Würzburg by way of Antwerp, Louvain, and Frankfurt (Ep 2128; AK III Epp 1314, 1324, 1341). In the winter of 1529–30 he matriculated at Freiburg, evidently following Erasmus, and now lived for some months under his roof (Ep 2303). He returned to Würzburg at the beginning of April when a canonry was bestowed upon him, taking with him Erasmus' glowing recommendation to his bishop, to which Thüngen replied by expressing his own appreciation of Stiebar (Epp 2303, 2314, 2361). In fact the canon was now frequently employed on important affairs and after Thüngen's death continued to enjoy the confidence of the new bishop, Konrad von Bibra. In 1532 he bought a large house, Hof Osternach, which enabled him to extend hospitality to many visitors.

In 1530 Stiebar attended the diet of Augsburg, where he gained the confidence of *Melanchthon (Epp 2357, 2358), and found time for a visit to Freiburg to see Erasmus (Epp 2363, 2365). In the summer of 1531 he spent a vacation, it seems, at Basel, but his further travels were mostly at the call of duty. In 1532 he attended the diet at Regensburg (Ep 2745), in 1533 he again passed through Basel, and in

1534 he undertook a mission to Saxony. In 1540 he attended the Haguenau conference and thereafter the diets of Regensburg (1541) and Nürnberg (1542). Stiebar, who also held benefices at Eichstätt and Bamberg, became provost of the Würzburg chapter in 1552. Attending again to diplomatic business in the autumn of that year at Augsburg, he fell out with Ambrosius von *Gumppenberg, who afterwards accused him of having thrown a notary down the stairs. Perhaps as a result of the excitement Stiebar suffered a stroke and remained partly paralysed. His moderation in the matter of religion is confirmed by his friendship with Camerarius and his patronage of the poet Petrus Lotichius, both Protestants. Among those whom he met through Erasmus or in his house were Christoph von *Carlowitz, Hieronymus *Jud, Karel *Uutenhove, and Andrzej *Zebrzydowski. His correspondence with Erasmus himself continued until the latter's death (Ep 3133).

BIBLIOGRAPHY: Allen IV 615 and Ep 2069 / Eva Mayer 'Daniel Stiebar von Buttenheim und Joachim Camerarius' *Würzburger Diözesangeschichtsblätter* 14–15 (1952–3) 485–99, relying frequently on letters in Joachim Camerarius' *Epistolarum libri quinque posteriores* (Frankfurt 1595) / Bierlaire *Familia* 81–4 and passim / *Matrikel Basel* I 361 / *Matrikel Freiburg* I 277 / *Matrikel Erfurt* II 291 / AK III Ep 1228, V 1316a, and passim   PGB

Wolfgang STÖCKEL of Munich, documented 1489–1540/1
Writing from Dresden on 13 March 1529 (Ep 2120), Johannes *Cochlaeus mentioned letters sent at this time from Dresden to Wittenberg, including one by his printer ('typographi mei'). P.S. Allen suggested this was the Leipzig printer Valentin *Schumann, who published Cochlaeus' *Septiceps Lutherus* mentioned in the same letter to Erasmus. It is more likely that Wolfgang Stöckel is intended, since he was in Dresden and around that time printed rather more of Cochlaeus' many pamphlets than did Schumann. Stöckel is also mentioned in a letter from Cochlaeus to *Pirckheimer dated 10 March and dispatched with Ep 2120.

Wolfgang Stöckel (Stöcklin, Müller, Molitor) matriculated at Erfurt in 1489; he printed in Leipzig from 1495 to 1526 and in Dresden from

1526 to 1540 and probably died there. In 1504 he went for a while to Wittenberg as the first printer to the university; subsequently he became a major distributor of *Luther's writings. Especially in Leipzig and for the most part anonymously he printed several German books and pamphlets derived from Erasmus' Latin version of the New Testament, such as the four gospels (1522), and also from some of his other works.

BIBLIOGRAPHY: ADB XXXVI 283–4 / Benzing *Buchdrucker* 83, 261–2, and passim / *Matrikel Erfurt* I 426 / Willibald Pirckheimer *Opera politica, historica, philologica et epistolica* (Frankfurt 1605, repr 1969) 395–6 / Martin Spahn *Johannes Cochläus* (Berlin 1898, repr 1964) 139, 346, 349–55, and passim / Heinz Holeczek *Erasmus Deutsch* (Stuttgart-Bad Cannstatt 1983–) I 52 and passim   PGB

Johann STÖFFLER of Justingen, 10 December 1452–16 February 1531
Johann Stöffler of Justingen, in Swabia, matriculated at the University of Ingolstadt on 21 April 1472. In 1477 he became the parish priest of Justingen. His knowledge of mathematics and astronomy was widely respected; he built famous clocks for Constance in 1496 and Ulm in 1499. Being very skilful in the computation of astronomical tables, Stöffler showed how the Julian calendar could be brought into harmony with astronomical data. His *Tabulae astronomicae* (Tübingen: T. Anshelm 1514) were preceded by his *Elucidatio fabricae ususque astrolabii* (Oppenheim: J. Köbel 1513). At the same time Stöffler was a prolific astrologer; later he had to defend himself against charges that his *Almanach* (Ulm: J. Pflaum 1499, many reprints) predicted a universal flood for 1524 and was spreading fear and panic among the people: *Expurgatio adversus divinationum ... suspitiones* (Tübingen: U. (1) Morhart 1523). In 1507 he matriculated at Tübingen, in 1511 he was called to a chair of mathematics in that university, and in 1522 he was rector. *Melanchthon was one of his students. However, after the expulsion of Ulrich of *Württemberg from his duchy, Stöffler no longer received the rent from his parish. In 1530 he and other members of the university moved to Blaubeuren to escape an outbreak of the plague, and there he died.

In 1528 (Ep 2081) Hubertus *Barlandus

showed great esteem for Stöffler, perhaps on account of his astrological skills, stating that he would like to study with him.

BIBLIOGRAPHY: Allen Ep 2081 / ADB XXXVI 317–18 / *Matrikel Tübingen* I 160 / BRE Ep 112 / AK II 526 / Karl Hartfelder *Philipp Melanchthon als Praeceptor Germaniae* (Berlin 1889, repr 1964) 37–8 and passim / Lynn Thorndike *A History of Magic and Experimental Science* (New York 1923–58) v 7, 181–2, 225–6, and passim   IG

John STOKESLEY of Collyweston, c 1475–8 September 1539

John Stokesley (Stockesley, Stocleus, Stocschleius, Stocsleius) was born at Collyweston, Northamptonshire, on 8 September, probably in 1475. From about 1495 he was a fellow of Magdalen College, Oxford – the college of many of Erasmus' English humanist friends. He was lector in logic in 1499, bursar in 1502–3, dean of divinity in 1503, lector in natural philosophy in 1504–5, and vice-president of the college from 1505 to 1507. His years as vice-president were marred by intense turmoil within the college, in the course of which Stokesley was accused of grave offences including adultery, harbouring a thief, and baptizing a cat in order to find treasure by magical means. The charges were unsubstantiated and Stokesley was exonerated. On 22 March 1505 he had been ordained, and in 1506 he was instituted to the vicarage of Willoughby, Warwickshire, and by 1512 to the rectory of Slimbridge, Gloucestershire, both college livings. He later travelled to Italy, and there is evidence that he borrowed books from the Vatican library in 1513.

After his return to England Stokesley received a succession of benefices, including the archdeaconries of Surrey and Dorset. He also became chaplain to *Henry VIII in 1518, king's councillor in 1521, and king's almoner in 1523. In 1525 he became an honorary member of Doctors' Commons, the association of canon and civil lawyers of London which included in its membership Thomas *More and many of the lawyer-bishops of Henry VIII. In 1529 he was sent to France as one of the English ambassadors; an important part of his mission was the collection of opinions against the validity of Henry's marriage to *Catherine of Aragon. Nominated bishop of London in July 1530, he

returned to England in October and was consecrated on 27 November. He assisted Edward *Fox, bishop of Hereford, in the compilation of a collection of university opinions in favour of the divorce, published in Latin in 1530 as *Gravissimae totius Italiae et Galliae academiarum censurae* (London: T. Berthelet; STC 14286), and in an English translation, probably by Thomas *Cranmer, in 1531 (STC 14287). In 1531 he summoned his clergy to contribute to the grant of money approved by the convocation of the clergy. In May 1533 he was at Dunstable when Cranmer pronounced the sentence of divorce against Catherine of Aragon, and on 10 September 1533 he baptized Princess Elizabeth, the daughter of *Anne Boleyn. He consented to the Act of Supremacy on 11 February 1534, with a proviso safeguarding the laws of the church and of Christ. In 1537 he helped Cuthbert *Tunstall write a remonstrance to Reginald *Pole on his *Pro unitatis ecclesiasticae defensione*, published in Bernard Garter's *A New Year's Gift* in 1579 (London: H. Bynneman; STC 11629). A conservative in doctrinal matters, he strenuously persecuted heretics in his diocese and resisted changes made in the church, thus incurring the hostility of Thomas *Cromwell. He was a member of the commission which prepared *The Godly and Pious Institution of a Christian Man* in 1537, joining *Tunstall in giving the work as Catholic an interpretation as possible.

Although Erasmus probably met Stokesley during one of his trips to England, or even when travelling in Italy, his first surviving references to him occur in 1518 and 1519: in letters to Paolo *Bombace (Ep 855) and Ulrich von *Hutten (Ep 999) he included Stokesley with Thomas *Linacre, Richard *Pace, and John *Colet among the ornaments of the court of Henry VIII. Stokesley may also be the bachelor theologian who in 1520 joined Thomas *More in defending Erasmus from the attacks of Henry *Standish at the English court (Epp 1126, 1127A). In his *De fructu* Pace described Stokesley as his 'great friend,' learned in theology and philosophy as well as in Latin, Greek, and Hebrew, and Linacre named him an executor of his will along with More and Tunstall. In May 1534 Juan Luis *Vives mistakenly reported to Erasmus that Stokesley had been imprisoned with John

*Fisher and More (Ep 2932). Erasmus passed this rumour on to Justus Ludovicus *Decius (Ep 2961) and to Guy *Morillon (Ep 2965).

BIBLIOGRAPHY: Allen Ep 855 / DNB XVIII 1290–2 / Emden BRUO III 1785–6 / LP III–XIV passim / C. Coote *Sketches of the Lives and Characters of Eminent English Civilians* (London 1804) provides the most available list of the members of Doctors' Commons / L.B. Smith *Tudor Prelates and Politics, 1536–1558* (Princeton 1953) 43, 53, and passim / Richard Pace *De fructu qui ex doctrina percipitur liber* ed F. Manley and R. Sylvester (New York 1967) 127, 179 / A.F. Pollard *Wolsey* (London 1929, repr 1966) 178

R.J. SCHOECK

Ambrosius STORCH *See Ambrosius* PELARGUS

Nikolaus STORCH documented 1520–25
Nikolaus Storch was a weaver in Zwickau who claimed prophetic powers and preached with considerable success in May 1521. He left Zwickau by the end of that year and went to Wittenberg with Marcus *Thomae (Ep 1258) and others. In January 1522 they had some immediate success with their sermons and also had discussions with Philippus *Melanchthon and Andreas *Karlstadt. Their agitation was stopped by the return of Martin *Luther in March 1522. From 1523 Storch was one of the instigators in the peasant uprising in Thuringia. According to one source he died in 1525 in a Munich hospital, but he may have continued to live peacefully in his home town (RGG VI 1951).

BIBLIOGRAPHY: Allen Ep 1258 / ADB XXXVI 442–5 / RGG VI 1951 / Luther w *Briefwechsel* II Ep 449 / Hermann Barge *Andreas Karlstadt von Bodenstein* (Leipzig 1905; repr 1968) I 400–1 / Nikolaus Müller *Die Wittenberger Bewegung 1521, und 1522* (Leipzig 1911) 135, 139   IG

Johann STORCK of Sélestat, documented 1482–1525
Johann Storck of Sélestat, Upper Alsace, received his early education in his native town and matriculated at the University of Basel in 1482, receiving a BA there in 1484 and a MA in 1487. Subsequently he was among the Alsatian clergy who served in the papal curia from 1518 to 1525, a period when there was a marked increase in Alsatian representation. Storck was well regarded by Jakob *Wimpfeling. This was

rather exceptional in view of Wimpfeling's critical attitude towards the Roman 'courtesans.' Storck enjoyed the reputation of a learned and able humanist. He may have met Erasmus at Sélestat in August 1514; at any rate he earned a mention in Erasmus' *Encomium Selestadii* (Reedijk poem 98) among the distinguished sons of that city.

BIBLIOGRAPHY: Reedijk 317 / *Matrikel Basel* I 173 / Francis Rapp *Réformes et Réformation à Strasbourg* (Paris 1974) 230–1

MIRIAM U. CHRISMAN

Johan STORE *See Johannes* MAGNUS

Caesar STRATEGUS
The only information about this Greek protégé of Marcus *Musurus comes from the manuscripts he copied. One of these (Paris, Bibliothèque Nationale, Graecus 2159) is dated 25 September 1492, but that is the only secure date in his life. His place of birth is also uncertain, though it seems most likely that he came from Crete. Manuscripts in the Biblioteca Laurenziana suggest that he began his career as a copyist in Florence and probably moved to Venice some time after the death of Lorenzo (I) de' *Medici in 1492. Venice provided ready employment for him: the names of sixteen patrons are known from his manuscripts, and a good deal of his work found its way to France in the 1530s and 1540s in the hands of the French ambassadors Jean de *Pins and Guillaume *Pellicier, who bought extensively in Venice for the royal library. Fra Urbano *Valeriani, Pietro *Bembo, Gasparo *Contarini, and Marino *Grimani all employed Strategus, who must also be the 'Greek by birth' mentioned by Erasmus among the regular members of the circle of Aldo *Manuzio (*Colloquia* ASD I-3 682).

BIBLIOGRAPHY: M. Vogel and V. Gardthausen *Die griechischen Schreiber des Mittelalters und der Renaissance* (Leipzig 1909) 224–5 / References to some of the relevant manuscripts and patrons in E. Mioni 'La biblioteca greca di Marco Musuro' *Archivio veneto* 93 (1971) 5–28

M.J.C. LOWRY

Govaert STRIJROY of Diest, d 10 November 1549
Govaert Strijroy (Strerode, Stryroyde, Stryrode) of Diest, in Brabant, matriculated at the

University of Louvain on 4 January 1516, apparently prior to joining the Dominican order. He was a MA in 1518, a licentiate in theology on 29 August 1528, and a doctor on 11 February 1533. In August 1537 and again at the time of his death he was prior of the Dominican monastery of Louvain, an office which he had also held at the time he helped to edit the Flemish Bible of Nicolaas van *Winghe published in 1548. He served the province of his order in the offices of definitor, to which he was appointed in 1535 and 1545, and inquisitor, with which he was entrusted in 1543. He died in Louvain.

In March 1525 the Antwerp printer Simon Cocus published an *Apologia* directed against Erasmus' *Exomologesis* (1523). The *Apologia* claimed to be the work of a theologian, Godefridus Ruysius Taxander. In August 1525 Erasmus believed that the *Apologia* had been produced by four Dominicans of Louvain (Ep 1603), and by December he seems to have realized that Govaert was one of them (Ep 1655). In *La Correspondance d'Erasme* IV ed M.A. Nauwelaerts et al (Brussels-Quebec 1970), it is suggested that Strijroy was Dominican prior of Louvain as early as 1520 and hence the nameless holder of that position mentioned by Erasmus in Epp 1144, 1147, 1164–6. However, other friars are recorded as Louvain priors on 3 May 1517 and 19 February 1523.

Strijroy is the author of *Een corte verclaeringe ... op de seven psalmen der penitencien* (Louvain: R. van Diest 1560) and *Dit sijn xv puntkens als xv trappen om op te climmen totten outaer Gods* (Antwerp: P. van Keerberghen n d).

BIBLIOGRAPHY: *Matricule de Louvain* III-1 523 / BNB XXIV 198–9 / H. de Jongh *L'Ancienne Faculté de théologie de Louvain* (Louvain 1911) 54*, 60* / de Vocht *Literae ad Craneveldium* Ep 148 / de Vocht CTL IV 437 / Geneviève Glorieux et al *Belgica Topographica, 1541–1600* (Nieuwkoop 1968–) nos 6806–7 / *Acta capitulorum provinciae Germaniae inferioris ordinis fratrum praedicatorum ab anno MDXV usque ad annum MDLIX* ed S.P. Woolfs (The Hague 1964) 25, 93, and passim / J. Molanus *Historia Lovaniensium* ed F.X. de Ram (Brussels 1861) I 242   PGB

Heinrich STROMER of Auerbach, 1482–26 November 1542

Heinrich Stromer (Stromerus, Auerbachius) of Auerbach, south-west of Zwickau, matriculated at Leipzig in 1497, obtained a BA in 1498 and a MA in 1501, and began to teach at the university. His first book, *Algorithmus linealis*, an introduction to arithmetic (Leipzig: M. Landsberg 1504) was reprinted several times. In 1506 Stromer edited *Lefèvre d'Etaples' introduction to Aristotle's *De anima* (Leipzig: J. Thanner; Stromer's epistle to the reader is reprinted in Rice *Prefatory Epistles* Ep 48). Prior to 1508, when he was rector of the university, Stromer had begun to study medicine, and in 1511 he obtained a medical doctorate. As a highly respected physician he was consulted by Duke George of *Saxony, the Elector Frederick of *Saxony, the Elector Joachim of Brandenburg, and Albert of *Brandenburg, archbishop of Mainz, to whom he dedicated his *Saluberrimae adversus pestilentiam observationes* (Leipzig: V. Schumann 1516). In 1516 Stromer was professor of pathology in Leipzig and had a number of close friends in that city, among them Petrus *Mosellanus. At the same time his connection with the courts of both Joachim and Albert of Brandenburg grew stronger, and by the end of 1516 he had joined Albert as a court physician.

For more than two years Stromer lived partly in Mainz and partly in Magdeburg and Halle, following the archbishop on his travels and attending the diet of Augsburg with him in 1518 (cf Ep 863). The beginnings of his friendship with Ulrich von *Hutten (Hutten *Opera* I Epp 85, 93), Gregor *Kopp, and Wolfgang Faber *Capito date from this time. Soon, however, Stromer grew weary of court life. He vented his dissatisfaction in a new edition of the *Libellus aulicorum miserias copiose exponens* by Aeneas Sylvius, later Pope *Pius II (Mainz: J. Schöffer 1517). Soon afterwards Hutten dedicated to Stromer his caustic dialogue *Aula* (Augsburg 1518). On 24 January 1519 in Leipzig Stromer married Anna Hummelshain, the sister of a former student (Ep 986), and obtained his release from Albert's service. Returning to Leipzig on 29 June 1519 from a lengthy journey, he attended the Leipzig disputation and was deeply impressed by *Luther's arguments. During an outbreak of the plague in August 1519 he moved with his wife to Altenburg but returned to Leipzig in 1520 and remained there for the rest of his life. He became a citizen of Leipzig on 13 February 1520, a member of the town council on 27

February 1520, and first councillor in 1526. When Mosellanus became rector of the university for the summer term of 1520, Stromer greeted him in an oration, *Sermo panegyricus Petro Mosellano ... dictus* (Leipzig: M. Lotter 1520). In 1521 Stromer had an opportunity to approach *Melanchthon on behalf of Albert of Brandenburg, who was short of cash and had ordered the resumption of the sale of an indulgence in Halle. For this measure Albert was strongly criticized by Luther. Stromer joined Albert's adviser, Capito, who was repeatedly his guest at Leipzig, and together they went to Wittenberg on 30 September in an effort to prevent a public attack on the archbishop (Ep 1241).

From 1523 Stromer was dean of the medical faculty; it was due to him that the teaching of anatomy was introduced in 1524 and improved methods of bookkeeping in 1525. Stromer was known to be a Lutheran, and in May 1524 the bishop of Merseburg, as chancellor of the University of Leipzig, attempted to have him removed, but by that time Stromer's influence was so strong that no measures were taken against him. Stromer did well financially; between 1520 and 1532 he built the Auerbachhof, later made famous by a scene in Goethe's *Faust*. He also owned several other houses. By 1538 one third of all the wine sold in Leipzig came from his cellars. In spite of many duties, Stromer found time for further publications on such medico-philosophical topics as alcoholism (*Utrum ebrietas ... morbus sit* and a similar work in German, both 1531) and death (*De morte hominis*). In April 1539, when the Reformation was introduced in Albertine Saxony after the death of Duke George of *Saxony, Luther came to Leipzig for the occasion and was hospitably received by Stromer. Three years later Stromer made his last will, providing for his two sons and six daughters. He died in Leipzig.

Stromer's contact with leading humanists began in 1516 and 1517, when he wrote to *Reuchlin (RE Ep 222) and Willibald *Pirckheimer, who became his close friend. In April 1517 Stromer wrote his first letter to Erasmus (Ep 578), soon followed by another (Ep 614), which Erasmus answered (Ep 631). A friendship based on mutual respect developed between them. When Erasmus was attacked by Edward *Lee, Stromer's admiration for him

found public expression in *Duae epistolae Henrici Stromeri Auerbachii et Gregorii Coppi Calvi* (Leipzig: M. Lotter 1520; cf CWE Ep 1083 introduction). In return Erasmus praised Stromer highly in a letter to Duke George of Saxony (Ep 1125). The exchange of friendly letters continued (Epp 1326, 1444, 1564); when Erasmus published his *De libero arbitrio* (1524) Stromer had the courage to defend Luther and the tact to do so in a letter (now lost) which almost pleased Erasmus. His remarkable answer to Stromer (Ep 1522) came to the attention of Melanchthon and Hutten, who both criticized it (Allen Ep 1523 introduction; ASD IX-1 400). There appears to be no solid evidence that Stromer was visiting Basel at the time of Erasmus' death (Ep 3134). At about that time, however, he sent his nephew, Sebastian Roth of Auerbach, a physician in Dresden, several copies of Erasmus' commentary on Psalm 14/15, *De puritate tabernaculi*. Roth distributed them among his friends and also translated Erasmus' work into German: *Von der Reinikeit der Kirchen* (Dresden: W. Stöckel 28 September 1536) with a dedication from Roth to Stromer.

BIBLIOGRAPHY: Allen Ep 578 / ADB I 638 / Gustav Wustmann *Der Wirt von Auerbachs Keller, Dr. Heinrich Stromer ...* (Leipzig 1902) / *Matrikel Leipzig* I 419, II 74–8, and passim / Luther w *Briefwechsel* I Ep 187 and passim / *Melanchthons Werke in Auswahl* ed R. Stupperich et al (Gütersloh 1951–) VII-1 Ep 57 and passim / Rice *Prefatory Epistles* Ep 48 / Heinz Holeczek *Erasmus Deutsch* (Stuttgart-Bad Cannstatt 1983–) I 272–5   IG

Ciriaco STROZZI of Florence, 22 April 1504– 6 December 1565
A descendant of the well-known Strozzi family (his father was Zaccaria Strozzi and his mother was named Maria), Ciriaco was born at Capalle, the family home near Florence. Skilled both in Latin and Greek, Ciriaco taught Greek language and philosophy at Florence. In 1536 he went to the University of Bologna, succeeding Stefano Salutati as professor of Greek, and remained there nearly eight years. At the end of the academic year 1542–3 he declined reappointment and was succeeded by Pompilio Amaseo. Summoned by Cosimo, Grand Duke of Tuscany, to the University of Pisa, Ciriaco enjoyed a prestigious position as teacher and

lecturer for the next twenty years. He numbered among his students and disciples leading humanists, nobles, and ecclesiastics. Jan (II) *Łaski included Ciriaco among his friends and described him as an admirer of Erasmus (Ep 2746).

Ciriaco composed a two-volume supplement to Aristotle's eight books of the *Politics*. This work, his outstanding contribution, was written in Greek and translated into Latin. It was published by the Giunta firm at Florence in 1562 and included in later editions of Aristotle's works.

Ciriaco died in Pisa, and his body was returned to his birthplace. A statue was erected in his honour in the Strozzi chapel in Santa Maria Novella in Florence.

BIBLIOGRAPHY: Allen Ep 2746 / Cosenza IV 3334 / 'Vita Kyriaci Strozae' in *Aristotelis opera omnia quae extant* (Paris 1629)

DE ETTA V. THOMSEN

Godefredus STRYRODE *See Govaert* STRIJROY

Jacobus Lopes STUNICA *See Diego* LÓPEZ ZÚÑIGA

Jakob STURM of Strasbourg, 10 August 1489–30 October 1553
Jakob Sturm (Sturmius) was a noble patrician of Strasbourg who played a central role in the humanist movement, in the religious reform, and in the political and diplomatic life of his city in the critical years 1520–53. He was educated for a clerical career at the University of Heidelberg (1501–3) under the personal tutelage of Jakob *Wimpfeling, who introduced the young patrician to humanism and to ancient literature. Sturm also absorbed from Wimpfeling a compelling belief in education as a means of social reform and was later instrumental in establishing in Strasbourg the publicly supported schools envisaged by his mentor. From 1504 to 1511 Sturm continued his theological studies at the University of Freiburg, graduating MA in 1505; he taught the humanities and eventually took up law, studying with *Zasius. He returned to Strasbourg and served from 1517 as secretary to the provost of the Strasbourg chapter, Henry, count *Palatine (Ep 612).

In 1523, however, Sturm broke with Wimpfeling's religious teaching, converted to the

Jakob Sturm

reformed faith, and began a career of public service. He entered the senate of Strasbourg and within three years had become a member of the prestigious Committee of Thirteen which was responsible for the military and foreign policy of the city. He took a leading role in shaping foreign policy. His epitaph, written by his brothers, records that he undertook ninety-one diplomatic missions for the city. He also served four terms as a *Stettmeister*, or member of the ruling executive.

Sturm recognized that the religious crisis had shattered the established foreign policy of the city-states. Traditionally the cities opposed the princes, in part by allying themselves with the emperor. The religious divisions required new alignments. The reformed cities would have to join the reformed princes to balance the threat from the Catholic emperor and the Catholic princes and cities. This meant, in turn, a rapprochement between the Lutheran and Zwinglian cities of South Germany. The focus of Sturm's diplomacy, until his death in 1553, was to forge a union of the evangelical forces in the Empire. This aim led him to gloss over doctrinal differences in an attempt to build on the similarities between *Zwingli and *Luther, minimizing their differences. He regarded the reformers' attempts to define their beliefs and incorporate them in formal confessions of faith as detrimental to the broader cause of peace. He gained the support of Martin *Bucer, and in 1530, at the diet of Augsburg and in the months thereafter, the two men working together forged the alliance between the South German cities and John, elector of *Saxony, which laid the groundwork for the Schmalkaldic League.

Sturm met Erasmus when the latter visited Strasbourg in 1514 (Ep 302). Erasmus recognized the quality of 'the incomparable young man ... who adds lustre to his distinguished family by his own high character' (Ep 305) and sent Sturm his greetings on several occasions (Epp 633, 883). In turn Sturm rose to defend Erasmus when a Dominican preached against Erasmus' New Testament soon after its publication (Ep 948). Erasmus maintained his good opinion of Sturm despite the latter's conversion to the Reformation. In 1529 he praised Sturm in a letter to Johann von *Vlatten as prudent, sincere, and candid. All Germany was in his debt, not just the citizens of Strasbourg (Ep 2088). Sturm, for his part, continued to be of service to his scholar friend. In 1531 he denied any connection with Gerard *Geldenhouwer and responded to Erasmus' inquiry with regard to a reprint of Erasmus' Epistola contra pseudevangelicos, a controversy which continued to rankle with Erasmus (Ep 2510). In 1535 Erasmus probably turned to Sturm, promoting the appointment of Franz (II) *Baer to a canonry of Jung St Peter (Ep 3065). Sturm was the only member of the Strasbourg community with whom Erasmus remained on close terms after the divisions of the reform. In his Epistola ad fratres Inferioris Germaniae of 1530, he pointed to Sturm as a man who accepted the reformed religion but was still able to discern the consequences of the tumultuous behaviour of the populace (ASD IX-1 382–4). This was, indeed, typical of Sturm's religious position. In every period of crisis he remained theologically neutral, never committing his religious beliefs to a written statement.

Sturm gave unstintingly of his time and energy within the city as well as on missions outside. He served as one of the four lay presidents of the synod of 1533 which drew up the Strasbourg Articles of Faith (later replaced by the Wittenberg Concord). He was one of the first men appointed to the city school board and a major force in the foundation of the Gymnasium (1538). Johann Sturm, the rector of the Gymnasium, and Johannes Sleidanus, the historian and diplomat, were drawn to the city by his patronage. At his death he left his books to the new Gymnasium. His collection served as the nucleus of what would become the university library. Sturm was the epitome of the patrician who gave his whole being to the city which he served. He was also the last of the breed.

BIBLIOGRAPHY: Allen Epp 302, 3065 / O. Winckelmann in ADB XXXVII 5–20 / Schottenloher II 314–15, VII 223 / Matrikel Heidelberg I 442 / Matrikel Freiburg I-1 157 / AK I Epp 385, 437, IV Ep 1810, and passim / Thomas A. Brady Jr 'Jacob Sturm of Strasbourg and the Lutherans at the diet of Augsburg, 1530' Church History 42 (1973) 183–202 / Thomas A. Brady Jr 'Jacob Sturm of Strasbourg (1489–1553) and the political security of German Protestantism, 1526–1532' (doctoral dissertation, University of Chicago 1968) / Thomas A. Brady Jr Ruling Class, Regime and Reformation at Strasbourg, 1520–1555 (Leiden 1978) passim / Georges Livet 'Jacques Sturm, Stettmeister de Strasbourg, formation et idées politiques (1489–1532),' Jean-Daniel Pariset 'Jacques Sturm ... son activité de 1532–53,' and Jean Rott 'Jacques Sturm ... son rôle comme scolarque de la Haute-Ecole' in Strasbourg au coeur religieux du XVIe siècle (Strasbourg 1977)

MIRIAM U. CHRISMAN

Andreas STÜRTZEL von Buchheim
d 2 December 1537

Andreas, the older brother of Jakob *Stürtzel, registered at the University of Freiburg on 11 June 1490. In 1500 he was a canon at Waldkirch, in the Breisgau. He also held prebends in Constance and Bressanone (Brixen, from 1506). In 1505 he was at Pavia and received a doctorate in canon law. Having been a canon at Basel from 1518, he was elected provost of that chapter on 28 April 1525 by the city council, which now claimed the right to make this appointment. He held his high office during the crucial years of Reformation unrest, and after leaving Basel in 1529 with the rest of the chapter, he helped negotiate an accommodation with the city which, among other things, permitted him to keep part of his revenues. Perhaps as compensation for the loss of status and income which had accompanied the exile of the Basel chapter, the Hapsburg government appointed him provost of the Waldkirch chapter in 1532. Thereafter he often resided at Waldkirch and was zealous in supressing reform movements. About 1535 his concubine, Ursula von Fürst, bore him a son named Christoph.

Andreas is mentioned in Ep 2505 in conjunction with his brother, Jakob, as wishing to purchase the house 'zum Walfisch' at Freiburg when it was vacated by Erasmus.

BIBLIOGRAPHY: Allen Ep 2497 / Matrikel Freiburg I-1 99 / Helvetia Sacra ed A. Bruckner (Basel 1972–) I-1 283 / J. Bücking in Zeitschrift für die Geschichte des Oberrheins 118 (1970) 253–5 / A. Münzer in Schau-ins-Land 33 (1906) 58–61 (reproducing a portrait at Waldkirch) / Aktensammlung zur Geschichte der Basler Reformation ed E. Dürr et al (Basel 1921–50) I 148, 465–6, 542, II 103–5, 182–3, 214–16, 461–2, IV 307–8, 316, 365–6, 388–9, 416–17, V 73, 76–7, 209, 221–2, VI 3–4, 80, 232–3, and passim / R. Wackernagel Geschichte der Stadt Basel (Basel 1907–54) III 392–3   PGB

Jakob STÜRTZEL von Buchheim d May 1538

Jakob Stürtzel (Stürzel, Stiertzel, Stertzel) was a son of Bartholomäus, a steward at Thann in Alsace, and a nephew of the better known Konrad Stürtzel, chancellor of *Maximilian I. On 26 April 1495 Jakob matriculated at the University of Freiburg. In 1497 he received a prebend at Speyer but subsequently married Elisabeth von Rathsamhausen and had seven children. He obtained a doctorate in law and on 3 July 1506 was co-opted to the Freiburg faculty of law, where he lectured in civil law until 1508. In that year he was appointed councillor of the Hapsburg government of Vorder-Österreich at Ensisheim. From 1519 he also undertook diplomatic missions for *Ferdinand I, negotiating frequently with the Swiss cantons. On one occasion he was expelled from Switzerland in the aftermath of the rebellion at Waldshut in 1525. From 1529 to 1533 he participated on behalf of his master in the

negotiations between the newly reformed city of Basel and the exiled cathedral chapter, of which his brother, Andreas *Stürtzel, was provost. He was again in Basel in 1536 and together with his two fellow ambassadors succeeded in mediating an end to the conflict between Bern and Savoy. From 1530 the various estates of his family were concentrated in his hands, including the principal holdings of Buchheim and adjacent villages near Freiburg. It seems that he often resided at Buchheim. At Freiburg he acquired citizenship in 1531 and at some point owned the house 'zur Trommel.' In Basel he owned the house 'Vessneck' from 1528 to 1534.

Jakob Stürtzel is mentioned alone (Ep 2497) and in conjunction with Andreas (Ep 2505) as having rented, with an option to buy, the house 'zum Walfisch' at Freiburg which was occupied by Erasmus until September 1531.

BIBLIOGRAPHY: Allen Ep 2497 / Matrikel Freiburg I-1 121 / J. Bücking 'Das Geschlecht Stürtzel von Buchheim (1491–1790)' Zeitschrift für die Geschichte des Oberrheins 118 (1970) 239–78, esp 256–8 / AK VII Ep 3172 and passim / Deutsche Reichstagsakten Jüngere Reihe (Gotha-Göttingen 1893–) II 379–80 and passim / Amtliche Sammlung der älteren Eidgenössischen Abschiede ed K. Krütli et al (Lucerne 1839–92) IV-1a–IV-1c passim / Aktensammlung zur Geschichte der Basler Reformation ed E. Dürr et al (Basel 1921–50) I 118, 187, 203, 545, II 131; III 191, 258–9, and passim   PGB

Hermann STUVE of Vechta, died c 1560

Hermann Stuve (Hermannus Vuestphalius, Stuvius, Stuvens, Stuwe) of Vechta, fifty kilometres south of Oldenburg, was a student of Johannes *Murmellius before he matriculated at Cologne on 29 October 1510. Between about 1517 and 1520 he taught at Zwolle, assisting Gerardus *Listrius (Ep 838), and extended hospitality to Murmellius, who had fled from Alkmaar with his wife and young son. Murmellius dedicated to him his Tabularum opuscula tria (Deventer: A. Pafraet 1517) and also his last work, Scoparius in barbariei propugnatores (Deventer: A. Pafraet c 1517). By 1520 Stuve had moved to Louvain and lived, like Erasmus, in the College of the Lily (Ep 1237). His move may well have been encouraged by his countryman Conradus *Goclenius, who had been his fellow student in Cologne and had recently been appointed to the Latin chair of Louvain's Collegium Trilingue. For a few years Stuve gave private lessons to students of the Trilingue. Later he returned to Westphalia as pastor in Wildeshausen, between Vechta and Bremen, where he remained for the rest of his life.

In Ep 1237 Erasmus praised Stuve's untiring diligence as a teacher.

BIBLIOGRAPHY: Allen Ep 1237 / de Vocht CTL I 480, II 84–5, 188–9 / Matrikel Köln II 666 / D. Reichling Johannes Murmellius (Freiburg 1880, repr 1963) 82, 107–8, 163–4   IG

Ambrosius SUAGRIUS See Ambrosius KETTENACKER

Lorenzo SUÁREZ de Figueroa documented 1519–28
Lorenzo Suárez de Figueroa was marquis of Priego and count of Feria. The piety of his family was well known in orthodox circles. His wife was a patron of Luis de Granada and of Juan de Avila, and his sons, Lorenzo and Antonio, became a Dominican and a Jesuit respectively.

Suárez de Figueroa sponsored the study of Luis de *Carvajal at the faculty of theology at Paris and received the dedication to Carvajal's Apologia monasticae religionis diluens nugas Erasmi ([Salamanca] 1528; LB X 1684A).

BIBLIOGRAPHY: Bataillon Erasmo y España 182, 318, 544   TBD

SUÁREZ physician of Madrid, documented 1528
In August 1528 Erasmus mentioned a certain 'Xuares,' a physician of Madrid, who had defended him in conversation with an ignorant Dominican (Epp 2029, 2045). This physician has not been identified. Allen thought that he might perhaps be identical with the Suárez mentioned as a common friend in a letter from Alfonso de *Valdés to Johannes *Dantiscus (dated from Toledo, 14 February 1529), but Boehmer suggested that the latter might be Cristóbal Suárez, a treasury official.

BIBLIOGRAPHY: Allen Ep 2029 / Bataillon Erasmo y España 342, 620 / 'Alphonsi Valdesii litterae XL ineditae ... ' ed Eduard Boehmer in Homenaje a Menéndez y Pelayo (Madrid 1899) I 385–412, esp 402   PGB

Gerard SUCKERAET of Deventer, d 1 February 1533
Gerard (Gerrit) Suckeraet (Suggerode, Suckerroe) of Deventer matriculated at the universities of Cologne (18 July 1489) and Bologna (1491), where he received a licence in canon law on 17 June 1497. In Ep 2633 he is called 'doctor medicus,' but this seems to be an error. In or before 1495 he was a canon of St Lebuin's, Deventer, and at the beginning of the sixteenth century he held a canonry of St Saviour's or Oudmunster, Utrecht. Pope *Adrian VI appointed him official and vicar of Utrecht on 10 December 1522. As inquisitor of Holland, he was among those who watched the execution of the first Dutch martyr of the Reformation, Jan de Bakker, at The Hague (1525). In 1527 Suckeraet succeeded Herman van Lochorst as dean of the Utrecht chapter; in the same year he was a member of an embassy to the court of Cleves. When the bishop-elect of Utrecht, Henry, count *Palatine, seized Utrecht in 1528, Suckeraet was arrested, but later that year he helped negotiate the transfer of the temporalities of the bishopric to *Charles V. From 20 December 1529 until 4 August 1530 he acted as vicar-general. He was buried at Montfoort.

Petrus Nannius dedicated his comedy Vinctus (1522) to Suckeraet. In 1532 Suckeraet sent Erasmus his compliments (Ep 2633); there is no other evidence of contact between them.

BIBLIOGRAPHY: Allen Ep 2633 / J. van Kuyk in NNBW II 1393 / Matrikel Köln II 264 / Knod 567 / C.A. Kalveen Het bestuur van bisschop en Staten (Groningen 1974); see index / J. Prinsen Collectanea van Gerardus Geldenhauer Noviomagus (Amsterdam 1901) 58, 79
C.G. VAN LEIJENHORST

Antoon (1) SUCKET of Mechelen, d 31 August 1524
Antoon Sucket (Sucquet, Sucquetus) was a son of Jan (d by 1490), the town physician of Mechelen from 1448, whose own father had immigrated from the diocese of Rouen. Antoon matriculated at the University of Louvain on 30 July 1488 and proceeded to study law. He joined the administration of the city of Bruges, where he married Isabella de Waele d'Axpoele (d 1533). After having been a legal secretary, he was promoted to the office of master of requests in 1515. In the summer of 1517 he accompanied the chancellor, Jean *Le Sauvage,

to Spain and was present when Erasmus' friend Jérôme de *Busleyden died at Bordeaux on 27 August. As one of the executors of Busleyden's will he collaborated with Erasmus in the realization of Busleyden's Collegium Trilingue. In 1519, if not earlier, Sucket was appointed to the privy council and returned to live in his native city of Mechelen. He was also a knight of the Golden Fleece.

Although none of their letters seems to have survived, there is much evidence for the warm friendship which united Sucket and Erasmus (Epp 1331, 1342, 1351). In *De conscribendis epistolis* (1522, ASD I-2 441–55) Erasmus inserted a formal letter of condolence to Antoon Sucket on the death of his son, Jan (II) *Sucket. When he learnt about Antoon's own death, he recalled him with deep regret and sincere gratitude (Ep 1556). In this letter he mentioned Antoon's children, who enjoyed an excellent education. In addition to the deceased Jan, he was no doubt thinking of Karel *Sucket, to whom he transferred his friendship for the father, and also of Antoon (II) *Sucket. Antoon also had a daughter and an illegitimate son, Frans. Other testimonies of Erasmus' friendship for Antoon are in Epp 2191, 2329.

BIBLIOGRAPHY: Allen Ep 1331 / de Vocht *Busleyden* 95–6, 121–5 / de Vocht CTL I 55–9 / *Matricule de Louvain* III-1 51

MARCEL A. NAUWELAERTS

Antoon (II) SUCKET of Bruges, d 18 November 1557
Antoon was the third son of Erasmus' friend Antoon (I) *Sucket. According to Erasmus he was still a child, or almost so, when his father died (Ep 1556). He studied at Louvain (1524–6) and Orléans (1530) and became a lawyer and a member of the grand council of Mechelen. The name of his wife was Maria de Hane.

BIBLIOGRAPHY: Allen Ep 1556 / *Matricule d'Orléans* II-2 186–7 / de Vocht *Busleyden* 125 / de Vocht CTL II 154–5

MARCEL A. NAUWELAERTS

Jan (I) SUCKET of Mechelen, d 1522
Jan, a son of the town physician of Mechelen and a brother of Antoon (I) *Sucket, matriculated at the University of Louvain on 30 July 1474. He studied law and on 22 January 1504 was appointed to the grand council of Mechelen. In 1519 and 1521 he undertook diplomatic

missions to *Christian II, king of Denmark. His successor on the grand council was appointed on 17 January 1523, so his death must have occurred by the end of 1522. It was mentioned in March 1523 by Pieter *Wichmans (Ep 1351). Jan was clearly an old acquaintance of Erasmus, who addressed a letter to him two years later, apparently oblivious of his death (Ep 1556). This letter paid tribute to Jan's recently deceased brother Antoon and asked Jan to take Antoon's place as a protector of the Collegium Trilingue in Louvain.

Jan Sucket had a daughter, Maria, who was married to Jan *Vrancx, a court physician and, like the Suckets, a loyal friend to Erasmus.

BIBLIOGRAPHY: Allen Epp 1351, 1556 / de Vocht *Busleyden* 122–3 / *Matricule de Louvain* II-1 307

MARCEL A. NAUWELAERTS

Jan (II) SUCKET of Bruges, d probably 1521/2
Jan, the son of Antoon (I) *Sucket, Erasmus' good friend, is documented only when he matriculated at the University of Louvain with his brother, Karel *Sucket, on 27 January 1519. In 1522 Erasmus specifically mentioned his death in *De conscribendis epistolis* (ASD I-2 441), calling him a youth of great promise.

BIBLIOGRAPHY: de Vocht *Busleyden* 96, 125 / *Matricule de Louvain* III-1 598

MARCEL A. NAUWELAERTS

Karel SUCKET of Bruges, d 3 November 1532
Karel, the first or second son of Antoon (I) *Sucket, matriculated at Louvain on 29 January 1519 with his brother, Jan (II) *Sucket. As he was then still a minor it may be assumed that he was born by 1506. As a friend of his father, Erasmus followed his progress from an early age (Ep 1556). In 1529 Karel was studying law at Dole in the Franche-Comté and encouraged *Viglius Zuichemus, his fellow student and friend for life, to address a letter to the much-admired humanist (Ep 2101). Sucket himself corresponded with Erasmus (Epp 2135, 2141), who was looking forward to having him as a guest at his table in Freiburg (Ep 2191), since Sucket was evidently considering becoming a student of the famous *Zasius. However, in the end he chose to go to Bourges, where *Alciati was teaching (Epp 2199, 2209, 2210). He continued to exchange letters with Erasmus (Epp 2356, 2373, 2464, 2682), who had agreed to recommend him to Alciati (Epp 2113, 2276,

2329). On 7 October 1530 Alciati reported that Sucket's doctorate was imminent and that he and Viglius would be equally suited to succeed to Zasius' chair in Freiburg (Epp 2394, 2418, 2468). Soon thereafter both left with Alciati for Italy; while Viglius went to Padua, Sucket remained in Turin, where he was appointed to a lectureship in law for a salary of one hundred crowns (Epp 2594, 2631). In 1531 Viglius expressed concern about Sucket's health and unease about his plans to marry a girl from Turin, and in January 1533 he had to inform Erasmus of his friend's untimely death (Ep 2753). He took steps to salvage Sucket's *Liber de interdictis*, which was in fact published at Turin by 1535.

Sucket was a friend of Maarten *Lips and a kinsman of Karel *Uutenhove (Ep 2209). Janus Secundus devoted some *Naeniae* to his memory and recalled him in other poems.

BIBLIOGRAPHY: Allen Epp 1556, 2191 / BNB XXIV 241–2 / de Vocht CTL II 150–4 / *Matricule de Louvain* III-1 598 / AK III Ep 1378 and passim

MARCEL A. NAUWELAERTS & PGB

Johann SUDERMANN of Cologne, died c 1537

Johann Sudermann was the son of another Johann who was a Cologne city councillor from 1472 to 1506. The younger Johann matriculated at Cologne on 13 June 1491 as a student in the faculty of arts and at Basel during the winter term 1493–4. Subsequently he earned a baccalaureate in both laws at Bologna and rematriculated at Cologne in September 1500, where he was granted a legal licence and a doctorate in canon law, both in 1508. From 7 April 1496 to his death he occupied a canonry at St Mary's in Aachen. In 1508 he was appointed to the office of precentor. After earning his doctorate the same year, he also held a professorship in law at the University of Cologne. He seems to have died in 1537, as his canonry was then assigned to Henricus de Milendock, while the office of precentor was occupied by Adam von Pirn on 7 December 1537.

Erasmus made Sudermann's acquaintance during his visit to Aachen in September 1518, when he dined at the precentor's table (Ep 867). Sudermann, who sent greetings to

Erasmus in 1519 (Ep 972), was one of the Aachen canons who formed a party of Erasmians around Leonardus *Priccardus.

BIBLIOGRAPHY: Allen Ep 867 / *Matrikel Köln* II 298 / *Matrikel Basel* I 227 / Anton Fahne *Geschichte der Kölnischen, Jülichschen und Bergischen Geschlechter in Stammtafeln, Wappen, Siegeln und Urkunden* (Cologne-Bonn 1848–53, repr 1965) I 426 (reproducing the Sudermann coat of arms) / *Nomina admodum reverendorum perillustrium atque generosorum dominorum canonicorum regalis ecclesiae B.M.V. Aquisgranensis* ed Antonius Heusch (Berlin 1892) 14, 16 / Hermann Keussen *Die alte Universität Köln: Grundzüge ihrer Verfassung und Geschichte* (Cologne 1934) 460 / 'Inventare und Regesten aus den Kölner Pfarrarchiven II' ed Heinrich Schaefer *Annalen des Historischen Vereins für den Niederrhein* 77 (1903) 195–6

KASPAR VON GREYERZ

SUFFOLK *See Charles* BRANDON, *Edmund de la* POLE

Gerard SUGGERODE *See Gerard* SUCKERAET

SULEIMAN I Ottoman sultan, 6 November 1494–7 September 1566

Suleiman I (Solymannus), known in the West as Suleiman the Magnificent, was the son of *Selim I and Hafsa Sultan, the daughter of Mengli Giray Khan of the Crimea. He became governor of Feodosiya (Kaffa) on the Crimea in 1509 and of Manisa, Western Anatolia, in 1513, and sultan on the death of his father in September 1520. Widely regarded as the greatest of all Ottoman sultans, he brought major accretions of territory and power to the Ottoman Empire. He personally took part in thirteen major campaigns, ten in Europe and three in Asia. He captured Belgrade in August 1521, making it possible for the Ottomans to penetrate more deeply into Europe. His capture of Rhodes from the knights of St John in December 1522 removed a menace on the flank of the empire. Victory over the Hungarians at Mohács on 29 August 1526 enabled Suleiman to occupy Buda and to overrun the greater part of Hungary. Here he first tried to set up a buffer state, supporting the claims of *John Zápolyai against those of Archduke *Ferdi-

nand for the vacant throne (Ep 3014). This
involved him in a long conflict with the
Hapsburgs which, complicated by other factors, such as Suleiman's alliance with France
(Ep 3119), extended to North Africa and the
Mediterranean. In 1529 Suleiman installed
John Zápolyai at Buda and then besieged
Vienna, but in vain. In 1532 he undertook
another Hungarian campaign in order to
maintain Zápolyai in power (Ep 3121). When
Zápolyai died in 1540, Suleiman established
direct Ottoman rule in Hungary, and his
campaigns of 1541, 1543, and 1566 were all
intended to consolidate the Ottoman presence
there.

Ottoman-Persian enmity, perpetuated by
defections and claims and counter claims in the
unstable frontier region, continued during
much of Suleiman's reign. He acquired Baghdad during his Persian campaign of 1534–6
returning completely victorious, despite excit-
ed and grossly exaggerated rumours of Turkish
defeats circulating in the West (Epp 3007, 3075,
3078, 3119). His campaigns of 1548–9 and
1553–5 strengthened the Ottoman position
along the frontiers, where the situation remained fluid. Relations with Persia improved
with the signing of the first Ottoman-Persian
agreement at Amasya in 1555.

Under Suleiman the Ottomans, who brought
into their service the Turkish corsair organiza-
tions of North Africa, developed into a major
sea-power. *Khair ad-Din Barbarossa's victory
over an allied Christian fleet off Prevesa in 1538
ensured their dominance of the Mediterranean. In 1551 Turgud Reis captured Tripolis, and
Piyale Pasha won a maritime victory over the
Christians off Djerba in 1560. However, the
Ottoman attempt to capture Malta from the
knights of St John in 1565 was repulsed. The
Ottomans also engaged the Portuguese, in the
process bringing Yemen and Aden under their
control but failing to prevent Portuguese
domination of the Indian ocean and the Gulf of
Persia.

Suleiman's reign was not free from internal
troubles. In 1520 Djanberdi al-Ghazali, the
governor of Damascus, and in 1524 Ahmed
Pasha, the governor of Egypt, rose in rebellion,
each seeking to establish his independent rule.
Both were defeated and executed. There were

Suleiman I

also uprisings in Anatolia (1526–8) induced by
economic grievances and Shi'ite influences and
a brief civil war in 1559 arising from the rivalry
of Suleiman's remaining sons, Bayezid and the
future Selim II. Bayezid, who incurred his
father's displeasure, was defeated and later
executed (1562). Suleiman's eldest son, Mus-
tafa, had been executed in 1553 through the
influence of Selim's mother, the famous Khur-
rem Sultan, and because he was suspected of
designs to secure the throne.

During Suleiman's reign state institutions
attained their classical form through his prom-
ulgation of Kanun (secular laws), which were
later codified in the different Kanunname.
Suleiman's legislative activity and his punctili-
ous respect for justice gained him the appella-
tion Kanunī, lawgiver.

Under Suleiman the Ottoman empire experienced a cultural advance that owed much to
his personal inspiration and initiative. He
built many mosques and edifices, Istanbul's
Süleymaniye complex, including mosque,
madrasa, and other buildings, being the
crowning architectural achievement of the

period. Suleiman, who died on 7 September 1566, is buried there. In *De bello turcico* (LB V 352) Erasmus gives a detailed summary of Suleiman's conquests and laments his victories.

BIBLIOGRAPHY: T. Gökbilgin in *Islam Ansiklopedisi* (Istanbul 1940–   ) XI 99–155, a good account with full bibliography / J.H. Kramers in *Encyclopaedia of Islam* (Leiden-London 1913–38) IV 522–7 / M. Süreyya *Sicill-i Osmâni* (Istanbul 1890–7) / *Kanunī Armaǧani* (Ankara 1970), containing papers commemorating the four-hundredth anniversary (in 1966) of Suleiman's death / The old biographies by R.B. Merriman *Suleiman the Magnificent* (Cambridge, Mass, 1944), H. Lamb *Suleiman the Magnificent* (New York 1951), and F. Downey *The Grande Turke* (New York 1929), contain errors.

FEHMI ISMAIL

Giovanni Antonio SULPIZIO of Veroli, b before 1450

Giovanni Antonio Sulpizio, editor, poet, and grammarian, was born at Veroli. Educated in his native city, he began there a teaching career which took him by 1475 to Perugia, thence to Urbino, and by about 1480 to Rome, where he was associated with *Pomponius Laetus. M.T. Graziosi has argued that Sulpizio is depicted in Antonio, the learned judge of humanist literary activity in Paolo *Cortesi's *De hominibus doctis dialogus*.

Sulpizio published together the *editiones principes* of Vitruvius' *De architectura* and Frontinus' *De aquaeductibus*, the latter in collaboration with Pomponius Laetus (Rome: G. Herolt c 1486). He also produced the *editio princeps* of the *Rei militaris scriptores* of Vegetius Renatus, Aelianus, and Frontinus (Rome: E. Silber 1487), a much-reprinted edition of Lucan's *Pharsalia* with commentary, and a commentary on Quintilian's *Institutiones oratoriae* published by Omnibonus Leonicenus with those of Lorenzo *Valla and Pomponius Laetus (Venice: Peregrinus de Pasqualibus 1494). Other editorial works are found in manuscript.

In his preface to Vitruvius, Sulpizio revealed that he had helped to revive classical drama in Rome by his teaching of acting and singing. Of his poetry, much survives only in manuscript, but his *Judicium Dei supremum de vivis et mortuis* was printed at Rome by Eucharius Silber in

1506, and a little poem on table manners for children, *Carmen iuvenile de moribus in mensa servandis*, was frequently reprinted and sometimes appended to Boethius and Quintilian.

Erasmus considered Sulpizio one of the best Latin grammarians of the age, linking him with Niccolò *Perotti (*De ratione studii* ASD I-2 148). In Ep 117 Erasmus mentioned favourably instructions on letter-writing found in one of Sulpizio's grammars. He was perhaps referring to an edition of Sulpizio's *Grammatica* which also contained his *De componendis et ornandis epistolis* (Venice: C. de Pensis 1489), normally published separately. The Newberry Library possesses such an edition, the *Regulae Sulpitii*, possibly printed at Venice by Johannes Tacuinus around 1495. Sulpizio also wrote *De constructionis octo figuris*, which was reprinted in several editions of Erasmus' *De constructione octo partium oratione* (Deventer, Cologne 1515), and a volume of treatises on poetics, *De versuum scansione: De syllabarum quantitate* ... (Rome c 1480).

BIBLIOGRAPHY: Allen Ep 117 / P. Cortesi *De hominibus doctis dialogus* ed M.T. Graziosi (Rome 1973) xxii–xxv / Cosenza V 441 / *Biographie universelle* ed L.-G. Michaud, new ed (Paris 1854–   ) XL 437–8 / B. Pecci *L'umanesimo e la 'Cioceria'* (Trani 1912) 29–111 / W.K. Percival 'Renaissance grammar: rebellion or evolution?' *Interrogativi dell'umanesimo* (Florence 1976) II 82–4, 87–9 / P.O. Kristeller *Iter Italicum* (London-Leiden 1965–   ) I 395, II 420, and passim / G.A. Sulpizio *Doctrina Mensae: Table Manners for Boys* ed H. Thomas (Oxford 1949) / G. Tiraboschi *Storia della letteratura italiana* new ed (Florence 1805–13) VI 874, 1086

JUDITH RICE HENDERSON

Simon SUNFELDUS (Ep 1260 of 16 February 1522)

In this letter Jakob *Ziegler replied from Rome to Erasmus' request for a manuscript containing Pontius' life of Cyprian. Ziegler stated that the manuscript belonged to the bishop or chapter of Wrocław and that he himself had seen it when it had been loaned to Simon Sunfeldus, a doctor of medicine, who knew Hebrew and Greek and was an old friend of Johann *Reuchlin. No trace has been found of Sunfeldus so far. Schottenloher suggested identifying him with the Leipzig physician

Christoph Sonfeld or Schönfeld who was a friend of *Mutianus Rufus and Heinrich *Stromer.

BIBLIOGRAPHY: Allen Ep 1260 / Karl Schotten-loher *Jakob Ziegler* (Münster 1910) 55–6

MICHAEL ERBE

Johannes SUTOR documented at Freiburg 1502–30

Johannes Sutor (presumably Suter in German) was a member of the Freiburg mercers' guild and received burgher rights there in 1502 when he was inducted into the town council as the master of his guild, the most prominent among the retailers' guilds. To qualify for denizenship applicants normally had to be residents of Freiburg for at least ten years. Sutor was again the master of his guild in 1510 and 1514; from 1516 he served continually on the town council. He thus belonged to the governing inner circle of guildsmen in Freiburg. He was also among the wealthiest of them, having an assessed worth of fifteen hundred florins in 1508, which rose to over thirty-one hundred florins in 1522. He is still found in the Freiburg tax lists for 1530. On 2 October 1515 he married Clementia, a daughter of Udalricus *Zasius. Erasmus was solicitously invited to the wedding but could not spare the time to go to Freiburg (Epp 357, 358).

Conceivably Johannes Sutor was a relative of Johann Suter (Sutor) of Zurzach, who had studied in Erfurt and Basel and began to teach arts courses at the University of Freiburg in 1464. Between 1472 and 1510 he served for nine terms as the rector of the university, and he was rich enough to endow a scholarship at Freiburg on 28 May 1506, to which he gave further funds in 1509 and 1515.

BIBLIOGRAPHY: Freiburg, Stadtarchiv MS B 5: 1b (Ratsbesatzungsbuch) ff 78 recto and following; MS E 1: A II a 1 (Bürgerbücher), respective years / For Johann Suter of Zurzach see *Matrikel Freiburg* I-1 30; *Matrikel Basel* I 30; AK IV Ep 1755   STEVEN ROWAN & PGB

Petrus SUTOR *See Pierre* COUSTURIER

Rutgerus SYCAMBER of Kirchberg, documented until 1516/17

Rutgerus was born between 1456 and 1461 in the village of Kirchberg, near Jülich, and adopted the name of Sycamber after the Sigambri, a Germanic tribe associated with that region. He was educated in Jülich and Venray and at a Premonstratensian convent near Neer, north of Roermond. Subsequently he entered the Latin school of Roermond and afterwards went to 's Hertogenbosch and Deventer before joining the house of Austin canons at Höningen, west of Speyer, where he made his profession. Next he moved to Basel, where he studied and became acquainted with Sebastian *Brant; from there he went to Beerenberg, an Austin priory between Pfungen and Wülflingen (Zürich), where he held the position of sub-prior for nearly two years. After residing for a time at the monastery of Molenbeke near Rinteln, on the Weser south of Minden, he moved on to the house of Vallis Gratiae in Bruges, and then returned to Höningen. At other times he visited Frankenthal in the Palatinate, the monastery of Kirschgarten near Worms, and *Trithemius' abbey of Sponheim.

Sycamber's life was not only itinerant but also marked by a lack of ease and comfort. In his only known letter to Erasmus (CWE Ep 65A) he mentioned frequent opposition from his fellow-monks. To keep his balance and self-control, he devoted himself untiringly to study and literary composition. He also maintained friendly contacts and correspondences with a great many fellow humanists, as is shown by the surviving documentation. Above all it was Trithemius who remained his close friend for many years and also encouraged his writing of poetry, as did Johann von *Dalberg to a lesser degree. Trithemius read his compositions and suggested improvements; he also advised Sycamber to study more Greek and frequently asked him to treat religious rather than mundane topics (Trithemius *Opera historica* II 499, 522, 524, 552). He finally honoured his friend by including him among the authors treated in his *Catalogus illustrium virorum* and his *De scriptoribus ecclesiasticis*. An evaluation of Sycamber's work will have to await a critical edition of his writings, his correspondence, and his autobiography. Trithemius said of him: 'He has his own fashion of making books and produces foetuses without number ... indeed, he is still at it today' (*Opera historica* II 555). But this somewhat patronizing statement must be contrasted with the positive evaluation of his

Dialogus de musica in a recent study. Sycamber's last known letter is dated 3 September 1507; according to Butzbach he was alive in 1508. His poem published in *Collectanea latinae loquutionis* and a reference to him in the famous *Epistolae obscurorum virorum* (Hutten *Operum supplementum* II 288) would even seem to indicate that he was still alive in 1516 or 1517.

Sycamber's letter to Erasmus (CWE Ep 65A) comes from a manuscript in Cologne (Historisches Archiv MS W 340), which illustrates the wide spread of Sycamber's connections; it contains unedited letters to Trithemius, Arnoldus *Bostius, Robert *Gaguin, Sebastian Brant, Jakob *Locher (Philomusus), Conradus Celtis, Jacques *Lefèvre d'Etaples, Johann von Dalberg, Matthaeus Herbenus, and many others. Two letters from Sycamber to Wigant Wirt, dealing with the quarrel about the Immaculate Conception, are in Strasbourg, Bibliothèque Nationale et Universitaire, MS L Lat. 103. Another letter to Trithemius is preserved in the latter's manuscript 'Quaedam de Sancta Anna' (Arnold 268). More letters are published in P.S. Allen 'Letters of Arnold Bostius' *The English Historical Review* 34 (1919) 225–36; *Der Briefwechsel des Konrad Celtis* ed Hans Rupprich (Munich 1934) Epp 78, 223; Robert Gaguin *Epistolae et orationes* ed Louis Thuasne (Paris 1898–1903) II Ep 81, 44–5; AK I Epp 72, 195, 355; Jan Oudewater (Palaeonydorus) *Liber ... de principio ... ordinis Carmelitani* (Mainz: P. Fridbergensis 1497).

The following works by Sycamber have appeared in print: *Dialogus de musica* (c 1500) ed Fritz Soddemann (Cologne 1963); *De quantitate syllabarum* (Cologne: sons of H. Quentel 1502); *Litania ad omnes sanctos* (Deventer 1514). A list of Sycamber's works, mentioning 110 titles, is included in *De quantitate syllabarum* (f A 1 verso–2 recto). They were divided into three manuscript volumes; the second of these is preserved in Cologne, Historisches Archiv MS W 340. The total number of Sycamber's writings may surpass 140 (AK I Ep 355).

One or more poems or epigrams by Sycamber are published in Theodor Gresemund Jr *Lucubratiunculae bonarum septem artium liberalium*; in four works by Johannes Trithemius, *De laudibus ordinis fratrum Carmelitarum, De laudibus sanctissimae matris Annae, Catalogus illustrium virorum*, and *De proprietate monachorum*,

all published between 1494 and 1495 in Mainz by Petrus Fridbergensis; and in Johannes de Lamsheim *Libelli tres* [Heidelberg: H. Knoblochtzer, c 1495–1500].

BIBLIOGRAPHY: CWE Ep 65A / Heinrich Hüschen 'Rutgerus Sycamber de Venray und sein Musiktraktat' in *Studien zur Musikgeschichte des Rheinlandes: Festschrift zum 80. Geburtstag von Ludwig Schiedermair* (Cologne 1956) 34–45 / Victor Scholderer 'Rutgerus Sicamber and his writings' in *Gutenberg – Jahrbuch 1957* (Mainz 1957) 129–30 / Johannes Trithemius *Opera historica ... ex bibliotheca Marquardi Freheri* (Frankfurt 1601, repr 1966) / Johannes Trithemius *Catalogus illustrium virorum* (Mainz: P. Fridbergensis 1495) / Johannes Trithemius *Liber de scriptoribus ecclesiasticis* (Basel: J. Amerbach 1494) / Klaus Arnold *Johannes Trithemius (1462–1516)* (Würzburg 1971) 100–2 and passim / Hutten *Operum supplementum* II 460–2, with an extract from J. Butzbach (Piemontanus) *Auctarium scriptorum ecclesiasticorum* / Cologne, Historisches Archiv MS W 340 (especially Sycamber's autobiography)

KONRAD WIEDEMANN

Martinus SYDONIUS *See* MARTINUS *Sydonius Transsylvanus*

SYLVAGIUS *See Jean (I), Jean (II), and Antoine* LE SAUVAGE

SYLVIUS *See François and Jacques* DUBOIS, *Johannes Sylvius* EGRANUS, SILVIUS

François SYMARD of Mondon, d 9 September 1554

A native of Mondon, near Vesoul in the Franche-Comté, François Symard (Simarius) was the son of Pierre, a high Hapsburg official. Having previously obtained the degree of MA, he was appointed rector of the chapter school of Besançon after due examination by the scholaster. Subsequently he went to Paris to study in the Collège de Bourgogne, where he was *boursier*. In 1521 he was regent in physics in the Collège de Calvi and on 22 October began to lecture on the *Sentences* of Petrus Lombardus. He was prior of the Collège de Sorbonne from 1525 to 1526, and on 26 October 1526 he received his doctorate in theology. Subsequently he left Paris to teach theology at the University of Dole. On 30 December 1531 *Charles v issued letters patent designating him a canon of Besançon. Amid the troubles of the church in Besançon his theological learning and his reputation as an excellent preacher were particularly useful, and on 17 September 1533 the archbishop of Besançon, Antoine de *Vergy, appointed him his suffragan with the nominal see of Nicopolis and a salary of two hundred francs in addition to his income from the canonry. In December 1536 Symard ordered the arrest of one Pierre Du Chastel for possessing a copy of the Bible translated by Robert Olivétan. The city council of Neuchâtel offered to debate Symard's contention that this translation contained errors and lies. In 1536 he sent greetings to Erasmus through Gilbert *Cousin (Ep 3080). On 11 April 1554 he resigned as prior of Notre-Dame de Bellefontaine. In his years at Paris he had begun to collect a library, and several incunables which were part of it are now in the public library of Besançon.

BIBLIOGRAPHY: Allen Ep 3080 / Farge no 447 / Augustin Castan *Catalogue des incunables de la Bibliothèque publique de Besançon* (Besançon 1893) 43 and passim / Augustin Castan 'Les évêques auxiliaires du siège métropolitain de Besançon' *Mémoires de la Société d'émulation du Doubs* 5th ser 1 (1876) 456–83, esp 472 / Augustin Castan 'Granvelle et le petit empereur de Besançon' *Revue historique* I (1876) 78–139, esp 86, 116 / Eubel III 258 / Gauthier 123, 126, 129, 130 / Besançon, Archives du Doubs MS G 250

JAMES K. FARGE & PGB

Jan SYMOENS *See Jan of* HEEMSTEDE

Jan SYNTHEN of Delden, d before December 1498
Jan Synthen (Synthius, Sintheimius, Zinthius, Delden), born at Delden, in Overijssel, was one of the Brethren of the Common Life at Deventer and served as a warden of the 'solarium publicum domus clericorum.' He also taught in St Lebuin's school, under Alexander *Hegius. In his *Compendium vitae* Erasmus credited Hegius and Synthen with introducing a more humanistic approach towards letters and learning at their school (Allen I 48; CWE 4 405). According to *Beatus Rhenanus, Synthen

had once predicted a bright future for Erasmus as a scholar (Allen I 57). That Erasmus mentioned him only once in his writings may have been due to beatings administered by Synthen to keep his gifted pupil humble. This, at least, is the view of Tracy, who cites a passage in *De pueris instituendis* to support his hypothesis (ASD I-2 56). Unfavourable comments about the Brethren of the Common Life in *De pronuntiatione* (ASD I-4 29) may also have been made with Synthen in mind. For the use of schools Synthen wrote *Regulae de accentibus* (c 1480), *Composita verborum* (c 1483), and *Verba deponentialia* (c 1483), all published at Deventer by Richard Paffraet. Synthen's best-known work, however, is his commentary on the *Doctrinale* of Alexander de Villa Dei, which was reprinted many times. Johann Butzbach (*Zeitschrift des Bergischen Geschichtsvereins* 7, 1871, 242) suggests that Hegius and Synthen were joint authors of this commentary but that they agreed that the first to die would lend his name to it. If Butzbach is correct, Synthen must have died before Hegius' death in December 1498, or even before 9 August 1488, when Richard Paffraet printed the commentary for the first time, and under Synthen's name.

BIBLIOGRAPHY: Allen I 48 / CWE 4 405 / F.S. Knipscheer in NNBW IX 197–8 / J.D. Tracy 'Bemerkungen zur Jugend des Erasmus,' *Basler Zeitschrift für Altertumskunde* 72 (1972) 221–30, esp 227–9 / H. Baudet et al in *Folium* 4 (1954) 27–8   C.G. VAN LEIJENHORST

László SZALKAY 1475–29 August 1526
The son of a cobbler, László Szalkay (Ladislaus Szalkai, Zalkay) was born at Mátészalka, in eastern Hungary and received his education at the municipal school of Sárospatak. His extensive school notes from 1489–90 have survived and are an important source for the educational history of Hungary in the fifteenth century. There is no indication that he ever went abroad in order to attend a university. His first employment was as a teacher, but his ambition drove him to seek a more lucrative position. By 1494 he was a scribe in the royal court at Buda. In 1496 he became an official of the treasury and four years later was in charge of the salt tax revenues from Transylvania. Thereafter his career, both secular and ecclesiastic, was spectacular. He received the bishopric of Vác

(1513–20) and exchanged it for the more lucrative bishopric of Eger (1520–24). In 1520 he was briefly archbishop of Kalocsa and in 1524 reached the highest ecclesiastical position in Hungary when he became archbishop of Esztergom (Gran) and primate of the kingdom, a position he held until his death. At the same time he was also royal treasurer (1515), chancellor (1521), and privy chancellor (1524).

Notorious for his boundless avarice and greed, Szalkay managed to accumulate an immense fortune. Not until 26 April 1525, when he was already archbishop of Esztergom, did he finally take holy orders. Although King *Louis II took steps in Rome to secure a cardinal's hat for Szalkay, Pope *Leo x politely declined, following the advice of Andrea da *Borgo. The disastrous political and economic conditions which prevailed during the reign of Louis II were blamed by the nobility on the incompetence and corruption of Szalkay. At the time of the diet of Rákos (April–May 1525) and the diet of Hatvan (July–August 1525) it seemed certain that he would fall from power and possibly even flee from Hungary (Epp 1603, 1606), but he was able to survive these political storms. When the Turks advanced upon southern Hungary in August 1526, Szalkay accompanied King Louis II and the Hungarian army on the ill-fated campaign which ended with the slaughter of the Christian forces at Mohács on 29 August. Leading his troops into battle, Archbishop Szalkay died along with the king and the flower of the Hungarian nobility.

Szalkay was dedicated to scholarship and learning and was part of the humanistic circle in Buda which had developed around Jacobus *Piso. He wrote some fine Latin epigrams, and several works were dedicated to him, among them poems by *Ursinus Velius, Martin of Nagyszombat (Trnava, Tyrnan), and Piso. His epigrams, as well as works dedicated to him, have been edited by J. Ábel and I. Hegedüs in Analecta nova ad historiam renascentium in Hungaria litterarum spectantia (Budapest 1903).

BIBLIOGRAPHY: Allen Ep 1603 / Magyar életrajzi lexikon (Budapest 1967–9) II 679 / Magyar irodalmi lexikon (Budapest 1963–5) III 138 / István Balogh Szalkay László esztergomi érsek (Kassa 1942) / István Mészáros A Szalkai- kodex és a xv. századvégi Sáróspataki iskola (Budapest 1972)   L. DOMONKOS

Krzysztof SZYDŁOWIECKI
1467–30 December 1532

Szydłowiecki (Schydłowiecz, Schiidłovietz, Schydłowyetz) came from a wealthy family of noblemen with estates in Szydłowiec, in Little Poland, and the coat of arms 'Odrowaz.' He was son of Stanisłaus, marshal of Casimir IV's court, and his second wife, Zofia of Goździkow and Pleszow. He was brought up at the court and was the classmate of the future King *Sigismund I. About the year 1492 he undertook a pilgrimage to the Holy Land, where he became a knight of the Holy Sepulchre. In 1498 he was made marshal of Prince Sigismund's court and accompanied him during his administration of Głogów in Silesia and other appointments in Bohemia and Hungary (1498–1506). After Sigismund's accession to the throne of Poland Szydłowiecki became his closest adviser and quickly climbed the administrative ladder. He was appointed castellan of Sandomierz on 24 December 1509, vice-chancellor of the realm on 15 February 1511, and grand chancellor on 4 March 1515. He advocated closer ties with the Hapsburgs and in 1515 promoted the meeting in Vienna between Sigismund and *Maximilian I, in which he took an active part. During this summit he received the title of baron of the Roman Empire from the emperor on 2 August 1515, while Sigismund named him prefect-general and voivode of Cracow on 6 August.

A capable diplomat, he was gladly welcomed at the emperor's court and was often sent on embassies to Austria and Hungary. Of special importance was a mission assigned to him in 1527, when he travelled to Prague and Olomouc to attempt to arrange a reconciliation between *John Zápolyai, and *Ferdinand of Austria. Appointed castellan of Cracow on 2 April 1527 he combined in his person the offices of chancellor and the most important senatorial dignitary in Poland. He exercised considerable influence upon the king and consolidated his power by co-operating closely with the vice-chancellor, Piotr *Tomicki. Szydłowiecki also signed private 'pacts of brotherhood' with the influential Hungarian dignitary György Szatmáry (1518) and Albert of *Brandenburg-Ansbach, duke of Prussia (1526). He strove to establish good relations with King *Henry VIII of England and his adviser Cardinal Thomas *Wolsey, with the king of France, *Francis I, and with the Emperor *Charles V.

Owing to his own acquisitive efforts and the generosity of the king, who gave him six prefectures, Szydłowiecki amassed a great fortune. He appeared in public with exaggerated magnificence and maintained splendid courts in Cracow and in his main residence, the castle of Omielow. Among the secular dignitaries at court he was the first great patron of literature and art. He established contacts with many humanists and lavishly rewarded the numerous works which were dedicated to him. He received praise in verse from Andrzej *Krzycki and Johannes *Dantiscus and dedications from Silvius Amatus Siculus and Rudolphus Agricola the younger, a professor of the University of Cracow. He also received poems from humanists such as Nicolaus Hussovianus. He collected a great library and brought illuminated manuscripts from abroad for his collection.

Around 1512 Szydłowiecki married Sophia of Targowisko, by whom he had four sons and five daughters. Only three lived beyond childhood: Sophia, who married the grand hetman of the realm Jan Tarnowski, Christine, who married the duke of Ziembice-Janusz, and Elżbieta, who married Mikołaj Radziwiłł, *voivode* of Wilno.

Szydłowiecki died in Cracow and was buried at the collegiate church at Opatow, where he had prepared his own tomb covered by a metal plate with his likeness etched on it. In 1536, on the initiative of his son-in-law Jan Tarnowski, the tomb was rebuilt by Italian master sculptors and became a work of art known as the Lament of Opatow.

Szydłowiecki was urged to establish contacts with Erasmus by Jan (II) *Łaski. It was at the latter's request that Erasmus dedicated his *Lingua* (ASD IV-1 233) to Szydłowiecki in 1525 (Ep 1593). Two of Erasmus' Polish friends, Hieronim *Łaski and Jan *Antonin, informed him of the great enthusiasm with which Szydłowiecki received the booklet (Epp 1622, 1660). Szydłowiecki immediately ordered it reprinted at Cracow (H. Wietor 1526), and in

addition to a letter of thanks (not preserved) he sent Erasmus a rich gift of gold: a watch and a spoon and fork (Ep 1698) made by the goldsmith Jan *Zimmermann (Ep 1660). In a letter of 9 September 1526 (Ep 1752) Erasmus thanked the Polish chancellor for his gifts, and from this moment they kept up friendly relations. Although no letters from Szydłowiecki to Erasmus have been preserved, we know of their cordial relationship both from Erasmus' letters to Szydłowiecki (Epp 1820, 1918, 2032, 2177, 2376) and from many remarks in Erasmus' correspondence with other Poles. Szydłowiecki's death was a personal blow to Erasmus, and he informed his friends in the West about it with great regret (Epp 2798, 2800, 2879).

BIBLIOGRAPHY: Allen Ep 1593 / *Korespondencja Erazma z Rotterdamu z Polakami* ed M. Cytowska (Warsaw 1965) / J. Kieszkowski *Kanclerz Krzysztof Szydłowiecki* (Poznań 1912) / W. Pociecha *Królowa Bona:Czasy i ludzie Odrodzenia* (Poznań 1949–58) I–IV / K. Morawski *Czasy Zygmuntowskie na tle prądów Odrodzenia* (Warsaw 1965)   HALINA KOWALSKA

Pieter TAELMAN (Ep 1458 of 30 June 1524) Pieter Taelman (Taelmannus) has not been identified. He was apparently a boy, perhaps associated with the household of Marcus *Laurinus at Mechelen, conceivably a young relative.

Benedetto TAGLIACARNE of Sarzana, d 18 October 1536
Born in Sarzana, near La Spezia, Benedetto Tagliacarne (Benedictus Theocrenus) associated himself with the powerful Fregoso family and by 1514 was secretary of the city of Genoa. When the troops of *Charles V took Genoa in 1522 he accompanied Federigo Fregoso, archbishop of Salerno, to France, where he tutored two sons of the *Robertet family, got to know Guillaume *Budé, and by October 1524 had just been appointed preceptor of the sons of King *Francis I. He accompanied the princes to Spain, where they were kept as hostages from 1526 to 1530, from the Peace of Madrid until after the 'Ladies' Peace' of Cambrai, and after his return he was rewarded with several benefices, an earlier marriage notwithstanding. On 2 January 1532/3 he took possession of

the Cistercian abbey of Fontfroide, south-west of Narbonne, and from 1534 to 1535 he was abbot of the Benedictine house of Nantueil, north of Angoulême. On 11 February 1534/5 he became bishop of Grasse (Alpes-Maritimes) on nomination by Francis I. In the year of his death he published a collection of Latin poems which he had composed in earlier years, *Poemata quae iuvenis admodum lusit* (Poitiers: Marnef brothers 1536), which included verses on the death of a daughter of Budé. He was succeeded as preceptor of the royal princes by Guillaume *Du Maine.

In 1527 Pedro Juan *Olivar wrote from Valladolid that Tagliacarne had spoken of Erasmus in derogatory terms while praising Christophe de *Longueil to the skies (Ep 1791).

BIBLIOGRAPHY: Allen Ep 1791 / EI XXXIII 180 / Cosenza IV 339 / *Gallia christiana* II 1294, VI 214 / Eubel III 205 / Louis Delaruelle *Répertoire ... de la correspondance de Guillaume Budé* (Toulouse-Paris 1907) Epp 152, 159   MICHEL REULOS

TAHMĀSP shah of Persia, 1514–76
Tahmāsp (Damas), the eldest son of Shah Ismail I, the founder of the Safawid dynasty and empire in Persia, ascended the throne as a boy of ten and actually began to exercise his authority by 1533. He lacked special gifts, however, and in his defensive wars against the Ottoman sultan *Suleiman I was forced to accept significant losses of territory and prestige. He even had to move his capital when the Turks occupied Tabrīz on 13 July 1534 and again in 1548. During the former campaign they also conquered Mesopotamia, and Baghdad remained in their hands from then until 1623. There was a good deal of exaggeration in the rumours about Persian counter-attacks and heavy Turkish defeats that circulated in Europe in 1535 and 1536 (Epp 3007, 3075, 3078, 3119). In 1555 Tahmāsp signed a peace with the Ottomans which remained in force for the remainder of his reign; however, in his later years he had to contend with Uzbek invasions, famine, and plague.

Tahmāsp played host to the Great Mogul Humāyūn, who was temporarily driven from his throne (1543–4) and to Bayezid, rebel son of Sultan Suleiman (1556–8), whom he betrayed. He himself is said to have died of poison. He was a patron of the arts and composed an autobiography.

BIBLIOGRAPHY: *The Encyclopaedia of Islam* (Leiden-London 1913–38) IV 588–9, 615–16 / M.G.S. Hodgson *The Venture of Islam* (Chicago 1974) III 31–3 and passim / Barbara von Palombini *Bündniswerben der abendländischen Mächte um Persien, 1453–1600* (Wiesbaden 1968) 66–95 and passim / *Die Denkwürdigkeiten Schah Tahmāsp's des Ersten von Persien* German trans by P. Horn (Strasbourg 1891)   PGB

Pierre TAISANT de l'Estoille *See Petrus STELLA*

Quirinus TALESIUS of Haarlem,
21 December 1505–27 May 1573
Quirijn Dirckszoon van Lipsen, better known as Talesius (a nickname derived from his father's trade), was the son of a comfortably-off clothmaker of Haarlem. He matriculated at the University of Cologne in the autumn of 1523 and subsequently was a student of Conradus *Goclenius at Louvain; Goclenius probably recommended him to Erasmus as famulus in succession to Lieven *Algoet. His name is not mentioned in Erasmus' letters until October 1527, when Talesius had apparently abandoned a plan to visit Holland (Ep 1890), but he must have entered Erasmus' service several years earlier, probably in 1524. In his will of 22 January 1527 (Allen VI 506) Erasmus set out a bequest of two hundred florins as a reward for his long and faithful service. While he was no longer remembered in Erasmus' subsequent will of 1536, Talesius did in fact receive a gift of 150 crowns in March 1529 (Ep 2113).

Early in February 1528 Talesius was dispatched to England (Epp 1955, 1959, 1960, 1964). By the middle of March he was at Louvain and at the beginning of April in Antwerp (Epp 1984, 1993). Subsequently in London he was put up by Zacharias *Deiotarus, who assisted him with the delivery of his letters (Ep 1990). He returned again by way of Antwerp and Louvain and reached Basel by the end of May (Epp 1993, 1994A, 1998, 2037), without having made a detour to his native Holland, as Erasmus feared he might (Ep 1966). Erasmus had nothing but praise for his famulus and recommended him warmly to Maximilian (II) of *Burgundy (Ep 2200). Talesius was like a beloved son to him (Ep 1955) and served him as a secretary capable of writing independent letters in his master's interest (Epp 2120, 2200;

AK III Epp 1464, 1469) and even prepared to act behind his master's back when Erasmus' well-being seemed to require it (AK IV Epp 1488, 1491). He also acted as Erasmus' valet (Epp 1966, 2349) and accountant (Ep 2352); his agent for the transfer of cash and letters of credit (Epp 2494, 2512, 2530, 2558, 2578, 2593); and the most trusted of messengers. In October 1529 he started out on a second journey to the Low Countries (Epp 2222, 2258, 2270) and England, where he remained until the end of November (Epp 2227, 2228, 2237). On 7 December he was at Tournai (Ep 2239) and on 13 December at Antwerp, where Erasmus *Schets handed him a considerable sum of money according to Erasmus' instructions (Epp 2243, 2270, 2286, 2558). On 26 December he was at Mechelen (Ep 2244), on 1 January 1530 at Cologne (Ep 2246), and a few days later back in Freiburg (Epp 2253, 2264).

In July 1530 Talesius was gravely ill from an attack of the 'English sweat' (Epp 2343, 2348, 2349, 2355, 2356) but recovered in time to be sent on a mission to the diet of Augsburg. He had arrived there by the middle of September (Ep 2386) and met Pieter van *Montfoort, a very well-connected young man from Haarlem, who told him that the post of pensionary in their native town was vacant (Ep 2389). After his return to Freiburg early in October (Ep 2393), he must no doubt have asked Erasmus to recommend him for this position. Erasmus would certainly have complied, as he had in fact previously undertaken steps to secure Talesius a comfortable future (Epp 2246, 2298). While the matter was under consideration at Haarlem, Talesius, that 'pillar' of Erasmus' household, went to fetch wine from Burgundy (Ep 2397) and also undertook a brief journey to the Low Countries (Ep 2404). From the turn of the year Erasmus announced Talesius' forthcoming departure (Ep 2412), and in April he left (Epp 2454, 2477, 2487, 2488). He travelled in the company of Karel *Uutenhove, whom Erasmus had paired with Talesius two years earlier as the speakers in his colloquy Ἀστραγαλισμός (ASD I-3 620–8). By mid-May they were in Antwerp (Ep 2494); Talesius then went on to Haarlem, and in July he wrote to Bonifacius *Amerbach about how quiet his existence amid law books had become (AK IV Ep 1539). Erasmus gave no signs of regretting his departure and even accused him of careless-

ness (Ep 2530). Talesius in turn asked Amerbach to intercede on his behalf with Erasmus (AK IV Epp 1539, 1554). He also kept on writing to Erasmus (Epp 2645, 2734, 2913), but the only extant letter is a friendly reply by Erasmus of 31 October 1532, in which he congratulated his former famulus on his marriage and commended his desire to go to Orléans, or to return there, for a spell of legal studies (Ep 2735). In 1534 and 1535, however, Erasmus' suspicions had won the upper hand again and he even accused Talesius of complicity with the 'traitor' *Quirinus Hagius (Epp 2496, 3052, 3061). Erasmus was wrong; Talesius kept among his treasured possessions a portrait of his former master for which his friend Cornelis *Croock composed an epigram. He did not, however, write a biography of Erasmus, as was suggested to him by Levinus *Ammonius. His only work appears to be an expurgated version of the Colloquia, which was never printed and appears to be lost.

In Haarlem Talesius married a widow by the name of Haasje Dircksdochter and was in fact appointed pensionary. It seems that Erasmus congratulated him on that appointment on 7 May 1532 (Ep 2647). As his family grew, he resigned from his position as pensionary and returned to the cloth trade. He was wealthy and between 1543 and 1570 was elected burgomaster of Haarlem for a total of ten terms. His end, however, was sad. He had remained a Catholic, and when Haarlem was occupied by a force loyal to William of Orange he was accused of conspiracy with the Spaniards who were besieging the city. In reprisal for some executions staged by the Spaniards, he was lynched by the aroused citizens on 27 May 1573, together with two of his daughters and other prisoners.

BIBLIOGRAPHY: Allen Ep 1966 / NNBW X 1013–14 / de Vocht CTL II 488–501 and passim / Bierlaire Familia 68–71 / AK III Epp 1292, 1464, V Ep 1468a and passim   FRANZ BIERLAIRE

Cyprianus TALEUS of Venice, documented 1510–32

Available information on Cyprianus Taleus (Talea) is as yet inadequate, and it is not entirely certain that all the following data concern the same person. A Venetian (rather than a Cypriot), Taleus is documented in Paris from 1510 but may have been there earlier. At

Ruard Tapper

---

any rate, he was personally acquainted with both Erasmus and Girolamo *Aleandro (Ep 2679). The latter formed an enduring friendship with him and used him regularly as an agent in financial transactions concerning his benefices. In his diary he always called him either 'dominus' or 'magister,' which may suggest that Taleus was a priest and that he held an academic degree. Taleus is also known for his contacts with young scholars from Germany and Switzerland such as Michael *Hummelberg (1516), Wilhelm *Nesen (Ep 768; z VII Epp 32, 35), who attended his lectures on Pliny in 1518, and Henricus *Glareanus (Ep 903). In 1530 he was principal of the Collège des Lombards; despite his advanced age and weak eyesight, he assisted in the preparation of an edition of St John Chrysostom for the printer Gerard *Morrhy (Ep 2311; cf Ep 2019) and to this end was in touch with Erasmus and Polidoro *Virgilio. Erasmus also remembered him or sent him greetings in letters to Germain de *Brie and Jacques *Toussain (Epp 1117, 1713).

BIBLIOGRAPHY: Allen Ep 768 / *Le Carnet de voyage de Jérôme Aléandre en France et à Liège*

(1510–1516) ed Jean Hoyoux (Brussels-Rome 1969) 55 and passim   MICHEL REULOS & PGB

Gulielmus TALEUS *See William* THALE

Konrad TANMAIR of Munderkingen, documented 1535
Konrad Tanmair of Munderkingen, on the Danube, south-west of Ulm, was a freight carter who had taken charge of a barrel at Augsburg which he was to deliver to Erasmus at Freiburg (Ep 2989).

Ruard TAPPER of Enkhuizen, 15 February 1487–2 March 1559
Ruard Tapper (Tappert, Ruwardus Nannonius or Enchusianus) of Enkhuizen, in Holland, matriculated at Louvain on 11 June 1503, obtained a MA with very high standing in 1507, and taught Aristotelian physics and logic while studying theology. He was admitted to the academic senate on 22 December 1511 and obtained a licence in theology on 3 June 1516 and a doctorate on 16 August 1519. He became a priest and in 1515 and 1517 was nominated for two benefices in keeping with the university's right of nomination. On 30 September 1519 the faculty of theology granted him the *venia legendi*, and on 21 November he succeeded Maarten van *Dorp as president of the College of the Holy Ghost, a position which he held until October 1533. In the mean time he succeeded Godschalk *Rosemondt (d December 1526) as professor of theology and canon of St Peter's. When Nicolas *Coppin died in June 1535, Tapper followed him as dean of St Peter's and chancellor of the university (Ep 3037). He was repeatedly elected dean of the theological faculty and also served for two terms as rector of the university.

Tapper, who had a speech impediment and lacked refinement in dress and manner, was made fun of in Wilhelm *Nesen's *Dialogus bilinguium ac trilinguium* (de Vocht CTL I 569–71). He was nevertheless a very able theologian who advocated improved education and discipline for the clergy. He trained scores of fine students and was highly respected by his friends, whether theologians such as Jan *Briart of Ath or humanists such as Petrus Nannius, *Alaard of Amsterdam, and Adrien *Amerot. He also proved his open mind towards the new learning when he served ex officio as a supervisor of the Collegium Trilingue. He took part in Inquisition proceedings but avoided excessive harshness. Tapper urged the Emperor *Charles v to form new dioceses in the Low Countries, and while attending the council of Trent (September 1551–April 1552) he took an active part in the discussions concerning penance and the mass. He also owned a valuable library. When he died in Brussels he left bequests for the poor and for scholarships.

Tapper's *Questio quodlibetica de effectibus quos consuetudo operatur in foro conscientiae* was twice printed in 1520 (Louvain: D. Martens, Antwerp: M. Hillen, NK 01140 and 3917); his commentaries on Louvain faculty pronouncements concerning dogma and heresy were published in 1554–5 (Lyon: M. Roy and L. Pesnot). Other works were published posthumously, and eventually his *Omnia quae haberi potuerunt opera* appeared in Cologne in 1582, published by the heirs of Arnold *Birckmann.

BIBLIOGRAPHY: Allen Ep 3037 / NNBW V 877–9 /LThK IX 1297 / de Vocht CTL I 571, III 575–9, IV 149–50 / de Vocht *Literae ad Craneveldium* 62 and passim / de Vocht MHL 571 / *Matricule de Louvain* III-1 256 / H. de Jongh *L'Ancienne Faculté de théologie de Louvain* (Louvain 1911) 180–6 and passim   IG

Evangelista TARASCONIO documented 1518–29
Evangelista Tarasconio was a secretary of Pope *Leo x who on 10 September 1518 composed a letter of approval for Erasmus' New Testament (Ep 864). He also served *Clement VII, addressing to him the 'Commentarii calamitatum Italiae' in four books (MSS in the Biblioteca Apostolica Vaticana and Archivio di Stato, Parma).

BIBLIOGRAPHY: Allen and CWE Ep 864 / P.O. Kristeller *Iter Italicum* (London-Leiden 1965–) II 452, 553 / Pastor VIII 155n   TBD

Guillaume TARDIF of Puy-en-Velay, c 1440–c 1500
Nothing is known about the early life and studies of Guillaume Tardif (Tardivus). He lived at Paris at least from 1467, as can be deduced from the dedication to him of a Latin *novella* by the Italian humanist Francesco Florio

(dated 31 December 1467). He may already have been teaching at the humanist-minded Collège de Navarre, but his activity there is attested to only from 1473 by a letter from Johann *Reuchlin to Jacques *Lefèvre d'Etaples.

Tardif's first publication was his *Grammatice basis* (n p, n d), with a dedicatory letter dated 1 January 1470 addressed to his pupil Charles Mariette. A second, enlarged edition, entitled *Compendiosissima grammatica* (Paris c 1475), contains the first French words printed in Paris, namely the conjugation of *aimer*. Perhaps in 1475 too the same press published Tardif's *Rhetorice artis ac oratorie facultatis compendium*, which summarizes the rhetorical principles of Cicero and Quintilian. A few years later Tardif synthesized his grammatical and rhetorical precepts in his *Eloquencie benedicendique sciencie compendium*, dedicated to *Charles VIII as dauphin and therefore published before 1483. He also edited Solinus' *Polihistor* and Vegetius' *De re militari*.

When Girolamo *Balbi arrived in Paris in the latter half of 1485, he dedicated his first volume of poems to Tardif. These poems, however, were not printed until later, and they appeared without the dedicatory letter and the complimentary poem to Tardif, for the very day after sending him these verses, Balbi began to attack Tardif. This must have occurred about the same time as his request of 14 March 1486 to the university that it examine Tardif's grammar, which he claimed to be useless and faulty.

Balbi's first volume of verses, with a new dedication to Guillaume de Rochefort, appeared in the first half of 1487. It was followed immediately by Tardif's *Antibalbica*, written within three days. Balbi replied with his *Rhetor gloriosus*, a satirical dialogue between Petrus Coardus, Charles *Fernand, and Guillaume Tardif (latter half of 1487), while Tardif published a substantially revised and enlarged version of his *Antibalbica* in 1489/90, and a third in 1495. Meanwhile Tardif had entered the king's service as his *domesticus lector*, and the character of his works changed completely. For the king's entertainment he published a French version of Poggio *Bracciolini's *Facetiae* (Paris: A. Verard c 1490); *Heures royales* (about 1488); *L'Art de bien vivre et de bien mourir* (Paris: A. Verard 1492); *Livre de l'art de faulconnerie et des* *chiens de chasse* (Paris: A. Verard 1493); and *Les Apologues et fables de Laurens Valle,* followed by the *Ditz des sages hommes,* a translation of Petrarch's *De salibus virorum illustrium* (Paris: A. Verard c 1495).

The place and date of Tardif's death are unknown. A woodcut on the verso of the title-page of *L'Art de faulconnerie* represents the author offering his work to the king.

In 1530 Erasmus recalled Fausto *Andrelini's controversies with other humanists and erroneously had him quarrel with Tardif (Ep 2379). No doubt he had in mind the controversy between Balbi and Tardif.

BIBLIOGRAPHY: Allen Ep 2379 / A. Claudin *Histoire de l'imprimerie en France au xve et au xvie siècle* (Paris 1900–1) I 151–8, II 371–9, and passim / S. Scholl *Guillaume Tardif und seine französische Übersetzung der Fabeln des Laurentius Valla* (Kempten 1903) / F. Simone 'Robert Gaguin ed il suo cenacolo umanistico ... : 1473–1485' *Aevum* 13 (1939) 410–76, esp 440–54 / L. Sozzi 'Le facezie di Poggio nel quattrocento francese' in *Miscellanea di studi e ricerche sul quattrocento francese* ed F. Simone (Turin 1967) 409–516 / P. Koj *Die frühe Rezeption der Fazetien Poggios in Frankreich* (Hamburg 1969) 125–89 / L. Sozzi 'Petrarca, Tardif e Denys de Harsy (con una nota su Francesco Florio)' *Studi francesi* 43 (1971) 78–82 / G. Tournoy 'The literary production of Hieronymus Balbus at Paris' *Gutenberg-Jahrbuch 1978* (Mainz 1978) 70–7 / E. Beltrona 'L'humaniste Guillaume Tardif' BHR 48 (1986) 7–39

GILBERT TOURNOY

Pierre TARTARET of Romont, d 1522

Pierre Tartaret (Tataret, Tateret) was born in Romont (Canton de Fribourg), in the diocese of Lausanne. He studied arts in Paris at the Collège de Reims under Jean Le Sueur, taking his BA on 4 March 1483 and his MA in March 1484 and incepting on 1 April 1484. He was the proctor of the German-English nation in 1484–5 and receiver in 1487–8, and was rector of the University of Paris from 15 December 1490 to 24 March 1491. He ranked seventh of thirty-two licentiates in theology promoted on 27 January 1496 and delayed reception of the doctorate until 1 April 1501. Tartaret was an active regent in arts and for twenty years was the leading interpreter of Duns Scotus and of

the logic of Peter of Spain. Among his pupils were Jérôme de *Hangest and Jacques *Merlin. Johann *Amerbach almost put his sons under Tartaret's tutelage in 1502 before finally opting for Nominalist teachers. By that time Tartaret had completed all his books, but they continued to be reprinted in several centres even into the seventeenth century.

Tartaret was one of the most active members of the Paris faculty of theology, presiding over numerous academic disputations and taking an interest in all its affairs. In 1514 he was on the faculty committee investigating the *Reuchlin affair. He regularly attended functions of his nation in Paris. He was a canon of Saint-Etienne-des-Grès, a canon of the diocese of Lausanne, and curé of Monte Acute (diocese of Liège?). In 1512 he was the vice-chancellor of Sainte-Geneviève (that is, of the faculty of arts). He died in 1522 (before 1 December). A record of bequests is extant, showing gifts to the abbey of Sainte-Geneviève, Saint-Etienne-des-Grès, the Collège de Reims, the faculty of theology, and various relatives in Romont. He was buried in the abbey church of Sainte-Geneviève. A notarized contract describing his tombstone is extant.

*Rabelais enjoyed a play on Tartaret's name, likening him to a barbarian Tartar, and Petrus Ramus also criticized him, while Erasmus mentioned him as a typical representative of Scotist scholasticism and dialectic concerns (Ep 1581; ASD I-2 285; LB IX 102 F). Tartaret's major works are *Expositio super textu Logices Aristotelis: Commentaria in libros philosophiae naturalis et metaphysicae Aristotelis* (Paris 1493; ed Wilhelm *Nesen, Basel: Johann Froben 1514, Paris: Gilles de Gourmont et al c 1514); *Expositio in summulas Petri Hispani* (Paris: André Bocard 1494, Pierre Levet, Geoffroy de Marnef 1501, Gilles de Gourmont et al c 1514, Jean Frellon et al 1520); *Questiones admodum subtiles et utiles totius materiae artium quatuor librorum Sententiarum Scoti* (Paris 1494); *Expositio totius philosophiae necnon metaphysicae Aristotelis* (Paris: André Bocard 1495); *Questiones super sex libros Ethicorum Aristotelis* (Paris: Jean Lambert 1496, Jean Frellon et al 1509, 1512, Pierre Gaudoul 1513); *Questiones morales in octo capita distincte ... discussae* ed Josse *Bade (Paris: Geoffroy de Marnef 1504, 1508, corrected ed Jean Frellon et al 1509, 1512, Pierre Gaudoul,

Jean Marchant 1513); *Doctoris Ioannis Duns Scoti Questiones quodlibetales familiarissime reportate* (Paris: Pierre Gromors, widow of Berthold Rembolt 1519); and *In quartum Sententiarum Scoti Dictata sive ... Reportata [cum textu]* ed Jean Champaigne (Paris: Claude Chevallon, Pierre Gromors 1520).

BIBLIOGRAPHY: Allen Ep 1581 / AK I Ep 154 and passim / *Auctarium chartularii universitatis Parisiensis* ed Charles Samaran et al (Paris 1894–1964) III and VI passim / Clerval passim / E. Coyecque *Recueil d'actes notariés* (Paris 1905) I no 418 / W. Ong *Ramus, Method and the Decay of Dialogue* (Cambridge, Mass, 1958) passim / C. Prantl *Geschichte der Logik im Abendlande* (Leipzig 1927) III 294–9 / Renaudet *Préréforme* passim / Paris, Archives de l'Université (Sorbonne) Registre 89 f cvi recto and passim / Paris, Minutier Central, Etude XXXIII 7 ff 365 recto, 365 verso–366 verso   JAMES K. FARGE

Jean de TARTAS documented 1525–34
Jean de Tartas (Tartesius) was born in Tartas (Landes), in Guyenne. In 1525 he succeeded Rogier Marbrasse as principal of the Collège de Lisieux in Paris (Ep 2065). In 1530 *Viglius Zuichemus wrote to Tartas that Andrea *Alciati had formed a most favourable opinion of him from the letters of Girolamo *Aiazza. Nicolaus *Clenardus praised Tartas and his direction of the college in 1531, stressing that not only were the three languages taught there but Tartas was also planning to add Chaldean and Arabic (*Meditationes graecanicae*, Louvain: Rutgerus Rescius 1531). Upon being invited by the town council of Bordeaux to revive the college there, Tartas laid plans for the Collège de Guyenne, intending it to resemble the Collège de Lisieux both in curriculum and in renown. After a preliminary voyage to Bordeaux, Tartas recruited twenty professors (among them Gentien Hervet, Robert Breton, and Jean Visagier), notably from Paris and Louvain, and returned to Bordeaux in February 1533. Lectures began in May 1533. But the council failed to provide sufficient funds for the curriculum and physical facilities demanded by Tartas, and his precipitate appeal to the Parlement of Bordeaux resulted in the council's sudden replacement of him with André de Gouveia on 15 July 1534. Tartas resumed the direction of the Collège de Lisieux in Paris. In 1539 Hubert

Sussanneau wrote that Tartas was three times principal of Lisieux. Both Sussanneau and Jean Visagier accused Tartas of serious personal and administrative defects. Petrus Nannius dedicated his Greek edition of Aristophanes' *Frogs* (Louvain: Rutgerus Rescius for Bartolomeus Gravius 1534) to Tartas.

BIBLIOGRAPHY: Allen Ep 2065, VIII xliii / P. Courteault 'Le premier principal au Collège de Guyenne' *Mélanges Abel Lefranc* (Paris 1936) 234–45 / NK I 135 / A. Polet *Petrus Nannius, 1500–1557* (Louvain 1936) 240–2 / R. Trinquet 'Nouveaux aperçus sur les débuts du Collège de Guyenne: de Jean de Tartas à André de Gouvéa (1533–1535)' BHR 26 (1964) 510–58 / de Vocht CTL III passim   JAMES K. FARGE

William TATE of York, d after 9 September 1540
William Tate (Taytt, Tatus, Taitus) graduated BA at Cambridge in 1490, proceeding MA in 1494. In 1496–7 he served as a junior proctor and later was nominated as the internal principal of Garret hostel. In 1500 (or in 1506) he was at Orléans and there met Erasmus, whom he had already met in England (Ep 1246). He departed for Italy around 1504 and the following year was registered with Robert *Fisher at the English Hospice in Rome. Most likely he received his doctorate in civil law from Bologna in 1505. By November 1508 Tate was back in England, for on 29 November he was admitted rector of Everingham, and in 1509 he also received a living at Thwing, both in Yorkshire. In 1520 he was appointed a canon of York and prebendary of Botevant, and in 1523 he was appointed a canon and prebendary of St George's Chapel, Windsor. By 1525 Tate was also an almoner of Henry Fitzroy, duke of Richmond, and a member of the Council of the North, offices he retained until the duke's death in 1536. Tate was also a member of Doctor's Commons and an amateur musician reputed as bearing 'a great stroke in such matters.' Tate's will was dated on 9 September 1540 and proved on 6 September 1544. The library of Gonville and Caius College, Cambridge, owns copies of Erasmus' Jerome (Basel 1516) and Guillaume *Budé's *Annotationes* to the Pandect (Paris 1508) which had belonged to him.

Tate is probably the 'humanissimus Dr.

Taitus' who is praised by Robert *Wakefield as a friend and a Hebrew scholar in the latter's *Oratio de laudibus et utilitate trium linguarum* (London 1524). In 1521 he arranged, with the king's approval, to send Erasmus a copy of *Henry VIII's *Assertio septem sacramentorum* against *Luther and also wrote to Erasmus, expressing his admiration for him (Ep 1246).

BIBLIOGRAPHY: Allen Ep 1246 / Emden BRUC 577, 684 / LP I 1355, IV passim / *The Acts and Monuments of John Foxe* ed G. Townsend (London 1847) / R.R. Reid *The King's Council of the North* (London 1921) 104, 113 / G.D. Squibb *Doctor's Commons* (Oxford 1977) 131 / G.B. Parks *The English Traveler to Italy* (Rome 1954–) I 627–8   MORDECHAI FEINGOLD

Pierre TAUAU de l'Etoile *See Petrus* STELLA

Juan Pardo de TAVERA of Toro, 16 May 1472–1 August 1545
Juan Pardo de Tavera was born at Toro, in the province of Zamora in León, and was a nephew of Diego de Deza, archbishop of Seville and inquisitor-general. He studied at Zamora and Salamanca. In 1494 he obtained a prebend in the cathedral of Zamora and in 1504 was rector of the University of Salamanca. Before 1513 he held a series of offices: judge of the Council of the Inquisition, precentor of the cathedral of Seville, and then vicar-general of that diocese. In 1513 he was appointed visitor to the royal chancery at Valladolid, which he completely reorganized, and in 1514 he was nominated to the see of Ciudad Rodrigo. He then undertook a successful diplomatic expedition to Portugal and was transferred first to the diocese of Osma and then, in 1524, to the archdiocese of Santiago de Compostela. At Santiago he launched an extraordinary legal action against his predecessor, Alonso de *Fonseca, then archbishop of Toledo and primate of Spain, suing him for failure to repair castles and other buildings damaged in the popular uprisings of the 1460s.

By the early 1520s Tavera was appointed president of the chancery of Valladolid, and during the later years of the decade he presided over several sessions of the Cortes. On 22 February 1531 he was created cardinal of San Giovanni a Porta Latina, and in 1534, again

following Fonseca, he became archbishop of Toledo. By this time he was one of the principal civil servants of *Charles V, together with Francisco de los Cobos and Nicolas *Perrenot de Granvelle. As president of the Council of Castile he was principal adviser to the Empress *Isabella of Portugal during Charles' frequent absences. He also became inquisitor-general, holding that office until his death, which occurred in Toledo.

In Ep 2163 to Erasmus, Alfonso de *Valdés mentions that opponents of his *Lactancio* (published 1529) had appealed in vain to Charles V, Tavera, and Alonso *Manrique, then inquisitor-general.

BIBLIOGRAPHY: Allen Ep 2163 / Eubel III 21, 173, 314 / Bataillon *Erasmo y España* 387, 467, 551 / *Enciclopedia universal ilustrada europeo-americana* (Barcelona, Madrid 1907?–) XLI 1447 / *Historia de España* ed Ramón Menéndez Pidal XVIII: Manuel Fernández Álvarez *La España del Emperador Carlos V* (Madrid 1966) *ad indicem*   DAVID MACKENZIE

Godefridus Ruysius TAXANDER *See* COR-NELIS *of Duiveland, Walter* RUYS, *Govaert* STRIJROY, *Vincentius* THEODERICI

Johann Baptista von TAXIS d 16 October 1541
Johann Baptista, the son of Roger von Taxis (Tassis), was descended from an old noble family of the region of Bergamo which had been in the service of the Hapsburg emperors for three generations. He was a nephew of Franz von Taxis, who in conjunction with other members of his family had developed the territorial mail service of Austria into an international one. Members of the family continued to operate the service collectively, and on 31 May 1512 all were confirmed by *Maximilian I as members of the hereditary nobility. On 12 November 1516 Franz and Johann Baptista signed an important agreement with the future *Charles V, by which the service was extended to include a number of Italian cities. After Franz's death in 1517 Johann Baptista was the recognized head of the family. In 1519 he personally delivered to the court of Brussels the news of Charles' election as emperor, and on 14 June 1520 he was confirmed by the monarch as 'chief et

maistre general des noz postes.' In 1530 he attended Charles' coronation at Bologna, and in 1535 he played host in his house at Brussels to the refugee sultan of Tunis, al-*Hasan ben Muhammad. It is possible that in 1529 Pieter *Gillis wished to refer to Johann Baptista personally when he mentioned a 'magister postarum' to whom he had entrusted a letter (Ep 2089).

Johann Baptista, who died in Brussels, was married to Christina van Wachtendonck. His eldest son, Roger, became provost of St Peter's and chancellor of the University of Louvain, and subsequently dean of Notre-Dame at Antwerp. Another son, Johann Baptista, chose a military and diplomatic career (NBW II 841–55).

BIBLIOGRAPHY: Allen Ep 2089 / J. Rübsam in ADB XXXVII 496–9, 792 / P.J. Goetschalckx *Geschiedenis der kanunniken van O.L.V. kapittel te Antwerpen (1585–1700)* (Antwerp n d) 36–45 / Götz von Pölnitz *Anton Fugger* (Tübingen 1958–   ) I 489, 505, and passim / F. Ohmann *Die Anfänge des Postwesens und die Taxis* (Leipzig 1909) passim

MARCEL A. NAUWELAERTS & PGB

Daniël TAYSPIL of Nieuwkerke, d 17–20 June 1533
Daniël Tayspil (Taispillus), of Nieuwkerke, near Armentières in Flanders, entered the Premonstratensian abbey of Saint-Augustin-lez-Thérouanne, making his profession there. On 1 September 1516 he was appointed suffragan to the bishop of Thérouanne and was granted an annuity on the bishopric; this was additional to another annuity on a priory in that same diocese which he had received earlier. His titular see was Byblos (biblical Gebal, modern Jebeil) in Lebanon. In the light of the numerous references to Tayspil contained in the *Régestes* of the diocese, it would seem that he carried out his pastoral duties with great diligence. In 1524 he was elected abbot of Voormezele, an Austin house near Ieper. He died after a stroke in June 1533, highly praised by Jacob *Hessele for his virtues and his faithful admiration of Erasmus (Ep 2843). His brother, Pieter Tayspil, was president of the council of Flanders in 1527 and of the privy council in 1531.

In the summer of 1521 Tayspil and Erasmus corresponded about an appointment for Agazio *Guidacerio to teach Hebrew at the Collegium Trilingue of Louvain (Ep 1221).

BIBLIOGRAPHY: Allen Ep 1221 / de Vocht CTL II 77–8 / U. Berlière 'Les évêques auxiliaires de Thérouanne' *Revue bénédictine* 55 (1907) 79–81 / O. Bled *Régestes des évêques de Thérouanne* (Saint-Omer 1904) I 10, II 130ff / Eubel III 202 / *Monasticon Belge* ed U. Berlière et al (Maredsous-Liège 1890–   ) III 728–30

ANDRÉ GODIN

Nikolaus von TECKLENBURG d 11 June 1535
The county of Tecklenburg, including the city of that name, west of Osnabrück in the Teutoburger Forest, remained independent until 1707, when it was incorporated into Prussia. Little is known about Count Nikolaus von Tecklenburg (Teckelenborch). He seems to have been a canon of Cologne (Ep 3041), and in April and May 1534 he participated in the siege of Münster with the army of Bishop Franz von *Waldeck. Subsequently he fought with the troops of Lübeck in the so-called Count's war and was killed in the battle near Assens, together with the commander, Count Johann von *Hoya (Ep 3041).

BIBLIOGRAPHY: F.C. Dahlmann and D. Schäfer *Geschichte von Dänemark* (Gotha 1840–1902) IV 287 / *Hanserezesse* ed Gottfried Wentz (Leipzig etc 1870–   ) IV-1 222, 411   PGB

Josephus TECTANDER of Cracow, c 1507–c 1543
Tectander (Zimmermann) was the son of the Cracow goldsmith Jan *Zimmermann and the brother-in-law of Jan *Antonin. He may be the Joseph who accompanied Antonin to Basel in 1524 (Ep 2031), then was in Hungary in the spring of 1527 (Ep 1810), and was preparing to travel to Basel a second time when Antonin fell ill (Epp 1916, 2031).

Tectander began his studies at the University of Cracow in 1527; in 1532 he received a MA and began to lecture on Aristotle and Ovid. At the same time he studied medicine, and in June 1534 he left Poland to continue these studies abroad. After short periods of attendance in Vienna and Padua he received a doctorate in medicine the same year from Ferrara. By mid-1535 he had returned to Cracow and was lecturing again at the university. Shortly after Christmas he interrupted his teaching and left for Basel, where he was well received by the printer Johann *Bebel and remained until the spring. He visited Erasmus and after his return to Cracow in August both Antonin and Tectander himself wrote to Erasmus, informing him of his safe arrival (Epp 3137, 3138). These letters were written after Erasmus' death. Tectander became the physician of the *voivode* of Cracow, Piotr *Kmita, and rendered medical services to the court of Queen *Bona Sforza and her daughter Isabella, who in 1539 became the wife of the Hungarian king, *John Zápolyai.

While in Basel, Tectander was asked by Bebel to translate Galen's *De venae sectione adversus Erasistratum*. He accepted and dedicated the work to Antonin on 12 March 1536; it was published in Galen's *Opera omnia* (Basel: A. Cratander 1536 and H. Froben 1542). He also took part in the preparation of a collective volume, *Morbi gallici curandi ratio exquisitissima* (Basel: J. Bebel 1536), and dedicated to Piotr Kmita his own *Elegiae III de peregrinationibus suis* (Cracow: Ungler 1542).

BIBLIOGRAPHY: Allen Ep 1810 / *Korespondencja Erazma z Rotterdamu z Polakami* ed Maria Cytowska (Warsaw 1965) / J.D. Janocki *Janociana sive clarorum atque illustrium Poloniae auctorum maecenatorumque memoriae miscellae* (Warsaw 1776) I 268–70 / *Bibliografia polska* ed K. Estreicher et al (Cracow 1870–1951) XVII 19, XXI 72–3 / H. Barycz *Historja Uniwersytetu Jagiellońskiego w epoce humanizmu* (Cracow 1935) / H. Brabant 'Erasme, ses maladies et ses médicins' *Colloquia Erasmiana Turonensia* I 539–68, esp 557, 568 / H. Barycz 'Die ersten wissenschaftlichen Verbindungen Polens mit Basel' *Vierteljahresschrift für Geschichte der Wissenschaft und Technik* (Warsaw) 5 (1960) Sonderheft 2, 45–6 / *Conclusiones Universitatis Cracoviensis ab anno 1441 ad annum 1589* ed H. Barycz (Cracow 1933) / *Liber diligentiarum Facultatis Artistae Universitatis Cracoviensis* ed W. Wisłocki (Cracow 1886) / Klemens Janicki *Carmina* ed G. Krokowski (Cracow 1966)   HALINA KOWALSKA

Luis de TEIXEIRA documented 1481–1534
Luis was the son of João Teixeira, who served as chancellor to King John II of Portugal. He studied at the University of Lisbon and then went to Italy. In 1481 he was in Florence, where he was a student of Angelo *Poliziano. In 1494 he became a doctor of law in Bologna and was appointed to a chair in law at the University of Ferrara, where he met Pietro *Bembo. After nearly twenty years Erasmus recalled close contacts in Italy between himself and the Portuguese (Ep 1800), but it is not certain where he made Teixeira's acquaintance. André de *Resende praised his rhetorical talents. In or after 1516 he returned to Portugal and taught the ancient languages to the future King *John III.

BIBLIOGRAPHY: Allen Ep 1800 / André de Resende *Oração de Sapiência* (Lisbon 1956) 54, 93–7 / Alfredo Pimenta *Dom João III* (Porto 1936) 5 / José Sebastião da Silva Dias *Instituto de Estudos Filosóficos* (Coimbra 1969) I 196–204
                                    ELISABETH FEIST HIRSCH

TERVISANUS (Ep 1989 of 19 April 1528)
In a letter to Gianfrancesco *Torresani in Venice, Erasmus sent his regrets for not writing to a friend of the addressee whose name he gave as Tervisanus. The latter has not been identified; perhaps he was a member of the patrician Trevisan (Trivisan) family from Venice rather than a man from Treviso.

Valentin von TETLEBEN d April-May 1551
Valentin von Tetleben (Teutleben, Tetenleben) was born of a noble family of Thuringia in 1488 or 1489. He matriculated at Erfurt in the winter term of 1502–3 and was appointed to a canonry of the Hildesheim cathedral chapter on 7 February 1506. In the same year he went to Bologna to continue his studies, obtaining a doctorate in civil and canon law on 23 May 1511. From 1513 to 1517 he was in Rome, attached to the household of Pope *Leo x and reaping further benefices, including a canonry of St Maurice's at Hildesheim. From 1519 to 1522 he was back in Rome as solicitor for Cardinal Albert of *Brandenburg but also performed legal work for dukes Frederick and George of *Saxony. He continued to seek more preferment and was appointed provost of St

Bartholomew's, Frankfurt am Main, in 1529. As vicar-general of Mainz he accompanied Cardinal Albert to the diets of Speyer (1529) and Augsburg (1530), keeping a written record of the proceedings.

On 30 September 1537 Tetleben was elected bishop of Hildesheim, on 22 February 1538 he was consecrated in Rome, and on 18 May he entered Hildesheim. The see was in a state of destitution because most of the episcopal estates had been taken over by the dukes of *Brunswick-Lüneburg with the connivance of *Charles v. Unable to improve matters substantially, Tetleben returned to Rome in the autumn of 1539 and continued to fight for the rights of his see at the diets of Regensburg and Speyer in 1541 and 1542. While the city of Hildesheim joined the reformed camp Tetleben travelled to Trent when a council was first convoked there in 1543. Despite failing health he continued his endeavours at successive diets.

Johann *Dietenberger addressed to Tetleben his treatise De divortio against Erasmus (1532), a fact which induced Erasmus to do likewise with his reply (LB IX 965D), although, refusing to name Dietenberger, he logically concealed Tetleben's identity too (LB IX 955A). Tetleben was connected with many of Erasmus' friends, including Fridericus *Nausea, and is not known to have been critical of the Dutch humanist.

BIBLIOGRAPHY: Valentin von Tetleben Protokoll des Augsburger Reichstages von 1530 ed H. Grundmann (Gütersloh 1958), especially 9–45 (biographical sketch) / Eubel III 210 / Epistolae ad Nauseam 72 and passim / Pflug Correspondance I Ep 112 and passim   PGB

Jodocus TEXTORIS See Jodocus Textoris de WINSHEIM

Jacob TEYNG See Jacobus CERATINUS

William THALE documented 1508–22
Nothing is known of William Thale (Thaleus, Thaleius, Taleus) before 1508, when he is found in Ferrara with Richard *Pace. In December of that year Erasmus entrusted Pace with a few manuscripts, including De copia, De ratione studii, and the two books of the

Antibarbari. Shortly afterwards Pace departed from Ferrara for Bologna, depositing the manuscripts with Thale. In 1509 Johannes *Sixtinus stated that Thale had given some of the manuscripts to him and others to John *Allen and Richard *Shurley (Ep 244). In 1511, while Thale was in Paris, he edited De ratione studii (Paris: G. Biermant 1511), substituting his name for Thomas *Grey's in the dedication (Ep 66; ASD I-2 147; CWE 24 665). The enraged Erasmus published the work again the following year, this time inserting a dedication to Pierre *Vitré instead of to Thale. Erasmus was never able to recover the two books of the Antibarbari. Irritated as Erasmus was with Thale during the following years, the two continued to remain in touch. A friendly letter (Ep 1224) of August 1521 from Erasmus survives, indicating that the two had met in England after the Ferrara incident. From the letter it also emerges that Erasmus had attempted to persuade Thale to move to Louvain, where the climate was especially conducive to studies. In the light of this letter it would seem that it was Thale himself, rather than a younger namesake, who matriculated at the University of Louvain on 3 December 1522 as 'Dominus Wilhelmus Taleus' of the archdiocese of York, although he had arrived earlier. In January 1522 Juan Luis *Vives mentioned that Thale had been recommended to him by Erasmus and was attending his lectures with Richard *Warham and Maurice *Birchinshaw (Ep 1256). In July 1522 Thale gave Vives two letters for forwarding to Erasmus and inquired about the fate of an earlier one; all three are missing (Ep 1303). Nothing is known so far about Thale's career in England.

BIBLIOGRAPHY: Allen Ep 1224 / CWE Epp 30:17n, 66 introduction / Matricule de Louvain III-1 688 / de Vocht MHL 4 / de Vocht CTL II 6–7, 404   MORDECHAI FEINGOLD & PGB

Joris van THEMSEKE of Bruges, died c 1535
Joris van Themseke (Georgius de Theimseke or Tempseca, Temsicius) was descended from a patrician family of Bruges and obtained a legal degree. Already an apostolic protonotary and chaplain to Philip the Handsome, duke of *Burgundy, he was elected dean of St Donatian's at Bruges in a contested ballot (29 May

1499) that was annulled by the Roman curia. He continued, however, to hold his prebend at St Donatian's, which he had received in 1505, and often resided in Bruges. Among his many other benefices were the provostships of the chapters of Cassel (1505–30) and Haarlem. Perhaps as early as 1491 he was dean of St Gudula's, Brussels; he also held the same office in the chapter of Notre Dame at Courtrai. On 8 March 1535 a cousin of his was appointed to his prebend in Bruges; therefore Themseke's death may have occurred at about this time.

Themseke was connected with the Burgundian court and carried out many diplomatic missions between 1508 and 1532. In 1504 he was appointed to the grand council of Mechelen with Jérôme de *Busleyden. He was a privy councillor from 1531. Erasmus met him in the summer of 1516 in Brussels at the dinner table of Chancellor Jean *Le Sauvage and thought highly of him (Ep 412). Shortly thereafter Themseke departed on an embassy to London, where he met Thomas *More (Ep 467), who praised him in his *Utopia* for his congeniality, diplomatic skill, and expert knowledge of the law. Themseke could well have been the trusted provost, who was also an old friend and a canon of St Donatian's, who took an important letter from Erasmus to Pope *Adrian VI (Ep 1352) when he went to Rome in the spring of 1523 on diplomatic business for the imperial court (Epp 1353, 1358). However no corroborating evidence for his journey has been presented so far.

BIBLIOGRAPHY: Allen Ep 412 / BNB VII 618–19 / de Vocht CTL I 516–17 / More Y IV 46, 298–9, 311, 371 / *Gallia christiana* v 258 / André Le Glay *Cameracum christianum* (Lille 1849) 123–4 / Michel Baelde *De collaterale raden onder Karel v en Filips II* (Brussels 1965) 317 and passim
ANDRÉ GODIN & PGB

THEOBALD, uncle of Erasmus See ERASMUS' family

Jan THEOBALD See Jean THIBAULT

Thomas THEOBALD d 1550
Thomas Theobald (Tybold) was the godson of Thomas *Boleyn, earl of Wiltshire, and possibly the Theobaldus mentioned by Guillaume *Budé as the bearer of a letter from Thomas

*More in 1521 (Rogers Ep 102). Possibly he was also the Tybbolde who graduated BA from Cambridge in 1527–8. He definitely departed from England early in 1530, for on 4 April he wrote a letter to Thomas Boleyn from Frankfurt (LP IV-3 6304). From that time onward he acted as an agent for various English prelates, combining such service with his pursuit of scholarship, unless the latter was merely a cover for his political activities. He is found matriculating at the University of Louvain on 23 February 1531. Nothing is heard of him until 9 January 1535, when a newsletter sent by him from Orléans to Boleyn is recorded (LP VIII 33). By July of that year he was in Antwerp informing Thomas *Cranmer of the latest continental news (LP VIII 1551), and for the following two years he travelled between France and Germany, providing regular intelligence to Boleyn, Cranmer, and Thomas *Bedyll.

By July 1537 Theobald was back in England, although according to Emden as early as 9 June 1536 he had been installed as a canon of Salisbury and as prebendary of Durnford. At any rate on 22 July 1537 Cranmer recommended Theobald to *Cromwell, requesting the latter to provide Theobald with new passports (LP XII-2 314). Theobald left England shortly thereafter and by late October had arrived at Strasbourg, where he delivered a letter from Cranmer to Martin *Bucer (LP XII-2 969). Theobald then proceeded to Italy, where he remained until 1540, informing his employers of, among other things, the movements of Reginald *Pole. After another brief visit to England he joined Stephen *Gardiner's embassy to the imperial court, and in a letter of 28 March 1541 to Justus *Jonas, Andreas *Osiander mentioned having met his 'old friend' Theobald in Wittenberg (LP XVI 667). Following the return of the embassy Theobald apparently remained in England for some time. By 1547 his relations with Cranmer had deteriorated, however, for Cranmer believed Theobald to be supplying information against him, even though Gardiner, who was equally suspect in this matter to Cranmer, tried to dispel his suspicions (*The Letters of Stephen Gardiner* ed J.M. Muller, Cambridge 1933, 327–8). By July 1550 Theobald had died in Flanders.

Theobald is mentioned in three letters

exchanged between Erasmus and Conradus *Goclenius in 1535. In the first, of 10 August (Ep 3037), Goclenius mentioned Theobald's stay with him and his suspicion that Theobald was a spy. Goclenius added that Theobald had informed him that Erasmus' pension was in Bedyll's hands, a fact which is reiterated in Goclenius' letter of 2 September (Ep 3052). Finally, on 28 September Goclenius identified Theobald as the person who informed him of Thomas *More's death (Ep 3061).

BIBLIOGRAPHY: Allen Ep 3037 / J. and J.A. Venn *Alumni Cantabrigienses* (Cambridge 1922–54) I-4 218 / LP VIII–XIV passim / *Matricule de Louvain* IV-1 49 / Jasper Ridley *Thomas Cromwell* (Oxford 1962) 90, 135, 158

MORDECHAI FEINGOLD

Benedictus THEOCRENUS *See Benedetto* *TAGLIACARNE*

Jacobus THEODERICI of Hoorn,
d before 10 February 1533
Jacobus Theoderici (Dierckx) was born at Hoorn, on the Frisian island of Terschelling, and was therefore also called Ceratinus. As a result modern scholars have often confused him with Jacobus *Ceratinus (Teyng), of Hoorn, North Holland. Theoderici went to school at Deventer before matriculating at the University of Erfurt in the spring term of 1500. Erfurt was traditionally popular with Frisian students; a scholarship was even reserved for them. Theoderici graduated BA in the autumn of 1501 and MA early in 1504; in the winter term of 1508 he was admitted to the council of the faculty of arts. At the same time he was studying theology, taking two of the preliminary degrees in 1509–10. For various terms between 1510 and 1517 he held the offices of dean, collector, and *taxator* or assessor of residential fees in the faculty of arts.

When Justus *Jonas set out to visit Erasmus at Louvain in the spring of 1519, Theoderici gave him a letter to take with him, to which Erasmus duly wrote an answer (Ep 940). Later that year Theoderici succeeded Jonas as rector of the university, being elected to the office for the winter term of 1519. In the same term he obtained his licence in theology and became a member of the Collegium maius. On 15 October 1520 he was promoted to the theological

doctorate and a readership in divinity at the Collegium maius in succession to the humanist Maternus Pistoris. His new position entitled him to membership in the theological faculty, but at the same time he remained a member of the arts faculty, serving as dean of the former in 1523 and of the latter in 1525. As dean of arts he reopened the preparatory school or *paedago-gium* which had remained closed for a while. From 1526 Theoderici and Ludwig *Platz were the only members of the Collegium maius; both may be considered Erasmians and largely responsible for the university's positive atti-tude towards humanism. Theoderici served again as collector for a term in both 1526 and 1528. He died in 1532 or early 1533, and on 10 February (St Scholastica) the university accept-ed a bequest set out in his will. He is not known to have produced any writings.

BIBLIOGRAPHY: Allen Ep 940 / Gustav Bauch *Die Universität Erfurt im Zeitalter des Frühhu-manismus* (Wrocław 1904) 153–5 / H.R. Abe *Die Universität Erfurt in ihren berühmtesten Persön-lichkeiten* (Erfurt 1958) 76 / Erich Kleineidam *Universitas Studii Erffordensis* (Leipzig 1964–80) II 310 and passim / *Matrikel Erfurt* II 214

ERICH KLEINEIDAM

Vincentius THEODERICI of Beverwijk,
1481–4 August 1526
Vincentius Theoderici (Dierckx, Dirks, Van Beverwyck, Vincentius Haerlemus) of Bever-wijk, north of Haarlem, joined the Dominican monastery of Haarlem in 1500. He was sent to Paris for study and there graduated bachelor of theology by 1513 and the following year taught in the house of his order. In 1517 he moved to Louvain and obtained his theological doctorate on 13 October of that year. He became director of studies (*regens*) at the Louvain monastery and on 31 August 1519 was appointed to the academic senate; on 30 September he was authorized to lecture in the faculty of theology. On 29 August 1521 he was elected dean of that faculty. In 1525 he was appointed *definitor*, or adviser to the provincial of his order; shortly before his death he was also named inquisitor for the diocese of Utrecht. In his Paris years Theoderici had helped produce an edition of the third part and supplement of Thomas Aquinas' *Summa theologiae* (Paris: for Claude Chevallon, preface dated 1514). He had also

edited Pierre de La Palud's commentary on the fourth book of Petrus Lombardus' *Sententiae* (Paris: for Jean Petit, François Regnault and Claude Chevallon 1514, reprinted in 1518).

Erasmus' troubles with Theoderici dated from 1520, as *Luther's following began to include Netherlanders. The conservative theologians of Louvain had long perceived affinities between Erasmus and Luther; encouraged by the papal bull *Exsurge Domine,* they now began a concerted and sustained attack upon Erasmus, who was himself a member of the Louvain theological faculty. From August 1520 Theoderici's attacks and intrigues are frequently mentioned in Erasmus' letters, at first without revealing his name (Epp 1126, 1144). In December, however, Erasmus gave up all pretence at discretion after Theoderici had taken his campaign to Dordrecht, where he found the authorities of Holland reluctant to support him (Epp 1164, 1165, 1186, 1196). In the spring of 1521 Erasmus vented his wrath in a long satirical letter to his detractor (Ep 1196) and another to the theological faculty of Louvain (Ep 1217), both of which he published without delay in the *Epistolae ad diversos* dated August 1521.

After Erasmus' move to Basel, Theoderici and his friends clearly continued their agitation in Louvain, and Erasmus never tired of denouncing him in his letters. He rudely charged him with stupidity (Ep 1342) and included him in any list of his worst enemies (*Spongia* ASD IX-1 205). There is little doubt that he was right in perceiving in Theoderici the driving spirit behind an *Apologia* against him published under the name of Godefridus Ruysius Taxander (Antwerp, March 1525; Epp 1603, 1608). He revenged himself by introducing a Dominican called Vincent among the wrangling, greedy friars of his colloquy *Funus* published in February 1526 (ASD I-3 540–7). Later that year he received the news of Theoderici's death of dropsy (Epp 1732, 1765) but continued to recall him with contempt and anger (Epp 2054, 2443).

BIBLIOGRAPHY: Allen Ep 1196 / de Vocht *Literae ad Craneveldium* Ep 148 / de Vocht CTL I 464–5, II 271, and passim / H. de Jongh *L'Ancienne Faculté de théologie de Louvain* (Louvain 1911) 171–2, 41*, 42*, 44*, 46*, and passim   PGB

THEODORICUS (Epp 673, 739, 761, 762 of September 1517–January 1518)
Theodoricus has not been identified. He was a bachelor of theology at Louvain who received help from Erasmus in the matter of a contested benefice.

THEODORICUS of Haarlem (Ep 1194 of 1521)
In the preface for his *De contemptu mundi* (Ep 1194) Erasmus stated that he wrote this work when he was scarcely twenty years old, on behalf of a monk named Theodoricus Harlemeus. Theodoricus and his nephew Jodocus, for whom the treatise was originally intended, are often thought to be fictitious characters. Assuming, however, that Erasmus did write *De contemptu mundi* on behalf of someone else, there is no reason to doubt that Theodoricus was that man and Jodocus his nephew. If they were fictitious, one might expect Erasmus to make some use of this imaginary family relationship, for instance to contrast the two men in terms of age, authority, and experience. Instead he stated in *De contemptu mundi* that both were then twenty-four years old (ASD V-1 57) and had been educated together (ASD V-1 40) – circumstances just unusual enough to reflect the truth rather than an invention.

No more is known about Theodoricus except that in Ep 1194 Erasmus noted that he was still alive in 1521. It is not clear why this statement should be thought to signal a 'pseudo-realistic' trick rather than be a candid expression of Erasmus' amazement at the fact – perhaps of recent discovery – that Theodoricus was still alive more than thirty years after he had composed the treatise for him. Moreover, by 1521 there were obvious reasons for not laying much stress on the person of Theodoricus; in fact his name might as well have been omitted, just as Erasmus did in the catalogue of his writings sent to *Botzheim (Allen I 18). A similar omission occurs in the introductory letter of an edition of *De pueris instituendis* (Basel: H. Froben September 1529), which had been revised by Erasmus himself. In short, circumstantial evidence points to the existence of Theodoricus and Jodocus rather than to their invention by Erasmus and thus corroborates his own account.

If the preceding argument is sound, it would

be rash to conclude that the girl Margareta, a protagonist of one of the liveliest scenes in *De contemptu mundi*, is entirely fictional. Erasmus' reader must assume that she was well known to Theodoricus and Jodocus, and again Erasmus mentioned that in 1521 she was still alive at Leiden, although her real name was different (ASD V-1 14, 78–9).

BIBLIOGRAPHY: Allen Ep 1194 / Albert Hyma *The Youth of Erasmus* 2nd ed (New York 1968) 167–81 / S. Dresden in ASD V-1 12–17

C.G. VAN LEIJENHORST

THEODORICUS Cortehoevius *See Theodoricus* CORTEHOEVIUS

THEODORICUS Monasteriensis *See Dietrich* KOLDE

Franciscus THEODORICUS of Gouda, d 8 September 1513
Franciscus Theodoricus (Theodorici, Trici, Franciscus Goudanus) was an Augustinian canon who lived at the monasteries of Sion near Delft and Steyn near Gouda before becoming prior of Hemsdonk near Schoonhoven. When he was at Steyn, Erasmus wrote at least three letters to Theodoricus (Epp 10, 12, 14), dated by Allen around 1488. Ep 14 suggests that Erasmus was on familiar terms with him, which may imply that Theodoricus had already moved to Steyn. Theodoricus was certainly at Steyn when Willem *Hermans wrote Ep 35 (c 1494). After he left the monastery Erasmus did not forget his old friend, sending him Ep 41 in 1494 and towards the end of 1505 asking him to collect as many of his early letters as he could (Ep 186). To Theodoricus' compliance with that request we owe the preservation of the important Gouda collection of Erasmus' letters (Allen I appendices 7 and 9). Franciscus Theodoricus might perhaps have been the Theodoricus who against his will joined Erasmus when he left Steyn to enter the service of Hendrik van *Bergen (Ep 33), and also the Franciscus who visited Erasmus at Courtebourne in the winter of 1501. A certain *Sasboudus informed Erasmus of Theodoricus' death (Ep 296), which occurred at Hemsdonk.

Theodoricus' only extant publication is the *Precatiuncule* (Gouda: Collaciebroeders [1512];

NK 1756) – a collection of short prayers, for the most part translated – which contained an introduction by his relative Reyner *Snoy and a dedication to Jacob *Mauritszoon. He dedicated to Snoy a 'Poematum liber unus' (c 1500) and a 'Volumen epistolarum familiarium'; both volumes were once in Boxhorn's library at Leiden but are now lost.

BIBLIOGRAPHY: Allen Ep 10 / Allen I appendix 3 / I. W[alvis] *Beschryving der stad Gouda* (Gouda-Leiden [1713]) I 244

C.G. VAN LEIJENHORST

Jean THIBAULT documented 1519–40
Jean Thibault (Tybaldaeus, Theobald) was probably born in Gournay-en-Bray (Département de la Seine-Maritime). He was active as a printer and publisher at Antwerp from 1519 to 1531, producing some twenty volumes by classical and humanistic authors. From 1527, however, he published medical works and prognostications as well as practising astrology and medicine. By 1531 or 1532 he was obliged to leave the Netherlands and moved to Paris, where he was the object of a series of legal actions brought by the faculty of medicine from 1532 to 1540. Nothing is known about the end of his life.

In 1519 Thibault printed works by Adrianus Cornelii *Barlandus and Erasmus (Ep 934); Edward *Lee accused Erasmus of dissuading the printer from publishing his attack on Erasmus' New Testament (Epp 1053, 1061; *Opuscula* 253).

BIBLIOGRAPHY: Allen Ep 1053 / H.D.L. Vervliet in NBW III 863–6 / Anne Rouzet *Dictionnaire des imprimeurs, libraires et éditeurs des xve et xvie siècles dans les limites géographiques de la Belgique actuelle* (Nieuwkoop 1975) 219–20

MARCEL A. NAUWELAERTS

Jacob van THIELT of Wervik, d 7 March 1541 or 1543
Jacob van Thielt (Tielt) was born around 1475 in Wervik, in Flanders, and became curate of Ledegem and St Martin's, Courtrai, successively. He was appointed to a canonry of Our Lady's chapter in Courtrai and was eventually elected precentor. Simultaneously with Pierre *Cotrel he served as vicar-general of three successive bishops of Tournai, Charles de Haultbois, Louis *Guillard, and Charles (II) de

*Croy. Early in November 1517 he shared a house at Courtrai with his good friend and fellow canon Jan de *Hondt, who succeeded him on 10 March 1541 as precentor. His influence and popularity with his fellow canons is reflected by many references to him in their wills. His funeral inscription is extant in the church of Our Lady in front of the altar of the Holy Sacrament.

Jacob van Thielt directed the education of a young man named *Soti, whom Jan de Hondt recommended warmly to Erasmus (Ep 1094).

BIBLIOGRAPHY: Allen and CWE Ep 1094 / *Monasticon Belge* ed U. Berlière et al (Maredsous-Liège 1890–) III 113 / F. de Potter *Geschiedenis der stad Kortrijk* (Ghent 1876) III 144–5, 230 / C. Caullet *Musiciens de la Collégiale Notre-Dame à Courtrai* (Courtrai-Bruges 1911) 57–69 / *Testaments d'une centaine de membres du Chapitre de Notre-Dame à Courtrai* ed Cercle historique et archéologique de Courtrai (Bruges-Courtrai [1922]) 32–72 passim / J.-P. Massaut *Josse Clichtove, l'humanisme et la réforme du clergé* (Liège 1968) II 33 / P. Declerk in *Horae Tornacenses* (Tournai 1971) 144, 153, 156 / *Chronologische Lijsten van de Geextendeerde Sententien berusten in het archief van der Grote Raad van Mechelen* (Brussels 1971) II 284, 475 / Paris, Bibliothèque Mazarine, MS 1068 f 280

GÉRARD MOREAU

Marcus THOMAE documented 1515–22
Marcus Thomae (Thome, Thomias), also called Stübner because he was the son of the owner of a bath house (*Badstube*) in Elsterberg, in Saxony, had studied at Leipzig in 1515 and at Wittenberg in 1518. Well read in the Scriptures, he joined Nikolaus *Storch, a weaver, in Zwickau and became one of the unruly 'Zwickau prophets.' In December 1521 some of them came to Wittenberg and had some success as preachers. They also had discussions with Andreas *Karlstadt and Philippus *Melanchthon, who received Thomae into his house to learn more about his views. Their agitation was stopped by Martin *Luther's return to Wittenberg in March 1522.

When reporting the arrival of the Zwickau prophets at Wittenberg to Frederick the Wise of *Saxony, Melanchthon mentioned two unschooled clothmakers and a third man who was educated. Thomae was evidently the latter

(*Melanchthons Briefwechsel* I Ep 192). Thomae may also be intended when Erasmus relayed the same news received from Wittenberg, speaking of two remarkably educated fullers (Ep 1258).

BIBLIOGRAPHY: Allen Ep 1258 / *Matrikel Leipzig* I 543 / *Matrikel Wittenberg* I 73 / RGG VI 1951 / Luther W *Briefwechsel* II Ep 449 / *Melanchthons Werke in Auswahl* ed R. Stupperich et al (Gütersloh 1951–) VII-1 Ep 64 / H. Barge *Andreas Bodenstein von Karlstadt* (Leipzig 1905, repr 1968) I 400–1   IG

THOMAS (Ep 36 of [early 1494?])
Thomas, a friend of Willem *Hermans and Cornelis *Gerard, has not been identified.

Georg THOMAS of Nordhausen, documented 1504–41
One Georgius Thomas, a priest at Eisenach, in Thuringia, wrote to Erasmus in August 1527, asking him to clarify his view of the Eucharist, just as *Luther had done. Thomas stated that he was not known to Erasmus (Ep 1868). The author of that letter is probably Georg Thomas, a son or relative of Heinrich Thomas (Thome), who from about 1503 to 1540 was burgomaster of Nordhausen, sixty-five kilometres east of Göttingen. Georg Thomas matriculated at the University of Leipzig in the winter term of 1504. A position at Eisenach in 1527 appears to agree well with the rest of his career, as far as it is known. In 1540 he had been parish priest at Northeim, twenty kilometres north of Göttingen, for a year, and in May 1541 he was preacher at Allendorf in Thuringia, thirty kilometres south of Göttingen.

BIBLIOGRAPHY: Allen Ep 1868 / *Matrikel Leipzig* I 465 / *Der Briefwechsel des Antonius Corvinus* ed P. Tschackert (Hannover 1900) Epp 84, 87, 90, 121 / *Der Briefwechsel des Justus Jonas* ed G. Kawerau (Halle 1884–5, repr 1964) I Epp 26, 99   MICHAEL ERBE

John THORNTON d by September 1516
Thornton (Thornden) first occurs as an Augustinian canon of Barnwell Priory, Cambridgeshire, which he left in 1480 to become a Benedictine monk of St Albans. Prior of Belvoir, Hertfordshire, and then of Wallingford, Berkshire, he received his doctorate in divinity at Oxford by 1503, and between 1506

and 1514 was commissary to the chancellor of the university, Archbishop William *Warham. In 1505 he was provided to the titular see of Syra or Cyrene, and from 1508 until his death served as Warham's suffragan in the archdiocese of Canterbury. He was prior of Dover in 1509 and by 1513 became prior of Folkestone. He also held a number of parochial livings, including that of Aldington, Kent, where he succeeded Erasmus by Warham's collation of 31 July 1512. The retiring rector was granted a pension of twenty pounds a year – an exception to the archbishop's usual prohibition of such arrangements. Thornton and his successor, Richard *Master, incurred Erasmus' displeasure by their attempts to withhold part or all of this annuity. In 1513 Thornton apparently tried to share with his pensioner the royal tenth voted by convocation on 7 July 1512. But Erasmus, writing to John *Colet, remarked that the suffragan had made no mention of this when the pension was agreed upon, although the tax had been imposed some three weeks before (Ep 278). Thornton resigned the living, and with it the responsibility for Erasmus' pension, by November 1514. According to Erasmus' report the suffragan's episcopal duties prevented him from attending to the needs of his parish (see Ecclesiastes LB V 811 E–F). His career was in any case drawing to a close, and he was dead by September 1516.

BIBLIOGRAPHY: Allen Ep 255 / Emden BRUO III 1867 / F.M. Powicke and E.B. Fryde Handbook of British Chronology 2nd ed (London 1961) 268

C.S. KNIGHTON

Alban THORER See Albanus TORINUS

Elizabeth THROCKMORTON d 13 January 1547

Elizabeth, the daughter of Thomas Throckmorton (Throckmerton), became the abbess of Denney, Cambridgeshire, in 1512. Renowned for her piety, Elizabeth was learned as well, and in 1528, when an alderman of London, Humphrey Monmouth, ran foul of the authorities for having distributed William *Tyndale's translation of Erasmus' Enchiridion, he recorded having lent a copy of the translation to Elizabeth at her request (LP IV 4282). Although a small abbey valued under two hundred pounds, Denney was granted a licence for

continuation under Elizabeth on 28 August 1536 (LP XI 385(35)). Nonetheless, by October 1539 Denney had been dissolved (LP XIV-2 435(49)), and the abbess, together with two or three nuns, had retired to Coughton, her family home. There the women maintained their orders as best they could until Elizabeth's death in 1547.

Erasmus' connection with Thomas *Grey led to his association with the abbey, for Grey, whose sisters were at Denney, had asked Erasmus to write a letter of salutation (c 1525). Erasmus complied and the abbey responded by sending him a gift which, however, was lost en route. Upon discovering the fate of the gift, Erasmus penned another letter to the nuns, this time a brief sermon on the theme 'in quietness and confidence shall be your strength,' the contents of which were published as Epistola consolatoria in adversis (Basel: H. Froben 1528; LB III-2 1874–9) and contained greetings to the 'most religious lady,' almost certainly Elizabeth. Allen published extracts of this letter as Ep 1925.

BIBLIOGRAPHY: Allen Ep 1925 / David Knowles The Religious Orders in England (Cambridge 1948–59) III 301, 412 / Victoria History of the Counties of England (London-Oxford 1900–) Cambridgeshire II 301–2, Warwickshire III 78, 85 / E.A.B. Barnard 'A 16th century dole-gate from Denny Abbey' Proceedings of the Cambridge Antiquarian Society 29 (1928) 72–5

MORDECHAI FEINGOLD

Konrad von THÜNGEN c 1466–16 June 1540

Konrad von Thüngen was descended from a family of Franconian knights. Little is known about his studies in Italy except that he made the acquaintance of Willibald *Pirckheimer between 1490 and 1497 in Padua or Pavia and acquired a taste for humanistic learning which was reflected later in his respect for and patronage of scholars. *Hutten, Pirckheimer, and Johann *Eck were among those who dedicated works to Thüngen; Erasmus too inscribed to him his commentary on Psalm 33 (1531), receiving in return a gift and a flattering letter (Epp 2314, 2428). On his return from Italy, Thüngen lived in Würzburg as a canon, and on 15 February 1519 he was unanimously elected prince-bishop of Würzburg. A faithful ally of the house of Hapsburg, he played an active role during the diets of the 1520s and the 1530s. After attending the diet of Worms in the spring of 1521 he negotiated Würzburg's membership in the Swabian League in November. From June to August 1525 he had to resort to a military campaign in order to reconquer his principality from the rebelling peasants; afterwards he had the rebels tried with regrettable, if lawful, severity. He was equally uncompromising in his opposition to the Protestant reformers and in his persecution of the Anabaptists.

In the summer of 1520 Erasmus addressed a letter of compliments to Thüngen (Ep 1124), apparently at the suggestion of Johannes *Draconites. The initial contacts were resumed and intensified from 1529 as a result of Erasmus' acquaintance with the Würzburg canon Daniel *Stiebar (Ep 2303) and the move to Würzburg of Augustinus *Marius (Epp 2164, 2321). Friendly relations continued until Erasmus' death (Epp 2457, 2942, 3133).

BIBLIOGRAPHY: Allen Ep 1124 / NDB XII 532–3 / ADB XVI 632–4 / Eubel III 208 / E. Hoyer 'Erzbischof Konrad III. von Thüngen als Richter' *Würzburger Diözesangeschichtsblätter* 14–15 (1952–3) 433–77 / B. von Bundschuh 'Die Stellung Würzburgs zur Christlichen Einigung 1538' *Würzburger Diözesangeschichtsblätter* 27 (1965) 5–28, esp 12–16 / A. Tausendpfund 'Der Beitritt des Hochstifts Würzburg zum Schwäbischen Bund' *Würzburger Diözesangeschichtsblätter* 37–8 (1975–6) 411–38, esp 416–31 / *Deutsche Reichstagsakten* Jüngere Reihe (Gotha-Göttingen 1893–) II 75–7, 149, and passim   PGB

Chunradus THURINGUS SALTZENSIS
(Ep 2802 of [c April] 1533)
While passing through Freiburg on his return from Italy 'Chunradus Thuringus Saltzensis' wrote to Erasmus, begging for money. He has not been identified; perhaps he came from Langensalza in Thuringia (Salza Doringiae), but Thuring or Döring could also have been his family name.

Alexius THURZO d 25 January 1543
Alexius (Elek), a son of Johannes (I) *Thurzo (Turzo) and half-brother of Johannes (II) and Stanislaus *Thurzo, was born around 1490 and

tutored by Jacobus *Piso. Following the death of his father in 1508 he represented the interests of the Thurzo-Fugger enterprises at the royal court in Buda. He became the protégé of the powerful chancellor, Bishop György Szathmári, whose niece Anna he married in 1510. The support of Szathmári and his immense wealth assured him of great influence at court. In 1515 he attended the gathering of monarchs at Vienna. Two years later he became the controller of the mining revenues of Kremnica (Kremnitz, Körmöc), while in 1515 he was named royal secretary and in 1522 treasurer. For the next four years he held the office of lord chief treasurer amid increasing financial difficulties. As the coffers of *Louis II and Queen *Mary were empty, he personally loaned large sums to the royal couple in return for extensive privileges and vast estates. In 1522 Queen Mary relinquished to him the revenues of the rich mining towns of northern Hungary in payment of debts. Blamed for the financial chaos which reigned throughout the kingdom, he was forced to resign his office as lord chief treasurer on 22 April 1525 (Ep 1602). The fiscal crisis, however, became even more severe and on 9 July 1526 Thurzo was reinstated and entrusted with the task of restoring fiscal equilibrium. The Fugger firm was secretly paying him a large salary.

A month later, when *Suleiman the Magnificent advanced with a large army upon Hungary, Thurzo accompanied Louis II on the ill-conceived campaign to the southern border, but a few days before the battle of Mohács he was sent back to Buda with orders to remain near the queen. Following the death of Louis II Thurzo helped the widowed queen in her flight from Buda. A loyal supporter of the Hapsburg cause, he worked for the election of *Ferdinand as king of Hungary and Bohemia and was amply rewarded with properties, many of them lands confiscated from *John Zápolyai, the king of the national party in Hungary. In 1527 Ferdinand appointed him lord chief justice of Hungary, and from 1532 he served as vice-regent of the areas under Hapsburg domination. The task was arduous and sometimes, it seems, sickening (Ep 2396) but he carried on. Ill health forced him to retire from all administrative positions in November

1542. He died on 25 January 1543 and was buried in the family vault at Levoča (Leutschau, Löcse).

A man of refinement and culture, Thurzo preferred the quiet life on his country estates to his court duties. A number of scholars dedicated books to him. With the encouragement of Jan *Antonin, a friend of the Thurzo family, Erasmus dedicated to Alexius his translation of two short treatises by Plutarch in 1525 (Epp 1572, 1602), but if he sent a present in return it apparently did not reach Erasmus (Epp 1660, 1810, 1825, 1916). The German humanist Valentin Eck, who around 1517 had tutored Alexius' daughter, dedicated several of his works to him, the most important of which was *De reipublicae administratione* (Cracow 1520). Alexius also established a school at Hlohovec (Freistadtl, Galgocz) and generously endowed the school and church of Levoča. The earliest surviving Hungarian love letter comes from his pen. It was written on 9 September 1528 to a certain widow whose husband had died at Mohács. His other unpublished letters are in the Országos Levéltár or National Archives, Budapest.

BIBLIOGRAPHY: Allen Ep 1572 / *Magyar életrajzi lexikon* (Budapest 1967–9) II 861 / Gusztáv Wenzel *Thurzó Zsigmond, János, Szaniszló és Ferencz négy egykorú püspök a bethlenfalvi Thurzó családból* (Budapest 1878) / Jozsef Fógel *II Lajos udvartartása* (Budapest 1917) / János Horváth *Az irodalmi müveltség megoszlása* (Budapest 1944) / Götz von Pölnitz *Anton Fugger* (Tübingen 1958–   ) I 69–75, 120–1, and passim / *Acta Tomiciana* (Poznań-Wrocław 1852–1966) IV–XVII passim / Valentin Eck *De antiquissima nominis et familiae Thurzonum origine et ... Alexii Thurzonis ... eminentia panegyris* (Cracow 1519) / The text of Alexius' love letter is printed in Gyula Zolnai *Nyelvemlekeink a könyvnyomtatás koráig* (Budapest 1894) 237 / The dedicatory epistle of Eck's *De reipublicae administratione* is in *Analecta nova ad historiam renascentium in Hungaria litterarum spectantia* ed J. Ábel and I. Hegedüs (Budapest 1903) 182–7   L. DOMONKOS

Johannes (I) THURZO 30 April 1437–
10 October 1508

Johannes (Jan, János) Thurzo (Turzo) was born in Levoča (Leutschau, Löcse, today in Czechoslovakia) to a family of Austrian origin. In his youth Thurzo spent much time in Italy, where he learnt smelting techniques. In 1464 he settled in Cracow and quickly made a huge fortune in the profitable copper trade and in the exploitation of copper and lead mines in Poland, later predominantly in Hungary. In 1494 he formed a partnership with the Fuggers and acquired a monopoly in mining, casting, and trading in copper from the mines and furnaces of Hungary, Slovakia, Silesia, and Austria. King *Vladislav II appointed him a commissioner of Hungarian mining and financial administrator (*Kammergraf*). He had the right to mint his own coins in Körmec Bánya and Nagy Bánya. In 1505 he received the title of baron of Bethlenfalva, in Szepes county. In Cracow, where he kept a stately home, he was an alderman and a supervisor in charge of the construction of the great altar in Our Lady's church, a work assigned to the sculptor Wit Stwosz. In this church Thurzo founded a private chapel for his family. He always maintained close contacts with the royal court and won praise for his interest in literature and art and also for his patronage of young humanists (Ep 1662).

Thurzo married twice, and both his wives – Urszula Behem and Barbara Beck – were daughters of wealthy Cracow burghers. From his first marriage three sons were born: Georgius (György), commissioner of Hungarian mining, Johannes (II) *Thurzo, bishop of Wrocław, and Stanislaus *Thurzo, bishop of Olomouc. The two sons from his second marriage were Alexius *Thurzo, treasurer of the king of Hungary, and Johannes, duke of Szepes.

Thurzo died at Rivoli, his manor near Levoča, and was buried in the church of St James, Levoča, where his sons erected a magnificent tomb in his memory.

BIBLIOGRAPHY: Allen Ep 1572 / L. Lepszy 'Turzonowie w Polsce' *Przeglad Polski* 96 (1890) 463–9 / E. Kovacs *Uniwersytet Krakowski a kultura węgierska* (Budapest 1965) 91–2 / B. Wapowski 'Kronika' in *Scriptores rerum Polonicarum* II (Cracow 1874) 85 / Götz von Pölnitz *Anton Fugger* (Tübingen 1958–   ) I 19 and passim   HALINA KOWALSKA

Johannes (II) THURZO 16 April 1464/5–
2 August 1520

A son of Johannes (I) *Thurzo, Johannes (Jan,
János) was a brother of Stanislaus *Thurzo and
a half-brother of Alexius *Thurzo. He was
educated at the University of Cracow, where
he received a MA in 1487 and also held the
office of rector (1498). He went to Italy, staying
in Rome for a few years and probably obtaining
a doctorate of laws. On his return to Wrocław,
he became a canon and in 1502 auxiliary
bishop. From 1506 to the end of his life he held
the bishopric of Wrocław (Breslau) and made it
into an important centre of Silesian humanism.
He maintained his ties with the intellectual
circles of Cracow and sent several young men
to study there at his expense, among them
Georg von *Logau. He was also in contact with
the scholarly group assembled by his brother
Stanislaus at Olomouc, in Moravia. Ties of
blood and friendship bound him to the royal
court at Buda, where Alexius was becoming
increasingly more powerful. A frequent visitor
to the Hungarian capital, Johannes was entrusted with important functions by King
*Vladislav II. In 1507 he was appointed
captain-general of Silesia, a position he held
for two years. On 11 March 1509 he was in
Prague for the coronation of young *Louis II as
king of Bohemia. A year later, Vladislav sent
Johannes on an embassy to Poland in efforts to
win King *Sigismund over to a common policy
against the Turks. On 8 February 1512 he was
again in Poland, representing his king at
Sigismund's marriage to Barbara, the sister of
*John Zápolyai.

In later life Johannes showed a definite
sympathy for the ideas of Martin *Luther. He
sent one of his canons to Wittenberg, who
brought back a letter as well as greetings from
both Luther and *Melanchthon. Johannes died
on 2 August 1520 at Nysa (Neisse) before the
letter could be delivered, but his secretary,
Johann *Hess, became a major figure in the
Reformation movement at Wrocław. Although
not himself a scholar, Johannes was, like his
brothers, a generous patron of humanists and
an admirer of Erasmus, to whose writings he
had been introduced by Jacobus *Piso in Buda
(Ep 1662). Together with *Ursinus Velius, who
had been supported by the Thurzo brothers in
his student days, Piso persuaded Johannes in

1518 to write to Erasmus (Ep 850), who sent an
affable reply (Ep 943). This led to another
exchange of letters in 1519 and 1520, the
bishop's being accompanied by gifts for Erasmus (Epp 1047, 1137), but Johannes' death cut
short this developing friendship. Erasmus was
saddened by the unexpected death and continued to remember Johannes' generosity (Epp
1242, 1544, 1754). Valentin Eck, a German
humanist, wrote an epitaph for Johannes as
well as addressing an *Epistola consolatoria* to his
brothers (Cracow 1520). Georg von Logau
dedicated several poems to his benefactor. In
1515 the Moravian humanist Stephanus Taurinus (Stieröchsel), a canon of Gyula Fehérvár
(Alba Iulia), visited the episcopal court of
Wrocław and was encouraged by Johannes to
write an account of the Hungarian peasant
revolt of 1514. The result was an epic poem
entitled *Stauromachia, id est cruciatorum servile
bellum*, a work of literary as well as historical
importance (ed J.C. von Engel in *Monumenta
Ungarica*, Vienna 1908).

BIBLIOGRAPHY: Allen Ep 850 / NDB x 482–3 /
C.A.H. Markgraf in ADB XIV 188–9 / Gusztáv
Wenzel *Thurzó Zsigmond, János, Szaniszló és
Ferencz, négy egykorú püspök a bethlenfalvi Thurzó
családból* (Budapest 1878) / Tivadar Thiene-
mann 'Mohács és Erasmus' *Minerva* 3 (1924) 1–
65 / János Horváth *Az irodalmi müveltség megos-
zlása* (Budapest 1944) 246–7 / Josef Macůrek
'Humanismus v oblasti moravsko-slezske a
jeho vztahy ke Slovensku v.2. polovine 15. a
počátkem 16. stoleti' in *Humanizmus a renescan-
cia na Slovensku* (Bratislava 1967) 332–55 /
*Analecta recentiora ad historiam renascentium in
Hungaria litterarum spectantia* ed I. Hegedüs
(Budapest 1906) 253–66 (Logau's poems) /
*Analecta nova ad historiam renascentium in
Hungaria litterarum spectantia* ed J. Ábel and
I. Hegedüs (Budapest 1903) 185–7 (Eck's
pieces) L. DOMONKOS

Stanislaus THURZO d 16 April 1540

Stanislaus (Szaniszló, Stanislav), a son of
Johannes (I) *Thurzo (Turzo), followed his
brother Johannes (II) *Thurzo to the University
of Cracow, enrolling in 1485. He took holy
orders that same year. In 1497 he became
bishop of Olomouc (Olmütz) in Moravia and
made his episcopal court a centre of humanism, encouraging the development of strong

ties to the scholarly circles in Poland, Hungary, and Silesia. To foster the growth of intellectual life in his diocese, he refused to appoint anybody to a canonry of his cathedral chapter who did not have a MA. Stanislaus enjoyed the confidence of *Vladislav II, king of Hungary and Bohemia, who sent him on a mission to Prague in 1508 to calm disturbances. In Prague Thurzo took part in the coronation of *Louis II as king of Bohemia on 11 March 1509. In 1515 he attended the conference of rulers at Vienna. During these years Stanislaus and his brother Johannes were frequent visitors to Buda and became members of the Erasmian circle which had developed around Jacobus *Piso (Ep 1662). Following the death of Louis II at the battle of Mohács (29 August 1526), Stanislaus became a firm supporter of the house of Hapsburg and participated in the coronation of *Ferdinand as king of Bohemia at Prague in February 1527. He administered his diocese of Olomouc for forty-three years in an exemplary manner, enriched it considerably, and met all Protestant influences with firm opposition.

Although not an active scholar, Stanislaus liberally supported men of learning and in return had a number of works dedicated to him. One of his protégés was *Ursinus Velius, who became the intermediary between Thurzo and Erasmus. Soon after his arrival at Basel in November 1521, Ursinus visited him, carrying a letter as well as a gift from Stanislaus (Epp 1342, 1343; AK II Ep 818). Other letters followed and Stanislaus again sent a present (Epp 1267, 1272). In 1525 Erasmus dedicated his edition of Pliny's Historia naturalis (Basel: J. Froben, Epp 1544, 1557) to Stanislaus and received a valuable cup in return, whereas *Beatus Rhenanus, who had inscribed to the bishop of Olomouc Froben editions of Tertullian (1521) and the Autores historiae ecclesiasticae (1523) apparently had to wait some time before receiving his reward, at least for the second dedication (Ep 1603; BRE Epp 207, 234, 266). Ursinus Velius continued to press Erasmus for another dedication to Thurzo, and this time of a writing of his own (Epp 1754, 2517). It was not, however, until 1532 that Erasmus dedicated his Enarratio on Psalm 38 to Thurzo (Epp 2608, 2699, 3049). While at Basel, Ursinus

Velius published a volume of poems in 1522 which he dedicated to Stanislaus. Jakob *Ziegler also dedicated a work to him (Ep 1260), as did Johannes Cuspinianus, Valentin Eck, Jan *Šlechta, Augustin of Olomouc, Johannes Dubravius, and the Polish writer Matthew of Mechov. Among those who enjoyed the hospitality of his episcopal court were Stephanus Taurinus, Vaclav of Vilhartice, Jan Zvolsky of Zvol, Georg von *Logau (Epp 2657, 2810), and the physician Jan *Antonin. A few of Stanislaus' letters have survived, scattered in Czechoslovak archives (Prague, Bratislava, Bánska Býstrica, and Kroměříž). A copy of his will, made by Dubravius, was sent to his brother Alexius and is now in the Hungarian Országos Levéltár or National Archives, Budapest.

BIBLIOGRAPHY: Allen Ep 1242 / Magyar életrajzi lexikon (Budapest 1967–9) II 862 / Gusztáv Wenzel Thurzó Zsigmond, János, Szaniszló és Ferencz, négy egykorú püspök a bethlenfalvi Thurzó családból (Budapest 1878) / Karl Wotke 'Der Olmützer Bischof Stanislaus Thurzó von Bethlenfalva und dessen Humanistenkreis' Zeitschrift des Vereines für die Geschichte Mährens und Schlesiens (1899) 338–388 / Josef Macůrek 'Humanismus v oblasti moravsko-slezske a jeho vztahy ke Slovensku v. 2. polovine 15. a počatkem 16. stoleti' Humanizmus a renescancia na Slovensku (Bratislava 1967) 332–55 / A number of poems by Georg von Logau dedicated to Stanislaus Thurzo are found in Analecta recentiora ad historiam renascentium in Hungaria litterarum spectantia ed I. Hegedüs (Budapest 1906) 247–67 / Poems by Ursinus Velius are in Analecta nova ad historiam renascentium in Hungaria litterarum spectantia ed J. Ábel and I. Hegedüs (Budapest 1903) 470   L. DOMONKOS

Stephan TIELER of Strasbourg, documented 1509–15
Very little is known about Stephan Tieler (Dieler, Diheler) of Strasbourg, who matriculated at the University of Heidelberg in May 1509, where he received his BA in the following year and his MA in 1511–12. After his return to Strasbourg he is listed as a member of the Strasbourg literary society in 1514 and 1515 and took part in the enthusiastic reception it accorded to Erasmus (Epp 302, 305).

BIBLIOGRAPHY: Allen Ep 302 / BRE Ep 54 / *Matrikel Heidelberg* I 470, II 433 PGB

Jacobus de TIELT *See Jacob van* THIELT

Gregorius TIPHERNAS 1413/14–c 1464

Gregorius Tiphernas (Gregorio Tifernate, or Tifernio, Gregorio da Città di Castello, Gregorio Castellano; not to be confused with Lilius Tiphernas) was born near Cortona. While still a young man he moved to Città di Castello, and he studied both there and at Perugia. He also went to Mistra, on the Peloponnese, studying with Georgius *Gemistos Plethon. Upon returning to Italy he taught Greek and medicine, living in various parts of Italy but also travelling to Tours and Paris (1456–9), where he taught at the university. His literary works consist primarily of translations from Greek into Latin, which were made especially during the papacy of *Nicholas v. These include versions of works of Aristotle, Theophrastus, Dion Chrysostom, and pseudo-Timaeus Locrus and books XI–XVII of Strabo's *Geography*, most of which remain in manuscript. The last of these is mentioned by Erasmus in *Adagia* II iv 7.

BIBLIOGRAPHY: G. Mancini 'Gregorio Tifernate' *Archivio storico italiano* 81 (1923) 65–112 / *Catalogus translationum et commentariorum* ed P.O. Kristeller and F.E. Cranz (Washington 1960–) II 230, 280, and passim

CHARLES B. SCHMITT

Frans TITELMANS of Hasselt,
1502–12 September 1537

Frans Titelmans (Franciscus Hasseltensis), born in Hasselt, in Limburg, matriculated as a poor student at Louvain on 12 June 1518, obtained a MA in 1521 and studied theology while teaching philosophy in the arts faculty. Some of his lectures were later published, such as *Libri duodecem de consideratione rerum naturalium* (Antwerp: S. Cocus 1530) and *Libri sex de consideratione dialectica* (Antwerp: S. Cocus 1533). On 28 February 1523 he was nominated by the faculty for a benefice, but soon thereafter he entered the Franciscan order at the Louvain monastery. He was chosen to instruct his fellow monks, at first again in philosophical subjects, but from 1527 he lectured on Scripture, in the traditional sense of moral and mystical interpretation. Again some of his expositions were eventually printed, such as *Elucidatio in omnes psalmos* (Antwerp: M. de Keyser for W. Vorsterman 1531), dedicated to *Charles v, and *Commentarii in Ecclesiasten* (Antwerp: S. Cocus 1536), dedicated to Cardinal Francisco de *Quiñones. Impressed with the stricter rule of the newly founded Capuchin order within the Franciscan tradition, he obtained his transfer to the Capuchins and in 1535 set out for Italy to meet the vicar-general, Bernardo of Asti, and to devote himself to works of charity. He taught theology in Milan and served in Rome in a hospital for the incurably ill. In 1537 he visited the Anticoli monastery in Lazio, where he died after a brief illness.

Among Titelman's teachers at Louvain was Jacobus *Latomus, who influenced him greatly. Although filled with scholarly ambitions and claiming to study Greek and even Hebrew texts, in his numerous lectures and publications Titelmans followed strictly the medieval technique of interpretation, preferring the pure fountain of St Thomas Aquinas to the troubled waters of humanist philology (Ep 1837A). Alerted by his friends at Louvain (Epp 1815, 1837), Erasmus warned Titelmans in May 1527 in a personal letter (Ep 1823). The friar replied, defending his views (Ep 1837A). In May 1528 Erasmus was first told by his friends of the existence of manuscript copies of a book in which Titelmans attacked him (Epp 1994, 1994A). In October he learnt that the friar had gone to Antwerp in search of a printer, while the theological faculty of Louvain, complying with recent injunctions issued by the papal curia and the imperial court, was trying to stop him. The result was that Erasmus' friends too were unable to intercept a copy of the work (Epp 2063, 2089). The book appeared (*Collationes quinque super epistolam ad Romanos*, Antwerp: W. Vorsterman May 1529), and presented the author in debate with Lorenzo *Valla, *Lefèvre d'Etaples, and Erasmus, who are all made to quote excerpts from their writings, albeit with distortions, only to be shown by Titelmans that the Vulgate was above criticism.

A brief but bitter controversy followed. Erasmus expressed his annoyance in numerous letters to his friends, especially in Epp

2205, 2206 of August 1529, both addressed to Johann von *Botzheim and published without delay in the *Opus epistolarum*. The second became the basis for a more comprehensive reply to Titelmans; *Responsio ad collationes* (Antwerp: P. Sylvius October 1529; cf Ep 2300). In December Titelmans replied with an *Epistola apologetica* (Antwerp: W. Vorsterman January 1530) and continued his attack with *De authoritate libri Apocalypsis* (Antwerp: M. Hillen 1530; Ep 2417). In February Erasmus reviled Titelmans, without naming him, in his open letter to the Franciscans (Ep 2275), a copy of which *Goclenius diplomatically failed to forward to the Louvain friars (Ep 2352), although the letter was quickly reprinted in Antwerp, together with the *Epistola contra pseudevangelicos* (Antwerp: M. de Keyser 1530). To this Titelmans did not reply, but he continued his own expositions of Scripture. His paraphrases of Job and the gospels of Matthew and John were published posthumously by his brother Pieter between 1543 and 1547. Among his other works one may note his edition of the chronicle of *Amandus of Zierikzee with an appendix on Ethiopia derived from Rui *Fernandes (Antwerp: S. Cocus 1534).

BIBLIOGRAPHY: Allen Ep 1823, VIII xliii / DTC XV-1 1144–6 / LThK X 210–11 / ADB XXXVIII 377 / *Matricule de Louvain* III-1 584 / de Vocht CTL III 57, 145–53, and passim / de Vocht *Dantiscus* 92–3 / H. de Jongh *L'Ancienne Faculté de théologie de Louvain* (Louvain 1911) 82, 249 / Pastor IV 630–4 / J.H. Bentley 'New Testament scholarship at Louvain in the early sixteenth century' *Studies in Medieval and Renaissance History* n s 2 (1979) 53–79, esp 69–79

IG & PGB

Piotr TOMICKI 1464–29 October 1535
Piotr Tomicki (Tomicius, Tomiczki), the son of Mikolaj, the standard-bearer of Poznań, who featured a boat in his coat of arms, was born on the family's estate at Tomice, in Great Poland. After the premature death of his father Piotr was educated at the court of his maternal uncle Andrzej of Szamotuly, the palatine of Poznań. When the latter undertook an embassy to the Emperor *Frederick III in February 1486, Piotr accompanied him and remained at Leipzig in the care of a private tutor until 1488. He matriculated for the spring term of 1489 at the

University of Cracow, receiving his BA in 1490 and his MA in early 1493. Later that year he visited the court of Vienna en route to the University of Bologna, where on 10 June 1500 he received a doctorate in canon law. Subsequently he was in Rome, where he participated in the jubilee celebrations and received some training in the papal chancery. Before the end of that year he had returned to Poland and joined the chancery of the bishop of Cracow, Cardinal Fryderyk Jagiełło. He undertook many missions in the cardinal's service and notably had the opportunity of meeting at his residence at Głogów the cardinal's brother, the future king *Sigismund I. After Fryderyk's death in March 1503, Tomicki was retained at Poznań by the bishop of Cracow, Jan Lubranski, but when Sigismund I ascended the throne on 8 December 1506, he became a secretary in the royal chancery.

Soon Tomicki was chosen to undertake some important diplomatic missions and thus went to Hungary in 1510, 1512, and from 1513 to 1514, and in 1511 he was sent to Silesia. At the same time he began to gather ecclesiastical preferment; among the benefices he owed to royal favour were canonries in Kujawy (1509) and at Gniezno (1510), while in 1512 he became *custos* of the Sandomir chapter, having been ordained priest the year before. He was bishop of Przemyśl from February 1514 and was appointed vice-chancellor of the realm by Sigismund in 1515; in 1520 he became bishop of Poznań and in 1525 of Cracow, a dignity which he retained until his death, declining the archsee of Gniezno in 1531. His dual functions as bishop of Cracow and royal vice-chancellor assured him of great influence in both domestic and foreign policies; however Queen *Bona was critical of the combination of the two offices.

Tomicki's approach to politics was characterized by caution and compromise. He was firmly opposed to Jan (I) *Łaski's aggressive pursuance of long-range targets deemed to be in the national interest and often managed to paralyse Łaski's endeavours. As the head of the pro-Hapsburg faction he supported King *Ferdinand against *John Zápolyai in the struggle for the crown of Hungary. Consequently he also opposed a policy of peace with the Turks and an alliance with France. In the field of religion he rejected the social and doctrinal ideas of the reformers and inspired Sigismund to promulgate several edicts to this end, prohibiting the importation of books from Germany (1523) and the departure of Polish students for German universities (1520, 1534). When he obtained papal authorization for certain Polish priests to read beyond the limits of Catholic orthodoxy, his concern was again the struggle against the reformers. In 1526 he demanded severe punishment for the evangelical rebels at Gdansk. In spite of his otherwise consistent policies, however, he opposed Łaski by advocating the treaty with Albert of *Brandenburg-Ansbach, who was to become the secular duke of Prussia and a Polish vassal.

Tomicki's life-style was marked by the formative years he passed in Italy, so much so that he was called 'the Italian.' He insisted on high standards of Latinity in the royal chancery, where he formed a generation of fine Polish statesmen and diplomats. He had documents and diplomatic correspondence gathered in proper archives, which form the basis of the published Acta Tomiciana. At his own court of Cracow he created a palace school which became a chief vehicle for the humanistic education of the sons of noble families prior to their enrolment in a university. Frankly elitist in spirit, his school employed foreign humanists as teachers, while Tomicki himself provided funds for gifted youths to study abroad. From 1523 he was also chancellor of the University of Cracow and, indeed, was called the 'maximus fautor' of that institution. In 1531 he decreed that the chair of rhetoric should henceforward be filled by election rather than by seniority, and that the occupant need no longer be a cleric. In 1533 he founded a chair of Roman law. Committed to the humanist ideal of 'trilinguitas,' he encouraged instruction in Greek and Hebrew. He tried to attract to Cracow such luminaries as Erasmus in 1525 (Ep 1652), *Melanchthon in 1530 (Ep 2911), and Lazzaro *Bonamico in 1535 (Cracow, Biblioteka Jagiellońska MS 6554). He induced King Sigismund to promulgate a decree by which a Cracow professor with twenty years of service was automatically raised to noble status.

Being devoted to the advancement of art and science as well as humanistic scholarship, Tomicki extended patronage to his nephew,

the poet Andrzej *Krzycki, the Hebrew scholar Jan van *Campen, the physician Jan *Antonin, and the Grecian Jerzy Liban. In several ways he sought to implement the specific ideals of Erasmus. He suggested that the education of Prince *Sigismund Augustus was to be based on the principles laid down in the Institutio principis christiani; he was also deeply interested in patristic studies and created a centre for their advancement at his court. The scholars responded by dedicating to him such patristic and exegetical works as Jerzy Liban's Antologia sanctorum patrum iussu Tomitii ... collecta (Cracow 1528), Jan van Campen's Proverbia Salomonis (Cracow: M. Scharffenberg 1534), Andrzej Krzycki's Commentarius in psalmum xxi (Cracow: H. Wietor 1527), and Valentinus Polidamus' Oratio in caput quartum Matthaei (Cracow 1531). With Tomicki's support Leonard *Cox published in 1529 his selection of the letters of St Jerome.

In further pursuance of his scholarly ideals Tomicki gathered a library of more than five hundred volumes, purchasing his books systematically through a number of agents and welcoming books as a gift from Polish and foreign dignitaries who wished to secure his good will for their political ends. Thus he obtained books from Albert of Brandenburg, duke of Prussia, and from István *Brodarics, chancellor to John Zápolyai. Apart from juridical, theological, and medical works, Erasmus is represented by many of his writings, some of which, such as a Querela pacis, are copiously annotated by their owner. Also included were some of Erasmus' polemical defences, sometimes received as a gift from the author (Ep 2600); among them were the Declarationes ad censuras Lutetiae and the Apologia adversus rhapsodias Alberti Pii.

Erasmus' contacts with Tomicki were maintained in part through his correspondence with Jan Antonin, Krzycki, and Justus Ludovicus *Decius. In December 1527 Antonin persuaded Erasmus to address his first letter to the bishop (Ep 1919). Although it consists of no more than a few polite lines, it is possible that Tomicki's support of Ferdinand's claims to Hungary had encouraged Erasmus to write. Tomicki's answer (Ep 1953), while equally short, was accompanied by sixty Hungarian ducats (Epp 1997, 2035). In return Erasmus dedicated to Tomicki in January 1529 the second edition of his Seneca (Ep 2091); he also lodged Tomicki's grand-nephew Andrzej *Zebrzydowski as a guest in his house and informed the bishop of Andrzej's progress (Epp 2035, 2173). With the passing of the years the correspondence between Erasmus and Tomicki became more personal and the contents of their letters more significant. They discussed the political situation, with Erasmus paying particular attention to the policies of the house of Hapsburg (Epp 2173, 2713, 2776, 2861, 3000, 3014, 3049); moreover they shared with one another their special concern for religion and the condition of their church (Epp 2173, 2861, 3000, 3049, 3066). They recommended to each other mutual acquaintances and protégés such as Marcin *Słap, Antonin, and Jan *Boner, and Erasmus frequently praised Tomicki in his letters to others (Epp 2176, 2178, 2299). He also dwelt on the state of his health (Epp 2377, 2776, 3000) and his literary undertakings (Epp 2377, 2600, 2776, 3049); both friends lamented the death of close friends; in particular it is in letters addressed to Tomicki that we find Erasmus' reaction to the deaths of *Warham and *More (Epp 2776, 2861, 3049). Erasmus let his friend know that *Paul III proposed to make him a cardinal (Ep 3049), and Tomicki, already on his deathbed, implored him to accept the honour for the sake of the church (Ep 3066). That letter, the last one Tomicki wrote, never reached Erasmus. It was found among the bishop's papers and not dispatched until 9 August 1536, when Erasmus himself had been dead for nearly a month (Ep 3137). He had, however, had the time to express his deep sorrow at the news of Tomicki's death in several letters (Epp 3089, 3095, 3104). The bishop had died at Cracow and was buried on 19 November 1535 in the St Thomas' chapel on the Wawel under a monument created to his own orders by Mario Padovano. Jerzy Liban composed a Sapphicon for the occasion which was sung and also published (Cracow: F. Ungler 1535).

Tomicki's friendship with Erasmus helped to bring about other connections, such as that with Johann *Sichard, who dedicated to Tomicki his edition of Sedulius Scotus' commentary on the epistles of Paul (Basel: H. Petri

1528). Tomicki was also in contact with Johannes *Cochlaeus, who sent the Polish bishop some of his books and wrote to him (Cracow, Biblioteka Jagiellońska MS 6554) about Erasmus, Luther, and *Melanchthon. Cochlaeus' influence was behind Tomicki's support for the royal edict of 4 February 1534 prohibiting Poles from studying at Wittenberg.

BIBLIOGRAPHY: Allen Ep 1919 / Bibliografia polska ed K. Estreicher et al (Cracow 1870–1951) 3rd part XXXI 218–19 / Nowy Korbut Piśmiennictwo staropolskie (Warsaw 1963–5) III 335–9 / H. Barycz Historia Uniwersytetu Jagiellońskiego (Warsaw 1935) 63–7 / S. Hozjusz Vita Petri Tomicki ed F. Hipler and W. Zakrzewski in Stanislai Hosii ... epistolae in Acta historica res gestas Poloniae illustrantia IV (Cracow 1879) clii–clxix and passim / S. Starowolski Vitae antistitum Cracoviensium (Cracow 1655) / F.J. Zacharyasiewicz Vitae episcoporum Premisliensium ritus Latini (Vienna 1844) 46–54 / K. Morawski Beiträge zur Geschichte des Humanismus in Polen in Sitzungsberichte der Kaiserlichen Akademie der Wissenschaften in Wien Phil.-Hist. Classe 118 (1889) / E. Zievier Neuere Geschichte Polens (Gotha 1915) I passim / S. Brzeziński 'Un bibliophile de la Renaissance en Pologne' in La Pologne au VIIe Congrès international des sciences historiques (Warsaw 1933) II / S. Łempicki Biskupi polskiego renesansu (Lwów 1938) / S. Kot Le relazioni secolari della Polonia con Bologna (Bologna 1949) 16–17 / L. Hajdukiewicz Księgozbiór i zainteresowania bibliofilskie Piotra Tomickiego na tle jego działalności kulturalnej (Wrocław-Warsaw 1961) / M. Krzyszkowska-Langertowa Działalność kulturalna P. Tomickiego, biskupa krakowskiego (Lwów 1939) / Korespondencja Erazma z Rotterdamu z Polakami ed and trans M. Cytowska (Warsaw 1965) / Diarius cuiusdam domestici Petri episcopi Cracoviensis ed W. Kętrzyński in Monumenta Poloniae Historica V (Lwów 1888) 897–904 / Acta Tomiciana (Poznań-Wrocław 1852–   ) I–XVI passim / Vetera monumenta Poloniae et Lithuaniae (Rome 1861) II 405ff / Budapest, Nemzeti Museum MS f lat 258 / Cracow, Biblioteka Czartoryskich MS Teki Naruszewicza 46–52

MARIA CYTOWSKA

Robert TONEYS of the diocese of Norwich, d July 1528
Robert Toneys (Tonnes, Tunnys) studied civil

law in Cambridge from 1479 and obtained his bachelor's degree on 16 February 1481. Subsequently he returned to his university to read for a doctorate in civil law in 1506–7. Being a cleric, he accumulated a rich harvest of ecclesiastical preferment, no doubt primarily through the favour of Cardinal *Wolsey, whose service he had entered by 1515 (LP II 336). He was a canon of Sarum and prebendary of Axford from 1494 and subsequently received canonries at Lincoln, Salisbury, and York, not to mention other benefices. He was also an apostolic protonotary.

In letters and documents his name is often associated with that of William *Burbank, another servant of Wolsey (Ep 1138). Toneys seems to have enjoyed the confidence of *Henry VIII as well. In August 1514 he drew up documents regarding the marriage of Princess *Mary Tudor and the peace with France (LP I 3101, 3142, 3146, 3176); in October 1515 he attested a treaty with *Ferdinand II of Aragon (LP II 1076), and in July 1517 one with the Emperor *Maximilian I and the future *Charles V (LP II 3437). He signed other documents as a notary public, and in 1520 he was one of the clerks of the court of chancery (LP III 1083).

Erasmus was personally acquainted with Toneys from his days in England (Ep 1138); in 1524 he sent him a brief complimentary letter (Ep 1492) and two years later greetings in a letter to Stephen *Gardiner (Ep 1745). Toneys died in July 1528 (LP IV 4463, 4592, 6184, pp 2765–6), and in the articles of accusation against Wolsey the cardinal was charged with having appropriated many of Toneys' rich possessions (LP IV 5749, 6075).

BIBLIOGRAPHY: Allen Ep 1138 / Emden BRUC 591 / LP I–IV passim   PGB

Arnold Luyd of TONGEREN d 28 August 1540

Arnold Luyd (van Luyde) was known in Latin as 'Tongrensis' after the city of Tongeren, in the Belgian province of Limburg, where he was born around 1468–70. His family probably came from nearby Lauw. On 2 November 1486 he matriculated at the University of Cologne and thereafter followed the regular course of study in arts and divinity, leading in 1509 to a theological doctorate. In 1513 he received a canonry at the Cologne chapter of St Marien-

graden and continued to serve the university for another twenty years as a professor and sometimes as rector. On 19 July 1533 he was elected to a canonry of the cathedral chapter of St Lambert's in Liège, and by this time he had returned to live permanently in the ecclesiastical principality of which he was a native. As inquisitor Tongeren took an active part in the preparation of an *édit général* against heretics which was published at Liège in 1545, or five years after Tongeren had died there.

During his years at Cologne Tongeren was best known for his part in the controversy around *Reuchlin. On the subject of Jewish mystical literature he published in 1512 (Cologne: heirs of H. Quentel) a *Tractatus propositionum alphabeticarum ... contra Iudaeos* and his *Articuli* listing suspect tenets extracted from Reuchlin's *Augenspiegel* (Ep 543). They prompted Reuchlin to respond with acrimony and secured for Tongeren a place of honour among the conservative theologians opposed to Erasmian humanism. It is thus not surprising that, Tongeren's attacks on Reuchlin apart, Erasmus showed little interest in the 'magister noster' (Epp 543, 1006). On the other hand, Tongeren had friendly ties with many outstanding men, among them Girolamo *Aleandro, Reginald *Pole, Gian Matteo *Giberti, Hubert Thomas, Dirk Loher, Jacob of *Hoogstraten, Hermannus *Buschius, Jan van Brusthem, Johannes *Murmellius, and also Theodoricus *Hezius, whom he appointed executor of his will. That will, dated 15 December 1539, is now in the archives of Liège, where Tongeren died the following year. He published numerous works in the fields of theology, pedagogics, and history. His portrait in ink (never published) is found on a document of 22 August 1549 preserved at Liège (see Poncelet).

BIBLIOGRAPHY: Allen Ep 543 / NDB I 381 / BNB XXV 430–2 / Matrikel Köln II 203 / Ludwig Geiger *Johann Reuchlin* (Leipzig 1871, repr 1964) 257–9, 266–8, 277–8 / J. Hartzheim *Bibliotheca Coloniensis* (Cologne 1750) 25 / L. Ennen *Geschichte der Stadt Köln* (Cologne 1875) IV 287 / N. Paulus *Die deutschen Dominikaner im Kampf gegen Luther* (Freiburg 1903) 95, 119, 122, 133 / F. Pijper *Bibliotheca Reformatoria Neerlandica* (The Hague 1905) III 382–5 / E. Poncelet *Cartulaire de l'Eglise Saint-Lambert à Liège* (Brussels 1893–1933) V 325–326 / J. de Theux *Le Chapitre cathédral de*

Saint-Lambert à Liège (Brussels 1871–4) III 70 /
L.-E. Halkin *Histoire religieuse des règnes de*
Corneille de Berghes et de Georges d'Autriche,
princes-évêques de Liège (Liège-Paris 1936) 109,
349, 375   LÉON-E. HALKIN

Louis de TONNERRE *See Louis de* HUSSON

Albanus TORINUS of Winterthur,
1489–23 February 1550
Torinus (Thorer, zum Thor, Turinus) matriculated at the University of Basel in 1516 and was
a MA in 1522. He taught at St Peter's school and
became a member of the faculty of arts in 1524,
occupying a chair of Latin in 1532. His
ambitions, however, tended to the medical
profession. In the summer of 1527 he studied
with *Paracelsus, and a year later he was a
member of the medical faculty. Early in 1529 he
visited Abbot Pierre de *Mornieu, perhaps in
Savoy on his way to Montpellier (Epp 2084,
2162), to offer him his recently published
translation of Epiphanius (Basel: A. Cratander
1529), which was dedicated to the abbot. By
1529 he had obtained a medical doctorate,
perhaps at Montpellier, where, according to
Allen, he became acquainted with Bishop
Guillaume *Pellicier. In May 1532 he visited
Erasmus in Freiburg and took Ep 2652 back to
Basel. From 1536 he held a chair of medicine at
Basel, and in 1542 he was rector of the
university. He eagerly sought a position as
court physician, and in 1533 he travelled to the
court of Würzburg after having dedicated his
translation of Alexander Trallianus (Basel: H.
Petri 1533) to Bishop Konrad von *Thüngen,
but he soon returned, disappointed in his
hopes (AK IV Epp 1727, 1746). In 1545 he lost
his position at the university for having gone
without leave to the courts of the margrave of
Baden and the dukes of Württemberg at
Montbéliard. Retaining his residence at Basel,
from 1545 to his death he was physician to
Duke Christopher of *Württemberg at Montbéliard. He published several Latin translations of Greek medical works including Paulus
Aegineta (Basel: A. Cratander and J. Bebel
1532), a version criticized by Andrea *Alciati
and others (AK IV Epp 1687, 1697). He also
translated Andreas Vesalius' *Epitome* into
German (Basel: J. Oporinus 1543) and wrote a
German treatise on the plague (Basel: B. Lasius

1539). His edition of Caelius Apicius (Basel
1541) is dedicated to Christopher of
Württemberg.

BIBLIOGRAPHY: Allen Ep 2084 / DHBS VI 553 /
AK III Ep 1396, VI Ep 2830, and passim / *Matrikel*
Basel I 331 / *Basler Chroniken* VIII 218–19 /
Albrecht Burckhardt *Geschichte der medizini-*
schen Fakultät zu Basel (Basel 1917) 38–42
                                                                        PGB

Jean TORNOND d 2 August 1547
Jean Tornond (Tournon), a doctor of civil and
canon law and a canon of Nozeroy, Franche-
Comté, was elected dean of the chapter in
succession to Jean Leclerc, who had died on 29
August 1525. When Jean Tornond was admitted a canon of Besançon on 5 January 1546 and
appointed official to the archbishop, he was
succeeded as dean of Nozeroy by his brother,
Etienne. In 1536 Gilbert *Cousin, himself a
canon at Nozeroy, praised his sincerity and his
determination to learn Greek regardless of his
age and duties (Ep 3123). But in April 1537
Tornond had to answer charges of heresy
before the Parlement of Dole. The investigation
dragged on until 1540, when the Parlement
referred the matter to the emperor's court and
Tornond succeeded in having it terminated at
the price of a journey to the Netherlands. On
the way he met the theologian Gentien Hervet,
who dedicated to him, with the date of 30
November 1540, part of his *Opuscula* (Lyon: E.
Dolet 1541). After his death Tornond was
buried in the cathedral of Besançon. The
Besançon public library owns an incunable
that had belonged to him.

BIBLIOGRAPHY: Allen Ep 3123 / Gilbert Cou-
sin *La Franche-Comté au milieu du* XVI*e siècle* ed
E. Monot (Lons-le-Saunier 1907) 42, 44 / Lucien
Febvre *Notes et documents sur la réforme et*
l'inquisition en Franche-Comté (Paris 1911) 84–5 /
Augustin Castan *Catalogue des incunables de la*
Bibliothèque publique de Besançon (Besançon
1893) 81 / Gauthier 136   PGB

Hermannus TORRENTINUS of Zwolle, died
c 1520
Herman van Beek or van der Beeke, called
Torrentinus, was a native of Zwolle, in the
province of Overijssel, and studied under
Alexander *Hegius at Deventer. He joined the
Brethren of the Common Life and taught at a

school at Groningen and subsequently at Zwolle, where he came under the influence of Wessel *Gansfort. He wrote several small books for use in his school, featuring texts by Virgil and *Sabellico. On Wessel's suggestion he pruned with ruthless severity the first part of Alexander de Villa Dei's standard Latin grammar, the *Doctrinale* (3rd ed Zwolle: A. Kempen 1504). His best-known work, *Elucidarius poeticus*, was published in 1498 (Deventer: R. Pafraet); though valuable in its own time, it did not satisfy the standards of the next generation of humanists. In a letter to Erasmus, Juan Luis *Vives made a contemptuous reference to the work of Torrentinus and *Kempo of Texel, his friend and colleague, who had edited the second part of the *Doctrinale* (Ep 1362).

By 1508 Torrentinus' eyesight was failing; he was succeeded as head of the Zwolle school by Gerardus *Listrius. His close friend Johannes *Murmellius dedicated an edition of *Poliziano's *Rusticus* (Münster: L. Bornemann 1510) to him.

BIBLIOGRAPHY: Allen Ep 1362 / de Vocht CTL I 198–9 / ADB II 245   CFG

Andrea TORRESANI of Asola, 4 March 1451–21 October 1528
Andrea Torresani was born at Asola, near Mantua, hence the frequent application of the name Asulanus to both himself and his sons. Andrea came to Venice at some time in the late 1470s, possibly learnt the printing trade with Nicolas Jenson, whose types he had acquired by 1482 (colophon to Panormitanus' commentaries on Books IV and V of the *Decretals*), and was operating independently by 1479. He printed 160 editions during the period up to his final merger with Aldo *Manuzio in 1507. The majority of these were on academic subjects such as law (53%), philosophy (23%), and Latin literature (9%), and found a stable market at nearby universities. From the fact that he was able to invest some thousands of ducats in Aldus' enterprise in 1495 and to enter more limited contracts with five other printers, we may assume that the humanists' view of Andrea as a successful and hard-bitten entrepreneur was close to the truth.

From 1495 until 1505 the partnership with Aldus was commercial only, and was marked by tensions which in some ways anticipate Erasmus' later attack on Andrea. By 1503 he seems to have been intervening more directly in the day-to-day operation of the company (preface to Origen's sermons, Renouard *Annales* I 1503, no 11), and this generated some resentment (Nolhac Ep 42). His concern for costs appears in a report of 1505 which shows his refusal to accept further responsibility for the sale of Aldine Greek texts (*Pirckheimer Briefwechsel* I Ep 86). But after Aldus' marriage to Maria, Torresani's daughter, and the fusion of the partners' assets in 1506 the alliance was never shaken. Aldus spoke of Andrea with both respect and affection in his will, and after Aldus' death Andrea declared that he would follow the same editorial program (preface to Ptolemy, Renouard, *Annales* I 1516, no 10). He adopted the symbol of the dolfin and anchor immediately (Ep 450).

During his visit to Venice in 1508 Erasmus lodged at Andrea's house in San Paternian, and both at that time and later relations between them were distant but cordial. Erasmus was paid promptly for editorial services (Ep 212) and was invited in the most friendly terms to return at any time or to send his writings (Epp 450, 628). In 1517 he still regarded Torresani as a possible alternative to Johann *Froben as his regular printer (Ep 628) and sent formal greetings to him via several other correspondents (Epp 611, 868, 1592, 1707, 1746). But though there is no sign of an open quarrel with Erasmus, it is plain that Andrea's reputation for greed and lack of sympathy with pure scholarship was widespread: Giambattista *Egnazio apparently referred to it in 1517 (Ep 588), and even when writing to Gianfrancesco *Torresani, Andrea's son, Erasmus commented that Andrea was kinder in deeds than in words (Ep 1592). In 1535 Paolo *Manuzio openly reproached the Torresani for their failure to maintain the standards set by Aldus (Pastorello Ep 288). We have no means of checking Erasmus' estimate that Andrea was worth eighty thousand ducats (ASD I-3 625), but it is significant that Sanudo noted his 'immense wealth' in his notice of the printer's death on 21 October 1528 (Sanudo *Diarii* XLIX 79).

Erasmus' posthumous attack on Andrea, who was pilloried as the grasping 'Antronius' of the colloquy *Opulentia sordida* in 1531, cannot, therefore, be seen as part of a personal vendetta and involves few problems of reconciliation with the earlier account of the Aldine circle in the *Adagia* (II i 1) of 1508. Erasmus probably composed the colloquy in response to the hostility of one or two Italians once loosely attached to the Aldine group (Girolamo *Aleandro, Alberto *Pio). Torresani was a convenient target for the riposte because he had long been unpopular even among the Italian humanists, and Erasmus had only to add a few superficial details like the sour wine, the limp lettuce, and the shellfish from the latrines (ASD I-3 676–85). The background of his description of the household – thirty people working with no more than half an hour's break until after ten o'clock at night – still conveys the same impression of industry as that presented in the *Adagia*.

BIBLIOGRAPHY: Allen Ep 212 / Numerous references to Torresani can be found in the collections of documents relating to Aldus, especially A.-A. Renouard *Annales de l'imprimerie des Alde* 3rd ed (Paris 1834, repr 1953); P. de Nolhac 'Les correspondants d'Alde Manuce' *Studi e documenti di storia e diritto* 8 (1887) 247–300, 9 (1888) 203–48; E. Pastorello *L'epistolario Manuziano* (Florence 1957); and *Aldo Manuzio, editore* ed G. Orlandi (Milan 1976) / For specific treatment of Andrea and his family see D. Bernoni *Dei Torresani, Blado e Ragazzoni, celebri stampatori a Venezia e Roma nel XV e XVI secolo* (Milan 1890, repr 1968); C.F. Bühler 'Some documents concerning the Torresani and the Aldine press' *The Library* 4th ser 25 (1945) 111–21   M.J.C. LOWRY

Frederico TORRESANI of Venice,
d 24 January 1561
Frederico was the younger son of Andrea *Torresani and the husband of Aldo *Manuzio's sister Paola. Frederico took little direct part in running the family business, being more eager to enjoy its benefits: on 28 March 1523 he was exiled from Venice for four years and fined a total of twelve hundred ducats for cheating at cards, a fact which was presumably known to Erasmus when he accused Andrea Torresani's sons of leading dissipated lives (ASD I-3 685). Frederico returned to Venice in 1527, took some indirect part in publishing both with his

brother and with Paolo *Manuzio, and died in 1561 as a comparatively rich man, able to bequeath a dowry of five thousand ducats to each of his two daughters. Erasmus twice sent greetings to him (Epp 1592, 1746), but both occasions fell during his period of exile and the relationship was purely formal.

BIBLIOGRAPHY: See under Andrea Torresani / Also C. Marciani 'Il testamento e altre notizie di Frederico Torresani' *La Bibliofilia* 73 (1971) 165–78   M.J.C. LOWRY

Gianfrancesco TORRESANI of Venice,
d after 1557
Gianfrancesco, the elder son and successor of Andrea *Torresani, was probably born during the early 1480s. Perhaps trained partly by Aldo *Manuzio, Gianfrancesco became a far better scholar than his father: his solid knowledge of Greek and Latin is documented in a number of surviving texts (Paris, Bibliothèque Nationale, Imprimés rés. Yb 484, Ms. gr. 1848, carry his signature). But in his dealings with intellectuals Gianfrancesco showed all his father's tactlessness. After reprinting Erasmus' Greek text of the New Testament in 1518 (Ep 770) he apparently complained about the monopoly of every revised edition of the *Adagia* which Johann *Froben had enjoyed since the Aldine text of 1508; but when Erasmus sent him a corrected copy of the most recent edition in 1523, he ignored it (Epp 1349, 1592). The incident seems to have been taken more seriously by *Casembroot and *Lupset (Epp 1594, 1595) than by Erasmus himself, who was soon pacified by a gift of the newly printed volumes of Galen (Epp 1623, 1628, 1746). But though still outwardly polite to Gianfrancesco, Erasmus refused to oblige him by taking care of some Italian students (Ep 1989) and was savagely critical of the text of Galen (Ep 1707). After his father's death Gianfrancesco quarrelled with Aldus' son and successor Paolo *Manuzio over the right to use the company's types. A temporary compromise was achieved, and they collaborated from 1534 until 1539 under the title of 'heirs of Aldus and Andrea'; then the company was dissolved and its assets liquidated over the next few years. From this moment Gianfrancesco's concern with printing was indirect and restricted to underwriting the editions of Antonio Niccolini or Paolo Manu-

zio. Bernoni dated his death to 1546, but a notarial act of 1557 shows that he was still active in business at that time (Marciani 168). In spite of his undoubted services in continuing the Aldine program of Greek publications both as printer and editor, Gianfrancesco seems to have been blighted by his father's reputation and received only the most formal tributes from contemporary intellectuals.

BIBLIOGRAPHY: Allen Ep 212 / Other information from the works of Bernoni, Bühler, and Marciani cited under Andrea and Frederico Torresani   M.J.C. LOWRY

Giovanni TORTELLI of Arezzo, d 26 April 1466

Giovanni Tortelli was born to Iacopo di Giovanni and Tita di Bartolomeo di messer Baldovinetto in Arezzo about 1400. He took a doctorate in medicine in 1433 and spent time in Florence as a client of the Strozzi. After a trip to Constantinople (1435–7), he entered papal service under the patronage of Cardinal Giuliano Cesarini. In 1449 he was part of the 'familia' of Pope *Nicholas v, with whom he co-operated in the establishment of the Vatican library. His most famous work was the erudite *Orthographia* (1449); he also translated classical and patristic Greek writings.

Erasmus mentioned Tortelli in the *Ciceronianus* (ASD I-2 661), where he is compared unfavourably with Petrarch.

BIBLIOGRAPHY: EI XXXIV 71 / Cosenza IV 3436–9 / M. Regoliosi 'Nuove ricerche intorno a Giovanni Tortelli: La vita ... ' *Italia medioevale e umanistica* 10 (1969) 129–96 / Maria Donata Rinaldi 'Fortuna e diffusione del *De Orthographia* di Giovanni Tortelli' *Italia medioevale e umanistica* 11 (1973) 227–61 / Alex Keller 'A Renaissance humanist looks at "new" inventions: the article "Horologius" in Giovanni Tortelli's *De Orthographia' Technology and Culture* 11 (1970) 345–65   JOHN F. D'AMICO

TOSSANUS See Jacques, Nicolas, and Pierre TOUSSAIN

François de TOURNON 1489–22 April 1562

François was the son of Jacques II, seigneur de Tournon (a Turnone), and of Jeanne de Polignac. The château of Tournon, where he was probably born, is eighteen kilometres north of Valence, on the right bank of the Rhone. As a younger son he was destined for the church and entered the abbey of Saint-Antoine-de-Viennois at the age of twelve. Confided by Boniface VIII to the Augustinian canons regular, this had become the mother house of an order of hospitallers whose commanderies and leprosaria were spread over a wide area. Tournon's career began with his appointment as head of a commandery, and then of an abbey. In the course of his life, he was abbot of some twenty-eight abbeys, all *in commendam*. In 1543 he became abbot-general of the order of St Anthony. Even more spectacular was his rise in the ranks of the secular clergy. He was archbishop of Embrun (1518–26), of Bourges (1526–38), of Auch (1538–51), and of Lyon (1551–62). The last office made him primate of Gaul and head of the episcopal hierarchy of the realm. In 1530 he was made cardinal by *Clement VII. As bishop of Sabina (1550) and Ostia (1560), he became dean of the Sacred College.

Erasmus saw Tournon repeatedly in Basel when the latter was there on an otherwise undocumented mission (Allen Ep 1342:550–5), which must have been towards the end of 1521 or early in 1522. Erasmus found him a 'iuvenis humanissimus.' Later in the year, Tournon, in association with Germain de *Brie, Guillaume *Budé, and Nicolas *Bérault, used his influence with *Francis I to obtain a passport for Erasmus to visit France. Erasmus expressed his gratitude in the one extant letter to Tournon (Ep 1319, 10 November 1522). Though the projected visit to France never took place, the letter shows that Tournon was at this time moving in the humanist circle around Francis I.

Tournon's loyalty to the crown was tested in 1523 by the conspiracy of Charles II, duke of Bourbon, but though the Tournons were his vassals, they remained loyal to the king. When Francis was captured at Pavia and taken prisoner to Spain, Tournon was sent by the regent, Louise of *Savoy, to negotiate his release (28 April 1525). It was while Tournon was in Spain that Louise, with the support of her daughter, *Margaret of Angoulême, future queen of Navarre, secured his election as archbishop of Bourges (5 June 1525). Having been a member of the council advising the regent during the king's absence, he became a

member of the king's council on his return to
France and retained this position during the
rest of Francis' life.

Tournon took a public stance on the issue of
reform for the first time as president of the
provincial council of Bourges (1527). Its decrees required parish priests to report Lutheran heretics, witches, and others engaged in
superstitious practices to their bishop and
forbad booksellers to possess, print, or sell
Lutheran books or any sacred works translated
into French during the past eight years. Such
measures seem relatively mild when compared
with the language of zealous extermination
issued by the council of Sens, meeting at the
same time under the presidency of Archbishop
Antoine *Duprat. In the summer of 1529
Tournon was a member of the French delegation which negotiated the peace of Cambrai
(signed on 5 August). The efforts which he and
Jean de *Selve had undertaken together as
ambassadors to Spain during the king's captivity to preserve Burgundy and the integrity of
France were thus finally realized.

In 1530 Tournon obtained the cardinal's hat
which Louise had been seeking on his behalf.
Her appreciation of him also found expression
when the Louvre was remodelled: a door was
cut to permit direct access from his room to
hers.

By 1535 Tournon was committed to the battle
against heresy, which he pursued at first,
however, with relative moderation. He recommended Mathieu Ory for appointment as
inquisitor-general and worked closely with
him in the years that followed. Being responsible for Lyon, Tournon put *Rabelais under
surveillance but, in deference to Margaret, did
not ask for his imprisonment. It was before
Tournon that Clément Marot had to abjure his
heresy, but according to François (p 459), the
role of Tournon was to reduce the abjuration to
a formality. By 1552 his attitude seems to have
become less moderate. Five Protestant students from Bern who were arrested as they
passed through Lyon were convicted of
heresy. As archbishop of Lyon Tournon
opposed appeals in their favour, and they
were burnt (16 May 1553). This case prompted
a citizen of Geneva to taunt Tournon with
harbouring a far more dangerous heretic
within his jurisdiction in the person of Michael

François de Tournon

*Servetus. Servetus was prosecuted by Ory
and would have been burnt in Vienne had he
not escaped to Geneva only to be burnt there.

Tournon had been out of favour at court
since the death of Francis I in 1547, but he
secured the recognition of *Henry II for his
services to the crown while resident in Rome.
Tournon was personally responsible for persuading the Sienese to place themselves under
the protection of France and to drive the
Spaniards out of their city (1551–2). By 1559,
however, he had become an advocate of a
Catholic peace which would enable Philip II
and Henry II to pursue the growing danger of
heresy in their respective territories. In 1560
Tournon supported the appeal of Pius IV for a
crusade against Geneva with the aid of Philip II
and in the interest of Emmanuel Philibert of
Savoy – the victors at Saint-Quentin. Until this
point Tournon had above all been a loyal
servant of the king's cause, but now the
politique had yielded to the partisan. He had
come a long way since his battles against the
Spaniard in Madrid and in Siena.

When it was proposed to hold a national
council of the church, Tournon fought strenu-

JAMES TUSSAN.

Jacques Toussain

ously against what he and Rome saw as a threat of schism. He agreed to attend the colloquy of Poissy (July 1561), but only as a preparation for the resumption of the general council at Trent. As primate of Gaul he presided over the colloquy and put to the vote the articles refuting the Calvinist position (9 October 1561). In 1550 he put his abbey of St Germain-des-Prés at the disposal of the Jesuits for the administration of the sacraments, although their entry into Paris was opposed by the bishop, the university, and the Parlement. The college which he had founded in Tournon in 1536 was turned over to them in January 1560. A supporter of humane letters throughout his life, Tournon did not share the university's jealousy towards a rival system of education. As a diplomat who had found service to the pope compatible with service to his king, Tournon was not troubled, as were so many defenders of the Gallican liberties, by the special oath Jesuits took to the pope.

BIBLIOGRAPHY: Allen Ep 1319 / Michel François *Le Cardinal François de Tournon* (Paris 1951) / *Correspondance du cardinal François de Tournon, 1521–1562* ed Michel François (Paris 1946) /

Gallia christiana I 1002–3 / *Sacrorum conciliorum nova et amplissima collectio* ed J.D. Mansi et al (Florence etc 1759–1962) XXXII 1141–8 for the council of Bourges / R.H. Bainton *Hunted Heretic: The Life and Death of Michael Servetus* (Boston 1953) 250 and passim

GORDON GRIFFITHS

Jacques TOUSSAIN d 15 March 1547
Jacques Toussain (Tusanus) was born in the diocese of Troyes and is documented in Paris from 1513. While completing his course of studies at the university with a MA received in 1521, he taught privately and for some years was living in the house of Louis *Ruzé, apparently until 1524 (Ep 810; Delaruelle Epp 84, 153). He was a student of Fausto *Andrelini and became a disciple, correspondent, and lifelong friend of Guillaume *Budé, who may have hoped to see him associated with the royal college as professor of Greek ever since plans for such an institution were discussed with *Francis I (Delaruelle Epp 77, 84). By 1526 such an appointment had been promised to Toussain (Ep 1842), and after a spell in the service of Ludovico *Canossa in 1529 (Ep 2421), the royal appointment materialized in 1530. Despite repeated difficulties (Epp 2421, 2810), it continued until Toussain's death, which occurred on the same day and in the same hour (AK VI Ep 2918) as that of François *Vatable, his colleague. His successor in this position was the famous Adrien Turnèbe.

From 1513 several books produced by the printer Josse *Bade reflect Toussain's association with his press. Moreover, in 1526 Bade published Toussain's own *Flosculi* gathered from Budé's *De contemptu rerum fortuitarum*, and probably in the same year his *Annotata* to Budé's letters. Toussain's name is also associated with a *Lexicon graecolatinum*, first published in 1552 (Paris: C. Guillard and G. Merlin), a Greek edition of Epictetus published in the same year (Paris: M. Le Jeune), and an edition of Janus *Lascaris' Greek epigrams (Paris: J. Bogard 1544), while a 1553 edition of Proclus' *Sphaera* included his annotations (Paris: M. Le Jeune).

In the light of their correspondence it does not appear that Toussain would have arrived in Paris early enough to meet Erasmus in person; he may, though, have known Erasmus' younger friend Henricus *Glareanus, who went to Paris in 1517, and seems to have corresponded with him too (Ep 2449). Known as a member of Budé's circle as well as the group of Erasmus' admirers in Paris (Epp 1407, 2340), Toussain was encouraged to write to Erasmus in 1518 (Ep 810), and their correspondence is preserved, with many gaps (Epp 1794, 1812, 2449), for the years 1526–31. In the first of these letters (Ep 1713) Erasmus suggested that Ciceronianism was threatening Budé's lifework as well as his own, but the publication of Erasmus' *Ciceronianus* in 1528 prompted Toussain to defend Budé's reputation with a Latin couplet which found wide circulation (printed in McNeil 72–3). Erasmus quickly came to believe that this attack had been far more consequential (Epp 2077, 2119, 2223, 2291) and also learnt about a number of specific instances in which Toussain had disagreed with him over Greek passages (Ep 2291). Germain de *Brie, a common friend, finally persuaded him that Toussain's offence was slight and that he deserved to be forgiven (Epp 2340, 2379). In the last preserved letter in 1531 Erasmus informed Toussain of the progress of the Collegium Trilingue in Louvain, the aims of which were comparable with those of the royal college in Paris (Ep 2449).

BIBLIOGRAPHY: Allen Ep 810 / Louis Delaruelle *Répertoire ... de la correspondance de Guillaume Budé* (Toulouse-Paris 1907) Epp 14, 77, 84, 153 / David O. McNeil *Guillaume Budé and Humanism in the Reign of Francis I* (Geneva 1975) 72–4 and passim / Rice *Prefatory Epistles* Ep 98 / E.V. Telle *L'Erasmianus sive Ciceronianus d'Etienne Dolet* (Geneva 1974) 59, 69, and passim / M.-M. de la Garanderie *Christianisme et lettres profanes (1515–1535)* (Lille-Paris 1976) I 95 and passim / Renaudet *Préréforme* 475, 640   PGB

Nicolas TOUSSAIN d 5 August 1520
Nicolas was an uncle of Pierre *Toussain, whom he supported during his studies and travels. He was a canon at Metz and from 22 November 1505 to his death was *primicerius*, presiding over the chapter. During his presidency Pierre too received a canonry in 1515. Nicolas died in Rome, where he had gone as a representative of Cardinal Jean de *Lorraine; his funeral monument in the church of

Sant'Onofrio was erected by Pierre and another relative.

There is also another Nicolas Toussain, a canon of Metz from 1522 to 1534.

Erasmus wrote to Toussain and the chapter of Metz in July 1519 requesting a catalogue of their rich library (Ep 997).

BIBLIOGRAPHY: Allen Ep 997 / John Viénot *Histoire de la Réforme dans le pays de Montbéliard* (Montbéliard 1900) I 40, 43 / *Gallia christiana* XIII 809 / V. Forcella *Iscrizioni delle chiese ... di Roma* (Rome 1869–84) V 300   PGB

Pierre TOUSSAIN of Saint-Laurent, 1499–5 October 1573
Pierre Toussain (Tossanus, Toussaint), the son of Jean or Richard, was born at Saint-Laurent, near Marville (Arondissement de Montmédy), on the northern border of Lorraine. He registered at the University of Basel in 1514–15 and later visited Cologne, Paris, and Rome, presumably for study. In 1515 he received a canonry at Metz, where his uncle, Nicolas *Toussain, presided over the chapter. After some quiet years at Metz he reappeared at Basel in 1524, living with Johannes *Oecolampadius (Ep 1559; cf Allen Ep 1538:50, ASD IX-1 394–6) and, like Oecolampadius, committed to radical opposition to the papal church, although in the course of many conversations he managed to persuade Erasmus that he was not a Lutheran (Ep 1559). At the insistence of his fellow canons he returned to Metz at the end of February 1525 but was thwarted in his efforts to preach in the new fashion. Disorders resulted (Ep 1559), and he returned to Basel once more, persuading Erasmus to complain to Cardinal Jean de *Lorraine about the way Toussain was treated in Metz. After another unfortunate experience at Metz in the company of Guillaume *Farel, he set out for Paris in October, provided with introductions from Erasmus, whom he had persuaded that his purpose was advanced study of the Greek language (Epp 1618, 1619). Throughout this period he managed to retain a degree of familiarity with Erasmus as well as Farel and Oecolampadius by supplying each with suitably offensive information about the others (ASD IX-1 394–6; Herminjard I Epp 121, 157, p 299), and he succeeded so well in this extraordinary role that in the end nobody bore him a grudge.

On his way to Paris or while returning from there to Lorraine, he was captured by the ecclesiastical authorities in February 1526 and imprisoned in Pont-à-Mousson. On his release he made his way to the French court at Angoulême (June 1526), where he met *Margaret of Angoulême, soon to be queen of Navarre, who showed him many favours, as did *Lefèvre d'Etaples and other members of the Meaux circle whom he promptly denounced for lack of courage. In February 1528 Erasmus knew that he was still attached to Margaret's entourage, was frequently in Paris, and enjoyed friendly relations with Louis de *Berquin (Ep 2042), about whose imprudent zeal he may have been warning Erasmus (Ep 2048).

Oecolampadius and Farel encouraged him many times to return to Switzerland, but not before the summer of 1531 did he leave France for good, first visiting *Zwingli at Zürich and then Farel at Grandson. Between 1532 and 1535 he was again in Basel, living with Simon *Grynaeus and complaining bitterly of his reduced circumstances. As soon as the French returned the county of Montbéliard to its rightful owner, Duke Ulrich of *Württemberg, Toussain was sent there in July 1535 to organize a Protestant church for the new governor, Count Georg von Württemberg. In preparation he had travelled to Tübingen, where he found Grynaeus in close contact with Duke Ulrich and also met Ambrosius *Blarer.

The remainder of Toussain's life was intricately connected with religious and political changes in the county of Montbéliard. Steering a moderately Calvinistic course, he was well aware of the need for compromise imposed on the one hand by the Lutheran faith of the Württemberg rulers and on the other by the growing militancy of the county's Catholic neighbours. In 1539 he married Jeanne Trinquatte, whose father was a respected barber of Montbéliard. In 1545, after another short exile at Basel, he met with Duke Ulrich, who now ruled personally in Montbéliard, and once more negotiated a modus vivendi for his church. The burning of Michael *Servetus at Geneva in 1553 led to vigorous protests on the part of Toussain which cast a lasting shadow on the relations between the churches of Montbéliard and Geneva. In 1571 the Calvinist principles finally had to yield to Lutheranism, partly because of the excessive zeal with which they were defended by Toussain's son, Daniel, and the father himself was induced to retire. He died at Montbéliard.

Toussain was an untiring correspondent; in addition to the hundreds of letters published by Herminjard and Viénot, many remain in manuscript at Basel, addressed mostly to his friends at Riquewihr, Matthias Erb and Sigismund Stier.

BIBLIOGRAPHY: Allen Ep 1559 / Herminjard passim / John Viénot Histoire de la Réforme dans le pays de Montbéliard (Montbéliard 1900) / Calvini opera ed G. Baum et al (Braunschweig 1863–1900) xx Ep 4166 and passim / Correspondance de Thédore de Bèze ed H. Aubert et al (Geneva 1960–   ) I Ep 58 and passim / AK VII Ep 3093, VIII Ep 3465, and passim / Matrikel Basel I 323 / BA Oekolampads I 293–4 and passim / Basler Chroniken VIII 236–7 and passim / P.G. Bietenholz Basle and France in the Sixteenth Century (Geneva-Toronto 1971) 93–4, 244–6, and passim / E. Droz Chemins de l'hérésie (Geneva 1970–6) II 331, 341, and passim / Öffentliche Bibliothek of the University of Basel MSS Ki.Ar. 22a, 25c etc   PGB

Bernardino TOVAR of Toledo, c 1490–c 1545
Bernadino Tovar was a half-brother of Juan, Francisco, and Isabel de *Vergara, all children of the same mother and in part at least of Jewish descent. Bernardino attended the universities of Alcalá and Salamanca, where he studied law in 1510. In Salamanca he joined the circle of devoted disciples around Francisca Hernández until 1524, when Juan de Vergara prevailed upon him to leave her. Instead he joined the following of María Cazalla, who from her home in Guadalajara exercised a passing influence upon the Erasmian churchmen of Alcalá, where Tovar was now residing. From 1525 he was at the centre of Castilian Erasmianism, maintaining on every occasion that the true service of God was inward and spiritual. In Alcalá he lived in the house of Juan de Vergara, which according to Bataillon he transformed into a sort of private academy devoted to evangelical humanism and unencumbered by the constraints regulating a university. No direct correspondence between Erasmus and Tovar has come to light, but

Erasmus was well aware of his great debt to Tovar (Ep 1875) and sent him greetings and compliments when writing to Juan de Vergara (Epp 1885, 2253). At least one exchange of letters between them has been lost (Ep 2004, 2133).

On 2 December 1529 Tovar was questioned for the first time by the Inquisition. On 27 July 1530 Francisca Hernández began to give testimony against him, charging him with heresy, and in September he was imprisoned by the Inquisition of Toledo (Epp 2932, 2965). For the humanists and Erasmians of Alcalá this was the signal to disband their circle. The record of Tovar's trial is lost, but in the course of the proceedings, which dragged on until October 1541, Juan de Vergara also was arrested in June 1533. It seems that in the end Tovar was compelled to abjure de vehementi (under strong suspicion of heresy, rather than as a notorious heretic) and to do penance for a stipulated period.

BIBLIOGRAPHY: Allen Ep 1814 / Bataillon Erasmo y España 177–80 and passim / Diccionario de historia eclesiástica de España ed Quintín Aldea Vaquero et al (Madrid 1972–5) IV 2587–92 / Eduard Boehmer Franzisca Hernández und Frai Franzisco Ortiz; Anfänge reformatorischer Bewegungen in Spanien unter Kaiser Karl V. (Leipzig 1865) / J.E. Longhurst 'Alumbrados, Erasmistas y Luteranos en el proceso de Juan de Vergara' Cuadernos de Historia de España 27–38 (1958–63) (for pages see Juan de Vergara) MILAGROS RIVERA

Johann TRACH See Johannes DRACONITES

Maximilianus TRANSSILVANUS d before 18 November 1538
Maximilianus Transsilvanus (Transsylvanus) should not be confused with Maximiliaan van *Bergen, heer van Zevenbergen (d 1522), whose name is also rendered 'Transsilvanus' in Latin. Nothing certain is known as yet about his origins. It is not impossible that he was, in fact, a native of Transylvania. His learning was later to impress both Erasmus and Alfonso de *Valdés, but again it is not known where he received his education, except that at one time Matthäus *Lang, the future archbishop of Salzburg, persuaded Pietro Martire d'Anghiera (Anglerius) to be his teacher. The first

known fruits of his literary talent can be traced to the diet of Constance in 1507: his moralizing poem Ad puellas Constantienses in conventu imperiali was later published in Ranutius Gherus (that is, Janus Gruterus) Delitiae centum poetarum belgicorum (Frankfurt 1614) IV 449–53. He is also mentioned in the preface of Heinrich *Bebel's Opuscula nova (Strasbourg: J. Grüninger 1508). By that time Transsilvanus must already have been employed in the imperial chancery, where he rose to the rank of permanent secretary and councillor to *Maximilian I. In 1511 he participated in an embassy to England and the following year he went to Italy, presumably on another diplomatic mission for his master. In 1515 he was secretary to Matthäus Lang, and by 1519 he was again a member of the imperial chancery.

On 30 November 1519 *Charles V received in Molins del Rey an embassy of German princes led by Frederick II, elector *Palatine, which had come to announce formally his election to the imperial throne. Transsilvanus, who was an eye-witness to the event, gathered a small collection of relevant documents, which he dedicated to his colleague Jean *Lalemand: Legatio ad ... Caesarem divum Carolum ... (Augsburg: S. Grimm and M. Wirsung 1519). When Charles V departed for Flanders and subsequently Germany, Transsilvanus was in the emperor's train. During the diet of Worms in 1521 it was his task to read out in the session of 17 April the titles of *Luther's works. He also edited an oration on the Turkish peril, which Girolamo *Balbi had given before the assembled estates of the empire: Oratio habita in imperiali conventu ... per inclyti regis Hungariae et Bohemiae oratores (n p, n d). The most notable of Transsilvanus' works was composed the following year. At the beginning of September 1522 the survivors of Magellan's expedition returned to Valladolid, under the command of Sebastian del Cano, having completed the first circumnavigation of the globe. Transsilvanus had returned to Spain with the emperor's court; he took advantage of his kinship with Christobal de Haro, who had in part financed Magellan's expedition, and subjected the crew to a thorough questioning. The result was his valuable report on this expedition, published in the form of a letter addressed to Matthäus Lang: De Moluccis insulis ... ad reverendissimum *cardinalem Saltzburgensem epistola* (Cologne: E. Cervicornus 1523). It aroused considerable interest and was reprinted several times. In addition Transsilvanus is sometimes credited with having designed a new globe, but this remains a matter of controversy.

Shortly after 1523 Transsilvanus left Spain for the Netherlands, where he spent his remaining years in the service of *Margaret of Austria and *Mary of Hungary, who entrusted him with a number of important diplomatic missions. For some years Diego *Gracián de Alderete was his secretary (Ep 1913). In 1530 he lost his first wife, Francisca, a daughter of the Spanish financier Diego de Haro. Thereafter he married Catherine de Mol, with whom he had two daughters, Jeanne and Marie. His considerable wealth enabled him to build a fine palace in Brussels as well as acquiring in 1522 the castle and lordship of Houtem, south of Ghent, and later, in 1537, the castle and lordship of Bouchout, near Brussels, for which he paid twenty-one thousand florins. At Bouchout he undertook an ambitious program of renovations and improvements but died before it was completed. On 18 November 1538 his two daughters entered into the inheritance.

It appears likely that Transsilvanus and Erasmus met in 1521 when the humanist was attending the court of Charles v. There is evidence of correspondence between them from the time of Transsilvanus' settlement in the Netherlands (Ep 1431). Three letters by Erasmus dating from 1525 have been preserved (Epp 1553, 1585, 1645), as well as two from Transsilvanus, written in 1527 (Epp 1802, 1897). These letters, and also some references in Erasmus' correspondence with others, show that Transsilvanus joined Alfonso de Valdés in repeated efforts to secure the payment of Erasmus' annuity from the imperial court and that he supported Erasmus in his conflicts with conservative theologians, especially the doctors of Louvain. Among their common friends was Cornelius *Agrippa of Nettesheim (Ep 2626), who dedicated his *De nobilitate et praecellentia foeminei sexus declamatio* to Margaret of Austria and Transsilvanus in 1529.

It is not known whether another member of the imperial chancery, *Martinus Sydonius

Transsylvanus, was connected with Maximilianus.

BIBLIOGRAPHY: Allen Ep 1553 / Alphonse Roersch in BNB XXV 521–7 / de Vocht *Literae ad Craneveldium* 167 / de Vocht CTL II 441 and passim / Bataillon *Erasmo y España* 231, 247, and passim / Alphonse Roersch 'Maximilien Transsylvanus, humaniste et secrétaire de Charles-Quint' *Bulletins de la classe des lettres de l'Académie royale de Belgique* 5th series 14 (1928) 94–112 / Alphonse Roersch 'Nouvelles indications concernant Maximilien Transsylvanus' *Revue belge de philologie et d'histoire* 7 (1928) 871–9   ALBRECHT LUTTENBERGER

Andreas von TRAUTMANNSDORF
last documented in 1556

The author of Ep 2398 (19 October 1530), who had probably gone to Augsburg to attend the diet, is most likely Andreas (III) von Trautmannsdorf, of the branch of that noble family established at Kirchberg, near Grafendorf, fifty kilometres north-east of Graz. There were, however, several namesakes. Born around 1500, Andreas (III) was a nephew of another Andreas, who rose to be dean of Salzburg (*Matrikel Wien* II-1 193); he was himself steward for the archbishop of Salzburg at Leibnitz in Styria and later cellarer of Styria. His brother, Wilhelm, who was a canon and eventually dean of Salzburg, seems to have taken an interest in humanistic learning.

BIBLIOGRAPHY: Allen Ep 2398 / Constant von Wurzbach *Biographisches Lexikon des Kaiserthums Österreich* (Vienna 1856–91) XLVII 64–5 (genealogical tables) / The information given above was supplied by Frau Dr Schuller and Professor Hermann Wiesflecker, University of Graz

Jan de TRAZEGNIES *See Johann POPPENRUYTER*

George of TREBIZOND of Heraklion, 3 April 1395–c 1472

Although his name recalls the original home of his great-great-grandfather, George of Trebizond (Georgius Trapezuntius) was born at Heraklion (Candia) in Crete, then under Venetian rule. Francesco Barbaro brought him to Venice, probably in April 1416, to serve as

Greek scribe for his new humanistic library,
and helped him to study Latin under Guarino
*Guarini of Verona and Vittorino da Feltre. In
1420, having become a Venetian citizen,
George took a Cretan bride, Galitia, who was
to bear him at least two sons, Andrea and
Jacopo, and five daughters. After spending
some time in Vicenza, George apparently went
back to Crete, perhaps as a Venetian official. In
1426 he returned to Italy, converted to Roman
Catholicism, and began teaching Latin publicly
at Vicenza. Late in 1427 he was expelled from
Vicenza because, he claimed, Guarino resented another school so close to his own at
Verona.

George taught privately in Venice until 1437,
with the exception of helping Vittorino da
Feltre in his school at Mantua in 1431 and 1432.
In Venice George composed the first comprehensive Renaissance treatise on rhetoric, notable for its use of Greek sources. However,
George's criticism in the *Rhetoricorum libri v* of
the style of Guarino led to a quarrel in 1437
with Andreas Agasus, purportedly a student
of Guarino but perhaps a pseudonym for
Guarino himself.

Recommended to Pope Eugenius IV by his
patron Barbaro and his former student Pietro
Barbo, the future Pope Paul II, in May 1437
George moved to Bologna, where the papal
court was in residence for the council of union
with the Greeks. After the court moved to
Ferrara early in 1438, George spent two years
at Bagno di Romagna as tutor to the children of
Gherardo Gambacorta of Pisa, dedicating to his
pupil Pietro his influential *Isagoge dialectica*, a
manual of simplified logic for the orator. By
mid-1440 George had joined the council again
at Florence. Vespasiano da Bisticci reported his
success teaching Greek and Latin there in both
public and private (*Le Vite* ed A. Greco,
Florence 1970, I 554). By 1441 George had
become a scriptor in the curia, as would his son
Andrea in 1442. In 1443 he moved with the
papal court to Rome and was sworn in as
apostolic secretary on 7 February 1444.

At Rome George continued teaching, but in
1450 Lorenzo *Valla began giving rival lectures
in rhetoric in order, he claimed in *Antidotum II*,
to defend Quintilian against George's censure.
After a lively six-month contest, George

George of Trebizond

withdrew from teaching, in part perhaps
because his energies were absorbed by his
Latin translations of Aristotle, Demosthenes,
Plato, Ptolemy, and the Greek Fathers Basil,
Gregory of Nyssa, John Chrysostom, Eusebius, Cyril of Alexandria, and Gregory of
Nazianzus. George had begun this work in the
early 1440s, encouraged by Cardinal *Bessa-
rion, who about 1442 had dedicated George's
translation of Basil's *Contra Eunomium* to Pope
Eugenius IV, and by Tommaso Parentucelli,
who employed George in many translations
after he became Pope *Nicholas V. In 1452
George refused to continue translating for the
pope because his commentary on Ptolemy's
Almagest had been critically reviewed by
Jacobus Cremonensis at the pope's request.
George was imprisoned for striking Poggio
*Bracciolini in a quarrel in the chancery on 4
May 1452 and was released on 9 May only after
writing an apology to Poggio. Soon after,
George was accused by Giovanni Aurispa of
having appropriated during the latter's ab-
sence fees due to him as papal secretary.
Unable to restore himself to favour with the

pope, George left Rome on 17 June for the patronage of King Alfonso I in Naples. There he lost more than four thousand ducats through unsuccessful financial speculation. In October 1453 George was reconciled with the pope through the intercession of Francesco *Filelfo, although he did not resume his duties in the chancery until the accession of Pope Calixtus III in 1455.

After George had left Rome in 1452, Bessarion encouraged Theodorus *Gaza to retranslate works of Aristotle which the pope had assigned to George, and after the death of his protector, Barbaro, in January 1454 Bessarion's circle became increasingly hostile to him. The completion of Gaza's translation of the *Problemata* forced George to publish his own late in 1454. Early that year Andreas Contrarius had presented to the pope a critique of George's translation of Eusebius' *De praeparatione evangelica*. When after the pope's death Gaza and Contrarius sought the patronage of King Alfonso, George retaliated with an invective *In perversionem Problematum Aristotelis a quodam Theodoro Cage [Gaza] editam et problematicae Aristotelis philosophiae protectio*, addressed to Alfonso, in which George claimed that Bessarion had deliberately sought his ruin. The two soon became antagonists in the debate over Plato and Aristotle which had begun in 1439 among the Greek delegates to the council of Florence. In 1458 George wrote a Greek letter on this debate to the monk Hesaia; Bessarion answered with *De natura et arte*. George's *Comparatio philosophorum Aristotelis et Platonis*, written in 1457, was published in 1458; Bessarion replied in 1459 with *In calumniatorem Platonis*. When the Latin translation of this last work was published (Rome: C. Sweynheym and A. Pannartz 1469), *De natura et arte* and a critique of George's translations of Plato's *Laws* and *Epinomis* were appended. George's *Annotationes* to *In calumniatorem Platonis*, written by mid-1470, were answered by Niccolò *Perotti in *Refutatio deliramentorum Georgii Trapezuntii Cretensis* the same year. While Bessarion received letters of congratulation from many humanists, George was attacked by Gaza, Domizio *Calderini, Andreas Contrarius, and Johannes *Argyropoulos.

During the pontificate of *Pius II, George retreated from Rome for a time because of a feud with his neighbour Giovanni Toscanella which resulted in street fighting. By June 1460 he had moved to Venice and for dedicating his translation of Plato's *Laws* to the Republic was rewarded with a teaching position, though he may have held it for a few months in competition with Giovanni Mario *Filelfo. Apparently a scandal concerning a Venetian girl resulted in George's brief imprisonment and in his return to Rome by May 1462.

As John Monfasani has recently shown, George considered himself a prophet of the Apocalypse. He interpreted the neo-Platonism of Cardinal Bessarion and his circle as an example of the apostasy which would precede the coming of the Ishmaelites, that is, the expansion of the Ottoman Empire into the Latin West. Since 1427 he had urged the rescue of Constantinople. After its fall in 1453 he undertook to avert the coming reign of terror by converting the sultan to Christianity, as his Greek treatise *On the Truth of the Faith of Christians to the Emir* shows. Having failed to interest Pope Pius II and King Ferrante of Naples in his plan, he finally persuaded Pope Paul II to send him to Greece and Turkey on this secret mission in 1465. In October 1466 he was imprisoned in the Castel Sant'Angelo while a Greek treatise addressed to Sultan *Mehmed II, *On the Eternal Glory of the Autocrat and his World Empire*, which he had written during his return voyage, was being investigated. Bessarion discovered two letters in which George sought the patronage of the sultan, but the pope released George after four months when the worst charges of treason proved groundless. George continued to believe in his prophetic vision, writing after his release a Greek treatise *On Divine Manuel, Shortly to be King of the Whole World*.

By 1469 George had resigned his office of apostolic secretary to his son Andrea. His son Jacopo would later serve as abbreviator in the chancery. Paolo Giovio depicted George in his last years as a senile old man wandering the streets of Rome (*Gli elogi degli uomini illustri* ed R. Meregazzi, Rome 1972, 59). He died there about 1472, having survived his wife by a few years, and was buried probably in the church of Santa Maria sopra Minerva, where the graves of his wife, his son Andrea, his daughter Maria, and two grandchildren are recorded.

Erasmus occasionally mentioned the works of George of Trebizond in his letters (Epp 36, 862, 2389). George's contest with Valla may explain Erasmus' interest in comparing the *Rhetoricorum libri v* with Quintilian (Ep 122). Erasmus judged George inferior to Theodorus Gaza as a translator (*Ciceronianus* ASD I-2 664–5), and in the preface to his Greek edition of Basil (Ep 2611) he wryly treated George's conventional apology for his translation (L. Mohler *Kardinal Bessarion* III 593–4) as if it had been intended literally. George's attack on Gaza's translation of Aristotle's *Problemata* exemplified for Erasmus the censure to which even the best scholars were exposed by the publication of their labours (Allen I 15 and Epp 1479, 2291).

The writings of George of Trebizond, many of which survive only in manuscript (P.O. Kristeller *Iter Italicum*, London-Leiden 1965–ㅤ), are too numerous to list here. Some have been published in *Patrologia Graeca* ... ed J.P. Migne (Paris 1857–1912) ser 2 XLIV 298–430, CLXI 745–908; *Epistolae Francisci Barbari* ed A.M. Querini (Brescia 1741) 290–303; E. Legrand *Cent-dix Lettres grecques de François Filelfo* (Paris 1892) 315–28; A. Gercke *Theodoros Gazes* (Greifswald 1903) 13–19; E. Walser *Poggius Florentinus* (Leipzig-Berlin 1914) 501–14; L. Mohler *Kardinal Bessarion* (Paderborn 1923–42) III 274–342, 593–4; and as appendices to John Monfasani's important *George of Trebizond: A Biography and a Study of his Rhetoric and Logic* (Leiden 1976).

BIBLIOGRAPHY: Allen Ep 36 / EI XVII 180 / R. Sabbadini *Storia del Ciceronianismo* (Turin 1885) 17–8 / R. Sabbadini 'Briciole umanistiche' *Giornale storico della letteratura italiana* 18 (1891) 230–41, 43 (1904) 253–4 / R. Sabbadini *La scuola e gli studi di Guarino Guarini Veronese* (Catania 1896) 60–1, 71–2, 76–8 / G. Castellani 'Giorgio da Trebizonda, maestro di eloquenza a Vicenza e a Venezia' *Nuovo archivio veneto* 11 (1896) 123–39 / P. Gothein *Francesco Barbaro* (Berlin 1932) 147–51 / R. Klibansky 'Plato's *Parmenides* in the Middle Ages and the Renaissance' *Mediaeval and Renaissance Studies* 1 (1943) 289–304 / A. Mercati 'Le due lettere di Giorgio

da Trebisonda a Maometto II' *Orientalia Christiana Periodica* 9 (1943) 65–99 / R. Cessi *Saggi romani* (Rome 1956) 129–85 / L. Labowsky 'Bessarion Studies IV and V '*Medieval and Renaissance Studies* 6 (1968) 173–205 / E. Garin *L'età nuova* (Naples 1969) 287–92 / S. Camporeale *Lorenzo Valla* (Florence 1972) 99–100, 132–4, and passim / On his rhetoric and logic see also H.S. Wilson 'George of Trebizond and early humanist rhetoric' *Studies in Philology* 40 (1943) 367–79; C. Vasoli *La dialettica e la retorica dell'umanesimo* (Milan 1968) 81–99 and passim; and C. Vasoli *Profezia e ragione* (Naples 1974) 520–3 and passim

JUDITH RICE HENDERSON

Andreas TRECESIUS *See Andrzej* TRZECIESKI

Gaspard TRECHSEL of Lyon, d 1570
Born in Lyon to the German printer Jean Trechsel (Drechsel), Gaspard was trained along with his older brother, Melchior *Trechsel, by Jean Schwab, alias Clein, who had married their widowed mother. Gaspard was already in touch with Erasmus by 1529, when he conveyed the humanist's greetings to Guy *Morillon in Saragossa and brought a message back to him in Basel (Ep 2083). In 1530 Gaspard took full control of the family printing shop with Melchior, and for a decade they printed for themselves or for other Lyon publishers the handsome humanist editions described in Melchior's biography. After 1540, when Melchior ceased working as a printer, Gaspard carried on the shop alone for another ten years, briefly in Vienne, then in Lyon. His editions included the *Biblia Sacra*, translated from Hebrew and Greek by the Dominican scholar Santo Pagnini and corrected by Michael *Servetus (1542, printed for Hugues de La Porte), and a splendid folio edition of the Vulgate, with glosses and other scholarly apparatus, edited by Servetus, and with the Bible pictures of Hans *Holbein (1545, printed for the Grande Compagnie des Libraires of Lyon). Gaspard married Magdelaine de Portunariis, the sister of Italian booksellers and the sister-in-law of the merchant-publisher Guillaume Rouillé. After 1549 he, too, abandoned printing and like his brother became an agent for Guillaume Rouillé for the Spanish

Johannes Trithemius

market. In 1559, Gaspard had debts to the publisher Laurent de Normandie in Geneva, which may indicate some Protestant interest on his part. He died in Salamanca in 1570.

BIBLIOGRAPHY: Allen Ep 2083 / J. and H. Baudrier *Bibliographie lyonnaise* (Lyon 1895–1921) XII 230–306 / H.-L. Schlaepfer 'Laurent de Normandie' in *Aspects de la propagande religieuse* (Geneva 1957) 187

NATALIE ZEMON DAVIS

Melchior TRECHSEL of Lyon, documented 1526–1564
Born in Lyon to the German printer Jean Trechsel, Melchior Trechsel learnt his trade from Jean Schwab, alias Clein, who had married his widowed mother. Clein's last edition before he died in 1530 was Erasmus' *Colloquia* but even before then Melchior Trechsel was in touch with the great humanist. He may already have met him in 1526 in Basel, where Melchior had arranged for the cutting of the blocks for Hans *Holbein's *Simulachres de la mort*. In early 1529 he brought a letter to Erasmus in Basel (Ep 2133), and later that year Erasmus mentioned that Hieronymus *Froben

had been considering sending his brother, Erasmius *Froben, to work for Melchior's 'cold' shop in Lyon, a decision Erasmus evidently did not favour (Ep 2231). In 1530 Melchior and his younger brother, Gaspard *Trechsel, assumed full control of their family's atelier. For ten years the brothers printed beautiful editions: Latin texts of Cicero, Horace, Terence, and other classical figures; works by Juan Luis *Vives; Erasmus' *Colloquia* (1533) and his edition of the works of Athanasius of Alexandria (1531–2); Ptolemy's *Geography*, translated into Latin by *Pirckheimer and corrected by Michael *Servetus; Holbein's Bible pictures and his celebrated *Simulachres de la Mort* (1538), with essays by the humanist priest of Lyon, Jean de Vauzelles. In 1540, a year after the strike of the Lyon printers' journeymen, Melchior stopped printing and became the agent in Spain for the Lyon merchant-publisher Guillaume Rouillé, who published many books for the Spanish market. He is last mentioned in Alcalá in 1564.

BIBLIOGRAPHY: Allen Ep 2083 / J. and H. Baudrier *Bibliographie lyonnaise* (Lyon 1895–1921) XII 230–306 / N.Z. Davis 'Holbein's *Pictures of Death* and the Reformation at Lyons' *Studies in the Renaissance* 3 (1956) 97–130 / AK III Ep 1448 and passim   NATALIE ZEMON DAVIS

TREVISANUS *See* TERVISANUS *(Ep 1989)*

TRIBELMANNUS *See* Georg TRÜBELMANN

Johannes TRITHEMIUS of Trittenheim, 1 February 1462–13 December 1516
Johann Heidenberg, who later called himself Trithemius, was born in Trittenheim, near Trier. Since his stepfather, Johann Zell, opposed his desire for further education, he ran away when he was seventeen, first to Trier, and then to Heidelberg, where he learnt Greek and Hebrew. In 1482 he entered the abbey of Sponheim, near Kreuznach in the Palatinate, a Benedictine house which had seen better days. On 29 July 1483 he was elected abbot. He collected a very valuable library and had connections with leading humanist scholars of his time. Conradus Celtis and Alexander *Hegius visited him at Sponheim. He tried to reform discipline among his monks according to the Bursfeld rule, placing greater emphasis

on studies; he also wrote such reference works as *Liber de scriptoribus ecclesiasticis* (Basel: J. Amerbach 1494), a scholarly dictionary of writers, past and present, and *Catalogus illustrium virorum Germaniae* ([Mainz]: P. Fridbergensis [1495]). In 1505 he went to Berlin at the invitation of the Elector Joachim of Brandenburg; in his absence the opposition to him that had been developing for some time at Sponheim gathered momentum. As a result he resigned the abbacy there in 1506 and on 12 October was elected abbot of the Benedictine abbey of St Jacob's at Würzburg, one of the few remaining 'Schottenklöster.' There he continued to work on his numerous writings until his death ten years later.

Trithemius' writings cover a wide range of subjects from traditional devotion to the occult. His major historical work, the *Chronicon Hirsaugiense* (Basel: J. Parcus for J. Oporinus 1559), is a universal chronicle to 1370, based on factual as well as fictitious sources. Although his fabrications were quickly recognized by Johannes *Stabius, *Beatus Rhenanus, and Konrad *Peutinger, Trithemius produced a greatly expanded version, the *Annales Hirsaugienses* (St Gallen 1690). In his *Steganographia* he followed the cabbalistic tradition laid down in Giovanni *Pico della Mirandola's *Conclusiones* (1486). According to D.P. Walker the '*Steganographia* is partly a treatise of cryptography in which the methods of encipherment are disguised as demonic magic, and partly a treatise on demonic magic.' It was never completed and was not printed until 1606, although it circulated in manuscript and was later placed on the *Index*. Trithemius' *Polygraphiae libri sex* ([Basel: A. Petri] for J. Haselberg 1518), a continuation of his *Steganographia*, dedicated to the Emperor *Maximilian I, did not impress Erasmus (cf Ep 1115). Trithemius is also mentioned in Ep 342 as a teacher of Nikolaus *Gerbel in 1504. Nicolaus *Basellius was also his student.

BIBLIOGRAPHY: Allen and CWE Ep 1115 / ADB XXXVIII 626–30 / J. Trithemius *Opera historica* (Frankfurt 1601, repr 1966) with a life by Johannes Duraclusius / Klaus Arnold *Johannes Trithemius (1462–1516)* (Würzburg 1971) / Paul Lehmann *Merkwürdigkeiten des Abtes Johannes Trithemius* (Munich 1961) / D.P. Walker *Spiritual and Demonic Magic from Ficino to Campanella*

(London 1958) 86–90 / F.A. Yates *Giordano Bruno and the Hermetic Tradition* (London 1964) 145–6, 258 / H. Rupprich in R. Newald et al *Geschichte der deutschen Literatur* (Munich 1957–) IV-1 666–8   IG

Agostino TRIVULZIO of Milan, d 30 March 1548

Agostino was the son of the Milanese nobleman and ducal councillor Giovanni Trivulzio and of Angiola Martinengo and a nephew of cardinals Antonio and Scaramuccia Trivulzio. Two of his close relations, his uncle Teodoro and his father's cousin, Giangiacomo Trivulzio, were marshals of France and governors of Milan. Support for France and association with her vicissitudes in Italy was the barometer of Agostino's own fortunes.

Having been abbot of the Cistercian house Acquafredda (Santa Maria Montisfrigidi) on Lake Como and subsequently protector of the order in Rome, Agostino became chamberlain and apostolic protonotary to *Julius II. He left Rome when the pope reversed his pro-French policy but returned after *Leo X's accession in 1513 to be created cardinal together with Scaramuccia in the great creation of cardinals in July 1517. During the pontificate of *Adrian VI he shared the family's impoverishment caused by *Charles V's decree annulling all favours received from France. In 1522 both he and Scaramuccia begged benefices, Agostino receiving the administration of the diocese of Bobbio (1522). During *Clement VII's pontificate he was appointed administrator of three French dioceses – Toulon (1524), Le Puy (1525), and Avranches (1526). In 1527 he was legate of the papal forces in the joint counteroffensive with France after the Colonna raid on Rome. When the imperialists sacked Rome in May, he was imprisoned with the pope in Castel Sant'Angelo and in November was taken hostage to the Castel Nuovo in Naples. After Scaramuccia's death on 3 August 1527 Agostino became the acknowledged protector of French interests in Rome. He accompanied Clement to Bologna for Charles V's coronation but left in March 1530 for the French court. He arrived for the release from captivity of *Francis I's two sons and witnessed the triumphal entry into Bordeaux of the king's new wife, *Eleanor, a sister of *Charles V, attending her at her coronation in March 1531. In October Francis I nominated him bishop of Bayeux. On the death of Clement VII, Agostino led the French faction in support of the candidature of Alessandro Farnese. In June 1536 *Paul III sent him as legate to Francis I (Ep 3121). In 1541 he accompanied the pope to Lucca to meet Charles v. He died in his Roman palace situated near Santa Maria in Vallicella and was buried in Santa Maria del Popolo.

Agostino's erudition earned him much respect. In 1530 Germain de *Brie described the learned contemporary he had known as a young man at Julius' court with such enthusiasm (Ep 2405) that Erasmus wrote to Trivulzio (Ep 2423), whom he himself had perhaps met at Padua in 1508 (Ep 2422). Dedications to Agostino include Scipione Vegio's *Historia rerum in Insubribus gestarum sub Gallorum dominio ab 1515 ad 1522* ed A. Ceruti (Milan 1876) and Filippo (II) *Beroaldo's *Carminum ad Augustinum Trivultium Cardinalem libri III* published posthumously by Dominicus Laelius (Rome: A. Bladus 1530). Agostino died before he could use his own material for a history of popes and cardinals, but a debt to his collections is acknowledged in the preface to Onofrio Panvinio's *Epitome pontificum Romanorum* (Venice: for G. Strada 1557).

BIBLIOGRAPHY: Allen Ep 2405 / P. Litta *Famiglie celebri italiane* (Milan 1819–85) I table 2 / A. Ciaconius *Vita et res gestae Pontificum Romanorum et S.R.E. Cardinalium* (Rome 1677) III 410–1 / P. Argelati *Bibliotheca scriptorum Mediolanensium* (Milan 1745) II-1 1519–20 / Eubel III 17, 136 / G. Moroni *Dizionario di erudizione storico-ecclesiastica* (Venice 1840–61) LXXXI 82 / Sanudo *Diarii* LIII 207, 211, 398, LIV 389, 397, 398 / G. Molini *Documenti di storia italiana* (Florence 1836–7) II 275–6 / *Corrispondenza segreta di Giovanni Matteo Giberti, datario di Clemente VII col card. Agostino Trivulzio dell'anno 1527* ed F.A. Gualterio (Turin 1845) / B. Varchi *Storia fiorentina* ed L. Arbib (Florence 1838–41) III 223

ROSEMARY DEVONSHIRE JONES

Felix TROPHINUS of Bologna, d 1527
Not a great deal is known about the life of Felix Trophinus (Troffinus, Trufino, Trofimo). Allen found evidence that in November 1516 he was in the service of Pietro Accolti, cardinal of Ravenna, and subsequently accompanied Cardinal *Cajetanus to the diet of Augsburg in 1518. In May 1519 they were in Koblenz, from where Trophinus wrote to Georgius *Spalatinus. Later he became chaplain and secretary to Cardinal Giulio de' Medici, the future Pope *Clement VII. In 1521 he was appointed apostolic collector for England in succession to Silvestro *Gigli. In March 1522, while on an errand from his cardinal to the newly elected Pope *Adrian VI in Spain, he was captured at sea by the French and had some difficulty in obtaining his release (LP III-2 2123, 2206, 2224). In the following year Cardinal Giulio himself ascended to the papacy, and on 24 August 1524 Trophinus was made bishop of Chieti in succession to Gianpietro Carafa, the future Pope *Paul IV. He took a former famulus of Erasmus, Johannes *Hovius, into his service and, no doubt at Hovius' request, Erasmus wrote him a short letter of congratulation in May 1525 (Ep 1575). In 1526 his see of Chieti was raised to an archbishopric. In 1527 he was apostolic datary for a while, but his health was failing and he died the same year.

Four letters to Trophinus by Girolamo *Aleandro have been published by Paquier. Paulus Grillandus of Castello dedicated to him as archbishop and datary a treatise, *De haereticis et sortilegiis* (Lyon: G. Giunta 1536).

BIBLIOGRAPHY: Allen Ep 1575 / Eubel III 311 / Sanudo *Diarii* XLV 418, XLVI 209, 299 / *Lettres familières de Jérôme Aléandre, 1510–40* ed J. Paquier (Paris 1909) passim / Cosenza IV 3478 / William E. Wilkie *The Cardinal Protectors of England* (Cambridge-London 1974) 122, 128

PGB

Georg TRÜBELMANN of Bamlach, documented 1513–56
Georg Trübelmann (Tribelmann, Truffelmann) of Bamlach, near Müllheim, Breisgau, is first mentioned among the Basel troops in the battle of Novara (1513), where he showed exceptional bravery and as a reward was given the citizenship of Basel and a pension for life. In 1516 he received an official rebuke for mercenary service in French pay and for 'sinning' with his brother's wife. In 1525 he was fined for having participated in the peasant war in the

Sundgau, probably again as a mercenary. In Basel he lived in the Petersgasse and is frequently mentioned (1529–35) in the sources as a carrier and messenger travelling between Basel and Freiburg (Epp 2554, 2747, 2827, 3051) and also occasionally to locations in Switzerland.

In June 1530 Trübelmann was investigated with other members of the 'Gartneren' guild who had so far failed to receive communion in the reformed fashion and promised to do so in future. In 1556 he was an attendant at the Basel staple and was fined for carrying a rosary on his person and for not having prevented his wife from performing a pilgrimage, although through a substitute only.

BIBLIOGRAPHY: AK III Ep 1331 and passim / Basler Chroniken VIII 296 / Aktensammlung zur Geschichte der Basler Reformation ed E. Dürr et al (Basel 1921–50) II 125–6, 141, IV 490, VI 583–4, 600 / R. Wackernagel Geschichte der Stadt Basel (Basel 1907–54) III 30, 36, 115, 383 / W.R. Staehelin Wappenbuch der Stadt Basel (Basel [1917–30]) III   PGB

Christoph TRUCHSESS von Waldburg
c 1509–1535

Christoph was the son of Wilhelm Truchsess the Elder (d 1557), a councillor of *Ferdinand I and governor of Württemberg. Christoph's relative Georg (1488–1531), perhaps an elder brother, commanded the army of the Swabian League; his younger brother, Otto (1514–73), became well known as cardinal and bishop of Augsburg. The family castle of Waldburg (Waltburg) is located near Ravensburg, north of Lake Constance. Christoph matriculated at Tübingen on 11 January 1519. Subsequently he continued his studies in Italy. In November 1525 he was at Padua (Ep 1649). After his return to Germany he chose a military career, like Georg, and in 1529 and 1532 was one of Ferdinand I's commanders against the Turks. In 1535 he accompanied *Charles V on his expedition to Tunis but died on his way back and was buried in Pavia. Johannes Alexander *Brassicanus dedicated to him an edition of Leonardo Bruni's De bonis studiis epistola (Strasbourg: J. Knobloch 1521). In October 1525 Erasmus was induced to write a complimentary letter to Truchsess, who sent an

elegant reply (Epp 1625, 1649). Erasmus was probably again referring to him the following spring when he sent greetings to an unnamed German count in Padua (Ep 1705).

A Christoph Truchsess von Waldburg who matriculated at Freiburg on 28 February 1495 (Matrikel Freiburg I 119) is probably not identical with Otto's brother.

BIBLIOGRAPHY: Allen Ep 1625 / Matrikel Tübingen I 224 / Christoph Scheurl's Briefbuch ed F. von Soden and J.K.F. Knaake (Potsdam 1876–72, repr 1962) II Ep 279 / Mathäus von Pappenheim Chronik der Truchsessen von Waldburg (Memmingen 1777–85) I 100–1
                                            ROSEMARIE AULINGER & PGB

Thomas TRUCHSESS von Wetzhausen
d 12 July 1523

Thomas was the son of Jakob Truchsess von Wetzhausen zu Dachsbach, a Franconian nobleman. He matriculated in Leipzig in 1484. Subsequently he obtained a canonry at Speyer and was in Rome on 24 March 1495 to pay the annates due on his appointment. In 1519 he also held a prebend in Würzburg and in 1513 the parish of Weibstadt. From 1500 Truchsess studied in Bologna and obtained a doctorate in canon law on 9 October 1504. At the same time he eagerly studied humanistic subjects, especially Greek under Filippo (II) *Beroaldo. He also went to Rome to obtain papal confirmation for Philipp von Rosenberg, who had been elected bishop of Speyer in September 1504, and in the summer of 1513 he rendered the same service to the next bishop, George, count *Palatine. On 5 September 1503 he was elected scholaster of the Speyer chapter, from about 1507 to 1513 he served as vicar-general of the bishop, and on 8 July 1517 he rose to be dean of Speyer. Truchsess was an old friend of Johann *Reuchlin, whose side he took in the controversy with the Cologne Dominicans. In 1514 he was one of Bishop George's delegates to examine Reuchlin's Augenspiegel and found it to be free of heresy. He was buried in the cathedral of Speyer. Both Erasmus and *Beatus Rhenanus composed epitaphs for him. Johannes *Cono dedicated to him his edition of Gregory of Nazianzus' oration in praise of Gregory of Nyssa (Strasbourg: M. Schürer 1512).

Erasmus enjoyed Truchsess' hospitality when passing through Speyer in 1514 or 1515, 1518, and 1521 and had nothing but praise for him (Epp 355, 867, 882, 1302, 1342). He also received other proofs of Truchsess' support of his cause (Ep 1289).

BIBLIOGRAPHY: Allen and CWE Ep 355 / G. Knod in ADB XXXVIII 683–5 / Knod 629 / *Matrikel Leipzig* I 340 / BRE Epp 162, 183 / RE Epp 67, 248 / Ludwig Geiger *Johann Reuchlin* (Leipzig 1871, repr 1964) 298–303   IG

TRUCKSESS (Ep 1374 of 6 July 1523)
Only a tentative identification can be offered for this acquaintance of Wolfgang *Capito and Johannes *Oecolampadius. The reference is perhaps to the petty nobleman Jakob Truchsess von Rheinfelden (documented from 1513, died by 1545), who for some time seems to have served Capito as a secretary. He owned a house in Basel and had connections with the *Amerbach family.

BIBLIOGRAPHY: Luther w *Briefwechsel* II Ep 451 (p 437) / AK V Ep 2484, VI Ep 2644, IX Ep 3686 / James M. Kittelson *Wolfgang Capito, from Humanist to Reformer* (Leiden 1975) 165 and passim   PGB

Andrzej TRZECIESKI d after 20 October 1547
Andrzej Trzecieski (Andreas Trecesius) came from a noble family in Little Poland; his father's name was Adam. In 1513 he began his studies at the University of Cracow, and in 1520 he graduated BA. At some undetermined time he continued his education in Germany and established close contacts with *Melanchthon, with whom he later maintained a correspondence. He lived mostly in Cracow, mixed with the booksellers, printers, and humanists, and collected a fine library. He was especially esteemed for his knowledge of Hebrew and was known as a 'vir multarum linguarum peritus simul et humanista.' As early as 1528 he was accused of spreading the teachings of *Luther. His home in Cracow was a regular meeting place for the supporters of the new religious currents. In 1546 a debate on the Trinity was held at his home, with a Dutch Antitrinitarian using the cover name of 'Spiritus' in attendance. Trzecieski maintained close ties with Jan *Antonin and Jan (II) *Łaski and especially with Justus Ludovicus *Decius, who

secured him the position of book purchaser for the library of the young King *Sigismund II Augustus.

Trzecieski had a son, also named Andrzej, who became a poet and Protestant activist. The identical names have on occasion caused some confusion. The only trace of Trzecieski's interest in Erasmus is a letter he wrote to him on 28 October 1527 (Ep 1895). He was then in Wrocław, having spent the summer on Greek studies at Leipzig and Erfurt. He regretted that his lack of funds had not permitted him to travel as far as Basel.

BIBLIOGRAPHY: Allen Ep 1895 / *Korespondencja Erazma z Rotterdamu z Polakami* ed and trans M. Cytowska (Warsaw 1965) / H. Barycz *Historia Uniwersytetu Jagiellońskiego* (Cracow 1935) / S. Kot *Andrzej Frycz Modrzewski* (Cracow 1923) / K. Hartleb *Biblioteka Zygmunta Augusta* (Lvov 1938) / A. Krókowski *Andrzej Trzecieski poeta-humanista i działacz reformacyjny* (Warsaw 1954) 10–25 / *Acta Tomiciana* (Poznań-Wrocław 1852–) x Epp 325, 326, 361 / S. Lubieniecki *Historia reformationis Polonicae* (Freistadt 1685) 18, 21, 23, 31, 52 / K. Piekarski 'Melanchtoniana Polonica' *Reformacja w Polsce* 4 (1926) 153–4 / *Lasciana nebst den ältesten evangelischen Synodalprotokollen Polens 1551–61* ed H. Dalton (Berlin 1898) Ep 34 / A. Frycz Modrzewski *Opera omnia* v: *Sylvae* (Warsaw 1960) 108

HALINA KOWALSKA

Peter TSCHUDI of Glarus, d 27 March 1532
The Tschudis were one of the leading families of Glarus (Switzerland), and Peter, whose father was Ludwig, was an older brother of Aegidius Tschudi, the statesman and famous historian. The two brothers and Valentin *Tschudi, their cousin, attended the school of *Glareanus at Basel (Ep 490) between about 1515 and 1517, and Peter and Valentin accompanied Glareanus to Paris (Ep 618). Of the three only Peter was registered in the University of Basel, with Glareanus and Fridolin *Egli, in the spring of 1514. After Peter had left Paris, before November 1521, he resumed his correspondence with *Zwingli, who seems to have recommended him for employment at Einsiedeln (February 1522). In July 1523 he was again at Glarus but subsequently moved to Chur, where he belonged to the evangelical party. In 1528 he was the town's treasurer and showed

courage and objectivity when translating documents to be laid before the judges of Abbot Theodul Schlegel, who was executed in 1529. On 27 December he sent Zwingli a survey of the political and religious situation in the Grisons and in Italy (z x Ep 949) and a year later reported to him after returning from the diet of Augsburg (z xi Ep 1147), although it seems that their relationship remained cautious (z x Ep 968). The Stiftsbibliothek Einsiedeln owns a Cicero (*Opera varia*, Venice: A. Manuzio 1514) which belonged to Peter and is annotated by him.

BIBLIOGRAPHY: Allen Ep 490 / *Historisch-biographisches Lexicon der Schweiz* (Neuchâtel 1921–34) VII 79 / ADB XXXVIII 730–1 / z VII Ep 18 and passim / BRE Ep 110 / *Vadianische Brief-sammlung* II Ep 199 and passim / *Matrikel Basel* I 319 / A. Büchi in *Aus Geschichte und Kunst ... Robert Durrer ... dargeboten* (Stans 1928) 382–4 / Oskar Vasella *Abt Theodul Schlegel von Chur und seine Zeit* (Fribourg 1954) 268, 299, 346 / W. Köhler 'Zwingli in Wildhaus und Einsiedeln' in *Zwingliana* 6 (1934–8) 1–4, esp 4

PGB

Valentin TSCHUDI of Glarus, 14 February 1499–8 December 1555

Valentin, whose father was Marquard, was a cousin of Aegidius and Peter *Tschudi. The boy's gifts were discovered by *Zwingli when he came to Glarus as the principal priest in 1506. In 1512–13 Valentin and Zwingli's younger brother, Jakob, studied together at Vienna under the care of *Vadianus. In 1513 he was at Pavia before joining *Glareanus' school at Basel two years later (Ep 490; z VII Ep 10). In 1517 he and Glareanus went to Paris, from where he wrote frequently to Zwingli. When Zwingli resigned his position at Glarus late in 1518 he recommended Valentin to be his successor. Tschudi was nominated but did not take up his duties until 12 October 1522 (z VII Ep 240), after he had left Paris in 1521 and spent some time with Zwingli in Zürich. His commitment to the reformed religion was only half-hearted, however, and was soon judged to be inadequate by Zwingli. He preached in an evangelical manner but also continued to say mass (z IX Ep 575, x Ep 1000) until his marriage in 1530, and even then he did not break completely with the old faith. His wife

was Anna Stucky, who came from a leading family of Zürich. He composed a German chronicle of the years 1519–33 (ed J. Strickler, Glarus 1888) which offers an impartial, if pessimistic, view of contemporary events in Switzerland. He died at Glarus of the plague.

BIBLIOGRAPHY: Allen Ep 490 / DHBS VI 695 / ADB XXXVIII 733–4 / z VII Ep 7 and passim / R. Feller and E. Bonjour *Geschichtsquellen der Schweiz* (Basel 1962) I 311–12 / *Vadianische Briefsammlung* II Ep 156 and passim / J. Winteler *Geschichte des Landes Glarus* (Glarus 1952–4) I 280–6 / O.F. Fritzsche *Glarean* (Frauenfeld 1890) 52 and passim   PGB

TUDERTINUS See Antonio PASINI

TUDOR See ARTHUR, EDMUND, MARGARET, and MARY Tudor

Arnoldus TUNGRENSIS See Arnold Luyd of TONGEREN

Cuthbert TUNSTALL 1474–18 November 1559

Cuthbert Tunstall (Tonstal, Donstall, Tonstallus, Tunstelus) was born at Hackforth, near Catterick in the North Riding of Yorkshire, probably the eldest and certainly the illegitimate son of Thomas Tunstall of Thurland Castle, Lancashire, a squire of the body to Richard III. His mother was a daughter of Sir John Conyers of Hornby Castle, which lies close to Hackforth. At some date subsequent to Cuthbert's birth, Thomas Tunstall apparently married his mother, and from all indications he was accepted as a member of the family. A legitimate brother, Brian, the 'stainless knight' of Walter Scott's *Marmion* (1808), fell at the battle of Flodden (1513) and, in a will made before the battle, asked that his brother Cuthbert – described as 'clericum fratrem' – become guardian of his young son and heir, Marmaduke. On 1 December 1514 Cuthbert was duly granted custody of the lands, wardship, and marriage of Marmaduke, aged six, who ultimately entered upon his inheritance on 15 February 1529.

Tunstall went to Oxford about 1491, according to the Oxford antiquary Brian Twyne, and would there have been a contemporary of Thomas *More, William *Grocyn, John *Colet,

Cuthbert Tunstall

and Thomas *Linacre, the last of whom became a very close friend. Some three years later he removed to Cambridge, where he was a scholar of the King's Hall (1496–7). About 1499 he left Cambridge in turn for Padua and remained there for six years. Linacre and Grocyn had preceded him there, and William *Latimer and Richard *Pace were contemporaries. He was a pupil of the professor of philosophy and Greek, Niccolò *Leonico Tomeo. Latimer in 1517 told Erasmus (Ep 520) that both Tunstall and Pace had been held back in their study of Greek by the 'ignorance or idleness' of their teacher at Padua. At all events, Tunstall became doctor of civil and canon law at Padua, where he may also have acquired his knowledge of Hebrew. Among the friends he acquired in Italy were Jérôme de *Busleyden, the Venetian Antonio Surian, future ambassador to *Henry VIII, Jacques *Lefèvre d'Etaples, and Aldo *Manuzio. With Busleyden in particular Tunstall was to have an important association, and in January 1516 he wrote to Henry VIII of the 'acquaintance and long familiarity' which existed between them 'when we were both scholars at Padua' (LP II-1 1383;

Sturge 13–14). He returned from Italy late in 1509 or early in 1510.

The first stages of Tunstall's clerical career were established before his return. On 25 September 1506 he had been made rector of Barmston, Yorkshire, a living in the gift of Lady Margaret Boynton, whose daughter married Cuthbert's brother, Brian, about this time (Sturge 16). Tunstall was not yet in major orders, but this did not prevent him acquiring three more rectories before the end of the year (see Sturge appendix xxv, Emden). He was ordained subdeacon on 24 March 1509 and deacon on 7 April, and was priested on 19 April 1511. That December he was made rector of Harrow-on-the-Hill, Middlesex.

Tunstall was now regularly resident in London, where he was a member of Doctors' Commons, the society of civilian lawyers whose members included Colet, Polidoro *Virgilio, Grocyn, More, and Edmund Bonner, among many other divines and men of learning. He was appointed chancellor to Archbishop *Warham in 1508, and in August 1511 commissary-general of the prerogative court of Canterbury. He apparently resided occasionally at Harrow-on-the-Hill, although he had a vicar there throughout his incumbency (Sturge 22). His next promotion was to the important post of master of the rolls in succession to John *Yonge on 12 May 1516. He resigned that office in October 1522 and on 25 May 1523 became keeper of the privy seal, a post he held until 24 January 1530.

During these years, Tunstall accumulated corresponding ecclesiastical preferments. He was admitted canon of Lincoln and prebendary of Stow Longa in succession to Thomas *Wolsey on 15 April 1514; archdeacon of Chester on 17 November 1515; canon of York and prebendary of Botevant in 1519; canon of Salisbury and prebendary of Combe and Harnham by collation on 26 May 1521, and finally dean of Salisbury in May 1521. These appointments were really an adjunct of his chief service to the government as a diplomatist. With Thomas More and others he was appointed envoy to the future *Charles V on 7 May 1515 to negotiate an agreement settling the terms of commercial intercourse between England and the Low Countries after the death of Philip the Handsome, duke of *Burgundy.

For most of the following year he was in the Netherlands, and apart from three brief visits to England he remained there until the autumn of 1517. During this time his friendship with Erasmus ripened. They had apparently met during Erasmus' visit to England in 1505 and 1506 and presumably frequently thereafter, but from the time of their meeting in Brussels about 3 June 1516 (Ep 412), their friendship grew swiftly.

After Tunstall's return from the Netherlands in September 1517 and the cessation of his dispatches, we know little of his activities for nearly three years. His sermon at the betrothal of the future Queen *Mary (not yet three years old) to the (still younger) *Francis, dauphin of France, on 5 October 1518 was printed by Richard *Pynson the same month and reprinted in Basel the next year. In June-July 1520 he attended the Field of Cloth of Gold and the Calais meetings (Ep 1107), where it was arranged that he should join the Emperor Charles v as ambassador to act as King Henry's spokesman in the marriage and other negotiations. He sailed for Calais on 13 September, arriving at Antwerp on 20 September, and thereafter was continuously in attendance on Charles v for six months, accompanying him by way of Louvain, Liège, and Maastricht to the coronation at Aachen on 23 October 1520. Subsequently he travelled with the emperor to Cologne (Ep 1155), Mainz, and Worms in time for the opening of the imperial diet in January 1521. While there Tunstall gained first-hand information about Lutheranism, and he wrote Wolsey a full account (Sturge 120–1, appendix x). He left Worms for England on 11 April. The following August he accompanied Wolsey, More, William *Blount, Lord Mountjoy, and Thomas *Ruthall to a conference at Calais with the representatives of the Empire and France, then to Bruges to meet with Charles in person. At Bruges he met Erasmus again (Ep 1233). He no doubt returned to England with Wolsey in November.

On 15 January 1522 Richard *Fitzjames, bishop of London, died, and the king at once named Tunstall his successor. On 19 October he was consecrated by Warham, Wolsey, and John *Fisher. His promotion was both a reward for his services and, as Warham pointed out, a recognition of his usefulness in entertaining visiting ambassadors in London (Sturge 71). However, his diplomatic career abroad was by no means over. In 1525, after the capture of *Francis I at the battle of Pavia, Tunstall was sent with Sir Richard *Wingfield on a special embassy to the court of Charles v. They left Cowes for Spain on 20 April 1525, disembarked at Ribadeo on 29 April, and arrived at Toledo, where Charles was in residence some twenty-five days after entering Spain. The complex negotiations lasted until the following January, and in the interval Tunstall and Richard *Sampson, the permanent ambassador, both fell ill, while Wingfield died. The English diplomats left for home on 26 January, travelling by way of France. Further missions followed. In 1527 for ten weeks Tunstall accompanied Wolsey to France, with More and Stephen *Gardiner; and two years later, on 30 June 1529, he was appointed chief English plenipotentiary with Thomas More to negotiate the peace of Cambrai (Sturge 107–9). Meanwhile, he had been appointed a counsel to Queen *Catherine of Aragon, with whom he showed strong sympathy (Sturge 171–87).

After his return from Cambrai in August 1529, and with the fall of Wolsey shortly thereafter, Tunstall was translated to the see of Durham on 21 February 1530. The following June he was also appointed president of the king's Council of the North. These related appointments entailed his surrender of the privy seal but bestowed on Tunstall, as bishop palatine, important authority for enforcement of royal policy in the north, as well as revenues two and a half times those of the see of London. They also removed a prominent opponent of the royal divorce from proximity to the court. Little record survives of his work in this period (Sturge 149), but his reaction to the Pilgrimage of Grace in 1536 was not a recommendation of his capacity as a royal administrator. In the Northern Convocation of 1531, he opposed the title of Supreme Head to designate the king's role in the church and continued in his loyalty to Catherine's cause until Archbishop *Cranmer annulled the king's marriage, after which Tunstall accepted the decision. On 1 June 1533 he attended the coronation of *Anne Boleyn, the new queen, and returned to the north almost at once. He does not appear to have returned to London until More was sent to the

Tower. On 2 March 1535 he made formal acknowledgement of Henry VIII as 'Supreme Head next after Christ of the Church in England,' renouncing obedience to the pope, and by the summer of 1536 he was apparently restored to full favour with the king (Sturge 203).

During the rest of Henry's reign Tunstall played the part of the conservative Henrician, probably the most erudite of the bishops who adhered to conservative positions in doctrine while practising obedience to the civil power. On Quinquagesima Sunday 1536 he spoke impressively in favour of Henry's new title at Paul's Cross and the same year wrote a firm reply to Reginald *Pole's *De unitate ecclesiae* (London: R. Wolfe 1560, STC 24341). He was one of the commissioners responsible for the 'Bishops' Book' of 1537, *The Godly and Pious Institution of a Christian Man*, in which Tunstall's knowledge of the doctrines of the Orthodox Church may have played some part (Sturge 212–13). In May 1538 he was one of three bishops appointed to confer with German Protestant envoys, a conference which extinguished all hope of doctrinal agreement (Sturge 213), and he had a prominent part in the promotion of the conservative Act of Six Articles, enacted on 28 June 1539. After the fall of Thomas *Cromwell he was instrumental in the annulment of Henry's marriage to Anne of Cleves, and in 1541 he accompanied the king on his progress through Yorkshire. For the rest of the reign he was employed chiefly in diplomatic negotiations with Scotland, France, and the Empire (Sturge 233–51). However, he also participated in the preparation of the last doctrinal formulary of Henry's reign, the King's Book, which appeared on 27 May 1543 after some three years of discussion.

The rest of Tunstall's long career must be dealt with very briefly. On the accession of Edward VI he was reappointed a member of the Council of the North. In 1550, with the fall of Edward Seymour, duke of Somerset, he was summoned to London by John Dudley, earl of Warwick, and at first confined, then later removed to the Tower (20 December 1551). He was deprived of his see on 14 October 1552. Queen Mary released and reinstated him in his bishopric, and Elizabeth appointed him a commissioner to treat with the Scots on 10 May 1559. However, Tunstall was apparently unwilling to be a party once again to the creation of a Henrician polity, and he declined to take part in the consecration of Matthew Parker. He then refused the Oath of Supremacy and was consequently deprived again on 28 September 1559. He was turned over to the custody of Parker in Lambeth Palace, where he died shortly thereafter, on 18 November, at the age of eighty-five.

Throughout their lives, Tunstall enjoyed the close friendship and admiration of More and Erasmus, both for his erudition and for his professional competence in the royal service. He was one of the scholars to whom Erasmus submitted his Latin translations of Euripides' *Hecuba* and *Iphigenia in Aulis* (Ep 207: 28 October 1507), and in May 1515 Erasmus praised him to Pieter *Gillis (as to others) as one of the best scholars in England (Ep 332). More described his pleasure in Tunstall's company during their first diplomatic mission in *Utopia* itself and in a letter to Erasmus (Ep 388); he praised Tunstall's learning, sagacity, and goodness even in his epitaph (Sturge 25). It is also apparent that More was particularly concerned to have Tunstall's opinion of the *Utopia*, where More's views on public service would have intrigued his chief-of-mission (Epp 467, 499; Rogers Ep 84). Erasmus again praised Tunstall's company during the winter of 1516–17, when he stayed with him in Brussels and described him to *Budé as an exceptional scholar, with unusual modesty, dignity, charm, and good humour (Ep 480; 28 October 1516). Although Erasmus was eager to promote a friendship between Budé and Tunstall, who was very interested in Budé's *De asse* and in ancient coinage, the correspondence languished after an initial exchange of letters, and it is unlikely that the diplomat had time for such a demanding correspondent (Epp 493, 531, 571, 583, 584). Erasmus was more successful in his introduction to Pieter Gillis, to whose new daughter Tunstall became godfather (Epp 477, 491, 516, 1726).

During these months there was a growing intimacy above all between Tunstall and Erasmus himself. He was deeply grateful for Tunstall's part in the revision of the text of the New Testament, through the loan of a manuscript and by consulting Greek codices on

Erasmus' behalf and suggesting emendations (Epp 597, 832). This collaboration occupied the later months of 1516 and the first half of 1517 in Brussels, Ghent, and Bruges. In July Tunstall removed to Middelburg, but by then the task was almost finished (Sturge 54–5). It was Tunstall's suggestion that the new edition (March 1519) should include the *Argumenta in omnes epistolas apostolicas nova* that Erasmus had composed over a decade earlier (Epp 886, 894). Three copies were printed on vellum, of which one was presented to Tunstall (CWE Epp 848, 886). Among other works of this period, Tunstall praised Erasmus' *De copia* and *Panegyricus* (Ep 584), and despite the friendly contact with Budé, in April 1517 he discouraged Erasmus from accepting any offers to remove to France, where there was too little esteem for education and theology was only a 'Sorbonian bog' (Ep 572). At the same time he supported Erasmus in his controversies with *Dorp and Lefèvre d'Etaples (Epp 477, 663, 706).

The next important phase in their friendship began with Tunstall's strong urging that Erasmus write against *Luther and the 'Lutheran poison' (Ep 1367, 5 June 1523). In his reply (Ep 1369) Erasmus resisted the appeal, insisting that some of Luther's views were good and might be lost in indiscriminate condemnation. The hardening of positions and Luther's own intransigence, however, alarmed Erasmus about the unity of the church and began to disillusion him with the German theologian's attitude. He was urged by Tunstall to address himself in particular to the issue of free will, where Erasmus had detected a difficulty for Luther (Ep 1342, 1 February 1523). By the end of 1523 he was planning his *De libero arbitrio* (September 1524), of whose publication he informed Tunstall, predicting that, despite his moderation, it would spark an uproar (Ep 1487). Erasmus' reply to Luther's subsequent *De servo arbitrio*, the *Hyperaspistes*, was first issued only in part to catch the spring book fair, and its completion was delayed for more than a year. Tunstall and More both continued to press Erasmus for further efforts, and Erasmus' reaction makes it clear that he did not share, even then, the single-minded determination of his English friends to make opposition to Luther the leading issue and was at least equally fearful of some of Luther's obscurantist

opponents (Ep 1804, 30 March 1527). Throughout this period Tunstall contributed generously to Erasmus' financial support (Epp 597, 651, 832, 1726, 1750, 1764, 1769, 1781).

In the last surviving letter from Tunstall to Erasmus, written from London on 24 October 1529 (Ep 2226), Tunstall's concern for his friend's reputation and welfare is still apparent. Erasmus had recently fled Basel, now in the hands of a Protestant government, and Tunstall urged him to make his position on the Eucharist clear, to publish more of the homilies attributed to Chrysostom on Scripture, and to imitate Augustine by purging his earlier writings of passages that offended his critics, especially the *Colloquia*. Erasmus had already heard a (false) report that an inhibition had been placed on their circulation in England and had written to Wolsey to ask that More and Tunstall might read them (Ep 1697, 25 April 1526). He replied to Tunstall's letter three months later (Ep 2263), again firmly determined not to give way merely for the sake of peace, and insisting that it was obscurantist monks who were responsible for fanning the flames of controversy. He added that he could find not only in the works of Augustine but also in those of St Paul six hundred passages that were by then branded heresies.

Despite these disagreements, the friendship between the two men was firm. Tunstall continued to support Erasmus against his critics, always urging him to be more circumspect (Epp 2443, 2459, 2468). At the end of his life, Erasmus restated a provision in an earlier will whereby he designated Tunstall one of those to be given a copy of his complete works as soon as they were published (Allen VI 505; Sturge 127).

Tunstall encouraged others besides Erasmus, among them John Christopherson, the future bishop of Chichester, and Polidoro Virgilio. He lent to Virgilio one of the two manuscripts used in his edition of Gildas' *De calamitate, excidio et conquestu Britanniae* (London: R. Ridley 1525; STC 11892). Rhabanus Maurus' *De sacramento Eucharistiae* was also edited in 1551 (Cologne: J. Quentel) from a manuscript belonging to Tunstall. Leonico Tomeo dedicated to him his *De varia historia*, and Virgilio his *Opus novum* of 1525, as well as a supplement to his own *Adagia*, apparently,

William Tyndale

which was never published (Ep 1366; Sturge 28–9). In 1533 Simon *Grynaeus dedicated his edition of the Greek text of Euclid, the first ever printed, to Tunstall, a complement in particular to Tunstall's *De arte supputandi*. This treatise on arithmetic, the first work on that subject printed in England (London: R. Pynson 1522; STC 24319) was composed during the busy years of Tunstall's early career and dedicated to Thomas More (Rogers Ep 111); it was reprinted several times in Paris and Strasbourg (Sturge 71–8). Erasmus sent a copy of it to Andrzej *Krzycki, secretary to King *Sigismund I of Poland (Ep 1629, 5 October 1525).

Tunstall's *In laudem matrimonii oratio*, delivered for the betrothal of the Princess Mary, was printed by Richard *Pynson in 1518 (STC 24320) and reprinted by Johann *Froben in 1519. His *De veritate corporis et sanguinis Domini nostri Jesu Christi in Eucharistia*, a restatement of the traditional doctrine of the Eucharist composed while he was imprisoned by the government of Edward VI, was published in Paris (M. Vascosan 1554) and twice reprinted the same year. His compendium of the Nichomachean Ethics, *Compendium ... ethicorum Aristotelis*, was published in Paris (M. Vascosan) the same

year, along with the *Expositio beati Ambrosii episcopi super Apocalypsin*, edited by Tunstall with a preface by him. His *Contra blasphematores Dei praedestinationis*, published in Antwerp in 1555, was his last theological work. *Certaine Godly and Deuout Prayers* were printed in London (J. Cawood 1558, STC 24318) before the death of Queen Mary, translated from the Latin by Thomas Paynell. A full account of these and other of his writings in print by 1580 appears in Sturge, appendix XXVI. For his gift of books to Cambridge University Library see Emden BRUO III 1915. His register as bishop of Durham was edited and calendared by Gladys Hinde (Surtees Society 161, Durham 1952). Of the several reputed portraits in existence (see Sturge appendix XXIX) that at Burton Constable in the possession of the Chichester-Constables is perhaps the most likely to have been executed during his lifetime.

BIBLIOGRAPHY: Allen Ep 207 / Emden BRUO III 1913–15 / DNB XIX 1237–42 (out of date) / Charles Sturge *Cuthbert Tunstal* (London 1938), the standard biography in which appendix VI contains a calendar of the correspondence between Tunstall and Erasmus / L. Baldwin Smith *Tudor Prelates and Politics* (Princeton 1953) passim / McConica 52–3 and passim
JAMES K. MCCONICA

Jan TURENHOUT *See Jan* DRIEDO

TURZO *See* THURZO

TUSANUS, TUSSANUS *See Jacques, Nicolas, and Pierre* TOUSSAIN

Jacobus TUTOR *See Jacob de* VOECHT

Johannes TYBALDAEUS *See Jean* THIBAULT

Thomas TYBOLD *See Thomas* THEOBALD

William TYNDALE d 6 October 1536
William Tyndale (Tindale) was born during the last decade of the fifteenth century. Having begun his studies at Magdalen Hall, Oxford, Tyndale proceeded MA on 2 July 1515, migrating shortly thereafter to Cambridge, where he remained until 1521. At both Oxford and Cambridge the writings of Erasmus proved an inspiration for the young Tyndale. The following year he was appointed tutor to the children

of Sir John Walsh, and the leisure time afforded by his post was devoted to, amongst other things, a translation of Erasmus' *Enchiridion* (1533; STC 10479). Tyndale's unorthodox theological views raised the ire of the local clergy, and in 1523 he moved to London in an unsuccessful bid to obtain *Tunstall's patronage. It was in London that Tyndale first became familiar with the teachings of *Luther, to which he was an immediate convert. Finding it impossible to proceed with his translation of the New Testament, Tyndale left England in 1524, and the remaining twelve years of his life were spent in continuous travel on the continent (Ep 2831) in an attempt to escape from his enemies. During this time he industriously proceeded with his theological writings, his main accomplishment being a celebrated translation of the Bible into English, for which purpose he mainly utilized the Greek and Latin editions of Erasmus. In 1535 Tyndale, then in Flanders, was betrayed into the hands of the imperial officers by Henry Phillips, an Englishman, and in spite of numerous attempts to obtain his release, he was tried for heresy and executed.

During the years 1531–3 Tyndale was engaged in a controversy with Thomas *More, which despite its importance does not appear to be mentioned in the extant correspondence of Erasmus. In a letter of June 1533 (Ep 2831) More did refer, however, to the English arch-heretic, who was the source of a rumour then circulating in London that *Melanchthon had recently conferred with *Francis I of France.

BIBLIOGRAPHY: DNB XIX 1351–8 / Emden BRUO 1501–40 567–9 / R. Demaus *William Tyndale* (London 1886) / J.F. Mozley *William Tyndale* (London 1937) / W.E. Campbell *Erasmus, Tyndale and More* (London 1949) / C.H. Williams *William Tyndale* (London 1969) / J.A. Gee 'Tindale and the 1533 English *Enchiridion* of Erasmus' *Publications of the Modern Language Association* 49 (1934) 460–71 / J.F. Mozley 'The English *Enchiridion* of Erasmus, 1533' *Review of English Studies* 20 (1944) 97–107 / More Y VIII
MORDECHAI FEINGOLD

Theodoricus TZOBEL *See Theoderich* ZOBEL

UDALRICHUS (Epp 2462, 2470) *See Ulrich* WIRTNER

Damianus UISSENACUS *See Damiaan van* VISSENAKEN

Nicasius de ULMO *See Nicaise* DELORME

Georg ULRICHER of Andlau, documented 1525–36
Georg Ulricher (Ulrichius) was established as a printer in Strasbourg from 1529 to 1536. The entry in the town record at the time of his purchase of citizenship (27 December 1525) indicates that he was from Andlau, in Lower Alsace. His main emphasis as a printer was on the works of the Protestant reformers, *Bucer, *Hedio, and the work of Otto *Brunfels. He is mentioned in Erasmus' correspondence as the reputed printer of Bucer's *Epistola apologetica* (Ep 2312) and because in 1535 he apparently sent to Basel *Sapidus' epigram attacking Etienne *Dolet (Ep 3069). In 1536 he sold his press to Crato Mylius and his whereabouts thereafter are not known.
BIBLIOGRAPHY: Benzing *Buchdrucker* 415 / *Short-Title Catalogue of Books Printed in German-Speaking Countries ... to 1600 now in the British Museum* (London 1962) 1199 and passim / François Ritter *Histoire de l'imprimerie alsacienne au XVe et XVIe siècles* (Paris 1955) 316–17 and passim / M.U. Chrisman *Bibliography of Strasbourg Imprints, 1480–1599* (New Haven 1982) 417 and passim   MIRIAM U. CHRISMAN

Frater URBANUS Bolzanius *See Urbano* VALERIANI

Henricus URBANUS of Orb, d October 1538
Heinrich Fastnacht of Orb, fifty-five kilometres to the north-east of Frankfurt am Main took the name of Urbanus after his native town. He registered at the University of Erfurt for the spring term of 1494 but soon entered the Cistercian abbey of Georgenthal, south of Gotha, where he was appointed procurator. From 1504 he was in contact with Conradus *Mutianus Rufus, a canon of Gotha, and soon became his closest and most trusted friend. The friendship that united them was extended to include Georgius *Spalatinus, who was appointed a teacher at Georgenthal with the help of Mutianus.

After misconduct with a nun caused Urbanus to lose his office, he went to Leipzig, where he resumed his studies in the spring term of 1508 and was a BA a year later and a MA in 1510. With the support of Mutianus he obtained the stewardship of a house Georgenthal maintained at Erfurt. Henceforward Urbanus was the principal link between Mutianus and the humanist circle of Erfurt. He wrote well and employed his talent in the cause of *Reuchlin; at the same time he maintained close contacts with *Eobanus Hessus and his circle. In 1525 Georgenthal was destroyed by the rebelling peasants and the abbey's possessions were taken over by the elector of Saxony; however, Urbanus was retained as steward of the Erfurt house. He faced a difficult position five years later when the city of Erfurt sequestered the 'Georgenthaler Hof,' but in 1534 (definitively in 1535) he was reconfirmed as steward by the elector. He died in the second half of October 1538. Although he had ceased to wear the Cistercian cowl in the course of 1525 and was a personal friend of *Melanchthon, he never adopted the teachings of *Luther. He gathered a large collection of Mutianus' letters and fortunately ignored repeated requests by Mutianus to destroy them. Thus it is to Urbanus that we owe our most important source of information on Erfurt humanism in its heyday.

Mutianus mentioned Urbanus to Erasmus in his letter of introduction for Martin *Hune (Ep 1425).

BIBLIOGRAPHY: Allen Ep 1425 / G. Bauch in ADB XXXIX 345–6 / G. Bauch *Die Universität Erfurt im Zeitalter des Frühhumanismus* (Wrocław 1904) 136–7 / Walter Schmid-Ewald 'Der Georgenthaler Hof in Erfurt' *Mitteilungen des Vereins für Geschichte und Altertumskunde von Erfurt* 46 (1930) 94–106 / *Der Briefwechsel des Conradus Mutianus Rufus* ed K. Gillert (Halle 1890) preface / RE Epp 167–9, 174

ERICH KLEINEIDAM

Antonio Codro URCEO of Rubiera, 14 August 1446–11 February 1500
Antonio Urceo was born at Rubiera, between Modena and Reggio. His family originally came from Orzi Nuovi, near Brescia, from which his surname was derived. He studied at Modena under Gaspar Tribaco and at Ferrara under Battista Guarini and Luca Riva, who taught him Greek. In 1470 he went to Forlì, where he was tutor to Sinibaldo, the natural son of Pino

de Ordelaffi, lord of the city. After the death of Pino a rebellion led to the siege of Sinibaldo and Urceo in the citadel of Forlì. Sinibaldo died during the siege and Urceo left the city, arriving at Bologna in 1480. There he taught grammar, rhetoric, and poetry, numbering Nicolaus Copernicus among his pupils. He corresponded with Aldo *Manuzio and wrote poetry, using the name 'Codrus,' possibly an allusion to the pauper in Juvenal 3. 203–10. Although his poetry was celebrated for its Epicurean, pagan flavour, Urceo, according to Ellinger, spent his last days in the monastery of San Salvatore of Bologna. His *Opera*, including letters, poems, and academic lectures, were published in 1502 (Bologna: J.A. de Benedictis) and thrice thereafter in the first half of the sixteenth century.

In the *Ciceronianus* Erasmus stated that Urceo, although a cultured man, skilled in Latin, was also an Epicurean who did not seek a prize difficult to attain (ASD I-2 664–6).

BIBLIOGRAPHY: Cosenza IV 3513–20 / EI XXXIV 780 / Georg Ellinger *Geschichte der neulateinischen Literatur Deutschlands im sechzehnten Jahrhundert* (Berlin-Leipzig 1929–33) I 98–102 / Martin Lowry *The World of Aldus Manutius* (Oxford 1979) 30, 191–2, and passim   TBD

don Lope de UREA *See* MICHAEL *don Lope*

Caspar URSINUS Velius of Świdnica, d 5 March 1539
Caspar Ursinus (Ursing, Bernhardi) also called himself Velius, perhaps after his address in the via Velia during his stay at Rome. Born at Świdnica (Schweidnitz), in Silesia, he matriculated at the universities of Cracow in 1505 and Leipzig in 1508. In 1509 he entered the service of Bishop Matthäus *Lang and in 1510 went with him to Italy. He matriculated at Bologna, where he was taught Greek by Scipione *Fortiguerra (Carteromachus). In 1512 he went to Rome and stayed there until the autumn of 1514. After his return to Germany he continued his service with Lang, who was now a cardinal, but also matriculated at Vienna in the autumn of 1515. In 1518 Johannes (II) *Thurzo, bishop of Wrocław, secured for him a canonry in that city (Ep 851), thus enabling him to continue his studies.

In 1517 *Maximilian I created Ursinus a

doctor and poet laureate. He taught Greek at the University of Vienna until an outbreak of plague in the summer of 1521. The desire to meet Erasmus led him to Basel, where the university registered him under the date of 1 August, although he may not have arrived by that date (AK II Ep 817 introduction). Soon he moved on to Freiburg, where he registered on 1 February 1522 and attended the lectures of Udalricus *Zasius (Epp 1252, 1266). He returned to Vienna, travelling by way of Stuttgart, where he visited the old *Reuchlin during the last weeks of his life and delivered to him a letter from Erasmus, to whom he subsequently reported in a hexametric *Epistola* (Vienna: J. Singriener 1524). After another visit to Rome (Ep 1557) he obtained the chair of rhetoric at the University of Vienna in 1524 (Ep 1514); in 1527 he was also appointed historian of King *Ferdinand I (Ep 1917), whom he accompanied on his Hungarian campaign in 1527 and 1528. In 1530 he attended the diet of Augsburg and in 1532 became tutor to the king's children (Ep 2664). In 1529 he left the clerical state and married amid the turmoil caused by the Turkish siege of Vienna (Ep 2313). He did not, however, abandon the Catholic faith. On 5 March 1539 he left his house at Vienna and never came back; it was said that he had drowned himself in the Danube, in a state of depression caused by domestic strife (cf Allen Ep 1514 introduction).

Erasmus probably first heard of Ursinus in March 1517 when another member of Lang's entourage, Riccardo *Bartolini, sent him a poem Ursinus had composed in his honour. Erasmus made a suitable reply and allowed the poem to be printed with his *Epistolae elegantes* of the same year (Epp 548, 549, reprinted among the preliminary pieces in LB I). This led to a direct exchange of polite letters and the publication by Erasmus of another poem by Ursinus (Epp 851, 944). When Ursinus came to Basel and they met in November 1521, Erasmus found himself confirmed in his liking of his young admirer, who brought him a present from Stanislaus *Thurzo (Epp 1242, 1243, 1252, 1256). He was genuinely sad to see Ursinus depart the following spring (Ep 1267). Ursinus' visit to Basel also led to a friendship and correspondence with Bonifacius *Amerbach. Moreover, Johann *Froben published Ursinus'

collected poems in March–April 1522 (AK II Ep 817 introduction). Ursinus encouraged Jacobus *Piso and Erasmus to keep in touch (Epp 1297, 1662). He also informed Erasmus about his difficulties in Vienna (Ep 1557) and the complicated affairs of Hungary (Ep 1917). He praised the exploits of Ferdinand and actually wrote a book on this topic, *De bello hungarico*, which was not printed until 1762. Erasmus praised this work together with Ursinus' poems in his *Ciceronianus* (ASD I-2 689), but Ursinus regretted that some of his friends, such as *Vives and *Haio Herman of Friesland, had not likewise received an honourable mention (Epp 2008, 2040, 2056; cf Ep 2453). While Ursinus attended the diet of Augsburg in 1530 (Epp 2339, 2392, 2402), Erasmus once again praised him in the most extravagant terms in a letter to Bernhard von *Cles (Ep 2383). In September 1531 Ursinus was able to pay another visit to Erasmus at Freiburg and to Amerbach at Basel (Epp 2543, 2546). An immediate result of that visit was Erasmus' dedication of a psalm commentary to Ursinus' former patron Stanislaus Thurzo (Ep 2608; cf Epp 2517, 2699). In June 1532 Ursinus wrote from Innsbruck the last extant letter of his correspondence with Erasmus (Ep 2664). He had taken up his duties as preceptor to the royal children and was looking forward to more peaceful days after his hectic life as a diplomat.

BIBLIOGRAPHY: Allen Ep 548 / Knod 591 / *Matrikel Leipzig* I 489 / *Matrikel Wien* II-1 425 / *Matrikel Basel* I 347 / *Matrikel Freiburg* I-1 257 / ADB XXXIX 367–9 / Reedijk 399–400 / AK II Ep 817 and passim / Schottenloher II 345 / Georg Ellinger *Geschichte der neulateinischen Literatur Deutschlands im sechzehnten Jahrhundert* (Berlin-Leipzig 1929–33) I 484–93 and passim / Ludwig Geiger *Johann Reuchlin* (Leipzig 1871, repr 1964) 471–2   MICHAEL ERBE & PGB

Johannes URSUS *See Jan Arentszoon* BEREN

Christopher URSWICK of Furness, c 1448–24 March 1522
Christopher Urswick (Hursewik, Orsewik, Urcewyk, Urseuuicus, Wreswyke, Wrsouyt, Wrswic) was born in Furness, Lancashire, to John Urswick and his wife, lay brother and sister of the Cistercian abbey of Furness, and

Christopher Urswick

educated at Cambridge University. He entered King's Hall, of which he was a fellow in 1470–1 and warden from 1485 to 1488. In 1479 he received a master's degree, probably in canon law; a doctorate of canon law followed in 1482. In 1499–1500 he was given a present by the university. In 1475–6 he rented a room in University College, Oxford, for six months; before 1474 he had also lived in Troston, Suffolk, and in London.

Urswick was ordained subdeacon on 16 April 1468 and priest on 23 May 1472 in York. A long career followed of pluralism and ecclesiastical preferment, reflecting his advancement in affairs on account of services to both *Henry VII and *Henry VIII (the career of Richard *Foxe is a parallel). Urswick was rector of Puttenham, Huntingdonshire (1482–5); canon and prebendary of St Stephen's, Westminster (1485 to at least 1489); canon of St Paul's, London, and prebendary of Chiswick (1487–?1522); canon and prebendary of Exeter (1488–1522), chancellor of Exeter (?1492–1522); rector of All Hallows the Great, London (1487), and of Chedzoy, Somerset (1487–8); canon of York and prebendary of Tockerington (1488–93), of

Masham (1494), and of Botevant (1494–6); archdeacon of Richmond (1494–1500); canon of Beverley, Yorkshire, and prebendary of St Martin's altar (1500–2); prebendary of Fridaythorpe (1502–22); canon of Lincoln and prebendary of North Kelsey (1488–95); archdeacon of Huntingdon (1496); prebendary of Milton Ecclesia (1501–22); rector of Bradwell-juxta-Mare, Essex (1488–97); canon and prebendary of Gnosall College, Staffordshire (1489–91); canon of Sarum and prebendary of Bedwyn (1490–1522); canon and prebendary of St George's Chapel Windsor (1492–6); archdeacon of Wiltshire (?1488–1522, Le Neve), of Norfolk (1500–22), and of Surrey (1501, Emden; but no evidence, Le Neve), and of Oxford (1504–22); canon of Wells and prebendary of Easton-in-Gordano (1502/3–1509); rector of Hackney, Middlesex (1502–22) and of Gedney, Lincolnshire (1504–19); canon of Southwell and prebendary of Norwell Palishall (1509–22); fellow of the collegiate church of Manchester (1504); and rector of Overton, Hampshire (until 1514), of Felpham, Sussex, and of Ashbury, Berkshire (both till 1522) (for exact dates see Emden BRUC 605–6). A Christopher Urswick was dean of Wolverhampton in 1500.

Urswick was dean of York (1488–94) and of Windsor (1496–1505), but there is, according to Le Neve, no evidence that he declined the see of Norwich in 1499. In 1509 he was a member of a commission to administer the diocese of York in the absence of Archbishop Christopher Bainbridge. His final twenty years were passed, in affluent semi-retirement and the enjoyment of revenues and pensions from benefices, as rector of Hackney. He rebuilt the church of St Augustine, Hackney, and was a notable rebuilder of St George's Chapel, Windsor, where a chapel bears his name. By 1492 he was registrar of the order of the Garter.

On 14 June 1474 Urswick received a pardon for all offences committed before 8 June. On 16 March 1480 he was in Rome and may have stayed there or elsewhere in Italy until 25 January 1481. About 1482 he entered the household of Lady Margaret *Beaufort, who presented him to his first living, made him her chaplain and confessor, and apparently involved him in the negotiations between herself and John *Morton, bishop of Ely, intended to lead to the marriage of her son Henry to

*Elizabeth of York. Urswick may have visited Morton during his exile in Brittany and may have fled to Flanders after the plot of Humphrey Stafford, duke of Buckingham, had failed. He was Morton's messenger to Henry at Vannes and fled with Henry to the French court; he was Henry's envoy to Henry Percy, the earl of Northumberland, and his chaplain and confessor; he crossed to England with Henry and went with him to victory at Bosworth (August 1485; Shakespeare *Richard III* act 4, scene 5). At once he was granted his prebend at Westminster, appointed Henry's royal almoner (24 September 1485), and soon afterwards dispatched to the papal curia (4 February 1486). After being admitted to the confraternity of English Hospice on 11 June, he had returned to England by November 1486. He was envoy to *Ferdinand II and *Isabella of Spain concerning the marriage of Prince *Arthur and *Catherine of Aragon (1488); to France (March and May 1488; 1492); and to Scotland (1491, 1492, 1493). He was again in Rome early in 1493; his commission to invest the future *Alfonso II, king of Naples, with the order of the Garter is dated 5 March. By 1 April he had left Rome but was there again in June. His last mission abroad as an envoy was to *Maximilian I at Augsburg in April 1496, but he was present at Calais at the meeting of Henry VII and Philip the Handsome, duke of *Burgundy (1500), and he served Henry's diplomacy at home, continuing to attend at court occasions and acting on commissions in later years. He was an executor of the wills of Henry VII and of Henry's mother, Lady Margaret Beaufort (1509), and of many lesser personages.

Urswick died in 1522 and was buried in St Augustine's, Hackney (destroyed 1798; tomb extant in St John's, Hackney). The memorial brass gives his age at death as 73, although on 14 January 1486 he himself said he was 50 (Gale 67). His will is dated 10 October 1521, with a codicil of 28 December 1521; it was proved on 11 April 1522.

Urswick was a member of the London-Oxford humanist circle, though as a patron rather than as an active scholar or writer. He was friendly with Polidoro *Virgilio, for whose *Anglica historia* he supplied information, John *Colet, Cuthbert *Tunstall (remembered in his will), and Thomas *More, for whose *History of*

Richard III he may also have provided first-hand evidence (More Y II lxxvi). His considerable means enabled him to be the earliest recorded, and with Colet the most substantial, English patron of Pieter *Meghen, who copied to his order Cicero's *De officiis* (1503), miscellany volumes of ecclesiastical texts (1504, 1504–5), a psalter (1514), and a Latin Chrysostom (1517), as well as undated manuscripts including texts by Celso Maffei, *Luther, *Savonarola, *Pius II, and Leonardo Bruni Aretino. Erasmus spoke of Meghen to Urswick as 'your protégé' (Ep 416).

Erasmus may well have encountered Urswick during his first English visit (1499–1500) – DNB is wrong in saying that they met in 1483 and 1503 – and must certainly have done so during Erasmus' second stay (1505–6). He dedicated to Urswick his translation of Lucian's *Gallus*, printed in 1506 (Ep 193) at the time when he was attempting to form a circle of English patrons via his renderings of Lucian. Perhaps in return for this dedication he received from Urswick a horse, which he greatly valued; it took him twice to Basel and back (Ep 416). From August 1516 he was writing to his London friends to help him get Urswick to fulfil his promise of another horse; he also sent the *Novum instrumentum* and his Jerome to encourage such patronage. Urswick temporized (Epp 451, 452, 455, 467, 468, 474, 481, 499), and in March 1518 Erasmus gave up the attempt to get a mount from Urswick (CWE Ep 785). Few letters from Urswick are known: a prefatory epistle to Henry, second Baron Daubeny (1503); letters to the fourth earl of Shrewsbury (?1517; London College of Arms, Talbot Papers, A fol 59); to Prior Thomas Goldstone II of Christ Church, Canterbury, before 1517, and to Thomas, Baron Darcy on 30 June 1521 (London, British Library MSS Add. 15673 and 24451 respectively).

Urswick made many gifts of manuscripts and printed books to individuals and to institutions: Cicero *De officiis* (Rouen, Bibliothèque municipale MS 929) to Henry, second Baron Daubeny (d 1508) and then to André Bohier, abbot of Fécamp; *Pius II *Historia bohemica*, Leonardo Bruni Aretino *De bello punico* (Princeton University MS Garrett 89), and St Augustine *De civitate Dei* (Venice 1475; Cambridge, Corpus Christi College MS 346 – an incunable annotated by Urswick) to St

George's chapel, Windsor; Albertanus of Brescia *De doctrina tacendi et dicendi* (Cambridge, Sidney Sussex College, MS Δ .3.3.), St Antoninus *Opus historiale* (Basel 1491; Bristol, Central Public Library), and Platina *Vitae pontificum* (Venice 1504; Bodleian Library) to the Black Friars, Lancaster; Celso Maffei *Dissuasoria ne Christiani principes ecclesiasticos usurpent census* (London, British Library MS Add. 15673) to Prior Thomas Goldstone II of Christ Church, Canterbury; Psalter (1514) and St John Chrysostom *Homiliae in Matthaeum* (1517; both Wells, Cathedral Chapter Library) to Hayles Abbey, Gloucestershire, in memory of Sir John Huddleston, whose executor Urswick was. He also owned a manuscript of Mandeville's *Travels* (Oxford, Bodleian Library, MS Bodl 841); and printed editions of Statius (Venice 1490; Cambridge, University Library), Quintus Curtius *Gesta Alexandri* (Venice 1494; Eton College Library), Justinian (Strasbourg 1491ff; York Minster Library), and Marcantonio *Sabellico *Res Venetae* (Venice 1487; Aberdeen, University Library); as well as the ecclesiastical miscellany manuscript volumes now in Washington, Folger Shakespeare Library MS v.α.84 (Maximus of Turin, Gregory of Nazianzus, Ambrose); Oxford, Bodleian Library, MS Douce 110 (Canonical Epistles, Ecclesiastes, pseudo-Ambrose, Augustine); Oxford Bodleian Library, MS Barlow 14 (annotated by Urswick; Jerome, Rufinus, Gregory of Nazianzus, pseudo-Ambrose, Celso Maffei); and Oxford, Bodleian Library, MS Univ Coll 40 (Chrysostom, Augustine, Luther, Savonarola).

There is no extant portrait; the brass on his altar tomb in St John's, Hackney, is a conventional representation.

BIBLIOGRAPHY: Allen Ep 193 / DNB XX 55–6 / Emden BRUC 605–6, 685 / Emden BRUO III 1935–6 / Thomas A. Urwick *Records of the Family of Urswyck, Urswick or Urwick* ed W. Urwick (St Albans 1893) 81–139, 223 / S.L. Ollard *Fasti Wyndesorienses: The Deans and Canons of Windsor* (Windsor 1950) / McConica 70–2 / Alan B. Cobban *King's Hall … Cambridge in the later Middle Ages* (Cambridge 1969) esp 288–9 / W.E. Wilkie *The Cardinal Protectors of England* (Cambridge 1974) 11 and passim / John Le Neve *Fasti Ecclesiae Anglicanae, 1340–1541* 2nd ed (London 1962–5) passim / Polidoro Virgilio *Anglica Historia* ed D. Hay (London 1950) xix and passim / J.B. Trapp and H. Schulte Herbrüggen *'The King's Good Servant,' Sir Thomas More, 1477/8–1535* (London 1977) no 18 and passim / D.S. Chambers *Cardinal Bainbridge in the Court of Rome* (Oxford 1965) 19 / W.K. Ferguson 'An unpublished letter of John Colet, Dean of St Paul's' *American Historical Review* 39 (1933–4) 697–9 esp 699 / F.K. Gale 'Christopher Urswick, Dean of Windsor, 1448–1522' (master's thesis, Warburg Institute, University of London, 1974) / J.B. Trapp 'Pieter Meghen, scribe and courier' *Erasmus in English* 11 (1981–2) 28–35　　　　J.B. TRAPP

Bartholomaeus Arnoldi of USINGEN c 1465– 9 September 1532

In a letter from Augustinus *Marius, Erasmus found a reference to a theologian whose name he could not read, though it looked to him like Vemgus. He asked Marius on 22 May 1530 to greet the theologian (Ep 2321). The name was very likely Usingensis, Usingerus, or Usingus, v equalling u.

Bartholomaeus Arnoldi of Usingen studied at Erfurt from 1484 and there taught scholastic philosophy and theology until 1526, acceding to the doctorate in 1514. He was one of the teachers of Martin *Luther, and around 1512 he entered the same Erfurt house of the Augustinian Eremites that Luther had entered some seven years earlier. Usingen, however, opposed the Reformation with great zeal, although he was sympathetic to the humanist movement and in 1523 called Erasmus 'studiorum nostri saeculi unicum decus' (Paulus 14). In the wake of the peasant rebellion and the triumph of the reform party, he left Erfurt early in 1526 for the Würzburg house of his order. Shortly after the date of Ep 2321 he went with Bishop Konrad von *Thüngen to the diet of Augsburg. Also accompanying the bishop were Marius and another friend of Erasmus, Daniel *Stiebar. That Marius, in particular, was close to Usingen can be seen from the fact that he put up a commemorative inscription to him in the refectory of the Würzburg monastery. Usingen published scholastic text-books and works of anti-Lutheran polemic.

BIBLIOGRAPHY: NDB I 388–9 / N. Paulus *Der Augustiner Bartholomäus Arnoldi von Usingen* (Freiburg 1893) / Erich Kleineidam *Universitas studii Erffordensis* (Leipzig 1964–80) II 300–1 and passim　　　　PGB

Christoph von UTENHEIM d 16 March 1527
Ruins of the castle of Ramstein, near Scherwil-
ler, Lower Alsace, which was occupied by the
Utenheim family from the early fifteenth
century, still survive. Christoph's father held a
high position in the administration of the
bishop of Strasbourg; his mother was Susanna
von Müllenheim. As early as 1452 a Basel
canonry was pledged to Christoph. In 1460 he
was registered at the University of Erfurt,
obtaining his MA in 1466. Having been a canon
of St Thomas' at Strasbourg, he was elected
provost of that chapter late in 1473 (he resigned
in 1494). At the same time his name appears in
the register of the University of Basel, where
he was rector for the winter term 1473–4 and
became a doctor of canon law in 1474. The
following year he became a canon of the Basel
chapter. He visited Rome in 1481 but otherwise
lived at Basel, becoming *custos* of the chapter in
1486. From 1499 he acted for the aged bishop,
ultimately with the title of coadjutor, before
himself being elected bishop of Basel on 1
December 1502 and consecrated on 2 May 1503.

A close friend of Johann Geiler of Kaysersberg and especially of Jakob *Wimpfeling – in
1497 the trio had planned to withdraw to a
hermitage in the Black Forest (Ep 2088) – and
also a patron of Sebastian *Brant, Utenheim
formed a dual commitment to ecclesiastical
reform and humanistic learning. In 1494 the
abbot of Cluny entrusted to him the reform of
the monastery of St Alban at Basel, but
whether his election as bishop was due to his
reforming views or to his social rank combined
with a reputation for personal weakness is
open to question. At any rate, he began his
episcopal tenure of office with a synod in 1503,
for which occasion Wimpfeling collected and
edited the statutes of the diocese. They were
splendidly printed (n p, n d) but could not
thereafter be enforced any better than previously. Nor were there any more annual
synods. Often the clergy resisted Utenheim's
attempts at reform, and in doing so was
supported in part by the Alsatian nobility and
also by Swiss cities like Basel that were eager to
enlarge their powers and territories at the
expense of the prince-bishopric. He did succeed, however, in bringing to Basel some very
able exponents of reform and humanism such
as Tilmann *Limperger in 1498, Johannes *Fabri
in 1513, Wolfgang *Capito in 1515, and

Christoph von Utenheim

Johannes *Oecolampadius in 1518. The presence of such men together with Utenheim's
cordial invitations and generous proofs of
friendship were bound to influence Erasmus'
decision to move to Basel. Thus together with
*Beatus Rhenanus, whom he often invited to
dine with him (Ep 594), Utenheim helped
create very fruitful links between the humanist
circles at Basel, in Alsace, and elsewhere. At
the same time some of his reform-minded
appointees began to adopt the views of Martin
*Luther. In 1520 Utenheim himself was still
being encouraged by Wimpfeling to support
Luther's stand at Rome, but by 1522 he had to
dissociate himself from the reformers, forbidding his clergy to attend the lectures and
sermons of Oecolampadius. This was no doubt
a grave disappointment to him. Worse, however, was the continued wrangling over rights
and powers with the Basel council and
sometimes with his own chapter – conflicts that
were distasteful to him and left him exhausted.
With the appointment of Nikolaus von *Diesbach as coadjutor in 1519 Utenheim began to
withdraw from the exercise of many duties and
powers. More and more frequently he resided
at the remote Porrentruy in the Jura. From 1526

he was prepared to resign, and the negotiations in this matter soon involved the court of King *Ferdinand. After submitting his resignation to the Basel chapter on 19 February 1527, Utenheim died at Porrentruy before a successor could be elected. Wimpfeling dedicated to him his *De concordia curatorum et fratrum mendicantium* [Strasbourg 1503] and Sebastian Brant his edition of a reforming speech of Jean Raulin (Basel: J. Bergmann 1498).

When Erasmus went to Basel in September 1514 Wimpfeling gave him a letter of introduction to Utenheim (Ep 305). In the course of that winter the bishop succeeded in making him feel especially welcome and honoured (Epp 412–14). He also wrote to William *Warham recommending Erasmus in view of his next visit to England (Epp 425, 456, 488). For his part Erasmus published in the first selection of his letters (1516) two pieces which noted amid generous compliments the bishop's approval of the New Testament (Epp 446, 456). In the *Auctarium* of 1518 he published the warm invitation to Basel that Utenheim had sent him in July 1517 (Ep 598), his answer promising the dedication of a forthcoming work (Ep 625), and several letters announcing to the world the bishop's virtues and his invitation (Epp 626, 756, 761, 809). More flattering comments appeared in the *Farrago* of 1519 with the publication of some earlier letters (Epp 412–14). When Erasmus returned to Basel in 1522 he was again given a warm welcome (Epp 1258, 1342) and afterwards saw or corresponded with the bishop on several occasions. At one time he attempted to excuse Hermannus *Buschius, who was moving closer to Luther (Ep 1496; ASD IX-1 368–9); he also exchanged reading matter with Utenheim (Ep 1332, receiving *Denis the Carthusian, sending Luther!). In 1524 he visited Utenheim in Porrentruy (Ep 1610).

The bishop's opinion clearly mattered to him in the case of the New Testament as well as other publications (Epp 1399, 1571). *De immensa Dei misericordia*, a work to be dedicated to Utenheim, was first sent to him in manuscript for his scrutiny (Epp 1456, 1464, 1474; Allen I 21). Much controversy followed the specific reforms advocated by Erasmus in his *Epistola de esu carnium*, addressed to Utenheim (Epp 1620, 1642, 1685; Allen I 33; ASD IX-1 1–50) and

published, Erasmus maintained in Ep 1581, at his request and against the author's earlier inclination. While Erasmus' praise of Utenheim's integrity and love of learning was no doubt sincere, he did not, as far as we know, comment on his administration of the diocese or on his death.

BIBLIOGRAPHY: Allen Ep 598 / NDB III 243 / *Helvetia sacra* ed A. Bruckner (Bern 1972–   ) I-1 199–200 and passim / *Matrikel Basel* I 121 / *Matrikel Erfurt* I 283 / E. Kleineidam *Universitas studii Erffordensis* (Leipzig 1964–80) I 376 and passim / R. Wackernagel *Geschichte der Stadt Basel* (Basel 1907–54) II-2 844, III 86–93, and passim / Schmidt *Histoire littéraire* I 23 and passim / *Aktensammlung zur Geschichte der Basler Reformation* ed E. Dürr et al (Basel 1921–50) I 76–7, II 79–80, 443–4, III 83–91 / *Basler Chroniken* VII 152–3 / BA *Oekolampads* I 20–1, 285–9, 458, II 6, and passim / AK I Ep 210 and passim   PGB

Karel UUTENHOVE of Ghent, documented c 1524–77

A son of Nicolaas (I) *Uutenhove, Karel was sent to Louvain by 1524 and attended the Collegium Trilingue. In June 1528 he set out for Basel; Erasmus received him into his household and took an immediate liking to the quiet youth (Epp 2001, 2015, 2062). Perhaps in the company of Andrzej *Zebrzydowski, he set out in the autumn for a brief visit to Paris, where he met Louis de *Berquin (Epp 2065, 2077, 2078), but soon returned to Erasmus (Epp 2078, 2089). Erasmus was happy to have him back and on 1 February 1529 dedicated to him his Greek edition of some *Opuscula* by St John Chrysostom (Ep 2093). Towards the end of that month, when Uutenhove left in Zebrzydowski's company (Epp 2161, 2173; AK IV Ep 2039) to continue his studies in Italy, Erasmus recommended him warmly to his friends in Venice and Padua (Epp 2105, 2106). Uutenhove remained in Italy until April 1531 and during this time regularly corresponded with Erasmus, who hoped to see him return as an accomplished Ciceronian and Greek scholar (Ep 2188) and reproached him for the careless style of his letters, which he attributed to a lack of diligence (Ep 2288). On his way home in the spring of 1531 Uutenhove stopped at Freiburg to greet Erasmus (Epp 2483, 2485) and in May he reached Ghent, where his mother had just died (Epp 2491, 2494). Erasmus recalled him with undisguised disappointment as a young man of good family and mediocre education, little given to study (Epp 2681, 2682), but their exchange of letters continued for some time, with Erasmus still eager to give advice, especially in view of Uutenhove's plans to get married (Epp 2700, 2799, 3019). In fact in 1532 Uutenhove married Anna de Grutere, niece of Willem de *Waele, a member of the council of Flanders and an old friend of Erasmus. Despite these additional ties Erasmus feared in 1535, no doubt without justification, that Uutenhove had turned against him under the influence of *Quirinus Hagius (Ep 3052).

Meanwhile Uutenhove continued to reside at Ghent, where he was elected an alderman in 1539, but he also spent a good deal of time at the family estate of Marckeghem. He played his part in Ghent's rebellion against the regent *Mary, queen of Hungary, in 1539 and 1540 and retired from public life during the ensuing repression. On account of his Protestant leanings he withdrew from 1556 to 1557 to Paris, where one of his sons, also named Karel, became a tutor in the house of Jean *Morel. The rest of Uutenhove's life is not well known. He remarried, corresponded with *Melanchthon, and apparently was obliged to leave his native country for good, retiring to the duchies of Jülich-Cleves, where his son Karel had established himself. The last record of the father seems to be a letter of 10 September 1577, in the hand of a secretary but signed 'Chas. Vtenhove, l'aveugle.'

Erasmus honoured Uutenhove by making him a speaker in his colloquy Ἀστραγαλισμός of 1529 (ASD I-3 620–8), and as late as 1587 his son was writing to Basel in search of unpublished letters by Erasmus.

BIBLIOGRAPHY: Allen Ep 2093 / de Vocht *Literae ad Craneveldium* 295 / de Vocht CTL II 465–73 and passim / de Vocht *Dantiscus* 94–5 and passim / Bierlaire *Familia* 86–7 / M.A. Nauwelaerts in *Commémoration nationale d'Erasme: Actes* (Brussels 1970) 157–8 / Primarily on Uutenhove's son Karel: Leonard Forster 'Charles Utenhove and Germany' in *European Context: Studies ... presented to Theodoor Weevers* (Cambridge 1971) 60–80 / P.G. Bietenholz *Basle and France in the Sixteenth Century* (Geneva-

Toronto 1971) 206 and passim / Rolf Kirmse 'Karel Utenhove – ein flämischer Emigrant am Niederrhein' *Jahrbuch Kreis Moers* 30 (1973) 142–55 / Johan Decavele *De dageraad van de reformatie in Vlaanderen (1520–1565)* (Brussels 1975) I 79, II 86–93, and passim

FRANZ BIERLAIRE

Nicolaas (I) UUTENHOVE of Ghent, d 11 February 1527

Nicolaas, the father of Karel *Uutenhove, was descended from a noble family of Ghent. The son of Rijkaert and Josine van den Vagheviere, he matriculated at the University of Louvain on 30 August 1480, proceeding in due course from liberal arts to the faculty of law. From 1498, if not earlier, he was a member of the council of Flanders, and in 1515 he was appointed its president. He was lord of Marckeghem. In 1496 or 1497 he married Agnes van den Varent, who bore him three children in addition to Karel. Two years after Nicolaas' death Erasmus recalled him with elaborate praise in a letter addressed to Karel (Ep 2093). It was accompanied by two epitaphs for Nicolaas, one in Latin, the other in Greek (Reedijk poems 121, 122).

BIBLIOGRAPHY: Allen Ep 2093 / *Matricule de Louvain* II-1 423 / de Vocht *Literae ad Craneveldium* 295 / Paul van Peteghem 'Centralisatie onder Keizer Karel (1515–1555)' (doctoral thesis, Rijksuniversiteit Gent 1980)

MARCEL A. NAUWELAERTS

Nicolaas (II) UUTENHOVE of Ghent, d 19 August 1549

Nicolaas was a first cousin of Karel *Uutenhove. Born probably at Ghent in 1499, he was the son of Rijkaert Uutenhove, knight, and Josine van de Woestyne. After studies at Orléans, Poitiers, and elsewhere, he graduated licentiate in law and from 1529 was councillor-in-ordinary of the council of Flanders and from 1547 of the grand council of Mechelen. On 2 September 1536 he married Elisabeth de Grutere. In Ep 2093 Erasmus praised him as a young man of great promise.

BIBLIOGRAPHY: Allen Ep 2093 / Paul van Peteghem 'Centralisatie onder Keizer Karl (1515–1555)' (doctoral thesis, Rijksuniversiteit Gent 1980) / de Vocht *Literae ad Craneveldium*

Joachim Vadianus

295 (with different indications as to descent and marriage)   MARCEL A. NAUWELAERTS

Johannes VACHANUS *See John* VAUGHAN

Ludovicus VACUS *See Luis* NÚÑEZ *Cabeza de Vaca*

Joachim VADIANUS of St Gallen, 29 November 1484–6 April 1551
Vadianus (Joachim von Watt) was descended from a leading family of merchants and magistrates at St Gallen. After attending the local grammar school he matriculated at the University of Vienna in the winter term of 1501–2 and graduated BA in 1504 and MA in 1508. With Nikolaus *Gerbel he belonged to the humanist circle of Conradus Celtis. From 1506 to 1507 he escaped from plague-infested Vienna, taught briefly at Villach, in Carinthia, and visited Venice and Padua. When he returned to Vienna he taught at the university, lecturing on various Latin authors but especially on geographers. In connection with his lectures he prepared commentaries on book VII of the older Pliny's *Historia naturalis* and on

Pomponius Mela which were published by Johann Singriener in Vienna in 1515 and 1518. In 1514 he was vice-chancellor of the university, and late in 1516 he was appointed to the chair of rhetoric, also being rector for the winter term of 1516–17. Meanwhile he pursued the study of medicine and obtained his doctorate late in 1517, perhaps in view of his intended return to St Gallen. He also published a study of poetry, *De poetica et carminis ratione* (Vienna: J. Singriener 1518), and in recognition, or rather anticipation, of his humanistic studies was made a poet laureate by *Maximilian I at Linz on 12 March 1514. In June 1518 he returned to his native city, but before he settled there for good, he spent some more time travelling, climbing Mount Pilatus because a passage of Pomponius Mela had aroused his curiosity, and visiting Leipzig, Poznań, Wrocław, and Cracow, returning by way of Vienna. On 18 August 1519 he married Martha Grebel, from a patrician Zürich family, a sister of Konrad Grebel, the future Anabaptist. Finally in the spring of 1520 he settled down at St Gallen as the town physician and a member of the inner council in succession to his father. His primary ambition was still to introduce his fellow-citizens to humanistic culture, and to this end he established ties with the humanist circle at Basel. On a visit there in the summer of 1522 he met Erasmus (Ep 1314), contributed to a new edition of *Glareanus' *Helvetiae descriptio*, and published with Andreas *Cratander a greatly enlarged edition of his Pomponius Mela. Soon, however, his concern for humanistic culture was overshadowed by his desire for religious reform. He had read *Luther's early writings and had long been acquainted with *Zwingli. From early 1523 he lectured on Acts, combining evangelical tenets with his old interest in geography (the latter reappearing in his *Epitome trium terrae partium*, Zürich: C. Froschauer 1534). He did not attempt to form his own theology and in some dogmatic positions remained closer to Luther than to Zwingli, but as a statesman he found the example of Zwinglian Zürich inspiring. After participating in a disputation at Zürich, 26–8 October 1523, he took the lead in establishing the reformed church in St Gallen and amid the process of change was elected mayor on 28

December 1525, filling this position to the end of his life as often as the law would permit, and encountering issues as difficult to deal with as Anabaptism, the conflict with the abbey of St Gallen, and the Swiss civil wars of Kappel. Nor did he allow the conduct of affairs to hinder his scholarly research, which was now increasingly directed to the field of history. His historical works, chief among which is a German chronicle of the abbots of St Gallen composed between 1529 and 1531, are characterized by careful gathering and critical evaluation of the sources. Throughout his life he conducted and preserved a voluminous correspondence with friends and scholars as far afield as Poland and Italy.

In the first edition of his Pomponius Mela, Vadianus found room for a complimentary mention of Erasmus which was not lost on the latter (Ep 1314) and was amplified in the second edition of 1522. Erasmus replied with similar compliments in the *Adagia* edition of 1526 (*Adagia* II iv 53).

BIBLIOGRAPHY: Allen Ep 1314 / ADB XLI 239–44 / Werner Näf *Vadian und seine Stadt St. Gallen* (St Gallen 1944–57) / *Vadian-Studien* ed Werner Näf et al (St Gallen 1945–   ) / z VII Ep 2 and passim / AK II Ep 668 and passim / R. Feller and E. Bonjour *Geschichtsschreibung der Schweiz* (Basel 1962) I 229–38 and passim / Vadianus' historical works in Latin are published in *Scriptores rerum Alemannicarum* ed M. Goldast (Frankfurt 1661) III; those in German by E. Götzinger (St Gallen 1875–9); his correspondence in *Vadianische Briefsammlung* / *Matrikel Wien* II-1 298, 432   PGB

Margarita VALDAURA of Bruges, 5 June 1505–14 October 1552

Margarita Valdaura, the wife of Juan Luis *Vives, was undoubtedly a primary model for the idealized female depicted in *De institutione feminae christianae* (Vives, *Omnia opera* IV 70–301), a literary initiative generally considered significant in sixteenth-century attitudes towards women and their education. Born in Bruges, she grew up amid the accoutrements of a fairly well-to-do merchant family. Possibly a dealer in gems (Vives had once seen him split a diamond with a hammer: *City of God* 842), Bernardo Valdaura belonged to a closely knit community of Spanish exiles of Jewish extrac-

tion. Clara Cervant, his wife and Margarita's mother, earned an eloquent eulogy from her son-in-law (too effusive for Erasmus: Ep 1830) as the totally dedicated nurse, wife, and mother, 'an ornament to her sex ... leaving to us a vast longing' at her death (de Vocht *Literae ad Craneveldium* Ep 248). Related to the Valdauras through his mother, Blanquina March, Vives joined their circle when he first went to Bruges in 1512 and remained closely involved with their fortunes over the years.

On 26 May, Corpus Christi Day of 1524, when he was thirty-two and she nineteen years of age, Juan Luis Vives and Margarita Valdaura were joined in marriage at St Donatian's cathedral, Bruges, by Jan van *Fevijn. The event caused a small flurry of letters among friends agreeing that the marriage was indeed felicitous (de Vocht *Literae ad Craneveldium* Epp 100, 107, 115). Erasmus had received Vives' letter of 16 June (Ep 1455) modestly describing the general approbation of their mutual friends; perhaps Erasmus chose to ignore the event, although his letter of September 2–6 with a possible answer has disappeared (Allen Ep 1513:24n). At any rate, he notified Juan de *Vergara in March 1526 (Ep 1684) without comment.

Margarita rarely left Bruges after her marriage. Once she was enticed without success by letter and gift to join *Catherine of Aragon in England, possibly a naïve gesture of the queen to keep Vives closer to the court at the impending divorce (de Vocht *Literae ad Craneveldium* Ep 252). Like the paragon described in his works, Margarita delighted her serious husband over sixteen years of marriage, never disturbing him in his study, caring for him in his illness, depending on him in time of trouble, journeying with him once to Lille to escape the plague (although returning earlier than he to nurse the victims of the Spanish quarter), and eventually pressuring Frans van *Cranevelt to publish posthumously her husband's last book. Like Alice *More, Elizabeth Cranevelt, and Roberte *Le Lieur (the wife of Guillaume *Budé), women whom Vives knew and admired deeply, Margarita enriched the life of a husband who was playing the new role of lay married scholar serving a new society.

As a widow, Margarita remained in Bruges until her death and was interred beside her husband in the cathedral where they were married. The memorial to the couple raised by her family featured their portraits; only ancient records attest to this monument since neither it nor the cathedral is presently in existence.

BIBLIOGRAPHY: Allen Ep 1455 / Adolfo Bonilla y San Martín *Luis Vives y la filosofía del renacimiento* 2nd ed (Madrid 1929) / Carlos Noreña *Juan Luis Vives* (The Hague 1970) 51, 89–92, and passim / Juan Luis Vives *Opera omnia* (Valencia 1782–90, repr 1966) / St Augustine *Of the Citie of God* ed and comm J.L. Vives, trans John Healy (London 1610) / De Vocht *Literae ad Craneveldium* Ep 102 and passim / Foster Watson *Vives: On Education, a Translation of the 'De tradendis disciplinis'* (Cambridge 1913) / Foster Watson *Vives and the Renaissance Education of Women* (London 1912)   ALICE TOBRINER

Alfonso de VALDÉS of Cuenca,
c 1500–6 October 1532
Alfonso and his younger brother Juan de *Valdés were the most famous of the six children of Fernando de Valdés, a nobleman of the New Castilian province of Cuenca. No records of Alfonso's birth, baptism, or studies have survived. Probably the Italian humanist Pietro Martire d'Anghiera was his private tutor. The only reference to Alfonso's education comes indirectly from the Spanish humanist Francisco de Enzinas, who in his *Mémoires* (1558) refers to Juan de Valdés as having been tutored by his brother: 'in disciplina fraterna praeclare instructus.' The first records of Alfonso's life date from when he went to Germany with the court of *Charles v in preparation for the imperial coronation. There are three personal letters of Alfonso to Anghiera dated at Brussels on 31 August 1520, at Aachen on 25 October 1520, and at Worms on 13 May 1521 (Anghiera *Opus epistolarum*, Alcalá 1530, Epp 689, 699, 723). Alfonso was attached to the secretarial staff of Charles v under the direction of Maximilianus *Transsilvanus, secretary for Latin correspondence. Alfonso's letters provide his personal impressions on the beginnings of Lutheranism, the imperial election, and the diet of Worms. In 1522 he returned to Spain with the court. Soon after the event he edited official reports on the battle of Pavia (24 February 1525) against the king of France, *Francis I (*Relación de las nuevas de Italia*, n p, n d). By February 1526 Alfonso himself was made secretary for Latin correspondence, and he was known as 'imperial secretary.' By 26 October he became a secretary to Mercurino *Gattinara.

It was in the mid-1520s that Valdés made his first known contact with Erasmus. On 15 December 1525 Transsilvanus wrote to Valdés from Brussels asking him to approach Charles v about the payment of Erasmus' pension (Caballero Ep 6; see Allen Ep 1645 introduction). In March 1527 both Gattinara and Transsilvanus referred to letters from Valdés to Erasmus (Epp 1790A, 1802), to which Erasmus replied in Ep 1807. Valdés became Erasmus' most enthusiastic supporter at the imperial court, frequently corresponding with him and establishing and maintaining contacts with Juan de *Vergara, Luis *Coronel, Alonso Ruiz de *Virués, Juan *Maldonado, and other Spanish Erasmians. When the attacks of Spanish friars led to the Valladolid conference of 1527, which was to hear objections against Erasmus, Valdés defended him and wrote to him to keep him informed of events (Ep 1839). On 23 November 1527 he advised Erasmus to proceed cautiously with the religious orders and encouraged him not to publish his reply to them as a sign of his moderation (Ep 1907). Later, when Erasmus was attacked by Luis de *Carvajal, Valdés was among those who gave him information and advice (Epp 2126, 2198).

Meanwhile through his writing Valdés stirred up a controversy of his own. On 6 May 1527 imperial troops began their notorious Sack of Rome. By July or August 1527 Valdés had written his first major work, the *Diálogo en que particularmente se tratan las cosas occuridas en Roma*, or *Lactancio*. It was circulated in manuscript, then published without place or date around 1529. The anti-papal theme of the *Lactancio* involved Valdés in a bitter conflict with Baldesar *Castiglione, the papal nuncio. On 14 May 1529 Valdés wrote to Erasmus describing the genesis of the *Lactancio* and the furore it caused (Ep 2163).

By 1529 conditions in Italy had stabilized to the point where Charles v could travel there to deal personally with *Clement VII. Valdés accompanied the emperor, disembarking at Genoa on 12 August 1529. There he met the two Spanish humanists Juan Ginés de *Sepúl-veda and Diego *López Zúñiga, an avowed enemy of Erasmus, who were in Cardinal Francisco de *Quiñones' escort to welcome the emperor on behalf of the pope. Valdés obtained from the pope a brief absolving him and his family of any ecclesiastical censure. He also obtained the privilege of having a 'portable altar.' He attended the emperor's coronation by the pope at Bologna and followed the imperial court through Italy and Germany. In April 1530 he was in Mantua and in June in Innsbruck. On 5 June 1530 Gattinara died, and on the following 9 July Erasmus wrote to Valdés commiserating with him on Gattinara's death (Ep 2349). Valdés took over Gattinara's role of mediator between Catholics and Protestants and at the diet of Augsburg acted in this sense. Alfonso's seven letters addressed to the cardinal of Ravenna, Benedetto *Accolti, deal with this subject and cover the period from 12 July to 24 September 1530. Valdés dealt with Philippus *Melanchthon as the Protestant representative and exercised an irenic and moderating influence. Also, at the emperor's request he translated the Augsburg Confession into Spanish. Ultimately the negotiations failed partly because of the impatience and lack of trust of the emperor and the papal legate Lorenzo *Campeggi.

Even after this failure Valdés did not completely lose his hope for a reunited Christendom led by the idealized, messianic figure of Charles v. He attended the coronation of *Ferdinand as king of the Romans and followed the imperial court in the Netherlands and Germany until the summer of 1532. He was present at the diet of Regensburg in the summer of 1532 but did not participate in the negotiations. Finally the plague overtook him, and he died in Vienna. His will is dated 5 October. On 24 March 1533 Erasmus wrote to Johann *Henckel about Valdés' death (Ep 2783; see also Epp 2798, 2800).

With Valdés' death Spanish Erasmianism suffered an irreparable blow and the imperial chancery lost an important moderating force. Valdés' connection with Erasmus is religious, political, and literary. The *Lactancio* is Erasmian in inspiration. It echoes the *Querela pacis* but is based on historico-political events closely associated with Valdés and the imperial chan-cery. It draws on its author's political experience, his Spanish messianism, and his imperial and Spanish antagonism to the papacy. It is in fact a theological vindication of the Sack of Rome and an apologia for the emperor. At the religious level Valdés advocated Erasmus' piety, and his critique of church abuses, externals, and ceremonies. Valdés' second work, the *Diálogo de Mercurio y Carón*, finished in the summer of 1528, also exemplifies his Erasmianism. The Erasmian sources of this book are the *Colloquia*, the *Moria*, the *Apophthegmata*, the *Enchiridion*, and the *Adagia*. But not everything in the *Mercurio y Carón* is Erasmian. Valdés' vision of the ideal Christian man has much in common with the ideas of the *alumbrados*. This made him, in the eyes of the Inquisition, even more dangerous than his Erasmianism, and is also the point of contact between the two Valdés brothers. At the literary level Alfonso also took Erasmus as a model. His Castilian prose is considered to be amongst the most accomplished before Cervantes. His correspondence is scattered in several works, but Caballero gathered most of it as an appendix to his book.

BIBLIOGRAPHY: Allen Ep 1807 / E. Boehmer *Bibliotheca Wiffeniana* (Strasbourg-London 1874–1904, repr 1962) / 'Alfonsi Valdesii litteras XL ineditas' ed E. Boehmer in *Homenaje a Menéndez y Pelayo* (Madrid 1899) I 385–412 / *Enciclopedia universal ilustrada europeo-americana* (Barcelona, Madrid 1907?–) LXVI 495–7 / E. Stern *Alfonso et Juan de Valdés, fragments de l'histoire de la réformation en Espagne et en Italie* (Strasbourg 1869) / M. Carrasco *Alfonso et Juan de Valdés, leur vie et leurs éscrits religieux* (Geneva 1880) / F. Caballero *Noticias biográficas y literarias de Alonso y Juan de Valdés* (Madrid 1875), with documentary appendix / M. Bataillon 'Alonso de Valdés, auteur du *Diálogo de Mercurio y Carón*' in *Homenaje ofrecido a Menéndez Pidal* (Madrid 1925) I 403–15 / Bataillon *Erasmo y España* 104, 111–2, and passim / Alfonso de Valdés *Diálogo de las cosas ocurridas en Roma* ed J.F. Montesinos (Madrid 1928), English version with introduction and notes by J.E. Longhurst in *Alfonso de Valdés and the Sack of Rome* (New Mexico 1952) / Alfonso de Valdés *Diálogo de Mercurio y Carón* ed J.F. Montesinos (Madrid 1929) / J.F. Montesinos 'Algunas notas sobre el *Diálogo de Mercurio y*

Carón' Revista de filología española 16 (1929)
225–66 / G. Bagnatori 'Cartas inéditas de
Alfonso de Valdés sobre la Dieta de Augsbur-
go' Bulletin hispanique 57 (1955) 353–74 /
Melanchthons Briefwechsel I Ep 936 / Domingo de
Santa Teresa Juan de Valdés 1498(?)–1541: Su
pensamiento religioso y las corrientes espirituales de
su tiempo (Rome 1957) / J.C. Nieto Juan de Valdés
and the Origins of the Spanish and Italian
Reformation (Geneva 1970, Spanish rev and
enlarged ed, Madrid-Mexico 1979)

JOSÉ C. NIETO

Juan de VALDÉS of Cuenca,
1509/10(?)–August 1541
Juan de Valdés was a son of Fernando de
Valdés, regidor of Cuenca, Spain, and deputy
for Cuenca in the Cortes. His mother's name is
unknown, but one of her brothers, Fernando
de la Barrera, a priest, was burnt at the stake
for relapsing into Judaism. Valdés too was of
Jewish converso origins. Early in his life he
probably had as a tutor the humanist Pietro
Martire d'Anghiera, as supposedly did his
elder brother Alfonso de *Valdés. Despite
Erasmus' ambiguous statement in Ep 1961 it is
unlikely that they were twin brothers.

The earliest reference to Valdés appears in
the Inquisition of Toledo's records of Pedro
Ruiz de Alcaraz's trial in 1525. It shows that
while he was a 'boy,' in the years 1523–4,
Valdés was a member of the household of
Diego *López Pacheco, marquis of Villena, an
enlightened nobleman sympathetic to Erasmus, in the town of Escalona (Toledo). There
Valdés attended the religious meetings of the
heretical alumbrados headed by Isabel de la
Cruz and Pedro Ruiz de Alcaraz (both of
Jewish converso origin). Here Valdés was
deeply influenced by the ideas expressed by
the alumbrados and probably experienced a
religious crisis or conversion. During the trial
of Alcaraz, Valdés was in Alcalá de Henares,
where he was probably studying at the
university by 18 November 1526; he remained
there until early 1531. It is there that he came
into contact with the Erasmian élite of Alcalá
such as Juan and Francisco de *Vergara, Juan
de Medina, and Hernán Vázquez. In Alcalá
Valdés received three letters from Erasmus.
The first was from Basel on 1 March 1528 and
confirms that Valdés was then a student at the

university (Ep 1961). In the second letter, also
from Basel, on 21 March 1529, Erasmus rejoiced
that Valdés had escaped the dangers in which
he had been involved with the publication of
his first work, the Diálogo de doctrina cristiana.
On this occasion Erasmus remarked on Valdés'
ability to couple the 'elegantia literarum' with
'pietatis christianae synceritatem,' something
that in Erasmus' opinion so far few Italians had
tried to accomplish (Ep 2127). The third and
last-known letter is dated from Freiburg on 13
January 1530 and contains the complaint that
Valdés did not answer Erasmus' letters (Ep
2251). Our knowledge of Valdés' stay in Alcalá
is very fragmentary, and it is not known what
kind of degree he received, if any.

From Alcalá Valdés moved to Rome, where
he appeared on 26 August 1531. He had left
Alcalá after learning that a second trial was
being prepared against him after he had been
exonerated in his first trial by the Inquisition
which accused him of expressing heretical
ideas in his Diálogo de doctrina cristiana. Very
little is known about Valdés' sojourn at the
papal court of *Clement VII. In a safe-conduct
he was given the title of 'chamberlain to the
pope' and 'secretary' to the Emperor *Charles
V; this safe-conduct was issued in view of his
intention to go and meet his brother Alfonso,
who was at Regensburg. Valdés stayed in
Rome as an imperial agent at the papal court.
He was a 'gentleman of sword and cape,' in the
words of Pietro Carnesecchi. Acting on behalf
of the emperor, Valdés handled the legal
matters of the scandalous case of the cardinal of
Ravenna, Benedetto *Accolti, for whom he felt
no sympathy. On 16 January 1534 Clement VII
conferred on Valdés the revenues of a church
in the Spanish diocese of Cartagena. While he
was still in Rome the city of Naples offered him
the post of archivist, a position that he
occupied briefly before returning to Rome.
Valdés finally settled in Naples in 1535, soon
after the death of Clement VII. In January 1536
Pope *Paul III conferred upon him the revenues of the church of St Clement in the diocese
of Cuenca. As a result Valdés enjoyed clerical
status in absentia and without receiving tonsure. For how long he enjoyed these revenues
we do not know, but in his last will Valdés did
not refer to them. While in Rome he made the
acquaintance of Carnesecchi, a protonotary to

Pope Clement VII, whom he met again at Naples in January 1540. In the end, on 30 September 1567, Carnesecchi would pay with his life for the views he derived from that friendship. In Naples Valdés also had, for a while, the title of 'supervisor of castles.' But his presence there is primarily related to the Spanish administration, in particular the secretary of state, Francisco de los Cobos, whom he served in some capacity.

In Naples Valdés came into contact with the Italian élite and aristocracy through his friendship with Giulia Gonzaga, a niece of Cardinal Ercole Gonzaga, with whom he was in correspondence on political matters. He established himself as the leader of a religious group to which Carnesecchi referred as the 'Regno di Dio.' The Valdesian circle became an important focus of religious ideas responsible for the beginnings of the Italian Reformation as well as Nicodemism. Valdés' religious ideas came very close to Reformation thought although no evidence can be produced to show that he was influenced in any direct sense by the Reformation. Justification by faith and the rejection of good works as a means of salvation are two of his most influential tenets. Around Valdés gathered figures such as Bernardino *Ochino, Marco Antonio Flaminio, Pietro Martire Vermigli, Donato Rullo, Apollonio Merenda, Carnesecchi, Jacopo Bonfadio, Galeazzo Caracciolo, and many other influential persons, as well as women of high society such as Giulia Gonzaga, Isabella Breseña, Roberta Carafa, Clarissa Ursina, and Vittoria Colonna. At his religious meetings Valdés expounded the Bible and theological ideas as well as humanist topics, as his *Diálogo de la lengua* well shows. He influenced deeply the prominent Italians gathered around him. He also helped shape the spirituality of the anonymous author of the *Beneficio di Cristo*, which was circulated widely among Protestants and Catholics alike. Celio Secundo Curione, the editor of Valdés' *Considerazioni*, refers to him in his 'Epistola del primo editore' as the 'dottore e pastore di persone nobili e illustri.' In Nicodemite fashion Valdés did not break openly with the Catholic church, but as regards his interior disposition there is no doubt that he was a heretic and died outside the fold of the Catholic church. The resumé of his last will (the complete text is lost) indicates

that his death occurred at Naples at the beginning of August 1541 and simply says of the funeral arrangements that 'all that he requested for his soul had been done.'

The relationship of Valdés to Erasmus is based primarily on two points: his student days at the University of Alcalá with its Erasmian climate, and his use of Erasmus' colloquy *Inquisitio de fide* for his *Diálogo de doctrina cristiana*, published without his name while he was a student at Alcalá. Like the colloquy, Valdés' book starts with an explanation of the Apostles' Creed in dialogue form; two of the characters' names, Antronio and Eusebio, are taken from other colloquies. Through Bataillon's research, Valdés' first book came to be known as a 'moderate Erasmian catechism,' although Bataillon also noticed that Valdés was moving 'irreversibly away from Erasmus.' More recently the Erasmianism of the *Diálogo* and the use of Erasmus' *Inquisitio* have been interpreted as a device or a mask to cover up Valdés' *alumbrado* ideas which were thought to be more dangerous than the Erasmian ones. Valdés used Erasmus to protect himself and attract the support of the Erasmians in Alcalá who would not have defended him if he had been charged with the *alumbrados'* heresies.

Valdés' writings, with the exception of his first work, were all published posthumously, although they enjoyed wide circulation in manuscript form both in the original Spanish and in Italian translations, first among the Valdesian group at Naples and, after his death, at Viterbo in the circle of Reginald *Pole. Many of them were lost. The Valdesian corpus extant today comprises several genres including catechisms, various theological writings, biblical commentaries and translations of biblical books, a linguistic study of the Castilian language, and a collection of letters: 1) catechisms: *Diálogo de doctrina cristiana* (Alcalá: M. de Eguía 14 January 1529); *In qual maniera si dovrebbero instituire i figliuoli cristiani* (n p [after 1540]); 2) other theological writings: *Alfabeto cristiano* (Venice: N. Bascarini 1545); *Modo di tener nell' insegnare et nel predicare il principio della religione cristiana* (1st ed, n p, n d, 2nd ed Rome 1545; it also contains the *Cinque trattatelli evangelici*); *Le cento e dieci divine considerazioni* (Basel 1550); 3) biblical commentaries and translations: *Commentario ó declaración breve y compendiosa sobre la epístola de S. Paulo a los Romanos* (Venice: J. Philadelphus 1556); *Commentario ... de S. Paulo a los Corinthios* (Venice: J. Philadelphus 1557 [both in Geneva, J. Crespin]); *Evangelio según San Mateo* (Madrid 1880); *Commentario a los salmos* [1-41] (Madrid 1885); *El salterio traduzido del hebreo en romance castellano* (Bonn 1880); 4) linguistic study: *Diálogo de la lengua* (Madrid 1737); 5) letters: *Cartas inéditas de Juan de Valdés al Cardenal Gonzaga* (Madrid 1931).

Valdés' first work was one of the earliest catechisms of the sixteenth century. It departed both in form and content from the tradition of the Middle Ages and appeared before *Luther's catechisms. It also influenced later catechetical literature in Spain. Valdés was also the first biblical commentator in the Castilian language. His commentaries are humanistic in method, based on the direct analysis of the biblical text in its original language. He made no use of the allegorical method. Valdés influenced both Spanish and Italian religious history as well as European thought. His *Diálogo de la lengua* was the first linguistic study of the Spanish language and gave him an exceptional place, together with Elio Antonio de *Nebrija, in the formation and evolution of Castilian.

BIBLIOGRAPHY: Allen Ep 1961 / E. Boehmer *Bibliotheca Wiffeniana* (Strasbourg-London 1874–1904, repr 1962) 65–130 / *Enciclopedia universal illustrada europeo-americana* (Barcelona, Madrid 1907?–) LXVI 500–3 / P. Paschini in *Enciclopedia Cattolica* (Vatican City 1948–54) XII 964–5 / D. Ricart in *New Catholic Encyclopedia* (New York-Washington, DC, 1967) XIV 514 / A. Márquez in *Diccionario de historia Eclesiástica de España* ed Q.A. Vaquero et al (Madrid 1972–5) IV 2685–6 / J.C. Nieto *Juan de Valdés and the Origins of the Spanish and Italian Reformation* (Geneva 1970, Spanish rev and enlarged ed Madrid-Mexico 1979) / F. Caballero *Noticias biográficas y literarias de Alonso y Juan de Valdés* (Madrid 1875), with documentary appendix / J. Heep *Juan de Valdés, seine Religion – sein Werden – seine Bedeutung* (Leipzig 1909) / Juan de Valdés *Diálogo de doctrina cristiana* (Alcalá 1529), reproduced in facsimile with introduction and notes by M. Bataillon (Coimbra 1925) / Bataillon *Erasmo y España* 181–2 and passim /

Juan de Valdés *Diálogo de la lengua* ed J.F. Montesinos (Madrid 1953) / J.E. Longhurst *Erasmus and the Spanish Inquisition: The Case of Juan de Valdés* (New Mexico 1950) / Domingo de Santa Teresa *Juan de Valdés 1498(?)–1541: Su pensamiento religioso y las corrientes espirituales de su tiempo* (Rome 1957) / D. Ricart *Juan de Valdés y el pensamiento religioso europeo de los siglos XVI–XVII* (Mexico 1958) / E. Cione *Juan de Valdés: La sua vita e il suo pensiero religioso* rev ed (Naples 1963), contains a complete bibliography / J.N. Bakhuizen van den Brink *Juan de Valdés reformateur en Espagne et Italie 1529–1541* (Geneva 1969) / J.C. Nieto 'Was Juan de Valdés an ordained priest?' BHR 32 (1970) 603–6 / J.C. Nieto 'Luther's ghost and Erasmus' masks in Spain' BHR 39 (1977) 33–49 / *Juan de Valdés' Two Catechisms* ed J.C. Nieto (Kansas 1981) / Benedetto da Mantova *Il Beneficio di Cristo, con le versioni del secolo XVI* ed E. Caponetto (Chicago 1972) 13–17 and passim

JOSÉ C. NIETO

Jacobus de VALENTIA *See Jaime* PEREZ

Urbano VALERIANI of Belluno, c 1443–1524 Fra Urbano Valeriani was born to the local blacksmith in Belluno, at the foot of the Dolomites, and was sometimes known as 'Bolzanius.' He joined the Conventual Franciscans and studied first in Treviso, probably with the eminent humanist Rolandello, then in Venice. Some time during the 1470s he attached himself to the future doge Andrea Gritti, who was then a corn-merchant in Constantinople, and travelled extensively in mainland Greece, Asia Minor, Egypt, and the Greek islands. Returning by way of Sicily, he studied in Messina at the Greek academy of Constantinus *Lascaris and climbed Mount Etna to investigate volcanic activity. From around 1484 he was tutor to Giovanni de' Medici in Florence but moved on some time after the future *Leo x had been elevated to cardinal in 1489. Fra Urbano then settled in Venice and opened the private school which he ran until the end of his life. Described by his biographers as a fascinating companion, he fitted easily into intellectual society, became an intimate member of the circle of Aldo *Manuzio, and helped Erasmus to prepare the Venetian edition of the *Adagia* in 1508 (*Adagia* II i 1).

His *Institutiones graecae grammatices*, commissioned by Manuzio and published by him in 1497, was the first Greek grammar written specifically for Latin readers: sought in vain by Erasmus as early as 1501 (Ep 159), it became one of the most popular introductory texts of the century and went through twenty-three editions. Fra Urbano's library, said to have contained an early manuscript of Homer's *Iliad*, was bequeathed to the monastery of San Niccolò in Venice but has been dispersed without trace.

BIBLIOGRAPHY: Allen Ep 159 / A. Castrifrancani *Oratio habita in funere Bellunensis* (Venice: B. de' Vitali 1524) / Gianpietro Valeriani *De litteratorum infelicitate* (Padua 1620) book II passim / G. Bustico 'Due umanisti veneti – Urbano Bolzanio e Piero Valeriani' *Civiltà moderna* 4 (1932) 86–103   M.J.C. LOWRY

Giorgio VALLA of Piacenza, c 1447–23 January 1500
Giorgio, the son of Andrea Valla of Piacenza, was a relative of Lorenzo *Valla. He studied Greek at Milan under Constantinus *Lascaris in the early 1460s, and later medicine at Pavia under Giovanni Marliani. He then taught humanities at Pavia, Genoa, and Milan. In 1485, through the influence of Ermolao (1) *Barbaro, he was appointed a public lecturer in the humanities at the school of San Marco in Venice, holding this post until his death. His tenure in Venice was marred in 1496 when he was imprisoned for several months on suspicion of betraying secrets to the Milanese government, but he was acquitted and freed.

Valla was a friend of the printer Aldo *Manuzio and played a prominent role in the editing and diffusion of Greek and Latin manuscripts, particularly in the areas of mathematics, medicine, and natural philosophy. He wrote commentaries on Cicero, Ptolemy, Juvenal, and Pliny the Elder, and translated into Latin works of Aristotle, Galen, Hippocrates, Euclid, and many others. His most important work – eagerly awaited by scholars – was *De expetendis et fugiendis rebus* (Venice: Aldo Manuzio 1501), a humanistic encyclopaedia of mathematical and scientific knowledge. Valla was also renowned for his extensive library of Greek and Latin manuscripts, which was purchased after his death by Alberto *Pio,

prince of Carpi, and is today found almost intact in the Biblioteca Estense at Modena.

Erasmus was critical of Valla's translation of the *Placita philosophorum* (Ep 2422). Valla's name also appears in the list of Italian stylists in the *Ciceronianus* (ASD I-2 667) and in *Adagia* I i 2. Ep 1479 contains a reference either to him or to Niccolò Valla.

BIBLIOGRAPHY: Allen Ep 1479 / Cosenza IV 3545–9 / Johan Ludvig Heiberg *Beiträge zur Geschichte Georg Valla's und seiner Bibliothek* (Leipzig 1896) / Eugenio Garin in *Storia di Milano* (Milan 1953–62) VIII 574 and passim / Martin Lowry *The World of Aldus Manutius* (Oxford 1979) 30, 181–4, and passim / Paul Rose 'Bartolomeo Zamberti's funeral oration for the humanist encyclopedist Giorgio Valla' in *Cultural Aspects of the Italian Renaissance: Essays Presented to P.O. Kristeller* ed C. Clough (Manchester 1976) 299–310 / G. Dalla Santa 'Nuovi appunti sul processo di Giorgio Valla e di Placidio Amerino in Venezia nel 1496' *Nuovo archivio veneto* 10 (1895) 13–23

JOHN F. D'AMICO & TBD

Lorenzo VALLA of Rome, 1407–1 August 1457
Lorenzo Valla (De Valle, Vallensis, Vallati) was the son of Luca Valla, doctor of civil and canon law and consistorial advocate, who was deceased before 1420; and of Caterina Scrivani, a daughter of the jurisconsult Giovanni Scrivani. Both parents were born in Piacenza (or vicinity). Lorenzo was born in Rome in 1407, as proved by R. Sabbadini (not 1405 as claimed by G. Mancini). He was not a member of the aristocratic Della Valle or Vallense family of Rome, to which he is sometimes ascribed. Lorenzo was brought up in Rome by his mother, who remained there after the father's death, and by his maternal uncle, Melchiorre Scrivani, a papal secretary of Martin V.

Valla received his early education in curial circles in Rome. It is possible but unlikely that he moved to Florence with the court of Martin V in 1419 and studied there, as Mancini thought. His higher education was also private, as the papal university in Rome, the Studium urbis, remained closed during his youth. According to Sabbadini he studied Greek with Aurispa in Rome in 1420–1 and with Rinuccio di Castiglione in 1425; he had learnt Latin on his own

Lorenzo Valla

ing versions of 1433 and the 1440s to *De vero falsoque bono* and then to *De vero bono*.

Valla was named lector in rhetoric at the Studio of Pavia and taught there for the terms of 1431–2 and 1432–3. There he came under important new intellectual influences and acquired new friends and enemies. In March 1433 he was forced to leave hurriedly for Milan because of the anger of the jurists at Pavia at his *Libellus* attacking Bartolus for ignorance of the ancient jurists. Through this controversial *opusculum* Valla acquired his reputation as a founder of 'legal humanism.'

While teaching privately at Milan in 1433, Valla paid a brief visit to Guarino *Guarini of Verona to enlist his support in his developing controversies. In 1434 and 1435 he taught privately at Genoa and visited Florence; he began a relatively long period of service as secretary to Alfonso I, king of Naples, in 1435. He accompanied the king on his campaigns until the conquest of Naples in 1442. He then based himself at the Neapolitan court until his definitive return to Rome and the curia in 1448.

During the early years of this period, 1435–43, Valla prepared drafts of a number of important works that were to remain or become influential in the sixteenth century, especially on such later humanists as Erasmus. A preliminary draft of Valla's *Elegantiarum linguae latinae libri sex* was completed in 1440 and prematurely circulated. Valla revised and added to this work over the years. Its importance as a major Renaissance study of Latin usage based on a large list of Latin authors was attested by the more than fifty manuscripts and 150 early printed editions still extant, though as yet no modern scholar has braved its intricacies to bring forth a critical edition. Erasmus, however, found it to be a work ideally suited to his own conceptions of language study and in about 1488 wrote a *Paraphrasis seu potius epitome in Elegantiarum libros Laurentii Vallae* (ed C.L. Heesakkers and J.H. Waszink, ASD I-4 187–351). The paraphrase was entrusted to Cornelis *Gerard, and perhaps with his connivance unauthorized editions were printed in 1529 by Johann Gymnich at Cologne and by Robert Estienne at Paris (Ep 2260). Erasmus (Ep 2416) then prepared his own edition of the work (Freiburg: J. Faber Emmeus March 1531), and in the

and had Leonardo Bruni as his 'corrector' of Latin in 1426. In all other respects Valla seems to have been an autodidact. That he was precocious and successful in his education is shown by his completion in 1428 at the age of twenty-one of his first work, the lost 'De comparatione Ciceronis Quintilianique,' in which he claimed greater importance for the rhetorical and philological studies of Quintilian than for Cicero's.

At the death of his uncle, Melchiorre Scrivani, in 1430 Valla attempted to gain appointment as his successor as papal secretary. His youth (he was twenty-four) and possibly the machinations of Poggio *Bracciolini led to his being denied the post. Valla then left for his ancestral city of Piacenza and remained there throughout 1430 and into the spring or summer of 1431 after the election of Eugenius IV as successor to Martin V. In 1431 at Piacenza he circulated *De voluptate libri tres* (written probably during his stay there, 1430–1). This was the first of three or possibly four continuously worked-over versions of Valla's major work in moral philosophy and theology the title of which was changed in the succeed-

next twenty years over fifty printings were made of the different versions.

In 1439–40 Valla completed the first version (as yet unprinted) of his 'Repastinatio dialecticae et philosophiae,' more generally known in its widely edited second version as *Disputationum dialecticarum libri tres*. A third slightly expanded version of the second also remains in manuscript. The *Elegantiae* was the first and possibly most widely diffused humanist analysis of Latin usage and served as a fundamental text in the fifteenth, sixteenth, and seventeenth centuries. The *Disputationes dialecticae* were a critique and revision of scholastic (Aristotelian) metaphysics and logic which were also widely diffused and influential.

In these same years (1439–40) Valla wrote or issued three other smaller works on moral theology and ecclesiology, two of which had an important influence on the Reformation period while the third remained hardly known until the nineteenth century. The *Dialogus de libero arbitrio* was praised by *Luther, dismissed by Erasmus (LB IX 1218F), and scorned by Calvin but was possibly misunderstood by all three. The *De professione religiosorum*, a critique of the claim of the religious bound by vows to greater merit than secular clergy and lay Christians, exercised no influence on either Erasmians or Protestants because its circulation was sharply restricted by Valla after his encounter with the Inquisition in 1444. The best-known and most influential of these works was his *De falso credita et ementita Constantini donatione declamatio*, which exposed the Donation of Constantine as a forgery and urged a pastoral conception of the papacy.

In 1443 Valla issued the first version of the work which had the most direct, acknowledged, and central influence on Erasmus: the *Collatio Novi Testamenti*. In 1505 Erasmus published this work of Valla with an introduction of his own; he gave it the title *Laurentii Vallensis viri tam graecae quam latinae linguae peritissimi in latinam Novi Testamenti interpretationem ex collatione graecorum exemplarium adnotationes apprime utiles* (Paris: J. Bade 1505). On the basis of recent manuscript discoveries, the work published by Erasmus proves to be the second version of the 1450s of Valla's work of 1443 called by him *Collatio Novi Testamenti*. The largest fraction of Erasmus' many references to Valla scattered through his works, and particularly through his editions of the New Testament (LB VI), cite Valla's scriptural criticism, either in agreement or opposition. Erasmus took from Valla the basic methodology which he developed and amplified, and, as he thought, deepened (Epp 182, 2172). The variations between Valla's two versions were numerous, though Erasmus utilized the more developed one; in general the original 1443 version contained a programmatically important *proemium* that must have been missing in the manuscript Erasmus published; it was also more philological and grammatical in its criticism of the Vulgate translation. The later version of the 1450s emphasized in several instances the theological implications of the different translations (something which Erasmus was keenly aware of in preparing his own translation a decade later). It also contained much of a philological and grammatical nature, as had the first. In this work Valla helped to lay the groundwork for philologically based scriptural theology to replace scholastic metaphysical analogy, something which he had already sharply criticized in his 'Repastinatio.'

Most likely as a consequence of Valla's challenges to established positions in the Christian tradition, he was subjected to an effort by the Inquisition at Naples to charge him with heresy in 1444. He was saved from an actual conviction by the intervention of King Alfonso, though there is some doubt as to whether he went through an authentic inquisitorial process or only through certain investigations preliminary to a formal trial. Contemporary scholars are inclined to accept Valla's own interpretation of this experience set forth in his *Antidotum secundum in Poggium* and his declarations of orthodoxy in his *Defensio questionum in philosophia* and his *Apologia* to Eugenius IV of November 1444 (Biblioteca Apostolica Vaticana MS cod. Ottob. lat. 2075, f 238–47). As a consequence the next four years at Naples (his last) were difficult ones for Valla.

Towards the end of 1445 or the beginning of 1446 Valla composed a first draft of his *Gesta Ferdinandi Regis Aragonum* (*Opera omnia* II 1–61) as a preliminary to a planned history of the reign of Alfonso which was never written. In the course of 1446 a rival humanist at the court

of Alfonso, Bartolomeo Facio, with the aid of
Valla's enemy, Il Panormita (Antonio Beccadelli), composed four invectives against Valla's
uncorrected draft history, to which Valla
responded in early 1447 with his *Antidotum in
Facium* (*Opera omnia* I 460–632), also in four
books. The fourth book is notable as containing Valla's important textual analysis *Emenda-
tiones sex librorum T. Livii de secundo bello
Punico*.

Having been stationed at Tivoli, near Rome,
the battle headquarters of his patron Alfonso,
during the spring of 1447, Valla made the
contacts with the newly elected Pope *Nicholas v which led to his settling in Rome as an
employee of the curia some time in 1448.
Although promised the office of *secretarius* by
Nicholas, he only received that of *scriptor* in
November 1448. In 1455 Calixtus III finally
awarded Valla the office of an apostolic
secretary. The long-standing hostility of Poggio Bracciolini towards Valla seems to have
been responsible for his being denied office
until after Poggio himself had left Rome.
Jealousy of Valla's increasing scholarly and
critical reputation seems to have motivated this
most influential of curial humanists, but
genuine scholarly and methodological issues
were also at stake. The quarrel culminated in
one of the most notorious humanist polemics of
the Renaissance. Poggio published the first of
five *Orationes in Laurentium Vallam* in February
1452; Valla's reply, his *Antidotum primum*, was
issued in July 1452. Poggio's second, third, and
fourth *Orationes* seem to have been completed
by the end of the same year, 1452. Valla
followed these with an *Apologus* I and II
(unfinished), replied to in Poggio's *Oratio v*,
followed by Valla's *Antidotum secundum* of
March/April 1453. The polemic retained its
fame and was much commented on in the
letters and writings of learned men for the next
century, partly because of the personal vindictiveness and asperity of both parties, but
possibly more for the confrontation of Poggio's
more traditional Ciceronian humanism and the
historical-analytical approach of Valla. Erasmus himself frequently mentioned the controversy, in which he favoured Valla (Epp 26; ASD
I-2 537; LB IX 283D).

During this last decade of his life, when
Valla was in the service of the curia, he
produced no major works. He did, however,
continue to issue revised versions of his earlier
ones: the *Collatio Novi Testamenti*, as has been
seen, the *Disputationes dialecticae*, the *Elegantiae
linguae latinae*, and possibly *De vero bono*. At the
request of Nicholas v he translated Thucydides
and Herodotus. Appointed to a chair at the
Studium urbis in 1450, he expounded the
philology of Quintilian. His commentaries on
Quintilian and Sallust are extant, as well as his
translations of Aesop, Homer, and Demosthenes, besides those of Thucydides and Herodotus just mentioned.

Three public discourses have survived from
these years, each of them important for its
statement of Valla's vision of language, history, and religion. His *Oratio in principio sui studii*
of 18 October 1455 argues the dependence of
civilization on the Latin language and extols
the importance of the Roman Catholic church
as a vehicle for the transmission of Latin. His
Sermo de mysterio eucharistiae, preached on Holy
Thursday of 1456 or 1457 at St John Lateran
(where he had been named a canon in October
1455), is perhaps his most important short
theological utterance, linking the dignity and
deification of man to the mystery of the
Incarnation daily re-enacted through the mass.
On 7 March 1457 he delivered *Encomium Sancti
Thomae Aquinatis* at the invitation of the
Dominicans of Santa Maria sopra Minerva.
Here he set forth his admiration for the piety of
the saint and his affirmation of patristic rather
than scholastic theology.

Valla died 1 August 1457 and is buried in the
basilica of St John Lateran. The following
epitaph could once be read by his tomb:
'Laurentio Vallae harum aedium sacrarum
canonico Alphonsi regis et pontificis maximi
secretario apostolicoque scriptori qui sua ae-
tate omnes eloquentia superavit Catherina
mater filio pientisimo posuit. Vixit annos L.
Obiit anno domini MCCCCLVII calendis Augu-
sti.' A sepulchral effigy is reproduced on page
6 of A. Wesseling's edition of Valla's *Antidotum
primum*. It seems incontrovertible that, of all
the Italian humanists, Lorenzo Valla's influence on Erasmus was the most complete and
most profound.

Valla's *Opera omnia* were printed at Basel in
1540 and 1543 by Henricus Petri; an anastatic
reprint was published at Turin in 1962,

introduced by Eugenio Garin and supplement-
ed by works missing from the Basel *Opera*.
Modern critical editions, a number of which
appear in the Turin reprint, include *De vero
bono, De vero falsoque bono* by Maristella De
Panizza Lorch (Bari 1970); *Dialogus de libero
arbitrio* by M. Anfossi in *Opuscoli filosofici: testi e
documenti inediti o rari pubblicati da Giovanni
Gentile* VI (Florence 1934); *De professione
religiosorum* and *Oratio in principio sui studii* by J.
Vahlen in *Laurentii Vallae opuscula tria* (Vienna
1869); *De falso credita et ementita Constantini
donatione declamatio* by C.B. Coleman with
English translation (New Haven, Conn, 1922)
and by W. Schwahn (Leipzig 1928); *Collatio
Novi Testamenti* by A. Perosa (Florence 1970);
Defensio questionum in philosophia by G. Zippel
in 'L'autodifesa di Lorenzo Valla per il processo dell'inquisizione napoletana' *Italia medioevale e umanistica* 13 (1970) 59–94; *Gesta Ferdinandi Regis Aragonum* by O. Besomi (Padua
1973); *In Pogium antidotum primum* by A.
Wesseling (Assen-Amsterdam 1978); *Encomium
Sancti Thomae Aquinatis* by J. Vahlen in
*Vierteljahrschrift für Kultur und Literatur der Re-
naissance* 1 (1886) 390–6 and G. Bertocci
(Rome 1888); and *Orationes* and *Prefationes* by
F. Adorno (Santiago 1954). Letters of Valla
were published by L. Barozzi and R. Sabbadini in *Studi sul Panormita e sul Valla* (Florence
1891) by G. Mancini in *Giornale storico della
letteratura italiana* 21 (1893) and by F. Adorno
in *Rinascimento* 6 (1955) 117–24.

BIBLIOGRAPHY: Gian Paolo Marchi in *Dizio-
nario critico della letteratura italiana* ed V. Branca
(Turin 1974) III 572–5 / Neal Gilbert in *The
Encyclopedia of Philosophy* ed P. Edwards (New
York 1967) VIII-2 27–9 / C. Carbonara in
Enciclopedia filosofica (Venice 1957–8) IV 1490–2
/D. Cantimori in EI XXXIV 923–5 / Girolamo
Mancini *Vita di Lorenzo Valla* (Florence 1891)
reviewed by R. Sabbadini in *Giornale storico
della letteratura italiana* 19 (1892) 403–14; Man-
cini's reply in *Giornale storico della letteratura
italiana* 21 (1893) 1–48 / Remigio Sabbadini and
Luciano Barozzi *Studi sul Panormita e sul Valla*
(Florence 1891) / Giorgio Radetti *Lorenzo Valla,
Scritti filosofici e religiosi* (Florence 1953) / G.
Radetti 'La religione di Lorenzo Valla' *Medioevo
e Rinascimento, Studi in onore di Bruno Nardi*
(Florence 1955) II 595–630 / Franco Gaeta
Lorenzo Valla, Filologia e storia nell'Umanesimo

italiano (Naples 1955) / F. Adorno 'Di alcune
orazioni e prefazioni di Lorenzo Valla' *Rinascimento* 5 (1954) 191–225 / Gianni Zippel
'Lorenzo Valla e le origini della storiografia
umanistica a Venezia' *Rinascimento* 7 (1956)
99–133 / Gianni Zippel 'La "Defensio quaestionum in philosophia" di Lorenzo Valla e un
noto processo dell'inquisizione napoletana'
*Bulletino dell'Istituto italiano per il Medioevo e
Archivio Muratoriano* 69 (1957) 319–47 / Gianni
Zippel 'L'Autodifesa di Lorenzo Valla per il
processo dell'inquisizione napoletana (1444)'
Italia medioevale e umanistica 13 (1970) 59–94 / J.
IJsewijn and G. Tournoy 'Un primo censi-
mento dei manoscritti e delle edizioni a stampa
degli "Elegantiarum linguae latinae libri sex"
di Lorenzo Valla' *Humanistica Lovaniensia*
18 (1969) 25–41 / J. IJsewijn and G. Tournoy
'Nuovi contributi per l'elenco dei manoscritti e
delle edizioni delle Elegantie di Lorenzo Valla'
Humanistica Lovaniensia 20 (1971) 1–3 / G.
Tournoy 'Lorenzo Valla en Erasmus' *Onze
Alma Mater* 23 (1969) 144–9 / Mario Fois *Il
pensiero cristiano di Lorenzo Valla nel quadro
storico-culturale del suo ambiente* (Analecta Gre-
goriana 174) (Rome 1969), extensive bibliogra-
phy / Charles Trinkaus *'In Our Image and
Likeness,' Humanity and Divinity in Italian
Humanist Thought* (London-Chicago 1970) chs
3, 12–14 / Giovanni Di Napoli *Lorenzo Valla,
Filosofia e religione nell'Umanesimo italiano* (Rome
1971) / Salvatore I. Camporeale *Lorenzo Valla,
Umanesimo e teologia* (Florence 1972) / Salvatore
I. Camporeale *Da Lorenzo Valla a Tommaso
Moro, Lo statuto umanistica della teologia* (Pistoia,
Memorie Domenicane, n s 4, 1973) / Salvatore I.
Camporeale *Lorenzo Valla, Tra Medioevo e
Rinascimento* (Pistoia, Memorie Domenicane, n
s 7, 1977) / Hanna-Barbara Gerl *Rhetorik als
Philosophie: Lorenzo Valla* (Munich 1974) /
Wolfram Setz *Lorenzo Vallas Schrift gegen die
Konstantinische Schenkung ... Zur Interpretation
und Wirkungsgeschichte* (Tübingen 1975)

CHARLES TRINKAUS

de VALLE *See Pierre* DUVAL, *Francisco de*
VAYLLE

Jean VALLIÈRE of Falaise, d 8 August 1523
Jean Vallière, an Austin friar born in the
region of Falaise, in Calvados, lived in a house
of his order at Livry, north-east of Paris. At the

age of about forty he was accused of blasphemy against Jesus and the Holy Virgin, sentenced, and burnt in Paris. Whether he was in fact a Lutheran is not quite clear. Erasmus reported the incident on 25 September (Ep 1388).

BIBLIOGRAPHY: Allen Ep 1388 / M. Mousseaux 'Note sur Jean Vallière' *Bulletin de la Société de l'histoire du Protestantisme français* 108 (1962) 18–27, publishing the text of the sentence / *Le Journal d'un bourgeois de Paris* ed V.-L. Bourrilly (Paris 1910) 397–8

MICHEL REULOS

Pietro VANNES of Lucca, d before 1 May 1563
Pietro Vannes (Ammonio) was the son of Stefano de Vannes of Lucca and a kinsman of Andrea *Ammonio, from 1511 Latin secretary to *Henry VIII of England. In 1513 he travelled to England to become assistant to Andrea. Silvestro *Gigli, bishop of Worcester and a native of Lucca, strongly recommended him to Thomas *Wolsey, whose secretary he became in 1514. Later he became Latin secretary to Henry VIII. On 12 November 1521 he obtained the benefice of Mottram, in the diocese of Coventry and Lichfield, and in 1523 he was incorporated bachelor of theology at Cambridge. In 1526 he was an unsuccessful candidate for the bishopric of Lucca.

In 1527 Vannes accompanied Cardinal Wolsey on a diplomatic mission to France, and on 28 November 1528 he and Sir Francis Bryan were sent to Rome to secure the annulment of Henry's marriage to *Catherine of Aragon. The mission was a complete failure, and in October 1529 Vannes returned to England. He continued to receive preferment and accumulated prebends at Salisbury, Worcester, York, and Wells, and finally the deanery of Salisbury. Although he was appointed collector of papal taxes in England on 17 July 1533, he subscribed to the articles of religion agreed upon by convocation in 1536.

During the reign of Edward VI Vannes resigned his deanery but continued to serve as Latin secretary to the king. On 19 May 1550 he was sent to Venice as ambassador, a post he continued to hold under *Mary I, who also reinstated him as dean of Salisbury. He was recalled to England in 1556, and retained his benefice under Elizabeth I.

After Andrea Ammonio died in August 1517

Erasmus asked Johannes *Sixtinus and Vannes to destroy or forward all his correspondence with Andrea and also any papers relating to dispensations which he had recently received from Rome (Epp 655, 656). When Vannes was negligent in doing this, Erasmus sent him a scathing letter, saying that he lacked the spirit and common sense of his kinsman (Epp 822, 828). Eight years later Erasmus' temper had cooled, and he sent Vannes greetings through Stephen *Gardiner (Ep 1745).

BIBLIOGRAPHY: Allen Ep 656 / DNB XX 134–6 / John and J.A. Venn *Alumni Cantabrigienses* (Cambridge 1922–54) I-4 294 / Clemente Pizzi *Un amico d'Erasmo, l'umanista Andrea Ammonio* (Florence 1956) 8 / William E. Wilkie *The Cardinal Protectors of England: Rome and the Tudors before the Reformation* (Cambridge 1974) 15, 145, and passim
TBD

Johannes VANNIUS *See Johann* WANNER

Aegidius VANNONIUS (Ep 2636 of 1532)
Aegidius Vannonius is mentioned as a servant of Jacopo *Canta, chamberlain to Cardinal Lorenzo *Campeggi. He visited Erasmus at Freiburg in 1532, bearing greetings and praising the virtues of his master. No more is known about him.

JOHN F. D'AMICO

Jean-Pierre de VARADE of Milan, d 1540
The son of a Milanese gentleman, Varade (Vérade, Lombardus) took refuge in Paris from the Italian wars before 1497, and learnt the trade of book selling. On 28 February 1508 he was named *libraire-juré*. When Varade died at the beginning of 1540, he left a widow, Eloyse Denise. One of his sons, Jacques, kept his title of *libraire-juré*.

Varade did not personally engage in publishing but instead took part in the international book trade and acted as an agent of Paolo and Antonio *Manuzio, to whom he was in debt at his death.

In 1512 Varade was involved in the purchase of books for Erasmus (Ep 263).

BIBLIOGRAPHY: Allen and CWE Ep 263 / Renouard *Répertoire* 419 / A. Parent *Les Métiers du livre à Paris au XVIe siècle (1535–1560)* (Geneva 1974) 154
GENEVIÈVE GUILLEMINOT

Nicolaus VARIUS *See Nicolas* WARY

Ulrich VARNBÜLER of St Gallen, 1474–1545

Ulrich Varnbüler (Farnbul, Varenbulerus) was descended from an influential and able family. His father, also named Ulrich, was frequently mayor of St Gallen until his career ended in political and military defeat. The son matriculated at Basel in 1489, moving on to the universities of Freiburg in 1490 and Vienna in 1492; he probably received a legal degree in Vienna. On 10 December 1507, at Regensburg, he was appointed protonotary in the chancery of the Reichskammergericht. His colleague in this position, Ambrosius Dietrich, was presumably a relative of Barbara Dietrich, who became Varnbüler's wife. As the court met in various locations he was often on the move. Erasmus was delighted to have him as a travelling companion from Worms to Mainz in September 1518 (Ep 867). In 1521 he was appointed chancellor to the Reichsregiment (1521–30) which was to exercise imperial powers in Germany in the absence of *Charles v. With the Reichsregiment Varnbüler at first resided in Nürnberg, where *Dürer sketched his portrait for a woodcut executed in 1522, and subsequently from 1524 in Esslingen and from 1527 in Speyer. At the termination of the Reichsregiment he attended the diet of Augsburg, in 1530, and then returned to the Reichskammergericht, becoming the head of its chancery, which was then in Mainz. He took his oath of office on 29 April 1531 and retired from this position before March 1540. In the summer of 1542 he was in the region of Ulm and Lindau and was given the title of councillor of the margrave of Baden, but in the same year he moved to Strasbourg, where he was employed by the government until the end of 1543 and where he died two years later.

As early proof of his admiration for Erasmus, Varnbüler translated into German the adage *Dulce bellum inexpertis* (iv i 1). The translation was published by Andreas *Cratander at Basel in 1519 with a preface dated from Mainz in 1515. In 1523 Varnbüler obtained authorization to issue in the name of the emperor an important privilege to protect Johann *Froben's publications against pirated editions (Epp 1341, 1344, 1353). In return Erasmus was eager to afford him satisfaction when he complained about the price he had been

Ulrich Varnbüler, by Albrecht Dürer

charged for one of Froben's books (Epp 1398, 1408, 1417). Cratander too was indebted to him for a protective privilege and dedicated his Cicero to him in March 1528. Other works were dedicated to him by *Pirckheimer and Peter (II) *Schöffer.

BIBLIOGRAPHY: Allen Ep 867 and iv xxix / AK vi Ep 2381a and passim / DHBS vii 48 (with Dürer's portrait) / Pirckheimer *Briefwechsel* ii Ep 351 / *Vadianische Briefsammlung* iv Ep 495, vi Epp 1234, 1243, 1264, and passim / *Neuer literarischer Anzeiger* 2 (1807) 254–60, 331–2, 438 / *Deutsche Reichstagsakten* Jüngere Reihe (Gotha-Göttingen 1893–   ) ii 756, 770 / *Matrikel Freiburg* i-1 100 / *Matrikel Wien* ii-1 226 (Hainricus Farenpüchler of St Gallen) / *Matrikel Basel* i 209   PGB

Thomas VARNET or VARVET *See Thomas WARNET*

Johann VARNOWER of Basel, documented 1528–9

Varnower is the baker mentioned by Erasmus in Ep 2054 with whom the priest Peter *Frauenberger once lodged. With Varnower's knowledge, Frauenberger gained access to his wife's bed, perhaps having used blackmail. Prior to the resulting scandal, in February and May 1528 the name of Hans Varnower, baker, appears in documents of legal transactions involving Frauenberger. On 27 May 1529 Varnower obtained a divorce from his wife, Margarete, who had borne a child assumed to be Frauenberger's.

BIBLIOGRAPHY: Allen Ep 2054 / R. Wacker-nagel *Geschichte der Stadt Basel* (Basel 1907–54) III 107* / *Basler Chroniken* I 445–6 / BA *Oekolampads* II 323, 332   PGB

Jean VASSEUR of Saint-Omer,
c 1440–18 January 1508
Jean Vasseur (Levasseur) was born at Saint-Omer, where his uncle, Chrestien Vasseur, was a canon of the church of Notre-Dame. On an unknown date he entered the Dominican convent in the town. He studied at Paris and on 12 December 1474 earned the degree of doctor of theology. He rose to prominence both in the Dominican order and in the hierarchy of the church: warden of Saint-Omer, vicar of the father-general and of the provincial of France for the Picard nation, inquisitor for the dioceses of Cambrai, Tournai, Arras, and Amiens on 30 January 1488, bishop *in partibus* of Byblos (Djebail), Lebanon, and suffragan to two bishops of Thérouanne, Antoine de Croy and Philippe de *Luxembourg. He was buried in the choir of the Dominican church of Saint-Omer, which he had himself been instrumental in constructing. A monument to him in black marble bears an inscription recalling the great events of his career.

Vasseur was without doubt the Dominican mentioned by Erasmus in Ep 130 in connection with the father of a family tried but acquitted of heresy. Erasmus detested the Dominican, describing him as 'the most corrupt, grasping and insolent fellow alive.' Erasmus' hatred was fuelled by Vasseur's conflict with Jean *Vitrier, warden of the Franciscan convent of Saint-Omer. Temperament, ideas, and goals separated the Dominican and the Franciscan. Educated in different universities and belonging to rival orders, the two men disagreed radically with one another: Vasseur, a conservative devoted to pomp and ceremony, was impervious to the mysticism and evangelism of Vitrier.

It is probable that Vasseur, being a Paris doctor of theology, played a role in the condemnation of Vitrier by the theological faculty in 1498. This was followed by the affair of the jubilee indulgences at Saint-Omer, reported by Erasmus in his biographical letter on Vitrier (Ep 1211). Vitrier judged the preaching of indulgences for the holy year 1500 simoniacal and indignantly refused when he was offered a substantial gift for the church of his convent in return for his silence. At the instigation of Vasseur he was excommunicated and twice cited to appear before the episcopal tribunal of Thérouanne. Vitrier was exonerated, but Erasmus did not cease to attack his Dominican opponent, accusing Vasseur of inspiring a homicidal attack on Vitrier by certain nuns of the convent of Ste Marguerite (Ep 1211). There is no decisive proof for the truth of this accusation. However, in their resistance to reform the recalcitrant nuns depended upon the spiritual and temporal powers of Saint-Omer, at the centre of which was Vasseur, who during the frequent absences of the bishop of Thérouanne controlled events in the diocese. He could cover abuses, give credence to questionable patents of morality prepared by his confrère Maupaie, the visitor and confessor of the nuns of Ste Marguerite, stop proceedings, and in short counteract in a thousand ways Vitrier's attempts at reform. Through his silences in the face of clerical abuse and his vainglorious behaviour he remained closed to the aspirations of an age that wanted to return to the purity of the Gospel.

BIBLIOGRAPHY: Allen Ep 130 / U. Berlière 'Les évêques auxiliaires de Thérouanne' *Revue bénédictine* 24 (1907) 62–85, esp 75–8 / A. Derville 'Jean Vitrier et les religieuses de Sainte Marguerite' *Revue du Nord* 42 (1960) 207–39 / A. Godin *Spiritualité franciscaine en Flandre au XVIème siècle: L'Homéliaire de Jean Vitrier* (Geneva 1971) / Saint-Omer, Bibliothèque municipale MS 782: 'Fondation du couvent des F. Prêcheurs de Saint-Omer l'an 1324 avec leur établissement au milieu de la ville l'an 1477 où l'on voit les plus grands hommes sortis de cette maison et plusieurs evenemens qui regardent les deux couvents etc ... par le R.P. Turpin ... l'an 1715' / Paris, Bibliothèque Nationale MS Lat 5657-A f 25 recto   ANDRÉ GODIN

François VATABLE of Gamaches,
c 1493–15 March 1547

François Vatable (Vatablus, Watebled) was
born at Gamaches, in Picardy. From his long
and intimate relationship with the Collège du
Cardinal Lemoine at Paris it seems likely that
he matriculated at that institution, probably in
1508. By 1511 he held a MA. Vatable mastered
Greek during the residence of Girolamo *Aleandro in Paris between 1511 and 1513. The
years 1513 and 1516 he most likely spent at
Avignon, where he learnt Hebrew.

In 1516 Vatable returned to Paris, where he
took up residence at St Germain-des-Prés as
assistant to *Lefèvre d'Etaples. In a letter to
Erasmus of 5 August 1516 Thomas *Grey refers
to Vatable as the 'discipulus' of Lefèvre (Ep
445). In the spring of 1521 he followed his
master to Meaux and became part of the reform
experiment being carried out there by Guillaume (II) *Briçonnet. In 1524 he most likely left
Meaux, exchanging his canonry there for the
rectory at Suresnes. In 1530 he was named
royal professor of Hebrew and was subsequently endowed with the abbey of Bellozane.

In 1511 Vatable published the logical works
of Boethius (Paris: H. Estienne). The next year
he brought out Manuel Chrysoloras' grammar
(Paris: P. Le Preux 1512). In 1518 he edited and
translated Aristotle's writings on natural philosophy (Paris: H. Estienne). Ten years later he
published a new edition of Lefèvre's *Aristotelis philosophiae naturalis paraphrases* (Paris: S.
de Colines 1528). In 1545 Robert Estienne published an edition of the Bible at Paris, the notes
of which were partly drawn from Vatable's
lectures on the Old Testament. Considerable
portions of these lectures survive in manuscripts formerly in the possession of Matthieu
Gauthier, abbot of Marmoutier (Paris, Bibliothèque Nationale MSS Lat 532, 533, 537, 538,
540).

BIBLIOGRAPHY: Allen III xxv / Rice *Prefatory
Epistles* Ep 83 / Abel Lefranc *Histoire du Collège
de France* (Paris 1893) 175–7 / Paris, Archives de
l'Université (Sorbonne) Registre 61 f 29 verso
                                        HENRY HELLER

Eligius de VAUGERMES (Ep 95 of 2 May
1499)
Vaugermes, a Picard, was rector of the
University of Paris from March to June 1499.

François Vatable

There is no evidence for his identification, as
suggested by Allen, with the 'Picardus' mentioned in Erasmus' letter; cf Allen and CWE Ep
95.

John VAUGHAN documented 1500–26
Vaughan (Vaghon, Vauhan, Vawen, Vicham,
Vichun, Voban, Waghan, Waugan, Waw-
ghan, Wawham, Wawhan, Wycham, Wyham)
was one of several minor figures at Queens'
College, Cambridge, whose company Erasmus
evidently enjoyed and subsequently recollect-
ed. He had taken his BA in 1500, proceeding MA
in 1503 and bachelor of divinity in 1511–12.
Between 1502 and 1504 he had been internal
principal of two university hostels – Garret
and St William's – before moving to Queens' as
a fellow in 1505. There he served as bursar and
dean of chapel, vacating his fellowship in 1518.
Erasmus referred to him as the copyist of
Andrea *Ammonio's 'Panegyricus ad Henricum VIII' when writing to the author in
December 1513 (Ep 283). He was one of a
number of Cambridge men mentioned by
Erasmus in writing to Henry *Bullock in the
years 1516–18 (Epp 456, 777, 826); similar

greetings occurred in a letter to Robert
*Aldridge in 1525 but elicited the reply that
Vaughan had by that time left Cambridge (Ep
1656, 1766). He was presumably the bachelor of
divinity named John Vaughan who unsuccessfully claimed the Cambridgeshire rectory of
Bartlow in 1526.

BIBLIOGRAPHY: Allen Ep 283 / Emden BRUC
608 (to be distinguished from the man of the
same name noted in Emden BRUO 1501–1540
591–2) / John and J.A. Venn *Alumni Cantabrigienses* (Cambridge 1922–54) I-4 295

C.S. KNIGHTON

Benoît VAUGRIS of Charly, documented
from 1518, d by February 1539
Benoît Vaugris (Vaugri) of Charly, south of
Lyon, was active in the book business,
co-operating in part with his brothers Jean and
Vincent. While Jean worked at Basel and Lyon,
primarily for Johann *Schabler, the husband of
a Claudia Vaugris, but also independently,
Vincent (Vincenzo Valgrisio; see perhaps
Allen Ep 2639:7) achieved the status of a major
publisher and bookseller in Venice and Milan,
trading under the 'sign of Erasmus.' Benoît
paid taxes at Lyon from 1518 to 1523. In the
latter year he opened a bookstore in Constance, travelling frequently to Venice, Milan
and Basel and later also to Freiburg, where he
visited Erasmus (Epp 1519, 1761, 2117, 2447).
He also did business with book men at
Nürnberg and Strasbourg. In 1526 he was
arrested at Bellinzona for carrying political
messages detrimental to Swiss interests, but
friends obtained his release. Because of the
connections between Schabler and the *Froben
family, contemporary sources sometimes refer
to Benoît Vaugris as a relative of Froben (Ep
1335; cf AK III Ep 1165).

Erasmus appealed in 1523 (Ep 1395) to the
city council of Basel to obtain the remission of a
fine for Benoît. Basel documents show that he
had been jailed since May 1522 after wounding
another man and that his sureties were
Schabler and his brother Jean. Another litigation at Basel, 1523–6, concerned the inheritance of his wife, Jacobe, which was contested
by relatives of her first husband, Lienhart
Zschopp.

BIBLIOGRAPHY: Allen Ep 1395 / Grimm *Buchführer* 1345–6 / T. and H. Baudrier *Bibliographie*
lyonnaise (Lyon 1895–1921) X 457–60 / AK III Epp
1103, 1157, 1165 / R. Wackernagel *Geschichte der*
Stadt Basel (Basel 1907–54) III 445, 92* / P.G.
Bietenholz *Basle and France in the Sixteenth*
Century (Geneva-Toronto 1971) 32 and passim

PGB

Johannes VAULTERUS *See Jan* WOUTERS

Pierre de VAULX (Ep 123 of [March 1500])
Pierre de Vaulx (Vaulg) was a common friend of
Erasmus and Jacob *Batt; Erasmus sent him
greetings when he wrote to Batt, who was at
the castle of Tournehem, between Calais and
Saint-Omer. A Pierre de Vaulx of Saint-Omer,
presumably a younger relative of Erasmus'
friend, matriculated at the University of Louvain on 22 December 1524 (*Matricule de Louvain*
III-1 736).

PGB

Joan VAUX d 4 September 1538
Lady Joan was the daughter of Sir William
Vaux, the sister of Sir Nicholas Vaux, and the
second wife of Sir Richard Guildford. In close
attendance at the English court, she accompanied *Mary Tudor, the bride of *Louis XII, to
France in 1514 as mistress of her maids of
honour. She received pensions for her services
in 1515 and 1516. After the death of her first
husband she married for a second time.

Sir Henry *Guildford was her son. In a letter
to Henry, Erasmus spoke of conversations
between himself and Lady Guildford, whom
he admired (Ep 966).

BIBLIOGRAPHY: Allen Ep 966 / DNB VIII 773, XX
192

CFG

VAYDOLEUSA (Ep 2961 of 22 August 1534)
Vaydoleusa appears to have been a visitor from
central Europe who brought Erasmus cash
presents from Justus *Decius and Johannes
*Dantiscus. He has not been identified.

Francisco de VAYLLE of Burgos, documented
1512–35
Francisco de Vaylle (Vaille, de Vaglio, de Valle)
was descended from a Burgos family that was
conceivably of Jewish *converso* origin. The
influential Fugger representative in Spain,
Caspar Vaylle (Weiler, Bailer, etc), was presumably a relative of his. Francisco's father,
Antonio, had moved to Antwerp by 1498 and

established himself as an important merchant and banker. When he died by 1512 his firm went to Francisco and his brother-in-law, Francisco de Moxica. The younger Vaylle married Maria, a daughter of the Antwerp merchant Nicolaas van Rechtergem. Maria's sister, Ida, was the wife of Erasmus *Schets, Erasmus' banker in Antwerp. In 1519 Vaylle was a master of the fraternity of Our Lady and from 1526 to 1529 he was an *ammanus*, a city official dealing with matters of civil law. Vaylle and his associates lent the Hapsburg government the sum of one hundred thousand pound groot of Flanders, which was apparently used to pay for the services of Franz von *Sickingen at the time of the election of *Charles v in 1519. The sum plus interest was to be paid back in Spain; however delay occurred which caused the creditors great anxiety. In 1526 Vaylle was involved in speculative real estate transactions at Antwerp.

Vaylle retained close connections with Spain, which he visited in 1525, writing from there to Schets, who passed on to Erasmus Vaylle's comments about widespread enthusiasm for Erasmus in Spain, adding that Vaylle himself was a well-educated man (Ep 1541). From the correspondence of Nicolaus *Clenardus it can be gathered that Vaylle returned to Spain around 1530. Perhaps in partial settlement of his claims he obtained the appointment of his son as prior of Salamanca, a benefice which brought a handsome income. Clenardus met the family in Salamanca and in 1534 helped to bring about the appointment of his friend Jan Was (Vasaeus) of Bruges as tutor to the prior, who was about fifteen. The last references to the Vaylle family in Clenardus' letters seem to occur in 1535 and are difficult to interpret. Perhaps both father and son contracted an illness, of which the son died while the father recovered.

BIBLIOGRAPHY: Marcel Bataillon *Etudes sur le Portugal au temps de l'humanisme* (Coimbra 1952) 53–4 / Bataillon *Erasmo y España* 161–4 / de Vocht CTL II 474 / Richard Ehrenberg *Das Zeitalter der Fugger* (Jena 1896) I 356–8, II 37–8, 41–2 / J.A. Goris *Etude sur les colonies marchandes méridionales … à Anvers de 1488 à 1567* (Louvain 1925) 374, 399–400, 550 / *Correspondance de Nicolas Clénard* ed Alphonse Roersch (Brussels 1940–1) I Epp 12, 19–21, 24, 26–7, 29 and notes / Ramon Carande *Carlos v y sus banqueros* (Madrid 1965–7) passim   PGB

Dionisio VÁZQUEZ of Toledo, 3 June 1479– July 1539
Dionisio Vázquez (Augustinianus), the son of Pedro Vázquez and María de San Pedro, was born in Toledo and made his profession in the Augustinian order in that city on 5 July 1500. He studied at Paris and received a doctorate in theology at Rome under the direction of Egidio *Antonini of Viterbo, the general of his order. He soon distinguished himself by his eloquence: he was preacher to Pope *Leo x and, on his return to Spain, to *Ferdinand II of Aragon and *Charles v. On 20 January 1532 he obtained the chair of Holy Scriptures at the University of Alcalá, which he occupied until his death, refusing to accept appointments to the dioceses of Mexico and Palencia. The universities of Alcalá, Toledo, and Paris awarded him honorary doctorates. His sermons in the vernacular were renowned during his lifetime: according to Alonso Orozco and other contemporary authors his expositions of the Gospel of St John were preached throughout Spain. He is numbered among the precursors of the Spanish mystics of the second half of the sixteenth century. A friend of the *alumbrado* Luis de Beteta, he testified for him at his trial before the Inquisition in 1538.

On 28 March 1527, when representatives of the religious orders in Spain were called to present specific objections to the teachings of Erasmus before the supreme council of the Inquisition, Vázquez spoke in praise of the humanist. These events were later reported to Erasmus by Juan de *Vergara (Ep 1814) and Juan Luis *Vives, who ranked Vázquez among the most fervent supporters of Erasmus in Spain (Ep 1847).

The works of Vázquez included the *Oratio habita Romae in apostolica sacri palatii capella* (Rome 1513), *De unitate et simplicitate personae Christi in duabus naturis* (Rome 1518), the 'Commentarium super Johannem ad litteram' (manuscript), and the 'Lectura sobre San Juan' (lost manuscript). A collection of *Sermones* was published by Félix G. Olmedo (Madrid 1943).

BIBLIOGRAPHY: Allen Ep 1814 / Bataillon *Erasmo y España* 238 and passim / David Gutiérrez *Ascéticos, místicos agustinos de Espa-*

ña, Portugal e Hispanoamérica (Rome 1956–9) II
156–8 / A. Manrique in Diccionario de historia
eclesiástica de España (Madrid 1972–5) IV
2715–16 / Gregorio de Santiago Vela Ensayo de
una biblioteca ibero-americana de la Orden de San
Agustín (Madrid 1913–31) VIII 103–6

                                    MILAGROS RIVERA

VEERE See Anna van BORSSELE, Adolph
of BURGUNDY

Hieronymus VELDT (Ep 2755 of [c 22 January
1533])
Bonifacius *Amerbach mentions the name of a
relative of either Johann *Gross or Anselmus
*Ephorinus. The decipherment of this name is
uncertain; Allen read 'Hieronymus Veldt'
whereas Alfred Hartmann (AK IV Ep 1711) read
'Florianus.'

Caspar VELIUS See Caspar URSINUS Velius

VEMGUS See Bartholomaeus Arnoldi of
USINGEN

Thomas VENATORIUS of Nürnberg,
d 4 February 1551
Thomas Venatorius (Gechauf) was born around 1488, but no further information is
available about his family and his education. It
may be that he acquired his humanistic and
theological knowledge in Italy. In 1519 he
addressed a letter to his patron and friend
Willibald *Pirckheimer, dating it from Kornburg, a small market town in the diocese of
Eichstätt. In 1520 he held the benefice of
Frühmesser in Kornburg, which was within the
gift of the Riedter family of Nürnberg. By this
time he had established a reputation in
humanist circles and was known both as a
follower of *Luther and as a great admirer of
*Reuchlin. On 16 June 1522 the Nürnberg
council appointed him preacher at the hospital
of the Holy Ghost. As early as 3 January 1523
the papal legate Francesco *Chieregati cited
him together with two other Nürnberg preachers, Andreas *Osiander and Dominik
*Schleupner, requesting their arrest and extra-
dition to Rome on account of their Lutheran
sermons (Ep 1344). The Nürnberg council,
however, protected the three men and thereafter consulted them repeatedly when forced to

deal with the religious divisions in the city. In
particular, Venatorius helped to draft Nürnberg's reform program, the 'grosse Ratschlag'
of December 1524, as well as participating in
the religious colloquy of March 1525 which
opened the way for the definitive victory of
Nürnberg's reform party.

In December 1525 Wenzel Linck was appointed warden and preacher of the Holy
Ghost hospital, while Venatorius continued to
serve as preacher to the hospital's Sutte
infirmary. From August 1533 to his retirement
in 1547 he was the minister of St Jacob's and
from 1534 he also served as school inspector. In
the summer of 1544 he was called to Rothen-
burg ob der Tauber to help introduce reform;
his mandate successfully completed, he returned to Nürnberg on 3 November. Since 11
August 1527 he had been married to a former
nun, Margarete Zeckendorfer, who died in the
spring of 1542. On 17 July 1542 he married
Margarete Kobolt.

Venatorius' Axiomata quaedam rerum christi-
anarum (Nürnberg 1526) presents in the form
of theses the principal tenets of evangelical
doctrine, reaffirming in particular Luther's
view of the Eucharist. In the same year he
dedicated to Pirckheimer his defence of infant
baptism, Pro baptismo et fide parvulorum (Nürnberg: J. Petreius 1527). A pastoral work about
death, Ein kurtz Underricht den sterbenden
Menschen gantz tröstlich geschriben (Nürnberg: J.
Stuchs 1527), was lauded by Luther, who in
1529 had it reprinted with a preface of his own
([Wittenberg]: J. Klug). The most important
among his theological writings, De virtute
christiana libri tres (Nürnberg: F. Peypus 1529),
was hailed by historians as the first Protestant
contribution to ethics. Venatorius defended
the Lutheran doctrine of justification against
Johann *Haner in De sola fide iustificante nos in
oculis Dei (Nürnberg: J. Petreius 1534).

In the 1530s Venatorius was able to devote
increased attention to humanistic scholarship.
Among his friends were Pirckheimer, *Eobanus Hessus, and *Dürer, whose death in 1528
caused him to publish a Monodia. Despite the
differences in their religious views, Pirckheimer had requested that after his death his
papers should be entrusted to Venatorius. There
is little evidence of contact with Erasmus (Ep
2606) except for a letter written in connection

with Pirckheimer's estate, in which he informed Erasmus inter alia of his decision to destroy part of Pirckheimer's correspondence (Ep 2537). Venatorius published in his own name a Latin translation of Aristophanes' *Plutus* (Nürnberg: J. Petreius 1531), a work in which Pirckheimer too had taken an interest, and edited Pirckheimer's Latin translation of Xenophon's *Hellenica*, which was published in Xenophon's *Opera* (Basel: A. Cratander 1534). His minor works of a humanistic character are numerous; special mention should be made, however, of his first edition of Archimedes' *Opera* in Greek and Latin (Basel: J. Herwagen 1544), which is dedicated to the Nürnberg council. Venatorius died in his native city.

BIBLIOGRAPHY: Allen Ep 2537 / ADB XXXIX 599–600 / RGG VI 1252 / Theodor Kolde in *Realencyclopädie für protestantische Theologie und Kirche* ed J.J. Herzog et al, 3rd ed (Leipzig 1896–1908) xx 489–91 / Theodor Kolde 'Thomas Venatorius, sein Leben und seine literarische Tätigkeit' *Beiträge zur bayerischen Kirchengeschichte* 13 (1907) 97–121 and 157–95 / Willehad Paul Eckert 'Erasmus von Rotterdam und Willibald Pirckheimer' in *Willibald Pirckheimer 1470/1970* (Nürnberg 1970) 11–22 / Niklas Holzberg *Willibald Pirckheimer: Griechischer Humanismus in Deutschland* (Munich 1981) 111–12, 362–3 and passim / Jürgen Lorz *Das reformatorische Wirken Dr. Wenzeslaus Lincks in Altenburg und Nürnberg (1523–47)* (Nürnberg 1978) 87, 90 ff, 237–8 / Andreas Osiander *Gesamtausgabe* (Gütersloh 1975–   ) I–III passim / Gerhard Pfeiffer *Quellen zur Nürnberger Reformationsgeschichte* (Nürnberg 1968) passim / Matthias Simon *Nürnbergisches Pfarrerbuch 1524–1806* (Nürnberg 1965) no 1439 / J.C.E. Schwarz 'Thomas Venatorius und die Anfänge der protestantischen Ethik' *Theologische Studien und Kritiken* 23 (1850) 79–142

STEPHAN FÜSSEL

Jean-Pierre VÉRADE *See Jean-Pierre de* VARADE

VERENA zur Meerkatzen documented at Basel 1526–9
In Ep 2153 (3 May 1529) Bartholomäus *Welser proposed as an agent capable of cashing a bill of exchange for Erasmus one Verena de Catomarino. No doubt she is the person

mentioned in a sales contract of 15 October 1526, when Basel acquired the village of Biel-Benken and had to pay off a mortgage belonging to 'derenn zur Merkazen.'

The name 'Meerkatze' applied to houses 19 and 26 and adjacent dwellings on the Petersberg, but independently also to house 10 on the Münsterberg. In the surviving documents concerning these locations, however, at the time in question no Verena could be found.

BIBLIOGRAPHY: *Urkundenbuch der Stadt Basel* ed R. Wackernagel et al (Basel 1890–1910) x 78 / Staatsarchiv Basel-Stadt, MSS Historisches Grundbuch   PGB

Francisco de VERGARA of Toledo, d 27 December 1545
Born at Toledo, Francisco was the brother of Juan and Isabel de *Vergara and the half-brother of Bernardino *Tovar. He was educated in the college of San Ildefonso at Alcalá, where he was a student of Demetrius of Crete and Hernán Núñez de Toledo, better known as el Comendador griego or el Pinciano. In 1522 he was named professor of Greek at the University of Alcalá, where he spent most of his life. He was a friend of Lorenzo Balbo de Lillo and Diego *Gracián de Alderete, with whom he corresponded in 1528 and 1529.

An ardent Erasmian like the other members of his family, Francisco was mentioned to Erasmus by Juan on 24 April 1527 as one to whom Juan had taught Greek and who had now surpassed his master (Ep 1814). At about the same time Francisco sent Erasmus a letter in Greek, unfortunately now lost, which Erasmus sent to the professors of the Collegium Trilingue of Louvain (Ep 1876) and replied to at length with Ep 1885. The two again exchanged letters in 1529 (Ep 2125), and on 13 January 1530 Erasmus addressed to Francisco a letter of introduction for Frans van der *Dilft, who was travelling to Spain (Ep 2254).

Vergara's works included two volumes in Greek: a small chrestomathy of Greek passages (Alcalá: M. de Eguía 1524) and an edition of the New Testament Epistles (Alcalá: M. de Eguía 1524), today lost. He also wrote *De graecae linguae grammatica libri quinque* (Alcalá: M. de Eguía 1537) and *De syllabarum graecarum quantitate* (Paris: J. Loys 1545) and translated nine sermons of Basil the Great (Alcalá: J.

Brocar 1544), which he dedicated to his brother Juan.

BIBLIOGRAPHY: Allen Ep 1876 / Bataillon *Erasmo y España* 12, 159, and passim /Nicolás Antonio *Bibliotheca Hispana nova* (Madrid 1783–8) 495 / Milagros Ezquerro *Diego Gracián de Alderete* (Toulouse 1968) / Emil Legrand 'Bibliographie hispano-grecque' no 49 in *Bibliographie hispanique 1915* (New York 1915)

MILAGROS RIVERA

Isabel de VERGARA of Toledo, documented 1528–33

Isabel was the sister of Juan and Francisco de *Vergara and the half-sister of Bernardino *Tovar. With them, she was part of a circle of Erasmians at Alcalá, where she resided. Lucio Marineo Siculo, who knew her there, placed her on the same intellectual plane as her brothers. She became familiar with the works of Erasmus, at first through Spanish translations, then in the original Latin (Ep 2004). The mystic Francisca Hernández denounced her to the Inquisition in July 1530 together with Juan and Bernardino. On 2 June 1533 Diego Hernández included her among the Lutheran faction in his declaration before the Inquisition calling her 'the devoted servant of the Lutherans.' It is not known whether she was arrested.

On 29 June 1528 Isabel sent greetings to Erasmus through Juan, who paid discreet tribute to her learning (Ep 2004). Erasmus returned the greeting, using the occasion to praise learned women (Ep 2133).

BIBLIOGRAPHY: Bataillon *Erasmo y España* 297, 342, and passim

MILAGROS RIVERA

Juan de VERGARA of Toledo, 4 September 1492–20 February 1557

Juan de Vergara was born at Toledo and was of Jewish descent on his maternal side. Francisco and Isabel de *Vergara were his brother and sister, and Bernardino *Tovar was his half-brother. He studied at the University of Alcalá, from 1508 at the latest. Between 1509 and 1512 he resided in the College of San Ildefonso as a 'familiar' or servant, and around 1514 he was chosen to be a fellow of the college by Cardinal *Jiménez de Cisneros, archbishop of Toledo. In January of that year he was a MA. He was not a professor at Alcalá, as Menéndez Pelayo and others have supposed, nor was he entrusted

with the chair of philosophy in 1512, as Nicolás Antonio affirmed. During his stay at the College of San Ildefonso he was involved in Jiménez's great project, the Polyglot Bible of Alcalá, published from 1514 to 1517. Vergara helped prepare the interlinear translation of the Greek text of Proverbs, Wisdom, Ecclesiastes, and Job. He also translated works of Aristotle, including the *Physics, Metaphysics*, and *On the Soul* (Toledo, Biblioteca del Cabildo MS). He stayed in San Ildefonso until the beginning of 1517, becoming a doctor of theology. His colleagues included Demetrius of Crete and Alfonso de Zamora.

In 1516 or 1517 Vergara became secretary to Cardinal Jiménez and thus entered the world of high politics. Jiménez gave him canonries at Alcalá and Toledo and various other benefices. In 1517, after the death of Jiménez, the archbishopric of Toledo passed to Guillaume (II) de *Croy. In the spring of 1520 Vergara sailed to the Low Countries with Alfonso de *Valdés to inform Croy about conditions at Toledo. It was there that his first, somewhat strained, meetings with Erasmus took place.

Soon after his arrival at Bruges in July 1520 Vergara was met by Erasmus, who inquired about a copy of the *Annotationes contra Erasmum* (Alcalá 1520), an attack on the first edition of his New Testament (Basel 1516) written by Diego *López Zúñiga, a theologian at Alcalá. Vergara had promised one of Erasmus' Flemish contacts in Spain, probably Pierre *Barbier, that he would take a copy to Erasmus. Great was Erasmus' consternation when he learnt that Vergara had accidently left the volume in Spain. He suggested to Vergara that López Zúñiga had deliberately failed to refer to his second edition of the New Testament (Basel 1518–19) when he composed the *Annotationes*. Vergara hastened to inform Erasmus that the second edition of the New Testament had not arrived in Spain when López Zúñiga wrote his book, and defended the latter as an assiduous scholar who loved both religious and secular authors of Latin, Greek, and Hebrew. Vergara later learnt, through a common friend, that Erasmus suspected that he had actually brought the book but had concealed it in order to give it to the supporters of Edward *Lee, who was also attacking Erasmus' New Testament, or else to delay any response from

Erasmus. Several days later Erasmus invited Vergara to dinner in order to learn more about López Zúñiga's *Annotationes,* and Vergara once again tried to allay his suspicions (Allen IV 623–4).

Vergara departed for Germany with Archbishop Croy to attend the Diet of Worms in 1521. On his return to the Netherlands in the summer of 1521 he learnt that Erasmus had obtained a copy of the *Annotationes* and was preparing a reply. After visiting Erasmus at Louvain, Vergara obtained a copy of his *Apologia contra Stunicam* (Louvain 1521) and sent it to López Zúñiga, who was then at Rome, on 10 October 1521. With the book he sent a long letter in which he tried to restrain his friend from making further attacks on Erasmus by informing him of the sagacity and industriousness of Erasmus and of the esteem in which he was held in Germany, England, and the Netherlands (Allen IV 623–5). Vergara's attempt at peacemaking failed miserably. López Zúñiga replied with a letter suggesting that Erasmus was an impious blasphemer in league with *Luther (Allen IV 625–8), and the next three years witnessed the publication of a series of polemical exchanges between Erasmus and the Spaniard.

Meanwhile a new problem arose for Vergara. Sancho *Carranza de Miranda, another professor of Alcalá residing at Rome, published what appeared to be a new attack on Erasmus, the *Opusculum in quasdam Erasmi Roterodami annotationes* (Rome 1522). Carranza had seen Vergara's letter to López Zúñiga and decided to dedicate his work to Vergara in the hope that he could persuade Erasmus of his good intentions. Vergara obliged by writing to Erasmus to warn him of López Zúñiga's hostile attitude and to inform him of Carranza's benevolence. Carranza, he said, was motivated not by hatred but by the desire for scholarly discussion (Ep 1277). Erasmus replied on 2 September 1522, expressing his gratitude for Vergara's letter, which he described as 'truly erudite, elegant and breathing a certain uncommon kindness towards me.' He added that he now realized that Vergara was a friend of the Muses (Ep 1312). From that moment Vergara became one of Erasmus' most loyal Spanish champions.

After the death of Guillaume de Croy in January 1521 Vergara entered the service of *Charles v as court chaplain. On his return to Spain in 1522 he was thrilled by the change he perceived in the intellectual climate. He jubilantly reported to Juan Luis *Vives that all Spaniards, learned and ignorant, ecclesiastics and laymen, were full of admiration for Erasmus. On 7 May 1523 he again wrote to López Zúñiga, informing him that the latter's reputation had been so severely damaged by the publication of the *Erasmi Roterodami blasphemiae et impietates* (Rome 1522) that he could no longer defend him, and once again begging him to make peace with Erasmus (Allen IV 631). Vergara had the opportunity to pursue his own humanistic interests through an academic career when, on the death of Elio Antonio de *Nebrija, he was offered the chair of rhetoric at Alcalá. However, he declined, suggesting instead his close friend Vives, who also declined. Vergara chose to remain near the centre of ecclesiastical power, accepting in 1524 the post of secretary to Alonso de *Fonseca, the new archbishop of Toledo. From this vantage point he was able to monitor and promote the cause of Erasmus in Spain. In March 1526 Erasmus wrote to Vergara inquiring about a certain Alonso de Olmedo who had written a series of admonitions to him, the 'Collationes ad Erasmum,' ostensibly on Vergara's advice (Ep 1684). Vergara, who did not know the man, made inquiries among his friends at the imperial court and elsewhere, and learnt that he was Alonso Ruiz de *Virués, a Benedictine monk of Burgos. After meeting Ruiz de Virués and exchanging many letters with him, Vergara assured Erasmus of his good intentions (Ep 1814), thus helping to bring about a lasting friendship between the two men.

However, not all was going well for the Erasmian cause in Spain. Members of the religious orders accused Erasmus of being a heretic and a supporter of *Luther. In March 1527 the inquisitor-general, Alonso *Manrique, met the representatives of the orders, then assembled at Valladolid for the Cortes, and renewed injunctions previously issued prohibiting attacks on Erasmus and his writings: if the monks had accusations against Erasmus they should present specific textual references to the Inquisition for judgment.

When the religious orders complied by presenting lists of their complaints, Manrique called a conference of theologians at Valladolid to assess the merits of their case. Vergara informed Erasmus about these events, and advised him to act with great prudence when dealing with the Spanish monks (Ep 1814). Erasmus replied with the comment that he intended to act cautiously, but added that if the monks continued their attacks he would turn their misdeeds against them (Ep 1875).

The conference of theologians began its meetings at Valladolid on 27 June 1527 but was suspended on 13 August without passing judgment for or against Erasmus. The Erasmian party appeared to be victorious, for they continued to enjoy the support of the court and of powerful ecclesiastics such as Manrique and Fonseca. As Vergara reported to Erasmus, the furore of the religious orders subsided after the conference (Ep 2004). The years 1527–30 witnessed what Bataillon has termed an 'invasion' of Spain by Erasmian works. Among other things, Vergara promoted the spread of Erasmian ideas by using his influence to defend Juan de *Valdés' Diálogo de doctrina cristiana (Alcalá 1529) before a commission of judges at Alcalá.

However, the triumph of the Erasmian party was short-lived. In 1529 Charles v and his court left Spain for Italy, thus removing for a time one of the greatest centres of support for Erasmus in Spain. In the early 1530s the Inquisition launched a series of attacks on prominent Erasmians. Bernardino Tovar, Vergara's half-brother, was among the first victims, imprisoned in September 1530 on the strength of evidence given against him by his former spiritual mentor, Francisca Hernández. Vergara, who had earlier tried to remove Tovar from Hernández's influence, was also accused of Lutheran sympathies and of accepting questionable teachings of Erasmus on the value of the religious life, the importance of fasts and pilgrimages, and other issues. On 19 April 1531 the opinions attributed to him by his accusers were examined by a commission composed of two Dominicans and two Franciscans, and all were deemed heretical or blasphemous. However, Vergara was still powerful, and proceedings against him were delayed. In the spring of 1533 the Inquisition intercepted letters written by him in invisible ink to the imprisoned Tovar. On 23 June he was arrested on charges of defending heretics, subverting the Inquisition, and suborning its members. Despite efforts made on his behalf by the inquisitor-general, Manrique, by Archbishop Fonseca (who died on 5 February 1534), and by the Empress *Isabella of Portugal, Vergara's trial lasted until December 1535. In his defence, in addition to denying any attachment to Lutheranism, Vergara reiterated his admiration for Erasmus. Of his bond with Erasmus he said: 'I tell you, sirs, that if this is a crime, it is common to many, even to great princes of all states and nations which value and esteem Erasmus for his teaching ... ' Vergara, however, was convicted of holding heretical opinions on indulgences, the nature of the sacraments, and the teachings of the church on oral prayer. On 21 December 1535 he was forced to abjure his errors on the scaffold at Toledo, where he held a prebend at the cathedral. His penalty was a fine of one thousand ducats and seclusion for a year at the monastery of San Augustín, where he was to do penance. He was freed on 27 February 1537, but his trial and imprisonment destroyed his career and undermined his health. He spent his last years as a canon of the cathedral at Toledo, devoting his time to his studies. The last known letter of Erasmus to Vergara was dated 19 November 1533 (Ep 2879). Vives informed Erasmus of Vergara's imprisonment on 10 May 1534 (Ep 2932), and Erasmus mentioned this event with sadness in a letter to Guy *Morillon (Ep 2965).

In addition to his work on the Polyglot Bible and on Aristotle, Vergara's most important work was the historical Tratado de las ocho questiones del templo (Toledo: J. Ferrer 1552, reprinted by F. Cerdà y Rico in Clarorum Hispanorum opuscula selecta et rariora, Madrid 1781). Vergara also began a biography of Cardinal Jiménez, now lost. The catalogue of manuscripts at the Biblioteca Nacional of Madrid includes a notice of a presentation made by Vergara in 1547 to the council of Castile against statutes on 'purity of blood,' but this too is lost. Juan Luis Vives made Vergara his main speaker in the Veritas fucata sive de licentia poetica (Louvain 1523).

BIBLIOGRAPHY: Allen Ep 1277 / H.J. de Jonge in ASD IX-2 44–7 and passim / Bataillon Erasmo y

España 39, 42, 96–9, and passim / Marcel Bataillon *Erasmo y el erasmismo* (Barcelona 1977) 171–4, 215–17 / A. Bonilla y San Martin 'Clarorum Hispaniensium epistolae ineditae' *Revue Hispanique* 8 (1901) 181–308 / J. Goñi in *Diccionario de historia eclesiástica de España* ed Q.A. Vaquero et al (Madrid 1972–5) IV 2737–42 / J.E. Longhurst 'Alumbrados, erasmistas y luteranos en el proceso de Juan de Vergara' *Cuadernos de historia de España* 27 (1958) 99–163; 28 (1958) 102–65; 29–30 (1959) 266–92; 31–2 (1960) 322–56; 35–6 (1962) 337–53; 37–8 (1963) 356–71 / M. de la Pinta Llorente *El erasmismo del doctor Juan de Vergara y otras interpretaciones* (Madrid 1945) / M. de la Pinta Llorente 'Una testificación del erasmista Alonso de Virués contra el doctor Juan de Vergara' *La Ciudad de Dios* 153 (1941) 354–5 / M. de la Pinta Llorente 'El humanista toledano Juan de Vergara' *La Ciudad de Dios* 154 (1942) 365–73 / M. de la Pinta Llorente *Aspectos históricos del sentimiento religioso en España, ortodoxia y heterodoxia* (Madrid 1961) / F. de B. San Roman 'El testamento del humanista Alvar Gómez de Castro' *Boletín de la Real Academia Española* 15 (1928) 543–66 / M. Serrano y Sanz 'Juan de Vergara y la Inquisición de Toledo' *Revista de archivos, bibliotecas y museos* 5 (1901) 896–912; 6 (1902) 29–42, 466–486   MILAGROS RIVERA & TBD

Pier Paolo VERGERIO of Capodistria, 1498–4 October 1565
Pier Paolo, a son of Girolamo Vergerio and a descendant of the humanist Pier Paolo Vergerio (1370–1444), was born in Capodistria, in Venetian territory. He received a doctorate in civil law at Padua on 21 May 1524 and by 16 October 1526, the date when he signed a marriage contract with Diana Contarini (d 1527), he was also a doctor of canon law. In the eight years after 1524 he practised law, as an advocate, a judge, and perhaps a teacher at Padua. In 1532 he travelled to Rome, where by mid-July he was a papal secretary. In October he was sent to Venice as a special envoy to work beside Roberto Maggio, the secretary of the recently deceased nuncio. In 1533 he was sent to the court of King *Ferdinand as nuncio. In 1535 Pope *Paul III sent him on a second nunciature to Germany, with the task of promoting a council at a location pleasing to the pope. In November 1535, while passing

through Wittenberg, he met Martin *Luther. He returned to Italy in December 1535 and the following May he was offered the remote diocese of Modrus in Croatia. Reluctant to accept Modrus, on 6 September 1536 he received Capodistria instead. His ordination to the priesthood and consecration as a bishop occurred between May 1536 and 1541.

In September 1536 Vergerio went to Capodistria intent on serving as a true pastor to his diocese. However he soon stirred up trouble through his attempts to reform the clergy and by trying to end payment of a pension from the revenues of his diocese. In the late 1530s he also came into increasing contact with proponents of evangelism who, inspired by Protestant reformers, called for an end to abuses within the church and a renewal of personal piety founded upon the Scriptures. He travelled to France in 1540 in the entourage of Cardinal Ippolito d'Este and there met *Margaret of Angoulême, protectress of French reformers. In November 1540 he went to Worms as an unofficial agent of King *Francis I to attend a colloquy between Catholics and Protestants. There he wrote and circulated *De unitate et pace ecclesiae*, printed at Venice (G.A. de' Niccolini da Sabbio) in 1542, in which he defended his view that only a general council, and not a local assembly, could cure the ills of Christendom. He left Germany in mid-March 1541, shortly before the commencement of the colloquy of Regensburg, and returned to Capodistria. However his efforts to reform the regular clergy led to resentment and to charges of heresy: specifically that he deprecated Catholic doctrines on purgatory and the veneration of the saints and that he encouraged the reading of heretical works. In 1545 he was refused a place at the council of Trent, and the following year proceedings were initiated against him in Venice before the representatives of the patriarch and of the papal nuncio. In May 1549 Vergerio fled to the Grisons, and on 3 July he was deprived of his diocese. He was the first Italian bishop to defect to the Protestant camp.

From the Grisons Vergerio moved on to Basel, where he enrolled in the university in 1549–50 and met Bonifacius *Amerbach, the executor of Erasmus' will and a supporter of religious refugees. He also came in contact with Italian reformers, including Lelio Sozzini and Matteo Gribaldi Moffa, who introduced him to Jean Calvin. Returning to the Grisons, he was nominated pastor of Vicosoprano in 1550. In 1553 he moved to the court of Christopher of *Württemberg at Tübingen, which became the new centre of his activity. In 1554 he condemned Celio Secondo Curione's *De amplitudine beati regni Dei*, which used a passage of Juan Luis *Vives' commentary on Augustine to argue that the observance of the natural law was sufficient for salvation. An enthusiastic propagandist for the Protestant cause, Vergerio visited Poland in 1556 and 1557, Bern, Geneva, and Basel in 1557, Friuli in 1558, and Poland again in 1560. In his last years he travelled to Chur, Zürich, and the Valtellina, but he was unable to establish himself as the leader of the Italian exiles. He died at Tübingen.

Erasmus wrote to Vergerio in 1533 during his first nunciature to Germany, commenting on peace negotiations with the Turks (Ep 2825). In 1535 Caspar *Hedio and Christoph von *Stadion informed Erasmus of the nuncio's attempts to win support for a council (Epp 3020, 3073). It is unlikely that Erasmus had much direct influence in the religious transformation of Vergerio. During his first nunciature Vergerio's attitude towards Erasmus was hostile: in a letter to King Ferdinand he denounced him as a heretic and a Lutheran. However he did try to dissuade Agostino *Steuco from attacking the humanist, lest another case of disagreement among Catholics cause scandal.

Vergerio's early works included the *Iuris civilis scholastici praelectio* (Venice: B. de' Vitali 1523) and *De republica Veneta liber primus* (Toscolano: Paganini 1526). After fleeing Italy his writings were mainly polemical and apologetical: *Le otto difensioni del Vergerio vescovo di Capodistria* (Basel: J. Parcus 1550), *Dodici trattatelli* (Basel: J. Parcus 1550), *De creatione Julii III* (Basel: J. Oporinus 1550), *De' portamenti di Papa Giulio III* (Zürich: C. Froschauer 1550), *Concilium ... Tridentinum ... fugiendum esse omnibus piis* (np 1551), *Retrattatione* ([Tübingen: widow of U. Morhart] 1556), and many others. He published a *Primus tomus operum adversus Papatum* (Tübingen: widow of U. Morhart 1563), but other volumes did not follow.

BIBLIOGRAPHY: Allen Ep 2825 / Eubel III 216 / D. Cantimori *Eretici italiani del cinquecento* (Florence 1939, repr 1967) / F.C. Church *The Italian Reformers, 1534–1564* (New York 1932) / M. Coglievina 'Pier Paolo Vergerio il giovane' *Pagine istriane* ser 3, 1 (1950) 61–73 / H. Jedin in LThK x 701–2 / P. Paschini *Pier Paolo Vergerio il giovane e la sua apostasia* (Rome 1925) / Anne Jacobson Schutte *Pier Paolo Vergerio: The Making of an Italian Reformer* (Geneva 1977) / Friedrich Hubert *Vergerios publizistische Thätigkeit nebst einer bibliographischen Übersicht* (Göttingen 1893)   MARCO BERNUZZI & TBD

Polydorus VERGILIUS *See Polidoro* VIRGILIO

Antoine de VERGY c August 1488–29 December 1541
A descendant of one of the great families of Burgundy, Antoine de Vergy (Vageyus) was elected a canon of Besançon on 10 October 1502 and at the same time archbishop in succession to François (I) de *Busleyden; papal confirmation followed on 4 November. He matriculated at Louvain in July 1505 and continued his studies at the Burgundian University of Dole. On 8 February 1509 he laid the foundation stone for the new church of Notre Dame at Dole. At the age of twenty-five, on 27 August 1513, he took possession of his see, although he was not consecrated until 1517. After some time spent at the court of Brussels, where he is said to have been a preceptor of the future *Charles v, Vergy returned to Burgundy, only to become involved, in 1518, in the continuing conflict with the city of Besançon. In 1520 he abruptly moved his court and entire administration, including the episcopal tribunal, to the castle of Gy, halfway between Besançon and Gray. For Besançon this meant loss of population and economic hardship. Ignoring the displeasure of Charles v, Vergy continued to treat the city, and sometimes his own chapter too, in a most highhanded manner until the conflict was resolved on 9 January 1528, partly thanks to the conciliatory attitude of Erasmus' friend, the archdeacon Ferry de *Carondelet.

Erasmus' connections with Vergy were slight. In 1523 Erasmus composed a mass in honour of the Virgin of Loretto at the request of his friend Thiébaut *Biétry, a priest in Porrentruy. Biétry apparently succeeded in drawing the archbishop's attention to Erasmus' mass and, coinciding with Erasmus' visit to Besançon in the spring of 1524, Vergy issued a diploma granting forty days' indulgence to any one in his diocese who used the mass (Ep 1391; LB V 1334–6). Erasmus later liked to refer to Vergy's diploma when accused of having spoken disrespectfully of the Virgin while at Besançon (Epp 1610, 1679, 1956).

BIBLIOGRAPHY: Allen Ep 1610 / Eubel II 106, III 134 / *Gallia christiana* XV 101–3 / Claude Fohlen et al *Histoire de Besançon* (Paris 1964–5) I 569, 605, and passim / A. Castan 'Granvelle et le petit empereur de Besançon, 1518–1538' *Revue historique* 1 (1876) 78–139, esp 91, 123, and passim / Gauthier 120, 123, 125, 133 / Besançon, Archives du Doubs, MS G 250

PGB

Jacques VÉRIER *See Jacobus* FABER

Gabriel VERINUS (Ep 2660 of 16 June [1532]) Gabriel Verinus wrote to Erasmus discussing the attacks on Erasmus from Catholic circles and proposing to write a dialogue in his defence, in which Erasmus would be represented in the person of Eloquence. He planned to dedicate the work to Lorenzo *Campeggi, of whose *familia* he may have been a member. If so, Erasmus may have met Verinus, who is not otherwise identified, during the years of Campeggi's legateship in Germany (1524–5, 1530–2).   JOHN F. D'AMICO

Louis de VERS d 5 December 1553 Little information appears to be available on Louis de Vers, who was descended from a noble family of Burgundy, the Vers-en-Montagne. He was jointly abbot of two Cistercian houses in the Franche-Comté; his appointment to Mont-Sainte-Marie, on the Doubs above Pontarlier, dated from 1509, and in 1529 he received La Charité, Haute-Saône, Canton de Gray.

Erasmus' connection with Vers was due to the fact that he was a relative of Gilbert *Cousin, who dedicated to him his Οἰκέτης (Basel: H. Froben and N. Episcopius 1535). It does not seem that Erasmus ever met Vers, but he wrote to him (Epp 2889, 3062) about a

benefice for Cousin and acknowledged a gift of excellent wine of which one barrel unfortunately turned out to be spoilt when it was opened (Epp 3095, 3102, 3115).

BIBLIOGRAPHY: Allen Ep 2889 / DHGE XII 417–18 / Gilbert Cousin *Opera* (Basel 1562) I 218 / Gilbert Cousin *La Franche-Comté au milieu du* XVIᵉ *siècle* ed E. Monot (Lons-le-Saunier 1907) 71, 76 / Henri Jougla de Morenas *Grand Armorial de France* (Paris 1934–52) VI 440

PGB

Bartholomeus van VESSEM d 29 April 1539 Around 1507 Bartholomeus van Vessem (Wessem) entered the household of Jérôme de *Busleyden, who knew Bartholomeus' elder brother, Arnold van Vessem, a Premonstratensian monk of Tongerloo abbey, and appreciated him for his musical skills. As Busleyden's chamberlain, Bartholomeus managed the servants and eventually accompanied his master on the journey to Spain. After Busleyden's death in Bordeaux on 27 August 1517, he brought the body back to Mechelen for burial. In Busleyden's will he had been appointed an executor (Ep 1051). He showed great diligence in the pursuit of this duty and sacrificed several years of his revenue as a canon of Aire, Pas-de-Calais, in order to travel through the Netherlands in search of suitable investments for the endowment of the Collegium Trilingue. He resided in Louvain while the college was being built, directing and surveying the work. A friend of Jan *Robbyns, the dean of St Rombaut's in Mechelen, he became a canon of that chapter and eventually died in Mechelen.

Erasmus referred to Vessem in December 1519 as the person who could inform Jan Robbyns about recent troubles at Louvain and the unjustified arrest of Rutgerus *Rescius (Ep 1046).

BIBLIOGRAPHY: Allen and CWE Ep 1046 / de Vocht *Busleyden* Ep 35 and passim / de Vocht CTL I 53–5, 293, III 379, IV 7–8, and passim

IG

Nicolaus VESUVIUS documented 1527–8 Nicolaus Vesuvius was chaplain to Michel *Boudet, bishop of Langres. No more seems to be known about him so far than what can be gathered from the correspondence of Erasmus.

They exchanged letters in 1527 and 1528, of which one by Vesuvius (Ep 1784) and three by Erasmus (Epp 1894, 2053, 2075) are extant. In particular, Erasmus sought to obtain through Vesuvius' good services a royal privilege protecting the *Froben edition of St Augustine. A reference in Ep 2065 may also be to Vesuvius.   MICHEL REULOS & PGB

Melchior Matthaei of VIANDEN
d before 25 February 1535

Melchior Matthaei of Vianden, in Luxembourg (Viandalus, Viandulus, Melchior Trevir) was born around 1490 and matriculated at the University of Louvain on 29 February 1508 as one of the 'poor' students of the College of the Castle. Two years later he graduated MA, standing second among 148 candidates. While pursuing the study of theology he taught classical languages so successfully that he came to the attention of Erasmus (Ep 1237). His colleagues in the faculty of arts too thought well enough of him to elect him procurator of the nation of Holland in 1518 and 1520. Early in 1522 Erasmus encouraged him warmly to accept a position of importance which had been offered to him, perhaps a chair at the University of Tournai which was then preparing to begin its activities (Ep 1257 and perhaps Ep 1292). Another three years would pass, however, before this project could be realized, and Vianden took this opportunity to continue his scholarly work at Louvain in close contact with Conradus *Goclenius and Maarten *Lips. He also entered into correspondence with Erasmus, who had meanwhile moved to Basel, and soon felt confident enough to suggest that Erasmus undertake a paraphrase of the Psalter. Erasmus was delighted, but he realized the magnitude of the task Vianden had proposed and was content to publish his Paraphrasis in Tertium Psalmum (Basel: J. Froben 1524) with a dedication to Vianden (Ep 1427; LB V 233–42; Allen I 21, 52). A few days later he resolved in the event of his death to leave Vianden the sum of 130 St Philip florins (Ep 1437).

On 20 June 1525 the University of Tournai finally inaugurated its programs, and Vianden, a special protégé of vicar-general Pierre *Cotrel (Ep 1427), was appointed to teach there jointly with Nicolaas van *Broeckhoven and Jacobus *Ceratinus. Although the university was

closed after only four months by order of the regent, *Margaret of Austria, Vianden remained in Tournai. He married twice and had several children (and thus may conceivably be the 'ille non sacerdos' mentioned in Ep 1292). He remained in contact with both Erasmus and Goclenius (Ep 1768), who later conveyed to Erasmus the sad news of Vianden's death from the plague (Ep 2998). As he had evidently been fond of Vianden, Erasmus was deeply grieved (Epp 3019, 3048).

BIBLIOGRAPHY: Allen Ep 1237 / Matricule de Louvain III-1 347 / de Vocht CTL II 350 and passim / de Vocht MHL 497 / Gérard Moreau Histoire du protestantisme à Tournai (Liège 1962) 61–2 / Claude Dufrasne and Marie-Thérèse Isaac in Ecoles et livres d'école en Hainaut du XVIe au XIXe siècle (Mons 1971) 126–8
                                        GÉRARD MOREAU

Willem of VIANEN d 20 November 1529

Willem of Vianen, south of Utrecht, (Guilhelmus Johannis Lamberti Vianensis, Vyanen) matriculated at the University of Louvain on 3 November 1478. By 1488 he had received his MA and was teaching elementary courses at the College of the Castle. He spent his entire life teaching at the university, which elected him rector for the spring terms of 1500 and 1508 as well as the winter term 1525–6. He was also dean of the faculty of arts for various terms to 1529. In 1505 he was appointed plebanus or curate of St Peter's, a benefice which was coupled to a theological chair. After the death of Jan *Briart in 1520 Vianen also exercised, at least on a temporary basis, the functions of a vice-chancellor acting for the absent chancellor, Adrian of Utrecht, the future pope *Adrian VI. As a theologian and scholar Vianen had no particular importance. In 1524 he was criticized, along with others, for some slackness in the exercise of certain teaching functions. After his death he was succeeded as plebanus and professor by Pieter de *Corte.

When Erasmus settled at Louvain in 1517 he mentioned Vianen along with Briart and *Dorp as three theologians who were showing particular sympathy for him (Epp 650, 651, 673). Later on Vianen was never mentioned among those Louvain theologians who opposed the humanistic Collegium Trilingue and were outspoken in their criticism of Erasmus himself. In 1525, when appealing to the theological faculty, Erasmus mentioned Vianen by name, evidently in deference to his rank as well as his open mind (Ep 1582).

BIBLIOGRAPHY: Allen Ep 650 / NNBW V 1019 / H. de Jongh *L'Ancienne Faculté de théologie de Louvain* (Louvain 1911) 155, 24*, and passim / *Matricule de Louvain* II-1 386, III-1 53, and passim / de Vocht MHL 412 and passim / de Vocht CTL I 532, II 257, 290, and passim   PGB

Georgius VICELIUS *See Georg* WITZEL

Marco Girolamo VIDA of Cremona, c 1485–27 September 1566

Marco Antonio Vida was born in Cremona to Guglielmo Vida and Leona Oscasale. He studied Latin and Greek with Lucari in Cremona and continued his studies in Mantua. In 1504 an elegy and an epigram of his appeared in the *Collectanea* in memory of Serafino Aquilano, edited by Filoteo Achillino and published at Bologna. In 1505 he returned to Cremona, where he studied philosophy and theology and entered the order of the canons regular of St John Lateran, in which he changed his name to Marco Girolamo and received holy orders. In 1510 he went to Rome, where he established a reputation as one of the greatest poets of sixteenth-century Italy. In 1511 he wrote an epicedion in 375 verses on the death of Oliviero Carafa, and in 1513 he published the *Carmen pastorale* lamenting the death of *Julius II. In May 1527 his first major publication appeared at Rome, a collection of earlier works including *De arte poetica carmen*, *De Bombyce*, *De ludo scacchorum*, and various hymns and bucolics (Rome: L. Vincentinus). Meanwhile before 1519 Pope *Leo X asked him to write a poem on the life of Christ modelled on Virgil's *Aeneid*. The *Christiados libri sex*, presented to *Clement VII in 1532, were first printed by Ludovico Britannico at Cremona in 1535 and earned Vida the name 'the Christian Virgil.'

Meanwhile Vida was rewarded with a series of ecclesiastical benefices. Around 1516 he received the priorate of SS Margherita e Pelagia and the vicarage of the church of San Lorenzo in Monticelli d'Ongina. Leo X later assigned him the priorate of San Silvestro in Monte Corno, near Frascati. Vida was made apostolic

Marco Girolamo Vida

protonotary around 1527, a canon of the cathedral of Cremona in 1531, and dean of the church of SS Maria e Dalmazio in Paderno in 1532. In 1533 he became bishop of Alba in Piedmont, where he initiated a campaign against heretical ideas and preachers. In the late 1530s the region was invaded by French and Spanish armies, and Vida addressed supplications to *Francis I of France. In 1542 he participated in the defence of Alba against a French expeditionary force, then retired to Cremona. He went to Trent three times between 1545 and 1547 to participate in the council. In 1548 he was appointed bishop of Cremona, where he resided from 1550. In 1564 he returned to Alba, where he died.

As a poet, Vida was a familiar figure in Roman literary circles and numbered among his friends Jacopo *Sadoleto, Paolo Giovio, Pietro *Bembo, Johannes *Lascaris, and many others. On 17 April 1533 *Viglius Zuichemus mentioned Vida's *De arte poetica carmen* in a letter to Erasmus, adding that Clement VII had made him a bishop for his *Christiados* (Ep 2791). Erasmus replied that he had not seen any of Vida's works (Ep 2810).

Vida also published two works of a political nature, the *Orationes pro Cremonensibus adversus Papienses in controversia principatus* (Cremona 1550) and the *Dialogi de dignitate reipublicae ... ad Reginaldum Polum Cardinalem, libri II* (Cremona: V. Conti 1556). In 1562 he published the decrees of a synod at Cremona, and in 1565 he prepared the decrees for the first provincial council of Milan at the request of Carlo Borromeo. In 1550 he published his *Poemata omnia* (Cremona: J. Mutius and B. Locheta).

BIBLIOGRAPHY: Ep 2791 / V. Cicchitelli *Sulle opere poetiche di Marco Girolamo Vida* (Naples 1904) / V. Cicchitelli *Sulle opere in prosa di Marco Girolamo Vida* (Naples 1909) / Georg Ellinger *Geschichte der neulateinischen Literatur Deutschlands im sechzehnten Jahrhundert* (Berlin-Leipzig 1929–33) I 206–8 and passim / Mario A. Di Cesare *Vida's 'Christiad' and Vergilian Epic* (New York-London 1964) / G. Mosca *Storia delle dottrine politiche* (Bari 1964) / Marco Girolamo Vida *The Christiad: A Latin-English Edition* ed and trans G.C. Drake and C.A. Forbes (Carbondale, Ill, 1978) / For an analysis of Vida's work with the text of his *De dignitate reipublicae* ... see G. Toffanin *L'umanesimo al Concilio di Trento* (Bologna 1955)

VALERIA SESTIERI LEE & TBD

Marco VIGERIO of Savona, 1446–18 July 1516
Emanuele Vigerio (de Vigeriis) was a grand-nephew of Francesco della Rovere, the future Pope *Sixtus IV, and joined the Franciscan Conventuals in 1462 or 1464, while the future pope became general of the order in 1464. In religion Vigerio received the name of Marco. He taught theology at Padua both in the university and at the Studio of the Franciscans. After Sixtus' elevation to the papacy Vigerio went to Rome, where he was a professor at the papal university (Sapienza) from 1474. On 6 October 1476 he was appointed bishop and prefect of Sinigallia, a position he held until his resignation in 1513. In 1484 he became master of the sacred palace and thus occupied a position of great influence. On 12 November 1503 he was governor of the Castel Sant'Angelo, and on 1 December 1505 he was among the early appointees of *Julius II to the college of cardinals. From then on he was commonly known as the cardinal of Sinigallia (LB IX 60C). At the fifth Lateran council he defended Julius

II against the accusations of the schismatic council of Pisa and promoted the reform of the calendar. His best-known work was a *Decachordum christianum* extolling the virtues of the holy family (Fano: G. Soncino 1507). The British Library owns a presentation copy with a manuscript letter from the author to King *Henry VII. The *Decachordum* was followed by a *Controversia de excellentia instrumentorum dominicae passionis* (Rome: M. Silber 1512), and both works were reprinted in Paris and Haguenau in 1517 and in Douai in 1607. A 'Dialogus de tollendis abusibus' was apparently never printed.

Erasmus mentioned the cardinal of Sinigallia as the author of a letter in defence of Jacques *Lefèvre d'Etaples which he had seen in Basel around 1514–17 (LB IX 60C).

BIBLIOGRAPHY: R. Ritzler in LThK x 785 / G. Odoardi in *Enciclopedia Cattolica* (Vatican City 1948–54) XII 1411–12 / Eubel II 235, III 10 / D.R. Campbell in *New Catholic Encyclopedia* (New York 1967–78) XIV 663   PGB

Fabio VIGILI of Spoleto, died c 18 February 1553
Fabio (Agatido) Vigili was born in Spoleto. He married and had two children. In 1498 he was in Rome in the service of Archbishop Juan Castelar of Trani and passed successively to the service of Cardinal Pietro *Isvaglies (1508), Cardinal Raffaele *Riario (1511), and finally Cardinal Alessandro Farnese (*Paul III). Pope *Leo x appointed him professor of eloquence at the University of Rome. When Farnese became pope, he made Vigili his private secretary (1534). Vigili was elevated to the bishopric of Foligno (1539) and a year later translated to the see of Spoleto (Blosius *Palladius succeeded him in Foligno). He died in Rome. He was learned in Greek and Hebrew and the law, and was respected as a poet. He was a member of the Academia Coryciana, and Palladius published a number of his poems in the *Coryciana* collection (Rome: L. de Henricis and L. Perusinus 1524). He translated Pseudo-Lucian's *Longaevi* and between 1508 and 1510 compiled a catalogue of the Vatican library (Vat Lat 7134–6). He numbered among his friends Palladius, Jacopo *Sadoleto, Christophe de *Longueil, and Tommaso Fedra *Inghirami.

The only known connection between Vigili

and Erasmus was an impersonal one. In 1535,
as secretary to Paul III, Vigili signed a letter to
Erasmus which praised him for his service to
the church and awarded him the provostship
of Deventer (Ep 3033).

BIBLIOGRAPHY: Allen Ep 3033 / G. Levi della
Vida *Ricerche sulla fondazione del più antico fondo
dei manoscritti orientali della Biblioteca Vaticana*
(Vatican City 1939) 34–9 and passim / M.-H.
Laurent *Fabio Vigili et les bibliothèques de Bologne
au début du* XVIe *siècle* (Vatican City 1943) /
Jeanne Bignami-Odier and José Ruysschaert *La
Bibliothèque Vaticane de Sixte* IV *à Pie* XI (Vatican
City 1973) 28, 40   JOHN F. D'AMICO

VIGLIUS ZUICHEMUS 19 October 1507–
8 May 1577

Viglius Zuichemus

Wigle Aytta called himself Viglius Zuichemus
after Swichum or Zwichem, the place of birth of
his uncle and patron Bernard Bucho van
*Aytta. Viglius was born in Barrahuis, near
Leeuwarden, Friesland, the second son of a
well-to-do farmer. Following the death of his
elder brother he was educated in the Hague in
the house of his uncle Bernard. After short
periods of schooling in Deventer and Leiden,
Viglius was entrusted to Jacob *Volkaerd, who
was also tutoring the sons of Nicolaas *Everaerts. Accompanied by Volkaerd, Viglius
went in the autumn of 1522 to Louvain and on
18 March 1523 he matriculated at the university. He read Latin and Greek authors with
Conradus *Goclenius and Rutgerus *Rescius
respectively and from 1524 he studied law.
From 1526 he continued his legal studies at
Dole in the Hapsburg Franche-Comté, where
he established connections with the family
of Anton *Fugger and may have begun to
tutor Johann Georg *Hörmann, who continued to be his charge in Avignon and
Bourges. On 8 May 1529 Viglius obtained a
doctorate in civil and canon law from the
University of Valence. Earlier that spring he
had gone to Avignon, where the famous
Andrea *Alciati had been teaching. The great
jurist was just preparing to take up a new
appointment at the University of Bourges, and
Viglius followed him there in June. After
two years he left Bourges, at first for a visit to
Orléans and Paris. Subsequently he called
on Bonifacius *Amerbach at Basel and on Erasmus at Freiburg. At Augsburg he stayed

with the Fuggers and in the autumn travelled
to Padua by way of Schwaz, where he visited
Georg *Hörmann, the father of his charge.
By the end of October 1531 he was at Padua.

In 1532 Viglius accepted a one-year appointment in Padua to lecture in civil law. In
February 1533 he visited the imperial court at
Bologna where Chancellor Matthias *Held
secured for him a pledge to a forthcoming
appointment to the imperial law court (Reichskammergericht). In October 1533 Viglius left
Italy, visiting Basel, Freiburg, and Cologne on
his way home. At Cologne early in 1534 Franz
von *Waldeck, bishop of Münster, offered him
the vacant position of official at the episcopal
high court at Dülmen. Viglius accepted; in
February 1535 he also received the deanship of
St Mary's chapter, Münster-Überwasser, having been admitted to lower orders fifteen years
earlier at Utrecht (19 September 1520). From his
judicial position at Dülmen he was able to
observe at close quarters and describe some of
the most dramatic phases of the Anabaptist
uprising at Münster. In the summer of 1535 he
was at long last offered an assessorship at the
Reichskammergericht in Speyer. He resigned

his office at Dülmen while retaining the deanship of St Mary's until January 1539.

Viglius remained at Speyer until the end of 1537, when he accepted a legal chair at the University of Ingolstadt. During his five years at Ingolstadt he served as rector of the university in 1539 and as dean of the faculty of law the following year. Meanwhile, on 12 October 1540 *Charles v named him to the privy council at Brussels and on 21 May 1543 he was appointed to the grand council of Meche-len. From the time of his departure from Ingolstadt in 1542, Viglius served the imperial court on a number of diplomatic missions. He was ambassador to William v, duke of *Cleves, and in 1544 he went to Speyer and Bremen to conduct peace negotiations between the Haps-burg courts, King *Christian III of Denmark, and the dukes of Schleswig-Holstein. In 1545 he attended the diet at Worms. As a close personal adviser he accompanied Charles v on his campaign against the members of the Schmalkaldic League and kept a diary in which he recorded the developments between June 1546 and January 1547 (ed August von Druffel, Munich 1877). As of 1 January 1549 he was appointed president of the privy council at Brussels, and five years later he was also given the presidency of the council of state. He continued in these high offices past the retirement of Charles v and remained one of the leading officials of the Netherlands in the era of Nicolas and Antoine *Perrenot de Granvelle. In 1559 he was also appointed prefect of the Burgundian library. As political tension in the Netherlands mounted he repeat-edly requested leave to retire from politics, but not until 1 September 1569 was he permitted to resign the presidency of the privy council, only to be called back to this office from 1573 to 1575, after the death of his successor. The presiden-cy of the council of state he held until his death, although he no longer carried any political weight with the governors, Fernando Alvarez de Toledo, duke of Alba, and Luis de Zúñiga y Requesens.

Among Viglius' many writings his Latin autobiography has retained particular signifi-cance (ed C.P. Hoynck van Papendrecht in *Analecta Belgica*, The Hague 1743, I-1). His juridical publications included commentaries to various parts of the *Corpus iuris* and above all an edition of Theophilus Antecessor after a

manuscript he had discovered in the library of San Marco, Venice: *Institutiones iuris civilis in graecam linguam per Theophilum Antecessorem olim traductae* (Basel: H. Froben 1534; often reprinted). Two of his political writings also continue to be of interest: one presented the claims of *Mary of Hungary against Duke William v of Cleves (*Iustificatio rationum ob quas regina Hungariae, Belgii gubernatrix, contra ducem Cliviae arma sumpsit*, Antwerp 1543), while the other defended the fiscal policies of Alba (*Commentarius ... super nova impositione seu vectigali decimi denarii rerum venditarum*, in *Analecta Belgica* I-2). Of his historical writings the diary of the Schmalkaldic war has been mentioned earlier, while two abstracts of the history of the Netherlands in the early reign of Philip II of Spain cover the years of incipient political unrest until 1573. They were not printed until 1858, when Alphonse Wauters published them together with related essays by Viglius' friend Joachim Hopper (*Mémoires de Viglius et d'Hopperus sur le commencement des troubles des Pays-Bas*, Brussels 1858). Viglius' correspondence with Hopper, together with a selection of his other letters, was published in 1661 at Leeuwarden and reprinted in *Analecta Belgica* I-1 and II-1. For other publications and manuscripts by Viglius see NBW.

In November 1528 Viglius is mentioned for the first time in the correspondence of Eras-mus, who was writing to Haio *Cammingha, a friend of Viglius and his fellow-student at Dole (Ep 2073). Perhaps Erasmus had been made aware of the talented young man either by Bernard Bucho van Aytta or by Goclenius. They had never met face to face, however (Ep 2329), when Viglius initiated their correspon-dence in February 1529 with a letter from Dole that expressed his profound and sincere admiration for the great scholar (Ep 2101). Erasmus' reply shows that he was delighted, although he declined Viglius' offer of support against his critics (Ep 2111). In May 1529 Viglius stated his intention to follow Alciati to Bourges (Ep 2168; cf Ep 2191), while in September he commented from there on Al-ciati's quarrel with Petrus *Stella (Ep 2210). Erasmus himself had recommended Viglius to Alciati, as can be gathered from the latter's letter of March 1530, in which he praised the excellence of the Dutch student (Ep 2276; cf Epp 2329, 2356). After Viglius had taken a short trip to Paris in the summer of 1530 (Ep 2373), Alciati informed Erasmus that Viglius was looking for a position in the Empire (Ep 2394). This was at a time when Alciati was suggesting Viglius as a successor for Udalricus *Zasius in Freiburg. Erasmus did in fact recommend him to Zasius, although he wondered whether the University of Louvain might not prove more congenial to Viglius (Ep 2468) and did not conceal from him his impression that Zasius himself favoured Bonifacius Amerbach (Ep 2484). These overtures were followed in the autumn of 1531 by Viglius' visits to Basel and Freiburg, where he finally met Erasmus in person, presenting to him an introduction from Amerbach and a ring with the signs of the zodiac (Epp 2551, 2586). In Freiburg Viglius also gained the favour of Zasius, whom he supported, as he had supported Alciati, in a feud with Stella (Stintzing 290–3).

Viglius continued his travels and after reaching Padua reported on them to Erasmus in November 1531 (Ep 2568). From Padua he continued to send frequent letters to Erasmus (Epp 2594, 2632, 2657, 2716, 2753, 2767, 2791, 2829, 2854), commenting on such matters as the agitation of the Italian Ciceronians (Ep 2632). Among Erasmus' answers, as far as they are preserved (Epp 2604, 2682, 2736, 2810), there is in turn an account of the attack Julius Caesar *Scaliger had launched against him (Ep 2682). During Viglius' years at Padua Erasmus' interest in and affection for him are also expressed in his letters to others; in July 1532, for instance, he recommended the Frieslander to Pietro *Bembo (Ep 2681; cf Ep 2768).

On his return from Italy Viglius carried a letter from Giambattista *Egnazio for Erasmus (Ep 2871), whom he visited at Freiburg. On 6 and 7 November 1533 Erasmus in turn gave him letters for Goclenius and Nicolaus *Olahus as well as a recommendation to Amerbach (Epp 2875–7). The former were not to be delivered for quite a while, however, since Viglius remained in Basel until February 1534 and prepared his edition of Theophilus Antecessor for the press of Hieronymus *Froben. In these months he again corresponded regularly with Erasmus, as is evident from his Epp 2885, 2888, 2891 and Erasmus' Ep 2878. In December Amerbach announced to Erasmus a forthcoming visit by Viglius and himself (Ep 2887); it

actually took place on 7 January, as Viglius recorded in his autobiography (p 13). Erasmus would have liked to retain Viglius in Freiburg, offering to make generous allowance for him in his will, and he regretted his departure accordingly (Ep 2913).

From then on only a few of Viglius' letters to Erasmus have been preserved (Epp 2957, 2962, 2999, 3060, 3071, and 3116). Most of these date from the period of Viglius' service with the bishop of Münster and deal predominantly with the Anabaptist uprising at Münster and the countermeasures deliberated upon at Worms in April 1535. Even though none of Erasmus' answers to these letters are extant, he continued to praise Viglius when writing to others (Epp 2915, 2925, 2956). While Franciscus *Rupilius expressed his satisfaction in March 1535 at Viglius' appointment to the Reichskammergericht (Ep 3007), Hector van *Hoxwier would have preferred to see him return to legal scholarship (Ep 3022), and Konrad *Heresbach likewise regretted that Viglius was lost to the Muses (Ep 3031A), a view Erasmus may well have shared. Viglius' admiration for Erasmus did not, however, end with the latter's death. In the troubled years after 1566 he belonged to the party among the members of the 'collateral' councils of Brussels which was working, albeit unsuccessfully, for reconciliation.

BIBLIOGRAPHY: Allen Ep 2101 / F. Postma in NBW VIII 837–55 / BNB I 590–4 / ADB XXXIX 699–703 / NNBW II 46–52 / Bernardus H.D. Hermesdorf Wigle van Aytta van Zwichem, hoogleraar en rechtsgeleerd schrijver (Leiden 1949) /de Vocht CTL II 145–50 and passim / Rudolf Schulze 'Der niederländische Rechtsgelehrte Viglius van Zwichem (1507–1577) als Bischöflich-Münsterischer Offizial und Dechant von Liebfrauen (Überwasser)' Westfälische Zeitschrift 101–2 (1953) 183–230 / Michael Baelde De collaterale raden onder Karel v en Filips II (Brussels 1965) 324–6 / AK IV Ep 1584 and passim / Roderich von Stintzing Ulrich Zasius (Basel 1857, repr 1961) 290–3 / Schottenloher II 412–13, VII 239, and passim   MICHAEL ERBE

Bartolomeo VILLANI of Pontremoli, documented 1523
The Villani family is found at Pontremoli, in the Apennines between Parma and La Spezia, from the fourteenth to the seventeenth centu-

ries, but to date it has not been possible to explain what Bartolomeo was doing in Locarno, from where he sent Ep 1372. Allen's hypothesis that he was a canon of San Vittore Mauro's in Locarno - Muralto, has not been confirmed.

BIBLIOGRAPHY: Allen Ep 1372 / On the chapter of San Vittore see *Helvetia sacra* ed A. Bruckner et al (Bern 1972–) II-1 105–20 / *Archivio storico ticinese* 24 (1965) 253–306; 43–4 (1970) 257–340; 50 (1972) 151–226, and passim

PGB

Simon VILLANOVANUS of Neufville, 1495–1530

Simon Villanovanus (Villeneuve, Neufville) was born in 1495, probably at Neufvilles, in Hainaut. After studying civil law at Pavia for six years, he arrived, impoverished, at Padua in 1521 and was befriended by Christophe de *Longueil, on whose recommendation and that of Giambattista *Egnazio he was employed as preceptor by François de Rosis, French ambassador to Venice. When Longueil died in September 1522, Villanovanus succeeded him as unofficial professor of rhetoric at Padua and after his own early death in 1530 was celebrated as a Ciceronian by Etienne *Dolet, Pierre Bunel, Jean *Salmon Macrin, Guillaume Scève, Jean Voulté, and François *Rabelais.

In his *Dialogus de imitatione Ciceroniana* (Lyon: S. Gryphius 1535), Dolet made Villanovanus, his teacher from 1527 to 1530, his spokesman against Erasmus' *Ciceronianus*. The interlocutor for Erasmus was Thomas *More, who, Erasmus complained, was made to speak 'timidly.' Further, More never visited Italy and, as Erasmus observed, More was in prison and Villanovanus dead when the *Dialogus* was published (Ep 3052).

Only one letter by Villanovanus has been discovered (see Christie 291), but there is some evidence that he wrote other works. His contemporaries circulated rumours that Dolet had published Villanovanus' papers as his own *Commentarii linguae latinae* (Lyon: S. Gryphius 1536–8). Most scholars now believe that the Villanovanus cited as the author of *De tribus prophetis* by Guillaume Postel in *Alcorani ... et Evangelistarum concordiae liber* (Paris: P. Gromors 1543) and accused by Jean Calvin in *De scandalis* (Geneva: J. Crespin 1551) of

denying the immortality of the soul was Simon Villanovanus and not Michael *Servetus. However, Villanovanus' reputation may have suffered simply by association with his religiously suspect student Dolet.

BIBLIOGRAPHY: Allen Ep 3052 / J. Bohatec *Budé und Calvin* (Graz 1950) 178–9 / Jean Calvin *Opera quae supersunt omnia* (Brunswick 1863–1900) VIII 44–5 / M. Chassaigne *Etienne Dolet* (Paris 1930) 11–15 / R.C. Christie *Etienne Dolet* rev ed (London 1899) 27–37 and passim / L. Febvre *Le Problème de l'incroyance au XVIe siècle* rev ed (Paris 1947) 111–2 and passim / T. Simar *Christophe de Longueil* (Louvain 1911) 88 / *L'Erasmianus sive Ciceronianus d'Etienne Dolet* ed E.V. Telle (Geneva 1974) 41–4 and passim

JUDITH RICE HENDERSON

VILLENA *See Diego* LÓPEZ PACHECO

Jakob VILLINGER of Sélestat,
d between 11 February and 25 August 1529
Jakob Villinger was taught by Crato Hoffmann (d 1501) in the famous Latin school of Sélestat in Alsace, where his contemporaries included *Beatus Rhenanus and Jakob *Spiegel, who was perhaps related to Villinger. In 1500 he is first mentioned as a finance official in the service of the Hapsburgs; in 1501 he was a member of the treasury and in 1510 the chief treasurer of *Maximilian I, trying to cope with the free-spending habits of his master and his limited resources. Gifted with a flair for politics, Villinger managed to borrow enough money for the crucial Hungarian marriages of 1515 and again played an important role in financing the election of *Charles V in 1519, working closely with Jakob *Fugger. Although gradually replaced by Gabriel de *Salamanca in his role as the chief financial adviser of the Hapsburgs in Germany, he continued in their service and took part in a diplomatic mission as late as February 1529.

Maximilian's preference for Villinger stemmed in part from a battle at Regensburg (11 September 1504) in the war of the Bavarian succession when he fought well and close enough to the emperor to be knighted by him. In about 1520 he acquired the coat of arms and title of the nobles von Schönenberg, a family of Alsace that had died out. His private financial and commercial dealings proceeded alongside, and were often closely related to, his service to the Hapsburgs. In 1509 he was a partner in a lumber transport venture in the Black Forest, and in 1511 he became a citizen of Freiburg. Soon he acquired three adjacent properties in order to build an imposing house, later called 'zum Walfisch' (Epp 2470, 2477, 2503). Originally built for the use of the Emperor Maximilian (Ep 2158; Allen I 69), it was Erasmus' home from 1529 to 1531. In 1512 Villinger purchased from Maximilian the estate called 'Heilig Kreuz' (Ep 2497) near Colmar, where he also owned a house. In the same period he married Ursula *Adler and settled at Augsburg. Among his highly speculative deals was a joint venture with the Höchstetter family in 1525 designed to acquire a monopoly on mercury mining at Idrija, near Ljubljana. It actually led to some losses for Villinger and his widow.

In 1520 Erasmus sent Villinger a letter of recommendation for the Dominican Johannes *Faber (Ep 1149). Spiegel, Johann *Gebwiler, Joannes Cuspinianus, and the entire Sélestat literary society addressed him in dedicatory letters for various publications (for details see Allen). In 1524 he and his wife donated stained-glass windows to the cathedral of Freiburg which portray the donors beside St James of Compostella with scenes of the legend of St Ursula in the background.

BIBLIOGRAPHY: Allen Ep 1149 / Clemens Bauer 'Jacob Villinger … Ein Umriss' in *Syntagma Friburgense … Hermann Aubin dargebracht* (Lindau-Constance 1956) 9–28 (reproducing Villinger's stained-glass portrait) / *Deutsche Reichstagsakten* Jüngere Reihe (Gotha-Göttingen 1893–) I–VII passim / BRE Ep 163 / LP III 84 and passim   PGB

Karl VILLINGER baron of Seyfriedsberg
The son of Jakob *Villinger and Ursula *Adler is mentioned, although not by name, in Ep 2497, in which his stepfather, Johann *Löble, refers to him as the owner of the house called 'zum Walfisch' at Freiburg. Karl retained his father's holdings in the mining region of Idrija and was an imperial councillor, but he had no public career and spent his life as a member of the landed aristocracy.

BIBLIOGRAPHY: Clemens Bauer in *Syntagma Friburgense … Hermann Aubin dargebracht* (Lindau-Constance 1956) 28   PGB

VINANTIUS (Epp 636, 722 of 1517)
Vinantius (Venantius) is the name of an unidentified man whom Erasmus expected to be in Cologne and to whom he sent greetings in letters addressed to Hermann von *Neuenahr (cf CWE Ep 636). It is possible that he was referring to Neuenahr's secretary, Gerhard von *Enschringen, whose name he evidently found troublesome; cf Ep 1078.   PGB

Augustin VINCENT Caminade *See Augustinus Vincentius* CAMINADUS

VINCENTIUS Cornelii *See Vincent* CORNELISSEN

Johann VINCHEL *See Johann* INGENWINKEL

Arnold VINCK *See Arnold* VYNCK

Tommaso de VIO *See Tommaso de Vio, Cardinal* CAJETANUS

Polidoro VIRGILIO of Urbino,
c 1470–18 April 1555
Polidoro Virgilio, a son of Giorgio Virgilio of Urbino, was educated at Padua and, less certainly, at Bologna, where he may have studied with Filippo (I) *Beroaldo. Before going to England in 1502, he enjoyed the patronage of the court of Urbino and the papacy; he was ordained priest before 20 December 1496. In England he took up the office of subcollector of Peter's Pence under Adriano *Castellesi, who had been collector since 1489 and was to be made cardinal in 1503. As Castellesi's assistant Polidoro played a significant role in Anglo-papal diplomacy, and as a native of Urbino he helped maintain a long-standing connection between the English and Urbinate courts. His work as intermediary between Italy and England evidently extended to economic affairs, for in 1504 he was charged with violating the exchange laws. His case was regularly postponed until 1509, when a royal pardon ended the matter. In the mean time Polidoro had begun to gather church preferments, most notably the archdiaconate of Wells in 1508 and the prebend of Oxgate in St Paul's in 1513.

*Julius II transferred the subcollectorship to Pietro *Griffi in the autumn of 1508, but

Polidoro resisted the loss of his office until 16 April 1509. He regained the office in 1512 and held it until 1515, a difficult year for him. By February 1514 he was planning a trip to Italy. Thomas *Wolsey's hopes for a cardinal's hat called Polidoro to Rome, and personal business, including his work on the *Anglica historia*, to Urbino. He returned to London early in 1515 to learn that Wolsey and *Henry VIII had begun to support Andrea *Ammonio's wish to be named collector of Peter's Pence. In order to ruin Castellesi, Ammonio charged that Castellesi's agent, Polidoro, had written letters unfriendly to Wolsey. The charges were not unfounded, and in the spring of 1515 Polidoro was imprisoned in the Tower, where he spent the rest of the year. Soon after his release *Leo x asked Wolsey to send him to Rome once again; he was back in England before the end of 1517.

For the rest of his life Polidoro avoided the political adventures which had punctuated his earlier career. There is reason to think, however, that his next journey to Italy must have involved royal consent, for it culminated in the publication of the *Anglica historia*, which dealt extensively with the dynastic and imperial ambitions of Henry VIII. In June 1532 (Ep 2662) Polidoro informed Erasmus that he had been called back to Italy and that he had been discussing his publishing plans with Johann *Bebel, who published the *Anglica historia* – which had been twenty years in preparation – at Basel in 1534. In the same year Polidoro drew up his will at Urbino; it is likely that he also visited Bebel in Basel and possible that he saw Erasmus as well, either in Basel or in Freiburg. Back in England, he conformed to Henry's reformation, signing the articles of religion of 1536 and the declaration in favour of communion in both kinds of 1547. He began preparations for his final return to Italy in 1546 but departed from England only in 1553. He died in Urbino two years later.

The outstanding issue in the relations of Erasmus and Polidoro was the question of whether Polidoro's *Proverbiorum libellus* antedated Erasmus' *Adagia*; another question is Erasmus' influence on Polidoro's later writings. To place the former in context, it is necessary to review Polidoro's first publications. In 1496 he published an augmented edition of the *Cornucopiae* of Niccolò *Perotti

(Venice: J. de Tridino). Although Polidoro never acknowledged his debt to Perotti, the *Cornucopiae* at least partly inspired his first original works, the *Proverbiorum libellus* (Venice: C. de Pensis 1498) and *De inventoribus rerum* (Venice: C. de Pensis 1499). Moreover, the obscure humanist Ludovico Gorgerio wrote an invective (Vat MS Urb. Lat. 1244) claiming that the *Proverbiorum libellus* plagiarized his own work. Although none of this information circulated widely during Polidoro's lifetime, he was sensitive about the question of the originality of his work. Erasmus' sensitivities on such questions are well known; it is noteworthy, then, that his dispute with Polidoro never led to a complete or final breach in their relations.

Polidoro and Erasmus shared many of the same friends in England and could have met there any time after Erasmus' second trip to England in 1505. The first hint of tension between them appears in Ep 531 of 15 February 1517, wherein Erasmus explained to Guillaume *Budé that he had brought out his *Adagia* (1st ed 1500) some years before he first heard Polidoro's name. Later, in 1520 (Ep 1175), Erasmus told Polidoro that rumours of his having plagiarized Polidoro's work had been spread by Lukas *Walters. Lukas had died in 1515, evidence that trouble may have been brewing for some time before the letter to Budé. Erasmus also mentioned (Ep 1175) that he and Polidoro had once joked at table about their rivalry, an event that must have occurred by 1517. It may also be significant that in the years before 1517 Erasmus grew close to Andrea Ammonio, who had helped end Castellesi's career and jeopardized Polidoro's. Whatever Ammonio's role in the quarrel, it was Polidoro who took the first important step for which clear evidence survives. He raised the issue of the priority of his work in a letter of 5 June 1519 to Richard *Pace, a letter which eventually appeared in Johann *Froben's July 1521 edition of Polidoro's book, by then retitled *Adagiorum liber*. On 6 December 1520 (Ep 1165), Erasmus remarked to Wolfgang *Capito that Edward *Lee in England was conspiring with Polidoro and preparing 'I know not what,' and when Erasmus wrote to Polidoro on 23 December (Ep 1175) he associated him once again with Lee, whose attack on Erasmus' New Testament preoccupied Erasmus during much of 1520.

Ranking Polidoro with Lee was the harshest gesture Erasmus made in the *Adagia* controversy.

Ep 1175 was also Erasmus' fullest statement of his differences with Polidoro. He explained to Polidoro (and later to Pace, Ep 1210) that Johann Froben was reluctant to publish the *Adagiorum liber* and agreed only after Erasmus pressed him, and that Erasmus saw to it that the book was printed on the best paper, in the finest type, and with the offending letter to Pace intact. He pointed out that he took some trouble to procure what he took to be the first edition of Polidoro's book through Jérôme de *Busleyden and that the volume in question had evidently come out in Italy several months after his own *Adagia* first appeared in Paris. Erasmus was mistaken, for he had probably seen the second edition of Virgilio's work (Venice: C. de Pensis November 1500), and seems never to have seen the original 1498 *Proverbiorum libellus*; as late as 1533, in the preface to the ninth edition of his *Adagia* (Ep 2773; see also Ep 2305), he still insisted that his book of proverbs was the first.

Along with the 1521 *Adagiorum liber* Froben brought out a new edition of *De inventoribus rerum* to which Polidoro had added five books. Though some of his criticisms of Christian institutions in this new material are Erasmian in spirit, they are neither as trenchant nor as elegant as those in the *Adagia* or *Colloquia*. Froben reissued both works in 1524 and 1525, and for this latter edition Polidoro prepared a *Commentariolum* on the Lord's Prayer which should be read with Erasmus' *Precatio dominica* of 1523 and his *Modus orandi Deum* of 1524. Erasmus continued his friendly interest in Polidoro's writing (Epp 1494, 1606, 1702), and Polidoro intervened in new eruptions of the Lee controversy (Epp 1606, 1796). Early in 1526 he sent Erasmus a gift, the price of a horse, 'qui te aliquo terrarum vehat' (Ep 1666). The book-dealer Franz *Birckmann was a common cause for complaint for the two humanists and may have instigated a momentary resurrection of the old tensions between them in 1527 and 1528 (Epp 1666, 1796, 1990). In the mean time Erasmus had dedicated to Polidoro an edition of some of John Chrysostom's sermons and had urged Polidoro to translate one homily himself (Ep 1734). He also asked Froben to undertake the publication of Polidoro's *De prodigiis* –

without success, however, for the first edition was Bebel's of 1531. Polidoro's translation of John Chrysostom's *Comparatio regis et monachi*, with its dedication to Erasmus, appeared at Paris (G. Morrhy) in the previous year (Epp 2019, 2311, 2379, 2466), but Erasmus did not use the translation in his edition of Chrysostom. Polidoro published his last book in 1545 (Basel: M. Isengrin), a collection of *Dialogi* on religious topics; one of them, *De vita perfecta*, is Erasmian in its outlook.

Polidoro is remembered today primarily for his *Anglica historia*, which scholars have seen as the beginning of modern English historiography, as an important piece of propaganda for the Tudor monarchy, and as an influence on Shakespeare's history plays. A modern edition and translation is by Denys Hay (London 1950). Polidoro's edition of Gildas ([Antwerp?] 1525) was another pioneering effort in scholarship. But in his own day he was best known as an author of reference works, the *Proverbiorum libellus* and *De inventoribus rerum*, which were frequently reissued in the sixteenth and seventeenth centuries.

BIBLIOGRAPHY: Allen Ep 1175 / W.A.J. Archbold in DNB xx 250–3 / C.H. Clough 'Frederigo Veterani, Polydore Vergil's "Anglica Historia" and Baldassare Castiglione's "Epistola … ad Henricum Angliae regem"' *English Historical Review* 82 (1967) 772–83 / Brian P. Copenhaver 'The historiography of discovery in the Renaissance: the sources and composition of Polydore Vergil's *De Inventoribus rerum* I–III' *Journal of the Warburg and Courtauld Institutes* 41 (1978) 192–214 / Denys Hay *Polydore Vergil: Renaissance Historian and Man of Letters* (Oxford 1952) / Richard Koebner '"The Imperial Crown of the Realm": Henry VIII, Constantine the Great, and Polydore Vergil' *Bulletin of the Institute for Historical Research* 26 (1953) 29–52 / F.J. Levy *Tudor Historical Thought* (San Marino, Cal, 1967) 31, 103, and passim / André Stegmann 'Le *De inventoribus rei christianae* de Polydor Vergil ou l'Erasmisme critique' in *Colloquia Erasmiana Turonensia* 313–22   BRIAN P. COPENHAVER

Hieronymus VIROMANDUS documented 1525–8
Viromandus, probably of Vermand, near Saint-Quentin, claimed to have received his training in the Collegium Trilingue in Louvain (Ep 1939). He then entered the service of Sir

Richard *Wingfield, English ambassador to Spain. After Wingfield's death on 22 July 1525 Viromandus became secretary to *George of Austria, the newly appointed bishop of Bressanone, who was in Spain at that time.

Viromandus wrote to Erasmus a letter now missing on behalf of George of Austria, inviting him to Bressanone. Erasmus replied on 3 February 1528 giving reasons why he could not leave Basel (Epp 1938, 1939).

BIBLIOGRAPHY: Allen Ep 1939 / de Vocht CTL II 132–3 IG

Alonso Ruiz de VIRUÉS of Olmedo, 1493–19 January 1545
Born in Olmedo, Virués was the son of Alonso Ruiz and Juana de Virués. In 1508 he entered the Benedictine monastery of San Juan at Burgos and was later sent to San Vicente, the Benedictine house of studies at the University of Salamanca, to take a master's degree in theology. In the early 1520s he returned to Burgos.

Virués was probably introduced to the ideas of Erasmus by Juan de Oria, the regent of studies at Salamanca. His first public intervention in defence of Erasmus was a letter written between 1525 and 1527 to the Franciscan warden at Alcalá de Henares. The letter was circulated widely and eventually printed by Spanish Erasmians (Ep 1838), and a Latin translation was presented to Erasmus by Juan Luis *Vives (Ep 1847). Later Virués used the letter as part of the introduction to his translations of eight of Erasmus' Colloquia. Virués' letter was almost contemporaneous with the 'Collationes septem' which he twice directed to Erasmus. These were a series of commentaries on points in Erasmus' writings which Virués felt could be better expressed or toned down somewhat to avoid the wrath of the monks. Erasmus received the 'Collationes' by March 1526. Since he did not know who Virués was and had not yet seen his letter to the Franciscan warden of Alcalá, he was suspicious of Virués and annoyed by his combination of praise and criticism (Epp 1701, 1717, 1804). Also he was still smarting from the attacks of Diego *López Zúñiga and the criticisms of Sancho *Carranza de Miranda. It finally took the combined efforts of Juan de *Vergara (Ep 1814), Juan Luis Vives (Ep 1836),

and Alfonso de *Valdés (Ep 1839) – in addition to letters from Virués himself (Epp 1786, 1838) – to reconcile Erasmus to the Benedictine (Ep 1875). Although Erasmus later apologized for his early suspicions (Ep 1968), his old irritation with the Benedictine would from time to time re-emerge (Ep 2644). In August 1531, however, Erasmus wrote Virués a long letter of consolation on the death of his brother, Jerónimo Ruiz de *Virués (Ep 2523).

Meanwhile, at Burgos, Virués supported Erasmus by reading publicly from the Enchiridion, by praising the humanist in his sermons, and by defending him from the attacks of the Dominican Pedro de *Vitoria (Ep 1836). From 27 June until 13 August 1527, at the conference of theologians held in Valladolid to investigate propositions from Erasmus' writings, Virués spoke in Erasmus' defence (Ep 1847). From 1526 onwards date the first of Virués' translations of and enthusiastic commentary on eight of the Colloquia, published anonymously in 1529 (Ep 1873) with three other translations as Colloquios familiares ... escritos por ... Erasmo ... traduzidos ... por un muy sabio varón (n p, n pr).

Virués moved to Valladolid and in the spring of 1531 to Salamanca as the prior of San Vicente. At an unknown date he was appointed court preacher to *Charles v, perhaps in part because of his support for Erasmus. In the winter of 1531 he was summoned to the court in Germany (Ep 2641), where he probably attended the diet of Regensburg (1532) and negotiations between Catholics and Protestants at Nürnberg. He returned to Spain in 1533 and the same year was elected abbot of San Zoilo de Carrión. Like other Spanish Erasmians in the 1530s, he soon became a victim of the Inquisition. In April 1534 he gave testimony against the imprisoned Juan de Vergara, but by the end of the year he was himself under arrest. His detention lasted until 1538, when he was sentenced to a public recantation, suspension from preaching for two years, and imprisonment in a monastery for a similar period. Almost immediately, on 29 May 1538, Charles v, who had intervened on his behalf throughout the case, obtained a papal bull absolving him entirely. Charles had Virués appointed bishop of the Canary Islands on 16 September 1538. He left Spain for the Canaries in 1540, and died there in Telde.

Other writings by Virués were *De matrimonio regis Angliae tractatus* (Salamanca 1530) and the *Philippicae disputationes viginti adversus Lutherana dogmata* (Antwerp: J. Crinitus 1541), chapter 20 of which contained excerpts from his 'Collationes' to Erasmus.

BIBLIOGRAPHY: Allen Ep 1684 / S. Giner *Alonso Ruiz de Virués en la controversia pretridentina con los protestantes* (Madrid 1964), repr as 'Alonso Ruiz de Virués (Estudio biográfico)' *Analecta Calasanctiana* 6 (1964) 117–201 / Bataillon *Erasmo y España* 219–23, 245–7, 294–309, and passim / V. Beltrán de Heredia 'Documentos inéditos acerca del proceso del erasmista Alonso de Virués' *Boletín de la Biblioteca Menéndez y Pelayo* 17 (1935) 242–57 / A. Bonilla y San Martín 'Erasmo en España' *Revue hispanique* 17 (1907) 379–548 / G.M. Colombás 'Un benedictino erasmista: Alonso Ruiz de Virués' *Yermo* 3 (1965) 3–46 / J. Feo y Ramos 'Don Fray Alonso Ruiz de Virués, obispo de Canarias (1539–1545)' *El Museo Canario* 3 (1935) 1–16 / 'Libro Becerro del monasterio de San Juan de Burgos' *Boletín de estadística e información del Excmo. Ayuntamiento de Burgos* 354 (August 1951) 109–18 / J.E. Longhurst 'Alumbrados erasmistas y luteranos en el proceso de Juan de Vergara' *Cuadernos de historia de España* 35–6 (1962) 337–53 / M. de la Pinta Llorente 'Una testificación del erasmista Alonso de Virués contra el doctor Juan de Vergara' *La Ciudad de Dios* 153 (1941) 345–55

PAUL J. DONNELLY & TBD

Jerónimo Ruiz de VIRUÉS of Olmedo, 1489–1530
Jerónimo Ruiz de Virués was a son of Alonso Ruiz and Juana de Virués from Olmedo and elder brother to Alonso Ruiz de *Virués. His date of birth can be ascertained from Erasmus' Ep 2523, addressed to his brother, Alonso. This letter is one of the main sources for Jerónimo's life. In 1508 he and his brother joined the Benedictine monastery of San Juan at Burgos. On 24 February 1524 he was listed among the community of San Vicente, the Benedictine house of studies at the University of Salamanca. That fact, together with the description of him in the monastic records as a notable theologian and Erasmus' likening of his education to that of Alonso, makes it almost certain that he took a master's degree in

theology there. On 28 March 1527 he was in Valladolid representing the Benedictines at a meeting of religious called to draw up a list of propositions taken from Erasmus' writings for investigation by a conference of theologians. Jerónimo's intervention in the debate and his advocacy of Erasmus' cause are described by Juan de *Vergara (Ep 1814). Virués did not participate, however, in the conference proper later that summer, possibly because he had already taken up a post at court at the instigation of the Empress *Isabella of Portugal. He served there for three years and died at Easter 1530. His reputation as a preacher is confirmed by Ep 2523, in which Erasmus showed a good knowledge of Jerónimo's life. There is no evidence, however, to suggest that Erasmus had any direct contact with him.

BIBLIOGRAPHY: Allen Epp 1814, 2523 / Bataillon *Erasmo y España* 237–8, 427 / S. Giner *Alonso Ruiz de Virués en la controversia pretridentina con los protestantes* (Madrid 1964), repr as 'Alonso Ruiz de Virués (Estudio biográfico)' in *Analecta Calasanctiana* 6 (1964) 117–201 / 'Libro Becerro del monasterio de San Juan de Burgos' *Boletín de estadística e información del Excmo. Ayuntamiento de Burgos* 354 (August 1951) 109–18

PAUL J. DONNELLY

Carolus VIRULUS of Louvain, c 1413–13 May 1493
Carolus Virulus (Menneken, Manneken) was probably born in Ghent and died at Louvain, where, in addition to holding other important university posts, he had been regent of the College of the Lily for fifty-six years. Matriculating at Louvain in 1432, he promoted licenciate and MA in 1435 and bachelor in canon law and in medicine before 1437, when he succeeded Jan Leyten of Hasselt as regent of the Lily. He became a member of the council of arts on 30 June 1435 and was chosen dean of the faculty of arts on 31 January 1442 and receiver of the faculty on 25 July 1446. He was twice elected rector of the university, on 31 August 1447 and 28 February 1465. Soon after 1447 he married Gertrude van den Dorne, who bore him his sons, Robertus *Virulus, Nicolaus, Henricus, Johannes, and Godefridus. She died before 1465. In addition to providing for his sons by his will of 16 January 1493 (with a codicil dated 6 February), Virulus be-

queathed the Lily to its poor students and *legentes* and his books and manuscripts to the library of St Martin's priory. He was buried in the priory church, which his gifts had helped to finish.

The first extant edition of Virulus' *Epistolarum formulae* was printed by Jan Veldener at Louvain in 1476, but if, as Henry de Vocht speculates, it had appeared as early as April 1474, it may have been the first book printed in that city. Frequently reprinted in northern Europe in the last quarter of the fifteenth century and admired by Virulus' contemporaries, it was held in contempt by the new humanist generation of the early sixteenth century. Erasmus commented unfavourably upon it in *De conscribendis epistolis* (ASD I-2 230–1, 265–6, 284) and in the *Dilutio* (ed E.V. Telle, 71). In Etienne *Dolet's reply to the *Ciceronianus* Erasmus was unjustly accused of preferring the letters of Virulus to those of Cicero.

BIBLIOGRAPHY: Valerius Andreas *Bibliotheca Belgica* 2nd ed (Louvain 1643) 128–9 / M.F.A.G. Campbell *Annales de la typographie néerlandaise au quinzième siècle* (The Hague 1874) 1201–11 and supplements 2, 3, 4 (1878–90) / *L'Erasmianus sive Ciceronianus d'Etienne Dolet* ed E.V. Telle (Geneva 1974) 33, 315 / J.F. Foppens *Bibliotheca Belgica* (Brussels 1739) 163–4 / J. Molanus *Les Quatorze Livres sur l'histoire de la ville de Louvain* ed P.F.X. de Ram (Brussels 1861) 473–4 and passim / J. Nève in BNB XXVI 778–80 / M.-L. Polain *Catalogue des livres imprimés au quinzième siècle des bibliothèques de Belgique* (Brussels 1932) 2591–7 / H. de Vocht *Inventaire des archives de l'Université de Louvain* (Louvain 1927) 1136–8, 1223, 1865 / de Vocht *Busleyden* 337–9 / de Vocht CTL I 85–98 / A. Gerlo and J. IJsewijn in *Classical Influences on European Culture A.D. 500–1500* ed R.R. Bolgar (Cambridge 1971) 105, 109–10, 117

JUDITH RICE HENDERSON

Robertus VIRULUS of Louvain, d after 1527
Robertus Virulus (Menneken or Manneken) was a son of Carolus *Virulus, regent of the College of the Lily at Louvain, and Gertrude van den Dorne. He matriculated in arts at the University of Louvain on 23 February 1476. He had studied law at Pavia before 4 September 1484, when his former master, the famous jurisprudent Jason a Mayno of Milan, replied

to his invitation to teach at Louvain. Virulus' first wife was Katrijn, the natural daughter of Jan van Winckele, and thus a half-sister of the younger Jan van *Winckele. She predeceased her father, who died on 17 June 1505. By his second wife, Katrijn van Vlaenderen, the widow of Golinus van't Sestich, he had a son.

Henry de Vocht speculates that Virulus died before 3 July 1522, when his wife and child were named in the will of Pieter van Thienen, professor of law, but Jan *Becker of Borsele wrote to Erasmus in 1527 from Virulus' house, where he was preceptor of Maximilian (II) of *Burgundy, a son of Adolph of *Burgundy, lord of Veere (Ep 1787). Carolus Virulus had bequeathed the rights and profits of the regent of the Lily to his eldest son, Nicolaus, and to Leo *Outers, one of his *legentes*, and houses to his other surviving sons, Robertus, Henricus, and Godefridus. At least Robertus and Henricus entertained well-to-do students as boarders, for Becker had lived with Henricus twenty years earlier when Cornelius Erdorf, a nephew of Jérôme de *Busleyden was in his charge.

BIBLIOGRAPHY: Allen Ep 1787 / J. Molanus *Les Quatorze Livres sur l'histoire de la ville de Louvain* ed P.F.X. de Ram (Brussels 1861) 558 / de Vocht *Busleyden* 337–41 / de Vocht CTL I 92–4 and passim / de Vocht *Literae ad Craneveldium* Ep 85

JUDITH RICE HENDERSON

Galeazzo VISCONTI of Milan, documented 1496–1531
Galeazzo Visconti was a Milanese nobleman, prominent in the political, military, and diplomatic affairs of his city. In April 1496 he undertook an embassy to the duke of Savoy at Turin. In 1500 Duke Ludovico *Sforza sent him to the Swiss diet at Zürich to obtain assistance against the French. After the French conquest of Milan he was for a time in the service of *Louis XII, but by 1515 he was prominent in organizing the resistance to France on behalf of Massimiliano Sforza, the son of Ludovico. After the victory of *Francis I of France at Marignano, Visconti served as a captain in the imperial army and as an agent of *Henry VIII of England in Switzerland. Around 1520 he again transferred his allegiance to the French, perhaps in an effort to wrest Milan from imperial forces. In April 1531 he was in Paris.

In December 1515 Erasmus sent Ep 378 to Andrea *Ammonio in England through Visconti. Andrea *Alciati dedicated his edition of Tacitus to the Milanese nobleman ([Milan]: A. Minutianus 1517).

BIBLIOGRAPHY: Allen Ep 378 / *Le lettere di Andrea Alciato giureconsulto* ed G.L. Barni (Florence 1953) Epp 4, 5, 154 / LP II 1193 and passim, III 1549 and passim, IV 1950 / *Calendar of State Papers, Venetian* II 301 and passim / Sanudo *Diarii* passim, but see especially I 180, IV 288, LIV 394 / *Amtliche Sammlung der älteren eidgenössischen Abschiede* ed J.K. Krütli et al (Lucerne 1839–82) III-2 10 and passim / G. Franceschini in *Storia di Milano* (Milan 1953–62) VIII 85 and passim   TBD

Damiaan van VISSENAKEN of Tienen, d after 1541

Damiaan van Vissenaken (Damianus Visse-nacus Tertius) was a physician from Tienen, resided at Ghent, and married Margareta, the daughter of Antonius *Clava after the death of her first husband, Willem Hannot. In 1532 Vissenaken's stepdaughter married Lieven *Algoet (Ep 2693), who had been Erasmus' servant and pupil for almost seven years beginning in 1519.

In the opinion of this writer, Vissenaken is possibly the 'medicus *Clavus' of whom Erasmus speaks in Ep 650. Erasmus' play on words can be explained by the fact that in medieval Latin *clavus* also meant *net*: the name Vissenaken without doubt suggested *vishaak* or *fishhook*. Thus *clavus* does not necessarily mean *nagel* or *nail*, as Allen suggests. Erasmus recommended Clavus to his friend Pieter *Gillis (Epp 681, 788).

In 1541 Vissenaken published his *Theoricae medicinae* (Antwerp: A. Dumaeus) dedicated to Nicolas *Perrenot de Granvelle with a preface dated by Vissenaken from the castle of Adolph of *Burgundy, lord of Veere.

BIBLIOGRAPHY: Allen Ep 2693 / de Vocht CTL II 138 / M.A. Nauwelaerts 'Erasme et Gand' in *Commémoration nationale d'Erasme: Actes* (Brussels 1970) 166–7 / P. van Peteghem 'Centralisatie in Vlaanderen onder Keizer Karel (1515–1555)' (doctoral thesis, Rijksuniversiteit Gent 1980)   MARCEL A. NAUWELAERTS

Alessandro VITELLI of Città di Castello, 1500–54

Alessandro belonged to the noble Vitelli family of Città di Castello, members of which

pursued military careers and then, in the sixteenth and seventeenth centuries, became prominent in the church. He was the illegitimate son of the condottiere Paolo Vitelli, who was decapitated by the Florentines on 1 October 1499 on a charge of treason. In 1526 he was one of the captains called upon by *Clement VII to defend Rome, but after disagreements with the other commanders he passed into the service of *Charles V. After the Sack of Rome in 1527 he remained in imperial service, and in 1530 he participated in the conquest of Florence, distinguishing himself in the attack on Volterra and in the battle of Gavinana. His attack on Pisa was repulsed by the Pisans. When Florence fell on 12 August 1530 Vitelli was one of seven witnesses who signed the city's capitulation. In 1532 Alessandro de' *Medici, the new ruler of Florence, made him captain of the guard, according to Varchi because it was believed he held a grudge against the republican elements of the city. In a letter of 16 August 1535 to Erasmus, Petrus *Merbelius reported that Vitelli 'governed' Alessandro, and that he was implicated in the suspected poisoning of Cardinal Ippolito de' *Medici, the focal point of opposition to Alessandro's regime (Ep 3039). In 1537, after the murder of Alessandro de' Medici by his cousin Lorenzino, Vitelli at first supported the plans of Cardinal Innocenzo Cibo to secure the succession of the natural son of the duke, Giulio. When Cosimo de' Medici was selected instead, Vitelli not only permitted the sack of the palaces of Alessandro and Lorenzino but also occupied the citadel of Florence in the name of the emperor, revealing the weakness of Cosimo's regime in its early stages. Vitelli then commanded the troops of Cosimo against a group of Florentine exiles, defeating them at Montemurlo and taking prisoner Filippo Strozzi, one of their leaders. However, he delayed turning Strozzi over to Cosimo, again under the pretext of holding him for the emperor.

In 1538 Charles V, under pressure from Cosimo to remove Vitelli from Florence, made him lord of Amatrice in the kingdom of Naples. Thereafter Vitelli became tied to the fortunes of the Farnese family, and was involved in the military plans of Pier Luigi and Ottavio, the son and grandson of Pope *Paul III. In 1540 he assisted Pier Luigi in the siege of Perugia, entering the city on 5 June. In 1546 he followed

Ottavio to Germany, where he joined campaigns against the Turks and then against the Protestants. When Pier Luigi, recently created duke of Parma and Piacenza, was killed by a conspiracy of nobles in 1547, Paul III sent Vitelli to Parma to help preserve the Farnese state. However the pope was suspicious of Vitelli's ties with the emperor and soon dismissed him. In 1551, under Julius III, Vitelli in fact helped lead the papal troops against Ottavio Farnese. In 1552 he commanded the imperial and Florentine forces in the siege of Siena.

Filippo Strozzi, who committed suicide in prison after he had been surrendered by Vitelli, dedicated to his 'saviour' his Italian translation of Polybius' work on the Roman militia (Florence, Archivio di Stato, Carte Strozziane III 50). Vitelli employed a number of artists at the family palace at Città di Castello, including Cola Calabrese, Battista della Billia, and Cristofano Gherardi, while Jacopo Pontormo painted a picture for him modelled on a design of Michelangelo on the theme 'Noli me tangere.'

BIBLIOGRAPHY: Allen Ep 3039 / C. Argegni *Condottieri, capitani, tribuni* series 19 of *Enciclopedia biografica e bibliografica 'Italiana'* (Milan 1936–7) III 380–1 / P. Litta *Famiglie celebri d'Italia* (Milan 1819–83) IV table 3 / P. Trotti *Ritratti ed elogi di capitani illustri* (Rome 1635) 231–2 / G.B. Adriani *Istoria de' suoi tempi* (Florence 1583) 46 / R. von Albertini *Firenze dalla repubblica al principato* (Turin 1970), trans of the German ed of 1955 / C. Bontempi 'Ricordi della città di Perugia dal 1528 al 1550' *Archivio storico italiano* 16-2 (1851) 321–401 esp 373 and passim / G.B. Cini *Vita del serenissimo signor Cosimo de' Medici* (Florence 1611) 85 / G. di Frolliere 'La guerra del sale ossia racconto della guerra sostenuta dai Perugini contro Paolo III nel 1540' *Archivio storico italiano* 16-2 (1851) 403–76 esp 428 and passim / F. Guicciardini *Storia d'Italia* ed C. Panigada (Bari 1929) passim / J. Nardi *Istoria della città di Firenze* (Florence 1858) II 176 and passim / P. Nores 'Storia della guerra di Paolo IV contro gli Spagnuoli' *Archivio storico italiano* 12 (1847) 63 / Alessandro Sozzini 'Diario delle cose avvenute in Siena dai 20 luglio 1550 … ' *Archivio storico italiano* 1-2 (1842) 101 and passim / G. Spini *Cosimo I e l'indipendenza del principato mediceo* (Florence 1980) 12 and passim

/ B. Varchi *Storia fiorentina* (Florence 1857–8) I 218, 230, II 154, III 3, and passim / G. Vasari *Le vite* ed C.L. Ragghianti (Milan-Rome 1942–9) II 409 / Francesco Vettori 'Sommario della istoria d'Italia' in *Scritti storici e politici* ed E. Niccolini (Bari 1972) 233   PAOLO PISSAVINO

Cornelio VITELLI of Cortona, c 1440–c 1500
Little is known about the early life of Vitelli (Vitellius), a native of Cortona, in Umbria. He perhaps studied at Bologna and Rome under Francesco *Filelfo, Domizio *Calderini, and Niccolò *Perotti. His first known work is a Latin epigram dedicated in 1474 to Federigo da Montefeltro and probably intended to secure his patronage. Four years later, on 1 April 1478, Vitelli pronounced the funeral oration at Padua for Angela, the wife of Paolo Leoni. In 1481 he lectured at Padua and also read Martial with the sons of patricians in Venice. He maintained contacts with Ermolao (1) *Barbaro, Giovanni Francesco Boccardo, Antonio Partenio Lazisio, Francesco Patrizi, and Girolamo Bologni. He dedicated works to Barbaro, Boccardo, and Partenio, while Bologni and Patrizi wrote some verses for him. Soon Vitelli began quarrelling with Giorgio *Merula, professor of eloquence at Venice, reproaching him for incompetence in expounding Pliny the Elder, Martial, and other classical authors. Not surprisingly, he had to leave the territory of Venice. He probably went to Oxford, where he may have been reader at New College in the period 1482–6. When the chair of poetics at the University of Louvain was vacated by Ludovicus Brunus, Vitelli was chosen to succeed him. He taught at Louvain from 1 February 1487 until the end of January 1488, and at the same time tried to establish contacts with the Hapsburg-Burgundian court, writing a letter and some poems to introduce himself to young Philip the Handsome, duke of *Burgundy, and his tutor, François (1) de *Busleyden. He also addressed two distichs to the Carmelite Arnoldus *Bostius. Perhaps it was his failure to obtain patronage that made Vitelli seek his fortune in Paris, where he arrived in the summer of 1488. On 5 September 1489 he and two other Italian humanists, Girolamo *Balbi and Fausto *Andrelini, were authorized to lecture publicly for one hour every afternoon. At first Vitelli appeared to be on good terms

with Balbi, who addressed a flattering Latin epigram to him and also succeeded in stirring him up against Andrelini, Balbi's rival. Andrelini answered with some biting elegies, published in his *Amores* (1490) and *Elegiae* (1494), and eventually also Balbi turned against Vitelli. These acrimonious controversies induced Vitelli to leave Paris at the end of 1489 or the beginning of 1490 and return to England. There he tried to win royal favour by composing a violent epigram against Robert *Gaguin, who had written some insolent lines about *Henry VII. This attempt was apparently unsuccessful, and in the autumn of 1490 he was back at Oxford. He taught privately and at the university, renting a room at Exeter College, where he stayed until the summer of 1492. Vitelli perhaps left England that year; in any case he is no longer heard of, and the place and date of his death are unknown.

Vitelli is mentioned by Erasmus in passing in the *Ciceronianus* (ASD I-2 667).

No works that Vitelli may have written in England have survived. Besides the letter and the poems written in the Low Countries and the little poem for the duke of Urbino, all his known works were composed in Venice or Padua. The funeral oration for Leoni's wife is preserved in the Museo Civico at Padua, MS B.P. 515, fasc 4. His brief *De dierum mensium annorumque observatione* and his *In defensionem Plinii et D. Calderini contra G. Merulam ... epistola*, both directed against Giorgio Merula, were printed together in Venice (B. de Tortis) in 1481 or early 1482. Vitelli's philological interest in Pliny is shown by two more works: an *Enarratiuncula*, introduced by a letter to Antonio Partenio, and first published by Nicolas *Bérault in *Marini Becichemi Scodrensis elegans ac docta in C. Plinium praelectio* (Paris 1519); and a tract in the form of another letter addressed to the same Partenio, following upon Niccolò Perotti's own commentaries: *Commentariolus in C. Plinii Secundi Prooemium, cum observationibus Cornelii Vitellii in eundem Commentariolum* (Venice 1480?; a manuscript copy is in Perugia, Badia di S. Pietro, CM 53, ff 172–6).

BIBLIOGRAPHY: E.C. Marchant in DNB XX 376 / E. Daxhelet 'Notes sur l'humaniste italien Cornelio Vitelli, professeur à Louvain à la fin du XVe siècle' *Bulletin de l'Institut historique belge de Rome* 15 (1935) 83–97 / H.L.R. Edwards 'Robert Gaguin and the English poets, 1489–90' *The Modern Language Review* 32 (1937) 430–4 / R. Weiss 'Cornelio Vitelli in France and England' *Journal of the Warburg Institute* 2 (1938–9) 219–26 / C.H. Clough 'Thomas Linacre, Cornelio Vitelli and humanistic studies at Oxford' in *Essays on the Life and Work of Thomas Linacre c 1460–1524* ed F. Maddison et al (Oxford 1977) 1–23 / G. Tournoy 'The literary production of Hieronymus Balbus at Paris' *Gutenberg-Jahrbuch 1978* (Mainz 1978) 70–7 / G. Tournoy 'New evidence on the Italian humanist Cornelius Vitellius (c 1440–c 1500)' *Lias* 5 (1978) 13–18

GILBERT TOURNOY

Erasmus VITELLIUS *See Erazm* CIOŁEK

Aegidius VITERBIENSIS, Giles of VITERBO *See Egidio* ANTONINI

VITERIUS *See Pierre* VITRÉ, *Jean* VITRIER

Francisco de VITORIA d 12 August 1546
Both the date and place of birth of Francisco de Vitoria have been disputed. The traditional date of 1486 has been set aside by some in favour of 1492, although the latter date leaves Vitoria five years younger than the statutory age for receiving his Paris doctorate. His parents, Pedro de Arcaya and Catalina de Compludo, moved from the Basque city of Vitoria to Castilian Burgos to take a position at the court. Both cities have claimed Vitoria, whose real name was Francisco de Arcaya y Compludo. He had two brothers, Pedro de *Vitoria, who also entered the Dominican order, and Juan, whose son Juan Alfonso de Vitoria became a Jesuit of some note.

Francisco de Vitoria joined the Dominicans at San Pablo, in Burgos, in 1505 and received the habit in 1506. He went to Paris, perhaps in 1507 but certainly by 1509; there he was influenced by the eclectic Nominalist Juan de Celaya and later studied theology under the Nominalist-turned-Thomist Pieter Crockaert. Among his contemporaries at the Collège de Saint-Jacques in Paris were Vincentius *Theoderici and the ill-fated Aimé Maigret. Other colleagues in the faculty of theology were Juan de Celaya, Gervasius *Wain, Nicolas *Maillard, and Jérôme Clichtove. Vitoria received his licence in theology on 24 March 1522, ranking sixth of thirty-six, and his doctorate on 27 June 1522. He was never active on the faculty of theology in Paris but returned to Spain, where he taught theology at the Dominican *studium* of San Gregorio in Valladolid. In 1526 he was elected by the students to the most prestigious chair in Spain, the 'prima' chair at Salamanca, which he held for twenty years until his death.

At the 1527 conference in Valladolid convened to examine the works of Erasmus in Spain, Vitoria took a middle position. He opposed a general censure or condemnation of Erasmus' works. Commenting on Erasmus' doctrine of the Trinity and of the divinity of Christ, Vitoria stated that Erasmus' works contained some false and heretical points (for example, that the Trinity cannot be proved from Scripture) as well as other phrases or ambiguous interpretations which should either be changed or struck out. Juan Luis *Vives had earlier written to Erasmus that Vitoria was a firm admirer who had defended Erasmus more than once in Paris (Ep 1836). This Erasmian position of Vitoria, probably delivered in academic disputations in Paris, had cooled considerably by 1527. Erasmus wrote a lengthy letter to Vitoria in November 1527 (Ep 1909) to refute the attacks of Edward *Lee and Noël *Béda and to ask Vitoria's help in Spain, particularly in restraining his brother Pedro. In later years, Vitoria called Erasmus a 'dangerous man' and even an 'advocate of heresies.'

Vitoria was a brilliant teacher and stylist who published nothing during his tenure at Salamanca. Nicolaus *Clenardus wrote that he had never received more beautiful letters than those of Vitoria. The foundation of Vitoria's thought and regular lectures was the writings of Thomas Aquinas, and, following the example of Crockaert in Paris, his commentaries on Aquinas were a radical pedagogical innovation at Salamanca. He is credited with the academic formation of hundreds of students who then dominated, through their students, the intellectual scene of Spain for over a century. Among Vitoria's auditors were Domingo de Soto, Melchor Cano, Alfonso de la Vera-Cruz, Diego de Zúñiga, Andrés Vega, Tomás Chaves, Bartolomé de Medina, and Martin de Ledesme. Vitoria is especially known

through the annual *Releccion*, a formal lecture to the whole university, recorded by students and published posthumously. His defence of the rights of the Indians in the New World influenced the 'New Laws for the Indies' of 1542 promulgated by *Charles v, with whom Vitoria corresponded on these matters. His innovative theories on war and international relations, as well as moral issues, have aroused much interest in the twentieth century. He was invoked as a kind of patron by the Pan-American Union in 1927 in Washington, where a bust of him was unveiled in 1963. Several learned societies and institutes bear his name.

Vitoria edited the following works: Thomas Aquinas *Liber nomine Secunda secundae a Petro Brussellensi castigatus* (Paris: Claude Chevallon 1512); Pedro de Covarrubias *Sermones dominicales* (Paris: Josse Bade 1520); St *Antoninus of Florence *Summa aurea* (Paris: Jean Petit 1521); and Pierre Bersuire *Dictionarium seu Repertorium morale* (Paris: Claude Chevallon and Berthold Rembolt 1521–2). Other works of Vitoria's are: *Relectiones theologicae* (Lyon: Jacques Boyer 1557; Salamanca: Juan de Canova 1565; at least eight other editions in the sixteenth and seventeenth centuries; see *Relecciones teológicas*, critical edition by L.G.A. Getino, Madrid 1933–); *Confesonario útil y probechoso* (Antwerp: Christophe Plantin 1558; at least eight other editions before 1580); *Summa sacramentorum ecclesiae ex doctrina Francisci à Victoria* ed Tomás de Chaves (Valladolid: Sebastiano Martinez 1560; at least thirty-seven other editions before 1630); and *Comentarios a la Secunda secundae de Santo Tomás* ed V. Beltrán de Heredia (Salamanca 1932–5, 1952). A list of published letters and other fragments is given in T. Urdánoz *Obras de Francisco de Vitoria* (Madrid 1960). The manuscripts of Vitoria are listed in V. Beltrán de Heredia *Los manuscritos de maestro Fray Francisco de Vitoria* (Madrid and Valencia 1928).

BIBLIOGRAPHY: Allen Ep 1909 / V. Beltrán de Heredia *Francisco de Vitoria* (Barcelona 1939) / V. Beltrán de Heredia and J.-G. Menéndez Rigada in DTC xv 3117–44 / Bataillon *Erasmo y España* 11, 222, and passim / Farge no 470 / J.A. Fernandez-Santamaria *The State, War and Peace: Spanish Political Thought in the Renaissance, 1516–1559* (Cambridge 1977) 58–119 / R. Garcia

Villoslada *La Universidad de Paris durante los estudios de Francisco de Vitoria, O.P. (1507–1522)* (Rome 1938) / R. Garcia Villoslada 'Erasmo y Vitoria' *Razón y Fé* (1935) 19–38, 340–50, 506–19 / L.G.A. Getino *El maestro Fr. Francisco de Vitoria: Su vida, su doctrina e influencia* (Madrid 1930) / R.C. González *Francisco de Vitoria, estudio bibliográfico* (Buenos Aires 1946) / P. Mesnard 'François de Vitoria et la liquidation de l'impérialisme' in *L'Essor de la philosophie politique au XVIᵉ siècle* 3rd ed (Paris 1951) 454–72 / C. Noreña 'Vitoria, Salamanca and the American Indians' in *Studies in Spanish Renaissance Thought* (The Hague 1975) 36–149 / A. Palau y Dulcet *Manual de librero hispanoamericano* XXVII (Barcelona and Oxford 1976) / J.B. Scott 'Francisco de Vitoria and his Law of Nations' in *The Spanish Origin of International Law* (Washington 1934) I / Quentin Skinner *The Foundations of Modern Political Thought* (Cambridge 1978) II passim / T. Urdánoz *Obras de Francisco de Vitoria* (Madrid 1960)

JAMES K. FARGE

Pedro de VITORIA documented 1526–7
According to Erasmus' informants in Spain Pedro de Vitoria was a brother of Francisco de *Vitoria. Like Francisco he was a Dominican, but in contrast to his brother's moderation in dealing with Erasmus he bitterly attacked the humanist in sermons preached at Burgos in 1526 and 1527 and engaged in controversies with the Erasmian Alonso Ruiz de *Virués (Epp 1836, 1902, 1903, 1909, 2205, 2371). Erasmus blamed Pedro, among other friars, for causing the uproar which led to the Valladolid conference of 1527. On 29 November 1527 he wrote to Francisco de Vitoria, at least in part to have him restrain his brother (Ep 1909). As Bataillon has pointed out, the Dominican whose conversation with Juan *Maldonado is reported in Ep 1908 was probably Francisco and not Pedro.

It has been argued, by L.G.A. Getino and others, that the Dominican brother of Francisco de Vitoria was named Diego and not Pedro. However, Bataillon has cast doubt on this theory by noting that a Dominican named Diego de Vitoria died in 1539, while a Dominican brother of Francisco was spoken of as still alive in 1545.

BIBLIOGRAPHY: Allen Ep 1836 / Bataillon *Erasmo y España* 225, 245, 274, and passim /

L.G.A. Getino *El maestro Fr. Francisco de Vitoria: Su vida, su doctrina e influencia* (Madrid 1930) 93 / C. Noreña 'Vitoria, Salamanca and the American Indians' in *Studies in Spanish Renaissance Thought* (The Hague 1975) 36–149 esp 37–8 and passim   TBD

Pierre VITRÉ of Paris, d 19 May 1540
Pierre Vitré (Viterius, de Vitry) took his MA at the Collège de Navarre before 1497 and probably succeeded Erasmus as tutor to the Englishman Thomas *Grey (Ep 58), with whom he remained in close contact in later years. He clearly was at one time intimate with Erasmus (Ep 768; Allen I 9); in 1532 Johannes Sphyractes forwarded from Paris a letter from Vitré to Erasmus and added that they had once shared room and board 'apud Britannos' (AK IV Ep 1674). Vitré taught for a while at Calais but was dismissed from there. On Erasmus' recommendation he returned to Paris, where he taught first at the Collège des Lombards and then, from about 1516 to 1536, at the Collège de Navarre, where he was regent in grammar. However, in February 1536 he informed Erasmus that business he conducted for Antoine de *La Barre, archbishop of Tours, had kept him away from Paris for the last three years (Ep 3101).

In 1512 Erasmus dedicated his *De ratione studii* to Vitré (Ep 66; CWE 24 665, 672, 691), and in 1518 he agreed to recommend his old friend to Etienne *Poncher, bishop of Paris (Epp 779, 817). Vitré frequently complained of his poverty (Ep 3101), and Erasmus put him into his last will and testament of 12 February 1536 (Allen XI 364) for a legacy of 150 crowns. It was perhaps in anticipation of this legacy that Vitré arranged on 22 September 1536 to retire from teaching and acquire lodgings at the Collège de Navarre for the rest of his life in return for payment of one lump sum of 120 livres tournois. Vitré was a friend of Philippus *Montanus, another legatee; they received and acknowledged their bequests jointly (AK IV Ep 2097, V Ep 2129).

BIBLIOGRAPHY: Allen Epp 66, 3101 / ASD I- 88 / AK IV Ep 1674 and passim / Jean de Launoy *Regii Navarrae gymnasii Parisiensis historia* (Paris 1677) I 980–1 / de Vocht CTL II 366 / Paris, Minutier Central MS XLIX 7, 22 September 1536   JAMES K. FARGE

Jean VITRIER of Saint-Omer, c 1456–
d before 15 June 1521

Jean Vitrier (Voirier, Veerier, Vitrarius, Viterius, Vitrius) was born at Saint-Omer to a family involved in the cloth trade. In his biographical letter on Vitrier (Ep 1211) Erasmus stated
that he entered the Franciscan order at an early
age, doubtless at the convent of Saint-Omer.
Endowed with a prodigious memory and a
lively intellect he studied at the University of
Louvain, where he matriculated in arts on 31
August 1475 and where he perhaps also
studied theology. Around 1486–8 he became
warden of the Observant Franciscans of
Namur, where he contributed to the rapid
growth of the convent and became embroiled
in conflicts with the Franciscan Conventuals.
He was already showing signs of the uncompromising mysticism and reforming intransigence which would lead him into three great
battles for the purity of the faith and a religion
founded on the Gospels.

The first occurred in 1498 at Tournai, where
Vitrier attacked the unreformed religious houses, the licentiousness of canons and other
ecclesiastics, and the superstitious cult of the
saints. The Paris faculty of theology censured
sixteen propositions drawn arbitrarily from his
sermons. It is not known whether he was
vindicated or forced to submit. In 1500,
however, he was the warden of the convent of
Saint-Omer. Although confronted with the
material needs of the convent, he behaved in a
fashion contrary to the general practice: on the
occasion of the preaching of indulgences for
the jubilee of 1500, which Vitrier judged
simoniacal, the commissioners attempted to
buy his silence by offering a gift for the
construction of the new convent church. The
warden indignantly refused the hundred
florins proposed. Excommunicated and twice
cited before the episcopal tribunal, the intractable Franciscan continued his sermons and
was eventually exonerated (Ep 1211). Vitrier's
third battle was for the reform of the nuns of
the convent of Ste Marguerite of Saint-Omer in
1501, described by Erasmus (Ep 1211) and
recorded in the judicial archives of the town. In
this case Vitrier, who was not above resorting
to force in order to make the recalcitrant nuns
leave this 'brothel,' narrowly escaped a murder
attempt by several of the nuns. In fact Vitrier

longed for martyrdom. In his radical commitment to his faith he was an heir to the
Franciscan spiritualism of the fifteenth century
which had absorbed the ideas of Joachim of
Fiore. This was the legacy he passed on to the
circle of religious that formed around him in the
Pas-de-Calais. His remarkable sermons show
the intensity of his mystical experience, his
debt to Origen, and his indifference to the
scholastic method.

Erasmus' meetings with Vitrier occurred
shortly after this last affair, when he resided at
Saint-Omer and Tournehem in 1501 and 1502.
The first contacts between the two men were
difficult (Ep 163), but as the months passed a
friendship developed (Ep 165). For a year the
friar helped the humanist deepen his love of St
Paul, first kindled by John *Colet. Above all,
Vitrier helped Erasmus solve his internal crisis
and converted him to the study of Origen.
Erasmus avidly read Origen's commentary on
the Epistle to the Romans and homilies during
his retreat at Courtebourne in the château of
Florent de *Calonne. One consequence of his
contact with Vitrier and Origen was the
composition of the *Enchiridion*, his first great
contribution to Christian literature. This masterpiece was filled with both direct and indirect
citations from Origen.

In 1502 Vitrier was forced to resign the post
of warden at Saint-Omer. The affair of the
refused gift of pork which Erasmus described
in Ep 1211 and other administrative 'errors'
merely provided a pretext for Vitrier's demotion. In fact the real causes included external
pressures – in particular that applied by the
Dominican Jean *Vasseur – accusations of
acting 'with heretics in the contempt of
ecclesiastical ceremonies, of scholastic doctors,
and of indulgences' (Saint Omer, Bibliothèque
municipale MS 782 93), and the hatred of
members of his own house who were jealous of
his brilliance and shamed by their own
mediocrity. Vitrier submitted with good grace.
At least until 1507 he humbly filled the pastoral
roles of preacher and confessor before finally
being relegated to the guidance of an obscure
convent of nuns at Courtrai (Ep 1211). He died
at an unknown date, certainly before 15 June
1521.

Thus ended in almost complete effacement
the life of a man who had done a great deal to

awaken Erasmus to his role as a Christian and as a theologian. For Erasmus, Vitrier was the equal of any saint: the ideal preacher (*Ecclesiastes* LB V 987C; also Allen Ep 1211:71–9) and a resurrected Origen (Ep 1211; *De vita, phrasi, docendi ratione ... Origenis* LB VIII 437E–440A).

BIBLIOGRAPHY: Allen Epp 163, 1211 / Alain Derville 'Jean Vitrier et les religieuses de Sainte Marguerite' *Revue du Nord* 42 (1960) 207–39 / Alain Derville in BNB XXXVIII 809–16 / André Godin *Spiritualité franciscaine en Flandre au* XVIᵉ *siècle: L'Homéliaire de Jean Vitrier: Texte, étude thématique et sémantique* (Geneva 1971) / André Godin *Erasme lecteur d'Origène* (Geneva 1982) 21–7 and passim / Jean Hadot 'Erasme à Tournehem et à Courtebourne' in *Colloquia Erasmiana Turonensia* I 87–96 / *Matricule de Louvain* II-1 333 / C. Du Plessis d'Argentré *Collectio judiciorum de novis erroribus ...* (Paris 1724) I-2 340–1 / Namur, Archives de l'Etat, 'Transports' nos 17, 27 / Saint-Omer, Bibliothèque municipale MS 782: 'Fondation du couvent des F. Prêcheurs de Saint-Omer l'an 1324 avec leur établissement au milieu de la ville l'an 1477 où on voit les plus grands hommes sortis de cette maison et plusieurs evenemens qui regardent les deux couvents etc ... par le R.P. Turpin ... l'an 1715'   ANDRÉ GODIN

Antonio de' VIVALDI of Genoa, documented 1511–46
The Vivaldi (de Vivaldis) were a Genoese banking family with agencies in Antwerp and London and interests extending as far as Spain. As early as 1483 they had participated in a loan to the English crown and as late as 1546 they were partners in credit arrangements providing large sums to the English crown, which also involved the city of London and the banking houses of Anton *Fugger and Erasmus *Schets. In 1519 they joined the firm of Benedetto de' *Fornari and his family partners as a minor source of the funds necessary for the election of *Charles V.

Antonio de' Vivaldi was resident in London and licensed to import silks into England in May 1511 (LP I 784:51). On 26 May 1513 he received papers of denization for life (LP I 2055). He was often involved in royal financial affairs, and even after his return to the continent and his native city in the early 1530s (LP IX 175–6) maintained contacts with the

English court through Thomas *Cromwell (LP X 403, 1130) and Richard *Pace (LP XI 779). In 1544 he and his family helped finance the latest war of Charles V against the French. He is mentioned in Ep 465 and conceivably referred to in Ep 1205.

BIBLIOGRAPHY: Allen Ep 465 / LP I–X passim / Richard Ehrenberg *Das Zeitalter der Fugger* (Jena 1896) I 103, 327–8 / J.A. Goris *Etude sur les colonies marchandes méridionales ... à Anvers de 1488 à 1567* (Louvain 1925) 394 and passim / Ramón Carande *Carlos V y sus banqueros* (Madrid 1959–67) III 40, 326, and passim / Götz von Pölnitz *Anton Fugger* (Tübingen 1958–) I 380–1, III 224, and passim

IG & PGB

Juan Luis VIVES of Valencia, 6 March 1492–6 May 1540
Juan Luis was born at Valencia to Juan Luis Vives Valeriola and Blanquina March, both converted Jews. By 1508 he was enrolled in the Gymnasium of Valencia, where he studied Latin grammar under Jerónimo Amiguet and Daniel Sisó and Greek classics under Bernardo Navarro. In 1509 he travelled to Paris, where he studied scholastic philosophy at the Collège de Montaigu under Jan Dullaert (Dullardus) of Ghent and the Aragonese Gaspar Lax de Sariñena. In 1512, dissatisfied with the rigid training offered by the University of Paris and inclined towards classical and humanistic studies, he left for Bruges, where he stayed at the house of the merchant Bernardo Valdaura, possibly a distant relative.

Although Vives returned to Paris in 1514 and 1520 and travelled frequently in later years, Bruges became his permanent home and the centre of his activities. Here he formed lasting friendships with Frans van *Cranevelt, Jan van *Fevijn, and Marcus *Laurinus. In his early years at Bruges Vives taught privately. Some time before Easter 1517 he was appointed tutor to Guillaume (II) de *Croy, the young cardinal and bishop of Cambrai who in December 1517 was appointed archbishop of Toledo. In 1517 Vives moved to Louvain with his pupil and obtained permission from the university to teach publicly within its halls, even though he lacked a formal degree. Croy died in a riding accident at Worms in January 1521 and Vives' financial situation deteriorated. Although he

Juan Luis Vives

continued to teach publicly at Louvain – other students included Honoratus *Joannius, Diego *Gracián de Alderete, and Jérôme *Ruffault – he desired a steady source of income which would free him completely for writing. In summer 1521 he sought the patronage of *Henry VIII of England through the offices of Thomas *More (Ep 1222), who had seen and praised several of his early publications (Ep 1106) and who possibly met him in person with Cranevelt at Bruges in 1520 (Ep 1145). When this project failed Vives attempted to attract Henry's attention by dedicating to him his commentaries on St Augustine's *De civitate Dei* (Basel: J. Froben 1522) commissioned by Erasmus. This too did not bear immediate fruit. By the end of 1522 Vives received the devastating news that his father had been apprehended by the Spanish Inquisition on a charge of resuming Jewish religious observances. In 1524 the elder Vives was convicted and handed over to the secular arm for execution. Although Vives' mother had died in 1509, she too came under the scrutiny of the Inquisition and after a trial in 1528 and 1529 her body was exhumed and burnt. Ironically, in the autumn of 1522, when

his father's trial was beginning, Vives received through Juan de *Vergara an offer to assume a chair at Alcalá vacated by the death of Antonio de *Nebrija, the father of Spanish humanism. Vives travelled to England in May 1523, intending to continue on to Spain (Ep 1362). However he never returned to his homeland, for he soon accepted an offer from Cardinal Thomas *Wolsey to lecture in Greek at Oxford.

For the next five years Vives divided his time between England, which he visited on six separate occasions, and Bruges, where he married Margarita *Valdaura, a daughter of his former host, in April 1524. In England he enjoyed the patronage of Henry VIII and of *Catherine of Aragon and cultivated friendships with Thomas More, John *Fisher, Thomas *Linacre, John *Claymond, and William *Blount, Lord Mountjoy. He also served as tutor to Princess *Mary in 1527 and 1528. In 1528, however, he lost the favour of Henry VIII by siding with Catherine in the matter of the divorce. Between 25 February and 1 April 1528 he was placed under house arrest at the instigation of Cardinal Wolsey, before being allowed to return to Bruges. In November 1528 Catherine recalled him to England to serve as her legal adviser and confidant, but Vives left almost immediately when the queen rejected his advice to remain silent during the divorce trial.

In the last decade of his life, the most productive from the literary point of view, Vives lived mainly at Bruges, travelling on occasion to Louvain, Breda, Paris, and other centres at the invitation of friends. He enjoyed patronage from a number of sources, including the Emperor *Charles V, Joris van *Halewijn, lord of Comines, and Dona Mencía de *Mendoza, the Spanish wife of Henry III, count of *Nassau-Dillenburg. He died at Bruges and was buried in the cathedral of St Donatian.

Vives met Erasmus in 1516 or 1517, possibly at Bruges. Erasmus was impressed with the young humanist and in 1519 recommended him without success as tutor for the young *Ferdinand of Austria (Ep 917, 927). In March 1520 Erasmus wrote the dedication for Vives' *Declamationes Syllanae quinque* (Antwerp: M. Hillen 1520) and, when this and other works drew compliments from Thomas More (Ep 1106), praised Vives profusely as one destined to place him in the shade (Ep 1107). Vives for his part was delighted to be an associate and protégé of Erasmus, who was then at the height of his fame and influence and resided close to Vives at Louvain. In June 1520, when visiting Paris, he sent Erasmus an enthusiastic report of the warm reception he had received from Johannes *Fortis and other friends, whom he feared he had alienated by writing *In pseudodialecticos* (1519), a scathing attack on the study of philosophy at the University of Paris (Ep 1108). Erasmus replied commenting on Vives' skill in winning back his former colleagues and expressing optimism at the favourable reception given humanism at Cambridge, Alcalá, and other universities throughout Europe (Ep 1111). In 1520, however, Erasmus' optimism was already being undermined by the uproar created by *Luther's Reformation. The theologians of Louvain were especially vocal in accusing Erasmus of inspiring the reformers, and in 1521 he left Louvain for Basel.

Before his departure, Erasmus persuaded Vives to edit Augustine's *De civitate Dei* for the projected *Froben edition of the Father's works. Vives began the task in January 1521, sending his text and commentary to Basel in instalments, the last in July 1522 (Epp 1222, 1256, 1271, 1281, 1303). Direct collaboration, however, placed a strain on the relationship of the two men, as Erasmus pressed Vives to complete the project quickly. In July 1522 Vives complained to Cranevelt of the harshness of Erasmus' letters and of his threats that Froben would publish an incomplete version of the work (de Vocht *Literae ad Craneveldium* Ep 8). Vives suffered from insomnia, and in August 1522, shortly after sending the last books to Basel, fell seriously ill. *De civitate Dei* was published in September, with an introductory letter by Erasmus (Ep 1309), a eulogy of Erasmus by Vives, and the dedicatory epistle to Henry VIII.

The edition of *De civitate Dei* behind him – at least for the time being – Vives embarked on his English adventures. He continued to correspond at length with Erasmus, sending him news of his personal life, seeking his comments on his *De institutione feminae christianae* (1524) and other works (Epp 1792, 1830), and informing him about recent events in England,

the Netherlands, and especially Spain, which in the mid-1520s was becoming increasingly receptive to Erasmus' books and ideas (Epp 1513, 1613, 1792, 2208). Vives was in frequent contact with Juan de Vergara, Alonso Ruiz de *Virués, Juan *Maldonado, and other Spanish Erasmians and kept Erasmus informed of the unsuccessful attempt by members of the religious orders in Spain to have the works of Erasmus censured at the Valladolid conference of 1527 (Epp 1836, 1847).

By August 1528, however, there were signs of a growing coolness in the relationship of the two humanists (Ep 2026). One reason for this was probably Vives' growing independence as a scholar. Another may have been Erasmus' reluctance to come to the defence of Vives' patroness, Catherine of Aragon, and his impolitic statement that he would rather allow Jupiter (Henry VIII) two Junos than try to take away one (Ep 2040). A third was continuing friction over *De civitate Dei*. Early in 1525 Erasmus had complained to Vives that sales of the edition were poor, blaming this on the length of Vives' commentary and pointing out that he had advised brevity (Ep 1531). In October 1527 (Ep 1889) he informed Vives that the Froben press wished to delay reprinting *De civitate Dei* for the new collected works of Augustine because many copies of Vives' edition remained unsold. When Vives countered that he had heard from the bookseller Franz *Birckmann that sales were going well, Erasmus harshly denied this claim, adding the cutting remark that Vives should write something useful, as did Lazare de *Baïf, author of *De re vestiaria* (Basel 1526) and other antiquarian works (Ep 2040). The quarrel appeared to be patched up when Vives sent Erasmus a conciliatory letter (Ep 2061) and the Froben press decided to reprint *De civitate Dei*. Erasmus sent advice for revisions and Vives was still working on the project on 30 August 1529 (Ep 2208). However, when *De civitate Dei* was reissued in December 1529 as the fifth volume of the Froben Augustine, it was in a version improved by Erasmus but without Vives' commentary and prefaces. When Vives' edition of *De civitate Dei* was next published (Paris: C. Chevallon 1531), Vives' eulogy of Erasmus was reduced to a matter of lines only (Allen Ep 1309). Despite Erasmus' negative reaction, Vives' commentary was a valuable contribution to the elucidation of Augustinian thought and was republished frequently, in English and French translations as well as in Latin. Vives was no longer printed at Basel in Erasmus' lifetime, whereas after his death the Basel printers revived their interest in Vives' work almost explosively.

After 1528 Vives' letters to Erasmus became shorter and less frequent; Vives excused himself by saying that their friendship did not depend on long letters (Ep 2502). When Erasmus complained that his opponent Luis de *Carvajal had included a letter of Vives in the *Dulcoratio amarulentiarum Erasmicae responsionis* (Paris 1530; Ep 2892), Vives replied in May 1534 protesting his friendship and stating that his letter for Carvajal was only one of general introduction. Vives' letter of May 1534 (Ep 2932) was the last to be exchanged between the two humanists and included the depressing news of the imprisonment of Thomas More and John Fisher in England and of Juan de Vergara and Bernardino *Tovar in Spain.

Although Vives did not place Erasmus in the shade, as the latter had predicted, he was the greatest Spanish humanist and educational theorist of the sixteenth century. His works were not limited to education but dealt with a wide range of subjects including religion, philosophy, social reform, and international relations. His earliest publications reflected his interests as a teacher and as a Christian: an edition of Hyginus (Paris: J. Lambert 1514); the dialogue *Christi Jesu triumphus et Mariae parentis eius ovatio* (Paris: J. Lambert 1514), the *Opuscula varia* containing the *Meditationes in septem psalmos quos vocant poenitentiae*, the *Praelectio in Georgica Vergilii*, and the *In pseudodialecticos* (Louvain: D. Martens, [1519]; NK 2172); the *Declamatio qua Quintiliano respondetur pro noverca contra caecum* (Louvain: D. Martens 1523; NK 1775); and the *Praelectio in quartum Rhetoricorum ad Herennium* (Louvain 1522). As the 1520s progressed his literary production expanded to include works on the theory of education, including *De institutione feminae christianae* (Antwerp: M. Hillen, 1524; NK 2167) *De ratione studii puerilis* (published with Thomas *Linacre's *Rudimenta grammatices*, Paris: R. Estienne 1536); and the *Introductio ad sapientiam* (Louvain: D. Martens 1524; NK 2168). He also

became interested in social and political issues, publishing *De subventione pauperum* (Bruges: H. de Crook 1525; NK 4066) – a work at least partly inspired by More's *Utopia* – *De officio mariti* (Bruges: H. de Crook 30 January 1529; NK 2171); and a series of works dealing with the question of peace in Europe and war against the Turks: *De Europae dissidiis et bello turcico* (Bruges: H. de Crook 1526; NK 2164), *De concordia et discordia humani generis* and *De pacificatione* (Antwerp: M. Hillen 1529; NK 2163). Other works from this period include the moral treatise *Satellitium animi sive symbola*, published with the *Introductio ad sapientiam* (NK 2168), and translations of Isocrates' *Areopagitica oratio* and *Ad Nicoclem*, published with *De Europae dissidiis ...* (NK 2164).

In the last decade of his life Vives completed his greatest pedagogical and philosophical works. These included *De disciplinis* (Antwerp: M. Hillen 1531; NK 4063), an encyclopaedic survey of the world of learning as it was in his own day and a program for its renewal; the *Latinae linguae exercitatio* (Paris: Foucher and Gaultherot 1540; Basel: R. Winter 1543), a collection of dialogues for learning Latin which became a standard textbook in schools, published fifty times in the sixteenth century; *De anima et vita* (Basel: R. Winter 1538), an innovative study of human psychology and philosophy; and *De veritate fidei christianae* (Basel: J. Oporinus 1543), the most thorough discussion of his religious views. In addition Vives published *De ratione dicendi* (Louvain: B. Gravius 1533); *De conscribendis epistolis* (Basel: B. Lasius and T. Platter 1536); *De Aristotelis operibus censura* (Basel: J. Oporinus 1538); *Ad animi excitationem in Deum commentatiunculae* (Antwerp: M. Hillen 1537); and *Interpretatio allegorica in Bucolica Vergili* (Basel: R. Winter 1539).

Vives' *Opera omnia* were printed at Basel by Nicolaus *Episcopius in 1555 and at Valencia by Gregorio Mayáns y Siscar between 1782 and 1790 (repr 1964). There are modern editions with translations of *Latinae linguae exercitatio* (London 1908, repr 1970) and *De disciplinis* (Cambridge 1913, repr 1971) by Foster Watson, *Introductio ad sapientiam* by Marian Tobriner (New York 1968), *De subventione pauperum* by Armando Saitta (Florence 1973), *De anima et vita* by Mario Sancipriano (Padua 1974), and *In* *pseudodialecticos* by Charles Fantazzi (Leiden 1979) and by Rita Guerlac (Dordrecht 1979).

BIBLIOGRAPHY: Allen Ep 927 / J.L. Vives *Obras completas* trans and ed L. Riber (Madrid 1947–8) / *Epistolario de Juan Luis Vives* trans and ed J. Jiménez Delgado (Salamanca 1979) / de Vocht *Literae ad Craneveldium* Epp 1, 2, and passim / Adolfo Bonilla y San Martín *Luis Vives y la filosofía del renacimiento* 2nd ed (Madrid 1929) / de Vocht MHL 1–60 and passim / de Vocht *Busleyden* 165 and passim / Bataillon *Erasmo y España* 17, 77, and passim / A. Salazar *Iconografía de J.L. Vives durante los siglos XVI, XVII, y XVIII* (Madrid 1953) / M. de la Pinta y Llorente and J.M. de Palacio *Procesos inquisitoriales contra la familia judía de Juan Luis Vives* (Madrid 1964) / Carlos Noreña *Juan Luis Vives* (The Hague 1970) / Carlos Noreña *Studies in Spanish Renaissance Thought* (The Hague 1975) 13–40 and passim / A. Guy *Vivès ou l'humanisme engagé* (Paris 1972) / D. Baker-Smith 'Juan Vives and the *Somnium Scipionis*' and J.C. Margolin 'Vivès, lecteur et critique de Platon et d'Aristote' in *Classical Influences on European Culture A.D. 1500–1700: Proceedings of an International Conference ... Cambridge, April 1974* ed R.R. Bolgar (Cambridge 1976) / P. Sainz Rodríguez et al *Homenaje a Luis Vives* Six papers read at the VI Congreso internacional de estudios clásicos, Madrid, September 1974 (Madrid 1977) / J. IJsewijn 'J.L. Vives in 1512–1517: a reconsideration of evidence' *Humanistica Lovaniensia* 26 (1977) 82–100   TBD

Margarita VIVES *See Margarita* VALDAURA

VLADISLAV II king of Bohemia and Hungary, c 1456–13 March 1516
Vladislav (Władysław, Ulászló, Ladislaus) was the eldest son of Casimir IV Jagiełło and a brother of *John Albert and *Sigismund I of Poland. He was elected king of Bohemia by the Bohemian diet on 27 May 1471, following the death of the 'Hussite king' George of Poděbrady. The coronation took place in Prague on 22 August 1471. In a protracted military conflict, the young ruler faced the Hungarian king *Matthias Corvinus, who made rival claims to the throne on the basis of an earlier election at Olomouc (Olmütz), in Moravia (3/4 May 1469) and coronation by a papal legate at Jihlava (Iglau) on 28 May 1471. By agreements

reached in 1478 and 1479 Matthias retained possession of Moravia, Silesia, and Lusatia (Bohemian crownlands previously occupied by him) for his lifetime. Vladislav controlled only Bohemia. When Matthias died in 1490, Vladislav was elected king of Hungary on 15 July 1490.

The unification of the Bohemian crownlands with Hungary laid the basis for the formation of the Hapsburg Danubian empire after 1526. The way was prepared by the peace of Bratislava (Pressburg) in 1491 and the treaty of Vienna in 1515 between Vladislav and the Emperor *Maximilian in which Vladislav agreed to the Hapsburg succession to the throne, should his own line become extinct. The hopes of the Hapsburgs were fulfilled when Vladislav's son, *Louis II, was killed in the battle of Mohács against the Turks (29 August 1526). In 1509 Vladislav joined the League of Cambrai directed against Venice in the futile hope of regaining Dalmatia for the crown of Hungary (*Julius exclusus*, Opuscula 112).

The reign of Vladislav was marked by increasing social, economic, political, and religious conflict. The Bohemian higher nobility, enriched by the confiscation of ecclesiastical properties during the Hussite revolution (1419–36) and hardly challenged by the weak and vacillating king, who resided mostly in Hungary after 1490, acquired further economic and political privileges at the expense of both the king and the royal cities (new constitution, *Landesordnung, zemské zřízení* in 1500, and the St Wenceslas Agreement in 1517). The increasing burdens of serfdom imposed on peasants provoked several violent uprisings (Moravia 1494, Bohemia 1496 and 1517, and Hungary 1514), and there were also revolts by miners in Bohemia.

The mounting tensions in Bohemia and Moravia were aggravated by the religious division between the Catholic minority, supported by the king, and the Hussite (Utraquist) majority. Violent confrontation was prevented by the 'Religious Peace of Kutná Hora' (Kuttenberg, Bohemia) in 1485 which guaranteed the right of individual choice, extended even to the peasants, and mutual toleration of the two parties. Valid originally for thirty-one years, the agreement was renewed in 1512 for perpetual duration. A similar agreement was reached in Moravia. However, neither statute provided for the toleration of other dissenting groups, such as the Czech or Bohemian Brethren (Unitas fratrum), who suffered sporadic persecution throughout the Jagiellonian period. Nonetheless their growth was assured under the protection of many lords (Epp 950, 1021).

Perhaps the only unifying force was generated by the humanist movement, which affected members of the nobility, burghers, and clergy regardless of their religious preference and social status. Paradoxically enough, the era of Vladislav represented a peak in the Renaissance art and architecture of Bohemia (the 'Vladislav gothic').

BIBLIOGRAPHY: Allen Ep 950 / Ottuv slovník naučný (Prague 1888–1909) XXVI 798–800 / For a list of sources and literature see Handbuch der Geschichte der böhmischen Länder ed Karl Bosl II (Stuttgart 1971) 99–143 and František Kavka Příručka k dějinám Československa do roku 1648 (Prague 1963) 254–360 / With no critical monograph on Vladislav available, the following general histories treat the Jagiellonian period: Ernest Denis Fin de l'indépendance bohème I (Paris 1890, repr New York 1971, also trans into Czech); František Palacký Dějiny národu českého (final ed Prague 1878, repr 1973; a German version: Geschichte von Böhmen, Prague 1836–67) V; Ferdinand Hrejsa Dějiny křesťanství v Československu IV (Prague 1948); Československá vlastivěda ed Václav Novotný IV (Prague 1932); R.R. Betts in The New Cambridge Modern History (Cambridge 1957–79) II 188–94, 468–75, and passim; Kamil Krofta in The Cambridge Medieval History (Cambridge 1911–38) VIII ch 3 / On humanism see Josef Truhlář Humanismus a humanisté za krále Vladislava II (Prague 1894) and Otakar Odložilík 'Recent studies in Czech humanism' Renaissance Quarterly 21 (1968) 248–53.   J.K. ZEMAN

Johann von VLATTEN d 11 June 1562
Johann von Vlatten (Wlaten) was descended from a collateral branch of the Merode family named after their estate of Vlatten near Düren, between Cologne and Aachen. As a reward for their tradition of service to the dukes of Jülich the Vlattens were hereditary cupbearers in the ducal household. Johann's father, Konrad, was bailiff of Düren. His wife, Anna von Velbrück, bore him seven children, of whom the eldest, Reinhard, succeeded to his father's office as well as serving as a diplomat and councillor. Johann, the second, and Werner von *Vlatten, the fourth child, entered the church. Born around 1498–9, Johann was made a canon of St Mary's, Aachen in 1511, but owing to his youth he could not take possession of his prebend until 20 June 1515 (Düsseldorf, Hauptstaatsarchiv, MSS Marienstift Aachen 11a f 41). On 17 July 1516 he matriculated at the University of Cologne, taking a BA on 2 November 1517. He then turned to legal studies; on 29 April 1520 he registered with the German nation at the University of Orléans, and probably on 13 April 1522 he matriculated at Freiburg, to study law under Udalricus *Zasius. Finally in 1526 he matriculated at Bologna and there received in the same year a doctorate in civil and canon law. Before his return to Germany he visited Rome, but in May 1527 he was present at the diet of Regensburg.

Vlatten was preceded in his studies at Cologne, Orléans, and Bologna by his later colleagues in the service of Jülich-Cleves, Johann *Gogreve and Heinrich Olisleger; it is possible that he was already in touch with them at that time. During his years in Cologne he may also have met some of Erasmus' friends there such as Johannes *Caesarius and Hermann von *Neuenahr; indeed he may have met Erasmus himself in 1518 at Aachen in the company of Leonardus *Priccardus (Ep 1170). In Freiburg he met Konrad *Heresbach, who dedicated to him an edition of Strabo (Basel: V. Curio 1523) and renewed his acquaintance with Erasmus, who visited Freiburg in March 1523.

Meanwhile, on 26 January 1517 Vlatten had been elected scholaster by the chapter of St Mary's, and on 23 December 1521 he was appointed provost of St Martin's at Kranenburg, near Cleves. At the beginning of 1524 he was named councillor to Duke John III of *Cleves, thus commencing his career in the service of the united duchies of Jülich-Cleves-Berg. He attended the imperial diets and appeared before the imperial vicar and his Reichsregiment at Esslingen as well as before the imperial law court at Speyer. With the rank of vice-chancellor from 1530 and chancellor from 1554, he had a large share in determining the policies of his masters, dukes John III and William V of *Cleves. In 1535 Vlatten was instrumental in forging a coalition of princes to suppress the Anabaptist 'kingdom' of Münster. On the other hand he spared no effort to prevent a military confrontation with *Charles V on account of Gelderland, to which Duke William had succeeded in 1538. However, Duke William, encouraged by the French, undertook a campaign in Gelderland and lost it (1543), as Vlatten had predicted. In the wake of these events Vlatten himself lost the provost-ship of Xanten, which he had held from 1536, to an imperial appointee. He was compensated with the provostship of the chapter of Kerpen, near Cologne. Three years earlier, in 1541, he had also been appointed provost of St Mary's, Aachen. In fact the conflict over Gelderland had done nothing to reduce his influence at the ducal court of Düsseldorf or his personal prestige at the court of Charles V. His responsibilities also extended to the sphere of dynastic marriages; he helped to negotiate the match between *Henry VIII of England and Anne of Cleves as well as the two marriages of Duke William. Among his many memoranda preserved in manuscript at the Hauptstaatsar-chiv of Düsseldorf, one advances a scheme for a defensive alliance designed to prevent Slavic encroachment and ensuing war in the Baltic region.

It was especially in the related fields of religious and educational policies that Vlatten worked towards the implementation of Eras-mian ideals, in conjunction with Gogreve, Olisleger, Heresbach, and others. Erasmus himself collaborated with them in revising the church ordinance for the duchies (1532). From the religious colloquy of Worms in 1540 to the 'Interim' settlement of Augsburg in 1548, Vlatten consistently took an irenic line, un-daunted by criticism from both the Lutheran and the papal camps. In 1545 he participated in drafting a major position paper clarifying the religious policy of the united duchies, while in 1548 he produced a careful exposé on the Augsburg Confession. In 1554 he did bring about the dismissal of the Lutheran preacher Hermann Hamelmann, but only after a collo-quy at Düsseldorf (14 August) had failed to produce a modus vivendi between the reli-gious parties. In 1545 he, Heresbach, and Gogreve together founded a college in Düssel-dorf, the 'gymnasium illustre.' The Erasmian curriculum of the new school proved so popular that it was viewed with misgivings by the Cologne Jesuits. The educational system of the united duchies was to be completed, and crowned, by the creation of a university at Duisburg. After years of patient endeavour Vlatten was able, only weeks before his death, to obtain papal approval for the university, but in the end the project could not be realized.

Following their meeting at Freiburg Erasmus dedicated to Vlatten his edition of Cicero's *Tusculanae quaestiones* (Basel: J. Froben Novem-ber 1523). The dedicatory letter (Ep 1390) is a text of great importance in revealing Erasmus' understanding of Cicero and classical antiquity in general. From then on Vlatten and Erasmus continued their correspondence until the latter's death; apart from ten extant letters written by Erasmus and nine by Vlatten, there is evidence for a number of additional exchang-es now missing. On 14 February 1528 Erasmus dedicated to Vlatten his *Ciceronianus* (Epp 1948, 2088; ASD I-2 599–710). Vlatten showed his appreciation with the gift of a silver cup (Ep 1964). In April 1528 Erasmus showed again how much he respected Vlatten's judgment and influence in that he instructed *Pirckhei-mer to brief the councillor of Jülich-Cleves on the progress of his quarrel with Heinrich *Eppendorf (Ep 1991). During the diet of Augsburg in 1530 Vlatten joined other friends of Erasmus in urging him to come to Augs-burg and subsequently kept in touch with him throughout the proceedings of the diet (Epp 2335, 2346, 2360, 2386). Later Vlatten urged Erasmus to undertake further writings on topics that would benefit the clergy of the united duchies in the performance of their office, and his encouragement may well be reflected in the composition of such works as the *Explanatio symboli* of 1533 and the *Eccle-siastes* of 1535 (Epp 2804, 2845, 3031). The need for works of this kind had impressed itself upon Vlatten in the course of his eccle-siastical visitations. Until the second half of the century visitation reports in the united duchies either mention the presence of the *Ecclesiastes* in school and parish libraries or recommend its acquisition.

In addition to his letters to Erasmus, only a few letter fragments of Vlatten's correspondence have survived, but numerous records of political and diplomatic activities exist in the Hauptstaatsarchiv of Düsseldorf. His influence as a patron of letters is reflected in twelve works dedicated to him between 1523 and 1564.

BIBLIOGRAPHY: Allen Ep 1390 / ADB XL 87–9 / Matrikel Köln II 767 / Matricule d'Orléans I 242 / Matrikel Freiburg I-1 258 no 60 (?) / Knod 601 / Anton Gail 'Johann von Vlatten und der Einfluss des Erasmus von Rotterdam auf die Kirchenpolitik der vereinigten Herzogtümer' Düsseldorfer Jahrbuch 45 (1951) 2–109 / Anton Gail in Rheinische Lebensbilder II ed B. Poll (Düsseldorf 1966) 53–73 / Hermann Hamelmann Geschichtliche Werke ed H. Detmer and K. Löffler (Münster 1902–13) II 283–5 and passim / Briefe von Andreas Masius und seinen Freunden ed Max Lossen (Leipzig 1886) 280, 323–5 / Otto R. Redlich Jülich-Bergische Kirchenpolitik am Ausgang des Mittelalters und in der Reformationszeit (Bonn 1907–15) passim / 'Freundesbriefe Konrads von Heresbach an Johann von Vlatten' ed Otto R. Redlich Zeitschrift des Bergischen Geschichtsvereins 41 (1905) 160–203 / Heinrich Lichius Die Verfassung des Marienstiftes zu Aachen bis zur französischen Zeit (Aachen 1915) 64, 94–7 ANTON J. GAIL

Werner von VLATTEN d 1573
Born perhaps around 1510, Werner seems to have lived largely in the shadow of his elder brother, Johann von *Vlatten. On 3 June 1527 he matriculated at the University of Louvain. Talented and well-educated, he appears in 1529 at Johann's side at Speyer, where Erasmus' famulus, Felix *Rex, met him and described him to his master as a promising youth (Ep 2130). On 23 April 1534 he was appointed a canon of St Mary's, Aachen, a chapter where Johann held the position of scholaster. When Johann advanced to the provostship in 1541 Werner succeeded him as scholaster. Five years earlier, on 23 October 1536, Werner had likewise been appointed scholaster of St Victor's, Xanten, another chapter where Johann held the provostship from the beginning of that year. Being thus responsible for the educational program of two chapters, Werner was well placed to support the Erasmian concerns and policies of his brother. In 1571 he owned the manor of Hohensand, near Krefeld, which at his death two years later passed into the hands of his nephew Johann, a son of his eldest brother, Reinhard von Vlatten. In 1561 a will by Werner had been submitted for approbation to the archbishop of Cologne: Annalen des Historischen Vereins für den Niederrhein 124 (1934) 129–31.

BIBLIOGRAPHY: Allen Ep 2130 / Matricule de Louvain III-1 777 / Anton Gail 'Johann von Vlatten ... ' Düsseldorfer Jahrbuch 45 (1951) 7, 9, 107 ANTON J. GAIL

Jacob de VOECHT of Antwerp, 1477–1536
Jacob de Voecht (Vocht, Voocht, Voogd, Tutor) was born at Antwerp. On 28 April 1491 he matriculated at Louvain, where he received a MA. On 28 January 1498 he matriculated at Orléans, where he received a licence in canon law in 1499. At Orléans he took in boarders (Ep 137), and Erasmus, having fled an outbreak of the plague at Paris, lodged with him during the last three months of 1500 (Ep 147). Erasmus remained in contact with his host (Epp 152, 157) and in 1519 dedicated a new edition of Cicero's De officiis to him (Ep 1013). From 10 February 1506 to 1536 Voecht was pensionary at Antwerp. He was a friend of Pieter *Gillis, who became town clerk at Antwerp. A mission to London in 1509 put him in contact with Thomas *More, who without doubt met him again at Antwerp in 1515. In 1514 *Margaret of Austria sent Voecht and Jaspar van *Halmale on an embassy to settle economic questions with *Christian II of Denmark. Elisabeth Mertens was Voecht's wife. He died at Antwerp.

BIBLIOGRAPHY: Allen Ep 152 / Matricule de Louvain III-1 72 / Matricule d'Orléans II-1 190–1 / H. de Vocht in BNB XXV 852–6 / de Vocht CTL II 110 / H. de Ridder-Symoens in NBW IV 936–8 MARCEL A. NAUWELAERTS

Thomas VOGLER of Obernai, d 4 March 1532
Thomas Vogler called himself Aucuparius but also used the names Didymus and Myropola. Like several of the Alsatian humanists, he was born in Obernai. He took holy orders and by 1501 was established in Strasbourg with an appointment as almoner to the cathedral

chapter. He also studied law, perhaps in Italy and certainly at Freiburg, where he received a degree in 1511. With the coming of the Reformation, Vogler remained a loyal Catholic. In 1524 he appeared on a list prepared by several burghers who hoped to organize a colloquy between the Protestant reformers and Catholic theologians. The colloquy, however, never took place. In 1525 Vogler is recorded as a canon of St Stephen's. At the end of his life he withdrew from the city and retired to the convent of Stephansfeld, where he died.

As a member of the literary society of Strasbourg, Vogler was honoured by his friends with the title of poet laureate. In June 1510 *Beatus Rhenanus dedicated to him a collection of poems by Baptista *Mantuanus. He was close to Jakob *Wimpfeling and defended him against the attacks of Thomas *Murner. Vogler met Erasmus when he passed through Strasbourg on his way to Basel in 1514. Wimpfeling included him among the members of the literary society of the city who admired and wished to serve Erasmus (Ep 302). Vogler wrote a poem in praise of Erasmus, calling him the son of Apollo, nourished by Minerva. When Erasmus replied to Wimpfeling (Ep 305) he paid tribute to Vogler's ability as a poet and sent a verse which he had 'scribbled' in Vogler's honour (Reedijk poem 96). In addition to writing poetry Vogler was active as an editor. He prepared an edition of Poggio *Bracciolini (Strasbourg: J. Schott for J. Knobloch 1513) dedicated to Sebastian *Brant, and an edition of Terence (Strasbourg: J. Grüninger 1511). He also wrote a preface for Lorenz Fries' edition of Ptolemy's *Geographia* (Strasbourg: J. Grüninger 1522).

BIBLIOGRAPHY: Allen Ep 302 / BRE Ep 17 / NDB I 428 / *Matrikel Freiburg* I-1 200 / Schmidt *Histoire littéraire* II 149–54, 407

MIRIAM U. CHRISMAN & TBD

Raphael VOLATERRANUS *See Raffaele* MAFFEI

Jacob VOLKAERD of Geertruidenberg, d before March 1528

Jacob Volkaerd (Volkert, Volcaerd, Volcardus) of Geertruidenberg, north of Breda, may have received a MA from Louvain in 1519. For some years he tutored the sons of patrician families

at The Hague. In October 1522 he went to Louvain with his student *Viglius Zuichemus, and they boarded together until 1525, when Viglius left Louvain, remaining in contact with his former teacher by correspondence. Volkaerd stayed on, teaching Latin and Greek to young men, among them probably Janus Secundus, who composed an elegy upon his premature death, and possibly Janus' brother Everardus *Nicolai. Volkaerd's *Oratio de usu eloquentiae*, delivered in 1525 before the faculty of arts, was very well received and printed in May 1526 by Michaël *Hillen in Antwerp. He also composed two epitaphs for his close friend Maarten van *Dorp, published in Erasmus' *De recta pronuntiatione* (Basel: H. Froben March 1528). Volkaerd himself is very likely the Jacobus who was a friend of Dorp and was commemorated in another of Erasmus' epitaphs (Reedijk poem 114) published in the same volume.

BIBLIOGRAPHY: Reedijk poem 114 / de Vocht MHL 505–6 / de Vocht CTL II 145–6 / de Vocht *Literae ad Craneveldium* Ep 189 and passim

IG

Paul VOLZ of Offenburg, 1480–6 July 1544

Paul Volz (Voltzius, Volsius) was born in Offenburg, near the Rhine, opposite Strasbourg, and received his early education at the Sélestat grammar school under the humanist Crato Hoffmann. He matriculated in theology at Tübingen in 1496 and then continued his literary pursuits at the Benedictine cloister of Schuttern, near Offenburg, after 1503. In 1512, as part of the Bursfeld monastic reform, he was appointed abbot of Honcourt (Hugshofen) near Sélestat. He was an active member of the Sélestat literary society, appreciated for his learning as well as for his spiritual sensitivity. *Beatus Rhenanus paid him homage by dedicating a collection of his writings to him in 1516 (BRE Ep 61). Erasmus followed in 1518 with the *Froben edition of the *Enchiridion*. The latter dedication was in the form of a long letter in which Erasmus pointed out to Volz the need to return to Christ as a model for life, particularly for ordinary Christians (Ep 858). Erasmus later noted that the dedication had increased the opposition of the Dominicans, thus making the *Enchiridion* more popular (Allen I 20).

The friendship between Erasmus and Volz

went back to at least 1515. On 30 October 1515 Volz wrote to Erasmus complimenting him on his letter to *Dorp (Ep 337), which he had been enjoying at the dinner table with Jakob *Wimpfeling and Johannes *Sapidus (Ep 368). A month later Volz asked Erasmus for help in interpreting a passage of Ezekiel (Ep 372). In February 1516 Erasmus, responding to a poem of praise from Sapidus, attempted to moderate some of the latter's flattery by noting that Sélestat had its own mentor of learning in Paul Volz: 'What a clear mind, what a frank, open nature, what simple wisdom, what a passion for study, and with all these gifts absolutely no opinion of himself!' (Ep 391A; Allen Ep 364). Erasmus maintained this opinion of his friend until his own death, despite the fact that Volz abandoned the Roman church for the Reformation. Few of Erasmus' friendships survived the change in religion.

Attracted to the reformers before 1521, Volz converted in gradual steps, first preaching in the evangelical style and later reading from Martin *Luther to the monks in his care. During the peasants' war he was forced to leave the cloister, and much of his scholarly work, which consisted mainly of antiquarian observations, was destroyed. He first took refuge in Sélestat, but by 1526, the year of his formal conversion, he was in Strasbourg. In 1530 he was assigned as preacher and chaplain to the nuns in the cloister of St Nicolaus in undis, where he built up a popular following. He was, however, independent of mind, more conservative than the Strasbourg reformers, but also deeply influenced by the spiritualism of Kaspar Schwenckfeld. Because of his persistent refusal to sign the Wittenberg Concord, he was removed from his pulpit on 13 January 1537. He was won back to communion with the Strasbourg reformers by Jean Calvin and read a full recantation of his previous views on communion before the assembled congregation of Jung St. Peter in July 1539. He was again installed at St. Nicolaus in undis and later permitted to preach in the cathedral.

The friendship between Erasmus and Volz was carefully nurtured by both of them. In 1524 Volz responded in shock to a false rumour of Erasmus' death (Epp 1518, 1525). Throughout the period of religious unrest they kept each other informed (Epp 1529, 1607). In 1532 Erasmus inquired of Caspar *Hedio what work Volz was engaged in, for there was no man who could compare with him in morals or in sanctity (Ep 2616). In 1536 Erasmus sent Volz a handsome gold cup in token of their long friendship (Ep 3114, BRE Ep 296) and in final recognition of his esteem Erasmus bequeathed Volz one hundred pieces of gold (Allen XI 364, BRE Ep 298). Volz responded to the cup and to Erasmus' death with two sincere, if laboured, poems (reprinted among the preliminary pieces in LB I). When Volz died Martin *Bucer preached the funeral eulogy.

BIBLIOGRAPHY: Allen Ep 368 / ADB XL 284–5 / Paul Adam L'Humanisme à Sélestat: L'école, les humanistes, la bibliothèque 2nd ed (Sélestat 1967) 25, 28, 56 / Marie-Joseph Bopp Die evangelischen Geistlichen und Theologen in Elsass und Lothringen von der Reformation bis zur Gegenwart (Neustadt a. d. Aisch 1959) / BRE Ep 61 and passim
MIRIAM U. CHRISMAN

Jacob VOOGD *See Jacob de* VOECHT

Hendrik VOS d 1 July 1523
Three Augustinian friars of the convent of Antwerp were condemned for heresy in 1523. Two of them, Hendrik Vos and Jan van den *Esschen, were burnt in the market place of Brussels, while the third, *Lambert of Torn, was imprisoned. Erasmus referred to these events in a letter to Huldrych *Zwingli (Ep 1384).

BIBLIOGRAPHY: Allen Ep 1384 / de Vocht Literae ad Craneveldium Ep 66
MARCEL A. NAUWELAERTS

Laurentius VOTICIUS documented 1520–65(?)
When the Czech Brethren sent Mikuláš *Klaudyán to visit Erasmus in the summer of 1520, he was accompanied by a second emissary (Ep 1183) whose name is given by Jan Blahoslav and Joachim *Camerarius as Laurentius Voticius. Unlike Klaudyán, this second visitor to Antwerp has not been identified. The Czech form of his name would have to be Vavřinec Votík. F.M. Bartoš suggested Vavřinec of Písek or Vavřinec of Žatec (Saaz), who graduated BA from the University of Prague in

1504 and 1509 respectively, or perhaps a member of the noble Votický family residing at Votice. In Blahoslav's account Voticius is described as a BA, while Camerarius added that he died in 1565 having reached old age.

BIBLIOGRAPHY: Allen Ep 1117 introduction / CWE Ep 1039 introduction / Jan Blahoslav 'Summa quaedam brevissima collecta ex variis scriptis Fratrum ... ' (1556) ed Jaroslav Goll in his *Quellen und Untersuchungen zur Geschichte der Böhmischen Brüder* (Prague 1878–82) I 124–5 / Joachim Camerarius *Historica narratio de Fratrum orthodoxorum ecclesiis in Bohemia, Moravia et Polonia* ed L. Camerarius (Heidelberg 1605) 124–6 / F.M. Bartoš 'Erasmus und die böhmische Reformation' *Communio viatorum* 1 (1958) 116–23, 246–57, esp 255
J.K. ZEMAN

Jan VRANCX documented 1523

Jan Vrancx (Van der Voirst), physician to *Margaret of Austria, was married to Maria Sucket (d 2 March 1551), daughter of Jan (I) *Sucket. He is mentioned by Pieter *Wichmans on 22 March 1523 as the son-in-law of Sucket and a friend of Erasmus (Ep 1351), and probably also by Joost *Vroye on 27 March 1523 (Ep 1355). On the death of Jan (I) Sucket late in 1522 Vrancx and his wife obtained a legal document absolving them from liabilities incurred by him. However, this did not prevent Antoon (I) *Sucket, Jan's brother from bringing a suit against them.

BIBLIOGRAPHY: G. van Doorslaer *Aperçu historique sur la médecine et les médecins à Malines avant le XIXe siècle* (Mechelen 1900) 79 / de Vocht *Literae ad Craneveldium* 536
MARCEL A. NAUWELAERTS

Arkleb VRANOVSKÝ *See Arkleb of* BOSKOVICE

Pieter de VRIENDT of Tholen, d 29 December 1556

Pieter de Vriendt (Amicus) of Tholen, in Zeeland, probably studied in Paris. Earning his livelihood as a tutor, he taught the sons of Gilles de *Busleyden (Ep 1173) and later those of Pieter van *Griboval (Ep 2716). On 13 February 1515 he matriculated at Louvain. In 1520 Erasmus recommended him for his knowledge of Latin, Greek, and law to Frans van

*Cranvelt (Ep 1173), who in turn recommended him to Louis *Guillard, bishop of Tournai. Soon thereafter de Vriendt was appointed to teach at the school of the Tournai chapter. In 1521 Erasmus wrote to him in an effort to silence a critic in Guillard's entourage; although the bishop replied in person, Erasmus found that he had little ground for satisfaction (Ep 1212). In the same year de Vriendt published his *Institutionis grammaticae ... libelli duo* (Antwerp: G. Vorsterman 22 June 1521, NK 116). Later he returned to Louvain, studied law, and obtained a doctorate on 13 September 1530. He lectured on feudal law in 1532 and succeeded Joost *Vroye as professor of civil law after the latter's death on 10 February 1533. De Vriendt, who held various offices at the university, was *dictator universitatis*, or writer of official letters, in 1533 and university notary in 1541. He died in Louvain.

BIBLIOGRAPHY: Allen Ep 1173 / NNBW V 1077–8 / de Vocht CTL II 126–7 / de Vocht *Busleyden* 19 / de Vocht *Danticus* 359 / *Matricule de Louvain* III-1 503
IG

Antoon VRIJE *See Antonius* GANG

Joost VROYE of Gavere, d 10 February 1533

Joost (Jodocus) Vroye (Vroeye, Gaverius, Laetus) matriculated at Louvain on 28 February 1499 and obtained the second place in the MA examination in 1505. While teaching, first languages, then logic and physics, he studied law and assisted Jan de *Neve, regent at the College of the Lily, whose health was poor at that time. Vroye was especially interested in the study of Greek lexigraphy and the syntax of Homer, which he taught in lectures that were greatly appreciated by his students. From 1509 Vroye, a priest, was a member of the academic senate. He obtained a doctorate of both laws on 22 May 1520 but continued his lectures until the end of April 1521; subsequently he was appointed president of the college of St Yves on 6 May 1521. On 16 November 1524 he was named to a chair of civil law and on 16 October 1526 he was also appointed extraordinary professor of canon law and canon of St Peter's. He was elected rector for the summer terms of 1521 and 1529, and on 28 February 1526 he succeeded his late friend Jean *Desmarez in the office of *dictator universitatis*, that is, writer of official letters. Vroye had already been in poor health in 1523 (Ep 1355); he resigned from teaching in 1532 and died a few months later.

Erasmus esteemed Vroye as a scholar and as a friend (Ep 717; colloquy *Epithalamium* to Pieter *Gillis, ASD I-3 416). Of their correspondence only two letters survive. Ep 1347 was an elaborate composition by Erasmus on the death of Jan de Neve, published in the *Exomologesis* (Basel: J. Froben 1524) and mentioned by Erasmus in his catalogue of works as 'De morte subita' (Allen I 40). In Ep 1355 Vroye responded to a request of Erasmus that he help recover several books and pieces of furniture kept for him by de Neve. In Ep 1668 Jan *Oem van Wijngaarden mentioned Vroye as one of his references.

BIBLIOGRAPHY: Allen Ep 717 / *Matricule de Louvain* III-1 183 / de Vocht CTL I 222–6, II 88 and passim   IG

Georgius VUICELIUS *See Georg* WITZEL

Petrus VULCANIUS of Bruges, c 1503–71
Vulcanius (de Smet) was born at Bruges, where he attended the school for the poor, the Bogaerdenschool. He registered as a 'pauper' in Louvain on 22 June 1523. Vulcanius studied Greek and Latin at the Collegium Trilingue under Rutgerus *Rescius and Conradus *Goclenius. Although it is not known when he became acquainted with Erasmus, in July 1533 Pierre *Barbier referred to him in a letter to Erasmus as 'antiquus tuus discipulus' (Ep 2842). Perhaps through the intercession of Erasmus, Vulcanius became preceptor to Charles *Blount, the son of William *Blount, Lord Mountjoy. He was in London at least during the period 1529–31.

A letter from Erasmus to Lord Mountjoy testifies to Erasmus' intention to write both to Charles Blount and to Vulcanius, if his health would allow it (Ep 2295). In March 1531 Erasmus praised Charles highly for his fine style (Ep 2459); this, however, was due rather to the qualities of his preceptor, as Erasmus found out after Vulcanius' departure (Ep 2794). Stressing Vulcanius' skill in languages, Erasmus recommended Simon *Grynaeus, who was travelling to England, to him (Ep

2460, 18 March 1531). But on 1 September of the same year Vulcanius was appointed a scribe or clerk in the government of his native town ('taelman en clerc van de vierschaere'), not at all the same office as pensionary, as suggested by Erasmus in his congratulatory letter of 20 April 1533 (Ep 2794). In the same letter Erasmus offered to write an epithalamium for Vulcanius' marriage which he contracted in this period with Adrianette Tuwaert. In 1543 Vulcanius travelled from Bruges through Germany to Italy. In October 1549 he moved to Louvain, but on 1 February 1550 he was appointed pensionary at Middelburg in Zeeland, in 1557 *patronus causarum*, or advocate, in the grand council of Mechelen, and in 1562 attorney-general (see Brussels, Bibliothèque Royale MS II 708/2). In 1562 Vulcanius bought a house and settled in Mechelen, where he died. His son, Bonaventura (b 1538), also called Vulcanius, became a distinguished scholar, teaching at Leiden for more than thirty years (1581–1614).

BIBLIOGRAPHY: Allen Ep 2460 / A. Dewitte in NBW VII 899–900 / Bruges, Stadsarchief 'Registers der Vierschaere, Register De Smet, 1531–1552' 2 vols / *Matricule de Louvain* III-1 700 / de Vocht *Literae ad Craneveldium* 614–15 / de Vocht CTL II 182–4 / H. de Vries de Heekelingen *Correspondance de Bonaventure Vulcanius pendant son séjour à Cologne, Genève et Bâle (1573–1577)* (The Hague 1923) 5, 28–31 / A. Dewitte 'Peter en Bonaventura de Smet, alias Vulcanius (1503–1571)' *Handelingen van het Genootschap voor Geschiedenis 'Société d'Emulation' te Brugge* 115 (1978) 17–42   GILBERT TOURNOY

Jan VULLINCK of Louvain, d 1530
Jan Vullinck (Vullinx alias de Winkele) matriculated at the University of Louvain on 28 February 1478. He was appointed secretary ('*scriba*') of the university on 2 August 1494 and was notary of the rector's court from 1496 and also of the conservator's court from 8 September 1503. At the same time Vullinck was the master of the school attached to the chapter of St Peter's and kept students as boarders in his house (Ep 1668). On 22 June 1500 he registered his son, who was perhaps too young to act independently, at the university. In 1524 he and his fellow-notary protested against the university's efforts to tax the notaries affiliated

to it. In March 1530 he resigned from his office and died later that year.

BIBLIOGRAPHY: Allen Ep 1668 / *Matricule de Louvain* II-1 372, III-1 201 / de Vocht CTL I 8, 368, and passim / de Vocht *Literae ad Craneveldium* Ep 111 / Henri de Jongh *L'Ancienne Faculté de théologie de Louvain* (Louvain 1911) 17* and passim   IG & PGB

Arnold VYNCK of Louvain, 1457–c 1537
In July 1517 Nicolas *Barbier informed Erasmus that part of his unpaid court pension was to be remitted through the receiver-general of Louvain ('receptor Lovaniensis'; Ep 613). A few weeks later Erasmus wrote to Pierre *Barbier that he had received the money from Adriaan, the treasurer ('Adrianus questor'; Ep 652). The first reference is probably to Arnold Vynck (Aert or Arnt Vinck), who from 1517 to 1519 was paymaster (*paymeester* or *rentmeester*) of the city of Louvain. Since the names of Arnold and Adriaan are quite similar and no Adriaan can be traced anywhere in the surviving records of the financial offices of either the city or the *béguinage*, the second reference may also be to Vynck. It should be born in mind, however, that there were other administrators of finance serving the university and other religious institutions, and for these no records survive for the period in question.

A member of a prosperous family, Arnold Vynck was thought of highly at the ducal court and at the end of the fifteenth century had been entrusted with the task of restoring order to the city's treasury.

BIBLIOGRAPHY: R. van Uytven *Stadsfinanciën en stadsekonomie te Leuven van de xiie tot het einde der xvie eeuw* (Brussels 1961) 12–13, 39–43 / M. Bourguignon *Inventaire des archives de l'assistance publique de la ville de Louvain* (Tongeren 1933) 151, 245, 349, 411, 434, 558, and passim / Louvain, Stadsarchief, MSS 55: 'Dienstboeck' (listing the holders of municipal offices) and 5140–1: 'Grote rekeningen' 1516–17 and 1517–18   LEO VAN BUYTEN

Willem de WAELE of Ieper, d 2 September 1540
Willem de Waele (Wale, Vala, Vuala, Vualus) was born in Ieper by 1479, the son of Pieter de Waele and Paulina van Axpoele. On 28 February 1495 he matriculated at the Universi-

ty of Louvain and later went on a pilgrimage to the Holy Land, becoming a knight of the Holy Sepulchre. He was lord of Hansebeke and Axpoele and resided at Ghent, where he was elected to the city council in 1515. In 1518 he was keeper of the archives of Flanders and on 4 June 1532 was appointed to the council of Flanders. His marriage to Gertrudis du Bosch remained childless. He belonged to the circle of Erasmus' friends in Ghent, where Erasmus first met him in 1514 (Ep 301). No exchange of letters seems to have taken place, but until 1533 Erasmus repeatedly sent his greetings and compliments to de Waele (Epp 1191, 1966, 2093, 2700, 2799), especially in his letters to Karel *Uutenhove, who in 1532 married de Waele's niece. Willem de Waele also was a patron of Uutenhove's friend Karel *Sucket.

BIBLIOGRAPHY: Allen Ep 301 / *Matricule de Louvain* III-1 117 / de Vocht CTL II 190, 469, IV 524, and passim / de Vocht *Danticus* 94–5 and passim / M.A. Nauwelaerts 'Erasme et Gand' in *Commémoration nationale d'Erasme: Actes* (Brussels 1970) 170–1 / P. van Peteghem 'Centralisatie onder Keizer Karel (1515–1555)' (thesis, Rijksuniversiteit Gent, 1980)
                                               MARCEL A. NAUWELAERTS

Pieter van WAELEM of Brussels, d 21 March 1567
Pieter van Waelem (Waelham, a Walem) was the son of another Pieter, who was master of the exchequer, and of Katrien Droogenbroodt. On 31 August 1498 he matriculated at the University of Louvain as a student of the College of the Falcon and subsequently became a licentiate in law. On 9 September 1528 he was appointed fiscal advocate of the council of Brabant at Brussels, and on 15 January 1531 he was promoted to councillor-in-ordinary. He also became a vice-lieutenant of the feudal court of Brabant. Pieter, who was lord of Machelen-Sint-Gertrudis, had several children by his first wife, Katrien, whose father was Hector van der Noot, a close relative of Jeroen, Adolf, and Joost van der *Noot. After her death he married Margriet van der Beken, and finally Margriet van Bredam.

Conradus *Goclenius referred to Pieter van Waelem as a colleague of Adolf van der Noot in connection with his efforts to secure a prebend of the Antwerp chapter (Ep 3111).

BIBLIOGRAPHY: Allen Ep 3111 / *Matricule de Louvain* III-1 176 / de Vocht CTL III 100 / J. de Azevedo-Coutiño-Bernal *Généalogie de la famille van der Noot* (n p 1771) 35–6 / Arthur Gaillard *Le Conseil de Brabant* (Brussels 1898–1902) III 351, 376 / V. de Ryckman de Betz and F. de Jonghe d'Ardoye *Armorial et biographies des chanceliers et conseillers de Brabant* (Hombeek 1956) II 524–6 / Alphonse Wauters *Histoire des environs de Bruxelles* (Brussels 1851–7) III 182 / Brussels, Archives générales du Royaume, MS Cour féodale de Brabant 134 f 4 recto, 64 recto, 447 recto, 354 f 12 verso / Brussels, Bibliothèque Royale, MS II 763 f 170 verso–171 recto
HILDE DE RIDDER-SYMOENS

Gervasius WAIN of Memmingen, d 14 December 1554

Gervasius Wain (Vaim, Waim, Weim) was born around 1491 at Memmingen, in Swabia, of a family with some claim to nobility. He came to Paris around 1505 and probably studied arts under Ludwig *Baer at the Collège de Sainte-Barbe, receiving his BA in 1507 and MA in 1508. An exchange of letters with Bruno *Amerbach in 1508 indicates a familiarity between them (AK I Ep 397). In 1511 Wain went from Paris to Freiburg to study under Johann Maier of *Eck (who dedicated his book against *Karlstadt in 1519 to Wain), but he was back in Paris by 1513, at which time he was a *hospes* of the Collège de Sorbonne and proctor of the German-English nation (the first of many offices he exercised for the nation). In 1516 he was a *socius* of the Sorbonne, where he was also prior in 1521. He was rector of the university in 1518. While still a bachelor in theology, Wain was involved in a heated academic quarrel with his colleague Juan de Celaya over Celaya's interpretation of Aristotle's *Posterior Analytics*, and Wain's *Tractatus noticiarum* (dedicated to Ludwig Baer) gave him the upper hand. He received his licence in theology on 24 March 1522, ranking fourth of thirty-six, and his doctorate on 12 June 1522. The faculty of theology expressed difficulty in reconciling Wain's claims to status as a regent doctor with his frequent absences. Wain continued to be active in the affairs of his nation and of the Collège de Sorbonne until about 1533.

Wain may well be the Gervasius whom

Maarten van *Dorp associated in August 1519 with *Beatus Rhenanus, who had been Baer's contemporary at Paris, and also with Baer himself and Wolfgang *Capito, Baer's colleague at Basel (BRE Ep 121). Wain visited Erasmus in the spring of 1527 (Ep 1827). Erasmus, who knew him already (Epp 1581, 1609), recommended him later to Cardinal Jean de *Lorraine (Ep 1911). Correspondence between them seems to have continued intermittently (Epp 1884, 1922, 2027, 2311), as Wain stood out among Erasmus' contacts in Paris as a source of succinct and accurate information.

In the mean time Wain entered the service of King *Francis I, notably in collaboration with Guillaume Du Bellay. Wain was active in Paris in promoting approval on behalf of Francis I of *Henry VIII's annulment proceedings, and a letter of Wain to Bishop Jean *Du Bellay in London was strategic in convincing Henry that Francis I was sincerely committed to obtaining a favourable decision from the faculty of theology in Paris. Wain successfully pleaded the cause at the University of Angers. In 1530 Wain was involved in negotiations with *Charles V for the release of Francis I's sons from Madrid. Between 1531 and 1534 Wain undertook at least seven different diplomatic missions to German princes and was instrumental in urging the creation of the Schmalkaldic League and its subsequent – if ephemeral – alliance with France. In 1534 Wain had to leave Augsburg secretly to escape imperial reprisals against him.

Wain's services were rewarded in 1533 with the Premonstratensian abbey of Cuissy (diocese of Laon) and in 1541 with the Benedictine abbey of Josaphat, near Chartres, where he was buried after his death at the age of sixty-three.

Wain edited with William Manderston and George Lockhart *Quaestiones et decisiones physicales* by Albert of Saxony, Christoph Thimon, Jean Buridan, et al (Paris: Josse Bade for self and Konrad Resch 1516, 1518; Lyon: Jean Moylin for Giacomo Giunta 1534). He also composed *Tractatus noticiarum [et] Quaestiones in libros posteriorum resolutionum philosophi* (Paris: Nicolas Des Prez for Konrad Resch 1519; Pierre Vidoue 1528).

BIBLIOGRAPHY: Allen Ep 1884 / AK I Epp 374, 397 / V.-L. Bourrilly *Guillaume du Bellay,*

seigneur de Langey, 1491–1543 (Paris 1905) 86
and passim / G. Bossert 'Gervasius Wain'
Blätter für württembergische Kirchengeschichte 9
(1894) 53–4 / *Catalogue des actes de François I*
(Paris 1885–1908) passim / Farge no 471 / J.G.
Schellhorn 'Etwas von Gervasius Waim, einem
Doctore Sorbonico' *Ergötzlichkeiten* (Ulm-
Leipzig 1762–4) I 270–94 / *Matrikel Freiburg* I-1
198 / P.G. Bietenholz *Basle and France in the
Sixteenth Century* (Geneva-Toronto 1971) 107
and passim   JAMES K. FARGE

Robert WAKEFIELD d 1537

Wakefield (Feldus, Wachefeldius, Wackasol-
dus, Wakefylde, Wakfeldus, Whafefeld) was
born in the archdiocese of York, perhaps at
Pontefract, and was educated at Cambridge,
taking his BA in 1513–14 and then studying
canon law. He subsequently went to Louvain,
taking his MA there before he incorporated in
Cambridge in 1519. From August to December
1519 he lectured in Hebrew at the Collegium
Trilingue at Louvain. He remained abroad
until 1523, spending some time in Paris; in July
1522 he was back in Louvain and later in that
summer went to Haguenau, where he arranged with Thomas *Anshelm for the printing
of some of his books. This led to the invitation
to succeed Johann *Reuchlin at Tübingen in
August 1522, where he introduced the study of
Arabic and Syriac. His presence there was
mentioned by Erasmus in a letter to John
*Fisher of 1 September 1522 (Ep 1311). Early in
the following year he was appointed by
*Henry VIII to lecture in Hebrew at Cambridge.
His popularity as a teacher of Greek and
Hebrew at Tübingen was such that the
university and Archduke *Ferdinand requested the king and Fisher, as chancellor of
Cambridge University, to allow him to remain
there. Fisher duly granted him two further
years' leave in 1523 and 1524, from which it has
been assumed that he was by this time a fellow
of Fisher's recently founded college, St John's
(he may have held this appointment as early as
1519–20). But he returned to his Cambridge
lectureship in 1523 and was admitted bachelor
of divinity in 1525. In 1529 he was supported
by the crown as a 'reader in Hebrew' and later
gave a lecture at Oxford, possibly in the hall of
King Henry VIII's College (subsequently Christ
Church), of which he became a canon in July

1532, shortly after supplicating for incorporation as a bachelor of divinity. He had been a
chaplain to the king since 1524 and in 1535 was
in similar service to Archbishop Thomas
*Cranmer. Wakefield's only known parochial
appointment was a curacy in St Albans,
Hertfordshire, held in 1535.

Wakefield's erudition in Hebrew and the
other ancient tongues was widely celebrated at
home and abroad. Among his pupils were
Reginald *Pole, whom he taught at the king's
request (Ep 1595), Richard *Pace (Ep 2287),
John Oliver, a leading civil lawyer, and
possibly Paschasius *Berselius (Ep 674). He
did, however, have his critics: he was accused
of removing books of interest to himself from
the library of Ramsey Abbey, and Erasmus
found him unfriendly (Ep 2287). His greatest
patrons were Fisher and Sir Thomas *Boleyn.
He was consulted by the king on the matter of
the divorce in 1527 and was at first a supporter
of *Catherine of Aragon. Later (though not, as
has been suggested, at *Cromwell's instigation) he changed his view and wrote a defence
of the king's cause, alleging the royal marriage
to be against divine as well as natural law. This
brought him into controversy with his former
patron Fisher. By his will dated 8 October 1537
he left his goods to his younger brother,
Thomas, also a Hebrew scholar, who became
regius professor at Cambridge in 1540. Robert
Wakefield's works include: *Oratio de laudibus
trium linguarum* (London: W. de Worde 1524,
STC 24944) notable as the first work printed in
England using Arabic and Hebrew type; *Syntagma de Hebreorum codicum incorruptione*
(London: W. de Worde c 1530, STC 24946), his
Oxford inaugural lecture; *Koster codicis*
(London: T. Berthelet c 1532, STC 24943) in
defence of the king; and *Paraphrasis in librum
Koheleth* (London: T. Gibson c 1536, STC 24945).

BIBLIOGRAPHY: Allen Ep 1311 / Emden BRUO
1501–1540 599–600 / McConica 66, 122–3, 127,
133–4 / G.R. Elton *Reform and Renewal*
(Cambridge 1973) 7, 61 / F.D. Logan 'The
origins of the so-called regius professorships:
an aspect of the renaissance at Oxford and
Cambridge' in *Renaissance and Renewal in
Christian History* ed D. Baker (Oxford 1977)
271–8 / de Vocht CTL I 379–86, 447, and passim,
II 357–8, and passim / Wakefield's will, proved
on 13 May 1538, is in London, Public Record

Franz von Waldeck

Office, MS PROB 11/27, ff 127 verso–128 (PCC 16 Dyngeley)
C.S. KNIGHTON

Marmaduke WALDBY documented 1505–40
Marmaduke Waldby studied at Cambridge, where he graduated BA in 1505. After proceeding MA he pursued a career in the church, becoming rector of Somerby by Brigg, Lincolnshire, a preferment exchanged in 1513 for the rectory of Trottiscliffe, Kent. In 1519 Waldby was admitted vicar of Sittingbourne and in 1520 of Brenchley, both in Kent. Quite possibly Waldby joined Reginald *Pole when the latter departed for Italy in February 1521. In any case in 1524 he is to be found in Pole's household, where he probably remained until the latter's return to England in 1527, for Waldby's next church preferment took place on 3 March of that year when he was admitted rector of Vange, Essex. Shortly afterwards Waldby is found as chaplain to Cardinal *Wolsey and the holder of a doctorate in theology, apparently acquired during his stay in Italy. In 1528 Waldby was again in Italy, while in 1534 and 1535 he rose still higher on the church ladder. He was installed as a canon of Ripon and prebendary of

Givandale and Skelton, becoming vicar of Thornton in Lonsdale and rector of Kirk Deighton, both in Yorkshire, the following year. Residing in the north, Waldby subsequently played a minor role in the Northern Rebellion. Owing to his many contacts with prominent men on the continent, the suggestion was made that Waldby be dispatched to the continent in 1537 in order to enlist the support of the Emperor *Charles v for the rebellion, but the suggestion was not acted upon (LP XII-1 1080, XII-2 292 (iii)). After the failure of the rebellion Waldby was imprisoned in the Tower for four months (LP XII-2 181) and probably forfeited all his preferments. In 1540 he was still alive (LP XV 382).

It is unknown whether Waldby and Erasmus ever met, although such a meeting might have taken place in Cambridge in 1505 or 1506. In a letter of 8 March 1526 (Ep 1675) Erasmus asked Reginald Pole to convey his greetings to Waldby.

BIBLIOGRAPHY: Allen Ep 1675 / Emden BRUC 610 / LP IV 3820, 3835, 4756, X 711, XI 60, XII-1 786, 789, 1021, 1079–81, 1130, XII-2 268 / Pietro Bembo *Epistolae* (Venice 1552) 596
MORDECHAI FEINGOLD

Franz von WALDECK 1491–15 July 1553
Franz was the third son of Philip II, count of Waldeck, south-west of Kassel, and Countess Katharina von Solms. In preparation for an ecclesiastical career he was sent to the University of Erfurt in 1506 and continued his studies from the summer term of 1510 at Leipzig. When he matriculated at the University of Leipzig he was already a canon of the cathedral chapter of Cologne. From 1521 he also held canonries at Mainz, Trier, and Paderborn. In 1530 he was elected bishop of Minden against the opposition of Henry the younger, count of Brunswick-Wolfenbüttel, who claimed the see for his son Philip, aged three. Franz von Waldeck's election was greatly helped by the support of John III, duke of *Cleves, who acted to protect his county of Ravensberg against the encroachment of the Brunswick dynasty. On 14 May 1532 Eric of Brunswick-Grubenhagen, recently elected bishop of Münster, died suddenly in the middle of a banquet, and on 1 June the cathedral chapter elected Franz von Waldeck to be his successor. By another lucky turn of events he was appointed bishop of

Osnabrück just a few days later, on 11 June (Ep 2687), and by papal dispensation of 16 August 1532 he was authorized to hold the three sees simultaneously.

Franz's elevation to the sees of both Münster and Osnabrück was largely due to the support of Landgrave Philip of *Hesse, who maintained personal relations with the counts of Waldeck and wished to enhance the safety of his northern frontier. In 1524 Franz's brother had introduced religious reform into the county of Waldeck, and Philip of Hesse knew Franz himself to be sympathetic to the Protestant cause. His tenure of the three ecclesiastical principalities of Westphalia did not, however, as one might have assumed, make Franz von Waldeck the most powerful lord in northern Germany. In order to secure his election by the canons of Münster he had been obliged to accept terms that left all political decisions in the hands of the chapter; in particular he was made to pledge a firm stand against the Reformation. These restrictions did not, however, prevent him from concluding a defensive alliance with the landgrave, which was signed at Kassel on 29 October 1532. In the event of any attack Franz was guaranteed the support of four hundred Hessian horsemen. In other ways too the landgrave was eager to assist his neighbour. His mediators brought about the treaty of Dülmen (14 February 1533), which settled outstanding conflicts between Franz and the city of Münster. The bishop retained his authority over the cathedral as well as some monasteries and chapels, while turning over to the Protestants all six parish churches. In the wake of this treaty Franz was finally able to hold his solemn entry into the city of Münster. The tensions, however, continued and were bound to increase progressively with the growing domination of Münster by the Anabaptist faction. Quite properly the bishop maintained that by favouring the Anabaptists the council itself had brought the subsequent disaster upon the city. By contrast, Konrad *Heresbach (Ep 3031A) blamed the bishop's intransigence for forcing the city to make common cause with the Anabaptists. By any count, the war which Franz begun on 3 March 1534 turned out to be a tragedy for both sides (Epp 3031, 3031A, 3041).

Franz von Waldeck was judged favourably by his former fellow-student, Ludolf *Cock,

who wanted Erasmus to write to the bishop (Ep 2687), and also by *Viglius Zuichemus, who was appointed his official (Epp 2957, 3060). He also found favour with the chronicler Dietrich Lilje, a monk of Iburg, and with the Lutheran minister Antonius *Corvinus of Warburg, who met him in the course of diplomatic negotiations. Generally historians have not judged him unfavourably, although Joseph Lortz calls him 'miserable' ('armselig'), censuring him for his political indecision and his concubinage. With regard to the latter, Franz was a child of his times. His political goals were reasonable and moderate, although it is true that by accepting the terms of his appointment to the see of Münster he had completely forfeited his freedom of action. He was bound to end in failure, a mere tool in the hands of others, and was denied the honourable exit that remained open to his superior, Hermann von *Wied, archbishop of Cologne.

BIBLIOGRAPHY: Allen Ep 2687 / ADB VII 290–2 / Eubel III 247 and passim / *Die niederdeutsche Bischofschronik* ed F. Runge (Osnabrück 1894) / *Die Schriften der Münsterischen Täufer und ihrer Gegner* ed R. Stupperich (Münster 1970) / Victor Schultze *Die Geschichte der Reformation in Waldeck* (Leipzig 1903) / Franz Fischer *Die Reformationsversuche des Bischofs Franz von Waldeck* (Hildesheim 1907) / H. Hoyer 'Untersuchungen über die Reformationsgeschichte des Fürstentums Osnabrück unter Erich II und Franz von Waldeck' *Zeitschrift für niedersächsische Kirchengeschichte* 32–3 (1927–8) 76–200 / F. Brune *Der Kampf um die evangelische Kirche im Münsterlande 1520–1802* (Witten 1962) / W.F. Dankbaar 'De reformatiepoging van bisschop Frans van Waldeck' *Nederlandse archief voor Kerkgeschiedenis* 47 (1965–6) 137–65 / K.H. Kirchhoff 'Die Belagerung und Eroberung Münsters 1534/35' *Westfälische Zeitschrift* 112 (1962) 77–170 / K.H. Kirchhoff 'Die Täufer im Münsterland: Verbreitung und Verfolgung des Täufertums im Stift Münster 1533–1550' *Westfälische Zeitschrift* 113 (1963) 1–110

ROBERT STUPPERICH

Humphrey WALKDEN d 1525–6

Humphrey Walkden (Walkenden) graduated BA in 1504 and proceeded MA in 1507 from Queen's College, Cambridge. That year also marked his election to a fellowship at Queen's, which he probably held until 1523. Subsequently Walkden served as a junior bursar in 1509–10, a mathematical lecturer – with his friend Henry *Bullock – from 1512 to 1514, and a university preacher in 1514. A priest from 1505, Walkden became a bachelor of divinity in 1517 and a doctor in 1520. Although Erasmus seems to have been quite fond of Walkden (Ep 456), no correspondence between them is known to exist except Ep 276 from Erasmus, requesting Walkden to translate a letter to Robert *Smith into English. Subsequently Erasmus conveyed greetings to Walkden via Bullock and Robert *Aldridge (Epp 456, 777, 826, 1656), but late in 1526 he was informed by the latter that Walkden had died (Ep 1766).

BIBLIOGRAPHY: Allen Epp 276, 1656 / CWE Ep 457 / Emden BRUC 611 / John and J.A. Venn *Alumni Cantabrigienses* (Cambridge 1922–54, repr 1974) I-4 315   MORDECHAI FEINGOLD

Lukas WALTERS of Chojnice, d 4 September 1515

Lukas Walters (Walteri, Vualterus Conitiensis) was born in Chojnice (Konitz), ninety kilometres south-west of Gdansk. On 2 December 1475 he registered at the University of Louvain as a 'poor' student in arts. In a colophon of 12 February 1495 he is mentioned as one of the correctors of Jacques *Lefèvre d'Etaples' edition of Johannes de Sacrobosco's *Sphera* (Paris: W. Hopyl). In 1497 he received a bachelor's degree in theology in Louvain and joined the university council on 2 October. He was appointed professor and canon of St Peter's in 1499 and from 1503 lectured on John Duns Scotus. On 6 July 1512 he obtained a doctorate of theology; he also became president of the College of the Holy Ghost. In February 1513 he was elected rector. For six years he had also taught theology at the Franciscan convent in Louvain. In his will dated 21 November 1514 he bequeathed books and sums of money to friends, students, and St Martin's, Louvain.

Erasmus apparently came to know Walters well while visiting Louvain from 1502 to 1504 but recalled him solely because Walters had accused Erasmus of plagiarizing Polidoro *Virgilio when composing his *Adagia* (Epp 531, 1175).

BIBLIOGRAPHY: Allen and CWE Ep 531 / *Matricule de Louvain* II-1 337 / de Vocht MHL 152–3 / de Vocht *Busleyden* 460 / Rice *Prefatory Epistles* Ep 8   IG & PGB

Hieronymus WALTHER of Leipzig, documented 1508–37

Hieronymus Walther (Walter, Valtherus) was probably descended from a Nürnberg family. At Nürnberg he went to school with Willibald *Pirckheimer. From 1508 he was at Leipzig as agent for the Welser firm of Augsburg. He acquired the citizenship of Leipzig and was a member of the city council from 1514 to 1536. In 1523 he built the Barthelshof (Markt 8), where he henceforward resided. He was a friend of Hieronymus *Emser (d 1527), for whom he erected a funeral monument in the church of Our Lady. He was also a close friend of Jan *Horák and Johannes *Cochlaeus, who in 1528 dedicated to him his German translation, *Funff Vorredde* ([Dresden]: W. Stöckel) derived from John *Fisher's *De veritate corporis et sanguinis Christi in eucharistia*, directed against Johannes *Oecolampadius. A convinced Catholic, Walther enjoyed the favour of Duke George of *Saxony until 1537, when he was accused of fraudulent business transactions and sentenced to a jail term as well as a fine. Hieronymus Walther apparently had a son of the same name, who probably matriculated at the University of Leipzig in 1514 (*Matrikel Leipzig* I 534; cf 632) and later seems to have succeeded his father, so that in later years some references may concern either the elder Hieronymus or the younger.

The elder Hieronymus arranged in 1530 for the forwarding of mail from Leipzig to Erasmus in Freiburg (Epp 2247, 2338).

BIBLIOGRAPHY: Allen Ep 2247 / ADB XLI 93 / Otto Clemen 'Beiträge zur sächsischen Reformationsgeschichte' ARG 3 (1906) 172–90, esp 184–8 / Rudolf Kötzschke and Hellmut Kretzschmar *Sächsische Geschichte* (Frankfurt am Main 1965) 170, 452 / Martin Spahn *Johannes Cochläus* (Berlin 1898, repr 1964) 103, 138–9 / Götz von Pölnitz *Anton Fugger* (Tübingen 1958–   ) I 379, 393, 463, 595, IV 700 / BA *Oekolampads* II 116–19 / Pflug *Correspondance* II Ep 355 and passim   MICHAEL ERBE & PGB

Johann WANNER of Kaufbeuren, d 1527/8

Johann Wanner (Vannius) came from an old family of Kaufbeuren, in Swabia, and matriculated at Erfurt for the summer term of 1506. In 1510 he was promoted MA together with Erasmus' admirers Justus *Jonas and Kaspar *Schalbe. He spent some time in Mindelheim, in Swabia, as a parish priest. In December 1521 the chapter of Constance appointed him preacher at the cathedral, an appointment that the humanists around Johann von *Botzheim had been pressing for. He joined their circle and took his oath of office on 1 March 1522, promising to give no support to the Lutheran faction. At first he was discreet about his interest in the ideas of *Zwingli and *Luther. Bishop Hugo von *Hohenlandenberg even appointed him as a member of the delegation sent to Zürich in April 1522 in an effort to restore the rules on fasting. In the winter of 1522–3, however, conservative opposition to Wanner was rising despite his efforts to show restraint in his preaching (Ep 1335), and he needed the support of populace and council to continue his mission from the pulpit (Epp 1382, 1401). On 16 January 1524 the bishop finally dismissed him on the orders of Archduke *Ferdinand. However, private citizens at first and later the city council provided a salary that permitted him to preach at St Stephen's. In March 1525 he married Agatha Mangolt, a former nun who had been the mistress of Paul *Ziegler, administrator of Chur. In January 1526 Wanner was preaching in Memmingen, while Johann *Zwick continued his work at St Stephen's. Wanner returned once more to Constance, but from January 1527 was back in Memmingen. He died there between 13 September and February 1528.

Erasmus met Wanner on his visit to Constance in the autumn of 1522. Despite two polite references (Ep 1342; Allen I 46) he expressed his concern over some questions Wanner had relayed to him through Botzheim in November 1522 (Ep 1331).

BIBLIOGRAPHY: Allen Ep 1335 / Matrikel Erfurt II 244 / F. Zoepfl in LThK x 955 / Rublack Reformation in Konstanz 213–14 and passim / Bernd Moeller Johannes Zwick und die Reformation in Konstanz (Gütersloh 1961) 67 and passim / Hermann Buck and Ekkehart Fabian Konstanzer Reformationsgeschichte in ihren Grundzügen (Tübingen 1965) I 186 and passim / Erich Kleineidam Universitas Studii Erffordensis (Leipzig 1964–80) II 126–7   IG

Richard WARHAM died c October 1545
In January 1522 Juan Luis *Vives stated that he was fond of two students recommended to him by Erasmus, William (II) *Thale and 'Varamus'

(Ep 1256). The latter was probably Richard Warham, although, unlike Thale, Richard did not matriculate at the University of Louvain until 9 October 1524. Perhaps a relative of Erasmus' patron, Archbishop William *Warham, Richard Warham (Waryn) received a bachelor's degree in civil law from Oxford in 1516. As a doctor of civil law of the University of Orléans he supplicated for incorporation at Oxford in 1527, and on 6 April of that year he was ordained by Cuthbert *Tunstall, bishop of London. He was rector of Clapham, Sussex, from 1516 to 1524, rector of Long Marston, Hertfordshire, from 1523 to his death, and a canon of Chichester and prebendary of Sidlesham from 1524 also to his death. He also obtained some other benefices.

BIBLIOGRAPHY: Allen Ep 1256 / Emden BRUO 1501–40 606 / Matricule de Louvain III-1 735 / de Vocht MHL 4 / de Vocht CTL II 404   PGB

William WARHAM c 1456–22 August 1532
Warham (Vuaramus, Waram, Wareham, Warhn), the last archbishop of Canterbury before Thomas *Cranmer and the break with Rome, and the last to combine that office with the chancellorship of England, had a long and conventional career in church and state but was also well disposed towards the new learning; his patronage of Erasmus earned him the permanent esteem of the Dutch scholar. Warham was born at Church Oakley, Hampshire, in about 1456: the exact date is unknown, but Erasmus was clearly not far wrong in believing Warham to be in his eighties by 1530 (Ep 2332). He was admitted scholar of Winchester College in 1469, proceeding in 1473 to New College, Oxford, where he was a fellow from 1475 to 1488. He took the degree of bachelor of canon law by 1484 and his doctorate two years later, incorporating at Cambridge in 1495–6. From 1506 until his death he was chancellor of Oxford University, though his influence was overshadowed for a time by that of Cardinal *Wolsey. On leaving Oxford in 1488 to begin a legal career as advocate in the court of arches in London he was presented to a New College benefice but did not take major orders until 1493. As well as holding several parochial livings he was precentor of Wells Cathedral from 1493 and archdeacon of Huntingdon from 1496. His principal occupation in these years was,

William Warham, by Hans Holbein The Younger

however, in legal and diplomatic service. He was master of the rolls in 1485 and from 1494 to 1502, and in 1490 seems to have visited Rome as proctor for John *Morton, archbishop of Canterbury, and John Alcock, bishop of Ely, in the curia. From 1491 he was frequently employed on commercial and political missions, mainly in the Netherlands. In October 1501 he was elected bishop of London, and in the following year resigned the mastership of the rolls to become keeper of the great seal. In November 1503 Warham was translated to Canterbury and in January of the next year was made lord chancellor.

Warham was not unnaturally one of the principal councillors in the early years of the reign of *Henry VIII; though he deferred to the opinion of Bishop Richard *Foxe of Winchester in some matters, the two episcopal councillors were united in seeking to guide the young king in a policy of peace. As archbishop, Warham is chiefly remembered for conducting a fairly acrimonious dispute with his provincial suffragans over probate jurisdiction and for suffering the humiliation of taking second place to Wolsey during the cardinal's legateship *a latere*

from 1518 to 1529. Warham had resigned the great seal in 1515, anxious to withdraw from a political scene which had become distasteful to him and hoping to concentrate on the administration of the church and the suppression of heresy. Erasmus heard of Warham's resignation from Thomas *More and heartily approved (Epp 388, 414). It is rumoured that he was offered the chancellorship again on Wolsey's fall (Ep 2253). In the last years of his life, though old and ill, he made a firm but ultimately fruitless stand against the progress of the Reformation, in both its political and its spiritual aspects. He is generally believed to have been responsible for the 'saving clause' by which convocation limited its assent to the king's supremacy in May 1531 with the words 'et quantum per Christi legem licet.' And in the following February he registered a bold formal protest at anti-clerical legislation past and contemplated. His longevity, which had so irritated Wolsey, was a major factor in delaying an internal settlement of the king's matrimonial problems. His eventual death in August 1532 opened the way for the appointment of Thomas Cranmer as archbishop of Canterbury and the Erastian settlement of the English church to which Warham was so firmly opposed. A primate in traditional mould, he failed to stem the spread of heresy and towards the end of his life had come to see himself in the role of Becket (cf Ep 1400).

Warham first met Erasmus in 1506, when the humanist was brought to Lambeth by William *Grocyn. Erasmus presented the archbishop with his translation of Euripides' *Hecuba* but was disappointed with the modest reward which Warham – seemingly unaware of the individuality of the gift – had offered. On his return to Paris Erasmus added the *Iphigenia* and dedicated the expanded work to Warham (Epp 188, 208). In May 1509, within a month of the accession of Henry VIII, Warham wrote to Erasmus offering him 150 nobles if he would take up permanent residence in England (Ep 214). Later in the same month William *Blount, Lord Mountjoy, first mentioned the possibility that Warham, said to be enthusiastic about Eramus' work, was to offer him an English benefice (Ep 215). Depite Erasmus' self-effacing assertion to John *Colet that he could accept nothing further from an already over-generous patron (Ep 237; cf Ep 240A), the rumour persisted (Epp 255, 256) and in March 1512 he was presented to the living of Aldington in Kent. He never visited his vicarage and resigned it four months later upon the grant of a pension – an arrangement which Warham did not normally favour, but which on this occasion he felt was justified on the grounds of Erasmus' service to the universal church (Ep 255; Allen I 62). The pension was thereafter a perpetual source of concern and trouble to Erasmus and his banker, Erasmus *Schets – and, no doubt, an irritation to Warham, who was besieged by complaints about the irregular or inadequate transmission of the money (Epp 387, 424, 425, 465, 467, 468, 474, 481, 513, and many others). In April 1512, in thanks for his benefice, Erasmus dedicated to Warham a group of translations from Lucian, 'scholarly trifles' as he called them, and referred to the archbishop as his 'one unrivalled Maecenas,' an epithet he frequently reiterated (though somewhat compromised by ascribing it also to Mountjoy; Epp 261, 293, cf Ep 211).

During these years Erasmus' letters are full of praise for the modesty, wisdom, and generosity of the English archbishop; indeed, Erasmus lost no opportunity to 'drop' the name of his illustrious patron when writing to his fellow scholars (Epp 252, 266, 269 among others). In addition to the Aldington pension Warham often sent Erasmus gifts from his private resources: 20 gold angels in 1512, 10 nobles in 1514 (Epp 240A, 286, 288). In 1514 he told Servatius *Rogerus that his Aldington living, worth 100 nobles, was exchanged for a pension of 100 crowns, and over the past few years he had received 400 nobles from Warham, including a single present of 150 (Ep 296). Warham helped Erasmus in other ways, such as with the loan of a manuscript from his library which Erasmus used in his edition of Seneca's Lucubrationes (Ep 325). In the preface to his New Testament of February 1516 (Ep 384), Erasmus acknowledged Warham as 'the one great patron' of his researches, though it was to *Leo x rather than the English primate that he eventually chose to dedicate the work (Ep 326; cf Ep 421).

At the same time Erasmus debated with his friends whether pope or archbishop should receive the dedication of his Jerome (Epp 333, 334), and on this occasion decided to honour Warham (Epp 396, 421). Writing to the pope in explanation, Erasmus described Warham as the unique patron of himself and all learning in England (Ep 335; cf Ep 384). In June Warham replied to Erasmus' gift of the New Testament volumes and the Jerome dedication; he also promised to attend to the problems with the pension (Ep 425). In the same month, John *Fisher, bishop of Rochester, alluded to Warham's warm approval of Erasmus' New Testament and his determination to do 'great things' for him; but in fact no further formal provision was ever made (Ep 432). Later in the year Erasmus visited England again and reported on the archbishop's continuing interest and benefactions; for once Erasmus declined cash but accepted other gifts including a horse and a gilt cup (Ep 457). In March 1517 Warham explained that he did not wish to interrupt Erasmus' current work by inviting him to England at that time but reassured him that his pension would be sent to him free of interest and commission (Ep 558).

In 1517 Erasmus moved to Louvain, allegedly for reasons of his health, but the move also strengthened his contacts with the court of *Charles v (of whom he was also a pensioner) and suggests that he had given up hope of more permanent patronage from his English friends (Ep 596). He had also become worried that if Warham should die his pension would be stopped; he therefore hoped to have it commuted to a single capital sum. Understandably reluctant to approach Warham directly on so delicate an issue, he sought to use More as a mediator (Ep 702; cf Ep 643). More pointed out that such an arrangement would be interpreted as the abandoning of Erasmus' concern for England and his friends there (Ep 706). Erasmus accepted More's argument (Ep 726), but thereafter his anxiety over the payment of the pension became even more pronounced (Epp 712, 736, 823, 892, 1205).

Erasmus resented the physical barrier presented by the English Channel (Ep 756) but in 1518 was contemplating a further trip to England to take place after he had been to Italy (Epp 781, 893). In the following year he told Cardinal Domenico *Grimani that Warham had asked him to translate Origen's In Psalmos, but there is no other evidence for such a commission (Ep 1017). Warham and Erasmus both attended the meetings of their monarchs in July 1520 (Ep 1102, CWE Ep 1106); perhaps Erasmus was struck by the evidence of his friend's advancing years, for in the following December he again expressed the hope for a more ample financial provision lest Warham's death should leave him pensionless (Ep 1176).

By 1521 Zacharias *Deiotarus of Friesland, formerly Erasmus' pupil, had entered Warham's service, and it was hoped that he would be able to assist in transmitting the pension payments (Ep 1205). Increasingly the menace of Lutheranism and the dangerous state of Europe became subjects of correspondence between Erasmus and Warham (Epp 1205, 1228, 1488, 1831). Between 1524 and 1526 the revised *Froben edition of Erasmus' Jerome appeared, dedicated again to Warham (Epp 1451, 1453, 1465, 1488, 1504). In the years 1525 to 1527 Erasmus frequently complained to Schets of the arrears of his pension and the loss in value which he sustained at the hands of agents and money-changers (Epp 1583, 1590, 1647, 1651, 1658, 1671, 1676). At the same time he was grateful for Warham's defence of his works, particularly his Jerome (Ep 1828).

In September 1527 Erasmus received an invitation from Henry VIII, underwritten by Warham, to go once more to England (Epp 1878, 1922, 1955), but he was reluctant to accept, fearing to be drawn into the now open controversy over the king's marriage (Epp 1926, 1977). Erasmus stayed away, appearing to exercise himself more over his pension (Epp 1999, 2014) than the scandal which was about to split the English church from the Roman see. By this time he had come to distinguish clearly between his pension, to which he felt entitled as of right, and the casual gifts which he received from Warham and other bishops (Ep 2072). When the pension was delayed in 1529 he felt that he must be out of favour with the archbishop (Ep 2159). By 1530 the matter had become almost obsessive – so much so that in March of that year, on reporting to Mountjoy a rumour of Warham's failing health, he expressed concern not for the impending loss of an esteemed patron but for his own probable financial distress (Ep 2295). In June he told

Christoph von *Stadion that Warham, now in his eighties was lame; and he feared the loss of two English pensions (the other has never been identified) worth two hundred florins – although a quarter was lost to the agents (Ep 2332). Warham's health and the consequent worry over the pension continued to occupy Erasmus' mind and pen during 1530 and 1531 (Epp 2370, 2413, 2459, 2487, 2488, 2490). Schets did his best, using various agents and merchants, and was able to report in July 1531 that Warham still lived (Ep 2511). Negotiations continued for another year (Epp 2576, 2620, 2704), but by October 1532 Erasmus had received definite news of the archbishop's death. He wrote to Charles *Blount extolling Warham's virtues and describing him as a 'sacred anchor' (Ep 2726) – a phrase which he repeated to two other correspondents (Epp 2735, 2745). Yet it is somewhat strange that Warham's passing is not mentioned in the many other letters which Erasmus wrote at this time. He was still fussing over his pension in 1533 and was evidently disappointed that Warham had left him nothing (Epp 2761, 2776, 2783). But on hearing the news of Cranmer's appointment he expressed himself confident that the pension would be honoured – a hope which More encouraged (Epp 2791, 2831, 2879). In this they were both right, for although Erasmus had once predicted that after Warham's death the English would not pay him a halfpenny (Ep 2488) the new archbishop did in fact continue the payments (Epp 2761, 2815, 2879). Only later did Erasmus begin to realize what he had lost at Warham's death; it was the beginning of a series of personal blows culminating in the executions of More and Fisher which finally severed Erasmus' English links and, on a wider scale, divided the international community of scholarship for which Erasmus had worked (Epp 2874, 3036, 3090, 3123).

Praise of Warham abounds in Erasmus' works (Allen I 5; *Adagia* I ii 55; ASD IV-1 342): Warham is credited with encouraging him to go to Italy (LB II 1050F–1051A), and there are long and celebrated accounts of his career and virtues in the *Ecclesiastes* (LB V 810E–811E) and in the commentaries on St Mark's gospel and 1 Thessalonians (LB VI 151–2, 903E–904E). Warham, though a patron of scholars, wrote nothing himself. But of his impressive library the law books were bequeathed to New College and his theological books to All Souls, while he gave his liturgial books to Winchester College.

Warham's portrait by Hans *Holbein, for which there is a drawing in the royal collection at Windsor Castle, hangs in Lambeth Palace. There is a copy in the Louvre.

BIBLIOGRAPHY: Allen Ep 188 / DNB XX 835–40 / Emden BRUO III 1988–92 / A.G. Dickens *The English Reformation* (New York 1964) 29 and passim / J.J. Scarisbrick *Henry VIII* (London 1968) 13 and passim / R.W. Chambers *Thomas More* (London 1935) 97 and passim / G.R. Elton *Reform and Reformation* (Cambridge, Mass, 1977) 12 and passim / P.S. Allen 'Dean Colet and Archbishop Warham' *English Historical Review* 17 (1902) 303–6 / H.W. Garrod 'Erasmus and his English patrons' *The Library* 5th ser 4 (1949–50) 1–13 / There has been no published life of Archbishop Warham, but important aspects of his primacy are dealt with in two unpublished Cambridge doctoral dissertations: J.J. Scarisbrick 'The conservative episcopate in England, 1529–1535' (1956) and M.J. Kelly 'Canterbury jurisdiction and influence during the episcopate of William Warham, 1503–1532' (1963)   C.S. KNIGHTON

Claes WARNERSZOON prior of Steyn, d 5 September 1504
Claes Warnerszoon (Nicolaus Wernerus) is first recorded as prior of the Augustinians of Steyn, near Gouda, in 1494. He was the seventh prior, succeeding Joost Claeszoon, documented as prior in 1491. While living abroad Erasmus made a point of keeping the prior informed about his daily pursuits, his health, and other matters of interest to those at Steyn (Epp 48, 50, 74, 77, 171). On one occasion Erasmus' outspoken language with regard to his critics at Steyn may have offended the prior (Ep 171), but normally relations seem to have been very friendly. Unlike Servatius *Rogerus, who was to succeed him, Warnerszoon approved of Erasmus' leaving Gouda, which gave Erasmus the opportunity for playing him off against Rogerus (Ep 296). Allen's suggestion that Warnerszoon was the N mentioned in Epp 81 and 83 is unconvincing.

BIBLIOGRAPHY: Allen and CWE Epp 48, 81 /

Dalmatius van Heel *De reguliere kanunniken van het klooster Emmaus* (Gouda 1949) 23
                                            C.G. VAN LEIJENHORST

Thomas WARNET of Cambrai, documented 1499–1517
Thomas Warnet (Varnet, mistakenly also Varvet) was from Cambrai. He probably studied arts at the Collège de Montaigu in Paris, where he collaborated with Jan *Standonck in the administration of the college and in his attempts to reform monastic and clerical discipline in Paris. Allen conjectures that he was perhaps the 'literary man of the name of Thomas' who accompanied Hendrik van *Bergen, bishop of Cambrai, to England in 1498. Warnet fled France in 1499 after publicly rebuking King *Louis XII for his divorce and remarriage, citing John the Baptist's words to King Herod: 'It is not lawful for you to have her' (Matt 14:4). During this exile he founded in Valenciennes the Collège des Bons-Enfants, sometimes called the Collège du Maître Thomas, as an affiliate of Montaigu. He returned to Paris in 1503 and was with Standonck when he died on 5 February 1504. On 19 February 1504, Warnet received his licence in theology, ranking eighth of twenty-two, and completed his doctorate on 12 December. In 1506 he presided over the doctoral disputations of Noël *Béda, and he was moderately active in the faculty of theology until 1514. Most of his efforts were devoted to continuing the reform movement of Standonck, gaining some success with the Benedictines of Chezal-Benoît, the Cluniacs of Saint-Martin-des-Champs, and the canons regular at Saint-Victor. Warnet was the curé of Saint-Nicholas-des-Champs in Paris from at least 1504 to 1517, the latest date known for him. His annual obit was celebrated on 17 May.

Warnet was probably the Thomas of Cambrai whom Erasmus knew at Paris by the end of 1498 (Ep 85), while his identification with Erasmus' good friend Thomas at Veere (Ep 139, December 1500) seems far-fetched.

Warnet collaborated with Noël Béda in the following works: *La Doctrine et instruction nécessaire aux chrestiens et chrestiennes* (Paris: Jean Trepperel c 1509); and *La Petite Dyablerie dont lucifer est le chef et les membres sont tous les ioueurs iniques et pecheurs reprouvez, intitule*

Leglise des mauvais, an adaptation of Sermon 42 *Quadragesimale de christiana religione* of San Bernardino of Siena (Paris: Jean Trepperel's widow and Jean Jehannot [1511]).

BIBLIOGRAPHY: Allen Ep 85 / Clerval passim / Farge no 472 / M. Godet *La Congrégation de Montaigu* (Paris 1912) / Renaudet *Préréforme* 302, 309, 569, and passim

JAMES K. FARGE

Nicolas WARY of Marville, d 30 November 1529

Nicolas Wary (Warry, de Warrity, Varius, Nicolaus Maruillanus) was born in Marville, near Longwy (formerly in Luxembourg, now in the French Département de Meurthe-et-Moselle). He matriculated at Louvain on 30 August 1508 as a 'poor' student and obtained a BA on 26 January 1510 and MA on 1 April 1511, with high standing. While studying theology – in which he was a bachelor by 1517 – he taught Aristotelian logic and physics in the College of the Falcon. Between 1515 and 1527 his colleagues nominated him to several benefices which were within the gift of the university, and he was elected dean of arts for a semester in 1517, 1520, and 1525, receiver in 1521, and procurator of the Gallic nation nine times.

In June 1522 Wary was sent to Rome to defend the university's right of nominating scholars to certain vacant benefices. His mission was at the point of succeeding when Pope *Adrian VI died in September 1523. New obstacles turned up, but after an intervention by Erasmus (Epp 1481, 1509) Wary eventually obtained the desired privileges and by September 1525 had returned to Louvain.

Wary had been associated with Jérôme de *Busleyden's Collegium Trilingue from the very beginning; in 1517 he had witnessed the founder's will with Jan *Stercke, who became the first president of the college. When Stercke resigned, Wary succeeded him on 21 January 1526, retaining the presidency until his death four years later. He was buried in St Peter's and Frans van *Cranevelt and Jakob *Jespersen wrote epitaphs for him (Ep 2570).

Wary certainly met Erasmus in Busleyden's entourage and had formed a connection with him before he left Louvain in 1521. Thereafter they corresponded, and the four preserved letters of Erasmus to Wary attest to a cordial

friendship. In Ep 1756 Erasmus gives a vivid description of the accidental explosion of gunpowder in Basel which had apparently given rise to new rumours about Erasmus' death. He was eager to advise the president of the Trilingue on matters that concerned the wellbeing of the college and intervened in *Rescius' favour when that professor was threatened with dismissal as a result of his marriage (Epp 1768, 1806A). Ep 1856 is the dedicatory preface to Wary of Erasmus' translation of St John Chrysostom's *De Babyla martyre* (Basel: J. Froben 1527), while in Ep 1973 Erasmus complained about the damage done to humanistic letters by the so-called evangelicals. Of Wary's letters none are preserved.

BIBLIOGRAPHY: Allen Ep 1481 / de Vocht CTL I 19–20, II 299–316, and passim / de Vocht *Busleyden* 92, 130–9, and passim / de Vocht *Epistolae ad Craneveldium* Ep 141 / *Matricule de Louvain* III-1 358   IG

John WATSON d 1537

Watson was a leading figure in the Cambridge of the 1520s and 1530s as master of Christ's College and twice vice-chancellor of the university. But accounts of his early life presented in the DNB and various college biographical registers are inconsistent, while Emden appears to conflate the careers of two men. His notice in BRUC first records him as a scholar of Eton around 1479–83 who went on to King's College, Cambridge, where he was a fellow from 1486 to 1493–4, taking his BA in 1486–7 and priest's orders in 1489. This follows Venn's entry, but the Eton biographer Sterry states firmly that this man was not the subsequent friend of Erasmus. For another Watson took his BA from Peterhouse in 1489 and his MA in 1492, and yet another was BA in 1497–8 and MA in 1500–1. One or other of these was admitted probationer fellow in 1500 and can therefore hardly have been the same man who had been a fellow of King's in the previous decade.

That the Peterhouse man was Erasmus' correspondent is clear from the address of Ep 576. He was a full fellow of his college from 1501 to 1516, during which time he held a number of college and university posts: bursar 1505–6 and 1509–13, junior proctor 1504–5, and select preacher 1505–6. In 1503 he was also curate of Little St Mary's, the parish church adjoining Peterhouse. He proceeded to the degree of bachelor of divinity in 1510–11 and took his doctorate in 1516–17. In 1515 he went on a pilgrimage to the Holy Land in the company of John Reston and Peter *Falck, the burgomaster of Fribourg who was a friend of Erasmus. En route he visited Italy and met others of the humanist circle (Ep 450). He moved from Peterhouse to become master of Christ's from 1517 to 1531 and was vice-chancellor from 1518 to 1520 and from 1529 to 1532. It is possible that he was the John Watson known to the Syon community as a Greek teacher (LP III-2 2062). In 1516 he had been appointed rector of Elsworth, Cambridgeshire, and from 1523 also held the living of St Mary Woolnoth, London. He may also have been rector of White Notley, Essex (which Emden claims he received in February 1537), but he mentioned only the two former parishes in his will. He made his will in January 1537 and this was proved in the following July. He made bequests to Peterhouse and Christ's, and also to the King's Hall, where he seems to have lived after resigning his mastership (Cambridge University Archives, MSS Ely Consistory Probate Records, Liber L, ff 84–6).

We first learn of Watson's association with Erasmus in October 1513 when the latter wrote to William *Gonnell, then in the fenland village of Landbeach because of plague in Cambridge, expressing a hope that he might visit him there in Watson's company (Epp 275, 276). In the following year Watson is mentioned by Erasmus as his intermediary with Gonnell (Ep 289). Watson himself wrote to Erasmus from Cambridge in August 1516, acknowledging a letter of the previous June which he wistfully claimed to value nearly as much as the fattest benefice. Among common friends he recalled Raffaele *Regio, Ambrogio *Leoni, and Pietro *Alcionio. He praised Erasmus' New Testament and looked forward to the appearance of his edition of Jerome. He asked for a full list of his writings and invited him to visit him (Ep 450). Erasmus had obviously not received this letter when he wrote a few days later to Henry *Bullock mentioning Watson, who he had heard was away from Cambridge (Ep 456). He replied to Watson's letter in January 1517 (Ep 512). Watson wrote back in April, dating his

letter from Peterhouse but inviting Erasmus to stay at his rectory of Elsworth. He described himself as neither Scotist nor Thomist, but 'a blockhead' (Ep 576). Erasmus sent him greetings again in 1518 (Ep 777). Watson was in fact a mild humanist, but no reformer. In 1520 he had been sent to London in a deputation from the university to refute *Luther's works. He was one of those who examined the teachings of the alleged heretic Robert Barnes in 1525 and was among the divines of the university consulted on the subject of the king's divorce in 1529. Although he was the king's chaplain, his conservatism was well known (as, for example, to *Gardiner), and he showed his position clearly when as vice-chancellor in 1530 he called on all graduands in divinity to denounce Wycliffe, Hus, Luther, and other heretics.

BIBLIOGRAPHY: Allen Ep 275 / DNB XX 924–5 / John and J.A. Venn *Alumni Cantabrigienses* (Cambridge 1922–54) I-4 348 / Emden BRUC 622–3 / W. Sterry *The Eton College Register 1441–1698* (Eton 1943) / T.A. Walker *A Biographical Register of Peterhouse Men* (Cambridge 1927–30) I 95–6 / J. Peile *Biographical Register of Christ's College* (Cambridge 1910) I 7 / J.B. Mullinger *The University of Cambridge from the Earliest Times to the Royal Injunctions of 1535* (Cambridge 1873) 499, 577   C.S. KNIGHTON

Joachim von WATT *See Joachim* VADIANUS

WATTENSCHNEE *See Johann* SCHABLER

Nikolaus von WATTENWYL of Bern,
d 12 March 1551
A descendant of one of Bern's most distinguished families, Nikolaus von Wattenwyl matriculated at the University of Basel in the spring of 1505 and studied in 1509–10 at Paris. From 1505 he began to receive plenty of ecclesiastical preferment, although he may not have been ordained priest until 1518. In 1509 he became a canon of St Vincent, Bern, and from 1520 he acted on behalf of the sick provost of that chapter, whom he succeeded on 5 March 1523. Meanwhile he was also provost of the cathedral chapter of Lausanne from 1514 to 1520, and from around 1517 he was a canon of Basel and as such closely connected with another Bern patrician, the coadjutor Nikolaus

von *Diesbach. From 1512 he was repeatedly in Rome collaborating with Cardinal Matthäus *Schiner and soon came to be considered by curial officials as their brightest hope in Switzerland. In 1522 a rumour circulated that he was to succeed Schiner as bishop of Sion. By that time, however, he had already established a connection with *Zwingli, some of whose letters to him have survived. From the time of his appointment as provost of St Vincent he worked energetically towards the reform of Bern, preventing a visitation by the bishop of Lausanne and instructing the clergy to preach according to the Gospel.

On 5 December 1525 Wattenwyl resigned all his ecclesiastical dignities and forthwith married Clara, the daughter of Claudius *May, a Dominican nun, while her brother, Jakob May, married Wattenwyl's sister Katharina, who was also a nun (z VIII Epp 357, 424, 462). Henceforward he lived in style as a lay patrician in his mansion at Bern and from 1529 in the castle of Wyl, near Bern, putting his town house at the disposal of Zwingli during the Bern disputation of 1528. In 1536 he presided over the disputation of Lausanne which set the stage for the reform of Vaud, which had recently been conquered by the Bernese. After meeting him at Basel in 1522, Erasmus sent him a spontaneous and warm-hearted letter (Ep 1264), anticipating cordial relations in the future. No subsequent contacts are recorded, however.

BIBLIOGRAPHY: Allen Ep 1264 / z VII Epp 214, VIII Ep 311, and passim / *Helvetia Sacra* ed A. Bruckner et al (Bern 1972–   ) II-2 159–60 / ADB XLI 249–50 / DHBS VII 234 / Richard Feller *Geschichte Berns* (Bern 1946–60) II 113, 121–2, 138 / *Aktensammlung zur Geschichte der Berner Reformation* ed R. Steck and G. Tobler (Bern 1918–23) 54 and passim / *Matrikel Basel* I 278 / *Vadianische Briefsammlung* II Ep 325, IV Ep 438   PGB

Chrétien WECHEL of Herentals,
d before 18 April 1554
Chrétien Wechel (Vuechel) of Herentals, near Antwerp, was probably the natural son of a priest, Jan van Wechele. He arrived in France about 1518 or 1519 and began to work as a manager for the Swabian bookseller Konrad *Resch, who had close connections with Basel.

On 1 August 1526, he bought Resch's shop and stock, in the rue Saint-Jacques 'sub scuto Basiliensi.' In 1528 he became a burgher of Paris, was named *libraire-juré*, and obtained letters of naturalization. At the end of 1529 he bought the press of Simon du Bois and from then on was simultaneously a bookseller, publisher, and printer. In 1539 he opened another shop, in the rue Saint-Jean-de-Beauvais. Named 'sub Pegaso,' it was located in the house of Jean Périer, whose widow Michelle Robillard, he had married. From 1546 the Pegasus was his only address. In his will, dated from 1550, he left his possessions in France to his nephew, André Wechel, who continued to do business at the Pegasus until the Saint Bartholomew's day massacre. His possessions in Germany were left to another nephew, Simeon, an engraver in Cologne. During his entire lifetime, Chrétien Wechel kept close personal and commercial ties with Germany and the Low Countries; he went to the Frankfurt fairs and published many German authors. He published text books, classical authors, and Greek medical works. He introduced into France some writings by minor German reformers and also published in 1546 the *Tiers Livre* by François *Rabelais.

Wechel was an important publisher of Erasmus' work, launching no less than thirty-one editions. He offered his services to Erasmus through the bookseller Gerard *Morrhy in 1530 (Ep 2311). In 1534 he was prosecuted for selling Erasmus' *De interdicto esu carnium*, which had been forbidden by the faculty of theology.

BIBLIOGRAPHY: Allen Ep 2311 / Renouard *Répertoire* 434–5 / H. Elie 'Chrétien Wechel, imprimeur à Paris' *Gutenberg-Jahrbuch 1954* (Mainz 1954) 181–97 / E. Armstrong 'The origins of Chrétien Wechel re-examined' BHR 23 (1961) 341–5 / A. Parent *Les Métiers du livre à Paris au XVIe siècle* (Geneva 1974) 160–2
                                        GENEVIÈVE GUILLEMINOT

Wilhelm WEIDOLT of Wrocław,
d summer 1539
Wilhelm Weidolt (Weidott, Weydolt) was descended from a family which had emigrated from Cracow to Wrocław. His father, also called Wilhelm, was a furrier and had obtained the citizenship of Wrocław in 1482. It was

there that the son established his earliest business connections, above all with Sigmund Pucher, with whom he was on good terms. By 1517 Weidolt had moved to Nürnberg; by 1520 he owned a house there, and by 1533 he was a citizen, and eventually he died there between 28 May and 17 September 1539. For certain periods, however, he lived at Frankfurt am Main, where in 1538 he purchased the house 'zum roten Kapaun.'

Among the international merchants of Nürnberg and Frankfurt few could match Weidolt's success. In 1515 Kilian Schedler of Isny and Konrad Barchanter of Nürnberg are mentioned as his fellow-creditors. In 1516 he did business with Anton Welser, Ambrosius Höchstetter, and their Augsburg partners such as Anton Koberger and Heinrich Knopf (Nürnberg, Staatsarchiv MS Rst Nürnberg, A-Laden-Urkunden 150). In 1520 he was the commercial agent of one Schilling, perhaps Jobst, who was also his kinsman. In 1521 he represented the interests of Jakob Baner of Cracow against Hans Koch of Nürnberg. His proxy for Baner's brother-in-law, Anton Pfau, and for Jakob Bensheimer of Landau is dated from Frankfurt, also in 1521. In the same year he did business with the Sauermanns, merchants of Wrocław and Cracow. In 1523 the Nürnberg council authorized him to collect a debt from the city of Wissembourg, in Alsace. In 1525 Veit Stoss is named among his debtors, and in the same year he transacted business with Johann Gerlich at Mechelen. In 1530 he joined Heinrich Stöcklin and others in negotiations with Jörg Langheimer and Sigmund Roth of Prague on behalf of the Nürnberg council (Nürnberg, Staatsarchiv, MS Rst Nürnberg, Landpflegamt, Gemeinakten S I L 598 no 201). From 1530 he represented the Schillings in their claims against the former Hungarian company of the Fuggers and *Thurzos, initially contacting Anton *Fugger from Cracow through the offices of Michael of Kaaden. In 1533 he represented the heirs of Andreas Streel of Nürnberg and Hans Zeh of Vach (Nürnberg, Staatsarchiv, MS Libri litterarum 46 ff 145, 174).

In Eastern Europe Weidolt was represented in the commercial centres of Lwów, Cracow, Wrocław, and Elbląg (Elbing). From Poland he imported beef, hides, and leather to Nürnberg and wax to Basel, while exporting

cloth to eastern markets. More than once his impetuous language got him into trouble; in 1528 he quarrelled with Heinrich Formschneider of Nürnberg, and in 1531 he was accused of causing unrest as a propagator of Zwinglian ideas (Nürnberg, Staatsarchiv MS Rst Nürnberg, A-Laden-Akten S I L 59 no 6 ff 16–17). Among his friends were Christoph Scheurl, legal consultant to the Nürnberg council, and Justus Ludovicus *Decius (Ep 2960). His portrait is preserved on a medal by Matthis Gerbel produced in 1535.

BIBLIOGRAPHY: Allen Ep 2960 / *Christoph Scheurl's Briefbuch* ed F. von Soden and J.K.F. Knaake (Potsdam 1872, repr 1972) II Ep 235 / Theodor Hampe *Nürnberger Ratsverlässe über Kunst und Künstler im Zeitalter der Spätgotik und Renaissance* (Vienna-Leipzig 1904) I passim / Carl L. Sachs 'Metzgergewerbe und Fleischversorgung der Reichsstadt Nürnberg bis zum Ende des 30-jährigen Kriegs' *Mitteilungen des Vereins für Geschichte der Stadt Nürnberg* 24 (1922) 77–8 / Adolf Jaeger *Veit Stoß und sein Geschlecht* ed Otto Puchner (Neustadt a.d. Aisch 1958) 73–4, 81–2 / Götz von Pölnitz *Anton Fugger* (Tübingen 1958–   ) I 539, 643 / *Nürnberger Totengeläutbücher III: St. Sebald 1517–1572* ed Helene Burger (Neustadt a.d. Aisch 1972) no 2008 / Hans Dieter Schmid *Täufertum und Obrigkeit in Nürnberg* (Nürnberg 1972) 96 / J.K.W. Willers *Die Nürnberger Handfeuerwaffe bis zur Mitte des 16. Jahrhunderts* (Nürnberg 1973) 209   FRANZ MACHILEK

Johann WEILER *See Johann* WILER

Pieter WELDANCK documented 1515–28 Pieter Weldanck (Weldock, Wyldanke) was a brewer (Ep 1931; LP IV 2881) and financial agent in London who by 1527 received the sum of ninety nobles from the coffers of Archbishop William *Warham with instructions to remit it to Erasmus. It seems that he tried to keep the money, which was finally recovered by Cuthbert *Tunstall after *Schets and Erasmus had mistakenly suspected the bookseller Franz *Birckmann, who apparently did some business with Weldanck (Epp 1866, 1931, 1955, 1993, 2001).

Weldanck is not by any means a common name. Although Erasmus once thought that Pieter was German (Ep 1866) he may be identified with the Pieter Weldanck who was paid by the royal exchequer for his services in March and April 1515. He was then in Antwerp and elsewhere and acted as an informer for England, perhaps while employed by *Margaret of Austria (LP II 323). On 20 November 1515 he received his letters of denization. There he was said to be a native of Zeeland and to exercize the trade of a blacksmith in Westminster.

BIBLIOGRAPHY: Allen Ep 1866 / LP II 323, III 3261, IV 2881   PGB

Thomas WELLES of Alresford, 1466–c May 1524

Thomas Welles was born in Alresford, Hampshire, the son of a tenant of Winchester College. He entered Winchester College in December 1478 and New College, Oxford, in January 1483. He was a fellow of New College in 1485 and there became closely acquainted with William *Warham, who did not resign his fellowship at New College until 1488. In 1520 Welles was elected warden of the college but declined the position.

Welles received his BA in 1488 and his MA soon after. Apparently he visited Italy, for he received a doctorate in theology from the University of Turin in 1503. He supplicated for incorporation to the same degree at Oxford in 1510 but was not accepted until 1521. Meanwhile, in 1497, he had been ordained deacon in St Frideswide Priory, Oxford, and in March 1498 priest at Oseney Abbey, Oxford. Welles also received many other benefices, including the rectory of Crayford, Kent, and canonries at Wells and St Crantock, Cornwall, all of which he held until his death. He was chaplain to Archbishop Warham from 1505 to 1511.

Welles was granted letters of fraternity by Christ Church Priory, Canterbury, in 1511. He gave many books to New College. Erasmus may have known him personally; in 1520 he greeted Welles in a letter to Thomas *Bedyll (Ep 1176).

BIBLIOGRAPHY: Allen Ep 1176 / Emden BRUO III 2008–9   CFG

Bartholomäus WELSER of Augsburg, 25 June 1484–28 March 1561

Bartholomäus Welser (Weltzer, Vuelzerus) was a son of Anton, a leading merchant-banker of Augsburg, and it may be assumed that he received the customary education given to the sons of merchants. It is likely that he joined his father's firm as a young man, paying special attention to the trade with East India and the American colonies of Spain. In 1505 he organized the earliest German trade link with India by dispatching his representatives with the fleet of Francisco d'Almeida. In 1511 he married Felicitas Grander, who bore him three sons. When his father died on 11 November 1518, Bartholomäus and his brother Anton jointly bought the house 'Auf dem Stein,' parts of which still exist today, and made it the headquarters of their banking and merchant firm, which did business from 1518 to 1553, when Anton died and Bartholomäus retired. Under their management the firm flourished. Branch offices were opened in Ulm and Nürnberg (1534 and 1535) and other family members were brought into the firm. Although Anton senior had established crucial business connections with the royal court of Spain, only his sons were able to profit fully from them. Loans to *Charles v brought in return privileges and favours of every kind, including a knighthood for Bartholomäus (22 November 1532), a universal safe-conduct (6 April 1541), and a privilege of exemption from some local jurisdictions (7 June 1546). The greatest success, however, was a charter (dated 27 March 1528) for the possession and development of Venezuela, complete with a monopoly on the import and export of goods; issued at first in the name of two agents, it was transferred to the Welsers on 17 February 1531. As they began to exercise their rights in Venezuela, often called 'Welserland,' difficulties arose between the Welsers and the Spanish governors. In 1546 Bartholomäus' son, also named Bartholomäus, was murdered in America. Thereafter his father allowed this enterprise to peter out.

On several occasions Welser acted as an adviser and envoy for his native city of Augsburg. Prior to the opening of the Augsburg diet in 1530, he and Wolfgang Langenmantel met Charles v at Innsbruck. While extending to him an official invitation according to established custom, they also took the opportunity to discuss various questions concerning trade and monopolies that had remained unsettled. During the Schmalkaldic war of 1546–7, Welser obtained Augsburg's permission to reside outside its boundaries for three years, so as to avoid any involvement in the city's war effort. From his temporary residence in Lindau he supported the emperor with large sums of money. After his victory in 1547 Charles V recalled him to Augsburg and later appointed him privy councillor (*Geheimer Rat*), one of the highest positions in the government of the city. In 1552 he lost this office temporarily during the Protestant revolt against the emperor, and in 1556 he resigned it for health reasons. From this time on Welser also appears to have taken an increased interest in scholarship, which is not surprising if one considers the scholarly tastes of his sister Margarethe *Welser and his brother Christoph. Although a Suetonius (1548) with marginal annotations by Welser has been discovered (Weyermann), Welser was a patron of learning rather than a scholar. He died in Amberg, Swabia, and was buried there, as was his wife, Felicitas.

Welser's connections with Erasmus appear to have been limited to financial transactions (Ep 2247). Difficulties arose over a remittance from Alonso de *Fonseca, archbishop of Toledo (Epp 2109, 2126), and like other financial agents Welser discovered that Erasmus was not an easy client to deal with (Ep 2153).

BIBLIOGRAPHY: Allen Ep 2153 / ADB XLI 684–6 / Schottenloher II 377–8, VII 233–4 / Götz von Pölnitz *Anton Fugger* (Tübingen 1958–) passim / Albrecht Weyermann *Nachrichten von Gelehrten und Künstlern, auch alten und neuen adelichen und bürgerlichen Familien aus der vormaligen Reichsstadt Ulm* (1798–1829) II 668 and passim / Franz von Wieser *Magelhaes-Strasse und Austral-Continent auf den Globen des Johann Schöner* (Innsbruck 1881) 98 / Paul von Stetten *Lebensbeschreibung zur Erweckung und Erhaltung bürgerlicher Tugend, Zweyte Sammlung* (Augsburg 1783) 214 ff / K. Klunzinger *Anteil des Ambrosius Dalfinger und des Nicolaus Federmann ... unter der Herrschaft der Welser von Augsburg in Venezuela* (Stuttgart 1857) / Juan Friede *Los Welser en la Conquista de Venezuela* (Caracas-Madrid 1961)

ROSEMARIE AULINGER

Margarethe WELSER of Augsburg, 14/18 March 1481–7 September 1552

Margarethe, the daughter of Anton and sister of Bartholomäus *Welser, was born in Augs-

Bartholomäus Welser

burg or in Memmingen, where her father held the office of burgomaster. On 20 November 1498 (RE Ep 66) she married Konrad *Peutinger. When praising his young bride in a letter to *Reuchlin, Peutinger mentioned her considerable knowledge of Latin (RE Ep 66). Through the years of her marriage Margarethe was able to pursue her scholarly interests. In addition to her duties as a housewife and mother of several children, she read classical authors in the original languages as well as studying the Bible and scriptural commentaries. When her brother Christoph Welser, provost of the Regensburg chapter, had gone to Rome, she sent him a letter on 1 December 1511 describing a statue of Mercury recently discovered in Augsburg and also coins and inscriptions in her husband's collection. The authenticity of this letter has been questioned, however, by Heinrich Lutz (*Peutinger* 101), and before him by Erich König (*Peutingerstudien* 26), but it remains a testimony to her reputation among contemporaries and posterity. In December 1521 a letter from her husband to Erasmus (Ep 1247) shows her comparing Erasmus' New Testament with a German version of the Gospels. What she found prompted her to add a note to her husband's letter, which has also been preserved. She may also be the housewife eager to discuss Romans whom Urbanus *Rhegius mentioned a month later (Ep 1253).

BIBLIOGRAPHY: Allen Ep 1247 / ADB XXV 567 / Johann Georg Lotter *Historia vitae atque meritorum Conradi Peutingeri* (Leipzig 1729) 20, 32, 58–60 / Franz Roth 'Zur Lebensgeschichte des Augsburger Stadtadvokaten Dr. Claudius Pius Peutinger' ARG 25 (1928) 99–127, 161–255, esp 102–3 / Erich König *Peutingerstudien* (Freiburg 1914) passim / Heinrich Lutz *Conrad Peutinger: Beiträge zu einer politischen Biographie* (Augsburg n d)   ROSEMARIE AULINGER

Andreas WENGI of Thurgau, d 3 February 1528
Andreas Wengi was a Cistercian in the abbey of Wettingen, near Baden, in the Aargau. From 1517 he held the position of *Grosskellner*, a regular stepping stone to the office of abbot, which he occupied from 7 March 1521 to his death. His life was a protracted and losing battle against the government of Zürich, which came progressively under the influence of *Zwingli. He attempted to retain as much as possible of the many rights and revenues that his abbey possessed in the city and especially the rural parishes of Zürich, but despite his appeals to the Swiss diet he could not prevent some Zwinglian preachers from being installed in parishes that depended on Wettingen. He was also unsuccessful in curbing, by withholding payments, the reforming zeal of Ambrosius *Kettenacker, the priest of Riehen, near Basel (Ep 1447). He played an important part in the Baden disputation of May 1526 and held a reception for the Catholic delegates in his abbey. In the same year he quarrelled with Laurentius *Merus, the parish priest of Baden.

BIBLIOGRAPHY: Allen Ep 1447 / Alfons Bugmann *Zürich und die Abtei Wettingen zur Zeit der Reformation und Gegenreformation* (Dietikon 1949) 5–34, 155–6 / *Amtliche Sammlung der ältern eidgenössischen Abschiede* ed J.K. Krütli et al (Lucerne 1839–82) IV-1a 257 and passim
                PGB

Roger WENTFORD documented at London 1506–18
Roger Wentford was the headmaster of St Anthony's School in Threadneedle Street,

perhaps the leading school in London during the period of *Henry VII and the early years of *Henry VIII, which Thomas *More had attended, under a former master named Nicholas Holt. Nothing seems to be known of Wentford outside the letters of Erasmus and More, and he does not appear in the registers of Oxford or Cambridge.

Even allowing for rhetorical expressions of friendship Wentford seems to have been something of a confidential friend of Erasmus in June 1506 (Ep 196), and he offered Erasmus money in 1511 (Ep 241). From this letter, in which Erasmus spoke of *Grocyn as patron and teacher to them both, it seems clear that Wentford had seen an early draft of *De copia*. In 1513 there is a letter entirely about John *Smith, who had been a pupil at St Antony's and whom Erasmus wanted to have as a servant (Ep 277).

In 1516 Wentford may have sent greetings to Erasmus in a letter of Thomas *Grey (Ep 445), and in 1518 an amusing incident occurred when Wentford wrote letters – apparently dull ones – to both Erasmus and More but confused them when writing the two addresses (Epp 688, 772). From Erasmus' reply it is learnt that in England he had consulted Wentford also over an early draft of the *Colloquia*, which had remained in the schoolmaster's hand. Wentford now returned it, as requested, but for reasons unknown kept back one dialogue, in which he may have played a role.

BIBLIOGRAPHY: Allen and CWE Ep 196
                R.J. SCHOECK & PGB

Georg WERNER of Paczkow, died c 1557
Georg, the son of Martin Werner (Vuernerus), was from Paczkow (Patschkau), in Silesia. After studies in Wittenberg (1511–12) he enrolled at the University of Cracow (1514) and in 1519 received a BA. He learnt the art of poetry from Valentin Eck, whom he apparently followed to Hungary in 1519. For a while Werner was the rector of a school at Košice (Czechoslovakia, then Kassa in Hungary), and later settled in nearby Prešov (Eperjes), where he became a town notary and then a judge. After the death of King *Louis II (1526) Werner was at first considered a partisan of *John Zápolyai. However, perhaps owing to the influence of Eck, he soon came to support King *Ferdinand, who rewarded his services by

appointing him councillor and castellan of Sowar and subsequently of Saros. Finally Ferdinand entrusted him with the office of royal vice-treasurer of Hungary (Ep 3137).

From Hungary Werner kept up close contacts with Cracow, where some of his Latin poems were printed from 1520. In 1527 (Ep 1916) Erasmus returned greetings from Werner which had apparently reached him in a letter from Jan *Antonin. Antonin also forwarded Werner's compliments in 1536 (Ep 3137).

Werner's principal publications were: De ... Joannis Thursonis episcopi Wratislaviensis obitu (Cracow: H. Wietor 1520) dedicated to the brothers Alexius and Johannes (II) *Thurzo; Elegiarum liber unus (Cracow: H. Wietor 1523); and De admirandis Hungariae aquis hypomnematia (Vienna: E. Aquila 1551). Poems by him were also printed in the first edition of Erasmus' Ep 1819 addressed to King *Sigismund I (Cracow: H. Wietor 1527), the second edition of Valentin Eck's De versificandi arte opusculum (Cracow: H. Wietor 1521), and the collective volume Pannoniae luctus (Cracow: H. Wietor 1544).

BIBLIOGRAPHY: Allen Ep 1916 / G. Bauch Deutsche Scholaren in Krakau in der Zeit der Renaissance 1460 bis 1520 (Wrocław 1901) 75–6 / H. Barycz Historia Uniwersytetu Jagiellońskiego w epose humanizmu (Cracow 1935) / E. Kovács Uniwersytet Krakowski a kultura węgierska (Budapest 1965) 90, 190 / I. Trenscényi-Waldapfel Erasmus es magyar barátai (Budapest 1941) 65–8 / Bibliographia polska ed Karl Estreicher et al (Cracow 1870–1951) XXXII 378 / Matrikel Wittenberg I 39

HALINA KOWALSKA

Johann WERNER of Nürnberg, 14 February 1468–c May 1522

Johann Werner (Vernerus) matriculated at Ingolstadt on 21 September 1484; he may be identical with a cleric of that name who in the autumn of 1492 obtained a benefice as Frühmesser in Kemnath, Upper Palatinate. Werner studied at Rome from 1493 to 1497 and there he took holy orders. In the summer of 1497 he seems to have been at Florence, for on 16 June Hartmann Schedel of Nürnberg requested him to purchase several books there. Subsequently he returned to Nürnberg, and on 29 April 1498 he celebrated his first mass at the church of St

Sebald. On 24 July 1503 Bianca Maria Sforza, the wife of *Maximilian I, wrote to the Nürnberg council, soliciting for Werner the first benefice within the council's gift to fall vacant. In December of that same year he is documented in the position of vicar in the Nürnberg suburb of Wöhrd, while efforts by his friend Conradus Celtis to have him appointed lecturer in Greek at the University of Vienna remained unsuccessful. By 1 October 1508 Werner was chaplain of St John's at Nürnberg, a position he was to retain until his death, between 12 March and 11 June 1522. When the imperial historiographer Johannes *Stabius visited Nürnberg during the spring and summer of 1512 he secured from the emperor a 'privilege' against the unauthorized reprinting of Werner's works, and in 1513 Maximilian referred to Werner as 'our chaplain.'

A member of Nürnberg's humanist circle, Werner had also many ties with scholars and humanists elsewhere, such as Johann von *Dalberg, Petrus *Apianus, Johannes *Cono, and Nikolaus *Kratzer. Werner developed a new method for determining longitude in nautical astronomy that was soon in general use. In 1514 and 1522 he published at Nürnberg two collections of his work in geography, mathematics, and astronomy, including several translations he had made of Greek texts such as the first book of Ptolemy's Geography, mentioned by Erasmus in Ep 2760. Other mathematical and astronomical writings are preserved in manuscript (a list is in Pilz 141–3), but some appear to be lost. Among these must be counted his German translation of Euclid's Elements prepared between 1505 and 1507. At least some of his horoscopes are extant in manuscript, such as the ones for *Pirckheimer, Scheurl, Bianca Maria Sforza, and Archduke *Ferdinand (Pilz 143–4). Werner's diary of meteorological observations appears to be unprecedented; his notes for the year of 1513 were edited by Johann Schöner: Canones ... complectentes praecepta et observationes de mutatione aurae (Nürnberg 1546). Apianus in his Introductio geographica (Ingolstadt 1533) drew extensively on Werner's work and *Dürer relied in large measure on Werner when describing the problems in the representation of spheres and cubes; see his Underweys-

sung der Messung (Nürnberg: J. Petreius 1525). Quite recently attention has been drawn to Werner's notebook of current events, which he kept from 1506 to 1521.

BIBLIOGRAPHY: Allen Ep 2760 / ADB XLII 56–8 / M. Folkerts in *Dictionary of Scientific Biography* ed C.C. Gillispie (New York 1970–80) XIV 272–7 / Karl Schottenloher 'Der Mathematiker und Astronom Johann Werner aus Nürnberg. 1466–1522' in *Festgabe Hermann Grauert* (Freiburg 1910) 147–55 / *Der Briefwechsel des Konrad Celtis* ed Hans Rupprich (Munich 1934) Ep 304 and passim / *Mittelalterliche Bibliothekskataloge Deutschlands und der Schweiz* III-1: *Bistum Bamberg* ed Paul Ruf (Munich 1939, repr 1961) no 149 / *Pirckheimer Briefwechsel* passim / A. Dürer *Schriftlicher Nachlass* ed Hans Rupprich (Berlin 1956–69) I–III passim / Hans Kressel 'Hans Werner ... ' *Mitteilungen des Vereins für Geschichte der Stadt Nürnberg* 52 (1963–64) 287–304 / Johannes Kist *Die Matrikel der Geistlichkeit des Bistums Bamberg 1400–1556* (Würzburg 1965) no 6570 / Siegfried Bachmann 'Johannes Werner ... als Chronist der Jahre 1506–1521' 102. *Bericht des Historischen Vereins Bamberg* (1966) 315–37 / Elisabeth Caesar 'Sebald Schreyer ... ' *Mitteilungen des Vereins für Geschichte der Stadt Nürnberg* 56 (1969) esp 110–11, 123 / *Albrecht Dürers Umwelt: Festschrift zum 500. Geburtstag Albrecht Dürers* (Nürnberg 1971) passim / Marian Biskup *Regesta Copernicana* (Wrocław-Warsaw-Cracow-Gdansk 1973) no 264 / Kurt Pilz *600 Jahre Astronomie in Nürnberg* (Nürnberg 1977) 132–48, 198–9

FRANZ MACHILEK

Nicolaus WERNERUS *See Claes*
WARNERSZOON

Johann WERTER documented at Erfurt 1511–18
Johann Werter (Werterius) matriculated at the University of Erfurt during the autumn term of 1511; the entry reads 'Johannes de Werter nobilis.' Little is known otherwise about this young nobleman, who received his BA in the autumn of 1513 and his MA in 1517, ranking fifteenth among seventeen graduates. He was a student of *Eobanus Hessus, with whose assistance he wrote some verse to be published in Jodocus *Winsheim's *Forma recte poenitendi* (Erfurt 1515). He was also Eobanus' companion in the autumn of 1518 when the two of them walked from Erfurt to Louvain in order to pay their respects to Erasmus. He was rewarded with a brief letter (Ep 875), which Erasmus himself published in the *Farrago* of October 1519. Werter is not mentioned subsequently in the Erfurt sources. He may have left the city by the time Eobanus published his *Hodoeporicon* in 1519. No more is known about him.

BIBLIOGRAPHY: Allen Epp 870, 875 / Carl Krause *Helius Eobanus Hessus* (Gotha 1879, repr 1963) I 289–90, and passim / *Matrikel Erfurt* II 272

ERICH KLEINEIDAM

Dietrich von WERTHERN 28 September 1468–4 September 1536
Dietrich von Werthern (Wertern, Wyrther) was a son of Hans von Werthern and was born on the family estate of Wiehe, in Thuringia. He matriculated at the University of Erfurt in the spring term of 1479 and from 1486 studied at Bologna, where in 1491 he was procurator of the German nation and on 9 April 1495 was promoted doctor of civil and canon law. In 1498 Frederick, the younger brother of George of *Saxony, was elected grand master of the Teutonic knights. Werthern accompanied Frederick to Prussia and henceforward served him as a councillor and diplomat, particularly in his negotiations with Poland and the Emperor *Maximilian I. From 1504 to 1512 he was chancellor of the Teutonic order, and after resigning the chancellorship he continued for a while to serve the next grand master, Albert (I) of *Brandenburg-Ansbach. From 1510 Werthern was also a councillor to Duke George of Saxony, who welcomed his diplomatic expertise and used him especially in the negotiations concerning Friesland. In January 1517 he accompanied Maximilian I on his last journey to the Low Countries and must have had several opportunities to meet Erasmus. He is mentioned in the autograph rough draft of Duke George's earliest letter to Erasmus (Ep 514), which may or may not have reached its destination. As late as 1530 Werthern undertook an embassy to Poland together with Christoph von *Carlowitz. Like Duke George he was a firm opponent of the Reformation, but he seems to have moderated his stand towards the end of his life. He died at his castle of Beichlingen, north-east of Erfurt.

BIBLIOGRAPHY: Allen Ep 514 / ADB XLII 116–19
/ Matrikel Erfurt I 376 / Knod 623–4 / Pflug
Correspondance I 190, 468, and passim / Walther
Hubatsch Albrecht von Brandenburg-Ansbach
(Heidelberg 1960) 41, 48   MICHAEL ERBE

Willem van de WERVE of Antwerp,
d after 1559
Willem van de Werve came from a prominent
family of Antwerp. His father, Raas van de
Werve (d 1517), was a city councillor; his
mother was Françoise Colins. Willem married
Margareta Scheyff, the widow of Karel van
Liere van Immerseel, who bore him two
children, Karel and Anna. Willem was an
alderman of the city from 1524, and from 1531 to
1550 he was the duke's margrave of Antwerp.
He was a knight and was made lord of Schilde
in 1559.

The 'Wilhelmus de Werma' who matriculated at Louvain in 1520 (Matricule de Louvain
III-1 622) was no doubt a namesake of the
margrave; there were at this time no fewer than
three Williams among the van de Werves of
Antwerp.

In January 1534 Erasmus complained in
letters to Brussels about a book of sermons by
Nikolaus *Ferber Herborn, which the Antwerp
printer Michaël *Hillen had published in 1533.
He received assurances that *Margaret of
Austria had ordered the margrave to punish
Hillen, but in December he had not learnt of
any proceedings against the printer (Epp 2912,
2915, 2922, 2948, 2981).

BIBLIOGRAPHY: Allen Ep 2912 / Floris Prims
Geschiedenis van Antwerpen (Brussels-Antwerp
1927–49) XVIII 85–6 / A. Bousse and A. Jamees
Inventaire van het archief van de familie van de
Werve en van Schilde (Brussels 1975) v–vi, xi
                    MARCEL A. NAUWELAERTS

Jan WESSEL See Wessel GANSFORT

Bartholomeus van WESSEM See Bartholomeus
van VESSEM

Matthias WEYNSEN of Dordrecht, d 9 March
1547
Matthias Weynsen (Wensen, Wenssens,
Wontsen) was descended from a patrician
family of Dordrecht and joined the Franciscan
order by 1508. He was warden of the Leiden

house when he published a devotional essay
on Christ's passion, Fasciculus myrrhae (Delft
1517). In 1518 he was appointed warden of the
Antwerp monastery and in 1529 of that of
's Hertogenbosch. Meanwhile, from 1521 to
1528, he was provincial of the Cologne
province of his order. Between 1527 and 1529
he carried through the separation from the old
Cologne province of a new province of the
Low Countries, of which he was subsequently
provincial from 1534 to 1535 and from 1538 to
1540. Known as a forceful preacher and a firm
opponent of Lutheranism, he died in his native
Dordrecht.

For most of his active life Weynsen resided in
Antwerp and there around 1520 he used in one
of his sermons a phrase which Erasmus
gleefully repeated in several letters (Epp 1188,
1192, 1196). In 1529 Erasmus learnt that
Weynsen was still in Antwerp and had begun
to stir up his fellow friars, telling them to attack
Erasmus in writing (Ep 2205). In December of
that same year Frans *Titelmans defended
Weynsen in his Epistola apologetica (Antwerp: J.
Vorsterman 1530; Ep 2245).

Matthias Weynsen published a revised
Dutch version of Jacobus de Milano's Stimulus
amoris (Antwerp: G. de Bonte 1535), a work
then attributed to St Bonaventure. Two of
Weynsen's sermons, dating from 1521, are
preserved in manuscript at Brussels (Bibliothèque Royale MS 11151–5), and some letters
written between 1518 and 1535 also survive.
Frans Titelmans (1534), Francisco Osuna
(1535), Jan Royaert (1538), and Johannes
Mahusius (1539) all dedicated a work to
Weynsen.

BIBLIOGRAPHY: B. de Troeyer in NBW I 967–8 /
B. de Troeyer in Franciscana 20 (1965) 19–25, an
article reprinted in his Bio-bibliographica Franciscana Neerlandica saeculi XVI (Nieuwkoop 1969–
70)   MARCEL A. NAUWELAERTS

Richard WHITFORD died c 1543
Probably a native of the eponymous Flintshire
village, Whitford (Whytford) was at Cambridge by 1496–7 and held a fellowship at
Queen's College from 1498 to 1504. Immediately on his admission he was licensed to study
abroad and accompanied the young William
*Blount, Lord Mountjoy, to Paris, where
Whitford himself took the degrees of BA and

MA. There he met Erasmus, who afterwards corresponded with him (Ep 89). Whitford returned to his college in 1499, incorporating MA, and held the offices of dean and bursar before leaving to become chaplain to Richard *Foxe, bishop of Winchester. Around 1507 he entered the celebrated Bridgettine monastery at Sion, Middlesex, where an uncle was already an inmate. There he achieved note as the author of devotional works and the translator of others (including the *Imitation of Christ*). In all he produced about a dozen books (some of the attributions have been questioned), mostly printed by Robert Redman and Wynkyn de Worde. Although his first efforts, translations of the rules of St Augustine and St Benedict, were directed to his fellow religious, his combination of medieval piety and humanistic interests reached a wider audience. In 1506 Erasmus had dedicated to him his declamation against Lucian's *Tyrannicida* (Ep 191); it is evident that Thomas *More, who essayed a similar piece, was also a friend of 'the wretch of Sion,' as Whitford was to sign his compositions. Whitford may also have met Ignatius Loyola on the Jesuit founder's visit to England in 1530. *The Pype or Tonne*, perhaps Whitford's most influential work, contained attacks on Lutheranism, and his staunchly conservative views brought him into conflict with the royal visitors of Sion in 1535. In a succession of letters to Thomas *Cromwell it was reported by Thomas *Bedyll that Whitford was one of the two most obstinate in the house; he had resisted the arguments of several court clerics and others sent to win him over and should therefore be 'weeded out.' But Whitford must have stayed at Sion because he received a pension at the dissolution of the house in November 1539. Thereafter he was protected in the London household of the Mountjoys, even escaping the requirement to take the succession oath. In 1541 he produced a new book which commended *Henry VIII's youthful and by then embarrassing defence of papal authority. He also complained that heretical pamphlets had been circulated under the covers of his own earlier publications. His pension was last paid in October 1543, and it is presumed that he died soon afterwards.

Whitford's writings reflect a wide knowledge of contemporary life as well as an acquaintance with law and classical literature. Cicero, Ovid, Sallust, and Bartholomaeus Anglicus (Glanville) were among the authors of books which he gave to the library at Sion.

BIBLIOGRAPHY: Allen Ep 89 / Emden BRUC 635–6 / DNB XXI 125–7 / LP VII 1090, VIII 1125 (both mis-dated 1534 for 1535), IX 986, XIV-2 581, XVIII-1, 436 (p 256) / P.G. Caraman 'An English monastic reformer of the sixteenth century' *Clergy Review* n s 28 (1947) 1–16 / W.A.M. Peters 'Richard Whitford and St Ignatius' visit to England' *Archivium Historicum Societatis Iesu* 25 (Rome 1956) 328–50 / McConica 56–7, 60, 115–16, 129, 173, 205, 266 / David Knowles *The Religious Orders in England* (Cambridge 1948–59) III 213–15, 218–19 / The most recent list of Whitford's publications is given in STC (2nd ed) 25412–25426; modern editions and books owned by Whitford are noted in Emden BRUC   C.S. KNIGHTON

Pieter WICHMANS of Brussels,
d 18 February 1535

Apart from his connection with Erasmus very little is known about Pieter Wichmans (Wickman, Wychman, Wijchmannus). He is first documented in 1482, when he matriculated at the University of Orléans. Eighteen years later, on 29 January 1500, he registered in the University of Louvain as a priest, presumably to study theology. From 1507 to his death he was a canon of St Peter's in Anderlecht, near Brussels; at one time he was also appointed scholaster of his chapter. In 1515 he built himself a fine mansion, the house 'de Zwane,' where he was later to play host to Erasmus. Nothing is known about the beginnings of their friendship; it is clear, however, that it was the rural peace of Anderlecht in the proximity of Brussels as well as Wichmans' congenial hospitality which caused Erasmus to stay with the canon for most of the summer of 1521 (Epp 1208, 1215, 1223, 1231, 1342). After his move to Basel Erasmus remained in touch with Wichmans, but in 1523 common acquaintances seem to have cast some doubt on Wichmans' loyalty to Erasmus' cause. In Ep 1351 the canon offers a sincere and engaging defence to Erasmus' reproaches. Wichmans' acquaintance with such men as Antoon (I) *Sucket, Adriaan *Wiele, *Goclenius, *Dorp, Nicolaas van *Broeckhoven, and Pieter *Gillis was presumably owed in part to his friendship with Erasmus.

'De Zwane' was acquired in 1931 by the municipality of Anderlecht and now houses the Erasmushuis Museum.

BIBLIOGRAPHY: Allen Ep 1231 / BNB XVII 278–9 /Matricule d'Orléans II-1 113–14 / Matricule de Louvain III-1 196 / de Vocht CTL I 59 and passim / de Vocht Literae ad Craneveldium Ep 49 / Wichmans' epitaph is in Le Grand Théatre sacré du duché de Brabant (The Hague 1734) I-2 297 / Gemeentemusea te Anderlecht Erasmushuis en Oud-Begijnhof, Catalogus (n d)

HILDE DE RIDDER-SIMOENS

Dietrich WICHWAEL See Theoderich
MICHWAEL

Johann Albrecht WIDMANSTETTER
of Nellingen, 1506–28 March 1557
Johann Albrecht Widmanstetter (Vidmestadius, Lucretius, Oesiander) was born in Nellingen, near Ulm. He received his first instruction from Gregor Bauler, the parish priest in Nellingen, who recognized the boy's unusual talent for learning languages. In 1526 at Tübingen he studied philosophy and law as well as Greek and Hebrew. In 1527 he travelled to Italy by way of Heidelberg and Basel; he later claimed as his teachers several Basel professors including Henricus *Glareanus and Bonifacius *Amerbach as well as the Hebrew scholar and cosmographer Sebastian Münster, who then taught at Heidelberg. In Turin Widmanstetter studied with Clement of Rhodes and his nephew Basil and himself lectured on Greek literature. In 1529 he went to Bologna and there attended the coronation of *Charles v in February 1530. From 1530 to 1532 he was in Naples, where he lectured on the Iliad. Adopting the name 'Lucretius,' he became a member of the Academy of Naples. He met Ortensio *Lando and above all Girolamo Seripando, who became his patron and close friend. In the summer of 1532 he seems to have joined the imperial fleet under Andrea *Doria for an expedition against Korone (Coron) before going to Rome at the invitation of Cardinal Egidio *Antonini of Viterbo, who had offered his support for Widmanstetter's study of Arabic. While learning Arabic and Syriac, he was

employed as secretary by Nikolaus von *Schönberg, who seems to have encouraged his biblical translations from the Greek. He also served popes *Clement VII and *Paul III as a diplomat. Among his Roman friends were Georg von *Logau, whose scholarly efforts he assisted generously, Agostino *Steuco, and Ambrosius von *Gumppenberg, who praised his knowledge of Chaldaic, Greek, and Hebrew in a letter to Erasmus (Ep 3047) but subsequently was embroiled in a feud with Widmanstetter that lasted until 1552.

After leaving Rome in 1539, Widmanstetter became a councillor to Duke Louis of *Bavaria, whose natural daughter Anna von Leonsberg he married in 1542 at Landshut. After another journey to Rome in the winter of 1543–4, in 1546 he became the chancellor of Cardinal Otto von Truchsess, bishop of Augsburg, whom he accompanied to Rome in 1550. In 1552 he was chancellor to King *Ferdinand I in Lower Austria. After the death of his wife in 1556 he became a canon in Regensburg and died there a few months later.

Widmanstetter collected a remarkable library which followed him in his frequent changes of residence and for the most part was eventually acquired by the ducal library of Munich. While most of the printed volumes were destroyed in the second world war or have otherwise left Munich, a valuable collection of manuscripts survives in the Bayerische Staatsbibliothek. It includes texts in Hebrew, Arabic, Turkish, Syriac, and Armenian, alphabetical lists of quotations extracted by Widmanstetter from Latin and Greek classics, and his commentary on the Iliad, as well as an anonymous manuscript volume by Guillaume Postel, which is dedicated to Widmanstetter as chancellor of Lower Austria, and Widmanstetter's scriptural translations. By 1533 Widmanstetter had translated parts of the New Testament from the Greek, using Erasmus' version for comparison and frequently criticizing him in marginal notes for inconsistent choice of words and other shortcomings. Far more important are Widmanstetter's pioneering contributions to oriental scholarship. In 1541 Martin *Bucer met Widmanstetter at the diet of Regensburg and was shown a Latin translation of the Koran which Widmanstetter claimed to be his own work and which he hoped to publish in Basel

(AK V Epp 2496, 2509). However, the famous Latin Koran published two years later by the Basel printer Johannes Oporinus reproduced the old translation made at Toledo in the twelfth century, although it did contain Widmanstetter's *Notationes falsarum impiarumque opinionum Mahumetis.* A Syriac version of the New Testament was published by him and Guillaume Postel in 1555, and a Syriac grammar, *Syriacae linguae prima elementa,* in 1556 (both Vienna: M. Zimmermann). Autobiographical details are contained in his *De iniustissimi odii origine et causis* (c 1552) against Gumppenberg.

In 1532 Widmanstetter appended a letter to Erasmus (Ep 2614) to the *Defensiones pro Erasmo* by his friend Alonso *Enríquez.

BIBLIOGRAPHY: Allen Ep 2614 / ADB XLII 357–61 / AK V Epp 2496, 2509 / Pflug *Correspondance* I Ep 101, II Ep 240, and passim / Hans Striedl 'Der Humanist Johann Albrecht Widmanstetter … als klassischer Philologe' in *Festgabe der Bayerischen Staatsbibliothek [für] Emil Gratzl* (Wiesbaden 1953) 96–120 / Hans Striedl 'Die Bücherei des Orientalisten Johann Albrecht Widmanstetter' in *Serta Monacensia: Franz Babinger zum 15. Januar 1951* ed H.J. Kissling and A. Schmaus (Leiden 1952) 200–44 / *Encyclopaedia Judaica* (Jerusalem 1971–2) XVI 487 / *Matrikel Tübingen* I 257 no 25(?) / Martin Steinmann *Johannes Oporinus* (Basel-Stuttgart 1966) 20–31   IG & PGB

Friedrich von WIED 1478–11 March 1551
Friedrich von Wied was the youngest brother of Hermann von *Wied, archbishop of Cologne; he is not to be confused with their nephew Friedrich von Wied (d 1568) who succeeded Hermann as archbishop. He matriculated at the University of Cologne on 18 December 1493 with Hermann. Little else is known about the course of his studies, and he does not seem to have obtained any academic degrees. He did, however, receive many benefices; from 1507 to 1517 he was dean of the chapter of St Gereon's, Cologne, and until 1537 provost of the Bonn chapter; likewise he held canonries of the cathedral chapters of Cologne, where he was *custos,* Münster, and Utrecht, where he was provost. On 6 November 1522 he was elected bishop of Münster. In his own day there were already critical assessments of his

qualifications to direct an ecclesiastical principality, and on 24 March 1532 he resigned the see of Münster and retired to his benefices at Cologne. There he was among the minority party of the cathedral chapter, supporting Archbishop Hermann in his attempts to introduce the Protestant Reformation. As a result Pope *Paul III deprived him of his benefices on 16 April 1546. He retired to Wied and died there five years later.

Friedrich is mentioned in passing in Ep 2957 as a former bishop of Münster.

BIBLIOGRAPHY: Allen Ep 2957 / *Matrikel Köln* I 349 / *Die Münsterischen Chroniken des Mittelalters* ed Julius Ficker (Münster 1851) passim / Leonard Ennen *Geschichte der Stadt Köln* (Cologne-Neuss 1863–80) IV passim / Conrad Varrentrapp *Hermann von Wied und sein Reformationsversuch in Köln* (Leipzig 1878) passim / Wilhelm van Gulik *Johannes Gropper (1503 bis 1559)* (Freiburg 1906) passim / Reinhold Schwarz *Personal- und Amtsdaten der Bischöfe der Kölner Kirchenprovinz von 1500–1800* Veröffentlichungen des Kölnischen Geschichtsvereins 1 (Cologne 1914) / Johannes Gropper *Briefwechsel* I 1529–1547 ed Reinhard Braunisch (Münster 1977) passim   ROLF DECOT

Hermann von WIED 14 January 1477–15 August 1552
Hermann von Wied was a son of Count Friedrich (d 1487) and Agnes von Virneburg (d 1478); his youngest brother was Friedrich von *Wied, bishop of Münster. As early as 14 January 1490 Hermann became a member of the cathedral chapter of Cologne. He matriculated at the University of Cologne on 18 December 1493, proposing to study law; at the same time private tutors provided him with the customary training of his class in the 'knightly virtues.' His knowledge of Latin remained rudimentary, and he does not appear to have earned any academic degrees. In addition to receiving a canonry at the chapter of St Gereon's, Cologne, Hermann was appointed chancellor to the archbishop, or *Domkeppler,* on 17 April 1503, and on 14 March 1515 he was unanimously elected archbishop. The episcopal consecration did not follow, however, until three years later, at the cathedral of Bonn. In addition to the ecclesiastical principality of Cologne, Hermann held the

diocese of Paderborn from 13 June 1532 as
administrator.

Owing to the influence of his chancellor,
Johann *Gropper, the archbishop convened a
diocesan synod in 1536 in efforts to reform his
clergy. However, the failure of the religious
colloquies of 1540–1 and the influence of his
councillor Peter *Medmann, a convinced Lutheran, caused him to move over to the
Protestant camp. Such leading reformers as
*Melanchthon and *Bucer and also Philip of
*Hesse entered into correspondence with him.
Bucer twice responded to his invitation and
visited Cologne in February and December
1542. The second visit led to a rift in the
cathedral chapter, with the majority of canons
headed by Gropper and Bernhard von *Hagen
opposing their Protestant archbishop and
those of their fellow canons who supported
him. The conflict came to an end when Pope
*Paul III deposed Hermann on 16 April 1546;
the measure was not publicly announced,
however, until August, and Hermann actually
resigned on 25 February 1547. He retired to his
estate of Wied, near Koblenz, and died there
five years later as a Protestant.

Hermann published under his own name an
ordinance for the reform of his ecclesiastical
principality which was actually the work of
Bucer and Melanchthon, *Einfältiges Bedenken*
(Bonn: L. von der Müllen 1543; new edition in
modern German by Helmut Gerhards and
Wilfried Borth, Düsseldorf 1972). Erasmus first
mentioned the archbishop in connection with
the crimes perpetrated by the 'Black Band' in
1517, singling Hermann out for his firm stand
against the marauders (Ep 829). Subsequently
it was his good friend the Cologne provost
Hermann von *Neuenahr who provided contacts between Erasmus and the elector, assuring Erasmus of Herman's admiration and a
warm welcome if he were to visit Cologne (Ep
1078); however, no personal encounter took
place when Erasmus stopped in Cologne for
three weeks in October and November 1520.
Later Neuenahr suggested an approach in
writing and in 1528 Erasmus addressed a letter
to the elector reiterating the merits of his
philosophy of Christ in the face of hardening
dogmatism in both the Catholic and the
reformed camps (Ep 1976). He received a
gracious answer (Ep 1995), and after the reform

Hermann von Wied

of Basel in February 1529 Neuenahr invited
Erasmus on behalf of the elector to settle at
Cologne (Ep 2137). Later Cornelius *Agrippa of
Nettesheim likewise emphasized Hermann's
admiration for Erasmus and again suggested a
visit (Epp 2626, 2790). In response Erasmus
resolved to dedicate his edition of Origen to
the elector (Ep 3128), but it was left to *Beatus
Rhenanus to compose the dedicatory letter
addressed to Hermann von Wied (Allen I 53–6)
after Erasmus' death. Some other letters in
Erasmus' correspondence deal with Hermann's role in suppressing the Anabaptist
kingdom of Münster (Epp 2957, 2990, 3031A,
3041).

BIBLIOGRAPHY: Allen Ep 829 / Robert Stupperich NDB VIII 636–7 / ADB XII 135–47 / *Matrikel
Köln* I 349 / August Franzen *Bischof und
Reformation: Erzbischof Hermann von Wied in
Köln vor der Entscheidung zwischen Reform und
Reformation* (Münster 1971) / Schottenloher III
nos 30837–30880 VII nos 61327–61333 / Leonard Ennen *Geschichte der Stadt Köln* (Cologne-
Neuss 1863–80) IV passim / Conrad Varrentrapp *Hermann von Wied und sein Reformationsversuch in Köln* (Leipzig 1878) / Reinhold

Schwarz *Personal- und Amtsdaten der Bischöfe der Kölner Kirchenprovinz von 1500–1800* Veröffentlichungen des Kölnischen Geschichtsvereins 1 (Cologne 1914)   ROLF DECOT

Adriaan WIELE of Brussels, documented 1498–1530
New research will be needed to add to P.S. Allen's account of the life of Adriaan Wiele (van der Wiele, Wiel, Vilius), who matriculated at the University of Louvain on 12 November 1498. His training appears to have been in the arts and Ep 2408 demonstrates his skill in the art of humanistic letter-writing. His career at the Netherlands court confirms his dedication to humanistic education. In a letter of 1507 he described himself as supervisor and tutor ('custos et pedagogus') of the children of Philip the Handsome of *Burgundy and *Joanna of Spain, that is to say the future *Charles v and his sisters *Eleanor and *Isabella, who were being brought up at the court of their aunt, *Margaret of Austria, in Mechelen. In 1513 he was the teacher of Charles' pages. On 27 July 1521, when *Christian ii of Denmark visited Bruges for meetings with Charles v, Wiele replied in his name to a welcoming address given by Frans van *Cranevelt. In March 1523 he was secretary to the council of Brabant at Brussels and belonged to the circle of Erasmians at court (Ep 1351). In 1530 he attended the diet of Augsburg and from there wrote to Erasmus in November about the hostile agitation of *Ferdinand's preacher, *Medardus. He offered his assistance in obtaining the payment of Erasmus' pension and suggested the address of their common friend Pieter *Gillis in Antwerp in case Erasmus wished to reply. The letter indicates a measure of familiarity between Erasmus and Wiele, who as a widower was worried about the care of his eight children and was translating Erasmus' *Vidua christiana* into French (Ep 2408).
    BIBLIOGRAPHY: Allen Ep 1351 / *Matricule de Louvain* iii-1 179 / de Vocht *Literae ad Craneveldium* 118, 372   PGB

Johann WILDENAUER *See Johannes Sylvius* EGRANUS

Johann WILER of Basel, 1491–1539
Johann Wiler (Hans Wyler, Johannes or Janus Wilerus, Wilerius) was descended from a

highly respected merchant family of Basel. His father, also named Johann (d 1499), was married to Elisabeth Oberried (d 1507), the sister of a rich Basel banker. The older Wiler owned an interest in several mines and lived for a number of years in London as a jeweller. He maintained a partnership with a merchant of jewels located in Basel and also kept a stock of the books produced by the Basel printer Michael Wenssler.
    The younger Johann was born in London and returned to Basel in the autumn of 1503. On 25 May 1513 he was declared of age and took over his inheritance. Little is known about his commercial activities, but he undertook several business trips to England, where his father, as he put it, had found happiness. On one of these trips he took Ep 581 to Antwerp. In 1512 he married Elisabeth Zscheckenbürlin, the great-niece of Hieronymus *Zscheckenbürlin and the heiress to much property including some manuscript chronicles to which her husband produced additions. He sat on the great council of Basel and in 1521 was one of the handful of magistrates who showed moral strength in refusing their share of the French pension money. His piety and integrity are emphasized by Albert Burer, the secretary of *Beatus Rhenanus. In 1522 he was losing his grip mentally and was placed under guardianship. After he had died a childless widower, Bonifacius *Amerbach remembered that he was his kinsman and gathered genealogical material for a possible claim to Wiler's estate (which was inventoried on 17 November 1539).
    BIBLIOGRAPHY: Allen Ep 581 / Rudolf Wackernagel *Geschichte der Stadt Basel* (Basel 1907–54) iii 119, 262, 285–6, 310, 52* / *Basler Chroniken* iv 395–408, vi 555, vii 355, 490 / BRE Epp 124, 125, 143 / AK i Ep 164, v Ep 2390 introductions and passim / W.R. Staehelin *Wappenbuch der Stadt Basel* (Basel [1917–30]) / *Urkundenbuch der Stadt Basel* ed R. Wackernagel et al (Basel 1890–1910) ix 374, x 277   PGB

WILHELM *See William iv, duke of* BAVARIA, *William v, duke of* CLEVES

WILLEM of Haarlem documented at Liège 1508–36
Little is known about Willem (Gulielmus Harlemus), evidently a native of Haarlem, who was a Brother of the Common Life attached to

the famous school of Liège. The registers of the Brethren of Liège list in 1508 'Wilhelmus Haerlen' and in 1536 'Wilhéaume Harlem.' As the name no longer occurs in the rolls of 1542 and thereafter, it seems likely that he died between 1536 and 1542. He is the author of two prayers published by Simon Verepaeus in his *Precationum piarum enchiridion* (Antwerp 1565). A marginal note in this book identifies him as 'Guilielmus Harlemius, rector domus Hieronimianae Leodiensis' ('William of Haarlem, rector of the school of the Brethren of the Common Life at Liège').

In May 1530 Willem visited Conradus *Goclenius in Louvain but would hardly seem to have been well acquainted with him. He complained bitterly that he had been maliciously reported to Erasmus as one of his enemies, swore to his innocence, and actually persuaded Goclenius to write to Erasmus on his behalf (Ep 2352). Three months later, on 27 August, Goclenius received a messenger from Liège with a note by Paschasius *Berselius concerning the machinations of Theodericus *Hezius, who had confiscated such books by Erasmus as were found in the school of the Brethren (Ep 2369). The unnamed messenger could perhaps be Willem of Haarlem, who was evidently eager to win back Erasmus' favour. In November 1531 Maarten *Lips, a friend of Goclenius, answered a query from Erasmus concerning Willem of Haarlem by stating that he had talked to the man. Willem, he said, implored Erasmus to forgive him and blamed the agitation against Erasmus entirely on some pupils of his school and also on a brother Christian (*Christianus Hieronymita), evidently a colleague of his (Ep 2566).

BIBLIOGRAPHY: de Vocht CTL II 616, III 92 / L.-E. Halkin 'Les Frères de la Vie Commune de la Maison Saint-Jérôme de Liège' *Bulletin de l'Institut archéologique liégeois* 65 (1945) 10, 22
LÉON-E. HALKIN

WILLEM of Louvain See Willem GHEERSHOVEN

Bridget WILTSHIRE
The daughter and heiress of Sir John *Wiltshire, comptroller of Calais, Bridget married Sir Richard *Wingfield as his second wife in or after 1513. They had four sons and two daughters. Erasmus greeted her in a letter to her husband in March 1518 (Ep 791). After

Wingfield's death in 1525 she married Sir Nicholas Hervey.

BIBLIOGRAPHY: Allen Ep 791 / DNB XXI 661 / LP III p 244 Wingfield, Sir Richard / Note: according to J. Anstis *The Register of the Most Noble Order of the Garter* (1724) I 233, at the time of her marriage to Wingfield Bridget was the widow of Sir Michael Harvey
C.S. KNIGHTON

John WILTSHIRE d after 5 July 1527
Wiltshire was knighted in 1504 or 1505 by command of the Emperor *Maximilian I. He lived at Dartford, Kent, where he once entertained Cardinal Thomas *Wolsey. In 1520 he was sheriff of Kent and treasurer of Calais and from 1503 to 1519 was comptroller of Calais. His daughter and heiress, Bridget *Wiltshire married Sir Richard *Wingfield in about 1513. Writing to Wingfield in March 1518, Erasmus conveyed his greetings to his correspondent's father-in-law (Ep 791).

BIBLIOGRAPHY: Allen Ep 791 / W.A. Shaw *The Knights of England* (London 1906) II 34 / George Cavendish *Thomas Wolsey, late Cardinal, his Life and Death* ed R. Lockyer (London 1962) 75
C.S. KNIGHTON

Jakob WIMPFELING of Sélestat, 25 July 1450–15 November 1528
Jakob Wimpfeling (Wimpheling) was born in Sélestat, Upper Alsace, the eldest son of Nikolaus, a saddler, and his wife, Katharina Bleger. After attending Sélestat's excellent Latin school directed by Ludwig *Dringenberg he studied from 1464 in Freiburg, from 1468 in Erfurt, and from 1469 in Heidelberg. After obtaining his MA in 1471 he turned to the study of canon law but soon switched to theology. At the same time he taught in the faculty of arts, of which he was dean in 1479, and in 1481 he was elected rector of the university. Apart from a short *De arte metrificandi* (Strasbourg: M. Hupfuff 1505) written for use in the schools and a number of historico-political poems, the most important literary fruit of his Heidelberg years was the dialogue *Stylpho* (n p [1495]). Though not intended for the stage, this dialogue initiated the genre of the Latin comedy in German humanist literature.

From 1484 to 1498 Wimpfeling lived at Speyer in possession of a benefice and served for a while as cathedral preacher. In these years he composed, among other works, a lengthy poem in praise of Speyer cathedral (1486, published in 1584) and two treatises about the rights and dignities of the clergy: *Oratio querulosa* (n p [1493–4]) and *Immunitatis et libertatis ecclesiasticae status ... defensio* (n p [1494]). These treatises express his basic faith in the traditional church, while in his poems about St Mary (*De triplici candore Mariae,* n p [1493]; *De nuntio angelico,* [Basel: J. Bergmann] 1494) he sided with the Franciscans in the dispute over the Immaculate Conception, a doctrine he was to defend throughout his life. At the same time he strongly advocated clerical reform and became the mouthpiece of German patriotic indignation over the marriage between *Charles VIII of France and Anne of Brittany. However, his pedagogical interests remained in the foreground. After writing *Elegantiarum medulla* (n p [1493]), an introduction to Latin composition, he presented the first comprehensive exposition of his views on education in the *Isidoneus Germanicus* ([Strasbourg]: J. Grüninger [1496–7]).

In 1496 Wimpfeling received a licence in theology, and two years later, at the request of Philip, elector Palatine, he returned to Heidelberg as professor of poetry and rhetoric. He joined the Sodalitas Rhenania which had been founded by Celtis in 1495 and counted *Reuchlin among its members. In 1498 his pedagogic-political dialogue *Philippica* (Strasbourg: M. Schott 1498) was performed in the presence of the Elector Philip; to the elector's son, the future Louis V, elector *Palatine, he dedicated his *Agatharchia* (Strasbourg: M. Schott 1498), a study of the model prince. During the same period he also composed the *Adolescentia* (Strasbourg: M. Flach 1500) his most significant educational work, which won him recognition and admiration in many circles and remained for decades the definitive work in Germany on humanistic education.

In 1501 Wimpfeling relinquished his lectureship in Heidelberg, and after an abortive plan to found a hermitage with his friends Johann Geiler of Kaysersberg and Christoph von *Utenheim, he retired to the Williamite monastery in Strasbourg, where he lived without fixed responsibilities and on a modest income. After that he left Strasbourg only occasionally, for instance in 1504, 1508, and 1510, to escort the sons of Strasbourg patricians to the universities of Freiburg and Heidelberg. For a few months in 1512 he became the priest and spiritual adviser of a nunnery in the Black Forest, but his old dream of a reclusive life failed to come true. Otherwise he dedicated himself to his studies and his plans for educational reform. His *Germania* (Strasbourg: J. Prüss 1501) and *Epithoma rerum Germanicarum* (Strasbourg: J. Prüss 1505) were followed in 1508 by a history of the bishopric of Strasbourg (Strasbourg: J. Grüninger). In addition he edited the eclogues of Baptista *Mantuanus (Strasbourg: J. Prüss 1503) and published *De integritate* (Strasbourg: J. Knobloch 1505), a protest against the accumulation of benefices and the immorality of the clergy. A year later he published a biography of Gerson (*De vita et miraculis Joannis Gerson,* Strasbourg: J. Prüss 1506) and the *Apologia pro republica christiana* (Pforzheim: T. Anshelm 1506). In 1510 the Emperor *Maximilian I, following a suggestion of Jacob *Spiegel, requested him to write a memorandum modelled after the *Gravamina* of the German nation (1457) which was to serve as a guideline for negotiations with the Roman curia. Greatly flattered, Wimpfeling complied, but Maximilian made no use of his treatise and it was not printed until the beginning of the Protestant Reformation (Sélestat: L. Schürer 1520).

Wimpfeling's great productivity in the Strasbourg years was due in part to his friendly contact with Johann Geiler and Sebastian *Brant, older men who had shaped the humanistic outlook particular to the Upper Rhine region. Wimpfeling himself became the central figure of a Strasbourg literary society (Epp 302, 305). The three men were united not only in their fight for better education and against corruption but also in their patriotic fervour and decidedly conservative principles. They maintained a position midway between *Hutten and other radical humanists of the next generation and the medieval tradition of moral theology: they believed in the Empire, followed Gerson's views on church reform, and conceded to the classical authors no more than a limited role in their educational and cultural program. These views involved Wimpfeling in numerous controversies. Thomas Murner in his *Germania nova* (1502) attacked the view that Alsace had always belonged to Germany, a thesis maintained in Wimpfeling's

Germania. On account of his hostile remarks against monks he also came in conflict with the Augustinians in Freiburg (1505–7) and as a result was twice summoned to Rome. He was saved by the intervention of his friends (Ep 333; Knepper 349–51). In 1512 he launched an indirect but desperate appeal to *Julius II, denouncing vice and corruption in the church (*Orationis Angeli anachoritae ... ad Julium II ... confirmatio* (n p, n d)).

Erasmus clearly wanted no part in Wimpfeling's tenaciously borne grudge against the Swiss for having fought Maximilian and forsaken the Empire in 1499 (Ep 858). Another dispute, however, affected Wimpfeling's relationship with Erasmus. When Jakob *Locher, since 1503 professor of poetry and rhetoric at Freiburg, publicly defended the value of poetry independent of theology, Wimpfeling and his friend Udalricus *Zasius effected his dismissal from the university. Locher avenged himself by deriding Wimpfeling and Zasius, and in 1510 Wimpfeling published a response, *Contra turpem libellum Philomusi* (n p, n d), in which he claimed that theology definitely took precedence over poetry and that secular poets simply corrupted youthful readers, a reversal of his previous position when he had conceded a certain educational value to ancient poetry. A year later, when the *Moria* was reprinted in Strasbourg through his efforts, he found himself obliged to append to his edition a letter to Erasmus indicating that he had never intended his verdict to apply to the *Moria* (Ep 224). Wimpfeling seems to have approved wholeheartedly of Erasmus' defence of the *Moria* against *Dorp (Ep 337), which he read over dinner with *Volz and *Sapidus (Ep 368).

In the *Diatriba* (Haguenau: H. Gran 1514), Wimpfeling's third important educational work, he expressly recommended that Erasmus' *Adagia* be read in schools. In the same year he made Erasmus' personal acquaintance: on his journey to Basel Erasmus had stopped in Strasbourg in August 1514 and was officially welcomed by the members of the recently founded literary society. In the name of the society, Wimpfeling sent a farewell address to Erasmus in Basel (Ep 302), which Erasmus answered with an elaborate letter of thanks (Ep 305).

For Wimpfeling Erasmus' visit was the climax and fitting conclusion to his residence in Strasbourg. A year later he returned to his native city of Sélestat and from then on lived in the house of his sister Magdalene *Wimpfeling, in modest circumstances and increasingly burdened by illness. Mostly because of his poor health he declined repeated invitations from his friend Utenheim, who had become bishop of Basel. The first of these he mentioned to Erasmus in January 1516 (Ep 382), reporting at the same time that he had praised him in his unpublished catalogue of the bishops of Mainz. Erasmus answered warmly (Ep 385). There is evidence for ongoing correspondence (Ep 612), but primarily the relationship was maintained thereafter through greetings and news related by common friends (Epp 575, 633, 858, 1063).

In Sélestat Wimpfeling was chaplain of the altars of St Anthony and St Catherine until 1524; he was also the focus of a literary society that counted among its members Paul Volz, *Beatus Rhenanus, Martin *Bucer, Johannes Sapidus, the head of the Latin school, and the printer Lazarus Schürer. Together with his nephew Jakob Spiegel, Wimpfeling supported the efforts of the city council to win control over Sélestat's parishes and thus prevent the accumulation of benefices. The *Oratio vulgi ad Deum* (n p [c 1517]) shows Wimpfeling on the eve of the peasants' war fully aware of the plight of the farmers faced with the avarice of the clergy. Thereafter Wimpfeling ceased to publish new works except for a dirge on the death of the Emperor Maximilian and was content to assist Schürer with his editions, to which he contributed some prefaces. Only once did he return to his former interests: in 1521 he wrote a thorough memorandum advocating the reform of the University of Heidelberg.

Wimpfeling did not take a public stand for or against Reuchlin, perhaps because of his aversion to Jews. Although he maintained a similar silence with regard to *Luther, his loyalty to the church of Rome was – for all his criticism of corruption – never in doubt. However, on 1 September 1520 he sent his friend Utenheim a copy of Erasmus' Ep 1033 to Cardinal Albert of *Brandenburg, which had been printed by Schürer among others. In his accompanying letter to Utenheim he expressed the wish that all German bishops might plead with *Leo X to treat Luther with mercy. After

Luther's breach with the church, Wimpfeling hardened in his opposition to him and brought his full authority to bear against the progress of the new faith at Sélestat. Since the majority of his friends accepted Luther, Wimpfeling found himself increasingly isolated. During his last years he frequently voiced complaints about his illness, the burden of old age, and the disloyalty of his friends. In 1520 he wrote in his last surviving letter to Erasmus that he longed for death and called Erasmus' *Enchiridion* and *Ratio verae theologiae* the only comfort left to him (Ep 1067). Perhaps because of Wimpfeling's complaints that all his friends had deserted him, Erasmus wrote him some affectionate lines, encouraging him, without success, to resume friendly relations with Sapidus, whose Lutheranism had caused a rift between the two men (Ep 1517). In the autumn of 1525 Wimpfeling was struck a further blow when three of his relatives were decapitated at Sélestat for their participation in the peasant revolt. He died three years later and was buried in the parish church. In a letter published with the second edition of the *Ciceronianus* (Ep 2088) Erasmus reacted warmly, though perhaps without the deep feelings expressed at the loss of some of his other friends. He had earlier honoured Wimpfeling with a mention in the *Ciceronianus* itself (ASD I-2 685–6). In comparing him with Erasmus, Otto Herding noted that Wimpfeling remained a stranger to the Greek language and civilization and often clung to scholastic theology. Stubborn, quarrelsome, and parochial in his devotion to Germany, he fell short of the Erasmian ideal of a humanist. Wimpfeling himself acknowledged the intellectual gap between Erasmus and himself in his appendix to Schürer's edition of Prudentius (1520). In the style of his time he used the adage of the elephant and the mouse (*Adagia* I ix 70; Knepper 306).

A critical edition of Wimpfeling's writings is progressing: I: *Adolescentia* and II-1 (life of Geiler, etc) ed Otto Herding (Munich 1965–   ). There is a modern edition of *Stylpho* by Hugo Holstein (Berlin 1892) and a German translation of *Pädagogische Schriften* ed Joseph Freundgen (Paderborn 1892).

BIBLIOGRAPHY: Allen Ep 224 / Ludwig Geiger in ADB XLIV 524–37 / *Matrikel Freiburg* I-1 29 / *Matrikel Heidelberg* I 328 and passim / Erich Kleineidam *Universitas Studii Erffordensis* (Leipzig 1964–80) II 56–7 and passim / BRE 621–2 and passim / AK I Ep 28 and passim / BA *Oekolampads* I 17–21 and passim / Joseph Knepper *Jakob Wimpfeling* (Freiburg 1902, repr 1965) / Schmidt *Histoire littéraire* I 1–188, II 317–40 / François Rapp *Réformes et Réformation à Strasbourg 1450–1525* (Paris 1974) 160–9 / Richard Newald *Probleme und Gestalten des deutschen Humanismus* (Berlin 1963) 346–68 and passim / Otto Herding 'Wimpfelings Begegnung mit Erasmus' in *Renatae litterae … August Buck … dargebracht* ed K. Heitmann and E. Schroeder (Frankfurt 1973) / L.W. Spitz *The Religious Renaissance of the German Humanists* (Cambridge, Mass, 1963) 41–60 and passim / Emil von Borries *Wimpfeling und Murner im Kampf um die ältere Geschichte des Elsasses* (Heidelberg 1926)   BARBARA KÖNNEKER

Magdalene WIMPFELING of Sélestat, d 15 August 1532
Magdalene, the younger sister of Jakob *Wimpfeling, was born after 1450. In 1483 she married the baker Jakob Spiegel, also of Sélestat. After Spiegel's death in 1493, Magdalene married another baker, Hans Meier (Meyer, Maier). When Wimpfeling returned to Sélestat in 1515, Magdalene was again widowed, and Wimpfeling made his home with her (Ep 2088), having finally obtained an appointment as chaplain in the parish church. Wimpfeling presented a manuscript volume of Latin sermons to the parish library in the name of his sister and himself. She was buried in the parish church next to her brother and was survived by her two sons, Jakob *Spiegel and Johannes *Maius.

BIBLIOGRAPHY: Allen Ep 2088 / Schmidt *Histoire littéraire* I 4, 13, 88, and passim / Joseph Gény *Die Reichsstadt Schlettstadt und ihr Anteil an den socialpolitischen und religiösen Bewegungen der Jahre 1490–1536* (Freiburg 1900) 30–1, 188–9   MIRIAM U. CHRISMAN

Conradus Coci de WIMPINA of Buchen, d 16 June 1531
Konrad Koch was born at Buchen, between Heidelberg and Würzburg, the son of a tanner; subsequently he called himself Conradus Coci de Fagis, after his native town, or de Wimpina

after Wimpfen, on the Neckar, where his family had originated and where he later held a canonry. In the winter term of 1479–80 he matriculated at the University of Leipzig, where he was a MA in 1484 and stayed on to teach in the faculty of arts while taking his degrees in theology. On 5 January 1503 he was promoted doctor of divinity. For the summer term of 1494 he had been rector of the university and in 1501–2 vice-chancellor. In 1506 he was appointed professor of theology at the newly founded University of Frankfurt an der Oder and also served as its first rector. From 1517 he was firmly committed to defending the traditional church against *Luther. It was with his help that in December 1517 Johann Tetzel drafted his reply to Luther's Ninety-five Theses for presentation to a provincial chapter of the Dominicans at Frankfurt. In 1530 Wimpina accompanied the Elector Joachim of Brandenburg to the diet of Augsburg, where he continued his opposition to the reformers. He died in the following year in the monastery of Amorbach in his native Franconia.

Wimpina composed a number of writings of humanistic-rhetorical and especially theological nature. His major attack on the Lutherans, *Sectarum, errorum, hallutinationum ... ab origine ... ad haec usque nostra tempora ... librorum partes tres* (Frankfurt a. O.: J. Hanau 1528), was no doubt the work of which he had a copy sent to Erasmus in the winter of 1529–30 (Ep 2247). Nothing is known about Erasmus' reaction.

BIBLIOGRAPHY: Allen Ep 2247 / ADB XLIII 330–5 / RGG VI 1728 / *Matrikel Leipzig* I 320, 403, II 17, III 410, and passim / *Matrikel Frankfurt* I 1, 48 / Ludwig Weiss 'Würzburger Bistumsangehörige als Weihekandidaten in Merseburg 1470–1556' *Würzburger Diözesangeschichtsblätter* 18–19 (1956–7) 148–95, esp 165–6 / Schottenloher II 392–3, III 19, V 283 / For a list of Wimpina's writings see Christian Gottlieb Jöcher et al *Allgemeines Gelehrten-Lexicon* (Leipzig 1750–1897, repr 1960–1) IV 2003–4

MICHAEL ERBE

Pieter WINCKEL documented c 1473–1505
Pieter Winckel was Erasmus' first teacher (CWE Ep 447:87ff; *Compendium vitae* CWE 4 405–6). The boy attended his lessons from the age of four until about 1477, possibly at Rotterdam

but more likely at Gouda. In 1485 Winckel was the second teacher of the school attached to the church of St John in Gouda; in 1487 he was the principal teacher and afterwards vice-pastor. In 1491–2 he went to Louvain and in 1496 to Mechelen, while an earlier trip to Louvain may well have given him the opportunity of transcribing a manuscript of Juvenal which may be identical with one preserved in the Bodleian Library, Oxford (MS Auct. F 5.2, dated 1478; Allen Ep 3:40n, VI xix).

According to the *Compendium vitae* Winckel was one of three guardians who took charge of Erasmus and his brother after the death of their parents. In Ep 1 Erasmus questioned Winckel's skill in managing their inheritance, and in Ep 447 he questioned his skill as a teacher, although he had to grant that the 'man was commonly regarded as pious and honourable.' He recalled how Winckel had once sent him a severe reply, probably to Ep 1 (cf *De conscribendis epistolis* ASD I-2 217). Being himself a priest, Winckel persistently encouraged Erasmus to opt for the monastic life (Ep 1436 and *Compendium vitae*). Winckel is last documented on 13 February 1505, when he witnessed the will of his fellow-townsman G.W. Raet.

BIBLIOGRAPHY: Allen Ep 1 and I 579 / A. Hyma *The Youth of Erasmus* 2nd ed (New York 1968) 59–63 and passim

C.G. VAN LEIJENHORST

Jan van WINCKELE of Louvain, d 27 March 1555
Jan van Winckele (Winckel) was the son of another Jan, who had prospered as a notary of the University of Louvain. On 28 February 1500 the son matriculated in the same university at a very young age and in 1506 he ranked first among more than one hundred MA graduates. At first he turned to legal studies, but in 1515 he received a doctorate in medicine. He lived at Louvain in a stately family mansion and since neither he nor his sister, Clara, had any offspring, under the terms of his father's will his home became a college for law students. In his own will of 20 December 1549 Winckele set out rules for the new college which prevented future inmates from studying the humanities and classical languages along with jurisprudence.

Some time after Erasmus' move to Louvain in

1517 Winckele seems to have entertained him and Maarten van *Dorp at a dinner where they met Frans van *Cranevelt, who was visiting Louvain. By the end of 1519, however, Winckele was sharply attacked in the anonymous *Epistola de magistris nostris Lovaniensibus* attributed to Wilhelm *Nesen. In the *Epistola* Winckele is given prominence amid the opponents of the new learning. Described as rich, uncultured, and conceited, he is said to be the inept physician of vice-chancellor Jan *Briart, who was then on his deathbed. Henry de Vocht suggested that Erasmus' blunt Ep 1042 of October–November 1519 might have been addressed to Winckele.

BIBLIOGRAPHY: CWE Ep 1042 / de Vocht CTL I 441–3, 585–6 / de Vocht *Literae ad Craneveldium* Ep 85 / *Matricule de Louvain* III-1 198   PGB

Ulrich WINDEMACHER *See Ulricus* FABRICIUS

Jodocus WINDSHEMIUS *See Jodocus Textoris de* WINSHEIM

Richard WINGFIELD c 1469–22 July 1525
Sir Richard Wingfield (Wimphildus) was a younger son of Sir John Wingfield of Letheringham, Suffolk, and Elizabeth, daughter of Sir John FitzLewis of West Horndon, Essex. What education he received is uncertain, but he is said to have attended Gray's Inn and the University of Ferrara. In 1497 he served against the Cornish rebels and became an esquire of the body to *Henry VII in 1500, thereafter taking occasional military commands. He was knighted by 14 November 1511, when he was appointed marshal of Calais, and in the next year undertook the first of many diplomatic missions which won him the confidence of *Henry VIII and the esteem of foreign rulers. From August 1513 to May 1519 he was deputy of Calais, where he was much respected and not too subservient to refuse orders he considered inept. In 1520 he became English ambassador to France in succession to Sir Thomas *Boleyn; the following year saw him as mediator between *Francis I and *Charles V. The emperor gave him an annuity and recommended him for the garter, which was conferred on 23 April 1522, in which year he also

arranged the emperor's visit to England. His high favour with the king earned him many grants of land including the manor of Kimbolton, in Huntingdonshire, where he built a seat. In 1522 and 1523 he was a justice of the peace for twenty-five counties. On 14 April 1524 he was appointed chancellor of the duchy of Lancaster; Thomas *More deputized for him when he was sent on his final mission, to Spain. Wingfield died at Toledo and was buried there. More succeeded him as chancellor of the duchy and also as high steward of Cambridge University – More had been a candidate for this office in 1524 but had stood down at the king's request to allow Wingfield's appointment.

Although there is little evidence of his interests outside diplomacy, Wingfield was a friend of Hugh Latimer, who commended him as having high regard for men of letters and the arts. He was known to Erasmus (Epp 375, 773), who, however, confused him with his brother Sir Robert, also a diplomat (Ep 362). In March 1518 Erasmus sent him a brief letter recalling his request to be told of a good physician (Ep 791). Wingfield married first Katherine Woodville, a sister of Edward IV's queen and widow of Henry Stafford, second duke of Buckingham, and of Jasper Tudor, duke of Bedford (Henry VII's uncle). After her death in 1497 he married Bridget, the daughter of Sir John *Wiltshire, by whom he had four sons and two daughters.

BIBLIOGRAPHY: Allen Ep 375 / DNB XXI 658–61 / C.H. Cooper *Athenae Cantabrigienses* (Cambridge 1858–61) I 32–3, 527 (which does not support the DNB allegation that Wingfield was educated at the university) / J.B. Mullinger *The History of the University of Cambridge from the Earliest Times to the Royal Injunctions of 1535* (Cambridge 1873) 584 / G.R. Elton *Studies in Tudor and Stuart Government and Politics* (Cambridge 1974) I 136, 140 / John Anstis *The Register of the Most Noble Order of the Garter* (London 1724) I 219–34 / J.M. Wingfield *Some Records of the Wingfield Family* (London 1925) 145–226 / G.E.C[ockayne] *The Complete Peerage of England* ed V. Gibbs et al (London 1910–59) II 73, 390 / C. Rawcliffe *The Staffords, Earls of Stafford and Dukes of Buckingham 1394–1521* (Cambridge 1978) 23, 36, 126–9   C.S. KNIGHTON

Robert WINGFIELD c 1464–18 March 1539
Robert was the seventh son of Sir John
Wingfield of Letheringham, Suffolk, and followed a military and diplomatic career similar
to that of his younger brother Sir Richard
*Wingfield. Both brothers served against the
Cornish rebels in 1497. In 1505 Robert went on
a pilgrimage to Rome and in January 1508
returned from the first of many embassies to the
imperial court. By the following July he was
knighted; other royal favours followed, and in
1511 he was styled a councillor and knight of
the body. Between 1511 and 1517 he was
mostly abroad, at Calais and on missions to the
Emperor *Maximilian I, but his fervent anti-
French prejudices made him the dupe of
Maximilian, and he was chastised by *Wolsey
and *Henry VIII himself. After some years in
semi-retirement in England he was sent abroad
again on a mission to *Charles V in December
1521, by which time he had become a privy
councillor and vice-chamberlain of the king's
household. In 1523 he was appointed to a
command in the English force to invade France
but remained at Calais as lieutenant of the
castle. After a final embassy to Brussels in 1525
he retired to Calais and was appointed deputy
there in October 1526. His reorganization of
the town's defences aroused considerable
hostility, but after vacating the post in March
1531 he continued to reside there, where he
had much property, and served as mayor in
1534.

Wingfield was brought up by his stepmother, Anne, Lady Scrope, and in 1520 was
specially admitted to Lincoln's Inn, London.
Otherwise nothing is known of his education
save that he became fluent in French and
German – a talent which may account for his
employment in diplomatic affairs, for which he
otherwise showed little aptitude. For long a
firm anti-Lutheran, in his last months he
expressed approval of the king's ecclesiastical
changes. Unlike his brother he is not known to
have shown much interest in learning, although *Pirckheimer described him as well-
read (Ep 326A). He edited a book entitled
*Disceptatio super dignitate et magnitudine regno-
rum Britannici et Gallici habita ab utriusque
oratoribus et legatis in concilio Constantiensi*
(Louvain: D. Martens 1517). The parallel

careers of the Wingfield brothers caused
Erasmus a moment of confusion in 1515 when
he wrote of Robert when he meant Richard (Ep
362), but elsewhere he was able to distinguish
between the two of them (Ep 375).

BIBLIOGRAPHY: Allen Ep 326A / DNB XXI
662–4   C.S. KNIGHTON

Nicolaas van WINGHE of Louvain,
c 1495–28 December 1552
Nicolaas van Winghe (Winghius, called Wi-
nantius by Erasmus), a descendant of a re-
spectable family in Louvain, was the younger
son of Nicolaas, a butcher and executioner.
He matriculated in Louvain on 27 October
1511 and had obtained a MA before joining the
Austin canons of St Maartensdal in Louvain in
1518. Winghe held several offices in the
monastery; he was librarian for several years,
procurator from 1532 to about 1540, then
sub-prior. In 1548 he left Louvain to become
rector and confessor of the Austin nuns of
Mishagen, north of Antwerp.

Van Winghe's great achievement was a
Flemish translation of the Bible (Antwerp: B.
Gravius 1548). In line with the medieval
tradition of vernacular renderings for private
devotion, it was remarkably successful and ran
through some twenty editions of the entire
Bible and some thirty separate editions of the
New Testament. Prior to printing, the transla-
tion had been read and approved by his friends
Ruard *Tapper, Pieter de *Corte, and Govaert
*Strijroy, who were all prominent theologians.
His Flemish translation of the *Imitation of Christ*
(Antwerp 1552) was dedicated to Theodoricus
*Hezius and ran through fifteen editions. He
also translated and edited patristic works; his
Flemish translation of Flavius Josephus' Jewish
history (Antwerp: S. Cocus 1553) was pub-
lished after his death.

Nicolaas van Winghe was on friendly terms
with Jacobus *Latomus. His friendship and
correspondence with Gerard *Morinck extended over many years (see de Vocht MHL, who
prints two letters), and afforded Morinck an
opportunity to defend Erasmus' Bible scholarship. At St Maartensdal van Winghe and the
sub-prior Rochus *Hyems were at the centre of
unswerving opposition to Erasmus, thus creating many problems for Erasmus' good friend

and their fellow-monk, Maarten *Lips. From Lips' reports to Erasmus (Epp 1837, 2566) it appears that van Winghe had written an attack upon Erasmus. Although Hyems wished to publish it, no more is heard about it.

BIBLIOGRAPHY: Allen Ep 1837 / W. Lourdaux in NBW VII 1086–8 / Matricule de Louvain III-1 434 / de Vocht MHL 556–72 / de Vocht CTL III 74–5 and passim   IG & PGB

Nikolaus WINMANN of Saanen, documented 1522–50

Nikolaus Winmann (Wynmann, Wimmanus) was born at Saanen, in the Bernese Oberland close to the boundary of the Valais. Thus he learnt to speak French and admire Cardinal Matthäus *Schiner. He learnt to swim at the age of thirteen when his mother took him to the popular spa of Leuk, in the Valais, and swimming remained a lifelong passion to which he devoted a book in humanistic style, the *Colymbetes* (Augsburg: H. Steiner 1538), describing various techniques and modes of instruction and relating many stories of feats and accidents. When he was sent to attend school at Zürich he found that swimming in the lake was a common practice among the boys. Later he continued his education at the school of St Elizabeth at Wrocław, no doubt following the precedent set by Thomas Platter from Valais. After his sojourn at Wrocław he lived with his family in Fribourg, Switzerland (Ep 2439). In March 1523 Winmann matriculated at the University of Vienna. *Ursinus Velius, who lectured there from 1524 became his teacher. After a vacation at Fribourg he visited Basel on his way back to Vienna and followed Erasmus on the street but was too shy to introduce himself. When Erasmus later learnt about the incident he responded with a warm letter (Epp 2439, 2486).

In December 1528 Winmann matriculated at Tübingen, primarily to study Hebrew; however he soon found time to explore the Nebelhöhle, a cave in the region of Blaubeuren. After another visit to Fribourg he went to Ingolstadt in the spring of 1533, teaching Greek from 1534 and both Greek and Hebrew from 1536. In 1538 he left Ingolstadt and after a visit to the abbey of St Emmeran at Regensburg went to Vienna in the autumn of 1539 to head Johannes *Fabri's college of St Nicholas. On

the way he fell in with Georgius *Loxanus, and their conversation inspired him to compose his *Syncretismus* (Cologne: J. Gymnich 1541) on the interrelated issues of religious concord and resistance against the Turks. This work gave him an opportunity to acknowledge his admiration for Erasmus, which he also communicated to Johann von *Botzheim (Ep 2977). After Fabri's death Winmann moved to Silesia, where his friends Loxanus and Georg von *Logau lived. He was appointed master of the school at Nysa (Neisse), and although it burnt down on 20 May 1542, he published in 1544 at Wrocław some *Dialogi* for use in the Nysa school. In 1548 he is documented as rector of the Protestant school of Elbląg (Elbing), east of Gdansk. In 1549 he sailed from Gdansk past Copenhagen and Jutland to Amsterdam. An account of this journey, *Navigationis maris arctoi ... descriptio*, was published at Basel [M. Isengrin 1550?]. The preface, dated from Speyer on 23 April 1550, is the last record we have of Winmann.

BIBLIOGRAPHY: Allen Ep 2439 / G. Bauch 'Beiträge zur Litteraturgeschichte des schlesischen Humanismus, v' Zeitschrift des Vereins für Geschichte und Altertum Schlesiens 37 (1905) 120–68, esp 131–68 / P. Beck 'Eine Quelle für Gustav Schwabs Gedicht: Der Reiter und der Bodensee' Zeitschrift der Gesellschaft für Geschichte, Altertums- und Volkskunde von Freiburg 22 (1906) 225–32 / DHBS VII 391 / Matrikel Wien III-1 30 / Matrikel Tübingen I 263   PGB

Jodocus Textoris de WINSHEIM of Windsheim, d 3 November 1520

Jodocus Textoris (Eckart) was best known by the name Jodocus Winsheim, which recalled his native city of Windsheim, fifty kilometres west of Nürnberg. In the spring term of 1502 he matriculated at Erfurt and there received his BA in 1504 and his MA early in 1507. He began to teach at the faculty of arts and was admitted to the faculty council in 1515; in 1517 he was appointed to the office of *taxator*, or assessor of residential fees. At the same time he pursued the study of theology and obtained his licence in the spring term of 1517, when he was appointed preacher to the chapter of Haug, near Würzburg, succeeding the gifted Johann Reyss.

Winsheim was in some measure attracted to

the humanist movement; as early as 1512 he had edited the *Bucolica* of Antonio Geraldini for the Erfurt printer Mathes Maler (von Hase no 347), but he did not belong to the humanist circle of either *Eobanus or *Mutianus. Rather he sympathized with the ideals of *Wimpfeling, and his advocacy of religious reform, which began at an early age, is reminiscent of Johann Geiler of Kaysersberg. In 1515 he published a *Forma recte poenitendi et confitendi ... Cantalicii poetae* (von Hase no 360), with introductory poems by Eobanus and Johann *Werter, who was one of Winsheim's students. This was followed by two sermons, *De passione domini* and *De humilitate*, both originally preached to a congregation of students (von Hase nos 290 and 362). Winsheim also contributed a preface to the *Summa in totam physicam* by Jodocus Trutfetter, published in 1514 (von Hase no 354). His association with Trutfetter's work may in part be responsible for the appearance of Winsheim's name in the first series of *Epistolae obscurorum virorum* (letter 38). When Eobanus and Werter visited Erasmus in Louvain in 1518 they brought him several letters and greetings from members of the Erfurt circle, including Winsheim. Erasmus returned Winsheim's greetings in his reply to Heinrich *Beyming (Ep 873), perhaps on account of the *Epistolae obscurorum virorum*. In Erfurt, however, this uncalled-for reference did no harm to Winsheim's reputation; his book on confession was especially popular. Johannes *Oecolampadius approached Wolfgang *Capito, then preacher at the cathedral of Basel, to have Winsheim's work reprinted by Johann *Froben. A Basel edition actually appeared in 1520, although from the press of Adam Petri. The correspondence between Oecolampadius and Capito was facilitated by Christoph Scheurl, who in turn came to engage Winsheim in a friendly correspondence. In the spring term of 1520 Petrus *Mosellanus, then rector of the University of Leipzig, proposed that Duke George of *Saxony offer Winsheim a chair of theology at Leipzig. As a result Winsheim obtained his theological doctorate at Erfurt on 15 October 1520, but he died unexpectedly on 3 November. Having been a vicar of St Severus, he lies buried in that church.

BIBLIOGRAPHY: Allen Ep 873 / Erich Kleinei-dam *Universitas Studii Erffordensis* (Leipzig 1964–80) II 308–9 (for a bibliography of Winsheim's writings) and passim / K.G. Scharold *Dr. Martin Luthers Reformation in nächster Beziehung auf das Bistum Würzburg* (Würzburg 1834) I 135 / Nikolaus Paulus 'Ein Beichtbüchlein für Erfurter Studenten' *Der Katholik* 19 (1899) 92ff, 382ff, 20 (1900) 94ff / *Akten und Briefe zur Kirchenpolitik Herzog Georgs von Sachsen* ed F. Gess (Leipzig 1905) I 129 / BA *Oekolampads* I 100–2 / *Christoph Scheurl's Briefbuch* ed F. von Soden and J.K.F. Knaake (Potsdam 1867–72) II Ep 209 / *Matrikel Erfurt* II 225 / Martin von Hase 'Bibliographie der Erfurter Drucke von 1501–1550' *Archiv für Geschichte des Buchwesens* 8 (1967) 655–1096 / F.W. Kampschulte *Die Universität Erfurt in ihrem Verhältnisse zu dem Humanismus und der Reformation* (Trier 1858–60, repr 1970) I 168–9

ERICH KLEINEIDAM

Johann WINTER Andernach *See Johannes* GUINTERIUS

Thomas WINTER d after 1543
Thomas Winter's celebrity rests solely on the fact that he was the illegitimate son of Cardinal *Wolsey, for despite education by some of the finest scholars in Europe and lavish ecclesiastical preferment, the boy appears to have been an untalented wastrel. His mother was most probably the daughter of a Thetford innkeeper, Peter Larke. Wolsey formed what was known as an 'uncanonical marriage' with the woman at about the time of his rise to power. Winter was first taught by Maurice *Birchinshaw, high master of St Paul's, London, from whom he learnt Latin, badly. On 30 August 1518 Birchinshaw and Winter both matriculated at the University of Louvain as students of the College of the Pig. Winter was too young at the time to take the customary oath. Erasmus, who continued to live in Louvain until 1521, was apparently in touch with them as he recommended Birchinshaw to Juan Luis *Vives (see also CWE Ep 1106). Vives' connections with Winter continued past the time of Wolsey's disgrace. In May 1523 Winter was in Padua under the care of Thomas *Lupset (Ep 1360) and probably went to Rome with Bishop John *Clerk. In September 1524 he had returned with Lupset to Louvain, at which

time Erasmus wrote to Wolsey about the boy's education (Epp 1486, 1491). In the following year, when the king's own bastard received recognition by being created duke of Richmond, Winter received the deanery of Wells. By the end of 1526 he was also provost of Beverley (of which his uncle Thomas *Larke was a pensioner), archdeacon of York, Richmond, and Suffolk, and canon of Wells, York, Salisbury, Lincoln, and Southwell, as well as the incumbent of several lesser livings including the rectory of St Matthew in his father's home town of Ipswich. To accommodate these preferments he was granted dispensations for age, non-residence, plurality, and, of course, bastardy.

Meanwhile Winter continued his studies in Greek in Paris under John Taylor, later master of the rolls. Everyone praised him for his father's sake. Lupset told Erasmus, rather oddly, that Winter was as dear to the cardinal as if he had been his legitimate son, while passing on a rumour that the young man was about to resign his benefices and marry the daughter of Henry *Bourchier, earl of Essex (Ep 1595). *Francis I patronized Winter, and Wolsey is said to have entertained the hope of having him elected pope with French assistance. He remained in France until October 1529, with Lupset as his tutor. His extravagance was becoming notorious; his livings (to which were added the mineral rights of his father's see of Durham) gave him about £2700 a year, but these were mostly retained by Wolsey himself, who left his son an allowance of about £200. Further grants followed, and he exchanged his Suffolk archdeaconry for that of Norfolk. When Bishop Richard *Foxe died in October 1528 and Wolsey was translated from Durham to Winchester, the cardinal attempted to secure the former diocese for his son; but by this time Wolsey's power was declining, and Winter never attained the episcopate. His pluralism and riches were criticized by John *Palsgrave and formed one of the accusations levelled by Thomas *More against the cardinal at his fall. Winter lost most of his preferments on his father's disgrace but retained those in the archdiocese of York, to which Wolsey himself proposed to retire. Once Wolsey was dead, Winter might have been expected to disappear from the record, but the king made

him his scholar and chaplain, and between 1531 and 1534 he was back in France and Italy, overspending as ever and writing begging letters to friends in England. Since 1530 he had been a member of the influential community of civil lawyers in London known as Doctors' Commons. By 1532 his tutor was Richard *Morison, Thomas *Cromwell's man. From Cromwell himself he obtained the archdeaconry of Cornwall (the lease of which to a layman led to prolonged litigation), but his true patron may have been Stephen *Gardiner. He eventually resigned his archdeaconry in 1543, whereafter nothing is known of him.

BIBLIOGRAPHY: Allen Ep 1360 / A.F. Pollard *Wolsey* (London 1929) 199 n 2, 306, 308–12, 323 / McConica 53, 110 / G.R. Elton *Reform and Renewal* (Cambridge 1973) 56–7 / J. Le Neve *Fasti Ecclesiae Anglicanae 1300–1541* ed J.M. Horn et al (London 1962–ㅤ) I 92, IV 30, 34 / *Matricule de Louvain* III-1 592 / J.L. Vives *Opera omnia* (Valencia 1782–90, repr 1964) VII 141 / de Vocht *Literae ad Craneveldium* Ep 136 and passim / de Vocht MHL 15–16 and passim / George B. Parks *The English Traveler to Italy* (Rome 1954–ㅤ) I 477, 481–2

C.S. KNIGHTON

Ulrich WIRTNER of Freiburg, d late April 1532

In March 1531 Erasmus reported on his dealings with 'Udalrichus tribunus' concerning his residence in the house 'zum Walfisch,' which belonged to the widow Ursula *Adler (Epp 2462, 2470). Although at this specific time he was apparently not *tribunus* (that is, 'Obristzunftmeister'), the reference is no doubt to Ulrich Wirtner, who had held this office, second only to the mayoralty, for several years in the past and was soon to hold it again. This identification is supported by a further remark late in February 1532 when Erasmus noted that the 'tribunus' – his title is given with a pun this time – had nearly died of the stone (Ep 2598). In fact, Wirtner died two months later.

Ulrich Wirtner (Müller, Molitoris) was born at Liestal, in the territory of Basel. He matriculated at the University of Basel in 1487 and received a BA in 1489 and subsequently a MA in 1492. He may have held the position of town clerk in Rheinfelden before he came to fill the same office at Freiburg from 1500 to 1504.

He was admitted to the citizenship of Freiburg and in 1504 joined the merchants' guild 'zum Falkenberg,' where he soon came to play a leading role. He served in various guild offices and on eight occasions between 1505 and 1532 was elected guild master for the term of one year; he held the position of vice-master for all but four years of that period. His influence was also felt in the municipal government, where he served with hardly an interruption on the Council of Twenty-four, was a member of the municipal court of law for nearly two decades, and held the office of *Obristzunftmeister*, or chief master of the guilds, for six terms (1512–13, 1515–16, 1518–19, 1521–2, 1528–9, and 1531–2). As *Bauherr* he supervised building activities (1507–14, with two interruptions). From 1522 to 1532 he was also bailiff of the Dreisamtal, which belonged to the city, and at various times he held the stewardship of one or another of Freiburg's monasteries. From 1504 to his death he was also one of the overseers of cathedral works; in this capacity he was portrayed with Sebastian von *Blumeneck and his other colleagues on Hans Baldung's predella on the high altar. Wirtner's coat of arms and the effigy of St Ulrich are shown on his panel of a stained-glass window in the central choir jointly donated by the overseers in 1511. In 1530 the Freiburg printer Johannes *Faber Emmeus dedicated to Wirtner his German translation of Erasmus' *Epistola contra pseudevangelicos* after the text had been revised by Erasmus personally.

Wirtner often represented Freiburg in negotiations with external authorities, in particular the Hapsburg government at Ensisheim. He also served the latter as a juror in trials for heresy (1524–30). Earlier he had been involved in negotiations with peasant rebels both during the 'Bundschuh' of 1516 and the peasants' war of 1525. In the course of two missions to Innsbruck (1518) and Worms (1520) he secured approval for a new code of by-laws for the city of Freiburg.

Wirtner was married to Ursula Rull of Freiburg and lived to his death in the imposing house 'zum Herzog' in the Salzstrasse.

BIBLIOGRAPHY: *Matrikel Basel* I 199 / F. Thiele *Die Freiburger Stadtschreiber im Mittelalter* (Freiburg 1973) 29, 128–9, and passim / F. Baumgarten *Der Freiburger Hochaltar* (Strasbourg 1904)

Ulrich Wirtner, by Hans Baldung

46 / J. Krummer-Schroth *Glasmalereien aus dem Freiburger Münster* (Freiburg 1967) 186 / H. Schreiber *Geschichte der Stadt und Universität Freiburg* (Freiburg 1857–60) III 302–3 / A. Buisson 'Der St. Blasienhof in Freiburg i.B.' *Schau-ins-Land* 29 (1902) 1–24, esp 3 / Heinz Holeczek *Erasmus Deutsch* (Stuttgart-Bad Cannstatt 1983–) I 228, 301 / Freiburg, Stadtarchiv MSS B 5 Ia no 2, B 5 XI no 14 f 35

HANS SCHADEK

Frans de WITTE documented 1518–30
Frans (Franciscus) de Witte, the son of Jacob, was one of the four mayors of Haarlem from 1518 to 1525 and from 1527 to 1529. In a letter to Erasmus of 20 September 1530 (Ep 2389), Pieter van *Montfoort mistakenly stated that de Witte was serving as mayor with his father, Jacob van *Montfoort, who was indeed mayor in that year. No doubt his error stemmed from the fact that the two had shared the mayoralty no fewer than seven times, from 1518 to 1523 and in 1527. De Witte may have donated one of St Bavo's stained-glass windows, the *Frans die wittenglas*, which needed repair in 1538 and is now lost.

Georg Witzel

BIBLIOGRAPHY: F. Allan *Geschiedenis en be-schrijving van Haarlem* (Haarlem 1874–88) III 275 / W.P.J. Overmeer in *Algemeen nederlandsch familieblad* n s 17 (1905) 206–7
C.G. VAN LEIJENHORST

Johann WITZ *See Johannes* SAPIDUS

Georg WITZEL of Vacha, 1501–16 February 1573

Georg Witzel (Vuicelius) was born in Vacha, in the Rhön hills, under the secular jurisdiction of Hesse and the ecclesiastical jurisdiction of the abbot of Fulda. In Vacha his father, Michael, kept an inn and was also the mayor. After attending school at Vacha, Schmalkalden, Eisenach, and Halle, Georg matriculated at the University of Erfurt for the winter term of 1516–17 and soon joined the circle of Erfurt humanists who received their inspiration from Erasmus. Having earned his BA Witzel returned to Vacha and took charge of the parish school. In 1520 he studied for a term at Wittenberg and, having taken holy orders, became a subordinate priest at Vacha, serving at the same time as town secretary. In 1523 he applied to the abbot of Fulda for permission to marry. This was refused, but he nevertheless married Elisabeth Kraus, the daughter of a burgher of Eisenach, and was compelled to resign his position in Vacha. He moved to Eisenach and became an assistant to the Lutheran preacher Jakob Strauss, whom he accompanied in 1525 on his visitation of the Eisenach district. His services were rewarded with the parish of Wenigen-Lupnitz. During the peasant troubles he took care to voice his complete rejection of Thomas Müntzer's position, but personal differences with the feudal patron of his church forced him to give up his parish.

With the support of *Luther Witzel was appointed to another parish, that of Niemegk, near Belzig, north of Wittenberg, where he found time to study the church Fathers, especially Vincent of Lérins, in the library of Werner von Stechau, a local nobleman. Another reader in that same library was Johannes Campanus, who started to profess antitrinitarian views. As a result, suspicion was cast upon Witzel too; he was arrested in March 1530 but soon regained his freedom and his parish. In the autumn of 1531 he resigned, however, on his own initiative and returned to Vacha with his wife and two sons. He hoped to obtain a Hebrew lectureship at the University of Erfurt, but his religious views had changed considerably during his years at Niemegk, so that Luther and Justus *Jonas intervened to have his application rejected. Landgrave Philip of *Hesse followed suit and banned him from his territories for alleged agitation against the Lutherans.

Witzel was rescued by Hoyer, count of Mansfeld, who appointed him as a Catholic preacher at Eisleben, a position in which he was not required to say mass. But he proved unable to stand up to the Lutheran minister who was backed by Jonas, and in 1538 was glad to follow a call to Dresden, where Duke George of *Saxony proposed to employ him in the pursuit of his policies aimed at reconciling the religious camps. Indebted to the spirit of Erasmus, the duke desired to have a statement drawn up that might serve as the basis of a new religious colloquy. Witzel formulated such a document and it was printed as *Typus ecclesiae prioris* ... (n p 1540 and several reprints).

However, the death of Duke George in 1539 and the ensuing reform of Albertine Saxony obliged him to move again, and he fled to the bishop of Meissen and subsequently to Berlin, where the Elector Joachim II of Brandenburg appointed him to a board created to prepare a new church ordinance for his state. He clashed with the Lutheran board members, however, and when the elector sided with the latter, Witzel's position became untenable. In 1540 he took his family to Würzburg and in the following year to Fulda, where the abbot, Johann von Henneberg, appointed him a councillor.

Friends and patrons laboured in vain to obtain a formal papal dispensation from his vow of celibacy; Pope *Paul III did not want to create a precedent, but he quietly condoned Witzel's marriage and even paid him an annuity. The vicissitudes of the Schmalkaldic war at one time compelled Witzel to leave Fulda again for Würzburg, but he returned, and in 1547 *Charles v invited him to the diet of Augsburg. Henceforward he served as a consultant to both Charles v and *Ferdinand I, who appointed him a councillor, and continued to serve under Maximilian II. With the arrival at Fulda of the troops of the Elector Maurice of Saxony in 1552 Witzel left for Worms and in the following year for Mainz, where he was to spend the last twenty years of his life, engaged mainly in writing and consulted by such princes as Duke William v of *Cleves and Erasmus von Limburg, bishop of Strasbourg. His literary activity came to a close with the famous *Via regia* (composed by 1564, but not printed until 1600), which used the Augsburg Confession as a basis to propose a 'royal' middle way between Scylla and Charybdis, the dangers inherent in both the Catholic and Protestant positions. Witzel died in Mainz and was buried in the parish church of St Ignatius.

In September 1532 and March 1533 respectively, when Witzel had left Ernestine Saxony but was still hopeful that the unity of the church might be saved by means of an ecumenical council, he twice wrote to Erasmus (Epp 2715, 2786). Erasmus failed to reply, using as an excuse lack of leisure and of Witzel's proper address (Ep 2918; LB X 1538B–C). Following a suggestion made by Count Hoyer

of Mansfeld, Witzel translated Erasmus' *De concordia* into German; an anonymous edition was printed in Erfurt in 1534.

Without quite realizing it, Witzel never really abandoned his hopes of seeing the Catholic church reformed along humanistic lines. His critical view of ecclesiastical abuses, which had once driven him into the Lutheran camp, remained unchanged in the days of the council of Trent. In joining the Lutherans he had assumed that Luther merely proposed to continue the reforms initiated by Erasmus. He never fathomed the depth of Luther's religious conviction and began to retreat when from 1530 the gulf between the religious camps continued to grow with the enunciation of the doctrinal position of each. In a letter to Jonas dated from Erfurt on 25 June 1532, Witzel defined his theological position. Then as later, he failed to grasp the full dimension of the religious cleavage and continued to believe that concord might be achieved on the basis of the teachings of the church Fathers. The concessions he was willing to make to the Protestants never went beyond the lay chalice and the right for priests to contract one marriage.

BIBLIOGRAPHY: Allen Ep 2715 / ADB XLIII 657–62 / RGG VI 1787–8 / Georg Witzel *Epistolarum libri quattuor* (Leipzig 1937) / G. Richter *Die Schriften Georg Witzels bibliographisch bearbeitet* (Fulda 1813) / Winfried Trusen *Um die Reform und Einheit der Kirche: Zum Leben und Werk Georg Witzels* (Münster 1957) / J.P. Dolan *The Influence of Erasmus, Witzel and Cassander in the Church Ordinances ... of Cleve* (Münster 1957) / Joseph Lecler *Histoire de la tolérance au siècle de la réforme* (Paris 1955) I 239–42, 266–7, and passim / Pflug *Correspondance* I Ep 39 and passim / Günther Franz 'Ein Gutachten über Georg Witzel und seine Lehre' in *Festschrift für Karl August Eckhardt* (Marburg 1961) 155–68   IRMGARD HÖSS

WLADISLAW Jagiełło *See* VLADISLAV II, *king of Bohemia and Hungary*

Reyner WOLFE d 1573
Reyner Wolfe (Reynold, Reginald Woulfe) is very probably the 'Reynerus quidam' from England whose letter to Simon *Grynaeus Erasmus mentioned in Ep 2997. Described as a

native of Gelderland in his letters of denization as an English subject (1533), he is documented as a bookseller in London from 1530. Early in 1536 he was admitted to the Company of Stationers, of which he was subsequently elected master in 1560, 1567, and 1572. In his younger years he seems to have made a practice of attending the Frankfurt book fair, for in 1538 it was noted that for once he did not do so because of the recent death of his wife. In 1537 he took a present from Thomas *Cranmer to Martin *Bucer in Strasbourg (LP XII-2 969; cf XIII-2 509).

From 1542 Reyner published books under his own imprint, using roman and italic type that was probably of continental origin and is claimed to be identical with material used by Johann Wolff at Frankfurt. In some of his productions he used a device quite similar to that of the *Froben press. The same sign of the Brazen Serpent was also displayed at his premises in St Paul's Churchyard. In 1547 he was appointed the king's printer in Latin, Greek, and Hebrew, but his annual fee of 26s 8p was negligible. Books printed in English prevail among his publications; they include several works by Cranmer as well as an English translation of Calvin's *Institutio* (1561) reprinted in 1574 by his widow (he had evidently remarried). In view of such undertakings it is not surprising that he produced little in the reign of Queen *Mary. He died by the end of 1573 and his will was proved on 9 January 1574.

BIBLIOGRAPHY: Allen Ep 2997 / G. Duff *A Century of the English Book Trade* (London 1905) 171–2 / H.S. Bennett *English Books and Readers 1475 to 1557* (Cambridge 1952) 23, 38, and passim / E.G. Duff et al *Hand-Lists of English Printers 1501–1556* (London 1895–1905) III / P.G. Morrison *Index of Printers ... in A.W. Pollard and G.R. Redgrave A Short-Title Catalogue* (Charlottesville 1950) 79 PGB

Thomas WOLFF of Basel, documented 1503–35

Thomas was the son of the printer Jakob Wolff, a native of Pforzheim, and of Dorothea David of Basel, a niece of Heinrich *David. In the spring of 1503 Thomas registered at the University of Basel. In 1515 he is documented as a printer, perhaps working for his father;

that same year the two men were involved in litigation over the bequest of Thomas' mother. Thomas became a member of the 'Safran' guild on 13 July 1518 when he was preparing to take charge of the press founded by his father in a house on the Heuberg. In 1522 he became a member of the 'Schlüssel' guild. Books produced by Thomas appeared from 1519 to 1535. At first he continued his father's emphasis on missals and works of scholastic theology, although he added humanistic titles such as a work by *Ficino and one on Roman topography and archaeology in 1519 and an edition of *Budé's commentary on the Pandects in 1534. More decisively still, he entered the lucrative field of Bibles and Reformation writings, publishing *Luther and *Oecolampadius, but also Kaspar Schwenckfeld and perhaps Balthasar *Hubmaier. In 1524 he printed some pamphlets by *Karlstadt for Anabaptist clients, as did Johann *Bebel. As a result both printers faced a short prison term (Ep 1523). Wolff often attended the Frankfurt book fair.

BIBLIOGRAPHY: ADB XLIV 54–5 / Grimm *Buchführer* 1361 / Benzing *Buchdrucker* 32 / *Matrikel Basel* I 270 / R. Wackernagel *Geschichte der Stadt Basel* (Basel 1907–54) III 441–2 and passim / *Aktensammlung zur Geschichte der Basler Reformation* ed E. Dürr et al (Basel 1921–50) I 138–9, 174–6, III 202, and passim / P. Heitz and C. Bernoulli *Basler Büchermarken* (Strasbourg 1895) xvii, 6–15 PGB

Thomas WOLSEY d 29 November 1530

Thomas Wolsey, archbishop of York, cardinal, and chief minister of *Henry VIII, was born in Ipswich, Suffolk. According to George Cavendish, Wolsey's gentleman usher who wrote an early life of the cardinal, Wolsey's father was 'an honest poor man.' It is usually said that he was a butcher. The date of Wolsey's birth is uncertain; different calculations produce estimates ranging from 1471 to 1475.

Thomas Wolsey was sent to Oxford at an early age. He received his BA at fifteen and was commonly dubbed 'the boy bachelor.' Remaining at Oxford, he became master of Magdalen School and bursar of Magdalen College, but he was forced to resign in 1500 after having applied funds to the construction of the college's tower without proper authority. He was ordained priest in 1498.

After a brief period as rector of Limington, Somerset, and chaplain to Sir Richard Nanfan, Wolsey gravitated to the court. He became a chaplain to *Henry VII in 1507 and continued in the service following the accession of Henry VIII in 1509. He served both kings in diplomatic and administrative capacities and accumulated ecclesiastical preferments, his earliest important acquisition being the deanery of Lincoln (1509). He became a canon of Windsor (1511), dean of Westminster (1513), bishop of Lincoln (1514), archbishop of York (1514), bishop of Bath and Wells (1518), bishop of Durham (1523), and bishop of Winchester (1529). Pope *Leo x created him a cardinal in 1515 – he greatly prized his red hat and had it borne in procession before him – and papal legate in 1518. He was almoner to Henry VIII from 1509 and succeeded William *Warham as chancellor in 1515.

Erasmus' translation of Plutarch's *De utilitate capienda ex inimicis*, undertaken in the summer of 1512, was dedicated to Wolsey in Ep 284 of 4 January 1514. Erasmus probably intended to give Wolsey a manuscript of this work as a New Year's present but was prevented from doing so by an attack of the stone which kept him at Cambridge (Ep 285). The plague in London later hindered Erasmus' approach to Wolsey (Ep 287). Soon after Erasmus' arrival in Basel the work was published by Johann *Froben in August 1514 with a fresh, more lengthy dedication (Ep 297).

Shortly before leaving England in 1514 Erasmus had paid his respects to Henry VIII and spoken with Wolsey, who encouraged him 'to be full of confidence and hope' (Ep 295). But he gave Erasmus no gift, showering upon him only the 'splendid promises' referred to in another letter (Ep 296). In 1515 Erasmus commented that Wolsey 'wields incredible influence, for he is so attentive to the business of the realm that the greater part of public affairs rests upon his shoulders' (Ep 333). He called Wolsey 'the sheet-anchor ... of my felicity' (Ep 348).

During the autumn of that year William *Blount, Lord Mountjoy, persuaded Wolsey to offer Erasmus a prebend at Tournai, which Henry VIII had conquered in 1513; but Wolsey later withdrew the offer, promising some preferment within England instead (Epp 360,

Thomas Wolsey

378, 388; LP II-1 899–90). In 1517 Erasmus wrote Wolsey a remarkable letter including some comments which the cardinal may not have appreciated (Ep 658). In 1518 Erasmus was again complaining that Wolsey's patronage had not so far materialized (Ep 775), and in 1519, hoping for a renewed offer (CWE Ep 964 introduction), he praised Wolsey for ridding England of beggars and vagabonds, reforming the monasteries and the clergy, and patronizing learning: 'I see a kind of regular golden age arising,' he wrote, 'if once that spirit of yours enters a certain number of princes' (Ep 967). In 1520 the paraphrases on the epistles of St Peter and St Jude were dedicated to Wolsey (Ep 1112). Despite illness Erasmus had managed to complete this work in time to present it to the cardinal in person when he saw him at Calais following the conference at the Field of Cloth of Gold; but Wolsey was too busy to receive the gift, and Erasmus had to send it to him later (Ep 1112 introduction). Erasmus saw Wolsey again in Bruges in 1521 (Epp 1223 introduction, 1342; LB VI 21F). In 1524 Erasmus wrote that he had intended to dedicate his paraphrase on the Acts of the Apostles to Wolsey, but in the end it was dedicated to *Clement VII (Epp 1415, 1418). At this time Henry VIII and Wolsey were urging Erasmus to write against *Luther (Ep 1683); when Erasmus completed his *De libero arbitrio* he considered dedicating it to Wolsey, but finally he left it without a dedication and sent copies to the cardinal and to the pope (Epp 1418, 1481, 1486). Erasmus had earlier interceded with Wolsey to prevent the burning of Luther's books in England (Ep 1113). In 1526 Erasmus wrote Wolsey concerning the *Colloquia*, for he had heard a rumour that they were banned in England as being heretical. He asked the cardinal to judge himself whether they were or not, adding that they contained nothing impure, irreverent, or seditious (Ep 1697).

As early as 1518 Wolsey had been interested in fostering humanistic learning at Oxford. Initially he founded six public lectureships, some of them held by Erasmus' friends *Lupset, *Vives, and John *Clement. In 1524 Wolsey undertook to establish a new college at Oxford, Cardinal's College, as well as a grammar school at Ipswich. The school disappeared following Wolsey's fall, but Henry VIII was persuaded to permit the college to continue, changing its name to Christ Church. Erasmus did not comment specifically on the foundation of Cardinal's College – indeed he confused it with *Foxe's college of Corpus Christi (LB IX 781F) – but a number of his earlier letters refer to Wolsey's efforts to raise the standard of learning at Oxford and praise his benefactions there (Epp 965, 967, 970, 990, 1111).

Wolsey was always interested in foreign affairs and was active in international diplomacy. It has been argued that his goal was to preserve a balance of power in Europe, or to become pope, or to maintain peace through international conferences and treaties such as the treaty of London (1518). In fact his motives may have been less elevated, and he may have responded to continually changing situations and to his sovereign's desires without developing any coherent underlying policy.

Between 1527 and 1529 Wolsey was charged with securing Henry VIII's divorce from *Catherine of Aragon, whom the king wished to put away so as to be free to marry *Anne Boleyn and, he hoped, beget a male heir to the English throne. During the summer of 1529 Wolsey and Cardinal *Campeggi conducted a trial at Blackfriars in London, but *Clement VII revoked the case to Rome and terminated the proceedings without a verdict. The king's wrath focused on Wolsey, who lost the position of chancellor and was ordered out of London into his archdiocese of York. Henry was further angered in 1530 upon hearing that Wolsey remained in correspondence with foreign powers despite a royal command to the contrary, and that he was making preparations for his enthronement as archbishop of York, a ceremony for which he had not previously found time. Wolsey was therefore arrested and ordered to return to London, where he would face treason charges, but he died on the way. Voicing regret that he had not served God as well as he had the king, he succumbed at Leicester Abbey on 29 November 1530. There are passing references to the cardinal's fall and death in a number of Erasmus' letters (Epp 2237, 2240, 2241, 2243, 2253, 2256, 2277, 2413). An illegitimate son, Thomas *Winter, is mentioned in correspondence between Lupset and Erasmus.

Although he wielded tremendous influence in both church and state Wolsey left little of permanent value in either sphere. Nor, despite his promises, did he provide significant patronage for Erasmus. His greatest lasting monument is perhaps Hampton Court Palace, which he constructed on the Thames west of London and where he lived surrounded by an enormous retinue of servants. Long a royal residence following Wolsey's fall, it remains one of the finest examples of Tudor architecture.

All the existing portraits of Wolsey are of one type, showing the cardinal's face in profile, and are very likely based on a single original. Examples are in the National Portrait Gallery, London; at Christ Church, Oxford; and at Hampton Court.

BIBLIOGRAPHY: James Gairdner in DNB XXI 796–814 / LP passim / George Cavendish *The Life and Death of Cardinal Wolsey* (1641, modern ed by Richard S. Sylvester 1959) / A.F. Pollard *Wolsey* (London 1929) / Charles W. Ferguson *Naked to Mine Enemies* (Boston 1958) / See also J.J. Scarisbrick *Henry VIII* (London 1968) passim STANFORD E. LEHMBERG

Johann Roman WONECKER of Windecken,
d before 8 February 1524
Wonecker (Wonacus, Wonnecker, Windecker)
of Windecken, in Hesse, registered at the
University of Erfurt in 1479 and there received
his MA in 1483. He may be identical with an
assistant barber-surgeon, 'Hans von Win-
deck,' documented at Basel in 1485. Further
studies led him later to claim doctorates in the
liberal arts, both laws, and medicine. From
1493 to 1523 he was town physician at Basel
and a member of the medical faculty. From 1500
he held a medical chair and in 1519 and 1522–3
was rector for a term. He practised law as well
as medicine and was much concerned with
astrology, publishing a number of annual
almanacs for Basel from 1495 on.

Wonecker's first wife, Margarethe Fätzbryn,
owned property in the territory of Mainz,
which may be the reason for his journeys to the
court of the archbishop in 1505 and 1520. After
her death on 26 November 1518 he married
Barbara Speyer, who after Wonecker's death
became the wife of Henricus *Glareanus. In
1508 Wonecker admitted in court to having
seduced and left with child one Ännchen
Gropp. He donated a painting to St Elizabeth's
church and composed distichs in honour of
St Jerome. Wonecker was fiercely opposed
to the reformers, and just before Christmas
1522 he posted on the Basel churches a list of
theses he was prepared to sustain in a disputation. They are noticeable for their obscurity as well as their clumsy scholastic
Latin, 'as elegant as the man himself,' according to Glareanus. No wonder that he was
ridiculed even after his death (mentioned by
Erasmus in Ep 1417) in an anonymous pamphlet. For good measure it also attacked Jakob
*Wimpfeling, who had been in touch with
Wonecker as early as 1505.

BIBLIOGRAPHY: Allen Ep 1417 / R. Wacker-
nagel *Geschichte der Stadt Basel* (Basel 1907–54)
III 131–2, 20*–1* / *Matrikel Erfurt* I 379 / *Matrikel
Basel* I 226, 339–40, 352–3 / Albrecht Burck-
hardt *Geschichte der medizinischen Fakultät zu
Basel* (Basel 1917) 16–18 / Schmidt *Histoire
littéraire* I 52, 97–8 / AK I Epp 392, 490, and
passim / Z VII Ep 264, VIII Ep 268, and passim /
Basler Chroniken I 440–3 / Erich Kleineidam
Universitas Studii Erffordensis (Leipzig 1964–80)
I 387, II 75   PGB

WOUTER of Gouda See GUALTERUS (Ep 13)

Jan WOUTERS 1484–1 February 1560
Jan Wouters (Vaulterus), lord of Vinderhoute,
near Ghent, was the son of another Jan, who
rose to be president of the Chambre des
comptes at Lille, and of Josine de Best, a
daughter of an important Ghent family. The
younger Jan matriculated at the University of
Louvain on 4 January 1502 and subsequently
obtained a licence in civil and canon law. He
began his career as first pensionary, or legal
consultant, to the city of Ghent. At the
beginning of 1509 he was appointed
councillor-commissary in the council of Flanders at Ghent, and on 9 September 1515 he was
promoted to councillor-in-ordinary. He retained this position until his death – longer
than any other councillor on record. The
presidency of the council, however, eluded
him, although on several occasions he was
acting president and a candidate for the top
position.

Jan was very rich and owned estates at
Bazel, near Antwerp and Wontergem, near
Courtrai, in addition to some other properties
near Ghent and Ieper; in Ghent he possessed a
beautiful mansion. In 1504 he married Maria
van den Nieuwenhuyse, who bore him several
children. In 1537 he married Peronne van der
Steenstrate, the widow of Jacob De Costere.

It is possible that Erasmus met Wouters in
the course of his repeated visits to Ghent
between 1514 and 1517. Wouters was a friend
of Juan Luis *Vives and through the latter sent
greetings to Erasmus in Ep 1303. A letter from
Vives to one of his sons is found in Vives' *Opera
omnia* (Valencia 1782–90, repr 1964) VII 216–17.

BIBLIOGRAPHY: Allen Ep 1303 / *Matricule de
Louvain* III-1 229 / E. Van Hende 'Notice sur
Jean Wouters … ' *Bulletin de la Commission
historique du Département du Nord* 16 (1883)
375–89 / C. Van den Bergen-Pantens 'Icono-
graphie d'une alliance: les Wouters et les Beste'
Le Parchemin 140 (1969) 389–401 / Paul van
Peteghem 'Centralisatie in Vlaanderen onder
Keizer Karel (1515–1555)' (doctoral thesis,
Rijksuniversiteit Gent 1980) II 56–62 / For
archival material in Ghent see J. Buntinx
*Inventaris van het archief van de Raad van
Vlaanderen (1386–1795)* (Brussels 1964–79) in-
dexes   PAUL VAN PETEGHEM

Ulrich, duke of Württemberg, by Hans Brosamer

Christopher, duke of WÜRTTEMBERG
12 May 1515–28 December 1568

Christopher, the son of Ulrich of *Württemberg and Sabina of Bavaria, was born in Urach. After the expulsion of his father from Württemberg by the Swabian League, Christopher, the heir to the duchy, remained in the hands of *Charles v and grew up at the court of Innsbruck, in Wiener Neustadt, and elsewhere in Austria. In 1530 he accompanied the emperor to the diet of Augsburg, but when Charles was preparing to take him to Spain in 1532 he fled to Landshut, where his uncle, Duke William iv of *Bavaria, helped him to pursue his claims to the duchy of Württemberg (Ep 2917). After his father's return to Württemberg in 1534 Christopher was sent to the court of King *Francis i of France. His right of succession to Württemberg and Montbéliard was confirmed in 1542, and in 1544 he married Anna Maria, a daughter of George of *Brandenburg-Ansbach. He became duke on 6 November 1550. Following Württemberg's participation in the war of the Schmalkaldic League (1547), King *Ferdinand raised legal claims to the duchy; not until the treaty of

Passau in 1552 was Christopher's rule secure. A convinced Lutheran, he retained Johann *Brenz, his father's superintendent, and introduced new ordinances for churches and schools in 1559. In the affairs of the Empire, however, he observed a policy of strict neutrality amid the opposing religious camps.

BIBLIOGRAPHY: NDB III 248–9 / ADB IV 243–50 / Karl Weller *Württembergische Geschichte* 5th ed by A. Weller (Stuttgart 1963) 155–67 and passim / Sigmund von Riezler *Geschichte Baierns* 2nd ed (Munich-Stuttgart 1927–32, repr 1964) IV 47–52, 257–60, and passim   IG

Ulrich, duke of WÜRTTEMBERG
8 February 1487–6 November 1550

Ulrich of Württemberg, the son of count Henry, who was born at Riquewihr, in Alsace, nominally began his rule of Württemberg in 1498. In 1511 he married Sabina of Bavaria. He accompanied the Emperor *Maximilian i in the Swiss war of 1499–1500 and supported his father-in-law, Duke Albert iv of Bavaria, in his war of succession against the Palatinate (1504); however, he turned against his former allies in 1512 when he left the Swabian League, a federation of south-west German townships and noblemen founded in 1487 under the leadership of the emperor. In 1514 high taxation led to peasant uprisings. When Duke Ulrich killed Hans von Hutten after a quarrel in 1515, Ulrich von *Hutten, a kinsman of the murdered Hans, became the duke's remorseless enemy (Epp 923, 986). In 1515 Sabina fled to her brothers William iv and Louis of *Bavaria. In 1519 the Swabian League, led by William of Bavaria, defeated Ulrich, and he had to flee his country. In 1520 the Emperor *Charles v took possession of Württemberg in exchange for his payment of the Swabian League's war debt and had the duchy ruled by his brother, *Ferdinand. From his remaining county of Montbéliard, Ulrich allied himself to *Francis i of France. He vainly attempted to regain Württemberg during the peasants' war in 1525 (Ep 1554) and had to seek refuge with his kinsman Philip of *Hesse, who confirmed him in his commitment to the Lutheran faith. King Ferdinand was formally installed as ruler of Württemberg in 1530, but with the help of Philip of Hesse and French subsidies Ulrich defeated the Austrian regent, Philip, count

*Palatine, in 1534. With the signing of the peace of Kadan in Bohemia, Ulrich was reinstated as duke. Lutheran reforms were introduced in Württemberg (Ep 3000), monasteries were dissolved, and church property was confiscated. After the defeat of the Schmalkaldic League in 1547, Württemberg was briefly occupied by Spanish troops. Ulrich had to accept humiliating terms in order to get rid of them, while Ferdinand renewed his legal claims to the duchy. The crisis was not resolved until after Duke Christopher of *Württemberg had succeeded his father.

Erasmus had no personal contacts with Ulrich but his correspondents frequently drew his attention to the turbulent affairs of Württemberg. In his own letters, too, he showed a fair measure of interest in Ulrich's fate. His friend Hutten participated personally in the Swabian League's war against the duke (Epp 923, 986, 1001, 1030), which also affected Johann *Reuchlin (Epp 747, 986, 1129). The developments of 1534 leading to the reinstatement of Ulrich were often discussed by Erasmus and his correspondents, especially those at Augsburg (Epp 2917, 2937, 2939, 2947, 2955, 2961, 3049).

BIBLIOGRAPHY: ADB XXXIX 237–43 / Karl Weller *Württembergische Geschichte* 5th ed by A. Weller (Stuttgart 1963) 90–4, 151–5, and passim / Ludwig Heyd *Ulrich, Herzog zu Württemberg* (Stuttgart 1840–1)   IG

Petrus WYCHMANUS *See Pieter* WICHMANS

Johann von der WYCK of Münster, d late April 1534
Johann von der Wyck (van der Wick, Wieck), who was descended from a patrician family of Münster, in Westphalia, is first documented in Rome about 1515. By that time he was a doctor of civil and canon law and a cleric of the diocese of Münster and was acting on behalf of *Reuchlin in his trial before the papal curia (Ep 615; RE Ep 201 and passim). His devotion to Reuchlin's cause is acknowledged in the *Epistolae obscurorum virorum*. On his return to Germany in the summer of 1520 he met *Luther at Wittenberg; the reformer afterwards expressed great confidence in his trustworthiness (w *Briefwechsel* II Epp 296, 310). From 1528 Johann von der Wyck is documented in

Bremen as legal consultant to the city council and a zealous Lutheran. He was instrumental in freeing Bremen from its isolation by way of diplomatic and legal steps that eventually led to its admission to the Schmalkaldic League and to the recognized status of a free city of the Empire. In 1532 he signed the religious agreement of the diet of Regensburg on behalf of Bremen and Duke Emil of Lüneburg. In 1533 he accepted a position in his native city of Münster similar to the one he continued to hold at Bremen. It seems that he hoped to strengthen resistance to the popular agitation of the Anabaptists. When the radicals triumphed at Münster he fled but was murdered by an official of Franz von *Waldeck, bishop of Münster, perhaps with the latter's consent.

BIBLIOGRAPHY: Allen Ep 615 / W. Bippen in ADB XLIV 381–2 / G.H. Williams *The Radical Reformation* (Philadelphia 1962) 366–7   PGB

Hans WYLER *See Johann* WILER

Nikolaus WYNMANN *See Nikolaus* WINMANN

XIMÉNEZ *See Francisco* JIMÉNEZ DE CISNEROS

YAHYA-Pasha-zade Mehmed Bey *See Yahya-Pasha-zade* MEHMED *Bey*

James YARFORD documented at London 1489–1527
Sir James Yarford was Lord Mayor of London for the year beginning 9 November 1518; he may be the Lord Mayor mentioned by Erasmus in Ep 1126.

BIBLIOGRAPHY: Allen Ep 1126 / *Acts of the Court of the Mercers' Company, 1453–1527* ed L. Lyell (Cambridge 1936) 200 and passim / LP I 1032 and passim   PGB

John YONGE d 25 April 1516
John Yonge (Young) was admitted to Winchester College on 29 September 1478 at the age of eleven. He subsequently studied at New College, Oxford, and graduated bachelor of civil law by 1494. Then he attended the University of Bologna for some years and received a doctorate in civil law from Ferrara in 1500. He was ordained deacon in 1495 and held many ecclesiastical offices and benefices, being appointed commissary of the prerogative to

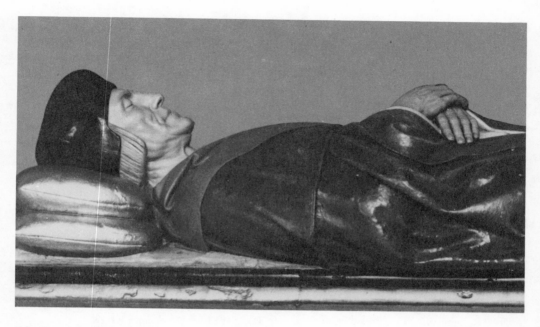

John Yonge, by Pietro Torrigiano

William *Warham, archbishop of Canterbury, in January 1504, then the archbishop's chancellor and auditor of causes in 1507. In January 1508 *Henry VII appointed him master of the rolls, an office which he held until his death. His monument in the rolls chapel has a recumbent effigy by Pietro Torrigiano.

Yonge was a friend of Erasmus, who dedicated to him his translation of Plutarch's *De tuenda bona valetudine praecepta* (Epp 268, 280, 283).

BIBLIOGRAPHY: Allen Ep 268 / DNB XXI 1242–3 / Emden BRUO III 2136–7 / F. Grossman 'Holbein, Torrigiano, and some portraits of John Colet' *Journal of the Warburg and Courtauld Institutes* 13 (1950) 209, 222, 225–6 / W.H. Garrod 'Erasmus and his English patrons' *The Library* 5th ser 4 (1949–50) 7 / R.J. Mitchell 'English students at Ferrara in the xvth century' *Italian Studies* 1 (1937) 78

R.J. SCHOECK

Antoon YSBRANDTSZ of Antwerp, documented 1474, d 1505
Antoon Ysbrandtsz (Ysebrant) matriculated in the University of Louvain on 30 June 1474 and served his native Antwerp as town secretary (1486–8) and pensionary, or legal consultant, from 1489 to his death. He married Wilhelmina *Beka, whose death preceded his own by a few years. Erasmus mentioned him in his epitaph for Wilhelmina (Reedijk poem 73), first published in the *Adagiorum collectanea* (Paris: J. Petit and J. Bade 24 December 1506–8 January 1507). Ysbrandtsz was succeeded in his office by Adriaan Herbouts and Erasmus' friend Jacob de *Voecht.

BIBLIOGRAPHY: de Vocht CTL II 74, 110 / Floris Prims *Geschiedenis van Antwerpen* (Antwerp 1927–49) XVI 207, 209 / H. de Ridder-Symoens in *Varia historica Brabantica* 6–7 ('s Hertogenbosch 1978) 106, 112 / *Matricule de Louvain* II-1 306

MARCEL A. NAUWELAERTS

YSSELSTEIN *See Floris and Maximiliaan van* EGMOND

Juan de ZAFRA documented 1529
The Franciscan Juan de Zafra (Zafranus) has remained obscure both in his origins and in most of his career. He is known only by his 1529 edition in Paris of Luis de *Carvajal's *Apologia* against Erasmus. In it Zafra deleted several of Carvajal's passages which might

have offended French readers. The edition carried a dedicatory preface to Francisco de *Quiñones, Franciscan minister general, and an exchange of verses with a certain Friar *Laxiangus. It was the cause for Erasmus' *Responsio adversus febricitantis libellum* (Basel: H. Froben, March 1529), where Zafra is mentioned at the end (LB x 1684A–B). He is probably the object of another, and slighting, reference in Ep 2134.

BIBLIOGRAPHY: Allen Ep 2110

JAMES K. FARGE

Willem Janszoon ZAGERE of Goes, d 4 December 1538

Willem Zagere (Sagarus, Sagher, Zagarus), a native of Goes, in Zuid-Beveland, matriculated at Louvain on 31 August 1507, as a student of the College of the Pig. He graduated MA under Adrianus Cornelii *Barlandus on 6 June 1510. In 1516 or 1517 he received a benefice at Ellemeet, on the island of Schouwen, which he resigned in 1519 when he went to study law in Orléans. After his return he was registered as a citizen of Zierikzee on 12 June 1521, and the following day was appointed pensionary of that town. He was also the first recorded rector of its Latin school. On 3 December 1528 the council of Holland at The Hague admitted him as a notary. On 13 April 1533 he resigned as pensionary and on 20 May his successor as a notary was appointed. Zagere moved to Leeuwarden, where he was made councillor in the council of Friesland on 17 June 1533. In September he sent greetings to Erasmus in one of Haio *Cammingha's letters (Ep 2866); they may have known each other from Louvain. Zagere died at Leeuwarden and was buried in the Grote Kerk.

A great admirer of Wessel *Gansfort, Zagere undertook a pilgrimage to Aduard and to Wessel's tomb in the church of the Poor Clares at Groningen, and even tried to buy his skull when it was shown to him. He was a friend of Frans van *Cranevelt, Gerard *Geldenhouwer, and Jason Pratensis, to whose *De uteris libri duo* (Antwerp: M. Hillen 1524; NK 1755) he contributed a complimentary letter. A 'Lex lecta intellecta digestis, interprete Guilhelmo Zagaro Selando' survives in MS 2769 of the Bibliothèque Royale at Brussels (f 285 recto–92 verso). His pupil Jacobus Zovitius of Dreischor dedicated to Zagere a drama, *Ruth* (Antwerp:

M. Hillen 1533; NK 9106), and Barlandus dedicated to him his letter *De ratione studii* and a *Carmen extemporale*.

BIBLIOGRAPHY: Allen Ep 2866 / NNBW VI 1215 / Matricule de Louvain III-1 342 / de Vocht Literae ad Craneveldium Ep 147 / M. van Rhijn Studiën over Wessel Gansfort en zijn tijd (Utrecht 1933) 163–9 / M. van Rhijn in Nederlands archief voor kerkgeschiedenis 30 (1938) 27–30 and 35 (1946–7) 85–90 / P.J. Meertens Letterkundig leven in Zeeland (Amsterdam 1943) 45–6 / E. Daxhelet Adrien Barlandus (Louvain 1938, repr 1967) 300–7

C.G. VAN LEIJENHORST

Jan ZAMBOCKI d 24 March 1529

Zambocki (Szamboczki, Zambolski, Samborkius) came from a poor family of the gentry which held the village of Zambock in Mazovia. In his youth he fell into the hands of the Tartars and was sold to the Turks, but after a few years of slavery he escaped and returned to Poland. In 1504 he joined the court of King Alexander, retaining his position under *Sigismund I. His abilities soon caught the eye of Piotr *Tomicki, who after assuming the office of vice-chancellor benefitted from Zambocki's many talents. Tomicki valued in particular his literary talents and employed him in composing the acts of chancery. In 1528 he was appointed royal secretary. Intelligent, well-read in classical literature, and a poet of some talent, Zambocki was able to surround himself with friends. Yet at the same time his religious indifference, his quarrelsomeness and his fondness of gossip brought him many enemies. Close ties connected him with Johannes *Dantiscus, and he also formed a friendship with Andrzej *Krzycki. His close and mutually respectful relationship with Tomicki lasted to the end of his life. Zambocki died in 1529 at Vilno.

There is no evidence that Zambocki had contacts with Jan (II) *Łaski, but they had many opportunities for meeting at the court or Tomicki's chancery. In 1527 Łaski showed considerable interest in Polish diplomacy towards Hungary, and it is known that Zambocki composed most of Tomicki's letters in this area. Thus Zambocki may well be the man who sent greetings to Erasmus through Łaski (Ep 1916).

BIBLIOGRAPHY: Allen Ep 1916 / K. Hartleb Jan Zambocki dworzanin i sekretarz JKM (Warsaw 1937) / W. Pociecha Królowa Bona: Czasy i ludzie

Odrodzenia (Poznań 1949–58) I–IV passim / K. Miaskowski 'Jugend und Studienjahre des Ermländischen Bischofs und Kardinals Stanislaus Hosius' *Zeitschrift für die Geschichte und Altertumskunde Ermlands* 19 (1916) 356 / A. Krzycki *Carmina* ed K. Morawski (Cracow 1888) / de Vocht *Dantiscus* 49

HALINA KOWALSKA

Giovanni Crisostomo ZANCHI of Bergamo, c 1490–1566

Panfilo, a son of Paolo Zanchi, was born at Bergamo. He entered the order of the canons regular of St John Lateran in 1524, taking the name Giovanni Crisostomo. In 1529 he was sent by his order to Padua, and in 1533 to Ravenna (Ep 2829). In 1540 he became prior of the convent of Santo Spirito at Bergamo, and in 1559 general of his order. He died at Bergamo.

Erasmus probably heard of Zanchi from *Viglius Zuichemus, who studied at Padua in the early 1530s. In July 1532 he informed Viglius that he had written to Zanchi (Ep 2682). Zanchi lent Viglius manuscripts of the sermons of St Ambrose against the Arians and of the life of St Cyprian by Pontius of Carthage (Epp 2716, 2791); Viglius copied the former for Erasmus, but not the latter, since Erasmus had already given a manuscript of it to Hieronymus *Froben of Basel (Epp 2829, 2885).

Zanchi's principal work was the *De Orobiorum sive Cenomanorum origine situ ac Bergami rebus antiquis libri III*, dedicated to Pietro *Bembo (Venice: B. dei Vitali 1531). Around 1536 he published a *Panegyricus* on the Emperor *Charles V, published again at Venice in 1560.

BIBLIOGRAPHY: Allen Ep 2682   TBD

van den ZANDE, ZANDERUS *See Levinus* AMMONIUS, Michael SANDER

Johannes ZAPOLYA *See* JOHN ZÁPOLYAI, *king of Hungary*

Clementia ZASIUS *See Udalricus* ZASIUS

Joachim ZASIUS of Freiburg, d 6 March 1540 Joachim was the oldest son of Udalricus *Zasius, the famous jurist. He should not be confused with his younger brother, also called Joachim, who died on 4 May 1569. The older Joachim matriculated at Freiburg on 18 April

1506. By 1519 he had left home and was temporarily estranged from his father (AK II Ep 705). In 1535 he was criticized for not having visited his father in nearly a decade (AK IV Ep 1964). It is not known when he entered the service of the dukes of Savoy, but he was in Savoy by 1524. He became ducal secretary and was given special responsibility for relations with the German states (Herminjard II Ep 285). In Turin he was a close friend of Jean de *Boyssoné (Ep 3082). In the course of his duties he visited Basel several times, probably meeting Erasmus in 1528 (Ep 2020). He returned to Basel in May 1533, but by August he had moved on to St Gallen and urgently needed to obtain copies of the works of Martin *Bucer. In March 1534 Joachim *Vadianus reported that Zasius had written from Turin how the gospel was freely preached there. The greater part of 1535 he spent at Basel, promoting the claims of Charles II of *Savoy to Montferrat. He obtained a legal opinion in this matter from his father and requested Bonifacius *Amerbach to translate its German passages into Latin (AK IV Epp 1969, 2011). In July 1536 he was at Baden (AK IV Ep 2034) to present to the Swiss cantons the plight of his master, who was being expelled from his lands by the French. Zasius then intended to ride to Milan for meetings with the duke, but instead spent the winter again at Basel (AK IV Ep 2073, V Ep 2101), supplying Amerbach with news about the war, as he saw fit. In 1538 he married into a highly respected Basel family. His wife, Katharina, a daughter of Franz Offenburg, returned to Basel after his death. He died in Savoy while visiting a mine which he owned there (AK V Ep 2412).

BIBLIOGRAPHY: Allen Ep 3082 / *Matrikel Freiburg* I-1 506 / AK II Ep 705, V Ep 2412, VI Ep 2691, VII Ep 3086, VIII xiv, xxii, and passim / Herminjard I Ep 76, II Ep 285 / *Vadianische Briefsammlung* V Epp 744, 757, VII Ep 38 / Some manuscript notes for this article were prepared by the late Henry Meylan   PGB

Johann Ulrich ZASIUS of Freiburg, 1521–27 April 1570

Johann Ulrich, a son of the jurist Udalricus *Zasius and his second wife, the former serving-girl, Barbara, was born at Freiburg im Breisgau. He was his father's favourite son and was thought to be destined for a brilliant legal career. He registered at the University of

Freiburg in 1534, and in 1536 his late father's patron, the Augsburg merchant Johann (II) *Paumgartner, sent him to Padua to study law (Ep 3129). He was sent back to Germany in 1538 for having neglected his studies, and he served Duke Charles II of *Savoy (the employer of his half-brother Joachim *Zasius) both before and after returning to Freiburg for his doctorate, which he obtained in 1542. In 1541 he published the definitive edition of his father's *Intellectus singulares* (Basel: M. Isengrin), and he was titular co-editor of his father's complete works along with Joachim Mynsinger von Frundeck (Lyon: S. Gryphius 1550). He carefully maintained personal ties inherited from his father, particularly with Bonifacius *Amerbach of Basel. His appointment as professor of Codex at Basel in 1543–4 was terminated after he refused to abandon his Catholic faith. Zasius then fell deeply into debt, and in 1545 he pawned his father's legal library and papers to Amerbach for a payment from the Erasmus estate. Although Zasius persuaded Amerbach to return the books in 1548, the papers (including considerable Erasmian materials) remained with Amerbach and are now in the Öffentliche Bibliothek of the University of Basel.

In 1546 Zasius entered the service of King *Ferdinand I as an all-purpose emissary. He became well known for keeping friends and clients informed of current events, and he was a supporter of church reform at the council of Trent. In the court of the Emperor Maximilian II he rose to be a councillor and imperial vice-chancellor, and he was ennobled as Zasius zum Rabenstein. He was seriously injured in an accident in 1565 and died in Vienna five years later.

Zasius married three times, and some children are known to have survived the second marriage. He is not to be identified with the Johann Ulrich Zasius of Bregenz who composed a *Catalogus legum antiquarum* edited by Johann Sturm at Strasbourg in 1551.

BIBLIOGRAPHY: Allen Ep 3129 / AK III Ep 1344, VI Ep 2685, and passim / ADB XLIV 706–8 / Winterberg 78–80   STEVEN ROWAN

Udalricus ZASIUS of Constance, 1461–24 November 1535
Udalricus (Ulrich) Zasius was born in Constance, the only son of Konrad Zäsi (Zäsy) and

Udalricus Zasius, by Théodore de Bry

his wife, Anna Sigwart, of a family which was of honourable status but had fallen into poverty. He was distantly related to the family of the later religious reformers of Constance, Ambrosius and Thomas *Blarer. He attended the cathedral school in Constance and began his studies at Tübingen in 1481, where he attended lectures in the arts and theology faculties and departed with a BA. He then entered the service of the bishop of Constance as a notary or court clerk and eventually rose to be head of the episcopal chancery, though he also performed tasks for the municipal government of Constance. In 1484 he applied for the position of schoolmaster of Überlingen and in 1485 for that of town clerk of Buchhorn (now part of Friedrichshafen). He seems eventually to have obtained the latter post. From 1489 to 1494 he was town clerk at Baden im Aargau, in Switzerland, and in 1491 he renounced his rights as a burgher of Constance. Even his earliest Latin letters from 1489 reveal the warm and earthy personality which always animated his work. After many attempts to find another position at St Gallen, Zürich, Constance, and even Milan, he was finally called to Freiburg im Breisgau as town clerk in 1494, where he at once became a burgher. Even before this time he had aided the Freiburg municipal government in litigation before the episcopal court of Constance. Henceforth his exclusive place of residence was to be Freiburg, then part of the Hapsburg dominion in the Upper Rhine region, and there he was to die. Although he occasionally went to Alsace or into Swabia to pursue litigation for his clients, he hardly ever seems to have visited the nearby city of Basel. Yet though Zasius' geographic world was very small, the circle of his literary, political, and scholarly contacts was very large indeed.

Zasius first took up formal studies in law only after he had begun work as town clerk in Freiburg. While serving in that post he inventoried the holdings of the municipal chancery and drafted a notable chronicle of the acts of the town council (as yet unpublished). In 1496 he left this post to head the municipal Latin school, which allowed him to dedicate himself to completing his humanistic and juristic training. In the mid-1490s he had close contacts with the poet Jakob *Locher and contributed prefatory letters for Locher's publications. In 1497 the Emperor *Maximilian I empowered the rector of Freiburg cathedral to promote Zasius to MA, but this promotion appears never to have been carried out. In 1499 Zasius resigned his office as schoolmaster to dedicate himself to full-time study, and in 1501 he was promoted to doctor of laws. Among his teachers the most important were Ulrich Krafft and Paulus de Cittadinis of Milan, who had come to Freiburg from Pavia and had been a student of Jason a Mayno. Zasius' formal study in law was, however, so brief that he can be considered to have been virtually self-educated. Zasius delivered his first legal lectures as a substitute for Paulus de Cittadinis in 1500, and he was called to lecture on the *Institutes* in addition to his regular duties as instructor of poetry and rhetoric when part of the university was in refuge from the plague at Rheinfelden in 1501. In 1503 Zasius repeated the course on the *Institutes* owing to the demand of the people of Freiburg. In 1502 he had re-entered the service of the town council as titular clerk of the public court, but he also served as legal counsel to the university. He was occasionally to find himself pulled both ways by his ties to the municipal government

on the one hand and the university on the other.

The university was pressured by both the town and the students to appoint Zasius to the ordinary professorship of law, which it finally did in 1506 despite numerous intrigues by hostile colleagues. Zasius could be a warm friend, but he was often a very difficult colleague. Since the conditions of his employment were not very favourable, he always had to supplement his salary by continuous work as a legal consultant and by taking in students as boarders. In 1508 Maximilian I granted him the title of imperial councillor, an honour which Zasius repaid with an oration greeting the monarch on his visit to Freiburg in 1510, and later by memorial orations for both Maximilian and his queen, Bianca Maria Sforza. His orations in praise of law, which he made it a practice to deliver at the start of courses or at promotional ceremonies, were eventually published as part of his *Lucubrationes* in 1518.

Zasius had agreed when he took the post of court clerk in 1502 to prepare a book of legal precedents describing the current practice of the municipal court of Freiburg, along with a legal code comprehending the customs, statutes, and rights of the town together with the relevant Roman law. Zasius never completed the first of these two assignments, though he had already collected a manual of precedents during his tenure as town clerk (Stadtarchiv Freiburg im Breisgau, MS B5: XIII, 4a). The second of the assignments, however, was carried out with singular success: the Freiburg law code of 1520, which is mostly his work, is rightly considered one of the most valuable legal codifications of its day, since it combined in an understandable fashion the traditional law of Freiburg and Roman law. The two legal traditions were here virtually fused together. This codification was Zasius' single most notable achievement, and it remained in legal force into the nineteenth century. It influenced later codifications in other German communities, some of which were compiled by Zasius' own students.

Zasius' reputation was spread at first by his friends and students, since he only started to publish his writings haltingly and late. His students at Freiburg rose rapidly to important

positions in the entourages of princes as well
as in ecclesiastical and municipal administra-
tions and courts, and they helped to publicize
their teacher and increase his influence. But
Zasius owed his fame most of all to the alliance
which he had made at the very outset with
humanism. He was in personal or epistolary
contact with many notable scholars far beyond
the bounds of his specialty, of his profession,
or of his nation. Whenever a devotee of
humanism visited Freiburg, he sought out
Zasius. In the first phase of Zasius' scholarly
development, he was very much a member of
the intellectual world which centred on Strasbourg. His ties with Johann Geiler of Kaysersberg, Jakob *Wimpfeling, Sebastian *Brant,
and Thomas Wolf the younger were very close.
He was also in early contact with Conradus
Celtis, Conradus *Mutianus Rufus, Willibald
*Pirckheimer, and Gianfrancesco *Pico della
Mirandola. Before the advent of Erasmus to the
Upper Rhine, Zasius' ties with Basel were
much weaker than those which connected him
to Alsace.

Bonifacius *Amerbach, Zasius' favourite
student, helped to bring Erasmus into direct
communication with Zasius. Amerbach, who
had already been in touch with Erasmus
through his father, the publisher Johann
*Amerbach, as well as the printer Johann
*Froben, did not hesitate to present his teacher
in the best possible light. Erasmus quickly
responded by sending Zasius a book, and
Zasius' acknowledgment (7 September 1514,
Ep 303) precipitated an intense correspondence. Even when one discounts the mutual
praise which was a staple in letters of this sort,
there remains sufficient evidence that each
respected the personality and accomplish-
ments of the other. Rudolf Wackernagel had
good reason for calling the correspondence
with Zasius the most important which Erasmus
had in Germany. Erasmus called Zasius 'the
only German who knows how to express
himself' (Ep 408). Zasius sent drafts of his work
in progress, and Erasmus replied by sending
Zasius his numerous publications as they
emerged from the presses in Basel. For a long
time they were unable to meet; an attempt by
Zasius to entice Erasmus to Freiburg for the
marriage of his daughter Clementia in 1515 fell
through (Ep 358). Only in the summer of 1518

did they meet – apparently in Basel – and
Erasmus declared that the jurist exceeded even
his highest expectations (Epp 857, 859).

Contact with Erasmus seems to have encouraged Zasius to publish his writings, and
Erasmus was a primary influence over his later
intellectual development. So far he had only
published a single monograph in Strasbourg in
1508, a controversial treatise on the forced
baptism of Jewish children. His next work, a
collection of legal essays entitled *Lucubrationes*,
did not appear until 1518, behind a prefatory
letter by Erasmus (Ep 862; cf Ep 904). In 1519 he
launched a polemic against Johann Maier of
*Eck on behalf of Erasmus' edition of the New
Testament (Ep 769 introduction). In 1526
followed Zasius' most important work, the
Intellectus singulares, which was published
along with a revised version of the works
already printed in 1518. This confirmed Zasius'
position as one of the leading legal scholars of
Europe as well as the premier German legal
humanist. All of this took shape with the
friendly advice and help of Erasmus and
Amerbach. Among the other members of the
Erasmian circle with close ties to Zasius were
*Beatus Rhenanus and Claudius *Cantiuncula.
Further-flung 'Erasmian' correspondents were
Andrea *Alciati and Guillaume *Budé (with
whom there were occasional differences: Ep
1407).

At first Zasius perceived Martin *Luther to
be yet another ally of Erasmus' proposals for
church reform. Very quickly, however, his
approval of him turned to antipathy and even
hatred once he saw Luther to be questioning
the foundations of the existing ecclesiastical
order. Erasmus' tactically balanced stance in
the early part of the Reformation crisis failed to
satisfy Zasius, causing him to express impatience with Erasmus' caution. Just as was the
case with Erasmus, however, Zasius repeatedly fell into conflicts with the radicals of all
camps due to his readiness to mediate. Zasius
risked public scandal and even serious penal-
ties by serving Erasmus a chicken during Lent
when the humanist visited Freiburg in March
1523 (Ep 1353), an incident described in
slightly veiled terms in the adage Ἰχθυοφαγία
(ASD I-3 529–30). For years Zasius defended the
Lutheran poet Philipp *Engelbrecht against
municipal and university authorities. The

pressure on Zasius was increased by conflicts between the university and the city and grew so intense that he even considered leaving Freiburg; in March 1522 he told Erasmus that he was considering taking a professorship in Mainz, seeing that all his pleas to both sides for restraint fell on deaf ears (Ep 1266). When a call to a position in Nürnberg actually did come in 1528, however, he declined owing to deteriorating health.

Curiously there is no reference to Zasius in Erasmus' extant correspondence between January 1524 and July 1529 (Epp 1407, 2196), but some letters may be lost, of course, and Zasius' correspondence with Amerbach shows no trace of any estrangement between Erasmus and Zasius. The latter greeted the publication of *De libero arbitrio* in 1524 with particular enthusiasm (AK II Ep 971) and for a time he toyed with the idea of translating it into German. Soon afterwards he scornfully rejected Amerbach's request that he translate a eucharistic treatise by *Oecolampadius, and in the autumn of 1526 he criticized Erasmus' *Detectio praestigiarum* for its overly cautious treatment of the eucharistic novelties at Basel (AK III Ep 1127). Zasius remarked then, 'Erasmus' writing on this is elegant, but others may determine whether it is strong enough in the face of such a threatening peril.' Soon afterwards he complained of Erasmus' 'coolness' and reluctance to use his divine gifts in the fight against the heretics: 'Oh, if only Erasmus had my courage, or I had the splendid spirit of Erasmus!' (AK III Ep 1134). Zasius' devotion to Erasmus as a Catholic reformer did not prevent him from making sport of the humanist's poetry on behalf of the cult of Loretto (AK III Ep 1030).

In April 1529 Erasmus moved to Freiburg from Basel, at least partly because Zasius was there to serve as an intellectual companion. Yet despite the fact that Erasmus was to live in Freiburg for six years, the two men actually had little personal contact in that time. Zasius' deafness (Ep 2196) and other physical ailments and the great differences in their personal life-styles contributed to this. Erasmus engaged in mild intrigues over a possible successor to Zasius, and Zasius in return sought to bring Erasmus into contact with his own latter-day patron, Johann (II) *Paum-

gartner. Despite occasional difficulties, Zasius continued to hold Erasmus in high regard, and Erasmus had an increasing influence over Zasius' own substantive thought, notably on his concept of equity. Erasmus repeatedly volunteered praises for Zasius in letters written in this period, such as the remarkable eulogy sent to Pirckheimer (Ep 2196; cf Epp 2209, 2329). When Zasius died, Erasmus composed an epitaph which reflected his respect (Reedijk poem 135).

Zasius had been married before he arrived in Freiburg, and this marriage produced four children. After his first wife died of the plague in late 1519, Zasius caused a great scandal by marrying his serving-girl, Barbara, who gave him seven children, of whom four survived him. The three children of the first marriage to survive him were one son, Joachim *Zasius the elder, and two daughters, Catharina, who married Georg *Funck, and Clementia, who married Johannes *Sutor. Of the sons of the second marriage, two stand out: Johann Ulrich *Zasius and Joachim the younger, who became a doctor of theology, a canon in the Basel and Constance cathedral chapters, and provost at Oelenberg. He died in 1569. Barbara died in 1566. Nothing further is known of his other children or descendents.

Zasius' most important works are: *Quaestiones de parvulis Judaeorum baptizandis* (Strasbourg: J. Grüninger 1508); *Lucubrationes* (Basel: J. Froben 1518); *Apologetica defensio contra Ioannem Eckium* (Basel: J. Froben 1519); *Intellectus singulares* (Basel: A. Cratander 1526; Freiburg: J. Faber 1532); *Defensio novissima contra Petrum Stellam* (Freiburg: J. Faber 1530); and *In usus feudorum epitome* (Basel: J. Bebel 1535). His *Opera omnia* ed Joachim Mynsinger von Frundeck and Johann Ulrich Zasius 7 vols (Lyon: S. Gryphius 1550) includes a large number of lecture courses and legal judgments (*Consilia*) published posthumously from Zasius' papers.

Manuscripts of unpublished Zasian letters, lectures, and legal judgments are primarily to be found in the Amerbach files, Öffentliche Bibliothek of the University of Basel, with a manuscript catalogue of the section C VI b by Hans Thieme. Letters of 1489–93 are in the Staatsarchiv of Lucerne, MS Formelbuch 1435/32, ff 79 verso–119 verso. German-language writings of 1494–6 and the drafts of the code of 1520 are in the Stadtarchiv Freiburg im Breisgau, and two lecture courses are found in the Universitätsbibliothek Freiburg im Breisgau, MSS 27, 232. A critique of Eck's arguments on behalf of interest-bearing contracts, 1515, is found in the Bayrische Staatsbibliothek, Munich, MS CLM 1470, ff 197 recto–9 recto. Also in the same collection, MS CLM 576, is a version of Zasius' 1521 lectures on *Rhetorica ad Herennium.*

BIBLIOGRAPHY: Allen and CWE Ep 303 / AK I Ep 51 and passim / ADB XLIV 708–15 / Schottenloher II 406, VII 238 / Roderich von Stintzing *Ulrich Zasius* (Basel 1857, repr 1961) / Erik Wolf *Grosse Rechtsdenker der deutschen Geistesgeschichte* 4th ed (Tübingen 1963) 59–101, excellent bibliography / Joseph Anton Stephan von Riegger *Udalrici Zasii epistolae ad viros aetatis suae doctissimos* (Ulm 1774), with a biography which is too seldom read / Hans Thieme 'Les leçons de Zasius,' 'L'Oeuvre juridique de Zasius' in *Pédagogues et juristes* ed Pierre Mesnard (Paris 1963) 31–47 / Hans Thieme 'Die "Nüwen Stattrechten und Statuten der löblichen Statt Fryburg" von 1520' in *Freiburg im Mittelalter* ed Wolfgang Müller (Bühl-Baden 1970) / Guido Kisch *Zasius und Reuchlin* (Constance-Stuttgart 1961) / Guido Kisch *Erasmus und die Jurisprudenz seiner Zeit* (Basel 1960) / Steven Rowan 'Ulrich Zasius and the baptism of Jewish children' *Sixteenth Century Journal* 6, 2 (1975) 3–25 / Steven Rowan 'Ulrich Zasius and John Eck' *Sixteenth Century Journal* 8, 2 (1977) 79–95 / Steven Rowan 'The German works of Ulrich Zasius' *Manuscripta* 21 (1977) 131–43 / Steven Rowan 'Ulrich Zasius on the death penalty for Anabaptists' BHR 41 (1979) 527–40 / Rudolf Wackernagel *Geschichte der Stadt Basel* (Basel 1907–54) III 195 and passim

HANS THIEME & STEVEN ROWAN

Andrzej ZEBRZYDOWSKI d 23 May 1560
Zebrzydowski (Andreas Sebridarius) was descended from a noble family with the coat-of-arms of 'Radwan' which owned estates in Więcbork, in Greater Poland. He was the son of Wojciech, steward of the archiepiscopal estate of Żnin. His mother, Elzbieta, was a sister of Andrzej *Krzycki, thus Zebrzydowski was the great-nephew of Piotr *Tomicki. He began his studies at the University of Cracow

in 1517 but left without receiving a degree. Krzycki and Tomicki, his patrons, hoped to prepare him for an ecclesiastical career. In 1527 he studied privately with Leonard *Cox, who asked Erasmus (Ep 1803) to write to the young man, encouraging him to pursue his education with renewed determination. Cox also mentioned Zebrzydowski's plan to visit Erasmus at Basel. Erasmus responded with a suitable letter to Zebrzydowski (Ep 1826), and in February 1528 Zebrzydowski was sent on his way to Basel (Epp 1954, 1958). He was to bring Erasmus a gift of money from King *Sigismund rewarding him for his Ep 1819 addressed to the king. Between 26 and 31 August Erasmus confirmed Zebrzydowski's presence in his home and acknowledged receipt of the royal gift (Epp 2030, 2031, 2033, 2035). Zebrzydowski made the acquaintance of Bonifacius *Amerbach, *Glareanus, and Johann *Sichard. To Erasmus' regret he left for Paris as early as the end of September (Ep 2052, 2173, 2201). In December Erasmus sent him an encouraging letter (Ep 2078), and in the spring of 1529 Zebrzydowski returned to stay with Erasmus for another short period. Then he left for Venice together with Karel *Uutenhove (Ep 2161, 2173), amid the beginnings of confessional violence at Basel. From Venice Zebrzydowski went to Padua, and there are no more traces of any contacts with Erasmus.

Thanks to the protection of his influential relatives Zebrzydowski was in possession of three rich benefices as early as 1520 (Ep 1803). On 23 August 1530 he was appointed a canon of Cracow, and he used his diplomatic skill as well as bribery to acquire additional dignities. On 30 March 1543 he was nominated to the bishopric of Kamieniec, and on 14 August he added to that see the provostship of Gniezno. He was appointed bishop of Chełm on 8 February 1545 but was soon transferred to the see of Włocławek. Finally on 23 February 1551 he obtained the rich and politically important bishopric of Cracow. Initially he cared little for church affairs and spent most of his time in pursuit of wealth. It was only after his advancement to the see of Cracow and owing to the pressure of his cathedral chapter that he began to combat the spread of the Reformation and to conduct numerous trials for heresy in his diocese. Although he never lived up to the intellectual promise shown in his youth, he was recognized, largely because of his high office, as a patron of scholars and men of letters. As bishop of Cracow he was also chancellor of the university.

Zebrzydowski died in May 1560 near Poznań while returning from his native Więcbork to Cracow. On 24 June he was buried in his cathedral, in the chapel of St Lawrence. On the magnificent monument set up by his heirs it was recorded in accordance with his own wishes that he was 'magni illius Erasmi Rotherodami discipulus et auditor.' Sichard dedicated to him his *Disciplinarum liberalium orbis* (Basel: J. Bebel 1528) and also paid him a compliment in the preface of his *Antidotum contra diversas fere omnium saeculorum haereses* (Basel: H. Petri 1528). Paolo *Manuzio sent Zebrzydowski a portrait of Aldo *Manuzio as a mark of esteem.

Zebrzydowski's correspondence from 1546 to 1553 is edited by W. Wisłocki: *Andrzeja na Więcborku Zebrzydowskiego biskupa włocław-skiego i krakowskiego korespondencja z lat 1546–1553* (Cracow 1878).

BIBLIOGRAPHY: Allen Ep 1826 / Bierlaire *Familia* 84–6 and passim / *Korespondencja Erazma z Rotterdamu z Polakami* ed M. Cytowska (Warsaw 1965) / T. Troskolański *Andrzej Radwan Zebrzydowski, biskup włocławski i krakowski* (Lwow 1899–1907) / J. Korytkowski *Prałaci i kanonicy katedry metropolitalnej gniez-nienskiej* (Gniezno 1883) IV 454–81 / H. Barycz 'Die ersten wissenschaftlichen Verbindungen Polens mit Basel' *Vierteljahresschrift für Ge-schichte der Wissenschaft und Technik* Sonderheft 2 (Warsaw 1960) 40–2, 100–1 / L. Hajdukiewicz *Ksiegozbiór i zainteresowania bibliofilskie Piotra Tomickiego na tle jego działalnósci kulturalnej* (Wrocław 1961) / *Petri Royzii Maurei Carmina* ed B. Kruczkiewicz (Cracow 1900)

HALINA KOWALSKA

Bartholomäus ZEHENDER of Cologne, c 1460–1516
Bartholomäus, or Barthold, Zehender (Bar-tholomaeus Decimator Coloniensis), was a pupil of Alexander *Hegius at St Lebuin's school, Deventer. He remained attached to that school, where he taught the fourth class beginning in 1489. From Deventer he moved to Zwolle, where he lived as a teacher until 1506.

In 1506 he succeeded Johannes Grovius as rector of St Mauritius' school at Münster and in 1511 Gerardus Bastius as rector of the munici-pal school of Alkmaar, where *Alaard of Amsterdam was one of his assistant teachers. In 1513 he entrusted the school to his successor, Johannes *Murmellius, and left Alkmaar for Deventer. He died at Minden. Erasmus listed him among the men of letters of his time (Ep 23), Hermannus *Buschius paid tribute to him in a poem, and Murmellius dedicated the fourth of his *Elegiae morales* (1508) to him. Zehender himself wrote *Epistola mythologica* ([Deventer: J. de Breda 1489/90]; Campbell 251), which was edited by D. Reichling in 1897; *Silva carminum* (Deventer: J. de Breda 1491; Campbell 257); *Canones* (Zwolle: P. Os [1500?]; NK 238); *Libellus elegiacus de septenis doloribus virg. Mariae* (Deventer: J. de Breda 6 November 1514; NK 241); and *Tractatus de diversis rebus ponderabilibus* (Deventer: T. de Borne 1515; NK 4123). Some poems of his Alkmaar period were edited by E.H. Rijken-berg and W. Lampen in *Haarlemsche Bijdragen* 21 (1896) 374–97 and 52 (1935) 107–27. Zehen-der also contributed several commendatory poems to other books.

BIBLIOGRAPHY: Allen Ep 23 / A.J. van der Aa et al *Biographisch woordenboek der Nederlanden* (Haarlem 1852–78, repr 1965) III 625–6 / W. Crecelius in ADB XVI 484–5 / J. Lindeboom in NNBW III 686–7 / 'Bartholomaei Coloniensis epistola mythologica' ed D. Reichling *Mittei-lungen der Gesellschaft für deutsche Erziehungs-und Schulgeschichte* 7 (1897) 111–72 / H.E. van Gelder *Geschiedenis der Latijnsche School te Alkmaar* (Alkmaar 1905) 86–8 / M.F.A.G. Campbell *Annales de la typographie néerlandaise au xve siècle* (The Hague 1874–90)

C.G. VAN LEIJENHORST

ZEVENBERGEN *See Maximiliaan van* BERGEN

Eustachius ZICHEMUS, de ZICHENIS *See Eustachius van der* RIVIEREN

Jakob ZIEGLER of Landau, d 1549
Jakob Ziegler (Zieglerus, Jacobus Landanus) was born by 1470 in Landau (Bavaria). He studied at the University of Ingolstadt (1491–1500) under the humanists Conradus Celtis and Jakob *Locher and formed a connection

with the mathematician Andreas Stiborius, who was a fellow student. He obtained a MA and in 1499 began to study and teach theology, but he left in 1500 to begin a life of intermittent travel in the course of which he became acquainted with Erasmus at an unknown date. He visited various parts of Germany before moving to Moravia (1508–11) and Budapest (1514–20), where he became a close friend of Celio *Calcagnini. Calcagnini recommended him, through his protector Cardinal Ippolito d'*Este, to Pope *Leo x. Thus prepared, Ziegler arrived in Rome on 1 March 1521, but Leo x, in whom he had hoped to find a patron, died in December 1521, while Ippolito d'Este had died the preceding year.

Ziegler seems to have found employment at the papal curia in an unknown capacity, and in February 1522 he wrote a substantial letter (Ep 1260) to Erasmus, urging him to prepare an edition of St Augustine and expressing his disgust with Diego *López Zúñiga, Erasmus' opponent, whom he had met twice. He promised to defend Erasmus in the introduction to a work on the Gospels he planned to write but was unable to finish. By the spring of 1523 his defence was in Erasmus' hands, and it was published as Libellus ... adversus Stunicae maledicentiam together with Erasmus' Catalogus lucubrationum (Basel: J. Froben 1523). Erasmus praised Ziegler in the preface (Ep 1342). Earlier he had replied to Ziegler's Ep 1260 and one other letter which is lost (Ep 1330) and sent greetings to him in Ep 1294. Another letter of Ziegler to Erasmus, dated 1524 but also lost, is mentioned in Erasmus' correspondence with *Ursinus Velius, who, like Ziegler, had belonged to the circle of Erasmus' supporters in Rome (Epp 1514, 1557).

Ziegler left Rome in 1525 and stayed partly in Ferrara and partly in Venice until 1531. He had followed the development of the Reformation in Germany with interest and gradually turned into a bitter opponent of the Roman church. In a series of unpublished invectives dating from this period he poured scorn and abuse upon individual popes and the papal church, censured *Charles v, that 'Fleming,' for selling out to Rome after the Sack, and also criticized Erasmus, that other 'Fleming,' for his anti-German stance in the colloquy Diversoria (Schottenloher Ziegler 238). This passage,

Jakob Ziegler, by Wolf Huber

however, was later crossed out in his manuscript, for when Ziegler returned to Germany in 1531 his high-spirited patriotic expectations once again gave way to disillusionment. He renewed his friendship and correspondence with Julius *Pflug and eventually came to favour Erasmian irenicism.

In 1531 Ziegler went to Strasbourg, where *Capito opened his house to him and *Bucer helped him secure an annual salary from the city council. But by 1534 his criticism of the Strasbourg ministers had become so outspoken that he thought it advisable to move on. He spent some time at Baden-Baden (1534–c 1539), where he tutored a son of Margrave Ernst of Baden, and in Vienna (1542–3), where he was a member of the theological faculty. He finally found a peaceful haven for his last years at the court of Wolfgang von Salm, bishop of Passau. There he died in 1549, perhaps in August.

During his years in Moravia Ziegler produced a polemic against the Czech Brethren in his Contra haereticos Valdenses ... libri quinque, published with related material by Melchior Lotter (Leipzig 1512). With his last work he returned to theological topics: Conceptionum in

Genesim mundi et Exodum commentarii, eiusdem super arbitrio humano exempla ... (Basel: J. Oporinus 1548). Intervening publications dealt primarily with cosmography and astronomy: *Quae intus continentur* ... (Strasbourg: P. Schöffer 1532), mostly descriptions of Syria, Egypt, and Arabia based on the Greek geographies, but also an excellent description of Scandinavia (Ep 2826); and *Sphaerae atque astrorum coelestium ratio* (Basel: J. Walder 1536). Ziegler's writings have failed to impress posterity, but their influence on some of his major contemporaries, while hard to assess, should not be underestimated.

BIBLIOGRAPHY: Allen Ep 1260 / ADB XLV 175–7 / Karl Schottenloher *Jakob Ziegler* (Münster 1910), an excellent study with a full bibliography of Ziegler's published and unpublished works / Pflug *Correspondance* I Ep 53 and passim / BA *Oekolampads* I 641–2 and passim

IG & PGB

Paul ZIEGLER of Nördlingen, d 25 August 1541
Paul was the son of Friedrich Ziegler, a cloth merchant, who had settled at Nördlingen, in Swabia, in 1471 and had been raised to noble status by *Maximilian I.

The Ziegler family must have had good connections with the curia of the bishop of Chur, which had long been offering careers to some clerical members of the noble families of southern Germany and the Hapsburg lands. From 1503 negotiations were conducted with both Paul and his brother Nikolaus Ziegler about a coadjutorship at Chur to relieve Bishop Konrad von Hewen, who wished to be free of his duties without losing all his revenues. On 6 June 1505 Paul Ziegler was confirmed by the pope as administrator, rather than coadjutor, of the diocese, which Hewen resigned against a handsome annuity. On 1 June 1506 Maximilian I officially invested Ziegler with the substantial lands in the Grisons that formed the secular dominion of the see of Chur, and at Easter 1507 he became a priest. On 18 August 1509 he was appointed councillor to the duke of Milan, and about the same time he was formally elected and confirmed as regular bishop of Chur, although his consecration did not take place until October 1517.

Meanwhile, in 1510 Ziegler had made

unsuccessful attempts to be appointed coadjutor of Speyer. In 1522 he received a papal annuity upon the provostship of Cologne. On the other hand, his close relations with the house of Hapsburg were watched with misgivings in the Three Leagues of the Grisons, and it was debated whether he should continue to be represented on their diets. This conflict came to a head in 1524, when the bishop refused to sign a new set of federal agreements and moved from Chur to his castle near Glorenza, Alto Adige. On 25 June 1526 the Leagues retaliated with the articles of Ilanz, which aimed at the termination of most episcopal rights and revenues, subjected the monasteries to secular control, and reserved all canonries for natives of the Grisons. For the following two years Ziegler was involved in secret negotiations for his resignation, which might have opened the way for a more forceful successor, but the manoeuvre failed and he continued to reside in the episcopal castle in Alto Adige, where he died.

In February 1530 Johann *Koler had returned from a trip to Italy undertaken in the company of Ziegler (Ep 2269).

BIBLIOGRAPHY: Allen Ep 2269 / *Helvetia sacra* ed A. Bruckner et al (Bern 1972–) I-1 493–4 / DHBS VII 435 / F. Pieth *Bündnergeschichte* (Chur 1945) 131–9 / *Deutsche Reichstagsakten* Jüngere Reihe (Gotha-Göttingen 1893–) II 812 / AK V Ep 2107

PGB

Amandus of ZIERIKZEE *See* AMANDUS *of Zierikzee*

Jan (died c 1540) **and Anna ZIMMERMAN** of Cracow
Jan Zimmerman (Czymerman) was a goldsmith in Cracow. He served on the city council and was an officer of his guild. Held in great esteem as a master of his craft, he worked for Queen *Bona, Erazm *Ciołek, abbot of Mogiła, the city council of Cracow, and many other patrons. Chancellor Krzysztof *Szydłowiecki chose him to craft his gift for Erasmus in appreciation of the *Lingua* dedicated to the chancellor (Epp 1660, 1698, 1752). Jan had several children, among them Jan, who succeeded him in his goldsmith's workshop. Another son, Josephus *Tectander, was a physician and correspondent of Erasmus,

while Jan's daughter Anna married (before 21 January 1526) Jan *Antonin, who was also a physician and friend and admirer of Erasmus. When her husband wrote to Erasmus Anna sent greetings which Erasmus returned (Epp 1660, 1698, 2176, 3137). She may well have selected a gift of special linen for him (Ep 1916).

BIBLIOGRAPHY: Allen Ep 1660 / L. Lepszy *Przemysł złotniczy w Polsce* (Cracow 1933) 128 / W. Pociecha *Królowa Bona: Czasy i ludzie Odrodzenia* (Poznań 1949) II 80, 110, 495–6 / *Zródła do dziejów Wawelu, v: Wypisy źródłowe do dziejów Wawelu z archiwaliów kapitulnych i kurialnych krakowskich, 1516–1523* ed B. Przybyszewski (Cracow 1970) 14

HALINA KOWALSKA

Joseph ZIMMERMANN *See Josephus* TECTANDER

Johannes ZINTHIUS *See Jan* SYNTHEN

ZIZIMUS *See* DJEM, *Ottoman prince*

Theoderich ZOBEL von Giebelstadt
d 6 October 1531
The Zobels were an ancient noble family of Franconia whose ancestral castle stood at Giebelstadt, south of Würzburg. Theoderich (Dietrich), whose parentage and date of birth are uncertain, was more than thirty years old on 28 May 1500 (Amrhein 119). From 12 February 1484 he was a canon of St Thomas', Strasbourg; on 19 May 1485 he matriculated at the University of Freiburg and on 21 May 1487 at Heidelberg. By August 1500 he had obtained a doctorate in civil and canon law. On 25 September 1497 he became a domiciliar and on 28 May 1500 a full canon ('canonicus capitularis') of the cathedral chapter of Mainz. He held additional benefices as provost of St Martin's, Bingen, and a canon of St Mariengraden, Mainz, having been authorized to hold three prebends simultaneously by papal dispensation of 3 April 1505. On 6 November 1506 he was appointed vicar-general 'in spiritualibus et ecclesiasticis' to the archbishop of Mainz, a position which he held to his death, serving successively the archbishops Jakob von Liebenstein, Uriel von Gemmingen, and Albert of *Brandenburg. He was also scholaster of St Thomas', Strasbourg (11

August 1517–November 1520), precentor of Mainz (23 October–13 December 1518), and scholaster of Mainz (11 December 1518 to his death). His tenure of these offices and additional evidence leave no doubt as to his being a priest, although his sacerdotal functions were exercised by a vicar (Herrmann *Protokolle* III 495–6). His residence at Mainz was the Arnsburger Hof in the Gräfengasse.

In addition to representing the archbishop in the ecclesiastical domain, Zobel also acted as a political adviser to his masters and from 1514 was one of the most influential councillors of Albert of Brandenburg. At the same time he represented the cathedral chapter in legal matters and on occasion mediated conflicts between the chapter and the archbishop, thus succeeding in serving both parties without any harm to his reputation. As one of the Mainz ambassadors he was in Rome in April 1505, and again from spring to December 1514 for negotiations about Albert's joint tenure of the archsees of Mainz and Magdeburg. Subsequently he helped supervise the indulgence deal arranged in these negotiations.

Zobel was present at the electors' meetings of Wesel in May 1517 and April 1519, the diet of Worms in 1521, and a conference of the Rhenish archbishops in October 1524 at Koblenz, which dealt with a crusade tax levied on the clergy and the progress of the Lutheran heresy. In 1522 he sat on the council governing the state of Mainz during the absence of Archbishop Albert. When the German estates were invited to prepare submissions to a national council to be held at Speyer in 1524, Zobel was a member of the Mainz committee on Lutheranism. Zobel shared his master's preference for a moderate stance; as a result few excommunications have been noted in the ecclesiastical principality of Mainz.

Zobel also enjoyed great prestige among humanist circles, where he had many personal friends. On 10 September 1508 he wrote to the theological faculty of the University of Cologne in support of Petrus Ravennas against his theological opponents (the letter is printed in Liessem 27). *Wimpfeling dedicated to him his edition of Dietrich Gresemund's *Historia violatae crucis* (Strasbourg: R. Beck 1512). Johannes Aesticampianus wished him a bishop's mitre in 1517, and in the same year Hermann von

*Neuenahr praised his support of *Reuchlin in the preface to Giorgio *Benigno's *Defensio Reuchlini* (Cologne 1517). In 1520 Johann *Huttich dedicated to Zobel the *Collectanea antiquitatum*, thus carrying out the intention of its deceased author, Gresemund, who had been a friend of Zobel. Erasmus was familiar with both of these works and may, in fact, have been personally acquainted with Zobel (CWE Ep 880 introduction). Acting no doubt on instructions received from his friends at Mainz, Erasmus paid Zobel a flattering compliment in his preface for Johann *Schöffer's edition of Livy (1518–19; Ep 919). *Hutten continued to think highly of Zobel and maintained personal contacts with him as late as the spring of 1519 (Hutten *Opera* I Epp 110, 120; AK II Ep 655), while *Capito referred to his support when dedicating his edition of John Chrysostom's *Paraenesis prior ... ad Theodorum lapsum* (Basel: J. Froben 1519) to Archbishop Albert. When *Charles V passed through Mainz in November 1520, it was Zobel who welcomed the emperor with an accomplished speech. Petrus *Mosellanus greeted him as a patron when writing to Capito on 27 July 1521 (Herrmann *Evangelische Bewegung* 63), and on 15 May 1522 Johannes ab Indagine dedicated to him his *Introductiones apotelesmaticae elegantes in chiromantiam* (Steitz 139–41). On 13 September 1525 Lorenzo *Campeggi recommended Fridericus *Nausea to Zobel, who supported Nausea a few months later for the vacant position of cathedral preacher at Mainz (*Epistolae ad Nauseam* 33, 43). Another connection with Erasmus dates from 1528, when Zobel promised Erasmus to let Hieronymus *Froben use the recently discovered manuscript of Livy which belonged to the Mainz chapter (Ep 1927).

In his *Exegesis Germaniae* (Haguenau: T. Anshelm 1518) Franciscus *Irenicus counted Zobel among the scholars and historians of Germany (signature h 3 verso), but very few compositions by him are known to exist. In addition to the letter in support of Ravennas and the one addressed to Erasmus, a letter of his to Archbishop Albert, dating from 1516, and two other documents signed by him and his fellow ambassadors (1514) were published by Schulte (II 103, 117–18, 150–2).

BIBLIOGRAPHY: Allen Ep 919 / *Matrikel Freiburg* I-1 81 / *Matrikel Heidelberg* I 386 / Johannes

Aesticampianus *Epigrammata* (Leipzig 1517) / 'Freiherrlich von Zobel'sches Archiv zu Messelhausen ... verzeichnet von ... Hugo Ehrensberger ... ' *Zeitschrift für die Geschichte des Oberrheins* n s 13 (1898) 124 / Gustav Bauch 'Aus der Geschichte des Mainzer Humanismus' *Archiv für hessische Geschichte und Altertumskunde* n s 5 (1907) 53 / *Geschlechts-Register der Reichs Frey unmittelbaren Ritterschafft Landes zu Francken löblichen Orts Ottenwald ... ed Johann Gottfried Biedermann (Culmbach 1751) table 36 / Johannes Burchardus *Diarium sive rerum urbanorum commentarii (1483–1506)* ed Louis Thuasne (Paris 1885) III xxxiii / Hans-Heinrich Fleischer *Dietrich Gresemund der Jüngere* (Wiesbaden 1967) 155 / Johann Heinrich Harpprecht *Staats-Archiv des Kays. und des H. Römischen Reiches Kammer-Gerichts* (Ulm 1759) III 31 / Fritz Herrmann *Die evangelische Bewegung zu Mainz im Reformationszeitalter* (Mainz 1907) 48, 63, 136, and passim / Georg Christian Ioannis *Rerum Moguntiacarum volumina tres* (Frankfurt am Main 1722–7) II 321 / Paul Kalkoff *W. Capito im Dienste Erzbischof Albrechts von Mainz* (Berlin 1907) 138 / Gustav C. Knod *Die Stiftsherren von St. Thomas zu Strassburg (1518–48)* (Strasbourg 1892) 38 / Hermann Joseph Liessem *Hermann van dem Busche: Sein Leben und seine Schriften* (Cologne 1884–1908, repr 1965) 27 / *Die Protokolle des Mainzer Domkapitels* ed Fritz Herrmann (Paderborn 1929–32) III xxvii–xxviii, 495–6, and passim / *Deutsche Reichstagsakten Jüngere Reihe* (Gotha-Göttingen 1893–) I 519, II 835 / Alois Schulte *Die Fugger in Rom* (Leipzig 1904) I 105–22 and passim / Georg Eduard Steitz 'Reformatorische Persönlichkeiten, Einflüsse und Vorgänge in der Reichsstadt Frankfurt am Main von 1519–22' *Archiv für Frankfurts Geschichte und Kunst* n s 6 (1869) 139–41 / Giebelstadt, Familienarchiv der Freiherren Zobel von Giebelstadt, MS 'Familien-Geschichte der Zobel von Giebelstadt' by August Amrhein   KONRAD WIEDEMANN

Lorenz ZOCH of Halle, 9 August 1477–1533 (?)
Lorenz (Laurentius) Zoch (Czoch, Zcoghe), born in Halle, matriculated in Leipzig in the spring of 1493 and obtained a BA on 7 March 1495 and a MA on 28 December 1498. He matriculated in Bologna in 1503, became

procurator of the German nation in 1505, and obtained a doctorate of civil and canon law on 20 March 1506. After his return to Germany he joined the law faculty in Leipzig after 1511. Subsequently he lived in his native Halle and acted as a councillor to Duke George of *Saxony and Archbishop Albert of *Branden-burg. As Albert's chancellor of Magdeburg he attended the diets of Augsburg in 1518 (Ep 863) and Nürnberg in 1522. In 1524 he also drew a salary as consultant to Albert's brother, the Elector Joachim of Brandenburg. On an un-known date he married Klara Preusser of Leipzig, who, like himself, was a Lutheran, and had been educated by the Benedictine nuns of Brehna near Bitterfeld together with Katharina von *Bora (Luther w *Briefwechsel* VI Ep 1879). His religious convictions may have been a factor in a demotion he suffered in 1527 when he lost his influential position in the government of Magdeburg, although he may have retained the title of chancellor. His complete downfall, and even a spell of confinement in his house, came about in the spring of 1531, when Cardinal Albert purged the Magdeburg administration of all Luther-ans. On 30 October 1531 he had regained his freedom of movement and wrote to *Luther to thank him for his support (w *Briefwechsel* VI Ep 1879). His wife died in the autumn of 1532 and he himself is said to have died the following year. If this is correct, another Lorenz Zoch, presumably his son, who matriculated at Wittenberg in 1529, later became councillor to the elector of Saxony and rector of the University of Wittenberg for the summer term of 1543. He died at Wittenberg on 27 February 1547. His sons, Lorenz and Hieronymus, matriculated in Wittenberg in March 1552.

BIBLIOGRAPHY: Allen Ep 863 / Knod 654 / *Matrikel Leipzig* I 396, II 38, 347, 365 / *Matrikel Wittenberg* I 135, 204, 273   IG

Hieronymus ZSCHECKENBÜRLIN of Basel, 1460/1–7 January 1536
Zscheckenbürlin was the last male descendant of a Basel family of rich merchants and powerful civic politicians. He matriculated at Basel in 1472 and was a BA in 1478; he moved on to Paris and then to Orléans, where he studied civil law together with Johann *Reuchlin, was procurator of the German nation, and gradua-

ted MA and licentiate of civil law on 21 April 1482. After his return home he suddenly decided to abandon his career and with much fanfare he entered the Carthusian monastery on 31 May 1487, taking his vows on 1 November. In view of his self-confidence and the amount of property he brought to the monastery it is not surprising that he became prior on 24 February 1502. Through his building activity and love of artistic decoration and beautiful books (each marked with an individually painted ex-libris) and also through his sumptuous hospitality, he led the monastery to a public prominence that was not matched by its spiritual life. At the time of Basel's reform in 1529 he went to Freiburg and embarrassed the Basel city council by claiming his large paternal inheritance which had gone to the monastery. Bonifacius *Amerbach, whose wife was Zscheckenbürlin's grand-niece, acted as his lawyer (AK III Epp 1424, 1425). Zscheckenbürlin's diplomatic and legal skill led to an understanding with the city on 16 July 1532 enabling him to return with some of his monks, but without the right to say mass. Of personal contacts with Erasmus there is surprisingly little evidence (Ep 2946; AK III Ep 1125) in spite of Zscheckenbürlin's close relations with the Amerbach family and the evident admiration for Erasmus at the Carthus-ian monastery (Allen Epp 1667, 1708; AK III Ep 1125).

BIBLIOGRAPHY: Allen Ep 2946 / DHBS VII 481 / R. Wackernagel *Geschichte der Stadt Basel* (Basel 1907–54) II-2 846–7, 904, and passim / AK II Ep 527 and passim / *Basler Chroniken* I 348–56 / *Aktensammlung zur Geschichte der Basler Refor-mation* ed E. Dürr et al (Basel 1921–50) II–VI passim / *Matricule d'Orléans* I-1 45, 47–8, II-1 102–3 / *Matrikel Basel* I 111   PGB

ZUICCIUS, ZUICCUS *See Konrad and Johann* ZWICK

Viglius ZUICHEMUS Phrysius *See* VIGLIUS ZUICHEMUS

Ulrichus ZUINGLIUS *See Huldrych* ZWINGLI

Francisco de ZÚÑIGA d 1536
Francisco de Zúñiga, third count of Miranda, was the son of Pedro de Zúñiga y Velasco,

count of Miranda, and a brother of Iñigo *López de Mendoza y Zúñiga, bishop of Burgos, and of Juan de Zúñiga y Avellaneda, commander of Castile. He was master of horses in charge of the household of the Empress *Isabella of Portugal. On 10 October 1528 he was named to assist the empress in the government of Spain in the absence of *Charles v, along with Alonso de *Fonseca, archbishop of Toledo, and Fadrique *Alvarez de Toledo, duke of Alba. This event was reported to Erasmus by Juan Luis *Vives (Ep 2208).

BIBLIOGRAPHY: Allen Ep 2208 / Bataillon *Erasmo y España* 329 / José M. March *Niñez y juventud de Felipe II* (Madrid 1941–2) I 96–7, II 97 and passim   TBD

ZÚÑIGA *See also Diego* LÓPEZ ZÚÑIGA

Pieter ZUUTPENE of Cassel, d before 1552
Pieter Zuutpene (Zuetpene, Zutpenius, Sutpene, Petrus Cassiletanus) of Cassel, near Saint-Omer, matriculated at the University of Louvain on 24 September 1502. In Louvain he quickly made friends with Maarten van *Dorp, his fellow student in the College of the Lily, and with Adrianus Cornelii *Barlandus, who was to be his guest in Veere in April 1521 and dedicated to Zuutpene his *Epitome* (Louvain: D. Martens 1521), a shortened version of Erasmus' *Adagia*, on his return to Louvain (Daxhelet Ep 44). Zuutpene seems to have studied civil law and went to live at Veere as legal and economic adviser to Adolph of *Burgundy. Erasmus too may have known him from Louvain, as he also arrived there in the autumn of 1502. He may have met Zuutpene again on his visits to Adolph of Burgundy and recalled him affectionately when Jan *Becker of Borsele went to live at Veere (Ep 952). In August 1519 he honoured Zuutpene with an elaborate letter of friendship (Ep 1005). Nothing is known now about some letters in fine Latin which, according to an early source, Zuutpene had written to Erasmus. That Zuutpene was also interested in history is evident from a dedication to him of the *Compendium chronicorum Flandriae* by Jacques Meyer of Bailleul. Meyer, who died in 1552, also wrote an epitaph for Zuutpene.

BIBLIOGRAPHY: Allen Ep 1005 / de Vocht CTL I 264 and passim / de Vocht MHL 351 / Etienne Daxhelet *Adrien Barlandus* (Louvain 1938, repr 1967) 20, 289–91 / *Matricule de Louvain* III-1; cf 419 for Karel Zuutpene of Cassel, matriculating in 1511   IG & PGB

Wigle van ZWICHEM *See* VIGLIUS ZUICHEMUS

Johann ZWICK of Constance, d 23 October 1542
Johann Zwick (Zuiccus, Zuiccius), the son of Konrad *Zwick (d 1523) and cousin of Ambrosius and Thomas *Blarer, was born around 1496. From 1509 to 1518 he studied law in Freiburg, where Udalricus *Zasius was one of his teachers. A fellow student, Bonifacius *Amerbach, became his friend by 1515. In 1516 he received holy orders at Constance and then went to Bologna. Subsequently he studied at Avignon and on 16 November 1520 he obtained a doctorate of both laws in Siena. On 7 July 1521 he matriculated in Basel, where he taught until 1522. From his boyhood he was intended to succeed his uncle, Magister Johann Zwick, a canon in Basel and parish priest in Riedlingen, on the Danube, who had died on 31 October 1521. Meanwhile Zwick had begun to study *Luther's writings. In September 1522 he secretly married Anna Tegerfelder at Constance and then took over the parish of Riedlingen. Zwick's interest in reform met with the disapproval of his bishop, Hugo von *Hohenlandenberg. In 1524 he visited the reformers of Strasbourg and Basel; later he received a citation to Rome, which he ignored (Epp 1519, 1574). By the beginning of 1526 he had to leave Riedlingen and returned to Constance, where he succeeded Johann *Wanner as preacher at St Stephen's (until 1538) and soon emerged as one of the leaders of the Constance reform movement. He was a member of the school board and taught catechism at the local Latin school as well as in Lindau.

Zwick corresponded frequently not only with Joachim *Vadianus but also with Heinrich *Bullinger and Conradus *Pellicanus. He went repeatedly to Zürich, while relations with the Strasbourg reformers had somewhat cooled by 1535. Under Vadianus' influence he also

engaged in humanist studies and together with
Thomas Blarer drew a map of Lake Constance
and surroundings for the *Geographia* of Sebastian Münster (Basel: H. Petri 1544). In 1541 he
went to Bischofszell, in Thurgau, where a
plague epidemic had struck and ministers were
needed; he died there of the plague.

Zwick wrote popular treatises such as
*Underrichtung warumb die Ee uss menschlichem
Gsatz in vyl grad verbotten sey* (Basel: A.
Cratander 1524); *Christlicher trostlicher under-
richt ... zu ainem säligen Stärben* (Constance: B.
Romätsch 1545); and a preface to the Frosch-
auer New Testament (Zürich 1535). He also
contributed hymns to the *Konstanzer
Gesangbuch*.

During his stay at Basel Zwick met *Beatus
Rhenanus and Heinrich *Eppendorf and generally belonged to the circle of Erasmus'
admirers, but as early as February 1522 his
sympathies had shifted to Luther. In the
autumn of that year he probably met Erasmus
when the latter visited Constance (BRE Ep 233).

BIBLIOGRAPHY: Allen Ep 1519 / ADB XLV 533 /
AK II Ep 539 / Knod 660 / *Matrikel Freiburg* I 188 /
Matrikel Basel I 347 / BRE Ep 233 / BA *Oekolampads*
I 278 and passim / Bernd Moeller *Johannes
Zwick und die Reformation in Konstanz* (Güters-
loh 1961) / Rublack *Reformation in Konstanz* 40,
90–1, and passim   IG

Konrad ZWICK of Constance,
d before 3 December 1523
Konrad, the father of Johann *Zwick, seems to
have been stationed in Spain between 1477 and
1480 as agent for the Ravensburg trade
company. After his return to Constance he
enjoyed the respect of his fellow citizens and
from 1485 to 1486 he was town councillor. The
success of his commercial activities is indicated
by the considerable fortune he left to his
children. At some point he entered the service
of Hugo von *Hohenlandenberg, bishop of
Constance, and was appointed steward of
Meersburg, on the lake across from Constance.
There he died late in 1523 (Ep 1401). It was only
after his death that the bishop took measures
against Johann Zwick on account of his
Protestant inclinations.

BIBLIOGRAPHY: Bernd Moeller *Johannes Zwick
und die Reformation in Konstanz* (Gütersloh 1961)

13–14, 64 / Rublack *Reformation in Konstanz*
334   IG

Huldrych ZWINGLI of Wildhaus, 1 January
1484–11 October 1531
Huldrych (Ulrich) Zwingli (Zuinglius) was
born in Wildhaus, in St Gallen, Switzerland,
the son of a well-to-do farmer and local official
or *Ammann*, Ulrich Zwingli, and his wife,
Margret Bruggmann. After initial instruction
by an uncle Zwingli attended Latin schools in
Bern, Basel, Vienna, and again Basel. In 1502
he entered the University of Basel and obtained a BA (1504) and a MA (1506); he also
studied theology in Basel, but only for one
semester before he became a parish priest in
Glarus (1506–16) and in Einsiedeln, an abbey
in the canton of Schwyz famous as a centre of
pilgrimage (1516–18). These years were decisive for Zwingli's development as reformer. On
the one hand they familiarized him with the
political and economic conditions of the Swiss
Confederation, such as the supply of mercenaries to foreign powers against pensions paid
to individual politicians and Switzerland's
own role as an independent European power
in the Italian wars; on the other hand they
introduced him to humanism, especially to the
Christian humanism of Erasmus. Not only did
Zwingli emerge as the leader of the Swiss
humanists; he also became an energetic advocate of church reform. His appointment as
parish priest at the Grossmünster of Zürich at
the beginning of 1519 permitted him to
translate his views into action. He did so in
close collaboration with the Zürich city council, which for decades had pursued an independent church policy 'for the honour of God
and the welfare of the commonwealth.' From
the first Zürich disputation (29 January 1523)
there emerged the groundwork for the first
reformed state church. At Zwingli's prompting
it was decided that henceforward the 'gospel
pure and unadorned' must be preached in the
territory of Zürich and accepted as a norm for
both church and society. In the following years
the cult of images and all monasteries were
eliminated in quick succession, and the traditional mass was replaced by daily sermon and
prayer services, while communion was to be
offered only four times a year. The Grossmün-

Huldrych Zwingli, by Hans Asper

ster chapter was transformed into a seminary
for evangelical ministers. New statutes were
passed regarding social welfare, marriage, and
moral conduct. A synod consisting of all parish
priests and professors as well as representatives of the council was to carry out and
safeguard the Reformation. Finally Zürich
committed itself to a new external policy
opposed to mercenary agreements. This new
order was soon imitated within the Confederation and in southern Germany. As a model for
the Reformed branch of Protestantism, it was
developed further by Zwingli's successor,
Heinrich Bullinger, as well as by Calvin in
Geneva, and became as decisive for western
Europe and the New World as Lutheranism
was for Germany and Scandinavia.

In this process Zwingli saw his own role as
that of a prophet and thus set out to compose
an impressive array of sermons, scriptural
commentaries, and theological treatises, the
importance of which is often not fully recognized by modern scholars. Among his principal
writings are *Auslegen und Gründe der Schlussreden* (1523); *Von göttlicher und menschlicher
Gerechtigkeit* (1523); *De vera et falsa religione*

commentarius (1525), the first manual of Protestant dogmatics; a sermon *De providentia Dei*
(1530); *Fidei ratio* (1530); and *Fidei expositio*
(1531). In addition he wrote numerous tracts in
opposition to Rome, the Anabaptists, and –
especially in the eucharistic controversy –
*Luther. As a prophet, Zwingli not only felt
responsible for the salvation of individual
souls and for the reform of the church and
society in Zürich, but because of his patriotism
he was led to seek not a formal theocracy, as is
frequently claimed, but a new deal for the
Swiss Confederation as a whole politically,
economically, and culturally. To achieve his
aims he worked hand in hand with the Zürich
council. Although not only Zürich but also the
cities of Bern, Basel, Schaffhausen, and St
Gallen joined Zwingli's reform movement in
1528 and 1529, he was unable to realize this
goal. The cantons of central Switzerland
remained loyal to Rome, and Zwingli's attempts to prevail by armed force, in keeping
with the spirit of the Old Testament, came to
naught. The reformer himself was slain in the
second Kappel war on 11 October 1531. The
subsequent peace treaty perpetuated the confessional divisions within the Confederation
but also led to mutual recognition and toler-
ance a quarter of a century before Germany
followed suit with the religious settlement of
Augsburg in 1555. It was also at the root of the
Swiss neutrality.

From the beginning the Zürich reform
movement differed from that of Wittenberg in
emphasis. Both Luther and Zwingli were
motivated by eschatological fear typical of the
late Middle Ages, but Luther's was rooted in a
concern for personal salvation whereas Zwingli's embraced the entire commonwealth. In
other words, the Zürich reform developed its
own identity because Zwingli and Luther were
working in different environments and because Zwingli's prevailingly pastoral responsibilities differed from those of the former monk
and professor in Wittenberg. The Swiss reform
obtained its characteristics from Zwingli, who
was humanistically educated and the leader of
a specifically Swiss *res publica literaria*, anxious
to reform his fatherland and the Christian
church through cultivating *bonae literae*.

It is in this context that the influence of
Erasmus became decisive for Zwingli. He

had read Erasmus' writings while he was still in Glarus: *De copia, De puero Jesu* with the poem *Expostulatio Jesu cum homine* (Reedijk poem 85), the *Adagia* (especially *Dulce bellum inexpertis*), the *Lucubrationes* with the *Enchiridion militis christiani* (Ep 164 introduction); in Einsiedeln and later on in Zürich he read the *Moria*, but above all, he read the theological works of Erasmus, the *Novum instrumentum* with its various prefaces, the *Annotationes*, and subsequently the paraphrases, as well as the *Querela pacis*. The impact of these readings was reinforced by a personal meeting with the prince of humanists in Basel in the spring of 1516 (Epp 401, 404) and their subsequent correspondence until 1523, of which six letters by Erasmus but only one by Zwingli are extant. Zwingli emerged from these encounters with the ideas of Erasmus as an advocate of pacifism and the *philosophia Christi*. His pacifism, which was really a kind of patriotism, Zwingli expressed in his fables in verse of the ox and the labyrinth (z I 1–22, 39–60), in his letters (eg z VII Ep 105), and more concretely in his preaching at Glarus, Einsiedeln, and Zürich, which called for an end to pensions and mercenary service. In 1522 he wrote to the same effect a *Göttliche Vermahnung an die Eidgenossen zu Schwyz* (z I 155–8).

Erasmus' *philosophia Christi* encouraged Zwingli to develop, independently of Luther, a Christocentric theology based on Scripture alone and replete with Paulinism. Together with the critique of the papal church and the shining example of Luther this brought about Zwingli's 'reformatorische Wende,' the intellectual turning point leading to his Protestant theology based on a doctrine of justification, predestination, and the corruptness of human nature.

To be specific, as early as 1514 or 1515 Zwingli had derived the principle of 'solus Christus' from his reading of Erasmus' *Expostulatio Jesu cum homine*. In 1523 he recalled: 'Eight or nine years ago I read a comforting poem by the most learned Erasmus of Rotterdam, put in the mouth of our Lord Jesus Christ who is complaining in many beautiful words that we do not seek our good in him although he is the fountainhead of all that is good, our sole cure and comfort and treasure of our soul'

(z II 217). About 1516 Zwingli added the principle of sole reliance on Scripture and his Paulinism when he began to copy Paul's letters in their original language and to learn them by heart. That far his views had evolved by the time he moved to Zürich. On 22 February 1519 he wrote to *Beatus Rhenanus that Erasmus' *Ratio* 'has found such approval with me that I cannot remember ever having found a richer harvest in such a small booklet' (z VII Ep 60). Beatus Rhenanus in turn hailed Zwingli on 6 December 1518: 'For I realize that you and men like you are putting before the people the philosophy of Christ in its purest form taken from the very sources, not corrupted by the interpretations of Scotists and Gabrielists but rightly and truly explained by Augustine, Ambrose, Cyprian, and Jerome' (z VII Ep 49).

The high value Zwingli placed on Erasmus' *philosophia Christi* is clearly revealed in his own statements. Repeatedly he specified that the starting-point of his work as a reformer had been the year 1516 and not his first acquaintance with Luther's writings late in 1518. In his *Auslegen und Gründe der Schlussreden* of 1523 he recalled: 'Even before anyone in our part of the world knew Luther's name, I began to preach the gospel of Christ' (z II 144–5). In the *Amica exegesis ad Martinum Lutherum* of 1527 he wrote: 'There were many and excellent men who long before Luther's name became famous realized what true religion depends on. They were taught by quite different teachers than you suppose. In my case, I testify before God that I have found the power and the substance of the gospel in my reading of John – and the treatises of Augustine and in my thorough scrutiny of the Greek text of Paul's epistles which I copied out in my own hand eleven years ago' (z V 712–14). Apart from other autobiographical notes in the *Apologeticus Archeteles* (z I 256), in *Von der Klarheit und Gewissheit des Wortes Gottes* (z I 379), and in a letter to Berthold Haller (z VII Ep 194), there is also the testimony of *Myconius, *Jud, and Bullinger to confirm the year 1516 as the breakthrough, reached through the study of Paul which was touched off by Erasmus.

It is not possible in this context to offer more than a summary view of Zwingli's progress from Erasmian to Protestant reformer. The crucial phase of this development, the 'refor-

matorische Wende,' occurred in 1520 and 1521.
Zwingli's new concepts of sin and grace took
definitive shape under the impact of a plague
epidemic and the papal bull threatening Luther
with excommunication, but above all as a result
of his intensive study of Paul's anthropology
and doctrine of sin as well as Augustine's
doctrine of predestination (z VII Ep 184). It is
likely that in this period Zwingli suffered
similar doubts and afflictions to those of
Luther. In the *Auslegen und Gründe der
Schlussreden* he commented on the fifth request
in the Lord's Prayer: 'Hence I conclude that no
other prayer has ever been given on earth
which puts man more truly to the test with
regard to faith and knowledge of himself than
the Lord's Prayer. For I believe that no one is
peace-loving enough that the words "forgive
us our trespasses" should not compel him to
recognize what is in himself and to submit to
the pure grace of God. And this is the fitting
prayer: that man should learn about himself
and become aware of what he is, and when he
has done so, that he should humble himself
[before God]' (z II 226). While Zwingli was not
influenced by Luther in reaching this conclusion, Luther's treatises, especially *De captivi-
tate Babylonica*, may on the other hand have
helped him to arrive at a new understanding of
Scripture as a means of salvation instead of the
sacraments (cf z VII Ep 194). In the second of his
sixty-seven *Schlussreden* (29 January 1523)
Zwingli put it this way: 'The sum and
substance of the gospel is that our Lord Christ
Jesus, the true son of God, has made known to
us the will of his heavenly Father, and has with
his sinlessness released us from death and
reconciled us to God' (z I 458). This led Zwingli
to reject the efficacy of works in favour of
justification by faith, which to him meant trust
in God's mercy and thus a new sanctity of life.
It further led to his rejection of free will and
acceptance of the will in bondage, and
therefore of the providence and omnipotence
of God, and to his rejection of the papacy in
favour of his new approach to worship,
baptism, and communion and to a thorough
reform of social life, as mentioned above. In
this context it is notable that as early as 1522
Zwingli anticipated and feared a dispute
between Erasmus and Luther over free will.

Zwingli's 'reformatorische Wende' inevitably caused the relationship between him and
Erasmus to cool: after the enthusiasm of the
years 1514–20 there was a growing alienation
between 1520 and 1522 and in the end, on the
part of Erasmus, frank hostility. While Zwingli
generally continued to respect Erasmus and to
mention him in his letters, at least in passing (z
VIII Epp 315, 371, 396, 401, IX Ep 720, XI Ep
1197), Erasmus' criticism of Zwingli's radical
stance became increasingly more impassioned.
In September 1522 he politely declined an
invitation to move to Zürich and admonished
Zwingli to 'fight not only bravely but wisely'
(Ep 1314); a few days later, after reading
Zwingli's *Apologeticus Archeteles*, he reacted
with genuine alarm, inviting Zwingli to show
in his actions the unassuming prudence
worthy of the gospel (Ep 1315; cf Epp 1327,
1331). A year later his last letter to Zwingli
showed a definite rift between the two men.
Erasmus indicated that he could not understand the riddles and paradoxes of Luther,
whose disciple Zwingli had obviously become
(Ep 1384). The same thought was expressed in
his dedicatory letter for the *Spongia*, addressed
to Zwingli (Ep 1378). No doubt Zwingli's grant
of asylum to Hutten was the last straw for
Erasmus. Subsequently open hostility was
reflected in Erasmus' letters as well as in his
works. He pointed to Zwingli's radical rejection of tradition and legitimate authorities,
indeed his use of force to reach his goals (Epp
1496, 1497, 1523, 2341), and the open disagreements within the Protestant camp over the
Eucharist and baptism, which discredited its
cause (Epp 1620, 1644, 1674, 1708, 1723, 1901;
Hyperaspistes LB X 1263D, 1268F, 1302D, 1308B).
In his *Epistola ad fratres Inferioris Germaniae* of
1530 he took exception to Zwingli's prophetism
(ASD IX-1 336) – 'some consider him a demi-god'
(ASD IX-1 352) – and described him as a
corruptor and agitator who had chosen the
motto 'The gospel wants blood.' It was in this
light that Erasmus saw Zwingli's death at
Kappel (Epp 2561, 2579, 2582).

In recent years Erasmus' theology has been
the subject of several new appraisals. As
pointed out earlier, Zwingli was indebted to it
for the development of his scriptural and
Christocentric principles and his Paulinism.

Beyond this, however, Zwingli scholars have not yet produced a comprehensive and systematic analysis of Zwingli's conscious and more often unconscious debts to Erasmus. The following is an attempt to sketch some important points in Zwingli's theology that are demonstrably influenced by Erasmus in the sense that they present a continuation of his *philosophia Christi* rather than a contrast to it.

Zwingli follows Erasmus in understanding Christ's death on the cross as the central message of the gospel: 'The gospel is the pledge and warranty of God's mercy ... had He given us any lesser pledge than Christ Jesus, His own son, we might have remained in the grips of doubt' (z IV 64–6). From this central tenet Zwingli develops his theology (in the specific sense of the term) as well as the anthropological and soteriological aspects of his system. With regard to theology, the terms 'summum bonum' and 'numen' characteristically used by Zwingli to refer to God are often found in Erasmus, as is the emphasis on God as the creator and preserver, on love as God's principal quality, on his combining justice with kindness, and on Christ as God's final and complete revelation. With regard to anthropology, Erasmus' thought determined Zwingli's view of the external and inner man, that is to say, the dichotomy of body and spirit (z VI-3 118), but also of man's corruption and need for salvation. Zwingli's concept of sin is derived from Erasmus not only in a general way but quite specifically with regard to original sin and its triple consequence of spiritual blindness, corporality, and weakness 'continually present in actual sin, and in the offence of resisting God's love, which demonstrate to the individual his personal guilt and responsibility' (Kohls *Theologie des Erasmus* I 155). With regard to soteriology, Zwingli's views of man's need of salvation and of faith as the only source of salvation can be traced back to Erasmus. To Zwingli faith is trust in God's mercy, is 'peace and reliance in Christ's merits' (z II 182), is the approach to Christ in the sense of Matthew 11:28–9. This may be compared with the importance to Erasmus of 2 Corinthians 12:9: 'My grace is all you need; power comes to its full strength in weakness.'

On this basis Zwingli and Erasmus share certain conclusions, above all that man cannot overcome sin in this life but ought to consider his entire life as a penance, a battle against sin, and a challenge to follow Christ's example as a believer and therefore be justified and saved. In thus stressing sanctification and responsibility, Zwingli owes a significant debt to the notion of 'militia' as developed by Erasmus in his *Enchiridion*. It must be admitted that he derived from Erasmus what has been termed his 'ingenious homiletic view of Christ as our captain,' the captain who sacrifices himself for his troops, whose actions constitute an example for his men, who opposes the corrupted doctrine of the established church and has come not only to save the world but also to change it (Gestrich 105). This idea, which is so characteristic of the Zürich reform movement and its prophet, is almost completely taken from Erasmus.

Zwingli's concept of law is likewise reminiscent of Erasmus, who, according to Kohls (*Theologie des Erasmus* I 69), in *De contemptu mundi* approached the notion of law from an evangelical point of view (based mainly on Matthew 11:29), equating it with *Paraklese* and recognizing the significance of commandments to Christians as an 'usus evangelicus.' In the same vein Zwingli wrote in 1523: 'The law is to them who worship God an evangel' (z II 232). Unlike Luther, he maintained this concept of law as expression of the Gospel throughout his life. Other points in which Erasmus influenced Zwingli included the latter's view of the salvation of chosen heathens, his attitude towards classical antiquity, and some elements of his sacramental teachings, especially those concerning the Eucharist.

BIBLIOGRAPHY: Allen Ep 401 / Georg Finsler *Zwingli-Bibliographie: Verzeichnis der gedruckten Schriften von und über Ulrich Zwingli* (Zürich 1897) / Ulrich Gäbler *Huldrych Zwingli im 20. Jahrhundert: Forschungsbericht und annotierte Bibliographie 1897–1972* (Zürich 1975)

Biography: Leonhard von Muralt in *Handbuch der Schweizer Geschichte* (Zürich 1972–) I 389–570 / Fritz Büsser *Huldrych Zwingli: Reformation als prophetischer Auftrag* (Göttingen 1973) / Oskar Farner *Huldrych Zwingli* (Zürich 1943–1960) / Martin Haas *Huldrych Zwingli und seine Zeit* 2nd ed (Zürich 1976) / Walther Köhler

Huldrych Zwingli 2nd ed (Leipzig 1954) /
George Richard Potter *Zwingli* (Cambridge
1976)

Sources: *Huldreich Zwinglis sämtliche Werke*
(Berlin-Leipzig-Zürich 1905–   , repr 1981,
Corpus Reformatorum vols 88–   ) / *The Latin
Works of Huldreich Zwingli* ed Samuel Macauley
Jackson (New York-London 1912–29)

Studies: Gottfried W. Locher *Die Zwinglische
Reformation im Rahmen der europäischen Kir-
chengeschichte* (Göttingen-Zürich 1979) / Abel E.
Burckhardt *Das Geistproblem bei Huldrych
Zwingli* (Leipzig 1932) / J.F.G. Goeters
'Zwinglis Werdegang als Erasmianer' *Reforma-
tion und Humanismus*: [Festschrift für] *Robert
Stupperich* ed M. Greschat and J.F.G. Goeters
(Witten 1969) 255–71 / Christof Gestrich
*Zwingli als Theologe: Glaube und Geist beim
Zürcher Reformator* (Zürich-Stuttgart 1967) /
R.C. Walton *Zwingli's Theocracy* (Toronto 1967)
/ Walther Köhler *Die Geisteswelt Ulrich Zwing-
lis: Christentum und Antike* (Gotha 1920) /

Ernst-Wilhelm Kohls *Die Theologie des Erasmus*
(Basel 1966) I 69, 155, and passim / Ernst-
Wilhelm Kohls 'Erasmus und die werdende
evangelische Bewegung des 16. Jahrhun-
derts' in *Scrinium Erasmianum* I 203–19 /
Gottfried Krodel 'Die Abendmahlslehre des
Erasmus von Rotterdam und seine Stellung
am Anfang des Abendmahlsstreites der Refor-
mation' (doctoral thesis, University of
Erlangen 1955) / Gottfried W. Locher 'Zwingli
and Erasmus' *Erasmus in English* 10 (1979/80)
2–11 / Henri Meylan 'Zwingli et Erasme, de
l'humanisme à la Réformation' *D'Erasme à
Théodore de Bèze* (Geneva 1976) 53–62 / Wilhelm
H. Neuser *Die reformatorische Wende bei Zwingli*
(Neukirchen-Vluyn 1977) / Jacques-Vincent
Pollet in DTC XV 3745–928 / Arthur Rich *Die
Anfänge der Theologie Huldrych Zwinglis* (Zürich
1949) / Joachim Rogge *Zwingli und Erasmus: Die
Friedensgedanken des jungen Zwingli* (Stuttgart
1962) / Johann Martin Usteri *Zwingli und
Erasmus* (Zürich 1885)   FRITZ BÜSSER

WORKS FREQUENTLY CITED

SHORT TITLE FORMS OF ERASMUS' WORKS

CONTRIBUTORS

ILLUSTRATION CREDITS

ILLUSTRATION INDEX

Works Frequently Cited

This list provides bibliographical information for works referred to in short title form. The reader should notice, however, that the text of certain biographies contains additional short title references to works listed in the bibliography of the specific article in question. That bibliography should be consulted in the first place. For Erasmus' writings see the short title list, pages 494–6.

ADB	*Allgemeine Deutsche Biographie* (Leipzig 1875–1912)
AK	*Die Amerbachkorrespondenz* ed A. Hartmann and B.R. Jenny (Basel 1942–)
Allen	*Opus epistolarum Des. Erasmi Roterodami* ed P.S. Allen, H.M. Allen, and H.W. Garrod (Oxford 1906–58)
ARG	*Archiv für Reformationsgeschichte. Archive for Reformation History*
ASD	*Opera Omnia Desiderii Erasmi Roterodami* (Amsterdam 1969–)
BA Oekolampads	*Briefe und Akten zum Leben Oekolampads* ed E. Staehelin, Quellen und Forschungen zur Reformationsgeschichte vols 10 and 19 (Leipzig 1927–34; repr 1971)
Basler Chroniken	*Basler Chroniken* (Leipzig-Basel 1872–)
Bataillon *Erasmo y España*	Marcel Bataillon *Erasmo y España: Estudios sobre la historia espiritual del siglo xvi* tr A. Alatorre, 2nd ed (Mexico City-Buenos Aires 1966)
Benzing *Buchdrucker*	Josef Benzing *Die Buchdrucker des 16. und 17. Jahrhunderts im deutschen Sprachgebiet* (Wiesbaden 1963)
BHR	*Bibliothèque d'Humanisme et Renaissance*
Bierlaire *Familia*	Franz Bierlaire *La familia d'Erasme* (Paris 1968)
Blarer Briefwechsel	*Briefwechsel der Brüder Ambrosius und Thomas Blaurer* ed T. Schiess (Freiburg 1908–12)
BNB	*Biographie nationale* (Académie royale des sciences, des lettres et des beaux-arts de Belgique, Brussels 1866–)
BRE	*Briefwechsel des Beatus Rhenanus* ed A. Horawitz and K. Hartfelder (Leipzig 1886, repr 1966)
Calendar of State Papers, Milan	*Calendar of State Papers and Manuscripts existing in the Archives and Collections of Milan* ... ed A.B. Hinds (Hereford 1912)
Calendar of State Papers, Spanish	*Calendar of Letters, Despatches and State Papers relating to the Negotiations between England and Spain preserved in the Archives of Simancas and elsewhere*, with supplements, ed G.A. Bergenroth et al (London 1862–)
Calendar of State Papers, Venetian	*Calendar of State Papers and Manuscripts relating to English Affairs existing in the Archives and Collections of Venice and other Libraries of*

Northern Italy, 1202–1672 ed R.L. Brown et al (London 1862–1940, repr 1970)

Clerval — *Registre des procès-verbaux de la faculté de théologie de Paris* ed J.-A. Clerval (Paris 1917)

Colloquia Erasmiana Turonensia — *Colloquia Erasmiana Turonensia* Douzième stage international d'études humanistes, Tours 1969, ed J.-C. Margolin (Paris-Toronto 1972)

Cosenza — Mario Emilio Cosenza *Biographical and Bibliographical Dictionary of the Italian Humanists and the World of Classical Scholarship in Italy, 1300–1800* (Boston, Mass 1962–7)

CWE — *Collected Works of Erasmus* (Toronto 1974–   )

DBF — *Dictionnaire de biographie française* ed J. Balteau et al (Paris 1933–   )

DBI — *Dizionario biografico degli Italiani* ed A.M. Ghisalberti et al (Rome 1960–   )

Delisle — Léopold Delisle 'Notice sur un régistre des procès-verbaux de la faculté de théologie de Paris pendant les années 1505–1533' *Notices et extraits des manuscrits de la Bibliothèque Nationale et autres bibliothèques* 36 (1899) 317–407. Offprint ed (Paris 1899)

DHBS — *Dictionnaire historique et biographique de la Suisse* (Neuchâtel 1921–34), simultaneously published in a very similar but not identical German version: *Historisch-Biographisches Lexikon der Schweiz*

DHGE — *Dictionnaire d'histoire et de géographie ecclésiastiques* ed A. Baudrillart et al (Paris 1912–   )

DNB — *Dictionary of National Biography* ed Leslie Stephen, Sidney Lee, et al (London 1885–   , repr 1949–50)

DS — *Dictionnaire de spiritualité ascétique et mystique, doctrine et histoire* ed M. Viller et al (Paris 1932–   )

DTC — *Dictionnaire de théologie catholique* ed A. Vacant et al (Paris 1899–1950)

EI — *Enciclopedia Italiana* ed D. Bartolini et al (Rome 1929–   , repr 1949)

Emden BRUC — A.B. Emden *A Biographical Register of the University of Cambridge to AD 1500* (Cambridge 1963)

Emden BRUO — A.B. Emden *A Biographical Register of the University of Oxford to AD 1500* (Oxford 1957–9)

Emden BRUO 1501–40 — A.B. Emden *A Biographical Register of the University of Oxford, AD 1501–1540* (Oxford 1974)

Epistolae ad Nauseam — *Epistolarum miscellanearum ad Fridericum Nauseam Blancicampianum … libri x* (Basel 1550)

Eubel — *Hierarchia catholica medii aevi summorum pontificum, S.R.E. cardinalium, ecclesiarum antistitum series* ed C. Eubel et al, 2nd ed (Münster 1913)

Farge — James K. Farge *Biographical Register of Paris Doctors of Theology, 1500–1536* Subsidia Mediaevalia 10 (Toronto 1980)

Gallia christiana — *Gallia christiana in provincias ecclesiasticas distributa* ed D. Sammarthanus et al (Paris 1715–1865, repr 1970)

Gauthier — Jules Gauthier *Département du Doubs: Inventaire sommaire des archives départementales antérieures à 1790: Archives ecclésiastiques série G I* (Besançon 1900)

Grimm *Buchführer* — Heinrich Grimm 'Die Buchführer des deutschen Kulturbereichs und ihre Niederlassungsorte in der Zeitspanne 1490 bis um 1550' *Archiv für Geschichte des Buchwesens* 7 (1965–6) 1153–1772

Herminjard   *Correspondance des Réformateurs dans les pays de langue française* ed
                                A.-L. Herminjard (Geneva-Paris 1866–97, repr 1965–6)
Hill   G.F. Hill *A Corpus of Italian Medals of the Renaissance before Cellini*
                                (London 1930)
Hutten *Opera*   *Ulrichi Hutteni equitis Germani opera* ed E. Böcking (Leipzig
                                1859–61, repr 1963)
Hutten *Operum*   *Ulrichi Hutteni equitis Germani operum supplementum* ed E. Böcking
  supplementum   (Leipzig 1869–71)
Knod   Gustav C. Knod *Deutsche Studenten in Bologna (1289-1562)* (Berlin
                                1899, repr 1970)
LB   *Desiderii Erasmi Roterodami opera omnia* ed J. Leclerc (Leiden
                                1703–6, repr 1961–2)
LP   *Letters and Papers, Foreign and Domestic, of the Reign of Henry VIII* ed
                                J.S. Brewer et al (London 1862–1932)
LThK   *Lexikon für Theologie und Kirche* 2nd ed by J. Höfer and K. Rahner
                                (Freiburg 1957–   )
Luther W   *D. Martin Luthers Werke: Kritische Gesamtausgabe* (Weimar 1883–   )
Matricule de Louvain   *Matricule de l'Université de Louvain* ed E. Reusens, A. Schillings, et
                                al (Brussels 1903–   )
Matricule de Montpellier   *Matricule de l'Université de Médecine de Montpellier (1503–1599)* ed
                                M. Gouron (Geneva 1957)
Matricule d'Orléans   *Premier Livre des procurateurs de la nation germanique de l'ancienne
                                Université d'Orléans, 1446–1546* ed C.M. Ridderikhoff, H. de
                                Ridder-Symoens, et al (Leiden 1971–   )
Matrikel Basel   *Die Matrikel der Universität Basel* ed H.G. Wackernagel et al (Basel
                                1951–   )
Matrikel Erfurt   *Acten der Erfurter Universität* ed J.C.H. Weissenborn et al (Halle
                                1881–99, repr 1976)
Matrikel Frankfurt   *Ältere Universitäts-Matrikeln* I: *Universität Frankfurt a.O.* ed
                                E. Friedländer et al (Leipzig 1887–91, repr 1965)
Matrikel Freiburg   *Die Matrikel der Universität Freiburg i. Br. von 1460–1656* ed
                                H. Mayer (Freiburg 1907–10, repr 1976)
Matrikel Greifswald   *Ältere Universitäts-Matrikeln* II: *Universität Greifswald* ed
                                E. Friedländer et al (Leipzig 1893–4, repr 1965)
Matrikel Heidelberg   *Die Matrikel der Universität Heidelberg von 1386 bis 1662* ed
                                G. Toepke (Heidelberg 1884–93, repr 1976)
Matrikel Köln   *Matrikel der Universität Köln* ed H. Keussen (Bonn 1919–31, repr
                                1979)
Matrikel Leipzig   *Die Matrikel der Universität Leipzig* ed G. Erler (Leipzig 1895–1902,
                                repr 1976)
Matrikel Rostock   *Die Matrikel der Universität Rostock* ed A. Hofmeister et al (Rostock-
                                Schwerin 1889–1922, repr 1976)
Matrikel Tübingen   *Die Matrikeln der Universität Tübingen* ed H. Hermelink et al
                                (Stuttgart-Tübingen 1906–   )
Matrikel Wien   *Die Matrikel der Universität Wien* (Publikationen des Instituts für
                                österreichische Geschichtsforschung VI. Reihe, 1. Abteilung,
                                Vienna-Graz-Cologne 1954–   )
Matrikel Wittenberg   *Album Academiae Vitebergensis: Ältere Reihe ... 1502–1602* ed K.E.
                                Förstemann et al (Leipzig-Halle 1841–1905, repr 1976)
Melanchthons Briefwechsel   *Melanchthons Briefwechsel: Kritische und kommentierte Gesamtausgabe*
                                ed Heinz Scheible (Stuttgart-Bad Cannstatt 1977–   )

McConica | J.K. McConica *English Humanists and Reformation Politics under Henry VIII and Edward VI* (Oxford 1965)
More Y | *The Yale Edition of the Complete Works of St Thomas More* (New Haven-London 1961–)
NBW | *Nationaal Biografisch Woordenboek* ed J. Duverger et al (Brussels 1964–)
NDB | *Neue Deutsche Biographie* (Berlin 1953–)
NK | Wouter Nijhoff and M.E. Kronenberg *Nederlandsche Bibliographie van 1500 tot 1540* (The Hague 1923–71)
NNBW | *Nieuw Nederlandsch Biografisch Woordenboek* ed P.C. Molhuysen, P.J. Blok, et al (Leiden 1911–37, repr 1974)
Opuscula | *Erasmi opuscula: A Supplement to the Opera omnia* ed W.K. Ferguson (The Hague 1933)
Pastor | Ludwig von Pastor *The History of the Popes from the Close of the Middle Ages* ed and tr R.F. Kerr et al, 3rd ed (London 1938–53)
Pflug *Correspondance* | Julius Pflug *Correspondance* ed J.V. Pollet (Leiden 1969–)
Pirckheimer *Briefwechsel* | *Willibald Pirckheimer Briefwechsel* ed Emil Reicke (Munich 1940–)
PSB | *Polski Słownik Biograficzny* (Cracow, etc 1935–)
RE | *Johann Reuchlins Briefwechsel* ed Ludwig Geiger (Stuttgart 1875, repr 1962)
Reedijk | *The Poems of Desiderius Erasmus* ed C. Reedijk (Leiden 1956)
Renaudet *Préréforme* | Augustin Renaudet *Préréforme et Humanisme à Paris pendant les premières guerres d'Italie (1494-1517)* 2nd ed (Paris 1953)
Renouard *Répertoire* | Philippe Renouard *Répertoire des imprimeurs parisiens, libraires, fondeurs de caractères et correcteurs d'imprimerie ... jusqu'à la fin du seizième siècle* ed J. Veyrin-Forrer and B. Moreau (Paris 1965)
RGG | *Die Religion in Geschichte und Gegenwart* 3rd ed (Tübingen 1956–62)
Rice *Prefatory Epistles* | *The Prefatory Epistles of Jacques Lefèvre d'Etaples and Related Texts* ed Eugene F. Rice, jr (New York–London 1972)
Rogers | *The Correspondence of Sir Thomas More* ed E.F. Rogers (Princeton 1947)
Rublack *Reformation in Konstanz* | Hans-Christoph Rublack *Die Einführung der Reformation in Konstanz von den Anfängen bis zum Abschluss 1531* (Gütersloh-Karlsruhe 1971)
Sanudo *Diarii* | *I Diarii di Marino Sanuto* ed N. Barozzi et al (Venice 1879–1903, repr 1969–70)
Schmidt *Histoire littéraire* | Charles Schmidt *Histoire littéraire de l'Alsace à la fin du XVe et au commencement du XVIe siècle* (Paris 1879, repr 1966)
Scrinium Erasmianum | *Scrinium Erasmianum: Mélanges historiques publiées sous le patronage de l'Université de Louvain à l'occasion du cinquième centenaire de la naissance d'Erasme* ed J. Coppens (Leiden 1969)
Schottenloher | Karl Schottenloher *Bibliographie zur deutschen Geschichte im Zeitalter der Glaubensspaltung* 2nd ed (Stuttgart 1956–66)
Schreiber *Universität Freiburg* | Heinrich Schreiber *Geschichte der Albert-Ludwigs-Universität zu Freiburg i. Br.*: second part of his *Geschichte der Stadt und Universität Freiburg im Breisgau* (Freiburg 1857–60)
STC | *A Short-Title Catalogue of Books Printed in England, Scotland, and Ireland and of English Books Printed Abroad* ed A.W. Pollard and G.R. Redgrave (London 1926); 2nd ed revised by W.A. Jackson et al (London 1976–)

Vadianische Briefsammlung	*Vadianische Briefsammlung* ed E. Arbenz and H. Wartmann : Mitteilungen zur vaterländischen Geschichte, vols 24–5, 27–30, and supplements (St Gallen 1890–1913)
de Vocht *Busleyden*	Henry de Vocht *Jérôme de Busleyden, Founder of the Louvain Collegium Trilingue: His Life and Writings* (Turnhout 1950)
de Vocht *Dantiscus*	Henry de Vocht *John Dantiscus and his Netherlandish Friends as Revealed by their Correspondence, 1522–1546* (Louvain 1961)
de Vocht *Literae ad Craneveldium*	*Literae virorum eruditorum ad Franciscum Craneveldium, 1522–1528* ed Henry de Vocht (Louvain 1928)
de Vocht MHL	Henry de Vocht *Monumenta Humanistica Lovaniensia: Texts and Studies about Louvain Humanists in the First Half of the xvith Century* (Louvain 1934)
de Vocht CTL	Henry de Vocht *History of the Foundation and the Rise of the Collegium Trilingue Lovaniense, 1517-1550* (Louvain 1951–5)
Winterberg	Hans Winterberg *Die Schüler von Ulrich Zasius* (Stuttgart 1961)
z	*Huldreich Zwinglis Sämtliche Werke* ed E. Egli et al, Corpus Reformatorum vols 88–101 (Berlin-Leipzig-Zürich 1905–)

Short Title Forms for
Erasmus' Works

Titles following colons are longer versions of the same, or are alternative titles. Items entirely enclosed in square brackets are of doubtful authorship. For abbreviations, see Works Frequently Cited, pages 489–93.

Adagia: Adagiorum chiliades 1508 (Adagiorum collectanea for the primitive form, when required) LB II / ASD II-5, 6 / CWE 30-36
Admonitio adversus mendacium: Admonitio adversus mendacium et obtrectationem LB X
Annotationes in Novum Testamentum LB VI
Antibarbari LB X / ASD I-1 / CWE 23
Apologia ad Fabrum: Apologia ad Iacobum Fabrum Stapulensem LB IX
Apologia ad Caranzam: Apologia ad Sanctium Caranzam, or Apologia de tribus locis, or Responsio ad annotationem Stunicae … a Sanctio Caranza defensam LB IX
Apologia ad viginti et quattuor libros A. Pii LB IX
Apologia adversus Petrum Sutorem: Apologia adversus debacchationes Petri Sutoris LB IX
Apologia adversus monachos: Apologia adversus monachos quosdam hispanos LB IX
Apologia adversus rhapsodias Alberti Pii LB IX
Apologia contra Latomi dialogum: Apologia contra Iacobi Latomi dialogum de tribus linguis LB IX
Apologiae contra Stunicam: Apologiae contra Lopidem Stunicam LB IX / ASD IX-2
Apologia de 'In principio erat sermo' LB IX
Apologia de laude matrimonii: Apologia pro declamatione de laude matrimonii LB IX
Apologia de loco 'Omnes quidem': Apologia de loco 'Omnes quidem resurgemus' LB IX
Apologia invectivis Lei: Apologia qua respondet duabus invectivis Eduardi Lei Opuscula
Apophthegmata LB IV
Appendix respondens ad Sutorem LB IX
Argumenta: Argumenta in omneis epistolas apostolicas nova (with Paraphrases)
Axiomata pro causa Lutheri: Axiomata pro causa Martini Lutheri Opuscula

Carmina varia LB VIII
Catalogus lucubrationum LB I
Christiani hominis institutum, carmen LB V
Ciceronianus: Dialogus Ciceronianus LB I / ASD I-2 / CWE 28
Colloquia (Familiarum colloquiorum formulae for the primitive form, when required) LB I / ASD I-3
Compendium vitae Allen I / CWE 4
[Consilium: Consilium cuiusdam ex animo cupientis esse consultum] Opuscula

De bello turcico: Consultatio de bello turcico LB V
De civilitate: De civilitate morum puerilium LB I / CWE 25
De concordia: De sarcienda ecclesiae concordia LB V

De conscribendis epistolis LB I / ASD I-2 / CWE 25
De constructione: De constructione octo partium orationis, or Syntaxis LB I / ASD I-4
De contemptu mundi: Epistola de contemptu mundi LB V / ASD V-1
De copia: De duplici copia verborum ac rerum LB I / CWE 24
De immensa Dei misericordia: Concio de immensa Dei misericordia LB V
De libero arbitrio: De libero arbitrio diatribe LB IX
De praeparatione: De praeparatione ad mortem LB V / ASD V-1
De pueris instituendis: De pueris statim ac liberaliter instituendis LB I / ASD I-2 / CWE 26
De puero Iesu: Concio de puero Iesu LB V
De ratione studii LB I / ASD I-2 / CWE 24
De recta pronuntiatione: De recta latini graecique sermonis pronuntiatione LB I / ASD I-4 / CWE 26
De tedio Iesu: Disputatiuncula de tedio, pavore, tristicia Iesu LB V
De virtute amplectenda: Oratio de virtute amplectenda LB V
Declamatio de morte LB IV
Declamatiuncula LB IV
Declarationes ad censuras Lutetiae vulgatas: Declarationes ad censuras Lutetiae vulgatas sub
    nomine facultatis theologiae Parisiensis LB IX
Detectio praestigiarum: Detectio praestigiarum cuiusdam libelli germanice scripti LB X / ASD IX-1
[Dialogus bilinguium ac trilinguium: Chonradi Nastadiensis dialogus bilinguium ac trilinguium
    Opuscula] CWE 7
Dilutio: Dilutio eorum quae Iodocus Clithoveus scripsit adversus declamationem suasoriam
    matrimonii
Divinationes ad notata Bedae LB IX

Ecclesiastes: Ecclesiastes sive de ratione concionandi LB V
Elenchus: Elenchus in N. Bedae censuras LB IX
Enchiridion: Enchiridion militis christiani LB V
Encomium matrimonii (in De conscribendis epistolis)
Encomium medicinae: Declamatio in laudem artis medicae LB I / ASD I-4
Epigrammata LB I
Epistola ad Dorpium LB IX / CWE 3
Epistola ad fratres Inferioris Germaniae: Responsio ad fratres Germaniae Inferioris ad epistolam
    apologeticam incerto autore proditam LB X
Epistola ad graculos: Epistola ad quosdam imprudentissimos graculos LB X
Epistola apologetica de Termino LB X
Epistola consolatoria: Epistola consolatoria virginibus sacris LB V
Epistola contra pseudevangelicos: Epistola contra quosdam qui se falso iactant evangelicos LB X /
    ASD IX-1
Epistola de esu carnium: Epistola apologetica ad Christophorum episcopum Basiliensem de
    interdicto esu carnium LB IX / ASD IX-1
Exomologesis: Exomologesis sive modus confitendi LB V
Explanatio symboli: Explanatio symboli apostolorum sive catechismus LB V / ASD V-1
Expostulatio Iesu LB V

Familiarum colloquiorum formulae (see Colloquia)
Formula: Conficiendarum epistolarum formula (see De conscribendis epistolis)

Hymni varii LB V
Hyperaspistes LB X

Institutio christiani matrimonii LB V
Institutio principis christiani LB IV / ASD IV-1 / CWE 27

[Julius exclusus: Dialogus Julius exclusus e coelis *Opuscula*] CWE 27

Lingua LB IV / ASD IV-1
Liturgia Virginis Matris: Virginis Matris apud Lauretum cultae liturgia LB V / ASD V-1

Methodus: Ratio verae theologiae LB V
Modus orandi Deum LB V / ASD V-1
Moria: Moriae encomium LB IV / ASD IV-3 / CWE 27

Novum Testamentum: Novum Testamentum 1519 and later (Novum instrumentum for the first
   edition, 1516, when required) LB VI

Obsecratio ad Virginem Mariam: Obsecratio sive oratio ad Virginem Mariam in rebus adversis
   LB V
Oratio de pace: Oratio de pace et discordia LB VIII
Oratio funebris: Oratio funebris Berthae de Heyen LB VIII

Paean Virgini Matri: Paean Virgini Matri dicendus LB V
Panegyricus: Panegyricus ad Philippum Austriae ducem LB IV / ASD IV-1 / CWE 27
Parabolae: Parabolae sive similia LB I / ASD I-5 / CWE 23
Paraclesis LB V, VI
Paraphrasis in Elegantias Vallae: Paraphrasis in Elegantias Laurentii Vallae LB I / ASD I-4
Paraphrasis in Matthaeum, etc (in Paraphrasis in Novum Testamentum)
Paraphrasis in Novum Testamentum LB VII / CWE 42–50
Peregrinatio apostolorum: Peregrinatio apostolorum Petri et Pauli LB VI, VII
Precatio ad Virginis filium Iesum (in Precatio pro pace)
Precatio dominica LB V
Precationes LB V
Precatio pro pace ecclesiae: Precatio ad Iesum pro pace ecclesiae LB IV, V
Progymnasmata: Progymnasmata quaedam primae adolescentiae Erasmi LB VIII
Psalmi: Psalmi, or Enarrationes sive commentarii in psalmos LB V
Purgatio adversus epistolam Lutheri: Purgatio adversus epistolam non sobriam Lutheri LB IX

Querela pacis LB IV / ASD IV-2 / CWE 27

Ratio verae theologiae: Methodus LB V
Responsio ad annotationes Lei: Liber quo respondet annotationibus Lei LB IX
Responsio ad collationes: Responsio ad collationes cuiusdam iuvenis gerontodidascali LB IX
Responsio ad disputationem de divortio: Responsio ad disputationem cuiusdam Phimostomi de
   divortio LB IX
Responsio ad epistolam Pii: Responsio ad epistolam paraeneticam Alberti Pii, or Responsio ad
   exhortationem Pii LB IX
Responsio ad notulas Bedaicas LB X
Responsio ad Petri Cursii defensionem: Epistola de apologia Cursii LB X
Responsio adversus febricitantis libellum: Apologia monasticae religionis LB X

Spongia: Spongia adversus aspergines Hutteni LB X / ASD IX-1
Supputatio: Supputatio calumniarum Natalis Bedae LB IX

Vidua christiana LB V
Virginis et martyris comparatio LB V
Vita Hieronymi: Vita divi Hieronymi Stridonensis *Opuscula*

Contributors

Danilo Aguzzi-Barbagli
Rosemarie Aulinger
Kenneth R. Bartlett
Marco Bernuzzi
Franz Bierlaire
Marjorie O'Rourke Boyle
Virginia Brown
Fritz Büsser
Leo van Buyten
Virginia W. Callahan
Anna Giulia Cavagna
D.S. Chambers
Miriam U. Chrisman
Brian P. Copenhaver
Elizabeth Crittall
Maria Cytowska
John F. D'Amico
Natalie Zemon Davis
Rolf Decot
Jan De Grauwe
Rosemary Devonshire Jones
L. Domonkos
Paul J. Donnelly
Richard M. Douglas
K.-H. Ducke
E.J.M. van Eijl
Edward English
Michael Erbe
Conor Fahy
James K. Farge
Mordechai Feingold
Felipe Fernández-Armesto
R.M. Flores

Inge Friedhuber
Stephan Füssel
Anton J. Gail
Marie-Madeleine de la Garanderie
Veronika Gerz-von Büren
André Godin
Frank Golczewski
Anthony Grafton
Kaspar von Greyerz
Gordon Griffiths
Hans R. Guggisberg
Geneviève Guilleminot
Léon-E. Halkin
John M. Headley
Gernot Heiss
Henry Heller
Judith Rice Henderson
Elisabeth Feist Hirsch
R. Gerald Hobbs
Eugen Hoffmann
Irmgard Höss
J. Hoyoux
Jozef IJsewijn
Marie-Thérèse Isaac
Fehmi Ismail
Denis R. Janz
William B. Jones
James M. Kittelson
Erich Kleineidam
C.S. Knighton
Alfred Kohler
Barbara Könneker
Georges Kouskoff

Halina Kowalska
Peter Krendl
Egmont Lee
Valeria Sestieri Lee
Stanford E. Lehmberg
C.G. van Leijenhorst
M.J.C. Lowry
Albrecht Luttenberger
James K. McConica
Franz Machilek
David Mackenzie
Louis P.A. Maingon
Peter Marzahl
Jean-Pierre Massaut
C. Matheeussen
Hansgeorg Molitor
Gérard Moreau
Marcel A. Nauwelaerts
José C. Nieto
John C. Olin
Arsenio Pacheco
Luis A. Pérez
Paul van Peteghem
Paolo Pissavino
Michel Reulos
Hilde de Ridder-Symoens
Dieter Riesenberger
Milagros Rivera

Steven Rowan
John Rowlands
Hans-Christoph Rublack
Gordon Rupp
Beat von Scarpatetti
Hans Schadek
Heinz Scheible
Charles B. Schmitt
R.J. Schoeck
Martin Schwarz Lausten
Harry R. Secor
Silvana Seidel Menchi
Heide Stratenwerth
Robert Stupperich
Hans Thieme
De Etta V. Thomsen
Alice Tobriner
Gilbert Tournoy
Godelieve Tournoy-Thoen
James D. Tracy
J.B. Trapp
Charles Trinkaus
Ronald W. Truman
Rainer Vinke
Hartmut Voit
Manfred E. Welti
Konrad Wiedemann
J.K. Zeman

Illustration Credits

Illustration Index

VOLUME 1

Adrian VI, Pope 6
Agricola, Johannes 14
Agricola, Rodolphus 15
Agrippa, Henricus Cornelius 17
Alaard of Amsterdam 20
Alciati, Andrea 24
Aleandro, Girolamo 29
Alexander VI, Pope 33
Alidosi, Francesco 36
Alvarez de Toledo, Fadrique 38
d'Amboise, Georges (I) 40
d'Amboise, Georges (II) 41
Amerbach, Bonifacius 43
Amsdorf, Nikolaus von 52
Boleyn, Anne 59
Apianus, Petrus 67
Argyropoulos, Johannes 71
Arthur, prince of Wales 73
Aventinus, Johannes 76

Bade, Josse 79
Bannisio, Jacopo 90
Bavaria, Ernest, duke of 102
Bavaria, William IV, duke of 103
Beatus, Rhenanus 105
Beaufort, Lady Margaret 110
Bembo, Pietro 121
Bentivoglio, Giovanni (II) 125 ·
Bergen, Anna van 129
Bergen, Antoon (I) van 130
Bergen, Hendrik van 132
Bergen, Jan (III) van 133
Bessarion, Cardinal 142
Binzenstock, Elizabeth, wife of
  Hans Holbein vol 2, 195
Blarer, Ambrosius 152
Blumeneck, Sebastian von 157
Boner, Seweryn 167
Bora, Katharina von 171
Borssele, Anna van 173

Bracciolini, Poggio 183
Brandenburg, Albert of 184
Brandenburg-Ansbach, George
  of 189
Brandon, Charles 189
Brant, Sebastian 190
Brenz, Johann 193
Briçonnet, Guillaume (I) 197
Brunfels, Otto 206
Bucer, Martin 209
Budé, Guillaume 213
Bugenhagen, Johann 218
Burgundy, Adolph of 223
Burgundy, Anthony of 224
Burgundy, Charles, duke of 225
Burgundy, David of 226
Burgundy, Philip (the Good),
  duke of 228
Burgundy, Philip (I) of 230
Busleyden, Jérôme de 236

Cajetanus, Tommaso de Vio,
  Cardinal 240
Camerarius, Joachim 247
Campeggi, Lorenzo 253
Capito, Wolfgang Faber 261
Carondelet, Ferry de 271
Carondelet, Jean (II) de 273
Carvajal, Bernardino López
  de 274
Castiglione, Baldesar 280
Catherine of Aragon 283
Catherine de' Medici 285
Chalcondyles, Demetrius 290
Chalon, René de 291
Chapuys, Eustache 293
Charles V 296
Charles VII 300
Christian II of Denmark 302
Claude, queen of France 306
Clement VII, Pope 308
Cles, Bernhard von 314

Cleves, William V, duke of 316
Cochlaeus, Johannes 321
Colet, John 324
Colster, Abel van 332
Contarini, Gasparo 335
Cousin, Gilbert 350
Cranevelt, Frans van 354
Cranmer, Thomas 356
Cresacre, Anne, wife of John
  (III) More vol 2 454
Cromwell, Thomas 360
Croy, Charles (I) de 364
Croy, Guillaume (I) de 366
Croy, Philippe de 369
Cusanus, Nicolaus 372

Dolet, Etienne 395
Doria, Andrea 397
Draconites, Johannes 404
Duprat, Antoine 412
Dürer, Albrecht 413

Eck, Johann Maier of 417
Eck, Leonhard von 419
Egmond, Floris van 422
Egmond, Joris van 423
Eleanor of Austria 426
Elizabeth of York 427
Eobanus Hessus, Helius 434
d'Este, Alfonso (I) de 444
Everaerts, Nicolaas 446

VOLUME 2

Fabri, Johannes 6
Farel, Guillaume 11
Farnese, Alessandro 13
Ferdinand I, Emperor 18
Ferdinand II of Aragon 20
Fernandes de Almada, Rui 22
Ficino, Marsilio 27

Filelfo, Francesco 31
Fisher, John 36
Foxe, Richard 47
Francis I 50
Francis, dauphin of France 53
Froben, Hieronymus 59
Froben, Johann 61
Fugger, Anton 65
Fugger, Jakob 67

Gaguin, Robert 70
Gardiner, Stephen 75
Gerbel, Nikolaus 90
Giberti, Gian Matteo 95
Giese, Tiedemann 96
Giggs, Margaret 97
Gillis, Pieter 100
Gois, Damião de 114
Gouffier, Artus 120
Greverade, Adolf 128
Greverade, Heinrich 129
Grimani, Domenico 133
Grynaeus, Simon 142
Guarini, Guarino 148
Guildford, Henry 150
Guildford, Lady Mary 151

Hedio, Caspar 170
Henry VII 177
Henry VIII 178
Henry II, king of France 181
Hesse, Philip, landgrave of 188
Hesse, Christina, landgravine of 189
Holbein, Hans, the Younger 194
Hörmann, Georg 203
Hosius, Stanislaus 206
Howard, Thomas 208
Hubmaier, Balthasar 211
Hutten, Moritz von 216
Hutten, Ulrich von 217
Huttich, Johann 220

Inghirami, Tommaso 223
Isabella, queen of Castile 227

James IV, king of Scotland 231
Jan of Leiden 233
Jiménez de Cisneros, Francisco 235
Joanna, queen of Castile 237
John, prince of Denmark 239
John III, king of Portugal 240
John Zápolyai 242
John Albert, king of Poland 243
Jonas, Justus 244

Jud, Leo 249
Julius II, Pope 250

Karlstadt, Andreas 253
Keck, Georg 256
Khair ad-Din Pasha 259
Kleberger, Johann 263
Kmita, Piotr 265
Knipperdolling, Bernhard 266
Koolman, Jan 272
Kratzer, Nikolaus 273

Lang, Matthäus 289
Lascaris, Janus 293
Łaski, Jan (II) 298
Latomus, Jacobus 305
Lefèvre d'Etaples, Jacques 316
Leo X, Pope 320
Loaysa, García de 337
Lorraine, Antoine, duke of 349
Louis XI, king of France 351
Louis XII, king of France 352
Louis II, king of Hungary 353
Lovell, Thomas 354
Luther, Hans 360
Luther, Margarete 360
Luther, Martin 361

Machiavelli, Niccolò 365
Manuzio, Aldo 377
Marck, Erard de la 383
Marck, Robert III de la 386
Margaret of Angoulême 387
Margaret of Austria 388
Margaret of Parma 390
Margaret Tudor, queen of Scotland 391
Mary of Austria 400
Mary I, queen of England 402
Marzio, Galeotto 404
Mathijszoon, Jan 407
Matthias Corvinus 408
Maximilian I, Emperor 411
Medici, Alessandro de' 415
Medici, Ippolito de' 416
Medici, Lorenzo (I) de' 418
Medici, Lorenzo (II) de' 419
Mehmed II 422
Melanchthon, Philippus 424
Merklin, Balthasar 434
Metsys, Quinten 438
Micault, Jean 441
Mil, Elisabeth de 444
More, Lady Alice 451
More, Elizabeth 452
More, Cecily 452

More, John (I) 453
More, John (III) 454
More, Margaret 455
More, Thomas 456
Morillon, Guy 461
Musurus, Marcus 473

VOLUME 3

Nausea, Fridericus 7
Navagero, Andrea 8
Nebrija, Elio Antonio de 9
Nicholas V, Pope 16

Occo, Pompeius 22
Oecolampadius, Johannes 25
Olahus, Nicolaus 29
Osiander, Andreas 35

Palatine, Dorothea, countess 41
Palatine, Frederick II, elector 40
Palatine, Henry, count 42
Palatine, Louis V, elector 43
Palatine, Otto Henry, elector 43
Palatine, Philip, count 44
Paracelsus, Theophrastus 50
Paul III, Pope 53
Paul IV, Pope 56
Paul of Middelburg 57
Paumgartner, Johann (I) 59
Pellicanus, Conradus 65
Perrenot de Granvelle, Nicolas 69
Peutinger, Konrad 74
Pfefferkorn, Johann 76
Pflug, Julius 77
Pico della Mirandola, Giovanni 81
Pirckheimer, Katharine 90
Pirckheimer, Klara 89
Pirckheimer, Willibald 91
Pistoris, Simon 96
Pius II, Pope 97
Platina, Bartolomeo 100
Pole, Reginald 103
Poliziano, Angelo 106
Pomponazzi, Pietro 109
Poncher, Etienne 111
Pontano, Giovanni 113
Pottelsberghe, Lieven van 117

Rabelais, François 128
Redwitz, Wigand von 133
Reuchlin, Johann 145
Rhein, Margarethe vom, wife of Nikolaus Stalburg 279
Riario, Raffaele 153

Roper, William 170
Rosenblatt, Wibrandis, wife of
    Oecolampadius 26
Rudolfinger, Johann 175

Sadoleto, Jacopo 184
Salviati, Giovanni 190
Sauli, Bandinello 198
Savonarola, Girolamo 200
Savoy, Louise of 201
Saxony, Frederick III, elector of
    203
Saxony, George, duke of 206
Saxony, John, elector of 208
Saxony, John Frederick, elector
    of 209
Scala, Bartolomeo 212
Scaliger, Julius Caesar 213
Schets, Erasmus 220
Schiner, Matthäus 222
Schönberg, Nikolaus von 229
Selim I 238
Servetus, Michael 242
Sforza, Francesco II 244
Sforza, Ludovico 245
Sforza, Gian Galeazzo 245

Sibyl of Julich-Cleves, wife of
    John Frederick, elector of
    Saxony 210
Sickingen, Franz von 248
Sigismund I, king of Poland 249
Sigismund II Augustus, king of
    Poland 251
Sixtus IV, Pope 256
Skelton, John 257
Spalatinus, Georgius 266
Stalburg, Nikolaus 278
Standonck, Jan 281
Staupitz, Johann von 283
Stewart, Alexander 286
Sturm, Jakob 293
Suleiman I 299

Tapper, Ruard 308
Tournon, François de 335
Toussain, Jacques 336
Trebizond, George of 341
Trithemius, Johannes 344
Tunstall, Cuthbert 350
Tyndale, William 354

Urswick, Christopher 358

Utenheim, Christoph von 361

Vadianus, Joachim 364
Valla, Lorenzo 372
Varnbüler, Ulrich 377
Vatable, François 379
Vida, Marco Girolamo 391
Viglius Zuichemus 393
Vives, Juan Luis 410

Waldeck, Franz von 424
Warham, William 428
Welser, Bartholomäus 437
Wied, Hermann von 445
Wirtner, Ulrich 457
Witzel, Georg 458
Wolsey, Thomas 461
Württemberg, Ulrich, duke of
    464

Yonge, John 466

Zasius, Udalricus 469
Ziegler, Jakob 475
Zwingli, Huldrych 482